READING DANCE

ALSO BY ROBERT GOTTLIEB

Balanchine: The Ballet Maker

Reading Jazz

Reading Lyrics (with Robert Kimball)

The Everyman Library's *Collected Stories* by Rudyard Kipling (Editor)

The Journals of John Cheever (Editor)

A Certain Style: The Art of the Plastic Handbag, 1949–1959

READING
DANCE

A GATHERING OF MEMOIRS, REPORTAGE,
CRITICISM, PROFILES, INTERVIEWS,
AND SOME UNCATEGORIZABLE EXTRAS

EDITED AND WITH AN INTRODUCTION BY

ROBERT GOTTLIEB

PANTHEON BOOKS, NEW YORK

All rights reserved. Published in the United States by Pantheon Books, a division of Random House, Inc., New York, and in Canada by Random House of Canada Limited, Toronto.

Pantheon Books and colophon are registered trademarks of Random House, Inc.

Library of Congress Cataloging-in-Publication Data

Reading dance : a gathering of memoirs, reportage, criticism, profiles, interviews, and some uncategorizable extras / edited and with an introduction by Robert Gottlieb.
p.   cm.
ISBN 978-0-375-42122-8
1. Dance.   2. Dance criticism.   I. Gottlieb, Robert S.
GV1600.R43 2009   792.8—dc22   2008024392

www.pantheonbooks.com

Printed in the United States of America
First Edition
2   4   6   8   9   7   5   3   1

CONTENTS

INTRODUCTION

Assembling an anthology is something like solving a puzzle, except that crosswords and jigsaws have predetermined correct solutions. Anthologies can only have ideal solutions, which are impossible to achieve since they depend on so many circumstances, beginning with the taste and judgment of the anthologizer: One man's ideal anthology is another man's mess.

This anthology is no more ideal than any other. It began with certain imposed (by me) limits, given the basic limitation of length—not that you could call it short. To help keep the length down I decided not to consider previously untranslated material, and because my aim was that everything here make sense to, and interest, the general reader, I haven't included the academic historical literature, treatises on technique, or writing on matters outside the range of today's dance-goers. The nineteenth century is represented by subjects we're all familiar with—*Giselle*, *The Sleeping Beauty*, *Swan Lake*; Bournonville and Petipa. The twentieth century focuses to a large extent on the achievements and personalities that dominated it—from Pavlova and Nijinsky and Diaghilev to Isadora Duncan and Martha Graham, from Ashton and Balanchine to Merce Cunningham and Paul Taylor and Twyla Tharp, from Fonteyn and Farrell and Gelsey Kirkland ("the Judy Garland of ballet") to Nureyev and Baryshnikov and Astaire—as well as the critical and repertorial voices, past and present, that carry the most conviction. There's also a modest smorgasbord of obscure, even eccentric, choices.

Anthologies pursue two goals that don't always coincide: They try to put forward the best possible writing, and they try to be inclusive. But some subjects have evoked almost too much valuable response, while others have required compromise if they were to be touched on at all—which is why books like this are almost by definition both unbalanced and uneven. On the other hand, pieces that may mean nothing to one reader may be the favorites of another. Obviously, I see virtue in every item I've included, or I wouldn't have included it.

The most noticeable imbalance is evident in the extent of material that touches on George Balanchine. This is partly a result of my belief that he is the most significant figure in the history of ballet. It's also a reflection of the vast range of writings about him, not only by his two finest critics, Edwin Denby and Arlene Croce, but also by the many other first-rate minds that have been inspired by him. In addition, he's been written about by countless dancers, musicians, associates, wives, and friends, and he's brought out the best in them. With Balanchine, there was no need to sacrifice quality for the sake of inclusivity.

In structuring this immense sampling of the dance literature, I've tried to help the reader along by arranging its two hundred–plus entries into coherent groups. Apart from the sections on major personalities and important critics, there are sections devoted to interviews (Tamara Toumanova, Antoinette Sibley, Mark Morris); profiles (Lincoln Kirstein, Bob Fosse, Olga Spessivtseva); teachers; accounts of the birth of important works from *Petrouchka* to *Apollo* to *Push Comes to Shove*; the movies (from Arlene Croce and Alastair Macaulay on Fred Astaire to director Michael Powell on the making of *The Red Shoes*). Here are the voices of Cecil Beaton and Irene Castle, Ninette de Valois and Bronislava Nijinska, Maya Plisetskaya and Allegra Kent, Serge Lifar and José Limón, Alicia Markova and Natalia Makarova, Ruth St. Denis and Michel Fokine, Susan Sontag and Jean Renoir. Plus a group of obscure, even eccentric, extras, including an account of Pavlova going shopping in London and recipes from Tanquil LeClercq's cookbook.

The assembling of *Reading Dance* has taken almost ten years of reading and rereading, structuring and restructuring—and soliciting and receiving the help of dozens of colleagues in the dance world. Joan Acocella not only opened up her library to me, generously lending me dozens of books and journals, but at a late stage she gave up many hours to go over the table of contents with me. Alastair Macaulay also spent half a day with me going through his dance library in London before he moved to New York to become the dance critic for *The New York Times*. Mindy Aloff was exceptionally ready with useful and perceptive suggestions, including the idea of inviting Christopher Caines to write about *Lilac Garden*. Tobi Tobias performed an invaluable service by entrusting to me the large portfolios in which she had preserved Nancy Goldner's remarkable and unfairly uncollected reviews.

Clive and Valerie Barnes, Holly Brubach, Mary Clarke, Robert Cornfield, Clement Crisp, Lynn Garafola, Leslie Getz, Robert Greskovic, Barbara Horgan, Julie Kavanagh, Keith Money, Claudia Roth Pierpont, Nancy Reynolds, Ellen Sorrin, David Vaughan—they all responded promptly to cries for help or comfort. Others helped simply by making available to me hard-to-find examples of their own work. Some of the contents of the book I already knew well, not only from a lifetime of reading about dance but also because I edited at Knopf at least fifteen of the books excerpted here. And two of the pieces (plus an interview) I knew particularly well since I wrote them myself; I included them on the principle, perhaps deluded, that they perform a useful service. I need to thank Chip McGrath, who commissioned my piece on Isadora Duncan for *The New York Times Book Review*; Barbara Epstein and Robert Silvers of *The New York Review of Books*, which printed my piece on Margot Fonteyn; and Ingrid Sischy of *Interview* magazine, who commissioned my interview with Allegra Kent.

The table of contents essentially constitutes my bibliography, but I want to draw the attention of readers to two essential collections that every dance-lover should own. One is the collected writings of Edwin Denby, edited by Robert Cornfield. The other, also edited by Cornfield, is Arlene Croce's *Writing in the Dark, Dancing in* The New Yorker. Fortunately, that book is in print, so I was able to supplement it by choosing important writings of hers that don't appear in it.

Another great service Arlene Croce performed for the world of dance was founding the journal *Ballet Review* in 1965. Much of the most important dance writing of our time would not have found its way to us without this initiative. Robert Cornfield and then Francis Mason followed her as the *Review*'s editor (Mason still serves in that capacity).

As anyone in the dance field can testify, a book like this could not exist without the cooperation of the Jerome Robbins Dance Division of the New York Public Library for the Performing Arts at Lincoln Center. Time and again, the staff, from top to bottom, came through—as they always do.

Finally, my gratitude to all my colleagues at Pantheon, most crucially to Altie Karper, the managing editor, with whom I've worked so happily for so many years, and who indulges me; to Meghan Wilson, the production editor; and to Kristen Bearse, the text designer. Warm, affectionate thanks to Diana Coglianese and Alena Graedon, my assistants during the long early stages of the book. And to their successor, Sarah Rothbard: Thank you for so consistently, capably, and good-naturedly going well beyond the call of duty.

ABOUT THE CONTRIBUTORS

JOAN ACOCELLA is a staff writer for *The New Yorker,* where she reviews dance and books. Her own books include *Mark Morris,* a critical biography of the choreographer; *Willa Cather and the Politics of Criticism*; and *Creating Hysteria: Women and Multiple Personality Disorder.* She also edited the first unexpurgated English edition of *The Diary of Vaslav Nijinsky.* With the publication of her collection of essays *Twenty-eight Artists and Two Saints* in 2007, she received the American Academy of Arts and Letters Award in Literature.

MINDY ALOFF is the editor of *Dance Anecdotes* and the author of *Hippo in a Tutu: Dancing in Disney Animation,* a study of the dance sources of historic Disney animated films. She teaches dance criticism and essay writing at Barnard College and serves as a consultant for The George Balanchine Foundation.

PETER ANASTOS'S original claim to fame was as the founding director and choreographer of the all-male Les Ballets Trockedero de Monte Carlo (The Trocks), for which he danced under his nom de danse, Olga Tchikaboumskaya. (His two best-known pieces for The Trocks were a Balanchine parody, *Go for Barocco,* and a Jerome Robbins parody, *Yes, Virginia, Another Piano Ballet.*) With Mikhail Baryshnikov, he choreographed a *Cinderella* for American Ballet Theatre and produced a TV special called *Baryshnikov in Hollywood.* He is currently artistic director of Ballet Idaho.

Educated at Oxford, CLIVE BARNES quickly became one of England's most prolific and influential dance critics. In 1965, he moved to New York to be, first, dance critic and, later, theater critic as well for *The New York Times.* Since 1977 he has reviewed dance, theater, and opera for the *New York Post,* as well as writing extensively for *Dance Magazine*. He is also the author of numerous books on dance and theater.

For many decades a revered figure in the world of British ballet, CYRIL BEAUMONT (1891–1976) was a renowned bookseller, writer, and scholar. He was at various times the editor of *Dance Journal,* the dance critic for the *Sunday Times* of London, and the chairman of the Cecchetti Society. Among his more than forty books is the *Complete Book of Ballets,* originally published in 1937.

TONI BENTLEY danced with New York City Ballet for ten years. She is the author of five books, including *Winter Season: A Dancer's Journal; Holding On to the Air* (co-authored with Suzanne Farrell); *Costumes by Karinska; Sisters of Salome;* and *The Surrender: An Erotic Memoir.* She writes for numerous publications, including *The New York Times Book Review, The New York Review of Books,* and *The New Republic.* She is the recipient of a 2008 Guggenheim Fellowship.

CAROLYN BROWN was for twenty years Merce Cunningham's leading female dancer and continues to work with the Cunningham company as an artistic consultant. She has been awarded the *Dance Magazine* award, five National Endowment for the Arts grants, and a John Simon Guggenheim Memorial Foundation Fellowship. Her writing has been published in *The New York Times, Dance Perspectives, Ballet Review,* and the *Dance Research Journal,* and in 2007 she published her widely praised memoir *Chance and Circumstance: Twenty Years with Cage and Cunningham.*

HOLLY BRUBACH began writing about dance when a knee injury put an end to her career as a performer. Her criticism has appeared in *Ballet Review, Ballet News, Vogue,* and *The Atlantic* (for which three of her pieces about dance won the National Magazine Award in Essays and Criticism in 1982). She is the author, with Alexandra Danilova, of *Choura: The Memoirs of Alexandra Danilova,* which in 1986 won the de la Torre Bueno Prize for the year's best book about dance. She has also written about dance for more than twenty television programs in the *Dance in America* series.

RICHARD BUCKLE (1916–2001) was one of England's cleverest and most provocative dance critics. He was the founder of the highly influential magazine *Ballet* and was for many years the dance critic for the *The Observer* and *The Sunday Times* of London. Among his books are two volumes of memoirs, *Adventures of a Ballet Critic,* and large-scale biographies of Diaghilev, Nijinsky, and (with John Taras) George Balanchine.

CHRISTOPHER CAINES is a choreographer and the artistic director of the Christopher Caines Dance Company, founded in 2000. He worked on the Balanchine Foundation's "Popular Balanchine" project, and his essays have appeared in the *International Encyclopedia of Dance,* for which he also served as assistant project editor; the *International Dictionary of Modern Dance;* the *American National Biography; The Village Voice;* and the *Movement Research Performance Journal.* He was a 2006 Guggenheim Foundation Fellow in Choreography.

ALAN CARTER joined the Vic-Wells Ballet in 1937, where he created a principal role in Frederick Ashton's *Harlequin in the Street.* In 1946 he choreographed his first ballet for Sadler's Wells, *The Catch,* and began a career as a painter, creating works based on dance steps and movement. He danced in the films *The Red Shoes, The Tales of Hoffmann,* and *Invitation to the Dance* and was director of several companies, including the St. James Ballet, London's Empire Theatre Ballet, the Munich Ballet, and the Wuppertal, Bordeaux, Helsinki, and Icelandic ballets.

The doyenne of British dance writing, MARY CLARKE is the author of the first detailed history of the Sadler's Wells Ballet and *Dancers of Mercury,* a similar work on Ballet Rambert and its founder. From 1977 to 1994 she was the dance critic for *The Guardian,* and from 1963 to 2008 she served as editor of *The Dancing Times,* England's most influential dance publication. (She remains a contributor and editor emerita there.) Clarke has written and contributed to many books, including *The Encyclopedia of Dance and Ballet* (with David Vaughan), and (with Clement Crisp) *The Ballet Goer's Guide* and *Ballet: An Illustrated History.*

A. V. COTON (1906–1969), a prominent English critic, was born Edward Haddakin. In 1935, while serving in the Metropolitan Police, he began writing ballet reviews. For fifteen years he was dance critic of *The Daily Telegraph,* and was active in organizing and managing several dance companies, including Antony Tudor's London Ballet.

Oxford-educated CLEMENT CRISP became ballet critic of *The Spectator* in 1966, and since 1970 he has been dance critic of the *Financial Times* (London), as well as the author of many well-regarded books. He is known for his enthusiasm—and his caustic outspokenness.

ARLENE CROCE, founding editor of *Ballet Review* magazine and, for twenty-five years, dance critic of *The New Yorker,* is the author of *The Fred*

Astaire & Ginger Rogers Book, Afterimages, Going to the Dance, Sight Lines, and *Writing in the Dark, Dancing in* The New Yorker.

NANCY DALVA has written about dance for numerous publications, including *The New Yorker, The Atlantic,* and *The New York Times,* and has broadcast theater and dance criticism for WNYC-FM. She is the director of the webcast series *Mondays with Merce* for the Cunningham Dance Foundation and writes "Letter from New York" for the online magazine danceviewtimes.

DAVID DANIEL (1942–2000) studied to be a concert pianist before beginning his distinguished career as an arts journalist. He wrote essays, reviews, and feature stories, as well as conducted interviews, for *The New York Times, The New Yorker, Vogue, Vanity Fair, Town & Country,* and numerous other periodicals. He also wrote the script for the 1995 documentary *Van Cliburn: Concert Pianist,* and was a much-admired photographer of ballet and opera stars.

RENÉE E. D'AOUST trained at the Martha Graham Center of Contemporary Dance and performed with the Kevin Wynn Collection, at The Yard, and with other companies. She subsequently graduated from Columbia University (BA) and the University of Notre Dame (MFA). "Graham Crackers" is a chapter from her book *Body of a Dancer.*

The great dance critic EDWIN DENBY was born in China in 1903 and died on Long Island in 1983. Profound, sensitive, and pleasing to read, his work was universally respected. Perhaps his deepest interest was reserved for Balanchine, Graham, and the dancers Danilova and Markova. He was also much admired for his poetry, and his modesty and gentleness drew the affection of everyone who knew him.

ANTON DOLIN (1904–1983) was born Sydney Francis Patrick Chippendal Healey-Kaye, but was universally known as Pat. He trained with Serafima Astafieva and Bronislava Nijinska, and in 1921 joined Diaghilev's Ballets Russes, in which his best-known role was as the lead in Nijinska's *Le Train Bleu.* His world-famous partnership with Alicia Markova saw them performing together in various companies, including the Vic-Wells, the Markova-Dolin Ballet, Festival Ballet, and American Ballet Theatre. His best-known work of choreography was his reconstruction of Jules Perrot's *Pas de Quatre.*

ANITA FINKEL (1950–1997) wrote about dance for *Ballet News* (where she was also an editor) and *Dance International, Stage Bill, GEO,* and *Connoisseur.*

In 1988, she founded *New Dance Review,* which she published until 1995. She was a contributor to Oxford University Press's *International Encyclopedia of Dance,* which she also helped to edit.

Best known as Genêt, her pen name through the fifty years she wrote for *The New Yorker* (beginning in its first year, 1925), JANET FLANNER (1892–1978) is considered one of the finest journalists of her time. As the magazine's Paris correspondent, she in essence brought sophisticated Europe to America both before and after the war. Her two essential books: *Paris Was Yesterday, 1925–1939,* and *Paris Journal, 1944–1955.*

One of Canada's leading journalists—a critic, columnist, reporter, and editor—JOHN FRASER played a crucial role in helping Mikhail Baryshnikov defect in Toronto in 1974. He has been the editor of *Saturday Night* magazine and the chair of the Canadian Journalism Foundation, and is the current master of Massey College. He wrote the text for *Private View: Inside Baryshnikov's American Ballet Theatre.*

LYNN GARAFOLA, a dance historian and critic, is the author of *Diaghilev's Ballets Russes* and *Legacies of Twentieth-Century Dance* and the editor of many books, including *André Levinson on Dance: Writings from Paris in the Twenties* (with Joan Acocella); *The Diaries of Marius Petipa; Rethinking the Sylph: New Perspectives on the Romantic Ballet; José Limón: An Unfinished Memoir;* and *The Ballets Russes and Its World.* She is the former editor of the series *Studies in Dance History* and a senior editor of *Dance Magazine.* She teaches at Barnard College/Columbia University.

ARTHUR GOLD (1917–1990) and ROBERT FIZDALE (1920–1995) were life-long companions as well as being one of the leading two-piano ensembles of their day. They were indefatigable musicians, travelers, cooks, and social figures, as well as the authors of biographies of Misia Sert and Sarah Bernhardt, and the invaluable *Gold and Fizdale Cookbook,* dedicated to their friend George Balanchine.

NANCY GOLDNER is a former dance critic for *The Christian Science Monitor, The Nation, The Philadelphia Inquirer,* and *Dance News.* She is the author of *The Story of Coppélia* (with Lincoln Kirstein), *The Stravinsky Festival of the New York City Ballet,* and, most recently, *Balanchine Variations.*

The editor of this volume, ROBERT GOTTLIEB, has been editor in chief of Simon and Schuster, Alfred A. Knopf, and *The New Yorker.* In recent years he has written extensively for *The New York Review of Books, The New Yorker, The*

New York Times Book Review, and *The New York Observer,* whose dance critic he has been since 1999. He is the author of *George Balanchine: The Dance Maker* and the editor of *Reading Jazz* and *Reading Lyrics* (with Robert Kimball).

HARRIS GREEN was fortunate to have arrived in New York in the fall of 1957, in time to see Margot Fonteyn in the Royal Ballet's *The Sleeping Beauty* at the old Metropolitan Opera House. While writing about theater and music for *The New York Times, Commonweal,* and *The New Leader,* he has also covered dance for *The Times, The New Republic, Ballet Review, Pointe,* and *Dance Magazine,* for which he was features editor from 1994 to 2000.

ROBERT GRESKOVIC covers dance for *The Wall Street Journal.* He is the author of *Ballet 101: The Complete Guide to Learning and Loving the Ballet,* associate at *Ballet Review,* consulting editor for *DanceView,* as well as a moderator of the Videos and Ballet History topics on the website Ballet Talk. He is New York correspondent for *Dance International,* dance essayist for *Britannica Book of the Year,* and a New York correspondent for *Dance Magazine Shinshokan* (Japan) and *Ballettanz.*

In the 1960s, ALMA GUILLERMOPRIETO took class regularly with members of the Martha Graham company, and with Graham herself. She also studied with Murray Louis and Alwin Nikolais at the Henry Street Settlement Playhouse. Between 1969 and 1972, she participated in several dance events staged by Twyla Tharp. A longtime student of Merce Cunningham, at his suggestion she taught dance at the National Art Schools in Cuba. In 1978 Guillermoprieto embarked on a journalism career, writing primarily for *The New Yorker* and *The New York Review of Books.*

B. H. (BERNARD) HAGGIN (1900–1987) was one of the most trenchant and influential of American music critics as well as a penetrating observer of ballet. Two of his heroes, with whom he was on close terms, were Toscanini and Balanchine. His two books on ballet are *Ballet Chronicle* (1970) and *Discovering Balanchine* (1983).

DALE HARRIS (1929–1996) was the dance critic of *The Wall Street Journal,* a music critic of the *New York Post,* and a frequent contributor to *Opera News, Opera Canada, The Guardian,* and to many other magazines and journals. He was best known, perhaps, for his brilliant lectures at the Metropolitan Museum of Art.

ARNOLD HASKELL (1903–1980) was the great popularizer of ballet in the interwar years, his 1934 book, *Balletomania: The Story of an Obsession,* probably the most successful of all books on ballet. He was one of the founders of the Camargo Society, in 1930, helping to change the history of dance in England, and was the first governor of the Sadler's Wells Ballet School, starting in 1947.

The leading American impresario of the twentieth century, SOL HUROK (1888–1974) arrived in America from the Ukraine at the age of eighteen. Both amiable and formidable, he won the confidence of the myriad performing artists whom he managed. The range of personalities he worked with included Isadora Duncan, Anna Pavlova, Feodor Chaliapin, Mary Wigman, Arthur Rubinstein, Marian Anderson, Isaac Stern, and Van Cliburn. And the organizations he imported or toured included the rival Ballets Russes companies, the Bolshoi, the Moiseyev, the Old Vic, and the Royal Ballet. His first memoir, *Impresario,* was made into the 1953 movie *Tonight We Sing,* with David Wayne as Hurok, Ezio Pinza as Chaliapin, and Tamara Toumanova as Pavlova.

As a columnist, essayist, and author, JILL JOHNSTON has championed the avant-garde and has been a radical feminist thinker and a pioneer in a personal style of nonfiction that helped reshape journalism. She has contributed to *The Village Voice, ARTnews,* and *The New York Times Book Review.* Since 1985, she has been a masthead contributor to *Art in America.* Her books include *Marmalade Me; Gullibles Travels; Mother Bound; Paper Daughter; Secret Lives in Art; At Sea on Land: Extreme Politics; Jasper Johns: Privileged Information; England's Child: The Carillon and the Casting of Big Bells.* Currently, she writes a syndicated web column.

DEBORAH JOWITT has written about dance for *The Village Voice* since 1967. She has published two collections: *Dance Beat: Selected Views and Reviews, 1967–1976* and *The Dance in Mind: Profiles and Reviews, 1976–1983.* Her *Time and the Dancing Image* won the de la Torre Bueno Prize for 1988. She edited *Meredith Monk.* Her *Jerome Robbins: His Life, His Theater, His Dance* was published in 2004. She lectures and conducts workshops worldwide, and teaches in the Dance Department of New York University's Tisch School of the Arts.

JULIE KAVANAGH trained as a dancer at the Royal Ballet School, and is the author of *Secret Muses: The Life of Frederick Ashton,* which won the de la Torre Bueno Prize, and *Nureyev: The Life,* shortlisted for the UK's 2007 Costa Biography Award. She has worked as dance critic of *The Spectator;* arts editor of *Harper's and Queen;* and London editor of *Women's Wear Daily, W, Vanity Fair,* and *The New Yorker.* She is married to ex–Royal Ballet dancer, now dance filmmaker, Ross MacGibbon.

ELIZABETH KENDALL is a dance and culture critic and author of *Where She Danced: The Birth of American Art-Dance, The Runaway Bride, Hollywood Romantic Comedy of the 1930s,* and two memoirs, *American Daughter* and *Autobiography of a Wardrobe.* She is working on a book about George Balanchine, Lida Ivanova, and ballet and revolution in Petersburg/Petrograd, Russia, 1904–24. She is currently an associate professor at Eugene Lang College of The New School; she also teaches at Sarah Lawrence College and has taught at Princeton, Columbia, Bard College, and Smolny College in Russia. She has written for many publications and worked on television documentaries.

Growing up in Cedar Rapids, Iowa, ROSANNE KLASS had a few weeks of tap lessons at age three and brief instruction in the fox-trot in her teens. At the University of Wisconsin she saw performances of modern dance and by Ballet Theatre. Coming to New York as an aspiring writer, she discovered the New York City Ballet. This constituted her background in dance when she conceived an idea for a ballet and called up George Balanchine. Her first book, *Land of the High Flags: Afghanistan When the Going Was Good,* published in 1964, has been recently reissued.

W. MCNEIL "MAC" LOWRY (1913–1993) was a major force in America's performing arts world through most of his life. For many years, beginning in 1957, he was director of arts and humanities for the Ford Foundation, making in 1963 a $7.7 million grant to a total of eight dance institutions, with by far the lion's share going to New York City Ballet and the School of American Ballet. Also in 1963, he won a special Tony Award for his support of the American theater. He was a journalist, editor, and writer for many publications, including *The New Yorker.*

ALASTAIR MACAULAY was chief theater critic of the *Financial Times* in London for more than thirteen years before becoming chief dance critic of *The New York Times* in 2007. In 1983, he was founding editor of the British quarterly *Dance Theatre Journal*; in 1988 and 1992, he served as guest dance critic to *The New Yorker.* His short biography of Margot Fonteyn was published in 1998; his book of intensive interviews with the choreographer Matthew Bourne was published in 2001.

Known to everyone as "Bill," P. W. MANCHESTER (1907–1998), born Phyllis Winifred in London, began her career as a dance writer in 1941, and in 1946 founded the periodical *Dance News.* She had already produced, in 1942, a successful book called *Vic-Wells: A Ballet Progress.* Leaving England for America, she joined Anatole Chujoy as associate editor of his *Dance News,* and co-editor of his *Dance Encyclopedia*. For twenty-eight years she taught dance history in Cincinnati.

FRANCIS MASON, editor of *Ballet Review* and dance critic for WQXR-FM radio since 1979, wrote with George Balanchine *101 Stories of the Great Ballets* and three editions of *Balanchine's Complete Stories of the Great Ballets*. In 1991 he edited *I Remember Balanchine: Recollections of the Ballet Master by Those Who Knew Him*. He was for a number of years Assistant Director of the Morgan Library in New York and was for many years chairman of the Martha Graham Company.

DON MCDONAGH, a dance critic for *The New York Times* from 1967 to 1977, has contributed reviews and feature articles on dance to *The Observer* and the *Financial Times* (London), and is the author of numerous articles in *Ballet Review, Dance and Dancers, Dance Magazine,* and *Les Saisons de la Danse*. His books include *The Rise and Fall and Rise of Modern Dance* (1970); *Martha Graham: A Biography* (1973); *The Complete Guide to Modern Dance* (1976); *How to Enjoy Ballet* (1978); and *George Balanchine* (1983).

KEITH MONEY began writing magazine articles (on equestrian sports) when he was just sixteen and still at college in New Zealand. His first book was published in 1960, and his first one-man show of paintings was in London's West End in 1961, when he was just twenty-five. With a continuous tripartite career in writing, painting, and photography, he has had a huge output in all these disciplines. A strong interest in theater resulted in eight coffee-table books concerning dance, including definitive assessments of the careers of Anna Pavlova and Margot Fonteyn.

DR. LIUBOV MYASNIKOVA is a senior scientist specializing in solid state physics at St. Petersburg's Ioffe Physical-Technical Institute of the Russian Academy of Sciences. She and her twin brother, Leonid, both a year younger than Nureyev, were close friends of the dancer's from 1958, when he was a student at the Vaganova Academy, until his defection in 1961. The three were briefly reunited twenty-eight years later, when he passed through Moscow on his way to visit his dying mother in his hometown of Ufa. As he was dying, Myasnikova traveled to Europe to help take care of him, spending more than a week by his hospital bedside.

BARBARA NEWMAN is a critic, essayist, and the author of eight books. She published *Striking a Balance*, her initial collection of interviews with distinguished dancers, when she was an associate critic for *Dance Magazine,* in New York. Her subsequent books include *Grace Under Pressure: Passing Dance*

Through Time and *The Illustrated Book of Ballet Stories,* a triple award-winner that has been translated into eight languages. Now living in London, she is the dance critic for *Country Life* magazine, reports on musical theater for *The Dancing Times,* and contributes regularly to the Voice of Dance website. She is currently preparing a sequel to *Striking a Balance.*

The exotically beautiful SONO OSATO was born in Omaha to a Japanese father and French-Canadian mother. She studied with Adolph Bolm, and was accepted into the Ballets Russes de Monte Carlo by Colonel de Basil at the age of fourteen. In 1940 she joined the new Ballet Theatre, and again danced many leading roles. Her career in the theater was spectacular: she was the lead dancer on Broadway for Agnes de Mille in *One Touch of Venus* and for Jerome Robbins in *On the Town* (as Miss Turnstiles). She also appeared to acclaim in the somewhat experimental *Ballet Ballads.*

A figure of immense authority, H. T. PARKER (1867–1934), theater critic of the *Boston Evening Transcript,* also wrote about dance with an understanding of the art unique in America in his time. His dance criticism has fortunately been collected in an invaluable volume, *Motion Arrested: Dance Reviews of H. T. Parker,* edited by Olive Holmes.

CLAUDIA ROTH PIERPONT is a staff writer for *The New Yorker,* where she has written about subjects ranging from Nietzsche to Mae West. A collection of her essays, *Passionate Minds: Women Rewriting the World,* published in 2000, was nominated for a National Book Critics Circle Award. She began her career writing about dance and published her first articles in *Ballet Review.*

STANLEY RABINOWITZ is Henry Steele Commager Professor and Professor of Russian at Amherst College, where he also directs the Amherst Center for Russian Culture. A specialist on nineteenth- and twentieth-century Russian prose fiction, he has recently devoted his energies to presenting the ballet writings of Akim Volynsky to an English-speaking audience; his volume of Volynsky's writings, *Ballet's Magic Kingdom: Selected Writings on Dance in Russia, 1911–1925,* has just been published.

NANCY REYNOLDS, a former dancer with the New York City Ballet, has been director of research for The George Balanchine Foundation since 1994. She conceived and continues to direct the foundation's video archives program. Her books include *Repertory in Review: 40 Years of the New York City Ballet,* *The Dance Catalog, In Performance: A Companion to the Classics of the Dance,* and (with Malcolm McCormick) *No Fixed Points: Dance in the Twentieth Century.*

MARCIA B. SIEGEL is an internationally known dance critic, historian, and lecturer. She is the author of *Howling Near Heaven: Twyla Tharp and the Reinvention of Modern Dance*; *The Shapes of Change: Images of American Dance*; *Days on Earth: The Dance of Doris Humphrey;* and three collections of reviews and commentary. A founding member of the Dance Critics Association, Siegel has written for newspapers, periodicals, and reference works. She is the dance critic of *The Hudson Review* and *The Boston Phoenix*.

SUSAN SONTAG (1933–2004) was possibly America's best known and most influential intellectual figure in the latter half of the twentieth century. Novelist, critic, essayist, theorist, and political activist, she enjoyed a wide range of interests, including avant-garde literature and theater, photography, and dance.

TERRY TEACHOUT is the drama critic of *The Wall Street Journal*, the music critic of *Commentary*, and the author of "Sightings," a biweekly column about the arts in America for the Saturday *Wall Street Journal*. He also writes about the arts on his blog About Last Night (www.terryteachout.com). His most recent books are *All in the Dances: A Brief Life of George Balanchine*; *A Terry Teachout Reader*; and *The Skeptic: A Life of H. L. Mencken*. He is finishing *Rhythm Man: A Life of Louis Armstrong* and the libretto to *The Letter*, Paul Moravec's operatic version of W. Somerset Maugham's play.

WALTER TERRY (1913–1982) was the popular and prolific dance critic of the *New York Herald Tribune* from 1939 to 1966 (with a wartime break, during which he was replaced by Edwin Denby). Later, he wrote (until his death) for *The Saturday Review*. He also wrote twenty-two books, including a fat and fascinating collection of his newspaper columns, *I Was There*.

TOBI TOBIAS is the New York dance critic for Bloomberg News. Much of her work has appeared in *Dance Magazine* (where she also edited the criticism for nearly a decade) and in *New York* magazine (where she served as dance critic for twenty-two years). In 1992, she was awarded a Danish knighthood in recognition of her extensive writing and her oral history project on the Royal Danish Ballet and its Bournonville tradition. In the course of a parallel career in writing for children, she has published more than two dozen books. For adults she has written *Obsessed by Dress,* a meditation on clothes.

CARL VAN VECHTEN (1880–1964), born in Cedar Rapids, Iowa, became a major cultural figure in New York as a critic, novelist, and photographer, and a propagandist for the Harlem Renaissance. In 1909, among the first American dance critics, he began writing reviews for *The New York Times*.

The best known of his novels were *The Tattooed Countess* and *Nigger Heaven*. His friendship with Gertrude Stein led to his being named her literary executor.

DAVID VAUGHAN has danced, sung, acted, and choreographed in London and Paris; on and off Broadway; in American regional theaters; in film and television; in ballet and modern dance companies; and in cabaret. He is the archivist of the Merce Cunningham Dance Company and the author of *Merce Cunningham: Fifty Years* and of *Frederick Ashton and His Ballets*. He was a member of the editorial board of the *International Encyclopedia of Dance*. In 2001 he received a New York Dance and Performance Award ("Bessie") for sustained achievement.

JAMES WARING (1922–1975) was a leader of the avant-garde in dance during the 1950s and 1960s, influencing not only choreographers of the postmodern movement, many of whom danced in his company, but also the painters and composers with whom he collaborated. From 1954 to 1969 his company presented such works as the evening-length *Dances Before the Wall, Poets' Vaudeville,* and *At the Hallelujah Gardens.* In later years he freelanced, choreographing for ballet and modern dance companies in the United States and abroad. He also contributed essays to *Ballet Review* and other journals.

LEIGH WITCHEL writes on dance for several publications, including *Ballet Review, Dance Now, DanceView, Pointe* magazine, and *Dance International.* He founded Dance as Ever, a chamber ballet company based in Manhattan, and has choreographed more than fifty ballets. He is the recipient of a Guggenheim Fellowship in Choreography.

FREDERICK ASHTON

 THE SCHOOL OF AMERICAN BALLET, INC.

LINCOLN E. KIRSTEIN, PRESIDENT & DIRECTOR
GEORGE BALANCHINE, CHAIRMAN OF FACULTY
EUGENIE OUROUSSOW, EXECUTIVE DIRECTOR
NATALIE MOLOSTWOFF, EXECUTIVE SECRETARY

February 26, 1960

Miss Mary Clarke
The Ballet Annual
4,5 and 6 Soho Square
London, W. 1
England

Dear Miss Clarke,

Thank you for your kind letter asking me to write a tribute to Frederick Ashton.

Freddy is my friend and knows very well that my English is not very hot. I think he would be terribly surprized if I managed to write 500 words in it!

I am sure he knows that I value his gifts and his achievements, and also how much I like him personally. I am certain that many beautiful things will be written about Freddy in the Ballet Annual with which I will agree, and I would like to be included among those who have joined in honoring him.

Yours sincerely,

George Balanchine

Sir Frederick Ashton, the greatest of English choreographers, was born in 1904 and died in 1988. Among his outstanding ballets are Façade, Les Rendezvous, Les Patineurs, Symphonic Variations, Scènes de ballet, Cinderella, Daphnis and Chloe, Sylvia, Ondine, La Fille mal gardée, The Two Pigeons, Marguerite and Armand, The Dream, Enigma Variations, *and* A Month in the Country. *Most of his career was spent with England's Royal Ballet (previously Sadler's Wells), of which he was director from 1963 to 1970 and where he worked in close collaboration with its founder, Ninette de Valois, and his leading muse, Margot Fonteyn. In 1962 he was knighted, and in 1971 he created the dances for the film* Tales of Beatrix Potter.

FREDERICK ASHTON
Notes on Choreography

With every new ballet that I produce I seek to empty myself of some plastic obsession and every ballet I do is, for me, the solving of a balletic problem.

But let me begin by explaining what I understand the function of the choreographer to be. First of all, he is to the ballet what a playwright is to a play; but whereas the playwright writes his play and generally hands it on to a producer who animates it for him and puts it on the stage, a choreographer does all this himself. Usually he is his own librettist also, so that in a sense the whole fount of the creation comes from him.

When I was younger I created ballets freely, spontaneously, and without much thought; the steps just flowed out of me and if they had any shape or form at all, generally it was because the music already had it, and not because I had consciously placed it there. Also, as befits the young, I wanted very much to please my audience and I thought it of great importance that I should entertain, amuse, and charm them. Now I don't think that way. Up to a point I don't care what the audience thinks, I work purely and selfishly for myself and only do ballets which please me and which I feel will both develop me as an artist and extend the idiom of the dance.

There are many different sources from which a ballet may spring to life. One can be affected by the paintings of a great master and wish to animate them; one may read a story which calls to be brought to life in movement; or one can hear a piece of music which somehow dances itself. And one can have strange ideas of one's own, or a theme may be suggested by some outside influence. In the course of my career I have responded to all these different forms of impetus.

As I said, one can be moved by the paintings of a great master and wish to animate them. This I have done in two or three of my own ballets, such as my very first which was *Leda and the Swan*. In this I was stirred by the paintings of Botticelli; I copied the postures and generally created, I think, the fresh springlike by morning of the world atmosphere of his paintings. I think this is a very good way for young choreographers to begin. Now that I am older I rather despise this form of creation, but it is certainly an absorbing way of working, for it necessitates the study of a whole period of painting and of manners, and this gives plastic richness and diversity to the pattern of the dance.

In my ballet *The Wise and Foolish Virgins*, which was arranged to the music of Bach, I went to eighteenth-century baroque but whereas previously in *Leda and the Swan* I had studied the paintings, in this ballet I not only studied baroque painting in general but also sculpture and architecture, and I tried to convey, with the bodies of the dancers, the swirling, rich, elaborate contortions of the baroque period. In this ballet no lines were spiral, everything was curved and interlacing, and the line of the dancers was broken and tormented, so to speak. That was a fascinating exercise for me.

As in the two ballets I have just described I studied the visual arts of painting, sculpture, and architecture, I would like now to tell you of another ballet I did, which was taken from a literary theme. This was called *The Quest*, and came out of the first book of Spenser's *Faerie Queen*, about the legend of Saint George, Una and the Dragon. It was an enormous canvas and I must say that I found it a struggle to give any idea in the ballet of the richness of Spenser's imagery, and quite frankly I don't think I really succeeded. The danger, in this kind of ballet, is that one comes upon situations which are purely literary and unballetic and are thus impossible to convey clearly to an audience without the use of words; for I personally do not like a ballet in which the audience has to spend three-quarters of the time with their noses in the program to try and find out what is happening on the stage. And I found it difficult, with allegorical characters, to convey clearly their humanity and to bring them to life on the stage as Spenser has brought them to life in his great poem. I personally am not fond of the literary ballet, because it seems to me that there comes a hiatus always in which one longs for the spoken word to clarify the subject. And these ballets seem to lead always more to miming than to dancing, thereby invading the functions of the drama or the cinema. In my balletic ideology it is the dancing which must be the foremost factor, for ballet is an expression of emotions and ideas through dancing, and not through words or too much gesture, though naturally these can play their part. But I am against the overlapping of one into the other, except in the case of intentional music dramas, when all the arts are welded into a whole.

This brings me to my third heading, which is taking one's lead directly from the music, and this is the method which I now prefer. Through it one gets the purity of the dance expressing nothing but itself, and thereby expressing a thousand degrees and facets of emotion, and the mystery of poetry of movement; leaving the audience to respond at will and to bring their own poetic reactions to the work before them. Just as the greatest music has no program, so I really believe the greatest ballets are the same, or at any rate have the merest thread of an idea which can be ignored, and on which the choreographer may weave his imagination for the combination of steps and patterns.

I consider that my own most successful ballets come under this category. The first ballet that I tried in this style was *Les Rendezvous* to the music of Auber. To this gay and sparkling music, and to the merest thread of an idea—it consists only of young people meeting and parting and meeting again—I wove, I think, a rich pattern of dancing which worked up to a climax, as did the music itself. And consciously, all through my career, I have been working to make the ballet independent of literary and pictorial motives, and to make it draw from the rich fount of classical ballet; for, to my way of thinking, all ballets that are not based on the classical ballet and do not create new dancing patterns and steps within its idiom are, as it were, only tributaries of the main stream.

Please don't misunderstand me and think that, by saying this, I mean there are not great ballets which are literary and pictorial. What I do mean to say is that they are isolated examples, and that if this line is pursued too strongly it will bring about the decadence of the dance. If the ballet is to survive, it must survive through its dancing qualities, just as drama must survive through the richness of the spoken word. In a Shakespearean play it is the richness of the language and the poetry that are paramount; the story is unimportant. And it is the same with all the greatest music, and dancing and ballets. In a ballet it is the dance that *must* be paramount.

—from *The Dance Has Many Faces,* edited by Walter Sorrell, 1951

CLIVE BARNES

Frederick Ashton and His Ballets

Perhaps the touchstone of choreography is its emotional expressiveness, and in all of Ashton's work his dances are particularly sensitive to overtones of feeling. The adolescent yearnings of *Valses Nobles et Sentimentales,* which shows, or rather hints at, the criss-cross of human relationships caught at the distilled abstraction of some strange ball, are revealed through the style of the actual choreography, with its languid arm movements contrasted with its impetuous entries. Even in such a slight work as *Les Patineurs,* Ashton, while partly concerned with the technical task of simulating ice-skating with ballet dancers, never fails to make the actual dancing emotionally expressive, and is constantly alive to the ballet's atmosphere. The perky choreography of the Blue Boy's solo, full of over-exuberant swank, the gracefully Victorian love of the White Skaters (he is all gallantry; she, all swoons) and the way in which all the dancing manages with its briskness to suggest the crispness of a winter morning, helps to give *Les Patineurs* a quality deeper than the thin ice of its surface charms, enabling it to bear the weight of any number of repetitions. This vigilance towards style and atmosphere is fundamentally a matter of craftsmanship, and naturally it is something which Ashton shares with all good choreographers. Even so it seems pertinent to insist that Ashton is an unusually fine craftsman, a quality that may perhaps be dissociated from his artistry. Thus while many choreographers can impose a generally coherent basic movement style upon a ballet, Ashton carries this quality to extreme lengths.

Sometimes he will slightly modify his whole mode of choreographic expression for an individual ballet. The glaringly obvious example of this is to be found in the plastic style he uses for *Dante Sonata.* More moderate, and more typical, is his procedure in *Ondine,* where for much of the ballet he adopts a peculiarly flowing type of choreography (based, he once claimed, on the movement of water), which gives the whole work a highly individual flavor. *Birthday Offering* he carried out in a style that suggested throughout, or perhaps "evoked" would be the better word, the Maryinsky ballet at the turn of the century, giving the work a sense of the Glazounov period, just as in *Sylvia* he has, particularly in his groupings, caught something of the Second Empire ballet prints, without sacrificing the contemporary tone of his choreography.

In giving individuality to a ballet, Ashton uses a number of varying devices. Sometimes this is as simple as sustaining a particular mood, so that *La Fille mal gardée* takes much of its flavor from a consistent suggestion of the countryside with its rustic simplicity and humors. But before discussing atmosphere in Ashton ballets, mention might be made of another of his favorite tricks that can be seen in *La Fille mal gardée*—the use of *leitmotiv*. Here he utilizes tap dancing (admittedly in some rather unusual guises) and various kinds of ribbon dances to give the choreography a sense of continuity. *Leitmotiv* also appears in *Cinderella,* where for example, soubresaut retirés first appear in the Fairy Spring variation, are later taken up by all the Seasons, and then are finally given in the second act by the Prince's friends.

"Atmosphere" is one of those jargon words so useful to hard-pressed journalists, because in ballet criticism it implies more than it means. It is always difficult to define precisely what is meant by atmosphere in a ballet, but perhaps one could call it the sustained suggestion or evocation of a particular mood, a particular period and place, or even a particular cultural background. The keywords are "sustained" and "particular." Personally I have never been able to understand why some ballets (and not always good ballets at that) should have this quality of atmosphere, while others have not, and I imagine that this is one of those mysteries that audiences and critics very rarely do unravel. Obviously atmosphere comes from a whole complex of sources, some combination of all the various constituents that go to make up a ballet, and however difficult it is to define, it is remarkably easy to recognize, or at least sense.

Ashton has the gift of evoking atmosphere to a pronounced extent. Sometimes, as in the examples of *The Wise Virgins* and *Dante Sonata* quoted above, this is achieved by allowing his choreography to be consciously influenced by painting, but frequently the method (and the result) is more involved and subtle. When he wants to give a ballet a literary flavor, Ashton has the remarkable facility for imbuing a whole work with just the right atmosphere. Comparatively few of his ballets fall into this literary category, and even when they do his approach and method vary considerably.

In *Illuminations,* his task was to suggest the burning symbolism of Rimbaud, and he achieved this with a series of short, descriptive charades (each evocative of a poem) through which the Poet himself wandered almost as a connecting link. These brief episodes—short, sharp flashes of insight, seen with the inner eye—have the fantastic artificiality of a dream, and the twisted beauty of Rimbaud was allowed to emerge through a formalized structure. Here Ashton is catching the author's spirit by giving a choreographic impression, perhaps even impersonation, of the author's style. In *Madame Chrysanthème* Ashton was basing his ballet on a novel by Pierre Loti, and on this occasion he evoked the literary original by adopting the author's approach to his subject, so that just as the novel is a delicately sensitive picture of Japan seen through European eyes, so Ashton's choreography aimed at the same effect.

In these two instances Ashton's intention (*inter alia*) appears to have been to allude to specific literary styles, but on other occasions he has created ballets that are instinct with a whole period, or if you prefer, a cultural climate. *Le Rêve de Léonor* was a deplorable ballet (one of his few total losses), yet it did succeed in suggesting the thwarted, out-moded ethos of surrealism far more cogently than did Massine in his equally deplorable *Mad Tristan*. In the same way, without comparing in detail the actual ballets, I feel that Ashton's *Apparitions* was also more successful than Massine's *Symphonie Fantastique* in its approach to its Romantic background. The shades of Walpole and Beckford haunting the elaborate fancies of Strawberry Hill and Fonthill, are never far from Ashton's scene. The Byronic, drug-taking Poet represents a somewhat later stage in the Romantic agony than the trappings of the rest of the ballet (he and his *femme fatale* alone are pure Berlioz), but the orgy in the cavern, clearly inspired by the activities of Sir Francis Dashwood's Hell-fire Club, like the funeral cortège deriving from Lewis's novel *The Monk,* helped to give *Apparitions* an exciting authenticity and a curiously pungent historical flavor.

Having now stressed the diversity found in Ashton's ballets I am left with the more difficult job of describing their kinship one to another, for underneath all their differences there runs his individual and quite unmistakable basic, choreographic style. What is the fundamental nature of Ashton's choreography? Two words suggest themselves to me—"fluent" and "lyrical." Fluency is an immediate characteristic of Ashton's work. The steps have a flow, and enchaînement after enchaînement pours out with an unforced originality. Smooth and effortless, the best of his choreography has a compulsive air of inevitability about it, almost as if it has not been created but only discovered. It has a wonderful sense of ease and freedom. Yet although it is undoubtedly fluent, I think I prefer the word "lyrical" to describe its essential nature. This word, carrying its suggestions of song, poetry, and spontaneity, seems to me to sum up very neatly the feel of Ashton's choreography.

Another characteristic quality of Ashton's work is musicality. The question of a choreographer's musicality is a factual thing that does not permit a factual answer. The nearest we can get is to apply the somewhat lame rule that choreography is musical which does not jar with the music, a yardstick that everyone can quote but no one can demonstrate. The matter is also complicated by musicality's having two distinct parts, in the choreographer's approach to the score's structure and also to its spirit. Then again disagreement can arise even on the purely technical aspect of the physical relationship between dance and music. Should the choreography seek to mirror the music (perhaps even to the extent where Miss X is dancing the

first subject and Miss Y the second) or should it run over the music like
the vocal line in an opera? How far should dancing seek to echo orchestral
color and texture—could an arabesque be, say, E flat, or a fouetté represent
a trombone? Can a crescendo be matched by increasing the number of
dancers, so that each member of the corps de ballet has, as it were, a decibel
factor? I raise these possibly frivolous questions because it seems to me that
too many people describe a choreographer as musical without describing
what they regard as musicality. Although I have seen a great deal of musical
choreography, for various reasons the only twentieth-century choreographers I would actually describe as instinctively musical are Fokine, Graham,
Balanchine, Lavrovsky, Tudor, Robbins, and Ashton.

Ashton does not tie himself to the quivering quaver, and to my mind no
really musical choreographer does adopt this minimal approach. He uses the
music's rhythm as a sheet anchor for his choreographic variations, a point of
departure and a point of return. He has a very sensitive feel for the shape
of the music—for example at one point in *Daphnis and Chloe,* the ballerina
is supported by her partner who turns slowly in time with the music; as the
music increases in tempo his turns get faster and Chloe floats upwards
into the air, this upward movement seeming to parallel the increasing volume of the orchestra, so that Daphnis is suggesting the quickening rhythmic
climax, while Chloe suggests the slow crescendo of sound. This instinctive
musicality—such an effect is unlikely to have been consciously planned—
shows itself time and again in Ashton's work. In the apotheosis to *Scènes de
ballet,* where Stravinsky's massive harmonies rise up and up to an infinite
grandeur, Ashton produces a magnificent peroration with a series of huge
lifts across the stage, one girl after another swooping over, carried in a mon-
umentalized grand jeté, as the brass pounds out its statement. In the male
variation devised for Idzikowski in *Les Rendezvous,* the dancer has to open out
with a series of pas ciseux set so that the accent of the musical phrase comes
on the apex of the jump. In *Symphonic Variations* the relationship between
male and female dancing on the one hand, and orchestra and piano on the
other, is amazingly complex and satisfying, and his use of concertante movement here has a marvellous spontaneity.

Ashton's regard for the spirit of the music as well as its letter is remarkable, and can perhaps be instanced by the different coloring he places on
Maurice Ravel's superficially similar *Valses Nobles et Sentimentales* (the apotheosis of Franz Schubert) and *La Valse* (the apotheosis of Johann Strauss). *La
Valse* is a particularly interesting example, because here he claims to have
tried "to keep as closely as possible to the idea which Ravel himself outlined
so clearly." Unfortunately the "idea outlined so clearly" on the score was not
the complete story, for during the course of the music's composition Ravel,
without changing his program note, linked it in his mind with "the fantastic

whirl of destiny." Ashton, it seems, to judge by what he said at the time, choreographed *La Valse* as nothing more than a vast concert waltz, and deliberately turned aside from any "dancing on the edge of a volcano." But fortunately the score governed him, and despite his intentions the music took over, and Ravel's "whirl of destiny" was manifested through almost every bar of the choreography.

Musicality apart, there are certain physical quirks to Ashton's choreography (his admirers call them "his style," his opponents call them "his mannerisms") that would probably make it instantly recognizable. He possibly produces his most typical choreography in pas de deux—the dance form in which he has done his best work. Apart from the mood which his pas de deux almost invariably evoke (rapt and intimate) they also tend to bear certain choreographic trademarks in common. There is "air-walking," where the girl is carried by the man, usually at his side, while her pointed feet describe what might almost be called supported jetés just above the ground, which they never touch. Less noticeable but no less significant characteristics are the girl circling round the man, or the man lifting the girl up and placing her to one side of him. The formal or semi-formal pas de deux is the crown of Ashton's invention, but his whole choreography reveals a considerable emphasis on double-work, some of it occasionally allegro and very frequently making use of highly ingenious lifts. It is for his double-work that he usually reserves his choreographic coinages, and the rest of his style tends to aim at a clean-cut simplicity. Naturally he has his favorite steps, so that chainé turns are fairly common in his work, fouettés are very rare, while unsupported pirouettes are not often used. There is a conscious and loving emphasis on all sorts of arabesques. His female choreography shows a marked tendency to be far more classical and quite often more spectacular than his arrangements for male dancers.

It is typical of the neo-classical choreographers for great importance to be placed on floor patterns, and Ashton is no exception in this regard. He appears to be particularly anxious to avoid the two-dimensional, frieze effect sometimes to be found in expressionist choreography, and it may be that it is his effort to combat this (even when his ballets are seen front-on from the stalls) that prompts him to make great use of diagonal patterns, semi-circles, and indeed any arrangement that will open up the depth of the stage for an audience placed at stage-level. For all this his ballets are best seen from above. In many ways the best position to view Ashton and Balanchine at Covent Garden is from the gallery right at the top of the house— this partly explains the situation found when the New York City Ballet visited London in 1950 and 1952 when the stalls (including the stall-borne critics) remained fairly detached, while the gallery went almost berserk with enthusiasm.

The last element in Ashton's basic style can possibly be best summed up under the word "ritual." Perhaps it was the influence of his early days in Peru when he came under the spell of Catholic ceremonials, perhaps more simply it is merely an orderly Englishness in his temperament, but for whatever reason Ashton loves the ritualistic aspect of ballet. Not all, but many of his works include ritualistic movement with processions of dancers, stylized gestures, and the slow unfolding of movement. Not only is this taste one of the factors that have placed him among Petipa's heirs (the framework of the nineteenth-century grand manner, with its discreetly gorgeous formalities rounded off by an apotheosis, being much to his taste) but it also leads to the most common flaw in his architectonics. Sometimes his corps de ballet dances are altogether too symmetrical, a quality which at its worst (notably in *Tiresias*) can make his choreography seem cold and dull. As a by-product of these occasional bouts of awful symmetry, there is his tendency to demand too difficult a degree of synchronization from his dancers. The sequential cadences in *Scènes de ballet* are rarely correctly performed, while the amount of togetherness he expected from the cast in *Variations on a Theme of Purcell* has never been forthcoming.

There is still one important aspect of Ashton's work that so far I have only hinted at. There is about all his ballets a very determined and deliberate lack of emphasis. He appears to care comparatively little for immediate impact, and even his most bravura choreography is aimed at the lustre of pearls rather than the brilliance of diamonds. It is largely for this reason that Ashton's ballets are notoriously difficult to assess at one seeing. They usually grow on their audience, and often show more of their qualities at each repeated seeing. As at a first sight his ballets occasionally are bewilderingly difficult to catch hold of, they are almost always far more popular with the regular ballet audience than with the casual visitors, and this lack of total immediate appeal has, I think, accounted in the past for more than a few critical cold-shoulders.

Ashton can be said to have contributed everything and nothing to the growth and development of British ballet. Although with *A Tragedy of Fashion* he created what is universally recognized as British ballet's inaugural work, and ever since has been its most prolific and consistently successful creative artist, the idea of his having anything positive to do with its ever-growing organization and administration is almost unthinkable. Where he would have been without Marie Rambert and Ninette de Valois is an interesting but unfruitful conjecture, yet he can justly be considered as the principal designer of the structure they eventually built.

His influence runs throughout every performance of the Royal Ballet, and even to a lesser extent through the other branch of the national ballet, the Ballet Rambert. The whole way the British dance owes an incalculable amount to Ashton's taste, and it is their distinctive way of performing the nineteenth-century classics to dance them as if they were performing a ballet by Ashton. Also as he has now been the dominating creative force in British ballet for about thirty years, his influence on his younger contemporaries has been very considerable. Even when they have reacted strongly against his personal choreographic style, many of them still show a disconcerting habit of suddenly slipping into Ashton's idiom, or unwittingly betraying an Ashton influence.

The first significant British ballet critic, J. E. Crawford Flitch, writing in 1912, said with prophetic wisdom: "Probably the real reason why England has failed to produce a great school of ballet is principally owing to the absence of a *maître de ballet* of genius." It is, I think, Ashton's presence more than anything else that has now made possible the "great school of ballet" for which Crawford Flitch hankered.

—from *Ballet Perspectives,* 1961

MINDY ALOFF
Enigma Variations

The choreographer Frederick Ashton—one of the greatest ballet masters in history—was born in 1904, in Guayaquil, Ecuador, to a couple who were natives of England. Around the age of three, he moved with his family (including three older brothers and a younger sister) to Lima, Peru, where he stayed until going to boarding school in England at the age of fifteen. Ashton never returned to Lima, yet over the course of his long career in the theater (which began rather late, at age eighteen, with ballet classes from Léonide Massine) he retained indelible memories of the dazzlingly stylish women on Lima's boulevards, of the public religious processions, and of the melancholy songs of his half-Inca nurse, which—as Julie Kavanagh recounts in her new life of Ashton—he recalled into old age.

Ashton's off-stage life was, from childhood, sexually complex, emotionally turbulent, and socially ranging. Yet even as he became an increasingly jaded critic of individuals, he demonstrated an innocent's captivation with feminine beauty, with grand public ceremony, and with societal allure. His ballets founded one fairytale kingdom after another—sometimes obviously, in ballroom settings, sometimes indirectly, as in the happy barnyard and farmhouse of what may be his wittiest and most ebullient work, *La Fille mal gardée* (1960).

By the end of his life, Ashton was ensconced literally among royalty. Shortly before his death in 1988, he found himself performing "a sort of mock belly dance" with the eighty-eight-year-old Queen Mother at a party during a week-long visit to Sandringham. His ballets contain few kings and queens as such; but when Ashton chose to portray them wearing crowns, he did so seriously and with unshadowed appreciation. But then, as a choreographer and, later, as the director of the Royal Ballet, he was entrenched in issues of governance and autocratic power. One can hardly oversee the making of ballets, and certainly not the day-to-day continuity of an entire ballet company, without pondering issues of private passion and public obligation, or of how to keep a kingdom stable against threats from without or, more difficult, dissension within.

Like Balanchine, Ashton had to wrestle with certain brutal facts: ballet, which is only good when it is great (as Arlene Croce once put it), is necessarily a meritocracy. By virtue of its physical challenges, it demands young bodies, and by virtue of its musical and allusive complexities, it demands old wisdom. Also like Balanchine, Ashton looked back to Petipa and Ivanov as his models, which meant that he was committed to the ballerina as the centerpiece of classical power. This, despite the fact that when Ashton woke up in bed with someone, that someone was usually a man. Kavanagh recounts his life exhaustively. To have been able to construct fantasy kingdoms ruled over by women while in the throes of love affairs with men was one of Ashton's triumphs, attesting to the strength of his devotion to classical ballet's tradition and technique. As Jerome Robbins said of Balanchine, who was able more easily to bring his emotional impulses and his artistic impulses together by marrying his ballerinas. Ashton's most enduring marriage was to ballet itself.

Within that marriage, Ashton's luck among women was nothing short of sensational. At the age of twelve, he saw Anna Pavlova dance in *The Fairy Doll,* and for the rest of his life she served him as the mother of all muses, prompting even Margot Fonteyn to say that "I always felt that Fred was seeing Pavlova and that I wasn't living up to her by any means." (Pavlova also predicted his success as a choreographer.) Like Balanchine, he saw Isadora Duncan perform late into her career, but fate permitted Ashton to recognize what was great about her, and to draw on those qualities of musicality and headstrong emotion over the full course of his career. His own initial ambitions as a choreographer were fondly and fertilely encouraged by Marie Rambert, who commissioned ballets from him for the Ballet Club at the Mercury Theater; by Bronislava Nijinska, who took him on as her student of classical technique and her apprentice in choreography while he performed for the Ida Rubinstein company in Paris during the late 1920s, where Nijinska was the resident choreographer; by the designer Sophie Fedorovitch, his long-time soulmate and colleague; by Lydia Lopokova, a former ballerina with Diaghilev's Ballets Russes, who, with her husband John Maynard Keynes and a handful of other intellectuals, among them the blisteringly brilliant conductor Constant Lambert, sponsored Ashton's choreography for the Camargo Society; and by the American-born millionairess Alice von Hofmannsthal, who introduced him to international high society, fell in love with him and, for a time, was his lover.

Ashton's long, generally productive, but frequently barbed relationship with Ninette de Valois, the indomitable founder of what was to become known as The Royal Ballet, can also be looked on in a positive light, since his clashes with de Valois seem to have strengthened his own sense of what he wanted from ballet. Kavanagh doesn't exactly indict de Valois for Ashton's forced retirement as the Royal's director in 1970, a position that he had taken over from de Valois in 1963, and in which he had served with high distinction: expanding the Petipa repertory, burnishing and expanding the Balanchine wing, overseeing the company's absorption of Rudolf Nureyev, bringing in Nijinska to stage her masterpieces *Les Noces* and *Les Biches,* bringing in the long-shunned Antony Tudor to make his first ballet, *Shadowplay,* for the Royal, as well as turning out some of the greatest ballets of his own career, among them a pristine staging of Satie (*Monotones*), a Victorian valentine to Mendelssohn by way of Shakespeare (*The Dream*), and a lambent homage to Elgar (*Enigma Variations*). Still, Kavanagh uses secondhand gossip to plant the idea that de Valois was the evil demon of the plan, which, from Ashton's point of view in later years, she was. This treatment of de Valois is one of the points in *Secret Muses* where Kavanagh is, in effect, attempting to prove that her biography is on Ashton's side. Given the murky nature of most theatrical feuds, however, one is advised to proceed to her conclusion with caution. De Valois, who is in her hundredth year, contests it.

Kavanagh's title can be interpreted, on one level, to mean those figures in Ashton's love life—most yet not all of them dancers, most yet not all of them men—who inspired the emotional and dramatic trajectories of his choreography. On another level, however, it can be interpreted to refer to his very way of thinking: to the secret signs of beauty and hope that characterize romance. And on another level it can be interpreted to mean *all* his sources of inspiration, which, to a new audience of balletgoers and readers, are secret in that they are no longer in the public eye, or topics in the gossip columns, or ready frames of reference in the theater.

For anyone under forty who attended the Royal's production of Ashton's two-act *Cinderella* at the Met during the company's exciting visit to New

York this past summer, Margot Fonteyn, the most frequently discussed proponent of the ballet's title role during Ashton's lifetime, would be a secret muse. A critic such as myself—who, of the two Cinderellas I saw, far preferred Darcey Bussell—cannot rely on memories of Fonteyn's shapely acting and her dramatically nuanced dancing to make the case as to why Bussell seemed generous and illuminating, while Leanne Benjamin, a limpid dancer, seemed to come to the character cold. One must begin one's statement of appreciation as if Fonteyn never existed, which, for much of the sold-out houses at the performances I attended, she doesn't. To hold a memory of Ashton's casts under Ashton's direction is indeed to be a keeper of secrets.

For a ballet master who did not regularly teach technique class (he appears to have lacked the scientific zest required for it), Ashton was very lucky in his ballerinas. They included Alicia Markova, Tamara Karsavina, Alexandra Danilova, Moira Shearer, Pamela May, Beryl Grey, Svetlana Beriosova, Antoinette Sibley, and Lynn Seymour. In at least one respect, in fact, he was luckier than Balanchine: in addition to being able to work with many ballerinas of distinction, Ashton was also able to rely on a *prima ballerina assoluta* for three entire decades. Margot Fonteyn was the protégée of both Ashton and de Valois, who recognized her potential well before he did.

For transcontinental theatergoers in the '40s, '50s, and '60s—as for Ashton's own dancers during that time—Fonteyn was more than Ashton's principal public muse and the standard-bearer of English classical style. She was something close to the spiritual queen of England, encapsulating the qualities of beauty, decorum, warmth, modesty, high spirits, and nobility that marked the culture of the Edwardian period at its best—that is, the culture of Ashton's mother's youth, to which he continually turned in his work. Ashton crystallized this image of Fonteyn in 1953, when, on the occasion of the coronation of Elizabeth II, he made a ballet called *Homage to the Queen,* in which Fonteyn, as Queen of the Air, was granted the prestigious crowning entrance, then lifted high over a living tableau formed by the corps, with her sister Queens—of the Waters, of Fire, and of the Earth—saluting her from the corners of the stage.

Unlike most historical queens, Fonteyn got to triumph as a princess, too, in her incandescent performances as Aurora in *The Sleeping Beauty.* Yet it was in the role of Odette, Queen of the Swans, that Fonteyn most fully articulated an ideal of monarchical authority. In 1963, Ashton rechoreographed the ballet's last act to spell this out. The heart of it is a passage in which Odette leads her flock away from the lake to safeguard them against von Rothbart's vehemence, guiding them, line by line, to safety. After each of these missions, she breaks off to comfort the figure of the stricken Siegfried, touching him each time with more enveloping tenderness and ardor. This is a queen of dreams, who attempts to rescue everyone according to his or her specific need, racing against the clock to provide now passion, now compassion. Alas, there is no one to mother her; the closest mother surrogate she has is the lake itself, formed of her dead mother's tears—the lake in which she and Siegfried merge.

If there is a more poignant emblem in ballet for the profound loneliness attendant on, and the emotional stamina required by, the position of full artistic responsibility, I should like to know it. For many dancegoers, Fonteyn's Odette has remained the standard of what a queen might be: at once fully vulnerable, an incarnation of beauty, and a student of Clausewitz. In a recent issue of *Ballet Review* Wendy Ellis, a notator of Ashton's ballets, is quoted as saying about this elegiac tone poem: "My father, who doesn't know anything about ballet, used to wait for the last act because he said it was the most magical thing he had ever seen."

Ellis's father appears to belong to a vanishing race of theatergoers. A new generation tends to treat the performing arts with a wariness about being suckered in that sometimes approaches cynicism, and an impulse to analyze and to "demystify" images in order to prove that they really add up to tricks of the theater, or to nothing. This has made for smart commentary, yet in its defiant disillusion it has also contributed to the decline of magic in ballet-making, especially the kind of necromancy in which Ashton excelled, where the very minutiae of geometrical formations, of upbeats and downbeats, of *épaulement* (carriage of the shoulders) and positions of the fingers, trail specific allusions and describable lyric suggestions, or, rather, secrete them: for instance, the moment at the end of another Fonteyn vehicle, *Scènes de ballet*, when most of the cast arrange themselves downstage in an architectural formation while, in an upstage corner, the ballerina stands on the thigh of her kneeling cavalier in a cameo quotation from *Swan Lake*.

Scènes de ballet, reportedly Ashton's favorite among all his works, is an impersonal syllogism of the Cecchetti brand of classical technique that he learned from Massine, Rambert, and Nijinska. (This rigorously structured and minutely classified pedagogy—on whose steps, phrasing, and postures Ashton drew throughout his career—is notable for its strict observance of ballet's five positions, for its textbook deportment, for its astonishingly faceted *petit allegro* vocabulary, and for the braided tensions it produces in the dancing body, giving it the look of late Hellenistic sculpture.) Like some of Nijinska's own classical ballets, *Scènes* is curiously inscrutable in its tone. Yet its references to the flowering of nineteenth-century Russian ballet, veined with courtliness and torrentially romantic love stories, lend it the shadow of depth. To my eyes, its style is emphatically artificial, with limbs changing position and heads rotating to correlate with the mathematics of Stravinsky's score, rather than to follow through physical impulses, as in an actual old classic.

And there are more puzzles. The costumes (by Ashton) are post-World War II glamour; the atmosphere, owing to André Beaurepaire's uncomfortably dark decor, is menacing. And yet the choreography, oddly stiff as it seems, bespeaks a language of sacred love. *Scènes de ballet* has remained in the Royal's repertory, a useful challenge in its technical terms alone; yet it is one of the rare Ashton works to have lasted which does not emotionally reveal itself on the sheer basis of its performances. Why was Ashton so delighted with it? What did he hope an ideal audience would see? (At its premiere, even the critics in his corner found the work cool, off-putting.)

A work such as Ashton's last act of *Swan Lake,* which is purely wonderful, does not require explanations. It is the puzzlement engendered by something such as *Scènes de ballet* that drives a dancegoer to the bookshelf, where the Ashton section now contains two indispensable volumes: Kavanagh's book, and *Frederick Ashton and His Ballets* by David Vaughan, which appeared twenty years ago. Although both books cover the same career, more or less, and sometimes overlap in their sources—Kavanagh's biography would not have been possible without Vaughan's pathbreaking research, as she notes—the stories that they tell, the information that they impart, and the conclusions that they draw are so polemically unlike that to read merely one is less than to read neither. . . .

Kavanagh tenders a painstakingly argued justification for shining a posthumous lantern on matters that Ashton sought to hide. Ashton, she argues, was a genius of a specific kind. "For me," she explains, "the most important discovery of writing Ashton's biography has been the extent to which his life *generated* his work. His genius was subjective, he lived by his heart and imbued his work with the sense of yearning and suffering that he himself experienced. 'I pour into it all my love, my frustrations, and sometimes autobiographical details. . . . In many ways, it has more reality than the life which I live.'" The ballet, she proposes, was not only Ashton's principal wife; it was principally his life. This is not the case for every choreographer. Indeed, it is quite rare. Balanchine, tempered as a teenager in the crucible of the Russian Revolution, and chastened by a year in a sanitorium, recovering from the loss of a lung to tuberculosis, knew that even when he had to give up studying ballet to forage for food in sub-zero temperatures, he could survive. Ashton's consecration to ballet seems closer to a performer's identification with his or her own art. In this essential way, he reminds one of Pavlova, who danced until she died.

Ashton was not initially a choreographer by choice, despite his gifts for it. He wanted to be a dancer, and began to explore the making of dances only when it became clear that he had started his training too late to meet his own standards of performing excellence. From a few films of his dancing during the 1930s that have miraculously been saved, one can see that he had everything necessary to be a marvellous dancer: the coordination, the intuitive kinetic taste, the amazing talent for mimicry (equivalent to an actor's ear for accents), the humility, and, most of all, the appetite. Everything but those blunt yet fundamental elements of execution, such as full turnout of the legs, that early childhood training would have given him.

Ashton's wound as a child at his father's impenetrable opposition to ballet study seems never to have healed, even partially. He died with the idea that his father was a monster, and his fans have been led to adopt that idea as well. One of the great coups of Kavanagh's biography is her independent curiosity about the motivations of George Ashton, the pursuit of which led her to travel to South America. The research that brings her to discuss him as a complex individual, to humanize him as his son never could, is a gift to both men, as well as to the history of ballet. (Kavanagh speculates that George Ashton "was a romantic, a fantasist, who without a creative outlet into which to channel his visions, had fictionalized his own life." She sums up his characteristically grim moods as a form of melancholia, and it was so severe it led him to take his own life.)

Kavanagh's extended discussion of *Scènes de ballet* shows up in the chapter entitled "Mr A Obsessed with Mr B," a chronicle of the years 1947–1950. The title, a Tiffany diamond of compression, refers to two relationships of Ashton's during that time. Most obviously, we are meant to think of Mr. A(shton)'s sense of inadequacy in comparison with Mr. B(alanchine). During these years, the choreographers were in relatively sustained contact. It was *Scènes de ballet* that led Balanchine to invite Ashton to choreograph for Ballet Society—an invitation that Ashton would later return when, in 1950, he helped to bring over Balanchine to set *Ballet Imperial* at Covent Garden. Balanchine hadn't even seen *Scènes*, which was given its premiere in London; he extended his offer based on secondhand accounts (one of them Lincoln Kirstein's, who wanted to import *Scènes* itself). Ashton's use of a score by Stravinsky may also have piqued Balanchine's interest. Ashton was proud of his staging of the score, remarking in a letter that "many people rave about it and say it's the best I've done, which I think, and Stravinsky's son adores it."

And also embedded in Kavanagh's chapter title is a reference to Ashton's love affair at the time with a much younger American dancer named Dick Beard. Kavanagh's biographical method puts pressure on this figure to serve as a secret muse of *Scènes,* although in a purely romantic rather than a specifically sexual sense. At the time *Scènes* was choreographed in London, Beard was in New York. The two corresponded, but an ocean separated them, and so the love that they professed was chivalric, despite its erotic expression in their letters. There may be an emotional allegory in the work; if so, it would be most complicated. According to Kavanagh, Ashton cast one or two other lovers as actual performers in it and embellished the geometry with static images of male love. These are not emphasized as such; they are sculptural postures, whose potential meanings cohere for those who care to seek them. The choreographic relationships, then, become a virtual cat's cradle of complexity, clarified only by the straightforward obeisance of all the male dancers to the ballerina Fonteyn.

On the other hand, since Kavanagh argues throughout *Secret Muses* that Ashton not only loved his ballerinas but also identified with them—that they *were* him, in effect—even this apparently simple paradigm of courtly devotion may be subject to reinterpretation. Does the ballet unnerve some audiences because of the quite Modernist sense it conveys that there is no final way to know it, no secret summation, no perfect vantage point from which all will coalesce into a revealing apothegm, as, in its very staging, the patterns are constructed so that anywhere can be the front? In that case, could it be that the road to appreciation of this unforthcoming yet fascinating Ashtonian experiment is the opportunity to see it periodically? After four decades in the repertory of the Royal Ballet, it has become a treasure for the balletgoers of London. Several generations have had the opportunity to learn how to look at it. They may not agree with the choreographer that it constitutes his best ballet of all, but they can accept it as an example of the highest stages of his craft.

So where does this leave Kavanagh's effort to get us to glimpse a connection between the cooling of Ashton's ardor toward Beard and the Arctic quality of the choreography—to whisper, in other words, that the tone of *Scènes* may in part be explained by biographical circumstances that have nothing directly to do with its creation? In the book's reflective afterword, she herself wonders, using a later Ashton ballet as a focus:

Does the knowledge that the Young Girl in *The Two Pigeons* is a reincarnation of the male chemistry student with whom [Ashton] was infatuated really add a valuable new dimension to the ballet's achingly sweet reconciliation duet? If anything, it is a distraction, diminishing the work's power of suggestion, the raison d'être of dance. It was this—the fear that exposure of the prosaic reality of the lived life would destroy the delicate subterfuge and poetry of his art—that, I believe, fuelled Fred's resistance far more than any sense of propriety. "Choreography is my whole being, my whole life, my reason for living," he once told an American journalist.

Her anxiety is even more profoundly revealed in the way that she has chosen to conclude the story. The last paragraphs of her last chapter about the life of Ashton quote from Fonteyn's tribute, written for his memorial

service. It is possible to take what she says as ceremonial; but if one considers her words seriously, they question the rationale for writing an Ashton
biography any longer than this passage:

> As a man I see a paradox: on the one hand sophistication and finely devel-
> oped taste in all things, yet on the other a very simple person at heart.
> One might expect a highly sophisticated person to make an effort to
> conceal some emotions. Not Ashton; like a child, if he was hurt, angry or
> even jealous he made no pretence. He was, above all, a very *human* human
> being, and for that, as much as for his extraordinary talents, he was beloved
> by all.

—from *The New Republic*, 1997

DAVID VAUGHAN
Ashton Now

The establishment of a national school of classical ballet depends on the
existence of three prerequisites: a great choreographer whose works provide a repertory and define a style; a company (preferably with its own theatre) to present that repertory; and an academy to codify and promote that
style and to provide dancers trained in it. The most obvious examples of
this combination of circumstances have been in Denmark, with August
Bournonville; in Russia, with Marius Petipa; in the United States, with
George Balanchine; and here in Britain, with Frederick Ashton.

The works of Bournonville, Petipa, and Balanchine have been maintained (with varying degrees of authenticity), but it is no secret that many
people believe that Ashton's work has been neglected by the company and
school whose first responsibility should be to preserve it. The number of
his ballets in the repertory of the Royal Ballet has undeniably declined,
and in the Royal Ballet School the Russian influence is in the ascendant,
while the Cecchetti system, the technical basis of the Ashton style, is in
eclipse.

Ashton, like Balanchine, his exact contemporary, was from the beginning
a prolific choreographer able to provide on demand works that could make

up a well-balanced program—the kind of program one used to see at Sadler's Wells or the New Theatre in the late thirties and early forties: ballets like *Apparitions, Nocturne, Les Patineurs, A Wedding Bouquet, Harlequin in the Street, Horoscope,* and later *Dante Sonata, The Wise Virgins,* and *The Wanderer.* More than that, these ballets, by their technical and interpretive demands, helped to turn young dancers into virtuosi, even into artists, and they formed the basis of what has come to be recognised as the English style of classical ballet, a style expressive of what we like to think of as the English national character—lyrical, precise, well-mannered, yet robust—but flavoured by Latin and Gallic elements in Ashton's own temperament and background, a certain chic, a certain flamboyance, which counteracted any tendency toward gentility or dowdiness. More seriously, Ashton's own dance experience—his adoration of Pavlova and Karsavina, his work with Massine and especially with Nijinska, and his study of the Cecchetti system—all contributed to the technical foundation of this English style, giving it greater freedom of épaulement, faster changes of direction, and more amplitude of movement.

In the years following the Sadler's Wells Ballet's move to Covent Garden, and especially during Ashton's tenure as director of what had become the Royal Ballet, from 1963 to 1970, the process continued. *Symphonic Variations,* which Ashton called his choreographic credo, and the ballets that came after it, constituted a contemporary repertory equalled in its number of masterpieces only by that of New York City Ballet. Margot Fonteyn, Ashton's muse, later acknowledged as prima ballerina assoluta, was joined by younger artists like Nadia Nerina, Svetlana Beriosova, Antoinette Sibley, Lynn Seymour, David Blair, and Anthony Dowell, most of them the products of the Royal Ballet School, as were the dancers who made up a corps de ballet unrivalled in the Western world.

Ashton's creativity after his premature, even enforced retirement was diminished in volume, but not in mastery. Yet he often used to predict that before long his works would be considered passé and that most would fall into oblivion. It is true that only a handful of ballets even by the greatest choreographers tend to survive, and that on the whole they are the best ones. But it is also true that in Ashton's case a number have disappeared too soon, and their neglect may have been due to a feeling among those who took over the direction of the company that these ballets were dated and irrelevant.

In other words, we were taken back to the kind of criticism that Ashton often suffered in his earlier years—that he failed to deal with sufficiently serious subject matter—to which was now added the further condemnation that he was out of touch with contemporary life and its problems. Ashton may have been aware of this stricture when he wrote that "ballets about current social happenings . . . [are likely] to date as quickly as yesterday's newspaper."

I would be the first to agree that Ashton was often on shaky ground when he tried to be trendy, as in *Jazz Calendar*. But it is naive at best to suppose that ballet is brought into the modern world when it concerns, say, the supposedly realistic depiction of sexual acts by people in jeans on a construction site. Apart from the fact that realism of that kind can be carried only so far in dance, the movement possibilities are limited. As someone once said: In ballet, people make love standing on their feet.

In his later years, Ashton's favourite subject was romantic love, a subject uniquely suited to dance expression. Who is to say that it is less representative of the human spirit than gang rape? I have often quoted Edwin Denby's observation that "the more trivial the subject, the deeper and more beautiful is Ashton's poetic view of it." The reverse is true of some choreographers, of whom one could say that the more profound the subject, the more trivial and prosaic is their treatment of it.

In any case, it is not seriousness of subject that makes serious choreography. In my view, the most important developments in the art form have come not from emotional expression but from formal innovation. What I am talking about here, clearly, is what has been called the Great Divide, or what Joan Acocella has termed the quarrel between the adherents of "expressive" and "pure" dance:

> One position is that dance is of value insofar as it is tells a story or at least expresses or portrays something in the way that literature or painting might. Opposing this is the view that dance has *autonomous* value, that it is capable of communicating something on the highest level of meaning through purely dance means, without resorting to imitation of the methods of painting or literature. According to this position, dance communicates as music does.*

It is generally accepted that this Great Divide is also between Europe on the one hand and America on the other, but it is interesting to note that the two choreographers whom Acocella names as embodying the "pure dance" view are Balanchine, who was American by adoption, and Ashton, sometimes called the most English of choreographers, who nevertheless felt more appreciated in America than at home.

In any case, expressive dance had once again reared its—dare I say?—

---

*Joan Acocella and Lynn Garafola: *André Levinson on Dance*.

ugly head in Britain as in Europe, and the damage to Ashton's reputation, and to the heritage of British ballet, was done. Certain works, of course, survived in the repertory, a handful of acknowledged classics: *La Fille mal gardée, The Dream, Cinderella, A Month in the Country*. True, *Monotones*, Ashton's purest distillation of classicism, also survived, but he himself kept *Symphonic Variations* out for a number of years for lack of a suitable cast. And this fact pinpoints one of the basic problems: Because Ashton's works were not being danced, nobody could dance them.

There were a few exceptions, of course—the dwindling number of dancers who had worked with him kept certain ballets alive when they were revived—*Scènes de ballet*, for instance. But too often revivals have looked like carbon copies at best. The last time *Enigma Variations* was performed by the parent company one saw dancers wearing the proper clothes and makeup and going through the motions they had learned, but the spirit of the ballet was gone. Roles like the mortal lovers in *The Dream* and the stepsisters in *Cinderella* have been performed in inexcusably broad and vulgar fashion. What is significant, though, is that in the hands of the few dancers I have mentioned, keepers of the flame like Lesley Collier and Nicola Roberts and Genesia Rosato, the ballerina roles remained pretty well inviolate. In other words, some part of the dance element survived. It is not the fault of younger dancers that even this dance element often eluded them: They were being asked for other qualities.

If Ashton's work is to live on as the patrimony of British ballet, it must be because the dance element will be kept alive through constant performance, careful teaching and coaching, and faithful staging. Young dancers must of course be allowed to interpret roles freshly, in their own way—one would not want them to dance them by rote, parrot-fashion, as it were—but at the minimum they will have to get the steps right.

Ashton was a master of structure, both in terms of what he called the "scaffolding," the matching of the action to the music, but also in terms of the dictionary definition, "the way in which parts are arranged or put together to form a whole," the bricks and mortar, if you like, of steps and transitions.

Alastair Macaulay reported in 1994 that people who saw the Birmingham Royal Ballet dance *La Fille mal gardée* in Turin "exclaimed with amazement that never before had they seen ballet with the harmony, structure, and fluency of music—that watching it was like reading a score." If you look carefully at *Scènes de ballet*, you will see that there isn't a single step in it that doesn't relate to the structure as a whole. This is equally true of unassuming ballets like *Les Rendezvous* and *Les Patineurs*—it is what has ensured their survival.

Ashton's genius is evident at every moment of *Daphnis and Chloe*, but I will just mention here Chloe's dance to the flute solo in the third scene, which is built on half a dozen steps, and variations on them: arabesque *piquée* into *failli* to fourth position *croisée*; the "folk" step of slapping the foot with the hand in front or in back, with *rond de jambe*; pas de bourrée with small *développé à la seconde* into *soutenu*; plié in fifth position *soussus*; little ballonnés on pointe—all varied with different ports de bras and gestures, such as the moment when she holds a pose in fourth position *croisée* with the arms in an "archaic" Greek position.

This leads me to another important truth about Ashton: We all know that he was a consummate storyteller when he wanted to be, but he told his stories and created his characters through the steps: you know what his people are like and what they are feeling because of how they dance. As Alan M. Kriegsman has written, "Ashton didn't subject the classical steps to the kinds of radical transfiguration that became Balanchine's signature." Ashton's great innovation was the extension of the classical vocabulary as a poetic language. I would add too that his use of space, especially in his purest dance works, *Symphonic Variations* and *Scènes de ballet* and *Monotones*, was as unconventional in its way as anything in Merce Cunningham. Of *Scènes de ballet* he said, "I . . . wanted to do a ballet that could be seen from any angle—anywhere could be front, so to speak."

Ashton's work, then, it seems to me, can speak to us as strongly today as it did thirty or forty or fifty years ago. It is classical, and it is modern. And indeed the situation now is more hopeful than it has been. This conference, and the gratifyingly large turn-out for it, are, I hope, both a symptom of and a stimulus to renewed interest in his work. The Ashton revivals at the Royal Ballet, plus *Enigma Variations* by the Birmingham Royal Ballet, move beyond the usual handful of ballets that have been danced in the past.

This is true with other companies, too: *Romeo and Juliet* is coming back into the repertory of the Royal Danish Ballet, thanks to Peter Schaufuss. *Two Pigeons*, which hasn't been in the Royal repertory lately, I believe, was revived in Turin. The Dutch National Ballet, American Ballet Theatre, and the National Ballet of Canada have acquired, or will acquire, *Symphonic Variations*. The Dutch National, where Wayne Eagling looks out for Ashton's interests, has also revived *Scènes de ballet*, a rarity among companies other than the Royal, and ABT also revived *Birthday Offering* a couple of years ago.

Since the death of Robert Joffrey, I'm sorry to say, the company he founded seems to have dropped most of its Ashton repertory, which was the most extensive outside the Royal Ballet—it even included *A Wedding Bouquet*. But I should like to see more Ashton ballets in American repertories—for instance, Pacific Northwest Ballet or Boston Ballet might have a stab at *Scènes de ballet* or *Rhapsody*. Alastair Macaulay wrote recently that the Russian companies should also acquire Ashton and Balanchine ballets that use Russian ballet scores, so that they could learn "how far their heritage has been absorbed in the West, and with what effect." There may, inevitably, be some loss of what we might think of as the pure Ashton style, but the gain for those other companies—and for Ashton's reputation worldwide—would surely be considerable.

The other, related question is that of which ballets could or should be revived. I am resigned to the fact that I will never again see *Harlequin in the Street* or *Mephisto Valse*, two ballets I loved—unless it's in heaven. The reconstruction of *Les Masques* shown at this conference, a ballet that gave me one of those moments of the shock of recognition of genius when I first saw it in the spring of 1939, gives hope that a revival might be possible. *Foyer de danse* could easily be revived from the film that exists, and might be an excellent choice for a smaller company like London City Ballet. *Les Rendezvous* has been out of the repertory for far too long, and I would hate to think that Ashton's fourth act of *Swan Lake*, that sublime elegiac poem, will not come back somehow, somewhere. Would it be worthwhile to try again with *Apparitions*, another ballet that meant a lot to me years ago? The ballroom scene, at least, is a masterpiece. Anthony Russell-Roberts has dropped a tantalising hint that the Royal Ballet may yet revive *Sylvia*. At all events, some important additions could be made to what one hopes would be the irreducible minimum of extant Ashton works—the Ashton canon. (Clement Crisp has written that he has made a list of thirty Ashton ballets that should be in repertory.)

Having introduced a personal note, I should like to end on it. Years ago, when I was serving in the army in World War II, I had the luck to be stationed in London for a while at the time when the Sadler's Wells Ballet was giving regular seasons at what was then the New Theatre. Needless to say, that was where I spent my free evenings. It couldn't last, of course, and before long I was shipped out to India. There I tried to assuage my feeling of deprivation by writing an essay, my first, on Ashton's work. There was another balletomane in the headquarters in Delhi, and I showed him what I had written. He said, "You're in love with Ashton's ballets!" And I realised that he had perceived an important truth about me. It's why even today I take pleasure in the mere naming of the ballets I have mentioned in the course of this talk—"title after title," as Virginia Woolf said, "to be laid upon the heart like an amulet against disaster."

E. M. Forster wrote in his essay, "The Raison d'Être of Criticism in the Arts":

I love music. Just to love it, or just to love anything or anybody is not enough. Love has to be clarified and controlled to give full value, and here is where criticism may help. But one has to start with love; one has, in the case of music, to want to hear the notes.

Or, to offer a paraphrase, one has to want to follow Sir Fred's steps.

—from the keynote lecture at the Roehampton Institute's
"Following Sir Fred's Steps" conference, 1994

POSTSCRIPT

In recent years, beginning in 1994, which would have been the year of Ashton's nineti-eth birthday, there has been a distinct improvement in the situation described here, when The Royal Ballet at last began the important task of reviving some important works too long absent from its programs. Also in 1994, the memorable conference "Following Sir Fred's Steps" took place at the Roehampton Institute in London (the text printed here was its keynote speech). The conference itself may have been a cata-lyst in the process of bringing his work back to the stage where it belongs. The process was accelerated in 2004, Ashton's centenary year, when The Royal Ballet presented a number of programs that included, among other things, a reconstructed Sylvia *(a co-production with American Ballet Theatre); two dances from the lost ballet* Devil's Holiday, *reconstructed by Frederic Franklin; and* Daphnis and Chloe, *with its orig-inal designs restored. In New York, the Lincoln Center Festival presented several pro-grams at the Metropolitan Opera House, danced by the Royal Ballet and Birmingham Royal Ballet, the Joffrey Ballet of Chicago, and K Company from Japan. In 2002 the Bolshoi Ballet finally acquired an Ashton ballet,* La Fille mal gardée, *as did Ameri-can Ballet Theatre in the same year and the Ballet of the Paris Opéra in 2007.*

ASHTON BALLETS

Enigma Variations
Nancy Goldner

One of Frederick Ashton's most cherished works, Enigma Variations *(1968) uses Edward Elgar's 1899 score, a set of fourteen variations dedicated to "friends pictured within." This is a ballet of character and relationships, of human encounters and frailties, rather than of technical virtuosity. The decor, by Julia Trevelyan Oman, movingly evokes the specific location of the ballet, in the Worcestershire countryside.*

If one were to choose the century's greatest ballet, it would be George Balanchine's *Agon.* The tour de force, standing with no precedent and no progeny, would be Frederick Ashton's *Enigma Variations.* Presented by Britain's Royal Ballet during a week's layover in New York, en route to the Far East, it was ample reward for an otherwise silly repertory, some of it, alas, by Ashton.

Enigma Variations achieves what no other dance has. Conceived in nonnarrative terms, it nevertheless plays like a novel, imparting the kind of information novels do, and using the novel's multi-faceted attack. In describing character, this ballet necessarily describes society, and vice versa. It exists in the present while successfully assuring the viewer it will move forward in time to a conclusion. We begin some novels with a slight panic: wanting immediately to know through which characters the theme will be stated, we reject the writer's staking-out of the territory as a false lead. In *Enigma Variations* Ashton's surveillance of the territory becomes, in a sense, the main theme, a fact that may alienate some from this masterpiece. But like the best of novels, *Enigma Variations* is immediately upfront about the protagonist's identity. When the curtain goes up he's standing alone in the middle of the stage while others stand at the sidelines in dimmer light.

Pondering a music score, his stance is suggestive, yet natural. The arrangement of the others around the garden set is drawn from real life, too. One lady reclines in a swing. At a table at the other side of the garden a man and woman converse over the last sip of tea. A few people stand at the back, chatting under a trellis leading away from the garden. A gentleman sits in a chair, doing, as far as one can tell, nothing. The illusion of reality is established at once and is never lost. That it is never lost is the miracle of *Enigma Variations*, for its structure is the antithesis of realism. *Enigma Variations* is a string of variations in which each character comes on and does his dance. The format is straight out of nineteenth-century convention, in essence no different from the third-act wedding divertissement beloved by choreographers because it was the moment they could forget story and get on with the dance. In *Enigma Variations* Ashton gets to eat his cake. He takes a convention profoundly antagonistic to realism and twirls it round to serve realism—at least, to cohabitate with it. In so doing he makes *Enigma Variations* a full dance experience as well as a dramatic one.

The man at stage center looking at a score is Edward Elgar. The people who drop by to visit, and to perform their variations, are his friends and neighbors. Each of them is triply described: in Ashton's choreography; in the Elgar score itself, which the composer called *Enigma Variations (My Friends Pictured Within)*; and in epigrams that Elgar wrote about his friends and which Ashton uses in the program notes. Much of the characterization, both musically and choreographically, is pictorial. Elgar's tricycle-riding crony circles the stage on his contraption, and that's it for that variation. A fellow fond of bulldogs prances with his hands curled like paws. Since their time on the stage is short, they function in the ballet as vignettes and in Elgar's life, one assumes, as acquaintances. Others are on stage when they're not dancing, and one can tell by their relaxed, unpredictable comings and goings that they're permanent fixtures in Elgar's life. One man, in fact, seems so comfortable in Elgar's garden that he feels free to sit in the chair (*his* chair it comes to be) and do nothing at all. The mutually felt intimacy between him and the home is verified later in the ballet, when he is a witness to a falling-out between Elgar and his wife, depicted as a variation in the form of a pas de deux.

But now I have given away a secret of the ballet's power. Although it matters how people dance, it matters more what those people do in the presence of other people. The order of the dances counts also. Why is it, for example, that Elgar and his wife are at odds now, when shortly before, in the musical and emotional climax of the ballet, they had pledged eternal devotion? The question is answered in the variation following the argument. A lady, not seen before, wafts into the garden on a bed of fog and dances before the entranced Elgar as a vision. The woman of the past she is, and evidently on Elgar's mind, as is everything at this point in the man's life.

Sequence of action and the context in which action is set are literary concerns. *Enigma Variations* accumulates the bulk of its meaning through them, even though it's a pure-dance work. Although each variation is interesting to look at in itself, each is a figurative variation on a theme that isn't entirely grasped until the ballet is over. The theme, of course, is the variety of species in Elgar's garden and the variety of experiences that can be had there. It's a place where kids can romp, where tricyclists can take a spin, where love affairs, some illicit, some imagined, and some socially sanctioned, may proceed, where a man can eat his lunch in peace and in his favorite chair, where a cellist may practice his craft, and where Elgar may worry about his future as a composer. For so small a place as Elgar's backyard to accommodate so much and many kinds of life is, to me, a depiction of earthly paradise. And it is for this vision of life, profoundly communal yet private, that I would return to *Enigma Variations* many times over.

But the ballet has art as well as life on its mind. Certainly the story takes on added significance because the hero is an artist, and added piquancy because he's drawn from real life by Ashton and *is* real life through his music. We don't read too much into the scenario to find in Ashton's earthly paradise a thesis on the conditions necessary for art-making. Yet as depicted by Ashton, the artist's final triumph isn't conceived "artistically." That is, when at the end of the ballet Elgar receives a telegram informing him that his *Enigma Variations* will be played by an important orchestra, thus ensuring him recognition, the choreography does not suddenly veer into an exploration of the music. It remains true to its representational style. All the friends gather round to cheer Elgar and his wife, and in the closing moment one of them takes a snapshot of the group.

Meanwhile, back in the structure department, the ballet proceeds as formally as ever. The gathering of the clan is conceived in strict finale form, its development and patterns as anti-realistic as the snapshot bit is realistic. Following the music's recapitulatory program, the characters each take a square of territory and repeat phrases from their variations. Four of the prominent ladies *bourrée* circles in the center of the stage, like the good fairies in *The Sleeping Beauty*. Then everyone joins in big unison jumps, like the crescendo of a Balanchine symphony. It's at the finale that Ashton's two-pronged attack comes to its most intense clash, with the garden suddenly transformed into ballroom and the motley crew into anonymous attendants. Then just as quickly, via the snapshot, does the ballet revert to real-life illusion. Ashton provides no resolution, no synthesis, and seems to enjoy not providing it. He'll have it two ways. The audience learns two things: how to build a life, and how to build a ballet.

—from *The Saturday Review,* July–August 1983

La Fille Mal Gardée
Nancy Goldner

Frederick Ashton's La Fille mal gardée *(1960) is without question the happiest, sunniest, most lovable of all ballets. The libretto is based on the original Dauberval staging of 1789 (the oldest ballet in the repertory), and the music is John Lanchbery's reworking of the Ferdinand Hérold version of the score. Osbert Lancaster designed the sets. The story is a simple, traditional one: the young heroine, Lise, is in love with the nice peasant boy, Colas, but her mother wants her to marry the idiotic son of a local bigwig. All this is transformed into a comic idyll, beginning with a bunch of chickens ushering in the dawn. The mother, more loving than threatening, is played by a male dancer in drag (and performs the wonderful clog dance); the mime scene and the ribbon dance were taught to Ashton by Karsavina, who danced Lise successfully at the Maryinsky. Kschessinska and Pavlova danced* Fille, *too. But they didn't have Ashton. Surely this is crowning glory of his career, and of English ballet.*

The Royal Ballet's visit at the Metropolitan Opera lasted only three weeks, and a good part of the time was given over to Kenneth MacMillan's new *Manon,* one of those besotted full-length extravaganzas that the Royal Ballet apparently feels it must produce to justify its royal charter and that management feels Americans expect from a foreign company. But we were also able to see a contemporary masterpiece, Frederick Ashton's *La Fille mal gardée.* This two-act pastoral comedy has gained the reputation of being a box-office loser here, perhaps because its length (neither short enough to be a "jewel" nor long enough to be "major") and its unimportant theme disqualify it from being the "grand ballet" that Americans associate with Royal Ballet fare. I do not know for a fact that *La Fille* is a financial liability, but if it is I would imagine that its biggest barrier to audience success constitutes its greatest achievement. In *La Fille* Ashton has the courage to pursue an utterly unprofound story and then to web it with so much humor, simple truth, and theatrical invention that it becomes a statement about the profundity of anti-profundity.

La Fille is a genre painting of farm life. Even though the story focuses on the love between Lise and Colas and the attempt by Lise's mother, Widow Simone, to thwart the romance so that she can marry her daughter off to a rich imbecile, the heart of the ballet's concern is milieu. The charm, and also spine, of it is that Ashton does not conceive of milieu as hazy background noise supplied by an ensemble, but in specifics. Thus the ballet begins with a dance for four hens and a rooster at dawn. Naturally the dance is adorable. It is also poignant because so truthful to its context: In a barnyard world, chickens are the most important "persons." Later on, when the farmers go to reap the fields, it's the chickens who lead the parade (a real parade, ending with a woman-made float) and the chickens to whom everyone bows when they get to the fields. The first thing we find out about Lise and Colas is that they both like butter; that is, they like the same aspects of the world they inhabit and so are natural-born lovers. Lise likes it so much that her first dance is a hymn to butter. We know that the farm is in France because, when Widow Simone frantically throws at Colas everything she can get her hands on to discourage him from hanging around Lise, she remembers to take the flowers out of the flower pot before hurling them over the balcony. Flower pots cost money.

The ballet is also filled with the sounds and rhythms of farm life. The scene where Lise and her mother spin yarn is a dance equivalent of the cozy, purring rhythm of the machine that will clothe them. Of course Lise almost strangles her mother with the yarn, but that is another part of the story, dealing with mother-daughter stuff and the theme of cheerful incompetence, from which *La Fille* draws much of its comic material. Churning butter is another rhythm. Lise is a typical teenager, lazy and moonily in love. She churns lackadaisically except when she wants to tease Colas with fake indifference, at which point she churns with some zip.

Much of the comedy is pure vaudeville; though *La Fille mal gardée*'s plot and locale is French, its spirit in many ways is English music hall. The most brilliant and lovable example is Widow Simone's soft-shoe routine (only the dance is done in sabots), complete with a four-woman chorus to fill in the gaps in taps. Except for the hero, who is conventionally heroic, if slightly doltish, the male characters have that music-hall ambiguity of sex, which is further complicated by the fact that Widow Simone is played by a man (the superb Stanley Holden). The humor is low, and the dumber it gets the more wonderful it becomes. There are double takes, glassy-eyed stares à la Jack Benny, and those silly modifications and explanations of gesture in mid-act when someone is caught in a foolish position.

The pinnacle of low humor is Alain, the nitwit in line for Lise's hand. We laugh at him for being a physical mess (his several solos reveal the kind of nervous disorder in which the shoulder jerks when the kneecap is thumped) and a mental case. He's a crybaby and has some sex problems. He lunges at girls with the grotesqueness of a man whose virginity has become a problem. In the original *La Fille*, Alain is a butterfly catcher. Ashton turns him into an Englishman by giving him an umbrella, with which Alain continually plays horsey. Ashton is not afraid to have us laugh at freakishness or even what at times is repulsive behavior, but *La Fille* is above all wrought with love and gentleness. Ashton creates a world where events end happily, where mothers change their motherly ways, lovers are united, and imbeciles are saved by their imbecility. At the very last moment of the ballet, after farm hands celebrate the mother's change of heart and the lovers' betrothal by hoisting them one by one above the crowd so that we in the audience can cheer them, Alain sneaks back into the house to claim his beloved umbrella. He dances off with it, happy. Curtain.

There are many other things to admire in *La Fille mal gardée*. For the most part it is one long stream of dance (rather ribbon of dance, since ribbons become a motif of Lise and Colas's bond). The ensemble dances are not masterpieces and could be shorter, but they are varied and full of verve. The love duets are characteristically Ashtonian in tenderness, intimacy, and sweet flow, yet Ashton still manages to insert virtuoso variations without upsetting the pastoral tone with Russian-style glitter. John Lanchbery's arrangement of the Ferdinand Hérold score is a model of usefulness, and Ashton makes some of the melodies more lilting than they might sound in concert. The work plays into every strength of the Royal Ballet, for it is a true ensemble piece, calls for great character dancing, which no other company can supply, and asks from the lead couple modesty and adeptness at characterization, which are two of the loveliest qualities of the Royal Ballet's stars. The ballet caught even the blue-blooded Rudolf Nureyev and Anthony Dowell in its spell of bucolic enchantment. The sight of these two *premiers danseurs* happily shooing roosters made one believe in the possibility of English democracy.

Yet I like *La Fille* best because of its answer to the question: What is more profound, smiles or frowns, fulfilled or unrequited love? The either/or construct is unfair, of course, but in *La Fille* Ashton gives tragedy a definitive run for the money and certainly extends one's notions of what profundity means. George Balanchine's *Apollo* asks the same question and answers it the same way. This is *Apollo*'s only similarity to *La Fille,* but it is an important one and may account for Balanchine's and Ashton's singular successes with ballet choreography.

The Royal Ballet performed *Apollo* twice this season, and never has any dance been so mangled by anybody. Everything went wrong—the Stravinsky score went six minutes over its prescribed length of thirty; the dancers do not know how to link Balanchine's steps; they do not know how to communicate abstract expression (a limitation that marred, to a lesser extent, Ashton's own *Symphonic Variations* as well); the weakest soloist was given the Terpsichore role, etc., etc. But the worst offense was that Nureyev and his three muses danced *Apollo* as though it were a tragedy. They saw dignity as ponderous movement and dead-serious demeanor, whereas Balanchine finds dignity in a dancer's sense of play and enjoyment of his and his partner's bodies. Apollo is happy because he is a god; Lise and Colas are happy because they are farmers. In their contentment with what is, in their utter peace with reality, the characters who live on Olympus and in the barnyard are related. Had the dancers spun through *Apollo* as they do in *La Fille,* they would have come much nearer the truth. Since *Apollo* is one of the all-time beauties, it is too bad for Anglo-American cultural relations that the beautiful Royal Ballet missed the connection between their dance by Ashton and ours by Balanchine.

—from *The Nation,* June 15, 1974

ASHTON'S ROMEO: A WISE VIRGIN
Joan Acocella

In 1955, Ashton created this version of Shakespeare's story for the Royal Danish Ballet, featuring Henning Kronstam and Mona Vangsaae. It was the first use outside Russia of the full Prokofiev score, but it's a more lyrical and less grand version than either the original Leonid Lavrovsky version or the later version by Kenneth MacMillan. This Romeo was danced for years by the Royal Danes and has been revived several times, most importantly by the London Festival Ballet in the eighties—so one can hope that it isn't really "lost" but is only hibernating.

Frederick Ashton's 1955 *Romeo and Juliet,* revived in July by London Festival Ballet, is a voyage in a time machine: Prokofiev without benefit of Lavrovsky. Which is not to say that if Ashton had waited a year and seen the Lavrovsky version (1940, revised 1946)—its first Western performance was during the Bolshoi's famous London season of 1956—he too, like other choreographers, would have filled his ballet with upside-down split-lifts and whores in striped stockings. (My guess is that he wouldn't have touched the subject at all.) Still, compared with the Bolshoi-influenced versions of Cranko and MacMillan, both much in evidence in New York last season, Ashton's looks like a virgin.

Ashton probably heard the music first in one of the three concert suites. Then, according to David Vaughan's biography, he went to Ninette de Valois with the idea of staging the ballet for Sadler's Wells. But de Valois already had a full-evening Ashton/Prokofiev ballet, *Cinderella,* and apparently felt that one was enough. Around the same time (early 1950s), Niels Bjørn Larsen became head of the Royal Danish Ballet and set himself the task, as he puts it, of "renewing the repertory." He asked for ballets from Lichine, from Balanchine. And he asked Ashton, who made him the offer that de Valois had refused. Larsen accepted.

Ashton went off to fulfill other commitments, then hurried to Copenhagen, where apparently he saw the full ballet score for the first time. Working with the score and a copy of Shakespeare's play—for the music, he claims, was sent to him with "no markings on it, no scenario, no indications of what was supposed to happen when"[1]—he mounted the ballet in just under seven weeks. (The crypt scene, says Larsen, was put together in two hours on the day before the dress rehearsal.) Meanwhile, Peter Rice, as befitted both the schedule and Ashton's conception of the ballet, designed an austerely simple set—basically just a colonnaded porch and a few moveables, such as Juliet's bed—and equally simple costumes, heavy on English pastels, light on Renaissance Italy.

Romeo og Julie had its premiere on 19 May 1955, with a cast that one would give a great deal to have seen: Mona Vangsaae as Juliet, Henning Kronstam as Romeo, Frank Schaufuss as Mercutio, Niels Bjørn Larsen as Tybalt, Flemming Flindt as Benvolio, and Kirsten Ralov as leader of the ensemble. The ballet was a big success, at home and abroad (e.g., Edinburgh Festival, 1955; New York, 1956, 1965). Of the English and American reviewers, most praised it highly; only A. V. Coton, it seems, hated it. Over a ten-year period it was given 105 performances, and then, after December 1965, it was dropped from the repertory. The reasons are not clear, but the dates are worth noting. Ten months earlier, England's Royal Ballet had unveiled MacMillan's plush *Romeo,* which in some minds undoubtedly made Ashton's look plain by comparison. And one such mind, to judge from his later career, was probably that of Flemming Flindt, who in January of 1966 took over from Larsen as director of the Royal Danish Ballet. Eventually, in 1974, Flindt brought in a new *Romeo,* John Neumeier's, and that was that.

In the meantime, of course, Ashton had acquired a company of his own, the Royal Ballet, where one of his earliest plans was to mount his *Romeo.* Larsen, it seems, already had a contract to come to London and set the ballet when Ashton, with that self-effacement so characteristic of him, bowed to MacMillan's wish to create a *Romeo* on the Royal. Hence the birth of MacMillan's version and the disappearance, for twenty years, of Ashton's.

Finally, in 1981, Peter Schaufuss, who is the son of Ashton's original Juliet and Mercutio and who had performed in the ballet as the Nurse's Page, managed to extract from Ashton permission to remount the ballet. Finding a troupe on which to set it was the next task—there were negotiations with the National Ballet of Canada and various other companies—but when Schaufuss became director of Festival Ballet last year, that problem was solved.

Crucial to Ashton's consent was Niels Bjørn Larsen. Ashton claimed that he remembered none of the choreography, but Larsen had the ballet recorded. In 1951, Larsen explains, he had to take over the Danish company "in a very quick way." (This was after Harald Lander's removal as director.) For this reason, and because he had no ballet master, he was nervous and overcareful. When Ashton came to do the *Romeo,* Larsen worried about preserving it properly, and so he notated it, using his own personal system, in two large graph-paper notebooks. (I saw them—verbal instructions in one column, neat little circles and arrows and lines in the other column.) Then he himself filmed the ballet. The camera he had could film only forty-five seconds before reloading, so he would film and reload, film and reload, as rehearsals and performances went on, filling in at the next performance (often with a different cast) what he had missed while reloading during the last. Eventually he had enough pieces to splice together a film of the whole ballet, albeit silent and with multiple cast changes. The only thing missing from the notebooks and the film was the mime, which he felt he could reconstruct from his own memory and that of his colleagues.

This, then, is what Larsen brought to Festival Ballet. "I told Fred, 'I can put it on, but I cannot shape it.'" (The ballet, he says, has "more épaulement than Bournonville.") In two periods of ten days, nine and a half hours a day, he put it on. Then Ashton, aided by Alexander Grant and LFB's ballet mistress Elizabeth Anderton, shaped it.[2] And on 23 July, at the London Coliseum, the revival was unveiled, to a public and a critical community so expectant that this reviewer, at least, could not get in until the second night.

ASHTON'S *ROMEO AND JULIET* is not one of his masterpieces, but it is a beautiful ballet and, in the way of submasterpieces, reveals the master's characteristics with unusual clarity. Two such characteristics have been heavily remarked upon by earlier writers. One is the structural loyalty to Petipa—Ashton's choice, for example, to make the Capulets' ball a suite of formal dances rather than the sort of extended *pas d'action* that one sees in MacMillan. The other is Ashton's interest in love and his consequent focusing on the lovers to the exclusion of the rest of Verona. I would stress another aspect of the ballet, and that is Ashton's extreme modesty—not, in this case, a self-effacing modesty but an almost aggressive modesty, in contrast to the immodesty of the score. Like an English host with a boisterous Russian guest, the choreography, by its insistent good manners, seems to be trying to teach the score how to behave.

To one who has seen this music in the hands of Lavrovsky, Cranko, MacMillan, Nureyev, it is hard to separate the score from the dime-novel features of those ballets: the violence, the windswept passion, the fated ruin— and all this, just as in *Gone with the Wind*, played out against a strife-filled "historical background" that further empurples the plot. Yet the music, with its doom themes and crashing chords, unquestionably invites such treatment. One should keep in mind the grim words with which Prokofiev, only lately returned from his modernist dalliance in Europe, defended his new score to his countrymen: "I have taken special pains to achieve a simplicity which will, I hope, reach the hearts of all listeners. If people find no melody and no emotion in this work of mine, I shall be very sorry."

In other words, MacMillan, in large measure, gives the score what it asks for. Ashton does not.

The violence, to begin with, he sharply undercuts. The first market scene, which in other versions is largely given over to premonitory hostilities, is here dominated by pleasant ensemble dancing. Yes, there are a few fistfights, and in order to give the Prince some justification for his entrance, Benvolio and Tybalt do a little dagger dance, but there are no deaths, no wounds, not even any swords drawn—nothing that, to my knowledge, would have drawn a Renaissance prince away from his dinner. At the same time, the play's (and score's) major repository of violence, Tybalt, has undergone a strange alteration. Taking his cue from a play on words in Shakespeare's text,[3] Ashton styles Tybalt the "King of Cats" (the character is listed thus in the program) and gives him a fairytaleish feline character, like something out of Act III of *The Sleeping Beauty*. While this Tybalt delivers a fine, horrible death (hurling himself downstairs), he elsewhere hovers a bit uncomfortably between reality and fantasy—a victim, I think, of Ashton's fondness for animal characters and perhaps also his distaste for real-life bullies.

Images of cruelty and betrayal are also exceedingly scarce. The Tybalt/ Lady Capulet incest business is absent (though without the Lavrovsky precedent there would be little reason for its being there). When Lady Capulet arrives on the scene after the double death, she arrives *with* Lord Capulet, and they go first to Mercutio's body, then to Tybalt's. It is death itself they rue, not just the death of their own. Likewise, working backward, the two big sword fights (Mercutio/Tybalt, Tybalt/Romeo), while fierce, are at least fair fights, not the dishonorable skewerings that MacMillan makes of them. Working further backward, no cruelty is even really prepared for. The big ballroom ensemble dance, which in all other versions I have seen is employed as a sort of town-without-pity symbol of clan hatred—all the Capulets, in ranked columns, stomping toward us in their blood-red brocades—is here divided up into two benign pieces. In one, Paris, backed by eight of his kinsmen, does a beautiful and rhythmically complex solo of leaps and beats. In the other, the party guests, led by Lord and Lady Capulet, perform a pretty ensemble number.

In the paring away of violence, some of the violence of Romeo and Juliet's love is also eliminated. In the ball scene there is a full-out *coup de foudre,* complete with spotlights, but Juliet is not so floored by it that she cannot, a few moments later, have a nice chat with Paris and join him in a pas de deux with no sign of mixed feelings. This civilizing of the passion goes further yet. Romeo and Juliet leave the stage together not once but *twice* before their empty-ballroom pas de deux. Thus, what is supposed to be their first time alone together, and what is danced as such (she pulls away at first, etc.), is actually the stage enactment—one might say the public enactment—of what has already taken place, with Attic discretion, offstage. And as the tidal-wave enormity of this love is reduced, so is its threatening aspect. The marriage scene, despite its ominous music, is genuinely happy.

Of course, choreographing against one's score has its perils. There are times when a clear gap opens between movement and music, making Prokofiev sound like a blow-hard or Ashton look ineffectual. When those thunderous chords sound at the end of the first scene and the Prince accordingly shakes his fists, you wonder what he's shaking them at. Conversely, when, in the absence of the incest business, Ashton stages a socially acceptable lament to the huge dirge that in other versions has Lady Capulet baring and pounding her breast, the Prokofiev seems excessive, bombastic.

Yet still, strangely, Ashton's *Romeo* is whole and lovely. Ballet does not have, at the moment, a great romantic artist, an Emily Brontë of choreography. (Nor, historically, is there any reason it should.) Hence there is no one who can give this neoromantic score a truly inspired as well as faithful reading. But we do have a great classical artist, and his handling of the score is precious for the classical values that he extracts from it—above all, the employment of the ballet vocabulary as "open symbol," expressive without literalism, without ceasing to be ballet.

An obvious example, already much commented upon, is the double manège in the balcony scene, where first, in an early, pitpat stage of love, Romeo supports Juliet in a circle of tripping runs and then, on the second go-round, they advance to proper lifts: love in full sail. A subtler example is the passage of parallel dance that occurs in this pas de deux. Imagine: parallel dance, with all its old-fashioned formality, and with all that *air* between the partners, in the middle of this *ne plus ultra* of coming together. Yet its effect is perfect, for it initiates a new meaning in the dance. As we see the lovers, side by side, kneeling and bending, we see that what has happened is not just their discovery of each other but their joyful discovery, through each other, of something beyond themselves, of life itself, to which they here pay an almost prayerful tribute. By the end of the dance, as they stand, again side by side, with arms raised to heaven, this latter discovery has become the dominant one. Life has flowered for them—a poignant development, considering how shortly it will end for them. But all this is achieved through steps, all symbolically, all via the oldest conventions of ballet.

It is actually amazing, after the other *Romeos,* to see how fully Ashton trusts in the expressive power of the purely classical vocabulary. When, in her first scene, he wants to show us Juliet escaping from her Nurse's skirts, trying out life, what does she try out? Steps. Little runs, arabesques, balances. "Look what I can do," she is saying to the Nurse. And that—boldness in *dancing*—is the image of her bold taking on of her future. Likewise, when, in the bedroom scene, she tries to induce Romeo to stay, she does not climb into his cloak but instead drops into arabesque, in which he is then forced to support her. With steps she detains him. This is not to say that naturalistic gesture is excluded. Indeed, in the midst of her arabesque, she points to the bed, with clear meaning. But the primary language is ballet, and Ashton is not afraid that we won't understand it.

This is in keeping with the striking formality, the antirealism, of much of this *Romeo,* at least in comparison with the others. In cutting the score, Ashton cut away much of the context of his drama, particularly in the market-square scenes. (As P. W. Manchester put it, Ashton had no interest in showing "ruffians throwing sides of meat at one another."[4]) His town square has no beggars, no fruit vendors, no local toughs—just an ensemble, the ballet ensemble. This formalist approach, combined with the spare abstraction of Peter Rice's set, effectively removes the drama from Renaissance Italy.

A good deal of plot is also removed, in keeping with the mother-in-law rule. Juliet is never introduced to Paris; she simply greets him and then dances with him. Romeo, Mercutio, and Benvolio never decide or prepare to crash the Capulets' party; they simply appear. Most remarkable of all, the central male characters are introduced, at the opening of the ballet, with no contextual support whatsoever. As the curtain rises, Romeo materializes on the porch (a wonderful effect—he seems to rise out of nowhere) and does a few steps indicative of his romantic temperament. On his exit, Tybalt appears, baring his talons and glaring (the "King of the Cats" business). Then come Mercutio and Benvolio, who do some jolly turns and exit flying. Thus, with a few strokes, does Ashton introduce his characters as *characters,* as people in a story. He does not need Rosaline[5] or whores or even Verona to validate their reality. He trusts our ability to suspend disbelief. And he politely assumes we've read the book.

When he wishes to supply detail, however, he does so with a full hand, using not just dance but substantial mime passages (in which, of course, his Danish dancers were world experts). What he fills in, above all, is the Capulet family, whom he imagines utterly differently from MacMillan et al. Ashton's people are no icons of rage and grief but decent ordinary folk who love one another. When Lady Capulet comes to tell Juliet it is time to marry, she does so with a sweet, brimming pleasure, hinting at a happy sexual history. When Tybalt expels Romeo from the Capulet ball, Juliet does not stand gaping but runs to her unhappy father and kisses his face ("It's nothing, Daddy, don't worry"), whereupon he pats her ("Okay, honey") and, his party having ended, kisses his wife's hand as the curtain comes down. Even in Act III, while he is angry at his daughter's intransigence, he is merely an angry father, not a personification of cold violence. And Lady Capulet, who in other versions of this scene stands torn between husband and daughter, here full-heartedly comforts Juliet—sits her on the bed, puts her arms around her—while still not taking sides against her husband. Indeed, with the exception of Tybalt (who, as noted, is largely derealized, deprived of moral force), all the people in Ashton's ballet are good people. When they can act well, they do. When they can't, they're sorry. As in Shakespeare, Romeo, having killed Paris in the crypt, grieves for him.

This world of ordinary goodness has a curiously Danish feel. One does not know how much Bournonville Ashton had seen (perhaps none, from what he has told biographer David Vaughan), but as the record shows, Ashton has a way of picking up things from his dancers, of using what they can best offer. At the same time, the world of the Capulets is unmistakably Ashtonian—part of the steady concern with moral values that runs through his work from close to the very beginning and which is his inheritance, I believe, not from ballet but from the English novel. (Ashton is the balletic continuation of the "Great Tradition.")

Why, then, with his refined moral sense, he should have fastened on this amoral score, which glories in the blood-letting, I do not know. But the English have always shown a taste for life lived on saltier terms than their own.

Here, in any case, is a classicist's *Romeo,* one in which ruin comes not as a sexy supernatural force in the world of unreason but merely as part of the *lacrimae rerum,* in a universe not otherwise cruel. Accordingly, it is a *Romeo,* the only one I know, that can—indeed, *must,* given its vision—entertain delicate considerations.

—from *Ballet Review,* Fall 1985

NOTES

1. John Percival, *The Times,* 20 July 1985.

2. In shaping the ballet, he also made some changes, and in view of the work's simplicity, it is interesting to note that they were all by way of elaboration. According to Larsen, Ashton, for the revival, added the following: (1) the pas de trois for Romeo, Mercutio, and Benvolio that opens the second market scene in Act II, (2) the sequence, in Juliet's first scene, where she runs off with the Nurse's handkerchief, and the reprise of this exceedingly English hanky business in the ballroom scene, (3) the reprise, in the bedroom pas de deux, of the tripping manège from the balcony scene, (4) Paris's entry and fight with Romeo in the crypt. In addition, he altered the character of the soloist who leads the ensemble. In the 1955 version she was named Rosaline, though according to Larsen she had no dramatic function. For the revival, Ashton, taking a name from the Capulets' guest list in Shakespeare's text (I, ii, 72), rechristened her "Livia, lover of Mercutio" and gave her a little interaction with Mercutio in the market scenes. Finally, Ashton elaborated the choreography of the balcony pas de deux: the turns in promenade are now more complicated in design, and the bends from the waist are bigger and more numerous. The only substantial cut was made while the ballet was still in the Danish repertory, and not by Ashton. The flag dance with which the ensemble opens Act II was edited to about one-third of its original length, a change made by Larsen at the urging of the RDB corps, to whom this number, which they found endless, was known as "flag hell."

3. Thibaut (also Thibert, Tybert) is a name for the Cat in the *Roman de Renart,* a medieval cycle of animal fables. Shakespeare makes the pun twice. Early in the play, Mercutio refers to Tybalt as "Prince of Cats" (II, iv, 19). Later, in their fatal duel, Mercutio addresses Tybalt as "Good King of Cats" (III, i, 80) and tells him that he's going to take one of his nine lives. But I do not think that Shakespeare's Tybalt is otherwise markedly feline.

4. Dance Critics Association conference, New York, June 1985.

5. See footnote 2. There was a Rosaline in the original version, but in name only, according to Larsen. She did not figure in Romeo's first entrance, as she does in Cranko and MacMillan.

Symphonic Variations

Julie Kavanagh

*Created in 1946, Symphonic Variations is often thought of as Frederick Ashton's
signature ballet. It seemed at the time of its creation a response to the end of the war,
to the restoration of peace and harmony to the world. Crucial to its effect are César
Franck's deeply felt score and the simple, elegant, and quietly suggestive decor by
Ashton's close friend Sophie Fedorovitch, a pale green backdrop streaked with thin
black lines. There are three couples (the original cast was led by Margot Fonteyn),
and there is no story. Symphonic Variations is simple, calm, pure, and very difficult
to dance.*

*S*ymphonic Variations was born out of five years' bitterness and despair, a lily-
flower "whatever horror nudge her root," and marked a new development in
British dance: a radical change in terms of scale and style. Like a film director
working with CinemaScope for the first time, Ashton was liberated by the
challenge of filling what seemed an infinity of space, even eliminating the
corps he had originally planned to use, in favour of six soloists on an empty
stage. "Quite unbelievable," says the choreographer Richard Alston. "I've
only ever once worked at Covent Garden, and it just filled me with awe . . .
you get lost in that space." Despite the feelings of inadequacy he confessed to
Billy Chappell, Ashton's confidence in his artistic capabilities was soaring. He
proved his new-found independence by disregarding Constant Lambert's
advice against using the César Franck score: "Constant said, 'It's complete in
itself,' which is what he told me when I wanted to do *La Mer*. In that case I
listened—I saw I'd have had my mouth full of seawater and drowned—but
with *Symphonic Variations* I didn't care what he thought and went on with it. In
the end he came to me and said, '*You* were right.'" Triumphantly so. Never
before had Ashton shown himself in such command of the music; the dance
visually enacted Franck's antiphonal writing and thematic variations, yet
sometimes departed from the score with a Cunninghamesque freedom. Soft
circuiting leaps juxtaposed with rapid stage-skimming enchaînements correspond to no detectable beat. Yet when Ashton does react literally to the
music, he seems to uncover extra subtleties: generating a flicker of wit in the
circling wrist movements that accompany a passage of semitonal semiqua-

vers; or in the fast backward diagonal for two girls, which is so attuned to the piano that it calls to mind the drolly synchronized dance of the Cygnets, or the Sapphic pair in *Les Biches* (which it deliberately echoes).

It was Sophie Fedorovitch with whom Ashton had a virtually telepathic collaboration throughout the making of the ballet. She was as much involved in the choreography as the dancers, sitting by his side at rehearsals and discussing the work way into the night. It was she who urged the economy of its final form—a result that came about through a process of elimination on both sides. While Ashton simplified and purified the dance, Sophie modified her original idea for the backdrop. Preliminary sketches that were recently discovered in the backing of the framed finished design (which Ashton owned), show the way in which faintly naturalistic imagery—a suggestion of the tree and slanting sun-rays—was refined into an abstract pattern of lines.*

When her friend Captain Goodliffe died in a Cambridge nursing home in 1940, Sophie moved from Marsh Farm to an adjoining barn, which she converted with characteristic simplicity, and where Ashton spent many a weekend. For her, too, the English countryside, especially in springtime, had a profound emotional impact, "refuel[ling] her spirit as it were" and formulating ideas for designs. The view, from the barn's large kitchen window, of foggy marshland merging with lowering Norfolk skies—mile after mile of open space—was the main inspiration for the empty panoramas of *Dante Sonata* and *Symphonic Variations*. "They were together in my mind," she told Simon Fleet. "Reaching for a higher plane, paradise really. In my mind there is a definite connection, using line . . ." (Fleet says she left the sentence unfinished, providing a suggestion and allowing the audience's imagination to fill in the rest.)

Sophie and Ashton were bicycling near Brancaster, towards the end of the war, when the idea for the colour of the design struck them like an epiphany: "We came up a hill and suddenly there was the most marvellous glade filled with sunshine, and this had the most terrific effect on us." So mesmeric and suggestive was the result—a backcloth washed "a sort of greenish yellow" and scored with sweeping, looping parabolas—that to Alastair Macaulay writing in *The New Yorker* its pastoral spirit evoked Marvell's garden, "Annihilating all that's made / To a green thought in a green shade."†

---

*See Beth Genné's article, "My Dearest Friend, My Greatest Collaborator," in *Following Sir Fred's Steps: Ashton's Legacy,* edited by Stephanie Jordan and Andrée Grau.
†There are several interpretations of these curving black lines: Fedorovitch told the dancer, Gilbert Vernon, that they were suggested by a weather chart with its high and low pressures; Ashton and Marie Rambert claimed that they reflected the outline of telephone wires patterned against the Norfolk moors; Pamela May remembered Sophie muttering something about the illustrations of patterns made by electrical currents she'd seen in a book. The critic Beth Genné believes that the original inspiration of a sun-filled country glade is reflected in the enclosing shape of the "protectively" bending lines.

When the curtain rises, the "sextet of perfect instrumentalists," on which Ashton always insisted (he never let this ballet, his signature work, out of his sight), stand like classical Greek statues in elegant repose: arms relaxed, head tilted and lowered, one foot crossed over and resting on its point. It is a continuing motif and the position to which the dancers return as the curtain falls—"In my beginning is my end" (it was one of three possible conclusions which Ashton finally chose at the dress rehearsal). The first cast has never been surpassed; in fact, they remain so intrinsic to the ballet that, even today, as Macaulay points out, the music seems to call out their names: "'Margot *Fon-teyn* . . . Moira *Shear*-er . . .'; then 'Michael *Somes;* Brian *Shaw;* Henry *Dan-ton.*' Though Franck quickly embroiders variations on the theme ('and *Pam-ela* May') he keeps returning to devout announcements of it." Once set in motion, the dancers never leave the stage; and, although the steps themselves are not taxing, the twenty-minute ballet is such a marathon that performers rehearsing it for the first time have sometimes been physically sick. During the initial run-throughs, the dancers would lie on the floor, panting and in tears, but Ashton was ruthless: "'Get up and do it again,' he'd say," until they were able to create the effect of effortless lyricism he wanted.

To begin with, there is a sense of dormancy on stage, as the trio of women—striking in the original cast, with their matching heights, and contrasting black, red, and blonde hair—are screened, purdah-like, by their outstretched arms. They are, Ashton has said, "like women waiting to be fructified, so to speak." He intended the ballet to progress from chastity to fertility, darkness to light, following the pattern of Shakespeare's last plays: death to rebirth was the obvious metaphor for the times. "It has that breathtaking quality of serenity, a sense of the morning of the world," a friend told Ashton, to which he replied, "Quite right."

The dominant theme of the seasons in the ballet held a perpetual fascination and mystery for Ashton. He endorses it in the ballet's four-part, cyclical structure and in the recurring circular patterns created when the dancers take hands and run in a chain, their "ringlets" evoking English May Day dances, while also alluding to the new international amity (traditionally, in court and country dances, held hands signified harmony). At the time of making *Symphonic Variations,* however, there were many other things on Ashton's mind. The original concept was far more complex, as these jottings from his notebook reveal:

a) *Poco allegro*—Part 1. The women, Winter, the period of waiting, the Moon period, the Underworld, the Darkness. The Earth, Venus mourning. The Virgin's faith.

b) *Allegretto*—Part 2. The arrival of the Men. The Sun's rays, the Summer, the World, the Heavens, the Light, Adonis returns to the Earth, Life, Love, the Lover excites the love of his Spouse.

a) *Molto piu lento*—Part 3. The Search, The Wound of Love and Rapture caused by the spark of love. The Dance of Union, Fertility.

b) *Allegro non troppo*—Part 4. The Call of the Bridegroom. The Festival. The Summer. The Marriage. The Heart's joy in union. "Art and Faith united in one unseverable bond."

The ballet is steeped in subliminal religious references. Ashton considered the notion of introducing a nun taking the veil, an idea he abandoned only to suggest it fleetingly when the ballerina kneels, as if in supplication, as the Bridegroom approaches. The medium, he felt, had become "anti-God, if you like," by which he meant that the symbolic power of dance "to whisper private and sacred things" was diminishing, while the literary, theatrical ballets of Helpmann and de Valois were taking precedence. "I am frankly bored with too much characterisation in ballet . . . I would personally prefer to see somebody moving beautifully and expressing nothing but 'line,' than all the characterisation in the world." *Symphonic Variations* was Ashton's manifesto, in which dance d'école is paramount. Yet, while it appears to be "simply steps, pure dancing," its emotional impact on audiences reveals another dimension: an atmospheric potency Ashton described as a "personal fount of emotion from which the choreography springs." "It's not abstract. It's not steps," Antoinette Sibley has said. "It's intoxication of everything that's beautiful on another, not human, plane . . . it's what heaven must be like."

Ashton was not only under the influence of the Carmelite mystics when he made the ballet; he was also responding to César Franck's "very religious" score. Franck's devout music, which, with its mystical ascent "towards pure gladness and life-giving light," is the progression to which the ballet itself aspires, an exultant expression of Ashton's renewed faith. Dazzlingly lit, *Symphonic Variations* possesses the clarity of a vision. Margot Fonteyn, as he said, gave "the clue to it": hypnotically still, she represents a soul in a state of grace, in that state of suspension during which, St. Theresa claimed, "visions so sublime" can appear. The ballet's main motif of stasis—anomalous in a medium which glorifies movement—is a direct reference to St. John of the Cross's teachings on Quiet: "The soul waits in inward peace and quietness and rest." Repose, of course, is crucial to the ballet, for mundane as much as mystical reasons: the dancers need to recover their breath. When Fonteyn stood as the other dancers swirled around her, a symbol of ever-fixed eternity contrasting with worldly flux, she was, in fact, saving her strength for a scherzo solo which immediately preceded her smooth, floating pas de deux with Michael Somes. And while the doctrine of St. John of the Cross is a major source for *Symphonic Variations,* Ashton keeps it submerged, in the same way T. S. Eliot does in *Four Quartets,* a work with its own "secret history" of mysticism. "Little Gidding" is particularly close in spirit to the ballet. Written under the shadow of the war, it, too, is lyrical and visionary, a poem "of greatest comfort and illumination." But, whereas Eliot embraced the via negativa, Ashton encompassed the sensuousness of the Spanish mystics, their baroque "indulgence of emotion" being fundamental to his background and sensibility.

A covert eroticism is also embedded in the ballet. When Franco Zeffirelli, "still bruised by the war," first saw *Symphonic Variations* at the Florence Festival in 1948, he was struck by its impact.

> At the times they touched one another you felt the *love* they had for each other. They had suffered, they studied hard then suddenly came into the world. They managed to make us feel all of that. At my age it was very important. It taught me that you can't achieve anything in the performing arts unless there is reciprocal love. It has to be an act of love.

Even the spatially cool pas de deux, where "male and female have become almost as impersonal as electrons," contains allusions to the sexual act: Ashton wanted the ballerina to "really stretch herself open on those high ecarté lifts, making an arc with delayed climax and arrival." And in a confessional subtext, Ashton dramatizes his life story to date. While remaining the cynosure among the three danseurs, Michael Somes is momentarily eclipsed by Brian Shaw, whose solo culminates in what Beryl de Zoete aptly described as a "breath-taking ecstatic renversé, winging a pirouette"—a feat which contemporaries say no other dancer has equalled. The ballet, as a friend told Ashton, is "almost Greek in feeling," emphasized by the women's white tunics (a variant of practice dress), and by its evocation of Grecian statuary. And like the Platonists, Ashton sees carnal love as a shadow of a higher, more spiritual devotion. Here, Michael Somes is once again the Ideal; deified in the original scenario as the Bridegroom of the Song of Songs—just as he was in *The Wise Virgins.* In the final version, he remains a magnetic force, drawing the three women around him in a tribute to Balanchine's *Apollo,* whose three muses curl round his body like tendrils. He is the life-giver, inciting the trio, "moving alone coldly, unfertilized" into dance, like dull roots stirred by spring rain. Later, he also reactivates the two sentinel men, leading them by his example.

Ashton would have discouraged an over-elaborate interpretation of *Symphonic Variations.* It is, after all, a simple ballet, devoid of story and character.

And yet, for him, as for Schiller, whose work he was then reading and transcribing, the human element was always inseparable from the abstract. None of the dancers—not even Somes or Fonteyn—knew of the existence of a libretto. He was reluctant to put his ideas into words, even to himself. "Perhaps I was afraid . . . I might deflect myself from creating the work in terms of dancing, and that it might become literary, and that the fluid nature of my inspiration might crystallize into something I did not really intend." Like Mallarmé, purging poetry of didactic content, Ashton made it his priority to reinstate the dance equivalent of poésie pure—steps and not ideas. But, at the same time, he recognized that choreography needed to be more than just an exercise in abstract dancing; that, without a basic idea behind it, a personal fount of expression, "a cold complexity emerges which ceases to move an audience." Similarly, in an early draft of "Little Gidding," Eliot acknowledged the lack "of some acute personal reminiscence (never to be explicated, of course, but to give power from well below the surface)."

Symphonic Variations is "a revelation of the power of classical dancing to evoke romantic reactions"—a fact proclaimed by the ballet's euphoric reception in April 1946. "Hardly have I read such unanimous praise in the press. There seemed not one dissatisfied critic to be found," wrote Adeline Genée, the famous, turn-of-the-century Swanilda, who remembered when Ashton and Georgie called on her in Hanover Terrace just as he was beginning to choreograph. "How she protested at [your] upsetting her drawing room with all your papers and drawings. Today she would be very proud of you." The ballet, as everyone agreed, was a landmark for Ashton and for English ballet. Arnold Haskell, recognizing *Symphonic Variations* as a masterpiece, also reminisced about the early days, commenting, "It has been a wonderful journey and a rapid one." Among other fan letters was one from Sacheverell Sitwell, who, likewise, declared the ballet to be Ashton's "best work . . . quite lovely and without one jarring or discordant note, a real classical creation and a wonderful test of your creative powers. . . ."

Symphonic Variations is a paradigm of native classicism: lyrical, idiosyncratic, yet true to its academic origins. Its personalized neoclassicism—a brilliant reminting of the language of Petipa—was not only a breakthrough in the development of English dance, but, at the time, spoke metaphorically of a brave new world. The ballet holds its own among the great war-generated works, including "Little Gidding," Evelyn Waugh's *Sword of Honour* trilogy, Henry Moore's Shelter drawings, and the paintings of Graham Sutherland and John Piper. In its celebration of the sanctity and eternity of the English countryside, it belongs in the neo-Romantic tradition, although it rejects the heightened realism that characterizes the genre. Charged with feeling, *Symphonic Variations* is a modern evolution of ballet blanc (in *Studies in Ballet,* Billy Chappell includes it in his chapter on Romantic Ballet). "Its emotional appeal expresses in some inexplicable abstract way, as much, or even more, of the human heart as any ballet with a definite plot or obvious theme." It is as subjective, in its way, as *Dante Sonata,* but "the emotional stream [which came] rushing out with all its rocks and stones and trees," as Beryl de Zoete wrote, has been distilled into "heavenly serenity."

—from *Secret Muses,* 1997

FRED ASTAIRE

Born in Omaha in 1899 (as Frederick Austerlitz), Fred Astaire, in the opinion of George Balanchine and Rudolf Nureyev among many others, was the greatest male dancer of the twentieth century.

He and his older sister, Adele, began as a child act in vaudeville when Fred was six years old, quickly established themselves as major vaudeville performers, and went on to star in a number of stage musicals, including George Gershwin's Lady Be Good *and* Funny Face. *Adele retired when she married Lord Charles Cavendish, and in 1933 Fred proceeded to Hollywood and the immortal ten-film partnership with Ginger Rogers (The Gay Divorcee,* Top Hat, Swing Time, Shall We Dance . . .). *Later, he danced with Rita Hayworth, Eleanor Powell (see page 868), Vera-Ellen, Judy Garland (Easter Parade), Leslie Caron (Daddy Long Legs), Audrey Hepburn (Funny Face), Barrie Chase (on television), and others, and eventually appeared in several successful non-musical films, beginning with On the Beach. He was also a favorite of the great songwriters of the period, introducing such songs as Cole Porter's "Night and Day," Irving Berlin's "Cheek to Cheek," Jerome Kern's "The Way You Look Tonight," Gershwin's "Fascinatin' Rhythm," and Johnny Mercer's "One for the Road." He died in 1987.*

FRED ASTAIRE
Beginnings

Ｗe arrived at the Pennsylvania Station on a gray day. It was unusual for us to see so many people, all in a hurry. The New York attitude as ever was to hurry whether you had to or not. We soon found that out, so we hurried too.

Mother parked us by the information booth in the middle of the vast station and told us to stay there while she saw about baggage and transportation. We did.

I said to Adele, "This is a big city."

She gave me a flat look and replied, "This is only the depot."

Mother arrived with a porter in a red cap and I asked him, "Which way is the business district?" He grinned, "Yassuh." I didn't realize, of course, that New York was nothin' else but.

We went to the Herald Square Hotel through jams of street cars, hansom cabs, and beer trucks.

There were a few days of sight-seeing and staring at new things, such as elevated trains, the Flatiron Building, and the subway. But we had come to town to work, as I soon found out, and the work, to my surprise, included me.

I can't say that I protested. I simply did not get the idea that dancing was for me. However, I took it as a matter of course. It seemed natural enough to go with Adele and do what she did.

Claude Alvienne's dancing school was in the same building as the Grand Opera House on Eighth Avenue at Twenty-third Street. To get to the dancing school we climbed a dark flight of narrow stairs to a small door which opened, surprisingly, into a big ball room. Rows of folding chairs lined three sides of the room and at one end was a stage.

This was a school that our parents had selected through a small advertisement they saw in a theatrical trade paper, the *New York Clipper,* to which my father subscribed. There we were. Alvienne was a kindly, fatherly man with white hair, quite the picturesque dancing master. We liked him at once and we liked Mrs. Alvienne. She was known as La Neva and had been a well-known toe dancer.

I can't remember much about my first dancing lessons but I know I didn't mind them. I think I did simple exercises along with other children. That phase is all quite vague to me.

What I do remember vividly is Mr. Alvienne beating time with a stick on the back of a wooden chair. On one side of the ballroom a lady played the piano. Mr. Alvienne stood in front of us, his right foot on a rung of the chair, that stick in his right hand, beating out the time. This got me.

When we made a mistake he would stop, lay his stick on the chair and say, "Now, we do it like so," as he demonstrated the step. He never scolded. He patiently showed how to do it "like so," then returned to his stick.

I still had no urge to dance, but I loved that stick.

Then there was acting, too. We were being trained in the drama.

Alvienne's was a good school and he was significant in the start of some very successful performers. Of those in our class, one to earn fame was Harry Pilcer, who became noted as a partner of the French star, Gaby Deslys, and also for his solo dance which he concluded by falling down a flight of stairs.

We usually hurried home after our classes to get at our grammar school work, which, as I mentioned before, Mother taught us. (We did not attend public school until several years later.) Between times we played, out in the street, with the kids in the neighborhood.

A part of Mother's curriculum also was to see that we went to the theatre occasionally. There were always many great stars appearing on the stage in New York. Lilly Langtry, Laurette Taylor, Maxine Elliott, Ethel Barrymore, DeWolf Hopper, Maude Adams, E. H. Sothern, William Collier, Weber and Fields, John Drew were known and loved everywhere not only on Broadway but in great and little theatres across the country, and in small-town opera houses. They were familiar names to us, of course, in a sort of oblivious kind of way.

We saw one musical comedy twenty-eight times, *The Soul Kiss* with Adeline Genée, the celebrated Danish ballet star. Mother hoped that some of Genée's dancing would rub off on us. This was the first really great dancing I ever saw. We all studied it intensely.

Adele and I danced from time to time in the school recitals. However, dramatic work was stressed just as much as the dance for these affairs and our first plunge in that direction came with Edmond Rostand. We were going to do *Cyrano de Bergerac*.

We asked who *he* was.

"A brave and gallant man in a famous play," Mother explained. "He has an enormous nose. In the play, Cyrano wears an artificial nose, made out of putty or something like that, and he fights anyone who makes fun of it.

"He is in love with a girl named Roxane," Mother went on. "She is beautiful and has long blond hair. This is a good part, too. Freddie, you will play Roxane."

This was news. Me play the girl?

But that's the way it turned out. I became Roxane in a blond wig, which tickled the back of my neck, and a satin dress rented from a costume company, which kept tripping me up. There was logic in the arrangement: I played the girl because I was three inches shorter than Adele.

My sister wore the pants, and swashbuckled in the balcony scene—only we had no balcony. We spoke Rostand's great poetry almost as if we understood what it meant.

Adele proclaimed:

> Roxane, adieu! I soon must die!
> This very night, beloved, and I
> Feel my soul heavy with love untold.
> I die! No more, as in days of old,

My loving, longing eyes will feast
On your least gesture. . . .

If I made any gestures they must have been from distress.

I was plagued by the wig, annoyed by the long dress, and embarrassed by the female impersonation. But Adele and I both looked on *Cyrano* as just another of those things we were supposed to do, like spelling. I didn't object. I was merely surprised that we did it at all. Why weren't we dancing?

Our *Cyrano* had a run of one night only, along with other dramatic and dancing skits by the various pupils, and was on stage seventeen minutes.

The next recital brought two large prop wedding cakes. This was actually a vaudeville act planned by Professor Alvienne, and he decided to give it a dress rehearsal at the recital. Mother bought all the props and effects for the act, most of which were built to order, not to mention the elaborate wardrobe and costumes. The wedding cakes were rather remarkable electrical and mechanical contrivances, about six feet in diameter and two feet high. They could be danced on and were equipped with musical bells which could be played with hands and feet. Electric lights were built into the structure so that at the proper moment they flashed on and off.

The purpose of these wedding cakes was to provide a background for a novelty miniature bride-and-groom number, Adele being the bride and I the groom. The costumes were fancy. Adele was in white satin and I was in full evening dress—black satin knickerbockers, white tie and tails. And naturally—a top hat.

There it was. The evil idea was planted way back there.

This was the first appearance of the top hat in my life. I've been trying for years to dispel the idea that I was born in one, but I guess I did come close to it.

Our act was "crazy." We not only danced on the cakes but up and down the musical stairs leading to them, while playing "Dreamland Waltz" with our toes.

After that specialty the cakes lit up, we made an exit, and Adele returned for a solo. Then I appeared in my solo, a buck and wing on my toes, bowed off in a hurry, and returned as a lobster. Adele, meanwhile, made a quick change and became a glass of champagne.

In these costumes we did an eccentric dance duet—then played more tunes on the musical cakes with our hands and feet. The act ran twelve minutes in full stage.

Actually, after only about a year at Alvienne's we were preparing to make our professional bow. And this was the act that did it.

I can remember being aware of coming up to the big event. It was not a nervous approach by either Adele or me. I don't think child performers are ever nervous.

We made our pro debut in Keyport, New Jersey. . . .

When we went on we were the opening act, the worst spot on the bill, placed there because it took so much time and made so much noise to set up our props.

Adele and I stepped out just as we had been taught. I think on the whole we did pretty well. I remember Mr. Alvienne's coming back after the matinee to comment favorably and give us encouragement. He told us we showed promise and just needed to keep working and practicing to become smoother and more professional.

My father, waiting hopefully in Omaha, was pleased to learn how we made out. The Keyport newspaper proclaimed: "The Astaires are the greatest child act in vaudeville." I think if two words had been added, "In Keyport," this might have been more accurate.

—from *Steps in Time,* 1959

Fred Astaire
Ginger's Dress

The dancing dresses of my partners have, for years, been a working problem, and in *Top Hat* I dare say it reached its dizzy peak.

I seldom discuss the style of a dress but I am concerned with how it will dance, or rather, react to the dance. Therefore, my partners are usually willing to let me help in choosing them.

Girls love to wear slacks when learning or rehearsing a dance. They are comfortable and convenient and allow complete freedom of movement. Ginger always wore them for rehearsal. In fact, Hermes and I were so used to seeing Ginger on the rehearsal stage in slacks that one day when she showed up in a dress we didn't know who she was.

What I'm getting at is that when putting on a dance, experimenting over and over with various steps, the slacks work perfectly, but when we finally have to get ready to shoot, it is necessary to try everything with a dress, the actual dress if possible, to see how things will go. That's when the awful awakening takes place, the realization that in some instances it is not possible to do the steps as planned with the dress. If the gown happens to be very full at the hem, for instance, it automatically becomes "our" dress instead of just my partner's, as it wraps around my feet, causing no end of trouble and hindrance to both of us. If it is too tight, the lady cannot negotiate the routined movement, necessitating an alteration of the choreography or a splitting of the skirt. Endless problems can arise out of this situation, and I made it a practice some years back to ask the lady to rehearse in a dress or in some sort of rehearsal prop cloth that behaved like a dress, so that we would not be confronted with impasses on the set at the last minute, holding up production and causing general consternation.

In *Top Hat,* Ginger and I had that wonderful song of Irving Berlin's, "Cheek to Cheek." I arranged a romantic, flowing type of dance to fit the situation in the picture and we took special pains to try for extra-smooth smoothness.

Ginger rehearsed the final few days before shooting in a prop dress. I had seen the drawing of the real one she was to wear—a feathered affair and very nice, too, I thought.

I asked Gin to get the dress on for one rehearsal to make sure about it with all those feathers. Gin tried to get it but was told that the feathers were not yet sewn on, and the dress would not be ready until the day we were to shoot the number. That was that.

The memorable day was soon on us, with nobody anticipating any unusual hazards in connection with a little thing like a dress. Well, Ginger finally arrived on the set after a delay of about an hour while she was getting into this thing. I thought it looked fine but it was somewhat fuller than I expected. We then got ready to rehearse the number right through with the playback for camera and lights. Everything went well through the song, but when we did the first movement of the dance, feathers started to fly as if a chicken had been attacked by a coyote.

I never saw so many feathers in my life. It was like a snowstorm. They were floating around like millions of moths. I had feathers in my eyes, my ears, my mouth, all over the front of my suit, which just happened to be a white-tie-and-tails outfit. (Now, wasn't that odd?)

I shouted out, "I thought these feathers were supposed to be sewn to this dress."

The wardrobe lady answered, "Oh, it's only because it was the first time the dress was moved around a bit. That won't happen again."

I suggested that we'd better start shooting the number pretty quick while there were still some feathers left on it.

Ginger didn't say much. I knew we were in trouble and that the feathers would never stop flying off that dress in dance movement, and we had plenty coming up.

We started by photographing the song, finished that, and stopped. So far so good.

We then went for the dance and again the feathers took over. The cameraman stopped us, saying he couldn't photograph the number that way, and also that the floor was covered with feathers. This went on again and again. Ginger's mama rushed on the stage to help—but even Lela couldn't. The feathers kept flying, the wardrobe lady shook the dress and the sweepers swept them up, but they kept flying and we could not get an OK take. It got to be funny after a while. The news went all over the lot that there was a blizzard on the *Top Hat* set. The sightseers poured in on us.

Finally, the fallout had run its main course. With just a minimum amount flying, the cameraman decided he would take a chance and photograph the number. We would see how it worked out in the rushes next morning.

When we finished shooting for the day, Hermes Pan and I sang a little parody on "Cheek to Cheek" to Ginger. It went (with apologies to Mr. B.):

> Feathers—I hate feathers—
> And I hate them so that I can hardly speak,
> And I never find the happiness I seek
> With those chicken feathers dancing
> Cheek to Cheek.

Next morning the rushes were good. Very few of the flying feathers picked up on the film and the glossy white floor showed none at all. What a relief!

We laughed about that episode for weeks afterward. It was sort of a running gag with Ginger and me. I used to call her "Feathers"!

—from *Steps in Time,* 1959

GINGER ROGERS
The Dress

One of the top movie stars of the thirties and forties, Ginger Rogers (1911–1995) got her start as a child performer in vaudeville before landing her first Broadway job. In 1930 she was featured in the Gershwins' Girl Crazy *(the show that made Ethel Merman a star). She was already making minor movies, and in 1933 she had her first real success:* 42nd Street. *That same year she made* Flying Down to Rio, *the first of the ten films with Fred Astaire which made them both tremendous stars. With her beauty and her spunky charm, her supple back, her talent for conveying feeling through movement, and a perfectionism that matched his, she was his perfect dance partner. Her career lasted for decades, and included many box-office hits, including* Kitty Foyle, *a weeper for which she won an Oscar. But the Astaire films are what guarantee her immortality.*

Bernard Newman, the dress designer, met with me to discuss the colors and shapes of the various dresses I was to wear in the film [*Top Hat*]. Unlike a lot of designers, Bernie was open to suggestions. He'd say, "Tell me what kind of dress you want to wear and what color you'd like." Then he'd show me swatches of all sorts of beautiful materials—lamé, chiffon, velvet, and brocade. I was particularly interested in the "Cheek to Cheek" number and made my preference known.

"I want a blue dress," I told him. "A pure blue with no green in it at all. Like the blue you find in the paintings of Monet. I would love the dress to be made of satin with myriads of ostrich feathers, low in the back and high in the front."

Bernie sketched as I spoke. It's funny to be discussing color when you're making a black-and-white film, but the tone had to be harmonious.

Bernie's final sketch had an extremely low back, as I had requested. The watercolor he had used was just the color I wanted. The dress was form-fitting satin encircled by ostrich feathers, lots of feathers. A specialist would be hired to extend the feathers and make them a consistent length. Bernie said it would take roughly $1,500 worth of feathers. . . .

In fact, I had already seen them. From here on, they would have to be okayed by the producer.

The setting for "Cheek to Cheek" was supposed to be a Venetian canal. As designed by Van Nest Polglase and Carroll Clark, it was most extravagant and the biggest B.W.S. (Big White Set) to date. But however beautiful it may have been, it was about as Italian as Pat O'Brien. The Lido canal set occupied two sound stages, side by side, put together to make room for the canals and gondolas. Where that water went after filming was done, I never knew.

On the day of shooting we rehearsed in ordinary clothes to mark the various positions for camera. We rehearsed before and after lunch until director Mark Sandrich called for a take. My beautiful blue feather dress was still up at wardrobe for its finishing touches. Argyle Nelson, our assistant director, called to have it brought over.

As I headed for my portable dressing room, I saw Clarkie, the wardrobe lady, walking through the stage door. She held my dress high above her head as she marched toward my dressing room. Mark Sandrich, Fred Astaire, Argyle Nelson, cameraman David Abel, Hermes Pan, and the technicians turned their heads to watch this blue apparition go by.

"What is it? A bird? A plane?"

"No, it's Ginger's dress!"

Clarkie paraded past the crew and their jibes and into my dressing room where she put the gown on a rack. Almost immediately there was a knock at my door; Mark Sandrich wanted to speak to me . . . alone.

What was this, I thought?

"Ginger," Mark started out. "You know that white dress you wore in *The Gay Divorcee*? Well, I would like you to wear that because I think it is a much, much prettier dress than this one."

My heart sank to my knees. "Do you mean—you don't like this dress?"

"Well, I don't really think it's right for this scene." As Mark talked, my suspicions grew. He was acting as a spokesman for someone else. I knew who it was who didn't like the dress.

"Mark, the white dress has already been seen by the public. They wouldn't want to see it again."

"They won't remember it, Ginger."

"I disagree with you, Mark. To accuse an audience of being stupid is risky. The critics would be on my neck and yours for being so shortsighted."

"Well, to tell you the truth," he said, "as we saw the dress being brought in, all of us around the camera immediately disliked it. I really would like to send upstairs to wardrobe and get your *Gay Divorcee* dress."

With that, he opened the door and made a director's exit. I was stunned, broken-hearted, disappointed, and angry! Had I been the type of actress to show my emotions, I would have cried, thrown something, or disappeared into the ladies' room for a few hours. I decided to telephone my mother.

"Mother, come over to the studio right away, please."

"What's wrong?"

"It's better to explain when you get here. Please hurry."

I returned to my portable dressing room. In a short while, the frayed white dress was brought to me. It was soiled and stretched from being on the hanger. It was a mess.

When Mother arrived, I explained the problem to her and showed her the blue dress.

"I think it's beautiful. What do you think, Mother?"

"It's gorgeous," she said. "You mean Mark wants you to wear that worn-out white dress instead of this lovely blue feathered one? Why, what's wrong with it?"

"All I know is, Mother, what I've just told you. The dress barely got in the door, and suddenly I became a villain."

Again there was a knock on the door, and Mark reentered.

"Ah, Lela," he said. "I'm so glad that you are here. You can help me convince Ginger to wear this graceful white dress she wore in *The Gay Divorcee* instead of this, this, this . . . feathered thing."

I could see he was holding back some impolite remarks about the dress. Knowing the sketch had to have been approved by the producer and shown to the director, I was puzzled. However, it was not up to me to remind them of studio policy.

"Well, Mark, I'm sorry, but I agree with Ginger. This blue feathered thing, as you call it, is a lovely gown, and I think she should wear it."

"Lela, perhaps you could come outside and talk with McDonough, Joe Nolan, and all the executives about this."

Mark ignored me and directed his whole argument to Lela. I opened the door and saw ten men, five from the front office, waiting to change my mind about the dress. By this time, I could see my mother bracing herself as Mark continued to protest the dress.

"Lela," he persisted, "why don't we call upstairs and have them find another dress that she has danced in?"

The words flew out of Mother's mouth like seven boomerangs: "Why don't you just get another girl!"

She took my hand and we both stormed past Mark Sandrich and out the stage door. The voice of Argyle Nelson stopped us. "Miss Rogers, would you come back onto the stage? Mr. Sandrich suggests that you rehearse once in the dress . . . the blue one."

Mother and I looked at each other to try to guess where the next bed of quicksand might be. He held open the door, and Mother said, "Don't go back unless you really want to."

"This much, Mother, I'll tell you. It's either that dress or home I go. So wait. You may have to take me home yet."

"Never worry. I'm going to wait," she said.

We went directly to my portable dressing room and were silent for the next ten minutes while I got into my beautiful blue satin dancing dress. I wondered how I was supposed to go out there and dance as though nothing had happened and listen to a love song being sung to me? Fred didn't like the dress. That was the root of the problem. When he approached me for the trial run, it was written on his face.

Our emotions were high-pitched. He didn't like my dress and I didn't like being put to the test. First he sang and then we danced. In our rehearsal for camera, it's true, some of the feathers did flutter and annoy Fred. He muttered to himself as he plucked the feathers off his tailcoat. Instead of "Cheek to Cheek," the song should have been called "Horns to Horns." I was determined to wear this dress, come hell or high water. And why not? It moved beautifully. Obviously, no one in the cast or crew was willing to take sides, particularly not my side. That was all right with me. I'd had to stand alone before. At least my mother was there to support me in the confrontation with the entire front office, plus Fred Astaire and Mark Sandrich. My 105 pounds couldn't have gotten me through the first round without her. The rehearsal was over and it was time for the take.

After the first take, I could feel that for one moment, they had conceded graciously. Fred's attitude was still cool and aloof, but Mark was not taking his losing with any grace. I was sad that they didn't see that that lovely dress would add to the number.

I appeared for the rushes the next day and was greeted by a cold silence. Rushes (unedited film takes) were usually seen at 6:30 or 7:00. This day they were shown at 4:00. The lights lowered, and *no one* in the projection room spoke to me. *No one* acknowledged my presence. I'd never played a specter before. The dance began. As I saw my beautiful dress in motion, I was pleased and happy. I was enthralled, just watching it move across the screen. When the lights came up, everyone filed out, speaking to each other sotto voce. I was the last one out of the room. As I reached the street, one of the assistants came up behind me and, as he passed me, said in a stage whisper while looking straight ahead, "I think it looks beautiful. So what's a loose feather or two." And he kept walking. That was the first kind word I'd heard from any of the group.

We returned to the set to film a few other scenes. Mark's attitude was stiff and businesslike. Fred's weather vane was aloof and cool. Everyone continued to ignore me. Only Argyle Nelson gave me a smile and wink at the end of the day. I didn't pout or sulk, even though I was bewildered.

Four days later, a small, plain white box with a tailored white bow was delivered to my permanent dressing room. I pulled off the lid and there was a note, which said simply:

> Dear Feathers.
> I love ya!
> Fred

Underneath the cotton layer was a gold feather for my charm bracelet.

—from *Ginger: My Story,* 1991

ARLENE CROCE
Notes on La Belle, La Perfectly Swell, Romance

Arlene Croce wrote this trailblazing piece on Astaire and Rogers in 1965, seven years before publishing her seminal The Fred Astaire & Ginger Rogers Book.

Fred Astaire, Ginger Rogers. I can feel a glow just thinking of you. Astaire's dancing made John O'Hara cry. Balanchine came to America in search of girls like Ginger Rogers. Nine films for RKO between 1933 and 1939 constitute the most remarkable musical series in screen history and the greatest dancing in movies. The tenth and last film was in 1949, when Metro reunited them in *The Barkleys of Broadway.* By way of celebrating, *The Barkleys* reprised "They Can't Take That Away From Me" from *Shall We Dance*—but they could. Astaire and Rogers remained thirties divinities. The great tunes, the scintillating steps, the grace and good looks, were heavenly chic perfume bottled, faceted, in Lalique crystal. Where these duets took place—casinos, ocean parks, deserted ballrooms, penthouse roofs under starry canopies or daylit bandstands in rainy weather—is now an abandoned playground, a Rainbow Room of the memory, or of the senses only. These were the most elegant seductions and, barring only the best of Griffith, Chaplin, and Garbo, the most elegaic partings in American cinema. Fred and Ginger were superseded by Gene Kelly and Cyd Charisse, aristocrats giving way to mass man. Like true aristocrats, in their final RKO film, *The Story of Vernon and Irene Castle,* Astaire and Rogers had looked back, not ahead, in a salute across time. Their perfect accuracy in the Castle style—the tango, Maxixe, Castle Walk— exceeds even the demands of authenticity to become biographical portraiture of a rare order. The continual surprise of the Castle film is how close the dance impersonations come, how *needlessly* good they are. Even Barrault as Deburau in *Children of Paradise* does not efface himself as Astaire does, playing Vernon Castle. But how, I wonder, would Gene be Fred, or Cyd, Ginger?

Astaire's style, for forty years a major criterion of masculine elegance the world over, does not admit of further definition. Like all formative influences that are both natural and great, it seems infinite norm; one cannot remember a time when it was not. In his prime he had a thrilling happiness like that of a young child. You've seen the port de bras Astaire uses at fast climaxes on three-year-olds, when they are at a vertiginous peak of excitement. Then, they too do not look out at the world, but down the vortex of their delight. Ginger's arms, not trained, were lovely, too; especially so in the noble upsweeping movement at the start of the last dance in *Swing Time.* Notice, too, her hands in "Pick Yourself Up." The raised shoulders, so widely criticized, was a feminine attitude of that era; they don't bother me in Ulanova either.

It's important to be very clear that "Fred-and-Ginger," as we speak of them, exist only in the timeless dimension of their dance. In this dimension they grow suddenly large and important in a way that isn't given to either alone. Fred, alone, is a known quantity. Adding him to anyone else was simple arithmetic. But with Ginger, as Cocteau said of the opium trance, one and one are no longer two, they are eleven. This, of course, is to say nothing of what they may "really" have been like, separately or together, in private life; or what they were in other films or different careers; or are now. It is only to note the glow of a beautifully conceived professional attitude.

At the core of their professionalism was a concentration upon dance as dance, not as acrobatics or sexy poses or self-expression.[1] Their absorption gave plausible life and seriousness to what remained generically lyric fantasy—the continuing lyric fantasy of which all their numbers were a part. Their confidence was such as to breed an almost mischievous gaiety. Notice how they watch each other throughout the two duets in the "Continental" sequence of *The Gay Divorcee;* it's impossible that the screen should ever again have captured such a delicious entre-nous sparkle of fun. To some observers the fun is a bit coldly technical; the dancing looks tricksy and too objective, like the challenge of a competition ("Beautiful music . . . dangerous rhythm . . ."). Just so. In an Astaire-Rogers film the dancing is often the only real serious business. Their way of dancing up to a song, rather than down to a plot, is what takes you by surprise; they gave each song all the emotion that belonged to it, and they gave the plot more than the shallowness of scripted characterization could allow for. So it is that, in *Carefree,* Astaire as a psychoanalyst "hypnotizes" his patient, Rogers, stepping directly from plot to dance in a way that would seem preposterous only if you hadn't been following the film for its exclusive lyric possibility—that of Astaire as a hypnotist. Audiences no longer know how to "read" Astaire's kind of musical; they are depressingly literal-minded. All that should matter in *Carefree* is that a dance emerge, and it does, one as wry and affecting, in its way, as the "Sleepwalker" pas de deux in *La Sonnambula*—at which audiences have been known to giggle, too.

Yes, the plots are awful and yes, there's never enough dancing. The perfect Astaire-Rogers film doesn't exist, but neither could one compose it by stringing together all the musical portions from all the films. *Swan Lake* is more than one white pas de deux and one black. I myself would gladly dispense with Fred's Benno, Edward Everett Horton, but not with the delirious comedy-script world he comes from, with its stale conventions and staler gags, its apparatus of door-slams, double takes, aspirins, and breaking glass. This may be very shoddy stuff but it is a functional necessity. So are the formula exhibitions of cheekiness, fatuity, and plain bad temper the scripts put the two stars through, much more convincing to my taste than the unctuous "me proud beauty" snortings of Jeanette MacDonald and Nelson Eddy at MGM. Nothing smarmy about Rogers and Astaire, especially when, suddenly tranquil, they become their angelic selves. Out of the agitated wreck of farce rises, somehow, the lyric act. In their dance all is redeemed. Subtract the wreckage and you have subtracted transfiguration and transcendence.

Often, one can even observe a quite subtle transfiguration taking place in the entire film. The dances are not about nothing. Frequently they have the most intimate connection with literal plot action. *Carefree* is only one example. The finale of *Shall We Dance* combines all the elements, symbolic as well as dramatic, of the plot. Coming at a plot climax in *The Gay Divorcee,* "Night and Day" begins in hostility and grows more and more serious. Turning at one point, she appears to strike him. The great "Never Gonna Dance" sequence recapitulates all the important action of *Swing Time* and sweeps it forward to a heart-rending climax as in a spasm of clenched anger she whirls out of his life. Yet, while there is a great deal that is being said in these dances, Astaire never once changes his choreographic style. It stays very dry. Nor do he and Rogers ever appear to be acting out meanings. Their smooth, informal, light objectivity continues straight across the lines of reference, so that you don't even have to notice them if you don't want to. And since the weight of gesture seems no more than what the music of the moment deserves, one is free to enjoy dancing unpossessed by extraneousness. This is, of course, the classical view, presupposing mastery of design, that one takes for granted in all forms of cultivated dancing. It's the difference, or one of the differences, between Astaire and Kelly. Where Kelly has ideas, Astaire has steps. Where Kelly has smartly tailored, dramatically apt Comden and Green scripts, Astaire in the thirties made do with obtuse formulae derived from nineteenth-century French farce. But of course the Kelly film is no longer a dance film. It's a story film with dances, as distinguished from a dance film with a story. When Fred and Ginger go into their dance, you see it as a distinct formal entity, even if it's been elaborately stage-managed and built up to, like the bandstand dance in *Top Hat*. In a Kelly film the plot action and the musical set pieces preserve a smooth continuity of high spirits, so that the pressure in a dance number will often seem too low, the dance itself plebeian or folksy, in order to "match up" with the rest of the picture. Wonderful as *Singin' in the Rain* is, it hasn't much to do with dancing. In time Astaire adapted himself remarkably to the new integrated expression, without ever being quite at home in it. (Minnelli's *The Bandwagon,* made in 1953, delightfully exploited his discomfort.)

Hard-core A&R stuff, what if you're the slightest bit susceptible you get high on, runs from '34 to '37. Already in *Carefree,* more screwball comedy than musical, the mould is cracking. Under Mark Sandrich's direction, the non-musical portions of the series often resemble a dream in which wax dummies come to life in a department store after dark. Still, and not only because of his gifted collaborators, I'd put the junkiest Sandrich up against the sleekest Kelly/Minnelli/Donen, as the greatest musical ever made. Perhaps it would be the odd, slightly fey and elusive *Shall We Dance,* with its Gershwin score, its strange use of dolls and masks, its counterpoint of "ballet" and "jazz"[2] with Ginger paralleling Harriet Hoctor in swooping backbends. Or maybe it would be *Follow the Fleet,* in which Fred dissuades Ginger from leaping to her death and refrains from shooting himself with a dear little automatic pistol, so that they can both perform Irving Berlin's "Let's Face the Music and Dance." Or *Carefree,* just for another Berlin tune, "Change Partners"—"Must you dance / Ev'ry dance / With the same / Fortunate man" (who else but Ralph Bellamy)? *The Gay Divorcee* has the divine "Night and Day," which if there could be only one dance I would choose above all the rest. This is the greatest, the most profoundly private, dance of seduction. Magnificently choreographed and scored, it changes the course of the entire film, and the moment at its end when Rogers gazes up, wordless, at her marvelous partner, is like a moment in Flaubert. (The corresponding dance in *Swing Time* is the "Waltz," and it too is followed, in a morning-after scene, by silence and gazing.) Some junk.

The champion Sandrich film is, of course, *Top Hat*. Its exuberant visual stylization makes it the favorite of film fans, but I find the dance fans prefer

George Stevens' *Swing Time,* and so do I. The year was 1936 and it was really swing, at least "Pick Yourself Up" is. The sudden switch in the coda to a broad, spacious, new riding tune and tempo couldn't be more in period, or more exhilarating. Delicate Jerome Kern swing makes a syncopated fantasy out of the "Waltz in Swing Time" and the luxury of the sound mixing is such that at one point, over the soft, stertorous murmur of cornets, one hears the brush of the dancers' feet on the floor. "A Fine Romance" is a touch Mamoulian in a setting of gently falling snow with that kind of music, and lyrics anything but gentle—a tongue-lashing in fact. Astaire's solo, "Bojangles of Harlem" begins with white chorus girls singing: "Ask anyone / Up Harlem way / Who that guy Bojangles is / They may not know / Who's President / But ask them who Bojangles is."[3] Astaire in blackface, in ragtime hoodoo, stays Astaire, stays white, but the dance he does is not race caricature. It has the dignity of homage. And through the supreme simultaneous glitter of both their styles, you realize Astaire is actually much closer in spirit to Bill Robinson than to Vernon Castle, even though his immersion in Robinson's characteristic style of virtuosity is much less.

What is left? The shampoo serenade to "The Way You Look Tonight," and last and almost best of all, "Never Gonna Dance." Where *Swing Time* finally shades *Top Hat* is in the unsurpassed beauty of the dancing and the special radiance in dance of the two stars. Both films have scores of dazzling abundance. Both have lemony Helen Broderick and limey Eric Blore. *Top Hat* is better balanced and more ambitious—it attempts comedy / romance / musical / satire, but it triumphs in the last two categories only, because of Irving Berlin's songs and Van Nest Polglase's gleaming Venice. The lines in *Swing Time* are funnier, but not by much. (Sample joke, *Top Hat:* "What is this strange power you have over horses?" "Horsepower." Sample joke, *Swing Time:* "You know, sometimes I should be left alone." "Always.") To be sure, there *is* Victor Moore, the "millions of no cuffs" tailor, and the sublime nuttiness of Moore's routine with Broderick, which today sounds like Beckett:

"Lovely, isn't it?"

"What is?"

"The music."

"What music?"

"The music they're playing."

"Oh. Yes. What made you think of it?"

"Oh, I don't know. My mind was wandering, I guess."

But as romance *Swing Time* is supreme, and stands among the greatest of all screen romances. In no other Astaire-Rogers film is there anything like so exact, so tender, and so magical a sense of the spirit of romantic love that is animated when he dances with her, and that is lost when for one plot reason or another he cannot dance with her. In no other film in the world is dancing used so persuasively as a simulacrum of adult passion and serious sexual commitment. It is not so much that these two people belong together, as that they belong together in the dance. Without the dance they are not. Without one another the dance is not. Hence the irony of Fred's song: "The wolf was discreet, he left me my feet, and so"—melancholy vow—"I'll put them down on anything but the la belle, la perfectly swell, romance—never gonna dance."

June-moon. Romance-dance. Trivial? In other movies the suspense is in whether the boy will get the girl in bed. Here we follow his need to get her onto the dance floor. The meaning is the same, only the language is different. In *Swing Time,* just this is the crux of the action: will they dance? Will Astaire, as Lucky the gambler,[4] win the orchestra back from the mobsters so that the dance can go on? One reiterated line becomes a kind of chord or refrain: "There isn't going to be any dance." We hear it time and again. "But there isn't going to be any dance . . . any music . . . any dance." Over and over we arrive at the impasse. By the time Fred does his sad song forswearing the dance, a mood of almost bitter frustration has set in. Not only has he lost the orchestra, he's lost Ginger, and he's feeling defeated on a grand scale. On two stage levels linked by two glistening staircases, a powerfully eloquent duet now moves through a succession of darkening emotions and abrupt rhythmic changes, in which we see unfolded in dance the story of the film. The dance lesson of "Pick Yourself Up" reappears as an extended, reflective walk around the floor. Actual steps from the "Waltz in Swing Time" are quoted. A sideways lunge face to face symbolizes blocked desire. Face to face without touching, and then side by side, they continue dancing. Finally the two staircases flanking the stage separate them in space. And at the top of the stairs, in the fiery sweep of an exit, all ends.

This is as grave a situation as any ever faced in the course of la belle romance. *Swing Time* was the sixth film for Astaire and Rogers, their fourth as co-starring principals. They were then at the dangerous peak of their fame. *Motion Picture Herald* had listed them in third place (after Shirley Temple and Clark Gable) among the Top Ten for 1935. The previous film, *Follow the Fleet,* had thought to vary the routine by casting Fred as a gum-chewing sailor and Ginger, veddy proper since that flight down to Rio, as a Times Square taxi dancer. For *Swing Time* glamor was back but the star vehicle had to keep moving in reverse. How? By keeping the dancers from their dance: "There isn't going to be any dance."

So far, so commercial. What makes *Swing Time* special is that in it the star system operates in the contriving of expedients that also make perfect sense, conscious or unconscious, as symbolic drama. It could be argued that this is the way it happens with all the Astaire-Rogers films and with other star vehicles as well. I merely suggest that if the continual conjuring of a large, credible fantasy life, different in each film, is the essence of the star package, then this essence becomes in *Swing Time* something like the apotheosis of Astaire-Rogers, the most brilliant variation on that great, stable theme. I do not say that the film balances between the commercial and the artistic, or even that by some alchemy it converts the dross of the one thing into the gold of the other. I say that the commercialism *is* art, that it is enough, without refinements. I don't think anything finer could be accomplished outside of the strict commercial context: how could the dancing be more beautiful, the exchanges more pointed than in this anciently obligatory passage?

SHE: Does she dance very beautifully?
HE: Who?
SHE: The girl you're in love with.
HE: Yes, very beautifully.
SHE: The girl you're engaged to, the girl you're going to marry.
HE: Oh, I don't know. I've danced with you. I'm never gonna dance again.

Fred's monogamous instinct is to quit dancing. It's unthinkable that he marry Betty Furness, a girl who doesn't dance, but if he must, how else be faithful to Ginger? The film is notoriously slow in starting; is it partly because it must await the appearance of Ginger before there can be any dancing? On meeting her, Fred's first act is to make her "teach" him how to dance. This is the dance of courtship. It also sets the theme of winning through over frustration ("Pick yourself up, dust yourself off, and start all over again," etc.), which is what has to be done in order to get to the big dance of seduction.

Worth just as much is the ironic note that tinkles through the film, the twist that starts things going in reverse. Fred's pretending he can't dance. The deliberate "anti-romantic" staging of "The Way You Look Tonight," built up, so legend has it, out of Mrs. Astaire's dislike of her husband's having to kiss anyone on the screen. The sarcasm of "A Fine Romance," neatly translating "La Belle Romance" into sour negatives.

The binding, overarching theme of reversal, like the theme of imposture in *Shall We Dance,* acquires its poignance, as I've noted, from the special luminosity of dance as an emblem of sexual union. It's hard to say just when this quite breathless transference of meanings becomes obvious in the film. What is necessary, though, is to note that it is there. Clearer than in any other film is this remarkably civilized and open awareness (Astaire's, or Jerome Kern's in his vision of Astaire) of dancing as the film's ritual of desire—not, vulgarly, Eros itself or any representation of it, but the soul of its honor, which cannot be revealed too often. At every nodal point connecting book, lyrics, music, and direction, a little click of intelligence registers this meaning distinctly. This intelligence works at a critical point to bridge a momentary blankness, and underpin what otherwise seems unmotivated excess, in the final scene when Ginger thinks she must marry the wrong man.

We cut to Helen Broderick, laughing. Why is she laughing? Because, she says, there isn't going to be any wedding. The more she thinks about it the harder she laughs. But she does not know that Astaire and Victor Moore have in fact put an end to the wedding by making off with the groom's pants— how could she know there has been a slip in continuity? Her reaction is utterly discontinuous in time. No matter. She laughs anyway. This is the privilege of poetic logic; it's script-proof. And there is nothing mystical about it. Here with a rush the logic of a metaphor becomes real, like an observable fact. Why shouldn't Helen Broderick, their best friend who is as close to them as the Nurse is to Romeo and Juliet, have known all along the truth about Fred and Ginger (which Ginger herself doesn't know as yet), namely, that they are all but "married" already?

Fred arrives. "There isn't going to be any wedding," he says. Now everybody laughs very hard at this superb joke, this punch line, this payoff to the running gag. Much too hard, surely, to be laughing at just poor Georges Metaxa without his pants. In the last reversal of the film, the tables are turned. Frustration dissolves. "What about the wedding?" asks a bewildered clergyman. "*There isn't going to be any wedding,*" Ginger answers, at last getting the point, and the moment when the beauty of it hits her, and she too collapses in laughter, is as brilliant a moment of truth and liberation as any in the entire cinematic repertory of romantic comedy, and I include such films as *The Rules of the Game* and *Smiles of a Summer Night*. At such a moment you can perceive the classic pattern of terminal symmetry slowly beginning to close. The film ends as it began, with a wedding (a misalliance) not taking place. Of course it doesn't look classical, it looks exactly like a routine Hollywood ending, which the implied touch of *commedia dell'arte* refreshes and seems to exalt. Instead of garlands, bow knots, the shaking of bells, there were in 1936 loud laughter and crowing, a festive mood of justice, and everybody joining in a sweetened reprise of the "la belle" song, "A Fine Romance."

But even this lucid finale is out-dazzled by Kern's summation of the film through his counterpoint of "A Fine Romance" and "The Way You Look Tonight." Like a miniature replica of the film's thematic world, or a scene in a paperweight, the final shot stands by itself. Both for what it recalls (visually, the snow pavilion of "A Fine Romance") and for what it accomplishes afresh, I'm full of admiration for this great shot of Fred and Ginger standing high over Manhattan against a panorama of falling snow—the snow of *Swing Time!*—each singing the other's song and finding that, not by accident, they blend to perfection. The sensation of the music, the snow, the sun that breaks through at the fadeout, and, not least, the Clinch in Waltz Time, is that of a rapidly lengthening emotional distance between us and the film, the equivalent of an Envoi.

As this sparkling film ends, it's not the interior meanings we think about and long to see again, it's the dancing. I enjoyed *Swing Time* for years without knowing why they all laughed their heads off at the end. Now that I do know I doubt if I shall be any more patient with what clever people have found to divert me, long minutes at a time, from the simple pleasure of watching great dancing. I'm grateful to *Swing Time* for delightfully converting the frustration of non-dance into dramatic rationale, for being blood and bone a dance film, the greatest of them all. Still it is some twenty-five minutes before "Pick Yourself Up" and an eternity between that and the "Waltz in Swing Time." Let us, then, go back to the Waltz when they are dancing it, so precisely, with that white magic that seems to collect in the air around them, the added pressure of the whole dance's being held in one take. The personal scale; the intimacy of the spectacle; the surprise of steps that are always intricate, varied, musical; the lovely dynamics of pressure, speed, texture, and motion; the mutual tact in partnering; the reposeful confidence at a flying tempo; the thrilling devotion to what is beautiful in all that is seen and heard—this is the greatest love story.

—from *Ballet Review*, Summer 1965

NOTES

1. "I have never used it [*i.e.,* dancing] as a means of expressing myself. I just dance."
—Fred Astaire, *Steps in Time*.
Harper & Bros., New York: 1959.

2. A truer counterpoint of ballet and jazz occurs in the Balanchine choreography for *The Goldwyn Follies* (1938).

3. "'Bojangles' was recognized among whites as a Negro leader in his day. And unlike the majority of the current claimants of that crown, he was solidly based in the esteem of the masses of his people. He knew them; they knew him."
—Frank Hercules, "The Decline and Fall of Sugar Hill,"
New York Herald Tribune, Feb. 28, 1965.

4. "And the cares that hung around me through the week/ Seem to vanish like a gambler's lucky streak. . . ." From this suggestive kernel in *Top Hat* grew Fred's cameo appearance as a gambler in *Follow the Fleet,* followed by the character of Lucky in *Swing Time.*

Nice Work, Darling, Nice Work

It does us all good to read the original reviews of enduring hits. "*Top Hat* is a vehicle . . . for Mr. Fred Astaire's genius," wrote Graham Greene in 1935. "It doesn't much matter that the music and lyrics are bad. Mr. Astaire is the nearest approach we are ever likely to have to a human Mickey Mouse; he might have been drawn by Mr. Walt Disney, with his quick physical wit, his incredible agility. He belongs to a fantasy world almost as free as Mickey's from the law of gravity, but unfortunately he has to act with human beings and not even Miss Ginger Rogers can match his freedom, lightness, and happiness."

Greene was so pleased with the Mickey Mouse point that he developed it in his 1936 review of Astaire and Rogers in *Follow the Fleet*. "If one needs to assign human qualities to this light, quick, humorous cartoon, they are the same as the early Mickey's: a touch of pathos, the sense of a courageous and impromptu intelligence, a capacity for getting into awkward situations . . . though Miss Ginger Rogers will never quite attain Minnie's significance (she is too brazen and self-sufficing for the part)."

Mickey and Minnie? Today, Fred Astaire and Ginger Rogers, in the nine black-and-white films they made together for RKO between 1933 and 1939, are archetypes just as standard as Disney's two characters. The "bad" music and lyrics in *Top Hat,* by the way, are by Irving Berlin; they include such songs as "Isn't This a Lovely Day (To Be Caught in the Rain)," "Top Hat, White Tie, and Tails," and "Cheek to Cheek." (When the film had been released two months earlier in the United States, all five of its songs went straight into the top fifteen of the hit parade in a week.) As danced by Astaire and Rogers, "Isn't This a Lovely Day" and "Cheek to Cheek" are classics as familiar as Disney's *Steamboat Willie*. We have to spend a little time puzzling over any Fred-Mickey Ginger-Minnie likeness ("many critics have noted the resemblance," wrote Greene), because Greene was missing the point. By the time *Follow the Fleet* filled the silver screen, Astaire and Rogers were living legends.

When John Travolta and Olivia Newton-John came together in *Grease,* when Jayne Torvill and Christopher Dean teamed up on ice, they excited hopes that Fred and Ginger had satisfied better. When a dance/love movie comes along like *Grease, Dirty Dancing, Strictly Ballroom,* pretty soon it gets compared to the RKO series: not to its advantage. Every few years, a season of all these Astaire-Rogers films comes around—maybe on TV, or maybe (as this February) at the National Film Theatre. To revisit Fred and Ginger is to return to the greatest archetype of danced romantic love in film, and one of the enduring archetypes of love in popular culture.

It often seems that, when Astaire arrived in Hollywood in 1933, he caught a wave. Musicals had just entered a peak era onstage—this was the era of Jerome Kern, Berlin, the Gershwins, Cole Porter—and all-speaking all-singing all-dancing movies had now begun to tackle them. Astaire made his screen debut as Joan Crawford's partner in MGM's *Dancing Lady* in 1933: his small contribution is the best thing in the movie. It was everybody's good luck that RKO teamed him with Ginger Rogers in *Flying Down to Rio* that year (fifth- and fourth- billing), and that RKO then built upon the success of their "Carioca" partnership. Their next film, *The Gay Divorcee* (a smash hit), arrived just as cinema happened to embark upon a rich new era of romantic comedy.

Astaire had been working hard for years to help create that wave. He had been a dance star in both London and New York (and on records) before Mickey Mouse was born, after all. Performing with his sister, Adele, he had helped to bring musicals to their peak in the 1920s: It was he who introduced such Gershwin numbers as "Fascinating Rhythm," "Funny Face," and "My One and Only" to the world. And he choreographed, or was choreographer-in-chief, of all his own dances. Records show how assiduously, between the 1920s and 1930s, his singing matured, in musicianship and in emotional command. The oh-gosh-oh-golly Puck became an authoritatively lyrical Berowne. Cole Porter wrote "Night and Day" (for the stage production of *The Gay Divorcee,* 1932) specifically for him. In it, he fluently covered a range of an octave and a half, a tessitura he would often span in the great songs he was to introduce in the following two decades. Songwriting was a major hobby of his own, and his input into the songs he launched was considerable. The romantic comedy of divorce and remarriage in *The Gay Divorcee* owed something to Noel Coward's *Private Lives,* but Coward already owed something in turn to Astaire, with whom he had taken dance lessons. Adele Astaire had just left the stage to marry into the British aristocracy; Astaire used *The Gay Divorcee* and his new partner, Claire Luce, to break out into a genre new to him, the dance duet as an expression of serious amorous attraction. As for Hollywood, Astaire had scarcely arrived there than—diverging completely from the Busby Berkeley model already established at Warner Bros.—he painstakingly set new directorial standards for how dance should appear on screen. "Either the camera will dance," he said, "or I will."

The main Astaire rules for filming dance went as follows: Show the dance from head to toe without close-up, film it in as few takes as possible, and run it from start to finish without reaction shots. Though the Astaire films didn't invariably follow all these rules to the letter, few subsequent dance films have even tried. It's dismaying to see how often, even when a ballet performance is being relayed to us live on TV, camerawork chops up the dancing. Fred and Ginger, by contrast, really do dance several of their duets in a single take, some of them almost three minutes in length. In the annals of cinema, these takes should stand beside the finest feats of D. W. Griffith, Ernst Lubitsch, Alfred Hitchcock, and Orson Welles. Yet here such is the art that conceals art that you may easily forget the camerawork altogether. What you can't miss is dance. And emotion. No films have ever trusted dance, and dancers, as did Astaire's.

"He gives her class and she gives him sex," said Katharine Hepburn, who appeared as co-star to Rogers in another well-known RKO movie, *Stage Door* (1937). Actually, such sex as Astaire ever really demonstrated on screen he had already discovered onstage dancing "Night and Day." James Agate, reviewing the West End premiere of *The Gay Divorcee,* enlarged on this: "Sex so bejewelled and beglamoured and be-pixied that the weaker vessels who fall for it can pretend that it isn't sex at all but a sublimated, Barriesque projection of the Little Fellow with the Knuckles in his Eyes. . . . It was said of Kean that he acted 'all around' people; Mr. Astaire dances all round Miss Claire Luce, now shepherding her, now buttressing, here giving her the floor, and there taking it with her in mutual rapture. It is legerdemain accomplished with the whole body, with the result that the eye endlessly follows that which in second-rate artists is second nature, but in first-rate talent is Nature itself." And class? Some sheer refinement did rub off on Rogers—along with so much else. Watching her grow as an artist on screen during her films of the 1930s is fascinating. But part of what's compelling about her in that period is how unclassy she remains. Even in their screen version of "Night and Day," which seems to have contained plenty of the stage original made for Luce, an element of what makes Rogers so refreshing is the tough Jean Harlow streak in her; it's even there in her stride. Dancing "Let's Face the Music and Dance" in *Follow the Fleet,* three films later, she had become sublime. She hadn't, however, become one of Hollywood's ladies. Like Barbara Stanwyck, she's classless.

We're among Americans in Paris. Lizzie/Rogers has just sung "I'll Be Hard to Handle" in rehearsal at the Café Russe. Huck/Astaire, who's been conducting her and his band of Wabash Indianians, throws away his baton and says "Nice work, darling, nice work." Then, while the band plays through the number again, they start to reminisce about the old days when they first worked together back in America. *She:* "You know, I think I was in love with you then, Huck." *He:* "I know you were. . . . And what's more I was madly in love with you." They stay casual. Mainly they banter; they're musical professionals. As they saunter onto the dance floor, she pulls up a leg by way of warm-up. He, whenever he reckons his teasing has scored a point, delivers a little "gotcha" tap burst. Once, rebuking him, she softly shakes her fists at him. Just as softly, he catches her wrists in his hands.

Now the camera shows them full-frame, head to heel; and the take that follows lasts to the end of the dance. Still holding her, but now with one hand moving surely to the back of her waist, he leads her into a walk. It's a don't-you-remember walk, until, at the end of the phrase, he suddenly arches right back, pulling her with him, so that they tip together, enough to make it a matter of risking her balance and his. From here on—though there remains a rich didn't-we-used-to-have-fun underlay—we're in the present tense, fast and funny. The stops and starts, the hesitations and sudden spurts, the fun of finding how well they work together again, even the little mime/dance quarrel, a whole series of suddenly-tipping-over-together steps, the excitement of finding they're together in rapid side-by-side hops and tap phrases, the whirling spin-turns: the alchemy of dancing with a partner has never been made more immediate.

The film is *Roberta.* It's the third they made together, it has a superb Jerome Kern score, and, when new in 1935, it made a strong impression. Alas, no Astaire-Rogers movie is less well known today. (MGM bought it in 1945 and withdrew it from circulation. The plan was to do a re-make, which came up in 1952 as *Lovely to Look At,* with Marge and Gower Champion replacing Astaire and Rogers. I derive this and much other information from John Mueller's 1986 study *Astaire Dancing.*) Since the 1970s, *Roberta* has emerged from obscurity. But it still crops up far less often than the other Fred-and-Ginger classics, and you have to hunt much harder to find a copy on video. (There is no DVD as yet.) So, if you show "I'll Be Hard to Handle" to a good many people who reckon they know about Fred and Ginger, you can still take many of them by surprise. I have never known the effect to be other than revelatory. Of their many great dances, this is the first that reached the screen in one take; and it still feels the freshest. The dance keeps catching them up in its own bliss.

It contains a particular bubble of spontaneity. Whereas earlier dances in Astaire films had been performed on red linoleum (in black-and-white, it looks grey), the dance floor here had been made, at Astaire's behest, from hard maple. And whereas usually he and his dance assistant Hermes Pan usually went over the soundtrack afterwards, to dub the taps in with full brightness, here the experiment was to record the sound of the dance live. So, though a few taps here sound, by Astaire's standards, a bit muzzy, the pay-off is that you can hear tiny laughs and soft giggles from Ginger, happy little gasps from both of them, and, as they tear into the top-speed highest-energy concluding section, even a happily roaring little "Oh!" from Fred. In that same passage, a lock of Ginger's hair comes loose and she even seems to try to blow it out of her eyes in high good humour while dancing. But the take continues till, at the end of some 2'51", they subside together onto some upright chairs. (In the next take, Ginger's hair is back in place.) The role of Lizzie was just what Rogers needed after *The Gay Divorcee*: this time, nobody could think she was just a substitute for Claire Luce. ("Glad you liked *Roberta*—it is dynamite in the box-office here in this country," Fred wrote to Adele. "You didn't say how you liked the dances. They're all new you know babe!")

"You must learn to walk first," says Penny/Rogers the dance instructor in *Swing Time* (1936) to Lucky/Astaire, who is pretending to be a hopeless student. And they just walk the dance floor, side by side, back and forth. Her precept is more satisfying in an Astaire movie than it could be anywhere else, because it applies to so many of his great dance duets. I love the old feminist joke "Remember that Ginger Rogers did everything that Fred Astaire did, only backwards and in high heels," but the truth is that they did a great deal of it side by side.

The most beautiful example of all occurs, again, in *Roberta*—their other duet, to "Smoke Gets in Your Eyes." Whereas in "I'll Be Hard to Handle" they were in high-waisted rehearsal trousers, here they're the epitome of glamour. He is in the white tie and tails that are part of his legend; she is a stunningly simple black shoulderless gown; their dance is the crowning event of the fashion show at Roberta's on the Avenue Montaigne. They are, as Astaire was to sing in his next movie, "Steppin' out, my dear, / To breathe an atmosphere / That simply reeks with class"; and instead they breathe it as if it were purest ozone. Slow, slow: the whole dance feels like a single glide around the floor. One can point to a number of highlights—the rich backbend Rogers does with one of his hands on the small of her back, their sudden chain of turns together, her glorious supported swan-queen fall, and the slow, sumptuous recovery—but the most bewitching passages occur while they're simply walking, side by side, in tempo. The first is as they descend four steps onto the dance floor. Without breaking the fox-trot-style flow, they take a little quick-quick step, back together up a step, before carrying on down, down. The other, after their most expansive passage, is when he, so gently, presses her head to nestle into his shoulder, an image of intimacy that Rogers, her eyes lowered, plays with an uncannily serious absorption, as he steers her back into a walk.

In three of their nine RKO movies—*Flying Down to Rio* (1933), *Roberta,* and *Follow the Fleet* (1935), you could excise Astaire and Rogers altogether and you'd still have the main narrative. But, secondary as their characters are in those films, their final duets achieve something else, embracing the emotion of the more central characters, while rising up above the story. In "I'll Be Hard to Handle" and, yet more astonishingly, "Let's Face the Music and Dance" (*Follow the Fleet*), they present a serious emotion that gathers up and embraces what's going on between the main couple and presents it in a transcendentally lyrical image. And the unaffected cool of their performance brings about another marvel. Watching and listening, we feel as if we *are* Fred and Ginger; their body-language is so direct, so unadorned.

On one level, it often seems that the nine Astaire-Rogers RKO films are all overlapping aspects of the same world, each a retelling of the same basic story. (Even their one colour film, *The Barkleys of Broadway,* made in 1949 for MGM, feels like a sequel, albeit best forgotten.) The stories tend to be similar, the same supporting actors turn up, Fred gets to dance in white tie and tails for at least one big scene in almost all, and there are harmless in-house connections from movie to movie. Because of these and other connections, it's almost impossible not to feel that, in their sixth RKO film, *Swing Time,* their ardently elegiac one last dance together, "Never Gonna Dance," is more than a farewell between Penny and Lucky, each reluctantly engaged to someone else. It feels as if Fred and Ginger themselves are saying good-bye to all that. At the end of their ninth, *The Story of Vernon and Irene Castle,* their final meeting is for one last waltz. Containing the feelings of Vernon and Irene at this point in their lives, this also embodies the great romantic secret of the whole series of films: they present the dance to the public, while focusing poignantly upon each other. Only in the *Castles* and the preceding *Carefree* did Astaire ever kiss Rogers. As he later remarked: "Saying 'I love you' was the job of our dance routines."

On another level, each Astaire-Rogers movie really is unique in the hue in which it views romance itself. Early on in *Flying Down to Rio* (1933), an American girl asks enviously, "What have these South Americans got below the equator that we haven't?" When Fred and Ginger join in the Carioca, they've got it beneath the equator too. The distance between their swaying pelvises is as charged, as delicious, as the contact between their two foreheads. In *The Gay Divorcee,* romance is heavily laced with intrigue. The story mixes seriousness about true feeling with a Wodehousian sophistication-cum-frivolity about everything else. The mix colours both the ardour of "Night and Day" and the glee of "The Continental." *Top Hat* exists in a kind of fantastic innocence, an idyll artificial right through to the adorable toy-Rialto bridges of its never-never Venice. Nobody save Fred and Ginger seems to be serious about marriage, sex, or love for a moment; and the romance between Fred and Ginger, even when at its most serious in the big whirls and falls of "Cheek to Cheek," seems Edenic. (There's even a running joke about Fred's character Jerry being Adam, "this gardener of Eden," with whom Ginger imagines wearing fig leaves.)

Even though *Follow the Fleet* has the crummiest plot of the whole series, the vitality of its West Coast demotic tone makes this their most intensely

American movie of all. The Navy comes into port, Fred chews gum in uniform, Ginger auditions for jobs, and bugle-call tap salutes abound. In a play-within-the-film climactic dance to "Let's Face the Music and Dance," they play characters-beyond-characters, transcendently elevated, and they make this little scene about despair not an escape from, but the overarching justification of, the movie. *Swing Time* is a never-gonna-dance never-gonna-marry Depression story set in a believable New York. Its laughter and anguish intermingle in a tender melancholy all its own, one that suffuses its audience. It's the supreme dance musical, dearly beloved of many—but this sad/happy emotion, constantly varied through the movie and crucial to its spell, is why it can't top *Top Hat* as the popular idea of the ultimate Astaire-Rogers vehicle. When *Swing Time* winds its plot up with an everybody's-laughing "There isn't going to be any wedding" solution, the audience laughs far less than the characters on screen. There's been memorable comedy earlier in the movie, but by now our response to the situation is too choked; and our distance from their laughter is part of the strange poignance that this comedy leaves in the mind.

Shall We Dance, whose basic plot is as farcical as any, suddenly tries in its last half-hour to capture the same big seriousness of feeling, most beautifully when Astaire sings "They Can't Take That Away From Me" to Rogers. But this is a story about two dancers, and they just don't dance together enough. I don't care greatly for *Carefree* (1938), but nobody could miss the strong new tones of its mixture of dream-fantasy and hypnosis-release. *The Story of Vernon and Irene Castle* (1939), by contrast, is thin, retro, and, after the first half-hour, so easy to love. Any little suspense about whether he will marry her is over in the first half-hour; any little suspense about whether they will enjoy success as a dance duo evaporates in the next half-hour. The film's spell lies all in the dances, along with the unlooked-for twist at the end. He dies: the only unhappy ending in the series.

It may seem that the "novelty" dances that occur in these movies serve little narrative purpose. But I find that the Carioca, the Continental, the Piccolino (in *Top Hat*), the Yam (in *Carefree*) become the epitomes of their respective movies. The beauty of *The Story of Vernon and Irene Castle* as a subject is that it's a bio-pic about a couple who, twenty years before Astaire and Rogers, had introduced one novelty dance after another to an exultant world: the Castle Walk, the Tango, the Maxixe, the Hesitation Waltz. Another novelty dance is the "Waltz in Swing Time," a rushing waltz richly overlaid with tap sophistication, and they dance it blithely. It's *Swing Time*'s true high, and the plot lays considerable suspense on whether they'll ever get to dance it. (After they've done so, it feels like the paradise they keep trying to regain.) Astaire and Rogers dance it in one take, and they never stop. Swirling, tapping, they pour themselves in a single spiralling path around the ballroom. They're never further from each other than arm's length, and the main image the dance leaves with us is that they're rapturously pinned to each other as they whirl around. Yet they're never close to *us;* they stay further away from the camera than in any other of their great dances. If Walter Pater was right that all arts aspire to the condition of music, the "Waltz in Swing Time" is where Astaire and Rogers most fully achieve that goal. Its music would seem incomplete without them. Part of its soundworld is its heart-stopping sudden hushes that allow us to hear their feet.

Astaire was an all-round musician. In these movies, you see him conducting, playing piano, singing, playing accordion, harmonica, and percussion, often with breathtaking stylishness and skill. As a singer, he was the first to perform a dazzling number of the last century's finest songs; and his phrasing as a singer loses nothing by comparison with that of Bing Crosby or Frank Sinatra, whose voices were so much more richly endowed. It was Astaire who, in the 1943 movie *The Sky's the Limit,* first sang the Harold Arlen/Johnny Mercer number "One for My Baby (and one more for the road)," later a Sinatra standard: a case in point. Though the arts of Jerome Kern and Irving Berlin had long been mature, Astaire brought them both to new peaks, and both composers acknowledged him as their best interpreter. For dance devotees, Kern's two Astaire-Rogers films, *Roberta* and *Swing Time,* can never be topped.

But it is principally because of his work with Astaire that I call Berlin the greatest dance composer of the twentieth century. The great musical career that spanned from "Alexander's Ragtime Band" to "I've Got the Sun in the Morning and the Moon at Night" never so perfectly encapsulated the moods of popular culture in imperishable songs as he did between 1935 and 1938 in "Isn't This a Lovely Day (To Be Caught in the Rain)?", "Top Hat, White Tie, and Tails," "Cheek to Cheek," "Let Yourself Go," "I'm Putting All My Eggs in One Basket," "Let's Face the Music and Dance," and "Change Partners and Dance." As singer, choreographer, and dancer, Astaire responded to the internal variety of these Berlin numbers, and to their sheer naturalness. He is the greatest dancer we have ever seen, and yet there are times when his singing of a Berlin song is yet more marvellous, to watch as well as to hear, than the dance that follows. Arlene Croce, in her definitive study *The Fred Astaire & Ginger Rogers Book,* describes "Cheek to Cheek" as an example of this. As another, I would suggest "Change Partners and Dance." Gently though he delivers it, the urgent undercurrent of his singing creates an insidiously alluring effect through the mid-line rests, as if beaming it through from his head into hers: "You have danced <rest> with him since the music began. <rest> Won't you change <rest> partners <rest> and dance with me?" In "Isn't This a Lovely Day," I would hold the way he carries his voice tenderly down through the words "rain" and "storm" beside the most beautiful portamenti of Caruso, Leider, and Callas.

And if there is one thing that can steal your attention from Astaire's singing of a classic song, it must be the way Rogers listens. She could put across a song vividly herself. (Her "I'll Be Hard to Handle" is irresistible, and my favourite Berlin song of all is her "Let Yourself Go," with its intoxicating shifts of metre and key.) But has anyone ever listened more beautifully than she did in the 1930s? She was his ideal partner not simply because of her beauty as a dancer, but because of her complete responsiveness. Which is present in the way she pays attention, sometime without moving a muscle, yet always in character. Rogers changed her hairstyles and, more startlingly, her voice from one film to the next; but her real acting occurs way beneath the surface: she has a different nervous system in each role. To watch her change from the impulsive deep-voiced heroine of *Carefree* (1938) to the loyal, still girlish muse of *The Story of Vernon and Irene Castle* (1939) is unsettling. By the seventh film, *Shall We Dance,* the makers of these films made almost too much of an event out of the brimming eyes with which she hears his delivery of "They Can't Take That Away From Me." The most haunting examples of her listening occur in the earlier movies, nowhere more wonderfully than in "Let's Face the Music and Dance." Here, though she paces across the stage, her face is almost numb, a mask drained of emotion. Only the eyes move. Her face remains cool when she's dancing the exalted duet that follows (another single take). Like Astaire, she trusts the medium to express everything: in this respect, they're both modernists in motion. The duet gathers a terrific pace through its many stops and starts, but the dynamics stay muted. It's like thick cream flowing fast.

One marvel of style in these movies is the way that Astaire moves from speech into song; a second is how he moves from song into dance. Did Berlin design two of *Top Hat*'s songs to showcase both these? Everybody remembers the explosive dance that Astaire does in the hotel room that wakes Dale/Ginger up in the room below, but just as marvellous is the introduction. "In me you see a youth who's completely on the loose," says Jerry/Astaire, sitting on the arm of a sofa, his hat holding a newly lit cigarette, to Horace/Edward Everett Horton. "No yens, no yearnings, no strings, and no connections, *no ties to my affections*": he's begun singing in mid-sentence! It's as if the idea of the rhyme is what's made his voice take wing. The same device occurs with "Cheek to Cheek," where he says to her, "All I know is: I'm in *heaven*," singing only as he reaches the noun. ("Heaven / I'm in heaven / And my heart beats so that I can hardly speak: / And I seem to find the happiness I seek / When we're out together dancing / Cheek to cheek.")

But the number he sings to Horace, "No Strings (I'm Fancy Free)," keeps steadily moving up from gear to gear. As the song gathers emphasis, he rises, clicks his fingers, does dance gestures—all, of course, in the same ongoing take. Now the camera cuts in for a new take that raises the excitement in the way he pours himself a drink while singing, putting down the decanter bang! like a loud tap. Better yet is the way he times two whooshes of the soda-syphon, and then, singing full-voiced, "So bring on the big attraction. . . ." suddenly he delivers what looks like an entrechat-six (an un-Astaire-like step), "my decks are cleared for action," and *now* he can't keep from dancing. The whole thing has been a crescendo, building since he was chatting; instead of a climax, Ginger knocks on the door to interrupt his flow; and then the sand number—whereby, dancing again on her ceiling, he puts her, Horace, and himself to sleep—is the enchanting diminuendo conclusion to the scene. (As late as the 1980s, revival cinemas would sometimes show ver-sions of *Top Hat* from which the whole sand dance had been cut; and in the NFT's 1983 Astaire-Rogers season, several of the films had infuriating lapses of sound-picture synchronisation. It's good to realise that some standards have risen.) Astaire's solos in these films are all endlessly rewatchable. You get lost in his rhythm: how he works around the music, against it, onto it. His arms can have as much punch as his feet—but mainly they stay amaz-ingly informal. And, even in those later solos where he confines himself to a narrow space, his whole body keeps changing outline. With him, a mere transfer of weight can be a major event in terms of shape, timing, and drama.

Before she joined him at RKO, Rogers had plenty of musical experience. Like him, she had introduced Gershwin songs on stage ("Embraceable You," "But Not For Me"); and in Hollywood she had already appeared in Busby Berkeley musicals. What the Astaire movies revealed in her, indeed devel-oped, was a body of breathtaking beauty. Whereas the legs of Betty Grable (who does bit roles in two of these Astaire-Rogers movies), so famous in the Second World War, no longer seem remarkable, and whereas most 1930s ballerinas exemplify physical types that are no longer quite our ideals, Gin-ger's physique is still gorgeous today: the ravishing slenderness of the legs, the lovely curves of the waist, the lush mobility of the back. And it's power-fully expressive.

Astaire went on to dance with other distinguished screen partners— Eleanor Powell, Rita Hayworth, Ann Miller, Judy Garland, Cyd Charisse, Leslie Caron, Audrey Hepburn, and others. He was always a model partner; some of his later duets are choreographically distinguished. You can argue that his best duets with Hayworth and Charisse are finely conceived as metaphors for serious emotion; certainly his duets with Powell are inven-tively brilliant outpourings of pure virtuosity. But in no important way has their quality of expression developed upon those he did with Rogers—whereas in the 1940s his art went on growing in his solos, which developed a remarkable new vein of abrasiveness. After Rogers, there is never quite a moment when the dance feels suffused by the love that the story at that point is usually about. Only with Rogers or when alone could Astaire unite feeling and form.

—from *The Times Literary Supplement*, February 27, 2004

FRED ASTAIRE
Letter to Adele

The older sister of Fred Astaire, Adele (1896–1981) performed with him first in a vaudeville act, then on Broadway and in London, where she was a particular favorite. In fact, she was probably more popular than he was, until she retired to marry into the British aristocracy and became Lady Charles Cavendish.

May 6, 1935

Dear Dellie:

Was delighted with your letter—and listen cutie—I know how you "slay 'em" over there—but it doesn't surprise me babe, you always have!! You seem to think it's unusual or something—listen kid you are terrific!!

"Little Dellie" thinks I've forgotten all about her—no fear babe—I know everything—I get loads of English clippings about you and they are swell!

I think your Cecil Beaton picture is beautiful—and I've just sent it to Margaret Case of *Vogue*—she wired me for it. She promised to send it right back.

Glad you liked *Roberta*—it is dynamite in the box-office here in this country and I think it will be in London too.

It stayed five weeks in Boston in a theatre that rarely holds anything for even two weeks.

It has been held over everywhere—and many places for three, four, and five weeks!

Isn't it nice! You didn't say how you liked the dances. They're all new you know babe!

I've got all new ones in *Top Hat* too—about five of 'em.

So far so good with this one—it looks alright and the numbers are swell. It's a goofy comedy plot and seems to be working out well—at least several things that I know you'll like. The next picture they're planning for me towards the end of the year—I'm a sailor!!!! . . .

George is with me now and is perfectly wonderful. He does everything. Serves table when I want him to—drives car—typewrites correspondence—and I even used him in one scene in this picture. He is thrilled beyond words. His quota number and passport etc. are all fine so he can stay permanently.

A lot of stars have press agents as you say in your letter—Bennett and G. Rogers I think too and many others—but I wouldn't have one as a gift. I have all I can do to keep the press department from bothering the life out of me at the studio. I refuse everything they ask me to do and still a lot of sappy stuff gets out—but it doesn't mean anything to those mugs that read the movie mags—however don't show this to anybody because if a mag got hold of it they'd love to print what I think!!!! Mother was swell here—do take good care of her—babe. . . .

Hope Charlie will not overdo the drinking thing—it's so wrong if his health suffers by it. I'm all for him getting a bit squiffed now and then but if it hurts the health!!! No!!

I'm bothered to hell by a fan club in my name. Some girl in Jersey City has got it going and they print a paper etc. and I have to write and wire every now and then and it's all such a lot of balls but I have to do it. They hold tremendous theatre parties and go in a mass when my pictures come there and they have pictures taken outside the theatre etc.

They want you to be an honorary member, so when they write—just answer and say, "thanks—of course I would" etc., etc., something nice. I get many other requests from people who want to start other clubs in my name but I say "No" because one is plenty. My fan mail totals about 17,000 letters a month which is supposed to be terrific—especially for me in pictures so short a time and doing few pictures. Fan mail gives me a pain in the neck. It's such a lot of balls—everybody wants to learn to dance etc., etc. I am publishing a book as soon as I can get time to edit it—there will unquestionably be a big sale for it if we get a good interesting and instructive set-up. They're calling me to the set—so I must run—it's lots of fun here—all the boys are swell—so much more amusing than the lousy stage. I hope I don't ever have to do stage again—except possibly a personal appearance tour for a few weeks.

Have already had an offer of $15,000 a week with Rogers—but I don't want to do any now—I haven't time and I would only consider it alone anyway—I know I can get $10,000 alone.

Thursday May 8th.

Well—I guess I'll get this off sweetie—I only have one shot this morning—the rest of the day I'll spend rehearsing "Cheek to Cheek," a swell tune—sort of different. It's a cross between "The Last Round-up" and "Night and Day," has no verse and the chorus runs something like seventy-two bars!! Figure that out. . . .

If you are in London when Ed Everett Horton is I told him to call you up. He leaves here in June and is the nicest person—so be sweet to him. He is in this picture and is so swell. I believe old Ed is a little bit of a pansy . . . doesn't quite know himself—however—do not camp with him—he is apt not to understand—I mean do not poke anything at him!!

You'll adore him.

Am sorry you were not there for Sam and Frances Goldwyn—they are so grand and we spend much time with them. She is swell and Sam is really a peach and funny!

Jimmy Cagney came over and watched me shoot part of my "Top Hat" number—he is a great guy! Sends me fan wires on each picture. Wish I could write more now—be good sweetie and take care of Ma—also Charlie—and yourself—no fancy autodriving by Chas. coming home from one of those Irish sprees at night.

Best love babe—

Phyllis is fine and sends love. . . .

—from *Fred Astaire: His Friends Talk*, 1988

GEORGE BALANCHINE

George Balanchine was born in St. Petersburg in 1904, and died in New York in 1983, leaving behind the largest and most important repertory of ballets we have. Trained at the Maryinsky school, and later a member of the company, he managed to get out of Bolshevik Russia in 1923, joining Diaghilev's Ballets Russes in Monte Carlo and quickly being appointed the company's ballet master. In 1928 he choreographed his first masterpiece, Apollo, *beginning his four-decade collaboration with Igor Stravinsky. Five years later he arrived in New York at the invitation of Lincoln Kirstein, and they quickly established the School of American Ballet, followed, in 1934, by Balanchine's first American masterpiece,* Serenade. *Until 1948, when the New York City Ballet came into official existence, he worked for Broadway (eighteen shows, including four for Rodgers and Hart, as well as* Cabin in the Sky *and* Where's Charley?); *for Hollywood (*The Goldwyn Follies *among others); and for various ballet venues, out of which came such works as* Concerto Barocco, Ballet Imperial, Theme and Variations, Symphony in C, *and* The Four Temperaments. *Later masterworks included another crucial collaboration with Stravinsky,* Agon (Stravinsky Violin Concerto, Symphony in Three Movements, *and* Duo Concertant *were to follow for the 1972 Stravinsky Festival), and his versions of* Firebird, The Nutcracker, Coppélia, *and* A Midsummer Night's Dream; *spectacles such as* Jewels *and* Vienna Waltzes; *works of upbeat Americana such as* Western Symphony *and* Who Cares?; *profound human statements such as* Liebeslieder Walzer *and* Robert Schumann's "Davidsbündlertänze"; *and that exquisite Mozart ballet,* Divertimento No. 15, *as well as his final masterpiece,* Mozartiana (1981). *By the end of his life, he had recapitulated the entire history of classical ballet while rethinking and revolutionizing classical technique and the very possibilities of ballet as an art form.*

GEORGE BALANCHINE

Marginal Notes on the Dance

I am so often told that my choreographic creations are "abstract." Does abstract mean that there is no story, no literary image, at best a general idea which remains untranslated in terms of reality? Does it mean the presentation of sound and movement, of unrelated conceptions and symbols in a disembodied state?

I said on another occasion* that no piece of music, no dance can in itself be abstract. You hear a physical sound, humanly organized, performed by people, or you see moving before you dancers of flesh and blood in a living relation to each other. What you hear and see is completely real. But the after-image that remains with the observer may have for him the quality of an abstraction. Music, through the force of its invention, leaves strong after-images. I myself think of Stravinsky's *Apollon,* for instance, as white music, in places as white-on-white.

For me whiteness is something positive (it has in itself an essence) and is, at the same time, abstract. Such a quality exerts great power over me when I am creating a dance; it is the music's final communication and fixes the pitch that determines my own invention.

Some choreographers seem to be so uncertain of their own medium that not only do they seek the ballet that "has a story" but they also have the story told in words. To me these are no longer ballets, they are choreographic plays. Any amplification necessary must come from the music which may, at times, make use of a chorus. Much can be said in movement that cannot be expressed by words. Movement must be self-explanatory. If it isn't, it has failed.

The dance has its own means of telling a story and need not invade the field of the drama or the cinema. The quality of the movement and the choreographic idea decide whether the story is understandable. In most cases, the criterion of success or failure lies in the choice of the subject matter.

Music is often adjectived as being too abstract. This is a vague and dangerous use of words and as unclear to me as when my ballets are described that way. Neither a symphony nor a fugue nor a sonata ever strikes me as being abstract. It is very real to me, very concrete, though "storyless." But

---

*"The Dance Element in Stravinsky's Music," *Dance Index,* Vol. VI, Nos. 10, 11, 12, 1947.

storyless is not abstract. Two dancers on the stage are enough material for a story; for me, they are already a story in themselves.

I approach a group of dancers on the stage like a sculptor who breathes life into his material, who gives it form and expression. I can feel them like clay in my hands. The minute I see them, I become excited and stimulated to move them. I do not feel I have to prepare myself. All I know is the music with which I am at least as intimately acquainted as a conductor of a symphony with his score. Of course, the contours of an outline, though sometimes only vaguely, exist in my mind—certain visualizations from listening to the score.

I am therefore greatly dependent on the rehearsal time at my disposal. When Tchaikovsky was once asked how he was able to compose whenever he had to, he is said to have answered: "My Muse comes to me when I tell her to come." Paraphrasing this answer of his, I often say that my Muse must come to me on "union" time.

My imagination is guided by the human material, by the dancers' personalities. I see the basic elements of the dance in its aesthetic manifestations, that is, in the beauty of movement, in the unfolding of rhythmical patterns, and not in their possible meaning or interpretation; I am less interested in the portrait of any real character than in the choreographic idea behind the dance action. Thus the importance of the story itself becomes reduced to being the frame for the picture I want to paint.

In the "storyless" ballet, the question of the costumes and sets gains importance. The stage designer has little to go by if he cannot derive his inspiration from the musical score, as the choreographer does. Then he must be present at the rehearsals and have the choreography furnish him with sufficient ideas. The "storyless" ballet is a great challenge to the designer's imagination, since he lacks any literary stimulation. On the other hand, there are the costumes and sets which can underline and help—with their composition of color and form—to make the visualization of music plastic and dramatic.

The designer must always be aware that the image he produces is part of the total effect with the only aim to create the necessary atmosphere for the dance composition with his sets and to stimulate the spectator's fantasy with his costume designs. This circumscribes his task. His contribution is by no means an accessory, but it must never be dominant. The sets must be in harmony with the idea of the dance composition and they can undoubtedly lead to new choreographic ideas. The costumes must not only fit the dancer, but also—what seems even more important—the dance action, that is, the idea and the movements which express it.

Whether a ballet has a story or not, the controlling image for me comes from the music. Stravinsky's music had the most decisive effect on my work and has always made itself felt in the direction of control and amplification.

My first real collaboration with Stravinsky began in 1928 when I worked on *Apollon*. I consider this the turning point of my life. This score, with its discipline and restraint, with its sustained oneness of tone and feeling, was a great revelation to me. It was then that I began to realize that to create means, first of all, to eliminate. Not a single fragment of any choreographic score should ever be replaceable by any other fragment; each piece must be unique in itself, the "inevitable" movement. I began to see how I could clarify by limiting and by reducing what seemed previously to have multiple possibilities.

Although my work has been greatly linked to Stravinsky's music for the last twenty years, I do not feel that one specific style of music lends itself better to the projection of sound into visible movement than another. But it may be difficult to fulfill certain composers' personal inspirations.

What I mainly expect from the composer whose work I am to visualize is a steady and reassuring pulse which holds the work together and which one should feel even in the rests. A pause, an interruption, must never be an empty space between indicated sounds. It cannot be just nothing, since life goes on within each silence. It must, in fact, act as a carrying agent from the last sound to the next one. The secret for an adequate rendering of the musical score into visualization lies in the dynamic use of silence and in the utmost consciousness of time.

The composer is able to give more life to a bar, more vitality and rhythmical substance than a choreographer, or a dancer for that matter. The musician deals with time and sound in a highly scientific way, his medium of creation lends itself to a strictly definable method, to organization and translation of a formula into artistry.

It is far more complicated for the dancer to recite a formula. The choreographer will never be able to achieve such precision in the expression of movement as the composer through sound effect. Not that we do not know what we are doing. Our technique certainly has method, but it is far more interpretive than subject to mathematical rules. Whenever I feel I have found the "inevitable" movement, I can never be as sure as in music that it might not need some clarification after all.

In my choreographic creations I have always been dependent on music. I feel a choreographer can't invent rhythms, he only reflects them in movement. The body is his sole medium and, unaided, the body will improvise for a short breath. But the organizing of rhythm on a grand scale is a sustained process. It is a function of the musical mind. Planning rhythm is like planning a house; it needs a structural operation.

—from *The Dance Has Many Faces*, edited by Walter Sorell, 1951

W. McNeil Lowry
Conversations with Balanchine

About four years ago, George Balanchine agreed to let me tape-record occasional conversations about ballet, about aesthetic and other influences upon his work, about dancers. I would do nothing with the tapes in his lifetime, I volunteered, though that proved to be a matter of complete indifference to him. My reason for this was a simple one, but not the most simple. I did not propose to raise questions about his personal life. And, from long experience, I did not expect him to talk about his choreographic process. I did propose to ask him all those flat, obvious questions I had learned to avoid in twenty-odd years of a quite particular, if sporadic association. Through those years, an unimpeachable witness to just how irrelevant most questions appeared to Balanchine was my friend Lincoln Kirstein, whom none has surpassed in the effort to make words throw light upon dance. My association with the two men began in 1957, when my objectives as director of the Ford Foundation's program in the arts were entwined with those of many American ballet companies and schools. This was twenty-four years after Lincoln Kirstein brought the choreographer and ballet master George Balanchine from Europe to found with him the School of American Ballet. It was nine years after Kirstein, as general director, and Balanchine, as ballet master, launched their third company, New York City Ballet. Their first two attempts had been the American Ballet (1935–1938) and Ballet Caravan (1936–1940).

What follows comes from four conversations scattered over approximately a year, beginning in February, 1979—in other words, when Mr. Balanchine still kept his accustomed schedule. I have not attempted to reproduce exact Balanchine English; neither my own technical competence nor my recording equipment would have been up to that. Here and there, I have improved my own sequence of topics or made my questions less verbose. The full transcript of the tapes is about twice the length of these excerpts.

LOWRY: *What do you understand other people to mean when they speak or write of "the Balanchine style" or "the Balanchine ballet"? When other people say that, what do you understand they mean?*
BALANCHINE: I don't.

LOWRY: *Does it interest you?*

BALANCHINE: No. I don't know what "they" mean. And they say "my style." I don't know what "my style" is. It's like—ask a horse why she is a horse, how she feels being a horse.

LOWRY: *But at some time in your own earlier adult life when you saw another chore-ographer's work, did you say, "I understand that because it's like Massine or Fokine"?*

BALANCHINE: That's right.

LOWRY: *So it's inevitable that people will say, "Well, I can tell that is Balanchine."*

BALANCHINE: Yes, naturally, but it's for somebody else to say it, not for me.

LOWRY: *Not for you?*

BALANCHINE: How could I know? I know that during my life I started cer-tain things: certain steps or certain combinations, or even acrobatics. I started this myself on my own body, because I was a dancer. And so now everybody uses this. And even if I do my own things that I used to do, it would look like I borrowed it from somebody else, you see. I don't know what I am. I know what I can *do*: I know how to teach, I know how to make people dance, and I like them to look a certain way. I force them. But it's very difficult. I don't know if you know yourself what you are speaking or thinking—that it's your way to think or your way to write.

LOWRY: *What artists in any field, dance or others, helped to shape your life?*

BALANCHINE: Ummm.

LOWRY: *Now, maybe you don't like the form of that question.*

BALANCHINE: Yes.

LOWRY: *One's life is shaped in his art—in your case, in his aesthetic and vision and creativity and what he does, what he makes, and that's also a question of influ-ences, you know. And people say "Balanchine, Petipa, Fokine, Massine"—I'm not asking that, but have there been artists who stood out from others and did you feel them and what they created and their work in your own life more than others?*

BALANCHINE: In my personal life or in dancing?

LOWRY: *Which one would you rather talk about?*

BALANCHINE: Well, personal life I don't know what it is even, you see. I'm not Humphrey Bogart or anyone like that. I guess I live like anybody else, you see. Of course, in dance—in music and in theatre, everything—of course I learned from lots of things. From childhood, we were already on the stage, not in the ballet only but in drama. And we had to memorize plays and speeches and poems, and some of us dancers became actors. The great actors in Russia were graduated as dancers first and then they went to drama school. We also did musical plays. Of course, at that time all the operas that I knew were almost all in Russian. I can sing "Aida" in Russian and Wagner in Russian. Also drama. We knew Shakespeare's "Midsummer Night's Dream" in Russian, and that's how I know "Midsummer Night's Dream" today—not in English, in Russian. So it's not that we were "influenced" but we were made. We were all in the Imperial School of Ballet. We were saturated with these things, you see.

LOWRY: *When you think of the visual arts—let's say, the plastic arts in your time—do you think of one artist or dwell on one in your mind or your imagination more than others? Or two or three? If we leave now music and dance for painting and sculpture, do you think of . . .*
BALANCHINE: Oh, yes, I do.

LOWRY: *Of whom?*
BALANCHINE: I would say the first time, really, I realized how beautiful painting was, it was Italian. When Diaghilev took me to Florence, I couldn't understand why it was good at first, but he told me, "Now you stare for hours. We're going to have lunch, and when we come back you'll still be here," in some chapel where Perugino was. And so I stared and stared and stared and stared, and they came back, and I said, "No, I don't know what's good about it." Later on, I went myself a hundred times. Then I realized how beautiful it is: the sky so pale blue and the way the faces . . . And from then on I somehow started to see Raphael and how beautiful it is, and then I found Mantegna, and then Caravaggio, and finally I realized how beautiful is Piero della Francesca. Also, I probably was a lot influenced by the church, or our church—the enormous cathedrals—and by our clergy: the way they were dressed, you know. And they also have a black clergy, these important ones that become patriarchs and wear black.

My uncle was also Archbishop of Tiflis, a monk—you know, gold and purple. It's like that somewhere in paradise; people wear the same. Music in the churches was fantastic. When I was a child, they gave me little things— holy articles and gold things—and I used to play priest, blessing the things. Also, I'd sign [he makes the sign of the cross], as in the church you sign. So that also to me was God. Not that it's "God invisible." I don't know what that is. God is this wonderful dress, you see. And always, and even now, I have to say I couldn't just *think* of God; you have to be really mystic or to work yourself, to sit down and meditate. But I can't do that. You know how people say

I'm involved with ballet and with moving, so that mostly through Christ I know that He'll talk, I know how He looks, I know His face, I know His beard and so on, and so we'll go to God.

LOWRY: *Let me see if I understand. You are saying that now, in your seventies, your visualization of God is still that of your childhood, with all the gold and purple and the holy articles you played with? But it is not mystical. You don't* think *God; you see* him *in the images of Christ and in other things?*
BALANCHINE: You see, that's how. I believe, and believe so fantastic! This whole thing is like art. Well, then came all these Italian paintings. And then in France I met for the first time Picasso and Braque. I worked with Braque, you know. And Derain worked on lots of ballets. Then there was Rouault, Utrillo, and persons like that, you see.

LOWRY: *Utrillo?*
BALANCHINE: Yes, Utrillo. So they were all there. We worked together. I didn't know even that Utrillo was important. They just were there. Rouault was— I don't believe people knew Rouault very well at that time. Now Rouault is great, but then Rouault—I don't know. . . .

LOWRY: *Bakst and Benois had not much to do with it when you came to Diaghilev?*
BALANCHINE: No. Bakst already was dead. Benois, Alex Benois, I knew, of course, in Russia. I knew his son, Nicola Benois. In Russia also, the painters who painted the scenery were great.

LOWRY: *Did you meet Tchelitchew in Europe or here?*
BALANCHINE: In Paris. That's where we made *Errante* together, I think. Tchelitchew was not very well known, I think. Also, Derain was not very well known. Cocteau. But we did things together. And Brecht and Kurt Weill were there, and they also were new to me. And Neher, the painter. This was the first time I met these Germans. Of course, you live where you're supposed to be.

LOWRY: *You live where you are?*
BALANCHINE: Where you are and who you are, you see. I don't know anything about Society. I don't understand what they're talking about. That's why I don't go to parties. I come in and see lots of well-dressed people— intelligent, nice-looking people. They talk about something. I *hear*, but I don't understand at all. I'm absolutely out of this. I can kiss the hand, say thank you—that's all I can do. But when they ask me questions about the people that are famous—names, great people—I know many, probably. Not all. Caesar I know, because I read Caesar's "Commentaries"—where

he went and things like that. Very interesting. Of course, you are saturated with where you live, where you are exposed to things. If you live in the water, you become a fish.

LOWRY: *What were your thoughts about your future artistic life when you first went to Hartford to start a school with Lincoln in 1933? What were your thoughts then about your future personal and artistic life?*
BALANCHINE: Well, when Lincoln asked me I already knew that it should be a school and a ballet company. I always wanted to have a start, with really clean, beautifully taught ballet people who could dance the way I want. And I told Lincoln, "This is a great opportunity." And I came here, and I expected that something would happen. When we went to Hartford, it was a very little place and nobody wanted us there, and there were, you know, already three teachers there that were against us. And the reporters immediately came, you know, and began writing things like "Why did he come here to spoil our life?" So, "Lincoln," I said, "let's go, because first of all it's too small. Let's go to New York." And always I had ideas, but first that it would have to be as big as possible, and as interesting.

The theatre we now have is a lovely theatre—only it's a toy. You cannot do magic here. You can do a little bit just like children who play at home, because it's like a box; you cannot move—it's built that way. They started well, but then they stopped Philip Johnson, because they wanted to build a smaller Rodgers and Hammerstein musical-comedy theatre. So the pit was made smaller, and they wanted to minimize and make it twenty feet by twenty, you know. The acoustics didn't matter, because it's all wired. They spoiled this theatre and didn't make it right. We're struggling here, and they keep asking me, "Why don't you do *Sleeping Beauty*?" You can't do it here. *Sleeping Beauty*, it's wonderful. It's quick. You need quick mechanics you can use to make more fantasy. *Nutcracker* is the maximum you can do here.

LOWRY: *When you first came and you went to Hartford and then to New York, how long did it take you to lose the feeling of an alien on this American scene, or did you really feel alien when you came?*
BALANCHINE: No, I never felt that I was a stranger here, you know. I always wanted to be American. I couldn't even speak English at that time, but I really wanted to be American. Somehow in Russia we read about America—about the prairies, about the things like . . .

LOWRY: *James Fenimore Cooper?*
BALANCHINE: Fenimore Cooper, yes, and another one. So I liked it. I thought it was a fantastic place.

LOWRY: *But New York didn't look that way?*

BALANCHINE: No, New York doesn't look that way, but New York still looks the way I used to see it. This cylinder and stars, you know—all that. Striped pants and people. Also black Negroes dressed for the cake-walk.

LOWRY: *You felt at home in New York City?*

BALANCHINE: That's right.

LOWRY: *I assume from what you said a little while ago you were feeling: This is where I am, and I'm with this. So really you were dancers and teachers and people helping make a school and a ballet, and, of course, you had a lot of friends. Maybe not right away—there were Russians here?*

BALANCHINE: Oh, absolutely.

LOWRY: *And you were very soon with them?*

BALANCHINE: That's right.

LOWRY: *But New York is a much more exotic and fantastic kind of city than Paris, London, or Berlin? It may not be as beautiful a city to some people or as important a city or whatever, but in 1934 it was more different from London, Paris, Rome, and Berlin than it is today, right? Because they have changed, too? It was a different place to be?*

BALANCHINE: Yes. Well, it was very nice to leave Russia and all that . . . London was wonderful, and I liked Berlin and the food and people and so on. Only, I could not stay in either place. You see, they did not allow you to stay; you could just go and work a little bit and then get out. You couldn't stay permanently. Our passport was a nonsense passport; you could travel with it, but you couldn't become a resident. Like if I wanted to stay in England before Lincoln invited me. Of course, in England I thought ballet was possible—probably more than anywhere else. In Paris, you. couldn't do anything. But in England you could. I lived with Lydia Lopokova and her husband, Maynard Keynes, the economist. She was sweet, and they were nice people. And finally I said I'd like to settle there, and he told me it was impossible to arrange it. You see, I couldn't get permission permanently to live there, to work.

LOWRY: *I should like to jump forward a little for one particular question. In 1935—the year you and Lincoln founded the company—the American Ballet was invited to be the resident company at the Metropolitan Opera. But after three years you left the Met, and the American Ballet was suspended. In 1940, after four short seasons touring new American ballets, Lincoln suspended Ballet Caravan. Did it ever*

*occur to you that the collaborative effort to build an important national ballet com-
pany had come to an end?*
BALANCHINE: I don't believe that I was really aware of what was going [on]
I really was not very sure what was happening. I always thought that we
must do something, and I always told Lincoln that, the beginning aside, it
eventually should be big, like the Imperial Ballet—a big stage, lots of
dancers. But I didn't know if this was possible. We started, of course, with
a failure: our first performances at the Adelphi. I mean, the public liked it,
but the critics didn't think it was good. I don't think Martin [John Martin,
dance critic of *The Times*] liked it or liked Lincoln somehow . . . You see,
at that time I really couldn't read; I couldn't understand what I read. I
knew only that they told me that Martin didn't like "Serenade," I think, or
whatever it was. But I'm not sure that this was true. Maybe now it would
be interesting to read what he said about our first Adelphi performance.

LOWRY: *Martin's enthusiasm was reserved for another work on the program,* Reminiscence. *He dismissed as only amusing* Errante *and* Alma Mater. *Of* Serenade, *he wrote that it was a "serviceable," not an "inspired," piece of work. He
acknowledged that Balanchine may have had his problems in devising choreography
for an inexperienced company. But he found* Serenade *lacking in spontaneity "to a
great extent."*
   *But what you're saying is that—even though for over two years nothing was
happening except in the American Ballet and your work as a choreographer for Hollywood and Broadway musicals—you weren't really questioning whether Lincoln
and you were going to come together again and try to make another company,
because it never was certain to you that it could be done anyway, that there was
going to be any continuous effort?*
BALANCHINE: Yes.

LOWRY: *But you never had any hesitancy whenever Lincoln said there's this money
or that opportunity—you never had any hesitancy in putting that first and saying
I want to make more ballets on the stage?*
BALANCHINE: I was doing a Broadway show at that time—I think it was *I
Married an Angel*—and I thought it was possible to perform on Mondays,
and Brigitte [Vera Zorina] was in *I Married an Angel,* you see, so I thought
maybe we could do concerts, and I asked Wiman [Dwight Deere Wiman,
the producer of *I Married an Angel*]. He didn't say no; he was trying to start
something to help me, but nothing happened. But what I did, I started *Concerto Barocco* with Brigitte, the first steps going around. I was planning to do
a small company on Mondays, like a touring chamber ballet—a chamber-
music *Barocco.* And I asked Hindemith to write something. I had some
money—about five hundred dollars—and I didn't know what to do with

it. I thought maybe to buy a cigarette case or to do something. But then I said maybe Hindemith would like to write something for that money. So I called his editor and I said that for the five hundred dollars would he like maybe to write me something for piano and just a small ensemble. And yes, sure, he said that he had time and he'd like to do it. I said anything he wants, and he says, "I don't know." So he wrote *Four Temperaments,* and I thought that this would be part of a small company. But meanwhile *I Married an Angel* closed, and nothing is happening. So right before we went to South America [on a tour arranged for Ballet Caravan by Nelson Rockefeller, who was then coordinator of Inter-American Affairs for President Roosevelt] I was already staging "Four Temperaments," with Pavel Tchelitchew on the scenery. He made very elaborate costumes, and we couldn't afford it. It was like twenty-five thousand dollars at that time—now it would be about a million. We couldn't afford it. I started, but Hindemith and I abandoned it until later, when Lincoln returned from the Army after the war.

LOWRY: *Can you give me your impressions of the principal dancers you first encountered here who had all their training in the United States? Lew Christensen, for example. Or Paul Haakon, or Nora Kaye? I'm interested in your talking about principal dancers that were—well, impressive enough to you: what you actually thought of them, and their training and their potential.*
BALANCHINE: Well, I think they were well trained—not all of them. Nora Kaye started with us. She was fourteen when she came to study. Annabelle Lyon already was a rather good dancer, because she was with Fokine. And Paul Haakon was a good dancer. He was professionally a dancer; he turned very well, and he was nice-looking, small. Lew Christensen was a very good dancer, a professional dancer. And they were—well, I thought they were very good dancers. Even compared to Europeans, I think they had a better texture, and they were easier to work with. They would understand me—I don't know, somehow.

LOWRY: *In comparison, let's say, with Tamara Geva or Toumanova or Riabouchin-ska—what about them?*
BALANCHINE: Well, you see, Toumanova and Baronova and Riabouchinska I knew when they were twelve years old—they just came out of school. They were still children; they danced rather well, and they mostly could turn very well at that time. They were very phenomenal twisters. But, you see, I was young. I was not sufficiently expert in teaching. I did rather well teaching, but not like now. Now I am absolute; I'm almost one hundred per cent sure that I know how it is, what is the matter with people, their possibility. Of course, you can't detect that at once, but for a while you wait, and then you see that something will happen or here maybe it's already the end.

LOWRY: *Is it probable that many of the American dancers I named you might have worked with because they were as good as what was available?*
BALANCHINE: I couldn't say that I was disappointed; I was not disappointed at all, I thought that people were very good. It was not exquisite as technique, or whatever it is, like now, because really we spend so much time now from childhood, and we really bring them along. Now, really, I choose. Now they have to follow that way, they are always monsters of perfection. Almost all, I would say, take anybody from the corps and they would be a very good soloist. But for a long time in the company there was, I would say, a maximum of eight girls. I don't speak about the boys— I couldn't get them at the school. It was rare when a really good man came in. But girls were everywhere, and there were really only eight. And Jerry [Jerome Robbins] used them, and I used them, and just eight; the rest was fill-in. And when you think of doing *Barocco* and after that two or three other things, you have already used your eight girls. Now I would say we have fifty; they are all excellent.

LOWRY: *But this had begun to change. When?*
BALANCHINE: It was slow.

LOWRY: *Early fifties, middle fifties?*
BALANCHINE: It slowly changed. The school started to give. We still at that time took some people who were ready, not only from our school but from auditions. People would come in. Now we don't audition professional dancers. We just take from the school. And the school gives our style, also because the children now participate in performances; they are ready. They are part of it. They dress well, they know the music, they know dance. So it's exactly what I thought we would have when I saw that the school was starting to give something like the Maryinsky. In Russia, there was nobody auditioned from the side; it all came from the school. Just as in opera in France they don't take anybody else.

LOWRY: *When you first saw Lew Christensen working in the things that you were able to perform and also taking more work in the School of American Ballet, what kind of a dancer did you think he was?*
BALANCHINE: He was excellent dancer, excellent dancer. He had first of all wonderful proportions, looked beautiful . . . And he also was wonderful partner, and the way he turns—his beats, whatever it is—he was . . . I wouldn't say he was a classical dancer, with classical feet like Eglevsky— like you would say danseur noble "classique." That's one thing. I would say Eglevsky had feet like Peter Martins, had really exquisite feet, and he used them . . . better than women.

LOWRY: *That Christensen was a first dancer in any of the companies he was in was obvious?*
BALANCHINE: Excellent dancer!

LOWRY: *And he didn't have all that competition at that time in those small companies, did he? There were a few other men, but . . .*
BALANCHINE: No, I would say the way he was when he was twenty years old he would be now. He would be probably one of the best.

LOWRY: *Yes. And he was musical. Not so musical as you, but musical.*
BALANCHINE: Well, I am different. I am not that musical, but I have a special idea what music is, and I was taught music. At home, we studied music, so I probably knew more about the technical part of music and the piano, because I was studying piano in the conservatory. If I didn't leave Russia, I think I might have become a better pianist. I don't believe that very many dancers of ballet and choreographers have specially studied. I think in old times, yes.

LOWRY: *Well, Christensen had a different situation—not as important as yours, but because of his father and uncles he had musical training in the home and in a cello class and so on. So he had more than most American dancers. What about others in those first years in America for you? Eugene Loring, for example—what kind of a dancer was he?*
BALANCHINE: Ummm, not very . . .

LOWRY: *Certainly not Christensen.*
BALANCHINE: Oh, no! Loring was not dancer.

LOWRY: *And William Dollar?*
BALANCHINE: Dollar was very good.

LOWRY: *Was he as good as Christensen?*
BALANCHINE: He was strange, but technically he was very able. He was . . . He had a strangeness; he was not really a classical dancer. He was an acrobat always.

BALANCHINE: If you want to know what we dancers talk about when we train, it's like speaking to a horse. When you want to persuade somebody to do something, you have to show them, you have to show them. You see, I used to show by doing it myself; now I can't show them. I ask Peter Martins to show to the boys. You have to show. You learn by looking, not by talking. I don't believe in a teacher who sits in a chair, I don't believe in it

126

.nd of an old-fashioned way to do it. I always say it's like you

.ther bird and you have little birds and they have to start. How do

it? Mother doesn't say, "Come on, move your tail five hundred

.es." Same thing with us. We don't say it. We do it. That's the only way

to ..each. There's no other way.

Jacques [D'Amboise], when he does choreography or moves, he comes to me and says, "Tell me, what do you think is wrong with this?" He feels that it's not right but doesn't know why. "Well, first of all, you stay too long in diagonal and you have people doing—you know, doing this and that. Why don't you shorten it and make it this way, forget this and that, O.K., and hit that little dip?" Now I look again and I say, "Well, that's a little better—only, you know, you imitate the tune, which is not right. Why do you imitate the tune, which already goes on by itself? It's like you put a piece of butter on cake and put a piece of butter on butter and you eat it, you see." We talk like that, and I advise him so it becomes a little better, and then he likes it.

Peter Martins is the same. "What should I do?" This and that, and we talk. Recently [March, 1980], he did one all by himself, and he dressed the dancers up, and all of a sudden they all disappeared. Somebody suggested to him to dress them in the period of Italian—something Renaissance, a little bit balletic, and so they made costumes, covering the bodies with lots of material. So I say, "Well, you look and you see material moving. Choreography disappears. It was very pretty before when they were doing some things, but now they're completely covered by material. You have to say to the designer, 'I want nothing—just *nothing*. A very little, bit here and nothing,' so that you can see the ballet." Because if it's a story, like if it's Iago or somebody trying to kill somebody, that I can understand. But I told him, "When you staged the dance you did now, you didn't need to have the dancers wear anything. You looked at them the way they were and you planned on the people's bodies and you liked it the way it was. But then after that somebody else—you believe that he's a good designer, somebody great, you know—he covers everything you've done." The same thing happened to my *Temperaments*. Seligmann came and covered everything completely from here to here with bows.

LOWRY: *Who came?*

BALANCHINE: Seligmann appeared. Kurt Seligmann. Remember that Surrealist? A very great name at that time. And so my ballet disappeared completely. I told him, "Can you take it out?" He said, "No, I can't." I say, "Well, Seligmann, *on ne voit rien—rien!*" I say, "Mary Ellen [Moylan]—we don't see Mary Ellen at all." And he said to me, *"Alors, et où est Seligmann?"* He doesn't give a damn what's going on.

LOWRY: *I don't come backstage very much now. I used to come a little bit, and sometimes I would see one of the dancers talking with you. Was it also pretty much the same: they were saying what about that and you'd take their leg or show them or you'd say good or not so good? It's not about* Serenade *or* Chaconne, *it's about a step, a movement, a jump?*

BALANCHINE: It's about the person. They're not interested in the corps de ballet or in some other dancer or a man. They're thinking how they did. So I watch. They know that I watch, because it may be the first time this person is dancing the part, or the second or third time, and I see. Even if it's not the third time, even if it is Suzanne [Farrell], then I'll come to her after the curtain's down. I'll say, "You know, that place you did this and that; you act too much, you started to play art instead of dancing," or something like that. And "Don't react at that moment—just dance, do this." Or she says, "I forgot the step, I don't remember if we do this or that." And I say, "Well, we used to go that way, now we do this way, probably." Sometimes, you see, they have a bad leg or knee, so we have to change the step sometimes right before a performance. They cannot turn on that side, they have to turn on the other side this way. We only analyze or talk just a little bit after. Or if it's a young person I let her do it the first time. I don't tell her everything—it's impossible to do that. I'll say, "If you do a little bit more turnout, then let's see what will happen." So next time she'll turn out a little more, and I say, "Now you're looking very good, but that's not everything. Why don't you look straight and go this way instead of that way?" That's what we do. We don't talk about beauty or *Serenade,* you know.

LOWRY: *The music? Do you talk about the music?*

BALANCHINE: If it's played too fast, sometimes they'll cry. "No, I couldn't do it!" I say, "You couldn't do it because he played too fast. You couldn't do it." And so when Robert [Irving, N.Y.C.B.'s music director] comes there, I say, "Robert, you know that was a little too fast." "Oh, no, they do it exactly the way I do it." I say, "But that's not very good, you know." So they cry and come to me to forget, you see.

I understand that talking about this is difficult, but for us also it's difficult. We stage ballet steps to music. The two must be very close; this is the thing. We analyze first. Also, it's conducting; we decide on the best way to do it. We use a metronome—you know all about this. We stage movements to this count. You can do lots of fast music, but you cannot do too many steps; you can play sixty-four notes quickly with your fingers, but you cannot do the same number of movements with your body, so if we take too many notes usually we put fewer steps. It depends on how it sounds. What's the illusion, what's it to look like? We don't do it like Mickey Mouse. You know.

[Makes sound of running up the musical scale and then running down.] You see, we don't do that.

LOWRY: *Each one is interested in himself or herself and how he or she did or might do better—each one? Then with some dancers there comes a time when they can also for some reason be interested in the group, the company, the ensemble, the other dancers—I don't mean just personally as friends?*
BALANCHINE: Yes.

LOWRY: *But they can?*
BALANCHINE: Yes.

LOWRY: *At one time in your life you became interested in working with another group of dancers, right? When you were quite young?*
BALANCHINE: Well, I put together friends and staged something for them.

LOWRY: *But there are dancers, perhaps, who never take an interest in the corps, or the company, or the ensemble—which means that obviously they are never going to try to be choreographers. There are dancers who are always simply doing the best for themselves as dancers?*
BALANCHINE: That's right. Mostly. Sometimes dancers go out front to see a ballet when they are injured or something, when they cannot dance. And then they come back and say, "Oh, it's soooo beautiful." [Imitates in a gushy voice.] "Beautiful. It's lovely." It's lovely, they like it. They also watch from the wings, they watch other dancers—how they dance. Young people go and look at somebody they like to look at. They all choose somebody they like to look at when they dance.

LOWRY: *You recently [November, 1979] made four more principals in the company. I'm interested in how your view of them and your decision to do that developed. How long had you been considering and thinking, Well, it's time for this one to be a principal? Does it normally happen over a long period of time, or how does it happen?*
BALANCHINE: You see, I've usually known them since they were children—every step that they have danced, since they were eight. Then they were nine, then they were children on the stage in *The Nutcracker.* So slowly you get an idea something will happen maybe, and yet you wait until the person gets developed completely. Sometimes it turns out that the legs are too short or the head is too big. Sometimes what happens to them is that they grow beautifully, the proportions are right. It takes a long time to develop a body for dancing—especially the feet. The points for girls have to be, I always say, like an elephant's trunk: strong and yet flexible and soft. The elephant's trunk looks like it's so soft, but in fact it is strong,

firm. Women's points have to be strong and also very flexible, pretty. It takes some time. Then suddenly if they work hard—for they have to work also . . . You cannot just give a lesson and believe that after one lesson something will happen. Some dancers don't believe in teachers. Or they go on to other teachers—they try to find somebody who will make them beautiful and great and noble and whatever it is, and they waste themselves. Sometimes they find that person, sometimes not. So we have special ideas about how a person should look, and she works to be that way, you see. And develops to a certain extent. It's not the way of the teachers anymore, it's already the dancers who make it happen. You know, it's like you want to be a priest, or you are a disciple of a great Sufi or someone like that, and finally you absorb certain things and then they leave you alone. It depends on what you've done, whether you understand, or if you have to go along. You cannot hang on to an adviser the rest of your life. So this is my theory: I abandon the dancer and say, "Now you do it yourself." I supervise, of course, and they always come to me. But you have to work yourself, because it's your body, your feet, your legs, your own whatever you have. And, strangely enough, it happens; it straightens itself out, sometimes fast, sometimes slow. Sometimes you look and you think, Well, my God, it's still a little bit heavy—clumsy and fat and not very interesting. Then suddenly something happens.

LOWRY: *Well, among these four, you announced them all at once, but you must have decided about one or two of them before you decided about the others—that it was time.*

BALANCHINE: Oh, yes.

LOWRY: *Over how long a period do you think? I know you've been watching them since they were children. I understand that. Then they're in the corps, or may even do a solo, but now you're going to make them a principal, and, as you tell me, I understand they're also working on themselves to try to develop. But they don't all come to the same point at the same month, or even six months . . .*

BALANCHINE: Well, you know, sometimes you watch a dancer and you already know that this someday will be an important dancer. And some you know never will be important dancers. They will be soloists, nice personalities, but never important. It's not only what I enjoy. I think of the public, of presenting to the public something that it will accept. That takes time. Of course, we feel a pressure, you know—all ballet masters do. Dancers always want to dance solo, and as soon as they dance one solo they want to become solo dancers. But we keep them, you see—we give them a solo and develop them that way, but they still have to do lots of other things. Otherwise, we wouldn't have any corps, any ensemble. But then let us say this person is Kyra Nichols. Now, Kyra became a very good soloist. She developed slowly. And then suddenly she became absolutely without any doubt . . .

LOWRY: *When did that happen?*

BALANCHINE: It happened in a year or so—like you're cooking something and you try it and say, "No, potato is not cooked yet," and all of a sudden it's cooked in a second.

LOWRY: *Here the company is and the school is, and though everybody has great personal interest in all the young people, there must be some limit to the young dancers being brought along. Are you that limit? Do you have to be a little objective and perhaps a little cool and ruthless about it?*

BALANCHINE: Yes. There is always the desire to have more, like people making money. Even today, I am going at two o'clock to see Danilova [Alexandra Danilova] give pointe class, because I want to eliminate already some people. Perhaps they have something: a certain look, a certain type of feet. Legs, maybe, and proportion. And some turn very well, some jump very well, whatever it is, but . . . it's very difficult to say. It's vibration. You see, it's like Koussevitzky when he had the Boston Symphony. And I believe also the Philadelphia with Stokowski. They chose a player because he had vibration that matches the rest of the strings, for instance. So I do the same thing— that's my privilege, you know. When the dancer is a child, she may be very good. But then later when she grows, you see, with a little bit more development, then the proportion develops, the whole thing changes. Well, today I'm going to see Danilova's class, and I have to eliminate, because there are probably thirty-five dancers there. I have to let them know who will have to go somewhere else.

LOWRY: *What are your goals—first, as George Balanchine, the ballet master, choreographer, everything? What are your own goals over the next two or three years? If you just thought of the next two or three years, what would be important for you at that time?*

BALANCHINE: I saw it yesterday [November 15, 1979]. Last night was the performance of *"ex-Ballet Imperial,"* I call it—now it's Tchaikovsky Piano Concerto No. 2—and I would say it had never been danced as well by the girls. They were absolutely fantastic. All of them, they looked beautiful. They moved . . . it absolutely never was like that. Even the lines were perfect, the hands were pretty, and everything, you see. So I don't even want anything better. The only need now, it's to develop men, boys: they are very good in comparison to what we had once. They are very good. They're young, they're also willing, they're very enthusiastic, you see, in comparison to the persons who used to take professional class—people who knew how to dance a little bit but were all a little bit disappointed in dance. But now we don't have any like that. They're all from school, they're all wonderful, but we have to develop better dancers that we can use. They can do whatever it is they have to do. Actually, they can support and so forth, but this is not the most beautiful, you know, the most wonderful thing. So we have to develop better men, like Martins, who is a really fantastic classical dancer. His feet, his legs are unusual, you see. And we need different-size boys. Not only very tall—we have lots of tall boys—but we also have to have medium-size boys who dance very well. I mean who dance, who will become very interesting dancers before the public. This will be important three years from now.

LOWRY: *To develop better men—they will be developed partly in rehearsal and performance on a stage and partly in continuing at the school?*
BALANCHINE: Andrei Kramarevsky, he's an excellent teacher and very like a lion, you know—lots of pep, enormous. You see, that's what we need. We need more life. I say that because Americans, and the English also—maybe it's an Anglo-Saxon trait—en masse they become sleepy. I call them zombies. And you have to shout and push them, you know, to make them more alive. Not that they are not, but it's a habit, maybe, or the way they think. Perhaps it's because of the critics, who always write that you have to be dignified or you're lacking good manners. In England, when you have tea with somebody you cannot just put in three pieces of sugar and start, you have to put just one little piece and hardly move your spoon, otherwise! you'll never be invited back. They give you a little toast, but you hardly touch it! If you eat the whole toast . . . But now I'm talking about the critics—like John Martin used to say that there was some kind of dignified allure needed to dance *Ballet Imperial,* because it's "imperial," because it's royal, because it's red carpet, I don't know what. Whatever it is, Americans have this laxity inside. You have to start pushing them and scream at them to make them more alive; you see what I mean. If you don't do that, they slowly will go to sleep. And they all imitate—all. Any company that I look at, they all think that *Giselle* is the example of beauty, of dance, of classicism—something like that. And they think that *Giselle* is a sleepy ballet. You know, like a—like Lincoln said—wonderful . . . disease. It's a new disease, called "Gisellitis." That is exactly what it is—it's "Gisellitis," you see. And I have to get something out, obviously. This is very important, and for now I wish that our own choreographers would have that pep. . . .

LOWRY: *Pep?*

BALANCHINE: Yeah, pep. Martins is very good. Now, Martins really makes them dance very well—a very good choreographer to start. So after all this I would say, I wish they would stay the way they were yesterday. The way they danced last night was excellent. I hope for three years they will be the same, so that they don't go to sleep again.

LOWRY: *You mean, they are now full of life, but it's easy for them to go to sleep, and you have constantly to keep them up?*

BALANCHINE: That's right.

LOWRY: *And that applies particularly to the men?*

BALANCHINE: No. To the whole company. Not individually. I mean . . . there are a few very good ones. I always compare them to horses. Even the race horses, even the wonderful horses, they're ready to go and win the race if somebody says so. The horse is not going to win the race alone, without anybody. If you leave horses alone, they're not going to run like man for pleasure—I mean, they play a little bit, but mostly they are quietly eating. They're born that way. And to move, this is up to something that you make yourself. You develop your muscles; and then you push to show what you can do. But, in reality, people don't want to do that. You're born to sit, or maybe to lie down or go to sleep: it was, I think, an Oriental idea. Why do we have to get up, stand up, run—why do we have to do this? It's good to sit down, it's better to lie down, and if you're lying down why not sleep, and if you go to sleep why be born even, you see?

LOWRY: *Are there other particular objectives or goals either for you in your artistic function or for the company that you can see as priorities over the next two or three years? Or trends?*

BALANCHINE: There is some kind of new balance, new style, new whatever it is—the idea that anybody can come in and use the dancers to do something, something different. I would say it will come to something. Because we are now in this period when people say, "Oh, my God, what will happen when you go?" But everybody goes. Roosevelt—people said, "What are we going to do without Roosevelt?" You see, everything finally will be different. It wouldn't be any good fifty years from now to do what we do now. It will be something else. Maybe we won't even need that technique. People will look different, they will move differently. Maybe they will want more at home, rather than in theatres. Who knows? But I'm not insisting now. You will ask how to preserve for posterity. I say, "Preserve what?" I mean, you make a movie. Look at the old movies. Look at Pavlova and it's ridiculous. Even Conrad Veidt—all these movies of UFA that I remember were fantastic. Now they're just silent movies, funny. Even the movies when I was with Goldwyn in 1937, when you look at them they're not very good.

LOWRY: *As movies, but the dancing still . . .*
BALANCHINE: But you would have to have the same people. Dancing doesn't exist; it's the people that make it. Last night again—last night was a beautiful performance, and that's what the company is. If they just walked around and danced badly, the ballet wouldn't exist. It doesn't exist.

LOWRY: *But you could imagine a really great performance of, let's say,* Serenade *or* Concerto Barocco *forty years from now—you could imagine it if it suited the dancers, if they wanted it?*
BALANCHINE: If they're developed the same way. If there is a leader to insist on that. If we are exactly the same way we are now, then why not? I mean, if you can preserve all the dancers, put them on ice and then melt them forty years from now, sure it will be. Probably people would like it, but it never will be.

LOWRY: *Are there isolated moments frozen like a frame in your own ballets, that when they occur you see like something thirty, forty, fifty years ago? Are there moments or movements or phrases in one of your ballets that, when you see them, have a reflection, an echo of something that you consciously feel or identify from way back in somebody else's work or in one of your early works?*
BALANCHINE: Oh, yes, naturally they come: Petipa's work and Fokine and . . . That's how we develop.

LOWRY: *I understand, but you said that, depending on when it is and who it is and the technique needed, people move differently and it's different. Well, there's been a lot of silly stuff written by people speculating about the origins of your work— right?—and your aesthetic and the classical theatrical dance that you do, and so on. And there's been a lot of stuff about derivation or whatever—that you took this or changed that, or then other people took from you, and so on. A lot of it is very interesting, but it's just like somebody beating his gums—it doesn't come out any- where. Yet sometimes I feel you couldn't always just rub out your memory—I don't mean when you're choreographing but when you're looking at something you've done. It's not a clean slate. There are all kinds of feeling, movement, attitude, music, the past of your own in there, right?*
BALANCHINE: Absolutely.

LOWRY: *So what I'm getting at, despite what you said a while ago—it is possible, is it not, that such a vast repertoire as you've had . . . There's no reason that some of those works shouldn't be as exciting and classical to dancers forty years from now as, let's say, Mozart is to an orchestra . . . Whenever you sniff like that I know you don't quite agree or you think I've gone astray somewhere.*

BALANCHINE: First of all, Mozart is great, you see. Also, it's printed, and also the technique needed to play it would always be there: if they don't develop it, they won't be able to play, you see. But we don't have anything like that; it never could be reproduced. We could only refer. For instance, we want to put back one ballet, and if we have movies we can do it, and then slowly I rearrange everything and see that the beats are right. But if you give these films to somebody else who never saw the ballet before it won't be any good. Something will be staged, yes, but it will be amateurish.

LOWRY: Yes. But, to take you and Danilova as an example, you can remember an awful lot of works.

BALANCHINE: Not the same, you know, because Danilova was already there; she was the past. She was, she is the past. She danced when Petipa was. I danced when Fokine was. With my whole body, no, but with her body she moves . . . For the children that learn variations now, it will be just a few steps that they will learn; it won't be any more. Critics now say, "Oh, that's not Petipa." How do they know? They don't know. I know what's Petipa, because during Petipa we lived there.

LOWRY: You mean one cannot transfer Petipa to Martins even though you're here?

BALANCHINE: You see, the steps, yes. But that's not all. Style is not conceptual. It's juice—it's whatever you're born with, you see. Now people are wearing beards. They're not supposed to wear beards. Beards are not in style today. When you see pictures of Debussy and Pasteur, my father, they were born with it—that was the style. Nobody shaved. They dressed a certain way, and that belonged to them. Now beards don't belong to people. All right, somebody wants to look like Christ, you know—the hair and all. But it's silly, it looks silly on people. It's all fake. I don't know. The taste of potatoes, the smell of flowers—these things have to be watched, but, of course, they develop. There are big farms that mechanically develop flowers that don't smell. They took the smell out of roses.

LOWRY: Today, you have said, "It's very good now and I hope it stays that way." Were you ever in the position to say almost that before? Were you in that position, or almost in that position, at any time before now?

BALANCHINE: There were a few ballets that I said, "This is the way it should stay always."

LOWRY: The way it's done?

BALANCHINE: Yes.

LOWRY: *And that could have been ten years ago or twenty years ago?*

BALANCHINE: I don't know twenty years ago; I would have to think about it.

LOWRY: *Every time I see* Symphony in C, *as I did this week, I of course think about the early 1950s, and even today when I see that I also see the people who danced each one of those sections in the fifties. Of course, it was very well done this week, and Suzanne, as you know, has for me a regal quality that she now knows she has, which gives an extra excitement. But I can remember people who danced that same part very, very well. Now maybe you would recall and say, "Well, OK, but overall the ensemble or the corps"—or whatever— "wasn't as good then as it is now"?*

BALANCHINE: I don't know. Actually, it was not very good. Really, they were sloppy a little bit.

LOWRY: *And wasn't it about that time that the number of principals was so small that it conditioned the works you could put on? When one of them went away somewhere or was injured, then you had to change, because you were working with about eight female principals?*

BALANCHINE: That's right. The only good decent dancers were eight. So they all danced all the time—in *Barocco* and everywhere they did this, because the rest were not very good. *Symphony in C* was Tanny [Tanaquil LeClercq] doing second movement; Tallchief [Maria Tallchief] was the first. And Pat Wilde was . . . I think she was third dancer. Or maybe sometimes was Janet Reed. These principals were good, you see. Also good partners.

LOWRY: *But now you are saying that, person for person, in the corps, soloist, and so on, it is much better, much stronger, more reserved—everything?*

BALANCHINE: Well, Tallchief was very good in the first movement—very strong, very good dancer. You see, if she would be twenty now she would be as good as anybody else. Tanny also would be as good as anybody else today. She could dance far away . . . [He waves his hand as if to say "inexpressibly— beyond everything."] This was the time when we started to be better, but before that it was very bad, because if Tanny was not there I couldn't find anybody to dance the second movement. Nobody could développé. So I went to Hollywood to try to find somebody who could do a higher développé. And I found somebody in school there and was very disappointed, because she really couldn't do it. That's how difficult it was. And then slowly it became better when Tanny started to dance, when Tallchief started. Then Pat Wilde came back—she was in England, then she came back.

LOWRY: *I think you said to me that you had no really great fears about finding the people to continue the school—the standards of the school—even after the elderly generation had gone. You're not pessimistic about that in the future?*

BALANCHINE: We have good dancers now that will teach.

LOWRY: *And you think the teachers will come ninety percent from your company?*
BALANCHINE: That's right.

LOWRY: *You do not have people out looking elsewhere at teachers?*
BALANCHINE: No.

LOWRY: *It's likely to continue to be a kind of extended family?*
BALANCHINE: Absolutely. But Martins has now been here for years and years. Martins is not anymore Danish. He's here and starting to choreograph.

LOWRY: *It's been so many months now, but earlier we were talking about all the different changes in roles, about ballet master, choreographer, régisseur, répétiteur, artistic director, you know, and so on. And I told you—you weren't very interested, there's no reason you should be—that most people a little farther away from the subject or from the ballet company when they think of George Balanchine think, of course, first of all about the choreographer historically, but when they think about George Balanchine in the company they think artistic director. They don't bother to look in the program and see that it says "ballet master." In all other ballet companies in the United States, when they think about the continuity of the company they'll talk about artistic director or artistic producer. What I'm saying is that in another company somebody like Martins might not have anybody like Lincoln Kirstein— that he'd have to be everything all by himself.*
BALANCHINE: It must be again one person. There has to be one person. One person to watch everything: leaking, it may be your plumbing is bad. Every day, all the time, and it's not only dancing. The dancing is good enough now; I don't have to tell them anything. As a matter of fact, I tell Rosemary [Dunleavy, assistant ballet master at N.Y.C.B.] when she says, "Shall I put this girl there? What would you like to do?" "No," I say, "just put anybody, because they're so good—anybody." I don't bother anymore, you see. I have other things to do—millions of things all the time. I mean, all the details: Why have we that green there, why is the color green so awful, why couldn't we have blue? We don't have any. Why not? I mean, there's millions of things. It's a part of the profession.

It's part of this profession also to economize. I'm economizing on this, on that. Like Lincoln tells Ronnie [Ronald Bates, the company's technical director], "You have to change the scenery, because it looks bad," and Ronnie, "It's hanging there and you have to do that, you have to do this," and I say, "No. Let's keep it the way it is." Or I say, "All right, but not the whole thing," you know. So I am the one that puts the screws on everything.

LOWRY: *So Peter Martins or Peter Smith or Peter Jones or anybody is likely in any situation, and even in this New York City Ballet situation, to have to be everything?*
BALANCHINE: You have to learn . . . not only learn, you have to be that way. I didn't learn anything, I didn't ask anybody. This is important what we did, Lincoln and I. I taught everybody how to dance. It was like teaching people how to cook, how to grow the food, how to eat it. Our ballet didn't exist before. So I have no title. I am myself. I mean, I'm ballet master, yes, because *Balletmeister, maître de ballet*—Petipa was *Balletmeister*. But we didn't have anything like that. So I am myself. What title did Einstein have? I'm not Einstein, but I mean, Einstein, what is he? I'd say—ah, he's director of advanced physics. No! He's Einstein: he does it. I only do this.

—from *The New Yorker*, 1983

EDWIN DENBY

Some Thoughts About Classicism and George Balanchine

The beautiful way the New York City company has been dancing this season in the magnificent pieces of its repertory—in *Serenade, Four Temperaments, Symphonie Concertante, Swan Lake, Caracole, Concerto Barocco, Orpheus, Symphony in C,* and the new *Metamorphoses*—not to mention such delicious small ones as *Pas de Trois, Harlequinade,* or *Valse Fantaisie*—made me want to write about the effect Balanchine's work has had in developing a largeness of expression in his dancers, and in showing all of us the kind of beauty classic ballet is by nature about. Thinking it over, I saw questions arise on tradition, purity of style, the future of classicism, and Balanchine's intentions in choreography; and I wondered what his own answers to them would be, or what he would say on such an array of large subjects. So one evening after watching an excellent performance of *Four Temperaments,* I found him backstage and we went across Fifty-sixth Street together to the luncheonette for a cup of coffee.

He began by mentioning the strain on the dancers of the current three-month season, dancing eight times a week and rehearsing novelties and replacements all day. After it was over, he said, smiling, the real job of cleaning up their style could begin; for the present it was like a hospital, all they could do was to keep patching themselves up just to continue. I assured him they had just danced very well indeed, and then told him about my general questions. He paused a moment. Then, taking up the issue of style, he answered that there were of course several styles of classic dancing; that he was interested in one particular one, the one he had learned as a boy from his great teachers in Petersburg—classic mime and character as well as academic style. He spoke as a quiet man does of something he knows entirely and knows he loves. He sketched the history of the Petersburg style. Then he took up aspects of other styles he did not care for—a certain sanctimonious decentness in that of Sadler's Wells, a note of expensively meretricious tastiness in that of the Paris Opéra—these are not his words, but I thought it was his meaning. He was not denying the right of others to a different taste than his own; nor did he mean to minimize the achievements of these two great bodies, but only to specify points of divergence. He said he believed in an energetic style, even a soldierly one, if one chose to put it that way.

Passing from the subject of style to tradition, he mentioned as an example the dance we know as the Prince's variation in *Swan Lake*. He told me that it used to be done all in brisés and small leaps, but that one time when Vladimirov was dancing it in Petersburg this great dancer changed it to big jetés; and now the big leaps are everywhere revered as tradition. I gathered he thought of tradition rather as a treasured experience of style than as a question of steps; it was a thought I only gradually came to understand.

At this point he noticed that Steve wanted to close his luncheonette, and so we went back to the theater and continued to speak standing in the backstage corridor. We got on the subject of notation. He emphasized the continuity of movement it could reproduce. I asked if *Four Temperaments* had been notated, adding that I felt sure the public in forty years' time would enjoy seeing it as much as we do, and would want to see it danced in the form it has now. "Oh, in forty years," he said, "ballet will be all different." After a momentary pause, he said firmly, as if returning to facts, that he believed ballet was entertainment. I realized he meant the word in its large sense of both a social and an attractive public occasion. But he looked at me and added, in a more personal tone, that when one makes a ballet, there is of course something or other one wants to say—one says what one says. He looked away, as if shrugging his shoulders, as one does after mentioning something one can't help but that one doesn't make an issue of in public.

At the far end of the corridor the dancers were now assembling for *Symphony in C,* the final ballet, and he returned to the subject of style and spoke of two ways of rising on toe—one he didn't like, of jumping up on pointe from the floor, the other rising from half-toe, which he wanted. Similarly in coming down in a step, he wanted his dancers to touch the floor not with the tip of the foot, but a trifle to one side, as if with the third toe, because this gives a smoother flexion. He spoke too of different ways of stretching the knee in relation to flexing the ankle as the dancer lands from a leap, and of stiff or flexible wrist motions in a port de bras. Details like these, he said, were not consciously noticed by the audience, nor meant to be. But to him they were important, and a dancer who had lived all his life in ballet noticed them at once. They corresponded, he suggested, to what in speaking one's native tongue is purity of vocabulary and cleanness of accent, qualities that belong to good manners and handsome behavior in a language one is born to and which one recognizes in it with pleasure. At that point I felt that he had, in his own way, replied to the large questions I had put at the beginning, though he had avoided all the large words and rubbery formulas such themes are likely to lead to. So I thanked him and went back to my seat and to the first bars of *Symphony in C.*

Balanchine had offered no rhetorical message. He had made his points distinctly and without insistence. It was several days before I realized more fully the larger ideas on the subject of style that his points had implied. He had suggested, for one, that style demands a constant attention to detail which the public is not meant to notice, which only professionals spot, so unemphatic do they remain in performance. The idea, too, of style as something a man who has spent many years of his life working in an art loves with attentive pertinacity. A classic dancer or choreographer recognizes style as a bond of friendship with the great artists he remembers from his childhood and with others more remote he knows only by name. For in spirit classic artists of the past are present at a serious performance and watch it with attention. And as I see Tallchief dance now in *Concerto Barocco,* I feel that they invisibly smile at her, they encourage her, they blow her little Italian kisses. They danced steps that were different but they understand what she means to do; her courage night after night is like theirs. And I think that they find a similar pleasure in the work of the company as a whole. For dancers have two sets of judges: the public and its journalists, who can give them celebrity, and the great artists of their own calling, who can give them a feeling of dignity and of proud modesty.

The bond between classic dancers is that of good style. But Balanchine in his conversation did not say that style in itself made a ballet, or that the entertainment he believed in was an exhibition of style. On the contrary he said that when he made a piece there was something or other he wanted to say. He was affirming the inner force that is called self-expression. And no doubt he would recognize it as well as an inner force in dancing. But for him there was no contradiction between creative force and the impersonal objective limitations of classic style. He knew in his own life as an artist—and what a wide, rich, and extraordinary life it has already been—that his love of style and his force of expression could not be divided, as they could not have been for others before him, and I am sure will not be for classic dancers of the future either.

That Balanchine expresses a meaning in a ballet is clear enough in those that tell a story. And he has made several striking story ballets even in the last decade. Among them are his recent vivid version of *Swan Lake; Night Shadow,* a savage account of the artist among society people; *Orpheus,* a large ritualistic myth of poetic destiny; and *Til,* a realist and antifascist farce. It took our bright-eyed young matinee audience to discover how good the jokes are in *Til,* and now the children have made it clear, the grown-ups see how touching are its sentiments.

The subject matter, however, of the so-called abstract dance ballets is not so easy to specify. On the point of the most recent, *Metamorphoses,* it happened that while it was being rehearsed, I met him and asked if what I had heard was true, that he was making a ballet on the Kafka short story, "The Metamorphosis." He laughed in surprise, and said no. But he added that as a matter of fact, about a month before, going down from his apartment one night to buy a paper, there on the sidewalk in the glare of the stand and right in the middle of New York he saw a huge cockroach going earnestly on its way. As for me, Olympic athletes, Balinese dancers, Byzantine seraphs seem all to have contributed images for this ballet, besides that Upper East Side cockroach. But onstage these elements do not appear with the expression they have in life. In the athlete section the explosive force of stops and speed makes a dazzle like winter Broadway in its dress of lights; hints from Bali are wildly transformed into a whirring insect orgy; the joyous big-scale nonsense of it and then the evanescent intensity of an insect pas de deux are as simple and childlike in their vitality as a Silly Symphony cartoon; and the end is a big sky swept by powerful, tender, and jubilant wings. What Balanchine has expressed is something else than the material he began with, something subjective; and I so respond to it.

His dance ballets each express a subjective meaning. I feel it as the cumulative effect of the many momentary images they present, dramatic, lyric, or choral. And the pleasure of them is seeing these images as they happen; responding to the succession of their brilliant differences that gradually compose into a structure—an excitement rather like reading a logically disjointed but explosively magnificent ode of Pindar. One might say they are dance entertainments meant to be watched by the natives in New York rather the way the natives of other places than this watch a social village dance in West Africa or watch a Balinese kebyar or legong.

I am supposing at least that natives take their dance forms for granted and watch instead the rapid images and figures. I like that way of watching best myself; and the closer I so follow a dance ballet, the more exciting I find it, and the more different each becomes. I do not enjoy all of Balanchine's equally, or all entirely. Some, like *Firebird* or *Card Game,* have disintegrated in large sections. Others, despite brilliant dancing and passages I enjoy, do not appeal to me in their overall expression—*La Valse, Scotch Symphony, Bourrée Fantasque.* So capricious is a subjective taste. And it is unstable too.

There is a perhaps less capricious way of following a dance piece. It is that of watching its formal structure. And the excitement of doing it is a more intellectual one. I am not sure that it is a good way to watch, but I will mention some of the discoveries one so makes, since they are another approach to the meaning of a piece.

An aspect of structure, for instance, is the way Balanchine sets the score, how he meets the patterns in time, the patterns of energy from which a dancer takes his spring. When you listen closely and watch closely at the same time you discover how witty, how imaginative, how keen his response at every moment is to the fixed architecture of the music. *Pas de Trois* and *Symphony in C* are not hard to follow in this double way, and their limpid musical interest helps to give them their light and friendly objective expression. More complex are the staccato phrasings of *Card Game;* or the interweaving of melodic lines and rhythmic accents in *Concerto Barocco;* or the light play— as of counterpoint—in the airy multiplicity of *Symphonie Concertante.* In this piece the so-called imitations of the music by the dancers, far from being literal, have a grace at once sophisticated and ingenuous. The musical play and the play of dance figures, between them, create bit by bit a subtle strength— the delicate girlish flower-freshness of the piece as a whole. But in relation to the score, the structural quality his ballets all show is their power of sustained rhythm. This power may express itself climactically as in *Serenade* or keep a so-to-speak even level as in *Concertante* or *Card Game.* It makes a difference in applause but not in fascination. Taking as a springboard the force of the extended rhythms—rhythmic sentences or periods—music can construct, Balanchine invents for the dancing as long, as coherent, and as strongly pulsing rhythmic figures; whatever quality of the rhythm gives the score its particular sweep of force he responds to objectively in the sweep of the dancing. And this overall rhythm is different in each piece.

Not that one doesn't recognize rhythmic devices of accent or of climax that he repeats—such as the rhythmic turning of palms inside outside; the Balanchine "pretzels," which I particularly like; or "the gate," an opening in the whirling corps through which in dynamic crescendo other dancers leap forward. He likes bits of canonic imitation; he likes the dramatic path of a star toward a climax to be framed in a neutral countermovement by satellite dancers. And there are some devices I don't care for too, such as the star's solo supported attitude on a musical climax, which (despite its beauty in Petipa) sometimes affects me in the way a too obvious quotation does. But to notice devices in themselves apart from the flow of rhythm and of images they serve to clarify tends to keep one from seeing the meaning of a piece.

Quite another surprise in his ballets if you watch objectively is the variety of shapes of steps, the variety of kinds of movement, that he manages to make classic. "Classic" might be said, of course, to include all kinds of movement that go to make up a three-act classic ballet: academic dancing, mime, character, processions, dancers in repose. And as folk and ballroom steps have been classicized in the past in many ways, so Balanchine has been classicizing movements from our Negro and show steps, as well as from our modern recital dance. In his more recent pieces, the shapes of the steps go from the classroom academicism of *Symphony in C* and the academic virtuosity of *Caracole* through ballroom and more or less traditional character dancing to the untraditional shapes of *Four Temperaments* with its modern-style jokes and crushing impact, or of *Orpheus,* or of *Metamorphoses* and its innocent stage-show style. What an extraordinary absence of prejudice as to what is proper in classicism these odd works show.

But in what sense can all his variety of movement be classical? It is so because of the way he asks the dancer to move, because of the kind of continuity in motion he calls for. For the continuity in all these pieces is that of which the familiar classroom exercises are the key and remain a touchstone. Classic dancing centers movement in a way professionally called "placement"; it centers it for the advantage of assurance in spring, balance, and visibility. The dancer learns to move with a natural continuity in impetus, and a natural expression of his full physical strength in the thighs—thighs and waist, where the greatest strength to move outward into space naturally lies.

Balanchine's constant attention to this principle develops in his dancers a gift for coherent, vigorous, positive, unsimpering movement, and a gift too for a powerful, spontaneous rhythmic pulse in action. And a final product of it is the spaciousness which their dancing—Tallchief exemplifies it—comes to have. Clear, sure-footed dancing travels through space easy and large, either in its instantaneous collective surges or in its slow and solitary paths. So space spreads in calm power from the center of the stage and from the moving dancer and gives a sense of human grandeur and of destiny to her action. In his conversation with me he had of course only stressed the small details of motion from which the large effects eventually can grow.

The final consistency that classical style gives to a performance comes from its discipline of behavior. Handsome behavior onstage gives to an entertainment a radiance Broadway dancing knows little of. Balanchine often builds it into the dance—even when he works on Broadway—by so timing the action that if it is done cleanly and accurately the dramatic color becomes one of a spontaneous considerateness among the dancers for one another and of a graceful feeling between the girls and boys. Further subtleties of behavior, subtle alternations of contact and neutral presence, are a part of the expression his pieces have. They seem, as is natural to Americans, unemphatic and usually even like unconscious actions.

But where drama demands more conscious relationships, these require a more conscious kind of acting. What Balanchine tries for as classic acting is not an emphatic emotional stress placed on a particular gesture for expression's sake. He tries instead to have expression present as a color throughout a dance or a role, sometimes growing a trifle stronger, sometimes less. It is as if a gesture were made in its simplest form by the whole body as it dances. This is a grand style of acting not at all like the usual Broadway naturalism. In ballet a realistic gesture if it is overstressed, or if the timing of it makes the dancer dwell on it "meaningfully," gets clammy; the grand style remains acceptable at any speed or intensity; and Tallchief often exemplifies it at a high intensity—in the writhings of Eurydice, for instance, or in the quiet lightness of her last entrance in *Firebird*.

What I have tried to say is that the meaning of a Balanchine piece is to be found in its brilliance and exhilarating variety of classical style. There is nothing hidden or esoteric or even frustrated about the expression of one of his dance ballets. The meaning of it, as of classical dancing generally, is whatever one loves as one watches it without thinking why. It is no use wasting time puzzling over what one doesn't love; one had better keep looking, and sharply, to see if there isn't something one does, because it goes so fast there is always a lot one misses. Pretty people, pretty clothes, pretty lights, music, pictures, all of it in motion with surprises and feats and all those unbelievable changes of speed and place and figure and weight and a grand continuous rhythm and a tumultuous sweep of imaginary space opening up further and forever, glorious and grand. And because they are all boys and girls doing it, you see these attractive people in all kinds of moments, their unconscious grace of movement, and unconscious grace in their awareness of each other, of themselves, of the music, of the audience, all happening instantaneously and transformed again without a second's reflection. That is what one can find to love. That is the entertainment, different in each piece. All these beauties may be gathered in a sort of story, or you may see them held together only by the music. It is up to you to look and seize them as they flash by in all their brilliant poetry. And many people in the audience do.

Classic ballet is a definite kind of entertainment, based on an ideal conception of expression professionally called "style." It does not try to be the same sort of fun as some other kind of entertainment. It tries to be as wonderful as possible in its own beautiful and voluntarily limited way, just as does any other art. What correct style exists for, what it hopes for, is a singular, unforeseen, an out-of-this-world beauty of expression. In our own local and spontaneous terms this is what Balanchine intends. I wish I had found a less heavy way of treating so joyous and unoppressive a form of entertainment; for a tender irony is close to the heart of it. But I hope I have made clear at least that neither classicism nor "Balanchine style" is, as one sometimes hears people say, merely a mechanical exactness in dancing or in choreography, no personality, no warmth, no human feeling. As for his dancers, this season in particular has shown us that the more correct their style, the more their individual personality becomes distinct and attractive onstage.

The strictest fans realize that his work in creating a company is still only half done. But though still unfinished, the result is already extraordinary. London, Paris, and Copenhagen have striking stars, have companies excellent in many ways, larger, wealthier, more secure than we know how to make them. This winter the hard-worked little New York City company has shown itself, both in style and repertory, more sound, more original, more beautiful than any you can see anywhere in the Western world.

In the last five years George Balanchine has come to be recognized as the greatest choreographer of our time abroad as well as here. Such a position has its drawbacks. But for my part, though his prestige may add nothing to my pleasure in his work, I have no quarrel with it.

—from *Dance Magazine,* 1953

B. H. HAGGIN
Personal Encounters

M y meeting with Balanchine in 1940 was the result of a number of happenings which began with my stay at Yaddo in the summer of 1931. One of the writers there was Clara Gruening Stillman, whom I continued to see in New York, and whom I visited one evening in the summer of 1932. When she asked what I had been doing recently I said I had broadcast, from a small station, a series of talks on the musical scene, for which I was hoping to find a publisher. This led her other visitor to say she thought the editor of the magazine she worked for would be interested in reading the talks and might be able to find a publisher for them. The magazine was *Hound and Horn;* its editor was Lincoln Kirstein; he *was* interested in the talks and liked them when he read them; and when I met him he was impressed by the fact that I had seen the Diaghilev company as early as 1916 in New York as well as in Europe in 1928 and '29, and that I was excited about the ballets of Balanchine. In addition to trying, unsuccessfully, to find a publisher for the talks, he asked me to write about the musical scene in his magazine—which I did until Kirstein, who had brought Balanchine here to start the School of American Ballet, decided in 1934 to divert to the school the money it cost to publish the magazine.

During the School's first year Kirstein now and then invited people to watch Balanchine's work with his students; and on a few of these occasions I was in the group that was introduced to Balanchine, whose members he would have been unable to recognize if he had passed them on the street ten minutes later. In June 1934 Edward Warburg, a financial backer of the school, arranged a demonstration performance for an invited audience on a lawn of his parents' Westchester estate; but soon after the performance began it was ended by rain; and the audience was asked to come into the Warburg mansion for a buffet supper. After a time there was talk among the guests about the fact that Balanchine was missing; and eventually we got the explanation that Balanchine, when he learned that the dancers were to eat separately from the guests, had elected to eat with the dancers.

The first presentation of his first performing group, the American Ballet, to the New York public occurred early in 1935; and having meanwhile become music critic of *The Brooklyn Daily Eagle*, I wrote some paragraphs on Balanchine and his ballets. I didn't write about ballet again until December 1940—this time in *The Nation*. Taking off from someone's statement to me that after a few minutes of a classical ballet he found the repetition of the same movements and positions boring, I pointed out that he failed to see how different these same movements were made in Fokine's *Les Sylphides*, for example, by the personal styles of the three ballerinas that were as different as the styles of three tennis players. And though he could appreciate the differences in the ways composers used the same musical sounds, he was unable to perceive the differences in the ways the same classical ballet movements were used in *Les Sylphides* and, say, *Swan Lake*. Nor did he consider the difference in vocabulary, syntax, and style of movement between Fokine's *Les Sylphides* and his *Petrouchka*, between *Petrouchka* and Balanchine's *Le Baiser de la Fée*, between *Le Baiser* and Balanchine's *Apollo*, his *Cotillon*. To me these differences were very clear and important; and I saw in Balanchine's work the operation of one of the most distinctive and exciting of artistic minds, with an extraordinary feeling for music: listening while one looked at the strange "Hand of Fate" pas de deux in *Cotillon*, one heard the related strangeness of Chabrier's music.

This *Nation* article brought a letter from Kirstein in which he said Balanchine would like to have lunch with me to thank me for the article, and suggested a day when I could watch a Balanchine class at the school and then go to lunch with them. It occurred to me that this might represent an idea of Kirstein's rather than a desire of Balanchine's; and in fact Balanchine, when we met, said nothing about the article (as he never spoke to me about any other writing of mine in the years thereafter). However, he did look at me as if curious about some oddity of mine; and what I thought might explain that look came out later when we were walking to the restaurant and I said I wasn't sure I had any business writing on a subject of which I had no technical knowledge. "Oh no!" he exclaimed. "You look; you see; you write what you see; and that's good." That was when he spoke of the critics in Europe finding in each new ballet of his a deterioration from its admirable predecessor—which they had said about the predecessor when *it* was new. If this was what Balanchine recalled as his experience with critics, one could understand his finding it an interesting oddity that I simply looked at a ballet of his and wrote what I saw in it and enjoyed. And another possible explanation was the concluding statement of my article. Balanchine, who had studied not only in the Maryinsky Theatre's ballet school but in the St. Petersburg conservatory, thought of himself as a musician, and of his choreography as a musical operation—a making visible in movement what he heard in a piece of music. It may therefore have been for him another interesting oddity that I was a music critic who perceived this about him and his work; and he talked to me thereafter as someone involved with music like himself.

Still on the way to the restaurant I mentioned the pleasure I had had from seeing *Cotillon* performed again by the De Basil company, which was then in New York. Balanchine answered that by now the work was very inaccurate because of all the things that had been forgotten or changed by the dancers in the course of the years; and when I begged him to restore it to accuracy he looked pleased but said nothing.

In conversation at lunch Kirstein asked him how his rehearsals of the new ballet he was doing for the de Basil company were going. "Oh, all right," Balanchine replied. "You must know what you are doing, because the dancers can tell if you know or you don't know. If you know, they will do whatever you say. If you say, 'Take off all your clothes,' they will do it. If you say, 'Lift both your legs and stay in the air,' they will do it." This introduced me to the quirky Balanchine mind, whose unexpected turns were not only surprising but on occasion devastating, as in his reply to the critic who demanded to know when anyone had seen Apollo on his knees: "When did anyone see Apollo?"

At one point he left the table to make a telephone call, and I asked Kirstein if there was any possibility of my watching the rehearsals of the new ballet. "Ask him," said Kirstein; and when I did ask, Balanchine's answer was "Certainly." One result of the meeting, therefore, was that from then on what I perceived in Balanchine's work and what I gradually came to understand about it were increased by what I observed at his rehearsals. I couldn't get to all of them; but those I did watch made me aware of details I might otherwise have missed; and it was the knowledge I acquired of the details of *Apollo* at the rehearsals for the Ballet Theatre production with André Eglevsky and later with Igor Youskevitch in the forties that gave them the significance and effect they hadn't had for me before. Moreover, in addition to what I learned about his work there were the things I learned at the rehearsals about Balanchine himself.

When I got to the first rehearsal I attended of the new ballet, *Balustrade*, I found Balanchine standing in front of a complicated grouping of dancers and studying it silently. After a few moments he said something which caused the dancers to separate and stand waiting while he turned to a portable phonograph and listened to a passage of the music, Stravinsky's Violin Concerto, then turned back to the dancers and began to arrange them in another grouping. As he had said, the dancers did whatever he asked; and that was true of the girl in the center of the group, who—silent, passive, in practice clothes, and without makeup—was only after some time recognizable as the glamorous and vivacious Baronova I had seen on the stage. When I arrived the next day I found Balanchine again standing in front of a complicated group, in which the girl in the center was not Baronova but someone else whom it took me even longer to recognize as the enchanting Riabouchinska, who, as the Mistress of Ceremonies in *Cotillon*, had spread a personal radiance over the entire stage. But the next day she too had disappeared; and in addition a flu epidemic caused Balanchine, each day, to find members of the *corps* missing whom he had rehearsed the day before. Whatever he thought and felt about these difficulties, he exhibited complete calm: each day he quietly chose replacements for the missing dancers from those in the studio, listened to a passage of music, and began to arrange the new dancers in a grouping. Thus I observed for the first time his way of working with whatever materials were available and under whatever conditions existed at the moment.

One of the male principals in *Balustrade* was Roman Jasinski, the outstanding characteristic of whose dancing was its sensitivity; and I perceived, first of all, how everything Balanchine invented for him exhibited this distinctive sensitivity. But since he demonstrated whatever he asked Jasinski to do, I saw also that each sensitive movement contrived especially for Jasinski and executed beautifully by him was even more beautiful and effective as it was done by Balanchine. And this I was to see again and again in his work with dancers.

At one rehearsal Balanchine said to me, in explanation of a sequence he was working on: "In Massine's ballets the dancers make some movements here; then they walk to another place and make some movements there. In my ballets the movements are all connected from beginning to end." And I got an impressive demonstration of this when, to my surprise and delight, Balanchine held two rehearsals of *Cotillon* to correct the inaccuracies he had mentioned to me; and the process of correction turned out to be one in which repeatedly the dancing was stopped for Balanchine and the dancers to search their memories and piece together the successive movements that originally had taken the dancers from one point to another in the sequence.

And there was an important fact that I learned about Balanchine's susceptibility to stimulation by music. Until then I had seen for the most part the results of such stimulation by music as attractive and affecting as the Chabrier pieces of *Cotillon*, Tchaikovsky's Serenade for strings and his Suite No. 4 (*Mozartiana*), Prokofiev's score for *The Prodigal Son*, Stravinsky's *Apollo* and *Le Baiser de la Fée*. What *Balustrade* revealed was that Balanchine could be stimulated also by what to my ears was and still is the extremely unattractive and inexpressive music of Stravinsky's Violin Concerto. And I was to find later that it could be stimulated by even worse music.

During the break of one of the rehearsals Balanchine told me he was having a birthday party that evening and asked me to come. I said I had no dinner jacket; he assured me it wasn't necessary; but when he opened the door of his apartment he was in white tie and tails. Since his wife at that time, Vera Zorina, was at the theater performing in *Louisiana Purchase*, and I was the first guest to arrive, we were alone, and he showed me some beautiful drawings by the painter Pavel Tchelitchew, who was designing the scenery and costumes for *Balustrade*. (He disrupted one rehearsal by rushing in excitedly to show everyone his costume designs: "For you, Tamaratchka [Toumanova], I made this costume with all stars!" And in the intermission after the first performance of the ballet, standing in the aisle with several people, he turned away from them every now and then to roar, "Balanchine is a genius!") The guests included—late in the evening, after his concert with the Boston Symphony in Carnegie Hall—Serge Koussevitzky, who at one point discussed with Balanchine the possibility of his working at Tanglewood in the summer. Their discussion was one in which Koussevitzky kept stating what *he* had thought Balanchine might do at Tanglewood, and Balanchine kept stating what *he* thought he might do, each with no regard for what was said by the other (and nothing ever came of the discussion). Still later Zorina arrived after her performance, bringing with her the conductor of her show, who handed Balanchine a birthday present which he said was a recording of Heifetz playing the Beethoven Violin Concerto with the Boston Symphony and Koussevitzky. When the parcel was opened there was a silence of embarrassment, which was broken by Koussevitzky. "With me he made the *Brahms* concerto," he said, adding sourly, "If it's Beethoven it's not with me—it's with Toscanini."

The rehearsals of *Balustrade* ended; and after three performances and the attack that Balanchine's every ballet got from John Martin in *The Times* (as I said elsewhere, his writing about Balanchine in those early years exhibited an unerring eye for greatness and an unrelenting hatred of it*) the piece departed with the de Basil company and was never seen in New York again. In the spring of 1941 Balanchine made, for a South American tour by the American Ballet, *Concerto Barocco*, at one rehearsal of which I recall his calling my attention to a phrase of movement by the *corps* that mirrored a phrase in Bach's score; and *Ballet Imperial*, now titled *Tchaikovsky Piano Concerto*, to that composer's Piano Concerto No. 2, a rarely performed but much finer work than the ubiquitous No. 1.

These were plotless dance ballets; and so was the *Danses Concertantes*, in September 1944, that Edwin Denby characterized as a "singular masterpiece"—made singular by the strikingly new invention that Stravinsky's music, with its *ostinatos*, elicited from Balanchine. In the opening ensemble one saw the elegant and witty movements of Danilova supported by Franklin, and behind them eight girls supported by four boys in an amusing *perpetuum mobile* of arabesques, turns, and leaps, with what Denby described as "changes from staccato movements to continuous ones, from rapid leaps and displacements to standing still," and the "separate spurts, stops and clipped stalkings" of individuals in a group that added up to a single long phrase. And the later dances by trios of two girls and a boy offered the amusing interaction with the music of the three dancers, their hands joined, in a continuous twisting under each others' arms, or the two girls supported by the boy in their continuously alternating *arabesques penchées*.

Writing about *Danses Concertantes*, I noted the objection of people accustomed to ballets with a plot—that they found plotless dance ballets mean-

---

*Later there was the change in Martin's writing about Balanchine that I reported in *The Nation* in 1952. Not that there was the slightest intimation in the writing that what Martin was saying now was different from what he had said in the early years: on the contrary, he wrote as if he had always been the benevolent admirer who, now, understood Balanchine's affection for *Apollo*, a "historical milestone," but had to point out that it was "a very young and dated effort" which would never be a popular ballet: who regretted having to counsel Balanchine to consign the wonderful invention of *The Four Temperaments* to oblivion for lack of the right music to carry it, and to return as beautiful a work as *Le Baiser de la Fée* to the storehouse until its technical problems were solved: and who, conceding the beauty of Balanchine's Act 2 of *Swan Lake*, nevertheless had to admonish him not to concern himself again with such old chestnuts—which was as though the director of a theater company were admonished not to concern himself with Shakespeare or Chekhov. "As a friend, and for your own good," said Martin to Balanchine, "I urge you to cut your throat." And years later, after his retirement from *The Times*, he carried this performance further in the article that appeared for several weeks in the New York City Ballet's programs, in which he wrote of the joy it was to see in the company's performances the fulfillment he had hoped for at the beginning. But impossible as it may seem, the writing in *The Times* by Martin's successor, Clive Barnes, was even worse—so outrageously worse that Balanchine instructed the company, he told me, not to quote Barnes's favorable statements in its promotional material.

ingless. And conceding that classical ballet movements, like other plastic materials—those of music, for example—could, certainly, be used in ways in which they meant nothing, I contended that they could also—like musical sounds—be used in ways which gave them the "eloquence of pure form" that Aldous Huxley talked about in his essay *Music at Night*. Some of my most exciting experiences of this eloquence, I said, had been provided by the "pure forms" of Balanchine's plotless dance ballets, which produced their effect in the same way as Mozart's piano concertos—with the play of mind and wit in the manipulation of the plastic material.

The singular *Danses Concertantes* was the first product of Balanchine's two-year association with the Monte Carlo Ballets Russes—some of the others that followed being revivals of *Le Bourgeois Gentilhomme* (originally made for the company in 1932), *Mozartiana,* and *Le Baiser de la Fée,* and in 1946 a new dramatic ballet, *Night Shadow* (now *La Sonnambula*). A rehearsal of *Le Bourgeois Gentilhomme* one morning on the City Center stage has remained in my memory. It began, at ten, with the company's rehearsal pianist missing, with workmen noisily installing the electronic devices Stokowski insisted he had to have for the concerts he was to conduct, and with Balanchine, undeterred by these difficulties, repeatedly going to the piano to play a passage of the music and returning to the dancers to show them what to do. Eventually the pianist arrived and, as she was seating herself at the piano, informed Balanchine that in an hour Danilova would have to have the stage to show Nicholas Magallanes how to partner her in *Swan Lake* that night in place of Franklin, who could not dance because of a knee injury. Balanchine said nothing and resumed work with his dancers. A little later I saw Danilova look in for a moment and disappear; and some time after that Balanchine signalled a break in the rehearsal, draping his jacket over his shoulders and lighting a cigarette while the dancers settled down around the stage. They were chatting when Danilova came in wearing a tutu which looked old enough to have been used at the premiere of *Swan Lake* in Russia, and stopping in the center of the stage to announce: "I want quiet. Those who want party go outside." Most of them stayed to watch as Danilova began to show Magallanes how "I go here . . . you hold me here—no, *here*! ['The Devil take him!' in Russian] . . . now I make three turns . . ." It was fascinating to see this placing of brick on brick of the structure whose splendid facade I would see that evening. But Balanchine, smoking his cigarette and watching with a professional's unfascinated eye, commented only, "Too slow."

In addition to the knowledge of the detail of *Le Baiser de la Fée* that I acquired at the rehearsals of this work there was the interest they had from the presence and active involvement of Stravinsky, whom I remember as a tiny man with a personal force that seemed to extend to his enormously outflowing breast-pocket handkerchief, and who, constantly consulted and deferred to by Balanchine, left no doubt of his satisfaction with what he saw. As for *Night Shadow*, I remember only the studio rehearsal at which Balanchine, waiting for Danilova to arrive, used the time to make the grotesque pas de deux for the couple in blackface with Ruthanna Boris and Edward Lindgren. Occasionally he took Lindgren's place to show him how to do something— which gave me pleasure to see, and led Boris to remark that she would give her life to dance in a pas de deux with Balanchine. He was still working with the two dancers when Danilova came in, dressed in a chic practice costume and sat down next to me. "I am late," she said, "because last night I was at party where a man gave me something to drink; and I wake up this morning with terrible headache. It shows you should not trust men." Balanchine now left the studio for a moment and returned with a coat hanger which he broke in two, giving one of the pieces to Danilova to hold as the candle in what he began to work out with her and Magallanes (in place of Franklin, who again was out with an injury): the work's climactic stroke of *fantaisie Balanchine*, the pas de deux of the Poet's encounter with the Somnambulist, in which his way first of expressing his wonder, then of attempting to establish contact with her mind, is to experiment with her moving body and control its motion—to send it now in this direction, now in that, to stop it, to spin it, to grasp the candle in her hand and use it to swing her now this way, now that.

Balanchine's two years with the Monte Carlo company were followed by the two subscription seasons of his own Ballet Society. One of the works of the second season, *Symphonie Concertante*, was not newly made for Ballet Society: Balanchine had made it a couple of years earlier for a program in which the advanced students of the School of American Ballet performed with the training orchestra of the National Orchestral Association in Carnegie Hall; and at that time I had seen, before the performance, a studio run-through with piano. Waiting for it to begin, I had watched the chattering girls milling around; then, when the piano had begun the orchestra's opening *ritornello* I had watched them in the formations leading to the entrance of the two soloists; and when the soloists had made their entrance I had been electrified by one of them. Ten minutes earlier a chattering student, now she had presented the image, in movement and occasional repose, of a matured and compelling ballet dancer. This had been my introduction to Tanaquil LeClercq, who two years later began to appear in the roles in Balanchine's works for Ballet Society that employed and revealed her extraordinary powers—not only the technique, style, and presence of a great ballerina in the slow movement of *Symphony in C*, but the dramatic vividness of her Bacchante in *Orpheus* and *Choleric Variation* in *The Four Temperaments*. She provided my first experience of what I was to see happen later with other dancers—the stimulation of Balanchine's creative imagination by a particular dancer's configuration of body and capacities for movement, on which his interest was concentrated.

In addition to the ballets of the second season, the society's subscribers saw a Balanchine demonstration of supported adagio, introduced by a lecture in which Kirstein, illustrating with slides, described what he said had been the change from the eighteenth century's one man dancing with several girls to the twentieth century's one girl with several men—the latter illustrated by a slide of the Siren with the Prodigal's Companions in Balanchine's *The Prodigal Son*. This had no relevance to the supported adagio Balanchine was to demonstrate; and Kirstein said nothing about the seduction pas de deux of the Siren and the Prodigal, whose details would have shown the audience Balanchine's imaginatively innovative use of supported adagio for dramatic purpose. When Kirstein had finished, Balanchine came onto the stage with LeClercq and Herbert Bliss and, smiling wickedly, confided to the audience: "I am going to show you what Lincoln doesn't know," after which he demonstrated the invention for LeClercq and Bliss of the successive phrases of a supported adagio.

For the New York City Ballet's eight performances a week, and its constantly expanding repertory, Ballet Society's group of dancers—principally Maria Tallchief, LeClercq, Marie-Jeanne, Francisco Moncion, Todd Bolender, Magallanes, and Bliss—was insufficient; and Balanchine brought in several from Ballet Theatre: Diana Adams, Janet Reed, Nora Kaye, Melissa Hayden, André Eglevsky, and Jerome Robbins. Eglevsky provided a virtuoso partner for Tallchief in display pieces like *Sylvia Pas de Deux, Capriccio Brillante,* and *Pas de Dix,* but also in works like Balanchine's new version of Act 2 of *Swan Lake* (in which, ignoring Balanchine's no-star policy, Eglevsky made a star's first entrance with a smiling greeting to the applauding audience) and *Scotch Symphony*; and unexpectedly he was very amusing as the amorous mustachioed French tennis player in *A la Français*. Robbins's gift for comedy served Balanchine well in the marvelous first movement of *Bourrée Fantasque* and in the title role of *Til Eulenspiegel*, but he was less effective in the revived *The Prodigal Son*. (He was replaced in this work by Moncion, whose powerful presence and dramatic mask, in addition to the continuous tension of his movement, achieved a performance in the last two scenes that no one has equalled. I might add that in Moncion's first season in *The Prodigal Son* the Father was Balanchine, whose presence and few movements were such as to make those of his successors in the role painful to see.)

At one of the rehearsals of *The Prodigal Son* Balanchine, having completed the seduction pas de deux, asked me if the end was correct. "It's not what I remember," I said; and when he looked at me inquiringly I added: "The end was a gradual interlocking of the two bodies, with the Siren's arm rising in triumph above them"—at which he nodded and got down on the floor with

Tallchief to work out what I had recalled to him. Later, when he had completed the last scene, he asked me if the final moment was correct. "No," I
said. "The Father stood motionless with the Prodigal prostrate at his feet, and
remained motionless as the Prodigal reached up to grasp his legs and began
to pull himself up into the Father's arms; then the Father brought his cloak
around the Prodigal's body and remained motionless as the curtain fell."
Again Balanchine nodded and worked this out with Robbins. It was astounding that he had not remembered these two extraordinary details.

Most interesting to me in those early years was what he was stimulated to
do with LeClercq by the capacities his interest was concentrated on—the
roles he contrived for her in *Bourrée Fantasque, Metamorphoses, Western Symphony, La Valse, Roma, Divertimento No.15*. It was not only her capacities in
dance movement that made her performances in these ballets memorable:
Balanchine could say he was not interested in dancers' personalities; but
what contributed to making LeClercq a fascinating and compelling dancer
for the spectator was the personality that irradiated her face and made it the
dramatic mask of a great actress. She was a delightful comic in the first
movement of *Bourrée Fantasque*, the last movement of *Western Symphony*, and
"In the Inn" of *Ivesiana;* and on the other hand, as the doomed girl in *La
Valse*—in her first entrance and her strangely perverse slow dance with Magallanes, her later encounter and dance with Moncion—she has never been
equalled. A rehearsal of that slow dance with Magallanes remains in my
memory; also the rehearsal for her first *Swan Lake*, in which, as she learned
the movements with Eglevsky in the adagio, she kept exclaiming "Such
fun!"; and the rehearsal of the 1951 *Apollo* in which she went through Polyhymnia's solo with her face radiating the joyous intelligence that contradicted Balanchine's remark at one point: "The muses were not intelligent."

LeClercq's response to my fascinated interest was a charming friendliness
which, after her marriage to Balanchine, she showed in ways that were as
moving as they were unexpected. Balanchine smiled his welcome at
rehearsals; but I had had no meeting with him elsewhere since the birthday
party in 1941. It was LeClercq who sent me the telegram inviting me to the
party celebrating their marriage, and the one inviting me to the party after
the final performance of the company's winter season. And I began to get
letters and postcards from Los Angeles or Rome with her news of the company and Balanchine. A letter in May 1954 informed me that he was doing a
new ballet with music by Ives that was a bit like *The Four Temperaments:*
"strange music, so the steps are sure to be queerish." And a letter in August
1953 relayed his comments on a matter which I must have expressed concern about to LeClercq—the disappearance of beautiful ballets from the
repertory. There was no Haieff *Divertimento*, she reported his saying, because
it had to have four wonderful boys and four terrific girls, without which

there was no point in doing it; there was no *Apollo* because there was no Apollo (Eglevsky, in the 1951 performances, had exhibited no god-like power in his delicate stepping about with upturned wrists, and no vital energy even in his leaps); *Symphonie Concertante* and *Jeu de Cartes* were not popular; and *Le Baiser de la Fée* would take lots of time because he wanted to re-do it. (He never did re-do it—not even for his Stravinsky Festival in 1972, when instead he used portions of the Stravinsky score for a new classical *pas de deux* with no relation to their dramatic significance in the original ballet. The company's manager, Betty Cage, told me this was because he remembered *Jeu de Cartes* and *Le Baiser de la Fée* as failures with the public. Not only did I remember them as successes, but LeClercq, whom I asked, also recalled that audiences "did like both ballets. No super hits . . . but nice applause, a few 'bravos' once or twice.")

In a letter in March 1954 LeClercq thanked me for a record I had given Balanchine, adding that their phonograph was "still on the blink." A performance of Berlioz's marvelous songs *Les Nuits d'Eté* had seemed to me exactly the right birthday present for someone who loved the music of Chabrier, Delibes, Lalo, and Bizet; but in a letter the following November she confessed that he hadn't liked it. We must all get together, she concluded: would I come to see *House of Flowers*, the Truman Capote-Harold Arlen musical show which Balanchine was staging and providing with dances. Denby and I did go to the last run-through without scenery and costumes before the rehearsals moved to Philadelphia; and soon after it began the seat next to mine was occupied by someone who turned out to be Balanchine. Whenever one of his contrivances in the action or dancing produced a roar of laughter in the theater I stole a look at him and found him staring at the stage impassively: he was there not to enjoy what he had contrived but only to see how it worked.

A week or so later he was dismissed by the producers of the show; but this resulted in some interesting moments at the Balanchine apartment on Christmas Eve. LeClercq asked me to come after nine; and when I arrived with a gift of a record for her I received a bulky gift that turned out to be the School of American Ballet's copy of Balanchine's book *The Complete Stories of the Great Ballets,* which he had appropriated for his purpose, and in which he had printed a limerick about "modest critic of Nation." The before-nine guests were Doubrovska and her husband Vladimirov; and a little later we were joined by the woman who had been the rehearsal pianist of *House of Flowers* and her husband. For a time she reported what had happened in the show in Philadelphia; then she and Balanchine began to recall things from earlier shows in which they had worked together, with Balanchine playing the songs on the piano; and from these, to our amazement, he switched to songs from shows of the '20s. Where did he get to know *these,* we exclaimed. "I was little boy in Russia," he replied with a grin.

A letter in March 1955 ended with a request that I call them the next week so we could get together for drinks, dinner—possibly at a "heavenly Italian restaurant." Actually the dinner was one Balanchine cooked at their apartment—the other guest being Natalie Molostwoff of the school's administration. While Balanchine was busy in the kitchen LeClercq told me how pleased she was by what I had written about Allegra Kent; and in conversation after the excellent dinner Balanchine expressed his *dis*pleasure at John Martin's inability to "see when anything is wrong," and at Martin's statement that Diana Adams had "what is more important than technique," when actually "Diana *has* technique." Also, Walter Terry had asked what was wrong with Eglevsky's *entrechats-six;* "and I said, 'You mean his *entrechats-huits*—and they are not wrong: they are tiny and delicate,'" as Balanchine demonstrated with his hands. But "Eglevsky hasn't worked in ten years," he went on. "I told him: 'Stop eating; work hard; dance wonderful *once*—then quit!' When I did the hoop dance in *Nutcracker* I was lazy; but I worked and worked and I did it this high; and at the end I jumped through the hoop so [he demonstrated the height] that I had to repeat it. And I never did it again." I mentioned my having seen him in the Spanish entrance in *The Ball:* "Ah, then you can say I was good dancer." I replied that I could say that also after seeing him show dancers movements that he did better than they, and I still remembered how he did Jasinski's movements in *Balustrade*—at which he looked surprised and pleased.

His recollections included the English critic Beaumont's having found everything in *The Prodigal Son* terrible except Lifar's dancing. "Lifar was very grand by that time," he said, "but when he first came from the Ukraine he couldn't dance at all. I showed him how to turn, and other things; and he said, 'Oh please, show me again.' " And he recalled that Olin Downes, in his attack on Balanchine's staging of Gluck's *Orfeo ed Euridice* at the Metropolitan in 1936, "wanted columns, which were introduced by Weber, and which were attacked *then!*" *Orfeo* was for him the most beautiful music in the world. "Yes," I said, "the second act." "And the *first* act!" he insisted.

In May 1956 I watched LeClercq at rehearsals of the two ballets, *A Musical Joke* and *Divertimento No. 15,* for the Mozart Festival that was to inaugurate the Shakespeare Festival Theater in Stratford. I went up to Stratford to see the performances, and wrote afterwards that LeClercq's movements—her unfolding *arabesques* in the long supported adagio of *A Musical Joke,* for example—had been made breathtakingly beautiful by their aura of her personal radiance. That was the last dancing of hers I saw; for at the end of that summer, in Copenhagen, she was stricken with polio.

Balanchine stayed with her in Copenhagen; and I wrote to her a few times and sent her a paperback volume of Bernard Shaw's music criticism, with no expectation of the reply a couple of months later: a huge fancy Christmas card on which she had managed to get her unsteady hand to write a few words. Next there was a long letter dictated to her mother, in which she reported that Balanchine was staging *Serenade* and *Apollo* for the Royal Danish Ballet and had found an Apollo whom he described as "beautiful boy, good face, could be movie star, Tarzan, you know, Weismuller." Then there were letters written with her by now steady hand—one of which began with a comment on my report of having had to resign from *The Nation* because of mistreatment by its new publisher, George Kirstein (Lincoln Kirstein's business-executive brother), and his new editor and literary editor, Carey McWilliams and Robert Hatch: that *she* was sorry about *The Nation* if *I* was, and "George says it will fold soon anyway (he usually is right)." Her amazingly undiminished gaiety in these letters could be taken to represent optimism about further recovery; but it was to continue when hope of recovery had been given up.

When they returned to New York in the fall of 1957 LeClercq, after a few weeks in the hospital, went to Warm Springs in Georgia, and Balanchine began rehearsals of *Square Dance* and *Agon*. At the end of a rehearsal one afternoon he inquired whether I had an engagement; and when I said I did not he asked me to have dinner with him. We went to the Russian Tea Room, where he was received as royalty and conducted to a table in a somewhat secluded corner. After ordering our meal he recalled the March of Dimes benefit performance in the '40s in which LeClercq had played a girl stricken with polio who was given a pair of ballet shoes that miraculously cured her, and said he was certain that this miracle would happen in the real situation now. And later he reported with vehemence how Herbert Bliss had asked for an opportunity to try his hand in choreographing a ballet, and had explained that choreography might provide a way of earning a living when he could no longer dance. "I said to him," Balanchine exclaimed, "*that* is no reason to become a choreographer! *I* became a choreographer because I wanted to move people around!" When we came out of the Russian Tea Room his eye caught the title of a Disney film at the Little Carnegie Theater, and he asked me to see it with him. After the film (about a woodchuck) I walked up Madison Avenue with him as far as his street; and a discussion of the marvels of Mozart's *Figaro* gave me an opportunity to say, "I've meant to ask you why you don't like Berlioz." "Because," he said, "his music is always the same"— which left me as dumbfounded as I had been when Toscanini had made the same statement about Mozart's symphonies.* It was extraordinary that someone with Balanchine's originality in his own art, and his interest in twentieth-century musical originals like Stravinsky, Schoenberg, Ives, and

---

* "But not G-minor," Toscanini had added. "*That* is great tragedy." And actually he had performed several of the others.

Webern, had no appreciation of one of the two great nineteenth-century originals (and twenty years later he would astonish me with his lack of appreciation of the other of the two, Mussorgsky).

The miracle Balanchine felt certain about didn't happen; and after 1956 he was stimulated by the particular capacities of other dancers than LeClercq: Adams (*Agon, Liebeslieder Walzer*), Kent (*Episodes, Bugaku*), Violette Verdy (*The Figure in the Carpet, Liebeslieder Walzer, Emeralds*), Patricia McBride (*Rubies, Who Cares?*), Jacques d'Amboise (*Who Cares?, Union Jack*), Edward Villella (*Bugaku, Tarantella, Rubies*), Suzanne Farrell (*Don Quixote, Diamonds, Tzigane, Chaconne*), Mimi Paul (*Emeralds*), Peter Martins (*Tzigane, Chaconne*). In those years I saw Balanchine and talked with him only briefly at rehearsals; and ten years passed before we had another extended conversation like the one at the Russian Tea Room.

After *Agon* he began rehearsals for *Gounod Symphony,* which was to have Tallchief dancing in the first performance and Adams alternating with her in subsequent performances. I recall only a rehearsal with Adams, at the end of which I saw Balanchine listening impassively as she said quietly, though her voice betrayed repressed emotion: "If Jacques [d'Amboise] rehearses only with Maria tomorrow and Wednesday I can't do the second performance." Balanchine was silent; then he said something I didn't hear, to which Adams replied: "If Jacques rehearses only with Maria tomorrow and Wednesday I can't do the second performance." And I don't think I'm only imagining another silence, then another comment by Balanchine that I didn't hear, to which Adams replied: "If Jacques rehearses only with Maria tomorrow and Wednesday I can't do the second performance." With this she turned to leave; and as she passed me she said hello and I asked her something— probably the time of the next rehearsal, for she replied: "I don't know. You just saw me having a fight about it." Thus I learned what constituted a "fight" in this backstage world apart in which, I had already suspected, the surface quiet concealed a lot of repressed emotion.

At a rehearsal in December 1963 for Villella's first performance in *Apollo*—with Patricia McBride, Suki Schorer, and Carol Sumner—Balanchine spoke with satisfaction about the fact that he now had this "short cast" for the work in addition to the "tall cast" headed by D'Amboise. It had been difficult to understand Balanchine's not having Villella dance in *Apollo* before this; and two or three years later, after Villella's beautiful performances in the work, it would be impossible to understand Balanchine's ending theme.

In February 1968, during a performance of *Firebird* with Melissa Hayden that I had chosen not to see, as I sat on a bench in the corridor reading something I became aware of someone standing in front of me; and looking up I was surprised to see that it was Balanchine, since his practice was to watch every performance. He surprised me further by sitting down beside me for a few minutes of conversation, chiefly about his ballet *The Figure in the Carpet,* which—after it had been out of the repertory for several years—he had made an unsuccessful attempt to revive. Both of us exclaimed enthusiastically about the Handel music; and I recalled two wonderful things in the choreography: Verdy's solos in the opening scene, and the courtiers' intricate dance to a fugal piece. Verdy, he reported, had remembered her solos, but no one could remember the other movements of the opening scene; and that had ended the attempt. Since the music was so fine, I said, how about using it again for a new ballet? An excellent idea, he replied; and I therefore wrote him an annual reminder of it a couple of times; but it never materialized.

About this time Mimi Paul disappeared from the company; and encountering Balanchine in the theater one evening I asked him what had happened to her. "She wants to dance *Sleeping Beauty,*" he said, "so she will go to Canada and dance *Sleeping Beauty*." But someone in the company told me she had resented Balanchine's concentration of his attention on Suzanne Farrell, ignoring the fact that it had not kept him from making effective use of other dancers—from assigning Paul, in particular, to the second movement of *Symphony in C,* and making for her the beautiful solo and wonderful *pas de deux* with Moncion in *Emeralds*. It was appalling, after these, to see the ugly misuse of her in Ballet Theatre's production of Nahat's *Brahms Quintet*.

In the fall of 1968—to teach young John Prinz elegance of style and skill in partnering in a classical *pas de deux*—Balanchine made the ballet *La Source,* to music of Delibes, with Verdy and Prinz. "He is like a lion," said Balanchine, making violent gestures, "and I'm trying to teach him to use his strength to do something small." At the rehearsals not only did I too learn something about elegance of style and skill in partnering, but I had the fascinating experience of seeing them demonstrated to Prinz by Balanchine. Repeatedly, taking Prinz's place with Verdy, Balanchine showed him that "you don't present yourself; you present *her*;" that when she was to be turned on pointe "you take her hand and show her off," and "you take only her fingers;" that when he set her down after a lift "you let her go and back away—on demi-pointe, not on heels." At one rehearsal, when Prinz suddenly stopped, exhausted, in a *pas de deux* and exclaimed, "I don't know about later, but it's too much for me now!", Balanchine sat motionless and silent for a few moments; then he walked to where Prinz and Verdy were standing, and said, "It's because you work too hard." And taking Verdy's hand he showed Prinz how easy it was to balance and turn Verdy on pointe as he walked around her. But then he discovered that she was trying to balance herself as he balanced her, with the result that they were working against each other. "You must do nothing," he said to her. "Just stand on pointe. The man must balance you and turn you." There were other corrections for Verdy—two of them puzzling. Recalling how her head was involved in her movement, I am surprised to find in my notes his admonishing her to "bend your head, not only your body. The head should move so"—and his demonstrating this to her. Even more surprising therefore is the request a few days later, "Less head movement. Just use your feet and your hands." And whereas Villella had admired her ability to understand and develop a new role immediately as she learned the steps, Balanchine said to her, "Don't perform. Just do the steps;" which, it seemed to me, was the equivalent of saying to an actress, "Don't perform. Just say the words."

At these rehearsals Balanchine occasionally took time out for an anecdote or an observation; and on one of these occasions he told of Massine's returning to the Diaghilev company to do *Zéphyr et Flore* at the time that Balanchine was choreographing *La Chatte*. Massine, when he was rehearsing, would not allow Balanchine even to walk through the studio; but he managed to be dressing in the studio when Balanchine was rehearsing, and saw some of the new movements Balanchine was inventing—among them Markova's turns on pointe with bent knee. The next day Diaghilev telephoned and told Balanchine that Massine had accused him of stealing a movement—the turns with bent knee— Massine had intended to use. "He said you stole his thoughts," said Diaghilev. "And I said, 'If someone can steal your thoughts, please don't think.'" "Massine did this again," said Balanchine, "when I put on *Swan Lake* for Diaghilev. This time the movement was Spessivtseva's *arabesque* after a double turn in the air. Diaghilev phoned me: 'Massine says you stole his *arabesque*;' and this time he was laughing."

The rehearsals of *La Source* took place after the break for lunch; and at Verdy's suggestion I watched several of the company classes that Balanchine gave before lunch. They began with exercises at the *barre* and away from it; then he invented extended sequences of ballet movements for the dancers to perform. At one point in the first class I attended he remarked, "Romanticism you have to get [pointing upward] from God. My business is to show you form." And later, dissatisfied with the performance of an extended sequence, he said: "You hear the words *port de bras;* but you never hear anything about the head and the neck. I want to remind you that you have a head and a neck." As he demonstrated by turning from an *arabesque* position in which he faced the wall on his right to one in which he faced the wall on his left, he said, "Your head turns first . . . and you see . . . [his face lighting up] . . . the clock [on the wall] . . . [laughter from the dancers] . . . Once more!" And after the repetition, "That's right."

It was after one of these classes that he inquired whether I had to go somewhere; and when I said I had nothing to do until the rehearsal of *La Source* he suggested that we go downstairs to the cafeteria. There we sat down at a table in a corner, and he talked first about Prinz—the fact that one of his associates had been dubious about his concerning himself with Prinz;

but "I saw possibilities, and I used him in *Don Quixote*." And he looked surprised and pleased when I said how excitingly novel and effective the *Pas de
Deux Mauresque* that he had made for Prinz and Suki Schorer had been in a
style I couldn't recall his having used before. He mentioned the old criticism
that his choreography was cold and mechanical; "but I say technique is
important—to learn to make a movement, a beautiful movement." When he
expressed anger about Clive Barnes's statement that the Joffrey Ballet had
performed his *Scotch Symphony* better than the New York City Ballet, I
reported to him Edwin Denby's palliating explanation of the irresponsibly
outrageous things Barnes said—that he said them to further the cause of ballet; and my reply to Denby—that *he* had furthered the cause of ballet by
writing what he saw, not what he invented. I went on to say that critics often
were not willing merely to report what they heard and saw, but instead
wrote what they thought would impress the public with their own performances—an outstanding example of this being Virgil Thomson's writing. In
reply Balanchine questioned whether Thomson, a composer, could deal
fairly with other composers; and I said that actually Thomson did deal fairly
with composers, but indulged in fantasy about performers—about
Toscanini, above all. Reverting to the statement about the Joffrey performance of *Scotch Symphony,* Balanchine said: "I gave them my ballets in the
beginning to help them; but no more. They have their dancers; they have
their Arpino; let them make their own ballets. I have beautiful dancers whom
I have trained; and my dancers will perform my ballets." Pursuing this train
of thought, he said: "I made everything myself . . . I with Lincoln [Kirstein].
He has ideas [Balanchine's hands made wild movements around his head];
then he disappears and leaves them to others." "You mean he leaves them to
you? " I asked. "That's right," said Balanchine. "He leaves them to me."

"I would like to go back and finish some of my ballets," he said later, "but
there are too many by now. I did it only with *Serenade*. In beginning I used
only two movements, because I made it to teach. Then, when I added I made
cuts. I was young, and thought I knew better than Tchaikovsky; so I left out
repetitions—for example at the end of the slow introduction to the third
movement [which he sang], and later in that movement [he sang a passage
with a sequential build-up]. Now I realized that Tchaikovsky was right. If
you hear first phrase only once you don't remember it; so Tchaikovsky
repeats it, and you say, 'Aha, that's first phrase again.' Then he repeats it a
step higher; and you know it's first phrase a step higher. So I put back all
those cuts. And none of the critics noticed it; nobody said a word!" (But
when he revived *Apollo* in 1979–80 he omitted Stravinsky's introduction.)

At one point he spoke of Gounod's wonderful writing at the beginning of
Faust. "Nobody in France wrote such music before Gounod; only after: Bizet,
then Chabrier." During a pause in that afternoon's rehearsal of *La Source* it

turned out that he had, the night before, attended the first performance of
Frank Corsaro's staging of *Faust* for the New York City Opera; and he
described indignantly how, when Marguerite had sung her beautiful aria in
her garden after her encounter with Faust, one had been distracted from it by
her Corsaro-directed struggle to take off her dress—of which Balanchine
gave a vivid imitation. (In an interview in *Opera News* he had stated his belief
that in opera "when a person sings . . . he should just stand and sing," and
there should be "minimum of gesture and movement, maximum of music.")

In the years that followed I recall Balanchine at a rehearsal, saying about
Liebeslieder Walzer, "This ballet I will not give to any other company. I will
keep it for my company" (it is no longer performed by his company; and to
see it one would have to go to Vienna, I believe); Balanchine and I, at a
rehearsal of *Who Cares?,* exclaiming to each other "What beautiful music!"
after one of the Gershwin songs; Balanchine, on some occasion, telling me
that in England "they say in America I lost my soul. And they say 'Come back;
we'll give it back to you.'"And I recall the only occasion when I argued with
him. After a matinee performance I had gone backstage, and finding a crowd
outside Verdy's dressing room I had started back toward the auditorium, and
came upon Balanchine reading the notices on a bulletin board. "Oh, hello,"
he said with a smile. "We haven't seen much of you." "I've been here
occasionally," I assured him. "Someone was talking about you the other
day . . . something about . . . maybe about Mussorgsky?" he said. "It must
have been my writing about the original version of *Boris Godunov,*" I replied.
"Yes," he said. Then, "What's original? It's the same thing!" he exclaimed,
meaning the same as the Rimsky-Korsakov version. "How can you say that? "
I asked in astonishment. "Rimsky didn't only re-orchestrate Mussorgsky's
Boris, as most people believe. He recomposed it—in melody, harmony,
rhythm. What he did was a scandal—the scandal it would be if Robbins were
to re-choreograph one of your ballets." "You like the Mazurka?" he asked,
meaning the Polonaise he had choreographed for the Metropolitan's production. "There is a great deal in *Boris* besides the Mazurka," I replied. "There are
wonderful passages for chorus; there are Boris's wonderful monologues in
the scene in his apartment." "You mean '*I have attained the highest power* [in
Russian]?" he asked. "Yes," I replied. "And as for the Mazurka, is every last
movement in one of your ballets as great as the greatest?" There was a
moment's silence; then "Yes!" he exclaimed. "Every movement. . . . And I
will tell you what is a scandal: they don't perform Glinka!" "But they do," I
protested. "You yourself staged one of his operas in Hamburg recently." "Yes,
but not in America," he replied; and seeing that the person he had been waiting for had arrived, he said goodbye with a smile and left.

By "argued" I mean only a continuous serious reasoning back and forth by
minds in contact. Very early I became aware of Balanchine's unwillingness to

engage in such reasoning and permit such contact, and the amusement he got from parrying a serious statement and throwing its maker off balance with an elusive or perverse answer; and in private conversation thereafter I didn't attempt to argue with him. His public statements I regarded as open to public comment, and commented on: since he had, for example, described his 1972 Stravinsky Festival to the press as one that would show Stravinsky's entire life as a composer, I wrote after the festival that I couldn't imagine the mental process by which he had arrived at the decision that this demonstration required the inclusion of an inconsequential piano sonata that Stravinsky wrote as a child, and his derivative and diffuse Symphony Op. 1, but not of the first monumental products of his matured powers, *Petrouchka* and *Le Sacre du Printemps;* the inclusion of minor matters of the '20s like the Octet and the Serenade in A, but not of the toweringly great *Le Baiser de la Fée*—i.e. the entire score with the choreography Balanchine made for it in 1937, not the few excerpts from the concert suite for which he devised a new choreography in 1972. But when in private conversation he said Berlioz's music was always the same I didn't feel any necessity of pointing out to him the striking differences in the six songs of *Les Nuits d'Eté*. And when I did argue with him about Mussorgsky's *Boris* it was because his questions to me indicated his willingness to have me do so. The private idiosyncrasies and eccentricities of genius, I believed, were entitled to such deference.

—from *Discovering Balanchine,* 1981

LINCOLN KIRSTEIN
Meeting Balanchine

A unique cultural figure in New York City and America, Lincoln Kirstein (1907–1996) is best known for bringing George Balanchine to America in 1933 to found the School of American Ballet and, eventually, the New York City Ballet. (Previously he had launched The American Ballet, Ballet Caravan, and Ballet Society.) Kirstein was born in Rochester, New York, and was educated at Harvard, where he founded the influential literary magazine Hound and Horn *and helped start the Harvard Society for Contemporary Art, which led to the founding of New York's Museum of Modern Art. He was a brilliant and spirited writer (and a fierce propa-*

gandist) on many subjects: his many books include Blast at Ballet: A Corrective
for the American Audience; Movement & Metaphor: Four Centuries of
Ballet; The New York City Ballet; Rhymes of a Pfc.; Nijinsky Dancing; *and
a memoir,* Mosaic. *As the scion of a wealthy family (his father was the chairman of
Filene's department store in Boston), he supported not only the ballet but many institutions and individuals in the dance and art worlds. He was the founder and publisher of the journal* Dance Index, *was responsible for the creation of what became
the Dance Division at the New York Public Library for the Performing Arts, and
helped launch the American Shakespeare Festival in Stratford, Connecticut. He was
deeply involved in the development of Lincoln Center in New York. His wide interests
ranged from photography to Japanese culture, but his deepest connection remained
his passion for the school and company he and Balanchine had founded.*

Very apprehensively, then, I squired Romola [Nijinsky] to the opening of
Edward James's *Ballets 1933* season at the Savoy. I was worried as to how she
might judge it, and whether or not, in a smaller theater than in Paris, with so
many new English dancers, the premiere might be disappointing. It was not
too bad. Toumanova danced like an angel and Tchelitchew's *Errante* with
Tilly Losch had genuine success. Afterward, Romola said that Tamarashka
was too big, too slow, not sufficiently musical, and should still be in school.
In fact, as far as she was concerned, the whole evening had the aspect of a
school graduation. To be sure, a few of Balanchine's *adagio* ideas in his supported duets were amusing, but the whole affair was a *salade russe*. During an
entr'acte she left a note for Serge Lifar with the Hotel Savoy's concierge and
then showed me the column behind which, twenty years before, she had
hidden, watching Vaslav go down to dinner with Diaghilev. After the show,
she took me backstage and I was introduced to Balanchine. He looked tired
and haggard but Romola was sympathetic, complimenting him on making
the scenery itself dance and his stage come alive, since he had few real
dancers to work with. She also allowed that old Sergei Pavlovich would be
pirouetting in his grave to see what had become of his Ballets Russes. I felt
let down, and left Romola to come back to her room alone. Whatever, however, I felt about my singular, personal future meant nothing to her, yet I was
still attached as if I was her keeper.

Shortly after, at a post-theater party at Kirk and Constance Askew's, the
new English dancer Frederick Ashton spoke of his project for a ballet number in a new Cochran revue: it would concern the love of an orchid for a
cactus. When I had drifted away from Ashton's enraptured group, the writer
Elizabeth Bowen questioned me in some detail about Romola and her preoccupation with spiritualism. I was astonished to learn that Bowen, too,

had known the trance-medium "Ma" Garrett, who had done some sort of research with Conan Doyle, and was not, she thought, entirely fraudulent.

Balanchine arrived with Diana Gould, one of his recently hired, native English dancers. After allowing things to settle down into individual personal groups, I managed to face him alone and then be seated, with drink, opposite. He began talking, saying he found it easier to make good dancers out of the English rather than the French, despite a lack of training and tradition. In Paris, too long a time was taken out for lunch; too much *vin rouge* and pastry; there had not been a great French dancer, girl or boy, for generations. The promising ones had to find careers in Russia. Nor had the Germans, Austrians, or even the Italians provided many notable performers. As for himself, he was scheduled to produce Beethoven's *Créatures de Prométhée* for the Grand Opéra. It was an orchestral score associated with a cult reputation but he felt it was not appropriate for dancing. Oh, he said, let Lifar have it to make an initial impression which the press might support. The music had never worked in a theater. At first Lifar had been a nice boy, with little training but a fine face and physique. But now as self-proclaimed heir of Russian male dancing he was spoiled and quite impossible to handle. He indicated down to the slightest degree how the choreography should frame him: had Diaghilev been around, this could never have happened.

I spoke of the Balanchine repertory I would so much like to see again, none of which was in current performance: *Barabau, Le Fils Prodigue, Le Bal, The Gods Go A-begging, Apollon Musagète.* But he said that one should be very slow to revive past work, and only after a decent interval had indicated a true value. *Le Bal,* for example, and *The Gods* too, were really only *pièces d' occasion,* run up quickly for the necessities of a weak season. Ballets existed as a breath, a mere memory, and there were sure to be opinions that revivals were never as good as debuts. Old ballets could seem laughingly *démodé* as for instance, *Schéhérazade,* now shabbily presented by the Monte Carlo company. Balanchine said he believed that the criteria of style changed from season to season, like the shifting waistlines of women's dresses. The vernacular of one decade faded for the next, and since fashion is a prime patron of the ballet, the up-to-date had its real significance. He kept using the adjective *"authentique"* or *"pas authentique,"* as if it had an ultimate criterion, qualifying what was possible to perform. I spoke such poor French that I probably grasped no more than half of what he intended, and imagined he noticed my failure to connect with an adequate response. But he went on expostulating, as if chiefly to himself.

This remained, even through later years, as my chief impression of him: never wholly discouraged, often depressed, absent as a tangible personality when not in actual labor onstage or in rehearsal. The classic dance was a concrete entity, almost a three-dimensional structure as he construed it. It must be reconstructed for service in our twentieth century, speeded up, its tempo accelerated, just as automobiles, once thought miraculous at sixty miles an hour, a mile a minute, now in the age of Sir Malcolm Campbell's "Bluebirds" were capable of almost five times that. Balanchine believed that ballet, as now taught, was at the mercy of petrified habit, chiefly instructed by retired dancers, seldom those of the first rank. In spite of this there had been considerable mechanical (and perhaps anatomical) progress in individuals. Today, Taglioni would seem inefficient compared to any well-trained technician like Danilova, Doubrovska, or his "baby-ballerinas." Most nineteenth-century dancers moved only on *demi-pointe*, without the snap and brilliance propelled by syncopation since Stravinsky and jazz. I had listened to this, as if to an oracle, and on reflection felt he must harbor some lurking curiosity about what I might ultimately propose, since my attention was genuinely rapt.

Back, alone in my room at Batt's Hotel, I tried to make sense of what Balanchine had meant for me to use—if such was the fact. I understood that Fokine, my previous basis for judgment, was no longer valid as a choreographer for the future. His taste was rooted in the aesthetics of Imperial Russia before World War I. Balanchine, despite his native origin, was a new sort of animal. I tried to define his particular role, which seemed at once that of repudiator and re-animator of the academic vocabulary. Stravinsky's innovation was an obvious companion and comparison, even if I was quite ignorant of any specific innovation. There was so much to digest, and although Balanchine had delivered an overwhelming bounty of suggestive indications— including hints that he might like to come to America, maybe with a group of twenty girls and five men, in a repertory of his own developed "modern-classicism"—he had made no sign that he cared to see me again. . . .

I began, quietly, to try to formulate for myself strategies as to how to get Balanchine to America, and what to do with him once he'd been landed. It could involve some kind of "educational" formula or "experimental" design, the establishment of a small model company which might be hired as a glamorous lecture-attraction, with myself as instructor. This could be built on, and I felt that sufficient interest would be shown for its novelty, particularly if it were presented as a serious, instructive event. Then there was the commercial theater; Fokine had mounted his own small numbers for Broadway revues, and Balanchine had worked well with Cochran in London. But I had no arrangement whatever with Balanchine, and so far had not been permitted to encounter Vladimir Dimitriev, his business manager, without whom, I had been universally told, no step could be taken. . . .

Then, abruptly, as an auspicious signal, Balanchine invited himself to lunch with me, alone. He spoke of the nightmare of the *Ballets 1933* season paid for by Edward James, and of its operation in Paris and now at the Savoy. The difficulties came not from too little, but too much money, mostly misspent. James, he said, had no notion of order or control and would barely let

Dimitriev act as a proper business manager. Meanwhile, James had slapped Lifar in the face, and was separating from Tilly Losch; clearly his real pleasure was not theater, but the drama of litigation. Things had come to such a pass for Balanchine that the vague promise of some odd American solution almost offered itself as salvation. The chaotic situation at the Savoy Theater allowed him to envision the projection of radical possibilities. Maybe, just maybe, there was the real chance for a New York adventure. Haunted by the lack of reality prompted by my closeness to Romola, I tried to explain to Balanchine the poverty of my own realistic position. But he seemed to prefer to take my disclaimers as modesty or discretion, which could even inspire a furtive, hopeful confidence. I realized our planning was artificial and unlikely, but hardly less promising than all the other elements which swarmed around our mutual needs.

The more we talked, the more specific were Balanchine's posited requirements. He would need his own team to found a school and a company. Absolutely necessary were Toumanova and her mother; hardly less so was Dimitriev. Then Pierre Vladimirov, the *danseur noble* who had followed Nijinsky at the Maryinsky Theatre, and Felia Doubrovska, his wife, still an important performer. The two could also teach and serve as the basis for a distinguished faculty. Then, there was Romola and the excitement her book would surely inspire. She would be an admirable hostess and could lecture with photographic documentation. Certainly, all this was possible, or impossible, as had been picturesquely proven by what theatrical history had seen fit to demonstrate over the last quarter-century. Balanchine swore that America had always been his dream since he had heard a jazz band as a schoolboy in Petersburg. His brief stint in Denmark had convinced him there was little chance for progressive work in Europe, what with the passive domination of the Paris Grand Opéra he'd helped, accidentally, to cede to Serge Lifar. He was now almost willing to gamble on a new continent. Romola would promise her dubious cooperation, with Vaslav's system of choreographic notation and what she could recall of his own ballets.

I was increasingly exhilarated by what he said, willing to suspend any negative judgment and to smother fright. Then Balanchine abruptly excused himself, intent on trying to find enough support to continue the season at the Savoy without the aid of Edward James, and perhaps with the appearance of Lifar as a surprising novelty. But before he went, he said he felt the need to explain to me why he'd been forced to quit the Monte Carlo company, and to found one of his own. It was not vanity, and he had lost much in the change, but he could not endure the oppressive tyranny of de Basil's sergeant-major, Grigoriev. Now de Basil was suing him for the breach of a contract which Balanchine said he'd never signed. Moreover, "Colonel" de Basil had called Balanchine a thief on account of Toumanova's defection. As for theft, Balanchine stated that de Basil, whose real name was Voskresensky, had been an ordinary policeman in Tiflis, and had no claim whatsoever to legitimacy as Diaghilev's successor. De Basil operated his troupe as if it were a police state.

While he spoke, I began to have a large and growing sympathy for Balanchine himself, not as an historic figure but as an individual, who, like others, depended on factors beyond his own extraordinary capacities, and whom perhaps I might have a real role in supporting. Perhaps it was this personal consideration, up until now quite lacking, that seemed to indicate my ultimate direction. An accumulation of self-confidence, almost amounting to a new peak of energy, enabled me to concentrate on a sixteen-page letter to Chick Austin, in Hartford, as a possible sponsor for a ballet school, a ballet company, and nothing less than an American renaissance of the arts through the collaboration of theater, music, and lyric poetry. At least, the museum held space for a studio and an auditorium for performances. Although the letter was fairly detailed and realistic in many respects, I did not venture into any guesses toward questions of money or maintenance. I knew little enough of the economic structure of Hartford, Connecticut, and its dependence on the great insurance corporations. Its Wadsworth Athenaeum was the oldest of American museums, Austin was the youngest of a new and volatile generation of museum directors, and I chose an optimistic style from which to project ambition, fate, ignorance, and something approaching passionate determination.

After I had finished, still at a peak of nervous tension, I went for a walk in Hyde Park to try to reach simplicity of mind again. There was a straggling parade of British Fascists, marching grimly along in columns of three abreast, since they had not enough men for military fours. I tried to soothe myself by isolating what one might recognize as the Fascist facial type, but failed. There were, among them, many good-looking working-class men and boys; the sight or threat of them did nothing to clear my head. Later, Romola made me take her to a séance conducted by the witch Garrett, with a few Hungarian hangers-on. A couple of metal picture frames bounced off a mantelpiece in the blacked-out room, but it all meant zero to me and led only to another sleepless night.

On the following afternoon, I spent from three o'clock in the afternoon until seven, just before curtain time at the Savoy, in my room at Batt's Hotel with Balanchine and Romola. Spread out on the cleanly swept, split-straw floor matting was a large map of the United States; I attempted to locate for them the distances from Hartford to New York City and beyond. There were towns with traditional interest in the arts, sites of museums and symphony orchestras, homes of possible patrons who might, somehow, at some future engagement, be sources of support. Balanchine spoke of his time in Copenhagen, and of how impossible as ballet music was Richard Strauss's

Josephlegende, in which he'd been forced to make deep cuts, much against his principles. He spoke of other disappointments, fatalistically, which made me sad. While everything lay in a spectacular future, the tactile presence of the big map on the clear, fresh floor exuded an aura of comforting promise. One could not deny the affluence of our East Coast or its commitment to American culture. Why could it not be attacked on frontiers which already had been successfully conquered in the past against heavy odds? . . .

I had a shower, re-read the draft of my letter to Chick Austin, and went downstairs to the lounge-bar. In a corner, dressed beautifully in long white evening dresses, three debutantes up from the country had white ostrich plumes in their headbands, as if costumed for a ballet. They were perhaps coming from the photographer's, having been presented at court, but they seemed to have strayed from Balanchine's ballroom in *Cotillon.* Three muses, three harpies, or three fates? This abrupt entrance of a wholly poetical vision, their actual presence at so unlikely yet traditional an occasion, served as a cheering signal. The marvelous thing about existence was that it seemed to prove the validity of an historical process despite the opposition of the ordinary. Ballet as fact once again interposed itself, not as an adornment or an accident, but as a constant, valid, and worthy element, allaying, at least for the moment, my more feverish animadversions.

I felt able to present myself backstage at the Savoy after the evening's performance. Balanchine showed me a telegram offering him a job teaching in New York, with a further year's option. He looked worn, tired, and he coughed a lot, but said he would let me know the next day what Vladimir Dimitriev thought of all this. Whether or not he had discussed me with this shady figure, I could not tell. Balanchine seemed almost as confused as myself as to any next step. The London engagement was ending, and he certainly needed a restorative period. He'd mentioned that French friends in the country, near a village I only remembered afterward as named Negrepelisse, had invited Dimitriev, Toumanova, and her mother for a fortnight's vacation. Backstage was filled with friends and hangers-on. I was finally introduced to Dimitriev, a solid figure resembling a stocky, gray tiger, with hard eyes and perfect formal politeness. I didn't think he'd even bothered to allow me a once-over inspection, and I took this as a sign to retire without further words. My sense of failure was almost final. Further contact with Balanchine seemed cut for keeps. . . .

[And then] there was a telegram from Chick Austin in Hartford in answer to my formidable letter. He had gained promises from Eddie Warburg, Jim Soby, Philip Johnson, and Paul Cooley for at least three thousand dollars, which he was depositing at my bank toward payment for Balanchine's steamship fare. This was more than half of what I had budgeted for transportation and a brief trial residence for Balanchine and his populous *équipe.*

I wired Balanchine at the Champs-Elysées Theater, the sole address I had for him in France. There was no response. A further cable from Hartford commanded: GO AHEAD IRONCLAD CONTRACT NECESSARY STARTING OCTOBER 1 5 SETTLE AS MUCH AS YOU CAN BRING PUBLICITY PHOTOGRAPHS MUSEUMS WILLING CAN'T WAIT. I decided that recklessness was required in my quest for Balanchine and I must rush to France and search for him. I began to sense that somehow I was now fatally aligned with a commanding historical process. The succession of similar indications as progressive steps forward seemed to project themselves into my immediate future, as if I was on a mobile stairway and was now unable to get off.

—from *Mosaic,* 1994

NATHAN MILSTEIN

My Friend George Balanchine

One of the most notable violinists of the twentieth century, Nathan Milstein (1903–1992) was born in Odessa, but by the early 1920s was playing throughout Europe. He and Vladimir Horowitz were friends with George Balanchine when they were all young men together in Monte Carlo, where Diaghilev's Ballets Russes had its residence. In 1929, Milstein came to America, and in 1942 obtained American citizenship. His autobiography, From Russia to the West: The Musical Memoirs and Reminiscences of Nathan Milstein, *was published in 1990.*

I met him in 1926, soon after Vladimir Horowitz and I came to Western Europe from Russia. It was in Monte Carlo. We quickly became friends: we had so much in common.

Balanchine had also recently emigrated from Russia. Except that when he left Petrograd in 1924 (just before it was renamed Leningrad) he knew he would not return, while Vladimir Horowitz and I still assumed that we were in Europe temporarily "for the purpose of artistic refinement and cultural propaganda" (as it said in our official mandate from the Revolutionary Military Council of the Soviet Republic).

Monte Carlo was a marvelous place for such refinement—for me, for Horowitz, and for Balanchine. He was with Diaghilev's ballet company then. In Monte Carlo, under the auspices of the countess of Monaco, Diaghilev found himself a refuge. His troupe occupied a small but beautiful local opera theater. On that stage he presented ballets featuring his current favorites: first Léonide Massine, then Serge Lifar.

Initially Diaghilev needed Balanchine to do fast choreography for the opera season—in Delibes's *Lakmé,* Offenbach's *Tales of Hoffmann,* and *Boris Godunov.* Georges (as we called him then, using the soft French pronunciation) also did some dancing.

I was engaged for several concerts in Monte Carlo, as was Horowitz. We went there for two or three weeks and stayed at the Palace Hotel. It was an inexpensive place but we thought it incredibly luxurious, especially after Russia. The comforts and food were incomparable! We were amazed and amused by everything—by the toy kingdom of Monaco, by the prince's guard (his miniature army parading around importantly in colorful uniforms), by the famous roulette wheels.

The musical director of the theater was then someone named Puttman. He was a severe gentleman and everyone feared him. No one had ever heard of unions in opera companies in those days, and Puttman bossed everyone around. He instructed Horowitz and me: "Don't play in the casino! If you want to watch others play, ask me, I'll give you passes. But no gambling!" We agreed readily, since we had no money to spare anyway. I walked around Monte Carlo. It was in January, and I remember wearing a coat. Monte Carlo isn't Nice.

It was easy to meet people at the Palace. All you had to do was reminisce out loud in Russian about the famous pirozhki of Petersburg: "Oh, how wonderful those pirozhki at Filippov's were!"

"I loved them too!" a voice would respond, and there you'd have a new friend.

Pretty ballerinas flitted through the hotel lobby. You could bump into Diaghilev himself, somewhat heavy but still with elegant bearing, or the businesslike Stravinsky (the composer lived not far away, in Nice). Huffy Lifar appeared frequently, and everyone bowed before Lubov Tchernicheva, Diaghilev's star. What a place it was, filled with life and glamour. And not because it was a deluxe establishment like the De Paris, but because of its clientele—young, talented, beautiful, brash. (I visited Monte Carlo recently and passed the Palace. It was empty, the windows boarded up.)

In our free time (and we had more than enough of it in Monte Carlo), Balanchine and I would sit in a café, observing the passersby and chatting about whatever came to mind, especially music. Balanchine made many subtle and original remarks. It turned out that we had much in common musically as well—we both had attended the same conservatory in Petersburg! People forget it now, but Balanchine studied piano at the conservatory. I can attest that he played not badly at all.

Of course, Georges was no virtuoso—he couldn't have given recitals—and I doubt that he could even have been a professional accompanist. When he sat down at the piano, he didn't play so much as "noodle," blurring over the hard parts. But, really, that didn't matter. Balanchine sight-read freely. And you could see immediately that he was a refined and responsive musician. I felt that quality instantly in his first ballets.

Yet Balanchine was far from a purist in music. For instance, he liked a popular *chansonnier* from Odessa, Leonid Utyosov, whom I also liked (it turned out we had both gone to his concerts in Russia). Balanchine retained that catholicity of musical taste. He not only wrote little songs himself, he freely used popular music in his staging—in particular, arrangements of songs by our mutual friend George Gershwin in the ballet *Who Cares?*

Animated and witty when the conversation was about music, Balanchine usually became much more reserved when the topic changed to women. Handsome and elegant, definitely a ladies' man, he gracefully avoided bragging about his conquests. When we met, his companion was Alexandra ("Choura") Danilova, soloist in Diaghilev's ballet company, a merry woman as cocky as a bantam rooster. No one ever knew whether Georges and Choura were married. The four of us used to get together: Balanchine, Danilova, Horowitz, and I. Horowitz tried courting Danilova, and she flirted with him charmingly.

Everyone around us fell in love, came together, broke up. There must have been something in the air of Monte Carlo!

Balanchine created in an ephemeral medium, he had no illusions about that. Yet his abstract ballets were nevertheless not abstract creations. He created them for particular dancers. Balanchine was inspired always by a given body, a given temperament, a given character. Theoretically those beautiful movements of his could have been learned by other dancers, but then in such cases George always made adjustments, often substantial ones, for specific performers.

Balanchine knew perfectly well that without him these adjustments would have been impossible. And that consequently, with time, his ballets would inevitably become more and more empty, and could eventually die. But this did not upset him in the least. He believed in a higher justice and, although a determined fatalist, he remained optimistic in any circumstances, even in misfortune, which abounded in his life.

This optimism was another thing that distinguished Balanchine from Stravinsky, who drenched everything around him with bitter sarcasm. I didn't like it, but for Stravinsky it was a natural way of confronting the world, and I don't reproach him for it at all.

Yes, it is likely that Balanchine's ballets will die someday, and that will be a great loss. But George left an inheritance that consists of more than his works. He left his moral example, a considerable legacy: the strength and wholeness of his character; his directness, adherence to principle, and lack of greed; his modesty and confidence in his abilities; his devotion to his art; his independence of fashion, fame, and trappings of success. All that is Balanchine. In difference to ignorant criticism, disdain for greedy managers—that's also Balanchine.

And in Balanchine's art, beyond the beauty of his ballets, there are lessons for us all. This is art with deep national roots, though not confined to them but open to the whole world. Balanchine was a brilliant master, a connoisseur of the classical tradition, yet he never stopped expanding the frontiers, constantly discovering something new. He was a revolutionary who created instead of destroying. Or, if you like, he was a conservative, capable of changing swiftly.

As I have said, culture today resembles a marketplace, like a mall where everything is bought and sold. Artists lose their sense of shame trying to force their wares, often second-rate and rotten, on the buyer. Balanchine was never a cheap vendor, even though he hardly pretended to be a saint. He didn't live up in the clouds. George liked beautiful and talented women, he savored good food, and he knew about wines (more than I did, even though my knowledge in that area is so modest that it isn't hard to surpass it).

And Balanchine did not attribute prophetic significance to his art. He hated snobbery. I recall how, when he spoke of the ballet, he readily used culinary metaphors. "I'm a chef," Balanchine often said, "making dishes for the audience to suit its taste. I only try to keep the menu varied." But it was real, healthful food—for the mind and for the heart.

When I think of Balanchine, I see him again. There he is—a real Russian personality. His face is sharply drawn; his body is lean, trained, flexible. He walks erect, confidently; quickly but without rushing. That impossible Texan string tie dangles from his neck (he has "regular" ties somewhere, but they're so much trouble). He exudes elegance, energy, joy.

That's how I remember him.

—from *From Russia to the West*, with Solomon Volkov,
translated by Antonina W. Bouis, 1990

VERA ZORINA

A Masculine Man

Born Eva Brigitta Hartwig (and called Brigitta all her life), Vera Zorina (1917–2003)—half Norwegian, half German—worked in the Ballet Russe for Léonide Massine, with whom she had a complicated personal relationship. She starred in the London production of the Rodgers-Hart-Balanchine musical On Your Toes *and came to the attention of Samuel Goldwyn, who brought her to Hollywood to star in* The Goldwyn Follies *(1938). Balanchine choreographed her* Goldwyn Follies *numbers—and married her. (They stayed uncomfortably married from 1938 to 1946.) Her film career fizzled out (her considerable beauty didn't translate to the screen), and she went on to star in other Broadway musicals, including* I Married an Angel—*also Rodgers, Hart, and Balanchine—and Irving Berlin's* Louisiana Purchase. *Beginning in 1948 she made frequent appearances as the narrator for the Honegger-Claudel oratorio* Jeanne d'Arc au Bûcher *and the Stravinsky-Gide* Persephone, *and in 1986 she published her autobiography,* Zorina.

George was a very masculine man in every sense of the word. He was a perfect example of the definition of *virile* in the *Oxford English Dictionary*: having procreative power of mind and character (in addition to the usual connotation). I refer to this in contrast to the present macho image, which is nothing more than swagger signifying nothing. Whatever he touched or was engaged in became creative, as if his perceptions were seen through a different prism. I imagine that it is so with all great artists. It is fashionable at present to insist that he is in the same orbit as Mozart, Picasso, and Stravinsky. Although it is meant as the highest accolade, I don't think he would necessarily consider it a compliment. Great artists know their worth long before the world gives its imprimatur. But Balanchine also knew that he was part of the artistic progression in the biblical sense of having been "begotten" by those who preceded him. If the public or critics did not understand him, that was their problem; he knew that they would one day. People said he was aloof or indifferent. He was not; he simply hid his disappointment better than anyone I know. Also, when you are miles ahead you cannot waste time waiting for people to catch up with you.

George was unique in his thinking, being, and manner of expressing himself. Fame meant nothing to him, money meant nothing to him either—at least not enough for a compromise. I remember how he confused a salesman who attempted to sell him a life insurance policy, pointing out, "When you are old, Mr. Balanchine, you will get all this income and—" George interrupted him and said, "Why don't you give me the money *now* to make beautiful ballets? When I'm old, all I will want is a cup of coffee." His pleasure lay in the realization of his labors. If his dancers executed his ballets the way he wanted them, he was happy.

He loved women and everything about them. He spoke of "wonderful blond hair," "beautiful blue eyes," "marvelous waist and hips," as lovingly as he talked about "wonderful feet," "beautiful legs," "high jumps," "moving very fast." Expressions like these sprinkled his conversation and were emphasized by gestures with his hands and a beautiful look of happiness on his face, tinged with a sly touch of wickedness. He loved perfume, jewelry, cars, dogs (especially German shepherds), and, of course, good food, vodka, and wine. In short, he was a sensuous man. He wanted his dancers to look beautiful— sometimes with their hair streaming loose, other times with sleek little heads topped by diamonds or delicate flowers at the nape of their necks. Above all, he wanted to show their bodies, unhampered by tricky costumes.

When we were married, he always supervised my costume fittings and insisted on the smallest details, and he did the same with my private clothes. He took me to the great Russian designer Valentina, who dressed me for years both on and off the stage. Though he loved that feminine world, he disliked feminine men. He admired "beautiful man" the way he would Michelangelo's David, but he wanted his male dancers to be cavaliers— courtly gentlemen gallantly escorting a lady or presenting a ballerina.

He admired physical beauty in an abstract form the way one might admire a painting by Seurat in terms of pointillism. He would discuss the particular tilt of the neck, those slender, fragile-looking stems actually having the strength of steel, as the "Maryinsky look"—after the famous school of ballet in St. Petersburg. This look, together with the upturned wrist like a fly-away bird, marked the dancer as an unmistakable Balanchine ballerina.

He would speak of the "suffering faces" of dancers, comparing them to saints, which reminded me of the angels in Rainer Maria Rilke's poem:

> *Sie haben alle müde Münde*
> *und helle Seelen ohne Saum*
> *und eine Sehnsucht wie nach Sünde*
> *geht ihnen manchmal durch den Traum.*

Fast gleichen sie einander alle;
in Gottes Gärten schweigen sie,
wie viele, viele Intervalle
in seiner Macht und Melodie.

Nur wenn sie ihre Flügel breiten,
sind sie die Wecker eines Winds:
Als ginge Gott mit seinen weiten
Bildhauerhänden durch die Seiten
im dunklen Buch des Anbeginns.

All of them have weary mouths
and bright souls without seam
and a yearning (as toward sin)
goes sometimes through their dream.

Almost they are all alike;
in God's gardens they keep silent
like many, many intervals
in his might and melody.

Only when they spread their wings
are they the wakers of a wind:
As though God went with his wide
sculptor hands through the pages
in the dark book of first beginnings.*

One would have to understand that in his mind "suffering faces" were not to be taken literally, or connected with a dancer's pain and bleeding toes, but meant spiritual suffering. To George dancers were saints because they worked harder and longer, were obedient, and never talked back, were always paid the least, and then went onstage and danced like angels.

—from *Zorina*, 1986

---

*Translation by M. D. Herter Norton.

BALANCHINE BALLETS

THREE SIDES OF *AGON*
Edwin Denby

Balanchine's groundbreaking modern ballet Agon, *with its commissioned score from Igor Stravinsky, had its premiere in 1957, featuring Diana Adams and Arthur Mitchell in its extraordinary central duet. It seemed at the time as radical an extension of classical technique as was possible, and like* Apollo *it remains a landmark in the history of ballet.*

ONE

*A*gon, a ballet composed by Igor Stravinsky in his personal twelve-tone style, choreographed by George Balanchine, and danced by the New York City Ballet, was given an enormous ovation last winter by the opening-night audience. The balcony stood up shouting and whistling when the choreographer took his bow. Downstairs, people came out into the lobby, their eyes bright as if the piece had been champagne. Marcel Duchamp, the painter, said he felt the way he had after the opening of *Le Sacre*. At later performances, *Agon* continued to be vehemently applauded. Some people found the ballet set their teeth on edge. The dancers show nothing but coolness and brilliantly high spirits.

Agon is a suite of dances. The score lasts twenty minutes, and never becomes louder than chamber music. Onstage the dancers are twelve at most, generally fewer. The ballet has the form of a small entertainment, and its subject—first, an assembling of contestants, then the contest itself, then a dispersal—corresponds to the three parts into which the score is divided.

The subject is shown in terms of a series of dances, not in terms of a mimed drama. It is shown by an amusing identity in the action, which is classic dancing shifted into a "character" style by a shift of accentuation. The shift appears, for example, in the timing of transitions between steps or within steps, the sweep of arm position, in the walk, in the funniness of feats of prowess. The general effect is an amusing deformation of classic shapes due to an unclassic drive or attack; and the drive itself looks like a basic way of moving one recognizes. The "basic gesture" of *Agon* has a frank, fast thrust like the action of Olympic athletes, and it also has a loose-fingered goofy reach like the grace of our local teenagers.

The first part of the ballet shows the young champions warming up. The long middle part—a series of virtuoso numbers—shows them rivalizing in feats of wit and courage. There is nothing about winning or losing. The little athletic meet is festive—you watch young people competing for fun at the brief height of their power and form. And the flavor of time and place is tenderly here and now.

Two

Agon shows that. Nobody notices because it shows so much else. While the ballet happens, the continuity one is delighted by is the free-association kind. The audience sees the sequence of action as screwball or abstract, and so do I.

The curtain rises on a stage bare and silent. Upstage four boys are seen with their backs to the public and motionless. They wear the company's dance uniform. Lightly they stand in an intent stillness. They whirl, four at once, to face you. The soundless whirl is a downbeat that starts the action.

On the upbeat, a fanfare begins, like cars honking a block away; the sound drops lower, changed into a pulse. Against it, and against a squiggle like a bit of wallpaper, you hear—as if by free association—a snatch of "Chinatown, My Chinatown" misremembered on an electric mandolin. The music sounds confident. Meanwhile the boys' steps have been exploding like pistol shots. The steps seem to come in tough, brief bursts. Dancing in canon, in unison, in and out of symmetry, the boys might be trying out their speed of waist, their strength of ankle; no lack of aggressiveness. But already two—no, eight—girls have replaced them. Rapidly they test toe power, stops on oblique lines, jetlike extensions. They hang in the air like a swarm of girl-size bees, while the music darts and eddies beneath them. It has become complex and abstract. But already the boys have re-entered, and the first crowding thrust of marching boys and leaping girls has a secret of scale that is frightening. The energy of it is like that of fifty dancers.

By now you have caught the pressure of the action. The phrases are compact and contrasted; they are lucid and short. Each phrase, as if with a burst, finds its new shape in a few steps, stops, and at once a different phrase explodes unexpectedly at a tangent. They fit like the stones of a mosaic, the many-colored stones of a mosaic seen close-by. Each is distinct, you see the cut between; and you see that the cut between them does not interrupt the dance impetus. The novel shapes before you change as buoyantly as the images of a dream. They tease. But like that of a brilliant dream, the power of scale is in earnest. No appeal from it.

While you have been dreaming, the same dance of the twelve dancers has been going on and on, very fast and very boring, like travel in outer space. Suddenly the music makes a two-beat cadence and stops. The dispersed dancers have unexpectedly turned toward you, stopped as in a posed photograph of athletes; they face you in silence, vanish, and instantly three of them stand in position to start a "number" like dancers in a ballet divertissement.

The music starts with a small circusy fanfare, as if it were tossing them a purple and red bouquet. They present themselves to the public as a dance team (Barbara Milberg, Barbara Walczak, Todd Bolender). Then the boy, left alone, begins to walk a Sarabande, elaborately coiled and circumspect. It recalls court dance as much as a cubist still life recalls a pipe or guitar. The boy's timing looks like that of a New York Latin in a leather jacket. And the cool lift of his wrong-way-round steps and rhythms gives the nonsense so apt a turn people begin to giggle. A moment later one is watching a girls' duet in the air, like flying twins *(haute danse)*. A trio begins. In triple canon the dancers do idiotic slenderizing exercises, theoretically derived from court gesture, while the music foghorns in the fashion of musique concrète. Zanily pedantic, the dance has the bounce and exuberant solemnity of a clown act. The audience laughs, applauds, and a different threesome appears (Melissa Hayden, Roy Tobias, Jonathan Watts).

For the new team the orchestra begins as it did for the previous one— first, the pushy, go-ahead fanfare, then the other phrase of harmonies that keep sliding without advancing, like seaweed underwater. (The two motifs keep returning in the score.)

The new team begins a little differently and develops an obvious difference. The boys present the girl in feats of balance, on the ground and in the air, dangerous feats of lucid nonsense. Their courage is perfect. Miss Hayden's deadpan humor and her distinctness are perfect too. At one point a quite unexpected flounce of little-girl primness as in silence she walks away from the boys endears her to the house. But her solo is a marvel of dancing at its most transparent. She seems merely to walk forward, to step back and skip, with now and then one arm held high, Spanish style, a gesture that draws attention to the sound of a castanet in the score. As she dances, she keeps calmly "on top of" two conflicting rhythms (or beats) that coincide once or twice and join on the last note. She stops and the house breaks into a roar of applause. In her calm, the audience has caught the acute edge of risk, the graceful freshness, the brilliance of buoyancy.

The New York audience may have been prepared for *Agon*'s special brilliance of rhythm by that of *Opus 34* and *Ivesiana,* two ballets never shown on tour. All three have shown an acuteness of rhythmic risk never seen and never imagined outside the city limits. The dangerousness of *Agon* is as tense as the danger of a tightrope act on the high wire. That is why the dancers look as possessed as acrobats. Not a split second leeway. The thrill is, they move with an innocent dignity.

At this point of *Agon* about thirteen minutes of dancing have passed. A third specialty team is standing onstage ready to begin (Diana Adams, Arthur Mitchell). The orchestra begins a third time with the two phrases one recognizes, and once again the dancers find in the same music a quite different rhythm and expression. As the introduction ends, the girl drops her head with an irrational gesture more caressing than anything one has seen so far.

They begin an acrobatic adagio. The sweetness is athletic. The absurdity of what they do startles by a grandeur of scale and of sensuousness. Turning pas de deux conventions upside down, the boy with a bold grace supports the girl and pivots her on pointe, lying on his back on the floor. At one moment classic movements turned inside out become intimate gestures. At another a pose forced way beyond its classic ending reveals a novel harmony. At still another, the mutual first tremor of an uncertain supported balance is so isolated musically it becomes a dance movement. So does the dangerous scoop out of balance and back into balance of the girl supported on pointe. The dance flows through stops, through scooping changes of pace, through differences of pace between the partners while they hold each other by the hand. They dance magnificently. From the start, both have shown a crescendo and decrescendo within the thrust of a move, an illusion of "breath"— though at the scary speed they move such a lovely modulation is inconceivable. The fact that Miss Adams is white and Mr. Mitchell Negro is neither stressed nor hidden; it adds to the interest.

The music for the pas de deux is in an expressive Viennese twelve-tone manner, much of it for strings. Earlier in the ballet, the sparse orchestration has made one aware of a faint echo, as if silence were pressing in at the edge of music and dancing. Now the silence interpenetrates the sound itself, as in a Beethoven quartet. During the climactic pas de deux of other ballets, you have watched the dancer stop still in the air, while the music surges ahead underneath; now, the other way around, you hear the music gasp and fail, while the two dancers move ahead confidently across the open void. After so many complex images, when the boy makes a simple joke, the effect is happy. Delighted by the dancers, the audience realizes it "understands" everything, and it is more and more eager to give them an ovation.

There isn't time. The two dancers have become one of four couples who make fast, close variations on a figure from the pas de deux. The action has reverted to the anonymous energy you saw in the first part. Now all twelve dancers are onstage and everything is very condensed and goes very fast. Now only the four boys are left, you begin to recognize a return to the start of the ballet, you begin to be anxious, and on the same wrestler's gesture of "on guard" that closed their initial dance—a gesture now differently directed—the music stops, the boys freeze, and the silence of the beginning returns. Nothing moves.

During the stillness, the accumulated momentum of the piece leaps forward in one's imagination, suddenly enormous. The drive of it now seems not to have let up for a moment since the curtain rose. To the realization of its power, as the curtain drops, people respond with vehement applause in a large emotion that includes the brilliant dancers and the goofiness of the fun.

The dancers have been "cool" in the jazz sense—no buildup, inventions that did not try to get anywhere, right after a climax an inconsequence like the archness of high comedy. But the dramatic power has not been that of jokes; it has been that of unforeseeable momentum. The action has had no end in view—it did not look for security, nor did it make any pitiful appeal for that. At the end, the imaginary contestants froze, toughly confident. The company seems to have figured jointly as the offbeat hero, and the risk as the menacing antagonist. The subject of *Agon,* as the poet Frank O'Hara said, is pride. The graceful image it offers is a buoyancy that mystifies and attracts.

THREE

A program note says that "the only subject" of the ballet is an interpretation of some French seventeenth-century society dances. The note tells you to disregard the classic Greek title *(Agon)* in favor of the French subtitles. It is a pity to. The title and the subtitles are words that refer to civilized rituals, the former to athletics, the latter to dancing. Athletic dancing is what *Agon* does. On the other hand, you won't catch anyone onstage looking either French or Greek. Or hear musically any reason they should. French baroque manners and sentiments are not being interpreted; elements or energies of forms are.

The sleight-of-hand kind of wit in the dancing is a part of that "interpretation." You see a dancer, rushing at top speed, stop sharp in a pose. The pose continues the sense of her rush. But the equilibrium of it is a trap, a dead end. To move ahead, she will have to retract and scrounge out. She doesn't, she holds the pose. And out of it, effortlessly, with a grace like Houdini's, she darts away. The trap has opened in an unforeseen direction, as music might by a surprising modulation. At times in *Agon* you see the dancer buoyantly spring such traps at almost every step. Or take the canonic imitations. At times a dancer begins a complex phrase bristling with accents and a second dancer leaping up and twisting back an eighth note later repeats it, then suddenly passes a quarter note ahead. The dissonance between them doesn't blur; if you follow it, you feel the contradictory lift of the double image put in doubt where the floor is. Or else you see a phrase of dance rhythm include a brief representational gesture, and the gesture's alien impetus and weight—the "false note" of it—make the momentum of the rhythm more vividly exact. These classic dissonances (and others you see) *Agon* fantastically extends. The wit isn't the device, it is the surprise of the quick lift you feel at that point. It relates to the atonal harmonies of the score—atonal harmonies that make the rhythmic momentum of the music more vividly exact.

At times you catch a kind of dissonant harmony in the image of a step. The explosive thrust of a big classic step has been deepened, speeded up, forced out farther, but the mollifying motions of the same step have been pared down. In a big step in which the aggressive leg action is normally cushioned by mildly rounded elbows, the cushioning has been pared down to mildly rounded palms. The conciliatory transitions have been dropped. So have the transitional small steps. Small steps do not lead up to and down from big ones. They act in opposition to big ones, and often stress their opposition by a contrariness.

The patterns appear and vanish with an unpredictable suddenness. Like the steps, their forms would be traditional except for the odd shift of stress and compactness of energy. The steps and the patterns recall those of baroque dancing much as the music recalls its baroque antecedents—that is, as absurdly as a current Harvard student recalls a baroque one. Of course, one recognizes the relation.

Agon shifts traditional actions to an off-balance balance on which they swiftly veer. But each move, large or small, is extended at top pitch. Nothing is retracted. The ardent exposure is that of a grace way out on a limb.

The first move the dancers make is a counter accent to the score. Phrase by phrase, the dancers make a counter rhythm to the rhythm of the music. Each rhythm is equally decisive and surprising, equally spontaneous. The unusualness of their resources is sumptuous, like a magnificent imaginative weight. One follows the sweep of both by a fantastic lift one feels. The Balanchinian buoyancy of impetus keeps one open to the vividly changeable Stravinskyan pressure of pulse and to its momentum. The emotion is that of scale. Against an enormous background one sees detached for an instant the hidden grace of the dancer's individual move, a chance event that passes with a small smile and a musical sound forever into nowhere.

—from *Evergreen Review,* 1959

Four Decades of *Agon*: The Pas de Deux
Leigh Witchel

This essay is taken from a much larger one that followed the performance history of Agon *from 1957 to 1997.*

When Bernard Taper was writing his biography of George Balanchine, the observation Balanchine made about the process was, "A racehorse doesn't keep a diary." Keeping to the modernist tradition that formed him, Balanchine disdained the idea of an unchangeable text, a ineluctable record. He fed on change, benevolent or perverse. It can be seen in his constant revisions and tinkering with ballets, even works like *Apollo* that unaltered were considered masterpieces. Barbara Milberg (Fisher), a member of the original cast of *Agon,* tells of a time when Balanchine was revising *Serenade* ("Mr. Tchaikovsky came to me in a dream last night and said it was all right") and adding a new section. Ann Hutchison, who had been engaged to notate *Serenade,* came up to him during the rehearsal and asked if he wished to know what came next. "No," he replied, referring to the dancer he was working with, "she moves differently. I'd rather change."

Another member of the original *Agon,* Barbara Walczak, relates another familiar line of Balanchine: "You know, dear, we can all be replaced, even me." What is the tension between these two statements? Balanchine insisted on a company without stars, but loved dancers with specific personalities. He knew that a ballet changed the moment it was recast but said no dancer was irreplaceable. If a dancer left a ballet, he would cast an entirely different type as a successor to the role or rechoreograph it. We see both in *Agon.*

We have now reached the fortieth anniversary of *Agon,* one of the greatest of Balanchine's achievements. This is a ballet with an unbroken performance tradition, which was almost always supervised by Balanchine during his life-time, yet it has undergone undeniable evolutions. What is the "text" of *Agon?* Balanchine began with the music and a type of movement and combined them with the physical possibilities of his dancers and the *Zeitgeist* of urban life in New York City during the 1950s to create a masterpiece. Altering any one of the elements alters the "text," and all of them have been altered, some irretrievably.

Talking about the "text" of a ballet is vaporous. There are the steps, but are we speaking of the steps as given or what they become when danced (and therefore interpreted)? Dancers may enrich or distort the "text"; in both cases their additions can become subsumed into the text as it is passed along. By consulting witnesses of the creation and continuing life of *Agon*, perhaps we can arrive at some answers. . . .

ALTHOUGH BALANCHINE explicitly said that the title *Agon* meant nothing and there was no contest, it becomes most apt when describing the pas de deux that forms the structural and emotional climax of the ballet. Although there is no literal contest, there is a dialectic of power exchange within the pas de deux. Does the woman place her leg to its extension, or is it placed there by the man? Arthur Mitchell said in 1974, "The one thing Bal-anchine kept saying was, "The girl is like a doll, and you're manipulating her." He said, "You must lead her." He didn't want her to do anything for her-self in the sense that she would take the initiative. I would take her and place her." Absolute passivity can be the most dictatorial stance of all.

Mitchell goes on to explain that Balanchine "started on the pas de deux first. He said, "This is the longest it's ever taken me to choreograph any-thing." We started on the pas de deux—Diana [Adams] and I—two weeks prior to anyone coming in. He said, "Because everything has to be *exactly* right." That's one of the few times—or the only time—I've ever seen him take things and throw them out. He experimented and he changed. Nor-mally he's just so prolific, and it's just there, it's so right, it just flows. . . . The whole pas de deux was built on Diana's body. The nervous intensity that Diana had made the whole pas de deux work because it's not so much the difficulty of the steps but the precariousness."

The pas de deux is the only section in the 1960 kinescope done entirely by the original dancers. It is easy to see why people attempted to tease hidden parables out of the different skin colors of Mitchell and Adams. Her demeanor is absolutely patrician. She is aware of his presence and manipulations, and at first it seems as if she remains politely indifferent to him: not an affectation, but so personal as to become apolitical—she simply cannot be disturbed. Yet there is also the intensity Mitchell mentions. She recalls Eurydice: one sees not that she isn't looking at him but that she *must not* look at him, as if the consequences might be awful.

By 1959 a new dancer, Allegra Kent, was also doing the role. Kent was a quirky dancer with a highly flexible body, the sort of dancer for whom Balanchine regularly made exceptions to his rules. In the 1973 film she is near the end of her career, but one can still see how much she extends the physicality of the pas de deux. Anatomy is destiny. Her greater pliancy makes the pas de deux naturally more sculptural. Her quirkiness can be seen in an incident at the beginning of the duet; when she gives her hand to Mitchell, she is seemingly unaware that it is too high and threatens to cover his face. As he takes her hand, Mitchell rather forcibly *yanks* it down, and she briefly registers surprise. Where Adams seems to avoid Mitchell, Kent seems unaware of him. Her focus is interior and diffuse. She seems only tenuously connected with reality.

Her heirs to this approach to the pas de deux were Suzanne Farrell and Darci Kistler. The young Farrell pushed the physicality of the duet still further, while adding a rather haunting childlike quality that appears in a truncated version of the pas de deux danced with Mitchell for a WNET telecast of 1965, *Dance: USA*. Her sheer physical power gives her innocence a frightening edge; she is not in control of her effects, and does not even seem to know that she can produce them. She is truly doll-like, or perhaps a Nabokovian nymphet. This quality is not part of the choreography; it is Farrell's "perfume" and her own physicality.

In the film *Peter Martins: A Dancer* we see Martins and Farrell performing the pas de deux sometime in the late 1970s. She is older and the Lolita quality is gone. Her performance is thoughtful, and her body has lost the plush childishness it had in the 1960s; she is thin and even slightly pinched-looking. It restores some of the "nervous intensity" seen in Adams's performances. Again, this is neither the choreography nor the "text"; but how often the thing we carry from a performance is not the text itself but the "perfume."

Kistler, of all recent dancers in the role, most recalls Farrell's eerie passivity. The difference is that while Farrell seems innocent of her place in the ballet, Kistler, like Kent, seems to be in a place totally different from her partner. As Nikolaj Hübbe drops her into splits, rather than angling her head away from him she arches straight back, focusing upward. She is not looking at him or away from him; he is not even a point of reference. He manipulates her into the most extreme positions, but he might as well be putting his hand through her, as if she were fog. She is unreachable. Her passivity is its own provocation.

Balanchine cast ballets for many reasons, often eminently practical: roles needed to be divided, dancers needed to be satisfied. Sometimes he cast a piece deliberately to erase the memory of the previous dancer. Was he reassessing the ballet through his casting? We see his ambivalence toward the dancers' additions to the "text." One imagines that through his casting, like an alchemist, Balanchine attempted at least minimally to contain and tame potentially volatile substances. He knew what the dancers added, but he needed to be in control of the process because it threatened to alter or obscure what was the "text."

The incredible plasticity of both Farrell and Kent also marked the gradual change of *Agon* from a ballet concerned with movement to a ballet concerned primarily with poses. The smallest changes to the choreography indicate it. For example, in the 1965 broadcast Farrell and Mitchell begin the actual pas from pointe tendu back facing out to the audience, rather than just standing and facing each other in à la seconde, as was done in 1960. It changes the emphasis from personal to presentational; the focus is the audience rather than each other. Farrell also touches her toe to her head in one of the back attitudes, which became part of the choreography. (This recalls Balanchine's alteration in the adagio of *Symphony in C* to have Farrell touch her head to her leg in the arabesque penchée. Why? Because she could.)

Adams' intentions in her performance are described by a letter she wrote to Francia Russell (quoted in Arlene Croce's "The Spelling of *Agon*" in the July 12, 1993, *The New Yorker*): "There are moments (when the two place hands on each other's wrists, for instance) which can be infused with deep sentimentality, can look motivated by "feeling." This drove Mr. B crazy. He really wanted it as cool and abstract as possible—*just* movement." Adams's coolness in the pas de deux was part of her character and her physicality, which were statuesque and patrician. That quality was not cast back into the ballet after she vacated the role, except perhaps when Darcey Bussell of Britain's Royal Ballet assumed the role for the 1993 Balanchine Celebration.

Another trace of Adams is in Russell's casting of Patricia Barker in the lead at Pacific Northwest Ballet. Russell cast the ballet as she remembered it—a tall woman with a cool, patrician demeanor in the pas de deux, and a soubrette in the second pas de trois.

While perhaps the woman with the most facility to do *Agon* to date, Bussell is also the most chilling. The contest has been won from the start. Even Kistler, who seems not to realize the partner is there, still physically relies on him. Bussell seems the opposite: she realizes her partner is there, and it is a nuisance. Physically, she seems to be doing the whole pas de deux by herself.

The 1982 performance for the Stravinsky Festival featured Heather Watts and Mel Tomlinson in the pas de deux. By this point, there was a distinct switch in emphasis throughout the entire ballet to a very sculptural style and a very placed, rather than off-balance, approach. Several members of the original cast mention the fascination of the black and white skin together. All mention it first as a sculptural fascination, of the designs made (for the first time) by Balanchine. Within this sculptural quality in the pas de deux, could an argument be made that a more "sculptural" approach to *Agon* has its roots in the pas de deux?

Even in 1960 much of what was done moved from pose to pose, from one fascinating shape that pushed the definable limits of a classical ballet to another. There is precedent for this in early ballets like *Apollo* and *Prodigal Son*, with poses so memorable and unlike others in ballet that they are known only by nicknames, like "The Swimming Lesson." Even so, the "steps between the steps" have a rhythmic and physical acuity to them. The way the woman moves her pointes through the man's legs when she is on his back at the beginning of the pas de deux, the way the man moves on his back when he supports her in penché; the steps may have an open timing, but they are not performed in isolation.

Balanchine was also responding to Stravinsky's cues in the score. From the beginning of the work's creation the dancers did not count the pas de deux, unlike any other part of the ballet, because there is nothing to count. The rhythmic pulse almost entirely drops out of the score in the pas de deux, not to return until almost its end before the coda. With its turgid harmonies, its lack of a driving pulse, the music suggests a slow procession of forms, almost like looking at underwater life through a glass. When the music returns to an allegro tempo, Balanchine also returns to an allegro style of choreography.

When Adams and Mitchell do the splits to the floor that follow, even in the cramped TV studio they travel forward and back on the stage and emphasize this, her pointed foot indicating the direction in which she will move. The emphasis of the step in 1982 is placed on the splits themselves, which stay in place. A more cryptic change is the deletion of Mitchell crouching in front of Adams immediately before the coda. It could be that Balanchine did not like the obvious implication or simply a question of spacing. Mitchell is exactly where he needs to be to begin the coda, whereas Tomlinson needs to move back several feet, so the time is spent walking to place. Mitchell does not do a slow développé at the beginning of the coda, and there is a movement switching arms that he does à terre which became a jump. Just before the coupé jetés to travel to Adams, Mitchell breaks into a little soft-shoe time step that is wonderful in its loose-footed timing. Even he does not repeat it in the 1973 film. Tomlinson does a much simpler "chug" in that spot.

These changes seem small (they are sometimes changes in steps, sometimes changes in detail), but they can have an almost homeopathic effect on the ballet, both rhythmically and on where the dancer directs the audience's attention. Adams and Mitchell point out the steps themselves; Watts and Tomlinson point out the shapes produced by the steps. Watts' looser-limbed body can push much farther than Adams'. The pirouette at the opening in 1960 ended with a tilt and Adams' foot resting near Mitchell's shoulder. Watts had pushed it by 1982 to a deep attitude penchée with her foot hooked around her partner's head. Still, Watts was following a precedent begun by dancers like Farrell and Kent, a precedent with Balanchine's approbation.

The Balanchine Trust tends to set the last version of a work, but assuming that Balanchine's best ideas were his last ones makes death the arbiter of his art. Going back to his earliest versions may retrieve lost ideas but also misses real improvements. He would have changed his ballets for as long as he lived; some changes would be applauded, and others deplored. Balanchine's ideas were in constant evolution, some of it linear, toward a long-term goal (such as how he wanted a dancer to look), some of it episodic and not to be revisited. (Barbara Walczak cites a period in the mid-1950s when Balanchine asked for no épaulement whatsoever; he wanted the dancer's head to be en face to the audience at all times.)

The present generation of dancers in NYCB has an ease in extension and a speed in getting to the extension's height that have been selectively bred into them. But such dancers, with a very different facility and who are being taught differently in class, dance with a different emphasis. Dancers selected for the purity, extremity, or amplitude of their line are taught daily in class to refine these qualities. They dance, understandably, to show the things for which they were chosen. Phrases are accented at the end. The shapes produced become as important as the movement and rhythm of the work.

This change in the facility of dancers altered *Agon,* but Balanchine may always have had at least some of those alterations in mind; he may have composed *Agon* presciently for the extreme abilities of contemporary dancers. His love of the possibilities of the body can be seen in the shapes he asked for and in the distortions that fascinated him. The danger is in becoming so obsessed with the physical shapes that their rhythms are forgotten. Balanchine loved jazz timing, especially in classical ballet. He wanted ballet danced by a dancer with classical form and facility but with jazzy timing, and a specific sort of jazz timing, the sort that was ubiquitous when his works were choreographed. This irregularity of timing is essential to *Agon,* but it is a musical timing, not merely physical.

There is pressure to standardize a ballet as it moves farther from the original cast. When there is a step out of the ordinary or irregular timing, especially seen on a videotape, should it be reproduced exactly as shown or are the tics of a previous performer being incorporated? Add to that the fact that reset ballets get much less rehearsal time than new choreography and the desire to standardize becomes even easier to understand.

Whither *Agon*? The majority of the original cast is still with us. The work is preserved in several different versions on film and by the dancers Balanchine coached. It is essential to recognize the flexibility of the "text," even during Balanchine's lifetime. Over two-and-a-half decades he coached the ballet as suited his taste and sensibility at the time. He threw out sections. He rethought others. He was artistically curious, even artistically perverse. And he was the final arbiter of what made his work "correct."

Will there be the same debates as there are among classical musicians about fidelity to performance traditions contemporary to the composition of the work? Will there be a latter-day Charles Marowitz or Mats Ek who will take the text and transform it for his or her own purpose? Possibly, but Balanchine's choreography, like the works of Shakespeare or Beethoven, is fertile enough to withstand alterations in performance. An educated, responsible audience, of whatever era, will also be curious about a baseline "text" before seeing variants. Rather than thinking of *Agon* as "text," with there somehow being an essential version, a better analogy for it, and all choreography, may be soil: one examines it, nourishes it, tends to it, and tries to make the most beautiful garden possible, but a different garden grows from it each time it is plowed. As Balanchine said in the 1965 telecast of *Dance: USA*, "They want to preserve. I am very selfish. I am having it *now*. I am having it and eating it, my own cake."

–from *Ballet Review,* Fall 1997

Holly Brubach

Created for a South American tour in 1941 sponsored by the State Department, Ballet Imperial revealed the exceptional virtuosity of one of Balanchine's favorite ballerinas, Marie-Jeanne. Now called Tchaikovsky Piano Concerto No. 2 *at New York City Ballet, it remains one of Balanchine's most thrilling deployments of grand classical technique.*

Balanchine's attitude toward music is respectful but never reverent. He sometimes takes the liberty of using the dance to improve on the music. Always, his choreography determines how we hear the score. He can even persuade us by the dancing to hear already familiar music in a way we've never heard it before, as he does in the *Nutcracker's* two most famous waltzes—of the Snowflakes and of the Flowers—which most people, whether or not they've seen the ballet, could sing in their sleep. Both pieces seem tedious on recordings but fresh in the theater, where Balanchine keeps them constantly moving. The Snowflakes, with only a handful of steps, fall into formation and scatter again. The Flowers fold and open, and, like a broom, sweep the Dew-drop offstage. This is Balanchine using the dancing to vary the score, to sustain our interest in the music, as he does in *Tchaikovsky Piano Concerto No. 2* (made in 1941 as *Ballet Imperial,* revised slightly and retitled in 1973): from a good, but by no means great, concerto, he has made a ballet that goes the music one better, a masterpiece.

As piano concertos go, Tchaikovsky's Second is an odd one—not well integrated, better defined as a symphony with piano obbligato. Balanchine justifies the boundary lines between piano and orchestra, which make for a standoff in the music, by drawing the distinction between the ballerina (or the soloist) and the corps in exactly the same places.

The dancers in this ballet are very clearly ranked. It is not a democracy. And, because the lead is such a technical obstacle course, it sets the ballerina apart from the corps. Balanchine sees to it that we recognize her superiority right off. A long trill alerts us to her entrance: she comes in on a scale that slides down four octaves into a piano cadenza, and whips off a virtuoso cadenza of her own—flat-footed pirouettes that stop on a dime, a circle of the stage in leaps out of one turn into the next.

If, upon close listening, this concerto sounds long-winded, even bombastic—as it never does during the ballet—it is most likely because the material doesn't quite support its huge symphonic treatment, and because of the liberties Tchaikovsky takes with the piano cadenzas. According to classical form, the cadenza is the movement's climax, customarily positioned just after the recapitulation and before the coda. Other Romantic composers played with this convention (Brahms put the cadenza up front in his Second Piano Concerto, Rachmaninov incorporated the recap in the cadenza in his Third), but the cadenza remained in their concertos the focal point. Here Tchaikovsky, however, scatters solo, cadenza-like passages throughout the first and third movements, and the effect is relentlessly climactic. Balanchine mitigates this by dealing a few of these passages to a soloist, the rest to the ballerina.

Tchaikovsky rather neatly links the three movements of this concerto thematically: the outer two, both *allegro,* are complementary. The first movement's main theme emphasizes the interval between the tonic and the dominant, and the main theme, the third, completes the scale from the dominant to the tonic. Balanchine treats the movements as three separate, but related, poems, as in a cycle. The cast of characters is the same—same ballerina, same cavalier, same corps, though the soloist and the men sit out the *Andante*—but the tone and the subject of each are quite different. As in the music, the third movement seems to pick up where the first left off; the second takes place outside time.

The opening, a march announced by the full orchestra and passed along to the piano, is the ballet's overture. The curtain rises on sixteen men and women in two facing lines. As a clarinet and a trumpet introduce a calm, all's-well theme, the men approach the women and bow. This ballet is full of these moments of acknowledgment, genuinely respectful. They are never cued by the music, as in Mozart, when the cadence so often begs a curtsy or a bow; in *Concerto No. 2* these gestures lend the music human detail. This ballet seems, as Balanchine's works on a grand scale inevitably do, to be about a society. It looks like a nice, well-planned place to live. The first movement unfolds in a very public-spirited way, with the corps filing into a circle, then staking out a square. When the man escorts the ballerina on a tour of the stage to review the troops, the corps pays her homage with a deep *révérence.*

Balanchine, at his most literal, may seize on a figure or theme in the music and magnify it in the dancing, with steps that perfectly conform to it, so that in the ballet it takes on more significance than in the score. In *Concerto No. 2,* as Tchaikovsky pushes the music uphill in insistent three-note phrases, Bal-

anchine assigns the soloist and corps a series of pirouettes that double back
on themselves on the same spot, alternating outside-inside-outside. The agitation these turns make with the music builds until the soloist exits and dis-
pels it, but not without having brought the entire ballet up to a new, higher
pitch of energy—higher than the energy of the music itself.

Tchaikovsky brings the all-hail march of the opening back for the first-
movement recap, but the ballet never flags: the theme, though familiar,
seems fresh because it's only now that we see dance steps set to it. The soloist
returns with a man on each arm, and, leaping, the men promenade her in
arabesque. The dance and the music gather steam. The melody, in the piano
part, is written to fall a sixteenth beyond the beat, so that the music lurches
ahead, carrying everyone along with it in a coda full of jumps and beats, in
unison. So vivacious and conclusive is this ending that it might otherwise signal the close of a whole ballet. Here, it seals the first movement.

Balanchine's *Concerto No. 2* is not the original score but a version abridged,
rewritten, and rearranged in parts by the pianist Alexander Siloti. Tchaikovsky, when consulted, apparently agreed to a few of these emendations and
disallowed the rest. Siloti published his version anyway, after the composer's
death. For years, when this concerto was performed, it was according to
Siloti. His revisions in the first and last movements are mostly pianistic, to fit
the music better to the hand. But the *Andante* is drastically altered—shorter
by 191 bars and dominated by the piano, as the original is not. Tchaikovsky
assigns the movement's main theme to a solo violin, then to a cello and violin
in counterpoint, and finally to the piano; Siloti gives it over to the piano right
off. (The violin and cello join in later, for the reprise.) Siloti deletes the contrasting material in the middle, a restless tossing-and-turning. It might be
argued that by doing so, he weakens the movement structurally: by his own
account, it consists of only the main theme, two times through, cadenza,
coda. On the other hand, his version keeps to the subject, a single melody.
(The movement is in *a b a* form, and he omits *b*.) It is one of the most beautiful melodies Tchaikovsky wrote—a long, sighing legato line that comes to
rest in what sounds like a benediction. With this theme entrusted to a trio,
the movement is set on an intimate, chamber-music scale.

Balanchine's second movement is accordingly as private as the first is public. He restores the original structure, *a b a*, in the dancing. The course of
events is this: The man takes hold of two lines of women who are holding
hands, and gently waves them back and forth, like streamers. He swirls them
one across the other, turns them inside out. The idea is playful, but the action
is somehow grave: because the stage is so large and the lines are so long, they
seem to swirl in slow motion, as if the air were very dense. The man rushes to
the downstage corners, with the women at his back. He stops—whatever
he was running toward has vanished. The two women flanking him stand

lookout, poised in *arabesque,* their hands on his shoulders. Then, ceremoniously, the women return to lines on either side of the stage, the same
columns that bracketed the *pas de deux* in the first movement. (This *Andante* is
Swan Lake in a nutshell: the rows for the corps, the vision of a woman, and the
male protagonist, searching.) The lines form a narrow alley down the center
of the stage, and at the far end we see the ballerina. The man kneels. She
comes to him, embraces him in a big *arabesque penchée,* then disappears
upstage, and the two lines of women, merging, cover her tracks for a
moment. Next we penetrate to the heart of this ballet, a brief *pas de deux,*
danced to the movement's main theme, this time shared by violin and cello,
with elaborate piano accompaniment. Balanchine leads us back out along the
route by which we came: the alley formed by the corps, the woman's
entrance, embrace, exit. When the man goes looking for her, asking the
women where she has gone, they look away—as in *Swan Lake*'s last act: the
answer is unspeakable. He takes hold of the two lines of women, waves them
back and forth again. They *bourrée* quietly away, leaving him alone. He kneels.

The final movement is back in broad daylight, but the sobriety of the
opening is gone, the stately march has given way to a boisterous mazurka.
The women jump in *arabesque,* and the men throw them into the air with a
boost at the hip. Tchaikovsky here puts his thematic material, which is not
very extensive, through a rigorous workout, and when the music stands on
its own, the themes begin to sound exhausted by so many key changes. Balanchine, however, borrows this harmonic momentum and, leaving Tchaikovsky to his own devices, pulls dance ideas out of the air instead of the
score. Throwing conventional arrangement to the winds, he tips the stage,
with the corps on the left side and the ballerina, by herself, on the right. Having assigned her a series of fouettés, ordinarily a scene-stealing technical feat,
he then washes the corps back and forth in lines around and in front of her,
obstructing the view. The melody again chafes at the beat, and dance and
music rush together headlong to the ballet's close, another full-cast finale.

Tchaikovsky's music is highly theatrical by nature: melodies come and
go, little episodes that suggest eventful choreography. *Concerto No. 2* is
astounding, because Balanchine has made so much happen in it—more than
most choreographers bring about in a full evening with the help of a plot—
and because he has built it all with so few steps: *sauté arabesque, cabriole, tour
jeté,* fouetté in *arabesque, arabesque penchée, jeté* in *arabesque,* turns of various
types. The extent of these steps is even more limited than this list suggests,
because so many of them pass through or land in *arabesque.* Of course, an
arabesque is probably the most familiar and the most fascinating position in all
ballet. It is the image of a ballerina that comes most readily to mind, the
pose held by those little doll dancers in music boxes. If *Concerto No. 2* seems
somehow surreal, I think it's because Balanchine has taken this ballerina

insignia and rubber-stamped it all over, everywhere. Like *Diamonds* (set to Tchaikovsky's Third Symphony) and *Theme and Variations* (to the last movement of his Suite No. 3), this ballet is redolent of the Maryinsky. But the picture it presents is heightened—a caricature of classical Russian ballet that fulfills an audience's innocent expectations or perpetuates the choreographer's nostalgia for a paradise he left behind.

—from *The Atlantic Monthly,* June 1981

CHACONNE
Nancy Goldner

Balanchine choreographed a number of versions of Gluck's Orfeo ed Euridice *before rethinking it for Suzanne Farrell and Peter Martins at New York City Ballet in 1976.*

One of the most hauntingly tinted *pas de deux* Balanchine has ever devised opens his otherwise all-white *Chaconne,* first introduced into the repertory of the New York City Ballet toward the end of its winter season. Suzanne Farrell and Peter Martins slowly walk toward each other from opposite sides of the stage; her eyes are cast down, his focus is on her. Upon meeting, their bodies revolve around each other and their arms intertwine. They make each other's acquaintance with the calm measure of foreknowledge; that's why these two figures immediately strike me as godly. To be sure, their measured embraces are more inquiring than Gluck's placid flute music from *Orfeo ed Euridice,* but not until Farrell embarks on traveling lifts and walks does the tension between aura and data develop into high drama. As Gluck's flutes amble about in the Elysian Fields, Farrell's powerful, long legs compel Martins to skim her through—the universe? Well, space will do. Those long, low strides are grandly serene, befitting gods in their element, but they are not accomplished without great will—Farrell's will. Everything about her presses forward. Like a real swan, without flutter and self-caressing fuss, her bottom leg tucks up beneath her lifted body and surges forward in fully acknowledged power. Her toe nips the ground, her wrists and neck press lightly down, and she's off again. Despite Gluck, the ground is always part of her world; indeed, parts of her journey are totally terrestrial. With Martins mooring her, she leans away from him and etches overlapping circles on the floor with the narrow tips of her toe shoes. The circular route from here to there is not the most economical, but the painstaking care with which Farrell works her feet renders this journey the most exquisite. Nor does Farrell avoid treacherous routes. She leans back into Martins's arms so that she is almost parallel with the floor, cranes her head backward, and with her partner as guide carefully extends one taut leg in front of the other.

Balanchine has a particular fondness for these not-so-enchanted walks in the enchanted garden. They seem to intimate that the dancers' effortless grace is hard won and precious; that sublime dance (and music) is necessarily tragic; that heaven is entered through a gate. By showing us in Farrell's walks the underside of the serene lifts and the dancers' serene demeanor, he also darkens and enriches the flute music. He makes dance and music painfully beautiful and so humanizes Gluck's paradise. In this duet Balanchine again discovers the point midway between the stratosphere and the empyrean. When Farrell propels herself and Martins across the stage and into the wings, one imagines them skimming that precarious line between supra-humanity and godhood for the rest of time.

As in *Agon, Apollo,* and *Stravinsky Violin Concerto,* whatever follows a *pas de deux* by Balanchine at the height of his powers is bound to jar. (In *Apollo* and to a lesser extent in *Agon* the ensemble seems to intrude purposely on the love dance.) The jar of the ensemble's entrance in *Chaconne* is more profound than in the other ballets because it involves not a level of intensity but of style. At the instant a small ensemble walks on stage and politely forms a semicircle, we know we are in a different climate. The ladies' white tunics and gentle-men's white silk shirts and tights are appropriate, whereas Martins's white costume looked contrived and Farrell's limp, dirty-white chiffon dress under-dressed. The ensemble stands at attention, the back scrim changes from blue to light pink, the flute gives way to the full orchestra, and four couples cross the stage in *arabesques,* buoyantly but not sweepingly. They are no more and no less than exercises as they would be executed in class (by very good dancers), beautiful only because they are *arabesques.* Not that Balanchine avoids working his art into them or into all the other rudimentary steps and phrases that form the next sections of *Chaconne.* In this entrée of the cast—first the ensemble, then the demi-soloists, and then the groups who will perform, we discover, separate variations—he slides each platoon into the frame in overlapping momentum, so that the canvas stretches, stretches and stretches some more—almost imperceptibly. However much one may sense his pupils' dila-tion, it is not until the entire cast falls into a tableau, the full-bodied sumptuousness of which could evoke only *The Sleeping Beauty,* that one fully realizes just how far and wide Balanchine has taken us—from a few modest *arabesques* and ladies' chains to the pinnacle of grandeur. That's the art. The materials, however, are the ABCs of school, and as I watched this and later sections I thought how delightful it must be for young dance students to see their daily struggles with *pas de bourrées, arabesques, ports de bras,* and even curtsies transformed into a divine masque. For clearly, this white-on-white exposition of steps and patterns is the empyrean Farrell and Martins skirted. If their duet was more thrilling because it was unbearably beautiful, and more provocative because Balanchine cannot use Farrell as a template for strict classicism, this grand entrée of *Chaconne* is more lambent for its a-tragic tone—in fact, for its utter lack of any tone, place, or climate. One could say it takes place in the court were court and stage not synonymous in Balanchine ballet. What I find so unusual about *Chaconne* is that it transcends even an intra-ballet association, the Russian Imperial connotations of *The Sleeping Beauty.*

Were *Chaconne* perfect, the links between the Farrell-Martins *pas de deux* and the following sections would have more depth than contrast. The duet would be subsumed by the whole. It stands isolated, a magnificent flaw in a magnificent ballet. Its inclusion—which, incidentally, does not appear in the program's schema—tells us that Balanchine is as interested in the unique qualities of his dancers as he is in ideas. If a dancer of Farrell's caliber cannot dance whitely, or cannot dance whitely and be true to herself, then Balanchine "accommodates" himself to the person. Consistency be damned.

The variations following the entrée are as translucent and simple and profound. Banking on the inherent strength of ballet technique, as a composer banks on scales, Balanchine shows us how baby talk may be eased into singing, supple sentences. Avoiding didactic simplicity, he drops dabs of color into the dances without subverting the whiteness. In the *pas de trois,* Jay Jolley carries his arms as though they held a lute; sometimes he plucks imaginary strings. Renee Estopinal and Wilhelmina Frankfurt swish their tunics as though they were long taffeta dresses. In the next dance, a duet, Susan Hendl and Jean-Pierre Frohlich remind one of clever court jesters via the broken lines of their arms and her attitudes perched on a bent knee. Whereas the *pas de trois* is nothing but transitional steps, this duet darts and spins with no transitional movement. Next comes a *pas de cinq* for cygnets—crisp and adorable. And then the big swan and consort return for a duet and variations. With Farrell and Martins, *Chaconne* again tilts into more vibrant colors, but in the context of the preceding dances, with their small coloristic signatures, the two stars do not carry *Chaconne* away with them. Rather, they lace essentially four-square choreography with coloratura dynamics. Farrell hops and bounces through even-spaced footwork; she scoops into normally gliding turns. Martins, on the other hand, smooths jumps, turns, and sudden directional shifts by means of that internal legato clock of his. Separately, they tat contrasting fabrics, which is one reason why they make such an interesting pair. With Farrell crinkling hers and Martins ironing his, there is no need to introduce stock competitiveness into their solos. The momentum they spark is more musical than intramural, and so can lead quite logically into the final chaconne for nearly the entire cast.

As Balanchine finales go, this one is a comparatively subdued version of his high-flying extravaganzas. To have organized its tides in more brilliant sequences and its clusters of dancers in brilliant configurations would have placed it in that very crystal palace Balanchine has been transcending; even at its conclusion *Chaconne* is white. Still, the finale could be a seedling of the one for *Le Palais de Cristal* (known here as *Symphony in C*). Certainly it will be as enduring as the Bizet symphony.

—from *The Nation,* February 28, 1976

Liebeslieder Walzer
Tobi Tobias

Balanchine's Liebeslieder Walzer *(1960), to the two "Liebeslieder" song cycles of Brahms, was greeted as a masterpiece by most of the critics, but it took years before it became a comparable audience success. Its length (over an hour) and its apparently modest ambition (four couples, waltzing, with no story, no climax, no message) left many watchers bewildered and even bored: In its first seasons, people would leave the theater when the lights were temporarily lowered after the first section ended. Today it's received almost religiously. The first part sees the couples in elegant evening clothes, the women in ballroom slippers and gowns. In the second half, the dancers are under the stars, in toe shoes and tulle. The two pianists and four singers remain onstage throughout. Somehow, by the end of the ballet, all of human feeling seems to have been conveyed. Anna Kisselgoff: "For Balanchine—or rather his admirers and critics—*Liebeslieder is a stunning confirmation that the great so-called antiromantic of twentieth-century ballet could reveal the depths of human emotions as well as, if not better than, anyone else."*

Balanchine's *Liebeslieder Walzer,* created in 1960 and given three luminous performances in the New York City Ballet's *Balanchine 100* centennial celebration, lasts for about an hour. It is so lovely and so infinitely inventive, you feel you could watch it forever.

A quartet of singers and a pair of pianists perform onstage for four couples who dance, the conceit being that they are all participating in a musical evening at home, a familiar pastime among the upper classes of nineteenth-century Europe. Their music consists of two Brahms song cycles whose titles translate as *Love Song Waltzes* and *New Love Song Waltzes.* Their setting, designed by David Mitchell and said to be inspired by Munich's Amalienburg Palace, is an elegant interior with filigreed paneling and furnishings to suit, the space gleaming bronze and pearly gray, as if softly lit by the candles in the wall sconces and the crowning chandelier. Dancers and singers wear similar period evening dress. Karinska's now legendary gowns for the women—cut with panache from luxurious low-gloss fabric, each in a different, barely perceptible, pale shade of off-white—are beautiful in stasis and ravishing in motion.

The choreography for the first half of *Liebeslieder* is an extension, along balletic lines, of social dancing, specifically the waltz, but it is no more like decorous social dancing than are the duets of Fred and Ginger. It constitutes a lexicon of movement, timing, impulse, and suggested emotion—all kept within the confines of waltz tempo and the situation that has been proposed. There are lifts, for example, but they skim the ground, never vault into the air; if on occasion they soar a little higher, the woman's partner still holds her vertical, as if she had just floated some inches upward from her erect dancing position. All the while, the tours de force of timing are coupled with mercurial shifts in mood. The tact, intelligence, and sheer theatrical genius with which everything is deployed seems nothing short of miraculous.

It's important to note, I think, that *Liebeslieder*'s four couples form a community of familiar friends. They gather regularly, one is led to assume, in each other's exquisitely appointed homes for an evening of music and dancing. They're more than acquaintances, surely, and perhaps, on occasion or merely through the mind's fugitive caprices, cross-couple intimates (though ultimately faithful to their partners). From time to time, two, three, or all four couples dance together, and this periodic deflection from the duet form that dominates the dance is perfectly calibrated, and frequently astonishing. Besides providing variety, the larger interaction roots the proceedings in the idea of social intercourse, proposing it not merely an amenity but as an element crucial to a life fully lived and fully felt.

When the first songbook comes to a close, the dancers throw open the room's three double doors and escape into the moonlit gardens that one imagines lie beyond—for a breath of fresh air, or perhaps to exchange sentiments that belong to two people alone. Some moments later, the artificial candles extinguished, the lighting given a blue cast that heightens the impression of night and mystery, the dancers reappear. The women who trod the floor lightly enough in their heeled ballroom slippers and voluminous ground-brushing skirts are now clad in pointe shoes and gauzy tutus with blossom- and dewdrop-studded ribbons lying just visible under the top layers of mist-tinted tulle. The flesh-and-blood inhabitants of the gracious room have been transformed into the creatures of their own dreams, launched into a space of uncertain boundaries.

In this part of the ballet, each couple has more time alone, unwatched by the others, because the illusion of a social occasion has been shed, and because the dancing has shifted to a fantasy world, a venue that—apart, of course, from folies à deux—is essentially private. The choreography for the latter half of *Liebeslieder* is, as you'd expect, more conventionally balletic than it was in the first—swifter, more daring, more intense—but it retains vestiges of social dance that link it to all that has gone before, and, as before, it is suffused with heady emotion. Eventually, pair by pair, the dancers flee even this less circumscribed space, and the stage is abandoned to the musicians.

The lyrics of the final song come from Goethe: "Now, you Muses, enough! In vain you strive to describe how misery and happiness alternate in a loving breast. You cannot heal the wounds that Amor has caused, but solace can come only from you, Kindly Ones." Slowly, again in couples, the dancers return, once more in mufti, to sit or stand meditatively, listening. When the music concludes, they gently applaud the musicians with their immaculately gloved hands as the curtain falls.

Liebeslieder has no narrative content, unless you count the precipitous shift from reality to ecstasy that occurs between its two parts as a specific event in time. (I don't; I think it's the kind of leap lyric poetry makes, independent of plot.) Neither is the choreography tethered to the lyrics of the songs. Its subject, apart from the music itself (as the choreographer might have argued), is, I would say, the many faces of love. If there is any aspect of civilized love that Balanchine hasn't treated here, I can't imagine what it might be. Charged with moods that fluctuate like spring weather, sometimes within a single brief duet, the ballet reveals romance to be, by turns, tender, joyous, pensive, flirtatious, wistful, tempestuous, angry, and conciliatory almost in a single breath, occasionally near-tragic. Love in *Liebeslieder* is imbued with nostalgia, existing as much in perfumed memory as in the ardent—often impetuous—declarations of a present moment. It is shadowed here and there by intimations of death, as if affairs of the heart could have no meaning without reference to the inevitable event that would annihilate them. If you're susceptible, the ballet stirs all your hidden feelings about love, perhaps even a few you've been keeping secret from yourself.

Innumerable leitmotifs weave through the ballet, surfacing and ebbing, according to the "climate" of a particular performance and the individual viewer's focus of attention. Over the years, observers have detected a theme they refer to as "the girl who is going to die." Her initial duet with her partner is happy and bounding, almost like a polka. But in their second she seems to be attempting to tell her lover some terrible secret, one that he already knows in his heart but can't bear to hear. He shields his face with the back of his white-gloved hand; her lips, ready, finally, to whisper the fateful words, nearly brush his palm. And all the while they go on dancing; none of the lightly etched gestures and poses of this little drama interrupt or override the momentum of their movement to the music. In a third duet, though, she swoons backward in his arms, hand to brow, the image of a person overtaken by faintness or fever. Regaining her footing, she moves away from her partner, as if illness likely to prove mortal had already isolated her from the consolation of his embrace. After a moment, they come together once more, but when she falters in his arms a second time, he lifts her extended body horizontally so that, for a brief but indelible moment, she is already a corpse. One of her arms is folded so that her hand rests on her breast; the lavish folds of her long pale skirt streaming away from her body resemble a winding sheet that has not yet been pinned into place. In Part II the relationship of the pair has almost no dramatic implications, but as the role is danced today, the young woman has become cousin to *The Sleeping Beauty*'s Aurora revealed to Prince Désiré as a vision and Giselle's doomed heroine returned to Earth as a spirit—in other words, impalpable.

Grace governs this ballet. The dancing, with the waltz as its heartbeat, is graceful. The behavior of the inhabitants of that exquisite room is as graceful in its sense of decorum's parameters as it is in its gestures. And the dancing figures, first experiencing a gamut of the subtle emotions that belong to the real life of people with high sensibility, then suddenly projected into the wilder world of their imagination and yet safely returned home, are surely in a state of grace.

At the premiere of *Liebeslieder,* in 1960, they took the house lights down to half for the extended pause between the two sections. I remember sitting in the hushed twilight and thinking, This is the most beautiful thing I have ever seen. I've had little cause to change my mind since.

—from artsjournal.com, May 10, 2004

A MIDSUMMER NIGHT'S DREAM
Anita Finkel

A brilliant piece of compressed yet transparent narration, Balanchine's two-act version of Shakespeare's great comedy, to music by Mendelssohn, opened at New York's City Center in 1962, featuring Melissa Hayden (Titania), Edward Villella (Oberon), and Arthur Mitchell (Puck). Five years later, Balanchine supervised a film version with most of the original cast members repeating their roles, but with Suzanne Farrell as Titania. (See Villella's account on page 1024.)

In Shakespeare's *A Midsummer Night's Dream,* five acts of moonstruck romantic confusion reach a peak when the fairy queen Titania is bewitched into making a fool of herself by falling in love with an ass. That odd pairing takes place on the fairy level, in the otherworldly domain of magic. It is brought about by King Oberon's desire for revenge and his servant Puck's deft way with the juice of a magical flower. When Puck and Oberon move into the human dimension, however, and attempt to untangle the loves of Helena and Demetrius, Hermia and Lysander, they create confusion where they meant to create order; and mismatched couples, thanks to that flower, proliferate. The plot is crammed with complication, with twists and turns and ironies, as it interweaves two completely different realms of action and understanding, the magical and the real. To translate such a network into a clear dance image is a challenge, and to capture the poetry and beauty with which Shakespeare depicts the conflict is a staggering one, yet Balanchine's work of 1962, *A Midsummer Night's Dream,* does this with an effect unparalleled in the tradition of dance.

Although Balanchine is more often acclaimed as the master of "abstract," or storyless, ballets, his genius flourished too when it took on narrative—in his much-loved *Nutcracker,* in *Harlequinade,* in *Coppélia.* These works share a lightness, a brightness, a sparkling affirmation that also characterize *A Midsummer Night's Dream.* In fact, because it is the most complex of Balanchine's narrative ballets, the one that dares to take on Shakespeare and emerge on a level of equal genius, this is probably Balanchine's greatest narrative work and possibly the greatest narrative ballet of all time. *A Midsummer Night's*

Dream is his most ambitious successful challenge to the tradition of nineteenth-century story ballets such as *Swan Lake* and *Giselle*.

To face the awesome task of abstracting Shakespeare from its verbal context, the choreographer chose one very simple, strong, basic dance image that would, without a syllable, convey the essence of confused love. He chose that one feature of classical dancing which is the cornerstone of ballet, its eternal subject matter: the pas de deux, the dance that embodies a real-life, human situation—romance—in a metaphorical, idealized, and timeless way. At the very end of *A Midsummer Night's Dream* is one of Balanchine's most lyrical and romantic pas de deux. But to reach this vision of perfect beauty and harmony, Balanchine takes us, delightfully, through a series of other pas de deux that illustrate stages at various distances from that ideal. And so, like Shakespeare, he takes us through images of misplaced and confused love before we see lovers reconciled and conflict resolved. In *A Midsummer Night's Dream*, Balanchine "translates" a play about a magical flower's ability to create unlikely romantic pairs into a ballet about unlikely romantic pairs. And he develops this not through mime or a detailed printed synopsis, but through very apparent and entertaining variations on the pas de deux.

By proceeding through such a method of exploring a dance convention, Balanchine was being in no way radical or revolutionary. Though we may not realize it, *Swan Lake* or *Giselle* are not about a sorcerer's bewitchment of a princess or the failing strength of a betrayed village girl. They are about the way ballet's conventions can suggest the yearnings and mysteries of the human heart, can make them theatrically vivid and compelling. To do so, these ballets explore the means generations of innovators found useful: a corps de ballet, various kinds of steps and tempos, costumes, lighting and set design, music, and the leading parts—the ballerina and the danseur noble, whose ultimate expression comes, in every ballet, in the pas de deux, when ballerina and danseur are at their most intense and committed. The plots, which can strike both fans and scoffers as window-dressing, are sequences of events that connect dance moments. And though *Swan Lake, Giselle,* and *The Sleeping Beauty* are sanctified by tradition, none of these nineteenth-century works represents the most advanced or "final" stage of entwining plot and ballet into profound theatrical statement. *A Midsummer Night's Dream* goes further and achieves more. It builds upon its predecessors and extends them.

In *A Midsummer Night's Dream* there are two pairs of human lovers—the fair-haired Hermia and her semblable Lysander, the dark Helena and the swarthy Demetrius. There is also a semi-human, semi-mythical pair, Hippolyta, queen of the Amazons, and Theseus. Surrounding them is the fairy kingdom led by its king and queen, Oberon and Titania. These four couples, all of whom are directed by Balanchine with perfect clarity and consistency, are placed in a forest filled with other beings. There are, in Act I—the "story" act—two corps de ballets, that of the butterflies and bugs who attend Oberon, and that of the long-legged, pink-clad nymphs who form Titania's retinue. In Act II, there are two completely different corps— the mass who dance the wedding march, and are led by the three bridal pairs, and the smaller corps of six couples who provide the frame for the crowning pas de deux.

Balanchine's method of creating characters is the key to the first act. Long before we notice that the ballet proceeds by exploring mismatched pas de deux, we respond to the characters. Though Oberon and Titania become angry at one another, and Puck certainly experiences vexation, feeling is not really a part of the fairy realm—we cannot for a moment imagine Titania or Oberon in tears. But the first human being we see, Helena, is weeping: she is in love with a man who has thrown her over for another woman. Helena is the softest-hearted creature in the ballet, the only soft-hearted one, in fact, and she is the heroine.

Her heartsickness goes unobserved at first; the fairies are preoccupied by their own spat, the dispensation of the "Indian" child whom both Titania and Oberon claim. Theirs is a debate of cold spite; they confront one another in frozen poses across the width of the stage. Oberon and Titania are in a sense inherently mismatched. Working, he said, from German legends, Balanchine built this couple around a short man and a tall woman, a reversal of human roles at the very outset. It is certainly an alignment that makes ballet impossible, but Balanchine avoids having this realization strike us at first because Oberon and Titania are too angry at each other to get close enough to hold hands.

Oberon and Titania may not dance with each other, but each *does* dance, and each has a partner—a partner in both cases so perfunctory as to be "not there." In Act I, Titania and Oberon dance what are in effect partnered solos. Titania, "at home" with her ladies-in-waiting, amuses herself with a cavalier whose sole function is to support her in her liquid extensions and glamorously prolonged balances. Titania's dance is self-indulgent and self-enclosed, lovely to look at, but ultimately unsatisfying because the man's role is confined to that of a prop, the "porteur" who might as well be a piece of furniture. The sense of a pas de deux as a love duet is absent.

It's likewise absent when Oberon dances, in the next scene, with *his* partner, the butterfly. While observers have been puzzled by the dance of Titania and the cavalier, they have at least noticed the man in green; virtually no one has noted that Oberon's dazzling bravura scherzo is not a solo but a dance with a female dancer who also executes difficult steps. This "pas de deux" reverses that of Titania and the cavalier—it is a duet in which the partners *never* touch, they simply spell each other. Again, while there is a triumphant virtuosity, there is a sterility to this dance, a missing dimension. Both Oberon and Titania fail to extend themselves into a level of dancing that would include reciprocity with a partner, taking as well as giving.

These two showpieces are followed by a "pas d'action," a section of dancing that carries the story line forward in a literal way. It is the scene showing the entanglements of the young Athenian lovers, and it develops, again, through incomplete pas de deux.

Hermia, who is rather smug and obnoxious about her popularity with the opposite sex, enters hand-in-hand with Lysander. The two bask in each other's devotion, executing a series of partnered moves based on embraces and yielding gestures, far less virtuoso than the sections that preceded them, more down-to-earth. After they stroll off, the sorrowing Helena pursues Demetrius onto the stage and tries to get him to repeat the same embracing lifts and poses that Lysander had performed. But he keeps pushing her away and refusing to "partner" her—that is, to listen to her. At one point he kicks her behind and runs offstage. The initial situation has been set: Hermia and Lysander can dance together, in a limited way; Helena and Demetrius cannot.

Later, while Hermia is alone, Demetrius runs on, seizing his opportunity to press his unwelcome suit. Again interest and rejection are played out in pas-de-deux terms: Helena had begged Demetrius to hold and lift her and he had pushed her arms away; here, he tries to lift and embrace Hermia, who flails her way out of his arms.

After Puck has gotten Lysander to fall asleep, applied the love potion to his eyes and reawakened him, the now-familiar gestures depicting attempts at a pas de deux and their frustration are employed by all four—all embraces are broken, all support is thwarted. The unifying theme of mismatched love conveyed through misaligned dancing is here developed in a different, burlesque key.

Yet look what happens when the love dust gets into Titania's eyes! This magical element turns her into something she is not. When the awakened Titania falls in love with poor, confused Bottom, suddenly she becomes a ballerina trying and failing to get a response from her partner—to get a pas de deux going with a creature that just wants to nibble grass. So, like Helena (and eventually Hermia, who tries to coax cooperation out of the suddenly Helena-mad Lysander), Titania tries to impose ballet, as a metaphor for love, on someone who does not feel it.

Because of the mad contrast between the queen and the ass, this unrealized duet is the most extreme and wittiest statement of the ballet's theme. But though it brings about the climax of the plot, it is not the center of the ballet. That comes through the resolution of the "human" plot. Demetrius, bewitched by Puck, does at last fall for Helena. Helena's love for Demetrius was, after all, the first emotion struck in the ballet, and it is the work's emotional center.

Act I cannot have a real pas de deux in it, or Balanchine defeats his thematic purpose. To keep the action from becoming frenzied, therefore, Helena and her suffering become more important than they are in Shakespeare. The expression of her true love is the first act's emotional punctuation. Puck, after he has (mistakenly) placed the love dust in Lysander's eyes, summons Helena and tries to get her attention so that she will stand in the awakening Athenian's line of vision. But loudly as he calls her, vigorously as he points and directs her, she just can't track onto Lysander until she stumbles over him. Later, though, when Puck directs her to the sleeping Demetrius, she sees *him* almost before she's close enough to really make him out. Her love, an important human value, is affirmed—even though it cannot, in this act, be affirmed in dance terms.

Before we quite reach the end of Act I, we get another example of the way a dance between a man and a woman can be prevented or blunted. We see another courting pair, Hippolyta and Theseus. In the play, it is the wedding of these two that provides the occasion for the plot, and let us not forget that theirs is a forced marriage—Theseus has won Hippolyta's consent at sword's point. Hippolyta is a cheerful, bravura version of the dreaming Titania, in that she is thriving in a partnerless state. But Hippolyta becomes subdued to the demands of the pas de deux (she's human, after all), while Titania, whose ability to love has been awakened, is confined to a world where that emotion cannot exist. When Act I ends, it is with the human lovers strolling through the woods, arm in arm, a sighing Helena happy at last, and Hermia happy in her way, her complacency restored.

Act II is impersonal and grand. The three sorted-out couples—Hermia and Lysander, Helena and Demetrius, Hippolyta and Theseus—celebrate their marriages in exquisitely formal pas de deux that subsume the need for a story. The story *is* the pas de deux. But the focus of interest in this act is the ultimate pas de deux: the dance between a star ballerina and danseur who have not appeared in Act I and are nothing and no one by themselves. Their dance represents the harmonious and complete reconciliation of all the lovers and suggests the lines which end another of Shakespeare's comedies, *As You Like It:* "Then is there mirth in heaven / When earthly things, made even / Atone together." Everything that was disjunction in the other couplings—height, spirit, nobility, devotion—is clarified and corrected here. Not only are the ballerina and her partner enlightened, they have never been confused.

But the ballet ends with a reappearance of fairyland, as if to emphasize that these two are almost gods, but not gods. The pair at the end exist in the human dimension; because of the angelic quality of their communication, their dancing, they are greater than anyone else—than the lovers, than the king Theseus, than the demi-mythic Hippolyta. And they are greater than

Oberon and Titania. Like Helena with her tears, the couple at the end of *A Midsummer Night's Dream* suggest that there is a higher nobility in humanity—which is capable of love and a duet of love—than in magical beings who are beautiful but cold. In Act II, the Athenians do their best dancing, and then they disappear. Oberon and Titania reappear—their reconciliation is expressed as at last they face each other across the dance floor to trace a formal minuet at arm's length; neither of them is at his or her fullest in the dance, but their acrimony is stilled—it's compromise. The most lasting and moving vision is that created by the pair of principals who perform the ballet's one real, complete pas de deux. They do not need magic. They are dancers, and for Balanchine that is a state of being above both the human and the divine.

—from *Pacific Northwest Ballet House Program*, 1985

Mozartiana
Arlene Croce

Balanchine's last major ballet, Mozartiana, was first performed in 1981, two years before his death. Its music—Tchaikovsky's homage to Mozart—had inspired him twice before. You could say that this third (and lasting) version was Balanchine's ultimate homage to both composers—and to Suzanne Farrell.

With its premiere last June clouded by injury and recasting, and all subsequent performances at the State Theatre cancelled, *Mozartiana* naturally became an irresistible magnet when the New York City Ballet announced it for the summer season in Saratoga. I saw it, at last, at a matinee. The amphitheatre of the Saratoga Performing Arts Center was flooded with daylight, the stage was noisy, and the orchestra, under Hugo Fiorato, played bumpily. The children in the cast were local recruits, who seemed younger and less well prepared than their School of American Ballet predecessors. Ib Andersen, who dances the lead opposite Suzanne Farrell, had not yet pulled his performance together. In general, the ballet's health is still fragile, but what a ballet. Set to Tchaikovsky's orchestrations of four compositions by Mozart, it is one of Balanchine's most bountiful creations, and he has achieved it with uncommonly narrow means. *Mozartiana* is the world in a bubble.

The cast is small and oddly chosen. Farrell and Andersen don't appear mated, the way Farrell and Peter Martins do, or Farrell and Jacques d'Amboise. Andersen has a stripling, asexual quality; he doesn't mate easily with anybody. Even the very young Darci Kistler looks better with Sean Lavery or Christopher d'Amboise than she does with Andersen. In *Apollo,* Andersen looks fine as the boy-god, but later, when he comes into his maturity and has to dominate the Muses, he's unconvincing, especially with Farrell as Terpsichore. Balanchine in *Mozartiana* uses Andersen's slightness in relation to Farrell as part of a scheme. It is, first, a way of accentuating the mild force of the music and its spiritual temper. Tchaikovsky, we may remember, revered Mozart as "the musical Christ" (compared with the Jehovah of Beethoven). Farrell's dances in *Mozartiana* are lighter, airier, more restricted in their sensuous range than in her dances in *Chaconne,* which she performs opposite Martins or Adam Lüders. She hurls no thunderbolts here; instead, one sees a fiery glow of pinpoints clustered in the sky. And then the feathery fall through space. Andersen's dances are also concentrated and aerial, but if he's light, she's lighter. Balanchine in his casting and use of Andersen has removed much of the gravity from the male end of the male-female partnership, but he hasn't upset the balance. The result lifts the whole ballet into an upper atmosphere; we breathe new air—the ether of *Mozartiana.*

The ballerina and her partner are, of course, a unit, but the ballet is structurally diffuse for most of its length. Andersen doesn't even enter until the final section—the Theme and Variations, which he dances with Farrell. The rest of the dancers—a male soloist, four women, and four little girls—aren't defined in their relations to each other until the finale. The little girls flank Farrell in the opening number, then disappear. The four women, who might be their grown-up counterparts, aren't identified with either of the men. Balanchine has avoided setting up the obvious correspondences and turnabouts. Although we sense the connection between the big and the small girls and between them and Farrell (for one thing, they're all dressed in black), it's an elusive and mysterious connection. And who is the second man? You might think that Balanchine would cast this lone male dancer in contrast to Andersen, but in fact it's Victor Castelli, another lightweight. Balanchine has used mirror symmetry before, but *Mozartiana* is a broken mirror; its parts don't come together until the end, and when they cohere it's not so much through the mutual gravitation of structural components as through the cumulative sense of the dancing. *Mozartiana* is transcendentally coherent. Castelli, in the finale, finds his place among the women, the little girls are relinked (literally) with Farrell, and Farrell is bonded to Andersen, but it goes beyond that. The ending of *Mozartiana* is more than a vision of ballet's great chain of being; the dancers are bound together by invisible skeins of movement. It happens because Balanchine, instead of just giving us his decisions about who belongs where, shows us how he arrived at them. In the working out of the dances, the casting proves itself. When the dancers stop and pose and the curtain starts to come down, they seem united in the totality called *Mozartiana*. In the Farrell-Andersen section, the sympathetic reverberations in the movement—he finishes a double pirouette as she begins a triple—create a kind of spiritual fusion. Balanchine's attack on *Mozartiana* is so unconcerted on the surface that the ballet seems to be going nowhere special. But the total effect is of an achieved process. I don't know if it's a great ballet—only that the quality it has is the quality of Balanchine's greatest.

This is the fourth version of *Mozartiana*. The first was produced in Paris by Les Ballets 1933. The following year, a revised and simplified *Mozartiana* was included in the repertory of the fledgling American Ballet alongside a new work to another Tchaikovsky score, *Serenade*. The revival a decade later by the Ballets Russes de Monte Carlo was apparently closer to the initial version; Christian Bérard reworked his original costumes and decor. In the fifties, a touring group led by the Monte Carlo's ballerina, Alexandra Danilova, performed the ballet in a reduction for four soloists. The current production is not a revival but a new creation. Although *Mozartiana* has never been a big ballet, it has had a more active ensemble, whose members took part in the variations of the closing section. In the Monte Carlo version, the ballerina and the danseur had two pas de deux but only one solo apiece. The Preghiera was performed by a soloist, who, veiled in black, was suspended between two shrouded figures. This curious passage, with its funereal overtones, has no counterpart in the new ballet, which modulates between temperate and winsome moods. Farrell's Preghiera, which is set at the beginning of the ballet, is an invocation rather than a dirge, but with no more liturgical suggestion than the Prayer in *Coppélia*. The choreography here and elsewhere magnificently exploits Farrell's long, slender points— their eager nibbling of the floor in bourrée, their slow or sudden flexions in relevé, their stalky elegance in parades and poses. In the Preghiera, she several times stands motionless on one foot, lifting a monumental thigh in second-position passé. Later, she walks or strides or hops on pointe, or beats, or draws her knees up in high, rich pas de chat, or she swivels into a blur of inside pirouettes still holding the knee in perfect second-position passé. There is more rapid small needlework in Farrell's variations than is customary in Balanchine's choreography for her, and the stitchery is invisible—you don't see the minute preparations. This is a Farrell specialty from early days, and it grows out of an emphasis in Balanchine's training. Besides that, Farrell seems to have mastered on her own another secret of control, which has to do with music and momentum. With her—and with almost no one else—a dance phrase is not a simple in-through-and-out but a complex set of subdivisions inferred from the music. Other dancers are more or less broad in their relation to music; Farrell is more or less subtle. The reason some people can't follow her is that they can't hear what she hears—they're unprepared for dancing that points out the broad musical sense of a passage only to dive inside the elastic mesh of its infrastructure. The way Farrell's transitions and recoveries are carried out, she's never not dancing. Yet she's not overactive—on the contrary. Because her dance impetus in its smallest and most gradual discriminations may make her appear almost stationary at times, one can't enjoy Farrell just by looking; one must look and listen. The supported adagio in *Mozartiana* may be the most finely worked one that Balanchine has yet made for her. Set to an extended violin cadenza, it's about the flowering of form within form. It isn't preciously delicate, and the scale it reaches is enormous; however, a descent from point to flat foot, a quarter-turn shift of weight, a change of direction are events of the greatest significance. It's this quality of expansion within restricted limits that Balanchine seems to be concentrating on just now in Farrell. He's made it the subject of *Mozartiana,* and his musical justification is the extraordinary Theme and Variations, in which the same melody is rendered over and over, with ever more inspiriting nonmelodic or submelodic invention. The musical process is very much like the one we hear in the Theme and Variations of *Divertimento No. 15* or of *Suite No. 3,* but the dance process in those ballets is not nearly so close a parallel to the music.

Ib Andersen has been handed a smashing role. He doesn't have to dominate or lead Farrell in this ballet, and his solos, which in their density might be described as Bournonville-baroque, represent a new peak in Balanchine's invention for male allegro technique. Not since he made Edward Villella's choreography to the Glinka "Divertimento Brillante" have we seen anything like them. Andersen's trouble is partly lack of preparation. As a newcomer, he's been put through the usual bewildering assortment of roles; in the Tchaikovsky Festival, he appeared in more new ballets than any other male dancer. But Andersen also suffers from a kind of overconditioning common among technicians of his grade; he can be blandly perfect. He looks "Mozartian," but he doesn't seem to be very responsive musically; he danced the principal role in *Divertimento No. 15* in a monotone. In *Mozartiana,* Balanchine lights a few small fires under Andersen. You can see moments of ignition, but I'm not persuaded that stamina and confidence are all this dancer needs to make a blaze. Castelli's performance, which I was seeing in Saratoga for the first time, is more unruly than Andersen's, yet it's exciting in a way that Andersen's is not. (If Castelli had Andersen's discipline, and Andersen had Castelli's dance sense . . .) In the Gigue, Castelli twists and leaps close to the ground. The style of the choreography, its swift jokes and deferential manner, suggests a comedian entertaining at court. Though all his dancing has been strikingly energized of late, Castelli has unusual intensity in this part. A lot of his steps are à terre, and the deep-black jagged ink line in which they are traced does provide a contrast to Andersen. It could be pushed even harder—Castelli's infernal gaiety against Andersen's "angelic" buoyance.

But it will always be Suzanne Farrell's ballet. The four women who appear toward the end of the Gigue and remain to dance the Minuet are all projections of Farrell; the resemblance, unmistakable, is what gives the ballet its mysterious amplitude. When Farrell enters in the Theme, strolling arm in arm with Andersen, she walks in air perfumed by now invisible permutations of herself, and she dances four variations, one for each member of the shadow quartet. As she returns, strolling, at the end of the ballet, the cast assembles for the first time, its tiny ranks expanding with cosmic implication. Thus does the master choreographer aggrandize the gifts and presence of a ballerina. Thus does he reveal her, sovereign in her reverberant kingdom of ballet—the one among the many who are one.

—from *The New Yorker*, August 10, 1981

ROBERT SCHUMANN'S "DAVIDSBÜNDLERTÄNZE"
Claudia Roth Pierpont

One of Balanchine's last major works, Robert Schumann's "Davidsbündlertänze" *premiered in 1980, a deeply felt work reflecting its creator's preoccupation with love, despair, and death. Four couples dance to Schumann's piano music, the central couple an echo of Schumann and his wife, Clara, as the composer slips into madness.*

That great romantic signpost and unlikely masterpiece, *Robert Schumann's* *"Davidsbündlertänze,"* has, like so many Balanchine works, revealed itself in ever increasing richness and detail since its first performances in the spring of 1980. The audience has overcome its initial confusion and become absorbed and responsive. Critically, though, objections have been raised: it doesn't have enough steps, it is choreographically thin, and much too long. How familiar these charges are—the criticism alone could date the ballet to the era of *Union Jack* and *Vienna Waltzes,* to Balanchine exploring theatrical and dramatic powers that spring from outside classical dancing and that remain uncompromised even as they flow into it. In these works, which almost disclaim formal ingenuity, Balanchine's genius seems to have grown ever more transparent. In their simplicity of means, they pay ardent homage to theatrical conventions even as they transform and renew them. *Davidsbündlertänze,* like its recent grand-scale predecessors, offers a heightening and apotheosizing of old and simple forms, made urgent with its even more advanced recoveries.

A work for solo piano in eighteen interdependent segments of abruptly changing key and mood, Schumann's music is set for four couples of unequal and uncertain, shifting pre-eminence. The romantic structure can be disorienting. It is not a concentric outgrowth from a sure center, as in a classical theme and variations, but a long sum of possibilities and contradictions. There is no predicting which of the dancers will emerge for each new section. They dance most often in individual couples, three times in solos, twice in two-couple groups of mirrored counterpoint, and twice in larger groups so consciously "public"—filled with bows of greeting, exchanges of partner—that they throw into relief the intensely private nature of all the rest.

The score is filled with theatrical suggestions and hovering characters: one or both of Schumann's imagined dual personalities is inscribed above each episode as the voice of its particular passion. It was dedicated "more emphatically than any of my other things" by Robert to Clara Schumann just after their secret betrothal, in late summer 1837, and described by Schumann as a "Polterabend" or magical wedding eve. The music brims with personal emblems and encoded intimacies, about or addressed to Clara, with memories and secrets and scraps of her music pressed into it like mementos into a diary.

Choreographed on Balanchine's return to the company from illness, and cast almost entirely with mature dancers with a long history and rich associations with him, the ballet has a corresponding sense of being extraordinarily personal to its maker. It takes on not only the biography immanent in the music but also its appearance of human susceptibility. In part this is prompted by the music's powerful suggestiveness, a result of the perfect projection of Schumann's desires upon the stage.

The ballet has roots in some familiar aspects of City Ballet: Suzanne Farrell's Terpsichore, Karin von Aroldingen's Eurydice, and even, it might be said, Adam Lüders' Don Quixote from the last performances of that ballet in 1978. There are familiar Balanchine motifs in it as well, such as the blinded fate of lovers and the transition from heeled shoes to pointe shoes, less dramatic here than in *Liebeslieder Walzer* but with a similar heightening of pitch, prose into poetry (and back—the first four sections, and the last, are danced in heeled shoes). Like *Apollo,* it is a story of artist and muse, a romantically refracted, lunar counterpart to that early classic radiance. Thematically, *Apollo* and *Davidsbündlertänze* frame a lifespan of genius, the artist taking over his powers in the flush of youth, choosing his muse, and moving toward the sun, the artist in final parting.

But rising out of the depths of elegy in *Davidsbündlertänze* is a high song of artistic control over new worlds of feeling. The ballet recaptures sensations that classicism rejects or overcomes—the spirit unseated, pouring out from the body. It accomplishes this with a formal economy that approaches the austere. The unity of tone that Balanchine said he learned to master in making *Apollo* is extended in *Davidsbündlertänze* over a perilous range of peaks and sudden drops. Throughout, there is a stressed simplicity of step, a graven repetition that counterbalances the work's feverishness, its sense of being all foreground, loaded with protagonists. There is no relief in it, only an intensity that seems always about to break but never does. It is a ballet in which distances collapse and the smallest gesture fills the proscenium.

Schumann's first annunciatory chords are taken from Clara's own music and are marked as her motto. Without preface or preparation Suzanne Farrell rushes on, pursued by her partner, Jacques d'Amboise. He entreats her to dance, but his role as partner is limited largely to approaching and beholding her as she spins away from him, hides her face, or arches into a deeply weighted backbend, a yearning shape that luxuriates in its own shapeliness. It could be an insignia for the ballet itself.

Karin von Aroldingen and Adam Lüders succeed them in the second section, to the plaintive, music-box melody in B minor that is the closest thing to a theme in the music. They are the biographical couple, Balanchine said, Robert and Clara Schumann. They have had other names in other of his ballets. The Schumann figure is an introspective hero, a visionary; as with Don Quixote, there is little of his nature that can be expressed in dancing. Lüders and von Aroldingen merely walk and touch, as though all but the most necessary gestures had already been consumed. Many of these gestures are descriptive of meaning, fulfilled not in themselves but in the mind—for Balanchine, this is a radical physical incompleteness. She takes his face between her hands, he wraps and binds her in her own arms. Finally she coaxes him, almost imperceptibly, into a small, halting dance, of a simple and brave gaiety, a delicate waltz step that looks blown by a light breeze.

From the initial exposition of these two sections, Balanchine opens a line of dramatic development and structural symmetry in the music. Neither of these couples is able to dance fully together, and the tension created by their attempts is resolved only in the ballet's last moments.

The other couples burst upon us headlong. They are the "minor" couples, more youthful, less programmatically bound, without any solos among them. Heather Watts and Peter Martins (later Joseph Duell) begin in separate entrances and bypassing leaps, a bravado of independence, matching steps with a fierce playfulness, and tearing off together. In the fourth pas de deux, Ib Andersen supports Stephanie Saland (originally Kay Mazzo, for a time Sara Leland) in a breathtaking series of turns back to back, he sweeping her into the air so forcefully that loving exaltation is indistinguishable from driving cruelty. The great tension of the ballet lies here, in these irreconcilable extremes of passion.

These latter couples seem carried by a love so encompassing and abandoned as to have achieved the status of a fate: infernal lovers caught on the wind in each other's arms. When they come together for a mirroring pas de quatre in the seventh section, their extremes of flight are matched by an eye-of-the-storm stillness. The melodic line falls away to a broken succession of chords as the couples move alternately into frozen poses of sculptural isolation, each with the compression and pitch of a drama contained in itself. The theme of each of these dramatic crystals is the womens' blindness and subjection in love, their helpless complicity. Balanchine has often used the metaphor of blindness. In *Davidsbündlertänze* there is an added twist. As each man steps back from his partner he draws her arm across her body and along behind her, so that it passes against her lowered head and eyes. He doesn't blind her with his own hand, as Martins did Mazzo in *Stravinsky Violin Concerto*. Under his power, she covers her own eyes.

The pose these women assume—leaning forward with slanting back and back leg, head lowered against one arm held out and drawn across the body—is beyond even the simply conventional. Balanchine has actually made light of this very pose before, in the "joke" section of *Donizetti Variations,* when one girl performs a jaunty, out-of-place solo against the background of an entire corps aligned in this "dramatic" position. To bring back such a pose and to mean it, to make it so powerfully felt, is a matter of context, of daring, and of an extraordinary will to expression. Convention is held over a flame until it reveals its essential outline, the moment when it first took shape. The images of this pas de quatre—the embraces exaggerated into pain, the women draped upon the men—have the extraordinary power of seeming to have abandoned artfulness itself in flares of great, artful beauty. Our stores of meaning are replenished. At one moment Watts hides her face in her hands, which are cupped in her partner's. She seems to wake, and moves away from him to look for the first time at their counterparts, posed in their own blind despair. She sees what we see, herself reflected. It is a moment of startling consciousness, made chilling when she lightly subsides again against her partner's shoulder.

Farrell introduces toe shoes to the ballet for the first time in the fifth section. Stepping out gingerly on her pointes, as though they were untried, she displays her attributes as surely as Terpsichore does when she paws the ground and twists her legs to show them from a vantage of angles at the start of her variation in *Apollo*. To a high, serpentine melody d'Amboise leads her in a promenade on pointe, supports her in turns in penché; low on a bent knee, she traces a circle on the ground with one pointe. She bourrées off, reaching out to him with undulant, beckoning arms as she pulls away, and the light tapping of her pointes over the quiet hush of the piano becomes a part of the texture of the whole.

In the pas de deux of the full-throated tenth section, Watts and Martins used to enter a beat before the music began, facing each other. He partnered her with a hand raised high above in a series of tightly closed turns, both her feet holding flat to the floor; as the register of the music climbed, one leg would by degrees rise until she was turning with a whipping force in attitude. The effect was of her tight control, her resistance, and her yielding. This beginning (and its mirror ending of the pas de deux) was changed after the first season, and now they enter moving from the wings, bound together with a single hand at opposing waist and shoulder, the other arm flung out, turning fiercely. The music is no longer opposed but given in to, the dancing transformed from a damming back of its rolling advance to a ride on its waves.

Later there are turns that bear a vestigial relationship to the vanished entrance; he controls her from a single raised hand, bringing her around and again in high whipping attitude. He drives her while barely touching her. In the same pas de deux Martins snatched Watts out of the air as she leapt past him. . . . There was an element of overmastery in Martins' performance that is part of the role, that made a terrible sense out of the recurrent images of this slight girl suspended against the crossing of those powerful arms and imposing head.

Farrell's dragonfly solo in the twelfth section is a frisky series of small jumps and smart taps of her pointes against the stage, all poised quick elegance and unentangled, unstoppable flow. She seems here like the ballet's classic memory. At the final moment all her skittering motion freezes into one pose, pulled tautly upward with one finger pointing. It is a muse's gesture, as we know it from *Apollo,* and a long-standing gesture of enlightenment, as we know it from Leonardo. It is a rare decisive moment in a field of wandering uncertainties.

Farrell's solo is followed by a party to which the Schumanns have not been invited. The other three men come bounding in and toast imaginary glasses high. Their wild spirits are subdued when their partners enter, a line of girls holding hands, to a tune that Schumann described as a wedding chorale played on an organ. There is a large, peaceful circling of the stage, and an exchange of partners, building to a moment of wild gesticulation as the men spin away. The women, at the front of the stage, circle slowly, arms raised and curved upward like candelabra, like the muses Apollo launches on a single linked journey come unmoored. Each man returns to his partner and rushes off in pursuit of her vanishing arabesque.

Lüders has a solo that dramatizes Schumann's madness. Its shapes are related to those of Melancholic in *The Four Temperaments*—close to the ground, with falls onto one knee and into deep back bends—but stripped down, stepless, with only the raw elements of force and rhythm left to it. His torment takes the form of five figures all in black, enormous inky silhouettes carrying giant quills, the Philistine Goliaths against whose criticism Schumann's Davidsbünd, a club of one, was formed. The murderous power of critics was not merely another personal phantasm of Schumann's but an article of romantic faith. The preface to Shelley's elegy for Keats, written in 1821, cites "the wound which his sensitive spirit had received from the criticism of *Endymion*" as the cause of the poet's early death by consumption. The figures who briefly appear and recede during Lüders' solo are well-outfitted for their roles in this tradition. They did not appear at the ballet's first performance, when only an abstract play of light drove Lüders from corner to corner. Perhaps their costumes were not ready, but this lighting display was obviously an easier, more comfortable, more modern solution. Instead, against the flickering lights, the figures emerge like Shakespearean ghosts, the visualization of the hero's inner terrors. Their physical presence must represent a considered commitment to theatrical convention, ironically and refreshingly scandalous to the audience.

The demons recede, and Lüders is joined by von Aroldingen. They are interrupted by the arrival of the others, all together for the first and only time. It is a social gathering, another exchange of partners and polite address, and the beginning of the great summing up. D'Amboise whispers in Farrell's ear, and they run off to pleasures elsewhere. Von Aroldingen coaxes Lüders away as though to begin another dance out of sight. The other two couples, remaining, rush and circle into place and pause expectantly.

The penultimate section of the ballet begins with a great dissolution of tension into the healing key of B major, a kind of aubade, a release into light.

Watts and Saland, supported by Martins and Andersen, step out onto pointe and into a high arabesque. Each pair moves in turn across the stage in a slow and undulating frieze. Their poses are fluid, softened echoes of the anguished tableaux of the seventh section. The passages for Watts and Martins are among the most beautiful in the ballet. He carries her forward on his extended arms as she inclines, long and streaming, against him, like some Daphne transfixed, all roots and runners, her head thrown back upon his shoulder, her hair cascading down, a hanging garden in his arms. Andersen runs across the stage to turn and offer his hand, from a distance, to Saland, who runs to take it, and they exit slowly, moving backward, in an echo of their earlier dances together, she stepping lightly on pointe while falling back in a deep curve over his arm. Alone, Martins and Watts move in a diagonal across the stage, he lifting her in supported jetés that rise slowly, she coasting on the upward pitch. They depart in a series of supported attitudes held and renewed across the back of the stage, a peace-at-last echo of their wild pas de deux of the tenth section. Far downstage, Farrell and d'Amboise enter for the last time.

The melody is about to break. Farrell opens from an echoing attitude into a huge supported arabesque, poised on the minute base of a single trembling note, three times repeated, like a diver on the brink. Suddenly the suspended phrase melts into the familiar B-minor refrain of the second section. She withdraws from him, but he shadows and intercepts her, insinuating himself into her languorous turns, drifting with her. He takes her hand after she has stepped lightly into a high arabesque, so that he doesn't seem to support her but to stop her. She moves away, averts her face. The refrain repeats, and he takes her by the hands, holding fast as she begins to strain against him. As the plaintive song rises into something more desperate, accelerating, the impulse of the dance bursts open. Farrell breaks away, spinning wildly as the music spirals up out of itself, and d'Amboise, thrown back by the force of her explosion, comes reeling after, snatching and flying at her flashing arabesque. She spins past him again, and as the music drops suddenly away, she stands, poised in momentary stillness, at the wings. The piano concludes its great building rush with this sudden stay, followed by a single drawn-out, slow-spun phrase, an expressive device that recurs in Schumann's music, like a final contemplation of something fast disappearing, almost gone. Farrell turns in place as though she might yet spin away, when a final tonic cadence opens like a door out of the B-minor theme. D'Amboise at last takes her around the waist and clasps himself to her as to the back of a great bird. Unfolding, she carries him away.

It is a blissful sigh into ease, and a false resolution. The audience is always fooled. The final section, the re-entrance of Lüders and von Aroldingen, draws a breath of surprise. Their final little waltz, at last achieved, is in

C major, the key initial meant perhaps as a final bow to Clara. (There is much pleasure, if not much sense, in this game of cryptography. The ballet, and the music, will stand in independent beauty when no one remembers the names whispered throughout, but we are richer for knowing them. What else does that incantatory, pulsed-out F of her final entrance in huge, hovering arabesque sing to us but "Farrell"?) There is a return to restlessness, fulfillment snatched away. To a delicate melody Lüders and von Aroldingen sway gently, to the side and together, or back to back, with encircling arms. Sorrow is worn so lightly in this bare little waltz. She brings her hands over her eyes, and, as he turns her, that too is brought into the dance. There are no separations between categories of expression. He kisses her hand and draws away into darkness. We are left with her still, white, columnar figure, standing closed and bowed on the dark stage, her head buried in her hands.

—from "Balanchine's Romanticism," *Ballet Review,* Summer 1984.

L a   V a l s e

Nancy Reynolds

La Valse's *Girl in White was the most famous role Balanchine created for the elegant and provocative Tanaquil LeClercq. The ominous Ravel score and Karinska's ravishing costumes—very much in the "New Look" mode of 1951—reflected the mood of death and corruption the ballet was meant to convey.* La Valse *was one of City Ballet's greatest early hits.*

*L*a *Valse, La Valse,* I'm falling in love with *La Valse,"* a young girl wrote in her diary half a century ago. Quite apart from the allure of Balanchine's ballet, the reason was not hard to find: its patrician ballerina, Tanaquil LeClercq, was also none other than the girl's first ballet teacher, surely one of the youngest and most glamorous in the profession. A willowy sophisticate in the first bloom of womanhood, Tanny was a bird of paradise, an orchid, a beguiling mixture of worldliness and innocence. Backstage, she showed the aspiring student her white tulle ball gown from *La Valse* and the black coat she dons in the course of her seduction by Death. "Isn't it lovely," she said to my mother and me. "Karinska took the black jets off an old dress." With that encounter, my everlasting love affair with dance began.

On February 20, 2001, *La Valse* celebrates its fiftieth birthday. At the time of its premiere, New York City Ballet had only been in existence for a little over two years, but the young company was already establishing a repertory known for originality and variety. In 1951 alone, audiences were treated to twelve new productions, including four by George Balanchine (*La Valse, Capriccio Brillante, À la Français,* and *Til Eulenspiegel*); two by Jerome Robbins (*The Cage* and *The Pied Piper*); one each by Antony Tudor, Todd Bolender, and Ruthanna Boris (the infectious *Cakewalk*); and revivals by Tudor (*Lilac Garden*), Ivanov (*Swan Lake,* Act II), and Petipa (*Minkus Pas de Trois*)—the latter two in Balanchine revisualizations.

With so little in the way of repertory history, each new success for the company was that much the sweeter. Although it was Balanchine's sizzling *Firebird* that had brought New York City Ballet to national attention two years before, making Maria Tallchief a star, in a more muted way something similar occurred with Tanaquil Le Clercq in *La Valse;* if Tallchief personified the Firebird for the company's small but avid public in those early years, LeClercq was *La Valse*'s doomed Girl in White.

La Valse may seem an unusual ballet in the Balanchine canon—exquisitely costumed in an era when New York City Ballet was becoming known for leotards; mysterious and unresolved at a time when "Balanchine ballet" stood for clarity and logic. It hinted at narrative. It exuded atmosphere. But as we now know, such qualities are to be found throughout Balanchine's oeuvre—he revealed his mystical side as early as *Le Bal,* with de Chirico designs (1929), and *Cotillon,* with its pas de deux "The Hand of Fate" (1931). *La Sonnambula*'s unseeing heroine is a creature who cannot be explained; in the "Adagio Lamentoso" from Tchaikovsky's *Symphonie Pathétique,* created in the choreographer's old age, a small child extinguishes the candle of life in Balanchine's vision of his own funeral. Suggestions of narrative can be found in *Serenade,* his first ballet in America; other works—*Ivesiana, Variations pour une Porte et un Soupir*—are ripe with fateful atmosphere.

The world of *La Valse* seems at first to be the gracious and well-mannered one of nineteenth-century society, but modernist accents of dissonance and ambiguity cut through it from the beginning. Ravel placed his *Valses Nobles et Sentimentales,* originally written for piano in 1911 (the music for the first section of the ballet), in "an imperial court about 1855. . . . At first the scene is dimmed by a kind of swirling mist, through which one discerns, vaguely and intermittently, the waltzing couples." LeClercq described the opening as "like going to a party. . . . I liked to watch in the wings before I came on, watch the other people, watch the costumes. I found that it got me

in the mood to look at the other people waltzing around, with the gloves—
they looked so pretty." Indeed, the Karinska ball gowns, with tulle skirts in
shades of red overlaid with a near-transparent layer of gray, are ravishing
(some of her most beautiful and elegant ever, although rivaled by hers for
two other Balanchine "waltz" ballets, *Liebeslieder Walzer* and *Vienna Waltzes*);
and the women's long white gloves virtually take on a life of their own.

But at this party, there is agitation in the air: the stage is a haunted ballroom, where the lights are always low. The first dancers are not even romantic couples, but three young women without partners. In their moods and
movements, the choreographic motifs of the entire ballet are presented in
embryo. They thrust the edges of their iridescent skirts above their heads,
while their angular arm gestures, accented by gloves, stand out like phos-
phorescent writing in the sky. They will reappear later in the ballet, sometimes hiding their eyes—like fates, or witnesses.

The ballerina enters alone. Like many Balanchine women, she barely
needs a partner. Even more than the three Fates, she seems lost in reverie,
bewitched by her surroundings and her own beauty. Her tulle skirt flies
higher, her long white gloves seem longer, than any we have seen. Her
abrupt, profile gestures in arms and torso recall, in Balanchine's own
description, the "plastique" of early modern dance—again, a world out of
whack. When her partner enters, they seek but do not see each other,
then reach but miss each other's arms. The scene dissolves as, through a
diaphanous veil, there is a glimpse of the specter of Death.

The onstage temperature rises. Of the score used for the second part of
the ballet, also called *La Valse* (1920), H. T. Parker wrote, "The chain of
waltzes seem[s] to break. Fragments of them crackle and jar, each against
each, in the tonal air. The harmonies roughen; . . . through a surface-
brilliance, harsh progressions jut; that which has been sensuous may, for the
instant, sound ugly. . . . Below the surface, and grating rude and grim upon
it, are stress and turbulence." Ravel appended a note to his manuscript quoting Comte de Salvandy: "We are dancing on the edge of a volcano."

It is into this gathering maelstrom that Balanchine thrusts the Girl in
White. Piece by piece, as if under a spell, she is reclothed in black by a dark
stranger. For Francisco Moncion, the original Death figure, "the quality
Tanny gave to the character was a kind of discontent and then an avidity for
reaching out to something new. . . . It is the allure of the unknown that tan-
talizes her. She clutches the [black] necklace, tries it on, and suddenly something fulfilling begins to happen." Edwin Denby wrote of her "fascinated
horror as she first views herself in Death's mirror." Le Clercq recalled for me
her frenzied and unnatural joy at putting on Death's garments, culminating
with the long black gloves. In an indelible image, Denby remembered that

"when [Tanny] put her hand into the glove, she threw up her head at the same time, so that it was a kind of immolation, like diving to destruction." After a final waltz—one "poisoned with absinthe"—the woman's now lifeless body is held aloft, as a crowd of dancers, almost crouching, races around her in a vortex. All traces of the romantic ballroom have vanished. We the audience revive from a waking nightmare, wondering what we have seen.

Five years after she first danced to her death on stage, Tanaquil LeClercq saw her career destroyed in glorious midstream by polio. After nearly a lifetime in a wheelchair and the partial use of only one arm, Balanchine's first Dewdrop, the nymph of Jerome Robbins's *Faun,* died in December 2000 at the age of seventy-one. As the possessor of immense courage and a sharp sense of humor in the face of the gravest affliction a dancer could be asked to bear, she will be mourned by all who knew her. For those who saw her dance, the memory of her theatrical chic, wit, and surpassing elegance must be forever vivid. For those who only knew her legend, she will remain a potent symbol of the early days of New York City Ballet.

—from *Stagebill,* 2001

WHO CARES?
Arlene Croce

In 1970, Balanchine created this carefree, splashy work to the songs of George Gershwin as orchestrated by Hershy Kay, with, at its heart, the solos and duets made for Patricia McBride, Marnee Morris, Karin von Aroldingen, and Jacques d'Amboise— three women and one man, in a deliberate reference to Apollo. *And is the title a snappy response to Suzanne Farrell's abrupt departure from the company a year before?*

The title of Balanchine's Gershwin ballet, *Who Cares?*, suggests that the piece is an elegant throwaway. That's how it looks, too—like nothing much. The curtain goes up while the orchestra is playing "Strike Up the Band," and we see a double exposure of Manhattan's skyline projected in a pinkish haze on the backcloth. An excellent idea, but it stops there. The rest of the stage looks bleak. The girls wear their very well-cut Karinska tutus, this time in turquoise and lemon yellow. The skirts have pleats and look 1920s and mod at the same time. So do the boys' black bellbottom slacks. Like the skyline, everything has a double impact, with one effect or style superimposed on another—Now on Then, ballet dancing on show tunes. The two planes of meaning are so shuffled that we're never completely in one world or the other; we're in both at once. Or, rather, we're in four worlds, since *Who Cares?* scrambles two elements, classical dancing and show dancing, and two eras, the twenties and the seventies, with equal paronomastic facility. And since the twenties was itself a period of classical revival, the play of references can grow almost infinitely complex. When Balanchine has five boys do double air turns (one boy at a time) in "Bidin' My Time," we're pleased with ourselves for thinking of the boys' variation in *Raymonda* Act III (the metrical swing of the music is pretty much the same) and even more pleased when we remember the masculine ensemble that made the song famous in the Gershwin show *Girl Crazy.* That's simple enough. But when toward the end of the ballet the four stars fly across the stage to "Clap Yo' Hands" in what is unmistakably a quotation from *Apollo,* we catch an unframable glimpse of the multiple precedents *Who Cares?* is made of. It's then that we see, for just the flash of the moment that he gives us to see it, how comradely the links are between the Gershwin of *Lady, Be Good!, Tip-Toes, Oh, Kay!,* and *Funny Face,* and the syncopated Stravinsky of *Apollon Musagète.* We notice that the dancers in the ballet wear necktie belts in homage not only to Astaire but to the Chanel who in 1928 knotted men's striped cravats around the waists of Apollo's muses. But the allusion to 1928 isn't end-stopped; it reverberates with *Apollo's* own recapitulations of the 1890s and Marius Petipa—high noon at the Maryinsky . . . and so we are borne back ceaselessly into the past. To the question "What is classicism?" Balanchine responds with a blithe shrug and a popular song. Classicism is the Hall of Fame viewed as a hall of mirrors. The Fun House.

The only thing I can't account for is the bleakness. (Well, I can: Poverty decor is the only decor at the New York City Ballet; the vulgar opulence of other productions is a form of poverty, too.) I hope they fix it soon, along with the opening ensemble dances, which look like a cheerless audition. These dances are standard pop Balanchine, which is to say a lot of jaunty, bright high kicks and pointwork—a little square, a little heavy with repeats, and too impressively ironical in the manner of *Western Symphony* and *Stars and Stripes,* two of the Fun House's major exhibits. It's a slow start and a wrong one. The ballet suddenly picks up, finds its own life, when the boys and girls start dancing out in pairs to " 'S Wonderful," "That Certain Feeling," "Do Do

Do," and "Lady Be Good"; the dance invention tumbles forth, so does the applause, and we realize that what we're going to see is not a clever foreigner's half-infatuated, half-skeptical view of a popular American art form; we're going to see the art form itself, re-energized. But this spectacle we see isn't like a musical comedy, it's more like a lieder recital with a few social mannerisms mostly in the pleasantly sappy style of Old Broadway. Just when you think that maybe the dancers do represent a musical-comedy chorus full of stock types (with Linda Merrill as the company's inevitable wild redhead), they vanish and another ballet or musical or recital begins.

The second half of *Who Cares?* has an *Apollo*-type cast—one boy (Jacques d'Amboise) and three girls (Patricia McBride, Marnee Morris, and Karin von Aroldingen). Each girl dances once with the boy and once by herself, and then the boy dances alone. They are all four together in the Apollonian coda. The music is the same parade of Gershwin hits that has been going on since the beginning, only now, with the lights blue and the stars out, we listen more intently. If this is a musical-comedy world, it's the most beautiful one that was ever imagined. In "Fascinatin' Rhythm," Patricia McBride holds a high extension in second and then in two or three lightning shifts of weight refocuses the whole silhouette while keeping on top of the original pose. It's so charming to see in relation to that unexpected stutter in the music which unexpectedly recurs, that it hits the audience like a joke, but that's fascinating rhythm, and that's *Who Cares?* Classical syntax, jazz punctuation. I couldn't begin to say what d'Amboise's solo to "Liza" is composed of, though—it suggests soft-shoe, virtuoso tap, and classical lift and amplitude all at once—and d'Amboise, whose style in classical ballet has characteristically a casual, crooning softness played against sudden monkeylike accelerandos and sharp bursts of detail, dances it in total splendor.

Everywhere, the tight choreography sustains an almost unbelievable musical interest. As if it weren't enough for Balanchine to give us dances of extreme tension and wit and elegance, he also gives us back the songs unadorned by their usual stagey associations. "Stairway to Paradise" isn't a big production number, it's one girl (Aroldingen) covering ground in powerful coltlike jumps and turns. And in the duets, the emotion is more serious (the sense of receding hopes, for example, in "The Man I Love") for not being acted out. It isn't emotion that dominates the stage so much as a musical faith that the choreography keeps, and this is what convinces us that the songs are good for more than getting drunk at the St. Regis—that they have theatrical momentousness and contemporary savor. Gershwin in 1970, in the age of Burt Bacharach, has no trouble sounding classical, and that is how Balanchine hears him.

I am also persuaded that Balanchine hears Gershwin the way Gershwin composed—pianistically; and this brings up the subject of orchestration and

Hershy Kay. Kay had been set the task of orchestrating sixteen of the seven-teen songs that Balanchine uses in *Who Cares?* (One number, "Clap Yo' Hands," is a recording made by Gershwin himself at the piano.) But because of commitments to the Broadway show *Coco*, Kay has so far orchestrated only the opening ("Strike Up the Band") and closing ("I Got Rhythm") songs. The remaining fourteen songs were played, with his customary sensitivity and attack by Gordon Boelzner, from arrangements based on Gershwin's pub-lished piano versions. These piano arrangements are unvaryingly simple: verse followed by chorus followed (sometimes twice) by chorus repeat. They are beautiful examples of Gershwin's highly developed keyboard tech-nique. Gershwin's pianism in his time was comparable to Gottschalk's in his, and I hope Kay's further orchestrations of Gershwin are as good as the ones he did for the Gottschalk ballet *Cakewalk*, by far his best orchestration for ballet. To my disappointed ear, his "Strike Up the Band" and "I Got Rhythm" were in the vulgarized idiom of his *Stars and Stripes*—hotcha added to heat; and while the musical format of *Who Cares?* precludes his "symphonizing" Gershwin in the style of *Western Symphony*, orchestral thickening could destroy the bone-dry delicacy, the tonal transparency of this music, and should be avoided like temptation. The more so as Balanchine has taken such evident delight in choreographing the counter-melodies, cross-rhythms, and abrupt syncopations out of which Gershwin built his compositions—it isn't all razz-ma-tazz. Not since the heyday of Fred Astaire have such felici-ties been observed. (In the title number, a loose-rhythmed pas de deux for d'Amboise and Aroldingen, there's an echo, for those who tune their echo chambers that way, of Astaire and Ginger Rogers.)

Fred and Ginger, Fred and Adele, George and Ira, George and Igor . . . it's easy to be seduced by the nostalgia of it all, but the remarkable thing about *Who Cares?* is how infrequently it appeals to that nostalgia. It certainly makes no appeal on the basis of period glamour or period camp. The mul-tiple images, the visual punning, the sense of a classical perspective—all of that sweeps by with a strength of evocation more powerful than any individ-ual moment of recognition. It's mysterious, the mythological intensity built up by a ballet that doesn't seem to have a thought in its airy head. No single cultural myth seems to be at the core of it. Manhattan in the Golden Twen-ties, penthouse parties where composers of brilliance entertained at the baby grand until dawn, are lovely to think about but aren't the subject of *Who Cares?* any more than a rainbow on a wet afternoon is. To put it as sim-ply as I can, this wonderful ballet enriches our fantasy life, as works of art are meant to do. It's tonic, medicinal, too. Its fresh, unclouded feeling seems to strike with special directness at the city's depressed spirits. Just before the premiere, Balanchine received New York City's highest award for cultural achievement, the Handel Medallion, on the stage of the State Theatre. He made a number of jokes in the disreputable manner of his hero on such occasions, Bob Hope, had what they call in show business a "good roll," and then rang up the curtain on a Gershwin march. The Higher Seriousness didn't have a chance, but who cares?—the ballet was a beaut.

—from *The Dancing Times,* April 1970

BALANCHINE LOST BALLETS

COTILLON
A. V. Coton

This plotless ballroom ballet—a predecessor to La Valse *and* Vienna Waltzes, *among others—was choreographed for the post-Diaghilev Ballet Russe in 1931. It featured the most glamorous of the famous "Baby Ballerinas," Tamara Toumonova (see page 816), giving her a chance to display her inevitable and relentless fouettés.* Cotillon *remained a staple of the company for many years.*

This is the most satisfying work of Balanchine of recent years. Whether a revival of *Apollon Musagète* could resurrect the fantastic beauty of that work as danced in 1928 by Lifar, Nikitina, Doubrovska, and Danilova, is difficult to guess; could Lichine today possibly effect the lovely statuesque and slow-moving patternings as did Lifar? And where is the trio to replace the Three Muses? Not that there is any instantly observable common factor between the two works, save the incidental one of their serving as exposition pieces of Balanchine's genius at opposite poles. Had Balanchine lived fifty years ago he might have created an *Apollon Musagète,* but only 1933, the air of the world today, its history, morality, and philosophy acting indirectly on the acute observation of a master choreographer could produce this vehicle of decadence. The aura of the fatal ballroom, the loveliness of corruption, the sense of sweet sin implicit in every move and gesture is the triumph of atmosphere building by indirection in all modern ballet. A complex and hazy scenario avoids direct plot progression. When the curtain rises we recognize the scene as a ballroom and the action is opened by the two hostesses—the one, a patrician hostess who is assisted by a professional, say, a mistress of ceremonies, who welcome the early arrivals and engage their attention until the master of ceremonies arrives, late of course; to have been in time would have been to establish a perverse note in this inverted sort of action. The items of the score—*Tourbillon, Minuet, Mauresque, Scherzo valse, Idylle, Valse romantique*—offer musical progressions against which the choreographer built correspondences in *pas seuls, pas-de-deux*, variations, and group movements; introduced against these patternings are the ceremony and pomp of the cotillion. The guests are a convocation of otherworldly figures, and in every dance figure created there is an expectancy implied but never defined, of some eventuality whose importance to these unreal figures is immense, but completely unguessable to us, the audience. The cotillion development, the solemn dances, the incident of the reading of hands, the tragic lyric of the lost couple who dance together in the absence of the other guests, the sudden confusing apparition of the Suitor, masked and drunk, imply a terroristic *motif* never directly expressed, or more than faintly suggested, by the sense content of the situation choreographically unfolded. By implication, infinities of action and contemplation exist in these shadowy figures. All the dreariness of elaborate pomp, the suave politenesses, the sensuous poetry of motion suddenly revealed in irrelevancies of beautiful action, the tragedy of unrealized love, and the agony of enforced solitude, all occur simply as illuminations to the plotless phases of action, as one watches the inevitability of the unfolding of a series of attitudes and reactions—never a plot progression—towards a never revealed conclusion.

As the coda is elaborated the guests wander off towards destinations which cannot be imagined, and as the last of them goes the Young Girl walks slowly into the centre stage, as the music winds into a fugue-like figure she spins a series of fouettés madder and swifter than any of the earlier movement in the work. The guests suddenly reappear, run to her, sweep into circular formation around her as she slows her spinning, then rises on to the pointes, and eases her movement exactly as the music elides from fugue to the final bars. The revolving circle slows and slows, precisely counterpointing her moves in an alternate direction; the visual and aural images are perfectly fused, as the final bars sigh away and the curtain gradually creeps down. . . . No commentary has been made, no story told, no explanation has been given for all these entries and meetings; the tragic interludes wherein these abstracted figures have revealed themselves more surely than could any novelist. The mystic revel is over, the guests are scattered to places beyond this world of men, outside the events and purposes of today. We can never know more than is revealed by the action; and nothing has been *explained* or taught. We shall remember the brocaded chairs and the discreet alcoves of the ballroom, the silk coats and knee-breeches of the men, the sea-green, lemon, cyclamen, rose, and lime of the brilliant net dresses of the women, their fans, their gloves—but we know nothing of any period or place to which they belong. As creation of atmosphere—in the absolute sense, not an atmosphere of a time or place—nothing else in ballet compares with *Cotillon*. Decor and dress have perfectly expanded the choreographic idioms of motion, gesture, stasis, into this revelation of a ghostly assembly going about its ghostly business, away from the comprehension of men. The choice of Chabrier's delicate and always sophisticated music accorded perfectly with the rest of the notation in depicting a beautiful and disturbing occasion beyond the vision or experience of ourselves.

—from *Writings on Dance*, 1938–1968

The Figure in the Carpet

Rosanne Klass

A highly elaborate and extended divertissement from 1960, filled with exotica and featuring almost the entire NewYork City Ballet. This ballet —its music by Handel— took its theme from the intricate patterns of Persian carpets. It was much admired but, according to Lincoln Kirstein, proved "too unwieldy to maintain"—or to survive.

When Balanchine's *The Figure in the Carpet* was first presented by the New York City Ballet in 1960 and in the seasons following at the City Center, those who saw it spoke of it with awe and affection, and regret that it was never revived when the company moved to the State Theater. Never filmed or notated, *Figure* seems to be another "lost" Balanchine ballet. Little is known about it even at the Dance Collection in the New York Public Library of the Performing Arts, Lincoln Center, New York, N.Y. (10023), which has more material on ballet than any other such place in the world. So when Genevieve Oswald, the collection's curator, received the following letter she was elated. I thank her for sharing Rosanne Klass's text with me and for giving *Ballet Review* permission to publish it.

—Francis Mason

Dear Miss Oswald:

The following footnote to ballet history, an account of the origins of George Balanchine's "lost" ballet *The Figure in the Carpet,* may be of interest to you for your files on the New York City Ballet. It is, as I say, merely a footnote; but it may still be useful. It is known to few people outside my immediate circle (although one of them, the late writer Ann Sperber, you may know) and, since I'm the only one who knows the whole story, I thought I'd let you know about it in case it is of interest.

I was the one who conceived the idea of a ballet based on the aesthetics of Persian art—specifically, Persian carpet art—and suggested it first to Arthur Upham Pope and then to Lincoln Kirstein and Mr. Balanchine in the fall of 1959.

It was an extraordinary experience for me, the more so since I have no personal background in dance—ballet lessons or such—except as a member of the audience of the NYCB since 1951. Needless to say, my contacts with Lincoln and Mr. B were among the memorable experiences of my life.

It all happened like this:

Sometime in the late autumn of 1959 an acquaintance, the musicologist Fritz Kuttner, asked me if I would be interested in doing some volunteer work by helping the famous scholar of Persian art Dr. Arthur Upham Pope, who was trying to organize the Fourth International Congress of Iranian Art and Archeology to be held in New York the following spring. At that time I was in the midst of a divorce (I was Rosanne Archer then) and eager to find a distraction; I had lived and traveled in Afghanistan and Iran, and Persian art was one of my interests; so I agreed.

A few days later, Dr. Kuttner introduced me to Dr. Pope, who was staying at a hotel in the West Fifties that he used as his base on his periodic visits to New York from Connecticut, while he was trying to organize his Congress. He was then about eighty-three, had a severe heart condition, and, as I vividly recall, greeted us propped up magisterially on his hotel bed, from which, using the telephone, he was conducting his activities. Pope expressed delight at being offered my assistance (in my spare time, of course; I was then working in the office of the chancellor of the Jewish Theological Seminary), since up to then he apparently had had no help.

He then turned to Fritz Kuttner and launched into a description of a program he wanted to put on as the climax of the Congress—a big, splashy public event to draw widespread attention, for which he wanted Fritz's help. Fritz was totally uninterested and speedily departed, and Dr. Pope asked me to join him for dinner at a nearby delicatessen.

Over a bowl of kreplach soup (which he insisted on praising as "splendid wonton soup"), Dr. Pope resumed discussion of his plan for what he thought would be a stupendous event—and what I privately thought would be an undoable catastrophe. He wanted to rent the Metropolitan

Opera House (the old house then, all red velvet and gold, down on Fortieth Street at Broadway) and hire the New York Philharmonic (presumably, I suppose, with some conductor or other; he didn't go into that). He, Dr. Pope, would stand on the stage of the Met and lecture on the aesthetics of Persian art and its relationship to Western baroque art while gigantic slide projections of the Ardebil Carpet would be shown on a vast screen behind him and, *simultaneously,* the Philharmonic would play the overture to *Die Meistersinger* full blast—which would, he thought, illustrate the points he was making.

It was all rather mind-boggling. But what to do? What to say? After all, he was a very old and very distinguished scholar; and besides, he was chairman of the whole shebang, while I was just a volunteer who had wandered in a few minutes ago with no credentials at all.

And then I had a brainstorm.

A few weeks earlier, at a performance of the New York City Ballet, I was talking with James Lyons, publisher of *The American Record Guide,* about his idea of Balanchine as "the Mozart of dance," and Jim had been discussing the abstract lines of movement in a Balanchine ballet on that evening's program. As Pope rattled along about the Met, the Philharmonic, the slides, and himself at the apex of it all, I suddenly thought, "Why couldn't one sort of linear movement be translated into another sort of linear movement?"

As delicately as possible, I suggested to Pope that the program he envisioned just might, perhaps, possibly, be a little difficult to carry out. But, I suggested, there might be an alternative: it might be possible to express the abstract linear movement of Persian carpet art in dance movement. And if in fact that was possible, there was only one man who could do it and that was George Balanchine—whom, needless to say, I had never met, and, as it turned out, Pope had never heard of.

Pope perked up. He was disappointed to lose the Philharmonic, the *Meistersinger,* and the spotlight; but, he now admitted, everyone he had talked to had turned thumbs down on that idea. I, however, was the only one to offer an alternative, something suitably grand and glorious. "I don't know anything about dancing," he said. "I'm the son of a Baptist minister—never even learned to do the two-step. I saw a ballet once in Moscow in the thirties—don't know anything about it. But if you know something about it, go ahead. Write me a memo. Proceed."

A couple of weeks later, he invited me to come down to a meeting of the board of directors of the Congress, at the home of Joel Barlow on Gramercy Park, to explain my idea to them. I was almost an hour late getting there—luckily, as it turned out. If I'd been on time, there would have been no *Figure in the Carpet.* Unknown to me, AUP—as Pope liked to be known to his admiring circle—had jumped the gun and told the board about the ballet idea before I got there, and they had turned it down flat as just another one of his grandiose fancies. But I didn't know that, because I wasn't there yet. (In fact, I didn't find out about the turndown till months later, after *Figure* had opened, when the writer Robert Payne, a member of Pope's board, told me. They had told AUP that the odds against doing any such thing were fifty thousand to one, and, Payne said, when the idea became reality they could hardly believe it.)

But when I got to Barlow's town house that night, everyone was very polite. Pope had me tell them about my idea, and then there was a sort of silence. I thought they were thinking about it; but actually, nobody wanted to hurt my feelings by telling me they had already rejected the idea. So I spent the rest of the evening listening to Dorothy Heyward tell me about the original production of *Porgy and Bess*.

I guess Dr. Pope was supposed to break the bad news to me, but he didn't want to do it either. We shared a cab uptown at the end of the evening, and I kept asking him what I should do next. Finally he just said, "Go ahead and see what you can do." And, quite blindly, I did.

If I hadn't been a naive kid, I would have known that you didn't just call up George Balanchine and say, "Hey, I have an idea for a ballet." But I was, and that's exactly what I did.

The next day, at my office, I looked up the phone number of the New York City Ballet, called, and asked to speak to George Balanchine. (Ann Sperber, at the next desk, listened breathlessly, awed, she later told me, at what she took to be my "savoir faire.") The operator put my call through to Robert Cornell, Lincoln Kirstein's assistant, who asked politely what I wanted to speak to Mr. Balanchine about.

I explained that I had an idea for a ballet that would transpose the aesthetics of Persian carpet art into dance terms.

He said thank you very much, he would pass the message on; and that was the end of the conversation.

I hung up, finally realizing just how naive and, well, dopey I had been, and, abashed and rather embarrassed to have been so foolish with some-body (Ann) around, I went back to work.

About fifteen minutes later the phone rang and a man asked for me. "Hello," he said, "this is Lincoln Kirstein. When can I talk to you?"

I was stunned.

He asked where I worked and said he would come up to Morningside Heights to have lunch with me the following day. I suggested that it might be more appropriate for me to come down to where he was. He said no, he would come up; and we arranged to meet in a little espresso café near my office. (You can see how vivid this all remains in my memory after all these years!)

That night (by now it may have been early December) we had a bliz-zard. The next day, half of New York had stopped functioning. Schools were closed. Offices were closed. But Lincoln Kirstein came up to West 122nd Street and met me for lunch.

What, he asked, was my idea? I explained it to him, explained some of the aesthetic principles in Persian carpet art—especially the linear movement—that I thought could be translated into dance. And then he said, "I like it. George will like it. We'll do it. Now I have to find the money for it."

I almost fell out of my chair.

Lincoln then began sketching out how he wanted to do it—all very abstract (not the way it turned out, but I'll get to that): movement, line, pure aesthetics—and told me something about the horrendous economics involved in producing a ballet: costumes, sets, meeting union requirements. For this one, he would use slide projections as backdrops to cut costs, and stick to simple abstract costumes, maybe just leotards. Carried away with excitement, I started to chime in with suggestions— and it may be worth noting that Lincoln never asked me what background, what training, what credentials I had. If he liked my ideas, he took them; if he didn't, he didn't take them and said why not. As straightforward as that. Lunch ended; I sort of levitated back to my office, and Lincoln charged off into the snow to take the idea back downtown.

So that's how it started.

Over the next couple of months, I was in fairly frequent contact with Lincoln and Mr. Balanchine. On one extraordinary afternoon I arranged a meeting between Lincoln and Dr. Pope. First Pope gave Lincoln a summary rundown of Persian art, its forms, their meanings, the aesthetic theories, etc. Then it was Lincoln's turn—and he gave Pope a concise history of dance, its aesthetics, its forms, etc. Oh, to have had a tape recorder that day! Lacking one, I just sat there, soaking up a lifetime's education in a couple of hours.

One day I got a call at my office. "This is George Balanchine," the caller said. There was a brief pause. Then he added, "Of the New York City Ballet," as though the world were full of George Balanchines and I needed to be told which one was calling. Mr. B wanted some information on Persian art, and could I meet with him? So on Saturday afternoon I went down to City Center, through the back door on West Fifty-sixth Street (for the first time) and upstairs, and spent the afternoon in a big room with an almost-as-big conference table in the middle, talking with Mr. B. He told me that he had a special affinity for Oriental carpets, that when he was a child in Georgia his home was filled with them. "I was a very naughty little boy," he said. "I took my penknife and cut one of the flowers out of the carpet. My parents were very angry."

By then, the concept of the ballet was changing. Instead of the purely abstract work that Lincoln had proposed, Balanchine had decided to do a court ballet. I don't know just when this happened or why, but I think the reasons were probably twofold. First of all, I recall being told in late January that *Panamerica,* the recent evening of ballets based on Latin American themes, had been a financial fiasco and that Balanchine,

Kirstein, or both felt they couldn't risk another financial flop; so they decided they had better do something colorful, theatrical, more surefire for the spring season. And then (although this is only my surmise) they may have been influenced by the problem of the music, which beset us from the beginning. No one wanted to use phony or pseudo-Oriental music of the "In a Persian Garden" sort, or even some of the Borodin pieces; and yet to use authentic Persian music would drive the audience out of the theater *toute de suite*. Lincoln called me a couple of times to ask if I knew of any music that would sound authentic or at least appropriate and yet workable in the theater, but I couldn't come up with any suggestions and neither could anyone else.

Eventually—possibly taking their cue from Pope's analogy between Persian and baroque aesthetics—either Lincoln or Mr. B or both together hit on Handel's *Royal Fireworks Music* and *Water Music* and the idea of the court ballet, though which came first I don't know.

Anyhow, at some point that wintry Saturday afternoon Mr. B started telling me what he planned to do, and then he was on his feet and showing me, dancing some of it, around the table. If I was overwhelmed by the afternoon with Lincoln and Dr. Pope, I was dazzled and dazed by this. (I must repeat: I had only sat in the audience. I had had no such contacts or experiences before. Others, in dance, doubtless had many. But I knew that I was with one of the geniuses of the age, and there he was discussing and dancing out something that had been an idea in my head just a few weeks before!)

I met with Mr. B several other times—he wanted photos and drawings for certain costume ideas, or he had this or that question about Persian art—and talked with Lincoln fairly often. But of course it was out of my hands by then. I could only stand on the sidelines and help when and if asked to—I had no professional skills to go further.

And besides, things had begun to get a bit sticky. Pope had told Lincoln that the Congress would put up the money for the ballet, or at least some of it. The premiere was scheduled to coincide with the opening of the Congress, and Pope had made assorted vague references to the Shah of Iran and his sister, to their very great interest in it all—very airy, very bland, never really specific but always very sure sounding. (The Shah and the princess did send AUP a number of tins of the finest Beluga caviar, which he took home—but not much else, it turned out.) In fact, Pope had very little funding at all. His allusions to money coming from the Shah were apparently pure fancy. Pope had no serious intention of paying any part of the costs of the ballet—or, if he ever did have any such intention, it was a pipe dream that soon vanished. He was the worst administrator I ever met, very lofty, grandiose, given to airy vagueness about any sort of practical details, concrete commitments, paying bills, keeping promises, etc., and was highly manipulative. But neither Lincoln nor I knew that in the beginning.

As the money began to be needed, and failed to materialize, this naturally created a certain degree of strain—with me caught in the middle,
asked by both Lincoln and Pope to convey messages from one to the
other. The atmosphere grew frosty. (It was made even chillier when my
then-husband, jealous of my involvement, tried to get into the act without my knowledge by gratuitously inviting Lincoln to consult him about
the music. That infuriated Lincoln—quite properly, I should say—and he
must have thought I had had a part in it.)

By early March, Lincoln finally realized that Pope and the Congress
were not going to contribute a cent. *The Figure in the Carpet* had been
announced for April. Early on, Lincoln had picked the title from the
Henry James story. Work had been proceeding for weeks, and the cost
had jumped from about $20,000 (for an abstract piece, using leotards,
with no sets) to around $120,000 (for a full-scale ballet, costumes, a big
water fountain gushing onstage, the works); it was to be the most lavish
ballet NYCB had mounted since *The Nutcracker* and, like *The Nutcracker,* a
full evening. And at this point, Lincoln discovered that he would have to
go out and raise every penny himself. And that's what he did.

Around that time, Kirstein and his staff stopped contacting me and may
have stopped contacting Pope as well. After all, Pope had forfeited any
claim to be consulted, and I suppose Lincoln thought of me only as Pope's
errand girl. Besides, Lincoln must have been outraged when he discovered that Pope had been stringing him along with pipe dreams and
excuses, and he may have thought I had knowingly participated in the
deception.

I don't know anything about the showdown between Kirstein and Pope.
AUP had brought in a former secretary, Lydia, who was extremely posses-
sive and secretive about him and his concerns. Unknown to me, Pope had
previously been involved in left-wing politics, and she had perhaps formed
the habit of secretiveness then. It became almost impossible for me (and
others) to talk to him directly, and completely impossible for me to get any
information through her. Although there must have been correspondence
and some sort of confrontation between Kirstein and Pope about the
promised funding, Lydia was quite capable of destroying anything that
might reflect unfavorably on AUP, and she certainly would not have let me
know about it. In fact, Lydia actually tried to prevent me from attending
the premiere of *The Figure in the Carpet* and the later special Congress performance, by commandeering and withholding the allotted tickets.

So, given the icecaps that had descended in all quarters, I never learned
much about what transpired during the six weeks before the premiere,
when the ballet was actually created.

But in spite of everything, Lincoln invited me to the dress rehearsal on
13 April, the morning of the premiere. I took a day off from the office. I
recall very clearly walking down Fifty-sixth Street past Carnegie Hall's

stage door on my way to City Center's stage door. I was literally intoxi-cated, really quite high and floating and lightheaded. It felt like three martinis, but I hadn't touched a drop—it was all sheer excitement. I saw Nicholas Magallanes walking toward me, away from the theater, and, knowing he was in *Figure,* I had an impulse to grab him (I'd never met him) and cry, "Why are you out here? Why aren't you inside getting into costume?" I didn't do it, but I sure wanted to.

It was the first time I had sat in on a rehearsal, so I was surprised when Mary Hinkson of the Martha Graham Company walked onstage. She had been brought in to do an African pas de deux with Arthur Mitchell. I had known her in college, and during a break I called to her, "Hi, Bunny!" She peered over the footlights, asking, "Who's here from Wisconsin? That's the only place they call me Bunny."

In the ballet, only the first scene, "The Sands of the Desert," contained anything of what Lincoln and I had discussed at that lunch in the blizzard—the pure abstract movement. And for that scene, the men's cos-tumes—brown leotards with blankets to wrap around the shoulders—had just arrived from Karinska and hadn't been tried on. The blankets, which Mr. B wanted for a touch of authenticity, after he looked at some old photographs and engravings, had mistakenly been made of a stiff fab-ric—felt, I think—and didn't drape, just stuck up rigidly, looking ridicu-lous. With the premiere just hours away there was no time to make new blankets, but these were really quite awful. Lincoln was sitting behind me in the darkness. I turned around and whispered, "The blankets are all wrong. You'll have to get rid of them."

"I'm not interested in scholarly authenticity!" he snapped. "This isn't an academic treatise—it's theater!"

(My memory gets a bit blurry at this point. Sometimes I like to think that I was bold enough to say, "I know it's theater, and that's why they won't work." But I probably just clammed up and said nothing and only wished I had the nerve to say it.)

When there was a pause in the rehearsal and the lights went up, Lin-coln came over and said, "I'm sorry I snapped at you. I'm under a lot of pressure." And then we talked about the blankets. By curtain time they had vanished, never to return.

That night *The Figure in the Carpet* opened. I levitated through that evening, too, although there was one disappointment: I was supposed to get a credit on the program ("Idea suggested by . . ." or something of the sort) but it wasn't there. That hurt, but never mind: the rest was glorious. The curtain went up, and they had a hit. After the curtain came down again to a thunder of applause, Lincoln was hugging me and hauling me around, introducing me to a multitude of celebrities as "the young lady who gave us the idea." I think I met Agnes de Mille, maybe Leonard Bern-stein—I don't know who else. I was too dazzled to keep track. And then there was a party upstairs where I danced (fox-trot, rhumba) with Jacques d'Amboise and Edward Villella, chatted with Diana Adams and Melissa Hayden—all the idols I had been watching for years.

A couple of days later the Congress of Iranian art opened. (As I recall, when the financing fell through, Lincoln decided to hold the premiere earlier, to meet the company's needs instead of the Congress's.) Later, there was a special performance of *Figure* dedicated to the Congress; and Pope, his board, and everyone else were thrilled—including, of course, the ones who had voted it down as impossible! . . .

P.S.: Oh, one last thing I almost forgot. . . .

On opening night of *Figure*, when he was rejoicing over having a hit, Lincoln leaned over and said to me, "This is wonderful. But I still wish we could have done it the way we originally planned it. I liked that even better."

And I should say that two of us *did* see that original ballet: Lincoln Kirstein and myself. On that snowy day when I met him and he said "We'll do it" and then started sketching out just how he wanted to do it, I *saw* the ballet he was describing—saw it as clearly as though it were being danced before my eyes. Obviously he saw it too. If no one else has recorded Kirstein's power to create in this way—to make you see what he sees in his mind's eye, literally to see it—then let this note be a record of it.

—from *Ballet Review,* Spring 1986

Opus 34
Edwin Denby

In 1954, within months of presenting his Nutcracker, *Balanchine created this dark and mordant work to Schoenberg's* Accompaniment Music to a Motion Picture, *op. 34). The music was played through twice without interruption, but with severely contrasting choreography and different casts. In its famous ending, the strong Klieg lights were turned on the audience, almost blinding them.*

*O**pus 34,* despite its press, is powerful theater, brilliantly produced and performed. Once more Balanchine has made a striking ballet different from any in the repertory, different from any anywhere. It is a powerful and it is a paradoxical ballet. It looks like modern dance, but it is entirely classical; it shows no sweeping discharge of physical energy, but it generates as much force as if it did; it is frightening in its pantomime, but the effects seem ludicrous. The fact is it combines the ludicrous and the tragic in a magnificent tragic glee. It is the same glee that is so intolerably enormous in *King Lear*. Children like it, but adults shudder. They wish *Opus* were meaningless, or even a joke at their expense; it isn't, its theater power is exact at every point.

Opus 34 is a piece in two parts not at all similar at first sight, but both set to the same darkly glistening and oppressive Schoenberg score. The first part is straight dancing in a peculiar range; the second is a fairy tale told in pantomime. The audience watches the first part absorbed and impressed; it watches the second fascinated, frightened, and giggling. Then the curtain comes down and there is a curious vacuum, the blank state of not knowing what hit you. One tries to get one's bearings; one can't seem to bring all one has seen in focus.

What has happened onstage has been peculiar. When the curtain goes up, thirteen dancers face you, dressed alike in plaster white, each standing alone. They quiver a knee and stop; they lunge forward and stop; they dangle their hands; crouching, they throw a hand wide, slip it between the legs, grab a knee and stop; they turn up their faces to you and stop; they stand erect again. They are not tense, but very alert. The gestures are swift and clear, done without any sentiment; they look a little comical—yet somehow like those of terror. Stops and movements build into phrases, complex classic figurations, sections. The dance develops a powerful rhythm. The dancers touch themselves, each other, sharply and without feeling and go on; groups start and stop in a narrow compass, they scarcely leave the ground, they stretch their strength oddly downward. By flashes the stops give a sudden supervisibility like a film close-up. It looks funny and dreadful, yet the movements are so elegantly done, the rhythm so strong, the variety so surprising, one has a sense of great dynamism. It is as if people were under an oppressive force, meeting it keenly and swiftly, using to the utmost the space left them. But the dancers come to a repeat, as if there were no issue from the trap. Then, very slow, they mysteriously merge into a close clump of people, and together they meet extinction candidly and without complaint. It is an image of strange tenderness.

At once the pantomime begins. A brother and sister stand with their backs to us at the footlights, facing the darkness upstage. They go forward into it, a witch beckons them aside. As they turn toward her, swooping creatures tear them apart, kidnap them, they disappear. Out of the dark comes a fat squad of nurses, two operating tables, a surgeon. An operation is performed. Bandages, bandages, bandages. Dumped off the tables are the brother and sister, horribly altered, dreadfully fascinating to see. They quiver fantastically, grovel in anguish, they reach for and find each other blindly, ludicrously. A slithery heap of something viscous appears, like a wave. The girl steps into it for relief, it slowly mounts, swallows her. A second wave absorbs the boy. In the heaving waves, the victims wriggle, they try to reach each other, they meet wallowing topsy-turvy, are separated. The brother is scooped wondrously upward, gone forever. The girl is stranded ashore and rises. She finds a frightening memento of him, she hoods herself in it; hooded, she paces forward to the footlights. She turns, finds herself where the two of them were once together, facing the enormous dark that bears down on her from everywhere. Alone she slowly paces into it. Blinding lights hit her head-on, set fire to her, and, erect, she paces on into them. Curtain.

The pantomime is clearly a fairy tale—the dark wood, the witches, the cruel wizard, the bewitched waves and lights. The grisly events are vivid but not naturalistic. They appear and disappear in an unnatural black void. And like a fairy tale, as we accept the truth of the story, we find ourselves back safe in a familiar domestic lamplit room, back in the familiar theater.

What I have described is what anyone sees who watches the stage. The action is lucidly shown and straightforward. The piece has no surrealist ambiguity; there is no mystification, no siding with the monster, no confusion or violation of personality. Still less is it a hoax, a "period" spoof. Both parts move steadily to a heroic ending, a moment of quiet for an image of final courage. Both show people meeting an overwhelming inhuman force with courage, without complaint. The destiny, savage and ludicrous, that they meet seems to be, as a friend said, "the end of everything"; but that is merely what none of us escapes.

The tragic horror of *Opus* is not a gloomy fancy the choreographer wants to make a personal point about. It is given by the score. You hear it insistently evoked by the music. And the program notes tell you the story Schoenberg had in mind. It is contained in the titles of the sections of his score: "Threat. Danger. Fear. Catastrophe." The choreographer has dramatized this four-word libretto as convincingly as he could and in two parallel ways. He has projected the rising horror it calls for through striking images of savage irony and human heroism. The glee and the tenderness of these make the unescapable catastrophe not a pessimistic defeat; no, they make it lift tragically in the midst of horror. And the dramatic impact it achieves is terrifyingly real.

As for the dramatic device of mingling the ludicrous and the tragic, that has long been legitimate, and even a glory of theater. Balanchine has used it before: in *Prodigal Son,* for instance, and in *Night Shadow;* used it without a story reference in *Four Temperaments.* And he has long hoped to make a *Don*

Quixote. He has certainly used a great many other and gentler devices when they were called for. The particular effect of this one is double: first it shocks one's stuffiness, then it delights one's sense of truth.

People shocked and puzzled by *Opus 34* have taken to the comfortable cliché that its devices and ideas are "the old-fashioned ones of the German twenties." This is nonsense for anyone who knows those twenties. Their characteristic was the protest, the resentful whine, the morbid self-dramatization. The ideas of *Opus* are consistently and clearly the opposite ones. It looks destiny in the face; it accepts catastrophe as a test of courage.

But what makes the ideas in the ballet appear with such expressive power is the way the stage action at every moment seems to fulfill the intense dramatic potency of the music. When the ballet is over you are convinced that you "understood" the score, you have felt its grandeur and theater. The music is Schoenberg's opus 34, "Accompaniment Music for a Motion Picture." Balanchine has set it twice: the first time he makes you see the forces of its tight logical form, the second the wide stream of its expressive rhetoric. In the first part of the ballet you watch the compressed phrases, the reversals, the intricate developments; wonderful how the dance reveals the hidden majesty of rhythm, reveals the intense spring of action left in the interlocking structure. In the second part, the music floods out like a soundtrack, weird as a spell of science fiction, inexorable in the timing of its dreadful stream. The sounds of it, the whirrs, squeals, reverberations, hums, and thuds, have frozen the first time on strictly limited dance movements, as if crystal by crystal their logic immured the dancers; then, the second time, the same sounds have liquidly lifted up a few solid gobs of nightmare, like the whisper of ghosts in a river that foretell what has happened already. Even if you don't look for the consistent narrative meaning *Opus* has, but follow it merely moment by moment as movements set to a particular score, the ballet makes its grand effect. That it offers two stage versions of the same very difficult music, each musically right and dramatically right, is a fantastic feat of choreographic virtuosity; but the expressive power, not the virtuosity, is what you feel as you watch.

In the pantomime the episodes become frightening because their exact timing projects them so forcefully. Note for instance the scary effect of the waits between when nothing at all happens. The gestures themselves are not those of psychological pantomime, nor are they stylized; they are the large simple factual actions that classic ballet has preserved from earlier theater. Note how real the effect is when the surgeon backs away from the tables, turns once, and then backs further away into the wings; or when legs wiggle without bodies out of the clasp of the waves; or the scare you feel when the sister picks up the piece of silk, though there is nothing special about the prop, and only a change of pace in her movement. The simple costumes and props by Esteban Francés, the complex lighting by Jean Rosenthal are to be sure marvels of theatrical imagination, so beautifully they suit every shade of the action.

The tense consistency of the pantomime's dramatic atmosphere might have been shattered at the point where the two dancers make a few startling dance movements; it isn't broken because these steps are in key with pantomime, they have the specific pantomime quality of movement. Similarly in the dance part of *Opus* the gestures derived from pantomime or modern dance do not jar with classic steps because they have been purposely given the specific quality of classic movement. They are made from a classic center, in classic balance, and in the classic rhythm of musical meter. They do not have a narrative continuity, but become—like classic steps—momentary shapes whose only urgency is that of musical rhythm and dance action. Such a shape will look oppressive not because the dancer dances it oppressedly, but because of its own visual and rhythmic nature. Whatever the look of the shape, a classic dancer can dance it clearly and securely; she keeps her swiftness, her elegance, her ease of bearing. And so the ballet allows for a steady confident brilliance in performance, and whatever it says is said nobly.

Brilliant the company looks as it performs, both girls and boys. No other company could duplicate the quickness of ear of these dancers; that they learned the piece in two weeks is an achievement unique in ballet history. Happily, the score is also played very handsomely and it is because the management provided for enough orchestra rehearsal—another admirable feat.

Opus 34 is a great ballet, and fans—even if they get angry—shouldn't miss it. It is in every way an exception among ballets, but it is legitimately classic wherever you test it. Such an exception is an honor to the company. It is worth a fight. It affirms the company's stand as the most adventurous anywhere, and it offers an adventure to the public.

My one objection is to the light that (if you sit in the orchestra center) shines in your eyes at the very end of the piece. It shines for nine seconds; the effect of the first four I like very much and wouldn't miss; during the last five seconds nothing more happens onstage, and I close my eyes and listen to the last grandiose whirrs of the music. If the light hurts your eyes too, you can try this solution. But just now a fan who has come into the room tells me he likes the whole nine seconds very much.

—from *Dance Magazine,* 1954

BALANCHINE DANCERS

DARCI KISTLER
Robert Greskovic

The last dancer Balanchine identified as a major ballerina, Darci Kistler joined City Ballet in 1980 and was made a principal two years later, having already been acclaimed for such central roles as Odette in Swan Lake *and the second movement of* Symphony in C. *She was to perform in dozens of Balanchine and Robbins works, as well as in a score of ballets created for her by Peter Martins, whom she married in 1991.*

Pace the pundits concerning the youth culture in this half of our century, most of us do not come to accomplish our work at any remarkably early age. The market must always, of course, supply necessary products, and a considerable group of youthful consumers will demand the goods of youth. But, compared to ages past with life spans shorter and adult responsibilities and accomplishments more readily found in teenage individuals, recent decades have seen many youthful consumers and few youthful creators.

The individual case of the contemporary ballet dancer is a complex one. Surely the physical demands of dancing give some advantage to youthful practitioners. Yet there remains a fairly pervasive myth that to dance "young" a dancer needs the experience only age can bring. Someone whom the critics call "the mature artist" is sometimes the performer whose confidence and authority on a stage are as undeniable as the off-peak condition of his technique.

As career lifespans of dancers increase, reputations grow along with sentiments and standards get set by artists whose performances are shaped with nuance but not free from technical compensations. The dance press publicizes and rhapsodizes on these longtimers to such an extent that the dance-watching public keeps its eyes peeled only for these revered and established stars and is incapable of recognizing anyone else in any way other than "pretty good *too.*"

Along with nearly every other example he's set, George Balanchine's lessons about dancers are only slowly being comprehended. As he has advanced and strengthened ballet technique, so has Balanchine reshaped ballet dancers. As he has created numerous original ballerina roles, Balanchine has constructed some as specially challenging for strong, new ballerinas.

By perceptively tailoring parts to the age and development of his company ballerinas, Balanchine provides decided alternatives to less suitable works from other eras in ballet's past. He has no use for what he is said to call "old-lady ballets." So, while a tradition, a press, and a resultant starstruck public reinforce the greatness of familiar stellar dancers, a separate advancement keeps going on.

There is no telling just how big a revelation sixteen-year-old Darci Kistler would have been had she come into the repertory out of the blue. To have gained this particular surprise/pleasure—and I feel insatiable wanting some other sensation in the face of so many Kistler gives—one would have had to be in the New York State Theater in the fall of 1980 completely unaware of various signs and portents.

Initially there had been her performances at fourteen-going-on-fifteen in the *William Tell pas de deux* (Bournonville staged by Stanley Williams) on the School of America Ballet workshop programs in May '79. Then her 1980 performances at fifteen-going-on-sixteen in the same surroundings as the Swan Queen in Alexandra Danilova's staging after Ivanov of *Swan Lake* (Act II).

Kistler had also served, in her first seasons on the company roster, in a few corps de ballet positions. I certainly recall her spindly presence in the Fourth Movement of *Symphony in C.* Just before the New York fall-winter season, Washington, D.C., had gotten the "sixteen-year-old kid" as Odette, Queen of the Swans, in Balanchine's after-Ivanov *Swan Lake* (on opening night, no less) for an October Kennedy Center engagement. There she also made debuts in the Intermezzo of *Brahms-Schoenberg Quartet* and the lead of *Valse Fantaisie.*

So even though company publicity focused no specific attention on Kistler or her assumption of major roles in the repertory, her New York debut can hardly be said to have lacked considerable "advance." Perhaps a case could even be made to define as truly extraordinary only talent that can be submitted to the glare of heated anticipation.

Hypothetically an unheralded Kistler debut would not only have surprised us, it might also have tempered the skepticism of certain in-the-know NYCB watchers who, given the pervasive (and sometimes lamebrained) excitement, chose to remain self-consciously aloof, to recall *other* flashes in the pan, to *wait* and see, or to report matter-of-factly that here was another *nice* young dancer. True, eager-beaver editors were likely raring to concoct and commission "Mr. B and Yet Another Baby Ballerina" fantasies, and excitable balletomanes were getting hysterical. But as the Baryshnikov episode had recently proven, fatuous views of the NYCB scene don't necessarily mean that the object is without significant importance.

Setting the true/false Kistler coin on its edge, I do wonder what the press reaction to Kistler would have been had there not been sufficient warning of something special waiting in the wings of Balanchine's company. When standards for judging dancers are so unsound and unformed, when a certain kind of slippery and rubbery contortionism keeps being called "strong dancing" (see: Cleveland Ballet, International Ballet of Caracas, Ballet Nacional de Cuba), there is no reason to believe that a truly talented and unknown young dancer will be recognized readily.

Whenever a younger dancer is specifically brought along according to Balanchine's advanced technical dictates—displaying long, open reach and simple unemoting straightforwardness—classifications such as "neo" and "personal" are likely to qualify the appraisal, implying that *not* being old-fashioned squared classical is somehow not being "correct." So long as the term "Balanchine dancer" signifies anything peculiar (anything other than highly accomplished, contemporary classical technique), Balanchine and his oeuvre remain grudgingly "acceptable" and basically misunderstood.

By virtue of her talents and her auspices, then, Darci Kistler's professional dancing career began in earnest during the 1980–81 fall-winter New York season. She began by leading other madly dashing maidens with loosed hair through the Scherzo of Balanchine's *Tchaikovsky Suite No. 3.* Beneath her long, iridescent metallic blue skirt you could sense her fine long legs, and in the frequent pauses in piqué effacée arabesque you could see the eagerness of her personality as well as the exactness of her school.

Her pose had the formality of balance and a tingle of excitement. And in spite of the kinetic center in her keenly arched lower back, you saw an equally potent focus in her uplifted head, beaming an openmouthed expression of release. Kistler could not only place herself completely in a pose, she could also project the feel of it to the farthest reaches of the theater. Running/twirling/jumping Kistler worked her thin, pale, long arms with bold, proud carriage; her large fine hands, with animated articulation but not exaggeration.

And, as if her thrilled accents were not embellishment enough, there was her honey amber hair of remarkable texture. Cutting and flaming through the air of her dancing, Kistler's long shining tresses added an extra, uncommon aura; as if in keeping with the image of a shooting star, her unbound hair detailed the afterglow of a trailing radiance. There even appeared to be a kind of calculation to the way her horsetail coiffeur was fixed in its barrette, at an angle: with each flick of her spotting through a turn, Kistler's hair flew away from her excited face in a slashing spiral path.

There followed an extensive series of new and important roles,* but in this initial display of her talent Kistler showed, if not everything in her technical range, then just about every one of the personal distinctions that make her an undeniable star. Scattered through my dozen-or-so years of NYCB watching had been some real and true fresh dance talents, but Kistler's performance in the Scherzo was not just (indeed, in some details, not *really*) a display of prodigious technical accomplishment. From her initial, energetic entrance she showed striking projection, uncontainable eagerness, and winning rapport with her audience. Looking back on this spectacular season one can plot Kistler's progress, pinpoint details, and evaluate her present range and state of development, but what remains a constant factor is that the magic and mystery of star-bright performing were hers, full force, from her first appearance.

The Scherzo of *Suite No. 3* has a single ballerina (in tandem with a danseur) leading an ensemble of eight sisters. Kistler's ensemble was danced by Michelle Bailey, Toni Bentley, Stacy Caddell, Susan Gluck, Julie Hays, Darla Hoover, Dana Lewis, and Roma Sosenko. During its frenzied concluding passage, this dance involves the ensemble maidens from both the Elegie and Valse Melancholique movements—here Evelyn Carton, Lisa Chalmers, Nina Fedorova, Florence Fitzgerald, Linda Homek, Jerri Kumery, Alexia Hess, Elise Ingalls, Cynthia Lochard, Melinda Roy, Barbara Siebert, and Noelle Shader. All of the dancers in this ensemble are older and more experienced than Kistler; most of them are accomplished technically, and many are noticeably gifted. But Kistler remained apart. And beyond her physical and technical attributes and distinctions, she remained in highest relief spiritually. Or is it that all aspects of Kistler the dancer are inseparable from Kistler the star?

When I'm watching her, I am thrilled by the full-blown avidity of her attack, and enchanted by her palpable exuberance. When I recall her, I recollect the open, beaming lift of her face as well as her reaching, stretching expansiveness. The stuff of Kistler's magic, however, is not limited to the charm of her smile or the gutsiness of her timing; at the center of her spirit is the formal solidity of a hardworking but not effortful dancer.

Kistler radiates tangible pleasure in the very act of accomplishment. The

---

*For the record, they are *Swan Lake* (Odette), *The Nutcracker* (Dew Drop and Sugar Plum Fairy), *Walpurgisnacht Ballet* (second girl), *Divertimento No. 15* (LeClercq's role), *Tchaikovsky Suite No. 2* (where several ballerina roles had been combined into one), *Tchaikovsky Suite No. 3* (Scherzo), *Raymonda Variations* (Sumner role), *Symphony in C* (Second Movement), *Suite from Histoire du Soldat, Coppélia* (Dawn), *Chaconne* (Hendl's role). *Brahms-Schoenberg Quartet* and *Valse Fantaisie* were not given in the 1980–81 fall-winter New York season.

forwardness we infer from her headlong urgent attack is a formal element in her weight-front uplifted carriage. Kistler doesn't just rest on top of a point of balance; she seems poised to go over the top. Even the radiance of her coloring is rooted in a fact of form. It glows from the flush of excitement that the physical workout of dancing brings to the translucent surface of her pale skin. Kistler's evident smiles, her wide-eyed looks and openmouthed breaths, are not premeditated, they are immediate and involuntary. The challenges that Balanchine's womanly ballerina roles put to her high-school age of innocence are far from beyond her: the grown-up pressures that go with them sometimes leave her almost giddy but never scared.

Kistler's musical acuity reinforces the edge established by her physical and personal individualities. The attentiveness with which she listens to her music (and here, her somewhat large ears add their own charming note) keeps her on top of every musical cue, and at times, even slightly ahead of them. As she goes through her dances, Kistler's manifest resolution to stay with every element of her enchaînements or every increment of her sustained moves exhibits an unflagging stamina. Her staying power, perhaps the most beneficial of her inherent, youthful attributes, is little short of amazing.

As *The Nutcracker*'s Dew Drop, she unleashed some of her tremendous powers with unaffectedly youthful ease. Executing with wonderful amplitude and barely discernible preparation the various grands jetés that are this role's hallmark, Kistler bounded through the center of the Waltz of the Flowers with a wildflower elegance. As she kicked open to soaring split each of the elementary effacés grands jetés, and grands jetés pas de chat, she rode through the air at a volatile diagonal. To accent the particularities of the grand jeté passé moves that leave the Dew Drop poised in a moment of tendu-front révérence, Kistler combined her forceful kick with a decisive raising of her knees and feet; by high-stepping en l'air before landing to nod en révérence, she marked the distinction between flying and billowing jumps.

She seems not to tire but rather to gain—or at the very least maintain—strengths, even in choreography that taxes her present skills. The tricky finesse of certain designs in the allegro passages of *Divertimento No. 15* obviously presented her with a challenge. Still, she sustained and kept pace with the entire sequence of combinations, even when the absolute execution of their complexities did not lie wholly within her powers. Galloping with her through an allegro combination, you find yourself pleasurably exhausted. Like some benevolent siren's, her keen sense of timing and commitment keeps her just atop the impetus of her moves, and just a touch ahead of our fixing a finished focus on them.

Of all the roles that constituted Kistler's baptism-by-submersion, the one in which any young ballerina would find herself going most against the grain of tradition is *Swan Lake*. Even if Balanchine's own version is less old-fashioned and more suited to contemporary dancers than many current stagings, the NYCB *Swan Lake* still has its own local lore. In it, Kistler scored perhaps her greatest triumph. As a naturally gifted adagio dancer, and a now somewhat restless (as if filled with dramatic "tension") allegro dancer, Kistler took on the challenge of this Odette, and invested it with her unique otherworldly and mysterious powers. Every move she made was large, every stretch long, every retard deep. Her pale skin, fair hair (here golden-looking), and linear, more boney than fleshy, limbs cut an all but translucent figure. Her hands, especially as her delicate wrists articulated them, were at once dance-step finishes and wing tips. Her impulses to open her mouth—and in correspondence to squint her eyes—were transformed without conscious accent into expressions of sighing release and inward reflection.

For every supported penchée arabesque the choreography demanded that she plummet into—all of them here securely and tenderly maintained by the prince-perfect partnering of Sean Lavery—Kistler went down deeply enough each time to touch her head to her knee. Needlessly? Perhaps, but when you see the ease with which she arrives at such deep/tall extremes as these, you realize that it would mean more calculation, not less, for a dancer as rangy and avid as Kistler to hold back from a full, head-down descent.

Kistler is not yet strongly or consistently turned-out in the thighs. The more thoughtful, supported passages of the Swan adagio allowed her to work on her turn-out and to hold her upper legs open. Kistler's limbs—as is characteristic of most adolescent physiques—are marked by more prominently jointed length than soft-curved form, and in much of her performance as the Swan Queen, Kistler's legs showed an additional articulation in the joints. In a simple développé out of a pirouette, she both accented the move and heightened its expansion by lifting her knee clearly *and* working her foot from a relaxed ankle. In pas de bourrée suivi in fifth position, she compensated for her unforcefully turned-over thighs by relaxing and accenting the parts played by her knee, ankle, and metatarsal joints in the move.

The effect, while less clean and fine than the full-leg suppleness achieved when the step is initiated primarily by the front of the pointes (see Suzanne Farrell produce the same move in her choreographies), does have its own drama. Especially since her pointes are so long of toe and so flexible at the metatarsal, Kistler's continuous bourrées exhibit a kind of triple tremolo. The work she does in her foot, her ankle, her knee, and—for that matter—in her hip, does more than permit her a unique mobility and speed; it endows the "broken" line established by these points of sensitivity with a kind of heroic fragility. Because the mechanism of her bourrée suivi moves is so multi-accented, Kistler's Odette travels on a wider base than most other Swan Queens at NYCB, and as she exits facing the wings of the stage, Kistler's open bourrée has a hobbling texture that invests her unwilling departure with a physical pathos.

The most thrilling of Kistler's Swan moments occurred during her entrance in the coda, when she executed some explosive élancés sissonnes that peaked in fearsomely open effacés arabesques. Kistler has a naturally huge jump, and the power and energy of her long feet and legs play a vital part in initiating and expanding all her pas d'élévations. And her diagonal entrance gained further urgency from her drive to stay with the speed *and volume* of Tchaikovsky's tempestuous coda.

For the record—and as food for thought—the Odette solo that Kistler danced is Balanchine's setting of the traditional Ivanov version, and not his own interpolation, which has been a customary feature of NYCB *Swan Lake* in my time. (I understand Maria Tallchief used to perform more or less the version danced now by Kistler.) The enchaînements here include several of those improvements Balanchine has been known to make in other traditional choreography. (Compare the enriched enchaînements in his *Pas de Dix* and *Cortège Hongrois* with the extant *Raymonda* recensions in the Kirov and Bolshoi repertoires.) In the diagonal that traditionally repeats twice two sissonnes leading to a relevé/developpé/arabesque pause, Balanchine saves the relevé/developpé/arabesque to finish only the second set of sissonnes. He substitutes a pas de bourrée on pointes through deliberate, high retiré, where the first pose in arabesque traditionally comes.

Kistler was seen to equally sumptuous advantage in the adagios of the Second Movement of *Symphony in C* and *The Nutcracker* grand pas de deux. The Bizet adagio was executed with thrilling physicality, but most memorable was its tone—Kistler sustained it as one long *happy* experience instead of as the more usual dreamy one. The Sugar Plum told us a great deal about the process and completeness with which Kistler works on a role.

In a performance at the beginning of *Nutcracker* season, Kistler was partnered by Ib Andersen. It was not a well-matched partnership. In repose, they were of complementary size, but when Kistler began to build and fill out the adagio moves with far-reaching extensions and impetuous timings, Andersen found himself outdistanced. Try as he would—and he did, valiantly—his medium frame could not encompass and secure the outgrowing amplitude of Kistler's scale. Their performance was a sequence of unsecured penchés, unsteady balances, and uncentered promenades. But did Kistler freeze or shrink? Not on her life! If anything, each missed moment sent her off to the next with even more reach and a bolder accent. And as if this example of fearlessness were not enough, she took the occasion of a later performance opposite a more appropriately scaled (and—one imagines—rehearsed) Peter Martins, to reveal what she'd learned from her performances with Andersen.

Nearly everything about this subsequent performance was rethought. Most striking was the moment when she's mechanically pulled along in arabesque. And it was not simply a matter of Martins' larger frame and hand being able to steady her. Her left leg—the working leg for this ride from stage left to stage right in first arabesque—is noticeably, imperfectly bowed out from the knee to the ankle. In the performance with Andersen, not only was her hip unsteadily held open, the line completing her arabesque was unpleasantly odd. By the time of this, her last performance as the Sugar Plum, she had *re*-placed her arabesque, and succeeded in holding it in a way that was markedly straighter and calm. No doubt Balanchine (and possibly Martins) took some part in helping her effect this change, but Kistler was the one who carried it off, and the triumph was properly hers.

Her formidable repertory has already offered up countless pleasures. The new challenges Balanchine has worked into her *Raymonda* variation (originally Sumner's) are of the more-difficult-to-accomplish variety—specifically, a series of grands jetés de côté that finish through renversé half-turns in attitude. Alas, what has gone are some straightforward grands jetés that—given Kistler's natural and easy elevation—used to be brilliantly light and breathtaking in their simplicity and largeness of design.

As the "Bergère" in the divertissement duet of *Chaconne,* Kistler was happy, delicate, and forthright. Particularly in the final daunting double attitude turn—the one on demi-plié pointe that begins with a push-off from her partner's outstretched arm—Kistler pulled the attitude into keenly lifted passé while she spun around on a confidently relaxed plié. And when stopped by her partner to pose and finish in fully extended position again, Kistler reopened her attitude at an even stronger height, balancing through a richer demi-plié and a more knuckled-over pointe, and capped it all with an almost laughing backward cast to her head and a Bolshoi palm-up flex for her hand.

As soloist (Heather Watts' role) to the ballerina in *Walpurgisnacht Ballet,* Kistler enjoys perhaps her most jeune fille part and gets to share her stage with Farrell. (I don't know what early Farrell was like, but without taking any originality away from either mature or baby ballerina, I wonder if the sly calm of latter-day Farrell grew out of an uncontainable delight like the young Kistler's.) In *Walpurgisnacht,* Kistler's luxuriant hair is tied back at first, then loose. When she prances in her chiffon shift and paces happily through her steps, it's with a special, informal radiance. The plain-faced relevé/grand battement steps Balanchine wants here become at once elementary and fantastic from Kistler. Given the astounding freedom of her hip for seconde position (and this in a company where sky-high secondes are a rule, not an exception) the climax of Kistler's kick must be called penultimate. As enlivened by her unaffected enthusiasm, Kistler's springing-and-kicking action is truly thrilling—to describe her working leg as "fly-away" is not exaggerated, nor even adequate.

Eventually, with cheerful nonchalance and aplomb, she hops through a series of elancés changements on pointe. And just as with her characteristic pas de bourrée suivi, in these sweetly spiky jumps, Kistler shows very delicately relaxed ankles and keeps her feet very heels-front, turned over. In effect these very turned-over-from-the-ankle steps keep Kistler's fifth so neat and sharp that each closed, changed position becomes as witty as it is virtuosic. All through this brief but by no means simple dance—a series of sautés passés also shows off the clarity and brilliance of her long, sharp feet—there is the feeling of playfulness between Kistler and her steps, Kistler and her choreographer, and Kistler and her audience.

There is no denying that some part of the exuberance and pride that Kistler projects stems from the great faith and interest Balanchine has shown in her. And the master ballet master will no doubt continue to show his interest as long as Kistler responds in kind. We cannot but see Kistler's early greatness in relation to Balanchine's enduring greatness. The future possibilities that exist between this dancer and her dancemaster are doubly promising and twice as unpredictable. If the ballerina in Kistler isn't wondrous enough already, maybe the wonder of ballet dancing holds no power over you.

—from *Ballet Review,* Summer 1981

PATRICIA MCBRIDE
Robert Greskovic

Patricia McBride joined New York City Ballet in 1959 and was made a principal in 1961. Immensely popular with the audience, she danced a huge portion of the Balanchine-Robbins repertory, often with her equally charismatic partner Edward Villella. Balanchine created the "Rubies" section of Jewels *on them, as well as* Tarantella *and the leading roles in* Harlequinade. *Among her other triumphs: Balanchine's* Who Cares? *and (as the girl in pink) Robbins's* Dances at a Gathering. *Her husband, Jean-Pierre Bonnefoux, was also a principal in the company.*

A skull-capped head of close-fitting hair, an unbreakable mask of makeup, bony arms, a slim torso fitted on an elongated, slightly S-shaped spine (where the po-po sticks out), flat thighs, knobby knees, and hyper-arched feet, and these are the physical qualities of a prima ballerina assoluta— Patricia McBride. Now a dancer at the beginning of her peak, McBride is unequaled; she is parts dancer/musician, flesh/steel, fragility/strength.

Certainly she is part of a perfect trinity—Balanchine/Ballet/McBride. McBride is post-Renaissance plastique, her configurations are at once Mannerist, Baroque, and Rococo. Architectural and painterly. Her physical distortions extend their classical form like a Madonna del Collo Lungo, her imposition and command on stage have the advancing and receding thrust of a marble staircase, and her delicately flourished façade has all the celestial arabesques of a gilded boudoir canopy. She is the perfect *example concrète* of the unlimited possibilities that Balanchine is creating with the ballet vocabulary. McB is a separate part of Balanchine's Ballet of the Twentieth Century.

McB produces choreography from her body, her way! Exposed and displayed with visible physical proud energy.

She is all joints, points and curves, and all lines. She uses her protruding knees and backside as positive elements of her filigree line. She can curve, curl, and straighten in any of Balanchine's most complex inventions, comfortably. Her points are not just for standing and posing, they're the ultimate end of an arc, her foot. She balances on them, rocks over them, digs with them, etches with them, or multi-flexes down from them.

In preparation from fourth position, especially as a finish from a jump, she is breathtaking. She doesn't adjust forward in her plié (downward) movement. In this fourth position plié or lunge preparation, her already forward weight smoothly sinks, angled down and back, resting until she springs perfectly to point and flashes through a multiple pirouette, tour, or jeté. Her spot sparkles each time her head times itself front. Aided by the flowers and glitter she often wears at the base of her neck, the effect McB gives is one of light refracting from the core of a faceted gem. She gives her audience acknowledgment as a bonus spot with her glance of glamour over her smooth and forward-leading épaulement.

Any manège of anything with McB is a totally undistracted, unblinking mesmerizing experience, till she lets you loose. Does anyone anywhere do more musical fouetté, chaîné, or piqué turns? These are the most hypnotic of McB's hypnotizing moments. She lets the music's speed spin her attack, note for note, with her exquisitely controlled turning ability. With McB it's not *turns* that excite, it's *these* turns that the music's moment describes that she sells. They're special in their moment in time. McB always sells *now*.

The upward curve of her body in sauté in arabesque traveling back would make watching her up close an impossibility. Two eyes plus two more would not be enough to follow the multiple directions and arcs her body takes in this simple jump.

Her point work is sharp, brilliant, and strong and, because of her hyper-arched feet, she can come off their minute base softly, with at least one extra metatarsal joint of transition. There is always that small amount of light under her points as she springs (jumps) sous sous, and "through the foot" is McB's first nature. In bourrées her legs ripple from toe through thigh. Energized by her incredibly workable front foot, they undulate through her crescent-shaped feet, cross fully at the heels and relaxed ankles, cushion in and out flexes of her concave, convex knees and re-re-cross through her flat thighs ending quietly in the lifted slight curve of her lower back.

All of this "technique" could have made her a kind of physical freak or phenomenon without her genius as a stage personality. Her makeup mask is unbreakable, her cheeks are smoothly blushed, her eye outlines and shadows are dark and strong. But her face is not frozen. She has three deliberate openings in her mask—eyes and mouth. Her eyes are framed and luxuri-ously lashed, but their light and life direct her attention outside, to our world. Her mouth is comfortably sweet in smiles or relaxations. These three lights give McB the openings that make her Columbine of "Harlequinade" a porcelain figurine with an impish soul. In this full-length role, she uses Balanchine's dictated movements as the character development he intended. She acknowledges her Harlequin with a different smile from the one that is an aside to her audience. Her focus shifts from those on stage to those off with her direct and clear lines of vision.

As the "Rubies" Woman, McB has no name, no specific character, she responds to the "red" of it all with a carefree good nature. It's a romp that she enjoys, and her flashing eyes and sweetly smirking mouth reflect the fun and games. Never a hint from her expression that it's all fiercely complex. She shows no tension to freeze her mask; she's without name but never without life.

As the *femme romantique* in the second movement of *Brahms-Schoenberg Quartet* she becomes less a person and more her movement. She lets her movement become the metaphor. Her trusting backbend, baring her chest to the audience, becomes the embrace. Her stillness in the arched pose caught on her partner's chest is not so much lifeless as anonymous. Her swoons to the lowest point of "his" support are that gesture, not *who's* doing it. McBride doesn't have an affair onstage; she presents the physical intima-cies of it. We don't know who she is, but we know what she's doing. She emphasizes the points of physical contact—her head on his shoulder, her torso against his, her back arching over his arm.

In Tchaikovsky's piano Concerto No. 2 McB is a leader. She's front and center expelling more energy than the combined-forces corps behind her. She leads them in a series of ballottés or brisés with their collected energies flowing through her movements. She acknowledges with calm bravery her position, and lets loose for everyone to know.

Through all these roles somewhere there comes an "I'm glad you love my love of dancing." At times when another dancer would be frantic, McB is excitedly content. She attacks the music with a complete knowledge of her body's range. In McB's oneness with music you can see muscle memory. She rarely thinks about her technical prowess, she actually seems to forget it. But she forgets everything only because she has learned everything. She entrusts herself completely to the music. Her fearlessness with her body is based in her total trust of the music.

Even in partnered sequences, McB acknowledges the music first. She's rarely "lifted" by a partner. He guides her jumps. Once at the crest of a lift, McB releases her energy, and poses a "lift" high and arched. She holds herself abandoned. She gives her partners no choice but to lift her high, she jumps to that height and trusts them to support her in finish, flight.

Or in her run-off exits, she breezes off stage with her legs lifting for the run but her heels remembering to lift front; thus McB runs and does emboîté.

McB is power and person. She brings to each moment on stage a pre-conditioned and trained body and abandons herself to it for the music's moment. Each performance is a new experience for me because she gives each time/space its moment's due. McB takes chances with forethought. She's never on a private trip but always a new one.

—from *Ballet Review*, 1978–1979

PETER MARTINS
Robert Greskovic

Born and trained in Denmark (his autobiography is titled Far from Denmark*), Peter Martins was already a major dancer when he joined New York City Ballet in 1970, partnering Suzanne Farrell in* Apollo. *That partnership became one of the most famous in world ballet, but his striking looks and superb skills would, on their own, have guaranteed Martins a leading position in the company. In the early eighties he assumed responsibility for running City Ballet, and has created scores of ballets for it, beginning with the striking* Calcium Light Night. *In 1991 he married ballerina Darci Kistler.*

Peter Martins is one of the dancers that I use to refute the "unnatural quality of ballet" argument. Of course it could be argued that his ideal physique is "unnatural" or at least "untypical," but certainly the ease and casualness of Martins' perfection of ballet movement is by and of itself "natural" looking. So much so that he is the perfect dancer-example for someone who has never seen ballet. Peter Martins is: turnout, placement, port de bras, épaulement, batterie, arabesque, attitude, pirouette, jeté, sauté, fouetté. He is: elegance, stretch, flex, point, noble, prince, classique. He is the finest male classical dancer in America today. He exemplifies the beauty, power, and mystique of the classical ballet vocabulary on its own (classroom) terms. The smooth perfection and control of his long body produce on stage a series of ballet pictures, perfect. He points and stretches his limbs with ease and casualness, extending his already towering physicality to superhuman lengths. He is an ideal of an ideal. He is what Americans think of as European, refined, bred, and aristocratic. He moves with an equal displacement of energy to all his body parts. He holds positions and executes steps with equalized coordination. Martins never attacks in the forceful sense of the word, he presents. He is aware of his positive physical command of space.

Part of the ease, simplicity, and casualness of Martins comes from his incredible ballon. Because of his tall physique he is able to get a lift from his long legs, but the careful and pliant use of his feet allows him to calculate his power in the air serenely and return through the softest plié one would ever want to see. His movement quality is soft and creamy; he lowers his chin and his glance; he exhales his épaulement and hovers from step to step. When he executes a series of beats in the air or crosses allegro changes on the ground, his total lack of tension or strain gives his arc or movement path a quality like a boomerang. I see the path all his activity makes rather than the activities themselves. His better-than-quintuple pirouette in plié in *Goldberg Variations* looks like a top whirring and accelerating from a hairline spiral axis. He takes the preparation into the stage with his plié and grows from it, spinning, and returns through deeper plié for a perfectly front still finish.

His free and easy hip joint gives him hip-level arabesques and attitudes with no visible amount of push to get there. His Bournonville background gives him not only perfect beats but also full-circled *ronds de jambes en l'air*. His elegance in performance is equally exquisite as dancer and as partner. He accounts in part for the heightened sense of elegance in his partner.

Here I admit Kay Mazzo, his frequent partner. Whenever he partners her he shows her off to her best advantage. His rock-solid placement and constant line enhance, anchor, and complement hers. When he points tendu while holding her in arabesque penchée, or promenade, as in *The Nutcracker* pas de deux, he extends his line by securing hers. She seems less timid, less sketchy, when he's securing her. She seems to trust him more than she trusts herself and gives more energy to her own body parts. It is these moments that make Mazzo a more rich and full dancer. Her placed trust in Martins's partnering seems to free her and give her body movement more life and energy.

As a solo performer Martins shows the varying degrees of impact that the energy of his dancing gives to a role. As Apollo (he *was* born to dance this role) he is superb, using his casual arrogance to execute the steps, poses, and partnering as a young god. He is aware of his regal being and nonchalantly breezes through the role, amused. He doesn't so much smile as look content, he basks in the ease with which he tosses off jumps and turns. His fair hair and light eyes complete any of his pastel costumes as an equal value that fills the space like heavy perfume. In the first movement of *Brahms-Schoenberg Quartet* or as *The Nutcracker* Cavalier, Peter Perfect Pastel Martins looks every inch the role even before he breathes and breezes through any of their intricate combinations.

Martins never stares his audience down, never snaps around any turns; he is never angled or sharp but always slightly croisé, slightly rounded or softened, like a finely serifed capital letter from the Trajan Column. His movements are clear and clean but not brilliant or hard, and this is perhaps all that is missing on occasion from a dancer of his ability. Sometimes his perfection of placement, casual turn and tilt of his head or downward glance leave me perfectly content rather than excitedly alive.

—from *Ballet Review*, 1978–1979

KYRA NICHOLS
Claudia Roth Pierpont

The career of Kyra Nichols, from 1974 to 2007, is one of the most illustrious in New York City Ballet's history. She was quickly recognized for her rock-steady technique and her aplomb—the most demanding roles, such as those in Tchaikovsky Piano Concerto No. 2 *and* Theme and Variations, *seemed effortless for her—but as her career progressed, she transformed herself into a noted dramatic dancer as well, in such ballets as* Davidsbündlertänze *and* Liebeslieder Walzer. *When she chose to retire, after thirty-three years, she was still a commanding presence.*

Kyra Nichols is justly celebrated as the current glory of the company. A genuine ballerina in the fullest flush of her dancing life, she is at that perfect conjunction of body and mind when youth just verges on maturity, and we are as struck by her performing intelligence as by the limitless technique that manifests it. When one speaks of the company's strength in the more traditional repertory these days, one could perhaps point more simply to the advent and development of Nichols. Although she dances a variety of roles, the heart of her repertory is in such works as *Raymonda Variations* and *La Source, Tchaikovsky Piano Concerto No. 2 (Ballet Imperial)*, and *Divertimento No. 15*, and as both Dewdrop and Sugar Plum in *The Nutcracker*—Balanchine's most direct re-creations of the ballerina tradition. In these roles she assimilates his most radical departures from that tradition—the speed, the complexities of phrase and rhythm, the flashing batterie—as so natural and so lightly won that they seem to have been there always, within the tradition itself. Her stylistic eloquence is royalist rather than revolutionary: she introduces and fulfills new standards in classical dancing in terms of absolute continuity with the old, without any threat of dissolution or of the breaking of bonds. She is the golden mean. By the generations-old standards of classical dance, Nichols is perfectly proportioned, perfectly centered and placed. Perfection is where her art begins, but only begins—her dancing has all the force of an original gift, not a learned reaction. This is the very thing that makes her succession to the position of exemplary ballerina at New York City Ballet so momentous a change. She is the first ballerina of our time to dance, in Balanchine's company, as though Suzanne Farrell had never happened, and she can do it now in some of Farrell's most personal repertory.

In the past few years, the great Farrell roles have been divided among the company's leading ballerinas. These are rich but problematic gifts—like jewels bought for a first wife, they are dangerously liable to summon loving memories of another. How to divorce Farrell herself—the body, the mannerisms, the inner music—from the roles is a challenge that has been met in a variety of ways; to generalize, Merrill Ashley (in *Chaconne* and *Diamonds*) often seems to go to battle with Farrell's effects, while Maria Calegari (in *Mozartiana* and *Davidsbündlertänze*) re-creates them. Both have given us moments of triumphant beauty in the midst of our longings for the great original. They have performed valiantly under a long shadow, and each delivers something new with every passing season. . . .

Nichols has been dancing her single Farrell role, in *Walpurgisnacht Ballet,* for several seasons now. This glorious teapot-tempest of a work was whipped up for the Paris Opéra's production of Gounod's *Faust* in 1975, about six months after Farrell returned to City Ballet. Balanchine may well have projected Farrell onto his Opéra exercise at the time, and he mounted it for her at NYCB in 1980. It is a role well suited to Nichols' gifts: its two ballerina solos are composed of the most purely academic stuff, made witty and "French" by a continual play of accent on and off the heavily stressed beat. Nichols performs all the steps with accents so different from Farrell's that nothing looks or even sounds the same; what was climactic once is now lightly passed over, and new climaxes emerge. In the series of développés à la seconde in the second variation, for example, Nichols does not hold the leg at the top of its height, as Farrell did with those enormous swinging steps, but pauses instead for a moment on the way down, with the leg in passé. The teasing rubato remains, but the emphasis is no longer on that highly unstable diagonal of leg poised overhead, threatening to topple the whole figure; stability is restored. And just when stability seems a comparatively homely virtue, Nichols finishes the variation with a series of turns made so dazzlingly light and fast—even terre à terre she is in the air—that the audience laughs in pleasure just as with Farrell's développés. All on her own terms, Nichols captures the wry exaggeration of effect that Balanchine and Farrell put into the work.

It is only in the fire-and-brimstone finale that Nichols' choices and inclination toward evenness of tone don't leave her room to make up for the sacrifice of drama: the driving diagonal of piqué turns that lances the stage from wing to wing is done without acceleration, and she doesn't dig into the ground and let rip as Farrell did in the great kick-line formation that follows. The ballet's final image remains stamped with Farrell's physical impress: at the head of a gathering wedge-formation of the corps, leading the charge, she leaps onto her partner's shoulder, one leg folded under, while the free leg swings out and around to lock behind in arabesque as her arm arches overhead. The rounded weight and length of Farrell's cantilevered leg, the extraordinary force of its rotation swinging out from the hip in an open arc, front to back, gave this isolated movement the power of a cannon maneuvering on a battlement. As one watched the ballet this winter, with an awareness of Farrell's catastrophic hip condition, it was almost a relief to see that Nichols does not reproduce that sense of sweep and might; the emphasis is again transferred, this time from the movement to the final pose, the arabesque aloft brightly pointing a direction as in the finale of *Allegro Brillante*.

Nichols took on a second Farrell role this season, a major one: *Diamonds*, the section of *Jewels* so specifically and idiomatically crafted for Farrell that it has long seemed less a role than an occasion to admire those unique gifts. *Diamonds* has seemed several sizes too big for other dancers who have tried it, slipping from their shoulders and leaving them bare, at a loss for occupation (Ashley) or else filling in with fussy details (Kay Mazzo). There was only one reason to think that Nichols would have better success: Tchaikovsky's music, his third and only major-key symphony.

Not that Farrell's Tchaikovsky is Nichols' Tchaikovsky. Farrell would doubtless have been the most contrary of Auroras, to judge by her performances in the nearest pendant in her own repertory, *Nutcracker*'s Sugar Plum Fairy. For all the glories of her performance, Farrell couldn't fit herself inside this role: she was too big, used up too much space, and her geometry veered off into spirals when it ought to have held to neat circles. A great Swan Queen, she was too bold and dangerous a dancer for Sugar Plum. When Balanchine choreographed *Diamonds* for Farrell in 1967, he added another mid-twentieth-century sister to the catalogue of Tchaikovsky heroines, one closest to the Swan in metaphor and shape and tragic sense, but incorporating the dangers and the exaggerations and the extended geometrics of Farrell. Nichols, with none of these qualities at her command, and a long list of nearly opposing virtues, took full possession of the role from her first performance. It was, however, a different role, recreated in her own image. Here was no Swan; the tragedy was gone. Instead, Nichols adapted another model from within the music, barely suspected before: in her open radiance and clarity she was, in type, a new Aurora. And in terms of the specific models of her own Balanchine roles, she was a new Dewdrop—it has been in that brief soloist role, conjured by Balanchine from Tchaikovsky's Waltz of the Flowers, that Nichols has given her most astonishingly buoyant performances up to now.

Dewdrop's role in the waltz is all flying entrances and exits, bursts of allegro punctuation, while the essence of *Diamonds* is an adagio of particularly cool grandeur. How does Nichols transfer the life of one to the other? By maintaining a carriage and a line so uplifted and taut that in *Diamonds* she quivered and shimmered even in stillness, so that expectation and impetus were part of every pose, every movement, and the inner flow of the adagio— even in the great sculpted images of flight—was quickened by the ceaseless pulse of her energy running through it. The plucked strings that resonate beneath the rest of the orchestra had their counterpart in her continuous vibration. Exultant, almost laughing, she brought out all the colors of the music—bursts of pinks and blues and yellows—where with Farrell what we saw was silver and whitest white. As with *Walpurgisnacht,* the accents and the geometry of the role became almost unrecognizable. When Farrell's partner would suddenly release her with full momentum into a single unsupported spin in low arabesque, we felt the vertiginous pull from the axis, the threat and exhilaration of the widening gyre. Nichols' axis is so surely vertical, even when swinging free in a loose and chancy turn like this, that she seems suspended from above by a golden thread, running right down her spine. One is reminded of how in Dewdrop's waltz she emerges from a series of tightly brilliant fouetté turns with a diminuendo into a lazy-susan of a turn in attitude, nearly lolling about her axis with an impudent ease. This ability to make changes in speed or direction or scale without interrupting the flow, as happens in music, is the essence of Balanchine's stylistic legacy; it unites his dancers under the skin, beneath all variations of body and temperament. It is what Nichols' dancing finally has in common with Farrell's, and what makes her *Diamonds* equally truthful. Only in the scherzo, of all places, does something seem to be missing, not because of a lack of brilliance but because of a lack of contrast. Farrell's quick keenness and edge, following upon her vast dream of an adagio, came as a shock; in Nichols' performance, the glittering qualities of the scherzo are already apparent in the adagio.

If the relentless sunniness of this description of Nichols seems too one-dimensional, it is important to note that it is only one aspect—albeit the most fully developed one—of the artist. Where she has ventured into another type of ballet, she has shown a darkly dramatic gift that is astonishing in its strength and honesty, as in *Liebeslieder Walzer* and *La Valse,* and most of all in her monumental, sorrowing performance in Karin von Aroldingen's role in *Davidsbündlertänze.* Who could have imagined that performance before it happened? It is also worth recalling for a moment that Nichols has performed all of her wonders almost entirely in other people's roles; Balanchine did not live to create for her. Peter Martins had the insight to try to fuse the dramatic and technical dimensions of her gift in the 1985 *Poulenc Sonata;* her role was a fine showcase, but Martins neglected to put a ballet around it. One of the most immediate and nagging of our boundless losses in Balanchine's death is that we will never know how he would have burnished this most golden girl.

—from *Ballet Review,* Spring 1988

VIOLETTE VERDY
B. H. Haggin

Having trained in France, where she was born, Violette Verdy danced for several companies before joining New York City Ballet in 1958. Balanchine, clearly impressed by her supreme musicality and wit, created for her a series of important roles in, among other ballets, Tchaikovsky Pas de Deux, La Source, Sonatine, Liebeslieder Walzer, A Midsummer Night's Dream *(the great pas de deux from the second act), and most famously the "Emeralds" section of* Jewels. *She was also in the original cast of Robbins's* Dances at a Gathering. *After her retirement, in 1977, she served as the director of the Paris Opéra Ballet.*

Wondering what the dancer's eye was aware of in Verdy's dancing, in addition to the elegance and style that enchanted the non-dancer's eye, I asked members of the company.* One of them, recalling Verdy's first movement of *Symphony in C,* said: "It was so elegant, with such quality; and the phrasing—the way she fell off those points! It's beautiful to see someone fall when she *wants* to fall and *controls* the fall; and it's one of the hardest things to do. It's hard enough just to find the balance; and some dancers just hit it and go on. But Verdy gets the value out of *reaching* the point, and *phrasing* it: of getting up to it, and hitting it, and then going off it. And that's finished dancing."

*Actually only Villella.

It was such details that the dancers spoke of—"these small, delicate things," as one of them put it. Thus, at the beginning of the Tchaikovsky *Pas de Deux*, "she steps back, back, back—and rests; then she begins the first phrase—pirouettes—and looks down; and just the tilt of the head is so sweet and right." Or, later in that piece, "she goes upstage and her partner pulls her: she goes just far enough—then turns and is back to him." Again, in that piece, "the skirt of her costume flows and floats in the same way she does; and it's an extraordinary thing that she can make her body act like this soft material." And in the *passés* she does at one point, there is the way she uses her eyes: "It's a very small thing to think of when you're making a performance; but it's a big thing from the audience's point of view. Very few realize it and understand it; but Verdy does. When she does this *passé, passé,* hold, it's not only the foot and the leg and the body and the arms, but the eyes too, with everything reaching the same point in time perfectly. And in the *passé* it's not just the foot and leg moving up from the stage to the knee: she brings them up as though they bounced right from the music. Another example of this feeling for music comes near the end of the piece, where she does some turns, then stops, but doesn't really stop: she hits that final pose with the music, but as the music continues and diminishes her arms and fingertips are still going with it, then the air just beyond her fingertips: her movement goes through her body, her arms, her fingertips, and pushes the air a bit, before it ends."

These last details come from someone for whom "the most distinctive thing about Verdy is the musical quality she has. It's an extraordinary, complete musical understanding, almost like Balanchine's in the way she can make you *see* the music. She did that with the first movement of *Episodes*. I didn't understand the score; but when I watched her I could understand the music and could see what Balanchine was after. Certain lunges didn't make sense—choreographic sense—to me when I saw someone else at rehearsal just lunge and turn, lunge and turn. Then I saw Verdy do them, and I said, 'Of course.' When she lunged and turned I saw a motivation for the lunge and turn—both in visual terms and in relation to the music."

This musical understanding, one dancer thought, had a great deal to do with "the amazing way Verdy understands a new role and develops it immediately, as soon as it is started. I have to learn the steps and the counts and digest them, and bring something to the role after that; but she brings something to it while she's learning the steps: you can see her doing it. I remember when a dancer was showing her the steps of a role: when Verdy repeated them they weren't just the steps any more, the way she suddenly brought them alive and made things happen and explode."

The musical understanding works with what she has as a dancer. "She has natural gifts for dancing," someone said. "Her feet are good, with a wonderful turn-out, which is so difficult to acquire. Her legs are good; her body is in good proportion, with the size and length of the legs right for the rest of the body; her head is the right size; the contour of the arm is nice. All these things make for the overall picture. In addition she knows her way, so to speak, around the stage—which is important. And she looks beautiful on the stage: she can make herself look absolutely lovely—and chic, really chic— on the stage. Whereas off-stage she's just not interested: she has her heart and her soul and her life in this thing called ballet—this theater business. In Russia, when we had a performance at eleven in the morning, she would be in the theater at eight, preparing, and doing her makeup for an hour and a half.

"Also, she is a thinking dancer; and because she works with her mind as well as her body, she works well by herself. It's important to take your classes—to feed on that steady diet of technique; but you also have to be able to work alone; and this is something Verdy does very well. She knows her body, and what she has to give it; and the only trouble is that she may get so involved in her work that she will go too far and knock herself out. She does a bar for an hour and a half, where ordinarily a bar is thirty-five min- utes. Then she does floor work; then she goes back to the bar with toe shoes. She has all this fantastic discipline, this fantastic dedication to the essentials that have to be worked at day in and day out. It's easy to get by on a slim diet of work, and many dancers do; but the really great dancers are the ones who work on absolutely everything, and who work with their minds as well as their bodies, like Verdy. Erik Bruhn is an incredible dancer; but he didn't just happen to get that way. The same with Verdy: she's not a great dancer because she just happened to become one, but because she faced and accepted the challenge, the demands of the endless thing that goes on day after day, with all the small details that are so hard to keep up and keep going. Just the carriage of the hand: it has to be worked on; and Verdy has the will to work on it. And everything else: the holding of the head, the ease here, the strength there, the stretch here, the pull there—everything."

What this endless work produces was described by a dancer to whom I spoke admiringly of Verdy's *Swan Lake*. "It's terrible when you are excited by someone who is dancing beautifully, and then you see a hand or a look of the head that is wrong. You want to see a complete performance: that's beauty! that's art! And a complete performance that isn't calculated—that is spontaneous, that just happens. Verdy gives you that. And she gives it to you in *Stars and Stripes* as well as *Swan Lake*. Some dancers are good only in certain things: they are lyric dancers, or dramatic dancers, or romantic dancers, or *demi-caractère* dancers. But Verdy is such a rounded dancer that I can see her doing any role. The remarkable thing, in fact, is that this French dancer, coming here to another style and another repertoire, has pointed up Balanchine's intentions in certain roles more than any of his other dancers. She's brought out things in roles that no one ever saw—that were always there, and that I'm sure Balanchine wanted to begin with, but that other dancers just didn't bring out. She made a great impression on the company because everything she did she made her own—she made a real performance of. She did it right from the start with the first thing she danced, the first movement of *Symphony in C:* it was *never* danced so well. She did it with *Firebird:* that was absolutely superb! She put it on and wore it: when she came out on stage she was that bird! And she did it with roles that were dull, that nobody wanted to dance, and that she made fantastic. The first movement of *Western Symphony,* for example: it's not very distinctive, but she completely understood it and took the western thing with her French flair, so that she got all the humor out of it that was intended and made it a scream. The same with *Stars and Stripes:* instead of just a bunch of girls running around with her leading them, she made it into a real parade, baton-twirling situation, and interesting thing, with her darting in and out and livening up the atmosphere."

There was more; but these are the most important things I was told about Verdy.

—from *Ballet Chronicle,* 1970

EDWARD VILLELLA
Arlene Croce

Edward Villella interrupted his studies at the School of American Ballet to acquire a degree from the New York Maritime Academy. He joined City Ballet in 1957 and became a principal in 1960, thrilling audiences with his virile athleticism. He was the original "Rubies" boy; Oberon in A Midsummer Night's Dream; *the Brown Boy in* Dances at a Gathering; *the central figure in* Watermill; *and the male lead (opposite his favorite partner, Patricia McBride) in* Harlequinade *and* Tarantella *and in "Rubies." His signature role, however, was as the Prodigal Son, which Balanchine revived for him in 1960 and after which Villella titled his memoirs. After retiring from dancing, Villella ran several ballet companies until, in 1986, he founded the Miami City Ballet.*

Edward Villella was an event from the moment he first appeared, a new member of the New York City Ballet, in the winter of 1957. His first solo role was in *Afternoon of a Faun*. Jerome Robbins is said to have based the Faun on Villella as a ballet student and the image he called up of Nijinsky. I didn't see that début; my first glimpse of the newcomer was in another Robbins ballet, *Interplay,* that same winter. Villella was the boy in the orange sweater—not one of the leads—and I shall never forget him sailing backwards through space in the hugest jump I had ever seen and landing quietly in his place in the lineup. The jump isn't in the choreography; at least, when I see *Interplay* today I never notice it. So Villella must have exaggerated or otherwise transformed some commonplace aerial step to produce the sensational effect I have remembered for twenty-five years.

Exaggeration in a young dancer of extraordinary gifts usually precedes a period of great growth. From the wild, happy excess that characterized the twenty-one-year-old Villella to the achieved artistry of Oberon in *A Midsummer Night's Dream,* it is only five years. What a joyride those years were—the City Center years. For $3.95, the top price, one could sit in the orchestra and not see the dancers' feet or sit upstairs, where latecomers blocked one's view of the opening ballet, which would be *Serenade* or *The Four Temperaments* or *Divertimento No. 15* or *Apollo.* Villella danced in none of these except the last. By the time he made his début in *Apollo,* in the winter of 1964, he was a mature performer, famous throughout the world. He had described, in his own progress as a dancer, the course Apollo takes from raw expression to full command of his art. Yet Villella's natural qualities were always apparent and did not change. He continued to enlarge, transform, reinterpret elements of classical style. But his effects were no longer specialties; they were part of a continuous demonstration of extreme capacity in the service of a coherent vision. He had grown up to his talent.

If Villella's art was reflected in *Apollo,* his life was reflected in *The Prodigal Son.* Villella had emerged during the period of Rebels Without Causes in America and Angry Young Men in England, and he made his first major début on the brink of a turbulent decade, when the term "generational revolt" would come to describe a stock attitude of political protest. Villella's revolt in *The Prodigal Son* was without petulance. You saw passion in the headlong drive to destruction. You saw the true innocence and natural elegance of the soul that was imperilled.* All this Villella showed vividly and

---

*Villella conveyed this point with great precision in the pas de trois for the Son and his two servants which comes in the scene where they are greeted by the gargoyles. The delicacy of Villella's dancing here, stepping from second into wide fourths and turning in attitude, and then sweeping into sautés pirouettes à la seconde, was a revelation after the near-brutal muscularity of his rebellion in the first scene.

easily. The last part of the ballet, The Return Home, was the part he worked on. Villella had bucked social convention to be a dancer; he had defied his parents for a number of years; to some extent, differing over goals and training, he defied his master Balanchine. The ballet *The Prodigal Son* had been created by Balanchine years before, for Diaghilev's Ballets Russes. The Prodigal is largely a mime role, and Villella had to learn how to play it. It says much for his intuitive understanding of the subject that he was able from the beginning to move his audiences using so little of the flashy athleticism they were by now paying to see.

Balanchine let the rebel work his way into the part without supervision. Not until after the début did he call Villella to rehearsal. The dramatic aspects of the role were never defined; Balanchine would watch Villella do the crawl home and say something like "Think of Russian icons."

"That idea began to solidify the style for me," Villella has recalled. "It led me to find a new way of holding my head or stretching my neck. There was a way to stylize the head and the hands in a moment of pleading. The look became a quality for me."

Balanchine's laissez-faire attitude turned out to be a blessing to Villella. It released the dancer's initiative and touched off his imagination. The role of the Prodigal as we see it danced today (even by so redoubtable a performer as Mikhail Baryshnikov) has been very largely shaped by Edward Villella.

In those years, while Villella was becoming a star, Balanchine tended to use his prowess in high jumps as a feature of spectacular closing ballets. In *Symphony in C*, Villella entered flying. For years afterward, at precisely the same moment in the third movement, audiences would respond clamorously not only to the height of the leap and its perfection of form but to the illusion of sustained flight: Villella just seemed to keep on climbing and riding air the whole time he was on the stage. He also danced the "Thunderer" section of *Stars and Stripes*—who can forget him flashing his grin and saluting as he bounded between the ranks of leaping cadets?—and, until it was deleted, the bronco cowboy in *Western Symphony*. The male role in the first pas de trois in *Agon* was mocking and ceremonious, an offbeat part for Villella; he gave it a quality of force which it retains to this day. In the revival of *La Sonnambula*, Villella was a memorable Harlequin, a world-weary cousin to the elfin charmer whom he later incarnated in *Harlequinade*. And how delicious his Candy Cane in *The Nutcracker*—what crackle and zest as he vaulted through his hoop and shifted his weight in the air. While audiences roared, critics sighed with pleasure. Even more remarkable than the vigor of his dancing was its continuing clarity and solidity as it changed shape—mercurial changes, as it were, frozen solid and cold as crystal. Villella took clean bites out of the air.

The first role that Balanchine made for this dynamo cracked the demi-caractère mold that had been shaping Villella's style. The Prince of Lorraine in *The Figure in the Carpet* was a purely classical creation cast in the eighteenth-century image of Vestris. (Among the several coincidences in the careers of Villella and Baryshnikov is the fact that each danced a Vestris early in his career.) The ballet, an extravaganza featuring nearly every dancer in the company, was short-lived. My memory of Villella in it is chiefly of a beautiful and luminous presence, strangely tender and exposed. Conceived the season after the revival of *The Prodigal Son,* Lorraine was the Son's classical counterpart. Beneath the Baroque dignity of the one and the blunt expressionism of the other lay the same quality of intense emotion. These were a young man's roles.

Between Lorraine and the great role of Oberon, which came two years later, there intervened another ill-fated Balanchine ballet, called *Electronics* after its score, which utilized then-fashionable electronic tape. Villella was cast as a creature of fantasy, a kind of science-fiction satyr. There may have been elements here that led to the exotic *Bugaku,* which lay just beyond. I refer to elements of characterization. Other elements, relating more specifically to Villella's unique qualities as a dancer, are traceable from then on in all the roles that Balanchine was to create for him—roles ranging from Oberon to Harlequin in *Harlequinade* and from *Bugaku* to *Tarantella* and "Rubies." What I chiefly remember of Villella in these roles is his rhythmic power. Villella's rhythm was a combination of attack and volume; he could compress a phrase to pinpoints or explode it from the inside. The attack was often exciting in itself: the quick relevé, the short takeoff. It was like a sharp jab that vanished into something huge and cushiony—that absorbed its own shock. All the Balanchine roles for Villella would capitalize on his unrivalled ability to sustain enormous bursts of movement at peak energy. Compared to the way men danced in other ballet companies, there would be no time for preparations and recoveries between step-sequences; there would be relatively little emphasis on line and pose.

Though physically small, Villella danced on a big scale. Balanchine sometimes cast him small, the better to reveal his gift for detail. He envisioned Oberon, king of the elves, as Villella, an artist of changes. So Oberon became an emulative, procreative force of nature. In the Scherzo, where he was surrounded by dozens of beetle-like elves, Villella performed one of his richest, most intricate and mesmerizing dances, darting and skimming like a dragonfly crossing the surface of a pond. In the flash of a single variation, Balanchine's poetry transformed a buoyant, virile young man into an image of scooting iridescent intelligence. Villella's attack became insectoid: a sting.

There was something demonic about the individual qualities of speed, brio, stamina, and finesse that Villella possessed, but there was nothing demonic or inhuman about his presence. Villella was a real man, warm and open, and his personality colored everything he did. His Oberon was the sunniest of Sun Kings. I remember one of his exits that used to hit the audience like a joke—a high jeté-flip in which he reversed his pose while soaring backwards into the wings. In another passage, he flew backwards at top speed, sitting on air and kicking air away like a tiresome footstool. This is an undying Villella image. (If a child ever asks you what it was that made Villella different, say "He could dance backwards.")

As Oberon, Villella mastered long passages of classical mime. In *Harlequinade* and "Rubies," the dance passages are saturated in character-color. "Rubies" may have been the closest to a full-length portrait that Balanchine ever made of Villella; it is also one of the few depictions we have in ballet of a fully sexed, civilized adult male. "Rubies"—so called because it is the second entry in the triptych called *Jewels*—used Villella's athletic stance to anchor an image of idiosyncratic masculine grace. (In college, Villella played varsity baseball and held the title in welterweight boxing for three years.) The other men in *Jewels* are cavaliers, poets, troubadours. Only Villella is non-romantic; he's jaunty, combative, debonair. He challenges as well as supports the ballerina. The role is infused with Broadway and circus and jazz club manners; its spiritual home is swing-time America. Villella's solos contained some superb comic moments. In one sequence, he pedalled about the stage, leaping and swerving ahead of a gang of men. In another travelling passage he seemed to play the piano mincingly before a sudden volcanic wind overtook him and he left the stage spinning with such velocity that you could almost see the air whizzing past his chest.

Villella partnered Violette Verdy and then, for many years, Patricia McBride. When Baryshnikov danced with New York City Ballet a few seasons ago, he inherited Villella's partner, McBride, along with Villella's roles. Baryshnikov is Villella's only possible successor; he has the timing, the punch, the virtuoso technique. Stylistically, of course, he is quite different. His assumption of the Villella repertory was largely a discourse on the differences in style between the American and the Russian classical schools and between their two greatest male exponents. (Strangely enough, the Villella role which fitted Baryshnikov best was in Robbins's *Dances at a Gathering*. Russian style was more easily accommodated by the American-born choreographer Robbins than by the Russian-born Balanchine.) When Baryshnikov left the company, the roles of Harlequin and the man in "Rubies" fell empty again. (Baryshnikov himself vacated Oberon owing to injury; the Prodigal he took with him to American Ballet Theatre.) The ballets are done but without the Villella spark. One can add other roles to the "unoccupied" list: *Donizetti Variations,* Third Movement *Brahms-Schoenberg Quartet.*

I have left out of this memoir an account of Villella's performances away from New York City Ballet, even though I saw and was stirred by quite a few of them. Like everyone else who watched him on television, I was grateful to Villella for broadcasting himself to the millions, showing those who could not see it live what ballet was like, inspiring and encouraging who knows how many American boys to become dancers themselves. Television brought Villella his greatest fame. But his glory as an artist lies in the ballets he left behind at his home company. The Villella repertory—both the roles he originated and those he assumed with special distinction—is the greatest corpus of ballets created for a male dancer in this century. When the final tally is taken and it shows American ballet in our time to have been largely a Balanchine production, there will be the honor roll of Balanchine dancers, name upon name. All those girls—and Edward Villella.

—from *Edward Villella in Photographs,* West Point, N.Y., May 1982

MIKHAIL BARYSHNIKOV

Born in Riga in 1948, Baryshnikov was trained in St. Petersburg's Vaganova school by the great pedagogue Alexander Pushkin, who had also trained Nureyev. On entering the Kirov (Maryinsky) company, he was immediately recognized as a phenomenon of ballet technique and style. In 1974 he defected from the Soviet Union and soon joined American Ballet Theatre, where he remained until, in 1978, he joined New York City Ballet in order to work with Balanchine. A year and a half later, he returned to ABT to be its artistic director, a post he held for nine years. From 1990 to 2002, now a modern dancer, he ran the White Oak Dance Project, and in 2004 he founded the Baryshnikov Arts Center in New York. Among the best-known of the many works created on him were Leonid Jakobson's Vestris, Tharp's Push Comes to Shove *(see page 1271), and Robbins's* Opus 19: The Dreamer *and* Other Dances. *He has appeared in a stage version of Kafka's* Metamorphosis *and in* Four Plays *by Beckett; in the films* The Turning Point *and* White Nights; *on television in* Sex and the City; *and is the author of* Baryshnikov at Work.

JOAN ACOCELLA
The Soloist

It is raining, and Mikhail Baryshnikov is standing in a courtyard in Riga, the capital of Latvia, pointing up at two corner windows of an old stucco building that was probably yellow once. With him are his companion, Lisa Rinehart, a former dancer with American Ballet Theatre, and two of his children—Peter, eight, and Aleksandra, or Shura, sixteen. He is showing them the house where he grew up. "It's Soviet communal apartment," he says to the children. "In one apartment, five families. Mother and Father have room at corner. See? Big window. Mother and Father sleep there, we eat there, table there. Then other little room, mostly just two beds, for half brother, Vladimir, and me. In other rooms, other people. For fifteen, sixteen people, one kitchen, one toilet, one bathroom, room with bathtub. But no hot water for bath. On Tuesday and Saturday, Vladimir and I go with Father to public bath."

I open the front door of the building and peer into the dark hallway. "Let's go up," I suggest. "No," he says, "I can't." It is more than a quarter century since he was here last.

AFTER HIS DEFECTION to the West, in 1974, Baryshnikov said again and again that he had no wish to return to the Soviet Union, or even to the former Soviet Union. Then, late last year, he accepted an invitation to dance at the Latvian National Opera, the stage on which he first set foot as a ballet dancer. Why he changed his mind is something of a mystery. Perhaps he just felt that it was time. (He will turn fifty next week.) Perhaps he wanted to show his children what he came from. To me all he said was "I am going to visit my mother's grave."

Baryshnikov, actually, is not a man for sentimental journeys. He is too resistant to falseness. Nor does he like being followed around by journalists. Interviews are torture to him: "You ask me what's happened in my life, why and how I did this and that. And I think and tell, but it's never true story, because everything is so much more complicated, and also I can't even remember how things happened. Whole process is boring. Also false, but mostly boring." He politely does not point out the journalist's role in this: how the questions are pitched, and the answers interpreted, according to already established ideas about the life in question—in this case, the life of a man who escaped from the Soviet Union at the age of twenty-six. It is hard to find an article on Baryshnikov that does not describe a look of melancholy in his eyes, supposedly the consequence of exile from his Russian homeland. This is the dominant theme of writings about him, but in his view it has nothing to do with him. He has lived in the United States for almost half his life. He is a United States citizen and regards this country as his home. He has lived with an American, Rinehart, for about ten years, and they have three children who speak no Russian.

Of course, when his return to Latvia was announced, the exile theme sounded with new force. The press in Riga was sown with sentimental formulas: the prodigal-son motif, the return-home motif, the ancestral-roots motif. He refused them all. For Russia, he says, he feels no nostalgia. Though his parents were Russian, he did not move to Russia until he was sixteen: "I was guest there, always." As for Latvia, it was his birthplace, but his parents were "occupiers" (his word) there. "The minute plane set down, the minute I stepped again on Latvian land, I realized this was never my home. My heart didn't even skip one beat."

* * *

WHAT HAS MADE Baryshnikov a paragon of late-twentieth-century dance is partly the purity of his ballet technique. In him the hidden meaning of ballet, and of classicism—that experience has order, that life can be understood—is clearer than in any other dancer on the stage today. Another part of his preeminence derives, of course, from his virtuosity, the lengths to which he was able to take ballet—the split leaps, the cyclonic pirouettes—without sacrificing purity. But what has made him an artist, and a popular artist, is the completeness of his performances: the level of concentration, the fullness of ambition, the sheer amount of detail, with the cast of the shoulder, the angle of the jaw, even the splay of the fingers, all deployed in the service of a single, pressing act of imagination. In him there is simply more to see than in most other dancers. No matter what role he is playing (and he has played some thankless ones), he always honors it completely, working every minute to make it a serious human story. In an interview prior to the Riga concerts, the Latvian theatre critic Normunds Naumanis asked him why he danced. He answered that he was not a religious person (quickly adding that his mother had been, and had had him secretly baptized) but that he thought he found onstage what people seek in religion: "some approximation to exaltation, inner purification, self-discovery." He may hate interviews, but once he is in one he tends to pour his heart out. (This may be why he hates them.)

Though Baryshnikov directs a company, the White Oak Dance Project, he went to Riga in October alone, as a solo dancer, and next week (January 21–25), at the City Center, in New York, he will again perform by himself—his first solo concerts, ever, in the United States. There is something fitting in this. The things he now seeks in dance—the exaltation, the self-discovery—are easier to find if one is not lifting another dancer at the same time. Furthermore, audiences these days don't want their view of him blocked by other people. But, basically, solo is his natural state, the condition that made him. The rootlessness of his childhood sent him into himself—made him a reader, a thinker, a mind—and the rule of force he worked under in the Soviet Union had the same effect: it made him cherish what could not be forced, his own thoughts. This became a way of dancing. It is not that when he is performing he is telling us who he is. Rather, he is telling us, as fully as he can, what truth he has found in the role, what he has thought about it. In many of his solos today, he seems to be giving us a portrait of thought itself—its bursts and hesitations, the neural firings—and this is something one must do solo.

IT WAS AS A PRESENTER of new work, not just as a dancer, that Baryshnikov returned to Riga. Most of the solos he brought were from his

White Oak repertory—works by people like Mark Morris, Twyla Tharp, and Dana Reitz. These pieces were far removed from the earnest Soviet ballets that the Latvians had last seen him in and that some of them would probably have liked to see him in again. (The Reitz piece, "Unspoken Territory," has him, in a sarong, stalking around the stage in silence—no music—for twenty minutes.) In his mind, he was going to Riga not as he was then but as he is today.

To the Riga press, however, it was what he was then—the man who had been one of them and had left—that was important. Also, as usual in the Soviet Union, former or otherwise, politics came to greet him. There is considerable tension between Riga's Latvian and Russian populations. (Though Russians outnumber Latvians in the capital, Latvian independence has made the Russians the underdogs now: Russians must pass a Latvian-language test to get a job in the government.) The Russians wanted to know why Baryshnikov had come to Latvia, not to Russia, and why, if he gave only three interviews concerning his visit (he wanted no press, no questions), he gave them to Latvian, not to Russian, journalists.

To such problems Baryshnikov applied his usual remedy: work. The happiest I ever saw him in Riga was in a studio in his old school, rehearsing works for the upcoming program. Perched on a folding chair, watching him, was the director of the school, Haralds Ritenbergs, who had been the leading danseur noble of the Latvian state ballet company when Baryshnikov was a child. ("To us he was like Rock Hudson," Baryshnikov says.) Next to Ritenbergs sat Juris Kapralis, a handsome, bighearted Latvian whom Baryshnikov had as his ballet teacher from age twelve to sixteen. What must these men have felt? Here was the dear, small, hardworking boy they had known, now almost fifty years old and the most famous dancer in the world, rehearsing before them steps such as they had never seen. There should have been some shock, some acknowledgment of the break in history—of all the years when so many things had happened to him, and to them, to make their lives so different. But there was none of that. What I saw was just three old pros working together. Baryshnikov would perform the steps. Then he and the two older men would huddle together and, in the hand language that dancers use, discuss the choreography. Yes, Baryshnikov said, this piece, no music. Yes, here I do arms this way, and he demonstrated a stiff, right-angled arm, the opposite of what ballet dancers are taught. I looked for raised eyebrows. There were none. The older men nodded, watched, asked questions. To them, it seemed, he was still their hardworking boy, and his business was their business, dancing. Baryshnikov showed them his shoes—jazz shoes, Western shoes—and Ritenbergs and Kapralis unlaced them, peered into them, poked the instep, flexed the sole. They were like two veteran wine makers inspecting a new kind of cork. Whatever feelings passed among the three men, they were all subsumed into work. Now, as had not happened when Baryshnikov showed me his old house or the hospital where he was born, time vanished. He had returned home at last, but the home wasn't Riga; it was ballet.

MIKHAIL NIKOLAIEVICH BARYSHNIKOV was born in Riga eight years after Latvia, in the midst of the Second World War, was forcibly annexed to the Soviet Union. Once the war was over, Russian workers streamed into this tiny Baltic country, the size of Vermont. Among them was Baryshnikov's father, Nikolai, a high-ranking military officer who was sent to Riga to teach military topography in the Air Force academy. With him came his new wife, Aleksandra, who had lost her first husband in the war, and Vladimir, her son by that first marriage. By Nikolai, she had Mikhail, eight years younger than Vladimir, in 1948. The parents' marriage was not happy. The father seems to have been a curt, cold man. The mother, Aleksandra, was another matter, Baryshnikov says—"softer, interesting." She had had very little education but was a passionate theatregoer. She went to drama, opera, and ballet, and she took Misha with her.

Misha was one of those children who cannot sit still. Erika Vitina, a friend of the family, says that when he ate at their house you could see his legs dancing around under the glass-topped dinner table. He himself remembers movement as an outlet for emotion. "One time I recall is when my mother first took me to visit my grandmother, on the Volga River," he told me. "Volga, it's a long way up from Latvia. We took a train through Moscow, and Moscow to Gorky, plus then you drive another seventy miles. We took taxi, or some car delivered us. It was very early morning when we arrived—little village, and very simple house, and there was my grandmother. And I was in such anticipation, because I was like five or so, maybe six. My mother said to me, "Mikhail, hug your grandmother." But I was so overwhelmed that I couldn't run to her and hug her. So I just start to jump and jump, jump like crazy, around and around. It was embarrassing, but same time totally what I needed to do. Mother and Grandmother stood and looked until it was over."

When he was about nine, his mother became friends with a woman who had danced with the Bolshoi Ballet in Moscow and who now gave ballet lessons in Riga. "Mother was very excited by this friendship," Baryshnikov says. She enrolled him in her friend's class. When he was eleven, he moved over to the Riga School of Choreography, the state ballet academy. (One of his classmates there was Alexander Godunov, who would also defect, and dance at American Ballet Theatre under Baryshnikov's directorship.) Soon he showed extraordinary talent. Erika Vitina stresses the mother's involvement in Misha's ballet studies: "The father had no interest whatsoever in the ballet school. The mother brought him to the ballet school, put him there. All this happened physically, hand to hand."

"I was mama's boy in a way," Baryshnikov says. He remembers how beautiful she was. (In fact, in the one photograph I have seen of her she looks uncannily like him. It could be Baryshnikov with a wig on.) "My mother was a country girl from the Volga River," he said in a 1986 interview with Roman Polanski. "She spoke with a strong Volga accent. Very beautiful, very Russian—a one-hundred-percent pure Russian bride. But to tell the whole story of my mother, it's a long story." The end of the story is that during the summer when he was twelve she again took him to the Volga to stay with her mother and then went back to Riga and hanged herself in the bathroom of the communal apartment. Vladimir found her. Baryshnikov never knew why she did it. "Father did not want to talk about it," he told me. Soon afterward, Vladimir left for the Army, and the father told Misha that now they would live together, just the two of them. The following year, Nikolai went away on a business trip and returned with a new wife, a new life. "I understood that I am not wanted," Baryshnikov said.

He looked for other families. He spent most summers with the family of Erika Vitina, and he stayed with them at other times as well. "Quite often," Vitina says, "he would ring our doorbell late at night, saying that he had run away. But a week later I would receive a call from the ballet school"—she, too, had a child enrolled there—"and would be told that unless I sent Misha home they would have to call the police. We spent two years in this manner. From time to time, he'd come to stay with me, and then his father would take him away again." Insofar as Baryshnikov has lived a life of exile, it had begun.

Erika Vitina recalls that his nights were often hard. Because he worried that he was too short to be a ballet dancer, he slept on a wooden plank—he had been told that this would help him grow faster (less traction)—and the blankets wouldn't stay tucked in. Before going to bed herself, Vitina would look in and cover him up again. Often, he would be calling out in his sleep, caught in a nightmare. But during the day, she says, he was "a happy, sunny boy." Now, looking back on those years, Baryshnikov is quick to dispel any atmosphere of pathos: "Children being left, it's not always like books of Charles Dickens. When you lose your parents in childhood, it's a fact of life, and, you know, human beings are extraordinary powerful survivors. My mother commit suicide. I was lucky it was not in front of me, OK? Which is truth, and Father was confused, and we never had any relationship, serious relationship. I never knew my father, in a way. But what? It's made me different? No. I mean, I blame for every fuckups in my life my parents? No."

"I got lucky," he adds. "I fell in love with dance." Every ounce of energy he had was now channelled into ballet. According to Juris Kapralis, who became his ballet teacher two months after his mother's death, he was a child workaholic: "Very serious boy. Perfectionist. Even in free time, go in corner and practice over and over again. Other boys playing, Misha studying. And not just steps, but artistic, as actor. He is thinking all the time what this role must be. I remember, once, *Nutcracker*. He was thirteen, perhaps. I was prince, and he was toy soldier. After Mouse King dies, Misha relax his body. No longer stiff, like wooden soldier. Soft. Our ballet director ask him, 'Who say you should do this?' And he answer, 'When Mouse King dies, toys become human. Toys become boys. Movements must change.' He devise that himself. Small boy, but thinking."

I asked Baryshnikov recently whether, after his mother's death, ballet might have been a way for him to return to her. He paused for a long time and then said, "In Russia, dancing is part of happiness in groups. Groups at parties, people dancing in circle, and they push child to center, to dance. Child soon works up little routine. Can do a little this"—hand at the back of the neck—"a little this"—arms joined horizontally across the chest—"and soon make up some special steps, and learn to save them for end, to make big finale. This way, child gets attention from adults."

In the case of a child artist, and particularly one who has suffered a terrible loss, it is tempting to read artistic decisions as psychological decisions, because we assume that a child cannot really be an artist. But, as many people have said, children are probably more artistic than adults, bolder in imagination, more unashamedly fascinated with shape, line, detail. In Baryshnikov's case, the mother's devotion and then the loss of her can help to explain one thing: the *work* he put into ballet. For the rest—the physical gift, the fusion of steps with fantasy, the interest in making something true and complete ("Toys become boys"), all of which are as much a part of him today as they were when he was twelve—we must look to him alone.

IN 1 9 6 4 , the Latvian state ballet went on tour to Leningrad with a ballet in which Baryshnikov, now sixteen, had a small role, and a member of the company took him to Alexander Pushkin, a revered teacher at the Kirov Ballet's school, the Vaganova Choreographic Institute. Pushkin immediately asked the director of the school to admit the boy. By September, Baryshnikov had moved to Leningrad and was installed at the barre in Pushkin's class. Thereafter, he rarely went back to Riga.

Next to his mother, Pushkin was probably the most important person in Baryshnikov's early life. Pushkin had begun his own ballet training in the studio of Nikolai Legat, who had helped train Nijinsky. Later, he studied with other famous teachers. When Baryshnikov joined his class, Pushkin was fifty-seven, and past dancing, but he had performed with the Kirov for almost thirty years, mostly in secondary roles. "Pas de deux, pas de trois,"

Baryshnikov says. "Sometimes substitute for a principal, but he was not principal type. Not very handsome—big nose, long legs, short body—and not very expressive. But classical, classical. Old-school, traditional, square. Academician. Usually, it's those kind of people, people who dance twenty-five years the same parts, who know more about technique than people who are advancing and trying out other sort of areas. Twenty-five years you come back after summer vacation and tune your body into same routine, you figure out timing, you figure out method."

Pushkin had begun teaching early, at the age of twenty-five, and he soon specialized in men. His classroom manner was famously laconic. He rarely offered corrections, and when he did they were of the most elementary sort. (It was said at the school that he had two: "Don't fall" and "Get up.") Rather, as Baryshnikov explains it, what made Pushkin so effective was the *logic* of the step combinations he taught—the fact that they were true not just to classical ballet but also to human musculature. They seemed right to the body, and so you did them right. And the more you did them the more you became a classical dancer. Another thing about Pushkin, his students say, is that he was a developer of individuality. He steered the students toward themselves, helped them find out what kinds of dancers they were. "Plus," Baryshnikov says, "he was extraordinary patient and extraordinary kind person. Really, really kind." If there is a point in classical art where aesthetics meet morals—where beauty, by appearing plain and natural, gives us hope that we, too, can be beautiful—Pushkin seems to have stood at that point, and held out a hand to his pupils. In any case, he was a specialist in calming down teenage boys, getting them to work, and making them take themselves seriously. Out of his classroom in the fifties and sixties came the Kirov's finest male dancers—notably Nikita Dolgushin, Yuri Soloviev, and Rudolf Nureyev.

PUSHKIN TOOK CERTAIN of his students very directly under his wing. The best-known example is Nureyev, who was ten years older than Baryshnikov. Nureyev had started studying ballet extremely late. "It was not until he was sixteen or seventeen that he came to Leningrad and put his leg in first position professionally," Baryshnikov says. "And he took this opportunity very—*errgghh*—like a tank. Very aggressive in terms of the education, in terms of the catch-up. And short temper. Sometimes in rehearsal, if he couldn't do certain steps he would just run out, crying, run home. Then, ten o'clock in the evening, he is back in studio working on the step till he will get it. People think he is oddball. And already his ambivalent sexuality was obvious, which in that conservative atmosphere was big problem. People were teasing him." So Pushkin and his wife, Xenia Jurgensen, another former Kirov dancer, took Nureyev into their home. He lived with them for a long time, not just while he was in school but also during his early years at the Kirov. The fact that Nureyev defected in 1961—that he was accomplished enough and brave enough to go—was probably due in large measure to them, though it broke their hearts. (When Baryshnikov first went to their house, he saw Nureyev's electric train, installed as a kind of relic, in their living room.) Sacred vessel of the Russian tradition, Pushkin bred dancers so good, so serious and ambitious, that they could not survive in Russia. Yuri Soloviev killed himself. Nikita Dolgushin was banished to the provinces. Nureyev and Baryshnikov defected.

PUSHKIN AND JURGENSEN took Baryshnikov in as they had taken in Nureyev. "I spent weeks, sometimes months, staying with them," he says. He also ate at their house almost every night. Jurgensen was a good cook. "Very upper-class Russian food," Baryshnikov says. "Winter food—veal, cream." Then Pushkin and his pupil would work together, sometimes for hours, often on arms: "Find my way of moving arms, coordination. Young dancers don't think about this, only think about feet." Then, very often, it was too late for Baryshnikov to return to the dormitory, so he slept on the Pushkins' couch.

Baryshnikov was still very worried about his height. Russian ballet companies follow a strict system, called *emploi,* whereby dancers are sorted by type into certain kinds of roles and remain there for the rest of their careers. Baryshnikov, though he was still growing (he eventually reached five feet seven), seemed too short for the danseur-noble roles, the grave, poetic leading-man roles. Not just his height but also his stage presence—he was boyish, vivacious, a personality—seemed to be pushing him toward demi-caractère roles, the quick, often comic supporting-actor roles. As he put it in his interview with Polanski, "I thought I would end up as a Joker or a Harlequin somewhere," and this was not what he wanted. But Pushkin believed that his pupil would be a danseur noble, and he got him just to go on working. In 1967, Baryshnikov graduated from the Vaganova school. At his graduation performance, in the "Corsaire" pas de deux, "the scene was unimaginable," his biographer Gennady Smakov writes. The crowd howled; the chandeliers shook. Baryshnikov was taken into the Kirov Ballet as a soloist, skipping the normal starting position in the corps de ballet, and now his troubles really began.

"I joined the company when it was falling apart," Baryshnikov told Smakov. In the late sixties and the seventies, the Kirov went through a period of repression from which it has never fully recovered. In part, this was due to a society-wide tightening up after the Khrushchev "thaw." But in the ballet world there was redoubled anxiety, the result of Nureyev's defection. Konstantin Sergeyev, the director of the Kirov, turned the company into a mini police state. The repertory consisted either of nineteenth-century classics, restaged by Sergeyev, or of socialist flag-wavers. (Sergeyev himself, in 1963, made a ballet, *The Distant Planet*, inspired by Yuri Gagarin's space-flight.) Any newly commissioned ballets were vetted to make sure they threatened neither government policy nor Sergeyev's primacy as company choreographer. The dancers were watched vigilantly for signs of insubordination. If they looked like defection risks—indeed, if they failed to attend company meetings or had the wrong friends—they were often barred from foreign tours, which were their only means of supplementing their tiny incomes. Typically, the list of who would be going on a tour was not posted until the day of departure. Shortly beforehand, meetings would be held at which the dancers were encouraged to denounce their colleagues, so that their own names, rather than their colleagues', would be on the list. Many cooperated. Cooperate or not, the dancers were brought to their knees. Righteous suffering can ruin you almost as fast as shame. Other privileges at the Kirov—roles, choice of partners, time onstage—were also awarded less on the basis of merit than according to one's history of cooperation. The careers of what were reportedly superb artists, people who were one in a thousand, and in whom ten years' training had been invested, were destroyed in this way.

Such were the circumstances in which Baryshnikov, nineteen years old and hungry to dance, found himself in 1967. He had to fight just to get onstage—at that time, even leading Kirov dancers performed only three to four times a month—and also to get the partners he wanted. Above all, he had to struggle over his casting. He was given danseur-noble roles eventually, but only eventually. (He waited six years to dance Albrecht in *Giselle,* a part he desperately wanted.) Worse was the problem of getting a chance to perform in something other than the standard repertory. Baryshnikov wanted to dance new ballets, modern ballets, and some were being created at the Kirov, with excellent roles for him. But again and again such ballets were vetoed by the company's *artsoviet,* or artistic committee, and dropped after one or two performances. Baryshnikov was sent back to dancing *Don Quixote.*

In 1970, midway into his seven-year career in Russia, things got a great deal worse, for in that year Natalia Makarova, the Kirov's rising young ballerina, defected while the company was performing in London. Baryshnikov was on this tour, and it was to him, not to Makarova, that the authorities devoted their special attention. As he sees it, they did not take Makarova seriously as a potential defector, because she was a woman: "They wouldn't think a woman would have guts to defect." Baryshnikov, on the other hand, sometimes had as many as three KGB agents tailing him as he walked down the streets of London. He says that at that time he had no thoughts of defection. If he was closely confined at the Kirov, that was because he was greatly valued there. He was one of the company's leading dancers. "Also," he says, "the Kirov was a home to me, and I had unfinished business. I wanted to do *this* dance, with *these* people." Indeed, when he got the news about Makarova, who was a friend and also a former girlfriend of his, he was terribly worried for her: "I thought it will be difficult for her to survive in the West, that people will get advantage of her, that she will be sorry. Can you believe how stupid?"

But the events that led to his own defection were already accumulating. Four months before the London tour, Pushkin had died—of a heart attack, on a sidewalk—at the age of sixty-two. At that point, Baryshnikov later told an interviewer, "I realized that I was totally on my own." A second important development was the London tour itself. The audience and the critics went crazy over him. (If he thought it would be hard for a Soviet dancer to survive in the West, his London reviews may have given him reason to rethink that conclusion later.) But London gave him more than good reviews: "You cannot know what it meant to travel. Just to see how other people react to you, and to *measure* your ability as an artist, as a dancer. And to see what's supposed to be your *life*—that your life is not just in cocoon, that other people in other countries do have same emotions." He met Western dancers. He became friends with Margot Fonteyn. He attended rehearsals at the Royal Ballet. He went to modern-dance classes. He saw American Ballet Theatre, which was performing in London at the same time.

He also met Nureyev, who was now living in London and dancing with the Royal Ballet. Nureyev went to see the Kirov performances and managed to get a message to Baryshnikov. "A man we both knew came to me and said, 'Rudolf want to see you if you want to.'" So the next morning Baryshnikov gave the KGB the slip and spent a whole day in Nureyev's big house, overlooking Richmond Park. They talked about ballet, he says: "Russian exercises, French exercises, teachers, class, how long barre—all technique, Rudolf's obsession." At lunch, Nureyev drank a whole bottle of wine by himself. (Baryshnikov couldn't drink. He was performing that night.) Then they went out and lay on the grass and talked about technique some more. "When I left, he gave me a couple of books—one with beautiful Michelangelo drawings—and some scarf he gave me. I was very touched by him." The two men remained friends until Nureyev's death, in 1993.

With Makarova's defection, the panic at the Kirov was even worse than it had been with Nureyev's. Sergeyev was removed from his post; a number of brief, fumbling directorships followed. Baryshnikov was watched more and more carefully. If Western dancers came to Leningrad and he went out to dinner with them, this was noted in his file, and the KGB came to talk to him about it. When Western choreographers got in touch with the Kirov to see if he could work with them, they were told he was sick. He was also under pressure to go to political rallies, and privileges in the theatre were made contingent on his attendance: "They'd say, if not this, then not this. Blackmail, you know?"

I N 1 9 7 4 , Baryshnikov staged what was called a Creative Evening—a favor sometimes accorded leading dancers. The dancer would commission an evening's worth of short works, often from young choreographers. (Whatever nonconformist ballets made it onto the Kirov stage were usually part of a Creative Evening.) The dancer would also choose the casts, assemble the sets and costumes, and star in the program. Then, after this display of open-mindedness, the administration would normally shelve the ballets. For his Creative Evening, Baryshnikov hired two experimental (and therefore extra-Leningrad) choreographers—Georgi Alexidze, based in Tbilisi, and Mai Murdmaa, an Estonian. There followed several months of anguish as, faced with harassment from the administration and apathy from the demoralized dancers, Baryshnikov tried to get the new ballets onstage. Cast members dropped out; costume designs were argued over (too revealing). Shortly before the premiere, Baryshnikov was pulled out of rehearsals to go to Moscow for another political rally. After the first preview, he met with the *artsoviet,* and they told him how bad they thought the show was. It was allowed a few performances anyway—all the tickets were already sold—but afterward, at a cast banquet, Baryshnikov burst into tears while he was trying to make a speech to the dancers. "He was talking and crying," Nina Alovert reports in her 1984 book, *Baryshnikov in Russia.* "Some people listened to him . . . while others continued to eat, scraping their plates with their forks."

The disappointments apart, Baryshnikov remembers Leningrad as a place of immense tedium: "The most interesting objects were people, saying what they would have done, if they could have. Which is what they talked about if they drank a little. But they didn't drink a little. They drank a lot." In a 1986 interview, Arlene Croce asked Baryshnikov's close friend Joseph Brodsky what would have become of the dancer if he had remained in Russia. "He'd be a ruin by now," Brodsky answered, "both physically and mentally. Physically because of the bottle. . . . Mentally because of that mixture of impotence and cynicism that corrodes everyone there—the stronger you are the worse it is."

Finally, he refused that fate. A few months after the Creative Evening, a group of dancers from the Bolshoi Ballet were leaving for a tour of Canada. The two Bolshoi veterans leading the tour, Raissa Struchkova and her husband, Alexander Lapauri, asked the Kirov if Baryshnikov and his frequent partner

Irina Kolpakova could join them, to add heft to the roster. The Kirov refused; at this point, the KGB was barely letting Baryshnikov out of its sight. But Kolpakova intervened, and she was a well-placed person—not just the Kirov's leading ballerina but a former administrator of the company and a member of the Party, with excellent connections. She apparently guaranteed Baryshnikov's safe return, and therefore they were allowed to go. That was the tour from which Baryshnikov did not return. Kolpakova somehow survived as the leading ballerina at the Kirov, but Struchkova and Lapauri were forbidden ever to leave the Soviet Union again. The following year, Lapauri got drunk one night, drove his car into a lamppost, and died. By that time, Baryshnikov was the new sensation of Western ballet, and if, with his fame, he also had a sad look in his eyes the cause was probably not nostalgia for the Soviet Union.

B A R Y S H N I K O V ' S   C A R E E R as a ballet dancer in the seventies and eighties has by now been the subject of hundreds of articles, and of half a dozen books as well. It had three stages: four years as the star of American Ballet Theatre (from 1974 to 1978), one year at George Balanchine's New York City Ballet (from 1978 to 1979), then nine years as the director of American Ballet Theatre (from 1980 to 1989). What he did during this time, above all, was acquire new repertory—the thing he had most wanted to do. In just his first two years in the West, he learned twenty-six new roles, more than he would have been given in a lifetime in the Soviet Union. And the process of working with new choreographers nudged his style in new directions.

Most important was his collaboration with Twyla Tharp. In the 1970s, Tharp was undergoing a transition from modern dance to ballet. Baryshnikov was also in transition, so he made a perfect subject for her. Starting with the hugely popular *Push Comes to Shove*, in 1976, she created for him a series of ballets that seemed to be about the project facing them both: how to marry the Old World dance to the new—in particular, how to join ballet, so outward and perfect, to the inwardness, the ruminations, of jazz. In Tharp's works, Baryshnikov's dancing became more shaded, with more hitches and grace notes, more little thoughts, tucked in between one step and the next. And it was these—the transitions, the secret places between the steps—that seemed to give the dancing its meaning. The big ballet moves were still there, but they were thrown off casually, like something taken for granted. Suddenly, out of some low-down noodling, Baryshnikov would rise up into an utterly perfect leap, and then land and noodle some more. This was surprising, witty, but it also seemed philosophical: a meditation on history, a memory of innocence in a mind past innocence. Appropriately, Tharp had Baryshnikov do this kind of dancing alone. It influenced all his future work, affecting not just him but the choreographers who worked with him after Tharp. The more he became that kind of dancer—inward, alone—the more they made that kind of dance for him.

At the same time, what Tharp made of Baryshnikov was in him already. He *was* a transplant, and alone, and he combined an exquisitely schooled classical technique with what seemed, even before Tharp, an increasingly ruminative quality, a deep sort of cool. He danced that way not only in Tharp's ballets but also in *Giselle,* and this gave him a special glamour. Soon he was more than an acclaimed ballet dancer: he was a celebrity, a dreamboat. Crucial to this development was the fact that in his hunger for new outlets he looked beyond live theatre. He made movies (*The Turning Point,* in 1977; *White Nights,* in 1985; *Dancers,* in 1987), and television specials, too, and he turned out to be extremely filmable. Now you didn't have to live in New York to be a Baryshnikov fan, any more than you had to live in Hollywood to be a Sylvester Stallone fan. He was an electronic-media ballet star, the first one in history.

The movies, of course, made use not only of his dancing but of his sex appeal. In all three of his Hollywood films, he was cast as a roué, a heartbreaker. The newspapers, meanwhile, were doing what they could to cover his love life: his rocky affair with Gelsey Kirkland, the ballerina who had left New York City Ballet to become his partner at ABT; his long liaison with Jessica Lange (which produced his first child, Aleksandra, named after his mother); his shorter stopovers with many others. "He goes through everybody, he doesn't miss anyone," the post-Baryshnikov Kirkland told a reporter. "I should have been so lucky," Baryshnikov says. But in a male ballet dancer even medium-level skirt-chasing makes good copy. Combined with all the other factors—his "exile," his famous melancholy, his tendency to flee interviewers, his hunger for new projects—it gave him a sort of Byronic profile, as a haunted man, a man of unfulfillable desires, unassuageable griefs. He did not fashion the image, but he fitted it, and nothing could have been more attractive. Posters of him hung in dorm rooms.

In 1979, only a year after he had made the switch from American Ballet Theatre to New York City Ballet, ABT asked him to come back, this time as the head of the company, and he accepted. The story of Baryshnikov's nine-year directorship of ABT is a long, messy, fascinating tale that has never been fully told. Briefly, he tried to modernize the company. He junked the star system and began promoting from within the ranks. He regalvanized the company's notoriously feckless corps de ballet. He brought in new repertory, including modern-dance pieces, plus crossover ballets by the most interesting American choreographers of the moment—people such as Tharp, David Gordon, and Mark Morris. Suddenly, the air began to circulate again at ABT. The corps moved with beauty and pride. The young soloists danced like demons. The new works were talked about, argued about. Before, what was interesting at ABT was merely this or that performance, usually by a foreign star. Now, for the first time since the 1950s, the company itself was a serious subject, an art-producing organization.

Not all of Baryshnikov's reforms were successful, and when they did succeed they weren't necessarily popular. Stars left in huffs. Critics deplored many of the new works. People accused Baryshnikov of trying to turn ABT into New York City Ballet, or into a modern-dance company, or, in any case, into something other than the plump, old-style, stars-and-classics institution that it had been, and which they still loved. The company's deficit swelled. The dancers went out on strike. There was constant friction between Baryshnikov and the board. He had ostensibly been hired as the company's artistic director, but the board also expected him to be its leading dancer and its No. 1 fund-raiser—roles that he declined. (He had repeated injuries; he could not dance as much. As for fund-raising, he loathed it. At parties for patrons, he was often the first person out the door.) And by insisting on a salary of a dollar a year as director—which, given his performance fees, he could afford—he felt he had given himself that right. But the wear on him was severe. In 1989, he gave notice that he would leave in 1990. A few months later, the administration went over his head and fired his second-in-command, Charles France. Baryshnikov resigned in a fury.

Why had he taken the job in the first place? He is not a natural leader. He can't press the flesh, give the interviews, settle the quarrels, or not willingly. Yet at the time when it came, the offer of the ABT directorship was something he could not refuse. Having seen at the Kirov how badly a ballet company could be directed, he was, of course, tempted to find out if he could run one well. At the same time, there was another factor—his year at New York City Ballet. It has often been claimed that Baryshnikov's experience there was a bitter disappointment to him because by the time he arrived Balanchine was already ill (he died within five years) and could not make new ballets for him. "That's nonsense, absolute nonsense," Baryshnikov says. "That one year was most interesting time in my American career." Part of the pleasure, again, was new repertory. In fifteen months at NYCB, he learned twenty-odd roles, and though he had trouble fitting into some of them—and not enough time—there were others, particularly Balanchine's *Apollo* and *The Prodigal Son,* that seemed to have been waiting all those years just for him. He was tremendous, utterly wrenching, as the Prodigal, and he was probably the best Apollo ever to inhabit that role. All the qualities needed to represent Balanchine's boy-god—childlikeness, aloneness, dignity, a sense of high mission—were already in him. He filled the ballet to its skin.

But Baryshnikov says that what was most important to him at NYCB was his sense that he had found a home. Balanchine had gone to the same school and made his professional début at the same theatre that Baryshnikov had, and, like him, had decided that to be an artist he must leave Russia. (Baryshnikov defected fifty years, almost to the day, after Balanchine left.) Balanchine had then created in the West what, in Baryshnikov's view, Russian ballet would have become but for the Revolution: modernist classicism. "I am entering the ideal future of the Maryinsky Ballet," he told reporters when he announced his switch to NYCB. (The Maryinsky was the Kirov's pre-Revolutionary name.) Also, Balanchine seems to have treated him like a son: "He told me, 'I wish I could be a little younger, a little healthier, that we could work more on new pieces, but let's not waste time. Let's do *Harlequinade,* let's do *Prodigal,* let's do this, let's do that, and think— whatever you want to do.' He cared what I will do."

The story is terrible. The homeless boy found a home, the sonless master found a son, but it was very late. Then came the invitation from ABT. Curiously, it was in part because of the gifts Baryshnikov was given at NYCB that he decided to leave. For one thing, Balanchine told him he could always come back. "I went to him and we talked for a long time," he recalls. "We talked for an hour one day, and he said, 'Come back tomorrow.' And he was very, sort of—not encouraging me, but said, 'If you can see what you want to do and can deal with people on the board and you have a clear vision, I think you should do it, take this chance.' He said, 'If it doesn't work, it doesn't work. You can come back, anytime. This is your home.'"

But it wasn't just the NYCB safety net that emboldened Baryshnikov to go to ABT. It was also what he saw as the moral lesson of NYCB, as taught to him by Balanchine and Jerome Robbins, the company's second ballet master. "Working with Balanchine and Jerry every day—just to see their *dedication* to the institution, the company, the school. Their seriousness, the seriousness of the whole setup, everything about it. Very different from the world which I come from, government-supported company, or commercially set-up company like Ballet Theatre. I learn so much. Something about dance ethics, about being a dancer, and the *quality* of the work. I learn how and why to respect choreographic vision and morale of theatre. And that was most important experience. On the surface I was just one of them, and that was fine. But deep inside I experienced extraordinary transformation, and I understand a lot of things, for my future work." Clearly, that was a major reason for his going to ABT. He felt he had learned something tremendous, and he wanted to use it. Those who accused him of trying to turn ABT into NYCB were partly right.

NEARLY TEN YEARS after Baryshnikov's departure from ABT, with the current administration trying desperately to restore the old stars-and-classics order, the company still reflects the changes he made: the corps still shows the verve he instilled in it, and the young soloist-level dancers still seem to dance with a sort of wild hope, as if they might actually be promoted. But these are things you can't discuss with Baryshnikov at present. The bitterness of the ABT years is still too keen. What he sees now as the "future work" to which he tried to carry the spirit of New York City Ballet is his present project: directing a modern-dance company. This troupe, the White Oak Dance Project, is a great curiosity. What is a Russian-trained ballet dancer doing directing an American modern-dance company? And why is a man who during the ABT years repeatedly said that he wanted to retire from the stage—that he had had it, that his knee was killing him (it has now been operated on five times)—still performing intensively: an activity that requires him to undergo two hours of physical therapy every day, and, on days when he is performing, four additional hours of warmups and rehearsal, not to speak of the travelling and the room-service dinners? "Well," he said to me in 1990, at the time of White Oak's founding, "I thought there is maybe a couple of years left, for fun." The late philanthropist Howard Gilman, a friend of his, offered to build him a rehearsal studio at the Gilman Foundation's White Oak Plantation, in Florida—in gratitude, Baryshnikov named the troupe after the plantation—and operations were set up in such a way that, unlike ABT, the company would not be a noose around his neck. He hired seasoned dancers—people who would not develop eating disorders—and he engaged them on a tour-by-tour basis. The company was not a company; it was a "project." It could vanish at any time. It had no board, no grants, no deficit. Either it paid for itself or Baryshnikov wrote a check. In other words, he set up the least institutional institution he could possibly create—one in which, for the first time, he could present and perform dance without the thousand circumstances that in his experience had compromised those activities.

White Oak has now been in existence for seven years. It is small, usually eight to twelve dancers. It is classy. (It travels with its own five-piece chamber orchestra. No taped music.) It tours for about four months a year, and it has been all around the world. For its first three or four years, the repertory was mostly by "name" choreographers: Martha Graham, Paul Taylor, David Gordon, Twyla Tharp, Mark Morris. (Morris helped Baryshnikov set up the company.) But in the last few years White Oak has begun dangling from the treetops, offering works by avant-gardists almost unknown outside New York and also by beginners—people who are making only their second or third pieces but whom Baryshnikov finds interesting. Still, the concerts regularly sell out, because he is performing in them. Two years ago, I sat in the Kravis Center, in West Palm Beach, Florida, with two thousand Republicans as they watched a big, ambitious, confusing piece called *What a Beauty!,* created by Kraig Patterson, a fledgling choreographer who is also a dancer with the Mark Morris Dance Group. The audience looked puzzled. But on this program there was also a solo for Baryshnikov; that is, the audience got to see, for perhaps twelve minutes, the most interesting dancer in the world today performing alone, and therefore they got their money's worth. In a sense, the situation is an artificial one. Baryshnikov probably knows this, but it doesn't seem to bother him. He is having an adventure, presenting new choreography. He is at last putting on his Creative Evening—night after night, with no *artsoviet* to tell him what they think— and if his fame can induce people to come and see it that is fine by him. Recently, I asked him the big question: In the West, had he got what he wanted? Had he found what he came for? "Oh, more than that, more than that," he said. "I never dreamt that I would work with so many extraordinary people." That was all he wanted, just to work with interesting people.

IN RETURN FOR TAKING only a nominal fee in Riga, Baryshnikov had arranged for the state opera's general-admission prices to be lowered for his performances, but the tickets were still beyond the means of most of Riga's ballet people. (The average salary in Riga is five hundred dollars a month.) So he opened his first dress rehearsal to the staff and pensioners of the opera house and the ballet school, and before the rehearsal began he came out in front of the curtain and addressed them. It was a strange moment—packed with history, like the session in the studio—and in parts of the audience there was probably some resentment against the local boy who made good. The people in that auditorium represented an old tradition, the one that had bred him and from which he had fled. Now they would see the new kind of dancing that he had preferred to theirs. But as he spoke, it was to their world, not his, that he addressed himself. He told them how this solo concert was dedicated to the memory of his mother; how happy he was, after so many years, to perform again on the stage where he had first danced; how pleased he was to present these dances to his theatre colleagues. And he choked up—the first time I ever saw him do so—and had to stop and pause repeatedly before speaking again.

Later, he said to me, "All those people who were sitting there, they were veterans of this society, this space. All these people that I saw when I was young, they were some very good dancers or not that good dancers, some of them good actors, or some of them just beautiful women, or some of them were great character dancers, or some very enthusiastic performers. I knew them by name, I knew their history. Half of those people are dead already, but the other half, in their sixties or their eighties, are sitting in that audience. And they're all of them in me, in my body, in my brain. You know, you learn to dance when you're very young. And in subconsciousness you take pieces from every person. Even worst dancers have two moves, one move, and you say, 'What was that? How did he do that?' And already it's in you. That's why I—that's why it was very moving—because, you know, I owe them." So again he did have a family, but it was dancers. In his second concert, he shared the program with the Latvian state ballet and its school—he did two solos, they did various dances, including some that he had appeared in as a boy (the Garland Waltz from *The Sleeping Beauty,* the "Corsaire" pas de deux)—and he donated the proceeds to his old school.

Both shows were a great success, but nothing was quite like the piece that Baryshnikov closed with on the last night. This was Tharp's *Pergolesi*—a smart choice, since, like the other pieces Tharp has made for Baryshnikov, it includes ballet, and so Baryshnikov was able to show the audience his old fireworks. Actually, though, *Pergolesi* includes just about everything: folk dance, eighteenth-century dance, quotes from famous ballets (*Le Spectre de la Rose, La Sylphide, Swan Lake*), shimmies, bugaloo, golf swings. He got a chance to do every kind of dance he knew—not just what he had learned in the West but also what he had been taught at the Riga School of Choreography. And I don't know what happened—maybe it was the bringing together of the two halves of his history, or maybe it was relief that this heavily freighted trip was nearly over, or maybe now, at the end, he just wanted to give these people everything he had—but he exploded. I have never seen him so happy onstage, or so wild. ("He's showing off!" said Lisa Rinehart, who was sitting next to me.) He gave them the double barrel turns, he gave them the triple pirouettes in attitude (and then he switched to the other leg and did two more). He rose like a piston; he landed like a lark. He took off like Jerry Lee Lewis; he finished like Jane Austen. From ledge to ledge of the dance he leapt, surefooted, unmindful, a man in love. The audience knew what they were seeing. The air in the theatre thickened almost visibly. Even the members of the orchestra, though their backs were to him, seemed to understand that something unusual was happening. Out of the pit, the beautiful introduction to Pergolesi's *Adriano in Siria* rose like a wave, and he rode it to the finish. By that time, we actually wanted him to stop, so that we could figure out what had happened to us. Latvians, I was told by the locals, almost never give standing ovations. And they never yell "Bravo!" in the theatre; they consider that vulgar. But they yelled "Bravo!" for him, and everyone stood, including the President of the Republic.

Baryshnikov took his curtain calls with the members of the Latvian National Opera Ballet, they in their dirndls and harem pants, he in his Isaac Mizrahi jerseys—messengers of the two worlds created when Europe broke in half. It will never wholly mend, any more than Baryshnikov, child of that break, was ever able to find an artistic home. But it is hard to regret his fate. Homelessness turned him inward, gave him to himself. Then dance, the substitute home, turned him outward, gave him to us.

—from *The New Yorker,* January 19, 1998

JOHN FRASER
Defection

O n June 29, 1974, Mikhail Baryshnikov was dancing with a visiting
Soviet ballet troupe in Canada, at the end of a week of performances at
Toronto's O'Keefe Centre. Shortly after 11:00 P.M., instead of boarding a
bus to go to a postperformance party with his Soviet colleagues, he bolted
through a crowd of well-wishers and headed for an automobile, parked near
the theater, in which he was whisked away from his Soviet past and into
a world of great expectations and beckoning horizons. *Defection* seems such
a corrosive and negative word for what was, in effect, the most positive act
of the young dancer's life, an act that was joyously received in the West. Yet
defection it was, and for several days—as he hid out at a country estate in
the middle of an Ontario forest—his fate became the focus of front-page
news across the world. . . .

Back in the early summer of 1974, the defection was widely hailed
for bringing to the West someone who had already been touted as "the
greatest Soviet male dancer since Rudolf Nureyev." Exceptional male
dancers are so few in number at any given time that their arrival by whatever
means is a major event, one that tends to define their own eras in ballet
lore, while their fame quickly spreads well beyond the confines of the
expanding but still specialized ballet audience. Baryshnikov's defection constituted a brave personal decision and an authentic historical moment, so it
would be appropriate if it could be reported that there was a due sense of
solemnity about it all. Appropriate, but inaccurate. There were too many
people laughing, one too many crying, a dance critic almost out of control,
and an overall scenario more appropriate for *Saturday Night Live* than
anything else.

I was then a young dance critic working for the Toronto *Globe and Mail*.
Like many other dance writers in North America, I had heard rumors about
a Soviet *wunderkind* named Baryshnikov, who had had the same teacher as
Nureyev. When it was announced that a provincial ballet troupe from the
Soviet Union would be touring Canada and Central America, there was little
reason for interest until it emerged that the company would be headed by
two stars of Leningrad's Kirov Ballet: Irina Kolpakova and one "M. N.
Barichnikoff."

The first performance on the cross-Canada tour was in Ottawa, and I made plans to go to the national capital to see the opening performance and to talk to Baryshnikov. An interview was denied, as it was pointed out that the "correct and polite" procedure was to request a meeting with the touring artistic director, Alexander Lapauri. When the correct request was made, it was quickly granted.

Lapauri was considered an outstanding character dancer in his day. He and his wife, Raissa Struchkova, were particularly well known for their joint appearances in two of the most overwrought of all Soviet choreographic works: *Walpurgisnacht* and *Spring Waters*. Struchkova was still being billed in the Soviet Union as a performing prima ballerina at the age of forty-eight, and to no one's evident surprise, she was along on this trip as a star attraction. She also came along for my interview with Lapauri, which got off to a very bad start when I asked if what everyone said about their "boy wonder" was true.

"Who are you talking about?" asked Lapauri, showing seemingly genuine perplexity. "We have many of what you call 'boy wonders' in the Soviet Union." Then, with a manly and self-effacing chuckle, he added, "Why, I myself was once called by such a title!"

He laughed again and looked at his wife, who smiled through clenched teeth that showed the glint of several stainless-steel caps.

"I mean Baryshnikov," I said.

"That one!" said Struchkova, and the great lady turned her head away from me in unfeigned disgust. Lapauri rushed in to get the conversation back on track.

"Mikhail Baryshnikov is, of course, a very exciting young dancer in our troupe, but he is only one of many. . . ."

Here Lapauri wandered off into a string of names and, enjoying the commanding lead he had taken in recapturing the interview, went on to discuss Soviet teaching methods and the perniciousness of the Western star system. As the interpreter droned on in a low monotone, I found myself fixated with the vision of Raissa Struchkova. Was she really going to perform? Would she actually dance with Baryshnikov as her partner? Such things surely weren't possible. It wasn't so much that her considerable age—for a ballerina—was against her. Margot Fonteyn and Alicia Alonso both managed to ride out their illustrious careers for decades on the strength of their well-preserved beauty, great fame, and the seemingly effortless distillation of their years of experience. With Struchkova it was somewhat different. Struchkova had been a beloved ballerina in her prime, and the memory of that prime in the Soviet Union—combined with Lapauri's and her own evident political clout—had been sufficient to mount this strange North American tour, which skirted the United States entirely. But the memory of Struchkova's earlier days was not enough for the mostly young audiences in

Canada, who tended to see only her current brawn and unrepentant bravado.

This was no ghostly sylph we beheld. Heaven and her husband alone knew what she tipped the scales at. The sight of her later that evening in full battle dress—spiked tutu, fingers like stilettos set menacingly at the end of her pudding-dough arms and hands, garish smile pasted on her face, her legs surely fashioned from the sturdiest heart of oak—was more than enough to make the strongest men tremble. Literally.

Struchkova's set piece on this tour was the lurid *Walpurgis Night,* the sort of choreography that convinces you finally that there is little point in trying to resist the Soviet menace. The high point in this meat grinder of a *divertissement* comes toward the end, when the leading ballerina flings herself into the waiting outstretched arms of no less than three male dancers. Interpreted by Struchkova, *Walpurgisnacht* is not so much a ballet about bacchanalia as it is a reenactment of the siege at Stalingrad. As she prepared to hurl herself into the air at the end, her feet pawed the stage floor. The knees of the three sacrificial males whose job was to safely catch the artistic director's cumbersome spouse were actually shaking. When she finally landed in their arms, the force of the full impact sent them reeling back several steps, and they looked like some potted version of the cygnets in *Swan Lake* trying to carry a steel girder.

Hardly had the full effect of this extraordinary scene sunk in when the curtain at the National Arts Center in Ottawa opened up to reveal Baryshnikov. In Ottawa the audience was not so aware of his reputation as they would be in Toronto and Montreal, where a palpable hush of expectation accompanied the first sight of him. Hundreds of ballet fans in New York were to come to the Montreal performances just to see him, and, as it was learned later, these included at least half a dozen with a special interest in getting beyond the KGB minders who were along on the tour to prevent what ultimately happened.

It was not necessary to know the intricacies of ballet technique to appreciate his brilliance, but those who had studied ballet were nevertheless left staggered at the feats he pulled off. In the pas de deux from *Don Quixote,* which he had to dance with Raissa Struchkova as the youthful Kitri, his solo variations—in which he appeared to be taking a walk in space, using his own technical innovations—caused one of those rare occasions when an audience momentarily did not know how to respond, mere applause seeming somehow inappropriate.

It was following the first night's performance at Toronto's O'Keefe Centre that I walked clumsily into Mikhail Baryshnikov's life. I wish this brief tale, which is not without elements of tension and intrigue, were less of a farce, but it isn't. It also set the mood for our subsequent friendship.

Following the performance at O'Keefe, I returned to my newspaper offices a few blocks away to write up a review of the evening. It was going to be an easy piece to write: Baryshnikov was brilliant, and this had to be celebrated; the Lapauri troupe, on the other hand, was dreadful, and the whys and wherefores had to be itemized. As I sat down at my typewriter, I noticed the message someone had left in the roller: "Mrs. Barnes from New York says it is extremely URGENT that you call her immediately."

With a deadline less than an hour away, I was inclined to put the call off until afterward, but curiosity got the better of me. Besides, Mrs. Barnes was Mrs. Trish Barnes, the wife (now divorced) of then *New York Times* dance critic Clive Barnes, and an influential figure in the ballet world in her own right.

"Do you speak Russian?" she asked after I dialed the New York number.

"*Nyet,*" I replied definitively.

"Well, maybe he speaks some French."

"Maybe who speaks French?"

"Baryshnikov," she said. "You have to get a message through to him tonight or tomorrow. It's absolutely crucial. I tried to do it in Montreal, but the situation was impossible. Use your ingenuity and see what you can do. Have you got a pencil to take down a phone number in New York?"

I got a pencil.

"Tell him his friends want to speak to him," she continued, her voice getting more authoritative as she realized she had me hooked.

"What's up?" I asked. "Is he going to defect?"

"Now look. Don't ask questions. Just get to him. There's no thought of defection. He has three very close friends here who simply have to make contact with him. Remember these names: *Dina, Tina, and Sasha.* Have you got them? *Dina, Tina, and Sasha.*"

"Who are they?"

"Just remember the names. And the phone number. And do be very careful. There may be some nasty people around him."

Right. Now, just *try* to write a review in thirty minutes after a conversation like that.

Somehow words formed themselves as an overactive imagination worked in another sphere altogether, transforming a humble arts writer into the James Bond of ballet. When I reread my review before handing it to the night editor, it was clear to me that I was going to have to strike immediately. The next day would be too late: After this piece was read by Struchkova and her laugh-a-minute husband, there would be no further chance of contact with anyone attached to this company. I think I even managed to say that the state of the corps de ballet represented a setback for Soviet-Canadian relations.

My best chance to nab Baryshnikov, however briefly, was at a reception for the Soviet troupe being given by Seagram's Distilleries in the downstairs foyer back at O'Keefe Centre, and it was there that I sped, faster even than Nureyev fleeing a female admirer. Careful preparations had all been made and I was full of Mountie-like resolve to get my man. To this end, I had written the New York phone number, complete with area code, on one side of a small sticky label. This was carefully anchored to the underside of a signet ring on my right hand. The intention was to shake hands with Baryshnikov at the appropriate moment—*after* turning the sticky side face outward. In this way the paper would stick to his palm as we unclasped. Where this utterly bizarre and foolish idea sprang from, I cannot say. Certainly, it was among the stupidest things I have ever done and came close to being the ruination of the whole exercise.

The reception was going full blast when I arrived—or at least as full blast as a party can go when it is comprised of people who don't understand one another's language. There were about two dozen large round tables set up, with the biggest reserved in the center for the Seagram hosts and their special guests. These included Celia Franca, founder and then artistic director of the National Ballet of Canada, Lapauri, and Struchkova, several translators who were considered part and parcel of the KGB—and Baryshnikov.

It was my first sight of him close up, and he looked tired, bored, and frustrated. You can catch exactly the same look on his face today if you pay hundreds of dollars to attend a gala performance of American Ballet Theatre and benefit party afterward. Look for an equivalent central table, the smiling and self-important visage of whoever happens to be chairman of the event, the gleaming countenances of the chief fund-raisers stroking the egos of their selected fund-givers, and then focus on the tired, bored, frustrated Russian expatriate beside them. On most occasions he tries hard to do what is expected of him at these events. Sometimes he doesn't fool anyone. It is at moments like these that I wonder if his life has changed all that much: If you spin on a stage fast enough, high commissars look remarkably like rich capitalists.

A presiding demon deep within me, which was in control of all my minor motor functions that evening, directed me to greet Miss Franca as effusively as possible, so that Baryshnikov would see that I was not some local dupe of his own security agents. If this seems silly in retrospect, it is nevertheless worthwhile pointing out that *glasnost* was not to rear its friendly face for more than a decade. Franca and I had an understanding. I suppose we liked each other well enough, but since I wrote about her company more often than anyone else in the country, I had to allow her periods in which she could dismiss me as an ignorant lunatic of surpassing irrelevance. For her part, she had to put up with my occasional comments about her "vulgar stylistic excesses" and "dictatorial spite." Other than these sorts of things, we had a wonderfully warm relationship during those years.

She was, of course, surprised to see me at the reception, for I never went to such affairs. To this day, I am sure she knew I was up to something.

"You must meet Misha," said Franca, pointing in Baryshnikov's direction. Even at that early date, people felt they had an automatic and immediate right to call him by the affectionate diminutive of his Christian name, Mikhail. At first this practice irritated him, since only his closest friends in Russia would have presumed to use it. In time, however, he got so fed up hearing his proper name pronounced either like a Nazi greeting to a Rolling Stone (Mick-Heil) or like some lost Hebrew prophet (Mick-high-el), that he began encouraging the active use of "Misha."

I had not planned on meeting the quarry quite so soon. Everyone at his table was watching us very closely, and there was no chance of passing anything whatsoever to him. I mumbled a desperate *"bonsoir"* and got one in return, just as a Seagram's official came up to escort me to my assigned spot—far, far away at the edge of the room. It would take me more than half an hour to figure out what to do. On one side of Baryshnikov sat Lapauri, and on the other a very unfriendly-looking translator-*cum*-KGB-minder. Eventually I managed to convince Lapauri that the translator was needed at my table, where a Canadian senator was having problems communicating with the Soviet conductor. When Lapauri himself soon afterward started table-hopping, I saw my best chance. I went straight to where Baryshnikov was sitting and put my hand on his shoulder. He looked at me quizzically as I started saying something in English, until I remembered I was supposed to speak French. Here was the first breakthrough. His French was worse than mine, and we understood each other perfectly. I said the magic three words—Dina, Tina, and Sasha—and his face lit up with the most wonderful amazed smile.

"Ici? Maintenant?" he asked.

"Non, non. À New York. J'ai ici le numéro du téléphone."

I coyly turned the palm of my hand to show him my clever plan. To my horror, the little strip of sticky paper had curled up into a tight ball and was now hopelessly attached to the ring. Trying to look as if I were picking at a wart, I eventually detached and uncurled the damn thing but realized the telephone number was now indistinct. Although I could just make out the figures, I was sure he wouldn't be able to. Baryshnikov laughed out loud. I have heard that laugh many times since and all over the world—in Beijing's Tien An Men Square beneath Stalin's dreadful memorial portrait, in southern Italy and northern Ontario, and all over the United States—but that first time it burst out with such spontaneity that I found myself laughing out loud as well, despite my nervousness. He reached into his jacket pocket and pulled out a notebook.

"Avez-vous un stylo?" he asked me, preparing to write down the telephone number.

Hmmm.

"Non."

A journalist without a pen or pencil, at the center of a great story, must expect to carry a certain amount of emblematic baggage. This was clearly a poorly planned escapade. I turned to the closest table and eventually cadged a stub of a pencil from someone. As Baryshnikov took down the last digits of the telephone number, Franca and Lapauri started walking toward us. Lapauri said something in Russian to Baryshnikov which made the dancer snort cynically and blurt out what I took to be swear words. Later I learned the Soviet artistic director had mockingly asked him: "How much has Celia Franca offered you to join her company?" To which he had replied, "Half a million dollars, but I am holding out for more."

This was all on a Monday evening in June. Four days later, having been contacted by the enigmatic Dina, Tina, and Sasha, he made his historic decision to defect. Even then, the mechanics of defection were not without elements of farce. Sasha, it turned out, was Alexander Minz, a former character dancer at the Kirov and a Jew who had been allowed to emigrate to Israel several years previously and was now part of the New York dance scene. Dina was Dina Makarova, a young woman who always seemed to be doing triple duty as a photographer, a translator, and a personal assistant. She had close ties to American Ballet Theatre and, especially, to the Russian ballerina Natalia Makarova (though they are unrelated), who had defected a few years earlier. Tina was Christina Berlin, the American "love interest," who was also the daughter of a senior Hearst Corporation executive. They had first met in London when Baryshnikov made his Western debut, and she had managed to keep up some sort of relationship with him during the ensuing four years. Together, these three and a small, hastily arranged network of other friends and acquaintances helped create a defection plan, once Baryshnikov had finished his internal struggle and made his decision. The date was to be Friday, June 29, and the defection would occur as soon as he could get dressed following the final performance at O'Keefe Centre.

As a plan it was simplicity itself—like all great plans that get screwed up. Dina Makarova and a good friend of mine in Toronto named Tim Stewart (whose involvement, like my own, was entirely coincidental) would be waiting in a car parked in front of a nearby restaurant. After the final curtain came down at 10:30 P.M. and Baryshnikov had changed, he would simply walk away from the company. The first leg of the journey would be a speedy drive to a Toronto safe house, where there would be a change of cars, and then the entire entourage would simply disappear into the neighboring country landscape to plan the immediate future in peace and quiet. At his leisure, Baryshnikov could consider his options, deal with the Canadian immigration and security authorities, talk to the artistic directors of ballet companies, and have a brief respite as he started the task of acclimating to his strange new world.

The plan started to go wrong when the stagehands couldn't get the O'Keefe Centre stage curtain open Friday night, delaying the entire performance by fifteen minutes. Then Baryshnikov complicated affairs by dancing too well, garnering curtain calls that stretched out the evening. By the time he got back to the dressing room at performance's end, he was already half an hour late. The couple waiting for him in the car were starting to get agitated and very concerned. One of the KGB minders informed Baryshnikov that he was expected to board a bus as soon as he was dressed, because the entire company was being taken to a civic reception.

In the end, Mikhail Baryshnikov's fans saved the day. A clutch of well-wishers and autograph seekers had blocked a clear passage to the waiting bus, and the dancer was able to use them as a foil to make his escape. While he was running through the adjacent parking lot toward the waiting car, he heard one of the minders shouting out, "Misha! Misha! Where are you going?"

—from *Private View,* 1988

ARLENE CROCE
Le Mystère Baryshnikov

He is a phenomenally gifted man who happens to have become a dancer. That he did not become the world's foremost soccer player or concert pianist is an accident of fate owing to his mother's interest in ballet and the presence, in the Latvian school curriculum, of courses in folk dance.

Baryshnikov's many blessings set him apart from even the greatest dancers we have seen, although it is important to note that he is not different from them in kind. The greatest dancers are born with the capacity to enrich their art, not merely their reputations. Some actually succeed in doing so, and most of these are women whose capacities have been explored by great choreographers in epochal roles. One thinks of Marie Taglioni in Filippo Taglioni's *La Sylphide,* of Carlotta Grisi in Jules Perrot's *Giselle.* Most recently, there has been Suzanne Farrell in a repertory of roles created by George Balanchine. Baryshnikov has incarnated many different images, prepared for him by many different choreographers. He is the most protean dancer since Nijinsky. But like Nijinsky and like Vestris before him,

Baryshnikov is largely self-produced. With or without benefit of choreography, he has generated shock waves that have swept the world of dance. By himself, he supplies the material for which ballerinas traditionally rely on choreographers—material which gives form and expressive meaning to creativity. This is not to say that he is immune to the disasters that can occur when choreographers fail him. And we cannot rule out the possibility of undreamed-of triumphs which might have been his if he, too, had had ballets made for him by Balanchine. But after twelve years in the West—years of discovery and exhaustive experimentation—Baryshnikov persists as an independent force, unique in stature, fertile in expression.

Baryshnikov, then, is the example in our time of the essentially procreative male genius in dance. Yet he is not another Nijinsky, still less another Massine or Lifar. For one thing, he abjures almost entirely the role of choreographer. It is easy to see how working in New York, which he calls "the city of a thousand choreographers and a thousand companies," could defeat any impulse he might feel to produce choreography in a formal sense. But a more compelling reason not to choreograph may be that he is not driven by a consummate ambition. Here is the greatest difference between Baryshnikov and all the others, great and small: though he may be possessed by a need to dance, he is not consumed by it. No white-hot flame burns in him, no unappeasable appetite for the stage. He will not die there, insatiable for applause or for whatever inner rewards performance holds. Baryshnikov is cool, very cool; he always has been, even when he first came bounding toward us with what the choreographer Twyla Tharp calls his "vast, naive energy." Even then, one saw how that energy was framed by a ceaseless effort toward self-control and away from excess. For all his prodigious technique, Baryshnikov is never ostentatious, he is never eccentric, and he is no *monstre sacré*. His energy is spiritual as well as physical. We know this because his every performance tells us so. What his performances do *not* tell us is how this undivided wholeness of expression can come about with no apparent involvement on the part of the personal Misha. The performances contain no self-explanations; it's as if the man who dances is somehow separate from the *being* who exists there on the stage. Where is the mortal man Baryshnikov? What motivates this impulse toward self-perfection? Where is the confessional element New York loves to see in every performer who ventures forth on its twinkling stages? Where are the revelations—the sweat, the sacrifice, the victimization? Where the naked need which only an audience can satisfy? Baryshnikov makes no concessions, no appeals, neither does he conceal himself. This is his mystery. This is why the most lucid classical dancer of our time is also the most enigmatic.

—from Paris *Vogue,* December 1986

JILL JOHNSTON
Baryshnikov Dancing Judson

In 2001, seven seminal Judson choreographers were featured in a touring show put together by Mikhail Baryshnikov and his White Oak Dance Project.

I went to see Mikhail Baryshnikov and his White Oak Dance Project at BAM the week of June because the work of seven so-called Judson choreographers was featured. The program was called "Past/*Forward*," meaning that post-Judson work by the choreographers, up in fact to the present, was included. I often put myself out to see the work of my time, or work by those of my time as it keeps evolving (or not), generally seeing little else. As a true old-timer, I tend to believe that all that came after is crap. In the case of the Judson revolution in dance-making, I may actually be right. Oh, I know there are individually brilliant works around, and of course there have been for years. But it takes a group to make a revolution. And revolutions happen probably only once or twice a century. And for those of us leavened on the art of revolutionary times, there can never be anything like it again. Not unless it comes again. And the 1960s will never come again.

Judson revisited under the auspices of Mikhail Baryshnikov is a sort of archival display, a retrospective exhibition, with differences so noteworthy as to make the subject new or unrecognizable. A fabulous displacement in context changes everything. The original performance space of the funky, cavernous, high-ceilinged, peaked-roof sanctuary room of Judson Church on Washington Square, with its woolly downtown in-crowd audience whose wild enthusiasm and educated interest were not least of what composed the revolution, was a setting integral to the work itself. Likewise, the grandly formal, corporate-sponsored proscenium stage at BAM, with its throngs attracted chiefly by the fame of a great ex-ballet dancer, is an arena that completely defines what we see there. This is Judson gone Hollywood, theatricalized in ways that fully contradict the tenets of Judson's origins and early performances in its heydays, 1962–64.

Anti-spectacle, anti-entertainment, anti–star image, anti–proscenium frontality, anti-expression or narrative, anti–dance movement itself as traditionally understood—here was a dissenting canon as insurrectional as the revolution in dance ushered in by the barefoot, ballet-hating Isadora Duncan in the late nineteenth century. Her pioneering work would be refined by Ruth St. Denis and Ted Shawn, then Doris Humphrey and Martha Graham (both schooled as Densishawn dancers in the 1930s), and in their wake by the Humphrey disciple José Limón. At last Merce Cunningham, formerly a Graham dancer, introduced in the 1950s a dance aesthetic that was entirely new. It was off Cunningham's back that the Judson choreographers leap-frogged. Among them were the seven represented by Baryshnikov at BAM: David Gordon, Steve Paxton, Simone Forti, Yvonne Rainer, Trisha Brown, Lucinda Childs, and Deborah Hay. Cunningham's studio at Fourteenth Street and Sixth Avenue was actually a launching pad. There Robert Dunn, a com-poser and follower of Cunningham's partner, John Cage, and the husband of one of Cunningham's dancers, Judith Dunn, taught the class in choreogra-phy that led to the first evening of performances at Judson Church, on July 6,1962. Much as Cunningham was admired and his aleatory method of com-position a class expedient, his maintenance of the old bedrock of dance in technical training, whether ballet or modern, was ditched entirely in the Judson experiment.

The new and unprecedented Judson look was movement lifted from everyday actions of ordinary people, including dancers when they are not dancing. "Pedestrian" was the word, and still is, for the new "dance." A pedestrian is a walker and there was plenty of plain walking in early Judson work. Steve Paxton, a Cunningham company member (1961–1964) all the while he was rebelling with the Judson group, particularly loved walking. And sitting and walking. In his 1964 solo *Flat* he sat and walked around and studiously removed his "costume" of shoes, jacket, shirt, and pants, hanging them on hooks taped to his body; then put his clothes back on, ever contin-uing sitting and walking. Sometimes he sat or stood still. It was very boring. Boring was tremendously exciting in the revolution. *Flat* is one of only three pieces transplanted intact from the Judson of 1962–1964 in Baryshnikov's Judson archive evening. And as its updated soloist, Baryshnikov makes it far from boring. Not because he doesn't follow its instructions to the letter, performing it in the required pedestrian "boring" manner. But because . . . well, because he is Baryshnikov. Just the question why he is doing this at all makes it pretty interesting.

Anyway, boring has long ceased to be exciting. A precise replica of an old Judson concert in its original or similar setting would make any old-timer sigh. We like simply the memory, and that being there was a sacred privi-lege. The new thing is what Baryshnikov is doing with it all. He's the real creator here. With techno-resources, financial backing, much experience as an artistic director (for nine years at the American Ballet Theatre) and a cultivated passion for dancing in the works of postmodern choreographers, he has forged an entertaining, commercially viable program out of an unlikely piece of history. For himself and his White Oak company of professionally trained younger dancers, he has dusted off several old, prosaic, Minimalist treasures, intact and/or adapted by the intrepid survivors, and integrated them superbly with examples of their work from the 1970s till now.

A downstage screen, dropped at intervals during the evening, is almost an "extra" performer, a "choral" auxiliary, helping to glue the parts together. The names of the Judson seven appear in succession on the screen while Baryshnikov in voice-over describes how he assembled the choreographers for this evening. A prologue video by Charles Atlas shows clips of them talking among themselves and includes fragments of work from that time. A fleeting image of artists Robert Morris and Carolee Schneemann in Morris's *Site* of 1965, one of Judson's most extraordinary pieces, reminds us that creators in mediums besides dance were participating, and that there were many more contributors than seven to that indelible scene.

Some of those who were left out, and who helped make it all happen, might at least have been listed by name on that all-purpose dropped screen. Not even the critics, essential scribes in any revolution, are noted, except by Rainer (speaking to a confrere on the Atlas video), who says guilefully, "And all the critics were outraged." Forgetting obviously, that Allen Hughes, filling in as dance critic at *The New York Times,* did a most commendable and charitable job of covering the group then.

Concerts continued at Judson Church until 1968, but by then they also abounded in art galleries, lofts, other churches, and different non-proscenium spaces. Such opportunities led inevitably to major independent careers. Sally Banes has described all this in her fine 1980 compendium of the era, *Terpsichore in Sneakers.*

The meeting of Baryshnikov and Judson was, it seems, a fortuity waiting to happen. He says that long before he formed White Oak (in 1990), while still a dancer at the Kirov in Russia, he was drawn to the work of the Judson postmodernists. He must have meant that he had heard or read about them, since he did not arrive in America until 1974, the year of his defection. He was an enthusiastic defector. Before long, and even as he was taking Westerners by storm—the most breathtaking ballet virtuoso since Nijinsky and Nureyev—he was dancing as a guest in works of modern choreographers, including Cunningham, Paul Taylor, Twyla Tharp, and even Limón and Graham. As director of the American Ballet Theatre during the 1980s, Baryshnikov upset and challenged the ABT trustees by commissioning difficult postmodern work. David Gordon, of the golden Judson age, was one of his choices. On the White Oak program at BAM, Gordon is listed as "director and writer"—in effect Baryshnikov's deputy organizer—and represented by three dance works. The earliest is dated 1975; the most recent, titled *Chair Intro 2000,* is a showboat solo opener made for Baryshnikov and a chair, set to the music of John Philip Sousa's *Stars and Stripes Forever.* It was quite thrilling indeed, designed no doubt to let us know that nothing we were going to see here would be "anti-spectacle" or "anti-entertainment." Even Lucinda Childs's uncompromising, soundless 1964 solo, *Carnation,* danced at BAM by White Oak company member Emily Coates, is divertingly updated with a live video enlarging the performer's projected image on screen behind her several times her size on stage. But this makes sense for such a big auditorium, where the small detailed gestures of *Carnation*—once so visible from, say, twenty feet at floor level in Judson Church—could be hard to make out.

Yvonne Rainer's signature solo work of the early period, *Trio A* of 1966, has undergone a number of transpositions since then, but surely none as concessional as its most recent manifestation in Baryshnikov's Judson evening. Here called *Tri A Pressured #3,* danced by the seven White Oak company members, its original soundlessness and famously uninflected movement—a long, deceptively simple, unpunctuated phrase—have been seriously compromised. With seven dancers facing every which way and performing the phrase contrapuntally to music of the Chambers Brothers (*In the Midnight Hour*), this once purest icon has been cast in a confusing Cunninghamesque space, and trounced additionally, sold out you could say, by rock-and-roll entertainment. Why not have bypassed *Trio A* altogether to bring back a much less boring Rainer artifact from the even deeper past, *Three Seascapes* of 1962?

Who would not love to see *Three Seascapes* again, or for the first time? The trouble is, who would perform it? It's got a lot of character, with weirdly restrained, as well as weirdly expressed, emotion. Rainer's screaming fit, which constituted the third of her *Three Seascapes,* was no doubt a clichéd commentary—shorn after all of narrative context—on the expressiveness that Judson, and Cunningham before Judson, banned. But it couldn't help functioning also as catharsis and release for all that repression—Rainer's and the group's—in their coded tyrannies. Her *Seascape* tantrum reverberates down through the Judson years and right into this page, decades later. Her stage presence altogether remains memorable. Even the bland constancy of *Trio A* as originally executed by Rainer was a commanding performance. Her controlled impassivity harbored an emotional intensity, a quality of pent-up fire and feeling, a volcanic reservoir of desire and ambition. We could see all that again, along with its reprieve, in *Three Seascapes,* if the right stand-in were enlisted. It's very much a girl's piece. But I could envision Baryshnikov doing it. He can do anything. (Except for the strenuousities of ballet; at fifty-two and with old occupational injuries, that's over for him.) He was beautiful in a blue velvet gown at BAM in 2000, doing a slow vampy solo made originally by Rainer for David Gordon's wife, Valda Setterfield, in 1972. This appeared in a thirty-five-minute collection of episodes strung, beadlike, or positioned for simultaneous performance, that Rainer culled for Baryshnikov's company from her pre-1975 choreography, titling the ensemble *After Many a Summer Dies the Swan*.

Rainer, alone among Baryshnikov's seven chosen Judson relicts, abandoned the field (in 1975) to pursue another career, in filmmaking. Her old Judson cronies have evolved as dance/choreographers in variegated ways. Some of the results have helped Baryshnikov enormously in concocting his audience-pleaser evening. Two artists, Trisha Brown and Lucinda Childs, needed no special introduction by Baryshnikov to dance-goers at large. Their reputations in fact exceed the limits of the dance world; they have companies, managers, publicists, and access to a slew of state-of-the-art designers and composers. Today, their roots in Judson seem truly archaic. By the early 1970s they had stopped sitting and walking (running was popular, too) or pushing objects around to begin dancing again—as dancing is commonly understood.

While Paxton and Hay also began dancing, they both fled New York in 1970 to live in a community in northernmost Vermont, never forming permanent companies to undertake tours or engage theaters for weeklong appearances or the like. In '76 Hay removed herself even further, to Austin, Texas, where she has led large group workshops that have ended up in local performances. Both Hay and Paxton have relied heavily on improvisation as a style or premise of their appearances. For Paxton, improvisation has been practically a science. That was clear on June 7 at BAM, the third night (there were five nights altogether) of the "Past/*Forward*" performances, when five of the seven choreographers, including Paxton, took advantage of an invitation by Baryshnikov to appear on stage and dance.

For Brown and Childs, who did solos, this was no novelty; they dance in the BAM kind of arena, here and abroad, all the time. Their works are completely set or determined, as is generally expected for large houses. Paxton's long solo improvisation, *O (for Simone),* frankly made me hold my breath. It was very nervy and intellectual. High puzzlement was his gambit, best befitting no doubt the incongruity of such a piece in front of the unwashed. A sort of lecture/dance questioning the nature of performance or performing at all, or presenting fixed choreography, it had several pre-set elements. First, just deciding to appear onstage; also, knowing that he intended to talk (however unscripted) about space; and having four bottles at hand to outline a performing space inside the proscenium space, within which he ultimately performed a dancerly improvisation. Paxton remains a fine dancer, in whatever context he devises. His message, in this instance, was not unfathomable. What do we really see or expect to see when we structure the frame that we find in the theater? Why do we have these barriers or borders? Why go to the theater?

Deborah Hay wisely chose to do a duet with Baryshnikov. So whatever was improvised about it—a program footnote says the dance, *Single Duet,* has a score that is interpreted differently in each performance—was absorbed utterly by the fascination of Baryshnikov, his every step or gesture a jewel of congruity and perfection. And Hay herself, at sixty, in a duet with a romantic trend, looked concordant with her celebrated partner, humbly seductive in her more alluring gender-specific part.

I'm an old-timer gone reactionary and rheumy. That's what happens. I loved the Baryshnikov show. (I take it that his elderly Judson captives did too.) And far from expecting anything so "democratic" as the '60s revolutionary inclusiveness to happen again, I look forward to the enthronement of the next woman in the great line of Duncan, St. Denis, Graham, and Humphrey. This is a heritage that Americans can be proud of. It carries the only creative medium in the world invented, evolved and heroized by the weaker sex. My present superannuation has its roots back in the 1950s while I was seated at the feet of Doris Humphrey, a choreographic genius who no longer danced due to an arthritic hip. By then the modernist movement was having its last hurrah. She and Graham were the inevitable combatants of their era. Now it looks like Trisha Brown and Lucinda Childs are the heirs to that earlier rivalry. Not that their work, and dancing personae, bear the least resemblance to those of Graham and Humphrey. Actually, Brown is physically not unlike Humphrey in her long litheness and open, airy dance style. However she is not the architect or disciplinarian of space that Humphrey was. Her work can sprawl incontinently, and it depends on some brilliant assists of music, set designs, lighting, and costumes. More critically, Brown dances too much, tend to be carried away by her dancing. There's a lot of "hooptedoodle" in the work, like prose that's too wordy. As if to make up for a lack of composition—a skill that Childs, by comparison, has turned into her signature.

So my candidate for enthronement is Lucinda Childs. Perhaps Baryshnikov thinks so too, since he crowned his Judson evenings with her 1993 *Concerto,* a stunning example of her obsessive group compositional style, one piece different from the next only by variation on a singular method of organizing her space. *Concerto* is accompanied by a score—Henryk Mikolaj Gorecki's *Concerto for Harpsichord and Strings*—as driving and exciting as the relentless pulverizing consumption of space by White Oak's seven dancers. At BAM and elsewhere, the dance has brought the house down with thunderous ovations.

Childs's approach, developed by the late '70s, is entirely mathematical and geometric. Her dancers are stick figures in schemes for moving them around the space in complex patterns. They are animated by very simple kinds of movement: walking running skipping, stopping, and turning, whatever gets them from one place to another, with some but not much arm action. Torsos remain mostly upright. The legs never shoot out or up or do anything "dancerly" that might distract from their main purpose of moving from here to there. It's an art of locomotion, and repetition. A permutational reordering of minimalist phrases creates a dense overlay of movement that keeps accreting, cumulating, into something much grander—and more stirring, finally—than you might expect from such slight units of composition.

Not unsurprisingly, Childs has frequently chosen accompanying sound scores by such minimalist composers as Philip Glass, John Adams, Terry Riley, and György Ligeti that best analogize, therefore advance and promote, the additive building effect of her dance geometries. Equally important in the work, and in keeping with its thorough abstraction, is the omission of gender distinctions—by size or role or traditional sort of coupling—and gender bending, such as David Gordon and Mark Morris have explored. But Childs's dancers are, after all, mere pawns in systems that absorb their individuality.

Baryshnikov's presence as one of the seven performers in *Concerto* is a challenge to that concept. He integrates himself perfectly, but you look for him nonetheless. Interesting questions form themselves around his appearance in this kind of work, and even in the solos that have either been made for him, or exhumed by him from the past. How much of his attractiveness is due to his investiture? Would he look special in the street in a crowd, or by himself? Is this a former god of the ballet descended to earth to grace our lowly modern dance tradition? To this I say resoundingly yes. He came from Russia with love—for America. Not with instrumentality, like Balanchine, imported by Lincoln Kirstein in 1933 to help establish the European court tradition here, which at length obscured our own indigenous high dance art form. But hey, without Balanchine, it's unlikely that Baryshnikov would have found a job in the United States in 1974. Anyway, by then the ballet and modern dance/choreographers had been infiltrating each other's mediums for some time. A vibrant crossover culture existed. Yet the ballet has persisted in America as the form *de résistance,* the premier money-maker, and dance trade of high visibility.

The eclipse of America's homegrown dance art by a form that flowered in Europe for the pleasure of royalty—a supreme irony as regards our constitutional origins as a nation—is under redress by a man who had grown up unhappy in a repressive regime at the Kirov. Bad things were going on there by the time Baryshnikov joined the company in the late '60s. The repertory was moribund. Good choreographers were lacking, and the Soviet authorities refused, on patriotic grounds, to invite Western choreographers to the Kirov. In 1974, Baryshnikov told Anna Kisselgoff of *The New York Times* that he had had no freedom to choose his own repertory and almost no opportunity to dance in new ballets, especially those created for him. "Roles are created for you open up new reserves in you that you didn't know about . . . it is very exciting." Under the Kirov's imperious rule, and at a time of worldwide restlessness, a crisis existed. With the desertion of Nureyev (1971) and several others, leading dancers were under surveillance for fear of more defections. On tour in London, Baryshnikov was wildly acclaimed; he made friends with the defector Nureyev, saw the ABT perform, and went to modern dance classes. According to Joan Acocella, writing in *The New Yorker* in 1998, his watershed moment occurred in Leningrad, after the London trip, when he staged what was called a Creative Evening. Here, apparently, is the precedent for Baryshnikov's Judson evening. By Kirov custom, a dancer would commission a program of short works, often from young choreographers, assemble sets and costumes and star in the production. The ballets thus contrived would normally be shelved by the Kirov administration. Baryshnikov met a worse fate when he was told how bad they thought his show was. It was allowed a few performances anyway. Then at a cast banquet, while he was trying to make a speech thanking his dancers, Baryshnikov burst into tears. A few months later, on tour in Canada with the Bolshoi Ballet, he defected.

Will his personal vindication, coming full circle in the smashing success of the Judson evening, and his embrace generally of the American-type dance, have any far-reaching consequences? Why not? Dancing with his White Oak company, Baryshnikov has created the most interesting thing to happen terpsichoreally in America since the very Judson revolution he has so imaginatively exploited. Possibly America will catch on and realize that right under its nose an indigenous tradition of great choreography bloomed and died out and is being born again under the sponsorship of a man who once starred in the medium that triumphed over it. A new expressionism may even be afoot. Baryshnikov is himself a touching performer, even in deadpan work. His ballet history, after all, includes narrative partnering and character roles. He has done Limón and Graham, the two masters of late modern thematic hyperbole. In the future he may choose postmodern work emphasizing affect or emotive context. Which is not to say that we want any storytelling again. I hardly loved it back when. What I find missing in work of any nature is inner depth, and maturity—the latent meaningfulness or lurking subtleties wrought, say, by that great soloist Katherine Litz.

A standout at BAM was Lucinda Childs's brush with ecstasy in her 2001 solo, *Largo,* to Arcangelo Corelli's *Concerti Grossi Op. 6,* performed the third evening, when the choreographers were invited to appear on stage and dance. In a contracted grammar of the structures that hold her group work, with the same precision and incisiveness, yet with a new-looking give in the torso, a greater generosity with the arms, she patrolled her space along that rarest of lines embracing the romantic and classical at once. Carried onward by the elegance of the composition, the systolic breath and exhalation of its perfect phrasing, the lushness of the Corelli, she generated a strange, unearthly, attenuated passion. A frontal moment near the end, when Childs's arms are outstretched, palms upward, was a vapor from a past age—Isadora as she appeared in all her glory, at the barricades in the tragic ardor of *La Marseillaise*. We don't seem ready yet for an unleashed Isadora, But in *Largo* we're looking at a pulsing resonance, possibly the figment of a new revolution. At the very least, we're looking at mature work, infused with a depth of feeling that simply a mastery of composition can inspire.

Baryshnikov himself may not have an ambition for the American dance such as I am gibbering on about. Asked by Acocella in her 1998 interview if he had got what he wanted in the West, he replied, "Oh, more than that—I never dreamt that I would work with so many extraordinary people." Acocella's comment: "That was all he wanted, just to work with interesting people."

—from *Art in America*, December 2001

MIKHAIL BARYSHNIKOV

Giselle

My formal preparation for the role of Albrecht in *Giselle* was not extensive. When I first joined the Kirov I made my debut in the Act I "peasant" pas de deux (usually referred to in Russia as the "classical" pas de deux) and continued to dance this bravura role right up until my debut as Albrecht. Consequently I was familiar with all the choreography and required very little preparation as far as the steps and mime were concerned. My coach for the debut was Vladilen Semyonov, one of the greatest *danseurs nobles* of the postwar Kirov generation.

It was in 1972 that I performed my first Albrecht; my partner was

Alla Sizova. I consider this the most important of all the debuts I made in the Soviet Union, a turning point for me. I had danced the principal parts in only two full-length ballets before this, *Don Quixote* and *The Sleeping Beauty.* I hadn't really been tested in a meaningful way until then. *Don Quixote* came very easily to me, and *The Sleeping Beauty* represented an exercise in classical style that was not the kind of dramatic challenge I was looking for. *Giselle* was important to me because the Kirov didn't really believe I could do it.

They didn't believe in "my" Albrecht for very specific reasons. The traditions, both physical and dramatic, in the way Albrecht is played are very strong in the Soviet Union. Two great interpretations of Albrecht—that of Konstantin Sergeyev at the Kirov and that of Alexei Yermolayev at the Bolshoi—established a standard from as far back as the 1930s. If Sergeyev's Albrecht was the more elegant and poetic and Yermolayev's the more ferocious, they both shared one quality that is basic to all Soviet interpretations: Albrecht is an aristocrat. His primary concern is his social position, and his love for Giselle is at best a somewhat serious bagatelle. Albrecht is by implication or intention a cad, and therefore a limited character. His social position and noble bearing are the most important aspects in the standard interpretation of the role.

There were two well-known exceptions to this standardization: the performance by Nikita Dolgushin, a very talented and gifted dancer from the Kirov (who incidentally made a double debut with Natalia Makarova), and by Rudolf Nureyev, who made his debut with Irina Kolpakova. Both interpretations departed significantly from the usual. Unfortunately, by the time I came along these two dancers were no longer with my company. My own models—Yuri Soloviev, Sergei Vikulov, Vladilen Semyonov, all gifted dancers—were still very much in the Sergeyev mold.

I wanted to do *Giselle* very much. I suppose most people consider it mainly a vehicle for a romantic ballerina, but of all the available classics it offers unequaled dramatic opportunities for the male lead. *Giselle* can, in fact, be a two-person drama, and it is the acting that makes the part of Albrecht such a great challenge.

The obstacles I faced in preparing *Giselle,* given the very strict tradition observed in the role, are obvious. I was very young, and looked even younger. My body did not fit the streamlined image of Albrecht. And nobody was convinced that I could do it. So I had something to prove to the directors and myself: I needed to find a way of dancing and miming that was believable and convincing—a way that was more spontaneous and less conceptually restricted.

I discovered for myself the key to a possible change in the entire dramatic architecture of the part. I would start with the premise that Albrecht *really* loves Giselle. This may not sound like such a radical departure, but it was, and I knew it was the only way I might succeed in the role and, by using my own native resources and instinct, resolve the inherent inconsistency imposed by tradition. My goal was to convince both the public and my director that I had a natural right to the part, that I had the ability to create a character I myself could believe in and who would be accepted.

Giselle is not perhaps the most extraordinary ballet ever devised, but it has wonderful opportunities for the dancer to develop. The outlines of the story are so clear, not just in detail but in atmosphere and intent. The steps are simple and effective. The basic material is so uncomplicated that within the given boundaries there are marvelous chances for improvisation. Because the public and the dancers are so familiar with this classic, there is an element of security at the outset that allows for great flexibility in interpretation.

As I said, I began to experiment with *Giselle*. In the past, the rigidly noble interpretation of Albrecht made the ballet into a social drama. *That* Albrecht, no matter where the emphasis was placed (he was either very elegant or very sinister), was basically a negative figure. He exploited Giselle, and then in the second act sought to lift his enormous cloud of guilt. But this interpretation always seemed to me inconsistent with his motives. Inconsistency can be interesting, but in this case it is disorienting. I began from another point entirely. For me Albrecht is so in love with Giselle that his love is his undoing. This love is so true, so perfect, that he does not want to jeopardize it by revealing his true identity. If Giselle knew who he really was, his passion could all too easily be taken to be a kind of *droit du seigneur*. It is the honesty of his feelings that leads him to his dishonesty. But fate steps in, and Albrecht is caught. I want the audience to know that Albrecht is innocent; not that he is not responsible for what occurs, but that his motives are pure.

Act I of *Giselle* is difficult because so much must be accomplished, and so much can happen. I want certain points in the characterization to be very clear. Albrecht knows he isn't what Giselle thinks he is, yet at the same time he is rather insensitive to the whole milieu in which he is moving. When Hilarion is played as a decent young swain also truly in love with Giselle, the conflict between the two men must be very clearly defined. Hilarion is jealous, and powerfully so. Albrecht is astonished that Hilarion would give him or Giselle trouble. After all, as the prince of the land he is used to getting his own way. It is Hilarion's aggressiveness that throws Albrecht off balance and leads to his first self-betrayal. Little by little he comes to realize that he and his love for Giselle are doomed. When he sees Bathilde's gift to Giselle he doesn't actually recognize it for what it is, but it gives him a jolt, it is a painful reminder to him that he has not told Giselle the truth. At this point the whole conflict is crystalized. Even though Albrecht's love for Giselle is the most important thing in his life, more important than the court and his princely duties, he cannot escape that whole other world. In the climactic final scene, when Hilarion triumphantly reveals Albrecht's secret, Albrecht's overwhelming instinct is to reassure Giselle of his love. This is much more important to him than taking revenge on Hilarion. In most versions of the ballet he tries to kill Hilarion. As I interpret the role, Albrecht suddenly realizes here that Hilarion, too, loves Giselle. He drops the sword. He wants to tell Giselle the truth and then is sickened when he sees that there is no point in doing so, that it is too late.

When Bathilde enters, Albrecht becomes stony with disappointment and regret. As he bends to kiss her hand, Giselle forces her way to him and Albrecht turns from her. He hasn't the strength to face her pain.

The traditional ending for Act I in Russia is for Albrecht to rush offstage. I have always chosen to remain, to try and seek comfort from those around me. There is no absolution, but this moment, performed in this way, creates an important bridge to the second act.

The dramatic material of *Giselle,* Act II, is not rich in substance, but with careful preparation and thought it can be meaningful. One basic consideration is that of maintaining a balance with the spirit, the Wili Giselle. The Act II Giselle demands a careful stylization and delicacy that precludes heavy dramatics, and it is very easy—and very destructive—for Albrecht to grab all the attention. The way I see it, Albrecht's task is now to adapt to the world of the Wilis. Once he realizes he is faced with another dimension, he desperately wants to communicate with it, to hold on to it in some way. So he must enter that world, believe in it, absorb it. He must also meet its standards. The Wilis express their power in dance. Their Queen's dance is bold and full of awesome strength. So Albrecht's dance must be strong too, as strong as possible. Once he sees Giselle as a spirit, he doesn't run away from her; he accepts her new state. He projects himself into her world. I want to make this transition clear. I know that many of these ideas do not translate literally to an audience, do not always come across, but they help me believe in the role as I feel it should be. The transition Albrecht makes from the real world to that of the Wilis begins the moment he dances *with* the Wili Giselle.

After that the task is relatively simple. The story makes the necessary demands. Albrecht fights to hold on to Giselle and fights to live.

It is difficult to maintain the sense of balance throughout, however. There must be no sharp turns, no radical departures once the mood is established. Albrecht must try to blend with Giselle. The flowers are crucial. They mean so many things to him: they are a symbol of his pain and they are a symbol of Giselle, too. Giselle expresses herself through flowers when she dances with the lilies, throwing them to him as if to say, "Yes, these flowers are a part of me. They are me. I know you must have them." And then later Giselle again uses the flowers to appease Myrtha, the Queen of the Wilis. Here it's as if she says, "See how strong my bond with this man is. Take these flowers and know it."

Finally, the flowers are central to the end of the whole drama. When Albrecht is saved and Giselle has forgiven him but must return to the world of the Wilis, Albrecht desperately tries to hold on to her. The way of that world cannot be halted, but in strewing the flowers in a straight line from her grave Albrecht tries to save her for himself, to hold on to the final link between them.

—from *Baryshnikov at Work,* 1976

AUGUST BOURNONVILLE

The great choreographer August Bournonville (1805–1879) was born in Copenhagen, where his father, Antoine, was a leading dancer. He studied in Paris with Auguste Vestris and danced there with Marie Taglioni, but returned to Denmark to become premier danseur and then ballet master, the director of the Royal Danish Ballet from 1830 to 1877. Among his most famous ballets are the version of La Sylphide *still performed today,* Napoli, A Folk Tale, Konservatoriet, The Guards of Amager (The King's Volunteers), The Kermesse in Bruges, Flower Festival in Genzano, *and* Far from Denmark, *most of which center on warm and human stories as opposed to the Romantic or exotic ballets of most European choreographers of the time. The style of dancing he created, "the Bournonville style," ranks lightness, buoyancy, and charm above technical virtuosity—not that it's an easy style to master (as generations of non-Danes can testify to).*

AUGUST BOURNONVILLE
Myself

BEGINNINGS

There is a kind of modesty that strongly verges on arrogance. I experienced an example of this with an actor who always arrayed himself in the garb of humility and designated his best as "the least bad," his ability as "feeble endeavor," the fruits of his labors as "modest attempts," etc. I asked him what he thought of another artist, and he heaped upon the latter the most favorable testimonials and placed him in the first rank. "But then," I was malicious enough to ask, "can this outstanding fellow equal you?" "I should certainly hope not!" replied the modest man, flushing with rage.

Noverre has done a very good thing in writing about himself, for without his *Letters* his name would by now be obliterated. But just as Mirabeau described his political ideal so remarkably like himself that Talleyrand added that it only lacked being heavily pockmarked, so too Noverre not only demands of the person he chooses to call "the balletmaster" a host of attributes but forbids him to possess certain others, such as being able to perform a role or a part. He also asserts that a beautiful voice is absolutely indicative of a bad dancer. Now, whether Noverre had truly stored in his head all the knowledge that appears in his work, I shall allow to remain unquestioned; but it is widely known that he always had a bad singing voice and was a mediocre dancer. Therefore, although I prostrate myself before the ballet's reformer, my whole nature conflicts with his demands too often for me to assume his viewpoint, which permits the light to fall upon him and the shadows upon everyone else. I therefore set forth my opinions not as dogmas but as the fruits of my experience. I offer my friends and country-men a remembrance of the Bournonville who has from time to time pro-vided them with happy moments, who has given the Danish theatre his best years and talents, and whom they once favored and honored with the name of artist. Should I tell them of my dancing and my ballets, the picture must be vivid; should I reveal to them the depths of my artist's soul, they shall bear witness that it must have been that way and no other. I do not intend to place myself on a pedestal but, rather, to fasten my image in the mirror of Truth.

One must distinguish self-contemplation from self-praise, just as one tells the difference between an exorbitant bill and an accurate account. I will pay my debt, but I also claim what is my due. Therefore, acknowledging that as a dancer I have never equaled Vestris's rapturous enthusiasm, Duport's perfec-tion, Albert's correctness, Paul's brilliance, or Perrot's lightness; that the compositions of Gardel, Milon, Didelot, and Henry stand before me as unsurpassable models; that Noverre's *Letters* have given me a lofty concep-tion of the artistic value of the dance, and my father's acting of the nobility of mime, I shall here venture to deliver a critique of myself, which no outsider *can* and no rival *will* give.

My father, Antoine Bournonville, was the youngest child of one of those alliances contracted between talent and beauty on the one hand, noble line-age and improvidence on the other. On his baptismal certificate, which I possess, it says that he was born in Lyon—with a *de* in front of his name—on May 19, 1760. However, I have reason to believe that my grandfather was not so much *noble* as *ennobled*, for after having been ruined in a theatrical venture, he deserted his wife and children, who were forced to seek refuge in the bosom of art. My aunt, Julie *de* Bournonville, was one of the most famous dancers of her day and shone at the Court Theatre in Vienna during the time of Noverre. My father entered *his* school in his ninth year, took part in all of his great master's ballets, and was present at the fantastic festivals which Hungary's magnates gave in honor of Empress Maria Theresa. He came to Paris in 1779, danced there and in London during a three-year period, and was summoned to Stockholm, where he remained until the death of Gustav III in 1791. In passing through Denmark on a journey, he made his debut in Copenhagen, married there, and was engaged as First Solodancer.

He was an extraordinarily handsome man, fiery, brave, and gallant; in short, a true *chevalier français* of the old school. Nevertheless, he became enraptured with the Revolutionary principles of Liberty and Equality, and he knew no greater hero than Lafayette. "In Virtue alone is true greatness found; in talent alone, valid claims." These lofty illusions constituted his life's fortune. He combined in his art all that he held to be noblest. He retained his ardent zeal for the dance until his last breath: I took leave of him in this life with *Polka militaire*, which I had to dance at his bedside, and he died a few days later in the firm conviction that both he and I had chosen "the most glorious career."

I was born in Copenhagen on August 21, 1805, and trod the stage for the first time as one of Lagertha's sons in October 1813. My years of apprenticeship were divided among dancing, singing, and acting. Because of the favor I won in several rather important roles, in works such as *The Little Shepherd Boy* and *The Judgment of Solomon,* for some time there was uncertainty as to which profession I should actually follow. A peculiar ease in aping people and in underscoring the comical elements in their voices and gestures even gave me a certain reputation as an actor, and many advised me to pursue the *opéra-comique,* which was so popular at that time. But my innate vocation, my father's example, the fact that this period of transition from boy to man is no good for singing and acting, together with a nervous and often quite troublesome stammer—which, as I have since learnt, was less a natural failing on my part than the result of physical exertion, and quite common among dancers and gymnasts—decided my fate, and when I accompanied my father to Paris in 1820, the die was cast. My enthusiasm was so great, in fact, that when in my twenty-first year Rossini perceived that I possessed a sonorous and flexible tenor voice and offered me instruction and engagement as a singer, I refused to abandon the Muse to whom I had offered my homage. At certain moments I have regretted this decision: as a singer I would have won more gold and greater glory with less effort, but perhaps I could not have done as much for my fellow artists as I have in my present sphere of activity. This should be a consolation to me.

Appointed Royal Dancer in 1823, the following year I traveled—at my own expense—to Paris, where I made my debut and was engaged until 1830, when I assumed the post at the Danish Royal Theatre which I am now leaving after eighteen years of completed activity.

As a dancer, I possessed a considerable measure of strength, lightness, precision, brilliance, and—when I was not carried away by the desire to display bravura—a natural grace, developed through superb training and enhanced by a sense of music. I also had a supple back, and my feet had just enough turn-out for me to be appreciated by even the severest master. The difficulties which I have worked hard to surmount, often with only partial success, were all connected with pirouettes and the composure necessary in slow pas and attitudes. My principal weaknesses were bent wrists, a swaying of the head during pirouettes, and a certain hardness in my elevation. (To conceal and combat these was my hardest task.) I have thrice altered the genre of my virtuosity to suit the demands of the time: in *The Sleepwalker* (1830), in Valdemar (1835), and in *Robert le Diable* (1841). There are dancers who possess greater aplomb, elevation, and ability to pirouette, who perform character dances with a greater measure of originality, but very few who have united more of the qualities of the dance or possessed greater variety than I. I danced with a manly joie de vivre, and my humor and energy have made the same impression in every theatre. I delighted the audience, and before they admired me, they liked me.

My talent for ballet composition had already begun to manifest itself in my childhood. Besides the fact that all my games centered around the arrangement of tableaux and the composition of ballets or so-called *entrées*, I also wrote my first libretto when I was fourteen years old (1819). It was based on Suhm's Nordic tale, *Habor and Signe,* and was followed by a dozen more, all of which were sacrificed to the stove.

I went to Paris, studied the profession of dancing for two years, and then became a soloist at the Grand Opéra, where I remained for four years. During these six years, I visited theatres and museums, studied history and languages, but never thought of composing even so much as sixteen measures of my own dance. I practiced, admired, or criticized the others, contemplated the intrinsic value of ballets with the insouciance of a true Parisian, and, like my comrades, aspired to earn money and praise without any real consideration of higher art.

I finally awakened from my careless attitude when, in the year 1829, I used my three-month leave of absence to make a trip to Denmark. I had to put together a repertoire and learn a good deal of it by heart. But when I came to mount it on the stage, I was forced to supply from my own resources what my memory lacked and to make those adaptations necessitated by local conditions. Here I came to know my strengths. By teaching roles to others, I obtained a clearer impression of my own part and for the first time, in a manner of speaking, came face to face with my art. Success crowned my endeavors, the confidence of others lent me courage, and in the enthusiasm of the moment, I made my first original [choreographic] attempts, which were, in fact, nothing but portions of my own life.

I consequently became a composer since I wished to appear as a dancer and mime; I became a teacher because I was forced to train subjects for my compositions; and I eventually organized one of the finest *corps de ballet* in Europe because through my struggle against repeated attempts to cut down and crush the dance, I developed a strength and persistence which up till then I had never believed to be part of my character.

With Galeotti's death and my father's retirement, there began a period during which the ballet steadily declined in the public's favor and esteem. A number of unsuccessful compositions further helped to downgrade the dance as an art. The Theatre regarded it as a troublesome burden, and it became the fashion for the audience to clear the house when the *entrée* began. Many other internal and external circumstances caused the public to consider a person who transferred from the ballet to the drama as having been saved from a fate worse than death. The ghost of a *corps de ballet* that still existed was used only as "padding" in spectacles. The humiliation reached its depth when an old *figurant,* who recoiled at the idea of being used as a footstool to a palanquin, was addressed in these words (whose tone contemporaries will surely be able to recognize): "Thank God you can be used for something!"

A great deal of hard work was needed in order to bring life back into an art which had lost its right to this name. After my first surprisingly success- ful attempts, people came to the conclusion that such a rapid transformation was but another proof of the unimportance of the thing. First it was said that dancing was not an art, and then that I was not an artist. In the beginning, the criticism was dignified though skeptical; later, it became angry and pee- vish, and, finally, knowledgeable but blasé (apathetic).

My strongest argument against the troublesome opponents of the Dance was a successful production. Foot by foot, I gained ground, which, however, was not exactly defended by the most loyal weapons. I loved my *corps de bal- let* as a shepherd his flock, and upon the whole we got along well with each other. They were interested in the work and were sincerely happy when it was successful. The tension under which I constantly labored often made me lose my temper with the less intelligent. My philanthropic ideas about the refinement of the heart through the influence of art were, more often than not, sorely disappointed and filled my soul with bitterness . . . nevertheless, I submit that the majority of my fellow artists learnt to appreciate my way of thinking, and I would have conquered those individuals who strayed from the fold, had they not been buttonholed by flattering backbiters *within,* and so-called advisory protectors *without,* the walls of the Theatre. They sowed many tares among the wheat, and often brought the harvest close to ruin. They manipulated the public and gave me coldness and contrariness instead of reward and recognition.

Twice during my career my perseverance failed. I tendered my resignation, which was turned down. I risked my future bread in order to obtain my freedom, but . . . I learnt to see things in a new and better light. Those scenes that once seemed so tragic now appeared laughable to me. I sensibly learnt to weigh advantages and disadvantages, and discovered that on the high-salaried Continent I could find just as much unpleasantness as I could here at home. If the Teatro San Carlo was more spacious, the Danish theatre gave me greater literary freedom; if it was uncertain whether my Nordic talent would please in the south, I could be sure that the store of ideas I had gathered in those southern climes would make my fortune here in the north; and finally, even though there were certain people in Copenhagen who could not tolerate me and my progress, I still had on my side writers, painters, and, above all, a whole generation of young savants who, by the letter they wrote in an effort to keep me in Denmark, gave me and my art a priceless diploma. Besides, I also had obligations to fulfill; what had been started had to be finished, and the course run out. I will soon arrive at this goal. . . .

I summarize my activity at the Danish Theatre in this way: In fifteen years I have performed in a variety of genres the most difficult, if not the most rewarding, roles in dancing and mime; but even though I have trained excellent pupils through instruction and my own example, I have up to now defended my post as First Solodancer. I have earned for the ballet a proper place in the Kingdom of Art, and I have made it an ornament for the very stage upon which I once saw it despised and neglected. In an age when there is looseness and distortion in dramatic literature, I have forged a new path and kept myself free from the excesses of Romanticism. Deprived of all the resources that a large and wealthy theatre has to offer, and working under many hampering conditions, I have been able to extract from art, nature, and history more than one successful idea, gladdened my countrymen, and provided for the Copenhagen Ballet a justifiable renown.

—from *My Theatre Life*, translated by Patricia N. McAndrew, 1979

MIKHAIL BARYSHNIKOV
La Sylphide

The first version of La Sylphide *was made for Taglioni in Paris, in 1832, by her father, Filippo. Four years later, August Bournonville created his own version of it in Copenhagen, but with new music, and that is the version still performed around the world. The tragic interaction of a mortal man with a supernatural sprite is a recurrent theme of the Romantic ballet, and* La Sylphide *is its purest expression.*

I had seen American Ballet Theatre's production of *La Sylphide* with Toni Lander and Royes Fernandez as well as the Royal Danish Ballet's version with Peter Schaufuss, and when I came to the West I immediately asked to dance it.

Everything about dancing Bournonville's ballets is different from what I have been trained to do. In Bournonville one is searching for a very reserved, refined stylistic voice, and yet one still wants to keep as much excitement as possible in the dancing. The technique is very unusual; it demands extraordinary flexibility in the legs and a kind of static torso. When I first began dancing this ballet my "classical habits" kept interfering; even something as simple as a run is different in Bournonville than in classical Russian style. When I had mastered the steps of *Sylphide* I still asked for an inordinate number of extra rehearsals because I felt it might not be as theatrically exciting as it ought to be. But as I became more and more familiar with the precision and cleanliness of the technique, as the rules which govern this world became absorbed into my body, I felt much better about it.

Just a few words on the technical aspects of this role: there are many, many jumps in Bournonville, many beats, entrechats, et cetera. The *épaulement* is extremely limited, so that as you move you feel you're dancing with your legs and nothing else. Erik Bruhn worked with me and gave me extremely good and detailed corrections, showing me how to reach the necessary balance of softness and strength in the many jumps and how to perform the role in general. For example, he showed me how to achieve what I would call a "soft startle" at the waking up of James in the first act.

There's enormous physical pleasure in dancing Bournonville. The style and the steps are so harmonious, so complete, that you instantly recognize in your mind and in your body a great classical tradition. The simplicity of it and the emotional tranquility are extremely satisfying.

On to the story. *La Sylphide* is a "realistic" fairy tale. James lives in a world that accepts sylphs and witches as a natural phenomenon. Good and evil are extremely conventional, much more conventional than, say, in *Giselle*. At the beginning of *La Sylphide,* as James sleeps, the Sylph is trying to get into his mind. When he moves restlessly in his chair as she dances so brilliantly around the room, she's "getting through" to him. He, of course, is not sure that it has really happened. He is still preoccupied with his first encounter with the Sylph when his mortal fiancée, Effie, kisses him. He remembers as if in a dream; he senses that something is happening and then when he sees the Sylph through the window his reaction is, "Oh well, she's *real.*" The Sylph is very unhappy that he is marrying Effie, but James is a responsible adult who has an obligation to Effie, even though he is completely fascinated with the Sylph.

In the long scene between James and the Sylph we see that he in fact begins to tire of her coquetry and jealousy, and feels that he must be honest toward Effie. And once again he's perplexed. The Sylph abandons her sad mood and says, "Let's dance." He is so surprised at this quick change in her mood that he is completely disarmed. The more she teases and tries to slip away from him, the more he wants her.

Perhaps the most interesting character in the entire ballet is the Witch. The whole story of *La Sylphide* unfolds as if it had been told by her. She is in complete control of herself and of the situation from the moment she enters. She has selected her victims, and she knows everything. James reacts more powerfully to her than to anything in his life—he knows instinctively that she is evil. When the Witch asks to warm her hands, James panics. He knows that she's dangerous and that he's got to get rid of her. He is terrified that she will do irrevocable damage. This whole scene is brilliantly conceived as a long pantomime between James and the Witch, both of whom know what's taking place. He goes through the charade of accepting her and letting her tell the fortunes, all the while terrified of her power. He knows that she is indeed a Witch. But when the Sylph returns at the end of the act he loses all sense of reason. His fear of the Witch and his love of Effie both pale as the delicious enchantment of this fairy creature mesmerizes him. (It is, after all, a romantic tale.) He leaves to go with her to the woods.

The second act begins on a delightful note—the Sylph takes James into her "house." And he thinks, "Oh, I've hit upon a nice upper-class sylphide." Hers is a very nice glade. She brings on her "sewing circle," teasing him, always slipping away from him, always putting something between him and herself. His frustration mounts. Then, of course, there's the long, brilliant dancing section and finally James's second scene with the Witch. He still rec-

ognizes her for what she is, but no longer fears anything. He has become the
great romantic egoist, spoiled and selfish like a child. He must have a present
to attract the Sylph, and he's too blind to see what's being done to him. The
Witch is in control. Of course, the whole thing ends in tragedy; the Sylph
dies from the poisoned scarf and James is left with nothing but an ugly sense
of reality as he watches Effie pass by. He has failed because of his romantic
notions. The power of his ideals, his need for perfection, have done him in
completely. James is always searching for the great romance, for poetry and
beauty in this life, and the Sylph embodied all that for him.

There's something else as well: the normal point of view is really set up
against James. From the way things work out we draw the conclusion that
one should not go after the impossible and the superficial.

The world of *La Sylphide* is a wonderful whole, with its great dancing
from a great tradition and with its marvelous score. The music is very good
dance music in the first place, and beyond that it contains *a secret*. It is naive,
but it has sudden and startling depths. It is also dramatically very accurate.

The dancing sections of *La Sylphide* are in many ways both parallel to and
independent of the story. You must be very careful when dancing not to use
too much dramatic emphasis in the "set" pieces, which are indeed very stylized. This doesn't mean that there isn't a general atmosphere to be maintained in which something of the drama can be expressed, but a very
delicate balance between drama and dance must be sustained. If I had to
decide between *La Sylphide* and *Giselle* as to which was the greater romantic
ballet or as to which was the most satisfying to perform—I just couldn't
choose.

—from *Baryshnikov at Work,* 1976

TOBI TOBIAS

A Folk Tale

A Folk Tale, *1854, was Bournonville's favorite among his works. On the surface, it's the old story of babies switched in the cradle—the troll child Birthe exchanged for the genteel Hilda—followed by eventual discovery and reconciliation. Underneath its fairy-story surface, it's about darkness and light, nature and nurture, restoration of the normal order of things—in this regard, a worthy cousin of* The Sleeping Beauty.

For all the richness of the world Bournonville creates, there are worlds apart that he pointedly ignored. Missing from Bournonville's theater is any sustained grappling with the elements of the erotic and the demonic with which most of the major Romantic inventors intuitively connected—and reveled in. Perhaps the vein of prudishness in his Biedermeier temperament that is acknowledged in his autobiography steered him away from the imaginative lures and presumed dangers of such material. *La Sylphide* belongs to a relatively early phase of his choreographic development.

There's no denying that, by following the path he did of sanguine sobriety, Bournonville cut himself off from a fertile area of creative investigation. I wonder, though, if an artist steeped in the turbulence and soul's jeopardy of the prevalent Romantic vein would have been capable of a work as singular and enchanting as Bournonville's *A Folk Tale*. It is as shimmering, delicate, and self-contained as a soap bubble—the product of a unique imagination.

The argument of the ballet is a fairy-tale staple: an exchange of infants from dichotomous backgrounds who grow up to uncover their true nature. Here a human child of the gentry is secretly replaced in her cradle with a baby of the troll colony that lurks, half-hidden, in its under-the-mountain (that is, subconscious) domain. The switched girls grow to maidenhood, each instinctively revealing or seeking her roots. Although the human Hilda is promised by the dowager troll to the more loutish of her two sons, she yearns for an ideal goodness, which the ballet symbolizes, endearingly, by Christianity and the handsome young hero, Junker Ove. On the other hand, despite the gentility of her upbringing, Birthe remains a troll at heart and, aptly, in body. In one of the ballet's most entertaining and psychologically keen sequences, she dances before a full-length mirror, in narcissistic, lyrical phrases—into which contorted troll-motions break uncontrollably.

The ballet contains a vestige of the themes of Romantic preoccupation—in the elf-maidens (a cross between the wilis and the nightgowned muses-with-flowing-hair in the *Élégie* section of Balanchine's *Tchaikovsky Suite No. 3*) who emerge from their mountain caverns and swirl through the dry-ice fog to entrap Junker Ove, and in Ove himself, a sketchy indication of the morbidly dreamy temperament of the model Romantic hero. But the ostensible villains of the piece, the troll folk, feel harmless—because they are so quaint. (The second brother eventually grows as lovable as one of Snow White's dwarfs.) This is a common folkloric device—subverting the potency of figures of mystery and fear by rendering them whimsically. But the real mark of Bournonville's genius is that, at the same time, he is able to make the entire troll community a riotously accurate personification of the human race in its less attractive guises. I'm particularly fond of the show of self-congratulatory indulgence in the minor vices revealed at their orgy, but Bournonville's deftest shaft may be in making the most characteristic attribute of these appalling creatures their bad manners.

Of course Bournonville, that inimitable proselytizer for joy, gives his story a happy outcome. What is remarkable about this closing scene in *A Folk Tale* is that one is wholly disarmed by the sweetness and purity of his means. The ballet ends, naturally, with the wedding of the lovers made for each other, Hilda and Ove. Imagine this sequence of images: six very young women (blond nymphets in pale green dresses, holding blossoming branches) softly waltzing; a slow processional, bland as a walk, for the wedding party, under wreaths of flowers; then, oddly slowed, the simplest of love pledges—the hand to the heart, then extended to the partner; a brief dance around a pastel-ribboned maypole; and the final assertion of the dulcet waltz motif accompanying a flurry of rose petals. Few artists could work with such trusting innocence.

—from *Dance Magazine,* 1980

NANCY GOLDNER

The Guards of Amager

In 1871, Bournonville created this lighthearted and popular ballet about a squad of volunteer guards stationed on the island of Amager, south of Copenhagen.

One of the delicious aspects of mime is that it takes a long time to say little. A typical mimed conversation goes like this: "I see." "You see?" "Yes." "What do you see?" "I see that over there." "You don't say." "Yes, I do say." Whereupon a pointed finger leads us "over there."

This conversation takes place somewhere in the first scene of *The Guards of Amager,* a Bournonville ballet presented by the Royal Danish Ballet at the tail end of their Metropolitan Opera season. Logically speaking, this build-up should mark the entrance of a Princess Aurora. Does this mime harken the entrance of the guards, then? Perhaps, but more likely the entrance of the soup tureen, which is carried across the entire length of the stage by a bouncy tea cozy of a woman. And yet it could plausibly refer to the wallpaper's pink roses. *The Guards of Amager* is that kind of ballet, with that kind of hierarchical scheme. Its tempo and content are like an ideal country weekend, when, with nothing to do and no place to go, one may dwell on the minutiae of one's surroundings, ponder which plates would be most appropriate for lunch, which for luncheon. And of course, the deeper one thinks about such matters, the quicker time flies. That it is difficult to remember where all the conversations fit is some measure of this scene's loveliness. Like a fine country holiday, an event in Bournonville's parlor defies reconstruction and time is unaccountably spent.

The Guards of Amager runs fifty minutes. The second half is easily accounted for: people dance. In the first half nothing happens—that is, assorted character types enter, make motions with their hands, bend their bodies a little this way and that way, walk quickly or not so quickly, gaze into space, eat, play the piano, flirt, play cards, remove their cloaks, exit. At one point the guards arrive with derring-do, but stay just long enough to send a yokel farmer into shy raptures of admiration. The eventfulness of their arrival is discordant, until one realizes that Bournonville brought them on only so that the farmer's reaction could be registered. This is the kind of event that consumes twenty-five minutes, and this time span was more fleet than any other during the Danish season. Unlike any other ballet performed in this country—with the exception of the party scene in Balanchine's *The Nutcracker*—time is unaccountable. It just rolls by as a jumble of domestic trivia, and it is sheer heaven.

Created in 1871, toward the end of Bournonville's career, *The Guards of Amager* presents to American audiences a lesser known aspect of this choreographer's work and a totally foreign style of theatre. In its relative absence of dance and in the way it pads about the stage, the ballet is at complete odds with our Balanchine-formed taste—although Balanchine occasionally relishes *mise en scène*—and is almost at complete odds with the Russian classics. *Swan Lake, Giselle,* and the others find much of their strength in important librettos; *The Guards of Amager* is consciously lightweight. The Russian works present mime scenes, to be sure, but as recitatives. There are no arias in the first scene of *The Guards;* hence, no recitatives.

The second scene bears a kinship to the Russian formula of last-act divertissement in that it is a string of dances, ranging from folk to a classical pas de trois, served up under the pretext of festive occasion, a carnival. Yet to call Bournonville and Petipa blood relatives is to overlook the modesty of Bournonville's classical ballet as compared to Petipa's deliberate exploitation of bravura; to ignore the consciously folk quality of Bournonville's folk dances, as opposed to Petipa's glamorization of them; and to dismiss the differing tonal intentions of all the dances. Russian divertissements function as a contrasting release from the constrictions of narrative; they get the ballet down to business. The dances in *The Guards* are a continuation of the first scene, in several ways. Although the medium of expression changes from mime to dance, one perceives the most basic change less in terms of movement style than of place and behavior. The characters we saw inside we now see outside. Whereas we saw them intimately in the first scene, we now see them behaving in a public forum, the bumpkins' ways transmuted into rustic formality, the urbanites' ways into citified formality. The folk element lives not only in the steps but in their presentation. As the dancers go through their paces with charming and somehow dignified deliberateness, one realizes that they have gone through this routine a thousand times. While the steps might interest the audience for their novelty, they enchant the participants through familiarity. Finally, our grasp of their contentment with the tried and true is infinitely more interesting than a folk dance could ever be in itself. The national dances of Russian ballet never show us folk dances through the eyes of the folk. They are conceived as novel diversions by urbanites for urbanites, and like all self-styled novelty acts can never be novel enough. They are holding actions for the classical *pas*. The inclusion of ballet proper in Bournonville's second scene does not relegate the folk stuff to second-class citizenship. It is of a different class, and the difference may be viewed as a continuation of a central theme in the first scene, where nuances of gesture, stance, and reaction indicate the differences between country (the people of the island Amager) and city (the volunteer troops stationed there and the wife and fiancées who come to visit them). It may also be noted that when the soldier who has been dallying with peasant girls embarks on a flirtation with a masked ballerina (who, unknown to him, is his wife teaching him a lesson), he is affirming his natural affinity to his class as well as to his wife.

Is this too fanciful a treatment of such a simple ballet as *The Guards of Amager?* Very likely. But I think it explains why Scene 1 is not a prelude to Scene 2, and why Scene 2 is not more interesting than Scene 1. It may also help to account for the rare unity Bournonville achieves between a directed first scene and a choreographed second scene. Unity of style is not to my mind the great virtue many critics hold it to be; indeed, it is in the interests of unity—modernity, realism, etc.—that so much bad dance pervades the MacMillan, Cranko, and Neumeier productions. Bournonville has it both ways. His dances are free of obsequious gestures toward meaningful dramatic content and, for what it's worth, sit comfortably beside mime. While modern-day choreographers find themselves in an impossible bind, drawn to nineteenth-century forms while detesting or fearing nineteenth-century conventions, Bournonville is delighted to exploit those conventions to the hilt.

Much as I enjoyed the second scene, it was the first that drew me back for a return visit, both for the virtuosity of its staging and the pleasure (and relief) of witnessing the Royal Danish in its single triumph of an otherwise unfortunate season. The scene is a perfect meeting ground for creator and performers. It hinges on a variety of stock character types, which the Danes have got down pat; delicately timed and accented gesture, and a flexible use of stage space—as flexible actually as Merce Cunningham's theatre. At certain moments the action is directed so as to appear nondirected; the dancer has the formidable task of wandering from here to there, rather than from point A to point B, but winding up "there" at precisely the right second. At other moments the action is self-consciously contrived, as when the children encircle a cookie jar that is deposited in the emphatic center of the stage, or when two bachelors and their sweethearts mime a squabble in exact accord with musical meter. The interplay and byplay between naturalism and artificiality gives this dumb show the tension it needs in lieu of dance or narrative pull, and it provides a superstructure of wit without which the ballet might well smother in its own feathers. Without stylistically nimble performers, the whole thing would sink at once. The Danes are master gaugers of stress and accent. They know how to take their time; they understand the difference between conversational and declarative gesture; they can modulate the emphasis of their gestures according to their place on the stage. Although they barely register beyond the first few rows of the orchestra when they dance, their mimed gestures fill an enormous opera house, using no more energy and no less refinement than actors summon to fill an Off-Broadway theatre. This feat was brilliantly demonstrated in the last moments of the ballet, when the masked ballerina reveals her true identity to her philandering husband. Upon realizing that he has been flirting with his wife, Henning Kronstam simply gazes at her, looks at the audience with bemused humility in modulated delayed-action tempo, drops his head slightly, and turns toward his wife. He is both sad and glad, both proud of and embarrassed by his embarrassment. Meanwhile, Vivi Flindt is standing absolutely still, but in the strained stretch of her neck we see all the hope she has put into the ruse and all the uncertainty she experiences for its outcome. Not able to bear the suspense of her husband's reaction anymore, she looks down. At precisely that moment, he mimes his devotion to her with a simplicity and weight of gesture new to the ballet. She catches only the end of his "speech," but evidently she senses the import of his dynamics, for we can see her neck and shoulders relax a trifle. In a flash, they embrace. In a flash, this noneventful wisp of a ballet attains a speck of truth most heavyweight contenders never graze.

—from *The Nation,* June 26, 1976

AUGUST BOURNONVILLE
Choreographic Creed

Dance is an art because it presupposes calling, knowledge, and skill.

It is a fine art because it strives for the ideal, not only in sculptural ways but also lyrically and dramatically.

The beauty to which dance ought to aspire is not dependent on taste and fashion but is based on the unchangeable laws of Nature.

Mime includes all of the emotions of the soul; dance, on the other hand, is most importantly an expression of joy, a desire to follow the rhythms of music.

It is the mission of art and particularly of the theater to sharpen thought, elevate the mind, and freshen the senses. Dance should above all beware of flattering the preferences of a blasé public for effects foreign to true art.

Gaiety strengthens, intoxication weakens.

The beautiful always retains the freshness of novelty; the amazing bores in the long run.

Dance, with the help of music, can raise itself to poetry but it can also sink to mummery through an excess of gymnastics. The so-called difficult has numerous adepts, while the apparently easy is only achieved by a chosen few.

The high point of artistic skill is to conceal mechanics and effort under a harmonious calm.

Mannerism is not character, and affectation is the decided enemy of grace.

Every dancer ought to consider his difficult art as a link in the chain of beauty, as a useful adornment to the stage and this in turn as a meaningful element in the spiritual development of the Nation.

—translated from the Danish by Henry Godfrey, 1978

COMMENTARY

PETER ANASTOS
La Bayadère

La Bayadère *was the ballet that sealed the success of Marius Petipa when it premiered in St. Petersburg in 1877. The score, by Minkus, is more than serviceable; the story encompasses both the opulent and exotic background and drama that audiences of the day demanded (it's an Oriental* Aida *on pointe) and the pure dance of the "Kingdom of the Shades" act.* La Bayadère *has been a crucial work for generations of great Russian dancers, from Kschessinska and Pavlova to Makarova, Nureyev, and Baryshnikov. It was first seen in the West (only the "Shades" act) in 1961, on a Kirov tour. Two years later, Nureyev brought the "Shades" to the Royal, and in 1980 Makarova staged the entire ballet for ABT. In 2001 the Kirov presented a laborious reconstruction of the 1900 revival.*

W̲e are too young in America to appreciate fully the levels at which revisionism lives in ballet. With our first generation of ballet choreographers still among us, we have yet to see the wholesale alteration of ballets we know and love by successive generations. If revisionism is still a dirty word in America, it is practiced in the Old World as a living theatrical tradition, and we might better prepare for it.

The hue and cry that went up after Balanchine's controversial revision of *Apollo* in 1979 may be some indication of our unpreparedness. Idealists have but to look down the pike another twenty years to see hundreds of little hands out there staging ballets, *after Balanchine.* Yes, Virginia, there won't always be a Rosemary.*

---

*Rosemary Dunleavy, New York City Ballet's ballet mistress.

For while Balanchine's work is now partially frozen by the technical wizardry of the "Dance in America" series, the old fox himself is far too experienced a revisionist to be pinned down by videotape. Balanchine has sought to spare himself the more deprecatory aspects of revisionism by providing us with so many revisions of his own. He has redecorated so many times for so many new tenants that latter-day "restorers" will have one hell of a time deciding which version to accept: the Art Deco, the Scandinavian, or the High Tech.

In revising himself Balanchine has set up a condition in which his ballets may be passed on and held up to the changing technical and stylistic future of dancers. His intent is protected from those who would later interpret him—the steps may change but the ballet remains.

Few other choreographers have had the smarts to get that jump on the revisionists. Take Fokine's *Les Sylphides:* he just got in under the wire after years of agonizing over its many bouts with surgery at the hands of interns. By 1940 he'd realized that "Changing Taste" was the name of the game and he'd better incorporate some revisions of his own or wind up a gouged and defaced monolith like Marius Petipa.

Old man Petipa, brilliant craftsman though he was, really wasn't up to slouching toward the Dance Explosion. Not that he didn't understand revisionism itself, having as he did such a grand time revising Saint-Léon and Perrot, rechoreographing here, revising there, multiplying personnel, juicing up the mime, interpolating new music, and adding specialty numbers. No, Petipa in his brilliance as courtier, politician, civil servant, and jovial maître en chef of the Twilight Spectacle of the Romanovs, overlooked his own invitation to Fairy "Changing Taste." Petipa was as much a prisoner of the Maryinsky as its chief magic-maker, the mechanic locked inside the jewelled egg. While he may have tinkered with his ballets or bolstered certain principal roles, he seldom (if ever) had a chance to make the kind of revisions that would protect his intent for future generations. And after all, his ballets were tribute to rigid Tsarism and not really adjustable to radical revision.

During his lifetime Petipa seldom had new productions, costumes were remade when worn out, scenery repainted from the originals; while set numbers were withdrawn or interpolated, they were never really rethought in new contexts; his ballets were never staged in foreign capitals for other state institutions, and there was never a touring unit through which he could assess their impact outside the court of St. Petersburg.

This grand and glorious monolith, this exquisitely tiered hierarchy of settings and gems, inexorably tied to the regime it served, contained no provisions for "Changing Taste." As both servant and commander, Petipa was a victim of state rigidity; he was not in a position to provide looseness or wearability, and he has left us no instructions or indications on how to revise. By the time of his death in 1910, he was a passive rallying post for the infighting of claimants to his "meaning." Herein lies the start of uncontrolled revisionism as demonstrated by the Soviets.

La Bayadère, the subject at hand, comes to us as a major exhibition of revisionism, Soviet-style. In its day it was one of the grand landmarks of the Petipa Era, residing far longer in the public and professional mind as a "typical" Petipa ballet than either The Sleeping Beauty or Swan Lake. Accustomed as we are in the West to considering Petipa a "classical" as opposed to a "dramatic" choreographer, La Bayadère is a major revelation into his aesthetic.

In 1900 Petipa revived Bayaderka for Matilde Kschessinska. In Tsarist parlance the difference between "revival," "restage," and "new production" is unclear. We know that the 1900 production was physically the same as in 1877, although Kschessinska in her memoirs calls it a "new production." But then she had reasons to overstate the circumstances in hindsight; having attained a kind of political supremacy within the company due to her proximity to the Tsar and his Imperial relatives, she treated her every appearance on the stage as a State occasion. It is unlikely that Petipa enlarged or amplified the role of Nikia for her. His personal opinion of her was so low that he referred to her (Diaries for April 1903) as "this human pig . . . a miserable dancer. . . ." but probably his political instincts kept them on friendly professional terms. In addition we have evidence from her contemporaries that she was not only a brilliant technician but a wonderful actress (her finest role was Esmeralda)—attributes shared by the original Nikia, Vazem, making it seem unnecessary for Petipa to much alter his conception of the part.

So little is known of performance style at this time it would be equally presumptive to know exactly what he did (if anything) for Pavlova when she assumed the role in the season 1902–1903. It would appear that Petipa admired her very much, having cast her as Nikia over the considerations of senior company members (she was not officially made ballerina until 1905). It is well known how daringly unusual Pavlova appeared next to her contemporaries; whether Petipa relished tailoring the role for her special talents or merely exhibited an old man's prerogative in suddenly elevating a beautiful young dancer to stardom remains to be answered. Through the personal triumph of Pavlova, and later Spessivtseva and Karsavina, and whatever inherent strengths the ballet held, Bayaderka remained a viable repertory production through the duration of the World War I period.

Until someone takes on the task of researching in depth the period from Petipa's death in 1910 to the advent of Soviet realism in the 1930s, the names of various directors, ballet masters, régisseurs, and production chiefs will continue to be spectral; except for Fokine, Nicholas Sergeyev, and Fyodor Lopukhov, no one emerges clearly. By 1919, however, a production of *Bayaderka* under the "supervision" of Lopukhov defines the start of major revisions in the ballet. Apparently due to the decimation of stagehands and supernumeraries brought on by war and revolution, the fifth act, with its destruction of the temple and apotheosis, was cut. Other changes in the production are harder to pin down. One thing is certain: Lopukhov provides the key to Soviet Revisionism. It must be stated clearly that the Soviet twenties roared with a more vicious sound than our Charleston and hot-cha. The "old ballet," i.e. Petipa, underwent virulent attack not only by Bolshevik cadres but by those wishing to keep whatever they had saved from the upheaval. Some indication of the enormous convulsions going on inside Russian theatrical institutions may be confirmed in Lopukhov's preposterous credos and manifestos. While Soviet historians hold that this man had a positive effect on the young Balanchine, it must not be overlooked that he found much of Petipa's choreography in *The Sleeping Beauty* "unmusical" and set about to "correct" it; he also "corrected" *The Nutcracker* (and who knows what else). Lopukhov's own famous creation, *Tanzsymphonia* (to Beethoven's *Fourth Symphony*) seems to mark the beginning of what we now call "Soviet junk"—whether it was itself junk is hard to say, for both Balanchine and Danilova remember its thrill and innovation.*

How much Petipa could have survived all this business is hard to verify. I would guess less than we generally assume. I would guess, too, that whatever Petipa choreography fit the new image of ballet (as defined by Lopukhov and, higher up, the Minister of Culture, Lunacharsky) was saved and the rest "corrected" accordingly. Much of the action of *Bayadère* makes a good example of this: all that talk about Nikia's suffering, her oppression and ultimate salvation through death's purge smacks more of Bolshevik dogma than the Tsarist ballet of Petipa, where peasants or slaves were presented as exotic creatures visiting the audience from faraway lands or distant times.

The great "corrective" thrust of the twenties seems to me to mark the divergence of ballet in Russia from the mainstream of twentieth-century dance. As Soviet ballet masters and teachers looked deeper into the "meaning" of Petipa's choreography, mining it for its store of moral content, they chose to detach or radically revise the "frivolous" dance element and concentrate on the dramatic. In the West we have sought to eliminate the trappings and expose the dance. I choose to see more Petipa in Balanchine's *Raymonda Variations* than in anything brought to us from Moscow or Leningrad simply because it dances, and continues to dance, unfettered by

*Editor's note: Revived in 2004 by the Kirov, it looked pretty junky to me.

theoretics. It speaks some kind of subliminal message I have never heard from a Russian company, it whispers ". . . had Petipa lived. . . ."

After Petipa now seems to be more a catch-all phrase that includes anything "classical" looking or dramatic in an "old-fashioned" way. *After Petipa* here is not like *after Petipa* there, nor are either like *after Petipa* elsewhere. Even the English, who were made privy to the master's notes through the work of Nicholas Sergeyev, take their Petipa from Diaghilev, and that is nothing if not editorialized.

After the 1920s there were two more important restagings of *La Bayadère*. A new production in 1932 by Agrippina Vaganova remains somehow mysterious—I can find little or nothing about it, nor did recent specific inquiries to sources in Leningrad yield anything of substance. Since we take it for granted that Vaganova was a teacher and technical pedagogue more than a political critic, we might assume that her staging of *Bayadère* sought purity of movement, or at least clarity of her new style. One wonders how she staged the Shades Scene. What is the origin of the second variation here, now called the "Vaganova variation"? Had she danced it herself with a particularly personal interpretation, or did she change the choreography to suit her developing technical methods? How did she handle the rest of the ballet? Was Lopukhov purged?

One element is telling: the coldness of the spectral bayadères was greatly improved upon by shortening their romantic tutus to classical length. This probably made the dance more crisp—it may also have provided reason to tighten or revise the choreography.

In 1941 Vakhtang Chabukiani and Vladimir Ponomaryov restaged *La Bayadère* after Petipa, Lopukhov, and Vaganova. The idea for the revival belonged to Chabukiani, who saw in it a vehicle for himself and Natalia Dudinskaya, although much of the restaging was done by Ponomaryov.* Both men have since been given program credits individually or together, depending on the political climate, for *Bayadères* at the Kirov or Bolshoi or elsewhere in the Soviet Union. But for all practical purposes this *Bayadère* is Chabukiani's. Let us first remember that he grew up and achieved stardom under Stalin—and if *La Bayadère* is any indication, he was really one of Uncle Joe's boys. His revisions of the ballet towed a certain line, a line not unknown even in Western theater, where political hipness (of whatever side) is the raison d'être; as the fifties gave us Shakespeare in turtlenecks, so the Soviet forties brought us realism, meaning, lessons, and codes of behavior. I suspect Chabukiani's strength as a male dancer/rhetorician contributed to

---

*Within the Kirov hierarchy, Ponomaryov was always the Number Two man: assistant artistic director of the Kirov Ballet from 1935 to 1938 and then acting director from 1941 through 1944, he wound up in the backwaters of Budapest, where he died in 1951. Chabukiani, after a brilliant career at the Kirov, was "exiled" to Tbilisi, where he "founded" the Georgian Ballet.

the increased importance of Solor (and the Fakirs) and expanded the role of men in the ballet in general (the Rajah, symbol of monarchy, could remain safely—purposefully—weak). Under Chabukiani's direction one imagines the postures of strong against weak, monarch against slave, privileged against dutiful became textually imposed. This sort of Method Revisionism has imbued the Soviet mentality since Stalin, and its usefulness has not been lost on the younger generation—the examples contained in Chabukiani have marked nearly every subsequent staging of a ballet in Russia, and the great artistic gifts we now receive from famous defectors in no uncertain terms reflect this conflict of "meaningful" realism over "decorative" abstractions. What's so unnerving about revisions of La Bayadère is the way the "old" is made to look "new" in conformity with a new audience's equipment to perceive the old.

In Chabukiani's Bayadère, as it is danced today by the Kirov, there is a wealth of information concerning his precise revisions. When Petipa's Act V was dropped in 1919, so too was a grand pas de deux therein for Gamzatti and Solor. Chabukiani choreographed this music in 1941, inserting it into Act II, thus making the entrée, divertissements, and pas de deux a unified pas d'action. Chabukiani's Act II begins with a grand march introducing priests, bayadères, fakirs, blackamoors, corps de ballet as celebrants, and the principals in various modes of conveyance (sedan chairs for the Rajah and Gamzatti, a magnificent stuffed elephant on wheels for Solor). Some of this may have been taken from the parade that filed in for Petipa's Act V Wedding Celebration. Chabukiani's pas d'action then follows:

(1) An opening short valse for the corps women, who carry Eastern fans and stuffed black parrots attached to their shoulders
(2) A grand valse for twelve women
(3) The entrance of Solor and Gamzatti, who then retire
(4) A pizzicato for four coryphées
(5) A dance for eight blackamoors played by children, who introduce a variation for the Bronze Idol
(6) Dance Manu, a variation for a bayadère balancing a jug on her head, assisted by two thirsty children
(7) A savage dance for the fakirs and a gypsy woman
(8) A variation for four taller and slower coryphées
(9) Entrée proper of Solor and Gamzatti
(10) Adage for this couple, backed up by two pas de trois
(11) Another variation for four coryphées
(12) Solor's variation
(13) Gamzatti's variation
(14) Coda
(15) Entrance of Nikia and solo

(16) Mime with a basket of flowers
(17) Nikia's death scene, and final tableau

This seems a typical Petipa formula—the difference lies partly in an increased importance for the male dancers. When Petipa featured academy students as blackamoors, they danced around a statue of a bronze idol. Chabukiani inserted a knock-out variation for a dancing idol, choreographed and performed by Nicolai Zubkovsky—and when you've got it, flaunt it. The Fakir's Dance is suitably animal and structurally includes a lone female (lapsed bayadère, gypsy, band-whore?) who whoops it up in the fashion of Kasatkina's *Don Quixote* Gypsy Dance. This is pure Soviet kitsch and reminds us of the underdeveloped sexual attitudes in socialist countries—things like *Walpurgisnacht* and the bacchanale in *Spartacus* always look embarrassingly dirty and harmlessly camp at the same time. This general mix of classical and character work seems a bit too concentrated for Petipa—he perhaps might have split them by acts, for example, by providing a Fire Festival in the Rajah Palace and then saving the classical divertissements for the Wedding Scene or the Shades Scene. In telescoping all these things, Chabukiani piles up a bumpy collection of *after Petipa* and heroic Soviet.

In Chabukiani's *Bayadère* there is a bit more mime than we see now in Act I; the friendly Fakir acts more as a go-between for Nikia and Solor. On the other hand, Chabukiani replaced a good deal of mime for the lovers by creating Nikia's second entrance with the pitcher of water and a pas de deux. The lifts here are a dead giveaway. Sources tell us that Chabukiani strengthened Nikia's two solos—her first entrance and her dance with the flower basket—by taking them from demi-pointe to full pointe. I cannot imagine a director, especially a "creative" one with choreographic aspirations, merely placing toe shoes on an old dance, so I believe Chabukiani probably made large changes for Nikia throughout Acts I and II. The Jampa Dance is performed for the Rajah alone just after the curtain rises, and there is extended mime for Nikia and Gamzatti in the confrontation. I have been told that up until the early 1960s the Shades Scene dissolved back into Solor's room where, in despair, he committed suicide, closing the ballet. I cannot pinpoint this to Lopukhov, Vaganova, or Chabukiani, but in 1941 self-liquidation was a popular Stalinist finale. Today the Kirov has dropped this, and they finish the ballet at the end of the Shades Scene. After World War II, *Bayadère* was restaged by Pyotr Gusev, artistic director of the Kirov, who only slightly cut some of the mises en scènes in Chabukiani's first act. When Konstantin Sergeyev took over the Kirov in 1951 he doubtless made further changes.

I am not at all convinced that the Shades Scene is a jealously guarded gem from the Petipa legacy. The 1941 Nikia was Natalia Dudinskaya, a prized product of the Vaganova Institute, and from the films and literature we have on her, a shining example of the new Soviet order (Order of the Red Banner of Labor, Badge of Honor, Stalin Prize, Honored Artist of the Republic). Since we look at the Shades Scene as an exhibition of academic classicism we might then ask, "Whose Academy?" When we cite how "modern" it looks, how much ahead of its time it seems, we are not merely looking at the structure of the piece (which is timeless) but at a certain openness in the upper body, a freedom in the port de bras, an ornamental back, a wide-open attitude—sound familiar? Structurally, I take Nikia at face value, and in her hierarchical place, and as I filter down through the three Shade variations and the corps de ballet, I begin to sense that the Petipa gem has been crudely recut for a new setting, cut to fit its place in a new academy with a new director.

The only other revision I can specifically pin down is an inserted pas de deux for Nikia and a slave featured in Act II as a kind of religious stamp of approval for the wedding of Solor and Gamzatti. It was choreographed by Konstantin Sergeyev in 1947 for Dudinskaya and Serebrennikov and has all the earmarks of the Tundra Circus.

The Kirov does, however, dance *La Bayadère* pretty much as Chabukiani staged it before the war. This is the version that Natalia Makarova grew up with and it is virtually set intact for ABT, excepting her recreation of a final scene in the temple. This is my main objection to Makarova's *Bayadère*—simply lifting a ballet this way and staging it for another company takes no more than a certain sum of money for the production. It takes little thought, really, and what work is involved centers on deciding what to cut and what to keep.

Miss Makarova has not done her homework here, and given her still viable contacts in Leningrad and her invaluable assistant on all matters of technique and style, Elena Tchernichova, one might even have expected more research, more digging, more uncovering, maybe even more Petipa. According to Tchernichova there are few sections of "pure" Petipa: Nikia's opening solo, with its strong *Giselle* referent in the révérénces and hops en tournant (these hops got even more referential in the fifties when Olga Moiseyeva began to straighten the tapped leg behind to low arabesque, thus exactly duplicating Giselle's Act II entrée), the mime throughout, Nikia's solo and scene at the close of Act I, and of course the Shades scene. Everything else in the ballet is later Sovietized material. When one compares the current Kirov production against Makarova's for ABT, one sees what very little work has been done. Not only is the credit line "World Premiere" incorrect (it only applies to Act III), it is spurious. What we have here is an editorialized version of a famous, watered-down classic in the repertory of the Kirov Theater, a translation made up for the impatience of an American audience. Its making required nothing more than three basically crude ingredients: a videotape, a blue pencil, and so many hours of toil by the ballet mistress.

I suppose audiences and critics are impressed with the length and size of the effort. For those of us who exist outside the ABT "Family," much more than this is expected. But for those within it, lowered expectations provide everything needed for a hit. Lowered expectations are in fact what keep ABT so attractive to the public. Long ago (when the Baby Moguls were really babies), ABT discovered how little content or quality was needed if ballet were just packaged and merchandized excitingly. Charles Payne's book *American Ballet Theatre,* for example, reads more like an *Esquire* piece on Twentieth Century Fox than a history of a ballet company—the Russian Package, The Great Collaborators Package, The American Package, The English Package, The Revival Package, Musical Packages, Star Packages, Gala Packages. Directors come and go, choreographers in and out, stars up and down—but isn't it all too wonderful, this great and glorious amalgamation of talent? . . . and after forty years of this razzle-dazzle let's stringtogether all the best clips, get the old gang back ("My, *she* looks good after all these years!"), tell a few stories, sing a few songs—now that's entertainment!

Today we have the Defector Package, or maybe it's the Russian Package II, or is it the International Package Strikes Back? Whatever it is, it is one of ABT's most successful merchandizing campaigns to date, full of all the glamour and thrill that brings people back season after season to cheer. This package features Baryshnikov's *Don Quixote,* and we all know what a lift that has been for American ballet; Makarova's 1974 staging of the Shades Scene (the Leningrad Shroud), Baryshnikov's *Nutcracker* (attention: psycho-history fans), a most interesting star-designer-story package in *The Sleeping Beauty,* and now *La Bayadère.* George Lucas could not have wielded a better deal.

In Makarova's *Bayadère* we have the famous English dancer Anthony Dowell in a new role, the up and comer from California Cynthia Harvey (attention: Debra Paget reincarnation fans), the ballerina herself as director and star, the exoticism of PierLuigi Samaritani's Imperial Ballet in the grand style, all of the above dressed to kill by Theoni V. Aldredge (Oscar for *Gatsby,* Tony for *Annie*). Only one unrealized aspect of the deal that might have elicited more thrills was Makarova's first choice as designer: Anthony Dowell.

The physical production is undeniably handsome, however, and does show off the ballet in a better light than does the Kirov (who, for their current production, still credit Allegri, the designer for the 1877 premiere). By finally rejecting whatever were Dowell's initial thoughts, and the subsequent complete designs of José Verona (both reportedly in flat Indian-printlike style), and opting for the grandly operatic designs of Samaritani, the period of the ballet certainly breathes more authenticity. *La Bayadère* is, after all, a nineteenth-century ballet set in the East and needs no more ethnic veracity than its operatic counterparts, *Lakmé* and *Turandot*.

The musical score for *La Bayadère* is, in spite of the low regard some have for Minkus, not without interest. I happen to enjoy his music for its period flavor, but he is not, as they say, another Mozart. John Lanchbery, ABT's Music Director since 1978, brings an impressive background to bear (directorships of the Royal Ballet, 1960–72, and the Australian Ballet, 1972–1978) in reshaping and vitalizing their heretofore woeful pit. Lanchbery is probably one of the best ballet conductors now working and his understanding and devotion are unquestionable. What doesn't really work is his taste as an arranger, and while his *La Fille mal gardée* for Ashton is a triumph of stylistic research, he gets less impressive as he goes along. *The Merry Widow* (overblown), Nureyev's *Don Quixote* (Kitri goes salsa-reggae), *Mayerling* (treatment problems), *The Turning Point* (tacky), and now *La Bayadère* (misguided). The worst thing about his arrangement of Minkus is the way he's pandered to its borderline camp. Where *Fille mal gardée* set us squarely in the period pastiche of Hérold and Rossini (did Ashton's singular influence temporarily correct Lanchbery's taste?), *Bayadère* misses the nineteenth century altogether and lands us in hoochy-cooch Hollywoodland. His takeoff seems to be a gigantic symphony orchestra in 1924 accompanying silent films in Grauman's Egyptian. Nikia and Solor are now Theda Bara and Douglas Fairbanks. Lanchbery's harmonic additives and juiced-up modulations (with Makarova reportedly giving often-grudging approval) don't help Minkus, they misplace him. The score played unadulterated by the Kirov orchestra satisfies by its clear and somewhat naive nineteenth-century ballet impression of a mysterious far-off land. By arranging the score *mit schlag*, Lanchbery has buried the natural flavor.

But the conductor is admittedly keen on movie music (see intermission interview with Pia Lindstrom during the *Bayadère* telecast in June) and once told Dick Cavett, in answer to a question on where Tchaikovsky might be today, that he'd be in Hollywood making a fortune!

The music for Act III is newly composed by Lanchbery "in the style" with the possible exception of the Candle Dance, which is interpolated from Pugni's *Esmeralda*. (In the Kirov version this music accompanies the Ritual Betrothal Pas de Deux in the Rajah's palace). The only other verifiable new music is the scene in Solor's room, which includes an opium-smoking theme Lanchbery improvised at the piano many years ago to accompany the showing of silent flicks in his flat (Lindstrom interview).

In staging *La Bayadère* for ABT Makarova has relied heavily on the judgment and diligence of her ballet mistress, Tchernichova. Although it will not be confirmed, I suspect both Makarova here and Baryshnikov in *Don Quixote* and *The Nutcracker* acted more as project directors and left the actual staging to Tchernichova. Compared to the Kirov *Bayadère* (which sadly is the only performance source we have), Makarova has cinched in most of the mime. In other places she has rearranged the order of the numbers; in Act I, Scene 3 (Chabukiani's Act II), she has eliminated all of the character dancing. In retrospect this was probably smart, although ideally one would see a mix of Chabukiani-Petipa spread over Acts I and III. Here one really misses the Dance Manu and then only for the accompanying children. But the regret is sentimental because this dance has a history of revealing future ballerinas. Among the children who once danced around the jug-balancing bayadère at the Maryinsky were Pavlova, Karsavina, Danilova, Ulanova, and probably others who "went on" (later as a teenager, Danilova would be the first Shade, leading the Imperial corps down the ramp in the Shades Scene, with Spessivtzeva her Nikia).

Markarova's staging of the Shades scene in 1974 was electrifying only because it took us by surprise. Who would have thought *that* corps . . . oh, well. ABT didn't have any soloist Shades then and it has none now. No company without a strong academy can put principals, soloists, corps, and children all on the same stage with any sense of unity. Now six years later the corps work is less impressive, but in the match dissolve in and out of Solor's room we at least have a context in which to see *his* grief. Nikia in context does little to change my perception of her as a Shade. She is equally holy in death and in life. Notwithstanding certain inadequacies and flaws in performance, Petipa's ghostly kingdom is still one of the most thrillingly timeless constructions in all the known literature. And its glory tugs at our imagination for what Petipa we will never know.

Makarova's Act III is the first attempt since the 1920s to complete *Bayadère* as originally intended. Zubkovsky's Bronze Idol Dance is strategically placed at the top of the act, followed by a processional march of priests, bayadères, and the wedding party. A Candle Dance for the bayadères kills time and its choreography looks too hard, too Soviet, too out of place. It's full of things like half turns in piqué attitude melting off pointe, which is not something one gives to sixteen girls in unison. Although the rest of Makarova's choreography for Act III is original, it does follow somewhat Petipa's outline. He stipulated a pas de quatre for Nikia's ghost, Solor, Gamzatti, and the Rajah in such a way, I imagine, that would tie the story together and at the same time remind the audience of both *Giselle* and *La Sylphide* in the manner of Nikia's appearances and disappearances seen only by Solor. This, anyway, is how Makarova has choreographed the pas de quatre, and it does make ballet sense. That it looks nothing like the rest of the ballet is its downfall. Further research might have helped, for example, with the music. At this point it is very weak, coming as it does after the Shades Scene, and seems to serve no purpose other than to set up the temple's destruction (itself something less than spectacular).

Makarova's casting of *La Bayadère,* as one would suspect given the material at hand, is hit and miss. The Europeans come off largely better than the Americans, but then they've had so much more experience in dramatic thinking, and rethinking, and rethinking. From the very first performance the role of Solor fit Anthony Dowell like a kid glove and as he continued he began to create some of the ballet's finest moments. Dowell comes to ABT one of the world's few remaining danseur nobles, and as he grows older he grows more noble. There is something even more exquisite about Dowell that we only glimpsed in *A Month in the Country*—through Solor we see it fullblown and magnificent, and that is his persona as a Romantic dancer. In *La Bayadère* he gives us the kind of ephemeral fragility and sensitivity nearly extinct in male dancing; his Solor is a kind of wistful fairy-tale prince all wrought up in incense and magic. In the Shades scene he is as much the vision as its creator and echoes qualities we only find in wilis, or sylphs, or naiads. Dowell's Solor recalls the words Gautier found to describe the dancing of Jules Perrot: ". . . the ariel, the sylph, the male Taglioni. . . ."

Patrick Bissell, on the other hand, made a gawky Solor who was apparently coached very carefully in noble posturing. He's just a nice American kid who probably lacks the sense of lost world princing needed for this part. He's not miscast, really, but he plays it so Jimmy Stewart I can hardly believe the turban.

With so much to take in from Dowell it is doubly disheartening to find so much lacking in the women. Starting right at the top it must be said that Natalia Makarova has now completed every aspect of the surgery and has finally become Giselle. She cannot dance any role now without the frail swooning that has transformed her every appearance into Further Into Beyond the Valley of the Wilis. From *Swan Lake* to *Contredances* to *Other Dances* it's all Giselle. I suppose that when something works you should keep it but this has really been carried too far. She now dances slower, more droopily, more seamlessly (some call this "musicality"). Her first act is by far the best—the Love Pas de Deux and the mime offer us a glimmer of this unfamiliar role, and the confrontation with Gamzatti is in many ways touchingly foreboding. But after this she tires and dons the veil. Her cancellation of Acts II and III for the national telecast was brilliantly conceived. Demurring at the peak, she left the audience her finest moments.

Martine van Hamel, on the other hand, has a rather more consistent interpretation throughout the ballet. She pays less attention to detail in shadings or characterization in the drama and goes for a technically through-danced Nikia. Van Hamel today is a much better dancer than she was five years ago, but she is a less interesting ballerina.

The role of Gamzatti is quite a plum. It's really sort of a Rosalind Russell part and the right ballerina could make a marvellous dish out of it. Unfortunately ABT has no one with range enough to seize it by the earrings and let fly. Gamzatti seems to lie somewhere between Effie (in *La Sylphide*), Myrtha, and Amneris, although she's neither dotty nor malevolent. In Petipa's production she wore heeled shoes and emoted, until the final act where she danced only an adage. Gamzatti is a princess, a great beauty, and a prize. She symbolizes everything a young prince could want but at the same time obstructs the path of true love between a nobleman and a temple dancer. Cynthia Harvey looks every inch a movie star in the costume but (who's kidding whom?) this girl simply can't dance. If she was chosen to eliminate competition with Makarova as Nikia, that's understandable at ABT, but rumors that Harvey is being groomed to become an important part of next season's lineup are too stupifying to consider. Van Hamel's Gamzatti was just like her performance as Nikia: well placed, stretched, pulled up. Good show, nice fouettés. And I must say it was fabulous to finally see Jolinda impersonate Maria Montez and for the company to give such a nice pat on the head to Janet Shibata (though she resembled a TV anchorperson glazing through the news). After all this it's *still* an interesting role—I only shudder at what Olga Tchikaboumskaya might have wrought in that confrontation scene.

Finally we are left with the outgrowth of Makarova's *Bayadère* for ABT. Will it end up as bedraggled as *The Sleeping Beauty* or will they simply play it out and then give us *The Kingdom of the Shades* on a bill with *Aurora's Wedding*? I saw five performances of *Bayadère* in its first run and by the third viewing I was enchanted, enthralled, and enveloped—not in this production, but in the larger significance of what Karsavina called "this holy ballet." I think despite the worst kind of corrections, revisions, and mediocre resuscitations, there is a great ballet imbedded in *Bayadère*. But unlike Excalibur, this ballet will never be freed; the hour is late and the image has forever faded and passed. Our fantasies are stirred by this production—we wonder still what the Imperial Ballet was like, for now it seems as distant as the performances through which it lived. Our age demands a speed-read comprehension that prepares us for the day after tomorrow and leaves no time for the fragrant nuances of yesterday. When old guard dancers speak of *La Bayadère* they do so not with any sense of historical moment but in an ecstasy of recollection that when the Maryinsky curtain rose—in Danilova's memory—and she and her Shades stepped down that ramp, they sent out to the audience all the perfume, the incandescence, the majesty of a faraway mountain pass in a strange unfathomable kingdom. Danilova's generation complains that all the old majesty and mystique is gone from modern revisions. In the ABT *Bayadère*, we Americans now see how great ballets can be revised into dim shadows of themselves.

—from *Ballet Review,* Vol. 8, Nos. 2 and 3, 1980

TONI BENTLEY

Costumes by Karinska

Born Varvara Zhmoudsky in Kharkov, Barbara Karinska (1886–1983) became the leading costume designer of her time. Her first job was with the new Ballets Russes in Monte Carlo in 1932, but the greatest part of her career was in collaboration with George Balanchine, who said of her, "I attribute to her 50 percent of the success of every ballet that she has dressed." All in all, she designed and/or executed nine thousand costumes for the New York City Ballet. Among the most spectacularly beautiful were those for La Valse, The Nutcracker, Jewels, *and—her last work—*Vienna Waltzes. *She and Balanchine worked together to create the soft "powder-puff" tutu he found essential to his vision of the female dancer. Karinska also designed for plays, musicals, and movies, sharing an Oscar for the 1948* Joan of Arc.

In late 1949, at the age of sixty-three, Karinska embarked on a new phase of her career. Balanchine asked her to not only make but design the costumes for a new ballet entitled *Bourrée Fantasque,* set to music by Emmanuel Chabrier. She produced lovely, jaunty black tutus flecked with bright colors and accessorized—in keeping with the lighthearted spirit of the ballet—with fans, gloves, and headpieces. While the honor and freedom of designing costumes herself were important to her, Karinska really had been "designing" throughout her career, each time she translated a sketch into fabric. "I think anything you designed became Karinska's. Otherwise, it just didn't happen," explained one designer. Karinska slipped into this new role easily and enthusiastically, and over the next several decades she designed over thirty ballets. In them, one can detect not only her characteristic brilliance of style and detail, but something more of her personal taste.

Karinska's conception of feminine beauty echoed Balanchine's, and it was here, with the female dancers, that they created what were perhaps their most inspired and influential images. The Balanchine ballerina that Karinska dressed was a woman on a pedestal, untouchable yet soft and vibrant—not an imposing goddess or empress with hard edges and uplifted bosom, but a real woman inhabiting her own body, draped in silk chiffon or cotton tulle that conformed to her true shape. In Balanchine's hands her movements became metaphors for her character—recognizably American, but classic, too. She was long, lean, young, athletic, energetic, and powerful, but she was dressed for some mythical court life, not for the gym. She was the Young Girl at the ball dressed in white in *La Valse*, the spiky, sexy insect in *Metamorphoses*, the tightly bodiced Dewdrop in *The Nutcracker*, the hip-swinging saloon girl in *Western Symphony*, the cheerful cheerleader in *Stars and Stripes*, the peach-and-pearl-veiled fairy in *A Midsummer Night's Dream*, and the shy, sheerly clad geisha in *Bugaku*.

But, whatever her role, the ballerina's own physique was visible and available for adventure, and this freedom was one of Karinska's greatest contributions. The dancer was never merely a mannequin for Karinska's virtuosic display, but remained, as for Balanchine, the focus of the whole endeavor. This celebration of female form reached a new peak in 1950 when Karinska recostumed Balanchine's *Symphony in C*. Here, in the forty identical white tutus, the aptly named "Balanchine/Karinska tutu" or "powder-puff tutu," was born, forever changing the way a ballet dancer could look.

One of the great inventions of theatrical costuming of all time, the tutu—probably derived from the French child's word "tu-tu" or "cul-cul" meaning "bottom," and thus seeming to relate to the panties onto which the layers of tulle are attached—first appeared in Paris, in a long version, in 1832, on Marie Taglioni in *La Sylphide*. As dancing became more virtuosic and modesty less prevalent, the skirt was gradually shortened to show more leg—first the ankle, then the knee, then the thigh. Before Balanchine and Karinska put their minds to it, the standard existing tutu, and still the most common around the world except at the New York City Ballet, was the British or Russian "pancake," so-called because of its deep, wide, and very flat skirt, supported by a wire hoop at the outer edges. Karinska had been making this type of tutu herself until she met Balanchine, although she preferred not to use a hoop but rather spokes that radiated out from the waist like an umbrella.

This type of tutu, however, had many qualities unsuited to Balanchine's vision of the way his dancers should move. The hoop or umbrella skirt often takes on movement of its own, echoing that of the dancer several beats later, in a way that is not always musically appropriate. And if dancers move quickly and close together, as they do in Balanchine ballets, their hoops can collide and tip, adding unchoreographed elements to the proceedings. Finally, because the skirts are wide and weighty they often reach to the knees, whereas Balanchine wanted to see more, see the legs, their arabesques and penchés moving easily, naturally, and freely, not fighting to get out from under a hoop. He did not like the sudden revelations of posterior that an extended leg would sometimes produce under a tipped pancake tutu. In short, Balanchine wanted a smaller, shorter, softer, lighter, more natural, and flattering tutu, and Karinska gave it to him.

Strictly speaking, this was not the first appearance of a short, fluffy tutu on the stage. Harriet Hoctor, the American toe dancer who performed on the vaudeville circuit during the 1930s, wore a similarly short tutu, with the obvious purpose of showing off her sensational legs. Curiously enough, though any direct influence is difficult to document, Balanchine may well have seen Hoctor dance when he arrived in America in 1933, and in 1936 he actually choreographed pieces for her to perform in the *Ziegfeld Follies*. Once again, as with *Star and Garter,* the vernacular, the popular, even the so-called vulgar may be seen to merge in Balanchine and Karinska's work. After all, Hoctor and Balanchine had the same motive in their costuming—to maximize the visual effect of the body.

The *Symphony in C* tutu, the prototype for the powder-puff tutu, had no hoop and only six or seven layers of gathered net (as opposed to the twelve or more used for the hoop tutu). The layers, each a half-inch longer than the previous one, were short, never precisely aligned, and tacked together loosely to give the skirt an unprecedented softness and fullness. The skirt fell in a natural, slightly downward slope over the hips to the tops of the thighs. But the skirt was only the most obvious of the changes and details that Karinska instituted. It was in her experiments with the bodice that Karinska really revolutionized the tutu.

Made before the panties or skirt are attached, the bodice is the foundation of the costume. Karinska's experiments with the cut, shape, seaming, and decoration of the bodice had begun in 1932, when she made her first one for members of the Ballets Russes de Monte Carlo. Using anywhere from six to fifteen panels of fabric, Karinska was a pioneer in the practice of cutting on the bias (the diagonal of the fabric, as opposed to straight up and down or across), for a highly fitted garment. Cutting on the bias was a much-admired technique in the couture world of Paris in the 1930s, where Karinska no doubt came across the idea. But there the beauty of the bias cut was usually found in loose-fitting garments, where the diagonal created its own kind of shape and sexy cling. Karinska's tremendous innovation was in using the bias cut for a tightly fitted bodice, where the give and take of the cut could be used to accommodate the aerobic requirements of a dancer's—or opera singer's—rib cage. "No one else knew how to do a bodice like that or even knew why you should do a bodice like that," says Broadway and ballet designer Patricia Zipprodt. "Most of them were so clumsy, straight-up-and-down bodices with seams, seams, seams, but never any alteration in the fabric, until Karinska. Her costumes were danceable things, singable things."

A typical Karinska bodice would be a mixture of panels, the back and center front usually cut the normal way, with various bias-cut panels in between, under, and around the ribs and diaphragm. Out of this extremely smooth and elegant-looking composition came another, less practical quality that epitomizes the sensual magic of Karinska's invention. She used only "living" fibers—ones made by plants or animals. These fabrics, unlike inert synthetics, give off an energy all their own, and, when complemented by stage lights, their various hidden qualities rise and shine. Thus, the ballerina's torso, wrapped in its straight and biased panels, would gleam as it moved around the stage, giving off alternately light and shadow, matte and sheen, like the facets of a precious stone. When ballerinas are described as glowing, or appearing chiseled like jewels, there is, therefore, real science behind the illusion.

Other Karinska touches can best be viewed by looking at examples— and there are many; Karinska made over nine thousand costumes for the New York City Ballet alone. In 1951 she designed the long tulle dresses for Balanchine's *La Valse,* and these mysterious, elongated, haunting ball gowns so perfectly complemented the cerie, pendulous tone of the ballet and Maurice Ravel's music that the ballet is unimaginable without them. Zipprodt attributes her own career decision to having once viewed these costumes.

> I had just come to New York and I was trying to figure out what to do with my life. I was painting and waitressing at Schrafft's—the whole routine of starving young people with dreams. I used to spend a great deal of time with Gjon Mili who was doing a big color story for *Life* and he dragged me to the ballet. It was *La Valse* and in comes Tanaquil LeClercq in this white dress. Bang. I went down to FIT [Fashion Institute of Technology] and beat on their doors and got a scholarship and went to school. I wanted to design for this company, for Balanchine. What Karinska had said with this dress changed my life.

(The white satin and tulle gown Zipprodt saw was, interestingly, not really white but rather a luscious cream color. Karinska knew that a true white has an empty, flat appearance onstage.) Later in the ballet, during her courtship with Death, this bride of youth dons a cape of sheer, black gauze and a beaded, black choker and carries a bouquet of dried black roses, thereby succinctly transforming her innocence into a poignant image of impending doom. The layering of dark over light gave an intangible sensation of the sinister that accentuated the essence of the music itself.

Layering of colors, often very disparate ones, was one of Karinska's specialties, and it was never more apparent or used to better dramatic advantage than in the other women's costumes in *La Valse.* Attached to heavy, silver-gray halter-cut bodices with low-slung backs, the long skirts were composed of up to six layers of color—red, orange, purple, and pink—all topped by a single layer of translucent gray. Balanchine took advantage of this unusual depth of color in his choreography when he had the women lift the edges of their skirts and fling them in the air to release a cascade of colors, each not quite looking like itself because of its neighbor's omnipresent glow. For the headpieces Karinska employed contradiction to perfection, sewing large, black-rimmed rhinestones into the wiry weave of black horsehair. They, like the costumes and the ballet, were sprightly and elegant but tinged with death. It was truly haunting elegance.

The subtler effect of layering similar colors can be found throughout Karinska's work, beginning with *Cotillon,* in 1932. For the Snowflake costumes for Balanchine's *Nutcracker,* in 1954, she juxtaposed beige, pink, and blue tulle for an airy, pale, not-quite-there feel—the feel of snow. For the "Emeralds" section of *Jewels,* in 1967, she covered three layers of yellow-beige tulle with one of dark green and one of light green. For *Raymonda Variations* in 1961, the overwhelming color of the tutus is bright pink, although the top layer is, in fact, of a pale blue. According to Karinska's canon, a single solid color is a dead event under the lights, inside a proscenium, and it is only by juxtaposing and combining that one can suggest the real blue-white of snow, the green of an emerald, or even the pink of a pastel ballet.

A different type of layering effect is apparent in Karinska's costumes for Balanchine's *Serenade.* First choreographed in 1934, this ballet set to Tchaikovsky's yearning score was Balanchine's first in America, and it had withstood various costuming styles for almost twenty years. There were leotards and skirts, then short tunics, then decorated ones, but when Karinska designed the pale blue gowns in 1952 for the New York City Ballet's production it was as if this great ballet had been through a long genesis and was only now in full bloom. So simple as to seem inevitable, the long-waisted, plain blue bodices ended in low-slung, diagonally placed (a very flattering line on a woman's hips that Karinska used frequently), ankle-length skirts of finely woven tulle. Each skirt was made of just one, much-gathered layer— twenty yards of fabric in all. Otherwise blue all around, in front of each leg, from hip to ankle, Karinska placed a sheer panel of beige tulle through which the dancer's legs would appear. The effect of this small detail is, like the ballet itself, subtle, yet exaggerated; sexy, yet demure. The overall effect of thirty-two of these windswept costumes on a moonlit stage, moving with Balanchine to Tchaikovsky, is one of the single most romantic atmospheres on any theatrical stage in this century.

Unlike many designers, who see a certain shade of color in their mind's eye and then proceed to stir the dye vats to reproduce it, Karinska disliked dyed colors. She knew that they were unstable and under the heat of the stage lights would inevitably change color and preferred to work within the "limitations" of what was available and what she could find on her numerous shopping trips to Paris. She would often buy hundreds of yards of a material she liked and put it on the shelf for a future ballet, and, with uncanny frequency, Balanchine would sooner or later come up with a ballet where she could indeed use it to perfection. To this day there remain drawers of new and antique lace, gold braid, silver roses, strings of bugle beads, and bolts of fabric that Karinska bought and never used. These treasures are kept in one of her old bureaus in the New York City Ballet costume shop, and sometimes, for a very special costume, a length of lace or a strand of beads will be carefully extracted from the stash. But mostly the bureau is kept under lock and key; what is in it is irreplaceable in today's manufacturing world. Ironically, the result of Karinska's insistence on using ready-made colors is a legacy of dyed ones. The browns and beiges and blues and pinks she used are no longer made and cannot be found at any price, so when the *Serenade* costumes need replacing, the vats of dye are filled and hundreds and hundreds of yards of tulle are plunged into the boiling liquid. Karinska would be horrified.

Dropped or diagonal waists were not the only figure-enhancing techniques Karinska used. While her famous *Symphony in C* tutu had a faceted bodice that reached to the hip, where the skirt began, many of her costumes—such as the beautifully tailored and somewhat more complex tutus for Balanchine's *Divertimento No. 15*—featured a yoke, an extra section of costume that reached from the skirt to the waist. The upper bodice section was shaped to meet the yoke at the waist on the sides and in a flattering V in the front. At the waistline, behind the joining of bodice and yoke, lies a series of invisible vertical elastics that together allow the dancer full movement from the waist and hips in all directions. The dancer does not feel them, and the audience does not see them; their presence is just one more detail that contributes to the overall fluid effect. Breaking a costume-making custom, Karinska often made the yoke in a different shade from the upper bodice, as in the 1966 ballet *Brahms-Schoenberg Quartet,* thereby recasting the appearance of the figure. The contrast, however subtle, creates depth, texture, and richness, qualities that correspond to and enhance the grandeur of Balanchine's ballet.

While these various details are of a visible and exterior nature, Karinska's innovations were not only for the audience but also for the dancer, and to peer inside one of her costumes is to view the matte side of luxury and the very loving dedication of this woman to the dancers she dressed. Made of cotton drill—a heavy, tightly woven fabric that gives shape and support to the satin it backs, and absorbency to the sweat and perfume of the human being it lays against—the bias-cut panels on the inside of a bodice are as beautifully cut, stitched, and finished as those on the outside. Seeing this, one can readily understand why a Karinska costume lasts three or four times longer than most others. With its delicate weaves, intricate seaming, and hand-stitched edges, each costume is made with the precision, quality, and strength of a military uniform.

Karinska's fittings were conducted for multiple purposes, of which physical fit and aesthetic beauty were only the most obvious. Fittings were tests of her laboratory results, and Karinska was interested not only in the static visual aspect of her work—and here most other designers cease their interest—but in the physical performance of her creations. "She understood the velocity of fabric," says Suzanne Farrell, a ballerina she clothed for almost twenty years. "Are you comfortable? Can you move?" she would ask, and if there was any hindrance, seen or felt, Karinska was known to tear out the entire garment on the spot and begin again. Her work attitude was notable for its extraordinary lack of ego, considering what a strong personality she did have. But her work was about the work, not about herself, and she would never insist on any feature or aspect of a costume just because she had designed it, or labored for days over it—especially if the dancer was restricted in any way or if Balanchine was not pleased.

—from *Costumes by Karinska,* 1995

ARLENE CROCE
Edwin Denby

The best dance critic living." That is what Edwin Denby, in 1940, called Serge Lifar. He thought Lifar, who had just published a book on Diaghilev, was good "because, first, he has the professional experience which turns dancing from a thing you buy ready-made into a thing you make yourself. And second, he sees dancing with the eyes of intelligence, as an ordinary person sometimes sees a friend or sees the weather; sees and believes at the same time. 'The eyes of a poet,' people say who know what poetry is about."

If today those words sound more generous than exact as applied to Lifar, it is because they strike us as a good description of Denby himself. He, too, had been a professional dancer (in Germany before Hitler), and he saw with the eyes of a poet—so much so that "people who know what poetry is about" were more than likely to have noticed the resemblance between the dance critic of the bimonthly *Modern Music* and the image he drew of Lifar. Denby by then had been at the craft of dance criticism for four years. He had already written, in *Modern Music,* the pieces on *Noces* and *Faune,* on ballet music, on Balanchine's *Poker Game* and *Baiser,* and on Ashton's *Devil's Hol-*

iday which would become immortalized in *Looking at the Dance.* He had addressed central issues in the work of Graham and Massine, identifying the qualities of pictorial tension which he found differently disturbing in each; and on Massine he had written one of the most luminous passages he would ever write: "As a pictorial arranger Massine is inexhaustible. But dancing is less pictorial than plastic, and pictures in dancing leave a void in the imagination. They arrest the drama of dancing which the imagination craves to continue, stimulated by all the kinetic senses of the body that demand a new movement to answer the one just past. Until a kind of secret satisfaction and a kind of secret weariness coincide."

This is the writing not only of a poet who sees but of a poet who feels, and who feels what we all feel. Denby gained from having been a dancer an incalculable advantage, but it is Denby the spectator who is the true artist of criticism. *Looking at the Dance,* the book that established his reputation as a critic, is very precisely named. Looking—perceiving with all his senses—is what Denby did. It is sometimes erroneously said that a School of Denby exists in American dance criticism. Schools are based on ideas and theories, and Denby's critical insight was a gift—his alone. The only idea he ever proposed (and it was more an article of faith than an idea) was that each of us should develop the critical insight he was born with. When he says that Lifar (read Denby) sees as an ordinary person "sees and believes," he is saying that the experience of dancing is a normal and subjective one—no special knowledge is needed in order to understand it—but also that this subjective experience is heightened by belief, by an unconditional acceptance of the truth of what one sees. Another way of saying it is that dancing appeals to the poet in us. But that still isn't all there is to it. Dancing is physical, a spectacle of grace in movement. The "kinetic senses of the body," more than the optic nerve, are what stimulate the imagination. I believe that Denby discovered these kinetic senses in his role as a critic, sitting there in the dark, and that the more he thought about it the more it seemed that kinetic excitement was what made viewing dancing a normal and subjective but by no means universal pleasure. Three years later, writing for the readers of the *New York Herald Tribune,* he arrived at a formulation both generous and strict: "To recognize poetic suggestion through dancing one must be susceptible to poetic values and susceptible to dance values as well."

This statement forms the cornerstone of *Looking at the Dance,* yet, because of the way that book was edited (it came out in 1949), it is extremely difficult to see how—by what cognitive process—the statement might have crystallized in Denby's mind. Not, in fact, until the publication, earlier this year, of a complete edition of the criticism was it possible to follow Denby's thinking as it evolved from one piece to another. The articles and reviews in *Looking at the Dance* were selected by the music and dance critic B. H. Haggin, who had championed Denby's work for years. Pieces written years apart were united under single headings—"Dancers in Performance," "Modern Dancers," "Dancers in Exotic Styles"—and the entries within each category were not always reprinted in their original sequence. The internal logic of the book (devised, I take it, by Haggin) is admirable. In the opening section, "Meaning in Ballet," an amalgam of various magazine articles and what appear to have been Sunday columns from the *Herald Tribune* actually creates the impression that Denby had composed a primer in dance technique and dance aesthetics for the popular audience. (Of course, he had done just that, but not systematically.) Grouping scattered reviews on specific topics also points up the variety of the dance scene in New York in the forties and the variety of Denby's response to it. But though *Looking at the Dance* remains a classic, it gives us an Olympian Denby, whose most decisive utterances are as casual and unpremeditated as bolts from the blue. *Dance Writings,* edited by Robert Cornfield and William MacKay, collects all but the most marginal critical work that Denby published, including the reviews and portions of reviews that were excluded from *Looking at the Dance,* adds some unpublished material, and presents the lot chronologically except where chronology would destroy some more significant order. Thus, although the *Modern Music* series (1936–43) overlapped for seven months the *Herald Tribune* series (1942–45), it does not do so here; all the pieces on Balanchine and New York City Ballet from 1946 onward appear in one section; and essays on matters unrelated to topical events appear in another.

The consequence of this new and complete presentation is the emergence of a Denby who is a more complex, more vividly real character than the deity of *Looking at the Dance.* We see him as a working critic and, when he joins the staff of the *Herald Tribune,* as a most improbably robust *hard*working critic. The dance calendar in those days was blank for long periods and insanely congested for brief ones; Denby filled out the year with ice shows, nightclub acts, and Broadway musicals. He went to modern-dance recitals in hellish places; he reviewed the Rockettes. Constitutionally a frail man, he seemed to thrive under the pressure. During the fall ballet season of 1943, he filed fifteen pieces in October alone, and among these were two major essays and six reviews of collectible caliber. It is the opinion of Minna Lederman, the editor of *Modern Music,* that Denby's newspaper pieces, written to tight deadlines, are better than the articles he labored over for her; I agree with this—no finer body of dance journalism exists. But except for a few places here and there the *Modern Music* series doesn't seem labored, and there is no break in style when Denby takes up his newspaper job. If anything, he grows more precise, his tone becomes more intimate still, and his communicative zeal is palpable. Even in the most crushingly routine assignment he is a good reporter. The conscientiousness with which he reviews cast changes, program fillers, conductors, costumes, and scenery comes as a revelation to those of us who were bred on *Looking at the Dance*. (I remember thinking that these things couldn't have mattered to Denby, because he never discussed them. Well, he did.)

In matters of opinion, too, there are some surprises. Ballets trounced in *Looking at the Dance* bob up restored by second or third viewings; a few personal reputations are sealed or unsealed. Normally the most benign of critics, Denby could be dangerous when provoked. Of Baronova's antics he writes, "She seems to want the title of 'Miss Ironpants.'" On the whole, though, fewer dancers than one might expect enter or leave the winner's circle. The famous portrait, verging on caricature, of "Miss Toumanova with her large, handsome, and deadly face," her "blocklike torso, limp arms, and predatory head positions" isn't radically altered by the addition of a few favorable comments, one of which—"When she dances it is a matter of life and death"—is reminiscent of a remark he'd made about Carmen Amaya: "She can dance as if nothing else existed in the world but dancing and death." But Denby's Lifar turns out to have been a very different creature from what we had thought him up to now—chiefly an object of satire: "Poor Lifar. He looks older onstage than Dolin or Massine," and so on, in a vein of malicious sympathy that becomes openly derisive with a description of Lifar's pomposities in *Giselle*. But this was in 1950. In 1940, not only was Lifar the best living critic; he was also, of all the dancers of the prewar period, the one closest to Denby's heart. The passages on Lifar the dancer and Lifar the critic (both omitted from *Looking at the Dance*) are cast in the same adulatory terms. Lifar in performance has a naturalness

> that goes beyond the gestures required, as though the character were as much alive as anybody living. As though on the stage, he seems to believe in the life that is going on outside of the theater in the present. He seems to believe that his part makes sense anywhere, that his part (in the words of Cummings) is competing with elephants and skyscrapers and the individual watching him. They all seem real at the same time, part of the same imagination, as they are really. There is something unprofessional about carrying reality around with you in public that goes straight to my heart.

Denby seems to be in love. He is, as we never again see him, at a loss, fumbling for words. And he realizes how he must sound; his very next sentence is "This is the kind of criticism it is hard to prove the justice of; I wish we could see Lifar more often so I could try." The echo of Lifar the dancer in Lifar the critic is, I think, brilliantly illuminating, but it tells us more about Denby—about the qualities he loved and valued—than about Lifar. The echo of Amaya in Toumanova is also illuminating, but there Denby is talking about something he saw rather than thought he saw or hoped to see. He doesn't draw a parallel, and, indeed, none should be inferred. But he didn't strike that chord twice by accident.

Nor is "pictorial tension" coincidentally a problem in the work of both Graham and Massine. From *Looking at the Dance* you might be able to tell that this business of visual and kinetic suggestion was on Denby's mind in 1937 and 1938—the Graham and Massine articles are both from that period. But they're placed under different headings, and the Graham piece, in which Denby *first* brings up the matter, comes ninety pages after the Massine. In *Dance Writings,* it comes eleven pages before. Again, I don't wish to suggest a parallel, still less an "influence." But photographs from the past reveal conventions of the era that were invisible at the time, and dances of past eras may do the same, even though they were composed and staged under very different auspices. Nothing is harder to spot than the unconscious patterns that connect the work of contemporaries. Yet Denby's eye saw something— probably the only thing—in Graham's work that was like Massine's. That he didn't make a critical point of the similarity is immaterial. He may not have had the chance. Companies didn't perform, and critics didn't write, often enough in those days for such tight connections to be made. Or he may not, so early in his critical career, have completely understood the implications of what he saw, or may have thought them self-evident—who knows? And who cares? The test of a critic is not how many points he can clinch but how transparent he is; unless we can see through him to the way it was, it won't help to know what he thinks it means. As Denby says, "It is not the critic's historic function to have the right opinions but to have interesting ones. He talks but he has nothing to sell." For Denby, a critic is functioning properly when his readers feel free enough to have interesting opinions of their own.

Denby expressed these views on the job of the critic in 1949, in an essay twice as long as it appeared in *Looking at the Dance;* he was by then the polished craftsman, the poet who became a journalist without losing his personal voice. It must have been with some misgiving that he forsook his privacy as a little-magazine critic for the public glare of a newspaper post. Newspapering is the most difficult work imaginable for a dance critic, and it was more so in Denby's day than in our own. The mood you were in when the curtain fell on *Pillar of Fire* was not the mood you had to be in to race to a typewriter and rap out a smart lead for the bulldog edition. Denby was exactly one year into the job, right in the middle of that congested 1943 season, when he had a mishap. He mistook Nora Kaye for Markova and wrote a glowing notice of the wrong ballerina. His apology was a characteristically elegant tribute to both ladies, but the episode embarrassed him profoundly; thirty years later he still spoke of it. Denby, who'd had no journalistic training, was proud of his professionalism. Then, too, as a proponent of ballet at a time when most intellectuals preferred modern dance, he had an evangelical mission. Denby's supporters formed up against the modern-dance legions behind John Martin, of the *Times*. But it was more than ballet versus modern dance. Virgil Thomson in his autobiography speaks of the appeal of the city's two leading newspapers to "the educated middle class," saying that the *Times* "has regularly in its critical columns followed a little belatedly the tastes of this group; the *Herald Tribune* under Ogden Reid aspired to lead them. It did not therefore, as the *Times* has so often done, shy away from novelty or elegance." With Denby on dance (and he certainly did not neglect modern dance) and Thomson on music, the *Trib* was a juggernaut of opinion. Martin and Olin Downes, on music, were no match for it. One can imagine how Denby's enemies used his mistake against him.

Denby was a professional, but he loved Richard Buckle's monthly *Ballet,* because, as he put it when the magazine folded, it didn't make him feel like "a harried fellow-professional." After 1945, he never wrote for a newspaper again. He relinquished his *Herald Tribune* post to Walter Terry, who reclaimed it after the war, and for the next two decades he concentrated on his poetry, writing dance pieces more or less when the spirit moved him. Some of the critical writing from that period appears to have been motivated more by a wish to satisfy friends and editors than by a need to get things said. Still, the publication, in 1965, of a second collection, *Dancers, Buildings and People in the Streets,* revealed a Denby whose pertinacity of thought was undiminished. Only the sporadic nature of the pieces keeps us from making cognitive connections among them. Connections are anyway more a matter of tone. Though the writing has a new, Jamesian density, the tone becomes more frankly confiding; he sounds like a man among friends and often writes as one, casting his reviews in epistolary form. It is a fair guess that the epistles were all addressed to Buckle, who published them. (It would have been nicer to be told who the "you" is, and where the "here" is in his letters from abroad.) But though Denby invoked the privileges of the form, he didn't abuse them. Far from writing for a coterie, as he was sometimes accused of doing, he was working to broaden access to the subject on its deepest levels, both for the reader and for himself. By the intensity of one's interest in dance one is made to feel a part of Denby's circle.

The editors tell us who some of Denby's actual friends were, and an imposing list it is: the poets Frank O'Hara, Kenneth Koch, James Schuyler, John Ashbery, Ron Padgett, Anne Waldman, Alice Notley, Ted Berrigan; the painters Willem and Elaine de Kooning, Franz Kline, Alex Katz, Red Grooms, Larry Rivers; the composers Virgil Thomson, Aaron Copland, Roger Sessions, John Cage; the photographer and filmmaker Rudolph Burckhardt; the choreographers Merce Cunningham, Paul Taylor, Jerome Robbins. This is the true School of Denby—his fellow artists, with whom, as the generations passed, he had more in common than with the pack of inattentive children who were trying to become dance critics. Gentlest of men, he bore our presumption with angelic patience and never presumed, in return, to educate us. Rather, he just talked and listened as if we were his equals. The only piece of practical advice he ever gave me was when, at the end of a long ballet summer in the city, he found me staggering: "Get a beach vacation." He also said that he used to prepare for Tudor's premieres by downing a steak at Gallagher's, then going home and sleeping for two hours. Edwin by then was part of the intellectual history of New York; he belonged to that artistic community which had made New York in the decades after the Second World War what Paris was in the decades after the first one. He was the chronicler of the great New York dance renaissance of the forties and fifties. He witnessed Graham's peak, Cunningham's and Taylor's emergence; he saw Balanchine (whose work had first impressed him in Paris, in the season of Les Ballets 1933) consolidate his powers on his New York power base.

Looking back on years we never knew, it's easy to think "Bliss was it in that dawn," and yet the reality of life as Denby lived it was not magnificent. It was a life of cafeterias, cigarettes, and stale coffee, of dancers, buildings, and people in the streets. (And the dancers were starving.) Denby took all this as part of his subject. If, as Cornfield says in his introduction, he changed the way we talk and think about dance, it was a change that could not have come about in any other city in the world. The artificial character of life in New York turns the natural world into an abstraction, something for the mind to contemplate. That is why abstract art is so intensely true an expression of New York—it is nature lived as a value. When Cunningham revived his 1953 piece *Septet* this season, he brought back those long-ago New York summers, with their mental weather, their intent street-corner conversations about painting and dance. Denby muses on a Markova performance in 1952: "Her dancing was queerer than anyone had remembered it. A few days later, meeting a balletomane usually far stricter than I on the street, I asked him what he thought of her this season. 'More wonderful than ever,' he cried aggressively." Once, Denby runs into Cunningham; they talk about Markova, naturally, and Denby goes home and writes. In *Septet*, it is possible to see traces of Markova, also Graham, also Balanchine, and to sense the spiritual presence of Denby. The young Paul Taylor was a member of the original cast. Later, it was Denby who introduced Taylor to Lincoln Kirstein and then to Alex Katz.

On the night of July 12, 1983, at the age of eighty, Edwin Denby killed himself with sleeping pills. The notes he left were clearheaded, but his faculties were failing, and he was miserable in his dependency on others. His last published remarks are sad. They concern Balanchine, who had died two months before. Denby begins, ominously enough, with the revival of *Symphonie Concertante* by American Ballet Theatre, which had upset him. Then, as he had done so often in the past, he concentrates on what makes Balanchine different from other choreographers, but having to go through it all again (he is being interviewed for *Dance Magazine*) seems to dishearten him. You feel him near to desperation in the effort to be clear, as if it were a once-and-for-all-time effort, and he keeps underlining his remarks with "This is a rare gift," or "Few choreographers have known how to do that." He wishes that the ballets—"Balanchine's butterflies"—could be preserved, but he seems to think they won't be.

Dance Writings does not end on this note of anguish. The last piece in the book is the great analytical essay "Forms in Motion and in Thought," in the concluding pages of which Denby comes closer to capturing the dance experience than any other writer ever has, even his beloved Mallarmé. The dance is in his mind, a replay of something he's seen (undoubtedly by Balanchine), or perhaps something he's made up, and it is conveyed to us—such is his virtuosity—in three distinctly different critical modes. First comes a description of how a classical ballet works, in writing that is entirely sensory, with no steps and no images, but so lucidly composed as to evoke continuous gestural force:

> But the action of a step determines the ramifications, the rise and fall of the continuous momentum. You begin to see the active impetus of the dancers creating the impetus moment by moment. They step out of one shape and into another, they change direction or speed, they erect and dissolve a configuration, and their secure and steady impetus keeps coming. The situations that dissolve as one watches are created and swept along by the ease and the fun and the positive lightness of it. They dance and, as they do, create in their wake an architectural momentum of imaginary weights and transported presences. Their activity does not leave behind any material object, only an imaginary one.

One of Denby's cherished beliefs about dancing had to do with the persistence of images as a key to comprehension. Dancing leaves behind "an imaginary object," "a classical shape," "a visual moment of climax," that goes on gathering force in the mind. From ballet in the theatre, then, he turns to ballet recollected in tranquillity:

> As you lie on the hot deserted beach far from town and with closed eyes recall the visual moment of climax, and scarcely hear the hoarse breathing of the small surf, a memory of the music it rose on returns, and you remember the prolonged melodious momentum of the score as if the musical phrase the step rose on had arrived from so far, so deep in the piece it appears to have been.

Finally, after all this so-to-speak disembodied language, he gives us an actual ballet in choreographic script and pictures, danced by cats and dogs on city streets. Every bit of it is wonderful. Here is an excerpt:

> And while cats one meets on different nights all like to follow the same adagio form, one cat will vary it by hunching her back or rolling seductively just out of reach, another, another night, by standing high on her toes as you pat her, and making little sous-sus on her front paws; a third by grand Petersburg-style tail wavings; a fourth, if you are down close enough, by rising on her hind paws, resting her front ones weightlessly on you, raising her wide ballerina eyes to yours, and then—delicate as a single finger pirouette—giving the tip of your nose a tender nip.

Only Denby's eye, only Denby's sweetness of wit, his deep understanding of the collusion of art and nature could have produced this incomparable fun. He left us a little too soon for friendship's sake. Still, his timing told us what we had known and feared to admit—that an era was really over. He had said his farewell years before, in the last poem in *Mediterranean Cities* (incidentally one of the few poems of his with a reference to dance):

> For with regret I leave the lovely world men made
> Despite their bad character, their art is mild.

The seasons roll on. The music starts, the dancers appear on the vast stage and begin to dance, "creating the impetus moment by moment." And, moment by moment, it is as if nothing had changed since the days when we would see him there, gazing pensively out at what he helped to establish and would not have abandoned without cause.

—from *The New Yorker,* April 13, 1987

Gelsey Kirkland: The Judy Garland of Ballet

Gelsey Kirkland, daughter of playwright Jack Kirkland (Tobacco Road), *studied at the School of American Ballet and, in 1968, at the age of fifteen, joined New York City Ballet. Her astounding technique was immediately recognized, and by 1972 she had been made a principal. (Edward Villella said that she had "steel-like legs that are doing the most fantastic technical feats while the upper body is soft and lovely as though nothing was going on underneath.") In 1974 she left City Ballet for American Ballet Theatre and a renowned partnership with Mikhail Baryshnikov. (Later, she was to dance Clara in his version of* The Nutcracker.) *Among the works created on her were Balanchine's revised* Firebird, *Robbins's* The Goldberg Variations, *and Tudor's* The Leaves Are Fading. *Unfortunately, she was emotionally unsteady, undergoing various plastic surgeries and suffering from anorexia and drug addiction. After a severe collapse, she returned to the stage, fragile but still a star, both at ABT and with London's Royal Ballet. Her autobiography,* Dancing on My Grave, *with its expressions of angry resentment at Balanchine, caused a scandal when it was published in 1986. In recent years she has been teaching and coaching, both in Australia and in America.*

HAD I NOT ALWAYS BEEN ASKED TO SELL MY BODY?

KIRKLAND

Gelsey Kirkland's best-selling autobiography, *Dancing on My Grave,* which she wrote with her husband, Greg Lawrence, churns up conflicting emotions in readers who saw her at her finest. To their dismay, they find exasperation and eventually scorn displacing the gratitude due a ballerina of her very special gifts. Few dancers that petite have so expanded the space around them in so dramatic, yet so lyrical, a manner. Surely we are still in her debt for the fleetness and clarity she bestowed upon us as the wunderkind of New York City Ballet, for the extra breadth her phrasing attained later, even after drugs and anorexia had made her appearances so unpredictable she had become the Judy Garland of American Ballet Theatre. The further one reads into *Grave,* however, the more uncertain one feels about how Kirkland would receive any expression of support at any time in her life. Still smoldering even today, she recalls one childhood ordeal after another when a

compliment annoyed her as much as a criticism. By the time she is twelve
and a fourth-year student at the School of American Ballet, she is so abristle
with hypersensitive antennae attuned to hostile vibes, real or imagined, that
not even Balanchine himself can approach as an admirer. Once, after she had
fallen during a demonstration of steps before SAB faculty and students, he
exclaimed: "You see, everybody, this girl is the only one who understood. I
ask for energy, and all you others were lazy, lazy, lazy. But Gelsey, she has
it—energy!" Little Gelsey's reaction is all too symptomatic: "I was astonished, uncertain whether or not he had just mocked me with his praise."

It soon becomes obvious that Kirkland is filled with something more than
the relentless self-criticism that young ballet students are rightly encouraged to practice in an art as demanding as it is narcissistic. Three pages later
she writes: "I gazed at my reflection with self-contempt." Twenty pages
further, still in her teens, she begins a self-imposed agony of plastic surgery
on her face and breasts so extensive it adds new meaning to the term "upper-
body work." By the time she is an international superstar (and thoroughly
miserable), she can perform such grands jetés of illogic as this conclusion
she leaps to after the management of the Vienna Staatsoper surprises her
with its traditional practice of paying artists their fees in cash in their dressing rooms just before a performance: "I understood at that moment the real
nature of my calling: I was a dancer and a member in good standing of the
oldest profession in the world." Still further, when she is assuring her book's
ascent on the charts by documenting her sensational addiction to drugs,
she writes of exchanging sex for coke: "Had I not always been asked to sell
my body?"

She displays, not surprisingly, a genuine gift for dramatics once she leaves
the neo-classicism of NYCB to perform the old classics and the contemporary works of Tudor, MacMillan, and Cranko abroad. These pages contain
virtually every instance of her having received any pleasure from dancing.
Unfortunately, the reader's relief at her happiness, as well as the delight
these interpretations gave, is tainted by learning how she approached her
roles. Her comments are as egocentric, and often as irrelevant, as what one
might hear at a rehearsal of *Hamlet* by lesser students at, say, Actors Studio.

"No explanation was offered as to the significance of the actions surrounding [Raymonda's] scarf," she complains. "Was I supposed to be fascinated that
this prop floated like an airy nothing? Was I supposed to be amused?"

"I instinctively rejected all the supernatural female creatures that inhabited
the nineteenth-century ballets: shades, sylphs, wilis, nymphs, swans. . . .
They had no power to move an audience unless I brought them down to earth
and made them human. They had to enter my reality."

"My conception of character [Odette/Odile] was contradicted by the
scenario [of *Swan Lake*]."

"I never allowed Giselle to become a wili. The stage directions never specified that she return to that world of evil, but to her own grave. . . ."

Occasionally, a genuine dramatic insight will remind us that Kirkland is, after all, a playwright's daughter. From what I've heard about Baryshnikov's choreography-by-committee, I can well believe that she created much of her role as Kitri in *Don Quixote*. More often, though, what she relates with such mystifying pride merely reminds us that her father, Jack, is best known for his adaptation of Erskine Caldwell's *Tobacco Road*. Her aperçu above about Giselle in Act II is particularly stupefying. Neither she nor any other ballerina has ever made Giselle a card-carrying member of Myrtha's rapacious pack: if Giselle were, there couldn't be an Act II. And the point about *her* Giselle's return to a grave at the dawn's first glimmering is meaningless. Where else do the dead reside during the day? Since nothing matters more in art than the result, and since nothing matters more in dancers than the quality of their movement, it may be unimportant whether what gripped us was Kirkland as Giselle or Giselle as Kirkland. It is significant, though, that Kirkland felt driven to remake her roles as fiercely as she was to remake her own body with plastic surgery, and that in both instances the longed-for difference obtained at such painful cost was usually unnoticed in the theater. What moved us was the way she moved.

Exasperation is balanced with sympathy once Kirkland turns inevitably to the specious comfort of drugs while a principal at ABT. She berates its management for doing little to help her fight addiction, but eventually one begins to sympathize with Baryshnikov and Chase. On the basis of her own testimony, Kirkland does not appear to be someone who would willingly respond to pleas, much less commands, to curb her self-destruction. Not until a couple of cocaine-induced brain seizures have set her to thrashing about like a hooked marlin does she consider what proves to be ineffective treatment. She soon resumes her harrowing crescendo of dependence: "By the time I returned to New York in April [1984], I was a speed freak, a Valium addict, a coke casualty, and a total wreck. Even my teeth were falling out."

Greg Lawrence enters her life at this low point. A writer and fellow victim of cocaine, he proves to be someone she can respect who also needs her—precisely the type of authority figure she seems to have been longing for all along. Propped against one another for mutual support, armed with recordings of classical music and the writings of Schiller, Plato, Shakespeare, and Helga Zepp LaRouche, they retire to a friend's house in upstate New York, then to their own place in Vermont, for a cold-turkey cure. She reports that writing this book, which she and Lawrence began in 1984, "has been the final therapeutic stage of my recovery." I do not intend to belittle their victory over drugs when I point out that, on the basis of this "therapeutic" book, Kirkland would seem to have more battles with herself to fight.

She is obviously still addicted to the bittersweet delights of avenging childhood wrongs, whether these occurred at age eight or twenty-five. Page after page is soaked with the kind of regurgitated grievance that a psychotherapist expects patients to bring up in the initial stages of treatment, but only occasional paragraphs give off the healthy scent of insight and acceptance, of the emotional maturity that should come with time. Whiffs of such understanding arise occasionally from passages about her undeniably difficult father. Virtually every comment about Balanchine emits an acrid reek. He too was someone she thought she could never please, so he became someone she had to defy as well as obey, someone to question as well as worship—someone whose slights she could avenge in this book because she had never been able to move *him* with her scorn in life.

The sole casualty of her kamikaze mission against Balanchine is Gelsey Kirkland. When she resorts to gossip and innuendo, she so diminishes herself that she suggests a peevish gnat buzzing about Balanchine's ankles, searching for his Achilles' heel. She is not indulging in Swiftian irony about a beloved's bowels when she writes of the jolt she felt upon learning Balanchine went to the toilet, like the rest of us: "I was utterly aghast. From that moment, he was transformed in my eyes, a god shaken from his hold on heaven."

There were, of course, unpleasant facets to the man's personality. He was not always a "nice person." Like Stravinsky, he could be petty about superstars who profited from his creations. But what do such gullies matter on the verdant terrain of his achievement? He was the greatest artist she ever met, yet this book so scants his choreography that those who buy it for the boudoir vignettes may well finish it convinced that Balanchine's chief contribution to dance was founding a horrid school where children's bodies are maimed for life. . . .

It would be difficult to find a more dismissive or inadequate account of Balanchine's and Kirstein's achievements than her capsule history of their decades-long battle against indifference, penury, hostility, and near despair: "After securing initial funding through the Warburg, Rockefeller, and Vanderbilt families, the Balanchine-Kirstein enterprise eventually consolidated control of American ballet with . . . millions of dollars of Ford Foundation grants. . . ." If an adverb can develop lower-back trouble from bearing excessive weight, "eventually" is patently doomed.

She is equally unenlightening about the working of Balanchine's mind: "To have a boyfriend jeopardized the possibility of dancing for Balanchine. Marriage was thought to be the kiss of death." Unlike Kirkland, who has only one witness (herself) to many of her encounters with Balanchine, I can produce two on this subject. Kyra Nichols and Daniel Duell informed me what happened when they approached him after they decided to get married.

They said they wanted to tell him something before he heard it from some-one else—but Balanchine stopped them. Leaping to the point, he said that everyone thinks he is against marriage, but what he objects to is that "woman marry bum" whom she must support while he spends all day "at O'Neal's" (a café near the State Theater). The defense now refers Ms. Kirkland to page fifty-nine of her memoir, where she describes her first big affair, a doomed grappling with a rock musician pseudonymously called "Jules": "His mar-riage broke up, and we lived together for two years, during which time I managed to support him and keep him out of Balanchine's sight." No doubt he and they visited O'Neal's at different times.

When she discusses artistic matters, we learn that Kirkland, like Disney-land, deals in fantasies: "Over the years, Mr. B derived a formula to fit what he saw as the essential speed of American life. This was his Evelyn Wood approach to classical dance." In *Far from Denmark,* an autobiography that errs on the side of reticence, Peter Martins perceptively states that mere speed was never the goal: "The word I'd give it is *energy.* Energy can be fast or slow, but what Balanchine is demanding is that all parts of the body be ener-gized. . . . In *adagio,* [he] asks for an energy that is slow, slow but intense and full." If further expert testimony is required, Kirkland can refer to the com-pliment Balanchine paid her at SAB when she fell down. (I'm presuming that it, like all the enlivening conversations she recalls years after they occurred, are accurate, of course.) As for her charge that he preferred dancers who were "zombies" or "automatons" to those with "personalities," I don't have the space to list the books, written by or about almost every major artist who ever worked with him, where that banality is contemptuously refuted.

To Balanchine, classical ballet was "a moral question." Ethics as well as aesthetics impelled classical choreographers and dancers to make difficult choices and meet rigorous demands when serving the composer. Only then would the spirit triumph over the body. *Dancing on My Grave* ultimately is so disheartening because it reveals Kirkland's brief triumph to have been far more physical than spiritual. Nothing could be more profoundly dispiriting than her book's dedication, which would have to be among the last passages she wrote: "In memory of Joseph Duell 1956–1986/that the cry for help might yet be heard." She must have plucked Duell's name off a headline in the New York *Post* as she returned her galley proofs to her editor. Duell appears nowhere else in the book. He and Kirkland were neither classmates at the school nor colleagues in, or out, of the company, yet she brazenly appropriates his personal agony because she presumes it suits her purposes: blaming ballet, and specifically Balanchine, for all her problems. Had she bothered to concern herself with fact rather than opportunistic fancy, she could have learned that Joseph Duell was not a man who cried out for help. Indeed, he did not need to during a youthful personal crisis years ago, when he was in the corps; unbidden, Balanchine offered advice and showed concern, and NYCB provided generous financial aid. In 1986, Duell wasn't confiding in anyone who cared about him. When I asked Nichols why no one had noticed how troubled he was, she replied that I must understand that Joe was an analytical, introspective guy always brooding about something. The company knew his mood was overcast, but they expected the sun to break through, as always. The demons of perfectionism that plagued him would have triumphed had he been a dancer or a CPA. Gelsey Kirkland would have had her problems had she been a milkmaid. That grave she dances upon was dug by herself.

—from *Ballet Review*, Winter 1987

ARNOLD L. HASKELL

Ulanova—A Tribute

One of the greatest of all twentieth-century ballerinas, Galina Ulanova (1910–1998) was the daughter of leading dancers at the Maryinsky and was automatically (and against her will) brought up in the family trade. Four months after graduating into the Kirov company, she was dancing her first Odette/Odile. A great favorite of Stalin's, she was transferred at his request from St. Petersburg to the Bolshoi, in Moscow. Among the many ballets created on her were the Leonid Lavrovsky Romeo and Juliet, The Fountain of Bakhchisarai, Cinderella, The Stone Flower, *and* The Red Poppy, *but she was also renowned for her interpretation of the classics, in particular* Giselle *but also* Les Sylphides, The Dying Swan, *and the double role in* Swan Lake. *She was forty-six when she made her debut in Great Britain and forty-nine when she first appeared in America, in both countries celebrated as the greatest of the great, her only rival being Fonteyn (who admired her immensely). Wherever she danced she was praised for the naturalism of her acting and the generosity of her personality. Offstage she looked like a drab middle-aged lady; on stage, she was the personification of youth—easily credible until the end of her career as Giselle or Juliet. After her retirement, at the age of fifty-two, she became a tireless and dedicated teacher and coach at the Bolshoi, having been awarded every honor the Soviet Union could bestow.*

I did not applaud Ulanova. The reaction to absolute beauty is definitely not a muscular effort. Indeed effort is its very antithesis. I resented the harsh, staccato noise that broke so crudely through the harmony that she had created. I realised that I had been waiting nearly forty years for such an experience, the confrontation with reality. I was deeply moved and infinitely grateful. This then is my belated tribute.

To see a dancer in the role of Giselle is to know everything she has to offer. Its challenge in technique and drama is tremendous, and it has increased in the century since its creation. What was then an emotion which an audience conditioned by Scott, Byron, Pushkin, de Musset, Heine, and Gautier could readily appreciate has now become something that, museum fashion, we label "romantic period." The music, such an innovation in its day, still has enormous charm but it does not move us of itself. Moreover, to the balletgoer of any experience the work has grown hackneyed. This fresh problem then of making a period-piece live and yet retain its style is added to the original difficulty of combining in one individual Sallé and Camargo, Taglioni and Elssler. It is obvious that comparatively few dancers in a generation are in any way equipped to dance it, though critics, realising the value to the dancer of making the attempt, have grown indulgent. That now will be at an end. Even among the finest contemporary Giselles there are the first act Giselles and the second act Giselles. Pavlova was up to now the only one I had seen who moved me equally in both acts. I did not, however, fully realize the possibility of yet another, more complete, Giselle where the character was a fully developed whole continuing the drama not merely contrasting the acts, though Chauviré in her interpretation had suggested this. Ulanova's Giselle is so complete and so magnificently simple that it is difficult to examine it in detail and impossible for anyone but a poet or philosopher to do it justice. When we first see her there is none of the customary foreboding that this poor girl is doomed. To me that was the flaw in Spessivtseva's moving performance. It is not merely a happy Giselle that we are shown but the abstract quality of happiness, not only Giselle in love but the essential spirit of love itself. Ulanova has risen above the banality of Gautier's charming story to reveal a universal truth. Gautier, essentially a materialist, would not have appreciated the point. How does a classical ballerina suggest that she is a naive peasant girl familiar with the cowshed and the chicken-run? If she is gauche and gawky, she betrays the dancer, if she is all dancing grace the character is lost. Ulanova's rendering of this is obvious to her audience but though it comes from minute gestures of the hands and from the eyes and mouth it defies analysis. The infinitely subtle revelation of Giselle's devotion to her mother, her deep love for Albrecht and her relationship to Hilarion, not the usual all-black villain but a jealous man from her own village, make a completely round character.

The second act is not merely the thistledown dancer, Taglioni as opposed to Elssler. It is, as the drama continues, another aspect of the same Giselle, spiritual as opposed to earthly love. The ballet is no longer the romantic episode of a betrayed girl; it becomes a tremendous love poem. To watch Ulanova at rehearsal is to see a series of old master drawings, brilliant sketches that are the raw material for the completed picture. There one can feel a powerful intellect at work while the performance itself is effortless and seemingly controlled by pure emotion; the master's pen and wash become glowing colour.

Ulanova's curtain call is a revealing study—very gradually, as that other world breaks in, one can see Ulanova taking the place of Giselle. The transition is awkward, the dancer naive, untheatrical and altogether moving. The off-stage Ulanova, therefore, does not come as a surprise in spite of the fact that she has been misunderstood in so many recent descriptions, innocently in this country, less so in France. She is not immediately forthcoming, partly to conserve the vast energy stored up for the performance, partly because she is extraordinarily shy and quite unaccustomed to the particular stresses and strains of western European theatrical life in which everything the artist does or does not do is of interest to the press. She takes neither her success nor her position for granted. She finds her reputation a very heavy burden. She was indeed so terrified of her appearance before a British audience that she would have given anything to have cried off and it took an immense effort of will for her to make the journey. Now she finds our audience as warm and understanding as that in Moscow and the atmosphere at Covent Garden completely homelike. As she put it, it was not she who had made a conquest but we who had enabled her to do her very best. No performance is mechanical, each one is built up for the occasion, "round a thought," as she said. She stressed the value of infrequent appearances so that dancing "did not become a trade." It is interesting to note that every performance of Giselle and Juliet was different in detail, though the sum total of the character was the same. When she relaxes outside the theatre or the formal occasion the first thing one notices are her wonderfully expressive eyes. They light up a face that has been strained and for the first time one realises how truly beautiful she is, with a beauty of expression that can never be seized by the camera. She has an immense sense of fun. Obviously she is a person of strong convictions but they are not expressed dogmatically. Like all good talkers she is an admirable listener genuinely interested in the other person's point of view. The main impression is one of extraordinary serenity. I would say that I had rarely met anyone more gentle though one can sense a will of iron. One of the things that amused her greatly was a report that she had asked for a match "with an imperious gesture." Nothing could be more out of character though the very shy often give an impression of abruptness.

I have no doubt that there will be people, as in the case of Pavlova, who will question Ulanova's technique. There are, especially in Russia, many far more spectacular dancers. Pavlova had the perfect technique in that it enabled her to express all that the role demanded. Any other interpretation of the word *technique* is complete nonsense. Ulanova's technique is flawless and unobtrusive. I had a wonderful proof of this in some extracts from an amateur film in which, out of context and without music, I was able to study her movement. It was, considered as abstract design, completely satisfying. Only then did technique become relevant.

Whether there is a direct lesson to be learnt from Ulanova I do not know. Such artists of genius who reveal new possibilities in the art they practise as distinct from great attainments are born at rare intervals. (Judging by what I have read the nearest approach to Ulanova seems to have been Sallé, a dancer centuries ahead of her period.) One may talk of hard work, as she does, but all dancers are hard workers, of technique, but that becomes irrelevant. It is a question, as she says, of knowing when to take liberties with technique in order to carry out one's individual conception of a role. That too does not explain genius. The word *humility* is more revealing. It is an attitude to life and to art that is quite distinct from modesty. It implies the purposeful surrender of a powerful personality that enables us to see Juliet and Giselle in the place of Ulanova. It was the quality that Duse brought to the stage. It comes from the surrender known to mystics in art and religion. "Aesthetic experience is the twin brother of mystic experience." The Indian writer on aesthetics, the late Ananda Coomaraswamy, in his fine collection of essays *The Dance of Shiva,* has many illuminating things to say on this subject. He talks of "a state of grace that cannot be achieved by deliberate effort." By this he does not, of course, mean that no effort is required in attaining craftsmanship. In other words the artist aims at perfection of craftsmanship but the resultant work of art is independent of the will.

A Jesuit told me that Ulanova gave him an impression of holiness. I think this would please her, irrespective of her views on orthodox religion, as it is very much her aim, as she told me, to leave people with an increased spiritual awareness.

It has been significant to note Ulanova's universal appeal; to the ordinary man in the street, if such a being exists, and to the trained aesthete as well as to the more exuberant *balletomane.* She rose to fame not through the ballet *habitué* as in the old Imperial days but through the large, changing proletarian audience of the present-day Moscow Theatre. "Those devoid of imagination in the theatre," says an Indian writer, "are as the woodwork, the walls

and the stones." They have been almost non-existent in front of this universal quality, this extreme simplification, this essential truth.

I can best end this tribute with a quotation from Clive Bell's *Art*—also
quoted by Coomaraswamy; nothing could be more to the point. "In those
moments of exaltation that art can give, it is easy to believe that we have
been possessed by an emotion that comes from the world of reality. Those
who take this view will have to say that there is in all things the stuff out of
which art is made—reality. The peculiarity of the artist would seem to be
that he possesses the power of surely and frequently seizing reality (generally behind pure form), and the power of expressing his sense of it, in pure
form always."

—from *Days with Ulanova,* by Albert Kahn, 1962

LINCOLN KIRSTEIN
Ballet in a Bad Time

THE GOLDEN AGE: 1909–1914

GODS AND HEROES

The success of the Russian ballet in Western Europe is a phenomenon so
familiar by virtue of the memoirs of Mme. Nijinsky, Svetlov, Prince Lieven,
Arnold Haskell, Gabriel Astruc, Jean Cocteau, and Calvocaressi, that there
is no need to push through it again. In 1909, only thirty years ago, Paris and
London had heard very little Russian music. Post-impressionism in painting
was still an unearned investment of the picture dealers, and dancing as represented by the ballet at the Paris Opéra, had all the bourgeois security of an
official finishing school for naughty girls. Three-quarters of the first great
success of the Russian ballet lay not in any of its inherent perfection of
music, decoration, choreography, or dancing, nor in any new social or moral
ideas, but rather in the *contrast* to everything accepted by Western Europe as
theatrical dancing at that time, and for the last forty years. As long back as
1892 Henry Adams had written "his heart sank to mere pulp before the dismal ballets at the Grand Opéra."

No one, of course, would recklessly attempt to underestimate the large
personal contributions of Stravinsky, Bakst, Benois, Fokine, or Nijinsky. But

let us at least grant them their historic due by considering them in their real place in their own time. There is no need to wrench them out of their realistic position and make them do double duty for all time and every place.

Petrouchka for example; let us take *Petrouchka*. Stravinsky's delectable orchestral score remains intact for concert at least, and the story in essence at least, is still useful. Benois' successive remountings of his original scenery seem thin, patchy, and creased today. As for Fokine's choreography: in the original production, he had Bolm, Karsavina, Nijinsky in the chief roles. The fragments of character dancing, the vignettes of coachmen and the moujiks were then brilliantly executed by top-rank character artists from the School of Moscow. Even the smaller parts, some scarcely more than walk-ons, such as the gypsy, the organ-grinder, or the drunken Barin, were taken by first-rate performers like Theodor Koslov, Bronislava Nijinska, and Ludmila Shollar. The holiday crowds in movement were organized, a sizeable crowd and not a stray handful of accidental supers picked up an hour before curtain time.

Now we have none of this former glory. To be sure, the best dancers available take the leading parts. But do they convince us as Blackamoor, as Ballerina, or as Doll? Do we see them as archetypes of tragedy we have been led by all the writers to look for? Are our hearts broken when Petrouchka's pitiful fluttering mittens crash through his paper house? We do not and they are not, at least if we're honest. We view with rapidly diminishing interest a vehicle once propelled by renowned artists. We see famous costumes nearly identical to those carried by Bolm, Karsavina, Nijinsky, covering dancers approximating the original gestures once electrified by Bolm, Karsavina, and Nijinsky. But now, it is all a ghostly double exposure, a spectral blackmail that the Golden Age of Russian ballet still exerts on our inert eyes.

The repertory of the Golden Age of Diaghilev still whipped like a staggering cart horse over the ballet trails of the world today, includes also besides *Petrouchka,* the dances from *Prince Igor, Les Sylphides, Carnaval, Papillons, L'Oiseau de Feu, L'Après-midi d'un Faune, Le Coq d'Or, Thamar,* and *Schéhérazade.* Of all of these, *Cléopâtre* alone, with its preposterous hobble-skirts and belly mirrors of the vogue of 1909, was howled off a Newark stage in 1937. The rest smugly remain. The indiscriminate, pot-flung color of Bakst, the caramel orchestration of Rimsky-Korsakov, Glazounov, or Tcherepnin, the old dancers' galvanic, drugging physicality has been something for our fathers and mothers to tell us about, like Dewey's triumph after Manila Bay, or their first automobile ride. Wonderful for them, but not for us. For us, if we leave off the rose-tinted spectacles obligingly provided by the Great Conspiracy of commercial manager, dance and music critic, and ballet patron, we will see only a dismal carnival in a theatrical storage warehouse. The fatigued world-worn troupes stamp out the mechanical tunes to which our ears have

long since refused to listen consciously. Yet these relics of the Golden Age of
Diaghilev are the very backbone, the chief mainstay of Russian ballet today.
When we see them again let us recognize them for what they are. We may harbor for them among other nostalgic souvenirs of our remote youth, an
affectionate warmth. But to think that there is anything here to instruct, nourish, or enlighten us for what we ourselves as adults will want to do or see, is
like going to be taught or advised by a darling old nurse, or a favorite scout-
master.

The silver age: 1917–1929

Experiment and "Modern Art"

This is the chapter of the Russian Ballet that isn't Russian, and it is the most
interesting chapter. That is, we assume *Petrouchka, Le Coq d'Or, Thamar,
L'Oiseau de Feu,* and *Prince Igor* are White Russian-Russian; *Schéhérazade* is
Russo-Persian; *Carnaval* and *Papillons* are Russo-Biedermeier, and *Les Sylphides* is Russo-ballet. For Russian, read Russian tearoom, with the tea in
individual tea bags and not a samovar in sight. The difference between
Diaghilev's *Ballets Russes* and Baliev's *Chauve Souris* was negligible at many
points of contact. The tearoom Russian soon enough tired even the Russians
themselves, and Diaghilev commenced an age of experiment which though
by far the most valuable contribution of his career both in paint, music, theatre, and poetry, is almost unrepresented in the present repertory of the
Russian Ballet companies. Many of these works, to be sure, might not
weather revival and, as we have recently seen, revivals are increasingly
exhumations. But as long as revivals pay on principle, let them revive this
period as well.

    With the departure of Fokine and Nijinsky passed Diaghilev's Golden
Age, and the youthful Massine was permitted direct contact with the international collaborators of the School of Paris. "Permitted contact" is correct,
because at that time there was no thought of a dictatorship by the choreographer, even by those as distinguished as Fokine or Massine. Diaghilev was
the only dictator of dance, decoration, or music. Massine and Nijinska
worked with Erik Satie, Matisse, Stravinsky, Juan Gris, Picasso, Prokoviev,
and Derain. Revolutionary cubism hit the ballet with its ton of bricks and
horrified the old-guard ballet-ballet lovers, which was Diaghilev's earnest
intention. Social-satire, American jazz, the everyday continental vacation,
and boulevard life of the 1920s; dada, neo-classicism, the falsely naive, the
falsely archaic, and decorative folklore no longer of Russia, but now of

England, Italy, France, or Spain were all exposed to the caprice of Diaghilev's ingenious combinations.

Why, with the exception of pieces deliberately old-fashioned at their very birth, such as *Le Chapeau Tricorne, La Boutique Fantasque, Cimarosiana,* or *The Good Humored Ladies,* is this experimental period unrepresented by the self-styled heirs of Diaghilev? Were the works of the Silver Age less amusing than those of the Golden Age? By no manner or means, and quite to the contrary. Nijinska's *Les Noçes* and *Les Biches,* Massine's *Parade, Mercure,* or *Ode,* Balanchine's *Le Bal, Barabau,* or *Le Fils Prodigue* would be a great deal more fun to see today than the rabble-scrabble and bobtail we're stuffed with instead. Only these ballets do not *represent* the *Russian* ballet of the "original" period. *Les Noçes,* it is true, was admirably revived in London and New York two years ago, but its starkness and the fact that it demanded a largish chorus were seized by the direction as an excuse to end its appearance once and for all. *Les Noçes* and these others are not considered sufficiently antique. They might destroy the picture carefully constructed by idolatrous historian, wise ballet manager, and lazy patron for the public's consumption. Remember the manager thinks the public is a stupid beast. *Russian* ballet, Russian *ballet, Russian Ballet*—repeat it ten times before each performance. What? A house party, a steel factory, a movie lot in *Russian* ballet? What would Petrouchka think, what Schéhérazade, what the Sylphs? The more sprightly inventions of Diaghilev's Silver Age, even lacking a large part of the original Imperial-schooled dancers, Bakst's decor, and the political prestige, were the real contribution of Diaghilev to contemporary theatrical art. These represented the institution of ballet faced with the world we lived in. Maybe some of the ballets were half-solutions, part failures, mere *succès d'estime* or scandal. They were, and still would be, however, neither as preposterous, muddy, or dull as the others which still stick like cinders in our eyes.

Don't think for a second all the Russian dancing artists themselves prefer the older repertory. Don't think their old-world hearts beat in dedicated sympathy to the tunes that pop concert, radio, and school band have worn bone-clean. Very often Zobeide's slave appears to be dying his death of ennui, a far deadlier sword than Shah Schariar's, and his ennui, dear manager, critic, and dear patron, is transmitted in its unadulterated wallop to us, blind as we are—the patient, hopeful watchers in the darkened house. Lord Chesterfield once remarked of two people dancing a minuet: "They looked as if they were hired to do it, and were doubtful of being paid."

—from *Blast at Ballet,* 1937

The Audience

The Vic-Wells Ballet has never been very well served by the critics, either amateur or professional. Over-praised in some quarters merely because it is British, it has been underestimated in others simply because it isn't Russian. And its audience—let's face it—hasn't on the whole been much help.

The reason perhaps lies in the fact that originally this audience was largely recruited from the ready-made audience who had been faithfully attending the Vic. and the Wells for the Shakespeare and Opera seasons for years. They knew little or nothing about ballet, but if Miss Baylis was going to sponsor it, then of course they must turn up and support it.

Now, as everyone knows, the applause at the Vic. always put that at an ordinary West End theatre to shame. It was a tribute we gladly paid, not only for the performance, but for the enjoyment we felt merely at being inside that delightful theatre. We applauded because we felt that the Vic. was another home, because we could there see plays we loved and which we rarely had a chance of seeing elsewhere. We applauded the loving care and efforts made by everyone there to see that the best possible was given us with the means at the management's command. This feeling was promptly transferred to the efforts of the ballet company, long before results really warranted it, and grew proportionately as the company improved.

Therefore today, when in many respects the Vic-Wells Ballet can stand comparison with any other company in the world, the applause has reached a pitch which is dangerously near hysteria and causes feelings of intense disgust amongst the serious ballet-goers, who, quite rightly, applaud strictly on merit but who, at the same time, are unconsciously prejudiced before-hand by the idolatrous atmosphere in front of the house.

This question of applause is in any case a tricky one, because every audience consists of people who are in various stages of balletomania, and this applies equally to the audiences at Russian ballet. I myself should be inclined to say that there are four stages of balletomania.

The initial stage is a state of awestricken delight, when we thrill at everything we see and think it is all too marvellous but are much too humble to let ourselves rip. We sit in numb delight, and envy those (we think) knowledgeable creatures who throw their weight about in the intervals and lead the cheering. The next stage comes when we ourselves have consolidated our positions as regulars and have a season or two behind us. Then it is our turn to make our presence felt, which we do in the most inordinate fashion, to our own intense satisfaction and, no doubt, the contemptuous amusement of the Old Guard. After a time we develop into the Old Guard ourselves, and then the *hoi polloi* who are just beginning to find *their* feet and their lungs, are objects of our deep derision and dislike. This is a stage when nothing is good enough for us. We don't know *what* the ballet is coming to, but really it was nothing like this in our young days; and where do all these frightful persons come from! The last stage is finally reached. We have acquired tolerance. We no longer expect every member of the *corps de ballet* to dance like Karsavina or Nijinsky; we don't utter loud moans at any of the mistakes or slips which inevitably occur from time to time; we don't even mind much if a lot of silly people are making themselves ridiculous shouting for a favourite who, in our opinion, has just given a not very noteworthy performance. In short, we are content to take ballet as it comes; we know that no one on earth can dance as well as the ideal which we carry in our heads, and we are thankful for the enjoyment we get without expecting perfection all the time.

Some balletomanes never get beyond the third stage, and a number of them who are safely in the fourth where the Russians are concerned, slip back a grade when they visit the Wells Ballet. They have adopted the Marxian (Groucho) ruling, "Whatever it is, I'm against it," and apply it to everything the Wells Ballet does. One feels that they would be highly indignant if they ever had to admit that they had enjoyed themselves. But they still come—oh yes, they turn up regularly, and undoubtedly get a great deal of gratification out of hating everything with such impartiality.

Unfortunately most balletomanes today seem to be in the second stage, and the indiscriminate applause from so large a section of the audience is a distressing feature of modern ballet-going, a situation which has grown more acute with the sensational war-time boom in ballet. No Russian company has been seen in London since 1939, and in the intervening period balletomanes in their hundreds have sprung up who have never had a chance of seeing anything but the English product. It is not their fault that they can have no standards of comparison, but their enthusiasm can have little value when it is applied to anything and everything. It is dangerous for the dancers to know that they will be greeted with identically the same ovation whatever their performance may have been like.

So far there is no sign of complacency in the Wells Company. Miss de Valois has obviously practised on them with good effect what she preached in her book, *Invitation to the Ballet,* about the meaninglessness of such applause. Yet one shudders to think what may be the reaction when this new audience is let loose for the first time amongst ballet on the grand scale as we have known it in the past.

Balletomanes have never before stood in such need of education. When the Diaghilev Ballet first burst upon the Western World the audience it attracted knew nothing of ballet as he showed it to them, but it was a far smaller one and, generally speaking, consisted of the intelligentsia of the day, with high artistic standards which they applied to this new art. Today ballet has reached a peak of popularity which would compare with that of the cinema were it not that ballet is still necessarily confined to the larger towns. It is therefore being seen by thousands of people who know nothing of any of the arts. Naturally they find it lovely and romantic, an escape from the drabness and strain of life as it has to be lived now.

Unless they can be taught to develop a critical appreciation of all that goes to make ballet, unless they can learn to recognise true artistry as opposed to surface tricks, then English ballet may find itself back in the dark ages of the old Empire days.

That will be a poor reward for the efforts of a sincere band of artists who have struggled so long and so faithfully, in the face of much indifference, hostility, and contempt, to establish a standard for English ballet far beyond anything that was ever even dreamed of ten years ago.

—from *Vic-Wells:A Ballet Progress,* 1942

SUSAN SONTAG

Dancer and the Dance

Lincoln Kirstein, the finest historian of dance and one of its master ideologues, has observed that in the nineteenth century what the prestige of ballet really amounted to was the reputation of the dancer; and that even when there were great choreographers (notably Petipa) and great dance scores (from Adam, Delibes, and Tchaikovsky), dance was still almost entirely identified for the large theatrical public with the personality and virtuosity of great dancers. That triumphant mutation in dance taste and in the composition of dance audiences which occurred just before World War I, in response to the authoritative intensity and exoticism of the Ballets Russes, did not challenge the old imbalance of attention—not even with the subsequent invention by Diaghilev of dance as an ambitious collaboration, in which major innovative artists outside the dance world were brought in to enhance this theatre of astonishment. The score might be by Stravinsky, the decor by Picasso, the costumes by Chanel, the libretto by Cocteau. But the blow of the sublime was delivered by a Nijinsky or a Karsavina—by the dancer. According to Kirstein, it was only with the advent of a choreographer so complete in his gifts as to change dance forever, George Balanchine, that the primacy of the choreographer over the performer, of dance over the dancer, was finally understood.

Kirstein's account of the more limited perspectives of dance publics before Balanchine is, of course, not incorrect. But I would point out that the exaltation of the performer over all else pervaded not only dance in the nineteenth (and early twentieth) century but all the arts that need to be performed. Recalling the effusive identification of dance with the dancer— say, with Marie Taglioni and with Fanny Elssler—one should recall as well other audiences, other raptures. The concert audiences ravished by Liszt and Paganini were also identifying music with the virtuoso performer: the music was, as it were, the occasion. Those who swooned over La Malibran in the new Rossini or Donizetti thought of opera as the vehicle of the singer. (As for the look of opera, whether it was the staging, the decor, or the often incongruous physique of the singer—this hardly seemed worthy of discussion.) And the focus of attention has been modified in these arts, too. Even the most diva-besotted portion of the opera public of recent decades is prepared to segregate the work from the performance and, within the performance, vocal prowess and expressiveness from acting—distinctions fused by the inflatedly partisan rhetoric of extreme reactions (either ecstasy or the rudest condemnation) that surrounded opera performance in the nineteenth century, particularly early performances of a new work. That the work is now routinely seen as transcending the performer, rather than the performer transcending the work, has come to be felt not just in dance, because of the advent of a supremely great choreographer, but in all the performing arts.

And yet, this being said, there seems to be something intrinsic to dance that warrants the kind of reverential attention paid in each generation to a very few dancers—something about what they do that is different from the achievements of surpassingly gifted, magnetic performers in other arts to whom we pay homage.

Dance cannot exist without dance design: choreography. But dance *is* the dancer.

The relation of dancer to choreographer is not just that of executant to *auteur*—which, however creative, however inspired the performer, is still a subservient relation. Though a performer in this sense, too, the dancer is also more. There is a mystery of incarnation in dance that has no analogue in the other performing arts.

A great dancer is not just performing (a role) but being (a dancer). Someone can be the greatest Odette/Odile, the greatest Albrecht one has ever seen—as a singer can be the best (in anyone's memory) Tosca or Boris or Carmen or Sieglinde or Don Giovanni, or an actor can be the finest Nora or Hamlet or Faust or Phaedra or Winnie. But beyond the already grandiose aim of giving the definitive performance of a work, a role, a score, there is a further, even higher standard which applies to dancers. One can be not just the best performer of certain roles but the most complete exhibit of what it is to be a dancer. Example: Mikhail Baryshnikov.

In any performing art which is largely repertory, interest naturally flows to the contribution of the executant. The work already exists. What is new, each time, is what this performer, these performers, bring to it in the way of new energies, changes in emphasis, or interpretation. How they make it different, or better. Or worse. The relation of work to performer is a musical-structural one: theme and variations. A given play or opera or sonata or ballet is the theme: all readings of it will be, to some extent, variations.

But here as well, although the dancer does what all executants of a work do, dance differs from the other performing arts. For the standard against which dancers measure their performances is not simply that of the highest excellence—as with actors and singers and musicians. The standard is perfection.

In my experience, no species of performing artist is as self-critical as a dancer. I have gone backstage many times to congratulate a friend or acquaintance who is an actor or a pianist or a singer on his or her superlative performance; invariably my praise is received without much demurral, with evident pleasure (my purpose, of course, *is* to give pleasure), and sometimes with relief. But each time I've congratulated a friend or acquaintance who is a dancer on a superb performance—and I include Baryshnikov—I've heard first a disconsolate litany of mistakes that were made: a beat was missed, a foot not pointed in the right way, there was a near slippage in some intricate partnering maneuver. Never mind that perhaps not only I but everyone else failed to observe these mistakes. They were made. The dancer knew. Therefore the performance was not *really* good. Not good enough.

In no other art can one find a comparable gap between what the world thinks of a star and what the star thinks about himself or herself, between the adulation that pours in from outside and the relentless dissatisfaction that goads one from within. The degree and severity of dancers' self-criticism is not simply a case of performers' raw nerves (virtually all great performing artists are worriers, skilled at self-criticism), of artistic conscience—a *défor-*

mation professionnelle. It is, rather, integral to the dancer's *formation profession-nelle.* Part of being a dancer is this cruelly self-punishing objectivity about one's shortcomings, as viewed from the perspective of an ideal observer, one more exacting than any real spectator could ever be: the god Dance.

Every serious dancer is driven by notions of perfection—perfect expressiveness, perfect technique. What this means in practice is not that anyone is perfect but that performance standards are always being raised.

The notion of progress in the arts has few defenders now. If Balanchine was the greatest choreographer who ever lived (an unverifiable proposition firmly held by many balletomanes, myself among them), it is surely not because he came after Noverre and Petipa and Fokine, because he was the last (or the most recent) of the breed. But there does seem to be something like linear progress in dance performance—unlike the other performing arts largely devoted to repertory, such as opera. (Was Callas greater than Rosa Ponselle or Claudia Muzio? The question does not make sense.) There is no doubt that the general level of dancing in unison in companies like the Kirov and the New York City Ballet (which have probably the two best *corps de ballet* in the world) and the prowess and power and expressiveness of the leading dancers in today's great ballet companies (the two just mentioned, the Paris Opéra Ballet, the Royal Ballet, and the American Ballet Theatre—among others) are far higher than the level of the most admired dancing of the past. All dance writers agree that, a few immortal soloists apart, the dancing in Diaghilev's Ballets Russes was technically quite limited by today's standards.

Raising the level is the function of the champion: a considerable number of people found they could run the four-minute mile once Roger Bannister had done it. As in sport or athletics, the achievement by a virtuoso dancer raises the achievable standard for everybody else. And this is what Baryshnikov, more than any other dancer of our time, has done—not only by what he can do with his body (he has, among other feats, jumped higher than anyone else, and has landed lower), but by what he can show, in the maturity and range of his expressiveness.

Dance demands a degree of service greater than any other performing art, or sport. While the daily life of every dancer is a full-time struggle against fatigue, strain, natural physical limitations and those due to injuries (which are inevitable), dance itself is the enactment of an energy which must seem, in all respects, untrammeled, effortless, at every moment fully mastered. The dancer's performance smile is not so much a smile as a categorical denial of what he or she is actually experiencing—for there is some discomfort, and often pain, in every major stint of performing. This is an important difference between the dancer and the athlete, who have much in common (ordeal, contest, brevity of career). In sport, the signs of effort are not concealed: on the contrary, making effort visible is part of the display. The public expects to see, and is moved by, the spectacle of the athlete visibly pushing himself or herself beyond the limits of endurance. The films of championship tennis matches or of the Tour de France or any comprehensive documentary about athletic competition (a splendid example: Ichikawa's *Tokyo Olympiad*) always reveal the athlete's strain and stress. (Indeed, the extent to which Leni Riefenstahl, in her film on the 1936 Olympic Games, chose *not* to show the athletes in this light is one of the signs that her film is really about politics—the aestheticizing of politics in totally ordered mass spectacle and in imperturbable solo performance— and not about sport as such.) That is why news of an athlete's injuries is a matter of general knowledge and legitimate curiosity on the part of the public, while news of dancers' injuries is not, and tends to be suppressed.

It is often said that dance is the creation of illusion: for example, the illusion of a weightless body. (This might be thought of as the furthest extension of the phantasm of a body without fatigue.) But it would be more accurate to call it the staging of a transfiguration. Dance enacts both being completely in the body and transcending the body. It seems to be a higher order of attention, where physical and mental attention become the same.

Dancers of unrivaled talents like Baryshnikov (among woman dancers, Suzanne Farrell comes first to mind) project a state of total focus, total concentration, which is not simply—as for an actor or a singer or a musician—the necessary prerequisite of producing a great performance. It *is* the performance, the very center of it.

Merce Cunningham and Lincoln Kirstein have both offered as a definition of dance: a spiritual activity in physical form. No art lends itself so aptly as dance does to metaphors borrowed from the spiritual life. (Grace, elevation . . .) Which means, too, that all discussions of the dance, and of great dancers, including this one, fit dance into some larger rhetoric about human possibility.

One practice is to pair off the greatest dancers as representing two ideal alternatives. The most astute dance writer of the nineteenth century, Théophile Gautier, so contrasted the reigning dancers of his era, Elssler and Taglioni. Elssler was pagan, earthy; Taglioni was spiritual, transcendent. And critics a decade ago, when absorbing the arrival of a second male Kirov refugee of genius in our midst, tended to compare Nureyev and Baryshnikov in the same way. Nureyev was Dionysian, Baryshnikov was Apollonian. Such symmetries are inevitably misleading, and this particular one does an injustice to Nureyev, who was a supremely gifted and expressive dancer and in the early years an ideal partner (with Fonteyn), as well as to Baryshnikov. For although Baryshnikov has perhaps never in his career been an ideal partner, it has to be said—without any disrespect to the grandeur of Nureyev's dancing and to his heroic tenacities—that the younger dancer proved to be a genius of another magnitude.

Of a magnitude without parallel. Guided by his generosity, his intellectual curiosity, and his unprecedented malleability as a dancer, Baryshnikov has given himself to more different kinds of dancing than any other great dancer in history. He has danced Russian ballet, Bournonville, the British recensions (Ashton, Tudor, MacMillan), Balanchine, Roland Petit, and a range of Americana from jazz dancing (a duo with Judith Jamison, choreographed by Alvin Ailey) to Robbins, Tharp, and Karole Armitage. He may, on occasion, have been abused or misused by his choreographers. But even when the role is not right, he is always more than the role. He is, almost literally, a transcendent dancer. Which is what dance strives to make actual.

—from French *Vogue*, December 1986

KONSTANTIN STANISLAVSKY
At the Ballet

Stanislavsky (1863–1938) came from a rich family—his father at one point was head of Moscow's merchant class. Konstantin wanted to act, and took "Stanislavsky" as a pseudonym to spare his family embarrassment. In 1897 he co-founded the Moscow Art Theatre, where he developed his new ideas about realism in acting and staging, in particular through his devotion to the plays of Anton Chekhov. Stanislavsky's theories of psychological truth in acting spread through Europe and America, leading eventually to the establishment here of both the Group Theater and the Actors Studio.

Things were going pretty badly in the Alexeyev Circle. My sisters and one of my brothers got married, became parents, burdened themselves with new cares and worries and found no time for acting. There was no possibility of staging a new production, and for quite some time I was inactive. But fate was kind and would not allow me to idle my time away. Pending some new presentation, it pushed me into the realm of Terpsichore. That art is indispensable for the dramatic actor. I had no special intentions when I started attending ballets. In this period of "interregnum" I could not decide definitely on anything, and so I went to the ballet to see how my friends, inveterate balletomanes, were "making fools of themselves." I went to laugh—and got stuck myself.

Balletomanes regarded going to the theatre as a sort of a duty. They did not miss a single performance, but they invariably arrived late in order to walk ceremoniously down the centre aisle to their seats to the accompaniment of ballet music. It was quite another thing if *she,* the object of the balletomane's affections, was on the stage from the very beginning. Then he would take his seat during the overture. God forbid that he be late, she might be hurt! And when *she* was through with her number and was not followed by a recognized ballerina, the balletomane considered it beyond his dignity of a connoisseur to waste his time on nonentities. While the latter danced, he would go to the smoking-room (especially opened for such people as he) and remain there until the usher (especially employed for this purpose) informed him that *she* was about to start her dance. It did not matter that the object of the balletomane's affections was not a talented dancer. It was his duty to watch *her,* his eyes glued to the opera glasses, when she danced and especially when she didn't. That is when they start "telegraphing" to each other.

To illustrate:

She was standing on the side while another girl was dancing. Looking across the footlights, at the seat where her admirer was, she smiled. That meant everything was all right, that she was not angry. If she had not smiled, but looked thoughtfully, sorrowfully over his head and then left with her eyes lowered, that would have meant that she was hurt, that she did not want to see him. Then everything would be wrong. The poor balletomane's heart would throb, his head would whirl. He would rush to his friend, feeling publicly insulted, and start whispering.

"Have you seen that?"

"I have," his friend would answer sadly.

"What does it mean?"

"I don't know. Were you in the alley yesterday?"

"I was."

"Did she smile? Did she blow you a kiss?"

"She did."

"Then I just don't understand."

"What should I do? Send her flowers?"

"You're crazy. Imagine sending flowers to a ballet school pupil. . . ."

"But then what?"

"Let me think. Wait! Mine is looking at me. . . . Bravo, bravo! Why don't you applaud?"

"Bravo, bravo, encore!"

"No, there won't be any encores. Listen, here's what we shall do. You buy flowers, I'll write a note and send it with the flowers to my girl and she'll pass them on and explain everything."

"That's perfect! You're a real friend, always helping me out. I'll do it right away."

In the next act *she* appears with a flower in her corsage, looks at the guilty balletomane and smiles. And he jumps up and rushes to his friend.

"She's smiled, she's smiled! Thank God! But why was she angry, I wonder."

"Come over after the show and my girl will tell you."

After the show the balletomane must take the object of his affections home. Those who are in love with the dancers of the ballet school wait for them at the stage door. And here is what happens. A stagecoach comes up for the girls. The young man opens the front door, i.e., the one nearer to the stage entrance. *She* jumps in and goes to the opposite side, i.e., to the back door, and bars it with her body. Then she lets the window down, *he* comes up and kisses her hand or slips a note or says something short but very important that will make her think all through the night. In the meantime, the other ballet school girls enter the coach by the front door.

But there were daring balletomanes who would kidnap the girl, put her into a waiting carriage, and order the coach to take them at breakneck speed through some streets. By the time the stagecoach arrived at the ballet school, the fugitives would be there. *He* would help the lady of his heart into the back door of the coach while the other girls were leaving by the front door, concealing the whole escapade from the chaperone. But that was a difficult thing and required from the balletomane to bribe the coachman and the doorman.

Having taken his lady love home, the balletomane would go to his friend's, or rather to his sweetheart's. And here he would get his explanation—and a very simple one. Why had *she* been displeased? On the previous day he and other balletomanes were in the alley adjoining the ballet school at the appointed hour and the girls were blowing them kisses and signalling to them. Just at that moment the instructress on duty appeared in the window below and the young men scattered away. The others returned a little later, but he did not and her friends laughed at her. That was why she had been displeased.

Unmarried dancers lived in furnished rooms and led a life that was very such akin to that of students in their attics. There were always many people, some would come with their own food, others would run and buy something, admirers would come with candy—and all that would be shared. It would be an impromptu supper or tea at a samovar. The gathering would criticize actresses and the theatre management, relate backstage incidents or—they always did that—discuss the latest shows. I loved such impromptu parties, for they gave me an opportunity to learn the secrets of ballet art. For one who does not intend to study a subject seriously, but just wants to get a general understanding of it because he may have to study it more thoroughly later on, it is useful and interesting to attend such discussions at which specialists analyze something they have just seen, heard, or personally experienced. These discussions and the arguments adduced did a great deal to acquaint me with the secrets of ballet technique. When a ballerina could not prove something by speech, she tried to do so with her legs, i.e., she danced. On more than one occasion I played the role of some dancer's partner and helped her to demonstrate her argument. Being clumsy, I sometimes dropped my partner and saw where I had erred in some technical method or trick. Add to that the eternal arguments that went on among the balletomanes in the smoking room, where I too was a habitué and where I met clever and well-read aesthetes—who discussed dances and plastique not from the angle of outer technique, but from that of how they impressed them artistically and creatively, and you will see that perhaps I had adequate grounds for considering myself amply equipped for research in this sphere. I repeat that I assimilated all this without having any aim in view, for I attended ballets not because I wanted to study them, but because I liked the mysterious, picturesque, and poetic life of the theatre.

Have you ever stopped to think how beautiful and quaint is the background on the stage, illuminated by blue, red, violet, and other lights? With a dreamy river "flowing" in the distance? A vast darkness rising endlessly, it seems, towards the roof; a mysterious depth in the trapdoor. Picturesque groups of actors and actresses, in costumes of different cut and colour, waiting to go on to the stage. And during the interval—bright lights, hustle and bustle, chaos, work. Canvases depicting mountains, rocks, rivers, seas, cloudless sky, stormy clouds, beautiful foliage, and the Inferno go up and come down. Stage hands push the walls of pavilions, colonnades, arches and other architectural parts, tired, perspiring, their faces grimy, and next to them an ethereal ballerina doing the last movements before going into her dance on the stage. Musicians in their tailcoats, ushers in their uniforms, slick officers, and well-dressed young balletomanes. The noise, the hum of human voices, the tension—a regular babel that fades away as the curtain goes up to give way to an orderly, harmonious picture. If there are any wonders on earth, they are on the stage!

How, in the circumstances, can one help falling in love? And I was in love too and for a full six months I ogled one of the girls from the ballet school who, they told me, was madly in love with me, and I too thought that she smiled at me and signalled to me. I was introduced to her when the girls were going home for Christmas holidays. But, to my horror, it turned out that for half a year I had been looking at one girl and talking about another. But this other was nice too and I immediately fell in love with her. Everything was childishly naive, mysterious, poetic and, what is more important, clean and pure. It is wrong to think that immorality reigns supreme in ballet. I didn't see any, and I always think with pleasure of the good times it afforded me, of my infatuations and loves. Ballet is a beautiful art, but . . . not for us dramatic actors. We need something else. Different plastique, different grace, different rhythm, gesture, gait, and movements. Different everything! But we can certainly emulate ballet workers' industriousness and ability to train their body.

—from *My Life in Art*, 1925

JAMES WARING

Three Essays on Dancing

1. ALEXANDRA DANILOVA AND OTHER UNSELFISH DANCERS

One of my first stage appearances was in a full production of Tchaikovsky's *The Sleeping Beauty* in San Francisco, staged in part by the late Anatol Oboukhov, with Vera Nemchinova, his wife, as Aurora. I remember her clarity, simplicity, strength, and musicality, but most of all I remember when she pricked herself with the spindle. She came all around the stage, trembling, holding the injured hand in the other, to show us what she had done, and to enlist our aid, somehow. I remember the look on her face, the concern of it, not simply with herself, but with herself as a part of the situation.

After a while, if you are lucky, you learn which way is front when you dance on a proscenium stage—sometimes I still have trouble—later, if you are luckier, you learn that there is no front, that the dancing has its roots and its repercussions in everything around one, and over and under, too.

In the "vision scene" in *Sleeping Beauty*, David Wall, as the Prince, walks at first lightly on the earth, as an aristocrat might, sensing his elevated status. Then, shown the specter of the sleeping Aurora, he moves as if growing from the ground, his torso and arms moving faster than, and ahead of, his feet. We watch him suddenly becoming solid, filling out, changing from air into earth or rock or tree trunk. He runs toward Aurora; she is gone, he stops, and the energy of the movement, instead of stopping, remains, charging his body like a battery. Electrifying: one may watch but not touch. The intention of the movement is completely realized in its energy, and like a ghost, remains vivid as an after-image, growing from the locus, or place, or particular world of its being.

The last time I saw Danilova in *Coppélia* I was in the front row of the family circle at the old Metropolitan Opera. She came out, her first entrance; I grabbed the balcony railing to keep from going over. What is this energy; what is its source? Danilova's gestures in *Coppélia* have the percussive quality of a whiplash. Her arm reaching in front of her in arabesque with fingers stretched apart is not the arm she uses in *Swan Lake,* or *La Boutique Fantasque,* or *Le Beau Danube,* or *Schéhérazade.* The *Swan Lake* arm is long and gothic, the fingers don't spread; the line of the arm suggests and relates to the spine, which, again gothic, seems to rise all the way from the pointes like a long sign-post indicating heaven. The torso is no longer square, as in *Coppélia,* but lengthened, lifted, and we are made aware of something in back of her (Rothbart?) and something above her, her destiny, perhaps.

In *Boutique Fantasque,* the difference between a live doll who dances, and the dancer in *Beau Danube* who performs with a street show: the flesh, pearly and cool with mists in *Swan Lake* is now like porcelain. I have no doubt but that the *Boutique* doll is made of china, in Danilova's conception. The street-dancer of *Beau Danube* is warm-fleshed, and somehow, vulgar without ever once becoming tasteless or offensive. The little finishing flourish of her arm when she ends a dance by climbing up on to the Strong Man's back is not a balletic gesture—but neither are the "balletic gestures" in her other roles.

It is difficult, and perhaps misleading, to talk about Danilova's arm or hand or back as separate things. In looking at dancers too often we are shown parts instead of the whole. The Street Dancer of *Danube,* with her proudly arched back, knows herself, her position in life, accepts her vulgarity, and goes on from there to deal with the changing realities of her situation from moment to moment. Thus, what we see of her is real. For Danilova, the reality is simply the understanding and acceptance of character, and the awareness of what happens to her in relation to the other people. Her attention is a balanced duality: in herself, and also in the situation. If the audience can be made to see what is happening on stage in terms of this kind of attention, alert, alive to one's own feeling and responsive to the stimulus of others, there is no possibility of boredom, nor of the unbalance of the dancer's private personality asserting itself. In short, the unselfish dancer creates the unselfconscious audience.

In the film *The Wizard of Oz,* Margaret Hamilton plays two roles, or two aspects of the same person. At first, in the small Kansas town, she is a prim, miserly villainess who kidnaps the heroine's dog. Then, in Oz, she is transmuted into the Wicked Witch, and is recognizably the same person, but somehow radically different. The device Miss Hamilton adopted was simple: in the Kansas role, she arches her spine—as the Witch, she rounds it into a long curve, which thrusts her chin and shoulders forward, and causes her hands to dangle in air suspended from her elbows. A friend of mine once directed a play that Miss Hamilton appeared in. I told him about her use of the spine in *Oz,* and he in turn mentioned it to her. She said: "Oh—is that what I did?"

Danilova's musicality is of such quality that one feels she is playing the music herself. In the czardas variation in *Raymonda* the free tempo of the "lassu" and the precision of the "friska" (the slow and fast parts typical of the czardas) are two aspects of the same thing, embodied and unified by a rhythmic understanding of the sort which encompasses a musical whole. This awareness, coupled with her power of attention, serves to focus the audience on any point desired. In the polka variation in *Coppélia* one's eye follows the unfolding of the hand gesture to its echo in the *rond de jambe* throughout a sequence of eight: each time more breathlessly. Thus, the dancer can lead the audience as a conductor an orchestra. This pleasant conspiracy, literally, breathing together, produces an ideal harmony: "just adaptation of parts to each other." So neither the dancer nor the spectator alone is enough. Neither, then, is sufficient unto himself. Each fulfills his purpose by losing his self, or by joining it with another self—and the breath of the conspirators reveals itself, finally, in its divinity and its truth, as spirit itself.

June 1967

2. GRACIE ALLEN AND THE WHEEL OF LIFE

Which is better, up or down? Do you remember Fred Astaire dancing on the ceiling, or the naughty child in *Blood of a Poet* wriggling up the wall? Is it naughty to go the wrong way? Remember "Wrong-way" Corrigan? Did you know that a corrigan is an elf? There is a ballet called *Les Korriganes*—what is it about? What is "about," anyway? Are you fond of prepositions? Where are we? Is the floor really the most useful mechanical device for dancers? Is the floor a machine? Do you know how to put your feet on the floor? Do you always put your best foot forward? How long is a Chinaman?

I don't know, but I remember Robert Benchley in the first version of Andy Warhol's sleep movie. It was funnier.

I guess I'm confused about direction. I'm invited to perform as part of *New Directions in Dance* and I'm not sure what is new, either. If there's no such thing as time (they're changing the measurement of time, by the way, this October) how can there be any dancing? And yet, there is dancing. Is it the arrow that moves, or the mind that moves? Is it the arrow that causes pain, or again, the mind? Someone said, "Pain is a matter of opinion."

First dance lesson: Put your feet on the floor. Now, put your mind in your feet. What's it like down there? What's it like, dancing on sharp knives? The same as any other dancing, no doubt. A floor is what's under you; footing; he has his feet on the ground. If I can be happy on stage standing on two feet, that's pretty good. If I can be happy standing on one foot, that's better. Next, on no feet, rising to heaven.

Where is heaven, if there is no earth? Where is up, if there is no down? Dancing is a description of an illusion. The more belief, the more dancing. Can you make a dance by destroying the illusion? I have seen Yvonne Rainer start to do this, in one dance, particularly. Does a new belief, then, come about? Short of death, it must. The dancer must live. The next illusion comes. Is this the movement of the mind? Some of us dancers are naughty, and we go the wrong way; we destroy things right and left, forward and backward. Right now I'm engaged in rapidly going backward. Is this my "new direction"?

When does extravagance become a necessity? Extravagance is exorbitant, outside the orbit, outside the circle. In *The Bald Soprano* Ionesco says, "Take a circle, caress it, and it will turn vicious." In *A Damsel in Distress,* a Fred Astaire film of 1937, in the amusement park sequence, Gracie Allen runs in a circle, on a great, turning wheel, for a very long time. Later, off the wheel, she still runs. Throughout the film, Gracie shows us her world, she talks, sings, dances, mimes: we don't know whether to laugh or cry. It is real, but it is not our illusion, it is hers. Suddenly, our knowing is changed, our circling no longer makes sense, only Gracie's does, such is her center. Her world is the only possible world; its rules are inexorable. She does not convince, she is convinced. Her motive, simply, is the movement of spirit, the movement of mind, the spiralling or radiation of her belief from its unshakeable center.

(Note: Gracie Allen died the 28th of August, 1964, at the age of 58.)

July–September 1964

3. Why I like the Rockettes, or, *Coppélia* revisited

Is a Rockette a little rock? Or, is it a little rocket? Is it *little*? Evidently. Can you like little things in a big way? Are questions more interesting than answers? Will I ever shut up?

During the last big snowstorm in New York City I asked myself, What happens when one of the Rockettes can't get to work? Do they close Radio City Music Hall? How many Rockettes are there, anyhow? Once I went to see a thing called *The Great March*; it was at Radio City. All it was, it was the Rockettes just marching, in these high heels; no high kicks for once, just marching, in all kinds of formations. It was pretty marvellous. At the back of the stage, which is big enough to contain the entire state of Rhode Island, were a lot of doors. The Rockettes kept marching in and out of these doors, like those figures on German clocks. Suddenly, after a while, all of the doors opened at once, and, Holy Christ, out came twice as many Rockettes as ever before. I was very confused, but it was wonderful. Later, somebody told me that the ballet girls had changed their costumes and had got themselves up to look like Rockettes. Of course, they don't really *dance* like the Rockettes do, but this was marching, after all, and I was confused, anyhow. So I still don't know just how many Rockettes there are, but if I look carefully I can usually tell them from the ballet, because in a way they are better dancers. I particularly like the one who looks like she is the mother of one of the others.

I like the Rockettes because they don't make any karma. Karma is the trouble you make for yourself by being nervous and worried, and by trying to do what you think is right. The Rockettes don't do this (when they dance), they just dance. And it's marvelous. They don't worry about it, so they can do it. Like the karate expert who can break a granite rock in two with the side of his hand; he just does it, and doesn't try to figure it out.

Dancing is quite a lot like breaking rocks: they don't want to break, and dancing doesn't want to be done. But, as soon as you don't care so much—or when you get interested in everything equally—things loosen up and start to happen. This is very un-Freudian.

So, you might say that what the Rockettes do, they do like machines. In an old ballet called *Coppélia,* the mad scientist makes this doll which he fools the hero into thinking is alive. He is pretty dumb, because then the heroine changes clothes with the doll, and he can't tell the difference.

What *is* the difference? Why are machines so mechanical—and, what's wrong with that? I was reading this science-fiction book about robots and thinking-machines, and in it it says that someday the thinking-machines will run everything, and make all the big decisions, and that they will do it perfectly; much better than people. And the thing is; it's true. Machines are very good. They can do things in less than a billionth of a second; I forget the word for it, but it's a nice word. They store away the knowledge of people—people die; machines just keep on adding more and more smartness; also they can put two and two together and get smarter than any of the people whose knowledge fed them. This is the same kind of learning process that natural-born brains use.

But, there is a great thing against machines on the part of people, most people, that is. Most people think machines are inhuman; they're not. There certainly are a lot of machines which seem pretty different from people; on the other hand, there are lots of people who are very different from each other, like, what cannibals do, for instance. And think nothing of it. Who is right? Well.

Actually, machines have many characteristics of people, and in time will have more. No two typewriters are alike. Pianists are very fussy about pianos; they take ages to find one that works for them. The more complicated a machine becomes, the more it becomes like a person—the more human, in other words. After all, machines are made by people; therefore, they are *like* people. The most mysterious things you find are always things in nature, that science is still trying to understand. Machines are understandable and sympathetic, being built to meet human requirements. But, we aren't fair to them, and we don't appreciate their qualities. We get angry at machines when they don't work, because we expect them to be perfect. We also get angry at them because sometimes they *are* perfect, whereas we are not— and we are aware of the difference, in a bad way.

Robots, eventually, will develop the characteristics of people, because of the tremendous increase in complexity. It is possible that someday you won't be able to tell them from real humans, except by their superiority. We have to face the fact of superiority. Not only in machines, but in anything. When we don't, we start making a lot of karma for ourselves. But, the Rockettes *are* little, because of that diminutive, and because there are so many of them all doing the same thing. Would it matter, if one or two were missing? It would change things, but I guess nobody would notice except the other Rockettes. Like, if it was the one that was the mother of the other, the other would notice.

Now, how *about* little things? Should you only like them a little? I like the Rockettes a lot. But, maybe the sum is larger than the total of the parts— I'm no good at arithmetic. Is it that when you get a lot of little things together, even if they are all alike, something better results? I don't believe it. I think I would like one Rockette all alone, except she would probably get nervous, or embarrassed, or something. Of course, they couldn't do what they do if they were self-conscious. The consciousness is not of self, but of what is being done. You don't have to be conscious of yourself, because you keep on going. You don't have to keep reminding yourself to breathe— unless you are pretty neurotic—or for the blood to go around. Blood doesn't get bored; it has lots of patience. The dance is the thing, as Shakespeare said. Did you know there are forty-four ways to spell Shakespeare? And all of them are right?

Well, what you are doing, is the thing. What you are doing right now, that is. You can't keep expecting that you will get happy next year; you won't. You have to be happy right now. I didn't say it was easy. Or obvious. You really have to do it, though. This way you avoid karma; it's like keeping your nose clear when you have a cold. Everybody knows it is necessary to keep breathing, but nobody knows why. But, as I said, we have this device inside us that does it for us. It doesn't *like* to breathe; on the other hand, it doesn't dislike it, either. It does it because that's its job—like those Radio City girls.

Merce Cunningham, the eminent hoofer, has a dance which is made up of things he saw people doing in the street. It is a pretty good dance. It is called "Minutiae," which means, little things. Merce Cunningham has also been known to make dances by mechanical means, tossing coins, and so on. In spite of this, they are pretty good, too. You could call this process getting rid of yourself, and getting on to the object. Or, getting rid of karma. You never really get rid of yourself, anyhow. I mean, there you are! What nonsense!

The best dancers are translucent. You see through them.

Later: Someone has just told me that a Rockette is a little Rockefeller.

ca. 1958

—from *Ballet Review*

JOAN ACOCELLA
L'Allegro, il Penseroso ed il Moderato

When Mark Morris moved his troupe to Brussels last fall and began
creating his first new work for the Théâtre de la Monnaie, he had almost
everything he could want at his disposal. To begin with, to make his two-
part piece, he had two and a half months—a generous time allowance that
included, at the end, six orchestra rehearsals. (By contrast, Balanchine at
New York City Ballet rarely had more than one or two orchestra rehearsals
for a new work.) He was able to add nine supplementary dancers to his
already enlarged company, for a cast of twenty-four. From Adrianne Lobel,
with whom he had worked on Peter Sellars' *Nixon in China,* he commissioned a complicated set, a series of twenty-one scrims and colored drops
hung from different depths in the flies, so that by raising and lowering them
he could control not just the color and lighting of the stage but also its size.
Christine Van Loon, a Belgian designer, costumed the dancers in silk chiffon—knee-length dresses for the women, loose tops with tights for the
men—and everyone had a change of clothes for Part Two (basically the same
outfit but in brighter colors). Morris used a full orchestra, a chorus of forty,
and five soloist singers, and he made a full-evening piece, two hours long.
Big and rich in all these ways, the new work is also big-spirited. With the
move to Belgium, Morris' resources had expanded many times over, and so
he made an expansive piece.

L'Allegro, il Penseroso ed il Moderato, which had its premiere on 23 November, is Morris' dance rendering of Handel's musical rendering of two companion poems, "L'Allegro" and "Il Penseroso," that John Milton wrote
sometime between 1630 and 1638, when he was in his twenties. While the
two poems are the works of a young genius, they are also typical products
of the Renaissance in the confident breadth of their embrace. In a short
space—"L'Allegro" is 152 lines long, "Il Penseroso" 176 lines—they allude

to, borrow from, and/or name most of the poets considered truly great by English people of the seventeenth century: Homer, Aeschylus, Sophocles, Euripides, Vergil, Ovid, Theocritus, Chaucer, Tasso, Ariosto, Spenser, Shakespeare, Marlowe, Ben Jonson. In other words, the poems round up the history of their own art. They also compass much of the physical world of Renaissance man: the towered cities, the theater, the cloister, the hearth, the cricket and the bee, the hound and horn. Finally, they are psychologically ambitious. Drawing on the tradition of humoral psychology that stretches from Empedocles down to Balanchine's *The Four Temperaments,* but which was especially strong in Milton's time. (Burton's *Anatomy of Melancholy* was published when Milton was a teenager, and Ben Jonson, who based much of his satire on humoral typology, was at that time England's most revered living poet.) "L'Allegro" and "Il Penseroso" are portraits of, respectively, the joyful and the contemplative states of mind, together with most of the intermediate stages. The furthest extremes they omit—passion, rage, grief—but otherwise they pretty much run the gamut of human affect.

Such inclusiveness, as I have said, was typical of the time. It was part of the Renaissance belief that the universe was knowable and worth knowing. Hence, it comes as no surprise that Milton's two poems, when you finish them, seem to leave behind a whole little world, green and buzzing, full of *things,* and all of them natural and beautiful. The surprise is that the same is true of Mark Morris' dance. Presumably, what defines the modern period is our loss of that Renaissance breadth and confidence: the belief that you could know the world and the mind and that in doing so you stood in an unbroken line of inheritance from artists past. Yet with no sacrifice of modern feeling—on the contrary—Morris gives back to us the old kind of beauty. It's as if, like Columbus, by sailing into unknown seas he returned home.

H a n d e l ' s   O r a t o r i o ,   w h i c h is Morris' score, takes Milton's poems not in their original form but in a revised, interleaved version devised for Handel by the poet Charles Jennens. As noted, the poems match. Each starts with the mood-struck speaker in question dismissing the contrary humor ("Hence, loathèd Melancholy," l'Allegro begins; "Hence, vain deluding Joys," says il Penseroso). Each then proceeds to an invocation of the appropriate goddess—Mirth and Melancholy, respectively—and a discussion of her birth, her pedigree, and her customary companions. Later each introduces the bird of his choice (the lark versus the nightingale), talks about the sort of nature walks he would take (daisy-dotted meadows versus twilight groves), and so on. Jennens' idea was to disassemble the two poems and put them back together in such a way that part answered part: l'Allegro's dismissal of Melancholy is immediately followed by il Penseroso's dismissal of vain deluding Joys; l'Allegro's invocation of Mirth is followed by il Penseroso's summoning of Melancholy, et cetera. The singers thus get to alternate, compete, and debate. And occasionally a third character, il Moderato ("the moderate one"), created by Jennens, chimes in with a stanza in defense of the *via media* that humoral psychology held to be the ideal mental strategy. Thus was created "l'Allegro, il Penseroso ed il Moderato," a sequence of arias, choruses, and recitatives, premiered in 1740. For his purposes Morris has deleted some numbers (including all but two of il Moderato's songs), shortened a few others, and in certain cases changed the order of the songs. The most important revision comes at the end, where he switched the placement of the two final arguments. Jennens gave il Penseroso the last word. Morris gives it to l'Allegro. He also prefaced each of the two parts of his dance with introductory music taken from Handel's 1739 Concerto Grosso No. 1 in G major. (Most of this information on the score comes from Roger Downey's helpful essay in the Monnaie souvenir program.)

So what you have here, in Morris's first evening-length work, is a suite of dances—one about a lark, one about laughter, one about church, one about cities, one about dreaming, one about hunting—almost thirty of them, and not a dull one among them. All of Morris's well-known qualities are here: his love of baroque music, his attention to musical structure, his fondness for cycling a set of gestures again and again through a dance, his way of producing narrative and abstract dance at the same time, his use of weight and ordinary movement, his use, in contrast, of the most elaborate art-dance images (Duncanesque nymphs, Humphreyesque votaries), his wit, his sexual latitudinarianism, his unembarrassed interest in the sacred. In other words, it's the same Mark Morris. But he has vaulted into a new sphere; his forces are deployed with a new freedom. Certain things that he has been very insistent, sometimes obsessive, about in the past—the musical structuring (*Marble Halls*), the recycling of gesture (*Stabat Mater*), the levelling of male-female differences (*Championship Wrestling*), the ironic confrontation of modern, vernacular ways of moving with refined "historical" styles (*Pièces en Concert*)—these things he is less strict about in *L'Allegro*. Somehow, things that once seemed opposites in his work have reconciled, made friends, at least for the space of this piece. *L'Allegro* has a new elasticity, a shapeliness, a sense of pacing, a relaxed and soaring confidence, an ability to bring many things together in just and vivid relation to one another.

You can see this already in the first few minutes. The opening of the piece is tremendous. In black darkness—nothing onstage, nothing anywhere—a tenor voice rises up out of the pit. "Hence, loathèd Melancholy, / Of Cerberus and blackest midnight born," it sings, and it goes on singing of the black world of Melancholy—the Stygian cave, the night raven, the ebony shades—for ten long lines. The effect is spooky, sepulchral, as if we too were in the Stygian cave, or some dark ditch in Dante's Hell, with someone addressing us from the inside of a tomb. The music adds to the tension. It is mostly strings, low and intermittent, sawing away beneath parts of the song but finding no melodic path. You hold your breath.

Then a dim, murky sort of swamp light goes up behind a black scrim, and dancers begin racing across the stage. Life! But inchoate at first: little groups form and vanish, trailing away like fog or cobwebs. This is day struggling to be born from night, and consciousness from dream, Creation from chaos. Then—bang! Up goes the scrim, on go the lights, toot go the woodwinds as they find their tune, and in answer to the singer's prayer—"Come, thou Goddess fair and free"—out onto the stage flies the goddess Mirth, Tina Fehlandt, her skirts dancing on the air behind her. Morris has never lacked for boldness, but the sheer simplicity of this image really takes your breath away. Here at the very opening is the patron saint of the piece, and her dancing tells you right away who she is and hence what the piece will be. She is history, and the history of art. As she leaps and prances, and as she is joined by her two sisters—together, they are the three Graces—you see before you the maenads of Attic sculpture and the three Graces of Botticelli's *Primavera* and Isadora Duncan, would-be maenad, who so much loved that Botticelli. (Whether you know it or not, you are also seeing Blake's illustration of Mirth from "L'Allegro." Blake made twelve watercolor illustrations, now in the Pierpont Morgan Library, of "L'Allegro" and "Il Penseroso," and these paintings supplied some of the ideas for Morris's dances. There, in a nutshell, you have his historicism: seventeenth-century poems, eighteenth-century oratorio, nineteenth-century paintings, leading into a twentieth-century dance.)

But whatever her historical antecedents, this Mirth is also modernity itself. With her big, healthy body and her short hair and frank demeanor, Fehlandt could come from nowhere but postmodern dance, with its challenge to ideas about artistic movement as opposed to ordinary movement and about femininity as opposed to masculinity. In the past Morris has repeatedly used Fehlandt as a kind of supra-woman, a woman who can do man's things. I will never forget the moment in *Dogtown* where she picks up David Landis and throws him across the stage. In both *Marble Halls* and *Strict Songs* the strength of her body was a central image of the dance. In the recent Poulenc *Sonata for Clarinet and Piano* Morris made her a stand-in for himself.

Some critics have felt that in using his female dancers this way, Morris denies them their femininity and thereby handicaps them and himself artistically. I feel differently. I think he can no more deny his female dancers their femininity than he can deny himself his masculinity. (Even in a dress, in *Deck of Cards,* he is unmistakably a man.) We live in a time when ideas about male and female are being questioned. For Morris the question is perhaps more pressing, but surely it is there for all of us. There are plenty of women who can pick up a man and throw him, and who might want to. Likewise, there are obviously men who wouldn't mind being picked up, if not thrown.

The point, however, is not that these facts exist but that Morris makes them interesting artistically. In *Love Song Waltzes,* for example, how much he made of the women's weighty strength: Ruth Davidson's big, wild pirouette, with her dress flying up, at the beginning of the piece, and the sense of community that came from the blurring of gender rules (who can lift whom, et cetera), and the air of sheer challenge—all of this enabling Brahms to speak to us again in a new way, as if those love songs were about our lives. Likewise, here at the opening of *L'Allegro* Morris is putting before us something very old and arty—nymphhood—but making it modern, by giving the steps the heft and thrust of modern life. And so we look at a nymph and see something that is ours.

Thus does he give us the message of his piece from the very start: "You will see old, archaic things here, things out of books, and they are all about us." I find it perfect and moving that the messenger he sent to tell us this is Fehlandt, who has done such hard battle for him in the modernization of gender. In turn, that effect is merely one aspect of his modernization of the symbol world of the past, and never has his devotion to the latter been clearer than in *L'Allegro.* He wants to make Milton as real to us as Vergil was to Milton.

Fehlandt's entry announces another trend as well: *L'Allegro* is a women's piece. It is strewn with great female solos, or dances led by women, most of them belonging to the women of Morris's original, 1980 company. Teri Weksler has the longest female solo: she is il Penseroso's nightingale, a bird whose strength is failing and who can't quite get into the air. Weksler, as is her habit, takes it utterly objectively—no tragic mask, no dying swan—and thus makes it lacerating. Penny Hutchinson, who is probably Morris' oldest artistic associate (they were friends in high school), has a complicated number where she goes from being one thing to the next; first she is a bee in a grove where il Penseroso wanders; then, when he dozes, she is his dream; then a monster in the dream; then the sweet music that he hears as he wakens; then "th'unseen genious of the wood," a sort of nature spirit watching over all this.

More goddesslike still is Ruth Davidson in the heroic solo that opens Part II of the piece. Il Penseroso, from the pit, sings of the joys of the mind—how when everyone else is asleep, he will sit alone in a dark tower, reading Neoplatonic treatises—and Davidson, all alone on the big Monnaie stage, does a dance where her arms seem to be the book that is opening. Meanwhile, however, her legs perform turns so exacting that she must surely be not any *thing* in this scene but rather the image of Penseroso's mental act as he scales the heights of thought: so beautiful and so difficult at the same time.

The partial use of mime in this dance—the opening of the arms like a book—is typical of *L'Allegro* as a whole and of Morris' work as a whole. For years he has given himself the freedom, when he chose, to use a gestural language as baldly literal as "Itsy Bitsy Spider." Think, for example, of "Robe of White" in *Songs That Tell a Story*—the mother taking the letter, signing for it—or *Love, You Have Won,* with the two dancers acting out all the metaphorical particulars (ship, star, bird) of the singer's love lament. But in these instances, as in so many, he is protean, changeable. What was introduced as representation soon wanders from that task and, like the little birds in a Tabriz carpet, becomes pure line, pure pattern.

A nice example in *L'Allegro* comes in the invocation of Melancholy. As in the invocation of Mirth, three women appear in response to the summons. Then the singer sings of how Melancholy's "saintly visage is too bright / To hit the sense of human sight," and the three women cover their eyes. Then, as the singer speaks of Melancholy's birth, the women take to the floor, and in an earthy bit of dumb show reminiscent of Balanchine's now-discarded prologue to *Apollo,* they give birth. So here are three more or less realistic actions. But I doubt that on first viewing most spectators will understand the words and their relationship to the action. And even once they do— once they buy the souvenir program, with the libretto, and say "Oh, that's what that was"—they are unlikely to hold for long onto the strictly mimetic sense. For one thing, that sense is undermined by the fact that, like Penny Hutchinson in the dance described earlier, the "actors" change roles: the three women are first the goddess (when they enter), then the mortals beholding her (when they cover their eyes), then her mother (when they give birth). So narrative identities travel *through* them rather than ever really belonging to them. (And anyway, there are three of them to represent one goddess, so how realistic was this to start with?) And as the dance proceeds and the gestures are repeated, their shapes and cadence become as important as their "meaning," just as the similarity of these three women to the three (Fehlandt and her sisters) who immediately preceded them, in the invocation of Mirth, becomes as important as their stated identity. The gestures never entirely come loose from their mimetic sense, but they have a lot of play, a lot of rope, and so we seem to see representation and abstraction at the same time, dancing together. The effect is very rich.

But the approach differs from part to part. In some of the dances, Morris fastens so hard on Milton's narrative that you cannot fail to understand it. There is a superbly comic hunt scene, done like a little school pageant, with horses (Susan Hadley, her chest held high, wonderfully vain and snooty as one of the lead horses), and trees (dancers in clumps, with gnarled arms sticking out this way and that), and dogs so eager that they bump into the trees, and two little foxes running for their lives.

Other dances are far looser readings of their text. The invocation to Melancholy breaks up into a number of dances, of which one has this text: "Come, but keep thy wonted state, / With even step, and musing gait; / And looks commercing with the skies, / Thy rapt soul sitting in thine eyes." But the dance has nothing to do with the goddess thus invoked. Two figures, Susan Hadley and Joachim Schlömer, are separated from one another by several lines of dancers crossing the stage laterally. The two look at one another, reach out for one another, and in the only direct connection between their story and il Penseroso's, they bob up and down on the soles of their feet, as if in excitement, when the singer speaks of "thy rapt soul sitting in thine eyes." Otherwise, they walk back and forth, gazing at one another, and the company walks between them ("with even step, and musing gait"), until the song is finished and they part, exiting in opposite directions. This beautiful little story—I think of it as the "Some Enchanted Evening" number— Morris has spun out of two simple ideas in his text, yearning and walking.

Elsewhere he takes other approaches. Sometimes, as in Weksler's nightingale number, the dance is more narrative than the text. Or he will follow the text word for word. Then sometimes he will pun on it, as when l'Allegro, speaking of going to the theater, mentions Ben Jonson's "learned sock"— that is, Jonson's learned comedy, "sock" being the soccus, or low-heeled shoe, worn by actors in Attic comedy—and Morris has his dancers sock one another. (They also stick their feet out, as if to show us their socks, but I think this pun was intended.)

My point, though, is not the genius of any one solution but the multiplicity of Morris' solutions. The same is true of spatial design. Between the variables of group size (solo, small group, tutti), gender (all male, all female), stage size (the action of the scrims), and line (curved and straight, diagonals and laterals, circles and semicircles and Xs and parabolas and wedges and tunnels), there seems to be almost nothing that he doesn't come up with, and still the variety is so unforced that you feel he could come up with a whole evening's worth more—that the man can go to the well as many times as he pleases.

And none of this variety is gained by small effects. Visually, everything is bold, clean, as readable as a STOP sign. You may get more out of it on the third viewing, but there's nothing you'll really miss on the first. The lark, for example, comes in and hops around the whole big stage all by himself, jerking his little head this way and that and picking up one little foot and then the other. (Jon Mensinger and Donald Mouton alternate in this role. I saw Mouton, and he is birdhood itself.) What a composition this is—all that space and this one small creature. This must be what the sky feels like to a bird: so big and yet not at all frightening. Then, suddenly, it all changes. As Mouton crosses the stage again, in flies the rest of the company behind him, their arms extended, winglike, and they swoop this way and that in those pulsing triangular formations that flocks of birds fly in. The pleasure here is not just to have the portrait of birdhood expanded on (one bird hopping versus a whole flock flying) but a purely formal joy—to have emptiness suddenly filled—and also a deep, half-mad kinesthetic thrill: to have something going pick-pick, sharp and little, give way to something huge and sweeping, like a tidal wave.

And this is just one small moment in a whole evening of such rich designs. Two circles of women give way to two lateral lines of men, and intimacy to formality. A men's circle dance that is all thrust and hop and kick is followed by a woman's circle dance that wafts like Kleenex in slow motion. Several times a dance at center stage is commented on by another dance transpiring upstage, behind a scrim. After Weksler's nightingale has struggled and struggled to get into the air, another bird—the excellent Olivia Maridjan-Koop, new to the company—takes off effortlessly, behind a scrim, into a blue sky. Just before that, two other women came through, held aloft by four men, in the joint role of the moon, who needn't ever worry about getting into the sky—she is always there.

What to my mind is the most breathtaking compositional effect occurs at the end of Part I. The dancers join hands to form six circles and run in those circles, when suddenly, before you can see what happened, they are four circles, and as you are trying to understand how they did it, they are now two circles, and then one, and still running, running, never missing a beat. And the fact that every time the break occurs it falls, from what I can tell, on a different count within the musical phrase makes it seem more thrilling, unstoppable, like a bomb exploding. Then peace. The dancers stand still in their big circle, holding hands: what was separate is now together, a human community. They lie down and, still in the circle, roll over one another (lovemaking). Then six pairs stay put on the floor; they are sleeping. Six others leave, as if their bedrooms were upstairs.

The elasticity that one sees in the spatial composition is there in mood and tone as well. Some dances are comic, others sad or sacred. The men's thrust-kick circle dance that I mentioned earlier is the funniest thing in *L'Allegro*. Just in case anyone ever accused him of eroding sex-role stereotypes, Morris here gives us a boys-will-be-boys number. All twelve men stand in a ring. First they embrace, then they sock one another in the face (the "Jonson's learned sock" business), then they do a nice, jolly, tripping circle dance. Then they start punching one another again; then they dance again, and so on.

So that's what boys are made of. Girls are different. The men's punchout is followed by a quintessentially wafting number for the women. This is another circle dance—we are meant to see the two as a pair—but instead of revolving forcefully, it flows and winds like a moving wreath: twelve enchanted princesses, perhaps, or twelve priestesses, descendants of Doris Humphrey, dancing around an invisible altar.

So the mood has swung from low comedy to a sort of pearl-tinted rapture, and then, once we have had our fill of these, in comes il Moderato, singing of how Reason dissolves Fancy, the sort of fancy we've just been tasting two varieties of. What is wonderful here is to see how Morris can find beauty not just in those two sexy extremes but in Moderato as well. To the steady, churning beat that Handel uses for Reason's march against Fancy, Morris creates a Thracian line dance, in which the twenty-four dancers form two lines and march toward, away from, and into one another in patterns that seem to multiply endlessly. Each time the two lines meet, center stage, a new surprise is born. Thus Reason, though steady, is no schoolmarm. Like the rule-bound poetic forms so popular in Handel's and Jennens's day, it can conceal miracles at its center.

So you have the whole range. And the aim is not just variety but comprehensiveness. This is the world, says Milton, and Morris intends the same—or so I read the conclusion of the piece. As I mentioned earlier, Morris in *L'Allegro* uses his beloved technique of cycling movement motifs, and among the motifs he uses here, probably the two most important are the group of three women and the circle dance. We see the group of three women at the very start—the three Graces, Mirth and her two sisters—and again in the next number, in the invocation of Melancholy. So both l'Allegro's goddess and il Penseroso's are visualized as three women. Soon another trio appears—Mark Morris's goddesses, the Muses (like Balanchine, he limits himself to three)—and as the singer tells us how "the Muses in a ring / Round about Jove's altar sing," these goddesses introduce the motif of the circle dance: they join hands and run ecstatically in a ring.

Part I ends in a series of circles, culminating in one big circle, the human community. Part II has more circle dances, notably the boys' "sock" dance and the Humphreyesque girls' dance. Then comes the final circle.

The end of *L'Allegro* is even more thrilling than the beginning. The stage is opened to its full depth, fully lit, and as the singers' voices go up in their final hymn to Mirth, the dancers, in ones and twos and threes, come leaping out of the back wings, join hands with others flying in from the other side, and race downstage toward us in a transport of joy. As one group exits, the next one enters, wave upon wave breaking. Then they all disappear, and after a moment's pause, like a delayed heartbeat, they reenter, forming three concentric circles. And as the drums pound and the trumpets raise their fanfare, the circles begin running: the outer one clockwise, the middle one counter-clockwise, and the inner circle—three women, just like the Muses—clockwise, as before, around Jove's altar.

Aside from being beautiful to look at, this image tells you everything. In its fusion of geometry and dynamism, it is the embodiment of Milton's and Handel's and Morris' meaning: the coming together of the two poles of the mind—reason and energy, contemplation and enjoyment, Apollo and Dionysus, seeing and being, Penseroso and Allegro. And in its echoes of pre-vious circles—the Muses' ring, the human community, the boys' dance, the girls' dance—we see that in this fusion of opposites, all the world is brought together. Indeed, the whole cosmos, for what we are seeing in this nest of spinning circles is a cosmological vision, with the planets and the suns and the stars revolving around the earth—that is to say, around man and man's mind—as the people of Milton's time still believed was the case. (Galileo's trial by the Inquisition for saying otherwise was in 1633, possibly the year in which Milton wrote these poems.)

L'Allegro is thus a world-loving work. Everything is there—the poets and the painters, the goddesses and the shepherds, youth and age, morning and night—and everything comes out pretty well. (In the hunt scene, the foxes get away.) And in the stupendous finale, the whole thing seems to lift off into a realm of rapture that recalls Dante and Joyce at the end of similar cosmo-logical enterprises. *L'Allegro* is a masterpiece. It will be counted as one of the crowning artistic achievements of the eighties. In addition, in its message of joy, it is perfect for its occasion: the move, the new job, the pretty opera house. It is like a big thank-you note. As such, it lacks the spiritual difficulty and the intensely private focus that have threaded their way through much of Morris' finest work. I would be sorry to think that I would never see this dark side again. (Those who have seen *Dido and Aeneas,* which Morris unveiled in March, three months after *L'Allegro,* have assured me that I needn't worry.) But *L'Allegro* is a day in the sun.

—from *Ballet Review,* Summer 1989

CYRIL BEAUMONT

Petrouchka

Premiering in 1911, Petrouchka *was the masterpiece of the ballets Fokine created for Diaghilev's Ballets Russes. The realistic crowd scenes at the Shrovetide Fair, the interplay among the three puppets, the tragedy of Petrouchka when his latent humanity breaks through his nonhuman condition—all combine to immense effect when a great dancer-actor is playing the central figure. The role was made on Nijinsky, of course, and no one who followed him, including Nureyev, Bruhn, and Baryshnikov, has surpassed him—or even equaled him. The original cast included Tamara Karsavina as the Ballerina, Alexandre Orlov as the Blackamoor, and Enrico Cecchetti as the Showman. Pierre Monteux was the conductor. The music was, with* Firebird, *one of Stravinsky's first great successes, and he was responsible for the libretto in collaboration with Alexandre Benois, who also designed the famous set and costumes.*

The ballet season opened on February 4, the program being *Thamar, Petrouchka,* and *Les Sylphides.* This was the London *premiere* of *Petrouchka,* the theme being by Alexandre Benois and Igor Stravinsky, the music by Igor Stravinsky, the scenery and costumes by Alexandre Benois, and the choreography by Michel Fokine.

The principal characters were: *the Dancer,* Thamar Karsavina; *Petrouchka,* Vaslav Nijinsky; *the Moor,* A. Kotchetovsky; *Old Showman,* Enrico Cecchetti; *Coachmen,* Semenov, Romanov, Rakmanov, Oumansky, Ivanovsky; *Grooms,* Kremnev, Gavrilov; *Bibulous Merchant,* Sergei Grigoriev; *Gypsies,* Mmes. Piltz, Astafieva; *Street Dancers,* Mmes. Jezerska, Gouluk; *First Organ-Grinder,* Tarassov; *Second Organ-Grinder,* M. Kobelev; *Old Father of the Fair,* Loboiko; *Picture-Showman,* Statkiewicz.

I well remember the startled expressions on the faces of the audience, and my own surprise, at the first hearing of Stravinsky's music, so wonderfully expressive of the raucous sounds and bustling movements of a fair, but which then sounded incredibly daring and uncouth to ears attuned to the melodies of classic composers.

The present generation who have long been accustomed to modernist music as well as the most strident forms of jazz, cannot imagine how novel and daring Stravinsky's score sounded in 1913.

Again, the setting, a Russian fairground in the 1830s, a charming composition in which primary colours, such as red, blue, and yellow, played a prominent part, was in striking contrast to the romantic settings of Oriental scenes typical of former productions.

Except for the *Polovtsian Dances from "Prince Igor,"* the previous ballets had romance or passion for their theme; *Petrouchka,* however, was a tragicomedy concerned, not with living persons, but with puppets, which their master, for a brief space, had endowed with human passions and emotions.

After the first shock of surprise had passed, I was soon captivated by the gay and ever-changing scene before my eyes—the nurses, in their full brightly coloured skirts, with one hand on hip, the other waving a handkerchief in the breeze; the coachmen, swinging to and fro to the well-marked rhythm of a dance, their long coats flapping as they stamped their feet and whirled round in time with the measure; the street dancers with their tinkling triangle; and all the motley crowd of stall-holders, cossacks, soldiers, policemen, ladies and gentlemen passing backwards and forwards, intent on seeing the sights. Suddenly the flow of movement was abruptly stayed by the appearance of the old Showman who, having collected about him an eager audience with the strange melody which he played on his pipe, drew back the curtains of his booth and revealed the three puppets—the Dancer, Petrouchka, and the Moor.

Every ballet-goer knows that the three puppets are supported from the shoulders by an iron stand set at the back of each cell, which enables the puppets to execute the curious mechanical dance with which the first scene draws to a close. When the Showman gave the signal for the puppets to dance, Nijinsky succeeded in investing the movements of his legs with a looseness suggesting that foot, leg, and thigh were threaded on a string attached to the hip; there was a curiously fitful quality in his movements, his limbs spasmodically leapt or twisted or stamped like the reflex actions of limbs whose muscles have been subjected to an electric current.

The whole production of the ballet was inspired. There was the blackout which brought the first scene to an abrupt conclusion, and the roll of drums that symbolized the passing crowd of sightseers outside the booth, and at the same time held the attention of the theatre audience, while the drop-curtain was lowered to permit of each change of scene, and then raised to disclose it.

There were four scenes, the first and last being the same, the scene of the fair; the other two showed Petrouchka's cell and the Moor's cell respectively. The second and third scenes were small ones set inside the main one, and since, in these, there were never more than three characters at one time, the contrasting gaiety of the outdoor scene with the comparative quiet of the indoor cells in which the puppets lived, was most effectively suggested.

The second scene, Petrouchka's cell, was the most unusual from the musical aspect, and at the first performance the members of the audience were considerably disconcerted by the piercing shrieks which conveyed Petrouchka's unhappiness. It was only gradually that it was seen how exactly right were those strident shrieks.

Nijinsky as Petrouchka dominated this and the last scene. He wore a thick white cotton blouse with a frilled collar edged with red, a red tie, satin trousers chequered in crimson and yellow, blue boots of soft leather, and a red and white hat with a tassel.

His features were made up a kind of putty colour, presumably a suggestion of wood; his nose was built up to have a thicker base; his eyebrows were painted out and replaced by a wavy line set half an inch higher; his lips were compressed together; his eyes seemed devoid of lid and socket, and suggested a pair of boot-buttons or two blobs of black paint; there was a little red on his cheeks. His features were formed into a sad and unhappy mask, an expression which remained constant throughout the ballet.

I have seen no one approach Nijinsky's rendering of Petrouchka, for, as I have said elsewhere, he suggested a puppet that sometimes aped a human being, whereas all the other interpreters conveyed a dancer imitating a puppet. He seemed to have probed the very soul of the character with astonishing intuition. Did he, in one of his dark moods of introspection, feel conscious of a strange parallel between Petrouchka and himself, and the Showman and Diaghilev?

Despite his set features he was, paradoxically enough, most expressive, his emotions being conveyed by the movements of his arms, the tilt of his head, and the various angles at which he bent his body from the waist. In general, his arms were stiff and extended like the arms of a puppet pivoted at the shoulder, but their meaning was plain. I well remember his dramatic entrance in the second scene when the double door leading to his cell burst open and he was propelled through it by the Showman's cruel boot. As if in acute pain, he tottered forward on his toes, flung up his arms, and threw back his head.

How vividly he presented his despair, his unhappiness, his misery, as he fingered and plucked at his clothes, the symbol of his servitude. Then he sank on his knees, and, with his stiff arms, now bent at the elbow, struck his neck first on one side and then on the other in a state of utter dejection at his pitiful lot.

Suddenly the folding door burst open and the Dancer appeared, to give him new hope. How excitedly he jerked his arms in greeting! But alas, the Dancer resented his strange manner of courtship and slammed the door in his face. Imagine his sorrow at this new affront. In a frenzy of rage and despair, he sought to escape from his cell and follow her.

Now I want to emphasize that this scene does not consist merely of Petrouchka kneeling at the bottom of the double door, making pattering movements of the hands up the wall and tearing at it until an opening is forced, through which his head and arms disappear, while his body remains within the room. To obtain the full dramatic value of this episode, the dancer must induce within himself a state of emotion such as a puppet temporarily endowed with life might feel under the circumstances, and then express it in terms of the movements designed by the choreographer. In most presentations of this scene I have been conscious of a certain casual approach, a "now I do the business of pattering on the wall and bring the scene to a close," the movements done as though prescribed, and not as the expression of a sudden mad moment of revolt on Petrouchka's part against the conditions which, when he was not performing to the public, made him a prisoner, confined within the narrow limits of his dark room.

Nijinsky gave an impressive performance of this episode. The Dancer's departure left him stunned for a brief moment, then he made you aware, through the almost imperceptible shaking of his head and body, and the twitching of his limbs, of the tumult of emotions stirring within him. Suddenly he flung himself on his knees by the doors, his gloved hands gliding ceaselessly up and down the jamb, higher and higher, as he tried to find an opening. Gradually he rose to his feet, still fingering the jamb more and more feverishly as his sense of frustration grew. Abruptly he rejected the door and passed his hands over the wall, faster and faster, while his head and limbs continually twitched from the intensity of his eagerness to escape. All at once his groping fingers found a weak spot and tore the paper apart—a piercing scream of triumph burst from the orchestra as his head and shoulders fell through the gap. His body went limp, curved in an inverted "v," as if he had fainted from exhaustion, while his arms, dropped in a vertical line, swung idly to and fro, as if still quivering from the violence of his efforts.

Another great moment occurred in the final scene when Petrouchka, struck by a blow from the Moor's scimitar, collapsed and sank on the snow-covered ground. He went inert like a broken doll. It was only with the greatest difficulty that he was able to raise himself from the ground. His head lolled to and fro as though attached to his neck by a piece of string. His arms jerked feebly. The green glare of a Bengal light turned his features a ghastly green. Then he fell back and rolled over on to his side.

Nijinsky's performance made a great impression upon me. As in all his creations, he absorbed himself completely in the character presented. His conceptions were illumined by genius; they were vital and memorable; and in the parts which he created he set a standard which his successors in those roles have never approached, let alone equalled.

Karsavina looked charming as the Dancer in her lace-fringed pantalettes, striped dull red and maroon, her pale mauve skirt, and her crimson velvet bodice with white sleeves trimmed with gold bands. Her hair, dressed in the short ringlets which became her so well, was crowned with a crimson velvet toque, trimmed with white fur. Her makeup was flesh-pink with a bright dab of red on each cheek. Her eyes were given an air of exaggerated surprise by short black lines painted ray-like about them.

She made the Dancer an impressionable, flighty young woman, and all her movements had a crispness and tautness which gave them a most attractively piquant quality. Her little dance with the trumpet was admirably timed and as gay and as sprightly as could be. Her daintiness made an excellent foil for the agitated, twitching, hypersensitive Petrouchka and the vain, lumbering, brutish Moor.

One of the most vivid of my recollections of Karsavina in this role is associated with the third scene, where she is captivated by the overwhelming personality of the Moor, so splendid a figure in his suit of emerald green and silver. When the Dancer paid him a visit, he dropped the coconut with which he had been playing, and, plumping himself on the divan, brazenly seized the Dancer and pulled her on to his knees. How delightfully she suggested by the particular tilting of her head and shoulders the nervous thrill she experienced from that bold attack. But when Petrouchka most inconsiderately burst upon the lovers and squeaked his indignation, her innate modesty returned and she quickly jumped to her feet, jerking up her hands to hide her burning cheeks.

Orlov created the role of the Moor when *Petrouchka* was first performed—at Paris; unfortunately, I never saw him. But Kotchetovsky, who played the Moor in the London premiere, has remained for me the best interpreter of that part, although Bolm ran him closely. Kotchetovsky's Moor was a big, burly, clumsy fellow, childishly vain of his physical strength and his imposing uniform. He made him a good-humoured lout with a child-like propensity for showing off at the slightest provocation, yet he did the simplest movements with such a smacking of his thick lips, such rolling of eyeballs, such gusto, that you could not help sharing in his extravagant delight.

And I must not forget Cecchetti as the old Showman, a mysterious, enigmatic figure, his every movement timed to perfection. How calmly and carelessly he followed the policeman come to acquaint him of the murder of Petrouchka, an absurd notion he quickly disposed of by his contemptuous shaking of the limp figure to prove that Petrouchka was nothing more than wood and sawdust. Then came the dramatic moment when, as he strolled homewards, dragging the puppet's limp body behind him, preparatory to returning it to its cell, there was a succession of eerie squeaks and Petrouchka's ghost appeared at the top of the booth, to mock his master, who, shaken and terrified by this unexpected and inexplicable phenomenon, hastily took to flight.

I can still see the abrupt end of Cecchetti's leisurely walk as he jerked back on his heels, his whole body tensed in an attitude of listening. Then, as Petrouchka's mocking squeaks were repeated, there flashed over Cecchetti's features a look of mingled bewilderment and surprise, which swiftly changed to abject fear. Full of apprehension, he half-turned his head in the direction of the sound, and, as he caught sight of the roof of the booth with the head and shoulders of that ghostly figure gibbering with its stiff arms, a chill sweat broke out on his forehead. He smoothed his brow with his trembling hand, shaking so violently that his hat fell from his head. The sound of that object striking the ground startled him into immediate action, and, filled with a frenzied desire to escape, he scurried away, as fast as his trembling legs would carry him.

—from *Bookseller at the Ballet: Memoirs 1891–1929,* 1975

CHRISTOPHER CAINES

Lilac Garden

Antony Tudor's most famous (and performed) work, Lilac Garden *(also called* Jardin aux Lilas*), was first seen in January 1936, at London's Ballet Rambert, featuring Maude Lloyd, Hugh Laing, and Tudor himself. The ballet made Tudor famous, and provided his calling card to America and the newly formed Ballet Theatre in 1940. Set to Chausson's richly romantic* Poème for Violin and Orchestra, Lilac Garden *is a quiet work of great psychological and emotional intensity, as it plays out the forced separation of "Caroline" from her young lover at a garden party, since she must marry her rich suitor.*

George Balanchine contended that a story ballet is only successful if you can tell, the moment the curtain goes up, who is who, and what is what, without any need for program notes. You can tell who the king is by the crown on his head—and there are no mothers-in-law in ballet.

Lilac Garden does not satisfy Balanchine's criteria in this regard. Neither characters nor story would be entirely legible without a program note, such as this one, used by American Ballet Theatre in its recent revivals of the work:

> Caroline, about to enter upon a marriage of convenience, tenders a farewell party to precede the ceremony. Among the guests are the man she really loved and the woman who, unknown to her, has been her fiancé's mistress. Quick meetings, interrupted confidences culminate with Caroline leaving on the arm of her betrothed, never having satisfied the desperate longings for the final kiss.

This note by itself is not enough, however; *Lilac Garden's* four main characters must also be identified in the program in a very special way. Caroline is the only character to whom Tudor accords the privilege of a name. Moreover, he takes care to give us only her first name, inviting us, the moment our eyes fall upon the ballet's program, to know Caroline as she knows herself, and as her friends know her. Unencumbered, for a moment, by the father's surname she has borne all her life, nor yet burdened by the husband's name soon to fall on her shoulders like a mantle of chains, Tudor offers us Caroline, and Caroline alone, as a *subject,* drawing us into empathetic intimacy the moment we see her, still, alone onstage with the Man She Must Marry, as the curtain rises. The other main characters, however, are initially *objects* of our interest (though they will not remain so, revealing themselves to us as they dance); Tudor defines them at the outset as types—but not as mere types. Her Lover, The Man She Must Marry: these descriptive phrases reveal the two men from Caroline's point of view (in his own mind, I imagine, her arrogant fiancé considers himself The Man She Is *Fortunate Enough* to Marry). Tudor's masterstroke is to call the fiancé's former mistress An Episode in His Past, to name her from the man's point of view, revealing the indifference, even contempt, he bears her. No longer a woman to him, she is nothing but an *episode*—left behind, best forgotten. Of the eight other characters, who represent Caroline's friends and relations, two have roles distinct enough that we might hazard names for them. One girl responds with special empathy to Caroline's distress; she seems to be her Best Friend (perhaps also a cousin), and, I imagine, the daughter of the party's hosts. And one boy, another cadet (all the boys but one are costumed as cadets from military academies) twice encounters the Episode in ways that suggest he has feelings for her, though she rejects him coldly—Her Admirer, perhaps. I have no doubt that Tudor himself devised detailed back stories for every dancer. In coaching sessions for an international group of students at Jacob's Pillow in the 1980s (preserved on video), for example,

Sallie Wilson emphasized that Caroline's lover has run away from his military academy to appear uninvited at her party; this is a detail no audience member could ever guess.

"All my ballets are about the bourgeoisie," Tudor is often quoted as saying, and many—including *Lilac Garden, Dim Lustre,* and *Pillar of Fire*—are moreover set around the turn of the twentieth century, the border between the Belle Époque and the Edwardian era, when Tudor's own mother was young, and when he was born. If the frequently reiterated claim by Tudor's admirers that he was the first to make ballets not about princesses and fairies but about "people like us—people we know" seems less and less plausible as the world that he documented recedes ever further into the past (and this is a problem that bedevils revivals of his ballets), the social background of his work is nonetheless entirely real, and nowhere more so than in *Lilac Garden.* Hundreds of "land poor" British families of the aristocracy and gentry—clans whose sometimes vast holdings provided ever less income in a post-agricultural society—were forced to peddle the imprimatur of their social prestige for infusions of cash by marrying their offspring to the spawn of wealthy industrialists. Caroline shares her melancholy match with countless other girls, especially in the decades around the two world wars.

However, we don't care about Caroline's story because it is historically real, but because Tudor makes it so emotionally real. *Lilac Garden* is a tragedy, although it is not tragic in the Aristotelian or Shakespearean sense: neither the gods nor God hover anywhere near Caroline's world (though there must indeed be a curate in the offing to perform the marriage rites, down his port, and take his customary fee). The ballet does not concern the death of a noble figure destroyed by the interweaving of fate and a fatal flaw in his character, but rather the death of hope in the heart of a girl who feels she has no choice but to accept the destiny her parents have chosen for her.

One aspect of *Lilac Garden*'s innovation and achievement is to compress—in only sixteen minutes—the tragic arc of fairy tale or folk tale that we know in *Swan Lake* or *Giselle* and confine it to the bourgeois world of the novel. Yet it is not so much the classic nineteenth-century novelists—Flaubert, Dickens—that Tudor's work suggests, but a modernist: Virginia Woolf. (It is worth noting too that both *Lilac Garden* and *Mrs. Dalloway* are set during parties and are, in very different ways, about what Woolf so charmingly called "party consciousness.") In its hushed and rushed and fleeting, overlapping encounters, *Lilac Garden* comes as close as dancing ever could to evoking the palpable ether of feeling that floats around and among the characters in Woolf's greatest works, *To the Lighthouse* and *Mrs. Dalloway*—as if emotion, even subjectivity itself, were like a vapor that we all emanate, drifting free of us and blending with the thoughts of others. (This aspect of Woolf's art is exquisitely analyzed in Erich Auerbach's essay on her work in his *Mimesis:The Representation of Reality in Western Literature*; in some passages, it could be Tudor's work he discusses.) Like Woolf, Tudor consciously turns away from the grand scale of his predecessors—in Woolf's case, from the epic origins of the novel and the vast canvasses of Eliot or Balzac or Tolstoy; in Tudor's case, from the sweeping narrative and spectacle of the Romantic and Classical narrative ballets—feeling the grand old forms to be inauthentic, hollow. Like Woolf, Tudor devotes himself to seeking a purely, piercingly, even excruciatingly, lyric truth.

Also like Woolf, Tudor will ultimately push his experiments so far that he will neglect fundamental laws of his own art form. *Dim Lustre* (which is in fact often said to recall the work of another modernist writer, namely Proust, based as it is on involuntary memory) "doesn't work" in much the same way that Woolf's *The Waves* doesn't work: each piece seems to wish it had been crafted in some other medium. *The Waves* wants to be a polyphonic radio collage (a form Glenn Gould would not invent until the 1960s), and *Dim Lustre,* with its flashbacks and split-screen effects, wants to be cinema. Indeed, watching some of Tudor's works—but not *Lilac Garden,* and not *The Leaves Are Fading* either—reminds me of Gould's remark on the keyboard music of Elizabethan master Orlando Gibbons (whom Gould often claimed to be his favorite composer, ahead even of Bach): an art of exquisite beauty that nonetheless somehow seems always to lack its ideal means of realization.

Lilac Garden also bears another, extratheatrical, dimension of tragedy. Tudor created the ballet in 1936, when he was not yet twenty-six years old, for Ballet Rambert in London. It is not a young man's ballet, but the work of an old soul, such as you often meet among dancers, and an artist already bracingly mature and assured, almost at one stroke, in his craft. *Lilac Garden* was Tudor's first significant ballet and it remains his greatest extant work, and very possibly his greatest work of all. Nothing for any artist could be more tragic than for his earliest work to be his best; you could just weep to think about it. *Lilac Garden* gave Tudor his voice and revealed to him his vocation. The ballet liberated him to do his life's work, yet it confined him too. In this sense *Lilac Garden* should be for choreographers who come after Tudor inspiring, but also cautionary.

Tudor's lack of productivity, especially in his last decades, is notorious. In at least one interview late in life, Tudor admitted that he had made "maybe ten percent" of the dances other choreographers might have made, because, he said, he wanted never to repeat himself. He is also said to have confessed privately to being afraid he had no more ideas for dances. David Vaughan, in his essay on Tudor for the *International Encyclopedia of Dance,* suggests that Tudor's failure to exercise his craft—to keep his creative muscles in shape, so to speak—may have been primarily responsible for his small output. But I think that the roots of Tudor's problem, in a way he himself perhaps never entirely understood—how intolerable such self-knowledge would be!—lie deep in his very conception of dancing as an expressive medium. And those roots are embedded in the soil of *Lilac Garden.*

Edwin Denby's trenchant critique of the "obvious weaknesses" in Tudor's ballets, memorably expressed in the *Kenyon Review* in 1948—"their shaping force is discontinuous; they have a weak and fragmentary dance impetus; they peter out at the end"—cannot justly be leveled at *Lilac Garden,* for here, and perhaps here alone in Tudor's oeuvre, the discontinuity, the persistent fragmentation of dance impulse, even the drastic diminuendo of the ending, are all utterly intrinsic, essential, to the dance's theme, manner, and mood, since in *Lilac Garden* the main characters' every inner impulse is interrupted, incomplete. As the curtain falls, we know moreover that the heroine's whole life will remain incomplete, for she will never know love fulfilled. *Lilac Garden* is a true masterpiece, a work in which theme, style, and form are perfectly united. But could Denby with justice have intended to include *Lilac Garden* when he wrote of Tudor, "His ballets are not primarily dance conceptions, but their sustained expressive intensity is clearly large-scale"?

To appreciate the peculiarity of Tudor's achievement in *Lilac Garden,* we might try to imagine what would have resulted if Ashton or Balanchine had been assigned the ballet's libretto and its score. When I picture Ashton's *Lilac Garden,* I imagine passages something like the exquisite central trio in the *Enigma Variations* (for the dancers representing composer Edward Elgar, his wife, and his closest male friend), which brims with Tudor-esque feeling— welling emotion scarcely acknowledged and only half expressed—and I realize how much in such passages Ashton owed to Tudor, or perhaps converged with the spirit of his work. Yet I cannot conceive an Ashton version of this ballet that is not utterly different from Tudor's. I think Ashton might have made a sharply observed social comedy, goodnaturedly satirizing the fiancé's social pretensions and Caroline's parents' bad faith. Perhaps, as in his *La Fille mal gardée,* Caroline and her cadet would have somehow outwitted their elders, and love won out in the end.

I am not sure Balanchine would have welcomed this imaginary commission: if there is indeed no place for mothers-in-law in ballet, *Lilac Garden* comes dangerously close to requiring them. At the least, in Tudor's ballet, we can readily imagine Caroline's and her fiancé's parents cooing together offstage right (where the drawing room of the house in which the party is held gives onto a terrace leading to the lilac garden itself), sipping their sherry or Pimm's Cup and toasting the suitability of the match. I also doubt that Balanchine would have approved of Chausson: I think he liked his French composers to be confidently, quintessentially French, like Ravel and Fauré, not self-consciously French in the vast, cold shadow of Wagner, like Chausson. But if Balanchine had accepted, I feel sure he would have threaded the action through dancing conceived as the featured entertainment at Caroline's party. Surely, in her social milieu, the family could have hired a few musicians, so the guests could enjoy waltzes and polkas and quadrilles on the lawn. Imagine the four main characters' encounters woven through and around a sequence of such dances, revealing their feelings to us and to one another as they dance figures that represent, first, *dancing.*

And here we collide with the weird paradox of *Lilac Garden,* and of all Tudor's work: that for him, dancing hardly ever represents, and in some way hardly ever *is,* dancing itself. In *Lilac Garden* dancing represents dialogue, interior monologue, fantasy, social behavior, and many layers of emotion, inner conflict, and underlying motivation. This is why with *Lilac Garden* Tudor is always credited with having invented the "psychological ballet" (in my view, an imprecise and inadequate formulation—but that's another essay). The closest in *Lilac Garden* that Tudor comes to the scenario I imagine Balanchine pursuing is one passage midway through the ballet that brings all the cast onstage briefly in a circling formation. Yet this moment represents social dancing only vestigially, really, it is more an image of the characters all conversing in the garden at the same time, and an abstract sign of the pressure of social conformity that constricts their behavior and emotional self-expression. But in Balanchine's ballets, no matter where they fall on a continuum with narrative and abstraction as its poles, dancing is always first and foremost dancing. Again and again, Balanchine builds a ballet on the foundation of a fictive occasion for social dance—*Cotillon, La Valse, Vienna Waltzes, Liebeslieder Walzer,* the *Davidsbündlertänze.* . . . The feeling of real social dances made sublime as Balanchine transforms them into theatrical dances graces even ballets, such as *Agon,* or *Emeralds,* or *Symphony in C,* that are not explicitly narrative. Above all, I am sure that if Balanchine or Ashton had made *Lilac Garden,* the dance would have been about some positive action, about something that *happens* in the course of the ballet onstage before our eyes.

The disquieting, almost eerie sense that dancing itself is secondary within Tudor's intuitive conception of the art of making dances—that dancing is always somehow overshadowed, or at one remove—infuses many of his exquisitely poetic titles: for Tudor, ballet is *echoing* trumpets, *fading* leaves, *dim* lustre, *dark* elegies, a play of *shadows*—or even this impossible chimera: a shadow of the wind. Something you can't see; something not there. Yet what Balanchine's whole art has to teach us above all is that dancing is something that *happens*—only here, only now. *Lilac Garden,* however, is ultimately not about an event that will happen—the wedding, which will take place soon after the curtain falls—but about things that *don't* happen. The discarded mistress never succeeds in confronting or unburdening herself to her former lover; the young cadet who is clearly attracted to her never has a chance to woo her; Caroline's fiancé does not permit her a proper farewell with any of her friends; and, most piercingly, Caroline and the boy who loves her never share the last kiss they long for.

It is a sign of Tudor's peculiar genius, his originality, and his wild courage, that he builds his ballet around a void. At its dramatic and musical peak, a great crescendo that recalls the bare solo violin theme with which Chausson's score begins—when any other choreographer would have filled the stage with motion—Tudor with exquisite skill sweeps the entire cast into that famous still tableau, with Caroline swooning in her fiancé's arms. For a moment, nothing happens onstage except the music—all the action is transferred into the anguished hearts of the audience. Then Caroline walks out of time, stepping through two-thirds of a small circle, reaching first toward the figure of her fiancé's mistress, then toward her true love. She hesitates, then retraces her steps, as if in a scrap of film run backward. Time starts again. Caroline stands still as her cadet rushes in and presses a sprig of lilac into her trembling fingers. Her fiancé reenters to wrap a short cape around her shoulders. With tiny gestures of one hand, she bids farewell to her friends, all lined up in couples to her right. The Man She Must Marry interrupts her goodbyes to lead her off into his life (films from the 1940s show Tudor in the role exiting with a smug smirk, patting Nora Kaye's arm patronizingly). Overcome by grief, the Best Friend collapses, dropping her face into her hands—just as Caroline has done earlier, in a trio during which the Best Friend literally hauls her up by one shoulder, as if to say, *Oh, don't give in!*— and is led off by one of the boys. Caroline's lover, his back to us, head turned and tilted down to one side, gripping one wrist in a soldier's "at ease" position, remains alone as the curtain falls.

I FIRST SAW *Lilac Garden* danced in a revival staged by the late Sallie Wilson for American Ballet Theatre in the company's fall 2000 season at City Center with Ekaterina Shelkanova—a beautiful soloist who unaccountably vanished from ABT not long thereafter—as Caroline. The ballet was programmed mainly that season as the middle ballet on weekend matinees, which many commented seemed to ill befit the work's dignity and its place in Ballet Theatre's history, and the family audiences that the company has tried to court for weekend afternoon shows since inaugurating its autumn seasons in 1997.

Nonetheless, the experience overwhelmed me. Never having seen *Lilac Garden* before, I could not say if it was a great performance; I think it was a pretty good one. Afterward, I could hardly speak. At intermission, standing uncomfortably close to several critics (including the editor of this volume), I dissolved in tears, and had to leave the theater. Somehow, I did not have it in me to stay for excerpts from *The Nutcracker*. I felt as though Tudor himself were standing in front of me, grasping me by the shoulders, shaking me hard, and saying in my face, *Do your work! Do your own work! Don't care what anybody else thinks!* (I have no idea what Tudor was in fact like as a mentor to younger choreographers.) That matinee remains the single most emotionally intense moment I have lived at the ballet, ever.

Lilac Garden, like many of Tudor's ballets, tells us that it does not make much sense for one woman or man to love another. Love is likely to be hopeless, agony. It makes even less sense, really, to love a work of art, which can never care for us, can never love us back. But at least if you love a poem or a novel you can often reread it; and if you love a painting or sculpture you can visit it in a museum, perhaps even keep it in your home. If you love a building, you can walk around it, or even inside it. If you love a piece of music, you can play it or sing it, and listen to recordings of it, which, with a little imagination, bring the score almost back to life.

To love a dance makes the least sense of all, for you can hardly ever see the dances that you cherish; they exist almost all the time only as afterimages; and video or film, compared to the living choreography on stage, is nothing. But I love *Lilac Garden* with all my heart, and I think I shall love it until the day I die.

—Previously unpublished

H. T. PARKER
Genée's Cool Charm

The most popular English dancer of the first years of the twentieth century, Adeline Genée (1878–1970) was actually Danish, becoming a principal at the Royal Danish Ballet at the age of seventeen. In 1897 she accepted a six-week engagement at the Empire Theatre in London's Leicester Square and stayed on, a huge star, for more than ten years, her most famous role being Swanilda in Coppélia. *She toured with great success in America—first appearing in a Ziegfeld hit,* The Soul Kiss; *the young Astaires saw it again and again—and in Australia. In 1920 she was instrumental in founding the institution that eventually became the Royal Academy of Dance, of which she remained president until her retirement in 1954. (Her replacement was Margot Fonteyn.) In 1950 she became a dame of the British Empire, the first dancer to be so honored. (See Max Beerbohm, page 1292.)*

Adeline Genée was to the very day of her retirement the dancer, par excellence, for cool and cultivated spirits. To the end she kept her hold upon the public that liked her devotion to the classic ballet and that was ever a little dubious over the newer and franker dancing of Isadora Duncan with her train of imitators, and of the passionate and thrilling Russians. Miss Duncan and her progeny danced in a fashion of their own that has widened the expressive scope and vividness of the dance, mated it to new rhythms and new music, subdued its virtuosity and increased its humanity. When the Russians danced, it was with the strange and exotic savor, the mingling of simplicity and sophistication, the passion and the mystery—to us of the Western World—that are in most of the applied arts of the Slav. Alone among the dancers of the first rank that we in America have known, Genée perpetuated the traditions of the classic school—of the dancing that descended from the eighteenth century into the nineteenth, that flowered in the golden years of Taglioni and Ellsler, Crisi and Cerito; fell away into the sterile and finical virtuosity that long flourished on the stages of Paris, Rome, and Petrograd; only to rise reincarnated for us of America and England in Genée.

By chance or design—much more probably the latter—she emphasized this descent and heightened this similitude by her choice of pieces. In one she danced and mimed as La Camargo, the illustrious dancer of the Paris of Louis XV, who widened the technical range of the ballet and who, beyond all her sisters of the eighteenth century, clothed her dancing in her own traits and spirit. In another, Genée danced in the ballet of the nuns' ghostly temptations from Meyerbeer's opera, *Robert the Devil*. It was a ballet of the thirties and the forties, a "real French ballet" in white tulle skirts and fleshings, as our grandparents would have called it. In such ballets did the dancers of the golden age move. Between whiles, too, Genée disported herself, with her own adept faculty as a comédienne, in light interludes, in fanciful or humorous dances of character.

For those that know and care for the classic technique of the dance and for those that only half suspect, out of quickened feeling, its exactions and felicities, Genée's dancing in the ballet from *Robert* was high, rare pleasure. She accomplished in it nearly every possible feat of virtuosity in a flawless perfection that seemed to rise with the difficulty of the achievement. Her light bounds, her graceful swirls, her rhythmed steps about the stage seemed aerial and bodiless. Her pirouettes were little rhapsodies in technique. Her poses flowed into beauty and grace of line that suggested no effort, that bore not a trace of stiffness. Artifice they were, but spontaneous and beautiful artifice. The subtler attributes and graces of the old dancing shone in her— in the varied poise of her head and shoulders, in the management of her hands, in the keeping of her body in flowing or arrested arabesque. She accomplished all these things with an ease, a sureness, an elegance, a completeness that were style in itself in conscious but unobtruded perfection. Then entered the personality of the dancer to glamour this dancing, in the narrow sense of the word, with beauty and with charm. Meyerbeer's ballet in spite of its elaborate program of temptations expresses nothing to the imaginations of the present but the beauty with which the dancer may clothe it. Dancing in it, nowadays, is "absolute" dancing existing for its own sake and making its appeal in its own right in the fashion of "absolute" music. Since there is no passion or mystery in the music or the imaginings behind, it was at one with Genée's own spirit. She sought the "absolute" and abstract quality of the dance—the body weaving beautiful patterns upon the air, then animating and illuminating them with the glow and the charm of the spirit behind. Of such disembodied beauty was her dancing in *Robert*.

The music of "La Camargo" was adapted from eighteenth century sources by Miss Dora Bright. The ballet was set on the stage in a boudoir wherein Boucher's fat and rosy nymphs looked down from the walls. It was diversified by entrances of Louis XV himself, a distressed mother, a half-grateful and a half-anxious soldier. It bade Genée mime as well as dance. She was La Camargo, momentarily melancholy and introspective, while over this disillusion she threw the wistful charm of face and motion which was the counterpart of merriment in the dancer's temperament. She had occasion also to make La Camargo arch, playful, merry, even with the great king who came to see her dance and who was fain to walk a smiling gavotte with her. As it happened, too, the distressed mother and the anxious soldier were no other than friends and companions of La Camargo's village youth, and so Genée could bubble with surprised pleasure at sight of them once more and play at being a peasant girl again.

Genée mimed with many of the conventional signs of the classic pantomime; but she softened and refined them with her individual charm, made her face the clear mirror of what they would reflect, and kept them flowing with an elegant and airy lightness. She could not mime deep and passionate moods, but she could fill surfaces with beautiful light and shade. She danced, too, as La Camargo, in the full flowing skirt and the high bodice that dancers wore in those days, danced in the very entrechats—the crossings of the feet in air—that Camargo herself invented, and in many another fashion that the eighteenth century may or may not have known. Over this dancing she wove the wonted beauty and charm that were in all she did; while costume, surroundings, the little tale, and the pleasant illusion of the eighteenth century touched both with elegance, with fragrance.

—from *Eighth Notes*, 1922

NANCY DALVA

Throw Tolstoy from the Train: Boris Eifman

Born in 1946, Boris Eifman went to ballet school in Kishinev (Moldavia) and then to the Leningrad choreographic conservatory. By 1976 he had founded his own company in St. Petersburg, focusing on dances intended to attract young audiences, often employing rock music (like Pink Floyd, for something called Bivocality). *He achieved international success with a series of highly sensational, full-evening ballets on mostly literary themes:* The Brothers Karamazov, Don Quixote, The Russian Hamlet, Pinocchio, *and* Anna Karenina, *among others, though perhaps his best-known work is based (loosely) on the tragic life of the ballerina Olga Spessivtseva (see page 1122). Critical opinion of his work is sharply divided between those who think it is a revolutionary antidote to the supposed staleness of classical ballet and those who, in the words of the critic Eric Taub, think of him as "kitsch masquerading as profundity."*

All good ballets are alike. Each bad ballet is bad in its own way. Or ways. For instance, the ballet Boris Eifman calls *Anna Karenina* is vulgar, meretricious, rapacious, and lewd, a low-brow spectacle cloaked in high brow pretensions. Rather than reminding the viewer of Tolstoy, the author of a novel of the same title, or even of Freud, with whom Eifman seems to confuse him (he notes, in the program, Anna's "psychoerotic essence"), the work is reminiscent of the MacMillan of *Manon* (though that louche ballet is a paragon of delicacy next to this one) tempered with the subtle elegance of the World Wide Wrestling Federation's genteel pageantry.

I admit I was vexed with the choreographer going into this, for I have not forgiven him for his portrayal of Tanaquil LeClerq in his ballet about—or I should say, "about"—George Balanchine, made for the New York City Ballet for the Balanchine centenary. But I resolved to emulate the open minded-ness of Tolstoy's concert-going Levin.

He, you will recall, is actually a character in the novel, although not in the ballet, where neither he nor his wife, Kitty, appears (sparing us a child-birth scene). There are, however, some characters in the ballet I could not quite place—for instance, two corps of leather queens and leather goons for whom I searched the novel's pages in vain upon returning home after the performance. But there, in Part Seven, Chapter V (which would be p. 684

of the recent Pevear/Volokhonsky translation, in the Penguin Classics edition), Levin attends a matinee. "Both pieces were new and in the new spirit," Tolstoy writes, "and Levin wanted to form his own opinion of them. . . . [he] resolved to listen as closely and conscientiously as possible. He tried not to get distracted and spoil his impression. . . ." Me, too, and it wasn't easy.

Eifman chooses to set the opening scene of his ballet to the same music Balanchine chose for *Serenade,* the first ballet he made in America, and well enough known to me that I could run it in my mind while watching the Eifman—or to be more precise, I couldn't not run it. At the opening, a little boy is playing with a train. (The whole thing takes place, basically, in a set that is variations on a train station. A ballroom that sees frequent service is an inversion of it, and the whole thing reeks of foretelling and doom and sexual imagery unknown to readers of the novel, who actually do not know in advance that Anna is going to kill herself, as neither does she.) A beautiful woman in a gorgeous velvet cocoon coat parts her legs and opens her arms, and drops the coat at the exact moment the girls in *Serenade* snap out of parallel position.

I doubt this is a coincidence. Eifman is smart, and Eifman is talented. He is also an extrovert, without any seeming self-knowledge, or indeed a sense of humor. (He is not, for instance, self-knowing in the way Liberace was, though certainly given to flash.) It probably hasn't occurred to him that but for politeness, one could fall out of one's seat laughing at some of his excesses, like the sex scene where Anna engages erotically with her bedframe, or the one where she drinks a potion the way Alice does in Wonderland and has a bizarre hallucination in which, seemingly naked (nude unitard, and, let's not forget, toe shoes), she dances a section of something not unlike Jerome Robbins's *The Cage,* if Robbins had included a chorus of the damned (also naked). After this, she gets carried off stage, stiff as a board.

These scenes occur after Anna, who in the Eifman ballet is married to the mob—or at any rate, to a domineering older man who looks like a mobster—has fallen in love with a younger man, a real hottie, who likes to paint her when not attending parties in variously hued tailcoats. Although he never scorns her that I could see, and her ominous spouse still seems eager to have her in his household and underwrite her lavish wardrobe, she quickly—and the second act goes pretty fast—falls into an inexplicable decline, ending with her suicide, but not before she despairs in a down spot, and some swirling snow.

There are two good scenes in the ballet. The first occurs when Anna and her lover, of course named Vronsky, are seen in their separate rooms, spotlighted on either side of the stage. Unfortunately, he is on a couch and she is on her bed and they are wracked with desire, but that does not diminish the impact of their moving, though apart, in exact synchrony. Then they dance out of their rooms and into the middle of the stage, and the moment is totally destroyed. The other really good scene is—I am not making this up—the scene in which the company depicts the train under which—or actually, into the midst of which—Anna is going to throw herself. For one thing, the score—a patchwork of Tchaikovsky, who like Tolstoy is conveniently long dead and thus unable to protest, or for that matter, sue—gives way to train sounds. Chugga-chugga, chugga-chugga.

To this inexorable sound, Eifman choreographs, very cleverly indeed, a little Constructivist ballet, quite forceful and, for a change, formal. Movement, and not a lot of expression layered on to it and into it and under it and over it, inspires a visceral response. Drama, not melodrama. Then Anna jumps from the train station platform, and the next thing you know, her corpse is being wheeled center stage on a luggage trolley. Curtain. And mad applause. Just, in fact, what Levin heard that day he went to the concert. "He was in utter perplexity when the piece ended," writes Tolstoy, "and felt great fatigue from such strained but in no way rewarded attention. Loud applause came from all sides. . . . Wishing to explain his perplexity by means of other people's impressions, Levin began to walk about, looking for connoisseurs. . . ."

These were not hard to come by at City Center, where one Eifman devotee, in from the suburbs, told me, "This is what ballet needs. Ballet needs passion." What could one say? To complain about this ballet is like complaining that *Oliver* distorts Charles Dickens, or that *Les Miz* misconstrues Victor Hugo, or that *Cats* is a misreading of T. S. Eliot, or that *The Phantom of the Opera*—well, you get the idea, though at least those entertainments don't pretend to be close readings. To take Eifman's *Anna Karenina* seriously is to give it too much credit. It isn't appalling, it is merely atrocious, and successful. The dancers, by the way, are very glamorous, and very good at dancing Eifman. They chew up the scenery. He chewed up a novel.

—from *danceviewtimes*, 2005

EDWIN DENBY

Against Meaning in Ballet

Some of my friends who go to ballet and like the entertainment it gives are sorry to have it classed among the fine arts and discussed, as the other fine arts are, intellectually. Though I do not agree with them, I have a great deal of sympathy for their anti-intellectual point of view. The dazzle of a ballet performance is quite reason enough to go; you see handsome young people—girls and boys with a bounding or delicate animal grace—dancing among the sensual luxuries of orchestral music and shining stage decoration and in the glamour of an audience's delight. To watch their lightness and harmonious ease, their clarity and boldness of motion, is a pleasure. And ballet dancers' specialties are their elastic tautness, their openness of gesture, their gaiety of leaping, beating, and whirling, their slow soaring flights. Your senses enjoy directly how they come forward and closer to you, or recede upstage, turning smaller and more fragile; how the boys and girls approach one another or draw apart, how they pass close without touching or entwine their bodies in stars of legs and arms—all the many ways they have of dancing together. You see a single dancer alone showing her figure from all sides deployed in many positions, or you see a troop of them dancing in happy unison. They are graceful, well mannered, and they preserve at best a personal dignity, a civilized modesty of deportment that keeps the sensual stimulus from being foolishly cute or commercially sexy. The beauty of young women's and young men's bodies, in motion or in momentary repose, is exhibited in an extraordinarily friendly manner.

When you enjoy ballet this way—and it is one of the ways everybody does enjoy it who likes to go—you don't find any prodigious difference between one piece and another, except that one will have enough dancing to satisfy and another not enough, one will show the dancers to their best advantage and another will tend to make them look a little more awkward and unfree. Such a happy ballet lover is puzzled by the severities of critics. He wonders why they seem to find immense differences between one piece and another, or between one short number and another, or between the proficiency of two striking dancers. The reasons the critics give, the relation of the steps to the music, the sequence of the effects, the sharply differentiated intellectual meaning they ascribe to dances, all this he will find either fanciful or plainly absurd.

Has ballet an intellectual content? The ballet lover with the point of view I am describing will concede that occasionally a soloist gives the sense of characterizing a part, that a few ballets even suggest a story with a psychological interest, a dramatic suspense, or a reference to real life. In such a case, he grants, ballet may be said to have an intellectual content. But these ballets generally turn out to be less satisfying to watch because the dancers do less ballet dancing in them; so, he concludes, one may as well affirm broadly that ballet does not properly offer a "serious" comment on life and that it is foolish to look for one.

I do not share these conclusions, and I find that my interest in the kind of meaning a ballet has leads me to an interest in choreography and dance technique. But I have a great deal of sympathy for the general attitude I have described. It is the general attitude that underlies the brilliant reviews of Théophile Gautier, the French poet of a hundred years ago, who is by common consent the greatest of ballet critics. He said of himself that he was a man who believed in the visible world. And his reviews are the image of what an intelligent man of the world saw happening on the stage. They are perfectly open; there is no private malignity in them; he is neither pontifical nor "popular"; there is no jargon and no ulterior motive. He watches not as a specialist in ballet, but as a responsive Parisian. The easy flow of his sentences is as much a tribute to the social occasion as it is to the accurate and elegant ease of ballet dancers in action. His warmth of response to personal varieties of grace and to the charming limits of a gift, his amusement at the pretensions of a libretto or the pretensions of a star, his sensual interest in the line of a shoulder and bosom, in the elasticity of an ankle, in the cut of a dress place the ballet he watches in a perspective of civilized good sense.

Ballet for him is an entertainment—a particularly agreeable way of spending an evening in town; and ballet is an art, it is a sensual refinement that delights the spirit. Art for him is not a temple of humanity one enters with a reverent exaltation. Art is a familiar pleasure and Gautier assumes that one strolls through the world of art as familiarly as one strolls through Paris, looking about in good weather or bad, meeting congenial friends or remarkable strangers, and one's enemies, too. Whether in art or in Paris, a civilized person appreciates seeing a gift and is refreshed by a graceful impulse; there is a general agreement about what constitutes good workmanship; and one takes one's neighbors' opinions less seriously than their behavior. Gautier differentiates keenly between good and bad ballet; but he differentiates as a matter of personal taste. He illustrates the advantages the sensual approach to ballet can have for an intelligence of exceptional sensual susceptibility and for a man of large sensual complacency.

Gautier assumes that all that people need do to enjoy art is to look and listen with ready attention and trust their own sensual impressions. He is right. But when they hear that ballet is an elaborate art with a complicated technique and tradition, many modest people are intimidated and are afraid to trust their own spontaneous impressions. They may have been to a few performances, they may have liked it when they saw it, but now they wonder if maybe they liked the wrong things and missed the right ones. Before going again, they want it explained, they want to know what to watch for and exactly what to feel. If it is really real art and fine great art, it must be studied before it is enjoyed; that is what they remember from school. In school the art of poetry is approached by a strictly rational method, which teaches you what to enjoy and how to discriminate. You are taught to analyze the technique and the relation of form to content; you are taught to identify and "evaluate" stylistic, biographical, economic, and anthropological influences, and told what is great and what is minor so you can prepare yourself for a great reaction or for a minor one. The effect of these conscientious labors on the pupils is distressing. For the rest of their lives they can't face a page of verse without experiencing a complete mental blackout. They don't enjoy, they don't discriminate, they don't even take the printed words at face value. For the rest of their lives they go prying for hidden motives back of literature, for psychological, economic, or stylistic explanations, and it never occurs to them to read the words and respond to them as they do to the nonsense of current songs or the nonsense of billboards by the roadside. Poetry is the same thing—it's words, only more interesting, more directly and richly sensual.

The first taste of art is spontaneously sensual, it is the discovery of an absorbing entertainment, an absorbing pleasure. If you ask anyone who enjoys ballet or any other art how he started, he will tell you that he enjoyed it long before he knew what it meant or how it worked. I remember the intense pleasure reading Shelley's *Adonais* gave me as a boy—long before I followed accurately the sense of the words; and once, twenty years later, I had two kittens who would purr in unison and watch me bright-eyed when I read them Shakespeare's *Sonnets,* clearly pleased by the compliment and by the sounds they heard. Would they have enjoyed them better if they had understood them? The answer is, they enjoyed them very much. Many a college graduate might have envied them.

I don't mean that so orderly and respectable an entertainment as that of art is made for the susceptibilities of kittens or children. But consider how the enormous orderly and respectable symphonic public enjoys its listening, enjoys it without recognizing themes, harmonies, or timbres, without evaluating the style historically or even knowing if the piece is being played as the composer intended. What do they hear when they hear a symphony?

Why, they hear the music, the interesting noises it makes. They follow the form and the character of it by following their direct acoustic impressions.

Susceptibility to ballet is a way of being susceptible to animal grace of movement. Many people are highly susceptible to the pleasure of seeing grace of movement who have never thought of going to ballet to look for it. They find it instead in watching graceful animals, animals of many species at play, flying, swimming, racing, and leaping and making gestures of affection toward one another, or watchful in harmonious repose. And they find it too in seeing graceful young people on the street or in a game or at the beach or in a dance hall, boys and girls in exuberant health who are doing pretty much what the charming animals do, and are as unconscious of their grace as they. Unconscious grace of movement is a natural and impermanent gift, like grace of features or of voice or of character, a lucky accident you keep meeting with all your life wherever you are. To be watching grace puts people into a particularly amiable frame of mind. It is an especially attractive form of feeling social consciousness.

But if ballet is a way of entertaining the audience by showing them animal grace, why is its way of moving so very unanimal-like and artificial? For the same reason that music has evolved so very artificial a way of organizing its pleasing noises. Art takes what in life is an accidental pleasure and tries to repeat and prolong it. It organizes, diversifies, characterizes, through an artifice that men evolve by trial and error. Ballet nowadays is as different from an accidental product as a symphony at Carnegie Hall is different from the noises Junior makes on his trumpet upstairs or Mary Ann with comb and tissue paper, sitting on the roof, the little monkey.

You don't have to know about ballet to enjoy it; all you have to do is look at it. If you are susceptible to it, and a good many people evidently are, you will like spontaneously some things you see and dislike others, and quite violently too. You may be so dazzled at first by a star or by the general atmosphere, you don't really know what happened; you may on the other hand find the performance absurdly stiff and affected except for a few unreasonable moments of intense pleasure; but if you are susceptible you will find you want to go again. When you go repeatedly, you begin to recognize what it is you like, and watch for it the next time. That way you get to know about ballet, you know a device of ballet because you have responded to it, you know that much at least about it. Even if nobody agrees with you, you still know it for yourself.

That the composite effect of ballet is a complex one is clear enough. Its devices make a long list, wherever you start. These devices are useful to give a particular moment of a dance a particular expression. The dancers in action give it at that moment a direct sensual reality. But if you watch often and watch attentively, the expressive power of some ballets and dancers will fascinate, perturb, and delight far more than that of others, and will keep alive in your imagination much more intensely long after you have left the theater. It is this aftereffect that dancers and ballets are judged by, by their audience.

To some of my friends the images ballet leaves in the imagination suggest, as poetry does, an aspect of the drama of human behavior. For others such ballet images keep their sensual mysteriousness, "abstract," unrationalized, and magical. Anyone who cannot bear to contemplate human behavior except from a rationalistic point of view had better not try to "understand" the exhilarating excitement of ballet; its finest images of our fate are no easier to face than those of poetry itself, though they are no less beautiful.

—from *Ballet*, March 1949

EDWIN DENBY

Superficial Thoughts on Foreign Classicism

Everybody knows that the principles of classicism are identical the world over. A ballet audience on any continent recognizes the same steps and the same elaborate theater apparatus, and knows what to expect in *Giselle* or *Swan Lake*. Everybody wants it that way and is proud of it, and with reason. And yet from experience everybody knows too that an American classic company as it dances a ballet has a general look that is not at all the same as that of a British company, and a Paris company is quite different from either. Different again is a Danish company, or an Italian, and further differences appear, no doubt, the farther you travel. It bothers the fans, this paradox.

It doesn't bother the general public. When a foreign company comes to a city accustomed to its own local one, the general public loves the exotic note, the picturesque stars, the novel repertory. Not so a fan. You can see him in any ballet capital, just such a real hard-shelled passionate fan hunched up morosely as a visiting troupe performs a piece he knows and loves. He can see that the company has gifts and works hard—but call that classicism! A few seats farther down is the other type of fan, the sociable kind, darting her sharp look brightly all over the stage at the funny foreigners, nudging her girlfriend and giggling, "Did you see his face when he offered that rose?"

When I first heard fans abroad bitterly resent our classicism, bitterly and inexplicably, I supposed they were being something like defensive or impe-rialist or chauvinist about their own; but later when I heard Americans com-plain as bitterly about European ballet, I realized it couldn't be the reason. The feelings of a fan about ballet anywhere in the world are deeper and sweeter than politics or economics. They are direct, more like the feelings of a passionate coffee drinker newly arrived in a strange country and for the first time tasting the brew that there is called coffee. Just as the cut of a pair of pants which is sheer heaven to an ardent sharpie in one country is merely risible to the sharpie in another, so the sociable fan can't help giggling at unexpected behavior in a familiar spot.

Unexpected for me was some of the behavior onstage when I saw a piece called *Suite de Danses* at the Paris Opéra. The orchestra was playing a familiar Chopin piano piece, and when the curtain went up I expected some sort of *Sylphides*. Sure enough there was the moonlight and there was a man dressed for *Sylphides*. But instead of his standing in a grove with the demented bevy of girls in white, there were a fountain basin, and steps rising, and platforms, and more steps—and high upstage center on a raised podium in a vivid white spotlight was this man by himself. He executed a few beautiful Fokin-esque ports de bras, rose on half-toe, and then, perfectly satisfied with him-self, walked offstage on the third floor. Below in the dry fountain basin a huddle of partly grown kids knelt in an undisciplined lineup with one gan-gling leg extended. A quarter of an hour later when they got up, their little knees had gone stiff. And as they began to dance they kept glancing down at their knees and then out at us with slumlike grimaces of disdain and shrugged up their little shoulders. Finally came a polonaise for all the big girls in white. But they weren't at all Fokine's moony young ladies. These self-respecting Parisian dancers each brought with her her own cavalier to keep her company. To supply so many hadn't been easy, and some of the part-ners looked neither youthful nor attractive in their walk; one tubby one, to give himself a more romantic look, had shadowed his cheeks so heavily that he seemed to have a three-day beard. Each man, regardless of shape, was dressed in a short *Sylphides* suit and wore a long pageboy wig of the loveliest hair. The older ones looked at the audience rakishly. And the audience applauded and cheered.

Evidently the audience had seen something quite different from what I had. And as I went home I imagined that to a Paris fan our own *Sylphides* might seem quite as ridiculous. He might point out that without changing a single sacrosanct step of Fokine's, our Anglo-American versions have

become—God knows how—as respectably dreamy as a bath-soap advertisement. No, they aren't always, but now and then they are, aren't they?
And I went on imagining a Paris fan's dismay at the sight of our clean-washed
girls, looking each one as like all the others as possible, instead of (as in
Paris) as unlike. How can you tell them apart, he might say—it was exactly
what I had heard in Paris at the first visit of Sadler's Wells—what fun can it
be to be a fan that way? I have heard the British answer: "We are perfectly
well pleased, thank you—so self-indulgent the French, such a pity too, great
institution, the Opéra." As for the Americans, when they see a huge gifted
company on the vast stage in Paris, they wonder that the Opéra public likes
its dance pleasure of so small a kind, inspected as though through an opera
glass, a limb or a waist at a time. At home we like the way a company looks
dancing as a company, a bold, large, and sweeping pleasure.

When I told a lady abroad that I thought it strange that classic dancing
should look so different from one country to another she said: "But everything else looks different too; it would be very strange if ballet didn't." And
when I returned, I heard Balanchine say: "When I first came to Paris from
Russia, Diaghilev took me to the best restaurants, famous for their fine food.
The waiter put before me a little dish with something particular on it. I
complained: 'You call this fine food? I want a big plate. And bring me potatoes and beef and pork and turnips and cabbage and more potatoes.' And
then I mixed them all up on the plate, and it was what I was used to. And I ate
it and said to Diaghilev, 'Yes, they have very fine food here.'" Ballet is like
that. People like what they are used to.

And people are used to changes, too. It is changing all the time. Americans used to be used to the Ballet Russe style, now they are used to the
American style—though a few fans still object to the change. Champs-
Elysées style has modified the Sadler's Wells. I have heard French dancers
sigh for the "great teachers" of New York, and Americans enthusiastic about
schools in Paris. The Danes are delighted to have Vera Volkova teach them a
style opposite to their own, the Italians and Turks have imported English
teachers, and the English swear by the Cecchetti method.

But an American fan who travels in Europe from one ballet city to
another sees, too, that the general look of the different companies in performance, different though it is, is more alike from capital to capital than the
general look of a crowd moving in the street in the morning; the movement
of the crowd, I mean, differs even more from one country to another. In
Copenhagen the crowd has an easy stride, strong in the waist, light on the
feet, with a hint of a sailor's roll. As they pass they look at one another briefly
and trustingly without moving the face. They enjoy walking. In Paris they
hate to walk. Each individual is going in an individual direction, at a different
speed. And they hate it, but they refuse to bump. They carry their bodies

with respect like a large parcel of dishes: sort of low. They jab their heels at the pavement, in short steps, each person differently; they trip, and strut, and jiggle, and waddle, and trudge, and limp; and every now and then a beauty passes among them sailing like a swan or stalking like a fine flamingo, completely isolated from the others. They notice her at once, but they refuse to look, and as she passes, every individual in the crowd from fifteen years old to sixty-five becomes more intensely himself or herself. That is their form of homage.

All over Italy half the population is constantly walking up and down hills carrying babies or parcels of food, a steady movement like breathing. The other half is in the street, the men leaning or relaxed in harmonious assurance, or lounging; the girls pass by just a little quickly, with an easy delicacy. Everybody enjoys everybody else's beauty—it belongs to everyone who sees it; they enjoy it all their life over and over with the same pleasure. One could guess that they had invented ballet. They know how to lift the waist imperceptibly as they turn half in profile, how to show a back, hold the head, raise an arm, point a foot, or extend a hand; they love doing it and seeing it. And they mistrust a person who won't make a scene; they all make them without getting confused or losing their sweetness; they do by couples, by threes, or by crowds at ticket booths, and breathe more easily for it. The only thing they will not tolerate is hurry and being hurried. They have no love for losing their habits of behavior; it makes them savage.

In London the crowd in the morning walks well, orderly, and the ears look delicious. Looking at the face isn't done. But then the beauties one would want to enjoy are in taxis, down from the country for the day. Truck drivers and dock workers have a curious autochthonous color sense—in subtle off-shade combinations—in their work clothes. After midnight, however, gentle monstrous creatures appear from underground, hideously primped and perfectly pleased with themselves, tell each other their secrets, and vanish, as natural to the soil as the creatures of Alice's dream.

As for the New York crowd, we all know it, and it doesn't resemble any of these at all.

How different the more consciously social movements are—coming into a room at a party, shaking hands, behaving at table, or sitting in a chair—everybody knows from foreign movies anyway. Dancers who grow up in a city naturally move in the way people around them have moved all their life. And that makes a difference in the overall or general look of a whole company, even if it doesn't show in one dancer doing a particular step. But classicism is so naked and enlarged a way of moving that any tiny unconscious residue in it of something else than the step—the residue of habit or of character—shows. And sometimes is beautiful. A dancer cannot intend such an unconscious overtone, for it is beautiful only if it is deeper than any intention. But a ballet fan can sense it and be moved. A faint reminiscence of a gesture seen with wonder as a child and long forgotten, an overtone characteristic of a city in the motion of someone one has loved and forgotten, returns sometimes in a dancer's innocent motion and makes its poignancy the more irresistible. Natural enough that an audience feels closest to the dancing of girls and boys of its own country. But the point of classicism is that local color is by an insistent discipline driven deeper and deeper into the unconscious imagination. There it becomes innocent, out of this world, unnationalist, and unsentimental.

I don't believe in an intentional local overtone in classicism. I believe that a good classicist should have less than as little as possible. But I never saw a homogeneous company that—besides tending to show a single style of teaching—didn't also in its general look show a common regional overtone. In a home company a fan becomes used to it and aware only of classicism; but when a foreign company first arrives the same fan is overpowered by its strangeness, its exoticism, and this keeps him from seeing the real classic dancing. It is very annoying. It takes time for this first confusion to wear off. That is why European fans respond more freely to our ballets with a local-color subject than to our classic ones: the general American look is plausible to them in an American number; in a classic number they want the unconscious regional overtone they are used to, as well as the conscious school style they are used to, too; that is the note which for them makes classicism plausible. Even Diaghilev, when he first came to Paris, had no success with *Giselle;* everybody adored the Russians when they were "barbaric" and "primitive," but in classicism these qualities seemed disturbing.

But I believe that fans here in New York are more and more ready to accept the initial shock of foreignness in classicism, curious to find out what a peregrine style may contain either of stimulus to our own or else of interest merely to widen a balletgoer's sense of the scope of international classicism. It was a similar curiosity that took me to Europe a few years ago to look around. Stay-at-home New Yorkers, however, have been able to see about as much as I. The only important Western company that has not been here is the Royal Danish Ballet, the importance of which I thought was its freshness and straightforwardness in presenting the touching (and soundly built) romantic ballets of Bournonville, of which no ballet fan can see too many. The choreography is simple, but original; the pace is easy, but sure; the dances are seen with a beautiful clarity; and the sentiment is both real and modest. It is a pleasure to see how simple, how chaste ballet can be and still go to your heart. A Galeotti ballet of 1786 (*The Caprices of Cupid and the Maître de Ballet*), in which a few steps have been, presumably at a later date, raised to real toe steps, but no other change has been made, is still alive and amusing as a piece, and even simpler in choreography. Their *Giselle* and *Coppélia* are the best one can see in their mime passages, but I don't care so much for the dance versions. I saw only two pieces of the modern repertory, and one of them, *Etudes,* seemed to me effective and clean, but not very distinguished. I imagine, however, that the full-length Bournonville ballets would have in New York the sort of gentle innocence we never see onstage, and that many of us would be happy not to resist.

But this extraordinary voyage back into the world of romantic ballet on which the Danish company can take one, refreshing though it is, is not an aspect of contemporary classicism. I wish one of their great mimes, Karstens or Larsen, could teach in New York. But the traditional atmosphere, the quiet ballet studios they work in, are very different from ours. What I wished very much, too, was that we could import the secure financial organization of those great European ensembles, which is founded on the practical experience of ballet as a long-term investment, analogous to the conception of our own cultural foundations. But the more an American looks at ballet abroad, where it is rooted in a city's life, the more he realizes that the most important way to improve our ballet is to keep it steadily and continuously living among us according to our local conditions, our own manners and behavior. In point of contemporary artistic interest our New York City Ballet is now in its own repertoire incomparably more exciting for me than any Western European company, larger and richer though they are, and brilliant though are some of their stars. And to my mind it is also in the dance style that it is close to achieving.

But I see no reason why one should dispute so unnecessary a question—which country's company is better; there is so much in all of them that is a pleasure, and particularly when one gets to know a company in its own home theater. The home audience responds so differently on points of manners, points that are unintelligible abroad, and that in fact have nothing to do with classic principles, but that become a part of the company's style. I was astonished and delighted watching a Parisian dancer save an awkward passage in performance. She seemed to be saying to the audience, "I'll tell you a secret: this is a passage of no consequence at all, and it doesn't suit my style either, such a stupid choreographer—oops, that elastic—again!—where was I? Oh yes, I'll just sketch in a few steps, I'm delicious at sketching in, you know—and then, just in a moment more, there's a bit—oh really so clever, you'll adore seeing how divine I am in it—ah, here goes now!" "How adorably alive," the audience whispered to its neighbor. A British dancer in a similar situation seems to say more decorously, "I should be happy if this weren't quite so undignified, but we must dance correctly, mustn't we, and it's such fun really, don't you think?" And her audience, staidly touched, breathes back: "Good old girl." I guess an American when the audience is losing interest goes on with her steps as if she muttered: "Don't bother me, I'm busy." She would seem rude to a foreigner, but, being an American, I know what she means, and I respect her for it. Better of course to go on dancing sweetly and not say anything at all; and I've seen dancers all over the world do that too, great dancers.

When you get to be familiar with any foreign style it becomes as misleading and absurd, as touching and delightful as daily life is abroad too. But I was curious abroad to find out if there was some particular regional style that was accepted as the best, and asking everywhere I found a general unanimity of opinion. The wisest fans were all agreed that, despite a few obvious defects, the one classic style that they felt in their hearts to be the most exciting, the most lovable and beautiful, was the style of their own country. I could not disagree with any of them, for I felt, so to speak, the same way, and so without going into particulars we parted with mutual expressions of sincere regard.

—from *Dance News Annual*, 1953

EDWIN DENBY

The Rockettes and Rhythm

The Rockettes at the Music Hall are an American institution and a very charming one. Their cheerfulness is sweet as that of a church social. Their dancing is fresh and modest, their rhythm accurate and light, and everyone can see that they accomplish what they set out to do to perfection. At the end of their routine when the line of them comes forward in a precision climax, the house takes all thirty-six of them collectively to its family heart. It is a very pleasant moment of contentment all around.

The Music Hall has a charming chorus of classic-ballet girls too, who, like the tap-dancing Rockettes, are perfectly accurate in their timing and exact in their motions. They too dance without affectation in a graceful and modest manner. Just as the Rockettes avoid what is "hot" and disturbing in taps, so the toe dancers avoid what is intensely expressive in ballet; instead they are phenomenally neat, they never blur anything they do, and everyone can see they fully deserve their applause.

The ballet doesn't, to be sure, establish a family feeling in the house as the Rockettes do, but then you rarely see toe dancing in the living room and you often see tap dancing there. Ballet is meant to be seen at a distance, it isn't relaxed or familiar in its bearing. But there is a further reason why the ballet is less effective at the Music Hall than the tap routine. In both of them the dramatic punch of the number lies in the unique (and apparently effortless) synchronization of all the dancers and of the entire dance with the music. While this feat heightens very much the sense of rhythm you get from the Rockettes, it doesn't somehow heighten the sense of rhythm you get from the ballet; though it's just as difficult a feat for the latter, it doesn't carry so in ballet.

The fact is that tap and ballet rhythm are different to start with, in the way they connect with the music. The tap dancer plays with the beat, he plays around it and he never leaves it alone. Whatever else he does in the way of elegant ornament, it's the beat that interests him, and each beat does. You see his relation to it in his motion and you hear it in his taps, and his relation to it is the excitement in the dance. The "hotter" he is, the more intimate and dramatic his relation to it becomes; but he can hold your interest just by showing a cool and a sure relation. And a tap-dancing chorus can by complete synchronization fix with a kind of finality the relation of the dance to the music and so reach a satisfying expression. You know what to follow and at the end you know where you are.

But you don't follow a ballet beat by beat. Ballet dancing probably once had a good deal of this percussive quality—so eighteenth-century dance music suggests. In 1890s ballet you can see a percussive dance number in the Cygnet quartet in *Swan Lake*. Contemporary American ballet tends to use this device more sharply—you see it in parts of *Rodeo* and particularly in *Concerto Barocco*. Here the sound of the dancers' toe steps is part of the effect. But these passages are details. More generally the rhythmic interest in ballet dancing isn't fixed on the beat or on the dancers' relation to it; the interest is in their relation to the musical phrase, to the melody, to the musical period. At such times their rhythm is a "free" one, more like that of a singer in its variety of emphasis than like that of a tap dancer.

Like the blues singer, the ballet dancer takes a freer emphasis for the sake of more intense dramatic (or lyric) expression, so he can change his speed against the steady music, so he can make more kinds of effects with his body and travel more freely about the stage. The spring that is the life and rhythm of taps is not tied to the beat in ballet; it has been extended, so to speak, into a lift in the expression of the dance; you follow the rhythm not by separate steps but by the rise and fall of extended phrases.

In taps you see and hear two different rhythms, both of them in the same strict musical meter. In ballet you often look at a free meter and listen to a strict one. Complete synchronization of ballet and music is a special effect that works by contrast to other rhythmic possibilities and it satisfies only when used for such a contrast. People accustomed to strict acoustic rhythm often take a while to get used to ballet rhythm so they can follow it, but there are many too who can't follow a tap dancer, who lose track of any dance rhythm unless it pounds the downbeat. Well, that's why there are several kinds of dance rhythm to suit different types of the human receiving set.

—from the *New York Herald Tribune*, February 20, 1944

NANCY GOLDNER

Alvin Ailey

The Alvin Ailey American Dance Theatre is enjoying huge box-office success. The City Center, which sponsored Alley's recent season, April 18–30, reports that the company set an all-time high in preseason sales. That is astonishing, considering that the theatre has been in business for a long time, has booked such a wide variety of attractions, and that the Ailey group does modern dance. Usually such successes are one-season affairs, when a choreographer is "discovered." Paul Taylor created a ticket flurry during the Christmas season six or seven years ago, and Merce Cunningham did the same in 1968. Now Cunningham is doing business as usual, while Taylor has not even appeared in New York this year, except for a lecture-demonstration. Ailey, however, has been doing well for the last two years. How does one account for this popularity in an art form for which public support is uncertain?

The answer ought to be that Ailey is a great choreographer, but he is a bad choreographer, if the usual standards are applied. His works are neither musical nor well constructed; indeed, many of them are unconstructed. He has no feel and perhaps no concern for lyricism. His themes are without metaphorical reverberations; in this sense, his ballets are not moving. Most important, he is not inventive. His dance vocabulary is so limited that one can predict what the dancers will do next. He adores arm movement, which is not only overused but intrinsically inane and corny, with its long, agonized stretches, reaching-out poses, and merely decorative, at times fussy, flourishes in the wrists, elbows, and shoulders. The amazing thing is that Ailey can keep turning out ballets. They look the same, but they do not bear the marks of a man pressured to create continually without the tools. One might surmise that he is content to produce the same spiritual "arm ballet" again and again, were he not also playing with so-called abstract ballets and with ideas that involve the whole body moving at full capacity. Yet these dances, like *Choral Dances, Myth,* and the new *The Lark Ascending,* are academic and anemic by comparison with Martha Graham, Doris Humphrey, and Lester Horton—and comparison is appropriate and inevitable. They are what might be termed classical modern dances, except that Ailey's classicism is imitative rather than in the quintessential spirit of its predecessors.

Artistically, there is nothing to cheer. But the fact is that in this case concerns about choreography and even dancing are beside the point. What one responds to, legitimately, in the dancers are stage presence, beautiful bodies and generous spirits—not technique. Although not memorable in themselves, the ballets strike up a remarkably warm and immediate relationship with the audience. The first thing one notices about that audience is its youthfulness. Many come in bunches, in casual mood and dress. Possibly the same crew went to a movie or rock concert the night before. A relatively large number of them are black. Ailey too is black, as are most of his dancers. His most characteristic and popular works are set to blues—in *Mary Lou's Mass,* to Mary Lou Williams' bluesy jazz score, and they have the blues's rambling, warm, and emotionally direct qualities. They are, first of all, ballets by a black man, for black people. That defines the company and triggers the feelings of rapport, which are then picked up by white people in the joy that comes from participating in a recognizable and common language, even if it is not one's native tongue. Humor is one touchstone. In *Mary Lou's Mass,* the parable of the beggar Lazarus who is scorned by the rich man and then gets the delicious satisfaction of revenge, once he is in Abraham's bosom, is told with an equally delicious, exaggerated simplicity and Biblical familiarity typical of black religiosity. The blacks get it, the whites recognize it, and in the end everyone loves it. This same ricocheting and intensification of response happens when the action gets sexy, as in Ailey's. *Revelations* and *Blues Suite* or Donald McKayle's *Rainbow 'Round My Shoulder,* revived this season. The encounters are extremely frank and provocative and at the same time kidding, teasing. The man eyes the rolling hips, knows he's done for, and relishes the thought of his undoing. It is a particularly black vision of sex, up-front, self-conscious, and mocking. Being so attitudinal, it strikes with incredible directness at the audience.

The blackness of the company's signature is not the only thing that gets the ball rolling. Ailey's dancers have soul that transcends color lines. They exude a sincerity and energy that sweep the audience into their wake. Having no intricate choreography to contend with—no fast footwork, balances in off-balance positions, or other virtuoso cares—they can put all their strength, mental and physical, into expressing energy itself, or the pure physicality of dancing. They do not evoke the ecstasy that Isadora Duncan talked about, for that was moral as well as physical, but the Ailey dancers do excite. The essence of this crude but powerful style is best seen in two solos that Ailey recently created for his two stars, Dudley Williams and Judith Jamison. The lines are sweeping, big, uncomplicated. Mostly, the dancers throw their arms outward and upward, their necks and torsos pulled along in the momentum created by their arms. Crescendo follows crescendo as the dancer spins into a deep arabesque, falls to the floor, throws an arm out, breathes deeply. Jamison's solo is called *Cry,* but every Ailey gesture seems to be a cry. One can forget that the dancers are dancing; they're just moving— with feeling. The illusion is thus created that anyone with enough of this "feeling" and lung power could approximate them. All of us are potential dancers, Ailey invites us to believe. The idea becomes irresistible and perhaps explains the tremendous sympathy and connection between audience and stage.

At the end of these exercises in blood and guts, the dancers line up for curtain calls. Most of them are exceptionally good-looking, while the tall Miss Jamison is no less than a phenomenon of bone structure. Their skin glistens with sweat. Their smiles of gratitude for the clapping are as straightforward as their dancing has been. It is impossible not to like them and very possible to love them, especially for people who can abandon themselves to the experience because they are not interested in choreography, or for those who choose to let choreography go hang for an evening.

I am always tempted, but ultimately unable to swing with Ailey, for that would involve a conscious effort to vacation. Yet the general audience reaction is genuine, and the Ailey success story might be one of the few examples of real, popular culture, in which audience and performers find each other on their own, without the aid of the professional vendors of culture. In the arts—most recently in dance, because it has just now joined the big time— critics and audience join in a complicated manipulative process which promulgates an opinion whose origin is obscure and not readily traceable to present reality, but is nonetheless omnipresent. It is just there, in the air, and the job of the audience and critics is to keep it there. The longer the image remains, the more powerful it becomes, until it is a self-fulfilling prophecy.

The acclaim that greets the Ailey company, however, is spontaneous and inspired by the moment. One might say the audience lacks sophistication. It does, which is too bad. But they do like Ailey for real—if not for what I think the most important reasons. Furthermore, they are impervious to the implications of sophistication, and that is their strength, for it is sophistication, or taste, that makes audiences nervous and vulnerable to the machinations of the taste makers.

—from *The Nation*, May 29, 1972

NANCY GOLDNER

Maurice Béjart

It was not Maurice Béjart's poor choreography that made his three-week season at the Brooklyn Academy of Music (ending February 14) so disturbing. After all, poor-to-middling choreography is what we usually see and, while it can disappoint or bore, it is rarely disturbing. But there was much more than plain bad craftsmanship and noncreativity connected with Béjart's Ballet of the Twentieth Century. The queasiness began, I suppose, when I got in the mail a button announcing that "Béjart is sexier." It was almost impossible to quell suspicions—was a ballet company coming, or a product of some Madison Avenue executive's outlandish imagination; were the Belgians going to be "sold" to us; and who was "us" anyway? Not those who understand enough about dance to realize that the art is intrinsically erotic. No, sexier Béjart would address himself to those ill-informed persons who thought that ballet was all frills, fluffy movement, and irrelevance—whatever that means.

Despite the suspicions, in fairness I had to reserve judgment on the sexy business, for the company had not even arrived in America. Now, after seeing them, I have learned to put more confidence in the publicity men. They do know what image they are conjuring up. Béjart not only confirmed the meaning of that button but surpassed it. The Béjart show was a sex show, but of a new mode; on the underside of the pop movement, perhaps. Many of the dancers were accomplished technicians, but that obviously was not what was on display. The women were used as automatons, including even the remarkable Suzanne Farrell, who until recently danced with the New York City Ballet. We saw her kick her legs, and we saw Maina Gielgud balance on one foot, but the choreography was not designed to show personality, that is, dancer's personality, or lyricism, the one aspect of the female personality that is best developed in dance. The women were treated as non-sexual (and by extension, nonhuman) entities. It might be argued that in the traditional structure men hold the same position. In the pas de deux, for example, the man is not as visible as the woman. But by partnering he fulfills a vital function as a dancer, and in deploying his strength to lift the woman he also functions as a man. Béjart's women had no function. Alas, there was luscious and willowy Miss Farrell, for whom Béjart could do nothing but have her ankle touch her nose.

Béjart's interest was the men. Had this interest manifested itself in dancing, there would have been a totally acceptable justification for his unorthodox preference, and a counterweight to the undeniable strangeness of seeing dance dominated by men. And yet by the time the season was over, I knew little about these dancers as dancers; I did not know if they could jump, turn, or beat their feet cleanly in the air. These technical feats are the dancers' character only in part, but it was even impossible to come to know their style of moving.

Béjart's failure to use his men as dancers was compounded by the fact that he used them as glamour boys. Faces tended to be thickly made up. Hair was noticeably long and shaggy, in that offhand but exclamatory manner that has become the symbol of hippiedom. Whether Béjart is responsible for such decorum is beside the point; evidently there is a company spirit in which such misplaced concern can flourish. When one considers what kind of movement Béjart gave to the men, however, their glamour takes on some peculiar overtones. The choreography consisted of undulating arm movements, body-beautiful torso configurations, and a couple of turns when nothing else was happening. It was all extremely self-conscious and calculated for effect, stemming not from the dancer but from an image, a visual picture, that Béjart imposed on the dancer. Imagine flipping quickly through some photographs of male models, and you will see a Béjart ballet. Effeminate movement combined with extravagant hairdos and makeup that emphasized the exotic all conspired to produce a freak show. It was freakish because the homosexual bent, though disguised in political themes and suggestions of the hip, became blatant and aggressive as it turned such female qualities as felineness, vanity, and prettiness into male virtues. In short, the men were acting sexy. Men may *be* sexy, but when they start to act sexy, which inevitably becomes a parody of femininity, the effect is grotesque—something akin to the Fellini types in *Satyricon*. Just as disturbing, though, was the fact that posturing took the place of dance. Virtuosity was apparently considered "irrelevant" when compared to the kinetic potency (male potency) of a wiggling hip or a dangling wrist.

Dishonesty was rampant in other areas. The audience was asked not only to identify with effeminacy but to respond to ideology rather than dance. The dancers embodied the romantic ideals of teenagers. Worse, those ideals were manipulated into a political context. In this way Béjart perpetuated the confused and ultimately birdbrained view that youth culture and political life are linked, and that to be a flower child or show other manifestations of fervency is somehow a meaningful political act. The dancers played either revolutionary partisans (*The Firebird*—yes, that's Stravinsky's *Firebird,* lifted from its magical Russian woods to the streets, where power belongs to the people), or alienated politicos (*Messe pour le Temps Présent*), or alienated lovers (*Romeo and Juliet*), or searchers of truth (*Les Vainqueurs*), or meditators (in the Eastern ballets, none of which were Eastern except that at times the dancers would just sit or stand; presumably thinking, but mostly breathing), or religious fanatics at the Western temple of Bach (poor Bach: he thought himself a musician; did he ever suppose that his notations would be worshipped by non-dancers?).

Dress was another conspiring factor in Béjart's coercive, not to mention adolescently conceived, ideological works. Sometimes a choreographer wants his dancers out of costume. Since the dance is on the stage and is choreographed—that is, since the dance is still a formal construction—the dancers cannot be literally out of costume if honesty is to prevail. An excellent convention takes care of this problem: the dancers wear the costume of the classroom, leotards and tights. This conveys the message while acknowledging that ballet is not everyday activity. On occasion (few occasions actually, but telling nevertheless), Béjart dressed his people in work shirts and dungarees, as if to say that we dancers with our flowing manes of hair, gorgeous bodies, and voluptuous faces are really just like you the audience—young, proletariat, even revolutionary. The assumption that this is the audience is presumptuous, but the message that the dancers are more than dancers is outrageous, particularly to those who like dance and ask no more than that dancers dance. It has become the fashion in the pop world to demand of performers that they have symbolic meaning as well as talent. To see the Béjart people take on that role without embarrassment, but with proud smugness, was terribly sad. For the implication is that if ballet must become a part of youth culture, if it depends on finding rapport with the audience through conventions that have nothing to do with dance, the art is in a state of decline.

Dance is not on the decline, and Béjart's efforts to liven it are therefore offensive. His premise is also a dead end for Béjart. It forces him to find a way of communication that is emblematic rather than real, in terms of actual

movement as well as subject matter. A dab of flexed foot and a pinch of alien-
ation and, presto—modern ballet. This is stuff for people who do not like or
trust dance. I wonder if Béjart is one of them.

—from *The Nation*, March 15, 1971

NANCY GOLDNER

The Bolshoi

S*partacus* and *Ivan the Terrible* are the only completely new ballets the Bolshoi is offering on this visit, its first since 1966. Both are the work of Yuri
Grigorovich, the Bolshoi's artistic director. Much can be said about the ballets, thematic content, and dramaturgy. To get to the bottom of them, however, one must look at the steps. Assuming that choreographing ballets may
be compared to knitting, Grigorovich works like a novice. Using thick
needles, his weave cannot possibly have the resilience, utility, and attractiveness of an expert knitter's fabric. The dancers in *Spartacus* and *Ivan the Terrible*
keep falling into the holes. There is nothing intrinsically wrong with the
space-consuming leap, the big one-handed lift, the broad sweep of the arm,
the little runs on pointe, a series of spins, a sudden collapse to the floor, a
chain of arabesques—except that Grigorovich must use this basic vocabulary to haul his dancers out of the holes. They always seem to be on the
rebound from a path to nowhere. Once the dancer has finished a diagonal or
circle, what then but to repeat the combination in the opposite direction or
drop it altogether and begin, as it were, a "new" dance. I doubt that any
dance in these ballets extends beyond five steps, which is one reason Grigorovich's choreography feels so choppy. The steps either ricochet off each
other or are glued by enormous glissades and intakes of breath, as though
the dancers were on the perpetual edge of a precipice. So much preparatory
signaling obliges Grigorovich to balance the scale with one hell of a lot of Big
Steps. Even when the step really is big (in contradistinction to the times
when the dancer must pretend it's big), it hardly justifies all the time taken to
get there. Nor are these moments graced with a follow-through in momentum. Spartacus uses half the length of the stage to get up in the air, and when
he comes down the dance is over. Then he, and we, must rev up again, for the

next climax. The audience is never given the pleasure of riding the crest of a climax. Grigorovich's intention, quite the reverse, is to sock the audience with sudden deaths.

To arrive at big moments, Grigorovich is safest, naturally, with jumps. But when he is choreographing for women, or when the man's solo is what he calls a monologue—a meditation on the current state of the protagonist's payche—he must by-pass jumps in favor of more "expressive" movement. Operating on the principle that the wow of technique resides in the legs and the emotional center in the torso and arms, these segments depend on the abilities of the dancers' upper halves to project what we have come to think of as Russian soul—the melancholic binges in which the arms gather at the breast and, palms up, fly spread-eagle at the audience in a grand invitation to share sorrow. These gestures are indeed eloquent and eloquently done by such heroes and heroines as Vladimir Vasiliev and Vyacheslav Gordeyev, Natalia Bessmertnova and Nina Sorokina, yet they would be more thrilling if they did not have to serve as proxies for the entire body. As such, they are to Russian ballet what tense pectoral muscles and swiveling hips are to our jazz ballet. Grigorovich is the Russian counterpart of our own Alvin Ailey.

With the women rarely touching ground in the duets, Grigorovich's pas de deux are actually *pas d'un*. As soon as the Khachaturian score for *Spartacus* or the Prokofiev conglomerate for *Ivan the Terrible* hits adagio, one knows that the man is going to lift the lady across his shoulder blades, slide her down the side of his leg, and then flip her head first over one shoulder so as to block her face and chest from view. (How telling that we rarely see the woman full-face and upside up at those very moments supposedly most expressive of the characters' deepest feelings.) Then, for the grand finale, he boosts her straight up into the air, as if she were the prize trophy of a turkey shoot. The woman, besides needing an infant's cast-iron stomach to weather her upside-down state of being, must play dead so that we may admire the man's strength in maneuvering her body so easily around his own; in the last duet of *Ivan the Terrible,* Anastasia actually is dead. Necrophiliac duets have long been tempting to the many choreographers who have done *Romeo and Juliet,* but Grigorovich does not need the excuse of plot to indulge his fancy. Necrophilia is the subject of all his duets, and the only confusion in the metaphor is that what looks corpse-like to me stands for passion in Grigorovich's eyes. During these duets, one notices that the woman's feet are always beautifully pointed and that one ankle is charmingly cocked on top of the other, so as to salvage the last shreds of long, clean line. One is grateful for these small points and for the dancers' interest in them. They are pros.

The other half of the choreographic story is the ensemble dances, those panoramas of movement against which the monologues and duets stand in relief. In *Spartacus* the ensembles are the armies, those of Crassus and those of Spartacus, and the Roman court of whores and satyrs. In *Ivan the Terrible* they are the bell ringers, Boyars, the Czar's secret police, and something which Grigorovich calls "Faces of Death" and "Heralds of Victory." (*Ivan* is the more allegorical of the two ballets.) The tactic is uniformly mass effect, unison dancing. Five people doing the same thing with extraordinary vigor yield so much electricity. Multiply the unit by five, and of course, the tactic is self-defeating because it produces an insatiable appetite. By the end of *Spartacus* nothing less than 250 soldiers charging with spears would have appeased me. Normally the movies give me a hunger for this kind of meal, and the best of the type serve up a satisfying one. Although Grigorovich has embraced the spectacular genre with more fervor and considerably more skill than his peers, he obviously cannot do on the stage what he could do on the screen. If only *Spartacus* and *Ivan* were the de Mille extravaganzas their debunkers claim them to be.

In fairness, it must be said that *Ivan* is better than *Spartacus*. (In truth, only the devil would propose such a comparison.) Russian folk movement, which forms the basis of much of the ensemble work in *Ivan,* is more attractive than any goose-stepping Roman legions. *Ivan* has one female lead instead of two, and consequently half as many duets. Ivan's first dance, in which Yuri Vladimirov thrusts his stiff legs up and down the stairs to his throne like a crazed epileptic, is a marvelous and lasting image, plus a telling comment on Vladimirov's crazily ungainly style in other bravura pieces. He has always danced like a maniac, and in *Ivan* he finally plays a maniac. He is wonderful, rolling eyeballs and all. Last but not least, *Ivan* is an hour shorter than *Spartacus* and is set to Prokofiev pieces, which, although plodding, are less excruciating than the music Khachaturian wrote expressly for *Spartacus*.

If *Ivan* and *Spartacus* were the soft apples in an ever growing collection of good ones, it would be easy to wish everyone better luck next time. They are, however, the major creative efforts of an entire decade in the life of the man who heads a very important institution. Moreover, they point to a situation larger than the ballets themselves. What is most disturbing about these epics is their failure to use the very technique developed by the Bolshoi, and the Kirov, in the nineteenth century, the very technology, if you will, that made *Swan Lake, Sleeping Beauty,* and twentieth-century ballet possible. The Mickey Mouse level of technique required of the dancers in Grigorovich's ballets is partly a result of, and partly responsible for, their flaccid choreographic weaves. The big breathing spells, the ricochet effect, and sudden deaths of movement that I have already described are some examples of easy-chair dancing. The fact that all the steps are done on the run instead of from proper, turned-out foot positions is another aspect of technique-less dancing and matrix-less choreography. The women suffer especially in pointe work, the most refined and unique aspect of ballet. Grigorovich does not allow them to use their pointe shoes as natural extensions of their legs. Instead of rolling up and off pointe, and instead of using pointe technique as an efficient way to express lightness and quickness in darting piqué movements, the women must always scoop themselves up onto pointe from a bent leg. Kinetically the effect is oom-pah-pah, constituting the ugly side of what is often called the heroic element in Bolshoi style. If one regards technique as an evolutionary process, this kind of dancing takes us back to the Dark Ages. To see the Bolshoi dancing at a contemporary level of technique, one must see Act II of *Swan Lake* and *Giselle*. (Another possibility might be *Sleeping Beauty*, but as of this writing it has not been done, and judging from what Grigorovich did to *Swan Lake*, one cannot assume that *Sleeping Beauty* will be Petipa.) Presumably, technique is still being perpetuated in class, if not on the stage. Watching the company hurl itself so passionately into *Ivan* and *Spartacus*, as though *Swan Lake* never existed, I could not help foreseeing a terrible schism. On stage, the company would be dancing nothing but Grigorovich and the like, while the lifeblood of the art would be incubating in the seclusion of the classroom. Petipa would be samizdat ballet. Gloomy thoughts, dispelled only by the sight of Gordeyev in anything and the company in Leonid Lavrovsky's vivid, straightforward production of *Giselle*.

—from *The Nation,* May 24, 1975

JILL JOHNSTON
Time Tunnel: José Limón

Recently someone I know turned to someone else I know and told them that my original entry into dance was through José Limón, or words to that effect. The tone of the statement was: "Can you believe it?" I can't believe it myself. But at that time I wasn't living in this century at all. I was living in a museum. Education is a museum game. The dance part of it for me ended quite naturally. One day I broke my foot and left the studio feeling greatly relieved of the necessity to go on. In that manner at least. When the foot mended I was happy to possess two good feet in condition for nothing better than getting myself from one place to another as I was accustomed to doing before seized by a zeal for astounding myself with feats of unusual locomotion.

Of course I didn't at that moment emerge from the dance museum I had entered upon delivering myself all innocent to be educated. No, I remained devoted. José was a King. I honored his presumption. I just waited, characteristically, for other accidents to indicate what century I was living in. Actually, I went back even further (I've placed José in the sixteenth and/or seventeenth century) and spent a lot of time in the library translating a book by a French musicologist called *The Court Ballet in France Before Louis XIV.* I was pretty hot to be educated. I'm not going to enumerate the accidents that led me eventually to the time I'm living. I've lost track of it all anyway. At some point travel accelerated and I think I woke up one morning and stepped out the door into the twentieth century. Nothing looked different. My head was just suddenly empty. Naturally one of the first things I did was to privately depose the King. Thereafter I viewed the master's concerts with clinical detachment and even conceived the idea of a thesis expounding the psychology of a man whose face was so often tilted in a position parallel to the sky. It seemed significant. Even off stage: my memory is of looking up at a chin upon a daily greeting.

I began to be very interested in the novel phenomenon of dancers looking me straight in the eye. A reasonable attitude. I didn't like to see them groveling around on the floor either. Up or down seemed excessive. The dead center thing was what I first remember liking about Cunningham. Of course he went up and down. His head too. But with a difference. He didn't have his head in the clouds and he wasn't hanging it between his legs either. I mean you didn't have to feel sorry for him on the one hand, or hope for his redemption from the powers above on the other. Quite considerate. With all this and other things in mind I'd go back to see José and puzzle over his intractable habit of looking so remote. He was certainly sincere. Well, I went through some changes. First I deposed him, as I said. Then I became an academic investigator. Next I denounced him as a stuffed museum piece. Then I saw what seems very good about him, never mind his century. At last I lost interest. And now the other evening I had another attack of curiosity (or responsibility) and went to the Brooklyn Academy of Music to see *Missa Brevis* and a new work, *The Winged*.

Both works are skyborne. *The Winged* is a kind of birdlore study set forth in a long series of divertissements (solos, duets, group, etc.) to a nice score of "incidental music" by Hank Johnson. The bird action is a lot of surprisingly inventive detail (especially for five girls in an angular predatory sequence) embedded in or welded onto the basic Limón vocabulary. Always the large fluid gliding weighted articulations of a body appearing in group form in swelling opulent, well-crafted symphonic orchestrations.

That applies to *Missa Brevis* though the dancers here move in the upper atmosphere without benefit of metaphor. The tilted heads were all there as I remembered. The group begins in a cluster stage center peering upward, possibly through a hole in the "bombed out church" where the dance takes place. José stands apart looking on his "flock" with paternal benevolence. José is sixty now. He doesn't look so much the King as the father-of-us-all type of thing. I'm still intrigued by his head. Imagine a history of the transition of style and attitude based on carriage. The proud Spaniard. The arrogant Conquistador. The stricken aristocrat. The Mexican-Indian underdog. The imperious matador. Jesus and Judas, Adam, Othello, Agamemnon, the Emperor Jones. He's played those roles. And he'd be delighted I'm sure to be a guest on TV's *Time Tunnel*—be sent back in time for tea and conversation with Bach, El Greco, and Michelangelo. He's a walking history book. The background might actually be more religious than I ever suspected. I thought of that as he lay prostrated in *Missa Brevis* in the form of a cross. He's probably simply a God-fearing man, but not in the American Puritan tradition, rather in another bygone manner of the exalted tragedies of saints and martyrs per Jesum Christum Dominum Nostrum.

—from *Marmalade Me,* February 8, 1968

JILL JOHNSTON
Charlotte Moorman: Over His Dead Body

I was privileged to be present Friday night, March 21, at Judson Church, at the most unusual manifestation of a performer-audience situation I have witnessed in a decade of attending a theatre in which the performer-audience relationship has been pushed in every conceivable direction. Unusual is a mild word for it. It was a kind of psychological trauma involving two principals and the rest of us in a spontaneous drama expressing the agony and the comedy of the condition called human. The occasion was the Destruction in Art Symposium preceded by Destruction events in Judson's backyard.

The atmosphere in the yard was a bit like a bazaar—the spectators milling around passing from one setup to another: an excerpt from Hermann Nitsch's Orgy-Mystery theatre; Lil Picard with plastic bags full of feathers set to flaming on a charcoal burner; Steve Rose standing by a frying pan on a hot plate cooking an orange and a banana; Bici Hendricks handing out ice picks to anyone wishing to hack at a large vertical hunk of ice surrounded by raw eggs; and preparations for Ralph Ortiz's chicken-killing event was the first presentiment of a rumble nobody expected. The two live chickens were strung up from trees several yards apart. John Wilcock calmly cut the chickens down and, assisted by Michael Kirby, made off with them to an adjoining yard to release them over a high fence. Ortiz later said he was delighted the chickens were rescued. He accepted the frustration of his plans as a worthwhile event in itself and re-programmed himself by subsequently attacking the two trees (he climbed one, Jon Hendricks the other), sawing a limb off each one after a preparation (pouring) of the cow's blood originally to have been part of the chicken scene. The attitude Ortiz assumed about the interference in his thing became relevant to the amazing drama that ensued inside at a scheduled panel of the artists involved. A soapbox orator from the yard, whose hysterical blather was punctuated with a few brilliant remarks, threatened to dominate proceedings in the lecture room. Hendricks, Ortiz, and Hansen accepted him without relinquishing their own purpose and somehow finally integrated him in the total situation.

Hendricks announced a performance by Charlotte Moorman of Nam June Paik's *One for Violin,* a piece dating from 1961. I knew the piece from Paik's performance of it in 1964 at a Fluxus concert. In a rather disorderly atmosphere Miss Moorman assumed the appropriate concentration and a courteous hush fell over the room. The piece entails the destruction of a violin after a long preliminary passage in which the performer raises the instrument in slow motion from a position at right angles to the waist to a position over the head in readiness to smash the thing on impact with the table. Miss Moorman got maybe one minute into the act when a man from the back tried to stop her. She dispatched him with a push and resumed the performance. And her more determined spectator approached the table and the war was on. Charlotte was angry. She demanded to know who he was (translated: who the hell do you think you are?). He said he didn't want her to break the violin. "By breaking a violin," he said, "you're doing the same thing as killing people." And something about giving it to a poor kid who could use it. Attempting to go on with the piece she said, "this is not a vaudeville routine" and "this is not an audience-participation piece." But he persisted and I think Charlotte slapped his face and suddenly there was a tragedy in the making and shock waves in the air and terrific agitation all around. Someone suggested he give her his coat in exchange for the violin. He removed his coat but she wouldn't have any of it. I was inspired by this suggestion and found myself hollering in the din: GIVE IT TO HIM. Charlotte accused her intruder of being as bad as the New York police. He announced that "we are sitting down and refusing to allow this violin to be broken." He forthwith stretched himself out on his back on the table in front of her. As Ortiz said later—she had to over his dead body. It happened very fast and there are probably as many versions of the climax as the number of people who were there. As I saw it, Charlotte's tormenter sat up and was sitting on the edge of the table and at some moment turned to face her at which point with malice aforethought she bashed him on the head with the violin and the blood was spilled. My description can't do justice to this extraordinary situation. The ramifications are extensive. It wasn't so much a question who was right or wrong (I thought, if pressed, both were right and both wrong), but what might have been done to avert the inevitable. That seems the ultimate political question so brilliantly posed by this little war right in the ranks of those so violently opposed to the war at the top.

The victim introduced himself as Saul Gottlieb. Charlotte was contrite and ministered to his wound. She explained the point of the piece is to show that we think nothing of killing people in Vietnam and we place a higher value on a violin. She said she didn't mean to hit him but he was in her performance area. Speaking of the therapeutic value of such actions Ortiz said Charlotte was trying to displace her hostility onto an inanimate object and Gottlieb wouldn't let her do that. Our soapbox man said that if "we the people want to come into the government" (represented here as artists) "we should be able to." He also told Gottlieb he was sick because he stood there and let her hit him with his back turned. Gottlieb said that Charlotte was determined to break the violin regardless of what happened and was unable to de-program herself. The adjustment Ortiz made in his chicken event became instructive. What were Charlotte's alternatives in the face of being robbed of her artist thing? Blowing her cool she was left with a literal destruction. The irony of a symbol converted into a reality. Yet why didn't Gottlieb honor her appeal for attention? "I request the honor of your presence at . . ." etc. At what? At the daily level, let's say, how we take turns in a conversation piece. Many more things were said at the Judson gathering. The last thing I saw was a touching demonstration by Steve Rose of a simple exchange based on respect. He requested the indulgence of his audience in a piece he wished to perform. He said it would begin when he finished talking and it would end when he sat down. He stood as he was and looked round slowly at the people there gathered with some slight perplexity I thought. And that was the piece. And the audience expressed their appreciation at a point well taken.

—from *Marmalade Me,* March 28, 1968

JILL JOHNSTON

Steve Paxton: Tornado in a Teacup

Last spring I was talking about hoping for a new funk dance. It may be upon us. A new metaphor might be sexier in the long run than the thing a metaphor is designed to conceal (among other functions) but there's no question that at certain historical moments the people can be heard to be yelling "Take It Off" so they can see what the metaphorical fuss is all about. Steve Paxton's comment on *Paradise Now* was that it didn't matter about the show too much, what you thought of it, when you were standing on stage there and happened to see one of the actors going down on the directress. Steve didn't pay for his ticket either. The best things in life are free. As for metaphors, you can get weak in the head thinking about what a metaphor is or isn't, or if there is such a thing, so I'll try to stick to the facts. A few weeks ago, visiting a couple of friends, I suggested or announced at random that there isn't a thing on television that isn't about fucking, so we promptly repaired to the bedroom to play with the set. First channel we got was one of those jungle dramas at a moment when the gorilla was squawking off a tree about to molest the young lady in a hammock. Next I think we spaced out on an advertisement for eye drops. The screen was filled with a big eye. The better to see you with my dear. And so on.

At the New School on October 15, 1968, Steve gave an *Untitled Lecture* on a mixed-bag program including Stuart Hodes, Margot Parsons, and John Wilson and the 1950 movie of José Limón's *Moor's Pavane,* which Betty Jones was on hand to talk about. Fortunately I'd been to Steve's rehearsal the day before—and saw the pornographic movie which was censored for the actual performance. Steve substituted a Biafran documentary. His piece consists of four simultaneously performed parts. It's a kind of illustrated lecture. Steve is talking on tape about sex and ballet; he stands downstage left making slight hand and pelvis gestures (also mouthing the lecture) stolen from Yvonne Rainer's *Body and Snot* piece from the week before (at the New School); and two films, several yards apart, are projected on the back wall. At the question period after the concert it seemed almost the whole audience was bending on Steve about his piece. Yvonne, for one, was outraged at what she thought to be a glib substitution of the Biafra film (notwithstanding the necessity), saying it destroyed the unity of the piece. I think she was really outraged at the theft of her *Body and Snot* material. Anyhow—the association of Biafran obscenity and *Swan Lake* (the other film) was certainly not as pointed or dramatic as the juxtaposition of *Swan Lake* with the pornography, especially since the lecture was about sex and ballet; but it was announced as a disappointed substitution, so I can't see how it mattered if you knew what it was supposed to be. My analysis of the great attention focused on Steve was that the audience felt deprived of the real thing, thus they were trying to find out what they missed exactly, and in detail, even if the question was about the weather.

If the definition of pornography is that which arouses prurient interests, I suppose the film was among the best of its kind. It's a Forty-second Street stag movie, nothing to do with tender sweet that I could see, just good old-fashioned mauling sucking and fucking. The way it worked with the *Swan Lake* film was staggering to my way of seeing it. There was nothing in between. Bang naked dirty funky low-down primal scene—next to the polite ethereal-ized de-corporealized all-dressed-up insanity of the good fairy godmother ballet. The balletomanes would have Steve's neck for this sort of proximity. I don't know if Steve had such a head-on impact in mind. I do know he already had the film (he used it in a rather obscured fashion last year in another context), and that he thinks a lot about all aspects of human physical qualities, in dance and otherwise. What interested him to explore here was a certain energy common to sex and ballet, as he sees it. The key sentence perhaps in the lecture is: "I speculate that some of the qualities which have made ballet, in spite of its practitioners, the second oldest professional physical tradition, is an early infusion of physiologically basic modes of energy use which I find similar to the ecstasy of stretching such as is experienced during certain types of orgasms . . . a positive and energized stretch." He seems to undo his little thesis at the end with the question: "Why are we in the West so hung up on orgasm?" The implied judgment throws the theory into a department of complaints, which may be more pertinent to the wild proximity (stunning) of two cultural physical extremes, one private and one public, than Steve himself realizes. I think any analysis of dance techniques in terms of basic sexual energies is both fascinating and important. Everybody knows what Graham's "contraction and release" syndrome is all about. A sex physiologist could probably make a critical contribution to dance literature with some scientific analogies. Anyhow, Steve upstaged me with his lecture, since I've been thinking for some time of developing the idea of ballet as a rigid erected phallic art. This is not what he had in mind in his lecture. We had a near knockdown controversy over it in Boston last week. For one thing, I said, how can you speculate on these matters without having read the classic essay on the orgasm by W. Reich. One's own experience may be sufficient for a theory (I accept it) but there's a point at which an experienced clinician can enrich a generalization by more inclusive evidence on a subject that's more scientific than poetic. Reich has been much criticized (before and after his death) for his single-minded concentration on full orgastic potency as the sine qua non of a healthy life; but his detailed description with diagrammatic support (regardless of opinions about his therapeutic conclusions) of the physiological process of orgastic excitation must be a masterwork of its kind in the field.

In our argument Steve said that although the motives are different, the pervasive "stretch" in ballet is similar to the orgastic stretch, not only in position but in the energy employed to get there and stay there. No question but what they both involve "a positive and energized stretch." Beyond that I disagree. I can't find anything not to agree with in Reich's description of orgastic potency as consisting of involuntary pleasurable contractions radiating from the genital to the whole body in a total surrender to the flow of biological energy. I'm not impressed with the ballet as an art of surrender. Our early modern dance technicians were much closer to an organic base for dance movement. Their revolt against the ballet, after all, was more than a historic rebellion in the interests of advancing a backward medium. Isadora set the scene. She predated Freud in her crudely expressed ideas about repression and liberation. Whether her successors knew it or not, they were expressing the temper of the new psychology. I think Graham was the only one to literally plunder the available literature. They all must have sensed that the ballet was a sick Western mode of physical discipline. Eventually they got trapped by it themselves—but that's another story.

What I see (and have felt) in the ballet "stretch" is a *rigor mortis* of painful extension. Those ballet dancers may have their ecstatic moments but nobody can convince me they don't in general suffer the tortures of the damned. There's no keener self-flagellation in any of our Western disciplines. If Steve were right I think they'd all look a helluva lot happier; furthermore they wouldn't be doing that in the first place. Ballet and pleasure are mutually exclusive activities. I can't think of a thing in the ballet repertoire of action that isn't an unrelieved exercise in phallic erected exhibitionism. There is a ballet here and there, like *Schéhérazade,* which deviates somehow into something sloppily organic. In any case, the classroom technique itself is nothing short of a borderline psychosis in rigid repressive control. The paradox of the ballet, by the way, is in its phallic nature masquerading as a pitifully romantic searching etherealized unearthly body. There's iron and steel and plenty of clenched teeth in every flight and facility. Another interesting paradox is that the ballet is rampant with representational orgasm. There are climaxes by the dozen in any one ballet. These are the traditional maneuvers of the choreographer to keep the audience awake with shifts in pace. An ascending accumulation of energy is a favorite device. The movement gets faster and bigger, etc., as the plot, the music, and the attention span of the audience all dictate. The ecstasy of the ballet is a giant put-on. A fanfare of unhappy instruments. A fountain of ice. A tornado in a teacup. But this brings me back to Steve's concluding question: "Why are we in the West so hung up on orgasm?" The *Swan Lake* and the pornography movies are hopelessly off base from opposite ends of the pleasure spectrum. Somewhere in the middle is the continuous uninterrupted pleasure of homeostasis best known to the Eastern mystics. Pornography is real hot stuff. The ballet is a frigid witch. The Eastern mystics know it isn't necessary either to have or to deny the orgasm to solve the anxiety of unrelieved tension. For them the surrender is total and constant . . . there's no such thing as unrelieved tension. They live in divine relief. The energy that Reich called orgone energy and which has been called diverse names for centuries is a cosmic energy coursing into and out of and through their bodies in a flow that can't be separated into states of tension (anxiety) and discharge (pleasure). This is the psychosomatic totality of a self-contained grace which we reserve for the ecstasy of a specific tyrannical experience known as orgasm. Definitely hung up.

Various writers have touched on or explored the broad changes in Western art since the turn of the century. An outstanding essay was by Leonard Myer in *The Hudson Review* a few years ago. He developed his thesis in terms of the end of teleological (purpose-oriented) art in the West, especially citing the chance methodology of the Dadaists and some contemporary composers as examples of the new purposeless, anticlimax art. In my opinion the most advanced art of the century is a conscious or unconscious attempt to eliminate not the orgasm but the orgasm anxiety complex. It's a complicated subject that I can't go on with here for reasons of space, except to throw out a few typical words used over and over to describe certain work in certain mediums: diffused, allover, ready-made, synthesis, defocused, equal value, etc.

—from *Marmalade Me*, October 24, 1968

ANDRÉ LEVINSON

The Significance of the Dance

The most influential European dance critic of his time, André Levinson (1887–1933) established himself as a critic in St. Petersburg. By 1921 he had fled the Soviet Union for Paris, where he wrote voluminously on many subjects, including literature and theater. Until his death, he also wrote for the American magazine Theatre Arts Monthly. *His range of interests in dance was wide—the classics, the Ballets Russes, modern dance, Asian, and jazz and Spanish dance—and his authority stemmed from a combination of theoretical perception and a fresh, keen eye for what was taking place on the stage.*

Taken in a general sense, the effort of the supposed reformers of the dance—be they named Fokine or Duncan—is above all an attempt to base the dance upon a rational or psychological foundation. One cannot move without reason; in order to hold interest the dance must have a subject. Thus, philosophical rationalism being already "dead and buried," some artists advance a sophomoric rationalism, a teleology which very nearly approaches a utilitarian conception of the dance—the freeing of the body from the limitations of a style, from the *immorality* of unnatural conventions, and Heaven knows what other humanitarian and pedagogical nonsense!

They would have the dance express definite emotions, be determined by rational motives. But what precise emotion does the overture to the *Magic Flute* express? What plausible subject inspired the trills from the "Queen of Night"? Why did El Greco exaggerate the length of limb in his saints and martyrs? Of what use are the fugues of Bach?

The apparent *irrationality* of the ballet, the absence of a passable bridge between the abstract spirit of its form and the superficial phenomena of our emotional life, aroused a profound distrust of the "dance for its own sake" in half cultured renovators, and orientated them toward pantomime, archeology, and folk dancing. They would sacrifice everything to a psychological realism, to an exact and intense evocation of the passions. They envy the drama, where everything is *motivated*. They seek the comprehensible, the explicable, the truth that can be proven; and they ask perplexedly, "What sense is there in spinning like a top?" *Naturalism,* having exhausted literature, seized upon the art of the comedian; now that the comedy has thrown it off, it menaces the ballet. The old doctrine—"Life is the law of art"—is again being preached to us. Let us consider it. Life is the raw material out of which art is made, but does this material (whether it be marble or the human body) contain within itself the law of creation? "The most important problem of architecture"—says Salomon Reinach in his splendid book—"is the victory over the suggestion of its medium."

What is then the aesthetic nature of the classic ballet? It is not easy to define, but the ancient sage frankly acknowledged that it was "difficult to define beauty."

It is easy to describe the technique, the gymnastics of the ballet dance, but who would think of establishing for each movement a corresponding psychological idea? The ballet dance, as we have already said, is not determined by any exterior motive. It includes its own law, its own logic, and any departure from that logic, pertaining to a body moving in space with the aim of creating beauty by *organized dynamism,* is perfectly apparent to the spectator.

One of the fundamentals of the ballet dance is equilibrium, the search for absolute balance. Hence the shape of the ballet slipper—flat sole and reinforced toe. "It is then the simple and irritating necessity of furnishing a balancing point for the ballerina which determines the shape of this shoe which you extol!"—jeer my adversaries. I find this necessity neither simple nor irritating. All architectural art is founded upon necessities just as simple. What is a buttress if not a force counterbalancing the pressure of the arch? What is a colonnade but a system of pillars supporting the weight of the cross beams?

In so far as it is possible to compare movement with immobility we find many points of analogy between architecture and the ballet. Like architecture the ballet is an emanation of geometrical and spatial conceptions. It is *Raum Kunst*—"the art of space," as the Germans call the arrangement of architectural interiors. It reduces its splendid and vibrant instrument—the human body—to its tectonic not plastic elements. For the plastic volume is autonomous, limited by the form. The framework of the dance is like the draft of a temple formed by lines—lines which are often ideally prolonged in space. This is why classic choreography can disregard certain plastic peculiarities of the human body which would break its unity of line.

Thus the leg of the ballerina with instep thrown out and toes rigid creates a vertical line of incomparable purity from which radiates a charming and delicate play of curved lines. In this position the shape of the leg, subordinate to the single movement of the whole body, loses its individual character and becomes conventionalized or generalized.

"You would like to synthesize the dance, then, but that is the opposite of art; you would achieve a dull uniformity; you would suppress creative development by doing away with individuality" and my adversaries would demand individual rights for each toe and finger, and tear the rose satin of Cinderella's slipper and the silken threads of her fleshings (for generally the first gesture of the modern dancer is to discard fleshings).

Every artist, painter, or sculptor begins with what is individual and works toward the typical, eliminating accidental and emphasizing essential elements. Creation is a constant deformation of empiric reality, a progress toward a superior reality, *de realibus ad realiora*. The path of the artist leads always from the concrete to the symbolic.

Who dares criticize the spirit of uniform synthesis found in Egyptian sculpture, in the Byzantine mosaics of Ravenna, or the primitive Siennese frescoes? Decidedly all these rebellions against the conventional formulae of the ballet must be relegated to the garret along with old-fashioned naturalist methods.

There is nothing more unnatural than the fundamental position of the ballet technique, the feet turned directly outwards, but the result of this habit achieved by years of gymnastic training is not only a balance which surmounts all difficulties but also an extraordinary *amplitude* of movement. Thus the *moving leg* can be raised until it forms an obtuse angle with the *pivot leg* without upsetting the centre of gravity. Natural movement acts upon a limited plane, while the ballet dancer can move with equal freedom in all directions.

Under the *old régime* with its great formal culture, a close relation existed between the theatrical dance and the dances of Court and Society. But with the decline of *mondaine* choreographic education not only the theatrical dance but even its elementary positions became impossible for the nonprofessional.

As it was more and more monopolized by professional artists, the artificial character of the dance became increasingly pronounced and at the same time more *spiritualized.*

The idealistic cult of the *toe dance* and the *élévation,* which determined the forms of our contemporary ballet, made its first appearance in the beginning of the nineteenth century. Noverre, the "Shakespeare of the dance," in the eighteenth century knew nothing of the whirling movements on the toe nor of balance prolonged in the *attitudes.*

This is not the first time that a crisis has occurred in the development of the ballet. They recur periodically and their usual symptom is the predominance of pantomime.

In the middle of the eighteenth century there was the *rationalist crisis;* in the beginning of the nineteenth the *romantic crisis.* Both menaced the ballet but it survived them enriched by new resources. The evolution of its technique has continued uninterruptedly. The different centuries through which the ballet has passed have left their impression upon its scenic arrangement. The libretto of 1830 is still its model and through this romantic veneer we catch glimpses of rococo affectations, the pompous allegories of the *French Baroque.* These echoes of the past may charm us—memories light as the pollen of flowers upon a butterfly's wing. But the living spirit of the ballet is not in these seductive futilities. She is not a marquise in powder and patches!

Today the ballet is passing through a third crisis. I do not know if it will prove as fecund as the other two, but I doubt not that the ballet will rise like the Phoenix from its ashes. It will adopt more profound modern theatrical conceptions. It will create for itself a new pictorial or architectural milieu. All the fortuitous elements, ephemeral and extraneous, which hide its true essence will fall by their own weight.

In this "twilight of the false gods" of dilettantism, of eclecticism, which would transform the dance into an ethnological or archeological exhibition, the classic ballet shines forth in all its splendor. For it presents unlimited plastic and dynamic possibilities. We have seen how the establishment of an artificial equilibrium multiplies these possibilities. Doubtless the number of fundamental movements is limited, like the colors of the spectrum visible to the human eye, or the sounds perceptible to human hearing; but the multitude of possible combinations, shades, and variations passes all imagination. It is only to the uneducated eye inapt to observe subtilties that the ballet appears monotonous, as is the measured verse of the poet to the uncultured ear.

These assertions are supported by incontestable evidence. And now the reformers admit the ballet scoffed at during a quarter of a century by the élite as well as the common herd, but they admit it only to combat it the better. Slyly they try to crush it beneath their respect and relegate it to the museum. "Very well," they say, "but can we attempt nothing new? Do you insist upon the monopoly of the dance by the ballet?"

And what if I do? Frankly these questions seem to me suspicious. Why should one so earnestly *seek* what one has *already found?* Why should one replace a thing which one publicly approves?

Two formidable armies are leagued against the ballet—those who do not see and prefer to touch, to hear, to feel, and those who *could* not if they *would.* But the classic ballet, strong in its tradition in accordance with the spirit of order and discipline which animates the élite of today, will triumph over this conspiracy of the blind and the paralytic, which I shall never cease to denounce.

May these few lines aid her triumph!

—from *Broom,* December 1922

ANDRÉ LEVINSON

The Spirit of the Classic Dance

Nothing is more difficult than to reduce the essential esthetic realities of the dance to verbal formulas. Our ordinary methods of analysis are of very little use in dealing with this art, which is primarily a discipline of movement. The dancer in motion is a harmony of living forms, masses, and outlines, whose relations to each other are continually varied by that "motion which causes the lines to flow." We are exceedingly ill equipped for the study of things in flux—even for considering motion itself as such. We cling to things at rest as though they were landmarks in a turbulent chaos. A modern engineer, for example, who wishes to study the mechanism of a revolving screw, would doubtless begin his studies by stopping the motor and taking it apart, in order to understand clearly the technical methods employed by the designer. The dancer has a fairly wide technical vocabulary, but it is one that is useful only to himself. Even the most expert spectator can decipher its hieroglyphics only with great difficulty—not because of ignorance nor unintelligence on his part, but because these technical terms invoke no corresponding muscular association in the layman's consciousness. It is because the art of the dance is so peculiarly inarticulate that it has never possessed a proper esthetic philosophy. Choreographic thought—and here we fall straightway into the use of an improper and misleading term—has always been condemned to expression through paraphrases—high-sounding but inaccurate. It has had to content itself with the shifting, uncertain expedient of the analogy, which is, according to Nietzsche, the surest way of falling into error. We approach the dance by aid of analogous hypotheses and the habits of thought employed in our consideration of other arts, with the inevitable result that we substitute the obvious facts of a static art for the elusive dynamics of the dance.

The great Noverre, called the "Shakespeare of the dance" by Garrick and "Prometheus" by Voltaire—who is still the most vital and thorough theoretician who has written on the subject—desired above everything to incorporate the dance into the group of "imitative arts." Carlo Blasis—the same incidentally who established the theory of classic instruction—struggled manfully to evolve some plausible connection between the spectacle of the dance and the poetry of the spoken drama. Others have conceived the dance as strictly limited to the expression of definite ideas—thereby sacrificing it to and confusing it with pantomime. It seems as though everyone had piled upon this art mistaken attributes or supplementary burdens in his efforts to redeem—even if only in a small way—the actual movements of the dance.

I can not think of anyone who has devoted himself to those characteristics which belong exclusively to dancing, or who has endeavored to formulate specifically the laws of this art on its own ground. Those famous dance historians whose names I have mentioned have listed, described, and analyzed a certain number of fundamental dance movements and set down the empirical laws which rule the execution of their elements. The grammar of Zorn is complete in its descriptive matter and the recent treatise of Cecchetti is invaluable as a method of instruction. But no one has ever tried to portray the intrinsic beauty of a dance step, its innate quality, its esthetic reason for being. This beauty is referred to the smile of the dancer, to the picturesque quality of his costume, to the general atmosphere surrounding him, to the synchronizing of his bodily rhythm with the beat of the music or again to the emotional appeal of the dramatic libretto of the ballet: but never is it shown to lie in the contours of the movement itself, in the constructive values of an attitude or in the thrilling dynamics of a leap in the air. All the other arts are foisted on the dance as instructors. Blasis even insisted that a dancer should, at any given moment, be a suitable model for the sculptor Canova. But a statue is motion captured and congealed, the eternal prison of one specific form. And while it is true that every movement does break up into moments of action and moments of rest, it is only these moments of rest, of stable equilibrium, and not the complete movement of the dance, that can be said to find an analogy in sculpture.

I am sure that an artilleryman, thoroughly familiar with the motion of projectiles, able to calculate accurately the trajectory of a shell, the force of the explosion that sets it in motion and the range of the missile released, could much more easily discover the principle of a dancer's leap than some loose-thinking poet, however magnificent his style. For the gunner operates with a knowledge of dynamics. Doubtless his aim is wholly material—destruction, pure and simple—while it is the desire of the dancer to create beauty which causes him to make use of his knowledge of mechanics and that finally dominates this knowledge. He subjects his muscles to a rigid discipline; through arduous practice he bends and adapts his body to the exigencies of an abstract and perfect form. In the end he brings the physio-logical factors—muscle contraction and relaxation—completely under the domination of the sovereign rhythm of the dance. This is what makes it so difficult to separate the gymnastic elements of the dance from its ideal essence. The technique of a dancer is not like the mechanical workings of a disjointed doll; it is physical effort constantly informed by beauty. This tech-nique is no supplementary reinforcement to his art, nor is it a mere device, designed to gain easy applause, like (according to Stendhal) the art of the versifier. It is the very soul of the dance; it *is* the dance itself.

Of all the various techniques it is that of the so-called classic dance—a term designating the style of dancing that is based on the traditional ballet technique—which has prevailed in the Western world. It seems to be in complete accord not only with the anatomical structure of the European but with his intellectual aspirations as well. We find this technique in all those countries where man is fashioned like us and where he thinks in our way. The little definite knowledge we have concerning the system of gymnastics of the ancient Greeks warrants our identifying certain of their "modes" with those of the contemporary dance. Today the universality of the classic style is disputed only by the oriental dance, that finds in the Cambodian ballet its highest and most complete expression. The superb efflorescence of the dance in Spain is in itself a vestige of an oriental civilization, repelled but not annihilated.

Opponents of the classic dance technique pretend to consider it an aca-demic code, imposed on the dance arbitrarily by pedants and long since obsolete. It is true that it does recapitulate the experience of centuries, for we find that certain of its fundamental ideas were accepted by the dancing masters of the Italian Renaissance. It was they who first broke away from the so-called "horizontal" conception of the dance, based on outlines and figures marked by the feet of the dancer on the floor—what you might call his itin-erary. The outlines of the choreographs of the seventeenth century, repro-ducing on paper the curving path drawn on the ground by the feet of the dancer, are the last vestiges of this "horizontal" idea, which was gradually displaced by the vertical conception of dancing—the configuration of motion in space. This important process, so fruitful in its developments, lasted throughout two centuries and strangely enough has never been even touched upon by any of those many chroniclers of the dance, who, as I have said before, invariably prefer to approach the subject as writers, musicians, or historians of folkways and manners. Inasmuch as the verbal formulas that serve to designate dance movements and attitudes have remained practically unchanged all this time, the superficial observer is apt to overlook this development.

As a matter of fact there is no question but that the meaning of these formulas changes with each generation. The five fundamental positions, which are the ABC of the dance, may seem to be the same for Feuillet, the choreographer of the "grand Siècle" and for Mademoiselle Zambelli—to mention one of the fairest flowers of contemporary classic dance. But this is not actually so. In the outlines of Feuillet that have come down to us, the feet in the first position make an obtuse angle. In the modern they are in the same straight line in the first position, and in the other positions in parallel lines. This may seem to be a trifling detail of growth and change, when one thinks of Isadora Duncan dancing a Beethoven symphony. But this almost imperceptible difference, this slight shift of a geometrical line, these feet pivoting at an angle of so many degrees, represents an enormously important acquisition, capable of infinite combinations and variety. This trifling detail is actually a realization of that essential principle and point of departure of classic choreography which took two centuries to prevail—that of turning the body—and more particularly the legs of the dancer—outward from its center.

I find myself at times looking at the history of the modern dance as though it were some charming but infinitely obscure romance, that needed a key to unlock its mysteries. This key is an understanding of what a dancer means when he speaks of turning out the body. The movement of the oriental dance is concentric. The knees almost instinctively come together and bend, the curved arms embrace the body. Everything is pulled together. Everything converges. The movement of the classic dance, on the other hand, is ex-centric—the arms and the legs stretch out, freeing themselves from the torso, expanding the chest. The whole region of the dancer's being, body and soul, is dilated. The actual manifestation of this can be readily seen or even better felt in the trained body of a classical ballet dancer. The dancer spreads the hips and rotates both legs, in their entire length from the waist down, away from each other, outward from the body's centre, so that they are both in profile to the audience although turned in opposite directions. The so-called five fundamental positions are merely derivations or variations of this outward turning posture, differentiated by the manner in which the two feet fit in, cross or by the distance that separates them. In the fifth position, where the two feet are completely crossed, toes to heels, you have the very incarnation of this principle of turning outward—that is to say, of the spirit of classic dancing. The fifth position is Taglioni; the third was Camargo. A whole century of experimentation and of slow, arduous assimilation lies between the two. The orthopedic machines, true instruments of torture, that were used to turn pupils out in the days of Noverre would not be tolerated today. But it does take several years of daily exercise, beginning at the ages of eight or nine years, to give a dancer the ability to perform this mechanical feat easily.

At this point, the reader may demand precisely what is gained by this hard won victory over nature. Just this—the body of the dancer is freed from the usual limitations upon human motion. Instead of being restricted to a simple backward and forward motion—the only directions in which the human body, operating normally, can move with ease and grace—this turning outward of the legs permits free motion in any direction without loss of equilibrium; forward, backwards, sideways, obliquely, or rotating. The actual extent of motion possible is considerably augmented, and since the feet are thus made to move on lines parallel to each other there is no interference and many motions otherwise impossible are thereby facilitated. As a good example of this, I might cite the *entrechat*—that exhilarating movement where the dancer leaps high in the air and crosses his legs several times while off the ground. This effective "braiding" movement necessitates the turning outward of the body—otherwise the dancer's legs would block each other.

What a tiresome recital, you may be saying, and all of this in trying to talk about so elusive and illusive a thing as the dance! But I assure you it is justified, for the very illusion of this enchanting art—which seems to ignore all natural laws—depends on an intelligent ordering of physical effort. The dancer then is a body moving in space according to any desired rhythm. We have seen how the turning outward of the body increases this space to an extraordinary degree, pushing back the invisible walls of that cylinder of air in the centre of which the dancer moves, giving him that extraordinary extension of body which is totally lacking in oriental dancing and multiplying to an infinite degree the direction of the movement as well as its various conformations. It surrounds the vertical of the body's equilibrium by a vortex of curves, segments of circles, arcs; it projects the body of the dancer into magnificent parabolas, curves it into a living spiral; it creates a whole world of animated forms that awake in us a throng of active sensations, that our usual mode of life has atrophied.

I have not tried to explain clearly more than one of the salient and decisive characteristics of the classic technique. The rich development of the dance that increases its sway from generation to generation corresponds to the gradual elaboration of this principle of turning outward.

If at the beginning of the classic period the dance served merely to give law and style to the carriage and deportment of the perfect courtier, or if at the time of the "*fêtes galantes*" it was still skipping and mincing, it has gradually become exalted and transfigured until it is now called upon to express the loftiest emotions of the human soul.

When once the enthusiasm of the romantic period had created the idea of the dance of elevation, it was only one step further to make the dancer rise up on his toes. It would be interesting to know at exactly what moment this second decisive factor entered in. The historians of the dance, unfortunately, are not concerned with telling us. It is however evident that this reform was at least a half century in preparation. The heel of the shoe raised up, the instep arched, the toe reached down—the plant no longer was rooted to the soil. What happened was that the foot simply refused to remain flat any longer. It strove to lengthen out the vertical lines of its structure. It gave up its natural method of functioning to further an esthetic end. And thus it is that when a dancer rises on her points, she breaks away from the exigencies of everyday life, and enters into an enchanted country—that she may thereby lose herself in the ideal.

To discipline the body to this ideal function, to make a dancer of a graceful child, it is necessary to begin by dehumanizing him, or rather by overcoming the habits of ordinary life. His muscles learn to bend, his legs are trained to turn outward from the waist, in order to increase the resources of his equilibrium. His torso becomes a completely plastic body. His limbs stir only as a part of an ensemble movement. His entire outline takes on an abstract and symmetrical quality. The accomplished dancer is an artificial being, an instrument of precision, and he is forced to undergo rigorous daily exercise to avoid lapsing into his original purely human state.

His whole being becomes imbued with that same unity, that same conformity with its ultimate aim, that constitutes the arresting beauty of a finished airplane, where every detail, as well as the general effect, expresses one supreme object—that of speed. But where the airplane is conceived in a utilitarian sense—the idea of beauty happening to superimpose itself upon it—the constant transfiguration, as you might call it, of the classic dancer from the ordinary to the ideal is the result of a disinterested will for perfection, an unquenchable thirst to surpass himself. Thus it is that an exalted aim transforms his mechanical efforts into an aesthetic phenomenon. You may ask whether I am suggesting that the dancer is a machine? But most certainly!—a machine for manufacturing beauty—if it is in any way possible to conceive a machine that in itself is a living, breathing thing, susceptible of the most exquisite emotions.

—from *Theatre Arts Monthly,* March 1925

ANDRÉ LEVINSON
Argentina

The recent unexpected renascence of Spanish dancing, an art whose creative power seemed to have been exhausted, is due primarily to the strange genius of one dancer, L'Argentina. Alone she has epitomized and regenerated a dance form long cheapened and falsified by the music hall gypsies turned out wholesale in Seville. And her phenomenal success has started a new initiative in Spanish dancing, the oldest and noblest of European exotics.

What is the miracle accomplished by this dancer of *boleros* and *alegrías?* That of having braved modern barbarism and made the sense of quality prevail. Her rise to fame has been slow and difficult, because her delicate and intense art, expressed in exquisite shadings, has been a standing challenge to the period. In a *genre* limited to a very few formulas, supported but also restricted by popular tradition, she has developed an incredible breadth and variety. Her intelligence has worked a subtle transformation of those curves, spirals, and ellipses, those interlaced ornaments and sinuous calligrams, which are the foundation of all Iberian *baile.* In her the spirit of the Occident triumphs over the lure of the Orient. She has once more reconquered Andalusia from the Arabs, and by that sign has triumphed.

There were some, at first, who contested the authenticity of this art, at once scientific and inspired. But Argentina, like any creative artist, was merely transposing the themes of Spanish folklore, the native dances which are the first rude stammer of primitive instinct, into style. She understood perfectly the two-fold nature of that dance—sense and spirit—which makes it so fascinating. Its paroxysmic beat—the animal passion which carries the popular dancer, twirling convulsively, around the Plaza de Rondas—she disciplined into form, by inscribing it in movements of a pure and highbred elegance and subduing it to perfection. Thanks to her, Spanish dancing has now entered a new phase and risen to hitherto unattained heights of sublimation.

Who is this woman to whom contemporary art owes so exquisite a surprise? Although born in Buenos Aires (whence her glorious surname), Antonia Argentina is a pure-blooded Spaniard, born of an Andalusian mother and a Castilian father. Her personality reveals the double influence of the Cordovan countryside and old Castile. At the age of four she began to study classic dancing under her father, *primer bailarín* of Her Most Catholic Majesty at the Opera of Madrid. At eleven she was engaged as *premiere danseuse* at the Teatro Real. The methods then prevailing on that stage were those of the Italian School, and the young girl had a long struggle before she could put into effect her own ideas of fusing virtuoso dancing with the spontaneous graces of the *bailaores de flamenca.*

She made her first appearance in France at the Jardin de Paris, and staged several ballets at the Moulin Rouge and the Olympia. Her reputation became world-wide, she visited England and Russia; from 1915 to 1920 she toured South America and Mexico. In New York, with the orchestra of the Little Symphony, she danced to the *Green Eyes* composed for her by Granados, the last page signed by that regretted musician. This composition is a slow *paseo,* a solemn and pensive parade. Two lectures on Spanish dancing given by the writer at the Comédie des Champs-Elysées, Paris, with illustrations by Madame Argentina herself, may have helped to discover the formula which ultimately established her reputation. Leaving the music hall, she toured Europe, giving exceptionally successful dance recitals. Such, briefly stated, are the facts. But the secret of her fascinating art remains to be penetrated.

Slender, sinuous, sheathed in a long, tight, triple-flounced gown that, in a foam of black spangled tulle, lengthens into a train, the dancer is like some heraldic serpent undulating on its tail. She carries her head high—a small head with a tilted nose, a narrow and purposeful brow, a sharply-modeled profile, and singularly luminous eyes. Argentina dances the *fandango,* that eternal pantomime of love, then the *corrida,* which is the representation of a bull-fight. But though she respects and achieves the figurative foundations of these dances, they are completely transformed by style. The *corrida* is, to be sure, a representation of life, a startling evocation of the tauromachic rites, with their magnanimous ardor and mannerly ferocity. But each of the matador's murderous movements, once subjected to rhythm, once incorporated into a group of moving forms, becomes a plastic symbol, a dance step. The living drama of the bloody arena is transformed into a divine game. The same is true of her treatment of the tango. The impassioned quality of such a dance is heightened by the absence of a partner. The isolation of the dancer, the impossible embrace, add a something indescribably melancholy to the desire of the flesh. A couple would be much less pathetic. This isolation is, in fact, a step toward abstraction.

Argentina gives an exquisite nobility to her passionate undulations, to the lure of hip and buttock. She lifts sensuality above carnal bondage. She distills and purifies it, without emasculating it. Even her own lithe body, like that of the classic dancer or some highly exact instrument, seems reduced to strict essentials; everything in her becomes a function of the dance. We might say that she has just enough of the woman—masses, lines, resources—to dance bewitchingly. What she gives us is not the total sensation, in its brutal or mixed materialism, but the essence of that sensation, its spiritual perfume.

You will never see Argentina dancing, tense and self-centered, on a single point of the stage. She moves about freely, broadly; she has much of the sweep of the classic dancer, for she has that training modified by Spanish formulas. Her rhythmic sense is marvelous. Her castanets show such a variety of *timbres* that they grow almost vocal, and such intensity of expression—impatience, defiance, triumph—that they are not merely a voice, but speech.

The essence of this art is the mutual inner-penetration, the parallel development, amazing in its precision, of the musical line and that drawn by the body in response to the melody. The same inner impulse seems to have produced both music and dance. Such movement, for example, as that in which she opens and slowly extends her arms, throwing herself backward, while the wooden clappers execute a subtly graduated crescendo, is unfolded, scaled, *filé* (to borrow a term from the singer) to raise our emotion to a climax. And, listening to the tap of her heels distilling anger or tenderness as they interpret the symphonic variations of the castanets, one is tempted to say with M. Paul Valéry of the Athenian dancer, Athikté, that "her ears are marvelously one with her ankles."

In certain scenes of Manuel de Falla's ballet, *El Amor Brujo,* Argentina has displayed her qualities with the greatest vigor. Her interpretation of this role at the Opéra-Comique in Paris was the crowning triumph of her career. The book is well-known: it inspired the master of Granada to conjure up all the demons of the dance.

Candelas is in love with Marco, but she is haunted by the ghost of a dead lover. This is the theme of a ballet, wrongly described on the program as a pantomime. It is in reality a ballet of magic for its steps and gestures are neither purely decorative dance-forms, nor the spontaneous and incoherent expression of passion: they are *incantations,* charms to repulse the disembodied spirit. This wonderful theme of the suffering spirit wresting itself from the clasp of chaos is interpreted by Madame Argentina, the protagonist of the ballet, and also the choreographer. The directors of the Opéra-Comique were intelligent enough to realize how apt and parallel was her manner to the intention of the great musician, who wrought a national lyric art out of the crude material of Spanish folklore.

The scene of terror, which serves as prelude to the struggle against occult instinct, derives, no doubt, from pantomime. We see her, with paralyzed body, bowed to the earth in fear. How, we ask ourselves, will this woman ever dance, unable as she is to rise or even to turn her head? Her creeping progress, cowering on inert hands and knees, from the glowing hearth to the cot, and her prostration, flat on the earth, like a worm cut in two, are poignantly pathetic. But Candelas recovers herself and begins the exorcism. She summons her companions and leads the ritual dance of fire around the brazier. An irresistible incantation: only Stravinsky has equalled its tension of rhythm, the insistence of its phrasing. A strident vibrato on the strings prepares this imperious, maddening hammer-beat, which the sorceress accents with her heels, as she glides sidewise, marking the measure with thumb and middle finger, the natural symbols of clapper and castanets. Or advancing with crossed steps toward the flame, and leaning over it, she fans it higher by the swirl of her skirts, that serve as a bellows, swaying with each movement of her hips. Then abruptly she throws herself backward, with outstretched arms and suddenly, around the rhythmic piston drumming harshly on the ear, rises a melodic phrase, twining in a light upward curve, and now, freed, released, the fluid body of the dancer winds in a graceful spiral.

A Negro "stepper" succumbs to the tyranny of rhythm: all his movements are reflex. But the Spaniard dominates and directs this fluid that penetrates her to the point of pain. She bears in her the intoxicating poison, but also the antidote, rapture and poise, folly and wisdom, the Maenad and the Muse.

—from *Theatre Arts Monthly,* October 1928

Sex, Violence, and Kenneth MacMillan

Several of the biggest scandals of the Royal Ballet's history attach to the choreographer Kenneth MacMillan. Scandals about matters integral to ballet: subject-matter, casting, music. The climax of his 1960 ballet *The Invitation* is a rape. What begins, disturbingly enough, as mutual attraction between an unhappily married man and an innocent, curious, teenage girl suddenly turns ugly as the man's attraction changes into merely brutal lust. The girl—wrapped belt-like around his waist as he, back to the audience, reaches sexual climax—mimes one of the many silent howls that mark MacMillan's choreography. In the early 1960s, this was shocking enough that audiences in the regions had to be warned in advance of its disturbing content. (The ballet outlived the scandal. It stayed in regular repertory until 1977, and it still made an impact when last revived in the 1990s.)

After the premier of MacMillan's *Romeo and Juliet* (1965), Margot Fonteyn and Rudolf Nureyev took a number of curtain calls unprecedented for a new ballet. But soon after the opening night it emerged that MacMillan had not made the title roles on them and had not wanted them to dance the premiere. "His" Juliet and Romeo in rehearsal had been Lynn Seymour and Christopher Gable—much more tearaway, angry, inspired by both Zeffirelli's famous 1960 Royal Shakespeare Company production as well as *West Side Story*—and *force majeure* had been applied to impose the most famous partnership in world ballet onto his new ballet as its first cast. When their turn came, Seymour and Gable were acclaimed too (unlike any other new ballet the company had seen, *Romeo and Juliet* was scheduled from the start the way the old ballet classics were, with no fewer than five star casts billed to take turns in the leading roles in its opening season alone); but this demotion was a harder knock than any rising star needs. Nureyev and the New York impresario Sol Hurok were probably the chief machinators behind it; but both Frederick Ashton, as the Royal Ballet's artistic director, and MacMillan himself could (should?) have fought for the important principle of giving an opening night to the dancers on whom the ballet had been made. In this case, MacMillan was both victim and agent. He had sacrificed his chosen dancers because Hurok et al. were guaranteeing him (aged thirty-five) a box-office smash hit on both sides of the Atlantic. Until then, *Romeo and Juliet* had been associated in London and New York with the legendary

Bolshoi production—and in fact he successfully encouraged even his fifth-cast Juliet to make a vividly individual interpretation of the role, quite distinct from either Fonteyn's or Seymour's divergent archetype; and his *Romeo* has remained a cornerstone of Royal repertory ever since. Nonetheless, once his success was sure, MacMillan went on complaining about his treatment up to the last years of his life.

Back in 1959, when MacMillan (born in 1929) had applied to choreograph Mahler's *Das Lied von der Erde* on the Royal Ballet, the board at Covent Garden had rejected the idea on grounds of the music's unsuitability for choreography.* This occurred despite the fact that Antony Tudor had choreographed his celebrated *Dark Elegies* to Mahler's *Kindertotenlieder* in 1938, and that it had been a staple item in the repertories of both Ballet Rambert and American Ballet Theatre ever since. So, in 1965, just months after the premiere of his *Romeo,* MacMillan made his Mahler ballet instead on the Stuttgart Ballet—and had such a triumph with it that, within the year, the Royal Ballet invited him to restage *The Song of the Earth* at Covent Garden, in whose repertory it ever since.† (The Royal Ballet's founder, Ninette de Valois, was moved to write a poem about MacMillan's ballet; Ashton, her successor as artistic director, said in the last year of his life that he thought it MacMillan's finest work.) MacMillan had achieved two of the biggest successes of the era—and had suffered two of the biggest rebuffs. He left the Royal Ballet in 1966 to work as artistic director of the Berlin Ballet. Seymour, the most original ballerina ever to have joined the Royal Ballet, went with him. Christopher Gable stayed, but in 1967 left ballet altogether.

When MacMillan came back to Britain, it was to succeed Frederick Ashton in 1970 as the Royal Ballet's artistic director. Ashton was as establishment as artists come, and his ballets were impeccably, brilliantly, crafted; MacMillan had been the Angry Young Man of ballet, and his ballets invariably contained various flaws of construction. Many people (especially in New York, where the Royal Ballet had been enjoying stellar biennial seasons since 1949) could not tolerate him at the company's helm; and he continued to encounter trouble at the highest level. In 1976, when he applied to choreograph Faure's *Requiem,* history repeated itself. The Royal Opera House board rejected his request as musically unsuitable (some of its Catholic members, led by John Pope Hennessy, were particularly alarmed). He choreographed the ballet on the Stuttgart and had another hit. Seven years later, he revived it on the Royal Ballet, where it has remained in repertory. For the Queen's Silver Jubilee in 1977, he used the choral dances from Benjamin

---

*My thanks for some of the details here to the critic Jann Parry, who undertook extensive archival research for her just published biography of MacMillan.
†In 1948, Tudor had also, though less successfully, made a ballet to *Das Lied von der Erde.*

Britten's *Gloriana* (an opera that the Queen was already known not to have enjoyed in her 1953 Coronation season) to show the first Queen Elizabeth (Lynn Seymour, again), in a skirtless farthingale frame, cavorting in sexually suggestive terms with a whole retinue of cavaliers. At the VIP reception afterwards, MacMillan was cold-shouldered by almost every bigwig except Denis Healey. His 1973 production of *The Sleeping Beauty* had not been a great success. Though he had always been encouraged by Ninette de Valois, he found in 1977 that she, aged seventy-eight, had gone to the powers at Covent Garden behind his back to submit her proposal for her own new production of this classic, and that it had been accepted. MacMillan resigned with almost immediate effect.

The scandals went on. Though he remained at Covent Garden as the Royal's resident choreographer, he went on making ballets that "the establishment" didn't want to see, and he often timed them to arrive at the least opportune moment. He was entitled to make a ballet about the Isadora "I am the enemy of ballet" Duncan, but why did he need to make his full-length *Isadora* to celebrate the fifty-year anniversary of the Royal Ballet's foundation? (It is the only ballet at Covent Garden whose premiere I remember being booed.) He not only choreographed the garden of the Finzi-Continis, he choreographed the gas-chambers too (*Valley of Shadows,* 1982). Not that they were a scandal: MacMillan had acclimatised his audience to uncomfortable subject matter by then. He had made a Diary of Anne Frank ballet (*The Burrow)* in 1958: since when he had gone on to cover the Russian Revolution and nervous breakdown (*Anastasia,* 1971), psychosis, syphilis, morphine addiction, and sexual double standards at the Habsburg court (*Mayerling,* 1978), and plenty more. He was particularly drawn to unromanticised aspects of heterosexual intercourse, to abnormal psychology, and to exposing the dark underbelly of royalist or oligarchical societies. And from early in his career—probably starting with his 1957 *Solitaire,* a beloved repertory item for many years—it was common critical currency (with his approval) to discuss many of the protagonists of his ballets as "Outsider" figures.

Today, these MacMillan scandals sound positively edifying. He's now widely spoken of as an artist of audacity and compassion, who enlarged ballet by deprettifying it and by forcing upon it new aspects of seriousness. But he shrank it, too. The palette of movement from which he drew became coarser, as did the strokes with which he employed it. By the mid-1970s, not even the old fogeys were seriously shocked by the sex and violence in MacMillan's ballets. One Colonel Blimp, bright-eyed on the opening night of *Mayerling,* was heard to say after Act One had ended on a scene of wedding-night gunfire, skull-wielding terror, and marital rape, "I normally fall asleep during this sort of thing—but not tonight!"

In time, scandal switched from MacMillan's seriousness of artistic intention to the embarrassing patchiness of his work and the paucity of his dance language. Some of his ballets contained acres of waste padding (if the Imperial scenes in the first two acts of *Anastasia* had gone on any longer, they would have had dances for the Imperial dog and the Imperial cat) while many of them simply couldn't express what they wanted to. Nobody looking at *Mayerling* can ever have thought that its four male Hungarian officers are successfully communicating the cause of Hungarian secession. The way they emerge from a curtain, waylay Crown Prince Rudolf on his way through the palace on his wedding night, catch him in successive half-Nelsons, and lean upon him while gesturing whispers into his ear, it looks as if they're blackmailing him about some sexual episode in his past: presumably one in which they participated.

MacMillan had some enemies and many detractors from the 1950s on, and the ineptness of such passages made him an easy target for them. You could turn from his work to that of George Balanchine, Frederick Ashton, Antony Tudor, Jerome Robbins, and, in modern dance, Martha Graham, all of whom were choreographing throughout most of MacMillan's career; and the comparison not only made MacMillan seem a more flawed and less substantial artist but also heavily in debt to all of them. Known to be morbidly sensitive to criticism, he made matters worse by sometimes rounding on even some of his most loyal supporters—biting the hand that had petted him for the last thirty years. Whereas the senior Ashton had been generous enough not to restage his own *Romeo* (made in 1955 for the Royal Danish Ballet) at Covent Garden once MacMillan had expressed an interest in creating his own new version, and whereas, when MacMillan announced his plan to choreograph Poulenc's *Gloria,* Ashton, an artist more akin to Poulenc in several respects, dropped his own ambition to choreograph that score, MacMillan was considerably less generous to younger choreographers. If there was even a rumour that a younger choreographer was interested in choreographing Stravinsky's *Pulcinella* or Britten's *Prince of the Pagodas,* he let it be known that, at Covent Garden, these scores must "belong" to him—even though he never did choreograph the former and though his eventual, long-delayed 1989 production of the Britten three-acter was very spotty in dance inspiration.

But, for all his flaws of execution and of character, you couldn't laugh MacMillan away. Ashton—though not above making bitchy remarks about MacMillan's more infelicitous choreography—certainly didn't. When he saw the weird and vicious characters of *My Brother, My Sisters* (a ballet in which the Brontë children overlap with the *Lord of the Flies*), he responded so fully that he recommended the ballet to everyone he knew. Even though *My Brother, My Sisters* (made on the Stuttgart Ballet in 1978, taken into Royal Ballet repertory in 1980) was one of the MacMillan ballets that

Ashtonophiles found easiest to knock, Ashton's own readiness to praise had a direct effect on its initial success in Royal Ballet repertory.

You still can't laugh MacMillan away. About his best work, there remains a kind of dignity, a lived sincerity of detail, that transcends his limitations. My own favourite is *Mayerling* (1978). This is a ballet that, in some dramatic respects, I care about in the way that I care about Verdi's *Don Carlos*—and not just because they're both full-length works about Habsburg crown princes with Oedipal problems and leftwing political sympathies. *Mayerling* is dedicated to Ashton, and, though it is mainly striking for its un-Ashtonian features, its most remarkable feature is one for which Ashton was famous: it seems astoundingly truthful to the real-life events it reports (cf. Ashton's 1968 tableau of Elgar at home in *Enigma Variations*), you're—mostly—persuaded by its interpretation of history, and its characters have a life that carries on in your head after the fall of the curtain. Like *Don Carlos* with Eboli, *Mayerling* has a second heroine, the prince's scheming ex-mistress Marie Larisch, who knows how dangerous she can be—and who ends up being banished. When I discovered that the real-life Marie Larisch is one of the voices in T. S. Eliot's *Waste Land* ("And when we were children, staying at the archduke's, My cousin's, he took me out on a sled, And I was frightened. He said, Marie, Marie, hold on tight"), it seemed only natural; in *Mayerling,* there is even an important snow scene in which Marie Larisch plays a vital part.

The interaction between secondary characters (reminiscent again of *Don Carlos*) makes *Mayerling* by far the most richly-textured of MacMillan's ballets. When Rudolf's mother, the Empress Elisabeth, finds Marie Larisch in her son's room, apparently in his arms, and finds that Marie has been (at least) condoning his morphine habit, she banishes her; and among the ballet's most loaded moments is Marie's quiet, slow, telling exit. Slowly, ruefully, ironically, even slyly, she curtseys to him—while placing her finger to her lips to indicate that his secrets remain safe. I have been crushed; and the fall of the Habsburg Empire will follow in due course; so let us set history in motion; and meanwhile let us preserve appearances. As Marie leaves the room (and the ballet), she pushes in Mary Vetsera to take her place: the young mistress (introduced to him by Marie, some scenes before) with whom he has already found the morbid erotic-psychotic relationship he craves and with whom he will now go to Mayerling to die. For such characters, such moments, we can readily accept a few misleading Hungarians earlier on.

MacMillan died in 1992, backstage at Covent Garden, during the performance of *Mayerling* with which the Royal Ballet opened its 1992–1993 season. His wife Deborah has now become a vigilant power widow in the manner of Cosima Wagner and Alma Mahler. Most MacMillan ballets remain in exceptionally good shape, and she has sanctioned or conceived posthumous revisions to some of them, so that they still seem works in progress. During the late 1990s, *Anastasia* was cut and redesigned; design revisions were made to *The Invitation; Different Drummer* (1984) has been relit; cuts have been attempted in *Manon* (1974); nearly-forgotten rarities, *Triad* (1972) and *Rituals* (1975), have been revived. The current 2002–03 season has seen an international celebration of his work. New productions of different ballets by him have been staged in Montreal, San Francisco, Milan, Copenhagen; existing productions have been revived in Paris, Washington, and New York; exhibitions have marked his work at both the Royal Opera House and at the Theatre Museum (the latter is called *The Outsider*); *Mayerling* was revived on the exact tenth anniversary of his death.

Full-length ballets are increasingly popular these days, and, in the absence of a living choreographer who can make new ones to catch the imagination, MacMillan's have become a boom industry. *Manon,* thought by many to have been a failure at its 1974 premiere, is now danced by ballet companies on several continents; *Mayerling* is now danced by the Royal Swedish Ballet too; and his *Romeo and Juliet,* now over thirty-eight years old and danced by companies from Russia to the States, has effectively become the world's definitive production.

To watch these and other MacMillan ballets again at Covent Garden this season has been to be struck anew by the essential difficultness of MacMillan's artistic character. The controversial nature of his work goes deeper than the scandals during his lifetime. MacMillan made one argue, still makes one argue, about the most crucial and enduringly controversial ingredients of ballet: its choice of music and response to music, its presentation of women and sex, its capacity to convey matters psychological or bluntly realistic. Just what was MacMillan trying to express? And what do the facts of his choreography actually express? The two things often seemed, still seem, very different.

There are extensive passages of *The Song of the Earth* where, the more MacMillan responds to Mahler's music and the words, the more feckless his dance looks. In the long final Farewell, the singer recounts a first-person-singular tale of how "My friend" arrives to announce his farewell from life. To the slowly delivered German words "Er sprach, seine Stimme war umflort: Du meine Freund . . ." ("He spoke, and his tones were veiled: "O my friend . . ."), MacMillan gives us very precisely timed mime gestures and a perplexing ménage à trois that show (a) that the person doing the speaking is not the protagonist's friend/lover but the spectral Messenger of Death (b) that his tones aren't muffled but repeatedly shouted, as if to the winds (c) that both the protagonist and her lover are nonetheless straining to catch his message. Yet, as the words proceed, the Messenger then stops being the teller; and indeed there's no message to be understood. (Except the one we've understood all along: You're going to *die*.) The lover has already made his dance farewell, in the strenuous, too metronomic, duet that MacMillan sets to the long Funeral March in the middle of this song. The best parts of this ballet are when MacMillan draws less close to individual words. When he depicts the loneliness of the protagonist, passing in bleak isolation through changing communities and landscapes (the changing perspectives, paths, and imagery of the choreography here include some of MacMillan's most haunting inventions), he catches a central image both of Mahler's song-cycle and of his own "outsider" motif.

After the original musical controversies of *The Song of the Earth* and *Requiem,* the powers that be at Covent Garden let him choreograph Poulenc's *Gloria* in 1980, and the ballet he achieved has widely been acclaimed as one of his masterpieces. Its basic concept, surely modeled after Britten's *War Requiem,* is eloquent enough. Ghosts revisit the trenches of the First World War and re-visit the situations of their sad lives—all ironically set against a liturgical text that says "Glory be to God." The main scenario of the ballet— principally in the relationship of the main heroine and the two men in her life—is inspired by Vera Brittain's *Testament of Youth* (at the time of *Gloria's* premiere, we had all just been following the TV adaptation). But when the music speeds up, MacMillan gives us happy choreography (the ballet's second heroine is cheerfully thrown about by men in some very chirpy acrobatic partnering) which dissolves the ballet's initial irony. On one occasion he actually stages a Calvary scene, with the main heroine and her two main partners being held aloft by others like Christ and the two thieves, each cruciform: an image that makes no sense in terms either of the music or the rest of the stage action.

More objectionable than that (and very far from Vera Brittain) is the terrible passivity of *Gloria's* chief heroine. She droops her way through the ballet, usually over the arm of one man or two, not because of any apparent grief but because she is from the outset a victim, a helpless, pliant, pretty doll. Both women in this ballet are further complicated by the uncertainty of the sexual implications of MacMillan's way with partnering. That second woman: is she sexually aroused or naive in the way she flings herself about with groups of men? We can't be sure, and we can be even less sure whether the main heroine knows what on earth she's doing when one pas de trois keeps manipulating her through various contorted figures until finally, held like open scissors with arms and legs apart, she is impaled between her two partners, their torsos pressing into, respectively, her crotch and head.

Danses Concertantes (1955) shows us that the twenty-five-year-old MacMillan might have become another artist altogether. By the highest standards, this choreography is rather too busy. Nor do its incidents add up powerfully in terms of overall architecture. But it remains a startling, impressive, academically virtuoso outpouring of pure-dance invention. The strokes in which it seems to have learnt from Ashton and Balanchine are always surpassed by those in which it makes witty effects of its own, and enduringly it catches the debonair chic of the mid-1950s. Watching this, his first professional ballet, one can't help asking: Has there been a single young ballet choreographer since 1955 who has announced his talent with such panache?

And then one asks: Why did MacMillan change? Some of the answers may become apparent when Jann Parry's biography comes out. But they won't stop the arguments. My own biggest problems with MacMillan have been to do with his sheer clumsiness, both with expression and with the medium of dance. But it is easiest today to argue about his presentation of women.

There are ballets in which MacMillan's women are rebellious, sympathetic, engaged. The main reason to see his *Romeo* is to see his Juliet. I have often sat out Act Two, during which she makes just one brief non-dance appearance, but in Act Three, during which she is hardly ever offstage, she carries the audience's heart with her impulsiveness, her decisiveness, her recklessness. Even so, especially in Act One, one has to cope with MacMillan's tiresome dualism of prudish, repressed townswomen versus fun-loving harlots—a dualism that occurs in far too many of his ballets. And there are other ballets—*Gloria* is among them—in which MacMillan treats women like plasticine.

Or like unresisting victims; or gluttons for punishment. During Act One of *Manon,* the heroine chooses des Grieux for love and then chooses to leave him for money; but in the next two acts others keep making her decisions for her. Act Two ends with a largely repetitive pas de deux about choice—does she want des Grieux, to whom she has returned, or does she want the sparkling bracelet she has earnt?–and what makes it especially feeble is that MacMillan then takes the choice literally out of her hands. Des Grieux, not she, makes her mind up for her; he rips the bracelet off her wrist, so that he is all she has left. When Lynn Seymour, the fifth-cast Manon, stepped into this ballet in 1975, she changed this episode, to the ballet's great gain. She, not des Grieux, made the crucial, angry, decision to tear off the bracelet and give herself up to love alone. (It was with a Seymour performance of *Manon* that MacMillan ended his regime as the Royal Ballet's artistic director in 1977.) But, even though Seymour now helps to coach the ballet, her interpretative decision on that point has been overruled or ignored. Today's Manons get bullied by des Grieux and by every other man. Maybe the victimhood of women is the point? But over three acts a nasty edge of masochism sets in.

One moment has more force today than when the ballet was young. It occurs during the final pas de deux. In the swamps of Louisiana, the dying Manon dances one last time with des Grieux. He lifts, spins, tosses, catches her. Here is another of MacMillan's acrobatic pas de deux, far more spectacular than substantial, but various ballerinas—Antoinette Sibley, Merle Park, Natalia Makarova, Seymour, Altynai Assylmuratova—have kept the dramatic tension going to the end in various ways: Manon can sail high in frenzy, cling to love as the one true value in her life, alternate between despair and my-will-be-done defiance, find *liebestod* transfiguration. (Sylvie Guillem today acts it with real force, but I find her dancing intolerably toneless.) But I have never seen any Manon go to death so limply as this season's debutante Alina Cojocaru; and Tamara Rojo was also distinctly passive. With both these Manons, I noticed here an incident when des Grieux, having flipped her body this way and that, suddenly rams his pelvis between her legs, as if taking her from behind. What makes this so weird is that this is the first sign of explicit sexual congress between them during the whole ballet. Now you're dying, now I'm throwing you about as never before, now I'll have you.

You can argue that MacMillan didn't intend these sexual or sadomasochistic aspects of *Manon* and *Gloria*. But he certainly did elsewhere. *The Judas Tree,* one of his last ballets, is the one that currently causes most argument. Set on a modern London building site (Canary Wharf visible in the background), it shows a girl variously goading men until they gang-rape her—during which assault she dies; the man most central to the rape then hangs himself; whereupon she rises from the dead, still lingering as he dangles from his rope. (Discuss.) An actor friend this season pointed out this ballet's resemblance to Harold Pinter's *The Homecoming;* here, as there, the woman is astoundingly complicit and provocative in her sexual dealings with the men. But Pinter's 1963 heroine survives, and though she lets her husband go, it isn't the death of him. By contrast, death is the idea MacMillan can't leave alone.

Characters in dance theatre have been dying for centuries. But even when you know the Sylphide's blind and wingless farewell to life, the Swan Queen's self-immolating leap offstage into the wings (i.e. into the lake), and whichever factors (madness, a weak heart, dancing too much, plunging a sword into her heart, betrayal in love) contribute to the still vexed issue of Giselle's death, it remains startling just how much death there is in MacMillan's ballets, and how much dancing the dying characters get to do. Romeo takes the dead-seeming body of Juliet, partners it, lifts it, drags it. The heroine of *The Song of the Earth* makes her prolonged farewell to life, reaching one climax in the intense funeral-march pas de deux with a lover who, it then emerges, will be claimed by the Messenger of Death before she is; the ballet reaches its close with all three—heroine, her now "dead" lover, and the Messenger—slowly advancing towards us in a tranquil limbo. The heroine of *Manon* finds her ambiguous death in the arms of des Grieux; in *Mayerling,* Crown Prince Rudolf eventually finds in Mary Vetsera the lover whose morbidity, passion, and psychosis match his, who will join him in the most

acrobatic of all sexual pas de deux before their double suicide. The characters of *Gloria* return from death to relive the loves and relationships of their
mortal lives before returning to their graves. In *Valley of Shadows,* the action
alternates between the garden of the Finzi-Continis (set to Tchaikovsky
music) and the gas chambers (set to Martinů); the former gradually emp-
ties, the latter gradually fills, its denizens all doing the same danced unison
shudder.

I think it's too crude to label all this (and there's more) as necrophilia, but
you can see why some ballet people do so. MacMillan choreographed like a
thanatomane, and sex and violence were natural ingredients to him. In *Mayerling,* all the elements came together in one heady brew. Romeo's behaviour
with the dead Juliet is relatively simple, and it's easy to find it romantically
affecting, especially if you notice echoes in it of the way he partnered her
when she was fully alive and responsive. Elsewhere, however, MacMillan's
preoccupation with the dying and the dead feels like a clumsy *idée fixe,* one
that adds up to a meaning beyond that of any individual ballet. It is, I think,
the angry wail of the true passive aggressive. You'll miss me when I'm gone;
you mistreated me right up to my death; when I was alive, I was the outsider,
but when I die I will be part of you; whatever love you had for me was the
wrong love and it couldn't keep me alive. This cumulative message, larger
than one's compassion for any individual MacMillan character, was often
deeply irritating when he was alive. Now that he has been dead for more
than ten years, it remains irksome. And yet, and yet: we do miss him. The
scene is smaller without him.

Act Two, Scene One of *Manon* occurs in an *hôtel particulier* where all kinds
of women are available, as is an ambiguous "garçonne" figure. She mainly
dances the same steps, on pointe, as the other harlots—yet she's in boy's
costume, and she dances a provocative mini-solo. The role was created for
Jennifer Jackson; this season, I asked her about it. She told me that, when
MacMillan had made it, she (then only in her second season with the Royal
Ballet) had assumed that she was just another of the scene's many loose
women. So, when she had received the boy's costume (designed for her by
Nicholas Georgiadis), she assumed that there was some mistake. She went to
MacMillan to inquire: What kind of role am I meant to be dancing? MacMil-
lan slyly took her aside and told her: "*You're* more expensive."

—from *The Times Literary Supplement* (London), 2003

MARCIA B. SIEGEL

Trisha Brown: Dancing Through the Language Barrier

Trisha Brown's image of the dancing figure is different: a woman, not conventionally pretty, neither thin nor fat, and without the taut muscle tone, the extra readiness of most other dancers. The Trisha Brown dancer, particularly Trisha Brown herself, is most of all *present;* she puts herself before you without comment and does what she does. When you first begin to look at what she does—moves rather than movements, separate shiftings of limbs or larger segments of the body into new shapes or positions, one after another in a fluid but mostly unaccented chain of events—it's a little like living where they speak a language you don't know. Out of the stream of German conversation around me I can identify only a few words, and even they are without the rationalizing structure called grammar. But I know the structure is there. And I listen to other things—to the rhythm and formation of the words, the modulation and blendings of voices, the different ways people use the same language. And I understand a lot—quite a lot.

Brown's *Locus,* the second of three dances shown last night at the Open House, eludes detection as a rational plan with specific meanings, although Brown has explained it somewhere and proved it is just that. But if you can't quite see the multiplicity of choices available to the dancers—they can move within imaginary cubes around themselves, cubes of different sizes, and can, in part of the dance, choose to do one of several designated portions of the movement sequence—still you can look at Locus for the peripheral information. During the part of the dance that's in unison you can enjoy the phrasing, almost hear the way the movements group themselves, because there's no music to make your eyes lazy or distract your attention. You can take pleasure in the organizing of the stage space into simple patterns and their subsequent disintegration and then the reforming of new patterns. At other times, you can get into the ebb and flow of energy through these loose bodies as they glide from arm gesture to shoulder swivel to displacement of the hip and back into alignment again.

Accumulation and *Group Primary Accumulation* are much easier to translate because the idea is simpler and more repetitive. The phrase accumulates, as one gesture at a time is added to what has been established. When Brown does it as a solo, the additions are sometimes simultaneous with parts of the existing phrase, the connections between gestures can smooth and round off the shapes so they're no longer distinct in themselves. But in the *Group Primary* version, with four women lying on the floor sideways to the audience, each gesture keeps its original shape clearly and enters the sequence consecutively. Since the phrase in this dance contains about forty accumulated small patterns, we get to see each one so many times that we begin to learn the sequence too. And when two stage managers come out and bodily pick up the dancers and move them into other positions—depositing them on their stomachs, sitting them in chairs—we mentally go on with the dance for them until they're settled and able to move their limbs again.

—from ORF Austrian Radio, October 21, 1976

MARCIA B. SIEGEL
Mauve Punk: Karole Armitage

If we have to start differentiating the varieties of punk now, Karole Armitage's *Do We Could* probably belongs somewhere at the soft end of the scale. The piece began with a slam and ended with a mannerly farewell. I figured maybe the punk was an affectation, a chance for some nice, clean dancers to get their hands dirty. The dancers—Armitage is a member of the Merce Cunningham company, Deborah Riley and Michael Bloom have both danced with Douglas Dunn—were dressed in those goofy, unbecoming clothes of punkdom. Armitage was all in black—tight cotton pants, a blouse, soft heelless boots. Riley wore black espadrilles, a black skimpy skirt slit way up on both sides, and a sleeveless white T-shirt. Bloom had on black basketball sneakers, black pants, a white shirt with the sleeves cut off, a black tie, and black-rimmed eyeglasses. All of them had their hair plastered down except for Armitage, who has a crew cut, and all their hands were freshly gloved in paint—yellow, blue, and purple.

They exploded out of that slamming door into the light and walked very fast around the room, the kind of racers' walk that makes your legs stiff and your torso gawk way out over them. The dancers looked a little like scared chickens, I thought. As they skittered around they made peculiar little hand gestures or jabbed at the air with their upper bodies. After a certain amount of time, they'd all come to a halt, rest a moment, then begin again. At each interval they seemed to be adding one gesture to the sequence, but their movements were so erratic and spastic that it didn't seem to count. They got a little winded during this section, but they didn't really push themselves. Paint started getting smeared on their clothes as their hands brushed against their bodies, and once Riley leaned on a pillar and left a good set of purple handprints.

In other sections of the piece, they stalked around like zombies, their hands flapping, their heads and arms jerking. They clustered indecisively together, sometimes appearing to lean on each other, sometimes pulling away, but how long they could sustain this supporting structure didn't seem to be an issue. For long periods of time they stood in one place, dropping into unresilient pliés and jerking their limbs and torsos. Again, sometimes I thought they were trying to hang loose from one particular joint or throw their weight just so far and stop it, but that didn't seem to be a consistent pattern either.

Another "theme" of the dance was to clutter up the space. The Kitchen space is permanently obstructed with pillars anyway, and I did think maybe Armitage was underlining a point there. The dancers would periodically interrupt their quasi-tasks to drag some unnecessary and inefficient-looking piece of equipment into the space where it would block their way—a two-by-four with a crude lamp on the end and a long cable trailing, a large reflector strung on a rope, stuff like that. But since they didn't seem particularly concerned with moving through the space in any special way, the junk just sat there and looked junky. Charles Atlas's patchy, low-wattage lighting made it all one piece with dingy Broome Street out the windows.

The dancers looked very different from one another. I sometimes thought they weren't all doing the same dance or that they were improvising or playing Follow the Leader Not Too Closely. Armitage is tall and spidery. Riley is strong and tense. Bloom's body doesn't settle properly into its skin when he finishes a move, he has to adjust it bit by bit, and it often fights him, giving off involuntary little flicks and knobby tremors on the way to an uneasy repose. Bloom was kind of the comic of the piece, peering around at the others as if checking their scene and perhaps finding it no more reassuring than his own.

While they were doing a long series of in-place thudding gestures, we could hear someone dragging something heavy up the Kitchen's back stairs and around the outer rooms, and finally knocking on the door near the audience. Armitage went and opened it. A man walked in with a hand truck, coats and a briefcase loaded on it. He unpacked while the dancers relaxed. He took out a water jug and glasses, paint can, paint thinner, paper towels, candles. He lit two candles and recited a few words of a possible poem. Then they all cleaned up the space, wiping the floor, painting over Riley's handprints on the pillar, putting the awkward props back where they'd been at the beginning. Armitage and Bloom toasted each other with water. Then they all put on their coats and left. It was the most resolute thing they'd done all night.

—from the *SoHo Weekly News,* December 20, 1979

MARCIA B. SIEGEL

Comforts of Hell: Bill Irwin

Somehow it seems right that Bill Irwin came to town on a night when New Yorkers had been more battered than usual by floods, blackouts, transit chaos, and political skulduggery. It seems right that an overflow audience arrived anyway to greet him. He's a sort of hero of the ashcans, a saintly version of your neighborhood bum. Irwin is the kind of clown who survives by persistence and sheer grit. The fact that he also happens to be clever, even intellectual, doesn't give him any advantage in his race with the Ultimate, it just prolongs the indignity. In his new piece *Not Quite / New York,* he's beset by challengers, loses to them all, but after the winners have left the ring he's still there, shuffling dejectedly in a fading light.

We see him first in running clothes. Confident as a young adman, he sprints into the room, stands center stage, and does a cool, efficient little movement combination—a hinge backward into an interrupted fall, a few tight gestures, a pivot into a loping circle around the space. He tries this a few times, then goes up to a wardrobe trunk and takes off his streamlined warm-up jacket. Underneath he wears a white dress shirt three sizes too big for him. He's ready to start again when the door opens and Charles Moulton comes in, dressed just as he is and carrying a suitcase. They eye each other; you think at first Moulton is late for a rehearsal and Irwin, in charge, is being patient but annoyed. With a long look and a cold nod of agreement, they both begin doing Irwin's running combination. Right away it's apparent that Moulton hasn't come to work with Irwin but to steal his show. Mid-course he takes a flying jump that isn't in the plan. Unnerved, Irwin keeps on going, but from that moment on you know he wants to keep this guy from getting the better of him.

Moulton leaves after he and Irwin put on identical white bow ties and pairs of baggy pants and hats the color of sludge. Irwin fiddles with a big box that looks like a crude homemade hi-fi and gets it to play some music, ragtime on a guitar. He starts dancing a rubberlegged version of the combination but the music fails him. While he's tinkering with the controls on the box, Moulton comes back and they do the routine again. They both put on matching too-big vests and suit jackets. The more daring Moulton is, the more Irwin comes unglued, tripping over his own feet, getting off on his timing, till Moulton swaggers out.

While Irwin is trying to practice a dance to Dixieland, another man (Michael Moschen) comes in and takes a white ball out of a black three-by-five card box. They start tossing the ball; then they're taking turns doing tricks with it. Irwin is a pretty good juggler but Moschen is a champ. Doug Skinner, the next rival, brings a ukulele, and they strum and sing a duet about the Charleston. But Irwin starts taking the words too seriously and Skinner lets him know he's screwing up—and in front of the hard-nosed New York critics, too. Irwin tries to ingratiate himself after Skinner's exit by doing a soft-shoe dance, but something horrible keeps dragging at his foot, threatening to suck him into the wings unless he scrambles with all his might to stay onstage. Tommy Sellars, who now arrives, plays the accordion while roller-skating. After a few go-rounds, Irwin's convinced Sellars is chasing him, decides to put on skates himself, thinks better of it when he see Sellars toss off some stunts. Left alone, he's driven into a fit by his own music machine.

The obsessive nature of this piece—always the challenger, dressed just like Irwin, the initial skirmish when it looks as if they might at least come out in a draw, then the humiliating defeat, the failure at even his own dance—lets us know this is the way life is. It's going to go on and on; only the acts will change. The more extravagant Irwin's alter egos get, the less it matters that he can't match them and the funnier his efforts at keeping up.

The idea that his adversary is himself seems an important part of Irwin's clown persona. In *Pantalone and Harlequin,* which is basically a series of skits accompanied on piano, toy xylophone, slide whistle, kazoo, and tambourine by Doug Skinner, he plays at least two sets of dual characters: the curmudgeonly old Pantalone and the street-smart Harlequin who trumps him; and two dueling Gentlemen from Verona, a tall, lordly one and a scrunched-up fat one. Irwin seems to be saying it's not just the faulty products of civilization that can defeat us, the recalcitrant pots of spaghetti or defiant sound systems, but our own grandiose ambitions. Staying alive, he seems to be saying, is the most absurd of our notions, and the most necessary.

When he's run out of skits, Harlequin subsides into a trunk and watches Moulton, Moschen, and Sellars glide by, assured, glamorous, and potent as ever. Irwin smiles sadly. He's wondering if he could parachute off the Empire State Building.

—from the *SoHo Weekly News,* September 22, 1981

MARCIA B. SIEGEL

Exhibit A and Possibly B: Meredith Monk

Meredith Monk's *Specimen Days* has been in the making for three years; maybe that's why the piece seems to have several unrelated themes. Monk's method of operations is fragmentary anyhow, and with elements of different scale, pitch, and character comfortably butted up against one another or laminated in sometimes baffling simultaneity, it doesn't much matter while you're watching that the ideas don't quite mesh. Nothing less expansive than entire cities, wars, or historical eras seems to satisfy Monk's panoramic vision, and this time she turns her attention to the Civil War. As usual she views it with the microcosmic eye of a poet, the sweep of a high-soaring bird. Images so familiar they're almost clichés seem new again in the sketchy, childlike outline or theatricalized miniature of her staging.

One possible center of the work is two families, one Northern and one Southern, who live similar lives though each has its own customs—gestures so well known they've become repetitive and barely functional. At dinner the Northerners spoon their soup toward the outside edge of the plate, make elaborate preparatory motions with knife and fork before attacking their food. The Southerners say grace with hands folded on the table and heads bowed, eat with many flourishes and gracious social asides. The children carefully copy everything their elders do, and later, when someone is dying, try to keep back their terror by reciting what they can remember from their lessons. Both families lose somebody in the war, but somehow both return intact to their dinner tables after it's over.

These are not any particular people, notable for their individual histories, but symbolic types, specimens I suppose. And they are observed and recorded in various ways. There's a photographer (Gail Turner, dressed as a man) who comes and sets up a big box camera on a tripod, ordering his subjects to hold still for fifteen seconds while he makes a picture. Monk herself plays the composer Louis Moreau Gottschalk, who lived in the South but was sympathetic to the Union side. Gottschalk made a great success touring as a concert pianist, and then wrote all the local color he'd seen, but almost none of the agony, into his light, danceable music. Monk, dressed in black trousers and a velvet frock coat, sits and ruminates at the piano, plays, writes a few notes, sings, but the music is her own chanting, rocking distillation of gut feelings—musical belly laughter, soothing murmurs, sobs. Once she dances a long shuffling journey accompanied by abstracted gestures of piano playing, receiving the applause of an audience, greeting well-wishers—duties of a touring celebrity.

Then there's a technocratic type in a lab coat (Pablo Vela), who's sometimes a lecturer demonstrating the statistics and assets of the actors. "Number one and Number three, step forward please. Incline from the waist. [Numbers one and three bow.] Thank you. You may retire." He brings on a black man (Cristobal Carambó), gets him to display his teeth, measures his head, reporting 16 centimeters ear to ear, 22.4 centimeters from crown to chin. Is he offering a slave on the auction block? Giving an anthropological paper? Suddenly Vela places his hands on Carambó's midsection, pauses dramatically, and pronounces, "Hunger." At the end of a long war scene, Vela coolly walks over the battlefield spraying the havoc with disinfectant.

Vela seems to represent the sanitizing, alienating effect of science on history—but then Monk's Gottschalk illustrates that art can do the same thing, and so does the objective journalism of Turner's Matthew Brady. From time to time a screen is brought in, once so that Vela can show a series of slides made of picture postcards—Paris, France; Peking, China; Easton, Pennsylvania. What begins as a travelogue suddenly incorporates those pictures of the families that were taken earlier, and also pictures of battlefields and exhausted troops.

It's mostly through Monk's music that the passions and sorrows of real people keep breaking through their fixed, flat tintype representations. From time to time the cast assembles to sing wailing, summoning, whimpering solos and choruses, sometimes from offstage, sometimes ranged in neat rows. Feelings flame to the surface, then quickly burn out. Robert Een sits completely still for a long time, as if posing for the camera, then he slowly gets up and smashes the chair.

Contrasting with the formality and stillness of these abstract characters is the montage of scenes showing the war itself. Turner and Vela, dressed like dime store Abe Lincolns, stand on soapboxes and orate silently while the chorus chants from different parts of the room. Een and Carambó, dressed as soldiers, dart in and out, shooting, falling, carrying one another off, managing to represent both the Union and Confederate armies by changing from blue to gray caps when they're offstage. Meanwhile stage managers are setting up tiny tents all over the space. Then the Abe Lincolns and the soldiers are gone, and from the wings big black rubber balls are rolled across the space, knocking over the tents. The effect of a room full of broken toy tents in a pale light is devastating, not at all cool or scientific.

After the war, the deathbed scenes, and the reassembling of the families, Monk has interpolated her movement-singing piece *Turtle Dreams,* perhaps simply as a return to severe formality. There *has* been a turtle in *Specimen Days,* actually—the star of three short films by Robert Withers. This engaging reptile is first seen plodding through a swamp, then hovering over a map of the United States, and finally blundering down the streets and over the elevated tracks of a miniature city. I couldn't figure out any way this went with the Civil War, though I enjoyed the films.

The last turtle film interrupts Monk, Een, Paul Langland, and Andrea Goodman in the middle of their dance, but their singing goes on behind it in the dark, with musical cries of pain and confusion and mourning. When the turtle's journey has finally taken it to the moon, the screen is cleared away to reveal an unfolding tableau in which the quartet continues singing, now with small fluorescent lights hanging across their chests.

Vela and Turner, now in modern dress, stand on soapboxes and exhort, sometimes clutching their sides as if they've been wounded, but continuing their silent orations. Four women in hoopskirts revolve at the periphery of the space. The other characters walk backward, slowly, across the rear of the space. At this point there are about three different sounds—the *Turtle Dreams* quartet singing, the chorus in the background, and Steve Lockwood's organ ostinato underneath it all. Nicky Paraiso leaves the other organ he's been playing and crosses to Monk's piano, where he sits and plays a lilting Gottschalk waltz. And that's the way the piece ends, in a cacophony of clashing sounds and people in motion, in which each sound, each group, has a distinct character and a clearly perceived pattern. Only a mind like Meredith Monk's could have no qualms about putting them all together.

—from the *SoHo Weekly News,* January 5, 1982

WALTER TERRY

Ballet on Ice

S*wan Lake* is about to freeze over, and the swans themselves are getting
ready for it. The old Tchaikovsky favorite has long given sanctuary to swan
maidens and their queen, but Catherine Littlefield has taken away their toe
slippers and put them on skates. If any one has a right to surprise swan lassies
with a change of climate, that one is Catherine Littlefield, for Miss Littlefield
is a classic ballerina in her own right, she has directed her own companies in
successful appearances here and abroad, she put dancers on bicycles in *American Jubilee* and she is a choreographer of recognized ability. Now she is
trying to unite spread eagles with arabesques in *It Happens on Ice,* the new
extravaganza coming to the Center Theater on the tenth of this month.

Fairly quivering with ideas on the possibilities of ballet on skates, Miss
Littlefield dashed into her first rehearsal and threw most of her young athletes on their faces with the intricacies of her skating steps. Soon she discovered that skates have a double edge and that an attractive arm movement
could throw the skaters' balance from one edge to the other so suddenly that
disaster was the only possible result. A little study cleared up matters, and
before long she had her skaters conscious of ballet line, group composition,
able to adapt their spins into ballet turns, their jumps into long ballet leaps.
Until he came under the Littlefield direction, one young man had supposed
that music was only to keep the audience's ears busy, but he soon learned
that ballet on skates meant that music and motion were destined to pay close
attention to each other.

At rehearsal the other day I saw some of the new works. Little, blonde
Catherine Littlefield kept warm with coat, mittens, a blanket, and coffee
while she shouted directions to her skaters. There was *Swan Lake,* with its
swan maidens, its queen, its prince, its hunters, and the evil magician. Hedy
Stenuf, the "prima skaterina" for the company, glided, soared, and swirled in
breathtaking fashion, while Gene Berg, as the magician, pursued her more
fleetly than man ever pursued fair lady. These two dancing skaters, along
with Skippy Baxter as the prince, are certain to win stellar positions for
themselves in the great field of ballet.

Before anti-classicists get worried, I want to assure them that Littlefield
has more tricks up her sleeve. A ballroom polonaise replete with elegance,
etiquette, and elan is on the schedule, and a Currier & Ives glimpse of a day

on the old skating pond is in production. This latter work is a gentle but hilarious satire on the naughty boys who trip every one up the bevies of girls being taught to skate by patient swains, the governess and her elite charges, the young lovers and the show-off skater who builds up to near-decipherable figure eight to the tune of ardent applause. A jazz number, *So What Goes*, splices its pep with all the appurtenances of love: a huge ring, a rose, angels, the lovers' knot, and the necessary lovers. A swing ballet and an iced version of a Negro spiritual will complete the Littlefield contributions.

I have always maintained that the American dance should and must partake of athleticism, for the simple reason that a nation's dance should honestly reflect the character of its people, and Americans are decidedly sports-minded. Great dancers have contributed richly to this union of sports with dance, but here at last is an actual fusion of the two, for ballet on ice possesses the rhythm, the patterns, the drama, and the characterizations of dance while it partakes of the skill, the speed, and the muscular prowess of the sport of skating.

The character of the rehearsal was typically American. No foreign yells, no posturing in front of mirrors marked the proceedings. Miss Littlefield issued terse, vernacular commands in a loud, firm voice. The skaters called her Catherine, the boys winked as they sailed by, but Miss Littlefield was boss, and the skaters snapped to attention when a reprimand was launched at them. The girls and boys have quickly learned the group spirit necessary to good sports of good dancing, and the men have managed to assume the grace of ballet without submitting to the effeminate gestures which curse so many males in the ballet.

It Happens on Ice should do several things for the American theater. It should help to carry those who profess disinterest in dance over the hurdle which separates athletics from dancing. It should influence American dancers who have failed to see the tie between dance and sports. It should, of course, open up a new field of entertainment, for the possibilities of ballets on skates are limitless. For the sake of upholding the supremacy of dance, I would like to mention in passing that skate dancing does possess certain limitations in the matter of movement: small gestures, subtle mime, and slow movements are practically out, detracting somewhat from the range and diversity of expression. But take skating, dancing, or theater entertainment in any form of motion as your criterion, and you will be convinced, I think, that Catherine Littlefield is becoming a theater figure of the first rank, a girl who is leaving her mark in the revue, in the ballet, and on ice.

—from the *New York Herald Tribune*, October 6, 1940

WALTER TERRY

The Nutcracker: Magic

The skyscrapers seemed to disappear, the roar of subways was hushed, surly looks vanished as New York, or a small part of it at any rate, was transformed into a fairyland of music and smiles and glorious magic. The magician responsible for this brief and delightful dream world was George Balanchine, whose new, evening-long production of *The Nutcracker* was given its first performance last evening at the City Center by the New York City Ballet.

But Mr. Balanchine, choreographic genius though he is, was not the only magician at work, for there was magic in the dancing of the company itself, in the sweet performing of forty children from the School of American Ballet, in the voices of the boys' choir from St. Thomas Episcopal Church.

And there was sorcery of the finest grade provided by Karinska, who created the fabulous costumes; by Horace Armistead, who designed the soaring scenery; by Vlady, maker of masks, and by Jean Rosenthal, who illumined this fairyland with her own magical lighting, just as Tchaikovsky had illumined (and he still does) the original "The Nutcracker" with his shining music more than sixty years ago.

In all respects, this new mounting of *The Nutcracker* constitutes a major event, for it represents the first program-length ballet produced by our own resident company—a sister company, the San Francisco Ballet, has its full-length *Nutcracker* and other such productions in its repertory—and it's the most lavish ballet yet attempted by the New York City Ballet. It is, indeed, a real spectacle, rich in excitement, impeccable in taste, and by all indications of audience response, a roaring hit.

Since American dancers rarely treat with the element of spectacle, it is appropriate to report first on such matters. Among other wonders, there is a transformation scene in which a living room fades from view and a sturdy Christmas tree commences to grow to gigantic proportions and while we are watching this with mouths joyfully agape, the little toys we have seen at the Christmas party become larger—including the wonderful Nutcracker itself—and giant mice invade the scene to do battle with the valiant toy soldiers.

Again there is a change and even the Christmas tree disappears to give way to a fairyland of snow in which flakes gently fall upon great branches already laden with whiteness. Later, we are carried to the Kingdom of

Sweets, supervised by the Sugar Plum Fairy herself, and here we meet danc-ing candy canes and marzipan, a lady with a hoopskirt so large that she can house a batch of children beneath it, flowers free of restraining roots, a flash-ing dewdrop, and other enchanting creatures.

Karinska, with her indescribably beautiful costumes; Mr. Armistead, with his scenes and transformations, and Leon Barzin and the orchestra, giving bright renewal to the Tchaikovsky score, cannot steal the glory away from the dancing. Once again, Mr. Balanchine has worked that miracle of using the traditional movements of the classical ballet and making them seem wholly new through the freshness of his sequences, through the imagery of his mass designs, through the evocation of hidden rhythms, through balanc-ing dance with silly humorous pantomime.

And the dancers do justice to Mr. Balanchine and his colleagues. Maria Tallchief, as the Sugar Plum Fairy, is herself a creature of magic, dancing the seemingly impossible with effortless beauty of movement, electrifying us with her brilliance, enchanting us with her radiance of being. Does she have any equals anywhere, inside or outside of fairyland? While watching her in *The Nutcracker,* one is tempted to doubt it.

And briefly, but with enthusiasm, one must note the charming perfor-mances of Alberta Grant, whose dream *The Nutcracker* is about, and Paul Nickel, the Nutcracker himself and a perfect little cavalier; Yvonne Mounsey and Herbert Bliss, who led a group in a Hot Chocolate episode with a dis-tinctly Spanish flavor; Francisco Moncion, as Coffee, in a lazy Arabian dance; George Li, as the chief figure in a Tea pas de trois, unmistakably Chinese; Robert Barnett, as the mercurial leader of the Candy Canes; lovely Janet Reed, good enough to eat as a Marzipan Shepherdess; Edward Bigelow, wearer of the mammoth hoopskirt; Tanaquil LeClercq as the Dewdrop; and Nicholas Magallanes as the Sugar Plum Fairy's gallant and expert partner.

—from the *New York Herald Tribune,* February 3, 1954

WALTER TERRY

Clytemnestra

O ne of the world's great ballet artists, currently deep in rehearsal, telephoned me last Tuesday evening as I was writing my review of Martha
Graham's new *Clytemnestra,* apologized for the interruption, and asked if I
had enjoyed the new Graham creation. I murmured something to the effect
that "enjoy" was not quite the word and the immediate response was, "Ah,
you were upset. It is important to be upset in the theater. Too much is simply amusing." Earlier, I had overheard a junior soloist of the ballet, who was
attending the performance, say, "Well, it's not entertainment in the usual
sense of the word but it's fascinating, disturbing, and I wouldn't have missed
it for the world."

Martha Graham, ever since she left her post as soloist with Ted Shawn and
later, the Denishawn Dancers, and completed a highly successful stint with
the *Greenwich Village Follies,* has achieved that presumably paradoxial position
of being an intensely dramatic and highly theatrical performer without
being an entertainer. *Clytemnestra,* which opened the Graham repertory
season at the Adelphi Theater, is upsetting, disturbing, stimulating, and
utterly absorbing dance-drama. It is not merely diverting, but then, neither
is *Death of a Salesman* or Richard Strauss' *Electra* or the great Oresteia (from
which *Clytemnestra* derives some of its material).

Indeed, Miss Graham's new, evening-long creation (in four acts) is, in a
very real sense, a monumental summation of her vivid and demanding
approach to dance. It is a revelation of "things felt," it is a dramatic analysis of
evil and the forces which permit evil to work, it is a psychological portrait of
a woman damned.

Like her Medea *(Cave of the Heart)* and Jocasta *(Night Journey),* her
Clytemnestra is not simply a dancing version of a classical figure as it moves
throughout the course of a drama or myth. Rather, does Miss Graham
concentrate upon one aspect of the character—Clytemnestra's necessity to
discover why she is dishonored and damned even among the dead of Hades—
and upon this single aspect, she builds her work. And by dancing, she can
communicate certain details of passion for which words are inadequate.

The choreography is cast in the style of a mighty ritual, unrushed, often
symbolic, relentless in its exposition of every factor pertinent to the fate of
the doom-ridden heroine. In fact, even elements of the Trojan War are intro-

duced, for the war itself had had a distant but inescapable (and disastrous) effect upon Clytemnestra. But throughout her work, Miss Graham has not sought to present only the acts of violence. She has presented us with causes, preludes, and plottings. Thus, the watcher, may wait impatiently (and suspensefully) as preparations are made for the inevitable. But then, when the inevitable comes, its impact is both climactic and releasing.

The archaic formalities of the work by no means obscure the vivid immediacy of Miss Graham's highly personalized movements. The crouched running steps speak of terror, the turns with a leg held high in back and the head close to the floor tell of restless waiting, the back falls to the floor are mirrors of despair, and the trembling hands and roving eyes reveal suspicion and doubt. These and other actions familiar to followers of Miss Graham are found here recharged and released to lay bare the elements of faithlessness, sacrifice, vengeance, murder, and revenge which mark the life, death, and doom of Clytemnestra.

Ageless in its ritualized form and in its theme and wholly contemporary and brilliantly theatrical in its method of presentation, this *Clytemnestra* would, I think, be as at home in an ancient Greek amphitheater as it is in a Broadway house. Part of this dual potency is due to the remarkable score by Halim El-Dabh, to the wonderfully stylized decor by Isamu Noguchi, and to Miss Graham's costume designs, based on drawings by one of her dancers, Helen McGehee.

The choreography, of course, comes first but the score is of importance because it serves that choreography. As independent music, it is often monotonous, and it wails, throbs, moans, and shrills, interrupted but rarely by snatches of luminous melody. But this is as it should be—in this case at least—for the dance itself demands neural sounds, music played upon the trembling nerves of the human body.

Obviously, in a creation of such size, in concept as well as in duration, not every moment of movement was equal to others. The first act seemed unnecessarily long, the very end (in which Clytemnestra finds hope in the promise of rebirth) was weakly keyed, and there were some other arguable elements.

Inarguable, however, was the majestic and dynamically vibrant performing of the star herself and the absolutely expert performances turned in by Yuriko, Helen McGehee, Matt Turney, Ethel Winter, Bertram Ross, Paul Taylor, Gene McDonald, David Wood, and other members of the company as they brought dance life to the figures of Electra, Orestes, Agamemnon, Aegisthus, Helen, Iphigenia, Cassandra, Paris, the Ghost of Agamemnon, Hades himself, the Furies, and others involved in a tragedy of heroic dimensions. Fine also were Bethany Beardslee and Robert Goss who spoke, intoned, sang, trilled, and cried out their notes in the El-Dabh score.

Given carte blanche (and sufficient newsprint), the critic would be
tempted to write a book about this *Clytemnestra,* but succinctness will have
to suffice and I will close by saying that Miss Graham has reached a new peak
of achievement in a long career in which triumphs have been the rule rather
than the exception.

—from the *New York Herald Tribune,* April 6, 1958

AKIM VOLYNSKY
Mathilde Kschessinska

*Akim Volynsky (1861–1926) began his career as a literary critic and journalist, hav-
ing edited the prominent St. Petersburg monthly* Northern Herald *from 1891 to
1898, after which he wrote a series of highly regarded books on Fyodor Dostoyevsky,
Nikolai Leskov, and Leonardo da Vinci (a volume on Rembrandt remains unpublished). Considered in Russia to be one of the most erudite men of his time, Volynsky
began focusing his scholarly interests on theater and dance in 1907, and between
1911 and 1925 he was St. Petersburg's most prolific and authoritative ballet critic.
He wrote more than four hundred reviews for the publications* The Stock Exchange
News *and* The Life of Art, *and in 1925 published his magnum opus,* The Book of
Exaltations, *based on the lectures he delivered on classical dance at his School of
Russian Ballet, which he directed from 1920 to 1925. That work, plus a large selection of essays and reviews including those reprinted here, has just been published in a
volume called* Ballet's Magic Kingdom: Selected Writings on Dance in Russia,
1911–1925, *edited and translated by Stanley Rabinowitz.*

Among the figures of contemporary ballet on the Maryinsky's stage,
M. F. Kschessinska constitutes a phenomenon of exceptional interest. Her
name enjoys great fame, her talent—unusually brilliant and of the highest
caliber—is recognized by all. Not only the technique of her dancing, for
which nothing is too difficult, but its overall character, produces a captivating impression: It excites and holds you in complete thrall, even though ballerinas of no less talent are dancing alongside of her. She is always at the

center of the ballet's action on stage. Something great and unique to her alone carries her artistic personality to extraordinary heights; it obliterates all fear and makes moot all competition and comparison with other forces in the ballet world. She is so much an individual, so unlike anyone around her, that in criticizing specific details of her choreographic art, one does not for a moment lose the sense of unfolding charm which characterizes her original talent overall.

There is no beautiful contour to her arch. A ballerina almost always dances facing the public rather than providing gliding, sharp, and sparkling lines of plastic action in profile.

Despite a blindingly beautiful take-off, Kschessinska's dancing appears to be concentrated on one spot and thus creates the impression more of a frozen frame than of an inspired quivering of forms to the melody and rhythm of the orchestra's music. One does not feel psychological impetuosity in her flight. Moreover, this dancer does depart from her toes, dancing all the time on pointes without either getting tired herself or fearing that she is tiring the spectator. Yet nonetheless, Kschessinska's dancing is a real marvel of balletic art with which no cliched or routine dancing can compare. She is more a brilliant orator of choreographic ideas and forms than an artist in the direct and exact sense of the word. Kschessinska is able to jolt the audience, as no one else on the contemporary stage can, by the purely external power of her art. Her dancing glistens with hues of rhetorical brilliance. It is not the rhythm of ideal form, restrained and precise, that has pride of place here, but precisely her hyperbolism, her inspired exaggeration, and her sweep—wild, crude, and brimming with passion.

Pavlova speaks and sings in her dancing. Her ebullient personality, full of fire and light, does not prevent her from magically falling into the flow of the pure and modern figures which flow one from the other with the same lightness and naturalness with which ideal similarities of mathematics conceptually grow and silently combine in their beautiful dance of elevated and looping truths.

Kschessinska prophesies. She lifts herself on her toe with such force, with such external passion, that the idea of slightly touching the floor, which is supposed to introduce an animation of gently universality into the dancing movements *terre-à-terre*, completely vanishes in her impulse to perform a movement or gesture on a collosal scale. With her plane foot, almost without an arch, her dancing—always on pointes—produces the impression of a smooth flow of forms, with no springy bending of the knee as she moves and with no gentle gracefulness and quivering surge on the surface, and it does so via the powerful and solemn play of its vigorous hues. Her double and triple turns create a genuine whirlwind on the stage. In her solo dancing, in her leaps en avant which are accompanied by the most difficult cabrioles,

Kschessinska is unmatched. At such times her face, with its features of captivating intellectualness and brand of special and magnetically attractive
beauty, and with its clever and penetrating eyes which are never silent, reflect
the poetry of the elevated moment. The mute plasticity of this remarkable
artist, who breaks all the canons and patterns of classical discipline, is full of
an inner noise and murmuring, full of thunder, full of great and subtle ideas
which are transmitted to the public and ignite it with unheard of ecstasy. It
sometimes happens that this public, seized by the rhetoric of her choreographic genius, gives itself up to the uncontrollable pathos of the impression
that it has experienced, forcing Kschessinska to repeat several times a certain
number which she has successfully performed. And with this the dancer's
enthusiasm grows and grows!

Pas fouetté is the apogee of Kschessinska's choreographic art. Left foot on
pointe, the dancer with her right foot makes complete circular rotations, not
stopping for a second and not moving from her place. Essentially uncomplicated, the pas, which consists of two tempos that are usually done to the
accompaniment of unpleasant, march-like music, takes on interest and significance only in connection with the quantity of rotations which the artist
produces. The frequent, rapid, cyclical movement—without interval—
produces an indissoluble whole that is not communicated by words, and
an irrational impression of momentary frenzy which can be beautiful.
Skalkovsky writes that the talented ballerina Bessone did fourteen fouetté
in *The Harlem Tulip* and Legnani in another ballet (I don't recall which)
did thirty-two circular rotations without moving an inch from her place!
Kschessinska, who certainly dances no worse than Legnani, is her equal in
the virtuoso execution of this difficult choreographic trick. She does it to
perfection, with a mastery that transforms it into a genuine masterpiece. This
is the power of an enormous stylistic talent which gives a final picturesque
touch to legendarily bold dancing. The artist here allows a gradually increasing quivering of dance rhythms into the movement, which, fixed on one
point, produces an impression of something endless. Without an internal
movement, which has the same irrational character, the fouetté would be
merely a trick of mindless acrobatics. But in Kschessinska this is the finishing
touch of her remarkable art, her rhetorical art which exists on a large scale.

In *Swan Lake* Kschessinska dances Odette, the queen of the swans, and
Odilliya, the daughter of the evil genius who looks like Odette. In scene two
of act one* there is a lovely grand pas of the swans in which the artist provides a whole series of beautiful and vivid plastic poses. She radiates here

---

*Volynsky refers throughout to a three-act version of *Swan Lake* in which the first scene with the White Swan (act
two in the four-act version) is scene two of act one, the Black Swan scene (act three in the four-act version) is act
two, and the White Swan finale is act three.

with unusually painterly pirouettes *avec attitude,* which create the impression of inspired statuesque figures. Kschessinska dances the final coda of this act in rapid tempo via which the passionate burning of her inner pulse is vividly conveyed.

In act two Kschessinska dances a *pas d'action.* Her pantomime is superb. In contrast to the dancing which does not always harmonize with the requirements of artistic measure, the play of her expressive face is of the most refined artistic quality. Nothing is superfluous and there is no affectation. This is not a demonstrative and naively graphic pantomime which substitutes for words, but rather the natural and simple kind which reflects emotion as it accompanies our speech no matter how it may be expressed. In Kschessinska's acting there is no conventional balletic pantomime: With the stylized gesture of her hand she is able to say everything that's necessary, everything required by the lyricism of the moment by means of the inner pathos of a balletic figure. In *Esmeralda,* for example, the artist's dramatic talent reaches extraordinary heights in this regard. I've never seen a more poetic expression of speechless love and jealousy on stage. The gypsy cries without tears via her darkening eyes. You feel her heart as if it's beating right next to you. In the artist's eyes that are raised to the sky there is so much faith, so much intelligence and resignation, that you unwittingly and boundlessly surrender to the scenic illusion of a suffering girl, though everything around her in the last act discourages you with its stiltedness. Once when I pointed out to an aging lover of ballet (and not a balletomane!) this beautiful moment in Kschessinska's acting, indicating the pious plastique of her marvelous genuflection, the cantankerous old man told me that the artist was copying the divine Zucchi.

Alas, I've not had the occasion to see the famous ballerina on stage. But I can explain such a lapse of critical judgment of a first-class dancer only by personal ill will: A huge number of lackluster people and an enormous amount of envy and spite surround Kschessinska's powerful talent. A similar storm at one point raged around the glorious name of M.G. Savina, when her talent was in decline. However, we can say with certainty that Kschessinska does not imitate anyone. Such complete creativeness, with its vividly individual stamp, develops from within, inspired by free thought and personal artistic temperament.

Several pas in act two of *Swan Lake,* the throwing of the body into its partner's arms; the quick and bold head-spinning fouetté which, by the way, was performed this time without the usual animation, and even not completely correctly, elicited tumultuous ovations from the entire theater. Here Kschessinska was at the height of that elevated and genuinely classical art, in which the rather crude Italian conceptions, brilliantly recast in the style of French exaltation, become the instrument for transmitting the real and ideal movements of the human soul. In her partnered dances, just as in her dances which are constructed on the ethereal rhythms of elevation, Kschessinska— for all the imperfections of the external structure of her legs—must be recognized as a great artistic figure of truly phenomenal power.

—from *Birzhevye vedomosti (The Stock Exchange News)*, 1911

AKIM VOLYNSKY

Olga Preobrajenska

Olga Preobrajenska dances beautifully in *Coppélia,* although the ballet in itself is old and not necessarily essential for the modern stage. Her talent, as she combines music and movement, is obvious at every turn.

The ballet opens with a waltz of passion. The simple dance on the toes, blended with leaps in arabesque and with the transferring of the body from one foot to the other, is full of gracefulness in her execution. The expression of despair in the gesticulation of the hands that convey the soul's tempest is incomparable. We observe this very brief variation with satisfaction, and it shows the artist in the splendor of her theatrical individuality. Primarily we have a dancer in the classical mold: The lines of her movements are maintained with mathematical precision, and even in combinations they provide forms of impeccable sharpness. Before us are dance patterns in the ancient sense of the word, and the physical manifestations of ideas onstage and in the beams of the footlights. And the dancing of Preobrajenska's hands wonderfully conforms to the dancing of her feet. It is as if they are playing on invisible currents. I've never seen even a fleeting stroke in Preobrajenska that departed from the musical line. But in the chaos of balletic forms that flicker before your eyes, you always feel the special energy of her hands. They accompany her feet, relaying not an external rhythm, but rather the beating of her soul which is in harmony with the orchestra.

In the first act of *Coppélia* Preobrajenska dances an adagio with Nikolai Legat. Standing in arabesque and holding her torso for several seconds, she suddenly turns her entire body forward and sideways, bending her right arm in the air almost to her waist. In general Preobrajenska succeeds wonderfully in these poses. The change of straight lines to those that are deeply bent lets us feel the intensification of the psychological motif. Then, going off to center stage, she does *attitudes,* leaning on her partner. *Attitudes* alternate with dances on pointe and with different kinds of new arabesques, concluding in a picturesque adagio. Though not rich in forms, this number nonetheless contains several beautiful moments. The groupings with the male partners are effected in lines of soft, warm sculpture.

The second act, with the exception of the comedy of the automation coming to life, gives us two dances with Preobrajenska: The semi-character Spanish dance with small pirouettes, and the Scottish dance with *battements frappés.* The entire act continues amid the gay uproar of the doll. Here the specific dabs of color smack of buffoonery. In the fast-paced rotations of the body you continually feel the dancer's lively smile, you sense her eyes, with their radiant beams, almost laughing. Giving itself up to the dancer's art, the entire hall quietly laughs to itself. Flashes of cheer fly across their faces.

In the third act Preobrajenska performs an adagio, a variation, and two codas. The adagio begins with dancing on pointes, with the right foot brought forward in a cross. Legat follows her along a straight line facing the audience. Then follow the usual arabesques for the adagio (low, with circular movements repeated several times with the help of her partner), and also charming *attitudes,* striving after the effect of a fleeting illusion. Amid the movement the dancer extends her right hand to her partner but, taking it back, she gives him her left one! Her whole body is turned sideways, with her back to the audience. The adagio ends as she jumps with both feet, brought down with heel toward toe, into the arms of her partner, palms extended forward prayerfully. And in the arms of a partner like Legat, Preobrajenska seems like a light doll.

The variation-pizzicato from *Sylvia** Preobrajenska dances alone. In the musical sense this number, as she performs it, is a model of choreographic art. Those headlong leaps and circular *sissones* joined with the *battements frappés,* those transfers of the body onto one foot (with the other moved to the side, half-bent in the air) produced so easily, freely, effortlessly, seem, in the final analysis, more musical than the very music of the orchestra. In any case, Preobrajenska's dancing is of a higher quality than Delibes's rhythmic creation, which is excessively vivid and flashy. The music of her movements is quiet and noble, like everything that is truly great, artistically polished, and full of ideas and inner ecstasy.

In conclusion Preobrajenska performs two codas. The first is developed by Legat. She does an arabesque, with her back to the audience, sideways, moving across the stage with quick jumps on pointes. Like a squall she rushes forward toward the wings, moving her foot along the floor with toe to heel and

---

*Presumably this variation was borrowed from *Sylvia* as a showcase for the ballerina Preobrajenska.

heel to toe. With that very arabesque in *La Fille mal gardée* Vaganova won over the public's sympathy.

Glory to Preobrajenska! Glory to her astounding talent! Glory to the genius of the work and to the music that makes her individualness a reality, an individualness which borders on magic and miracle. Only in art can one encounter such plasticity, such transubstantiation of the personal principle, such an ability to fuse oneself so completely and absolutely with beauty, sound, and theatrical myth!

—from *Birzhevye vedomosti (The Stock Exchange News)*, 1912

AKIM VOLYNSKY

Lida Ivanova

Lida Ivanova's body has still not been recovered. One gets the impression that the girl has not died but has disappeared without a trace. But already one wants to correct the word that has slipped from my pencil: For the ballet Lida Ivanova has not disappeared without a trace. I see a deep furrow that has been drawn on our theatrical field by the sudden departure of this still not-quite-mature but extraordinarily remarkable dancer. To make one's debut and immediately enter the history of ballet is not something that is fated to happen to every talent. There are brilliant debuts, after which the artist's activity acquires a fatal character of systematic decline—at its zenith, in the heyday of its fame, this small glory feeds on the glow of sweet, far-off days of possible promise. There are other careers which are tranquil and even. The issued promissory notes are not great, it's easy to pay one's debts, everything flows smoothly and calmly ahead under well-arranged sails with a favorable wind. If a favorable current is added to this favorable wind— artistic connections through the father or influential sister—the little boat successfully docks at the final harbor where it will disarm for a long while. This is perhaps the best kind of fame in the world. Such fame a caring father wishes for his daughter, thinking of her warm, comfortable, and joyful days. Of just such fame different types of solicitous mothers dream, starting from those who overflow with love to Madame Cardinale inclusively. Fame is conceived here as something sweet and simple, as concrete as an orange on a plate or as a good income with a predictable return. One wishes such fame for all beginning dancers. But let us give pride of place to the rapture we experience when we think of the beauty that enveloped the dancer on her short and tragic course. I must say firmly and staunchly "the dancer who disappeared," because no one heretofore has seen Lida Ivanova weakening, extinguishing, or dying. Her career was still at the stage of debut. But this debut was somehow special: With each minute the girl was more and more etched in strength and talent, in that true frame which befits great natures.

From her first artistic steps this young girl was enveloped in an atmosphere of anxiety. Two years ago a rumor circulated that a carriage had severed her leg. I remember the confusion, my telegram, and the comforting response I received. This was right after she finished school, before she became a great artist; yet though the sensitive and highly talented Olga Preobrajenska highly valued her, there gathered around her certain unstable elements, the air around her almost shook with anxious whispering, fearful pride, growing envy, and convulsed reputations, which was the way it remained up until the last minute. But not only the air shook. An epoch of intrigue began, toxins were prepared, and Florentine knives were sharpened. It is too early to name names. If Lida Ivanova had fallen while she was dancing, I would have been the first to think this was done deliberately, by a spiteful hand, as occasionally has happened on theater, opera, and ballet stages. The power of envy is dark and threatening, especially when a bright and genuine talent comes to the fore among the chaos of degradation and decline. I am ready to believe that the motor of the fateful boat really did malfunction. But I would also not be surprised if, with another group of passengers and in other circumstances, the catastrophe could not have been avoided.

The word motor brings Ivanova's internal motor to mind. I remember her as a girl, tranquil and balanced. It was pleasant to talk to her. She strung her words in a quiet voice like large pearls on the thread of a free-flowing conversation. Her comments were thoughtful, and she asked questions in the slowly burning fire of her inquisitive temperament. Of late, and especially last winter, Ivanova was unrecognizable. Suddenly everything changed. A fervor appeared, along with an expectation and edginess, that sometimes produced an unhealthy impression. Her internal motor had moved from its equilibrium and began fussing about. Everything excited and irritated her. Her every step was followed, and everyone talked about her indiscriminately. One couldn't laugh out loud—that would be an admission of suspicious extravagance. One couldn't simply and innocently carouse a bit, that would be acknowledged as engaging in inadmissable liberties. Not everyone can imagine how hard it is to live when a hundred hearts wish you dead and when a hundred eyes follow your every action with wily malice. All of this spoiled Ivanova's emotional motor and hurried it to death. . . . If her history had turned out somewhat more successfully, if her internal motor had run more normally and peacefully without having to push through the obstacles accumulated on her path, we would see a flourishing Ivanova before us.

Her talent grew with every hour. I shall long remember the impression I took away after her last performance this season. She made a brilliant display of her unusual elevation. Elevation was in general the major element of her fledgling art. I have already written on this subject and now I mention it only to delineate one special feature of this young artist's talent. When people generally speak about elevation, they have in mind something light, high, and beautifully airborne. A person is carried through the air with the grace of a butterfly. But in this instance we have something entirely different. Genuine artistic elevation is not like this at all. We know Pavlova's elevation to be something uniquely inspired, with wings powerfully spread in the air, in the glow of vigorous flames and in the light of a glowing dream. One important feature always caught your attention. Pavlova's elevation was never burdened by the determined will that was raging within her, or by the liquified gold of a newborn person. No matter how highly I value this talent, this hurricane-like glory of our time, we are dealing here with the mindset of former, anti-quated times, a classical figure in the museum of the past.

In Lida Ivanova's elevations other traits and qualities manifested themselves. Another era has blown in like a storm on our scene. What a remarkable being Adrienne Lecouvreur was in the world of intrigues and machinations! [Ivanova], small in stature, with a high forehead and a pure, bright face without wrinkles and their possibilities; big-eyed; stridently monumental in her port de bras and very much like a sketch in an album of a future great artist, she soared in the air with a spectacular take-off. Our epoch demands that the iron and copper—the true grit of the popular masses—ascend to the stars, and not the ethereal reveries of individuals. Man himself has grown more severe, but even weightier: He yearns for the heights. And that's where Lida Ivanova's mission lay. She did not spread her-self in the air like Pavlova, but performed *en tournant* in the arms of her part-ner like no other dancer before her. It's senseless to compare her *terre-à-terre* with that of today's miserable dancers. In *The Little Humpbacked Horse* she demonstrated a phenomenal rotation of her body in the air. Her arabesque was almost monstrous in terms of academic design. Her legs were stretched too widely. But there was no way to deflect your attention from the plastic figure. The theater rocked with applause. The willful enthusiasm that lifted her body glared like an entire sun high in the air. There was something even terrifying in the young dancer's take-off. Worried by this marvelous picture, I immediately whispered to her mother: "Tell Lida it's not done this way. But I adore her art!" "Not done" because at that very second the compositional design didn't call for it. But one can still do it because the ecstasy that lifts us to the sky prevails over all canons of beauty.

I recall another incident which lovers of classical dance can never forget. Spessivtseva was performing *Le Corsaire*. The audience grew alert because, prodded by a blind faith in the reputation of an accomplished artist, it expected to see something completely perfect. There's a moment in the first act when the ballerina is sitting and waiting, while on stage the wonderful duet of the slave girl and her partner unfolds. The remarkable adagio, corrected and reconstructed by Johansson, takes place. Spessivtseva and Lukom enjoyed well-deserved success in this duet at the beginning of their careers. But times change. In the above-mentioned performance, Spessivtseva could only hope to retain her former reputation, but Lida Ivanova needed to acquire fame for herself, to burst into the future through her new talent. And something extraordinary happened. The underaged girl created a movement that was purely elemental. When, in her wild leap, she found herself in her partner's arms—high and unattainable, and filled with a determined fire in the spirit of the new historical moment—all that surrounded grew dim, except her. A beautiful star was ignited. True fame was born, for no artist can have it without elevation.

I shall not analyze any other performances by Lida Ivanova. In several roles she revealed an astonishingly expressive talent. Dancing the Fisherman's Wife in *Pharoah's Daughter* she demonstrated all the little wheels and little screws of her miraculous mechanism. Her little motor rushed about the stage, spreading around its ardent emotional excitement. Her acting was utterly talented, unfeigned, cheerful, and far from being routine. But in the current repertoire she still had not gotten the chance to prove her worth in all her brilliance. Of course, we would not have seen Lida Ivanova enter the pantheon of ballet idols in Stravinsky's *Petrouchka*—that musically and choreographically pretentious piece of nonsense with its annoyingly false drum and exhausting fanfares. She was a purely classical dancer whose soul contained the music of exalted moods, adequate only for similarly serious forms of dance. I urged her father to send Lida to Milan as soon as possible, where her growing talent would have received the appropriate stamp. Oh, if that little motor had been in Milan right now!

If the sea returns Lida Ivanova's body to us, the entire city will take part in her funeral. Are there enough white roses in the flower shops for this occasion? Something strangely intoxicating flashed by us in the evanescent fate of this virtual child, who embodied the entire destiny of our now-orphaned ballet. Her appearance inspired us with hope. Her death will add another pathetic page in the history of art, where posterity will separate the artificial diamonds from the genuine ones.

—from *Zhizn' iskusstva (The Life of Art)*, 1924

AKIM VOLYNSKY

Olga Spessivtseva

(See page 1122)

It is my duty to provide a brief evaluation of Olga Spessivtseva's dancing. But let me say at the outset that to write about the classical art of this dancer apart from the personality itself, to isolate choreographical issues from this artist's charm, is well nigh impossible. This is a talent completely harmonious, balanced, and consummate in its design, which is where all of its wealth has gone. With regard to her art, we are dealing with a person who is so special and delicately individual that she has deeply impressed the public with the features of her unique and original beauty. Her gentle and slightly protuberant forehead—somewhat in the spirit of Carlo Dolci—is feminine and charming, like an oval of a delicate plant. And, of course, it is poetic. This is Cecilia Dolci, but not St. Cecilia, in a realistic likeness—as if reduced to an affecting miniature. The permanent stamp of undying childhood lies in this artist, and this is all the more remarkable since we are dealing with a brunette in whom the traits of childhood ordinarily disappear quickly, often at the earliest age. And for this reason Spessivtseva's eyes also produce an unusually favorable impression. A little tear glistens in them, just as a note of weeping resounds in her voice, even in her laugh, to all those who know her. Nevertheless her face is entirely dramatic in the elevated, innermost meaning of this word, and, perhaps, it is precisely this attribute wherein resides the characteristic that most interests us about her appearance. Spessivtseva need only stand and then smile with her mouth and eyes, and an unexpected radiance pours forth in all its gypsy-like, Spanish charm. Some years ago, at the beginning of her career, Spessivtseva suddenly revealed this quality of her mimetic character in the role of Pieretta, when she smiled her special smile and glided her childlike hand through the hair of her kneeling cavalier. The hall quivered with delight. At the time I thought, and said so in print, that before us was not only a talented dancer but a rare jewel of dramatic art in ballet, the likes of whom the Russian stage had heretofore never seen.

What is dramatic acting, dramatic mime in ballet? This is yet another issue which begs careful resolution. Extolling Zucchi, the late Skalkovsky loved to underscore the Italian's sustainedly and incredibly expressive acting. She could show passion in all of its authentic features. She was able to play and create roles in the ordinary sense of this word. But if we hold to the features described by Skalkovsky, then we would have to believe that there was comparatively little material in Zucchi's acting that could be deemed balletic and classical in nature. In the best case she was an artist of high caliber, but in the style of Duse or Sarah Bernhardt. However, this kind of expressive talent, no matter how valuable in itself, demands in ballet a complete transformation and adaptation to the peculiar conditions of the classical stage. On this stage there is no real, everyday decor. Everything is silent. There are no peals of laughter, no crying. The very theme of the action is provided not by the libretto, which is usually stilted and banal, but by the musical suggestion of the orchestra and by the immanent content of the classical staging. One who cannot read and translate these figures of classical apparatus, these immeasurable and diverse *battements,* these overhead leaps with circular rotations in the air, will never accurately understand what is really happening in ballet. And the dancer finds herself in the same position.

I ask myself: Was the vaunted Zucchi a mimic interpreter of the music's audial and figurative material, and of the dance's internal themes? I do not see this in Skalkovsky's numerous descriptions, and I myself never saw Zucchi dance. But what we see before us in Spessivtseva's mimetic talent gives a striking illustration of the idea I am trying to defend. Of course, all faces must be animated on the ballet stage. All lips must smile. All eyes must burn with rapture and artistic emotions. But between the iridescent expression of the heroes and heroines of ballet's magic kingdom and the musical-choreographic motifs of every individual performance, there must exist absolute harmony. One must not only dance to the music, one must smile to it; one must mimic and gesticulate to the tempos of the orchestra that is being conducted. All the body's acting in dance is subservient not to the verbal material, of which there is none, but to the two key distractions—music and plastique, which constitute the essential content of classical ballet.

In this regard Spessivtseva represents a rare phenomenon. All of her acting is classical in the best sense of the word. There is not a single feature from run-of-the-mill drama. We have instead a direct reflection of the plastic motif of dance assumed in its most basic, internal form. Her face is usu-

ally focused in on itself, serious and pensive, as if preoccupied with a presentiment of approaching darkness or an imminent tear. She goes out on
stage and takes up the fourth position, and without any apparatus the entire
scene is ready. Nowadays such lovely moments in her art are becoming rarities, slightly past their prime in the growing richness of her natural talent.
But the overall ability to carry with her the coming sound, the silent tangle
of emotions which is just on the verge of unfolding, the anguish and anticipation of artistic inspiration and intellectual wonder—this the artist has
fully preserved. This is a spirit that weeps children's tears, that weeps almost
in her sleeve, with the capriciousness and angry little voice of a child who is
unable to immediately become an adult and is powerless to allow its inner
"I" to completely master itself. This is a spirit that weeps about its limits. In
ballet terminology this is the purest *croisé*, the bud of a beautiful talent which
has not yet experienced its complete flowering, and which, despite its frequent appearances, has still not presented to the public its consummate
éffacé. Every ballerina has her invincible charm. Pavlova exhibits her spirit in
grandiose proportions; the whole theater blazes from her art. The flutter of
her wings is heard from high altitude. Spessivtseva is all promise, all upsurge
to the unrealizable, all oohs and ahs of a kind of insatiable sadness with which
she is also able to captivate the public. She does not ignite the audience with
the fire of her talent, but she extends over it the palpitating sheath of all
those tears, as yet unborn but already tormenting her heart. Eternally
young, she does not face the bitter fate of a flower past its bloom. And I pity
anyone who has never seen this everlasting bud of beauty and talent.

How well Spessivtseva's unique artistic talent is reflected in *Giselle*! On
stage is a little girl, eternally dancing and dying from the disappointment
which has overtaken her. In the second act she is aleady Wilis who continues
to dance even in the world beyond the grave. I don't want to speak about the
separate numbers of this marvelous ballet. From the point of view of choreography, Spessivtseva's performance in both acts stands up to the strictest
criticism. She dances with Semenov, currently unequalled in the world in
terms of the power, beauty, and lightness of his elevation and *ballon*. And
what a captivating combination of two different talents we have in this
unforgettable pair: The airiness of their leaps and the most delicate clinging
to the ground. Much air is displaced from the powerful surge of masculine
energy. Semenov is able to unhinge the magic of genuine art, but what truly
special earthliness, what unique realisticness there is in Spessivtseva's performance! This is the earth—and really not the earth: Something unsteady,
unstable, and smokily incandescent ties her to the far-off sky. The impression
is enormous. The couple's fame abroad, especially in Italy, would be indescribable. In spite of my wish to refrain from details, I cannot help but note
Spessivtseva's first dance with Semenov. A classical *ballotte* is brilliantly

mounted, as only Petipa could mount it. This is the innocent play and frolic of two young people in love. There's one moment—an imperceptible little feature, an instant, a point—when both artists seem to be hanging in mid-air. Now beyond this moment is the repetition of slight *battements* after a firm strutting of the leg. The number as performed by the artists comes off incomparably. Roulades of sweet-scented laughter pour from the stage. Of the other numbers I will not write, except to praise enthusiastically Spessivtseva's acting, especially the scene of grief, madness, and death in act one. This is utterly splendid. Suddenly the gait slackens, the steps grow numb. The entire gaunt body folds into a white ball. What teary, childlike eyes, darkened with fiery specks of fright that are under her thickly coiffed hair that is now untangling! This is a wounded bird falling helplessly from a tree. Something very miniature distinguishes this Giselle. But in its totality this miniature is marvelous, like the enamel work of a great master, it is a miniature which has already taken its rightful place in the showcase of the choreographic art's greatest jewels.

—from *Zhizn'iskusstva (The Life of Art)*, 1923

MERCE CUNNINGHAM

Born in 1919 and still creating dance works in 2008, Merce Cunningham is one of the most influential dance maker of his time. He was born in Centralia, Washington, and from 1939 to 1945 danced for Martha Graham, creating such roles as the Revivalist *in* Appalachian Spring *and* March *in* Letter to the World. *His brilliant speed and elevation as a dancer made him famous, but his more or less two hundred choreographed works have made him a crucial figure in the world of dance for more than sixty years. His life companion, the composer John Cage, was a determining influence on his art, which has always focused on pure body movement. He and Cage developed the idea of chance to determine aspects of his choreography, and he has been a pioneer in the use of computers in creating works of dance.*

Nancy Dalva

Merce

That's what everyone calls him. It doesn't seem improper, we just do it. Merce's work, Merce's studio, Merce's dancers, Merce's performances. Christened Mercier Philip Cunningham, known as Merce.

Why? First, because the name so suits him, suggesting, as it does, both the element mercury—quicksilver, changeable, unpredictable—and the god Mercury, fleet-footed messenger from Olympus. Second, fans (and isn't that what we are, at heart?) often call their favorites by their given names: Rudy, Martha, Misha, Twyla . . . Merce.

But that is not all. Merce is called Merce because his manner is unaffected and direct; because he is held in great affection, as well as esteem; and because he is so clearly our contemporary—if we can catch up with him. This man who has kept dance apace with the other arts of the twentieth century—music, painting and sculpture, literature—is now busy whisking it into the twenty-first. His work is not merely reflective, *it is predictive.* He is the least *dated* person imaginable, and the most acute observer of natural phenomena.

Here are a few things about Merce that you won't find out from his dances: He has a beautiful speaking voice, melodious and low, and the most marvelous laugh. He likes good red wine. He has a black leather jacket. His mother, a woman of considerable independence, loved to travel. His father was a lawyer. He is a Chevalier de la Légion d'Honneur, appointed by President François Mitterrand. He doesn't like to celebrate his birthday.

Here are some things you will find out: There is no greater choreographer, no braver or more truthful performer. There is no one more innovative; his dances encompass a technique and a philosophy yet are full of the everyday.

Here are the best things about Merce's dances: They are commanding and rigorous, and submit themselves readily to explication and analysis. Recollected in tranquillity, they absorb all thought, all conjecture—a strange and wonderful power common to all profound works of imagination. They offer a proposition about the function of dance, and a suggestion for how to go about looking at it. One might even come to think, after a long time of looking and thinking, that these dances offer a proposition about the nature of life, and how to go through it. Yet *none* of this matters at the moment of seeing the dance.

In the theater, all you have to do is open your eyes and your mind, and let the dance in. Everything you need to know is in it. There is no secret. You can enjoy figuring out the dance—there is much fun and reward in this—or, when the time is ripe, you can let the dance transfigure you. How this happens is a mystery not easily expressed in words, for dance comes in at the eye. One can say this much, at least. It is not something that happens with every dance of Merce's, or at every performance, and yet there is this possibility, this necessity: you will find yourself in the dance.

Some years ago, the Merce Cunningham Dance Company performed a season of eleven Events at New York City's Joyce Theater. (These ninety-minute works, unique at each performance, are paradigmatic Cunningham—made up of fragments, short and long, from the repertory; indifferent as to accompaniment, decor, and costuming; dance for its own sake.) At that time, John Cage, Takehisa Kosugi, and David Tudor were in the pit. (Their music is a whole story—a separate story—unto itself.) One night, Cage waxed oracular, sending forth garbled messages that directly addressed the very issue at hand, as it were. That is, how to partake of the dance before us.

"It gives you all thought," Cage intoned cheerfully. "My advice: Where are you in it? To give more time for the trip than oooh, aohhh, geraghhh . . ."

Where are we in it? We are with Merce. There is no better company, and there's no need to worry about where we are going. We learn by going where we have to go. Or, as Merce puts it, "The only way to do it is to do it." All we have to do is look.

—from *Dance Ink Magazine,* Spring 1994

MERCE CUNNINGHAM
The Dancer and the Dance

in conversation with Jacqueline Lesschaeve

J.L. *Merce Cunningham, how did you become a dancer?*
M.C. I didn't *become* a dancer, I've always danced. I always had an appetite for dancing. I should say, though, that it didn't just suddenly occur to me either, at the age of five, that I could become a dancer. There is nothing in my family history that suggests that I would be a dancer. My father was a lawyer, and so are my two brothers. One of them is now a judge. Both of them have always lived in the same town in the State of Washington.

J.L. *You felt different from the beginning?*
M.C. That's difficult to say, and understand. The only thing that I can think of is that my father had a certain theatrical talent in the courtroom. I don't see anything else or at least anything obvious.

J.L. *If he was a lawyer, I imagine he took pleasure in the arts of language.*
M.C. Yes. He also had a great sense of humor and loved good stories. He was an astonishingly open and generous person, broad minded in a quite amazing way for someone who lived all his life in a small town. For him it didn't matter what profession you followed as long as you really worked at it. He loved very different people. He just didn't care for phony people, "windbags" as he called them. So there I was at the age of eight, already dancing, going to the little dancing school in Centralia. I had wanted to go there without knowing what it was all about, and my parents let me do it.

More than dancing it was the idea of being on stage, in a theater that attracted me. Later, still without having any idea of what I would become, dancing was always an integral part of theater for me.

When I was eight, I remember dancing a sailor's hornpipe. It was a common dance in vaudeville and music hall in America. You learned it in small schools.

My dance classes didn't last long because the school soon closed down, and then there was nothing. So, for several years I went on studying without studying dance. But when I was thirteen I asked my mother if I could learn tap dancing with Mrs. Maud Barrett who had opened a dancing school in Centralia. Mrs. Barrett went to the same church as my mother which we all attended since we were brought up as Catholics. I didn't know her but I knew she was a friend of my mother. I'm sure my parents were very surprised at what I was asking but they let me have my way. In fact, I had seen, probably two years before, around the age of eleven, an evening that Mrs. Barrett had organized. She gave a recital every year in a theater in town that was used as a cinema but had been originally a vaudeville house. There was a stage, small, but still a good stage. She'd have her students there and they'd do all kinds of dances. She knew tap dances and waltzes and soft shoe and lots of other dances. And the audience was filled with the parents of the children who were performing. I remember the little kids doing dances wearing all kinds of costumes that she kept year after year.

Then, at one point, she came on stage dressed in a yellow gown with white pantaloons and little black patent leather shoes, swinging Indian clubs. I'd never seen anyone do that, and she was also talking to the audience because they were all her friends; that was quite a sight. Then she put the clubs down on the side of the stage. She didn't really stop talking. And she put something over her skirt. I couldn't figure out what it was at first, but I later realized it was a big rubber band. Then she got up on her hands and walked around the stage and didn't stop talking. It was such a sight to see this woman, who was no longer young, with this kind of energy. It stunned me. I thought, I have to study dancing. And my parents let me study with her. My father had a good feeling about letting people do what they want to do. His idea was that as long as you worked at it, it was all right. And he rather liked Mrs. Barrett. She'd been in a circus, in vaudeville as well. She must have been close to fifty then, a marvelous woman, full of energy and spirit. As a little kid I was fascinated by her. She would teach us a tap dance and then we would shuffle around and try to do it. Then she would get up in that nervous energetic way she had, and say: "No, that's not it." She would do it, and her feet would just fly and it was wonderful. You could hear it, I can hear it still. It was perfect, and what we were doing wasn't. I can hear the kind of sound she made, the rhythm was remarkable. After a few years she began to ask me to dance with her daughter Marjorie who was two or three years older than I was. She would make tap routines for the two of us. We would go and do them in little halls. I was in high school by then, and we did that for several years. Then one summer when I was still in high school she proposed that we all go to California on a tour. She would go with her daughter and me, and she also wanted to bring along Mrs. Fail, who played the piano for these shows. She also took her small son Leon along. Of course we didn't have any money or anything, that was perpetual. I thought the whole idea was marvelous, of course, though I never knew what was really going on. We set out. Mrs. Barrett had this funny old car, and the five of us (Leon was very small) got into it. I remember my mother wanting to see us off, so Mother took the car down to have it filled up with gasoline before we started off. I'm sure my parents thought this was just hopeless, the whole idea. But off we went, I don't think we had any engagements, if you could call them that, before we left. It was real adventure. But Mrs. Barrett was determined and by this time Marjorie and I had a sort of act, first a duet together, then she did what Mrs. Barrett called a single, then I did a single and we did a routine together, then Marjorie did some other kind of tap dance and I did a Russian dance, sometimes sitting on my heels with my legs going out from under me. We did an exhibition ballroom dance as a finale. Then we would bow and that was it. While Marjorie was dancing alone I had to change into a full dress suit, and I only had two minutes. It was very funny. Anyway, Mrs. Barrett got us some engagements in three or four clubs, and sometimes we played in movie houses where they had shows—we'd play in between the movies. We got to Los Angeles. I don't remember playing in San Francisco, though we may have. It's a long time ago. We stayed for at least a month and we finally found our way back.

J.L. *That was your first experience of having a public.*
M.C. Playing that way was quite strange because ordinarily we'd played in the fair grounds and little clubs around Centralia.

Then I went to school for a year at the University of Washington in Seattle, which I didn't like at all. I did some dancing, went to some classes. It was like musical comedy dancing, not strict classical ballet. It was clear enough but it wasn't as interesting to me as Mrs. Barrett. Just after that, I really wanted to study theater. I couldn't get it out of my mind. So I went back home and told my parents that I would like to go to New York. Of course they wouldn't hear of that. It was out of the question.

J.L. *At that age you could almost do whatever you wanted?*

M.C. That's true, but they suggested I go to a school in Seattle which they knew about, because they knew of the lady who ran it, whose name was Cornish. The school was named after her, The Cornish School for Performing and Visual Arts. I did go there for two years. It was a wonderful school. Miss Nellie Cornish was a remarkable woman, with a real sense about young people being trained in the arts. We went to school from eight in the morning till six at night. As Aunt Nellie said, you make your own schedule here. At eight o'clock we had a dance technique class. It was Martha Graham's work, taught by Bonnie Bird, who'd been in her company. She was a very good teacher. Then at 9:30 there was a eurythmics class two or three times a week. There was a theater class which was why I went, I was going to be an actor, but I liked dancing, so I took dance classes also. There were acting classes, diction and singing classes, a workshop about making dances, composition, theater history at some point, and another dance class.

J.L. *You were lucky.*

M.C. Yes, I later realized how lucky I was. At first I thought, if this is what school is in Seattle, a school in New York must be marvelous.

J.L. *You were eighteen or nineteen then.*

M.C. I never had serious dance training before that. For months I could hardly crawl up the stairs, but I did it. Day after day at eight o'clock in the morning. We had two technical classes a day, almost every day, plus all the rehearsals.

The first summer, I went to Mills College in Oakland, California. Bonnie Bird at the Cornish School got me a scholarship. I hitchhiked down there, but I didn't have to pay for the classes, which was fortunate as I didn't have any money. I went back to the Cornish School for the second year and that was the year John [Cage] was there. He had come to play for the dance classes. And he also started a percussion orchestra and asked me to be in it, which I thought was marvelous. The school was the same; that is, Miss Cornish was still in charge of it. The second summer I went again to Mills College, where the entire Bennington School of the Dance was in residence. Martha Graham, Doris Humphrey and Charles Weidman, and Hanya Holm were there. I'd heard about them for years but I had never seen them. Martha Graham asked me to come to New York and be in her company. I just said yes. Because I knew I didn't want to go back to the Cornish School, and although I didn't quite know how, I knew I was going to go to New York. It was simply an excuse: in a way, I had no idea what I was going to do—absolutely none. I had never seen her dance, not even at the summer school. They just came and taught, they didn't give any performances. I was asked to join two other companies but they didn't seem as interesting. Besides I was prepared for her by Bonnie Bird. So I went. I mean I came back to Centralia and just said to my parents, I'm going to New York. My mother's mouth fell open. My father looked at me, then looked back at her and said, "Let him go, he's going to go anyway."

I left for New York. I went on a train and sat up all the time for as many days as it took. At that time you could go all around the United States for the same price, so I went to San Francisco and Los Angeles where I knew some people, and I stopped in both cities. Then I went across to New York. I went to the Graham studio and Martha said, "Oh, I didn't think you'd come." I didn't say anything, but I thought, "You don't know me very well, lady." She was astonishing, very beautiful, and a marvelous dancer. I thought she was amazing to watch. In a few years she became a large public figure. In her company she had up to then only women, then she got one man, Erick Hawkins, who came to dance with her. He was the first man. I'm sure it was just by accident that I became part of her company, simply because I appeared. But she didn't really know very much about dancing for men. I began to study in her school and to see other things. And every day there was a class. I had no money—in terms of that, I could barely survive and simply eked out a living. I didn't have to pay for classes, so it was all right as long as I could find a way to survive every day. I got a job for that first year teaching in a school for a few hours and we did go on a tour during the year. For that time it was a fairly long tour, about six weeks. We also had two or three performances in New York.

After a time, I went to study at the School of American Ballet. Actually Martha suggested I go there. Lincoln Kirstein who directed the school was a friend of hers and I think she thought it would be good for me to go to another place where there was a technique which would push my body in a different way than her particular work did. I'm guessing, because actually . . .

I remember Lincoln Kirstein saying, "What do you want to study ballet for? You're a modern dancer." I said, "I really like all kinds of dancing," which was true. I had no strong feeling about it one way or another. Somehow they fixed it so I could study there, I had to pay a little bit of money, I managed it and they were very nice. I studied on and off for a year or so, probably more than that but not steadily, because I would be working with Graham as well.

J.L. *How did you turn from theater to dancing?*
M.C. Well, the first year I was in New York, I was with a small theater group, and we did some plays. I was involved with two of them, one of them was a play by e.e. cummings called *him*. We presented it twice, not in a theater but in somebody's living room. I even had trouble getting to all the rehearsals. I realized that the next year it wasn't going to work, I either had to do the dancing or something else, and I decided to do the dancing, but I think the choice had already been made at the Cornish School because I had even there by the second year been doing more dancing than drama. I was also interested in the possibility of being in musical comedies in New York. First of all, that was a way you could dance as a job instead of eking out a living, but I gradually lost interest in it.

There were a number of short tours with Graham. In 1944 John Cage and I gave our first program. I began working on my own dances probably the second year I was there, just to work at making pieces. I was still with the Graham company but it was just the same as when I had decided to go to New York: I knew the time would come when I should leave the Graham company, though that didn't happen for another year, but I had made up my mind about that. I did six solos altogether—and we presented them in the Humphrey Weidman Studio. The solos were two or three minutes. One was five or six minutes long. I changed costume between each one. I change very fast. It was a legacy from my vaudeville days with Mrs. Barrett. The theater on Sixteenth Street that Doris Humphrey and Charles Weidman had was small but the dance space was fairly large. It was not impossible and there were a few seats, 150 or so. We decided to give our one performance there. It was such a problem to just manage to pay for that and to do it. The next year, although I was still with Graham, I did a solo program in another theater, at the Hunter College Playhouse, which is bigger than the one we had the year before. I had been trained up to that point in composition classes with Louis Horst and the Cornish School, with all those ideas about nineteenth-century forms being variation, sonata, chaconne, ABA, and so on. I didn't find these very interesting and from the beginning of my solo dances I began to work with John Cage, who already had ideas about structure which were both clear and also contemporary.

I started with the idea that first of all any kind of movement could be dancing. I didn't express it that way at the time, but I thought that any kind of movement could be used as dance movement, that there was no limit in that sense. Then I went on to the idea that each dance should be different. That is, what you find for each dance as movement should be different from what you had used in previous dances. What I am trying to say by that is that in looking for movement, I would look for something I didn't know about rather than something I did know about. Now when you find something you don't know about or don't know how to do, you have to find a way to do it, like a child stumbling and trying to walk, or a little colt getting up. You find that you have this awkward thing which is often interesting, and I would think, "Oh, I must practice that. There's something there I don't know about, some kind of life." Then maybe something would come which I would think lively. And I would see how it worked within the structure but, as I say, the structure is not something that pinned us down. It was something underneath, that you had to play with.

J.L. *It's rather difficult to get rid of what you're supposed to know.*
M.C. Oh, absolutely, it's hard. First of all, it is difficult to do it anyway, because of habits and growing up. Most of all dancers are terrified about losing what they've practiced. Whereas I really think I didn't express it this way, but I had a feeling there always must be something else, there must always be something more. Different kinds of movement. At the same time like every other dancer I went every day to class. Or rather I did it myself because at that period I was already teaching class. I worked alone as I still do in the morning.

J.L. *It's very difficult to work alone.*
M.C. It's terrible, the most difficult thing being to keep up the endurance and rhythm, without someone else to compete against. I'm sure that over the years that's why I have a kind of structure in the class, because I had to have that for myself or I never would have kept it going; without it one dissolves. I wouldn't say everybody has to but I had to. Your whole energy builds and you keep it up if you work at making a structure. One has a tendency when one works alone to do either what one knows or do a lot of, say, one exercise one day and then not do it the next. But my idea always was "Oh, I have to do everything, every day, even though it's only a little bit." Even now, on tour, I get up very early and go to the theater before the other dancers and I work an hour, an hour and a half if there's time, before I give them a class, because I know that most of them can't— some of them could do it themselves—but most of them can't. They would not understand how to do it right. I had to learn. And it might deteriorate too.

J.L. *At the time we're talking of, you were training yourself already and not taking classes anymore at the School of American Ballet or at Graham . . .*
M.C. No, I did my work and worked on my dances and I would go to the Graham rehearsals while I was still in the Company. But shortly I was out of it, and then I was simply on my own.

J.L. *How did you feel using the two styles of training: Graham and classical ballet?*
M.C. In Graham's Company I looked probably like a ballet dancer because my legs were straight and I had a certain lightness. Yet I had not had ballet training when I first went there. When they would say, "Oh, you must have studied ballet," I didn't understand why they thought I had because my experience was so limited at that time. But as I watched and looked I began to understand. I could see how they might think that. But I wasn't turned out enormously. I had to practice all the time. I was not elaborate in any sense. Nor did I really understand ballet. There were so many technical details in it which were unfamiliar to me that it was simply a question of learning how to do them. The major teachers at the school at the time taught the Russian style. Two of them had been with Pavlova. It was this Russian style that became popular from 1910 on. I learned it and that was confusing to me because I had some technique, and I didn't go in as an elementary student. I tried to grab onto those exercises never knowing what they were about. But I worked at it and began to get some sense of what I was doing. I worked by myself and tried to think what were the basic principles behind those exercises, or those of Graham. What were they about? What's the back doing when the leg is horizontal and so on? And I spent hours trying to puzzle that out.

J.L. *Where did you work then? Where did you do this?*
M.C. In a very small loft on Seventeenth Street, in a place which was falling to pieces, of course. I had a little living space up front and I worked at the back. I had a small, what do you call it, potbelly stove, round, with a big pipe which runs up the back and that gave most of the heat. I used to collect wood from the street and put it in to keep warm. Actually there was some heat during the day, but nights it was freezing. It was an old building, it was bitter, really bitter, but if I sat close and had enough wood I could manage.

I'm sure that it's really at that time that something gradually began to happen, even though I couldn't know what it was. They were detailed exercises, and I wanted to keep this idea of the use of the back somehow with the legs. I had a great facility with my legs, with the speed, precision, and all of that. I had no trouble with rhythm at all, and I never understood when some people were having trouble. Mrs. Barrett once said, "Oh, your rhythm is great."

Apart from that, in the Graham style, they kept talking about the heaviness in the work. I understood what Martha was about. I could see it. The gravity. I thought the way she moved was very beautiful. Even when I was first there, I thought she was amazing, but I didn't think the rest of it was interesting at all. Those exercises that they do sitting on the floor, I could do them but when I left Graham I never did them anymore. I just tried to see what the movement was, not to expect it to be like she did it, not in the least. The same with ballet exercises: if I put my leg out there and it's supposed to go out at a 180 degree angle and your back's supposed to be straight, how do *I* do that? And you're supposed to have your arms wide. How do *I* do that? Not just an ego trip, but to find out, since I didn't have anyone else to work with but myself. At the same time, not just to get a position, but how do you go from one step to another? Which is one of the key questions of dancing. I would think that is what makes up dancing. At the same time, the position, once you get where you're going, has to be clear.

It was difficult for me at that time—probably still is—to talk with dancers. Not that I don't like them. They would mainly talk about the way somebody did something: they didn't like this or did like that, it always had to do with personalities. It's like gossip. That's entertaining and I like it too, but I also wanted to talk about ideas and there wasn't anybody I could talk with, except John. I couldn't talk with dancers. Graham's dancers all thought she was marvelous and if I said anything against her work, that was the end. The ballet people didn't know who I was and they wouldn't talk to me anyway at that point.

What I was trying to find out was how people move, within my own experience, which I kept trying to enlarge. If I saw something that I didn't understand then I would try it. I still do. There are lots of things I can see I don't understand, things for the feet, fast things, jumping things, which though I did them easily I never could quite understand when I was doing them. Now I can understand them. I mean, I can give them to my dancers and make them do them—at least it looks like it. What I'm trying to say in all this is that it remains always interesting if you get outside yourself. If you are stuck with yourself you stay with what you know and you can never attempt anything outside that.

At that time, Lincoln Kirstein who had founded the Ballet Society (which later became the New York City Ballet) asked me to make a ballet for one of the four programs he did every year. Balanchine was involved in them, naturally, but Lincoln wanted to also have young choreographers. With seven or eight ballet dancers, including Tanaquil LeClerq, and I was in it, I did a ballet called *The Seasons.* John wrote the music for it. It wasn't long, probably fifteen or twenty minutes, but it seemed long to me. When I accepted, I thought, I'll try and find out how to work with ballet dancers. And I worked very hard on it. Isamu Noguchi did the costumes and the decor. I've always found that when I work with people who are not trained directly with me I have simply to make compromises. In other words, as I later did with the dancers from the Paris Opéra, I try to make clear what I want and then see how to get that without making them feel fake. Or uncomfortable. If I did, I found it might work. And in this case it did. It was the first ballet that I had ever done, so there were movements that nowadays if I were working with them I could make clearer to the dancers. Then I didn't know how, but now I do.

This ballet was also done two or three times later on at City Center, when the Ballet Society had become the New York City Ballet.

J.L. *Could we date the first time* The Seasons *was shown?*
M.C. 1947.

J.L. *Just after the war, then. In New York at the time did you feel any effects from the war period?*
M.C. During the war, two large companies were in residence and performed in New York: the American Ballet Theater and the Ballets Russes de Monte Carlo. Quite apart from the war, there weren't many possibilities for dancers to perform, as there are now; the only companies that performed for an extended period of time at all were the ballet companies, and their seasons lasted no more than two weeks. If they happened to play at the same time they split the public. A modern dancer would give a single program once a year.

When Lincoln Kirstein started the Ballet Society in the autumn of 1946, his idea was to sponsor new works, particularly ballet works. The first programs were given in theaters with inadequate stages, but in the spring of 1947 he managed to get the Ziegfield Theater, where *The Seasons* was first presented. The Ziegfield Theater no longer exists but it had a very good stage. It was big and was quite a beautiful theater. Then the Ballet Society went to the City Center.

J.L. *The reason I asked about the war period is that at that time many European writers, poets, and painters came to New York and it probably created a different milieu, though they knew each other more or less, each one was mainly doing his own work.*
M.C. That's right. As a matter of fact it was during that war period that I saw (I didn't have much to do with them in the sense of friendship or anything of the kind) the paintings of Max Ernst and Marcel Duchamp and Piet Mondrian. But sometimes I would go to parties at Peggy Guggenheim's where they would be (John and Xenia Cage were staying with her and Max Ernst), and there were other artists who had come from abroad. That was a totally different world from the one that I knew through the Graham circle, and I expect that probably prompted me in some way to go and look at their work. Peggy Guggenheim had a gallery on

Fifty-seventh Street and I remember very often seeing shows there. She showed not only the surrealists but also younger artists, and I began going to art exhibits. It's funny because the School of American Ballet was on Fifty-ninth Street and Madison Avenue, and at that time the important galleries were on Fifty-seventh Street, so one could go to class and then go and have a look. I began to do that. Because there were so few performances we were not always rehearsing or concerned with something being prepared the way we are now, so we had time to look around the city.

I always had the feeling when I was with Graham that it was very confined. I don't mean that her work was confined, but it was a kind of closed circle, so to speak. It changed later, I'm sure, but at this time, it was closed, as were the other modern dance groups, like Doris Humphrey's. It was simply assumed that you had nothing to do with anything else. When I went to study ballet, many of those modern dancers thought that this was very odd and strange, and almost mad, which was of no concern to me because I was simply interested in studying ballet.

I began to know the painting world and, through John Cage, the music world. By the time we gave that first program together in 1944, the audience who came to see us was very small of course, but was composed of many of these painters. Very few dancers came, perhaps some of the Graham people came, I don't remember exactly. I do remember a number of painters coming and young composers, people interested in new possibilities. Right from the start there was a difference between what I did and what I had been doing with Martha, even though I was still in her company. There was a fair difference. The Graham dancers were loyal to Martha naturally, and had very strong feelings about her. I was doing something you weren't supposed to do, and not at all as Louis Horst, whom we all had some sort of experience with, said we ought to.

For the dancers, Louis Horst was quite a remarkable man. I didn't like his ideas but he had an extraordinary eye about dancing. He really *looked* at it. When he died I wrote Graham a note and said I thought he was remarkable in his absolutely fierce devotion to dancing for all those years. I'm not sure that he liked what I did, but he wouldn't *not look* at it. He would look at it and years later after he was dead, I remember a friend of mine, Drusa Wilker (her married name is Sherman) who had played the piano for dance classes for many years—she became a great friend because she is such as a warm-hearted person—she told me she wanted to see *Winterbranch* because she had read all the criticisms saying that it was impossible and it sounded to her absolutely marvelous. So she saw it, and did find it marvelous, and said, "You know what? Louis would have liked it." That may be. Maybe. Anyway, as I began to do my own work, I grew more and more separate from that modern dance situation, which was probably bound to happen.

J.L. *Did the link with painting develop at that time?*

M.C. Yes, I remember, for instance, hearing painters talk, not about dancing of course. I didn't know them well so I didn't say anything at these parties or gatherings, but whether there were a lot of them or a few, they would talk about painting and this was interesting even though I knew nothing about it. I'd seen very few paintings of any kind other than some reproductions in books, and so this was all totally new to me. But I began to realize who these people were in terms of art history, and I would listen and they would talk about their work, or somebody else's work and the kind of talk was so different from anything I knew in the Graham world where talking was about technical things or what Martha might be doing or not doing.

J.L. *At the time Martha Graham was engaged in some kind of war, wasn't she, that had almost been won?*

M.C. She was a very strong woman who demanded or felt she needed that kind of objective to keep going, because of course there had been a great deal of animosity toward her work.

I began to see another world, and the taste for it grew also through the School of American Ballet. I began at the same time in New York to go to ballet. I hadn't seen very much. There weren't that many programs and I didn't have much money but you could go for very little and sometimes get in free at the intermission for the second ballet. I did that as often as I could the first year I was in New York. I went to see as many dance programs as possible. At the time I knew very little about ballet history. Looking at all these programs and trying to make sense of all this to myself, I began to read about it.

Because of the war, the Ballets Russes de Monte Carlo was stationed in New York and toured the States. They had a season in New York in the fall and in the spring. Some of those dancers studied at the School of American Ballet. So you could see them work there. I remember seeing Alexandra Danilova in class once, a wonderful dancer. I don't mean her technique, but the quality, the way she was on stage, a warmth she radiated. Seeing her in class, not knowing who she was—I'm sure I'd seen her but I didn't make a connection. The whole thing was so bewildering to me—I thought she was absolutely beautiful to look at. I asked who she was and when I found out, I felt foolish: "But that's Danilova!"

J.L. *Was John Cage in New York then?*

M.C. John was not there for the first year or so when I had come to be in the Graham Company. But when he came he suggested we do a program together. He said we must do something. I began to see that was what you had to do, but it was so difficult—and still is of course. You had to do everything: rent the place, get the tickets printed, print the program, do the publicity, sell the tickets, answer the phone. We made a list of names and sent out cards, got the money to mail them. In terms of now the money was nothing, but then it was gigantic. Two hundred dollars was like ten thousand now, because I was probably living on fifty dollars a month. But we just did it, and I, not being very bright about any of all this, just plodded on. I think if I'd thought half a second I would never have done it. It was so difficult and also it was—what do you call it?—in a way, forward—as though I were pushing myself in a way that someone else wouldn't have.

I remember the same thing when I first came to the Graham studio. I began with classes and Martha was planning two or three programs at Christmas time. I had come in the fall, and she put me in one of the pieces. I can't remember the name of it now, but we just went ahead and rehearsed it and when we were performing in it, suddenly here we were in this elaborate New York theater—a Broadway house it was—a very good theater, and just before I was to make my first entrance in this piece, I suddenly realized that here I was coming on and that this was New York. I had never thought of it before, and I thought, Good heavens, what am I doing here!

Anyway, there is so much in life, if you ever stop and think, you simply wouldn't do it. I remember a girl who was in my company for a number of years; she was a wonderful person. We were having class one day and she asked me how to do a certain movement, and finally I said, "Marianne, the only way to do it is to do it," and I think that's the only answer I've ever been able to figure out. You just go ahead and do it.

Not long ago, we were in Amherst giving a program, that's where she lives now, and she told me that story, and said, "You know, I never forgot that. When you said that to me I was dumbfounded but that was the only thing to do, just go ahead and do it."

I think in my case it was *naiveté*. That may not quite be the right word because someone bright about that kind of thing could also have the drive to do something. But I didn't know a great deal. I just pushed on, tried to work at things, and then present them, so to speak. If there's something that you have to do, if that needs to be done, you'll find a way to do it. At least that's been my experience.

J.L. *When John Cage arrived in New York, did he know other musicians?*
M.C. He got to know them through Davidson Taylor at CBS and Minna Lederman, who was the editor of *Modern Music*. He had been involved with music in Chicago, but also he knew a lot of artists and had met some of the people who were in New York. He came to New York then because so to speak it was time for him to come, because of his own work and situation—just perhaps as it's necessary for a French artist to come to

Paris. You may not stay but you have to come and find out whether it's where you belong or don't belong. It's the same with dancers. If they are really serious about dancing, they will at some point come to New York. They may not stay, but they have to come and find out what it is.

—from *The Dancer and the Dance,* 1985

CAROLYN BROWN

At the Theater de Lys

I was once again dancing at least five or six hours a day—two classes at the Met, plus class and rehearsal with Merce. In November, Merce added Saturday and Sunday rehearsals. No one complained or wanted to. Those of us who didn't have outside jobs—and I was one of the lucky ones who didn't, that fall—worked on publicity for the de Lys, typing releases for newspapers and magazines. Remy [Charlip] decided that what was needed was an article in Dance magazine, so he wrote "Composing by Chance" and the magazine accepted it for its January issue, which was on the stands by the time the company opened at the Theater de Lys on December 29. In mid-November Merce got the flu, but it didn't keep him away from work except for one day, and that day we rehearsed ourselves. We rehearsed Thanksgiving Day, then a dozen or so people went to Merce's loft to address flyers for the season while John [Cage] and M.C. and Nick made a glorious dinner. The Thanksgiving turkey—mammoth size—was a gift from Remy and the A & P. The design for the flyers was a gift from Remy, too, and everyone was delighted with them: they were 17 × 5½, on heavy, high-gloss colored paper (orange, green, yellow, turquoise, sea-foam) with bold type and a clean, clear layout. Seeing the printed flyer was a sudden jarring confirmation of the reality that lay ahead; reading it made me weak in the legs and caused my innards to heave up against my diaphragm. For the month that followed, a horrible feeling of fright and near-paralysis alternated with happier, more positive emotions. Working really hard alleviated the stage fright, but when I was away from the studio, should my eye fall on a poster or newspaper advertisement or a sheaf of flyers, my panic would return. At Black Mountain classes, rehearsals and performances were in the same familiar space in the midst of an audience of people we saw and conversed with every day. There was a sense of wholeness about that experience, a sense that art and life were really one. But the Theater de Lys was alien territory: its stage proportions were radically different from our studio's proportions, the surface was unfamiliar and slightly treacherous, and the audience—for the most part—was that unknown enigmatic thing, the New York Audience, which holds nameless terrors for all performers from whatever discipline, of whatever nationality.

I felt our professional status even more when, on December 10, I signed my first dancers' Standard Artists Agreement, an AGMA (American Guild of Musical Artists) contract. "The DANCER shall be paid $87.50 per week for performance week and $47.00 for the first five rehearsal weeks. . . ." We rehearsed for at least ten weeks before the season, but there was no way Merce and John could pay us union wages (or *any* wages) for that length of time, so our contract—one week of rehearsals, one week of performances— met the barest, most minimal union requirements and still allowed us to play the Theater de Lys, a union house. Once again Paul Williams appeared, like a benevolent genie, to provide the necessary funds. Without him the season could not have taken place. John took on the job of administrative director and fundraiser, even going door to door to get advertisers for the program. He'd arrive in the middle of rehearsal, beaming, jubilant over the newest catch: Pantheon Books or Salabert Music Publishers or Tibor de Nagy Gallery. It was an elegant group of advertisers that John succeeded in enlisting. It included art galleries, bookstores, book publishers, music publishers, dancers, a couple of Village restaurants and specialty shops, and Morty Feldman, whose advertisement simply gave his name and phone number.

The flu went the rounds of the company. For a while David Tudor was sick, unable to play for our rehearsals, but by mid-December my letters to my parents were reassuring: "All goes well. We rehearse daily—work very hard—but things are going smoothly," but they also included words of warning: "Have no doubt you and [your students] will be *shocked* by the music for some of the dances. I don't think you'll have much trouble with the dancing itself—although you may be shocked there too. I've grown so accustomed to this kind of movement that it is no longer strange to me."

The stage for the Theater de Lys was minuscule. Merce's dances couldn't possibly be seen to advantage in such a cramped space, so it was decided to build an extension, a large apron jutting out into the house, which would give us more depth, even though it meant losing some of the three hundred seats. We had almost no rehearsal time in the theatre and everyone was uneasy about the two different floors under our bare feet. Not only were the two surfaces unfamiliar, but the sense of solidity changed from backstage to front, and each floor resonated differently, too. On the day of opening night,

I woke up with a stiff neck and an upset stomach, and spent the predawn hours throwing up or huddled shivering uncontrollably under the covers. Earle was more amused than worried; he was sure I was suffering from nothing more serious than a case of stage fright. That infuriated me! *I* blamed Simple Simon, the hamburger restaurant in Sheridan Square where the company often went after rehearsal. I'd never had stage fright of that sort before, not even as a college sophomore when I'd done the lead role in two versions of *Antigone* in a single day: Sophocles' at the matinee and Jean Anouilh's French adaptation in the evening. This *had* to be mild food poisoning! I would not accept any other explanation! By noon I rallied and made my way to the theatre. Though my skin was ashen, my knees were weak, and I was thoroughly frightened, I was also angry at my body for letting me down, and this anger roused my determination to get through rehearsal and the performance without revealing my malady to Merce. For the next twenty years, I rarely performed without experiencing some degree of stage fright, but I was never again physically ill with it as I was, apparently, on the day that Merce's fledgling company made its New York debut in 1953.

The week flew by. I remember almost nothing. The essence of performing is its "nowness"—no mind, no memory. Just that brief time when one has the chance to be whole, when seemingly disconnected threads of one's being are woven and intertwined into the complete present. No other. No past. No future. No mind as an entity distinct from the body. Certainly I've experienced memorable performances—but what made them memorable was extraneous to the dancing. And, unfortunately, there are all too many remembered performances—the ones I call "supermarket performances"—when one's mind and body are functioning, but separately, each on a different course, the mind preoccupied with dreary details as mundane as today's grocery list or as self-involved as a catalogue of criticisms of one's own dancing, while the body goes through the motions, executing the steps like a windup toy.

What I best remember about that week is sitting out in the house watching Merce rehearse his solos. Until then, he had always rehearsed them when the company was absent. *Two Step. Root of an Unfocus. Totem Ancestor. Collage. Solo Suite in Space and Time. Untitled Solo. Variations.* A solo in *Suite by Chance.* Plus the brief, hilarious solo in *Dime-A-Dance* called "The Eclectic," set to Beethoven's *Bagatelle* (opus 126, no. 4) which was a sendup of modern dance and dancers and a parody of current mannerisms. These solos encompassed an enormous range of physical and emotional expression. The early ones, *Totem Ancestor* (1942) and *Root of an Unfocus* (1944), appeared to be narratives—"telling" specific stories. *Untitled Solo* (1953), so powerful in its dramatic intensity, was not *about* something, it *was* that thing—raw, direct, immediate, in itself dynamically real. When Viola Farber, Paul Taylor, and I were reminiscing about the early days some twenty-seven years later, we all agreed that *Untitled Solo* was, of all Merce's solos, still our favorite. *Solo Suite in Space and Time* (1953) was just that, but no Cunningham solo is ever devoid of drama. *Two Step* was a tour de force of mercurial exuberance, breathtaking to watch and looking as if it was fun to do. I think *Variations* was an attempt to present basic academic ballet vocabulary in a new way, by reordering the rhythms and phrasing and continuity that one comes to expect in conventional ballet, but it never succeeded with me—it lacked the clarity of truly *classical* ballet, so the intentions of the dance were never satisfactorily realized. I quite agreed with Louis Horst, who wrote that *Variations* "was disappointing and seemed to have no place on a modern dance program. While it showed that Mr. Cunningham knows his ballet principles, it also showed that performance of a dance such as this should be left to some great ballet virtuoso." The *Collage* solo, I read as a kind of medley of personae, contrarily heroic as it celebrated the ordinary and the commonplace: James Joyce's "H.C.E." in motion.

For Merce the de Lys season was a grueling labor of love: eight performances, including matinee and evening on both Saturday and Sunday. In addition to the six group works and our duet, *Amores,* Merce danced eight different solos, at least two at each performance, with each solo performed at least twice during the week's run. By the middle of the week he'd injured himself. He kept rubbing or feeling his foot and ankle in rehearsal, and he limped noticeably when he taught company class, but I saw no indication of any injury when he performed. Thinking about it now, reading over the program and realizing what fierce demands he'd made on himself, I was made acutely aware that the Theater de Lys season was very nearly a one-man show, with Merce on stage dancing nonstop from the moment the curtain rose at 8:40 p.m. until it fell at the end of each performance about two hours later. But he showed little pleasure, as I recall, and for most of that week he seemed depressed. On the last evening, when it was over, I saw him sitting motionless, alone in the men's dressing room after everyone else had cleared out; he looked dispirited and hollow-eyed. I asked if he was all right; his reply was direct and devastating: "My jump is gone. I'll never be able to jump again as I used to." He was thirty-four years old, and for him at that moment, this was a tragedy. It was his nimble-footed jump that had won him accolades in Martha Graham's company ("Dear March, come in!" in *Letter to theWorld*). It was his phenomenal bounding elevation when he leapt halfway across the City Center stage in *Two Step* that had made the audience gasp in amazement. Now he was convinced that he'd never jump like that again. Merce had been onstage at least 95 percent of the time in all eight performances of the de Lys season. For someone with such a voracious appetite for performing, an appetite that abated only slightly in the succeeding forty-plus years, the loss of any movement possibility would seem a calamity. And he was right about his jump. That special aeriality he'd become famous for did not return. But he didn't stop jumping; he found other ways, new accents, and different rhythms when choreographing for himself.

—from *Chance and Circumstance,* 2007

TERRY TEACHOUT

Pale Horse, Pale Rider

I see the shaman is in residence tonight," a skeptical-sounding balletomane remarked drily after looking over the program of a performance by the Merce Cunningham Dance Company during its last City Center season. Translation: Merce Cunningham was dancing in *Enter,* thus allowing veteran Merce-watchers to engage in the umpteenth annual discussion of whether or not his increasingly wobbly onstage appearances still have some artistic validity. Merce-watchers always argue about his cameos (I like them), just as they continue to debate the merits of the organized sound that accompanies his dances. But these are family arguments, amiable pseudo-quarrels hardly more serious than the yearly wrangle over whether Aunt Suzy should put more sage in the dressing next Thanksgiving. No minds are changed, and nothing is at stake. At least in New York, there is rarely anyone in attendance at a performance of the Cunningham company who doesn't already know he'll like what he sees.

Those who venture into City Center unwittingly are generally driven from it quickly, most often by one of the high-voltage electronic scores Cunningham likes to deploy from time to time. This season there were two, for *Sounddance* and *CRWDSPCR,* and a handful of people stalked out of every performance I saw of both dances. Yet this, too, is considered part of the Merce Cunningham experience. You don't have to wander very far at intermission to hear Cunningham fans chattering happily, even complacently, about how Merce can still drive the Philistines out of the theater, even at the ripe old age of seventy-five. It occurred to me—not for the first time—that there is something unattractive about the attitudes implicit in such talk. Snobbishness is a venial sin, but it tends also to be a two-way proposition. In the case of

Merce Cunningham, it's hard to spend much time watching his company on stage without getting the feeling that somebody up there is intensely interested in cultivating the perception that the genius of Merce is simply not accessible to every Tom, Dick, or Harry who stumbles in off Fifty-fifth Street.

On one level, of course, this is perfectly true: Merce Cunningham is not Bob Fosse. But it is also true that most of the great geniuses of art have sought, and ultimately won, a popular following. This is particularly true of George Balanchine, the choreographer to whom Cunningham is most often compared. There was a time when Balanchine was widely viewed as difficult—not difficult as Shakespeare is difficult, but as Joyce is difficult. Yet Balanchine wanted to please the largest possible audience—on his own terms, to be sure, but those terms were far more generous than was commonly supposed in, say, 1940. New York City Ballet is the institutional embodiment of that desire, a place where tens of thousands of people come every year to see *Agon* and *Concerto Barocco* and *The Four Temperaments* and *The Nutcracker* and *Slaughter on Tenth Avenue*. It offers masterpieces to suit every taste, including the common. Merce Cunningham, by contrast, has made little or no impression on those people for whom dance is an occasional entertainment rather than a central concern. Just prior to the company's City Center season, Mikhail Baryshnikov's White Oak Dance Project danced Cunningham's *Signals* at the New York State Theater. It was clear to the most casual eavesdropper that the house was full of people who had no idea who Merce Cunningham was (and who, at evening's end, were firmly resolved to keep it that way). The interesting thing is not that he has failed to reach a general audience but that, as far as I can see, he doesn't want to. Perhaps I do him an injustice; it may be that in his secret heart, Merce would like his company to perform in sold-out arenas. But the fact remains that the atmosphere of a Cunningham season is not just serious but esoteric—cultic, if you like.

I took three Cunningham first-timers to City Center this year, and questioned them afterward. To a woman, they were mystified by the monolithic repertory: three dances a night, all plotless, all structureless, all fitted out with impenetrably gnomic titles. John Martin's famously idiotic line about *Symphony in C*—"Balanchine has once again given us that ballet of his, this time for some inscrutable reason to the Bizet symphony"—not infrequently comes to mind when I see a Cunningham premiere. Similarly, the company is full of good dancers, but it is impossible for a novice to tell them apart. The dancers are listed alphabetically, both in the company roster and for every individual dance. There are no photos in the program, or in the lobby. Even when specific dancers are featured, as Alan Good and Jenifer Weaver were in *Beach Birds,* it's anybody's guess who they are. The printed slip identifying the cast of *Sounddance* in order of appearance had the feel of a last-minute concession, as if Cunningham had to be strapped down and tortured before finally given permission to put in the program. As it happens, this approach does rough justice to far too many of Cunningham's dancers, most of whom are individual only in the sense that identical twins have different finger-prints. There isn't a woman in Paul Taylor's company I wouldn't recognize on the street. Not so Merce's troupe. Night after night, the curtain goes up on a stageful of pretty-but-not-too-pretty WASPs. (Even the company's lone black dancer seems white in retrospect.) Fine as the overall level of the dancing was this season, there were only two company members, Good and Weaver, who made strongly individual impressions.

Cunningham's style of presentation reminds me of the way Walt Disney used to do the credits for his animated features. Every artist who worked on the picture, no matter how briefly, got screen credit—in small print, at the end of the last reel. Needless to say, you came away remembering only one name. Anyone who knows anything about Merce Cunningham knows that the studied facelessness of his ensemble is a reflection of his larger philoso-phy of Eastern egolessness. But anyone who knows anything about history knows that those who claim to be egoless usually have the biggest egos of all. I suppose it doesn't really matter. Merce is a genius—we all know that. But there is something just a little bit pat about his wanting to have it both ways.

THIS IS ONLY one of the many elements of the Cunningham aesthetic in which theory and practice seem out of kilter. To spend an evening with the Merce Cunningham Dance Company is to leaf through a fat scrapbook of twentieth-century nonsense. As we look at the self-consciously alphabetical listing of dancers, we are reminded of the communal ideals of the sixties, the decade in which the props were kicked out—perhaps permanently—from under Western culture. As the curtain goes up, we find ourselves face to face with two of the most absurdly rigid theories ever foisted upon a dance audi-ence: the idea that dance and music ought to take place simultaneously but not synchronously, and the idea that large choreographic structures can be meaningfully determined by rolling dice. As the "orchestra" starts to play, we are confronted by the ghost of John Cage, the man whose harebrained notions probably did more to damage Western music than anyone since Schoenberg. (Fifty years from now, Cunningham's dances will keep Cage's music alive in exactly the same way that La Bayadère keeps the music of Minkus alive.) And then we forget the theories, and are enthralled. The superficial foolishnesses recede quickly into the background; even the music becomes unimportant, a distant clatter one quickly learns to tune out. The dances are all that matter. Of all the lessons Merce Cunningham teaches us, this is the most important one: theory is meaningless to a genius.

I don't mean to deprecate the power of theory to carry even the finest artist across slack stretches of inspiration. It is absurd to suggest that Balanchine ever played it safe for one instant in his creative life, but it is certainly true that he did his high-wire acts over a safety net. Two nets, in fact: the twin disciplines of classical ballet and classical music. Not that these disciplines can make bad steps good, but when you submit to them, you're betting with the house, not against it. Cunningham always works without a net, and always bets against the house. He does not rely on music, on a libretto, or a strong scenic conception, or the structural conventions of classical ballet, to give shelter to his dances. He makes steps and strings them together according to a method of his own devising. Under normal circumstances, only one aspect of his dances is predetermined: there will usually be three of them on a program, meaning that they must last somewhere between twenty and forty minutes. After that, all bets are off.

That Cunningham's method works at all, much less that it works so often, is an extraordinary tribute to his fertility. He is, in fact, so fertile that we have thereby been deprived of a clear understanding of the growth of his art. For the last decade or so, the Cunningham company has mostly performed new and newish dances. As a result, those who started watching Cunningham after about 1980 are inescapably limited in their knowledge of how Merce got from there to here. Though there are books to read, some of which are illuminating, the most important book, a *catalogue raisonée* of Cunningham's dances, has not yet been written. Until David Vaughan finally does for Cunningham what he did for Frederick Ashton,* we are forced to rely primarily on the films Cunningham has been making since 1973. Sadly, Cunningham's films tell us little about the first half of his career. The earliest of his dances to have been filmed in its entirety is *Septet* (1953). There is nothing earlier, and not all that much later—he didn't get serious about filming his work until the late 1970s. But this season, in addition to having access to Cunningham's complete filmed oeuvre, New York dancegoers were able to augment their sketchy knowledge of Cunningham's middle period with two rare and supremely important revivals: *Signals* (1970), danced by White Oak, and *Sounddance* (1975), danced by the Cunningham company. For Cunningham's younger fans, it was catch-up time.

The most valuable of Cunningham's films from the period before he began to work with director Charles Atlas is the beautifully legible *Septet* shot in 1964 by Hakki Seppala for a Finnish TV broadcast. To see it is to see the Cunningham that might have been—a conventional Cunningham. Though the body language of *Septet* is as idiosyncratic as anything the Cunningham company dances today, the tone of the dance is startlingly "normal." It isn't just that *Septet* derives its structure (and counts) from a piece of

---

*He did so in 1998 with *Merce Cunningham: Fifty Years.*

music, Erik Satie's *Three Pieces in the Form of a Pear.* It's the style, the cheery atmosphere of accessibility, that startles. The Finnish audience laughs happily at the handshake scene, and even goes so far as to applaud one especially virtuosic combination. Don't they know this is modern dance?

Septet came at the end of a long string of works, most of them to Cage's pre-chance music for prepared piano, which one gathers from contemporary accounts to have been more or less problematic. Had Cunningham continued to work in the vein of *Septet,* we would doubtless now see it as his "breakthrough" work, in much the same way that *Aureole* was Paul Taylor's breakthrough work—the point at which his creative conception stabilized, allowing the audience to begin the long process of catching up with his imagination. In Taylor's case, that process culminated thirteen years later in *Esplanade,* the dance that made him popular. But Cunningham treated *Septet* as an end, not a beginning. Starting in 1953, he abandoned conventional music and the dance structures that arise from it, opting instead for structures determined in part by the use of chance operations.

The film of *Crises* (1960), shot at a 1962 rehearsal, shows how quickly Cunningham sloughed off convention. The music, by Conlon Nancarrow, takes place in the same time frame as the choreography, but does not generate it. (Nor could it. Nancarrow's player-piano etudes are based on irrational rhythmic relationships that make *Le Sacre du printemps* look like freshman algebra.) Hence the dance, convincing from point to point, seems somewhat aimless when viewed as a whole. This is a problem that Cunningham has never consistently managed to solve, except by claiming that it isn't a problem. But it is, at least for the audience. By abandoning both tonal music and what Vaughan calls "the usual principles governing dance structure—cause and effect, conflict and resolution, building to a climax," Cunningham tears down the signposts that allow the viewers of a dance to orient themselves in time—to know, among other homely but relevant things, that a dance is almost over. (One gets the feeling that a great many Cunningham dances end when the alarm clock goes off.)

The only thing missing from *Crises* is the dadaist scenic element that Cunningham had begun to incorporate into his work in the late fifties. This aspect of middle-period Cunningham we know more by description (and from some of the earlier films) than anything else, though *Signals,* with its stick and chairs, gave a hint of what it was like to see the Cunningham company in the days when its members used to dance *around* the set pieces created by Robert Rauschenberg and his associates. Once again, theory comes into play, in this case Cunningham's celebrated theory of "multiplicity of centers." As the choreographer explained to Jacqueline Lesschaeve in *The Dancer and the The Dance:* "The three arts don't come from a single idea which the dance demonstrates, the music supports, and the decor illustrates, but rather they are three separate elements each central to itself." And once again, theory and practice diverge: Cunningham has not kept in his active repertory any of the dances that make use of elaborate set pieces like Andy Warhol's helium-filled pillows of *RainForest* or Jasper Johns's Duchamp-inspired decor for *Walkaround Time*. His sets are now for the most part purely decorative backdrops. In late Cunningham, the steps are the thing.

The "new" Cunningham—the only one today's audiences can know in any kind of detail—makes two kinds of dances. One kind is pure: no plot, no concept, no metaphors, nothing but steps in time. This is the Cunningham of *CRWDSPCR,* the more impressive of the two new works danced at City Center this season; this, too, is the Cunningham that novices, however fascinated, tend to find intimidating. And not just novices, either. *CRWDSPCR* is a very exciting dance, but it is also a very busy dance, one that I found impossible to grasp on first viewing (and far from easy to grasp when I went back a second time).

The other Merce Cunningham is the maker of *Sounddance* and *Beach Birds* (1991), to my mind the highlights of the company's current repertory. *Sounddance* is, on its surface, a quintessential specimen of the Bad Cunningham, the one who accompanies his dances with earsplitting music and crams in so many steps that you get a headache trying to tease them apart. But *Sounddance,* far from being inaccessible, is actually as close as Cunningham has come to making a crowd-pleasing applause machine. The reason is simple: *Sounddance* has an immediately intelligible structure. The dancers make their entrances, one by one, through the "door" in the center of the canvas backdrop; they exit, in a different order, through the same "door." Regardless of what happens in between, the twin bookends of those marvelously individual entrances and exits are what make *Sounddance* add up.

Nor is this structure purely arbitrary. Cunningham has furnished us with a clue, an epigraph from *Finnegans Wake:* "In the beginning was the sounddance." It is a very openended clue, and only a crudely literal mind would leap to the simplest explanation, that *Sounddance* is "about" the life cycle. It is no more about the life cycle than *The Four Temperaments* is about astrology. But the controlling visual metaphor of the dance is bound to evoke varyingly sophisticated mental images of that kind. This gives *Sounddance* an expressive force that transcends the sum total of its steps. Even David Tudor's score contributes significantly to the overall effect. Its sheer loudness is very much in keeping with the highly charged energy of the onstage action. Random though the correlation of music and dance necessarily is, the final impression left by *Sounddance* is congruent and convincing—even theatrical.

Many of the same things could be said about *Beach Birds.* Like *Sounddance,* it is dominated by a frankly theatrical concept: Cunningham's steps and Marsha Skinner's costumes clearly suggest that we are viewing a colony of water birds. And though the structure is less conventional than that of *Sounddance* (there is never any sense that one choreographic event need necessarily follow another), *Beach Birds* rests unequivocally on a dramatic fulcrum: a man comes on stage, plucks a woman from the ensemble, and dances with her. For Balanchine, this is standard operating procedure; for Cunningham, it is wildly heterodox. Cunningham rarely places a pas de deux at the center of his dances, and even more rarely charges it with romantic implications: "You see a man and a woman dancing together, or being together, it doesn't have to be thought of this way, but you make a gesture which can suddenly make it intimate, and you don't have to *decide* that this is an intimate gesture, but you do something, and it becomes so." But it is hard to view the *Beach Birds* pas de deux as other than romantic, an impression strengthened by a viewing of *Beach Birds for Camera* (1992), Cunningham's latest and most satisfying film.

Beach Birds for Camera is the first film in which Cunningham and his current director-collaborator Elliot Caplan have completely solved the vexing problem of "where" a dance film takes place. Most of Cunningham's films are shot in his New York studio, and no attempt is made to conceal the fact that we are watching dancers in a studio, or to create the illusion of stage space. Looking at the earlier films, one felt that Cunningham took this line because he didn't have the money to do anything else; the results usually seem cheesy and, occasionally, coy. But *Beach Birds for Camera* was filmed in two different locations, a dance studio and a sound stage. We are carefully distanced from the former by the subtle use of soft focus, translucent light, and handsomely grainy black-and-white cinematography. Then, just as Alan Good begins to dance with Victoria Finlayson, the film abruptly changes locales—and switches to color.

This jolting transition is obviously intended to mark off the main structural event of the dance. But it also reinforces the romantic atmosphere of the pas de deux. It is as if Good, entering into a sexless, Edenic community of bird-dancers, carries with him the charge of sexuality that brings Finlayson to life (i.e., full color). The climactic phrase of their mating dance, so memorable on stage, becomes almost unbearably intense on film: Finlayson slowly spreads her slender arms over Good and brushes the back of his bowed head with her face. It is an oddly solemn act of tenderness, almost a benediction. Then Good turns to look at her, a gesture of utmost simplicity that nonetheless makes the remainder of *Beach Birds,* lovely though it is, seem like an afterthought. The whole film is wonderfully intimate—Cage's all-but-silent score leaves plenty of room to hear the dancers move and breathe and grunt—but the pas de deux, mostly shot in close-up, raises this intimacy to an unexpectedly high level.

In the black-and-white section of *Beach Birds for Camera,* we also get a brief but memorable glimpse of Jenifer Weaver, by far the most interesting of Cunningham's new crop of female dancers. Weaver lacks the austerely athletic beauty of Finlayson. Seen at rest (as we see her briefly in *Touchbase*), she makes no special impression. Her hair is lank, her face plain and sober. But as soon as she starts to move, she seizes the eye. Her large feet strike and pierce the stage; her legs become taut with certainty; her face radiates the ecstasy of action. She is a *big* dancer—the only woman in the company of whom this can be said—and she makes out of the *Beach Birds* pas de deux, which she now performs on stage, something so bold that the first time I saw *Beach Birds for Camera,* Finlayson actually looked a bit wan by comparison.

Though that impression gave way on successive viewings, it reminded me of the thing about Cunningham's dances I find least appealing: they have a way of seeming pale, even safe, when viewed in bulk. This may sound like a bizarre thing to say about a man who at the age of seventy-five can still make people run screaming from City Center. But the Cunningham aesthetic is one of renunciation: renunciation of conventional structure, conventional music, even the conventional effect of distinctively individual dancers. Renunciation is a religious act, a means of putting temptation behind you. Yet it is precisely because dances like *Beach Birds* and *Sounddance* yield to temptation—because they incorporate theatrical effects about which Cunningham usually seems dubious—that they make much of the company's current repertory look flat.

"Grace," says Cunningham in an oft-quoted remark, "comes when the energy for the given situation is full and there is no excess." This is a beautiful aphorism, and a revealing one. Cunningham's excesses are invariably ones of energy, not passion. The opening tableau of *CRWDSPCR*, an explosion of complex movement enacted by a stageful of seemingly frenzied dancers, is a deliberate act of excess—there is simply too much to see. But other kinds of excess are rigorously shunned. Try to imagine a *vulgar* Cunningham dance. It is impossible precisely because Cunningham never risks vulgarity, or exhibitionism, or sentimentality. To praise this restraint as a manifestation of his classicism is to confuse form with content. Cunningham's classicism is an act of concealment. It is supremely characteristic of the Cunningham aesthetic that his dancers almost never smile on stage.

The remarkable thing about Merce Cunningham is not that his aesthetic should occasionally fail to satisfy, but that it works as well as it does. I can't imagine him as my desert-island choreographer any more than I can imagine going on a macrobiotic diet. But if I could have three choreographers for my desert-island company, I suspect he would be one of them. There is no doubt in my mind that he would be a better artist (and a more popular one) if he were more willing to embrace than renounce. Still, this sort of criticism is valid only at the very highest level of achievement. I wish he were warmer, but I love him as he is.

—from *New Dance Review,* 1994

SERGEI DIAGHILEV

The greatest of all ballet impresarios was Sergei Diaghilev (1872–1929), who founded the Ballets Russes, thereby changing the history of dance. Coming from a rich family, he was able to please himself by studying singing and music at university, then joined a group of like-minded young intellectuals and aesthetes who founded an important journal, Mir Iskusstva (World of Art). His deep interest in ballet was rewarded when he was appointed assistant to Prince Volkonsky, who had become the director of the Imperial Theater, but his artistic differences with the prince led to his being fired. In successive years he brought to Paris a huge exhibition of Russian art, a series of concerts of Russian music, a season of Russian opera (Chaliapin in Boris Gudonov), and finally, in 1909, the first season of the Ballets Russes. For the next twenty years the company represented everything that was new, exciting, and influential in ballet. Among the composers from whom Diaghilev commissioned new work were Debussy, Ravel, Strauss, Satie, Prokofiev, and of course Stravinsky—the scores of Firebird, Le Sacre du Printemps, Les Noces. His leading dancers were his lover Nijinsky, Pavlova (for a short while), Karsavina, and on through Massine, Dolin, Lifar, Markova, Danilova, and others. His ballet masters: Fokine, Nijinsky, Massine, Nijinska, Balanchine. Among the artists he commissioned for decor: Picasso, Matisse, Derain, Rouault. His death, in 1929, led to the great diaspora of the dance world: Ninette de Valois to England, Lifar to Paris, Balanchine eventually to America, and his dancers everywhere. Diaghilev remains a legend of creativity (although he created nothing directly), taste, authority—and of genius.

ARNOLD L. HASKELL

Sergei Diaghilev

Even during Diaghilev's lifetime a legend surrounded him, which has now grown to such enormous dimensions that it has become impossible to see the real man, or to form a correct estimate of his achievement, and that of his many brilliant collaborators. His work and vast knowledge drew him into so many different circles that each person, almost, has a distorted picture of his particular Diaghilev, coloured through distance—pictures that it is generally impossible to reconcile. I have attempted this sketch of him from innumerable conversations with his collaborators, friends and enemies, members of his company, and also from my personal knowledge. I knew him but slightly, and he disliked me from the moment that I began criticising the ballet, though he agreed with so many of the conclusions I reached. He was always intolerant of any independent criticism, and on one occasion, it is said, visited Levinson's editor, demanding his instant dismissal. I had an intense admiration for him, and he was the only person of whom I have ever been a little frightened. This distance has given me the possibility of gaining a true perspective; so overpowering was his personality that anyone at all intimate with him would naturally have coloured views. "I could never talk to him without feeling like crying, and many others were the same," said a usually well-balanced member of his company to me. That makes an approach very difficult. We are immediately on an emotional plane, and it is his intellect that it is valuable to assess.

It is first necessary to destroy some of this legend that gets between us and him. The best known portrait, now, is that by Romola Nijinsky,* and it is all the more misleading through being on so many points nearly accurate, and always highly plausible. It is of course only natural that the wife of Nijinsky should see in Diaghilev the brilliant villain of the Middle Ages; *her* Diaghilev must have assumed some of those aspects, but it cannot be allowed to persist in its entirety as a true portrait. I could balance it with as many clearly established acts of goodness, that would, by substituting Santa Claus for Cesare Borgia, form a portrait equally misleading.

We must first admit his abnormal views on love, an undisputed fact.

Nijinsky, by Romola Nijinsky

He had only once, early in life, tried normal relations with a woman, and the occasion must have been unfortunate. It left him with a deep disgust, amounting to terror. He had never forgotten the incident, and talked of it at times. However, women played a large part in his life. Because of these views, he could meet them as equals, select them for their intelligence, and admire their beauty, coldly, as if they were museum exhibits. Women were attracted by him, and helped him from the very start. Some of the most remarkable women of the day were his allies, and made his triumphs possible. His deep loves made of him a lonely man, certain to be constantly disillusioned and disappointed, deliriously happy at one moment, dejected the next. He was only attracted by the virile, normal man, who was certain with maturity to attract and be attracted by the opposite sex, and to prefer the company of some witless little girl to the brilliant Sergei Pavlovitch: situations that one could not expect him to accept. Once that fact is admitted and understood, without condoning it in any way, it is not difficult to imagine his feelings on receiving the brief and unexpected telegraphic announcement of Nijinsky's marriage. To Sergei Pavlovitch, it was obviously quite impossible to retain him in the company, to work and to remain in daily contact with him and the intruder, his wife. The dismissal of him at once was no beginning of a dark mediæval plot to wipe him out of existence, but merely the very normal reaction of a very abnormal man. Once one admits this conception of love—and it has never been disputed—what other course was open to him? Also there was much more in it. It had its idealistic aspect.

Nijinsky as a choregrapher was Diaghilev's own creation, and it was through the opportunities that Diaghilev gave him, the careful nursing, the development of his personality, and the all-important intellectual contacts, that he could compose. Nijinsky was famous in Russia first, but in the old repertoire, and without Sergei Pavlovitch his fame would have remained local—just that of another brilliant dancer among brilliant dancers. Diaghilev must certainly have realised, aside from any feelings of jealousy, that however much Nijinsky was now living the normal life of a normal man, those opportunities would cease and his whole dream of creation would be shattered. Nijinsky was exceptionally receptive material, but needed the constant stimulation that Diaghilev alone could provide. When he left Diaghilev he immediately deteriorated as a dancer, and his choregraphy also failed, in the opinion of many. Another point that must have weighed with him was the fact—and the whole company knew it—that Nijinsky was highly strung and unbalanced from the very beginning, and that he needed the most extraordinary care and a total freedom from responsibility, a care that Diaghilev had always given him. It would be tragic to see him grow worse before his very eyes, without the means or the right to try to save him.

There is no suggestion that Diaghilev seduced him. Nijinsky was not a child. He had an enormous respect and admiration for him, and profited both materially and as an artist from the friendship. As events proved, his one hope of sanity lay in remaining with Diaghilev. While his desire to marry was natural, it must not be looked upon as an escape from some ogre, from an entirely unmitigated evil. The balance between the two men was, up to this point, very even; materially Nijinsky had certainly gained the most.

Such a separation, therefore, is not only understandable; anything else was quite out of the question. Then came the demand for the payment of arrears of salary—the first unfriendly act, and from the other side. To a man already suffering, this must have been a heavy blow. It is certain from all sources of evidence that Diaghilev was scrupulously honest; strangely avaricious in small things, generous, even lavish, in large. Many dancers, during the war and after, remained with him for years without ever having felt the need for a signed contract. For at least two of his dancers he deposited money in the bank in addition to their generous salaries, as some compensation for having taken them away from the guaranteed livelihood of the Maryinsky. This was done without any compulsion. Another dancer, who had refused his advances, he offered to send to a sanatorium in Switzerland, when he was threatened with tuberculosis. When it came to a reckoning between him and Nijinsky, he had looked after all Nijinsky's personal needs, had gratified his slightest wish, and had made him many costly presents. It must surely have been tacitly understood that the large salary was but a "paper" one, for the sake of appearances and publicity. Diaghilev could not stoop to reckon up all these favours, and here at any rate Nijinsky and his wife were the aggressors. A woman older and more experienced than the headstrong young girl, Romola, who knew so clearly what she wanted, and pursued it through so many difficulties, would have persuaded him to leave matters alone instead of taking the lead. She clearly felt her power, and there was a certain thrill even in the duel with her defeated rival—this great man whom her husband still worshipped. Between the two, Nijinsky, sighing for peace and the opportunity to serve his art, must have been both mystified and unhappy.

As to the tale of subsequent persecutions, one cannot for a moment believe them: they are altogether too fantastic and out of keeping with the whole of Diaghilev's known character. Once his dreams had been shattered he would have been bitter and disillusioned, but he would have let so painful a subject alone. Subsequent stories show this to have been the case. Many times disappointed, he still retained a friendship on a non-emotional basis when the other party made it possible. It was while they were still with him that he fought tooth and nail to retain their affections, was jealous to the extent of having them shadowed by detectives day and night, and adopted all the petty tricks that jealousy inspires even in the greatest minds.

The charge that Fokine sought to prevent Nijinsky appearing in *Le Spectre* *de la Rose* in London, or that Diaghilev even tried to influence him to do so, is indignantly denied by Fokine. One cannot conceive of these men as joint conspirators. Neither does it show any plot, that Bakst refused to collaborate with Nijinsky in his efforts to rival Diaghilev. Bakst, as a loyal and grateful friend, must have resented the whole thing, and held back not through fear or compulsion, as is suggested by Madame Nijinsky, but through common decency. The notion that Diaghilev incited two men to drive Nijinsky mad, by putting vaguely pseudo-Tolstoyan ideas into his head, is the most fantastic of all. Nijinsky himself was already unbalanced, obviously sought the company of other unstable men, and one of these "conspirators" died insane a little time later. The other, whom I know well, was young, impressionable, and soon threw off such ideas, which must have come at one time or another to so many adolescent Russians, who can ill digest so rich a literature. Also there is not a doubt that, at the time, he had an axe to grind, and enjoyed his influence over Nijinsky. It was not for nothing that he was called "Nijinsky's Rasputin" by the rest of the company. The thing undoubtedly happened as Romola Nijinsky describes it, but quite spontaneously and without the knowledge of Diaghilev, who, when he heard of it, strongly disapproved.*

I have investigated, too, the story of the attempt on his life. It was just one of those frightening episodes that, in spite of all precautions, occur from time to time on the stage. The object fell just behind Nijinsky and in front of Leon Woizikovsky, for whom it might equally well have been intended. I have myself witnessed almost the identical thing—the falling of a huge weight from the flies. Nijinsky may have been unpopular—all successful dancers are; it is part of the game—but the game does not include murder.[†]

We know that, throughout Nijinsky's unfortunate malady, Diaghilev showed, not remorse, but a very natural solicitude. He could be remorseless in pursuit of his aims, extremely jealous, and quite capable of strong hatred—every fault and quality in him was exaggerated—but this aimless vendetta is entirely out of keeping with his essentially creative character, and is not supported by anything more than the vague conjectures of a loving imaginative wife and her delicate husband. Diaghilev had his petty side, but it was shown by such things as making it indirectly difficult for someone he did not like to remain in the company, through passport troubles and the like, but he never pursued them or tried to damage their livelihood.

Nijinsky's own action in keeping Diaghilev away from the American tour, and assuming responsibilities for which he was so obviously unfitted, must certainly have damaged the artistic results of the entire enterprise, and jeo-

---

*He never quite forgave the unfortunate stage manager of the tour, who was quite powerless to intervene. —A. L. H.

[†] Editor's note: Except, of course, in Balanchine's *Slaughter on Tenth Avenue*.

pardised its very existence. The ballet could live perfectly well without Nijinsky, as events have proved, but without Diaghilev it was aimless. In this whole unpleasant episode Diaghilev showed the very greatest magnanimity. It was his ballet and he need not have consented to the tour. He wished for its success, and it was Nijinsky himself who selected the artists, omitting Grigoriev, whose help would have been invaluable. Apart from any sentiment, Diaghilev would never have tried to bring about a costly failure; it would have been cheaper to put his foot down from the very start.

In this whole story of the friendship and enmity of these two men, once the unfortunate basis, that made it delicate from the very start, has been admitted, it is clear that Diaghilev was more hurt than hurting.

His *manie des grandeurs,* another important part of the legend, certainly existed, and with some justification. His superiority was felt and admitted by others, who were themselves by no means toadies. He shone in any company, and it was not unnatural to play up to it at times. On one occasion he told me, after some trouble in the company, "I can get rid of all these people and have just as good a Ballet within three weeks. Dancers will pay to say they have been with me." Perhaps this was not strictly accurate at the time, 1925, but it was near enough to the truth. I had heard many of the offers that he turned down.

In one case a very large sum of money was offered him to "star" a young dancer whom he admired, but did not yet think ripe for such responsibility. He badly needed the money, but refused without hesitation, and felt himself insulted. He never forgave her. He had largely made the present company, the Maryinsky supply was exhausted, and he could form others, if not in three weeks, then within the year. On another occasion, at supper, I heard him reprimand one of his dancers for eating peas with a knife. "But, Sergei Pavlovitch, you are doing precisely the same thing." "I can, because I am Diaghilev"; which was true, and is a very old story that has always been true.

Lydia Sokolova has told me that apart from England, where each dancer has always had groups of friends and admirers, they always danced for Diaghilev and for Diaghilev alone. I have often heard them debating earnestly, when he had gone on one of his trips, as to what train he would take. "Ah, the 8:30, then he will have dinner at once and won't be there for the first ballet," in a tone of relief. His presence made an enormous and obvious difference to the whole quality of the performance. He noticed every single detail of dancing, makeup, and costume, from the placing of a safety-pin, and his opinions would reach the dancers via Grigorieff day by day, often in the form of a fine. Diaghilev had a hyper-sensitive eye. One of his *bêtes noires* was a big head. "I have a big head and there isn't going to be another one in the company." He was on that account most particular about the style of hairdressing. Another saying of his was: "There is nothing uglier in the world than a woman's thighs," and he never permitted the short revealing classical *tutu,* except in boyishly slim figures, such as Alice Nikitina's in *Zéphyr et Flore.*

This fact, of Diaghilev as an *audience,* can give us a first positive clue to his character; it reveals, and is explained by, his heredity. Ballet in Russia first took root through the nobles having private troupes of their own, brought over from the Continent or composed of their own serfs, performing not for profit but for their amusement and that of their guests. Diaghilev by breeding was such a nobleman. However much a showman he was, educating and cultivating his public, this precedent persisted, and was a part of him. He was Diaghilev the autocrat, and never in any sense an impresario, though he could and did outdistance them all at their own game. His ballet danced for him, for his gratification and his greater glory. Everyone in the theatre worked for him, even carpenters and electricians. On some occasions the dancers would leave the theatre in the evening, and find him still seated there the next morning, worn out, with deep bags under his eyes, surrounded by the technical staff. They earned big sums in overtime, but for no one else would they ever have done the same thing. He graciously shared his pleasure with the public, and with him pleasure largely consisted in watching the reactions of others to anything that moved him deeply. That is the essential picture that one must have first of all. Otherwise the position of the man who was not an impresario, and neither dancer, painter, nor musician, but who influenced all three for a quarter of a century, is impossible to understand. We can think of him as a Lorenzo the Magnificent, never a dilettante, but an artist in appreciation, and, in many interpretations of the word, a fully creative mind.

Our view of Diaghilev as a creator depends largely upon the particular period in his career. One of the very best studies is that of A. Benois, his first mentor, and collaborator of the early days. He tells how Diaghilev, the young provincial, of good county family, joined their little circle of artists, sponsored by his cousin Filosofov, and of the impressions he made, beginning as the timid outsider on sufferance, and soon becoming the dominating force. One episode he recalls in particular, the sudden interruption during a picnic of a long abstract discussion on Wagner:

> Lying as I was on my back, looking at the clouds, I could not see what was happening. . . . Sergei took advantage of this to creep up to me, seize hold of me and start pummelling me, laughing heartily all the while. Never before had such a thing happened in our group. We were all quiet and well brought up . . . real mother's boys. . . . Also I soon felt that big Sergei was much stronger than I, and that, although the eldest, I risked a humiliating defeat. I had recourse to a ruse, screaming lustily so as to persuade him that

he had broken my arm. He was impressed, released me with regret at having been unable to follow up his advantage and even helped me to get up, which I did, groaning and rubbing my arm energetically.

This childish scene has remained fixed in my memory with extraordinary vividness and I think that the reason for it is that suddenly I had a vision of the true nature of Sergei, the nature of a fighter. Although we soon became fast friends long before any collaboration, a sort of fight was always mixed up in our relationship, which gave our friendship a particular zest.

Diaghilev, the fighter, was to overcome all the difficulties and intrigues of the twenty-five years that surrounded his venture. Only a fighter and an absolute autocrat could have succeeded. Diaghilev was born a dictator, but that rare thing, the dictator of discrimination and intelligence.

"Only one thing," says Benois, "was lacking in that generation of Russian artists who contributed to the creation of all these fine artistic manifestations—it was just that, the will to create, that same will to create that Diaghilev possessed to the full."

In the years immediately before the ballet, Diaghilev shows magnificent scholarship in a monograph on the Russian painter Levitzsky. He dabbles in music, tries his voice as a singer, and is dissuaded by Rimsky-Korsakov from composing, after a first effort had been heard. That is the end of dilettantism. Then comes the organisation of art exhibitions, the editing of a review and the sponsoring of a whole new movement. This means fighting and diplomacy. The young provincial has found himself. The first few years of the ballet are an exploitation of that will, but it is still clearly the Fokine ballet, and we are told that the only suggestion he ever made to Fokine was during a rehearsal of *L'Oiseau de Feu,* when he pointed out that the heart was on the left side. Fokine is fully justified in all that he says: the real Diaghilev was still to appear.

It is with the ripening of the Nijinsky friendship that we first see him. The results of that friendship had deprived him of a permanent headquarters, and had made him almost an outlaw. Now he had to rely from season to season entirely on his diplomatic skill. Nijinsky, as an artist, was the result of the opportunities provided for him by Diaghilev, who did not create his ballets or ever claim to do so, but who surrounded him with the necessary ingredients and waited.* When Nijinsky left him, he was immediately ready with Massine, a truly brilliant mind, who profited by the opportunities to the full, and soon found his own direction.

Then Diaghilev was ready to enhance those creations. Forsaking for ever

---

*In all the discussions I had with him, never once did he lay claim to a creation or even to ideas that I knew had come from him. His autocracy and leadership were understood things; it pleased him to be generous; it was the prerogative of being a Tsar.

ready-made music, and the decor of those artists who had started out with him, he commenced the Diaghilev Ballet, and it is of this second period, the Massine period, that he was proudest. Choreography, music, decor, all must be commissioned, and the result must show no gaps, and, however bad any of his rare failures may have been, there never was a gap. Much subsequent ballet has been more important, but there have always been some flaws in its presentation, one of the partners struggling to express something different. While it is quite clear that Diaghilev himself was a man of few ideas or direct suggestions, he could inspire ideas in his *entourage,* and then act. He himself never laid claim to ideas and avoided personal publicity. Never on any occasion did he appear on the stage. All the extravagant claims were made by his over-enthusiastic admirers.

"What exactly do I do? Well, you can say that I superintend the lighting," was his invariable reply. He could play with light like an artist mixing paint on his canvas, and patiently persisted until the crease in the old drop curtain of *Petrouchka* was completely washed away.

It is not true, either, to go to the other extreme and to believe the jibe that painters admired his knowledge of music, musicians his knowledge of painting. "If you placed twenty scores before him, he would pick out the best, and give his reasons, too," Auric told me, while Larionov used the identical phrase to describe his knowledge of painting. I have seen him interrupt an orchestra rehearsal to make some criticism, when Stravinsky himself was conducting, and the suggestion was readily accepted. If he appeared to interfere but little in the actual choreography, it was because he had picked his men with the greatest care, and had influenced their whole minds and manner of thinking, previously. He did not just commission a work as a mere financial transaction. His collaborators stayed with him months at a time at Monte Carlo, and he actually watched the work in progress, criticising it bit by bit. The greatest artists of the day listened to his criticism with respect.

"Creative?" says Larionov, one of his brilliant collaborators. "In one respect at any rate, admirably so. He created his audiences. For months ahead, before each new departure he arranged for inspired talk to circulate in the salons, and listened carefully to opinions. Even the head waiter in a restaurant was worth influencing. This preliminary 'provocation' was part of a deliberate system."

Did he always believe in his own works? At times that is a little doubtful. Once when I asked him what he really thought of a new ballet, he replied: "I cannot tell yet. I haven't read the papers." A *boutade,* of course, but ever since the scandal over *L' Après-midi d'un faune* he realised the full value of controversy and enjoyed it. It meant a fight. Such a work as *Romeo et Juliette* was boosted far above its merits, through the demonstration and quarrel amongst the *surréalistes,* which Diaghilev definitely anticipated, if he did not foster it. His own personal taste in music was for melody, and in Switzerland, during the war, Stravinsky teased him for his excessive admiration for Tchaikovsky. Stravinsky subsequently revised his opinions; Diaghilev remained firm, though publicly for a time he left Tchaikovsky far behind.

His taste in dancing was for classicism, though he could admire something totally different. I remember his urging me to see the acrobatics of the Gertrude Hoffman girls. This was a superficial momentary interest of a man whom everything interested. Olga Spessivtseva was his favoured *ballerina*. He said of her: "Olga Spessivtseva and Anna Pavlova are like two halves of an apple, but the Spessivtseva half has been in the sun." Unjust, of course, but he never could forgive Pavlova for having made a success away from his influence. The Maryinsky *ballerinas* he admired wholeheartedly, and could talk for hours about Kschessinska, her art, charm, and intelligence. He was far less of a revolutionary than Fokine, though the results associated with him were so much more extreme. The failure of *The Sleeping Princess* affected him more than people can know. It was a return to his own taste, and its rejection in the nature of a personal rebuff. Other failures he could talk of light-heartedly, as "successful failures" or the reverse. His deliberate policy after that, in his own words, shortly before his death, was to sicken the public gradually with the grotesque, and the "*dernier cri,*" until he had educated them sufficiently to return to the purity of classicism. Both his choregraphers of the ultra-modern period were themselves sickened, and longing for the return. When he died this was fully planned. Dolin was engaged, Lifar nearly ready, and his beloved Spessivtseva waiting. Often, too, he tried to induce Kschessinska to return to the stage. The change of direction, which took place after his death, was in a sense due to him. Lifar danced *Giselle* and *L'Oiseau Bleu* with Spessivtseva; to see this would have given him the greatest joy. Massine discovered the new symphonic classicism.

All this shows clearly that Diaghilev could not initiate artistic movements without years of preparation; he seized them at their birth, and showed them to the public at large. The era 1909–1929 was the Diaghilev era, because he crystallised what was going on, and not because he actually created it. This does not detract from him; it puts his genius on another plane, and at the same time allows full credit to his collaborators.

Diaghilev has been called, by many, an excellent business man, and if the keeping alive of an expensive company for so long deserves the description, he was, though in point of detail the artist plus nobleman in him always won. *The Sleeping Princess* would have needed a record run to meet its expenses. Each costume in one brief scene cost over £50. Others have profited by this lavishness, for today the original costumes are still being worn in *Petrouchka, Prince Igor,* and *Le Chapeau Tricorne,* still in admirable condition. Not a penny would be spared either on entertaining or on the smallest detail once an idea had entered into his head. He had no fixed home and very few personal wants. Only in the last few years he collected books, chiefly Pushkiniana, that followed him round in crates. The unique collection of pictures that he formed was all given away. He collected deliberately for others. He paid a friend's doctor's bill in the finest Baksts I have ever seen. His business ability would be more correctly summed up as infectious personal charm and enthusiasm. I can never conceive of his balancing a budget or attempting to do so. If his guarantors lost their money, as they invariably did, they found the results well worth the expenditure, and were ready to lose and gain once more, the next year.

Enfin, en 1913, pour la saison inaugurale des Champs-Élysées, il me tint la dragée haute et me fit payer ses spectacles un demi-million! Cette folie, que je n'avais pas le droit de ne pas commettre, permit la création du *Sacre,* mais coûta la vie à ma direction.

A remarkable statement from even so enlightened a theatrical manager as Gabriel Astruc.

Often in small expenses he was close. I have seen him haggling with a chauffeur in Monte Carlo over two francs, and at times his dinner-jacket was sadly frayed. Every penny went into his dreams. He handled millions, and died poor.

For so brilliant a man, Diaghilev was strangely superstitious. When a black cat crossed his path I have known him go ten minutes out of his way to take another route, and on one occasion, at the Prince's Theatre, when a black cat jumped on the stage during a rehearsal of *Le Sacre du printemps,* he was first frantic and then resigned and miserable. Incidentally that season was one of his rare failures. A hat on the table meant sorrow; a hat on the bed, death. He was also frightened of being photographed. He needed much persuading, and considered it most unlucky. There are few photographs of him, scarcely any that are posed.

Strangely enough, this fighter, who could face a moral situation with hero-ism, was a physical coward. He was terrified of the idea of pain in himself or in others. Once at the Savoy, when a small boil in his mouth required lancing, he shrieked so hysterically at the sight of the instrument that the doctor had to abandon his attempt. It was agony for him to cross the Channel, especially as a gypsy had once predicted that he would meet death on the water. He loathed the very sight of a vast expanse of water, and would remain locked in his cabin; while at times he waited days for a favourable crossing, letting the company go on ahead. It can be imagined how much he suffered during a wartime crossing to the United States, when there was actual danger. Day and night he wore his life-saving jacket. Once during ship's drill, not satisfied with standing by his station, he clambered into the lifeboat, and was snapped in that undignified position. Then later, when, in a fog, the sirens blew, after shivering in his cabin, he rushed on deck prepared for the worst, but the journey was over, and they were well past the Statue of Liberty.

These anecdotes of weakness are not told to detract from a great man; they are an indisputable part of a true portrait, that must take all such things into account.

His relations with the company are interesting. With a few exceptions none of them knew him. He did not suffer fools gladly, politely, or at all, except where his affections were engaged, and if they were not unusually clever or talented, then they were—just dancers. For their part they admired him: it almost amounted to worship; but at the same time they were thoroughly scared. The fear of secessions on an important scale played a large part in these relations. He was constantly on the look-out, and no one was allowed to assume too much power. It was not a question of megalomania, but of solid common sense. Where he recognised brains or unusual talent—and he was always generous in recognising intelligence in others—there was no service he would not render. He once told Lydia Sokolova, "Remember I am your friend; if ever for any reason you need me, I will come. You can always rely on my help. Consider me as a father." These were not just words. When she was so dangerously ill in Paris, he brought his own surgeon for her, and, on the tour that followed, cabled every few hours. He was frantic and asked the company to pray for her. That is an aspect of him that is little known, but it is very much a part of him, the true friend.

He was always, except with his special favourites, where he was blind, able to separate the individual he liked from the artist who served him. It was quite impossible to ask him for roles, equally impossible to drop a role that had grown wearisome. He disliked intensely any fishing for praise. One artist after an unexpected triumph in a difficult role went up to him expectantly. "Not at all bad," he told her, "but let us hope you will do it much better next time."

He kept a careful eye on the company's morals from an æsthetic point of view. If any girl went out repeatedly in company that he found common or unsuitable for the Russian Ballet, without saying anything definite, he took steps to dismiss her from the company. He was no hypocrite, he did not preach a morality foreign to himself, but the whole tone of these servants of art must be maintained. Nothing could be allowed to interfere with the quality of their work.

Fortunately when the end came it was in Venice, a final wish fulfilled. His almost childish greed and love of sweet things certainly hastened the end. I have seen him eat almost a whole box of chocolates, chuckling at this defiance of the doctor's orders, strange contradiction in one so afraid. When it came, he was surrounded by those he loved, and who loved him. He, who was so terrified of suffering, went out quietly, all fears calmed by nature's soothing anæsthetic of unconsciousness.

"I feel fuddled, drunk," were his last words.

So passed this superman.

—from *Balletomania*, 1934

LYNN GARAFOLA

Coming Home
DIAGHILEV IN PERM

For years, Perm was a "closed" city. In Soviet parlance, that meant off-limits to foreigners: tourists, diplomats, correspondents, and scholars. Not that many people itched to see this Urals capital. With its chemical plants and munitions factories, Perm was a city of smokestacks, gray, modern, and charmless. Until Gorbachev, moreover, it was a center of the Gulag. In the surrounding penal colonies, prisoners "of conscience" like the poet Marina Tsvetaeva had died or spent years at hard labor.

The last time I arrived in Moscow, I learned that, thanks to glasnost, Perm had been "opened." To get there, one had to be on "official" business, but for the first time since the 1930s, foreigners were welcome. I made up my mind to go, and a few months later, with an invitation from the Perm State Art Gallery, boarded the Aeroflot flight from Moscow. Two hours and two time zones later, I was in Perm.

My reason for going was curiosity. I wanted to see where Sergei Diaghilev had grown up. I had written a book about him, and the geography of his life had become an obsession. I knew where he ate lunch in Madrid and ordered winter coats in London, where he recited Pushkin in Florence and "insulted" Ravel in Monte Carlo. I had walked the former English Prospect in Leningrad where he once lived and had stood in the lobby of the hotel in Venice where he died. And in Paris, Turin, Milan, and countless other cities, I had visited the theaters where his Ballets Russes performed.

Yet, like other Western scholars, I had never seen the city of his youth.

Although Diaghilev was born in the province of Novgorod, he lived in Perm from the time he was two until he was eighteen. This upbringing set him apart from the friends and future colleagues he met in St. Petersburg when he settled there as a university student in 1890. One of these, Alexandre Benois, recalled his impressions of the young collegian in *Reminiscences of the Russian Ballet:* "[Diaghilev] was very much of a provincial when he first arrived in St. Petersburg and Valetchka [Walter Nouvel], Kostia [Konstantin] Somov, and I were even shocked by his rather uncouth manners and primitive views, though this was only natural to one who had lived all his life in the depths of the Perm countryside."

On the drive from the airport, I learn that Perm today is an industrial city of one million. In Diaghilev's time, it was a mercantile and administrative center with only a fraction of the current population. In the taxi with me is Nadezhda Vladimirovna Beliaeva, director of the Gallery and my host, and Natalia Sergeevna Ginsburg, the museum's curator of foreign art, who is acting as my translator. We could be in the American rust belt. On both sides of the road are factories with peeling walls and corroded fittings. Although it's only eight-thirty at night, the streets are deserted.

At the hotel, a high rise on Komsomol Prospect, Nadezhda Vladimirovna outlines my program. It's a full one: talks, tours, performances, a visit to Diaghilev's house. Then she describes what the Gallery has done to "bring Diaghilev home." She begins with the 1987 exhibition "Sergei Diaghilev and Artistic Culture of the Late Nineteenth and Early Twentieth Centuries." Did I know this was the first show about Diaghilev since the Revolution? No, but it wasn't hard to believe. For years he had been a nonperson, and even today, eight years after the publication of Ilya Zil'bershtein's two-volume collection of documents, *Sergei Diaghilev and Russian Art,* he remains in the shadow of the artists he revealed to the West. Then, there was the three-day conference that dovetailed with the exhibition, and the volume of papers on topics ranging from Diaghilev's career as a student to his activities as a critic and historian of art. She talks about the 1987 show, rich in biographical materials and documents of life in old Perm.

The next morning, with Natalia Sergeevna, I get my first glimpse of the nineteenth-century city. It's just across the hotel's carless parking lot and beyond the steel-girdered "univermag" (Russian for department store). But it's another world entirely; taking leave of the Soviet present, you enter the Russian past. Within minutes, we reach a promenade. Below lies a river, serene and glassy in the morning light. This is the Kama; it winds north through the Perm oblast (district) and south past Kazan to the Volga. In Diaghilev's time, paddlesteamers traveled the river, discharging their passengers at the old boat station. This morning, a mist hangs over the water, and on the embankment remain patches of last night's snow. Above us rises a

steeple. That's our Gallery, Natalia Sergeevna tells me. Before the Revolution, it was the Cathedral of the Transfiguration, attended by all the best
people, including the Diaghilevs. In 1922, it became a museum. I later learn
that of the dozens of churches that existed in Perm before the Revolution,
few survived the 1930s.

At the Gallery, the curators are waiting. I am to give a talk, an informal
one, and for once in my life I do it off the cuff. Today, I can't remember a
word I said, but I know I will never have such an audience again or feel the
reality of Diaghilev's life meshed with so many impossible dreams. Think of
him: *barin,* patron, collector, captain for twenty years of an enterprise
dedicated to beauty, a man who could move mountains to get what he
wanted, and did, on three continents. He loved pleasure and found it everywhere, in good food, fine tailoring, rare books, handsome faces. He ate
chocolates and cream puffs with gusto, without a care for his waistline or the
diabetes that eventually killed him. If ever a figure was larger than life, it was
Diaghilev.

Yet, in the faces around me that morning in Perm, I discern no irony, no
sense of the incongruity between his privileged existence and their own. In
this city of factories and housing projects, where people have forgotten the
taste of chocolate and never known the feel of silk and where a trip to the
West is an unimaginable luxury, Diaghilev gives leave to imagine another
kind of world—a lost paradise of beauty, pleasure, and ease.

Significantly, my audience is all women. Warm, capable, with the toll of
double-burdened lives showing on the older ones, they are typical Russian
women, conjuring suppers from empty supermarket shelves and touches of
elegance from drab, ill-fitting clothing. None has traveled abroad, and few
have met a foreigner before. But they dream, finding in the past an escape
from the present and in nostalgia a means of giving focus to their yearnings
for a better life. For Diaghilev's admirers in Perm, the reality of his life pales
before the liberating power of his myth.

That evening, I am taken to the Tchaikovsky Theater, where the Perm Ballet is to give *Don Quixote*. Before the performance, however, we have a date
with the theater archivist. A jovial man with a passion for local history, he
guides me through the exhibition on the gallery level of the theater. The
show is about old Perm, and he happily points out the treasures: a ten-foot-
long map of the Kama from its source all the way to Kazan, panoramas of
the nineteenth-century city (in which I spot the Gallery's steeple), period
photographs of notable buildings, including the Assembly of Nobles, the
Meshkov mansion (a merchant palace on the embankment), and the Opera
Theater. There are also pictures of leading citizens, including members of
the Diaghilev clan.

Back in the office, he sits me down. You know, he tells me, it's not true what they say, that culture came to Perm with the Revolution. Not true at all. In the old days, this was a cultural center. All the best people made music; they gave concerts, they formed an orchestra, they organized benefit performances for charity. The Diaghilevs were very musical; they had a chamber group that was the pride of the city and performed several times a year at the Assembly of Nobles, just down the street from where the family lived. It was these same people, he continues, who built the opera house we're sitting in now. A subscription was taken up, and everyone pledged something; the Diaghilevs gave five thousand rubles. That was in the 1870s. By the 1890s, touring opera companies, with dancers, were giving full-scale performances.

At intermission, his friend Galina, a designer at the theater, takes me backstage. In the left wing, she points out the remnants of an old wall, left standing as a souvenir when this part of the theater was rebuilt in the 1950s. Then, she relates a piece of old lore about Diaghilev. In his day, the theater was off-limits to students. But he used to sneak here anyway, roaming the corridors and getting into trouble for it. So this, I thought as we rejoined the crowd, is where it all started, in a theater his family helped to build. No wonder proprietorship came easily to him.

Like St. Petersburg, Perm is a city of white nights, and at eleven, when we leave the theater, it's still light. In front of us is Komsomol Square, the heart of what remains of the old town; people come here to stroll in the park, my guides tell me, because it gives them a sense of the past. Although it's hard to believe, until the 1930s the square was covered by a complex of shops. To my surprise, I learn that a Diaghilev had built this emporium; I hadn't realized that the family, apart from one vodka-producing maverick, was "in trade." Other sights are pointed out: the corner-wrapping building with a balcony where Dmitrii Vasil'evich Diaghilev, Diaghilev's great-grandfather, once lived, and across from it the former *gymnasium,* or preparatory school, that Diaghilev attended from 1883 until 1890, when he graduated. No wonder Nadezhda Vladimirovna is badgering the city fathers to rename this Diaghilev Square.

Among my guides is Evgeniia Ivanovna Egorova. A woman in her sixties, she grew up in the countryside, not far from the village of Bikbarda, where the Diaghilevs had an estate. To the south of Perm (today, about five or six hours by bus), Bikbarda was a beautiful spot, with flowering orchards and woods. In the summer, the whole Diaghilev family gathered there. As a boy, she adds, Sergei Pavlovich loved to swim, a piece of information I find astonishing given Diaghilev's later horror of crossing even the calmest waterway.

She also fills me in on the history of the clan. The first Diaghilev to settle in Perm was Pavel Fedorovich. He came from Tobolsk, in Siberia, where his boyar ancestors had been sent by Ivan the Terrible, and he died in Perm in

1767. His son, Vasilii Pavlovich, administered rural metalworks and, like most of the Diaghilevs, married into a merchant family. His son, Diaghilev's great-grandfather, was the Dmitrii Vasil'evich with the house on Komsomol Square. A musician, writer, and painter, he was the first Diaghilev to display the artistic proclivities that henceforth distinguished the family.

In a torrent of forenames and patronymics, the chronicle moves forward to Diaghilev's day. She tells me about Elena Valerianovna Panaeva, his step-mother, whose father built railroads and opened a theater in St. Petersburg for Italian opera that burnt to the ground in 1905; her sister, Alexandra Vale-rianovna, a singer who studied in Paris, performed in Milan, and married a nephew of Tchaikovsky. She tells me about cousins who painted and gradu-ated from the Conservatory. And, leaping into the Soviet era, she tells me about nieces and grandnephews who carried on the family musical tradition.

I press Evgeniia Ivanovna for information about Diaghilev's immediate family. Did they remain in Perm? What happened to them during the Revo-lution? After Sergei Pavlovich left for St. Petersburg, she tells me, the house was robbed, and the family went to live in lodgings. Then, they moved to Poltava, a city in the eastern Ukraine, where Diaghilev's father resumed his military career. When Pavel Pavlovich died in 1914 (on the day World War I broke out), Elena Valerianovna moved to St. Petersburg, where she died in 1919 at the age of sixty-eight.

There is pain on Evgeniia Ivanovna's face as she continues the story. Diaghilev's brother Valentin followed his father into the army. In 1917, when the Revolution began, he was a general and the father of four sons, two of whom perished in the Civil War. Then, in 1927, Valentin was arrested and sent to Solovki, a bleak island prison off Archangel, where he died two years later. His wife, Alexandra Alekseeva Peiker, was also arrested and sent to Siberia. The children were left to fend for themselves; Sergei was sixteen and Vasilii fourteen, and they had to sell off the family books and furniture to eat. As for Iurii, Sergei Pavlovich's other brother, he too was sent away, to middle Asia near Tashkent, where he died in 1957. (His wife, Tatiana Andreevna Lugovskaia, was a painter who participated in the early exhibi-tions of the *Mir iskusstva* group.)

As Evgeniia Ivanovna relates this sorry tale, I recall some letters I had read at the Dance Collection in New York. They were dated January 1928 and written by one Jean Herbette to Philippe Berthelot, a high-ranking offi-cial in the French ministry of foreign affairs. What the Dance Collection had were copies made for Diaghilev by his assistant, Boris Kochno. Their import was the following: In late 1927, presumably at Diaghilev's behest, the French approached Maxim Litvinov, the Soviet Commissar of Foreign Affairs, for information about the whereabouts of Valentin and his wife, Alexandra Alekseeva, both of whom had disappeared. An inquiry was made, but as Herbette reported to his superior, the secret police "found no trace of an arrest." The timing of the enquiry had always puzzled me. Now I understood. Diaghilev had lost his closest relations not in the Revolution, but in the first wave of Stalin's purges.

It is with Evgeniia Ivanovna, too, that I finally lay eyes on Diaghilev's house. Located at the corner of Karl Marx and Pushkin streets, it is now elementary school number eleven. At first, I am struck by the modesty of the building; only one-story, it has neither the columns nor balconies of Perm's statelier monuments. Then I notice its elegance: the French windows, the classical cornices, and the rhythmic effect produced by their repetition. Today, the walls are pinkish-beige; the windows and cornices white. In Diaghilev's time, the façade was livelier, with loops and edgings painted in high contrast to the walls. We arrive a few minutes before ten. The principal, Raisa Dmitrievna Zobygeva, is finishing a science lesson. She motions us into the classroom and introduces us; "foreigner," I hear the ten-year-olds whispering as she writes out their assignment.

Raisa Dmitrievna shows us around. Except for the eighteen-foot ceilings and the windows that flood the administrative offices with light, little remains of the building's original layout. Only the parlor is intact, a huge corner room with a piano at one end, where today, as in Diaghilev's time, concerts are given. On the walls are blowups of family photographs: Diaghilev, in a high chair, with Elena Valerianovna, and as a *gymnasium* student, his right hand thrust Napoleon-style into his overcoat; his father, as a dashing officer; the three brothers, Sergei, Valentin, and Iurii, as children; the family's chamber music group. Though the chandelier, the pier glass, and all the old furniture are gone, it's not hard to imagine this room as the setting of Diaghilev's introduction to civilized pleasure. Or, on a grimmer note, to imagine that from the windows facing the Siberian Way, as Karl Marx Street used to be called, he had his first glimpse of prisoners setting off on foot to Siberia. The tsars had their Gulags, too.

In the journey from Perm to Paris, Diaghilev remade himself as a cosmopolitan. Yet, always, he remained deeply Russian, attuned to the ways and arts of a country that belonged fully to Europe only at its westernmost borders. This sense of Russia was surely a legacy of Perm; here, even the Westernized elite was surrounded by popular tradition. At the Gallery, behind what was once the iconostasis, I am shown a remarkable collection of icons "rescued" from abandoned churches in the Perm region. Few are as beautiful as icons I have seen in Moscow, but they display the robust imagination of genuine folk art, the "primitivism" that Diaghilev brilliantly exploited in works like Le Coq d'Or. Even more remarkable is the museum's collection of religious sculpture: polychrome saints and crucifixions unique to Orthodox churches of the Urals.

Although Diaghilev was not a religious man, he had a keen appreciation for Russian religious art. In the 1906 exhibition that marked his debut on the Paris art scene, he included no fewer than twenty-six examples of the successive schools of icon painting. Among the unrealized projects that occupied his thoughts in 1914 and 1915 was *Liturgie,* a cubo-futurist "mystery" inspired, in part, by the icon tradition of Russia's north. Doubtless, his first encounter with popular religious art came in the country churches of Perm.

Examples of these have been reconstructed at Khokhlovka, the Gallery's outdoor museum about forty kilometers from the city. Dark, wooden, crowned by a single onion dome, they are typical of the churches that once dotted the Russian countryside. What strikes me most about Khokhlovka, however, is the setting. Here is the Kama as Diaghilev knew it, sparkling, majestic, unpolluted. As far as the eye can see are timberlands of birch and pine, thick forests where people come in the fall to gather mushrooms and where I imagine the Dashas and Mashas of Russian fairy tales adventuring among the bears. The quiet and the boundless space are overwhelming. Only a will as titanic as Diaghilev's could survive the encounter with this nature undiminished.

Time and again, the Gallery curators who were my guides lamented their isolation within the larger Perm community. When it comes to dance, however, the city is far from a wasteland. Now the best of the country's regional troupes, the Perm Ballet began as a small ensemble in the 1920s. Until World War II, influence flowed from Moscow; then, with the arrival of the Kirov (now St. Petersburg) Ballet, which spent the war years in Perm, the technical and stylistic baseline was oriented to Leningrad. Kirov versions entered the repertory, while Kirov teachers revamped the company's feeder school, training the teachers who have made the Perm Choreographic Academy (to give the school its full name) justly famous.

Today, Ninel Pidemskaia runs the school, and she kindly allows us to visit some classes. We begin with Ludmila Pavlovna Sakharova's, an advanced one for girls. Sakharova (who has taught at Oleg Vinogradoff's Universal Ballet Academy in Washington) is the school's most celebrated pedagogue, and in her newest crop of seventeen-year-olds you see the line, plastique, and coordinated use of the upper body that distinguishes the best Russian dancing. In Yelena Vladimorovna Bystritskaia's fourth-year class, I see how that coordination is achieved. She's working on an adagio, and after a few bars she stops the pianist. What's wrong with you today? she asks a blond girl in the tone of an offended lioness. No eyes, no head; you look terrible. The scene is repeated not once, but six times, with Yelena Vladimirovna pleading, threatening, cajoling, until the details of the preparation are correct.

Although he never abjured the technique of ballet, Diaghilev made his reputation as a promoter of choreographic experiment. How fitting, then, that the best of the handful of innovators on today's Russian dance scene should live and work in Perm. I meet Evgenii Panfilov in the tiny room of a local palace of culture that serves as headquarters of his Experimental Modern Dance Theater. We are not a ballet company, he announces straight off, and we're not subsidized by the state; the Perm Electrotechnical Plant, which sponsors us, gives us the studio down the hall where we rehearse and this room where we do everything else. Panfilov never went to ballet school. Deciding at nearly twenty to be a choreographer, he enrolled in the dance department at GITIS, a Moscow institute that specializes in training actors and directors. Returning to Perm before he graduated, he began to choreograph.

In the studio, he leads the company's dozen dancers through a typical warm-up. He has told me he doesn't have a "system," but all the exercises he gives work the torso, while encouraging freedom in the arms and upper bodies. I am impressed by the commitment of the dancers and by their diversity; one woman is black. After the warm-up, we repair to the auditorium for a run-through of Panfilov's most recent work, *The Armchair*. It's a dark piece, a succession of fantasies and deadly acts dominated by the image of a general in tsarist-style epaulets. Some of Panfilov's devices recall Pina Bausch, whose work, he says, he has never seen. But what distinguishes *The Armchair* from most examples of German dance-theater is the choreographer's commitment to dance; with Panfilov, movement is far more than the glue of a mixed-media collage. He does not eschew ballet, although he uses its steps selectively, assimilating them into an open-ended, idiosyncratic idiom that incorporates gesture, pedestrian movement, ritual, acrobatics, and occasionally speech.

I leave Perm on Tuesday afternoon. The morning is devoted to leave-taking, a last walk through the old streets, good-byes to the women of the Gallery who have become friends. In the hotel, waiting for the taxi, Nadezhda Vladimirovna sits me down. It's our custom, she says, when people leave, to keep a moment of silence. So, in the quiet, I sit, thinking of the city Diaghilev left and the benighted one he has come home to, and wondering, as I have so often these past days, at the spell of memory and its mysterious hold on the imagination.

—from *Ballet Review*, Summer 1996 (written in 1990)

NICOLAS NABOKOV

Diaghilev and Music

Born to an upper-class Russian family (Vladimir Nabokov was a cousin), Nicolas Nabokov (1903–1978) was living in Paris by 1923, pursuing his career as a composer. His ballet Ode *was presented by Sergei Diaghilev in 1928, and thirty-eight years later, his friend George Balanchine commissioned the score for* Don Quixote *from him. In 1939 he became an American citizen, and for many years he served as the secretary-general of the Congress for Cultural Freedom. He was also a learned and sophisticated lecturer and writer.*

Diaghilev had never written a single piece of music, yet he knew more music, and in a way more *about* music, than many an erudite musician. Since his early youth he had developed a voracious appetite for all kinds of music—light and serious, old and new, romantic and classical. As a result of this profuse and polyglot diet he had accumulated a vast store of data (he knew a staggering number of compositions of various styles and historical periods) and had acquired a professional's grasp of musical techniques. What was quite exceptional in his knowledge was its intuitive, its immediate aspect; in other words, Diaghilev had the gift of detecting, after one incomplete and cursory hearing, the quality of a piece of music.

This gift, so simple and yet so infinitely rare, made it possible for him not only to determine the intrinsic value of a new work of art, but also to relate it to other works and thus to evaluate the extent and the quality of artistic discovery present in it. Diaghilev's personal taste (and he had a definite taste for the monumental works of late Romanticism) never interfered with his interest in music of all periods and styles. He was always on the lookout for something new—a new work, a new composer, a forgotten score by an eighteenth-century master dug up from some dusty French or Italian library. In this search it was his primary concern to determine right away whether the music was good or bad, and hence whether it was suitable for use by his company. The astonishing thing, of course, was not that he asked himself those obvious questions ("Is this good? Can I use it?") but that after hearing a new work only once he was able to make up his mind unhesitatingly and appraise the specific qualities or defects of the work with masterful precision.

I remember arguing with him about my own ballet after I had played it for him for the first time in the midsummer of 1927. The subject of the ballet was taken from a poem—an "Ode to the Majesty of God on the Occasion of the Appearance of the Great Northern Lights"—by the eighteenth-century court poet and physicist Mikhail Lomonosov (referred to in Russia as the "father of Russian science"). It is a famous example of Russian didactic and "encyclopedist" court poetry inspired by French and German examples. Written in the flamboyant and archaic Russian of that period, it represents a thinly veiled allegory on the enthronement of Empress Elizabeth—the aurora borealis of the poem.

Diaghilev, of course, knew the poem and liked its oddly baroque metaphors and its resonant language (although normally he was quite indifferent to poetry); but chiefly what pleased him in it was its reference to Empress Elizabeth. According to a rumor (which he may well have started himself), Diaghilev was, on his mother's side, a descendant of Elizabeth—a great-great-grandson of one of the Empress's natural children. He was flattered by this illicit relationship to the Imperial house of Russia; it made him a direct descendant of Peter the Great, and gave him a kind of "morganatic" halo. There was, in effect, a slight physical resemblance between him and the puffy-faced daughter of Russia's first Emperor. As for Diaghilev's character, what could be more like that of the dynamic, quick-tempered, and despotic Peter?

But quite apart from this, Diaghilev liked the whole idea of a Russian "period piece." Boris Kochno and I concocted a two-act ballet libretto, the second act of which was supposed to represent the "Feast of the Northern Lights"—in other words, the coronation of Empress Elizabeth. I had written a short introduction to this second act; Diaghilev wanted a longer and more "ample" one. He objected to my introduction and called it a "meager pot of Conservatory porridge." I felt hurt, and defended myself by saying that the way I had written it was right, that it was a good fugato in the style of the eighteenth-century French overtures. Diaghilev smiled mockingly and replied, "Maybe, *mon cher,* it *is* a fugato, maybe even a fugue, but it certainly isn't any good. You know I don't really care whether you write a fugue or a fugato, a French or a Brazilian overture; what matters is that you write good music." He concluded, "This goes equally for Richard Strauss and the waltz-Strauss, for Bach and Offenbach. It is a simple but a very golden rule."

On another occasion I remember him discussing a new ballet score by a young protégé of Prokofiev. Prokofiev, Diaghilev, and I had just finished listening to it in the rehearsal room of the Monte Carlo Theater. Diaghilev was in one of his most explosive moods; he ranted and shouted at Prokofiev, "How can you like this, Seryoja? Don't you see that it's drivel? It's stupid, it's dull; worse than that, it's eely and slimy; it sounds like Arensky. There is only one page of it that seems acceptable. Here, give it to me." He took the score out of Prokofiev's hands and started to turn the pages angrily. "Here it is. You see . . . this melody. It's the only piece of light in this dusty piece; but unfortunately it only lasts five measures."

Many years later Prokofiev and I played that piece over again; it was utterly inept and dull. When we came to the page which Diaghilev had pointed out, Prokofiev muttered, "Damn it, Diaghilev was right. This is certainly very 'dusty' stuff."

His knowledge of music of the past was both broad and detailed. One would ask him a question about a composer, say for example about Méhul, a forgotten French opera composer and contemporary of Beethoven. "Oh yes," he would answer, "Méhul was a first-rate opera composer, but he did not know how to handle big scenes (as did Mozart). Nevertheless he had an excellent melodic gift and his operas are full of attractive arias." And then he would quote an aria from a totally obsolete opera by Méhul and maybe even sing a tune from it. "You know," he would say, "Méhul wrote at least twenty operas; one of them, *The Epicure,* was, I believe, written in collaboration with Cherubini. He also wrote several ballets which contain superb examples of classical dance music." He would conclude sententiously, "Why don't you look at Méhul's music? Some of it is in music stores but most of it is at the Bibliothèque de l'Opéra."

I remember the way he listened to a new work, always earnest and respectful. If he liked it, he would discuss it page by page and point by point, and make you play sections of it over and over again. If, on the contrary, he did not like the piece, his face would immediately take on a sour and worn expression; he would look bored and sleepy. As soon as the composer had finished playing Diaghilev would thank him with that icy, exaggerated politeness with which French courtiers brushed off importune commoners, and leave the room without saying another word. Sometimes he would interrupt in the middle of the performance and shout, "Wait, wait! Play that over again!" And having heard it once more, he would say, "This comes straight from the tenor aria of X's opera." If you disagreed, or said that you did not know the opera or the particular passage, he would order one of his minions to get the score, and then he would make you play the aria. He was usually correct; the measures he had pointed out and the aria would bear a noticeable resemblance.

His remarks about music were always clever and penetrating and revealed a profound understanding of the particular characteristics of certain composers. I once arrived unnoticed in the apartment of Misia Sert (the wife of the Spanish painter) and found Diaghilev at the piano, with his glasses on, painstakingly deciphering the *Davidsbündlertänze* by Schumann. When I asked him why he was playing this particular piece, he said, "I always wonder what makes Schumann's music hold together. Look how he repeats and repeats the same phrase," and he started playing the third part of the piece very slowly and clumsily. "And yet, you see, it is never dull. It is filled with a peculiar kind of lyric nervousness. Of course, I am only talking about his piano music; his symphonies are at times terribly dull and boringly repetitious." He looked at the music again and added pensively, "Schumann's music is best when it is played in a very small room with no people in it at all, when it is just between you and him."

It sometimes seemed to outsiders (and even to some of his collaborators) that Diaghilev's taste for music was too eclectic, too lacking the indispensable "positive partisanship" to make a real dent in the annals of music history. It is true that the musical inventory of his ballet company for the twenty-five years of its existence represents a remarkable mélange. It is a hodgepodge of styles, of musical traditions, and of aesthetic attitudes. In it, you jump from the musical perfection of Stravinsky's *Les Noces* or his *Apollon Musagète* down to the grotesque inanities of a score like *Cléopâtra* (an Egyptian extravaganza of about 1909–1910 made up of stale tidbits from the music of eight-odd Russian composers) and from the admirable pages of Prokofiev's moving and lyrical *Prodigal Son* (a work so unjustly forgotten by present-day ballet companies) to the banalities of Georges Auric's *Pastorale,* probably the silliest ballet produced in the twenties by the Diaghilev company.

This lack of a specific line in the choice of music was quite disconcerting at times and made one think of Diaghilev as a kind of director of a musical zoo, as someone who wanted to own every species of animal under the sun from the platypuses to the pandas. Yet Diaghilev had a very definite personal musical taste, different from, if not contrary to, those of some of his younger contemporaries.

During one of my last conversations with him in the winter of 1928, he vituperated against the light and easy *musiquette* of young Parisian composers. "All this fake little music," he shouted, "doesn't mean anything at all. I've had enough of it. *Merci!* I can have a ballet by X every year, and next year it will be as stale as an old *blin* [Russian pancake]. Only the snobs and *les limités* (a favorite expression of his) like that. No, no. There is no one now who has *le souffle, l'élan* of Wagner, of Tchaikovsky, or of Verdi—those were real, full-blooded, great men."

"But Sergei Pavlovitch," I asked, "what about Stravinsky and Prokofiev? And what about your new 'discovery,' Paul Hindemith?" (He had just commissioned Hindemith to write him a ballet.) "Hindemith . . . yes, probably he is good . . . perhaps very good . . . but we'll hear him and judge him next year."

To Diaghilev a contemporary composer existed only by virtue of his having written music for the Ballets Russes. His peculiar egocentricity and megalomania made it seem that a composer who had not written for his ballet company was a composer whom he did not want, either because he considered his music bad or because the composer had not come around to be given a commission. Even if this were not the case, he wanted it always to appear as if he had "discovered" his composer, which in the case of Hindemith (who by then was already a famous man) seemed particularly comical.

"And Stravinsky?" I asked again.

"Stravinsky is a great composer . . . the greatest of our time; even the stupid British critics have learned their lesson and know that Stravinsky's greatness is a settled issue. To me, however, his best works are those of the beginning, those which he wrote before *Pulcinella;* I mean *Petrouchka, Le Sacre, Les Noces.* This does not imply that I don't admire *Oedipus Rex* and adore *Apollon;* both are classically beautiful and technically perfect. Who else can write like that nowadays? But you see—" He stopped abruptly and changed the subject. "You were speaking about Prokofiev?" he said in the tone of a man who is answering his own question. "Yes, of course, his *Prodigal Son* is in its way a masterpiece; it has a lyrical quality new to Prokofiev, and what is particularly good about it is that it is his own and no one else's." He underscored each word by knocking the floor with his cane. "Have you heard it?" he continued. "Did he play it for you?" And without waiting for an answer he said, "You know, Prokofiev is furious at me for wanting to cut a few pages. Did he talk to you about it?"

Few things seemed to give Diaghilev more pleasure than to make cuts in a new score; it was a kind of delightful ritual with him, and he surrounded the "operation" with exquisite politeness and princely formalities. Usually he would invite the composer to lunch; then, using all his charms, he would tell the story of how he cut eighteen pages of Rimsky-Korsakov's *Schéhérazade* and *x* pages of Richard Strauss's *Joseph's Legend.* After reciting a list of equally famous musical appendectomies, he would finally come to the point. "Don't you think," he would say, "that the second act of your ballet is too long? Don't you think it should be cut?" And before you could say yes or no, one of his helpers would hand him the score and he would point to the spot he wanted cut, saying, "I looked at it carefully yesterday and I think the cuts should be made here and here . . . don't you agree?" All the questions in this speech were purely rhetorical and, together with the unusually sumptuous lunch, provided the preparatory anesthetic before the inevitable operation.

"Few composers today," Diaghilev went on, "have Prokofiev's gift of inventing personal melodies, and even fewer have a genuine flair for a fresh use of simple tonal harmonies. You know, Prokofiev has never fallen prey to all such rubbish as atonality, polytonality, and *tout ce fatras de l'Europe Centrale.*" He is much too talented and much too genuine for that. He doesn't need to hide behind inane theories and absurd noises. His nostrils are big and open; he is not afraid of breathing fresh air wherever he finds it. He does not have to sit in cluttered rooms and invent theories. But even in Prokofiev's music there is a lack. I don't know what it is, but something is incomplete . . . some measure of greatness is absent."

Yet it appears that during the last days of Diaghilev's life, in a hotel roomon the Lido, he returned completely to the musical passions of his adolescence. He spoke with excitement and fervor of the greatness of Wagner's *Parsifal* and *Tristan* and the majestic splendor of Beethoven's *Ninth Symphony,* and he hummed the familiar tunes of his beloved *Pathétique* of Tchaikovsky.

These, then, were the true musical loves of Diaghilev throughout his life. He certainly admired and loved classical music, but his unswerving devotion went to the massive works of the masters of the Romantic period; it was their art which had formed his taste and in many ways molded his approach to music.

—from *Old Friends and New Music,* 1951

VERNON DUKE

Auditioning for Diaghilev

The composer Vernon Duke (1903–1969) was born Vladimir Dukelsky in what is now Belarus. By the time he was eighteen he had made his way to New York, where he became a close friend of George Gershwin's. (Years later, he would complete the film score of The Goldwyn Follies *when Gershwin died suddenly.) As Vernon Duke, he wrote a number of popular hits—"I Can't Get Started," "April in Paris," "Autumn in New York"—as well as the Broadway production of the all-black musical* Cabin in the Sky, *collaborating with his friend George Balanchine. As Vladimir Dukelsky, he*

was commissioned by Diaghilev in 1925 to write the score for Massine's ballet
Zéphyr et Flore, and continued his career as a classical composer under that
name.

A few days later Valitchka [Walter Nouvel] telephoned and in a slightly pompous voice announced that I was invited to Diaghilev's box that night and should I pass the inspection, would most likely be taken to a supper party for Stravinsky after the performance. I was to wear tails or, at least, a dinner jacket. Did I own one? I most certainly did. "All's well, then," Valitchka said. "Oh, youth, youth! khe, khe, khe . . ." and rang off.

Could this be happening to me? I was to meet the great man, the aesthetic dictator of the century, in his own lair—and so easily, so painlessly—only within a few weeks of my arrival in Paris. Life was good and so was Valitchka Nouvel. "Just you wait, Pavlik," I said gaily to Tchelitchew. "I'll get a ballet commission and you'll do the sets." "No, I won't," Tchelitchew replied. "I hate the theater."

I, for one, loved the theater that evening. It was a Stravinsky gala and featured *Les Noces,* with the music of which I was only vaguely familiar. In the box sat Misia Sert, covered with glittering jewels, a square-headed important-looking woman with a massive jaw and rather a mean mouth; a young-old man in tails with an Italian accent; and Koribut-Kubitovitch (nicknamed "Pavka"), a benign sexagenarian of the type known as "venerable"; he had the whitest of white beards, the pinkest of pink lips, an expression of infinite benevolence, and turned out to be Diaghilev's cousin. Diaghilev was busy back-stage, settling a quarrel between two dancers, as I overheard Koribut say. Decked out in my inoffensive Eighth Avenue dinner jacket, I was overwhelmed by the distinguished company, who paid not the slightest attention to me, and, modestly tucked away in a corner, became absorbed in the proceedings on the stage. Gontcharova's black-and-white decor for *Les Noces,* the choreography, shrewdly mixing paganism and geometry, and best of all, the luminous "undressed" uncannily persuasive music, the four pianos clashing and clicking their teeth, the constantly changing rhythms chasing each other without stopping for breath, fired my whole being. At the final curtain I screamed "Bravos" with the rest of the Stravinskyites, with such undisguised abandon that even the majestic Misia rewarded me with a smile and studied me with mild interest through her tortoise-shell lorgnette.

Shortly afterwards the door behind me opened and in walked a man of an appearance so remarkable that it will be hard to give the reader a faithful pen portrait of him. Sergei Pavlovitch Diaghilev was a big man—slightly over six feet tall—broad and big-limbed, but not corpulent; his head was enormous, and the face—a world in itself; you hardly noticed the rest of his body. The still-abundant graying hair was parted meticulously on the side and displayed the oft-described silver-white patch in the middle—no crafty coiffeur's trick but, from all accounts, something of a birthmark. When I first gazed at Diaghilev's face, I thought instantly of a decadent Roman emperor—Caligula, perhaps—although Diaghilev was allergic to horses among other things, then the Tartar in him—possibly Genghis Khan—or even a barbarous Scythian, became visible—and lastly, what he really was: a Russian *grand seigneur* of Alexander III vintage. The eyes had a piercing, mocking intensity about them, softened by unusually heavy eyelids, and he was fond of closing them slowly, as if persuaded by some unseen Morpheus, but only for a moment; they were soon peering at you again, not missing a thing. The mouth was cruel and soft at the same time, the mustache even more close-clipped than Valitchka's, the smile irresistible and oddly feminine. Sergei Pavlovitch carried monocles in all his pockets and had a habit of dropping one into his left hand, producing another with the right and screwing it into his eye languidly, making a lazy chewing motion with his mouth the while, as if munching spinach. He was well, although not conspicuously well, dressed and wore his Davis dinner jacket as if it were a dressing gown. His voice seemed monstrously affected at first—the Imperial Page's voice of aristocratic St. Petersburg—but you soon knew that he must have, too, been born with it. Diaghilev spoke French superbly, and English adequately.

He walked straight up to Misia, took her head in his hands and kissed her on both cheeks. "*Mon Sergei! Mon ange!*" cooed Misia, and started an excited and unpunctuated monologue. She had the rare knack of talking to one person in a room full of people in a loud and even booming voice, but with intonations so intimate and a vocabulary so special, that the monologue was unintelligible to all but the person addressed. That was an essentially Paris-snob stunt and I was being treated to it for the first time. Little Valitchka soon appeared, emerging from the dark of the *avant-loge,* with Boris Kochno on his heels, handsomer than the dancers on the stage and smiling at no one in particular. Boris patted me on the back, somewhat tentatively, and then ran up to Mme. Sert, bowing low to kiss her bejeweled hand; Misia went right on talking, with barely a nod to Boris. Diaghilev soon turned to Nouvel, exclaiming: "Heavens, hadn't we better go off to supper? Stravinsky is in a good enough mood, but he must be starving." Valitchka adjusted his pince-nez, obviously nervous, and muttered: "Seriozha, this is Vladimir Dukelsky, the young composer I told you about." Diaghilev then noticed me, dropped his monocle, adjusted another in its place and did the spinach-munching routine, the three actions permitting him to examine me minutely. "Ah, a good-looking boy," he drawled. "That in itself is most unusual. Composers are seldom good-looking; neither Stravinsky nor Prokofiev ever won any beauty prizes. How old are you?" I told him I was twenty. "That's encouraging, too. I don't like young men over twenty-five; they lose their adolescent charm and sleep with any woman who gives them the nod. I fire most of my male dancers when they reach that age." More spinach-munching, then an amused smile. "This is all very simple. If your music is bad I can always hire you as a dancer. *N'est-ce pas, Misia?*" Misia smiled thinly, wrinkling up her small nose, and surveyed me again through the lorgnette. I was embarrassed by this initiation, well aware of the fact that I'd never do as a dancer—my body was too thin and unmuscular. "Oh, so you still can blush," Diaghilev went on. "Valitchka, I think him a very pleasant young man and I want him to come to supper with us. Come with Boris—I believe you two already know one another. *Viens, Misia.*" The regal Mme. Sert nodded, permitted herself to be enveloped in her evening cloak by the taciturn old-young man, whose name I never learned, and they went out, followed by Diaghilev, Valitchka traipsing daintily behind him, Boris and I the last to leave.

Supper at Pré Catalan in the Bois was a very Parisian affair. I recall the crimson-and-gold decor of the room, the excellent champagne and the superlative food—Diaghilev was an accomplished gourmet, but his palate was so jaded that he had to pour virtually a whole shaker of salt and another of pepper on whatever he ate, and then cover the dish with a thick layer of Savora, his favorite condiment, in order to taste anything at all. Five or six *élégantes* were present—including Misia, Daisy Fellowes, Daisy de Segonzac, Lady Abdy, and one of the d'Erlangers; Stravinsky, in tails, was not unlike an emaciated Pickwick, accompanied by the faithful Winkle and Snodgrass—George Auric and Francis Poulenc, two husky and amiable youths, one fair, the other dark—and the amorous Tupman, Valitchka Nouvel. To continue with the possibly farfetched analogy, these gentlemen were soon joined by an overdressed Jingle—Jean Cocteau of the fallen-angel face, sleeve-cuffs unbuttoned to permit the bourgeoisie to feast their eyes on the firemanred lining (a sartorial must with him) and the fanciful, if not always intelligible, line of gab. These people, including Stravinsky, talked of Stravinsky and I drank in every eloquent word.

I wasn't asked, but managed to tell Igor Fedorovitch how transported I was by *Les Noces,* which effusion was graciously received. Coco Chanel walked in, looking like a jockey in drag, and demanded to know who the new young man (me) was, and whether, by chance, I wasn't a new dancer. When told that I wrote music, she looked at me without interest, and turned an appreciative ear to Cocteau's newest epigram. I was too happy to care. My departure was as unspectacular as was my entrance and I went back to Montparnasse in a cab and in a daze.

Two days later the ever-punctual Valitchka telephoned again and told me that Diaghilev desired me to play my concerto for him; and would I come to the Baron de Meyer's house that afternoon, as the baron had an especially good piano *and* it was in tune?

So the big moment had come, though, in the anticipation of it, my new self-assurance vanished. It was all working out too well; to a young man already used to the bitterness of bad breaks, such persistent good fortune appeared suspicious. "What does he want with my concerto?" I thought sadly. "Nouvel doesn't really like it and I myself think it reminiscent in spots." I made up my mind to at least play it well and, pushing the indignant Alan off the piano stool, went on a four-hour practice jag.

The de Meyers lived in *un hôtel,* which, in this instance, meant a private dwelling (*hôtel particulier*), not an inn. The house and its owners were typical of the all-powerful *tout Paris* set—Louis XV and Marie Laurencin with *Vogue* trimmings. There was a faint tinge of violet in the beautiful white hair of both de Meyers—a decorative pair, aggressively agreeable, as people of their class are, when receiving; the class that labels everything that comes their way as either *divin* or *d'un ennui mortel*—be it music, a new novel, a new restaurant, or a new concubine. I was brought by Diaghilev, the magician and explorer, therefore there was a good chance of my being *divin.* I don't think they knew that the frail youth with jet-black hair was in their home "on approval" and that his fate hung perilously in the balance.

I was the first to enter the de Meyer drawing room—a regrettable mistake, as no one *divin* is ever punctual. My embarrassment was somewhat relieved by the cordiality of my hosts and the perfection of the dry Martini I was offered, a drink still misunderstood by Parisians, who call it *un dry*— pronounced "dree"—and make it almost entirely of vermouth, using gin as sparingly as if it were Fernet Branca. Some small talk followed, very small indeed on my part, and then Sergei Pavlovitch entered with Boris in tow, both splendidly shaven and eau-de-cologned.

I was much too nervous to listen to the gossip that made up the general conversation. I drank two more Martinis and, just as I emptied the second, was asked by Diaghilev to show him the concerto I had brought with me. After carefully wiping and then adjusting one of his monocles, he began perusing the manuscript, humming to himself in a strange catlike voice and conducting with a pudgy index finger. I watched the performance with awe and astonishment. Diaghilev, who never missed anything, smiled indulgently and put down my music. "Few people know it, but I'm a *compositeur manqué,*" he remarked. "I was always behind in my harmony lessons with Rimsky-Korsakov, but once managed to write a piano piece, which I showed him. It was very bad and he said so." Sergei Pavlovitch then rose brusquely and led me to the piano. "Let me hear your concerto: I'll turn the pages for you."

With the determination of despair and, encouraged by the excellence of the instrument, I gave a creditable account of my "Passport to Paris." I remember vividly thinking as I played on: "I don't care, here it is. It's the best I can do, take it or leave it." When I hit the last crashing C-major chord, there was a moment of dreadful, complete silence—I didn't turn around but knew that the two de Meyers and Boris were looking at Diaghilev, awaiting his verdict. To my astonishment, the great man began clapping his hands thunderously and with such determination that the others soon joined in the applause. "*Bravo, jeune homme,* and congratulations. Best new music I've heard in years. Now—what shall we call your ballet?" he inquired suddenly. I was completely taken aback. "*What* ballet, Sergei Pavlovitch?" I queried. "The one you will write for me, of course. You *will* write one, won't you?" Kochno now intervened. He got up, embraced me and, smiling knowingly, declared that he already had an idea for "my" ballet and that the idea was certain to please Sergei Pavlovitch. I dimly remember that I was then made much of by the de Meyers and that a bottle of champagne appeared mysteriously and toasts to the new Diaghilev composer were drunk by all, including the toastee.

I was taken home to 150 by Diaghilev himself—Kochno stayed on to dinner at the de Meyers'—in a large chauffered limousine. My discoverer had his arm around me and talked softly and earnestly about my talent, the future before me, the task he was entrusting me with, and his hope that I would fulfill his expectations; I was so dazed and drunk with the Martinis, the champagne, and my crashing, complete success, that I only understood half of what Sergei Pavlovitch said, but loved every word of it. He deposited me in Boulevard Montparnasse, kissed me heartily on both cheeks Russian fashion, and departed. Both Alan and Pavlik were out; I dined alone extravagantly on a corner terrace, paying eleven francs for a copious meal, and, exhausted by the events of the day, went off to bed. That night I cried my first, and probably last, tears of happiness and realized that Victorian novelists had something there, for never did tears taste so sweet to me.

—from *Passport to Paris,* 1955

ISADORA DUNCAN

Isadora Duncan (1877–1927) and Mary Pickford were the most famous American women of the early twentieth century. Duncan was born in San Francisco and worked her way across the country to New York, where she became well known for the "modern dance" concerts she inaugurated, all flowing Grecian draperies and apparently improvisational movements. In 1899 she set out for Europe in search of larger fields to conquer, and quickly attained an enormous reputation and vast audiences, who received her rapturously. Blessed with natural charm and great charisma, she went from triumph to triumph until her two children—one by the avant-garde theatrical designer Gordon Craig, the other by the Singer sewing machine heir Paris Singer— were drowned in an accident in 1913, a trauma from which she never completely recovered. In 1922 she left Western Europe for the Soviet Union, having been promised every possible resource to found schools there to train young children—her life-long goal. Two years later, having married the poet Sergei Esenin (who committed suicide after abandoning her), she returned to the West, and to a rapid deterioration that lasted until her tragic death in 1927, when a long scarf she was wearing caught in the spokes of a wheel of a moving car and broke her neck. She remains the most famous and influential of all the founders of modern dance.

Isadora Duncan
In Russia

It is impossible, is it not, to believe in a Providence or Guiding Destiny when one takes up the morning newspaper and reads of twenty people dead in a railway accident, who had not thought of death the day before; or of a whole town devastated with tidal wave or flood. Then why be so absurdly egotistical as to imagine a Providence guiding our small selves?

Yet there are things in my life so extraordinary as to make me believe at times in predestination. For instance, that train to St. Petersburg, instead of arriving at four in the afternoon, as scheduled, was stopped by snowdrifts and arrived at four the next morning, twelve hours late. There was no one at the station to meet me. When I descended from the train the temperature was ten degrees below zero. I had never felt such cold. The padded Russian coachmen were hitting their arms with their gloved fists to keep the blood flowing in their veins.

I left my maid with the baggage and, taking a one-horse cab, directed the driver to the Hotel Europa. Here I was, in the black dawn of Russia, quite alone, on the way to the Hotel when suddenly I beheld a sight equal in ghastliness to any in the imagination of Edgar Allan Poe.

It was a long procession that I saw from a distance. Black and mournful it came. There were men laden and bent under their loads—coffins—one after another. The coachman slowed his horse to a walk and bent and crossed himself. I looked on in the indistinct dawn, filled with horror. I asked him what this was. Although I knew no Russian, he managed to convey to me that these were the workmen shot down before the Winter Palace the day before—the fatal January 5, 1905, because, unarmed, they had come to ask the Tsar for help in their distress—for bread for their wives and children. I told the coachman to stop. The tears ran down my face and were frozen on my cheeks as this sad, endless procession passed me. But why buried at dawn? Because later in the day it might have caused more revolution. The sight of it was not for the city in the daytime. The tears choked in my throat. With boundless indignation I watched these poor grief-stricken workmen carrying their martyred dead. If the train had not been twelve hours late, I would never have seen this.

> O dark and mournful night without one sign of Dawn,
> O sad procession of poor stumbling forms,
> Haunted, weeping eyes and poor hard worked rugged hands
> Stifling with their poor black shawls
> The sobs and moans beside their dead—
> Guards walking stilted on either side.

If I had never seen it, all my life would have been different. There, before this seemingly endless procession, this tragedy, I vowed myself and my forces to the service of the people and the down-trodden. Ah, how small and useless now seemed all my personal love desires and sufferings! How useless even my Art, unless it could help this. Finally the last sad ones passed us. The coachman turned wonderingly and watched my tears. Again he crossed himself with a patient sigh, and spurred his horse toward the Hotel.

I mounted to my palatial rooms and slipped into the quiet bed, where I cried myself to sleep. But the pity, the despairing rage of that dawn was to bear fruit in my life thereafter.

The room of the Hotel Europa was immense and high-ceilinged. The windows were sealed and never opened. The air came through ventilators high in the wall. I awoke late. My manager called, bringing flowers. Soon my room was filled with flowers.

Two nights later I appeared before the élite of St. Petersburg society in the Salle des Nobles. How strange it must have been to those dilettantes of the gorgeous Ballet, with its lavish decorations and scenery, to watch a young girl, clothed in a tunic of cobweb, appear and dance before a simple blue curtain to the music of Chopin; dance her soul as she understood the soul of Chopin! Yet even for the first dance there was a storm of applause. My soul that yearned and suffered the tragic notes of the Preludes; my soul that aspired and revolted to the thunder of the Polonaises; my soul that wept with righteous anger, thinking of the martyrs of that funeral procession of the dawn; this soul awakened in that wealthy, spoiled, and aristocratic audience a response of stirring applause. How curious!

The next day I received a visit from a most charming little lady, wrapped in sables, with diamonds hanging from her ears, and her neck encircled with pearls. To my astonishment she announced that she was the great dancer [Mathilde Kschessinka]. She had come to greet me in the name of the Russian Ballet and invite me to a gala performance at the Opera that night. I had been used to receiving only coldness and enmity from the Ballet in Bayreuth. They had even gone so far as to strew tacks on my carpet so that my feet were torn. This change of sentiment was both gratifying and astounding to me.

That evening a magnificent carriage, warmed and filled with expensive furs, conducted me to the Opera, where I found a first tier box, containing flowers, bonbons, and three beautiful specimens of the *jeunesse dorée* of St. Petersburg. I was still wearing my little white tunic and sandals, and must have looked very odd in the midst of this gathering of all the wealth and aristocracy of St. Petersburg.

I am an enemy to the ballet, which I consider a false and preposterous art, in fact, outside the pale of all art. But it was impossible not to applaud the fairy-like figure of Kschinsky as she flitted across the stage, more like a lovely bird or butterfly than a human being.

In the entr'acte I looked about me, and saw the most beautiful women in the world, in marvellous décolleté gowns, covered with jewels, escorted by men in distinguished uniforms; all this display of luxurious riches so difficult to understand in contrast with the funeral procession of the previous dawn. All these smiling and fortunate people, what kinship had they with the others?

After the performance I was invited to supper in the palace of Kschinsky, and there met the Grand Duke Michael, who listened with some astonishment as I discoursed on the plan of a school of dancing for the children of the people. I must have seemed an utterly incomprehensible figure, but they all received me with the kindest cordiality and lavish hospitality.

Some days later I received a visit from the lovely Pavlova; and again I was presented with a box to see her in the ravishing ballet of *Gisèle*. Although the movement of these dances was against every artistic and human feeling, again I could not resist warmly applauding the exquisite apparition of Pavlova as she floated over the stage that evening.

At supper in the house of Pavlova, which was more modest than Kschinsky's palace, but equally beautiful, I sat between the painters Bakst and Benois, and met, for the first time, Sergei Diaghilev, with whom I engaged in ardent discussion on the art of the dance as I conceived it, as against the ballet.

That evening, at supper, the painter Bakst made a little sketch of me which now appears in his book, showing my most serious countenance, with curls sentimentally hanging down on one side. It is curious that Bakst, who had some clairvoyant powers, read my hand that night. He found there two crosses. "You will have great glory," he said, "but you will lose the two creatures whom you love most on earth." At that time this prophecy was a riddle to me.

After supper the indefatigable Pavlova danced again, to the delight of her friends. Although it was five o'clock in the morning before we left, she invited me to come at half past eight the same morning, if I would like to see her work. I arrived three hours later (I confess I was considerably fatigued) to find her standing in her tulle dress practising at the bar, going through the most rigorous gymnastics, while an old gentleman with a violin marked the time, and admonished her to greater efforts. This was the famous master Petipas.

For three hours I sat tense with bewilderment, watching the amazing feats of Pavlova. She seemed to be made of steel and elastic. Her beautiful face took on the stern lines of a martyr. She never stopped for one moment. The whole tendency of this training seems to be to separate the gymnastic movements of the body completely from the mind. The mind, on the contrary, can only suffer in aloofness from this rigorous muscular discipline. This is just the opposite from all the theories on which I founded my school, by which the body becomes transparent and is a medium for the mind and spirit.

As twelve o'clock approached, there were preparations for luncheon, but, at the table, Pavlova sat white and pale, and hardly touched food or wine. I admit I was hungry and ate many *podjarsky* cutlets. Pavlova took me back to my hotel and then went to one of those interminable rehearsals at the Royal Theatre. I, very weary, fell upon my bed and slept soundly, praising my stars that no unkind fate had ever given me the career of a ballet dancer!

The following day I also arose at the unheard-of hour of eight o'clock to visit the Imperial Ballet School, where I saw all the little pupils standing in rows, and going through those torturing exercises. They stood on the tips of their toes for hours, like so many victims of a cruel and unnecessary Inquisition. The great, bare dancing rooms, devoid of any beauty or inspiration, with a large picture of the Tsar as the only relief of the walls, were like a torture chamber. I was more than ever convinced that the Imperial Ballet School is an enemy to nature and to Art. . . .

As much as the ballet had filled me with horror, so the Stanislavsky Theatre thrilled me with enthusiasm. I went there every night that I was not dancing myself, and was received with the greatest affection by all the troupe. Stanislavsky came very often to see me and thought that by questioning me thoroughly, he would be able to transform all my dances into a new school of dancing in his theatre. But I told him that could only be done by beginning with children. Apropos of this, on my next visit to Moscow, I saw some young, beautiful girls of his troupe trying to dance, but the result was deplorable.

As Stanislavsky was exceedingly busy all day in his theatre with rehearsals, he was in the habit of coming to see me frequently after the performance. In his book he says of these talks: "I suppose I must have tired Duncan with my questions." No: he did not tire me. I was bursting with enthusiasm to transmit my ideas.

In fact the keen, snowy air, the Russian food, especially the caviar, had completely cured my wasting illness . . . And now my whole being longed for the contact of a strong personality. As Stanislavsky stood before me, I saw such a one in him.

One night I looked at him, with his fine handsome figure, broad shoulders, black hair just turning to grey on the temples, and something within me revolted at always playing this role of Egeria. As he was about to leave, I placed my hands on his shoulders and entwined them about his strong neck, then, pulling his head down to mine, I kissed him on the mouth. He returned my kiss with tenderness. But he wore a look of extreme astonishment, as if this were the last thing he expected. Then, when I attempted to draw him further, he started back and, looking at me with consternation, exclaimed, "But what should we do with the child?" "What child?" I asked. "Why, our child, of course. What should we do with it? You see," he continued in a ponderous manner, "I would never approve of any child of mine being raised outside my jurisdiction, and that would be difficult in my present household."

His extraordinary seriousness about this child was too much for my sense of humour, and I burst into laughter, at which he stared in distress, left me, and hurried down the corridor of the hotel. I was still laughing at intervals all night. But, nonetheless, in spite of my laughter, I was exasperated, and angry too. I think I then thoroughly understood why some quite refined men might slam on their hats after certain meetings with the highly intellectual, and betake themselves to places of doubtful reputation. Well, being a woman, I couldn't do this; so I twisted and turned the rest of the night. In the morning I repaired to a Russian bath, where the alternate hot steam and cold water retoned my system.

And yet, in contradiction, the young men I had met in Kschessinka's loge, who would have given anything to be allowed to make love to me, bored me so by the first words they said to me, that they even froze my senses to the very centre of desire. I suppose this is what is called a "cerebrale." Certainly after the inspiring and cultured society of Charles Hallé and Heinrich Thode, I could not possibly stand the society of the *jeunesse dorée!*

Many years later, I told this story of Stanislavsky to his wife, who was overcome with merriment and exclaimed, "Oh, but that is just like him. He takes life so seriously."

Attack as I might, I received some sweet kisses, but otherwise I just met with a callous, solid resistance which there was no disputing. Stanislavsky didn't risk coming to my room again after the theatre, but one day he made me very happy by taking me out in an open sleigh to a restaurant in the country, where we had lunch in a private room. We drank vodka and champagne and we talked of art, and I was finally convinced that it would take Circe herself to break down the stronghold of Stanislavsky's virtue.

I had often heard of the terrible dangers which young girls risked by going into theatrical life, but, as my readers can see from my career so far, it was just the opposite. I really suffered from too much awe and respect and admiration, which I inspired in my admirers.

—from *My Life,* 1927

MARY DESTI

How I Met Isadora

Born Mary Dempsey to an Irish immigrant family in Quebec, Mary Desti
(1871–1931) was a complete self-invention, beginning with the faux-aristocratic
Italian name she assumed. Her second (or third) husband, Solomon Sturges—a rich
Chicago stockbroker—adopted her son, Preston, who became the famous Hollywood
director. Sturges's money allowed Mary to lead much of her life in Europe, where in
1901 she met and became the lifelong friend of Isadora Duncan. Along the way, she
had a series of lovers, including the notorious necromancer Aleister Crowley, with
whom she played at clairvoyancy. She also created a line of cosmetics—the most successful was a youth cream called Secret of the Harem—for her business, Maison
Desti. As a writer, she was not particularly devoted to the concept of accuracy.

In January, 1901, after a disastrous runaway marriage and later divorce, I
tucked my little year and a half old babe under my arm and started for
Paris to study for the stage. This I did under the advice of Dr. Ziegfeld, Flo
Ziegfeld's father, who had the Conservatoire of Music in Chicago. At this
moment I had rather an extraordinary voice and, as I was scarcely more than
a child myself, great things were hoped for from my Paris trip.

We arrived in Paris at ten o'clock at night and, not knowing anything
about the hotels, I took a room at the Hotel Terminus, located just where the
boat train arrives. Paris at this time, twenty-eight years ago, was not the
Paris of to-day, and very few comforts and accommodations could be found,
even at the first class hotels. I was given an immense room with a great
canopied bed in which everything felt damp, the sheets, covers, and pillow
cases, but I finally succeeded in having the hotel maid make a roaring fire in
the fireplace and insisted that she air the linen in front of this.

As I had come without a maid or nurse, I had to take entire charge of my
baby. So, asking the chambermaid to arrange a bath for us and not being able
to leave the baby alone, I took him with me.* You could not believe the
distance the bathroom was from this bedroom. It seemed like half a mile, and
then I was shown into an immense room with a great marble bath in which a

---

* This baby was Preston Sturges.

sheet had been draped. So uninviting and cheerless! Taking off my baby's night clothes and my own, together we got in this bath and never will I forget the shivery feelings I had and the baby was almost blue. Wrapping every towel I could find around him and myself, I dashed back to my room. By this time the maid had arranged the bed and we crawled in, shivering, I holding him tight to my breast trying to warm him. The maid, feeling sorry for us, got some hot bricks and put two or three of them into the bed.

By this time four or five of the passengers who had been most kind on the trip (especially old Mr. King) came flocking to my room, saying it was the night of the great Opéra Ball, which is only held once a year and one of the greatest sights of Paris and nothing would do but that I get up and dress and go to see this ball. They gave the maid about a month's wages to stay and take care of the baby, who was by this time asleep, and she promised faithfully not to leave him for a second.

Off we went to this ball. Such a gorgeous, resplendent sight! Its equal I have never seen since. It was held at the Grand Opéra and all the artists of Paris tried to outdo one another in magnificence and originality. In a few hours it became pandemonium and only with the greatest efforts did my escorts find me, as one Frenchman after another swept me off my feet, crying, "Oh, la belle Américaine, la belle Américaine." This was my first glimpse of Paris. We finally returned at four o'clock in the morning.

The next morning about ten o'clock I awoke to find my baby very restless and a little bit feverish. After breakfast, with its delightful chocolate, brioche, and confiture, I asked for an American paper, and looking through its columns found an advertisement saying "If you want rooms or apartments or anything, come to Donald Downey, 3 Rue Scribe."

I at once took a cab, my baby with me, and was so amused at the sight of the overstuffed cocher. He seemed to have five or six overcoats, one over the other, and talked a continual stream to his horse and to me, naturally none of which I understood. We arrived at 3 Rue Scribe which to-day forms the entrance to the Scribe Hotel, but at that time was a funny little office where three or four clerks headed by Donald Downey were leading Americans a merry chase in search of Paris homes.

I explained to Mr. Downey what I wanted—a room in a private family with a piano where I could study. He said he had just the very thing, but "My dear," he said, "you must come upstairs and meet my wife and have a cup of tea with us. There is the most delightful American lady with her at present, whom I am sure you will enjoy meeting."

He took me up a little spindly iron stairs which shot you immediately into the floor above the office, and on entering, he said to his wife, "My dear, here is a sweet little American with her baby. We must look after her." (This really meant taking everything you had if he could.) I had scarcely time to speak, before one of the most lovely women I have ever seen, tall and majestic, came over and wrapped her arms around me, saying, "Oh you darling! What is your name?" And I said, "Mary."

"Is this your baby?" Whereupon she took the baby out of my arms and we all sat down while Mrs. Downey poured tea. "Why, Mary, you darling, I am going to take you both right home to Isadora."

Mrs. Duncan's suggestion did not fit in at all with Mr. Downey's plans, so he insisted upon taking me to the most marvellous rooms he said he had found. Mrs. Duncan, having just rented a studio from Mr. Downey, knew what an old fox he was and insisted upon accompanying us, much to my delight. We drove to the Rue de Douie in Montmartre which really meant nothing to me then, as I didn't know one quarter of Paris from the other.

The landlady had already been telephoned and she had prepared a bright fire and all the lights were gleaming in this very charming room which she showed us. This house had formerly been the home of a great writer and now was a sort of a school for fine literature, gymnastics, and stage deportment. The room was a large back parlor with immense folding doors covered by heavy curtains shutting out the adjoining front room. I never questioned why the lights were lit so early in the day but after arranging and paying for a month's rent I went with Mrs. Duncan who was still holding my baby, to 45 Avenue de Villers. This was Isadora's studio.

After mounting the stairs Mrs. Duncan threw open the door with a great flourish, crying, "Isadora, Isadora, look what I have brought you, Mary and her baby."

Isadora and Raymond both ran forward, clasping me in their arms and dancing around in a circle as though I were some person they had been waiting for. At this moment, with a great flash of understanding, my heart went out to Isadora, and she still has it with her in eternity.

Isadora, Isadora, when the greatest writers and artists of the world have vied with one another to describe or portray you, how can I with my poor stumbling pen dare to give even the faintest outline of your grace and unearthly beauty! You, an antique goddess reborn that man might again catch a glimpse of pure beauty, and for this daring act the gods have sent you heartaches and sorrows beyond the scope of human comprehension, and which you bore like a martyr.

Had I never suspected before your goddess origin, I should have sensed it one minute before your cruel death, when you, in perfect health, waved to us crying, *"Adieu, mes amis. Je vais à la gloire!"*

Your championship of all that was brave and heroic, your hatred of all hypocrisy and deceit, your courage and fortitude in openly and fearlessly blazing the path of woman and her right to bear children irrespective of man-made law!

How to describe Isadora? Had I been ushered into Paradise and given over to my guardian angel, I could not have been more uplifted. Isadora was in her little dancing tunic, a colorless gauze of some sort, draped softly about her slender, ethereal form; her exquisite little head poised on her swan-like throat and tilted to one side like a bird, as though the weight of her auburn curls caused it to droop; a little retroussé nose that gave just the slightest human touch, otherwise I should have thrown myself on my knees before her, believing I was worshipping a celestial being. My head swam with ecstasy when a very nasal American voice brought me to earth. Raymond, who at this time was a beautiful, enthusiastic, charming young American, dressed like the young French artists of that time with loose flowing collar and great bow tie, and still wearing ordinary shoes, although he was beginning to occupy himself creating sandals.

There were several famous studios in this same building.

Emma Eames had the one right in front of Isadora, and later, d'Annunzio's wife had the one above, from the window of which one day the dear lady threw herself to the pavement and I believe remained a cripple ever after.

Isadora and Raymond caught me by the hands and we all danced around in a ring, for all the world like little children, while Mrs. Duncan, seating the baby on the piano, gaily played some marvellous dance tunes. Here began the friendship which lasted all the rest of our lives.

—from *The Untold Story,* 1929

MARY DESTI
Isadora's Death

Just as we were finishing our very simple dinner, an immense dark cloud seemed to descend on our table between Isadora and me. I gasped, "Oh, My God, Isadora, something terrible is happening."

Isadora cried, "Mary, for Heaven's sake, what's the matter? I never saw so tragic a face. What is it? Why are you trembling? Waiter, bring a glass of brandy." I said I didn't want any brandy and would be all right in a moment. The waiter brought the brandy, and Isadora insisted that I drink it. This was just nine o'clock.

Isadora said, "It's just nine o'clock, we must hurry." She took my arm and said, "Now, Mary, what is the matter?"

And I answered, "Please, Isadora, don't go in that auto. My nerves are terribly unstrung; I'm afraid something might happen to you."

"My dear, I would go for this ride tonight even if I were sure it would be my last. Even then, I would go quicker. But don't worry, Bugatti is not coming."

We went into the studio, and she turned on all the lights, and the gramophone, and began to dance wildly. Suddenly from the window she saw Bugatti drive up with his car. She started for the door. I pleaded, "Isadora, please put on my black cape, it's quite cold."

"No, no, my dear, nothing but my red-painted shawl."

I went out first, and Ivan followed her, also throwing her own red woollen shawl, in spite of her protests, around her. (The one in which she always danced the "Marseillaise.") I ran out ahead of her, and said to Bugatti, "I don't believe you realize what a great person you are driving tonight. I beg of you to be careful, and if she asks you to go fast, I beg you not to. I'm terribly nervous tonight."

"Madame, you need have no fear," he replied, "I've never had an accident in my life."

Isadora came out; seeing her red shawl, he offered her his leather coat. She threw her red-painted shawl about her throat, and shook her head, saying: *"Adieu, mes amis. Je vais à gloire."*

Those were the last words Isadora Duncan ever spoke. One minute after she was dead.

H o w c a n I explain just what happened? As the car started slowly, it had hardly gone ten yards, when I noticed the fringe of her shawl, like a streak of blood, hanging down behind, dragging in the dirt. I called, *"Isadora, ta chale, ta chale."* Suddenly the car stopped and I said to Ivan, "Run quickly to Isadora and tell her her shawl is hanging down and will be spoiled."

I believed they had stopped because I called, and I rushed towards them. Several machines had stopped, and Bugatti was screaming, *"J'ai tué la Madonne, j'ai tué la Madonne."* I ran to Isadora, and found her seated just as she had left me two seconds before, except that her beautiful head was drawn down against the side of the car, held fast by the shawl.

This powerful racing car was a very low, two-seated affair. The seat of the driver was a little, in advance of the other occupant, so that Bugatti would have to turn around to see her. There were no mud guards on the car, and as Isadora threw her shawl around her neck and across her shoulder, the heavy fringe hanging down behind caught in the rear wheel on her side. Naturally a few revolutions of the wheel dragged her poor beautiful head forward, crushing her face against the side of the car and holding it as in a vise. The very first revolution of the wheel had broken her neck, severing the jugular vein, and as she had always wished, had killed her instantly, without one second's pain or knowledge of what was happening.

Not realizing that she was dead, but believing the shawl was strangling her, I instantly tried to loosen it from her warm, soft neck. Calling for a knife, I ran to the balcony of the restaurant, snatched a knife and ran back. Realizing its uselessness, I called for a scissors, which somebody handed me instantly. I ran cut the fringe and part of the shawl from the wheel.

I called frantically for a surgeon, for help, but people seemed dazed. A car had stopped just beside us and I begged two or three of the men to lift Isadora in, not knowing to whom the car belonged nor caring. I sat beside her in the backseat, and held her in my arms, while the driver and his wife sat in the front.

I urged and urged them to go their fastest, remembering never to lose my head for a second, realizing, that Isadora's only hope was my being calm. We had been on our way to the hospital about five minutes, when the police stopped us. Begging them not to interfere but to come with us, they stood one on each running board, and we continued straight ahead like mad for the hospital. All the while I was trying to get Isadora to breathe but when I saw her dear eyes blinded from the blow against the side of the car and her beautiful little nose which she so prided herself on, destroyed by the sudden impact and disfigured forever, somewhere deep within me, I never wanted her to come back to all that horror and suffering.

A peculiar change had come over her face. I felt her pulse, but in spite of its stillness, I couldn't realize, I couldn't, that there was even a possibility that she was dead.

At last we arrived at the hospital, where they did not want to let us in, believing she was dead and they are not allowed to take dead people in. But I so insisted and even took one end of the cot myself on which they had placed her, that almost unconsciously the attendants helped me, and we carried her inside. I begged them to get the best surgeons and doctors immediately, to spare no expense; but already there was a doctor kneeling beside her who said, "Madame, calm yourself; there is nothing to be done. She was killed instantly."

Oh, God! oh, God! There was I alone, and Isadora lying dead. I tried so hard to be brave, to hold on to my senses, which were swimming. The chief of police, taking me by the arm, asked me if could give him any information about the accident, and at the same time, giving instructions to have Isadora taken to the morgue. "I will do anything you ask, answer all questions, if you will permit me to stay beside Isadora."

He told me that was impossible; she had to be taken to the morgue. At this I became frantic, saying, "No, never, over my dead body. I will never allow you to take her to the morgue. I couldn't endure it; it's a sacrilege to take Isadora Duncan to the morgue. But if you will permit me to take her back to her studio, I will do anything you like. For God's sake do this. Can't you see I'm all alone and I must stay with her?"

Never will I forget the kindness and courtesy of all these people. The Chief said, "If the landlord will permit her to be placed in her studio, I myself will attend to everything for you."

. . . When the coroners and doctors had finished, I dressed Isadora in her red dress and her dancing veils, and there, in the midst of her great couch, surrounded by myriads of the flowers she loved best, she looked like a little Tanagra figure lying in a garden. We lighted the studio with hundreds of candles, and with flowers everywhere, it was like a blue chapel. Across her feet I had thrown her purple mantle, which made a pool of light like a reflection from heaven.

People told me afterward that it was so beautiful that they stood breathless when they entered. She would love it so, that was what made it possible. After they had made arrangements to take Isadora to Paris, they placed her in a zinc-lined box. Across her breast I placed one solitary red rose, with just my heart's blood, and three sprays of lilies of France, one from Augustin, one from Elizabeth and one from Raymond. Then a single flower from each of her dearest friends across the sea—Mary Fanton Roberts, Ruth Mitchell, Eva Le Gallienne, Mercedes D'Acosta, Preston Sturges, Edward Steichen, Arnold Genthe, and a little bunch of roses from her school, her adopted children. Then they solemnly closed it and soldered it fast. I threw her purple mantle over it all. This was the mantle she always wore when she danced the Resurrection.

. . . As it was American Legion Day in Paris, there was great celebration, and the cortège had to make many detours which brought us through all the weird French quarters of Paris. How Isadora would have loved this! These were the people who knew and loved her. Thousands lined the streets, most of whom had seen her dance. The populace of Paris adored her, and there was scarcely a dry eye all along the road.

Paris was wildly decorated with American flags. Every one thought they were meant for the soldiers, but I knew that America unconsciously had decorated Paris for one of its greatest Americans. She had brought her American art to all parts of Europe, and while all Europe bowed in sorrow for this great artist, old Glory waved her a grand farewell.

Just as we passed in front of the Trocadero Theatre, where Isadora had danced to five thousand people at a time and where many more had acclaimed her from outside because they could not gain entrance, there on the very pinnacle waved the Stars and Stripes of her native land, at the same instant, going in the contrary direction and right in front of the Trocadero, was passing the contingent from California. When they saw the Star-Spangled Banner, which Raymond had so sweetly and thoughtfully thrown over the casket at the last moment, they stopped to ask, "What American was passing?" We told them California's pride. Hundreds of years from now California will be known as the birthplace of the greatest dancer—the greatest artist—and the greatest American of all time.

As we reached the cemetery, Pére La Chaise, over ten thousand people were there, crowding the alleys so it was impossible to move. Whole cordons of police tried to make way for the cortège. Old people hobbled near who had seen her dance twenty years before. Mothers held their children up, telling them to remember that they had seen the funeral of the great dancer, the great Isadora Duncan, and everyone spoke in whispers of the cruel accident to her children.

The students of Beaux Arts sobbed aloud. Young soldiers stood with their heads bowed and it took a very long time before we reached the crematory. The last time I had entered there was to accompany the remains of Isadora's wonderful mother and once before that, when I had accompanied Isadora to cremate her two little children and their poor nurse.

Memories, memories, memories! I will never enter that crematory again alive.

At last we had arrived at the steps that lead to nowhere—the crematory steps. The cordon of police with the greatest difficulty begged the surging crowd to give way to permit the family to pass. Elizabeth held my arm and somehow we mounted the steps and found ourselves within the chapel whose altar is a purifying furnace, leaving nothing but a handful of silvery ashes.

Albert Wolfe, the great conductor, who conducted Isadora's last performance in Paris, had promised me he would carry out Isadora's oft-repeated wish. She had always said, "My spirit will never leave this earth until it hears the strains of Bach's great aria in 're.'" Edouard Mauaselin sang the "Ave Maria" with a wistfulness that almost broke one's heart, while outside the great masses watched the spiral of grey smoke which later turned to white and wafted away to melt into the clouds. Raymond during this ceremony went outside to speak a few words to the multitude.

When he had finished, Elizabeth and I accompanied him up the steps. Then the most extraordinary ceremony took place. Behind the heavy curtain, and there before our eyes, they drew from the glaring furnace the asbestos coach containing the last remains of Isadora. Oh, God! How wonderful it was! Her ashes just formed a trace of her figure dancing. It looked like a white drawing of her. The only earthly thing left was the dome of her exquisite little skull. At once Byron's act in snatching Shelley's heart from the flames came to me, but at the same moment the whole thing dissolved into ashes.

I wish I could describe the effect seeing that few handfuls of ashes had on all of us. Sorrow dropped from us like a garment. You could no longer mourn Isadora in these ashes. We felt instantaneously the nothingness of all earthly flesh, and that she was not and never could have been of this clay. Isadora, who was always all spirit, had now come into her own and the crowd outside who had seen the smoke ascend, had seen more of the real Isadora than we who now beheld her ashes.

If only all people would be brave and have the courage to cremate their loved ones, and look afterwards at their ashes, all the horror of death would pass away. True, nothing can help the void left in their lives, but their eyes and hearts will be lifted up to the skies, instead of shuddering at the horrible barbarous thought of the cold clay and worms.

We placed Isadora's ashes beside those of her children and her mother, but she had made me promise that one day I would take these ashes and scatter them in the sea.

The great fearless brave spirit had passed away, but the message she left behind will live forever.

"*Adieu, mes amis. Je vais à la gloire!*"

—from *The Untold Story*, 1929

When Mother came back to this country, early in 1928, I got the simple and horrifying story again from her own lips. Actually, said my mother, who by then had recovered from the first shattering shock, it was a good thing. Isadora was drinking heavily, had become as fat as a balloon and was daily destroying the legends of her past loveliness and the dignity of her great position among the artists of the world.

—from *Preston Sturges on Preston Sturges*

Isadora

Like a ghost from the grave Isadora Duncan is dancing again at Nice. A decade ago her art, animated by her extraordinary public personality, came as close to founding an esthetic renaissance as American morality would allow, and the provinces especially had a narrow escape. Today her body, whose Attic splendor once brought Greece to Kansas and Kalamazoo, is approaching its half-century mark. Her spirit is still green as a bay tree, but her flesh is worn, perhaps by the weight of laurels. She is the last of the trilogy of great female personalities our century produced. Two of them, Duse and Bernhardt, have gone to their elaborate national tombs. Only Isadora Duncan, the youngest, the American, remains wandering the European earth.

No one has taken Isadora's place in her own country and she is not missed. Of that fervor for the classic dance which she was the first to bring to a land bred on "Turkey in the Straw," beneficial signs remain from which she alone has not benefitted. Eurythmic movements now appear in the curricula of girls' schools. Vestal virgins frieze about the altar fire of St. Marks-in-the-Bouwerie on Sabbath afternoons. As a cross between gymnasia and God, Greek dance camps flourish in the Catskills, where under the summer spruce, metaphysics and muscles are welded in an Ilissan hocus-pocus for the female young. Lisa, one of her first pupils, teaches in the studio of the Champs-Elysées. Isadora's sister Elizabeth, to whom Greek might still be Greek if it had not been for Isadora, has a toga school in Berlin. Her brother Raymond, who operates a modern craft school in Paris, wears sandals and Socratic robes as if they were a family coat of arms. Isadora alone has neither sandals nor school. Most grandiose of all her influences, Diaghilev's Russian Ballet—which ironically owed its national rebirth to the inspiration of Isadora, then dancing with new terpsichorean ideals in Moscow—still seasons as an exotic spectacle in London and Monte Carlo. Only Isadora, animator of all these forces, has become obscure. Only she with her heroic sculptural movements has dropped by the wayside where she lies inert like one of those beautiful battered pagan tombs that still line the Sacred Road between Eleusis and the city of the Parthenon.

Isadora arrived in our plain and tasteless Republic before the era of the half-nude revue, before the discovery of what is now called our Native Literary School, even before the era of the celluloid sophistication of the cinema, which by its ubiquity does so much to unite the cosmopolisms of Terre Haute and New York. What America now has, and gorges on in the way of sophistication, it then hungered for. Repressed by generations of Puritanism, it longed for bright, visible, and blatant beauty presented in a public form the simple citizenry could understand. Isadora appeared as a half-clothed Greek. . . . A Paris couturier recently said woman's modern freedom in dress is largely due to Isadora. She was the first artist to appear uncinctured, barefooted, and free. She arrived like a glorious bounding Minerva in the midst of a cautious corseted decade. The clergy, hearing of (though supposedly without ever seeing) her bare calf, denounced it as violently as if it had been golden. Despite its longings, for a moment America hesitated, Puritanism rather than poetry coupling lewd with nude in rhyme. But Isadora, originally from California and by then from Berlin, Paris, and other points, arrived bearing her gifts as a Greek. She came like a figure from the Elgin marbles. The world over, and in America particularly, Greek sculpture was recognized to be almost notorious for its purity. The overpowering sentiment for Hellenic culture, even in the unschooled United States, silenced the outcries. Isadora had come as antique art and with such backing she became a cult.

Those were Isadora's great years. Not only in New York and Chicago but in the smaller, harder towns, when she moved across the stage, head reared, eyes mad, scarlet kirtle flying to the music of the "Marseillaise," she lifted from their seats people who had never left theatre seats before except to get up and go home. Whatever she danced to, whether it was France's revolutionary hymn, or the pure salon passion of Chopin's waltzes, or the unbearable heat of Brahms' German mode, she conspired to make the atmosphere Greek, fusing *Zeitgeists* and national sounds into one immortal Platonic pantomime.

Thus she inspired people who had never been inspired in their lives and to whom inspiration was exhilarating, useless, and unbecoming. Exalted at the concert hall by her display of Greek beauty, limbs, and drapes which though they were two thousand years old she seemed to make excitingly modern, her followers, dazzled, filled with Phidianisms, went home to Fords, big hats, and the theory of Bull Moose, the more real items of their progressive age.

Dancing appeals less to the public than the other two original theatrical forms, drama and opera (unless, like the Russian Ballet, dancing manages to partake of all three). Nevertheless, Isadora not only danced but was demanded all over America and Europe. On the Continent she is more widely known today than any other American of our decade, including Woodrow Wilson and excepting only Chaplin and Fairbanks, both of whom, via a strip of celluloid, can penetrate to remote hamlets without ever leaving

Hollywood. But Isadora has gone everywhere in the flesh. She has danced before kings and peasants. She has danced from the Pacific to London, from Petrograd to the Black Sea, from Athens to Paris and Berlin.

She penetrated to the Georgian States of the Caucasus, riding third-class amid fleas and disease, performing in obscure halls before yokels and princes whom she left astonished, slightly enlightened, and somehow altered by the vision. For twenty years her life has been more exciting and fantastic than anything Zola or Defoe ever fabricated for their heroines. Her companions have been the great public talent of our generation—Duse, d'Annunzio, Bakst, Rodin, Bernhardt, Picabia, Brancusi, and so on. Her friends have run the gamut from starving poets down to millionaires. She has been prodigal of herself, her art, illusions, work, emotions, and funds. She has spent fortunes. After the war her Sunday night suppers in the Rue de Pompe were banquets where guests strolled in, strolled out, and from low divans supped princi-pally on champagne and strawberry tarts, while Isadora, barely clad in chif-fon robes, rose when the spirit moved her to dance exquisitely. Week after week came people whose names she never knew. They were like moths. She once gave a house party that started in Paris, gathered force in Venice, and culminated weeks later on a houseboat on the Nile.

In order to promulgate her pedagogic theories of beauty and education for the young, she has legally adopted and supported some thirty or forty children during her life, one group being the little Slavs who are still danc-ing in Soviet Russia. During her famous season at the New York Century Theatre where she gave a classic Greek cycle, "Oedipus Rex," "Antigone," and the like, she bought up every Easter lily in Manhattan to decorate the theatre the night she opened in Berlioz' "L'Enfance du Christ," which was her Easter program. The lilies, whose perfume suffocated the spectators, cost two thousand dollars. Isadora had, at the moment, three thousand dol-lars to her name. And at midnight, long after all good lily-selling florists were in bed, she gave a champagne supper. It cost the other thousand.

Isadora, who has an un-American genius for art, for organizing love, maternity, politics, and pedagogy on a great personal scale, had also an un-American genius for grandeur.

After the lilies faded, Isadora and her school sat amid their luggage on the pier where a ship was about to sail for France. They had neither tickets nor money. But they had a classic faith in fate and a determination to go back to Europe where art was understood. Just before the boat sailed, there appeared a school teacher. Isadora had never seen her before. The teacher gave Isadora the savings of years and Isadora sailed away. Herself grand, she could inspire grandeur in others, a tragic and tiring gift. There have always been school teachers and lilies in Isadora's life.

In the three summer programs which Isadora recently gave in her studio at Nice, one with the concordance of Leo Tecktonius, the pianist, the other two with Jean Cocteau, French poet and *éphèbe,* who accompanied her dancing with his spoken verse, her art was seen to have changed. She treads the boards but little now, she stands almost immobile or in slow splendid steps with slow splendid arms moves to music, seeking, hunting, finding. Across her face, tilting this way and that, flee the mortal looks of tragedy, knowledge, love, scorn, pain. Posing through the works of Wagner, through tales of Dante, through the touching legend of St. Francis feeding crumbs and wisdom to his birds, Isadora is still great. By an economy (her first) she has arrived at elimination. As if the movements of dancing had become too redundant for her spirit, she has saved from dancing only its shape.

Where will she dance next? In one of her periodic fits of extravagant poverty and although needing the big sum offered, she once refused to dance in Wanamaker's Auditorium, disdaining for her art such a "scene of suspenders." She has refused other theatres because they contain restaurants. She has just refused to appear at the Champs-Elysées because it is a music-hall. She talks of giving some performances in Catalonia. She might dance in a castle in Spain.

There is also much ado about her now in the Paris journals because of the recent sale of her house in Neuilly, a sale she was forced to make to pay a debt of ten thousand francs, and her refusal of a legacy valued at 300,000 francs from her one-time husband, Esenin, the Russian poet. The Neuilly house has just been repurchased by a group of friends who will make it into a school as a memorial to the dancer's two children so tragically drowned in Paris in 1913.

All her life Isadora has been a practical idealist. She has put into practice certain ideals of art, maternity, and political liberty which people prefer to read as theories on paper. Her ideals of human liberty are not unsimilar to those of Plato, to those of Shelley, to those of Lord Byron which led him to die dramatically in Greece. All they gained for Isadora was the loss of her passport and the presence of the constabulary on the stage of the Indianapolis Opera House where the chief of police watched for sedition in the movement of Isadora's knees.

Denounced as a Russian "red" sympathizer, Isadora does not even receive a postal card from the Soviet Government to give her news of her school which she housed in its capital. For Isadora has had a fancy for facts. As she once told Boston it was tasteless and dull, so, when they were fêting her in triumph in Moscow, she told the Bolsheviks she found them bourgeois.

Great artists are tragic. Genius is too large; and it may have been grandeur that proved Isadora's undoing—the grandeur of temporary luxury, the grandeur of permanent ideals.

She is too expansive for personal salvation. She has had friends. What she needed was an entire government. She had checkbooks. Her scope called for a national treasury. It is not for nothing that she is hailed by her first name only as queens have been, were they great Catherines or Marie Antoinettes. Isadora is now writing her memoirs. Her private life, which always aroused public interest, is therein detailed. By her, the truth can then be told.

—from *The New Yorker,* January 1, 1927, published only months
before Isadora's death

ANDRÉ LEVINSON

Isadora Duncan: In Memoriam

A two-fold danger threatens the memory of the dead artist. Before amnesia wipes him from memory, posthumous glorification sets in; even more than the "communicative warmth of the banquet halls," the august meditation of funerals favors the birth of panegyric. Few things are as frivolous as the eloquence of certain obituaries, and for the buffoons who pirouette upon the printed word what better pretext than the death of an illustrious dancer, when her name is Isadora Duncan!

Still, it is pointless to deny either my past objections to her doctrine or the endless arguments I have used to combat her influence, in acknowledging my grief before the horrible and abrupt end of that great existence.

Those, like myself, who contested the intrinsic value of her reforms bow before the heroic character of her action and the exceptional breadth of her personality. Here her influence was universal. The prodigious enterprise of this young American, missionary of a new aesthetic sent to evangelize the world, remains without a doubt embedded in the history of dance and theatre. Nevertheless, deceptive illusions have come about.

In reality the dreadful accident that brought an end to her prodigious existence did nothing but cut short the slow agony of her art, the distress, where her soul crawled in pain, artless and fervent. Isadora had outlived her apogee. Today, no one in even pious delusion would know how to galvanize the work from totally negative material that became irremediably decayed and fatally consecrated to decrepitude through the absence of constructive and lasting virtues. Before she had succumbed personally, this was evidenced in her doctrine and later in her mystique, because her subversive apostasy lay in the negation of all doctrine. The immense universal prestige that, not long ago, surrounded her, the enthusiasm of electrified crowds and the conquered élite who attached themselves to her everywhere, endured as long as the body flourished. This was, after all, the blossoming of this instinctive being. The physical diminution that followed close to maturity could not but cut into an art which was like the expression of a biological plenitude; once this overflow of living forces dried up, nothing was sufficient to nourish the extinguished fire.

The idolatry of the body, the cult of spontaneous emotion and chance reflexes placed that artist at the mercy of implacable forces of nature. Alone, the primacy of the spirit and the power of abstraction preserve in art forms a durable youth. The art of Isadora Duncan had aged with her. Those who had not seen her when she was twenty had not seen her. It was at the Trocadero, in May of 1923, that these inexorable ravages were apparent to me for the last time. Here was the heartbroken echo that I found in my critical account of "that which was Isadora." "How I remember from the upright and noble carriage of her small head, to the torso of a robust amazon. . . . Yesterday, tortured, I sought those traits in her heavy face, the nape of her neck, and her massive thighs, revealed by an overly short tunic. Nothing survived of the malleable personality that so impressed us formerly. Her play appeared monotonous, impoverished, her march heavy, her running tired. The arms, the wrists had lost their suppleness. The fingers alone were gestures of a conductor indicating the beat to invisible musicians. From all this agonizing spectacle, where naturalism direct from expression has supplanted all rhythmic or plastic inclination, a single memory stays with me. I see the dancer, again with arms crucified as on an imaginary cross, the body weighed down, knees bent, legs broadly, brutally split apart. Then the head rolls back, the chest follows and the short head of hair sweeps the floor. These two positions achieve a sad grandeur while treading close to the grotesque. They muse upon the parodies of théàtre classique, where Daumier remains monumental in the same derision, or again on the ferociously sincere nudes of "Gynecée" of Andre Rouveyre."

But time heals all wounds. It will erase the humiliating memory of such decrepitude and forever will change Isadora herself. Her legend will survive, because no other dancer will know the same apotheosis.

The singular, incredible adventure! This young lady coming some thirty years ago from San Francisco, armed with a candid faith and an energy that a single doubt could not weaken, traversed "the Europe of ancient parapets" and implanted there, brushing aside all resistance, an entirely new conception of the dance, which was also a conception of life. She ventured for thirty years to establish by herself a new order—or disorder—by breaking with all forms of traditional art.

She was the product of a race that had no past. One can conceive the advantages and the dangers of such a situation. She braved everything, risked everything. In renouncing the contribution of theatrical illusion, the prestige of decor, and the artifices of scenery, she walked the bare stage barefoot, naked herself beneath her silk tunic (the inevitable concession to decency). Certainly she deplored hypocritical constraint. Her intention was not to reform theatrical dance. She decided to ignore everything that preceded her. Without the least hesitation, strong in her private conviction, the daring American made a clean sweep of time-honored tradition; she disavowed totally a choreographic heritage that was an integral part of our own civilization. Confident in her mission, she broke with the past, and for her own part began to dance anew. Her bare soles trod virgin ground from the outset. She would dance as the bird sings, according to her heart's impulses, the emotion of her body, the inspiration of the hour that passes, and without knowing how, listening to nothing except her spirit. It was not only the reasoned discipline of classical ballet that was trampled by her white feet. It was the general effect of the social and intellectual conventions upon which civilized society lives. She freed herself not only from tights and corset, the equipment of the ballerina, but from all fetters capable of constraining the full scope of her sovereign whim. Her quasi-nudity wasn't an outrage to modesty but an act of faith. There can be no question of modesty for this body in a state of paradisiacal beatitude that ignores good and evil. That the persuasive candor of the young barbarian had been seconded by a genius of propaganda worthy of Barnum is not sufficient to explain her extraordinary hold on an immense public or before long the worldwide fame of her art. While running from capital to capital across Europe, alone, unknown, she faced the numerous armies of corps de ballet from the Opéra. She crossed over the belly of these dormant troupes as they wallowed in self-satisfaction or idleness, deserting their posts at the first alert; her surprise attack caused trouble among the élite as well as the dancers d'école. They were disconcerted, frustrated, and seduced by the dazzling candor of the intrepid amazon and the singular physical attraction of her robust and gentle youth.

In Russia, where ballet survived in its ancient splendor, Anna Pavlova adopted and coddled the intruder with the generosity that marked a genius; Michel Fokine directly imitated her. Elsewhere an immense public, strangers to dance until then, acclaimed the advent of the barefoot dancer. Everywhere, her example aroused the ardor of imitators; soon there was a mass of disciples. Isadora was the initiatrice, the first master of a vast movement.

Nothing that we call rhythmic dance or plastique today would be possible without her. We owe to her even the principle, be it contestable, of this novelty. All that a generation wished for or dreamed about in dance was accomplished thanks to her—or against her; never outside of her. These lines are written by one who had dedicated himself to the restoration of French classic dancing. Where did he begin? By attacking Isadora Duncan! Because, by a miracle of will and faith, she had imprinted her seal on an entire epoch. Whether the future dance historian appreciates this epoch as a period of renaissance or of decadence, he will have to inscribe the name Isadora at the head of a chapter consecrated to our time.

But how do you explain this extraordinary effervescence, this seemingly psychic contagion that made the élite as well as the mass of people feverish to see this noble feminine form running across the stage! What was the substance of this choreographic messianism that was to beat in so many hearts? And what is the philosophy of this astonishing destiny?

One cannot so stir masses, heretofore indifferent to dance, solely by modifying types of steps or certain habits in costume. And it wasn't the coming of this woman that accomplished this miracle of collective fervor. The attraction of her robust body, bather in the sweat of the palestra, was more chaste than sensual. Her barefoot evolutions on the stages of Paris, St. Petersburg, or Vienna to the sound of music by Beethoven or Grieg, aroused the same emotion. Her coming responded by necessity to some kind of anticipation, some expectation. Everything in her became for the audience the living symbol of their most secret aspirations.

The arrival of Isadora was like the fulfillment of a dream that often has consoled humanity in dark hours: the return of the golden age, the promise of paradise regained, that "state of nature" which had been fallacious fiction when imagined by J. J. Rousseau. She came to free instinct from the constraints that inflict civilization; she was to exalt spontaneous emotion over conventional reasonableness; she spurned elaborate artifice, denounced it as a blemish along with all those who opposed inspired improvisation. Through her, dance became the free flight of the being left to his own impulses, to the bewildered muscular reactions of the body. As an immediate expression of the self, this art was emancipated from all premeditated discipline.

Like all romanticism, the Duncan revolution was destructive. In breaking with accepted ideas, she caressed anarchy. In abolishing an order, even though it was only an aesthetic order, she delighted malcontents. Her rebellion tore the monopoly of theatrical dance away from an aristocracy and from an oligarchy of professional dancers educated by the rules of their art, in order to deliver it up to the masses.

Such a demagogy made light of caste privileges and exclusivity. The example of Duncan seemed to institute universal suffrage through dance. It was permissible for each spectator to recognize in himself a virtual dancer. This illusion was borne out from one day to the next, in countless vocations; Isadora's rivals are legion. No one could wait to express what was, in its essence, nothing but the manifestation of an outstanding personality, a unique originality. One had thought that instruction by the innovator would provide free access to this ecstatic salutation. But there was no one with this key except Isadora.

"He who is the most beautiful," wrote Eupalinos, the architect of Megara as imagined by Paul Valéry, "is by necessity tyrannical." Isadora crushed tyranny and instituted her own rigor. She opened the floodgates to dilettantes; in this way the naked feet of the dancer served as a revolutionary emblem. She was barefooted like the *sans-culottes* in 1793. Her famous escapade in Bolshevik Russia is consistent with the logic of her character. She hoped to rediscover there the lost paradise promised by Rousseau to man, the state of nature delivered from the taints of civilization.

Like all romanticism, the Duncan revolution united the utopia of the golden age to the nostalgia of a legendary past. Like the soul of Goethe's Iphigenia exiled on Tauris, Isadora's soul sought out the country of the Greeks. Hasn't the antique ideal been exalted since Brutus in 1793? But what is important, above all, is that, inevitably, there must have been a certain cohesion and continuity necessary for this blossoming of such a sensitive being—for this negation of form to have forcibly taken form; it was necessary that a glorious precedent be conferred on the endeavors of this young stranger. This formal and ideal framework Isadora found in the example presumed by the Hellenes; she wished to revive Greek dancing out of figurative monuments which preserve its vestiges.

In all ages, this selfsame aim has enflamed innovators of the dance. Mlle Sallé had, in *Pygmalion,* given up the dress of the day to wear Grecian drapery. Less than a century later, Emma Hamilton, the *grande amoureuse* of which M. Albert Flament has told us, composed many dances based on antique bas-reliefs. Loie Fuller and also Raymond Duncan pointed the way for Isadora. Soon you see it, this action of symbolic attitudes, danced beneath the eyes of the gods, in the empty orchestra of the theatre of Dionysus.

With a certain number of borrowed gestures from ancient dancers, it was, before everything, the cult of the transfigured flesh, the religion of the body, the habitat of the gods which she brought back from her trip to Greece. Great memories nourish the best inspirations of this "pagan mystique." Certainly, the image she takes from Greek beauty remains scanty indeed, warped, her interpretation of the documents arbitrary. Through a generous illusion, Isadora thought she found on bas-reliefs and the sides of vases those gestures which she used to stylize her hazardous course, to formalize her obscure emotion. In Isadora's Hellenism and in her cult of the deified body, one catches a glimpse of an ideal acquired through books, through the atavism of the race, the ancestral heritage. In the pugnacious warmth and severe nudity of Diane the huntress, one encounters the form of the sportive American and the puritanism of the Presbyterians of Scotland. In the unstarched fabric that drapes Isadora, one anticipates, with memories of Tanagra, this disdain for vain artifice and worldly pomp, this Protestant rigor which opposed Cromwell's roundheads to the cavaliers of Charles Stuart. Rather than voluptuousness, there was something ascetic, almost monkish, in Isadora's feet dirtied by the dust of the stage, flattened and deformed by rough contact with the floor.

Having repudiated the "sterile precepts" of academic dancing, humbled long ago by Noverre, Isadora was disposed to nothing but a very restrained repertoire of movements, varying in steps and course, augmented with the play of a supple wrist, a leaning or tossing up of the head and torso. This paucity of form was compensated for by an intensity of expression, a degree of muscular tension, a vigor in spirited accents, from lively skipping on half point to frenzied stamping in bacchic ecstacy. If her admiration for the Greeks supplied the plastic side of her danced monologues, it was her sovereign charm that made the movement spring up and connect the strides of her fantastic motion. To these graces and raptures a stimulant was needed. She demanded this impulsive force from music—music acting like a magnetic force upon the skin-deep sensibility. Each dance was born from the spirit of the score.

We touch here on the greatest surprise that Duncan's innovation produced. Isadora renounced the symmetrical breath and regular pulse of so-called proper dance music and plunged resolutely into the flood of the symphony. She danced Chopin; she danced Brahms and Beethoven symphonies; she danced Gluck opéras and the lieder of Richard Wagner. Voluptuously, she floated on the sonorous wave, obeying rhythmic suggestions, subjugated like a somnambulist by the musical flow. I side with those who consider such a complete subjugation of dance by another art error. But that error measures the extent of a vast ambition! Isadora saw things on a large scale, if not from the correct viewpoint.

Homage or sacrilege, conquest or infringement, this choice was, to begin with, a mistake. To be sure, one easily finds in the full movement of a symphony the suggestion of a choreographic theme, a latent ballet. But to make the musical development regress to its physical origin in the dancer's corporeal rhythm is a vain endeavor. Beethoven composed thirty-three admirable variations on a melody from a soothing waltz proposed by Diabelli, which under the circumstances, is nothing.

"Dance can reveal everything that music conceives," wrote Baudelaire. It was toward this revelation that the efforts of Isadora Duncan constantly strove. This interpretation was the gift, renewed every day, from her to the crowds with whom she communed. We have said that three principles guided Isadora in her revolt against tradition. She wished to be natural, she tried to imitate the ancients, and she subordinated dance to music. These theoretical principles are worth what they are worth. But the flame that inhabited this exceptional being illumined them with an ephemeral splendor.

—translated by Jill Silverman for *Ballet Review,* 1978–1979; original French
Publication, 1929

ROBERT GOTTLIEB
Free Spirit

The most famous woman of the first quarter of the twentieth century may have been Mary Pickford, but the most influential, and the most notorious, was Isadora Duncan. She was the progenitor and soul of a new art form, modern dance. She was the prototype of the uninhibited young American whose freshness and originality charmed jaded old Europe. And for decades she startled respectable society—even as she helped transform it—with her flouting of conventions, both onstage and off. You would have to go back to George Sand or Byron to find a comparably galvanizing figure. Early in 1927, in the fledgling *New Yorker,* Janet Flanner identified her as "the last of the trilogy of great female personalities our century produced," along with Duse and Bernhardt. But those two supreme actresses were dead ends; no one could follow in their footsteps. Isadora's accomplishments reverberate through the history of dance to this day.

Isadora Duncan was born in San Francisco in 1877, the youngest of four children. Her father regularly made and lost fortunes, and eventually was gone from the family (he was to die in a shipwreck—nothing the Duncans did was ordinary). The children and their mother lived from hand to mouth; there is more than a touch of Micawberism in the way they got by—high spirits in the midst of semi-penury. But already Isadora was demonstrating the vigorous independence that was to carry her to world fame.

From the start she was clearly the Chosen One within what the family called the Clan Duncan. At eighteen, with her mother in tow and $25 in her pocket, she started east and soon wangled a job with Augustin Daly's prestigious stage company, spending months in various demeaning (to her) roles and developing "a perfect nausea for the theater." She confronted Daly:

"What's the good of having me here, with my genius, when you make no use of me?" By the time she was twenty-one, she was established in New York, appearing in concerts, dancing to Chopin at special matinees, providing entertainment in private salons (including Mrs. Astor's, in Newport). She was young, slender, very pretty with her vivid red hair and Irish button nose, and exceedingly charming—a Botticelli figurine. She was also highly respectable, with her formidable mother at the piano and her brothers and sister accompanying her dancing with recitations, often from "The Rubaiyat." Yet she was already shocking people with her "unobscured limbs." And she was already lecturing—hectoring?—her audiences about The Dance.

In May 1899, after a typical Duncan calamity (a near-fatal fire in their hotel), Isadora set out for the larger opportunities of Europe. Her reputation grew as she succeeded in London, then Paris, and was sealed in Budapest in 1902—twenty sold-out performances, ovations, roses thrown at her feet. She was also no longer a virgin. Oszkar Beregi, a handsome young actor, was performing Romeo, and very quickly she was his offstage Juliet, only without benefit of Friar Lawrence. She had waited a long while to discover sex—she was twenty-five—but she would make up for lost time.

Not for long with Beregi, however; soon he tactfully suggested that she proceed with her career, and, having fantasized about marriage, she felt as if she had "eaten bushels of broken glass." On she went, though, to Vienna and Munich, where she had an even greater triumph. It was there, her latest biographer Peter Kurth tells us,* that "the German 'cult of Isadora' was born, a national craze that took her beyond success and notoriety into the realms of literature, philosophy, feminism and even science . . . as the realization of Darwin's dream, the 'Dancer of the Future,' whose coming proclaimed the triumph of beauty and the liberation of women in the final perfection of the race." In *My Life,* her more readable than accurate autobiography, she recalls that it was in Berlin at this time that "on my return from performances where the audience had been delirious with joy, I would sit far into the night in my white tunic, with a glass of white milk beside me, poring over the pages of Kant's 'Critique of Pure Reason.'" Her blue-stocking earnestness had found its perfect match in Germanic high-seriousness. It was also in Berlin that she was invited by Cosima, the Widow Wagner, to perform in the bacchanal from "Tannhäuser" at Bayreuth. This experience proved to be a mixed blessing, but a passion for Cosima's son-in-law helped distract Isadora from the loss of Oszkar.

Through these years, she was constantly studying the sources of movement and refining her own liberating approach to dance, which she claimed

---

*In *Isadora: A Sensational Life.*

to have discovered in the waves breaking on California shores, in the art of ancient Greece, in the ideas of Whitman, Nietzsche, and Wagner. Wherever she went, she proclaimed her aesthetic, both from the stage and in writing. Her costumes were scant, but she was shrouded in her lofty ideas: "Art which is not religious is not art, is mere merchandise." Within a short time she was being acclaimed everywhere as a profound revolutionary spirit.

But what was her dancing really *like*? She never allowed herself to be filmed, so all our evidence is secondhand. In a 1992 article, Anne Hollander, having studied the numberless photographs and artistic representations that constitute the massive Duncan iconography, reported that they "tell a fairly consistent story, showing the thrusting knee, the bowed or thrown-back head, the open arms, the whirling colored stuffs veiling the torso. None show Duncan in midair. Along with running, she seems to have done a great deal of skipping and prancing, with her bare knees pushing up through slits in the drapery, but no high or broad leaping, no extended legs. Instead, she used the floor, kneeling and reclining, collapsing and rising. The face in the pictures is always blank—attention is riveted on those flashing naked legs and feet, those sweeping bare arms, that rounded exposed throat." In other words, throw in Isadora's radical insistence that movement must come from the solar plexus, and here is modern dance. We also know how musical she was, responding spontaneously rather than analytically to her beloved Chopin, her Gluck, her Beethoven, her Brahms, her Wagner. In this, too, she was radical—critics violently disapproved of her presumption in dancing to symphonic masterpieces.

In 1903 Isadora temporarily abandoned her career so that the Duncans could fulfill their dream of setting foot in Greece, which—in order to make the trip "as primitive as possible"—they approached in a little sailing boat, at dawn. On the beach, Isadora and her brother Raymond knelt down and kissed the soil, Raymond declaiming poetry. "The inhabitants all came down to the beach to greet us, and the first landing of Christopher Columbus in America could not have caused more astonishment among the natives." Soon the clan had rejected their already unusual garments to don "tunic and chlamys and peplum"; they had already substituted sandals for shoes. (Isadora was to dress this way for much of her life, and Raymond for all of his.) They bought land and started to erect a temple, but alas, the land they had acquired had no water within two and a half miles. Still, "we were living under the reign of Agamemnon, Menelaus, and Priam." (Priam, presumably, was on a visit from Troy.) After a year of the simple life, she was touring again, to the usual acclaim.

Soon Isadora met the man who was surely the great love of her life, the avantgarde stage designer Gordon Craig, who was the illegitimate son of England's most treasured actress, Ellen Terry. Craig was handsome, he was brilliant, and he was a ruthlessly selfish womanizer. (He was not only married but was the father of eight children, only four of them with his wife.) Craig brought Isadora the sexual and intellectual companionship she craved, the satisfaction of being linked with a great man (as she and he both saw him), and her first child, Deirdre. He also brought her anguish, as their passion and their competing obsessions with their work turned them into characters out of Strindberg. (The evidence is all there in Francis Steegmuller's invaluable edition of their correspondence, *Your Isadora*.) As usual, Isadora held nothing back: "O I tell you I have no caution or care," she wrote to him, "& if I don't see you soon I will pull myself up by the roots & throw myself in the Sea. . . . Come nice growly Tiger—Eat me up . . . Come Eat me—Put your lips to mine & begin that way." Her need to give too much had found its fatal counterpart in his bottomless need to take.

Late in 1904, in the flush of her early happiness with Craig, she arrived in St. Petersburg on her first trip to Russia—a crucial moment in ballet history, given the liberating influence her dancing was to have on the young Michel Fokine's experiments. There has been endless discussion as to exactly how great an influence this was, but according to Diaghilev, she dealt the Russian ballet "a shock from which it could never recover." Despite her animadversions against ballet—"an expression of degeneration, of living death"—she was warmly welcomed by the ballet establishment and, of course, by the public. And she made a powerful impression on Stanislavsky, who later wrote, "It became clear to me that we were looking for one and the same thing in different branches of art."

It was around this time that Isadora began her lifelong struggle to establish a school for children. The first one was in Berlin, and was run mainly by her sister, Elizabeth; there were to be others. Wherever she went, Isadora battled to convince not only rich patrons but governments to back her grandiose plans. These schools were Isadora's obsession, reflecting both her determination to spread her word—that to live was to dance—and her fierce need to mother. For years she spent the fortune in fees she was earning to support them.

In her endless pursuit of money for the Berlin school, Isadora often joked about acquiring a millionaire, and as usual she had her way. In 1909, she encountered the astonishingly rich Paris Singer, an imposing, well-educated, and generally amiable forty-year-old who was one of the heirs of the Singer Sewing Machine Company. She reports: "He entered, tall and blond, curling hair and beard. My first thought was: Lohengrin." A second thought: "I realized that this was my millionaire, for whom I had sent my brain waves seeking." Lohengrin was instantly smitten, and soon was providing jewels, yachts, a magnificent chateau in which she could start yet another school, and a second child, Patrick. She loved Singer, was grateful to him, and then perversely and repeatedly treated him so badly that he backed away. The last straw came in 1917 when he offered to buy her Madison Square Garden. "What do you think I am, a circus?" she snapped. "I suppose you want me to advertise prizefights with my dancing!" At that, he was finally gone.

But by then she was no longer the Isadora the world had celebrated. Four years earlier had come the great tragedy of her life. Deirdre and Patrick, five and three years old, were drowned when their car slid down a muddy embankment and into the Seine. It was a death blow to Isadora: "When real sorrow is encountered there is for the stricken no gesture, no expression. Like Niobe turned to stone, I sat and longed for annihilation in death." She fled to Greece with her brothers and sister; to Turkey, Italy, Switzerland, Paris, back to Italy, finding solace nowhere.

What eventually brought her back to life was, of course, dancing. Her most famous work during this period was "Marseillaise," which ended with "her left breast bared in evocation of Delacroix's 'Liberty Leading the People,'" and she was to bare her breast in Europe and across North and South America throughout World War I. Agnes de Mille, who saw her at this time, described her as a "prematurely aged and bloated woman," yet added, "Isadora wore a blood-red robe which she threw over her shoulder as she stamped to the footlights and raised her arms in the great Duncan salute. . . . This was heroic and I never forgot it. No one who saw Isadora ever forgot her."

After a period of relative calm, the final significant episode of Isadora's life began in 1921 with an extended stay in the Soviet Union, which had promised her an official school. (She now saw herself as a Communist, insisting to the startled Russians on being called "Comrade.") This was the trip that kindled her last full-blown romantic liaison, with the brilliant but dangerously unstable poet Sergei Esenin. She was forty-five when they met; he was twenty-six. It was another case of love at first sight, followed at once by every kind of trouble—yet, presumably to ensure Esenin safe passage to the West, she married him, after decades of proclaiming herself above marriage.

To call this relationship a fiasco is to fail to do it justice. Disaster? Debacle? Catastrophe? He was violent, alcoholic, and untrustworthy, but also extraordinarily talented and famous—essential for Isadora. Besides, with his baby face and golden hair, he reminded her of her poor dead little Patrick. (There's a recipe for marriage!) He loved her, needed her, sponged from her, abused her. They racketed around Europe and America creating bedlam wherever they went—drunken scenes, unpaid bills. (As one observer put it, "Every intelligent person, in Moscow and everywhere else they went, from Paris to Kansas City, knew that this blind union was a disaster to them both, as well as to the hotel furniture.") She got him back to Russia, where he dumped her; she saw him only twice more. A year later, he hanged himself in a hotel room, having first slit one of his wrists so that he could write a final poem in his blood.

By then she was back in France, and for the rest of her life she lived mainly in Nice and Paris. She was in a dire state. Friends loyally denied that she was a drunk, but she was one. And she was fat. The seventeen-year-old George Balanchine had watched her perform in Petrograd in the early twenties, and, with all the heartlessness of youth, saw her as "a drunken, fat woman who for hours was rolling around like a pig." (He did add, though, "She was probably a nice juicy girl when she was young.")

She was equally far gone emotionally. She had grown sexually rapacious and undiscriminating, and was living precariously, with occasional hand-outs from friends and a few francs earned from makeshift performances. There were pawnshops, dispossessions; always one step ahead of the sheriff. (On a train trip to Paris—the deluxe train, of course—the porter had to pay for her dinner.) Then, flings and extravagant generosity when money came through. Economy and moderation were, needless to say, alien to her nature. In 1927, desperate for cash, she finally settled down to write her memoirs. (Her publishers had insisted that she spice them up; well, maybe they were right—*My Life* is still in print.) Her last lover in residence was a young Russian musician, but she also became involved with the notorious Mercedes de Acosta, who later took up with Garbo and Dietrich, among others. The evidence points to a passionate affair. (Until then, Isadora had presumably been too busy with men, as she lurched from the great and the near-great—Picabia, Steichen, the pianist Harold Bauer, the war ace Roland Garros, to name a very few of her scores, even hundreds, of conquests—to just plain Joes, like the stoker, the boxer, and the gigolo she dallied with on the steamship that took her to South America in 1916.)

By the fall of 1927 she had little to look forward to; at fifty, and given her physical condition, she could not realistically count on a dance future. The famous death came swiftly. Flirting with a young garage mechanic from Nice, she demanded that he take her out in a racing car that she announced she was thinking of buying. (Isadora had always loved fast cars.) She stepped into the car, wearing a large shawl that her closest friend, Mary Desti, had designed for her. *"Adieu, mes amis, je vais à la gloire,"* she cried. The fringes of the shawl caught in the spokes of the left rear wheel, the car started forward, and within seconds Isadora's neck was broken and she was dead. It is certainly tempting to see her instantaneous and painless death as a merciful release.

How to make sense of this immense, complicated, beautiful, and grotesque life? Many have tried; the Isadora Duncan literature is a tidal wave of loving reminiscence, obfuscation, self-glorification, infighting, and supposition by those who knew her, followed by a series of generally worthy biographies and extended commentaries on her work. Yet we are left with questions. First, how good a dancer was she? There is so much testimony to her performing genius, her irresistible stage charisma, that they can hardly be doubted. Consider: Edith Wharton ("That first sight of Isadora's dancing was a white milestone to me. It shed a light on every kind of beauty"); Tamara Karsavina ("She moved with those wonderful steps of hers with a simplicity and detachment that could only come through the intuition of genius itself"); Frederick Ashton ("I got an impression of enormous grace, and enormous power in her dancing—she was very serious, and held the audience and held them completely"); Sergei Koussevitsky ("She incarnated music in her dance"); Ruth St. Denis ("For Isadora, I would do battle. To reject her genius is unthinkable"); Rodin ("The greatest woman I have ever known. . . . Sometimes I think she is the greatest woman the world has ever known"). If we can't trust witnesses like these, whom can we trust?

It is her life that presents the unanswerable question. Why did this glorious girl, with the world at her feet, turn into the ghastly wreck who could say toward the end, "I don't dance anymore, I only move my weight around," and "There are only two things left, a drink and a boy"? The easiest explanation is that the death of the children permanently unhinged her. But the seeds of her destruction must always have been there, and two of her early New York friends suggest what they may have been.

Arnold Genthe, who took superb pictures of her, wrote in his memoirs: "Where her work was concerned she had integrity and patience, knowing no compromise with what she felt to be the truth about beauty. In her personal life she had charm and a naive wit. Of tact and self-control she had very little, nor did she wish to have. She was the complete and willing tool of her impulses."

And the socialist writer Max Eastman, who knew her intimately, confesses that "despite her beautiful and triumphant deeds," her "courage, kindness, wit and true-heartedness," he did not like her. "She had made a cult of impulse and impracticality, rapture and abandon. . . . She had confused caprice with independence, heroics with heroism, mutiny with revolution. . . . How embarrassed I always was by the admirable force of character with which Isadora insisted on being half-baked."

In other words, she demanded total, untrammeled freedom. "I am the spiritual daughter of Walt Whitman," she had declared, and indeed "Song of Myself" could stand as a motto for her entire life. She is an extreme example of the American spirit of self-reliance that believes only in itself and refuses all limits. For Isadora there were no rules, there was only the Song of Herself; she lacked the discipline, the emotional and moral resources, to keep liberty from collapsing into license.

It was this that Max Eastman grasped and deplored. Yet he could also say,

"All who have escaped in any degree from the rigidity and prissiness of our once national religion of negation owe a debt to Isadora Duncan's dancing. She rode the wave of revolt against Puritanism; she rode it, and with her fame and Dionysian raptures drove it on. She was—perhaps it is simplest to say—the crest of the wave, an event not only in art but in the history of life."

—from *The New York Times Book Review,* December 30, 2001

SUZANNE FARRELL

Suzanne Farrell was born Roberta Sue Ficker in Cincinnati in 1945 and as a young teenager was seen there by Diana Adams, who recommended her to Balanchine and the School of American Ballet. Joining City Ballet in 1961, she quickly became Bal-anchine's dancer of choice—he created many ballets for her, beginning with Medi-tation *and including* Don Quixote, "Diamonds," *the Gypsy movement of* Brahms-Schoenberg Quartet, *the final sections of both* Union Jack *and* Vienna Waltzes, Chaconne, Tzigane, *Robert Schumann's* "Davidsbündertänze," *and his last major work,* Mozartiana. *She also danced almost all the ballerina roles in the standard Balanchine repertory. (She was Titania in Balanchine's film of his* A Midsummer Night's Dream.*) During her five-year break from the company in the early seventies, she performed with Maurice Béjart. Now she directs the Suzanne Farrell Ballet at the Kennedy Center, and has been awarded a Kennedy Center Honor as well as the National Medal of Arts.*

SUZANNE FARRELL
Audition

Mother was more nervous than I about the prospect of my audition at Balanchine's school; she had decided by now that Balanchine was the top, and starting at the top seemed like a dangerous thing to do. It was against her midwestern work ethic; if you failed, the only place to go would be down, probably with shattered confidence. Despite the New York City Ballet Juniors and Symphony in C in Indiana, I remained realistic about where I might dance. American Ballet Theatre had a school, and Radio City had a ballet company, and both were on our agenda. But Diana [Adams] had told us to call the School of American Ballet, so we did that first. Afraid that we might not understand New York habits, we enlisted our friend Nelle Fisher, the choreographer for the Cincinnati Summer Opera, to phone for us. I was told to come at eleven-thirty the next day.

Even though everything depended on this audition—and since the Canadian fiasco, auditions seemed to me like tortures designed to break my spirit—I had not taken a ballet class for a month. Frantically, I took a class at American Ballet Theatre's school, but in 1960 teenage dancers were not obsessive, and I didn't worry about being out of shape. Nevertheless, I took the audition very seriously: I went into the basement of our friends' house and did another barre.

That morning, we took the train into the city and rented a studio at the since demolished Columbus Circle Studios so that Miss Fisher could give me a warm-up. At eleven o'clock Mother and I climbed into a taxi and told the driver the address—2291 Broadway. There was a canopy over the door that said in painted letters "School of American Ballet." Inside was a long, steep stairway—I counted twenty-nine steps. Since then I have always sewn on my toe shoe ribbons with twenty-nine stitches, which is far too many. At the top of the stairs was a fire door that read "School of American Ballet," this time in big black stick-on letters. I turned to my mother and said with quiet gravity, "Here goes."

Inside it was very gray and empty. I heard piano music playing but saw no one, just a long corridor lined with red vinyl couches, like a coffee shop. We found a woman behind a desk and I said, "I'm Suzanne Ficker, and I have an audition." I was usually Suzi Ficker, but we had decided that Suzanne sounded more official; to us it meant the difference between Cincinnati and New York. I was rather surprised when all they said was, "Go and get changed," and pointed to a door. I didn't expect red-carpet treatment or blaring trumpets, but since this was my big moment in the big city, I was a little shaken that they were so matter-of-fact about it. But I obediently went into the dressing room to change. I thought my black scoop-necked leotard with cap sleeves and my pink tights were very chic—at least they were in Cincinnati—and besides they were the only ones I owned. I wore old soft toe shoes instead of leather ballet slippers, because I had seen in pictures that professional dancers always wore toe shoes.

Outside the woman pointed to the end of the corridor and said, "Have a seat." We passed a door with a typewritten note on it saying, "Do not open the door while class is in progress." But I heard music and couldn't resist peeking at what I already considered my competition. I saw girls at the barre doing ronds de jambe on the floor. They all looked terrific, and I turned to Mother and said, "I don't stand a chance."

Now I began to worry. When you're from a small town, you don't know what big time is, you only know big-time small time, and that is a far cry from big-time big time. It was scary, so many tapered turned-out legs, straight knees, and arched feet all in a row. I had been the star in Cincinnati, and here I already knew I was not.

Mother and I sat, as we were told, in the far corner of the hallway, frozen like stone. Still no one else appeared and except for the tinkle of piano music from the studio it was silent. Click, the front door opened, and like marionettes Mother and I turned. There at the far end of the corridor was George Balanchine.

I had never seen him in the flesh, but I knew it was him, and he looked just as I knew he would. That year *Dance Magazine* had run a two-part article on Balanchine and the New York City Ballet, and in one issue was a picture of him, very austere in his embroidered cowboy shirt and black string tie. It was my only vision of him, and it was exactly what came through the door of the School of American Ballet that day—the jacket, the shirt, the tie, everything.

As he came toward us, all I saw was the photo getting bigger and bigger in front of me, only this was in color. Mother and I grabbed each other, and she said, "Oh my God, there he is."

"I'm Suzanne Ficker," I said, "and this is my mother." Mr. Balanchine did not introduce himself. He clasped his hands, did a little bow, and motioned toward a closed door. I jumped up and went with him. My mother says all she could think was, "There goes my baby—with that *man*." It was my fifteenth birthday.

I didn't know at the time how unusual it was for Balanchine to audition me himself, although I knew he was a famous ballet company director and didn't presume that he had time for everything.

We went into an empty studio. I briefly wondered where all the other kids for the audition were but soon resolved the question—this was how they did it in New York. I also expected that he would tell me what to do, as in my previous experience, so when he asked me if I had a routine, a number, to show him, I said, "No." I knew this was not a good beginning, and I didn't want it all to end right there, so, hoping to salvage the situation, I quickly told him that I knew a dance from my June recital. He said, "Oh, all right, do that," leaned on the barre, titled his head back, and looked down his nose. "I'll sing the music," I explained, hoping to fill the loud silence echoing in the empty room, and proceeded to hum Glazounov's *The Seasons* and dance Miss La Cour's choreography. He just watched.

I don't know what he thought, but as the years went by I often asked him, "What did you ever see in me that day?" He never answered; he only laughed.

It seemed like an eternity that I was there singing and dancing. Finally he held up his arms and said, "Stop, stop, stop. Come over here." He had me sit on the floor and take off my shoes. He wanted to examine my left foot, because, as I found out later, Diana had been concerned about it. It had been kicked by a horse and totally crushed, leaving me flat-footed on one side. It could easily have meant that I would never be a professional dancer, but I think by then Providence had taken over. . . .

In Mother's baby films of me I can see that once upon a time my feet were equally arched. It had been a beautiful foot, and I often worried that it wasn't as developed as the other one and would say so to Mr. B. He would only grin and say: "Oh, dear, but you know, if it was a beautiful foot, you'd be perfect."

When Mr. Balanchine held my foot in his hands that day, I felt that he was holding my life. I wasn't sure what he was thinking, but he had strong, warm hands. He asked me to point my right foot and saw that it was nicely arched, and when he asked me to point my left, he saw that it wasn't. Then, still holding my left foot, he tried to bend my toes back in the opposite direction.

I didn't know what he wanted, so my instinct took over and I resisted. I gritted my teeth and wouldn't let him bend my toes. He sniffed in his inimitable way, let go, and said, "Fine." He helped me up from the floor and led me to the door, very much the gentleman. As we went out into the corridor where Mother was waiting, he said, "Thank you," and I said, "Thank you." He disappeared down the hall. It was over.

I changed back into my street clothes, and we left the way we came. No one said a word to us. We walked down the twenty-nine steps and went next door to Schrafft's for ice cream. My diary entry for that day was not hopeful:

> Today my audition was terrible. I could hardly understand a word Balanchine said. The school is very nice.

The next day the phone rang, and the lady at the other end said I had a scholarship.

—from *Holding On to the Air,* with Toni Bentley, 1990

A Conversation with Suzanne Farrell

BALLET REVIEW: *Did you always want to be a dancer?*
SUZANNE FARRELL: No. Not in the very beginning.

BR: *How did you get started?*
SF: My mother took me to class. I just went because that's the way things were. It was part of life and I accepted it. I didn't mind going once a week to the ballet studio. Fortunately, though, my teacher included acrobatics, which I enjoyed a lot. I was very supple and liked daring, even dangerous things: backbends, walkovers, cartwheels, flips, and so on. That's what kept me interested at first.

BR: *Did you enjoy ballet more when you began to have a little something to dance?*
SF: A bit. My first recital was fun. I was a cat and wore a pretty white costume. For the next recital my cat costume was dyed gray and I was a mouse. Then I did a little something with Ballet Russe when they came to Cincinnati.* Even though I enjoyed that, I still wasn't an addict. I didn't live to dance.

BR: *Did you gradually realize you wanted to be a dancer, or was there a moment?* . . .
SF: There was a moment. I was twelve and I was to dance with my class in a lecture/demonstration of *Les Sylphides* on the stage of the Cincinnati Music Hall. The theater was cold and dark and we were to perform on a little apron built out in front of the stage, with the orchestra behind us. Everyone was complaining about the lack of heat, the mustiness, the bad floor, the cramped space. But I felt life in all that. I stood there on the empty stage, looking out at all those empty seats and knew I was a dancer—that I had to dance. As a little private token, I knelt and picked up a splinter from the stage to commemorate that moment. I still have it. There had been many people in the Music Hall and on its stage; I felt something of them had remained. As a dancer I knew I was part of that

---

* Clara in *The Nutcracker* with Alicia Alonso and Igor Youskevitch.

existence. Even today I feel as much life in an empty theater as I do when every seat is filled.

BR: *Someone once said of you that you seem as if you'd dance the same whether or not there was an audience.*
SF: I have to because I dance for God, who gave me the gift of dancing. I also want to be true to the choreographer, and I like to please and surprise my partner. If I manage all that, I'm pleased—not too pleased and not for long. I have to be dissatisfied to keep going—I mean, you can't keep repeating yourself just because you pleased yourself or even someone else. I can't say I don't care about the public, but that's not my first consideration.

BR: *Getting back to the Cincinnati Music Hall . . . after that moment, did you make drastic changes in your life, in your habits?*
SF: By that time I was taking class every day. And we lived across the street from the Cincinnati Conservatory of Music where I studied—my mother planned that. I began to spend every available minute in ballet class. I took class every day, and on Saturday. I also demonstrated for the other classes. I even demonstrated the barre exercises standing in the center of the floor. I began to listen to as much music as possible. I organized a ballet club, the New York City Ballet Juniors. I was the boss because I was the tallest. Then I realized if I was the boss, I'd have to give my people something to dance. So I began to make up dances for us to perform. What free hours I had I spent at the library looking at old pictures of dancers and ballets.

BR: *Were you seeking models?*
SF: No. I was just curious to know what they looked like.

BR: *Did you find any inspiration in any of the dancers who came to Cincinnati?*
SF: No. I'm not a spectator. I'm not particularly interested in someone else's dancing. My inspiration comes from my own work. Though I admire professionalism in other dancers. And I'm curious and interested to see how they solve problems.

BR: *I know you went to a Catholic girls' school. Perhaps you sought role models in the lives of the saints? Or perhaps the Blessed Virgin?*
SF: All those statues did impress me. At our school there was a celebration of Mary every year on May Day that always thrilled me. We had a procession and sang hymns and a girl was chosen to climb a ladder and place the crown on the Virgin's head. I was never chosen, although it was always what I wanted most. I guess I was too rowdy, not elegant enough. Once I remem-

ber thinking during the ceremony, Gee, why do they keep talking about temptation and things going wrong and needing faith to get you through? I haven't sinned; life is a breeze. What temptations do they mean? But no, I never identified with the Virgin Mary. I would never aspire that high. I thought she was pretty, and blue is my favorite color. And I did envision her as a blonde, which I was. Her statue stood atop the world which was half encircled by a crescent moon. She had such beautiful feet; one was crushing the head of a snake. I found those images were very real and very alive with meaning—like music, which has meaning, but not verbal meaning. Or like *Serenade,* whose meaning is impossible to put into words, to name, and because of that its reality is even grander, more sublime. I also liked Joan of Arc very much. She was a young girl and needed lots of strength for what she had to do. Karinska was born near St. Joan's birthplace in France, and it was she who began to talk to me about St. Joan. It was just about the time Mr. Balanchine and I were working on *Don Quixote.* She gave me medals and pictures and told me stories. Years later I found myself turning to Joan of Arc, especially when I didn't know what to do and needed strength and faith to go on. I don't know who has meant more to me, though. I was in a church in Paris recently where there were dozens of places to light candles, but I found myself lighting a candle in front of the Virgin Mary. Mostly I go by what's in my heart. I don't think these things out.

BR: *Were you a good student at school?*
SF: Not particularly good or bad. I liked all the things girls weren't supposed to like–such as math, reading, and diagramming sentences. The grade wasn't important. I liked tests a lot because I liked the challenge of figuring things out and trying to do my best under pressure. I liked Latin, reading and translating myths. Actually, I liked the pictures better than the stories: pictures of gods and goddesses in flowing drapery, friezes from the Parthenon. My favorite story was about a girl named Pyrrha. She was very lonely. Everybody else had been wiped out because they'd sinned. One day the oracle told her to go to the river bank, gather up all the rocks she could find, and throw each one over her shoulder into the river without looking back. This was a test of her faith. Each time she threw a rock, a person would spring up from the water—saved. I was moved by her ability to trust and to believe. I guess if she'd looked around, the spell would have been broken. Just like in Sodom and Gomorrah— even Orpheus.

BR: *One of your sisters played the piano and the other was a dancer. There must have been a lot of music and dance around the house.*
SF: Oh, sure. Our favorite game was ballet.

BR: *You mean putting on a show?*

SF: No. It was a game the three of us played. Donna was The Teacher, Beverly was The Mother, and I was The Promising Young Student. The Teacher was very strict. The Mother always made sure I did whatever The Teacher asked. And I, as The Promising Young Student, was obedient and full of surprises. We put on shows, too. Carnivals, revues—singing, dancing, baton twirling, acrobatics, you name it. We were very professional about it. We picked out the music, made costumes, rehearsed, and then had final dress rehearsals. I composed dances to songs like "Just One of Those Things," "I Cover the Waterfront," and "I'm Looking Over a Four Leaf Clover." We'd draw pictures, too, and hang them in the trees and be stupid enough to think somebody would buy them. Then we'd make out our invitations and put them in the neighbors' mailboxes. Sometimes nobody came to our performances, or maybe nobody except our parents. But we did it for real. It was having a fantasy and making it come true with your own hard work. The preparation, the work, and the performance were all for real. It wasn't make-believe just because nobody showed up.

BR: *Fantasy and hard work?*

SF: Sure. If you are going to have the guts to dream, you have to have the guts to pay the price. You have to be prepared for them to come true. But you can't go around hoping wonderful things are going to drop out of the sky. There are forty girls in the New York City Ballet. I'd be a fool to assume my dreams are more farfetched than theirs. So it's not enough just to be prepared professionally. You can keep your job by going to class, knowing your part, and arriving at rehearsal on time with your ribbons tucked neatly into your shoes. But if you're presumptuous enough to have dreams and expect to realize any, you have to know how to make one opportunity be the base of another. When I danced my first lead—the Dark Angel in *Serenade*—you know, the girl who enters with her hand over the boy's eyes—it was my first year in the company and we were at Ravinia, just after the spring season at City Center. Somebody was out or had to do something else that night and Mr. Balanchine said casually, "Oh, let Suzanne do it. She hasn't got anything else to do." However, I didn't take his remark casually. I was determined to be the very best I could possibly be. And I had less than twenty-four hours to prepare. I didn't know the role, except for what I'd been able to pick up from watching. I knew I wouldn't have a rehearsal with all the other people in the ballet, because rehearsal time had to be spent on another ballet. So first things first. The ballet mistress showed me the steps, which I learned as quickly as I could. Then I realized something very important, I thought, about being a professional dancer: there would never, ever, be enough time to practice a thing physically as many times as I would like. And I think it changed my mind, too, about what rehearsal is really for. It's good to practice things physically, but it's good to think about them, too. I don't mean pondering over psychology and motivation, because as a dancer you are supposed to be presenting a ballet, not your personal reaction to Tchaikovsky's music. So, after going through my part a few times physically, I began to go over and over it mentally. This helped to calm my nerves and make me feel more secure. Having memorized both the steps and the music and being able to think them through, I realized then that one doesn't necessarily always think that way in an orderly sequence. Suppose there was a slip, a mistake, some distraction—would I be like a tour guide with a memorized speech who has to start over at the beginning if interrupted? Then I began to think through the music, picking out a spot at random, and making sure I knew exactly what was happening with my whole body, at any point on the stage, at any place in the ballet, I even reversed the ballet in my mind, and learned how to dance it in any direction, entering, for example, from the opposite wing, or from any other wing for that matter. That was an invaluable piece of discipline. Because later on, when I began to dance music of greater tonal and rhythmic complexity, I could, within hearing two or three notes, know exactly where I should be on the stage, the exact position of my body, the phrasing, everything. Consequently, I'm freer to take risks, to be spontaneous, to respond to the conductor, rather than repeating the same performance night after night.

BR: *Had you ever prepared a role that way before?*
SF: No. That's what I mean about being prepared as well as knowing how to get prepared. I was already prepared in a way—Mr. Balanchine had seen fit to try me out in the role. But once having been assigned the role, I knew I had to do even more. I wanted to be worthy of his trust, especially so since I knew he wouldn't be able to attend the performance. Since my preparation and work had given me the opportunity of being tried out in a big role, I had the freedom to use what little time there was to learn the role in the most productive way. You know, that's something lacking in a lot of dancers today—they know all the tricks of the trade and none of the trade. Meeting a challenge head on is just part of my personality. I was a tomboy when I was a kid. I liked games and competition. Something was already there in my character and I put it to use. Although sometimes I don't realize things like that about myself until they are needed. Things which, unless tapped, might not surface until the need or opportunity arises.

BR: *How much time do you usually like to spend rehearsing a performance of a new role?*

SF: Rehearsal and performance are two entirely different things. When you rehearse, you only need to learn the steps and the music and the shape and dynamics of a piece. You can't "rehearse" a performance.

BR: *You often hear of a dancer rehearsing or working on a role for weeks and weeks, sometimes even for a year. Obviously it can be done.*

SF: I can't imagine what on earth they are doing for all that time or even how they expect such work to benefit a performance. Maybe they are not only memorizing the steps and the music but every single effect they intend to make during a performance. What they wind up doing in that case is finally giving a rehearsal to which the public is invited. You cannot rehearse a performance, because a performance is a process, an enactment that must be done in accordance with the speed and dynamics of the music on a given night. You have to be attuned to your partner. There are a million things that happen in performance that cannot be anticipated in rehearsal. You have to remember everything you did in a performance so you'll know where you were weak and where you were strong—but even that has to be done carefully, because the next time you dance the dynamics of the music and everything else might not dictate that you even attempt the effects you attempted in the previous performance. I know some dancers who if they've rehearsed three pirouettes are going to try and do three in performance, come hell or high water, just because they've rehearsed it. But you should be able to do doubles or quadruples, because it should depend on the dictates of the moment, not on what you've rehearsed. A few weeks ago we were rehearsing *Vienna Waltzes* and we'd just finished the finale so I thought we were through. After I'd already taken off my long practice dress, Mr. Balanchine asked to see my solo. So for the first time I danced my solo just wearing tights and leg warmers. I found myself taking tiny, tiny balancés. It felt so delicate, so beautiful. I said to myself, "Mmm, Farrell. Remember this. It's a nice effect. Something you haven't done before." I was so excited about my discovery. But that evening when I put on the costume and felt the weight of it, I knew I couldn't do those tiny steps because they wouldn't produce enough momentum to move the dress as dramatically as I'd like. I just stored away the memory of that effect and told myself, "Some other time, Farrell. Some other ballet."

BR: *It does seem to us that there are indeed certain effects you can be relied upon to make. For instance, the falls in the Adagio of* Symphony in C.

sf: I don't always do them the same way. How I do them depends on the tension and the speed of the music—how much room there is to fill up. I do like for the first fall to be rather a surprise. I might linger over it a bit. For the next one, well, we've seen it, and so why linger over it? I might linger over the next one because it's the last one we'll see. Or I might increase the lingering in each one—a kind of visual crescendo. I could also reverse the order. It all hinges on the present.

br: *This "lingering," as you call it, makes the fall look like it's being done in slow motion. Do you know how you do it, or is it just an instinctive reaction to the music?*
sf: I don't believe in "instinctive reaction" to music. I may find myself producing an effect sometimes that I didn't plan. But I'm never unaware of it. Afterwards, I'll analyze it and decide if it's worth keeping. Then I'll work on how to amplify or diminish it so it can become part of the palette I have at my disposal. Who knows? Maybe the effect you're talking about in *Symphony in C* I originally did instinctively. But I know exactly how to produce it and how to modify it. The music rises. I slowly take a deep breath—this raises the rib cage and the upper chest. My head is up and tilted back slightly. I turn the head slightly to make a softer line in the neck—falling with the neck and head completely straight looks corpselike to me. Then I fall, and when my partner catches me I exhale slowly. It all happens on one very, very slow breath that must be visible to the audience. Any number of people may have the same "instinctive reaction" to that moment—but it doesn't matter what you feel. You've got to produce something visually and physically to indicate what you feel.

br: *You mentioned earlier about things you've learned about yourself when the need arose. Tell us more about that.*
sf: When I was still sort of new in the company, Jacques d'Amboise and I were dancing his *Irish Fantasy.* After my variation I stood on the side of the stage while Jacques danced his. After the performance a friend said, "Gee, you have the cutest way of licking your lips while you're over there in the corner." I was mortified. The mouth tends to get dry when you dance, so after my variation I'd moistened my lips a bit while standing in place. My friend's remark made me realize something so simple yet so vital: even if you aren't center stage and dancing, you are never invisible. Just that helped me a lot in learning to present a presentable picture on the stage at all times. I was able to take that even further when I danced for Maurice Béjart in arenas and on thrust stages. In those situations, you are always facing some part of the audience. What a challenge that was—knowing you had to be at your best from every angle at every moment. There's no such thing as turning your back to the audience, no hidden moments to

lick your lips as you walk upstage. It reminds me of something Mr. Balanchine says in class: "If you must look in the mirror, make sure what you see is worth looking at." I had to make myself "worth looking at" from all sides—all the time.

BR: *Do you think your experience with Béjart was productive?*
SF: Indeed; I learned a great deal. Needless to say, before I went to Béjart I danced only the best choreography. One masterpiece after another. I know the word "masterpiece" is thrown around like loose change, but nevertheless it's true. Take it or leave it. Anyway, most of Béjart's choreography for women is, well, a bit thin. I'm a performer. I've invested my whole life in performing. I want to look good on the stage, to be interesting to look at. So I was forced, challenged, to make the most of the material given me, to make myself noticed even when I didn't have much to do. I learned how to completely saturate a role, how to get everything out of it. I became more and more conscious of presence and how to maintain it. Just before I went to Brussels, I'd had a bad knee injury while dancing *Swan Lake* with the National Ballet of Canada. I was afraid I might have to have an operation. Fortunately, neither the schedule nor the ballets in Brussels were as strenuous as what I'd been accustomed to at NYCB, so the knee was able to heal itself naturally. Had I been dancing Balanchine works every day, it's unlikely I could have avoided a serious operation. I also had time to experiment. For example, Béjart liked my high, off-balance battement. So he used it frequently. I knew I couldn't keep on doing the same old step over and over again. So I learned to do it with different inflections: faster, slower, changing speeds, and finally with a back bend. When I returned to NYCB, I was able, I think, to add brilliance to such pieces as the Scherzo in "Diamonds" and Act III of *Don Quixote*.

BR: *Were you close to Béjart personally?*
SF: Yes. I have to be close to the choreographer I'm working for. I like Béjart personally. He's an honest man, not at all pretentious, and he is extremely kind and considerate. Although I know his ballets seem pretentious at times.

BR: *Were there differences of opinion? Arguments?*
SF: Once I refused to wear a costume. It was a black body stocking with cutouts so the flesh showed. It was so vulgar, so unfeminine. I told him I couldn't dance in it, and he changed it. I didn't do it to be temperamental, spoiled, or assert my will over the choreographer. I simply could not have walked onto the stage wearing that costume. I never demand selfishly; I demand because I am willing to give everything. If a condition

arises in which I feel my will to give everything has been hampered, then I feel I must speak up.

BR: *You obviously know there's a difference between Balanchine's and Béjart's choreography, yet you always danced Béjart's pieces as conscientiously as you did Balanchine's. Was this difficult?*

SF: No. To have done otherwise would have been pointless and vulgar. I'm a dancer, not a critic; it's not a dancer's place to comment on the choreography she is dancing while she is dancing. That's tasteless and an affront to your own art. I consider myself the servant of the choreographer and the composer, but I am also me. Out of respect for ballet, the choreographer, and myself, I will always give my last ounce of energy to present myself and the choreography I'm given in the best possible light. I couldn't do otherwise. And just for the record, let me add that Béjart has some very nice ballets. His *Le Sacre du Printemps* and *Bolero* are good pieces. Naturally, you always hope for perfect circumstances: ideal choreography, good music, a good conductor, good stage, beautiful costumes. Even that impressive list leaves out the most important thing of all: the commitment a dancer brings to her art. Commitment is neither controlled nor elicited by the choreographer. For that reason, Mr. Balanchine cannot, for all his gifts, create an artist; neither can Mr. Béjart destroy one. You can dance a hundred Balanchine ballets without becoming an artist. Many have. In fact, you can choose easily to hide behind his choreography and never reveal anything of yourself. When Mr. Balanchine first asked me to dance *Ballet Imperial,* I thought the piece was too big for me. I couldn't believe its size, scope, speed, or intricacy. Yet I did everything I could possibly do to make a success of it, and I learned immensely from the experience. It was good for me to leave my pride behind. I learned artistically, too—pacing and control, speed and economy of means in a big ballet; things I was able to apply to other ballets immediately. But whatever the circumstances— no matter what company, which choreographer, whether I think the ballet above or beneath me—I'm not going to wink at the audience to let them in on anything. I'm a big card player, you know. And whatever the hand I'm dealt, I play for blood.

BR: *Did you take Béjart's class?*

SF: Yes, when he taught. It was a good class, precise, thorough. I preferred the men's class; it was stronger. Shortly after we arrived in Brussels, Paul, my husband, made me a tape of music from Balanchine ballets: *Gounod Symphony, The Nutcracker, Symphony in C, Scotch Symphony,* and some other things. Every day after company class we would do our own Balanchine barre and

I would practice my Balanchine ballets. I'd work at refining my technique, my feet—whatever needed work. I worked a great deal on speed—you lose it if you don't use it daily. Stamina, too. You have to work as hard as you can to build and maintain stamina, which you need in order to be feminine on the stage. Who wants to see a woman gasping for breath, sweating, and tapping around in her toe shoes?

BR: *So you practiced your Balanchine repertory in order to be ready to return to NYCB eventually?*
SF: No. I practiced it because I needed it. My body needed it, and I needed it spiritually. Had I worked solely with the idea of coming back to NYCB, that would have been brooding. I don't brood, because it makes the moment you are living in unavailable. A dancer lives in the present. I was working for Béjart, and that's what I did. I insist on getting the most out of whatever conditions I'm working in. Looking forward or backward robs you of the only moment you have: now. However, when the time came to return to NYCB, I was ready.

BR: *Can you tell us something of the circumstances around your coming back to NYCB?*
SF: It's very simple. I went to a performance of NYCB at Saratoga—it was July of 1974. I saw *La Valse* for the first time. I'd danced it many times, but had never seen it from out front. I was terribly moved. I wrote Mr. Balanchine a note which said something like, "As wonderful as it is to watch your ballets, it is more wonderful to dance them. Is this impossible?" It was short and to the point. He sent for me. We met, and the topic of discussion was "When do we get back to work?" Nothing more. Or perhaps I should say nothing less.

BR: *It has been noted elsewhere that other dancers have left NYCB and returned only to find that the company and Mr. Balanchine have left them behind. Yet Mr. Balanchine has continued to compose for you. How do you account for this?*
SF: I've kept myself useful to him.

BR: *How?*
SF: As a dancer becomes more famous or successful, the tendency is to think This is the way I look best or This is what the public expects me to do, then to hold back a little from trying something new. I don't necessarily mean new roles, but new approaches, new ways of moving, steps that aren't your favorite or most comfortable. Even though one holds back only a little, it only takes a little to stifle Mr. Balanchine. He isn't inter-

ested in presenting you the same way every time with no more than a costume change. When you reach the point where you absolutely *must* look a
certain way, you are no longer useful to Balanchine. Remember how wonderful Mimi Paul was in *Valse-Fantasie?* She didn't jump very well, so Mr.
Balanchine choreographed a lot of jumps for her. Because she was willing,
Balanchine brought out a facet of Mimi we had never seen before. And it
was exciting. When he did *Don Quixote* for me I had lousy bourrées, and he
wanted me to improve them. Consequently every act of *Don Quixote* contains a different problem in bourrées. He knows if he makes you do something in front of people, you'll practice and get better, that is if you are
interested in getting better. When you aren't, he isn't interested in you. So
if you care, you practice to achieve ease and fluency in what you can't do.
You must always be willing to put your ego and your reputation on the
line. By not trusting Balanchine, you simply limit yourself.

BR: *Did you ever not trust Mr. Balanchine?*
SF: Yes, once. My second year in the company I had to replace Diana
Adams in the premiere of *Movements for Piano and Orchestra* on less than a
week's notice. And I wasn't even the understudy. Time for the performance came and I just didn't think I was ready. So I said just that to Mr.
Balanchine. His reply was, "My dear, just leave that to me. Let me worry
about that." So I put my fate in his hands—not without, of course, doing
everything I could possibly do myself. He has never failed me. I will always
trust him to present me well, even when he asks me for something I've
never done before.

BR: *Do you ever do any reading to prepare for a new role?*
SF: What does reading have to do with dancing?

BR: *Apparently a lot of people do it in preparing for a role. They read about character, period, costume, manners, and so forth.*
SF: I'm sure they must gather a lot of interesting and useless information. Reading has nothing to do with dancing. It doesn't matter
what I think about a role. What matters is how and when I move. Dancing
is not a translation of words to movement. Actually, I did read about
Nijinsky when I was doing Béjart's ballet. I got all twitchy and neurotic in
my performance because I knew about facts and theories which had no
counterpart or realization in movement. I should have known better.
I tried to read *Don Quixote* while Mr. Balanchine was preparing that ballet.
I read some of the passages about Dulcinea, but I was very busy and I
couldn't concentrate. Then the book seemed to me long-winded and

boring. I knew, though, that anything I needed to know about Dulcinea would be in Balanchine's choreography. If you go with him, you can't go wrong.

BR: *When you know he's planning a new ballet, do you listen to the music he is thinking of using?*
SF: No. I'm a musical person, and if I hear music, naturally I'm going to think of steps and cook up my own ideas and possibilities of what can be done. In the dance I made up when I was a kid to "I Cover the Waterfront," I decided to do a big split kick to a marvelous passage in the music—a big crescendo, drumroll, cymbal crash. . . . Every time I danced that I wasted a lot of time going chassé, chassé, chassé just so I'd be on the right foot for the kick. A complete waste of time. I'm not going to waste a second when I work for Balanchine. I want to come to a ballet fresh and let the choreography happen. That way I don't have to adjust upward or downward because of preconceived notions of my own.

BR: *When the two of you are working together on a new ballet, do you ever make suggestions?*
SF: Only if he asks. Usually such questions have to do with steps, not choreography, because Balanchine choreography does not reside in the steps. The choreography is in the process and the structure. The steps just show it. The steps can be anything. He's proven that dozens of times when he forgets part of a ballet or changes it for a particular dancer. Sometimes he sees me doing something I didn't realize I could do, like dancing off balance. When we were preparing *Don Quixote* he saw I could pirouette, lose my balance, and keep turning without falling. He'd say, "Do that again." I might have broken my neck if he'd just said, "Turn off balance." He just used what he saw, and when I realized what he'd done I was able to bring more variety and color to it. My off-balance turns and battements are much more precarious and dangerous now than when I first began doing them. A lot of the steps in the first part of *Tzigane* are my improvisation. He set it and arranged it, but I dreamed it up. At one point I was standing there in a penchée arabesque and he said, "Yes, dear. We know you can do that. What else can you do? Can you do something from that position?" So I turned the torso over and brought down the arabesque leg in piqué attitude front. Some of the hand gestures and backbend things in *Vienna Waltzes* are mine. When Mr. Balanchine comes to a rehearsal for a new ballet, he knows what he wants in terms of order, structure, how and when things are going to happen. Sometimes, though, maybe he doesn't have a step in mind, or the step he thought of doesn't exactly fit or look

right, and I'll know he's looking around for something. I'll dance up to that point and "fall" into a step or a pose and maybe he'll say, "Hm. Do that again."

BR: *Have there been any significant changes in the way you and Mr. Balanchine work together?*
SF: When he teaches class now, sometimes I think I don't understand him as much as I used to. I try to look more deeply into what he says: his examples, analogies, etc. The deeper you look, the more you find, and the more you find, the harder it is to do. If you go through that process, though, the longer you remember what he says. Before I left the company, I always stood in front in class. People knew he wanted me in front. They would look to see how I did a step. I was the first to do a step down the floor. He wanted me to. He knew I knew what he wanted, and the others expected it. On the rare occasion I might not be in class, no one stood in my place, I'm told. Physically or symbolically, I was there in front. But now—I realize many more things about his class. Many more things to be tried, digested, tested. In attempting to assimilate all that, I am not secure in class. I don't stand in front anymore. I'm embarrassed to go down the floor. I'm the last one to go. But I'm not proud. Class is not a performance. The aim of class, as I now see it, is to attempt to understand Balanchine's ideas and the principles behind them, not to try to perform a step perfectly according to your own standards. Class is the place to make mistakes and fall on your face, not where you prove yourself. But on the stage I know I do what he wants.

BR: *You take yourself pretty seriously, don't you?*
SF: I certainly do. Why do you ask?

BR: *We were just thinking of a remark by a famous ballerina. She said something like "I don't take myself seriously, but I take my work seriously."*
SF: Maybe she was just being witty.

BR: *We don't think so. We think she meant it.*
SF: Maybe she thought she meant it. Maybe the idea works for her, but not for me. I believe pride (not in the arrogant or stupid sense) in oneself is the means by which a performer conveys his respect for the audience. A performance is like a contract between performer and audience. They've paid their money and dressed up to come to the ballet. They've come to be entertained or transported. I have worked all my life to dance as well as I can. It's my pride in my work and my taking myself seriously that makes me want to deliver my best. I have to live up to my end of the bargain. I respect

the public, but I don't let them dictate to me. I love applause, too. Who doesn't? But if I get a lot of applause one night for a quadruple pirouette, I'd be cheating myself and the public by doing no more than repeating night after night what I knew was guaranteed to get applause. You can't let yourself be limited by the audience's expectations. Besides, do four pirouettes two nights in a row and then they want five, and then how far can you go? It all becomes pointless. Anyway, I think a ballerina has to take herself seriously. Although I don't think for a second that I *am* Terpsichore, I am the medium through which she is seen. I hope my seriousness about myself shows the audience my seriousness about my work.

BR: *You've said you know you do what Mr. Balanchine wants onstage. Do you know how much of what you do is what he wants and how much you do is simply what he likes?*
SF: Yes.

BR: *Well?*
SF: Balanchine likes what he wants and wants what he likes. A performance should be seamless. You shouldn't think, This part is Balanchine's idea and this is Farrell's contribution to it. He has done his work and I mine. You should simply see a beautiful ballet danced to beautiful music. I still haven't given you the answer you want, have I?

BR: *No.*
SF: Well, it's all you're going to get.

—from *Ballet Review,* Vol. 7, No. 1, 1978–1979

DAVID DANIEL
A Conversation with Diana Adams

DAVID DANIEL: *You've probably heard it before:"Balanchine can make you into a star." One ballet mother told me there's a saying among her tribe that if your daughter can walk, Balanchine can make her dance. A variant of this belief is often invoked (by people you wouldn't otherwise think nutty) to explain*

Farrell's stature and prominence:"It could've been anyone; he just happened to like Suzanne."

DIANA ADAMS: Yes, I've heard that. It's maddening. I don't believe that people who say it realize what they're saying. They're not just maligning Suzanne and Mr. Balanchine. They're also insulting every other serious artist who ever worked for Balanchine. It's absurd to believe that his personal interest can make you into an artist or a star. Or that the lack of it could prevent you from becoming one. What interests Balanchine is dancing. Anyone who believes "It could've been anyone" should also test his theory by doing what Suzanne did and see what happens. The opportunity is there; it always has been. But the simple fact remains that no one has ever worked for him the way she has. I remember saying to Mine [Nathalie] Gleboff [of the School of American Ballet]—it was toward the end of Suzanne's third year in the company—"No wonder he wants her to do everything. All you have to do is look at a class. She's the only one who does everything he asks."

The only real answer to the question of "Why Suzanne?" was, and still is, right there before your eyes, in her dancing. The public probably dates her career from the period following *Movements for Piano and Orchestra* [1963] when she began to do literally everything. Perhaps it seemed that she'd just happened out of nowhere. But she hadn't. She'd already been in the company for a year and a half. Before that she was a student at the School. He was aware of her from the very beginning because I'd asked him to take a look at her when she came to audition at the School. When she joined the company and began to take his class she proceeded to consume everything he had to say about dancing. Nothing he ever said went by her, even corrections he gave to other dancers. None of this escaped him.

DANIEL: *Were people in the company aware of the kind of work she was doing?*
ADAMS: Very few had any idea of what she was doing until one day everybody realized here was a corps member who was dancing nothing except principal roles and adding one new one after another. Suzanne is a very private person. She's not very sociable or outgoing; she never talked to anyone about her work or ambitions. And her work was so quiet and unostentatious you could've easily not noticed her. People who work hard often do it rather noisily, to attract Balanchine's attention, which, in turn, attracts everyone else's attention. Suzanne didn't work that way, so naturally no one spotted her as someone who was possibly on the way up. They were barely aware that she existed, let alone that she was doing anything unusual. Jacques d'Amboise and I, and a few others who'd worked with

Balanchine for a long time and knew what he admired in a dancer, were aware of the impact she was making on him.

DANIEL: *And of course you were the one responsible for bringing Suzanne to the School in the first place. How did you happen to find her?*
ADAMS: The Ford Foundation gave the School a grant. They were testing a program designed to raise the level of dancing and dance teaching in this country. Their aid made it possible for us to travel about, audition students, and give scholarships for study in their hometowns or at the School. Marian LaCour, Suzanne's teacher at the Cincinnati Conservatory, heard about the program and asked that someone from SAB come and audition her pupils.

DANIEL: *Did Suzanne make an immediate impression on you?*
ADAMS: It's more complicated than that. That's why it was so difficult for me to decide what to do with her. Let me explain. My method of auditioning was to watch a class. I'd begin to eliminate while the kids were at the barre. Sounds cruel, I know, but it's absolutely necessary. By the time they get to the center of the floor you've weeded out those without acceptable feet and body proportions. Then you can concentrate on those remaining to see whether they have any talent for moving. At the barre, I'd looked at Suzanne and ticked off "not scholarship feet."

There was another girl, much stronger than Suzanne, who'd quickly gotten my attention, and I was watching her closely. She could turn well, which I could see even though she was having a bad day. But as the audition went on, I began to see that this girl was naturally awkward. Then when I gave an adagio exercise, Suzanne began to dominate my attention. She was naturally *not* awkward; in fact, she was naturally quite graceful, uncommonly so. You couldn't miss it. Her movement had a special quality: finer, nicer, something extra. This is already something unusual, you see. Grace or the lack of it isn't affected one way or the other by training.

DANIEL: *And besides a gift for moving beautifully?*
ADAMS: Again, something impossible to teach: she could make any step, no matter how difficult, look harmonious and natural. She could make very difficult and sophisticated transitions—from one phrase to another, from a difficult step to an easy one, etc.—and make them look logical and fluent. This is so rare many professional dancers never learn to do it.

DANIEL: *Obviously you're talking about musical talent. The ability to hear music and organize choreography according to the music's accents and gradations of stress.*

ADAMS: Yes. You can develop it to a high degree in someone who already has it. But you can't instill it in anyone.

DANIEL: *Did her technique have any other highlights, say, of physical dexterity that you thought could be profitably developed? Turning, for example, or speed?*

ADAMS: I couldn't tell. That's why she was so perplexing. Her training had obviously been sound. She just seemed to have had so little of it that I couldn't tell what she might be able to do with more. She had no faults that would've needed years of retraining to correct. But she was physically rather weak and lacked the sustaining control of sheer muscular strength. In spite of that, everything she did was very refined; it looked like *dancing*. And yet you couldn't see it from more than ten feet away. I had no way of estimating if there was enough time left to prepare her to dance professionally. She needed strength to make those marvelous qualities visible on a big stage. She was fourteen, which is young, of course, but it's also old in terms of training a really fine dancer. My problem was sort of like wondering how to get a tablecloth onto a table that was already set without moving anything. I didn't know if it could be done. The training at the School of American Ballet is the most stringent in this country (or any other). It's so difficult you have to figure it'll take someone at least two years just to adjust enough to begin to be able to absorb what's going on. If that proved the case with Suzanne she would already be in her late teens or early twenties before she could think about getting started professionally. And that would've been too late to have made it worth the effort.

DANIEL: *We know that she did get to the School. So you took a chance and gave her a scholarship on the basis of her fluency and musical ability?*

ADAMS: Heavens, no. There was a lot to consider. I'd never be reckless with someone's money. I felt accountable, morally and professionally, to everyone: to the youngsters, to SAB, and the Ford Foundation. I didn't want to be responsible for Suzanne's and her mother's moving to New York if Suzanne's prospects for succeeding were no more than dim or questionable. And after all, the aim of the program was very precise: to provide training for dancers who could reasonably expect to become professional.

DANIEL: *How did you reach your decision?*

ADAMS: After the audition I had a long talk with Suzanne's teacher—this was in April—and she told me that Suzanne's mother had already planned to move to New York as soon as the school year was over. This news relieved me. Since they were going anyway, I wouldn't be guilty of sending them on a futile chase. So I decided to have Balanchine look at her once she got to New York under her own steam.

DANIEL: *You didn't gave her a scholarship?*
ADAMS: No. Balanchine did it himself. I only asked him to take a look at her and see what he thought.

DANIEL: *Surely no one in his right mind would've expected you to predict accurately one hundred percent of the time. Was her talent so problematic that you felt you needed another opinion?*
ADAMS: There was no question of whether or not she had talent, but whether we'd found it in time to make it usable. Suzanne presented me with a case I didn't feel equipped to deal with properly. I had never taught youngsters; in fact, I was still dancing. I could look at a student and tell if she had good proportions, well-developed feet, and if, for her age, her physical and musical development were sufficiently advanced for her to benefit from study at SAB. But Suzanne's gifts were out of kilter with her physical development; very advanced in some areas, not so in others. I wanted Balanchine to see her because he had a fund of experience to draw on that I didn't have. I knew he could tell how much more Suzanne could benefit from training. Her gift was too rare to lose if it could be developed in time. That's why I felt his judgment was necessary.

It's always gratifying to know your work is taken as seriously as you'd intended it.

DANIEL: *Afterwards, when Suzanne enrolled at the School, did your relationship become that of mentor and protégée?*
ADAMS: No, I felt my responsibilities to Suzanne and the School were discharged when I delivered her to them. I wasn't a member of the faculty and had no official status at the School. It would've been highly inappropriate for me to have made suggestions to her or to have interfered in any way with her training. She was in the hands of professionals who knew what she needed, and I assumed that her progress would happen if the talent and determination were there.

Remember, too, that Suzanne is not someone who communicates very readily or easily. She's a very reserved person, and I think it's not easy for her to express her feelings and inner thoughts. Whatever the reason, she just doesn't do it. You can be sure she never came to me to unburden herself emotionally. However, I did continue to feel a personal concern for her, knowing, as I did, the pressures of moving to New York and the intensity of her regimen at the School. I kept in touch with her on the basis of my personal affection for her, but otherwise I felt no responsibility to guide her through her training; it simply wasn't my province. And she didn't ask for help either.

DANIEL: *Earlier you spoke of Suzanne's relative weakness for her age with regard to how soon she might begin to benefit from the demands of SAB training. You said it could take two years or more to adjust enough to begin to assimilate profitably. Yet Suzanne spent only a little more than nine months there before she was invited to join the company. How do you account for this?*

ADAMS: Suzanne's tremendous single-mindedness. Nothing deterred her, and she never wavered. She's extraordinarily strong-willed, and she allowed no distractions to interfere with what she had set out to accomplish. She never got sidetracked by boys, sightseeing, the glamour of New York, Broadway shows, imitating other ballerinas, or even going to the ballet, for that matter. She just buckled down and went ahead with her work. She was a smart girl even when was fourteen. I'm not talking about intelligence, but wisdom. She's also able to draw on enormous reserves of strength of character; I think she gets this from her religion. These qualities are the intangibles, things you can't estimate or measure in an audition.

DANIEL: *Did you, through your contact with the teachers at the School, keep apprised of her rate of progress?*

ADAMS: It was common knowledge among the teachers that you only had to tell Suzanne something one time for her to possess it. Her progress was visible from one day to the next.

DANIEL: *Miss [Muriel] Stuart and Mme [Antonina] Tumkovsky both said the same thing: "You only had to mention something to Suzanne once." I take it this is unusual?*

ADAMS: Part of the philosophy behind daily class is that you learn and reinforce through repetition. What the student doesn't "hear" or understand today, she may comprehend tomorrow, the next day, or three months from now. Then, having gotten it, she forgets and must be told again. And in her zeal to incorporate one new correction into her work she may concentrate so hard she'll forget the dozen or so given her before that. That's why the teacher has to repeat everything over and over. But Suzanne never forgot anything. That's why she was such a pleasure to her teachers. When she was given a correction she could incorporate it into her work immediately. She might not achieve it that day or the next, but she never had to be told again. The rate at which she learned was double or triple that of even the most gifted, simply because she lacked the need for repetition. Let me assure you that this fact became quite well known throughout the School.

Later on, when Mr. Balanchine was thinking of doing *Meditation* [1963], he worked with Suzanne a few times. Afterwards he came to me and said, "She's like a stone to lift!" She was still so young she hadn't yet lost her baby fat and slimmed down. I mentioned this to her very gently and subtly, and she lost weight quick as a shot. All it took was a mention.

DANIEL: *The need for repetition—I suppose this is what Balanchine is referring to when he calls his work "pouring water through the sieve"?*
ADAMS: When you teach ballet you have to resign yourself to the fact that every time you walk into a class, yesterday never existed. With Suzanne yesterday wasn't something to be forgotten, but exceeded. This is one of the prime reasons, I think, why working with her was so gratifying to Balanchine. Everything he said to her counted; it made a difference.

DANIEL: *After a few weeks at the School, when she was promoted to Mme [Felia] Doubrovska's Special Class, Suzanne wrote in her diary: "I'm one of the youngest in my class. But my goal is to be the best."*
ADAMS: Anyone could tell you that her progress was due to more than ambition and hard work, not that these things are by any means trivial. But there was a quantitative and qualitative difference in Suzanne's work. I mentioned her single-mindedness before; it's worth mentioning again. She has an ironclad will. She has a keen analytical intelligence and enormous personal power. Once she'd mastered something, a triple pirouette, say, she'd move on to a step she couldn't do as well. You see, already that's unusual. She wouldn't waste valuable time by repeating what she knew would bring a compliment from the teacher. She was always placing her ego at risk. Everybody needs compliments and feedback; Suzanne, though . . . I'm not suggesting that she was unusual in that she lacked the basic human needs we all have, but that she won't spend time giving in to them. She's very stoical and hard-minded toward herself. This reminds me of something Jacques always says about her—that she's always one hundred percent *there;* she makes every second count.

DANIEL: *After she joined the company did she look to you for assistance, or as a role model? Did you coach her in any of the ballets you had danced?*
ADAMS: Oh, no. I delivered her to the School, and they delivered her to Balanchine. That's how it works. The company is Balanchine's province entirely. She was taking his class, and he was telling her everything she needed to know. And no one has ever, ever worked in his class like she did. Nothing he ever said went by her. Balanchine became aware of that very quickly.

DANIEL: *Please tell me more about her work in his class. For years I believed, and I think this is a common belief, that her authority in dancing Balanchine came from some special knowledge she'd gotten from him in private lessons and rehearsals. Suzanne says this is not so, that everything she knows about dancing Balanchine is what she learned in his classes.*

ADAMS: First you must understand something about Balanchine's class. Many people resented his classes because they were so impossibly difficult. I was a real disciple maybe more so than most. I believed every word he said, and yet I used to get furious at his barre. He'd give a combination and I'd mumble to myself, "It can't be done. Nobody can dance that fast." We used to say, as a sort of shared joke among the ballerinas, that the purpose of his class was to make you feel clumsy. Joking like that took the edge off things, even though we were all trying very hard to do what he asked for.

But Suzanne! She just did it—everything—as if she didn't know or care that it was supposed to be difficult. She stood at the barre like a horse wearing blinkers and never once looked around to see what anyone else was doing—never mind whether they found it difficult. And she certainly didn't crack jokes about it. If Balanchine said to do something, she never bothered to consider its difficulty or impossibility. She assumed it was possible, and did it. If he made a suggestion to her she applied it immediately and without question. She didn't hold back, didn't argue. She never even said "But . . ." Now that may not seem unusual to you, but I've seen dancers argue with Balanchine about the correct way to do a plié.

Finally you could see—anybody could see it—watching him teach her was like seeing an engineer tuning and revving up a fantastic new machine. The intensity of her concentration was almost terrifying to watch. He'd give one of his paralyzing combinations; you'd be exhausted even before the music started. But Suzanne would zip through it without batting an eye. She didn't even sweat. Whatever quirky movement or odd rhythm he gave, she'd take it in and feed it back to him. He began to make things harder and harder. Suzanne inhaled and kept going. Balanchine was thrilled to have a dancer like that, and he often said so.

DANIEL: *Surely these qualities and attitudes can't be said to be unique to Farrell in that they could be claimed for her and no one else. Balanchine has developed and nurtured many great artists, all of whom have been willing to lend themselves without stint to following his instructions. And surely ambition and hard work are no more than the daily bread of the successful artist.*

ADAMS: I'm not trying to belittle the accomplishment of any of Balanchine's other dancers. But the combination of Suzanne's qualities, their intensity and degree, these things are unique. No one has ever worked as hard for Balanchine or extended herself to him in the way she has. There's no getting around that fact.

DANIEL: *Do you think that Balanchine might've interpreted Suzanne's devotion to him as a kind of malleability or passivity and that it appealed to the Pygmalion / Svengali side of his nature?*
ADAMS: No, no, no. A thousand times no. There's no Pygmalion/Svengali aspect to Balanchine's character. I can't imagine that passivity would be attractive to any choreographer, certainly not to Balanchine. And no one who has worked as hard as Suzanne did could ever be called passive.

DANIEL: *Suzanne has said to me that it's not enough for a dancer merely to follow Balanchine's instruction, that the dancer herself must take charge of what she does. She says, "Style is what you are." Therefore she considers it her task to do what he asks for, then take it a step further to make it her own, and to achieve her originality within the compass of how he likes dancing to look. This brings up the paramount question for every NYCB dancer: what Balanchine wants. Suzanne addresses this issue by distinguishing a difference between what Balanchine says and what Balanchine wants. To do the former, she has said, all you need is a sound set of eardrums; his directions are so precise you don't even need to be a trained dancer to follow them. I once asked her how you could tell when someone was doing "what Balanchine says." And she said, "Easy. Some look like they're dancing in a plaster cast. Others may look like they've got lockjaw. When you see someone doing something exactly the same way every time, you know they're doing exactly what Balanchine said; just that and no more." Of course she believes that a dancer must do what he says, but as a means of achieving what he wants, not as an end in itself. To her, what he wants is to see what is special in each dancer. When you've shown him that, she says, you've engaged him at the highest level of his imagination; you've given him something to compose. Otherwise, you're asking Balanchine to reinvent out of his own memory and experience; to do what she calls "rearranging furniture."*
ADAMS: She has earned the right to say that, and it's an accurate description of what she has done. However, it's no small feat to do what Balanchine says. But there you are—it's her willingness to dare and take something a step further; I think this hits at the very heart of why she became so important to Balanchine. You see, I never liked to move quickly. Balanchine used to get exasperated with me and tell me I was resisting him. I'd say, "But you don't understand. I'm a lyric dancer." And he'd say, "No you're not. You're a lazy dancer."

DANIEL: *Tell me more about that. How did your own estimate of yourself run counter to Balanchine's expectations of you?*

ADAMS: I was tall, and he liked my dancing because it was legible and musical. He wanted me to extend my range by combining it with the speediness of an allegro dancer. But I didn't think of myself as a virtuoso dancer, and didn't feel comfortable in that range. I didn't even like to dance the fast finales of ballets I had adagio parts in.

DANIEL: *You said earlier that it was Suzanne's adagio that first caught your eye. So I guess she's a natural adagio dancer. Did she have to work extra hard to develop allegro speed and brilliance?*

ADAMS: There's more to it than that. Suzanne is unusual for the sheer quantity of her physical gifts. Yes, she's a natural adagio dancer, but she's also naturally very speedy. She could have gone either way, but she didn't.

DANIEL: *What do you mean—"could have gone either way"?*

ADAMS: I'm not talking about Suzanne's physical gifts now but her attitude, the temperament she brings to dancing. Almost any dancer, regardless of her gifts, begins her career by accepting a limitation about herself. By the time she has discovered what she is (or wants to be) in terms of her physique and personality, she has typed herself as a soubrette, or an allegro, lyric, dramatic, adagio, or whatever, kind of dancer; she has decided that's that. Then she grooms herself according to that image and seeks roles in which she can express it. It's only natural, and everybody does it. Suzanne didn't; she bypassed the idea of self-classification according to type as if the idea never existed, which meant that every ounce of her talent was available to Balanchine. She refused to limit herself. Whatever Balanchine thought was possible, she thought was possible. She never said something wasn't her type of role, that it was too fast, too slow, too hard, too anything. There wasn't anything she wouldn't risk for Balanchine. It happens all the time to him: a girl says she wants to do more, tells him she wants to develop; he gives her a role, and she says it isn't her cup of tea. Simply because once a dancer decides who and what she is, she won't budge. But Suzanne kept going. Finally, there wasn't anything she couldn't do. Her range is unheard of.

I remember once, a few years after I'd stopped dancing, I remarked to Balanchine that in one week Suzanne had danced ballets from the repertories of virtually every important dancer he'd ever worked with, besides dancing pieces he'd made for her. He just sort of nodded and said, "Well, you see, dear, Suzanne never resisted."

DANIEL: *In the spring of Suzanne's second year in the company, Balanchine composed* Movements for Piano and Orchestra *for you. You fell ill a few days before the premiere. Balanchine didn't believe the ballet could go on without you. The status of the ballet went into limbo for a few days. Finally, Jacques, the male lead, persuaded Balanchine to let him teach your part to Suzanne. He taught her as much as he could remember, but he simply didn't know all of your part. He asked you for help; you agreed, even though you were confined to bed and forbidden by your doctor to move. Suzanne and Jacques arrived at your house to find you lying in bed. . . .*

ADAMS: I wasn't in bed. I was lying on the couch in the front room. But no, I wasn't supposed to move about at all. It was extraordinary how we managed to get that ballet put together. I wouldn't have believed it could be done. Many of the movements were things Jacques and I did together; he had already taught her all of that. Thank God for Jacques. I taught her the stuff he didn't know: the girl's solos, instructions for her head and arms, pointe work.

DANIEL: *How did you teach it if you couldn't move? How could you show her what to do?*

ADAMS: I described it verbally and used my hands. Dancers use a kind of shorthand—literally—to show things to each other. We know what we mean; a revolution of the finger is "pirouette," you show pointe work with the hands. Then there's the vocabulary—croisé, effacé, etc. Even so, I must say I kept thinking that this ballet, so difficult, so far outside balletic conventions, would be impossible to convey that way. I didn't see how it could be done unless I could get up and show it. If you've seen *Movements* you know how hopelessly inadequate words like "glissade" and "pas de bourrée" are. Nevertheless, we pressed on. I'd lie there and give counts and tell them which hand or foot to start on. And finally I began to see we were going to get through it. Of course there were other terrific problems. The parquet floor was so slippery Suzanne couldn't put on her pointe shoes, so she had to memorize the pointe work separately and then graft it onto the rest later. The room was so small she had to memorize distances and directions, too—you know, downstage about ten feet, left for eight feet, turn upside down, etc.

DANIEL: *Did she seem flustered at the prospect of all this? That same week she was getting ready to dance the premiere of John Taras' Arcade [1963], preparing your role in* Liebeslieder Walzer *[1960], and dancing all her corps parts. And she was still more or less a full-time high school student.*

ADAMS: Suzanne is shy, but the moment she starts dancing something else takes over. She was very quick and smart that day. I was very impressed with her for several reasons. For one thing, she didn't have much experience with Stravinsky or that quirky kind of movement. And for another, she had to learn the ballet in a fragmented way, then she had to glue everything together. But a few days later, when I was able to move about, I went to check it out at the dress rehearsal for Stravinsky and she had it letter-perfect.

DANIEL: *How many sessions did she and Jacques have with you?*
ADAMS: We did it in one session, about forty-five minutes. I must give a lot of credit to Jacques. It couldn't have been done without him. A lot of the ballet was double work, and he had learned what I was doing because he was partnering me. He wasn't required to know my part; a lot of partners wouldn't have known anything except their own part. But Jacques did know, and he knew the structure of the entire ballet. He understood its style and what the piece was supposed to look like.

DANIEL: *It seems to me that the simple logistics of playing the tape back and forth to find the right place in the music would've taken longer than forty-five minutes. The music was relatively new and somewhat hard to hear; it's Stravinsky's late, "difficult," serial style. Even today some people think it sounds like a giant cigar box full of blips and squiggles.*
ADAMS: We didn't have a tape. Like you said, the music was relatively new, and I don't think it had been recorded. If it had, we didn't have a copy. Jacques and I counted out loud. We knew it more or less by heart. Of course, knowing Balanchine's structural counts helped, too. His choreography is always such an astute analysis of the score you can't help but remember the music.

DANIEL: *In the months and years immediately following the premiere of* Movements, *as one of her contemporaries put it, "Wherever you looked, there was Suzanne." She was still a member of the corps de ballet [she was promoted to the rank of principal dancer following the 1965 spring season], but she danced only lead parts from then on, and, as you've noted, she kept adding one new one after another. During the 1964–1965 season, for example, she danced in ninety of the company's ninety-five performances; on every program that didn't have* Harlequinade *on the bill. She began to enjoy an enormous public and critical success. But there was another response to her, too; people—that is, reviewers (some), the public (but not all), many in the company itself—seemed to sniff heresy in the air. You could attribute this reaction to a number of things, but there was never any one thing you could put your finger on that would explain it. It wasn't just her youth and relative inexperience, or the frequency with which she appeared in hallowed roles or that many viewers (and dancers) were baffled when she danced parts they thought should be assigned to another "type" of dancer. She had other strikes against her, too: her manner was unlike a debutante's in that she didn't seem grateful or diffident toward the audience: she didn't take her cues from the audience before pulling out her big effects, neither did she acknowledge their applause with even bigger ones; she showed nothing in her manner, however implicitly, that asked or waited for affirmation. The combination of all this threw everything off balance. She was seen as uppity; she lacked credentials, if not credibility. She had violated the rules of apprenticeship and apostolicity. And for those who saw Farrell's presence on Balanchine's stage in that light, it all added up to something even worse: this child had somehow beguiled Balanchine, whose works they'd seen performed by the great dancers of the day—the likes of Diana Adams, Melissa Hayden, Allegra Kent, Tanaquil LeClercq, Maria Tallchief, Violette Verdy, Patricia Wilde. . . . When you walked into the theater during those years, words like "presume" and "has gone too far this time" hung in the air like motes; you didn't need to ask of whom they were said. One of the major New York daily papers devoted space to a flurry of mail from viewers who argued whether or not Farrell deserved such attention, if Balanchine's concentration on her kept older, more experienced artists off the stage, and if his interest in her precluded his developing other young dancers. In private, people said Balanchine was capricious and that Farrell was an Eve Harrington.*

ADAMS: I don't think I danced anymore after *Movements,* at least not enough to speak of, so I wasn't around the company itself very much. Even at a distance, yes, I began to hear about all this and was very aware of what was happening. All you heard was flak and more flak about what she was dancing, how often she danced, and of people's resentment of Balanchine's attentions to her. I grew very concerned for her; it's one thing to be a loner but quite another to become ostracized and isolated the way she was. People often said she was aloof and formidable; well, she was. But she hadn't changed. She was exactly the same way when she was fourteen. She's simply not a sociable person. I don't think she likes to be around people very much. Her manner doesn't invite contact or communication. But nobody deserves what Suzanne got. The jealousy and resentment she has had to live with is the most terrible kind there is. Not that there's a good kind.

Now of course no one blossoms into a completely finished artist overnight; there was still work to be done—there always is, no matter who you are. But Suzanne was no raw recruit onto whom Balanchine was pinning fond hopes. It wasn't as if he found her attractive, gave her a lot of stuff to do, and then just hoped she could manage it somehow. She didn't spring out of nowhere.

In the end, though, it's one of the oldest stories in the book. She was a dramatically original artist, and no one knew what to make of her. They saw her going beyond old limitations, and I guess they thought she was breaking the rules, too. But she wasn't; she was reaffirming them in a new way. She confused people. I remember talking to her early in her career when the critics were beginning to write about her. She was stunned because they'd begun to say, in a disapproving, dismissive way, that she was cold, distant, and reserved. I could sympathize with her here. They used to say it about me, too, but I probably deserved it; I never had her courage. I remember her saying in a puzzled way, "I think I'm rather flamboyant." And of course she was right. Although there was also something about her dancing that was reserved and private. Naturally the critics were confused; they thought you had to be one or the other. Suzanne was both. She gives you everything physically and at the same time seems to savor some secret for herself. It's a marvelous, fascinating quality. I think it has to do with what dancing means to her. For anyone to work as hard as she does, some part of it has to be for herself alone. And I think it's a remarkable act of grace and dignity that she doesn't involve the audience in these personal considerations. She withholds nothing physically from her dancing, and what she seems to withhold personally isn't the absence of anything so much as it is the presence of a personal mystery.

DANIEL: *Like you said earlier, "No wonder he wants her to do everything."*
ADAMS: Let me add one more thing. I hope I haven't made Suzanne sound like a completely self-made woman, and that the only reason she has succeeded is that she worked hard. She succeeded because she brought all those qualities of character and determination to serve what was to begin with an exceptional gift. Hard work alone could not have produced an artist of Suzanne's radiance.

—from *Ballet Review*, Winter 1982

Suzanne Farrell

The simultaneities of contrasts that Farrell combines in her performing are present in her very being. Her head is small, her coloring fair-to-delicate, her eyes large and gently angled. Her mouth, narrow and neat, has a prominent overbite that serves to emphasize it definitely and delicately. Her exceptionally long and fine neck lifts in harmonious opposition to her fine-boned narrow shoulders and her long narrow arms and hands. Her torso with its natural waist and wide hips contrasts with her long, smoothly tapering, but nowhere muscle-bound, legs. Her ample (even at her thinnest) thighs taper at her legs, funnellike, steadily to her feet (her calf is just noticeable enough to define itself without undue accentuation). And oh, her feet! Their tapering continuation of her leg is clear and steady, until it reaches her metatarsal and toes; it's then that you note the extralong plunge that her straight, strong length of toes gives her pointes. What makes the length of the tip of her pointes so unique is their straightness. Other ballerinas have toes similarly long, but I've never seen any so long maintain so vertical a front to the curve. Just as Farrell's legs taper smoothly from her hip to her toes without a noticeable accentuation at the calf, so her foot (on pointe) tapers and curves (long, from ankle to tiptoe) without an accentuated bulge or shift of a knuckle. Thus the phenomenal strengths that Farrell manifests seem to come not from obvious curves of muscles bulging with power, but from some armature structure at the core of a tapering, delicate, pale frame. I do not mean to imply that Farrell is wraithlike or spectral in her delicacy. Farrell is not pencil slim. Her naturally wide hips can become plumply full when she's in a weight-gaining state of health. In her trimmest state Farrell still has noticeably broad hips that give her thigh a distinctly full rise, and in her weightier forms her midrift silhouette might more appropriately describe our notions of a classical odalisque rather than a classical ballerina. But changing many of our notions about ballet seems one of Farrell's happiest tasks; and watching her pirouette, penché, or kick with untold facility and playful power makes you see beyond the steps and shapes you expect her to accomplish and leaves you awestruck by the newfound extremes and advancements she reaches instead.

So while a funnel-tapered thigh and wide hips may not become the permanent standard of ballerina build, neither are they at all detrimental to

Farrell's rightness onstage. The "girl" who so often comes to mind when one observes the ballerina onstage is more likely the "young woman" when Farrell is there in all her un-muscle-bound, woman-wide physicality. Setting and defining as she does her personal standards of physical aesthetics, Farrell is formally captivating even when she's slightly overweight—only in certain ruffly, poofy tutus does her amplitude around the middle (thighs and waist) go beyond the acceptable.

Without swallowing whole the cliché reduction that ballet is woman, there is still something specially revealing about Farrell's womanliness in Balanchine's ballets. If "quintessential" is too exclusive a word, then perhaps "exemplary" defines the concentration, complexity, and comfort Farrell gives in performing Balanchine. While I mean neither to claim that she's ideal in every Balanchine role nor to limit her powers only to Balanchine, it's more important to recognize the exceptions than to dwell on them. Farrell became the ballerina she is under Balanchine's tutelage (a dual process worked both in his ballets and in his classes), and combining her double development with her own physical and mental gifts, she is a Balanchine ballerina. The qualifiers, though, should be read not as a restriction on her scope but rather as a pedigree of her advanced abilities. She can do more than the average ballerina not only because her gifts are far above average but also because her Balanchinian challenges bred her that way.

When she's performing her feats of legerdecorps, Farrell is exercising her own part in Balanchine's enriched school of ballet. Looking at *Meditation,* the pas d'action from *Don Quixote,* and *Chaconne,* you can see early, middle, and late Farrell work, respectively; and when you pause to study the respective designs Balanchine created with Farrell ("on" Farrell or "for" Farrell, if you prefer) you note, granting the shades of difference in their musical (and dramatic) moods, their interrelationships of poses, lifts, and steps. In all three views, Farrell is dressed in a chiffon shift, and while each one of these dances calls in some part for duet work, what you see predominantly is Farrell—long, articulate, and strong even while she's lifted by, leaning on, or carried by her partner. Balanchine's well-loved effacé positions are described and held by Farrell with an astonishing breadth (those wide hips—lifted and opened to fullness—serve to dramatize Balanchine's intended design). The consciousness and far-reaching abandon that Farrell imparts to her reposes (in a partner's grasp) or to her poses (self-supported) depict at once an exposed vulnerability and a potent heroism. Naive eyes swept up in a compassion for the drama of this Tchaikovskian vision or this Dulcinean ideal or this Euridice might see a figure driven by or surrendered to her destiny, but another viewer (and listener) might also recognize a Farrell courageously trusting and taking chances with her remarkable technique. Fair Maiden Farrell, as these three roles might be categorized, not only trusts her partner and expands in poses, she also moves unsupported in solos and in so doing executes turns, kicks, and jumps with few of the standard preparatory moves that we are accustomed to seeing from other (i.e., other than NYCB) dancers. And the signature Balanchinian method for streamlining or actively de-emphasizing preparations is practical because of dancers like Farrell. Watch her in enchaînements such as those in *Chaconne,* where she steps, piqué, into a manège of soutenu turns, demi-plié on pointe, and finishes with a specialty all her own, a multiple (unheard of!/?) soutenu twirl. Or watch her in the same role enrich a series of relevé (to full pointe) grand battement strokes by sinking, plumb-line perfect, a demi-plié shock-absorber-retard move to her supporting leg just as the kick reaches its apex, and then notice her effortlessly maintain her vertical strength as she lowers (not drops!) her kick back down again.

Chaconne is good evidence for a "dancer before the vehicle" argument. There are some scholars, I suppose, who would not list it as a Farrell-created role, since Balanchine set the dances elsewhere (Hamburg and Paris) before he mounted this set on his own company. Still, until I see some other dancer perform the part with anything like Farrell's finesse, you'll have a hard time unconvincing me that this Euridice moves her distinctive (choreographic) ways precisely because she came to our light through Farrell's prismatic medium. Likewise, the similarity to the poses of lifts in *Meditation* and *Don Quixote* makes me want to admire Balanchine's invention while recognizing Farrell's specific, physical inspiration. Minuter, less specific touches in *Chaconne* strike me as Farrell notes, whether or not they were originally conceived for her. There is the profile look of her figure in the foot-spragging walk she does with her escort Martins. Coming as it does just after Martins has picked her up and put her down (twice)—the first time she's lifted in tight fifth and lands in sharp échappé second; the next reverses the invention and snaps her échappé position closed and sets down again in clean fifth— Farrell's slouching walk then underscores the formal, calculated playfulness of the lifts with the relaxed, informal locomotions of the strides.

The fullest range of Balanchine's kinetic dynamics gets quintessentially shaped through Farrell's protean delivery. Fresh, enriching details appear all through her performances of "her" roles, and here is one of her most delectable: Just before she sets into her striding slouch, she prepares us for its changed tone by sinking a dippy demi-plié while still in fifth on pointe and shading it all with a slight side-bending frisson before she sashays to another part of the stage. In her parallel-positioned knuckled-over prancing (where the foot spragging has a kind of throwaway elegance—similar to a gown's train's or a fur wrap's dragging over the ground), Farrell becomes a specific presentation of a notably Balanchinean look. The same specification as recognition comes when she finishes the driven delicacies of her enchaînements in the chaconne proper with a simple turned-in, one-leg-flexed stance, with her head lowered in harmony with one hand going to rest at her side after passing through a finishing move in front of her upper body. Once arrived at through this subsiding gesture, her pose—a *croisé*, plainly relaxed attitude—makes me see the design of this stance (where the one flexed and turned-in knee rests, rocked over, on pointe), so signature Balanchine, as a resetting of a maiden's or goddess's posture from classical Greek sculpture. Perhaps it's the Euridice theme or the Temple of Amor setting, but very likely it's Farrell's pale-pink-marble coloring in her fluted Grecian tunic, and the exquisite line of the back of her neck to the back of her lowered head in profile, that make me read this paused, posing woman in terms of the asymmetrically flexed gesture of the legs that relaxes the thigh, tilts the hips, leans the torso, and softens the shoulders, and recognize it as a fleshed-out insight to the theory of archetypal *déesse* design. Farrell's confidence in repose makes us conscious of this pose, and her spragging-prancing (which is essentially a croisé/effacé alternating view of the same pose) details two casual yet typical instances where Farrell's distinctive hips and thighs and Balanchine's use of them exemplify both broken and newly set traditions. A combination of youthful innocence and powerful articulation catalyzes in Farrell and shows us Balanchine and ballet in their essential particular perspectives.

Farrell is an original who establishes standards and makes advances for the art she champions. While her astounding accomplishments put us in awe of her, her seemingly frail pastel delicacy soothes us to our ease. Her remarkable impact comes from a process of counteractions. The immediacy of her attack is both playful and powerful. Similarly, while her performing concentration rests in her music she still finds moments to go for the step—she's a mistress of rubato. And her "robbing of time" often means pouring out energy to whirl through yet another revolution of an already multiple pirouette, or to "hold" the pinnacle pose of a grand battement while she throws back her head and swathes its reclining air of abandon with the embellishment of a preening port de bras. See all the playful and bold considerations with which she executes the scherzo in *Diamonds,* all the sustained clear poses and balances, the sudden reversals, the momentum-gathering turns—all telling of incredible ease while they arrive at newfound extremes of potency.

The radiance that Farrell exudes is of a luminosity that no single source could effect. Take her moment in the finale of *Diamonds* when out of a supported multiple pirouette she is guided around in penchée arabesque pose. As if the extraordinary mechanism of her turning weren't hypnotic and amazing enough, when she blossoms the gossamer funnel of her pirouette into an arabesque and then tips into the penchée pose that lengthens in two directions at once as she extends an épaulé arm (to establish a second arabesque), we not only see a wonderful feat of turning and balance, we're deeply touched by the expression of sweet ecstasy that shines out from her uplifted gaze and gently tilted head. Concentrated there in her fair, warm coloring, her velvety gray eyes, and her fine, overbite-clarified smile (which gives a rabbitlike tweak to her kitten's face) is a kind of literal highlight: Farrell riding the crest of her art, her talent, and her fame.

A parallel yet contrasting sample of her ability to gauge and vary her effects comes at a similar moment in the Adagio of *Symphony in C*. There too she moves from supported pirouette, arms en couronne, into an arabesque-to-épaulé-penché pose promenade. And in this similarly designed move she also uses the upcurved angle and tilt of her head to present a central concentrating focus to her move, and her face does look radiant, but it's a different ecstasy. To Tchaikovsky's crescendoing finale she shows the move more lightheaded and bright with her smile; to Bizet's sustained, echoing tensions she expresses more dreamy intensities with her gaze. Both instances show how the move—where the pirouette seems the preparation for the promenade—elicits a "surfacing" lift of her head from the depth of the plunge; but in the former her face expresses "whee!" to the "ride" of the promenade, while in the latter it seems to exhale the release of a sigh.

Attenuating the length and sustaining the breadth of her moves are special concerns of Farrell's, and their potency begets increased concentration from her audience. A related example is the long, deep effacé penchée arabesque she calculates in *Symphony in C*. With the additional axis described by her outstretched arms (her lunging partner supports her by the hands), she extends and grows in three directions at once. Her descending torso and her ascending leg cleave through the line described by her balance-pole port de bras, and she details the directions of three dimensions in long, clean strokes. But she finishes her radial calculation with the curling hook of a move—at what seems the very bottom of her tilting descent, she continues the bowing line of her torso with a curving nod of her head that aims to touch her knee. This finishing element exposes the especially exquisite length at the back of her neck and acts like the lode-origin of an endlessly ongoing arc. The golden spiral constructed according to the golden mean couldn't be of more harmonious energy. When she begins the "recovery" that brings her up again, she arises in reverse concentrated order: She unhooks her head, then upcurves her spine, and finally relowers her arabesque leg. If the results of her intense concentration weren't so finely shaped, her calculated process might be overwhelmingly fatiguing to watch.

The full scope of Farrell's contributions to the school of ballet in general and to the oeuvre of Balanchine in particular is not likely to be grasped by the dance world until the distance of time allows us to scrutinize carefully what now nearly dazzles overwhelmingly. To be more fully understood, Farrell's effect needs to settle—which means, in its way, being brought down to earth from the heights she tends to travel. Undeniable Farrell facts and indelible Farrell features will continue to filter down through to ballet's less enlightened academies as long as Farrell continues to accomplish and acclaim Balanchine's theories, though by the time their impact is felt, even in reasonable proportion to Farrell's performing contribution, she may well have stopped performing. Historians will probably try to accumulate and evaluate her widespread importance, but if they haven't seen her dance, they won't have a clue to what they've missed.

—from *Ballet Review,* Vol. 7, No. 4, 1978–1979

FIRST PERSON

CECIL BEATON

First Designs

*Famous as a fashion photographer and theater designer (*My Fair Lady*), the ultra-chic Cecil Beaton (1904–1980) also designed a number of ballets. Among them were several for Frederick Ashton—*Apparitions *and the Fonteyn-Nureyev vehicle* Marguerite and Armand—*and, for New York City Ballet,* Illuminations, Picnic at Tintagel, *and Balanchine's* Swan Lake. *Beaton won Academy Awards for the film versions of both* My Fair Lady *and* Gigi.

I t was during de Basil's 1936 season at Covent Garden and just after the premiere of *Symphonie Fantastique* that I had my first taste of what life was like back-stage with a company of Russian dancers. I had been called in to photograph the new ballet after a matinée performance, and I had the first glimpse of "ballet temperament" as I was soon to know it to my cost, when, later in the same season, I was asked to design the sets and costumes for a new ballet.

I knew by experience that photo-calls are always extremely unpopular with any theatrical company. To the performers the whole thing always appears to be a waste of precious moments of relaxation, and the sense of anticlimax that must follow the final fall of the curtain makes the dancers both sulky and uncooperative. To add to the general atmosphere of irritation and impatience on this particular occasion, there had been some trouble with the stage-hands (who, of course, were cursing me and longing to get off to their tea), and my first sight of Massine on that afternoon was of a being transfigured by fury. Always highly nervous and taut, the dancer was white as a sheet, and his body, lips, and legs were trembling uncontrollably in spasms of terrifying rage. Somehow or other I got through the ordeal of photographing this highly complicated ballet and was left wondering whether life with the Russian Ballet was always so exhausting. I was soon to learn.

When Boris Kochno approached me and asked whether I would like to do the decor and costumes for a ballet I was stunned and delighted. Apart from anything else, I knew that I was the first English designer to have been asked to work with a Russian company. This was not my first attempt at ballet decor, for earlier that year I had designed the scenery and costumes for a ballet devised by Osbert Sitwell and Frederick Ashton for C. B. Cochran's revue *Follow the Sun*. It was called *The First Shoot: a Tragedy* and starred the American actress and dancer Claire Luce.

The ballet, in one scene, lasted ten minutes, and all the action took place in a glade or clearing of a wood during an Edwardian shooting party which consisted of some fifteen or twenty Edwardian notables, Austrian counts with American wives, Parsee merchants, and all the rest of that lost world. . . . The women were tweed-clad, engine-turned, all except our prima ballerina Lady de Fontenoy, who according to the synopsis was formerly Connie Winsome, the famous leading lady from Daly's or the Gaiety, who had married a year or two previously Lord de Fontenoy, a rich young nobleman, late of the Horse Guards. The other leading dancer in our ballet was "Lord Charles Canterbury, the comparatively poor but fascinating younger son of the Duke of Dashton."

Osbert Sitwell, explaining his ballet, said, "We want to observe in everything that *faint* line of parodied resemblance to the *Lac des Cygnes* (pheasant feather opposed to swans), though that, I see, is more to be done by sudden bursts of idiot mirth in the middle of melancholy, love-soaked passages, than by the clothes. Anyhow, we must make it magnificent, and not to be forgotten!"

To my surprise the whole thing had turned out to be delightfully straightforward. To begin with I had worked out the general scheme with Frederick Ashton on a piece of notepaper, sketching in the dancers in conventional ballet skirts. But the choreographer said at once, "No tutus!" I simply removed the skirts on the designs, and the effect was charming.

I was fortunate in that the costumes were made by Madame Karinska, the dressmaker who had made tutus for all the Diaghilev dancers, and for Pavlova herself. Karinska has that rare genius for being able to interpret an artist's sketches in such a way as to produce exactly the effect required, while at the same time making costumes in which dancers can perform without the freedom of their movements being in any way hampered.

When I saw what she had made of my sketches, I was both astonished and delighted. The caped coats and suits of plus-fours worn by the male members of the balletic shoot were of theatrically interpreted tweeds which Karinska fabricated with large painted checks and bold stripes, emphasised by heavy stitching in coarse wool. On the dresses worn by the chorus, who represented pheasants, she stitched pieces of mica (her own idea) to reproduce the sheen of feathers.

From first to last things went smoothly in the creation of this ballet, and the result, as far as I was concerned, was very gratifying. I may say that it in no way prepared me for what was to come.

The moment chosen for the creation of my ballet, *Le Pavillon,* was very inauspicious so far as the de Basil company was concerned. All the dancers were thoroughly exhausted by the work on *Symphonie Fantastique,* and they had not been given any break to recover their strength. *Pavillon* was a little trifle, with choreography by David Lichine and music by Borodin. It had no specific theme, showing merely a collection of dancers representing birds, flowers, butterflies, and other insects disporting themselves in a glade, apparently attracted by the lights glittering from a small glass pavilion on a hillock in the centre of a wood.

In a setting of hydrangea blues, I designed the dancers' dresses on a basis of underskirts in many shades of clear blue. Over these they were to wear gauze skirts, wings and flowers in all the brightest colours imaginable, but when Kochno saw the half-finished dresses hanging in the wardrobe, a positive riot of blue, he was enchanted with the effect, and said that they must be left as they were. Being new to the business and uncertain of my own judgment I foolishly said "Yes," and the final result on the stage was just blue upon blue upon blue. The setting, too, was a failure, for during the time it was being painted in the workshops I agreed to its being painted in flat washes instead of having the rough texture of the original designs, and I altered certain other things without referring to my sketches. I have since learned that, having achieved the desired effect on paper, it is imperative to refer constantly to the original, and to be extremely chary of last-minute alterations.

From the very first the corps de ballet were as uncooperative as they could be. They absolutely refused to wear the headdresses that I had designed for them—little caps upon which were sewn feathers, antennae, and flower petals, saying, quite unreasonably as I discovered, that wearing them they could not hear the music. When they discovered that they were expected to wear bird-wings over their tutus you would have thought that it was the end of the world. I pleaded with them in French, and they replied by talking among themselves in rapid Russian. It was like fighting feathers. The very second my back was turned they did their own designing, pulling everything to pieces and altering my ideas to suit themselves. Lichine remained neutral but was completely evasive, and instead of explaining to me that it was hard for a dancer to turn pirouettes wearing the high collar that I had designed, he appeared quite suddenly on the stage in the lowest décolleté.

I gave up the fight in the end, but I had learnt my lesson.

There was, however, one exception among the dancers, one for whom I have always had a soft spot—Irina Baronova. With her lovely *boule-de-suif* quality which makes her a kind of placid descendant of Lopokova, she is a genuine artist who always respects the rules of the game. On this, and on every other occasion, I found her enchanting to deal with.

On its first showing at Covent Garden *Le Pavillon* was given the place of honour in the middle of the program. This was a great mistake, for it was essentially an "unimportant" ballet, and should have come at the beginning of the evening. One ballet critic described it the next morning as "a little trifle in Oxford and Cambridge blue"—which it was.

I was in a state of almost suicidal depression about the whole experience. I realised that I should have stuck to my guns and insisted upon my original designs for the costumes being carried out. It was then that, quite unconsciously, I took a most unethical step. Having appealed to de Basil, who refused to allow any changes in the costumes after the first night, I went to my friend Karinska and said, "You know how I planned this. I will pay for any alterations myself, but will you help me to carry them out?" She agreed, and immediately got to work on the brilliant bird-wings, flowers, and overskirts. When they were ready she surreptitiously removed the costumes from the dressing-rooms, completed the alterations, and returned them only ten minutes before the ballet was due to start. I enjoyed watching the consternation among the corps de ballet when they saw their new costumes. Some, in fury, tried to wrench from the skirts the glittering bird-wings that had been added. But Madame Karinska had done her work thoroughly; the new additions were made with the idea of a long tour in view and were fastened securely. It was too late. The ballet dancers must go on-stage looking the way I wanted them to look. I hurried through the pass door to the back of the dress circle, saw the curtain rise and my original conception of the ballet come to life. The difference in atmosphere was remarkable. The superimposed colours had brought the stage to life; as the different dancers were introduced, a variety and novelty that had been lacking saved the ballet from monotony. I beamed with satisfaction. But not for long. De Basil was also in the audience that evening, and when he saw the transformation his fury knew no bounds. He became white with rage—even whiter than usual. I was sent for; the Russian stage-manager intimated to me on the way to the office that *scandall*—the Russian word which means every kind of appalling "to-do"—had well and truly broken loose. My reception was glacial. I was told, among other things, that I had behaved in a disgracefully undisciplined manner—quite unlike that expected of an English gentleman—and that my conduct as a whole had been totally unprofessional. But I did not care. I had salvaged my own integrity as a designer. In the future I need not be ashamed at the appearance of my ballet.

—from *Ballet*, 1951

IRENE CASTLE

Dancing with Vernon

The partnership of Vernon (1887–1918) and Irene (1893–1969) Castle was a sensational success in America from 1912 to 1916. They created a number of dance crazes—among them the one-step and the fox-trot—and taught them through their Castle House dancing school. On Broadway they appeared in a series of musical shows, ending with Irving Berlin's Watch Your Step *in 1914. Two years later, Vernon enlisted in the RAF and was killed in a training accident. Their story was recreated by Fred Astaire and Ginger Rogers in the ninth of their films together,* The Story of Vernon and Irene Castle. *Perhaps Irene Castle's most famous moment came when she bobbed her hair, influencing millions of women across the nation.*

By the fall of 1913 America had gone absolutely dance-mad. The whole nation seemed to be divided into two equal forces, those who were for it and those who were against it, and even the champions of the cause had to compromise to stay in business. When "ragtime" swept the country the one-step came right along with it, killing off the waltz and the two-step. A list of the popular dances of the time reads like a table of contents for a zoo, with the Turkey-Trot, the Grizzly Bear, the Bunny Hug, the Camel Walk, and the Lame Duck.

The battle of the newspapers began. Half of them condemned the new dances as not only unsightly, but downright immoral. When I had my appendix out the doctors got into the act. Half of them tried to prove that dancing had damaged my appendix and caused the attack. The rest of them stoutly defended both my appendix and my dancing. Dancing was good clean exercise, they said, and definitely therapeutic.

One newspaper conducted a survey of leading ministers and bishops of many denominations and then printed their cautious replies on the ethics of dancing. Most of them denied seeing such dances and they were about equally divided as to whether or not it was a sin.

If it was a sin, half the population of the large cities was in danger. New places were opening daily to cater to the businessmen who dropped everything early in the afternoon and trotted off to the nearest dance parlor for a lap or two around the floor. The practice began to cut into working hours and a prominent magazine editor fired fifteen girls for doing the Turkey Trot during lunch hour.

One of my favorite newspaper stories concerns the New Jersey girl who was hauled into court for singing "Everybody's Doing It Now" and Turkey-Trotting down the street in a residential neighborhood. When the case came to trial a small riot ensued as the defense attorney insisted on singing the song and the spectators joined in when he reached the chorus. When the jury requested an encore the lawyer sang it again and did a fast Turkey Trot in front of the judge's bench, to great applause. The jury found her not guilty.

It was against the law to dance too close to your partner at the time and bouncers in restaurants tapped their patrons on the shoulder when they get closer than nine inches. One inventor went so far as to try to market a pair of metal belts with a nine-inch bar connecting them, to teach people how to dance with the right space between them.

The one big target for the crusaders was the tango. I suppose its opponents objected to the man bending the woman over backwards and peering into her eyes with a smoldering passionate look.

As I look back on the tango battle, it doesn't seem possible that so many people could have been so worked up over something so very foolish, but I can remember quite vividly the furor it caused. A public school in Brooklyn split down the middle over the tango when one educator suggested adding it to the curriculum. Another promoter arranged to have a folk dance called the *furlana* done in front of the pope, hoping to substitute it for the tango in America with papal sanction. There were no takers in jazz-smitten New York and the attempt brought an icy denial from the Vatican.

I am more amazed to find, in going back over the newspapers of the day, that in the midst of the battle Vernon and I were never attacked. I think now it was because both sides regarded us as their champions. We were clean-cut; we were married and when we danced there was nothing suggestive about it. We made dancing look like the fun it was and so gradually we became a middle ground both sides could accept.

Gilbert Seldes, one of the outstanding critics of the time, spoke of Vernon and me this way:

That these two, years ago, determined the course dancing should take is incontestable. They were decisive characters, like Boileau in French poetry and Berlin in ragtime; for they understood, absorbed, and transformed everything known of dancing up to that time and out of it made something beautiful and new. Vernon Castle, it is possible, was the better dancer of the two; in addition to the beauty of his dancing he had inventiveness, he anticipated things of 1923 with his rigid body and his evolutions on his heel; but if he were the greater, his finest creation was Irene.

No one else has ever given exactly that sense of being freely perfect, of moving without effort and without will, in more than accord, in absolute identity with music. There was always something unimpassioned, cool not cold, in her abandon; it was certainly the least sensual dancing in the world; the whole appeal was visual. It was as if the eye following her graceful motion across a stage was gratified by its own orbit, and found a sensuous pleasure in the ease of her line, in the disembodied lightness of her footfalls in the careless slope of her lovely shoulders. It was not—it seemed not to be—intelligent dancing; however trained, it was still intuitive. She danced from the shoulders down, the straight scapular supports of her head were at the same time the balances on which her exquisitely poised body rested. There were no steps, no tricks, no stunts. There was only dancing, and it was all that one ever dreamed of flight, with wings poised, and swooping gently down to rest.

I have a great fondness for that description because it describes the way it was, or at least the way I felt when I danced. Vernon *did* invent the steps, often on the spur of the moment, and by keeping my eyes firmly fixed on the stud button of his dress shirt could anticipate every move he was going to make and we made together, floating around the floor like two persons sharing the same mind. It was intuitive dancing, to be sure, because I never practiced if I could help it, and if it had been difficult, I'm sure I never would have had the patience to carry on with it.

If I can criticize his criticism, there is one thing he left out, a very important thing, the sense of humor that permeated all our dancing, the great sense of bubbling joy we shared together when we danced. It was impossible for us to be serious when we were dancing. If Vernon had ever looked into my eyes with smoldering passion during the tango, we would have both burst out laughing.

—from *Castles in the Air,* 1958

NINETTE DE VALOIS

Escape from Holland

Dame Ninette de Valois (1898–2001) was born Edris Stannus in County Wicklow, Ireland. She was a popular child dancer in England, then joined Diaghilev's Ballets Russes in 1926 and left two years later, with the ambition of creating a classical ballet company in England. With the support of Lilian Baylis, head of the Old Vic, she formed the Vic-Wells company, or Sadler's Wells, which after the war became the Royal Ballet; she also founded the Royal Ballet School. Known to everyone as "Madam," she remained a formidable presence at the Royal and throughout the dance world until her death. Her most successful efforts as a choreographer were Job, The Rake's Progress, *and* Checkmate.

It was in the early spring of 1940 that the British Council and the Foreign Office decided to present Holland with a little cultural propaganda in the form of the Sadler's Wells Ballet. The late Lord Lloyd, a great ballet lover, and head of the British Council at that time, was the prime mover in the plan. The venture was considered important enough to justify the call-up due for any male dancers that spring being deferred for two months.

On May 4 we embarked for Rotterdam. We were the only occupants of a small Dutch boat; we travelled tourist and were crowded into as small a space as possible. The dining table was squeezed into a large cabin, with bunks from floor to ceiling; it was here that the male members of the ballet were to sleep. We women had similar sleeping accommodation, but were spared the canteen trimmings. The first-class saloons, cabins, and deck promenades were all barricaded off, an arrangement that made it impossible for us to move freely about the boat. It was an un-adventurous journey made mainly by night; at boat-drill just before dark we saw the gloomy spectacle of sunken trawlers with their funnels and masts still above water.

Rotterdam greeted us with scintillating sunshine setting off its Dutch cleanliness in the clear morning air. It was, I think, a national holiday: cyclists seemed to be everywhere, with circlets of tulips round their necks and entwined across the handlebars of their bicycles. Life seemed leisurely, and the comforts of life exceedingly plentiful. Our Dutch agents, the Beeks, packed us into a motor bus for the thirty-minute drive to The Hague, where we were to live during the entire ten days' tour of Holland.

It was not unlike coming out of a long, deep sleep: for a brief space of time we had emerged from a country responding to the rhythm of war. Our English nights were governed by an intense blackout, made bearable only by the weapon of the torch, which must be shone on the ground, just a little ahead of each footstep taken. The days were given to coping with rations, restrictions, and over-crowding; endless bill-posters appeared saying either: "Have you got your gas-mask with you?" or "Is your journey really necessary?"

"Lovely Holland," we thought, with its bright lights that made our eyes blink at such unaccustomed brilliance. "Beautiful food!" we exclaimed, at the plates of deep pink ham and the smooth thin-cut slices of Dutch cheese: the butter left us dazed and the sugar ecstatic.

It is our opening night at the charming Hague theatre. How friendly is the audience, and how startling the sight of the Opera House foyer! I find myself suddenly confronted with the delicious formality of full evening dress, a convention already discarded in England to the lumber room of our nostalgic past. Full, voluminous evening dresses in rich, heavy silks, encase Dutch dowagers; they crown their smooth decorous hair-styles with suitable tiaras, and long, luxurious, white kid gloves stretch their way opulently up their well-upholstered arms. Shy, plump daughters in virginal tulle accompany these worthy ladies, escorted by prosperous-looking Dutch fathers, resplendent in tails. Standing at the corner of the foyer I suddenly find myself very near tears: I have been long enough in the country to recognize the outward signs of courage everywhere. I know that every thinking Dutch man and woman is aware that life can change overnight for them, and in a way that years of war may not change England. Tonight they paid their tribute, and express their innermost thoughts for England and her welfare: no matter that these feelings are expressed prosaically in tulle, silk, tiaras, and immaculate kid gloves.

A little later in the evening the signs of friendship take on a more poetic note: at the close of the performance a heavy shower of tulip petals falls on the dancers from the roof of the theatre: the cascade seems without end; one imagines those orderly fields of tulips outside breaking ranks and casting themselves from the skies in a gesture of friendly self-abandon . . . the scene has become, with time, a curtain-call that is a shining moment in memory, kept bright and alight by the spirit that prompted it.

Each day found us in our bus travelling along interminably long and straight roads, on our way to some other town where we were due to give a performance: we returned to The Hague, by the same means, in the very early hours of the morning. As the week progressed the general situation appeared to worsen, and this was manifested in a tension and a general rest-lessness, not to mention alarming rumour. From conversations with the Dutch themselves, it was difficult to make out anything; there was either a fatalistic shrug of the shoulders, or an optimistic allusion to the history of the first world war.

I received my first shock the night that we played in Hengelo. This was a border town situated in a part of the country that, in case of invasion, was not to be defended. The performance was preceded by a dinner given by that indefatigable institution—the English-Netherlands Society—and I had been invited to be their guest of honour. Just before dinner I was informed by the now very anxious Beeks that all railways were closed. I asked the chair-man, a Dutchman, if he considered that it would be wiser for us to depart immediately after the performance. (The British Council had arranged for us to stay the night in this town as it was hours by car from The Hague.) He assured me that there was no need to worry, the closing of the railways in towns so near the German border was a very common occurrence. Never-theless, I decided on a short night's rest and we left very early in the morn-ing for The Hague.

The week progressed; anxiety mounted; the British Government fell; scraps of news were picked up on the radios, but still we continued to carry out our mission. The Dutch still gave us their full attention and showed, at every performance, their enthusiastic appreciation. At the lovely little the-atre of the Phillips' factory the entire audience stood to applaud us at the end of the performance . . . and once more the tulip petals rained down on the dancers' heads.

It is Thursday, May 9; our objective was Arnhem. On our way the bus passed by a great number of people trudging in the opposite direction . . . peasants dragging children and carrying large bundles of belongings. We gave our performance, and once more, with its steady defiance of gathering clouds, the English-Netherlands Society entertained me before the show. The chairman, a charming Dutch Baroness, was accompanied by an enchant-ing small daughter. This eight-year-old child had a distinction and person-ality rare in one so young. Her mother spoke of the child's wish to become a dancer. I remember my reaction: that here a star was born—no matter in what guise. In an ankle-length party dress this child presented me with a bouquet of red tulips; but the tulips are over-shadowed by the elfin grace of the donor and the small face lit up by its promise of character, at present shining forth from a pair of sensitive dancing eyes. I can see her as clearly today in that indelible impression of her youthful yesterday as the world sees her now in the full flowering of her young womanhood: her name is Audrey Hepburn.

Concerning our Dutch adventure, memory has now become a torrent of pinpoint flashbacks: even trivial incidents press urgently for a hearing: their influence is such that it compels me to record some of these happenings in chronological order.

Earlier in our Arnhem day I had sat with the wardrobe mistress, and, to help her, had patched most carefully one of the legs of Frederick Ashton's *Façade* trousers: it was a large, carefully sewn patch, just over the knee, for it was executed with a due regard for the importance of its longevity. However, I have never known how long my patch did last, or what Germanic dancing knee may eventually have worn it out. I never saw the garment again.

Supper after the Arnhem performance: I can recall how hastily we ate it and that it consisted of large plates of wonderful ham and generous helpings of salad. I can remember looking out of a window, straining my eyes across the flat countryside to the not very distant horizon, which was German territory. We were bidden to hurry and to board the waiting bus so as to start our long trek back to The Hague with all possible speed. The drive was ominous: the roads full of the Dutch populace deciding on a move towards the coast, and full equally of Dutch soldiers tramping in the opposite direction to take up posts of more sinister significance.

It was a dark night that seemed preoccupied with heralding in Holland's dark tomorrow.

By 3 a.m. we were back at The Hague. By 4 a.m. I was awakened by a sharp fusillade. From my window, in that cold touch of dawn on Friday, May 10, I could discern two planes seemingly trying to get above each other: even then I did not recognize a dogfight in progress: I returned to bed faintly irritated by what I presumed to be Dutch early morning manœuvres. But there was no more sleep, for the noise increased. I arose, donned a dressing-gown, and went out into the passage. The hotel was slightly astir, and I ran into a member of the Company. I expressed some annoyance with Dutch preoccupation with war, and with one of those masterly examples of British understatement, Fanny Spicer made the following reply: "Excuse me, Miss de Valois, but I really think it must be the Germans." I went down to the hall porter who left me in no doubt as to the nature of the noise. Holland, he said, had been invaded, and, he added rather cynically, "You are in for a long stay in my country."

The rest of that day is fragmentary in my memory: for instance, the arrest of the large German blonde in our hotel, and her descent, an imposing Valkyrie, down the main stairs escorted by two small Dutch soldiers. We were all delighted with our uninhibited view from chairs in the hall lounge! For some days we had eyed her with curiosity in the hotel dining-room. She did not even deign to look our way; one felt that she somehow considered our existence on earth to be no more than a matter of momentary irritation. She had reminded me of a rhododendron in full bloom: now, between two stocky grey-clad figures, I witnessed the fall of her over-luscious petals.

Somewhere about 10 a.m. I was able to get out and visit the British Embassy, where I was greeted with an atmosphere of kindliness and patience, not to mention an intense pre-occupation with bonfires. There were bonfires in the grounds and bonfires in all the fireplaces throughout the reception and secretarial rooms. A modest number of serene, grey-haired ladies of the chancellery appeared to accept the invasion as they might an ambassadorial garden party; both cases naturally meant much extra work to do—with the garden party there would be numerous domestic details to attend to, with an invasion there was the constant feeding of the bonfires with documents and correspondence ensuring that only efficiently charred remains would eventually become the property of the enemy. I returned to the hotel to await, with assumed patience and no bonfires to distract me, news of how and when we might hope to get away.

On my return I heard that early in the morning some of the Company, huddled round a wireless set, had made great efforts to get the BBC. They eventually succeeded. England, though, was living according to plan: over the radio was to be heard a bright, female voice coaxing the British housewife to stick to her daily dozen. "Up—down—up—down—little bounce—little bounce—little bounce—up!" she merrily chanted. Only a little time earlier I had chased the Company off the hotel roof where they had gone to witness a fine exhibition of the little bounce—the German parachutists coming down in the immediate surroundings of the town; and on the same roof had been found the following leaflet, fluttering down in its thousands over The Hague from enemy aircraft:

> Strong German troop units have surrounded the city. Resistance is of no use. Germany does not fight your country but Great Britain. In order to continue this battle the German Army has been forced to penetrate your country. The German Army protects the life and goods of every peace-loving citizen. However, the German troops will punish every deed of violence committed by the population with a death sentence. Every citizen is obliged to carry on with his work as usual. Thus he will serve the interests of his own nation.

A curious lightening in the town's atmosphere came about midday. The morning had been grey and stormy; the loneliness of the deserted streets in sharp contrast to the noise of the dogfights in the air, shrapnel descending, and military motor-bicycles and lorries rushing through the town to other destinations. Now the sun was out and the cafés filled up; the Dutch bicycle traffic was suddenly in evidence again in its full force. I sat in the hotel's pavement café with Lambert and Ashton—but we were driven inside by a stray bullet which, ricocheting unpleasantly from the pavement, passed between our heads and crashed through the plate glass of the café window directly behind us. The bullet had come from a German plane that had just swooped low over the little square.

Friday night found a tired company sleeping anywhere on the ground floor of the hotel and up the stairs, for the position was deteriorating rapidly. By Saturday morning German planes were roaring over the town, dipping low and sending us all continually to the ground, flat on our faces: the destruction of Rotterdam had started; we were aware that this town was only thirty minutes by car from The Hague and about the same number of seconds by plane. Rotterdam had a death roll of twenty thousand inhabitants, The Hague merely got the occasional bomb that was meant for its unhappy neighbour. We gauged the devastating, systematic horror of the attack from the unceasing roar of the planes, passing over in their close, sinister formation.

We were by now confined to the hotel; it was no longer safe outside and we had been informed by the Embassy that we must be ready to leave at a moment's notice. Just before the situation had deteriorated so sharply, I had been once more to the Embassy to collect some money for the journey; I saw Lord Chichester, who was one of the secretaries, and he gave me all that he had—£25. We discussed the situation and studied the map on the wall, which showed how far the Germans had penetrated by land at that moment. During the day several false alarms followed as to when and how we were to leave. At one moment we were informed that we would leave in a fishing smack from Scheveningen, a seaside resort very near The Hague. The fishing smack would be under the command of Admiral Dickens, and, as a matter of interest, we were informed that he was a grandson of Charles Dickens. Nothing came of this plan (which held all the ingredients of a first-class musical comedy), for by the time the crazy venture was decided on, the German parachutists had landed in a series of buoyant little bounces on our precious beach—thus effectively cutting us off from a taste of the Admiral's seamanship. I met him at the end of the war and he confirmed the authenticity of the story, one that, till then, I had never quite believed!

Late on Saturday afternoon our devoted concert agents came to see us and said that we must immediately make ourselves packets of food; we were also told that one tiny hand suitcase was all that we could take with us. Our main luggage and all personal belongings were to be left behind. It was odd how much consternation this caused! I parted with a silk dressing-gown with more misery than my evening dress, for I knew which of the two I would find the more useful in the ensuing years. Ashton was distraught about his brand-new dinner jacket. I decided that this expensive item of the male wardrobe was large enough for me to wear over my light summer coat and skirt—so one solitary dinner jacket saw England again. We cut our own sandwiches in the hotel kitchen, for the Dutch staff had long left the hotel in a last bid to get back to their homes and families.

Late in the afternoon a man arrived at the hotel and announced brusquely that there was a bus at the door and that everyone was to board it immediately—it was our last chance to get away. It was a horrible moment: I had received strict instructions from the Embassy that on no account was I to accept any form of transport other than that arranged through them. I could see the mute appeal on the still stoically disciplined faces of the Company, yet I had to tell him (with outer conviction but no inner courage) that the Company could not go without the sanction of the Embassy. He asked me irritably what I was waiting for as he was from the Embassy; in fact he happened to be the military attaché. I snapped back, equally irritably, that I could not possibly know that as he was in mufti: I added that he could have said so at the beginning, and saved an argument. Tempers were short by now.

The bus awaited us, complete with an armed guard. It was about six o'clock in the afternoon when we set off for an unknown destination. The deserted streets had about them an unearthly silence and we passed many houses with rifles protruding from their windows. We were all very quiet, for we had just taken a sad farewell of our kindly Dutch agents who had shown such selfless devotion towards the problem of our safety. They stood on the pavement with Lord Chichester waving us good-bye: brave people now facing a future that we had undoubtedly made very much more difficult for them: it was known to everyone how hard they had worked to assist the escape of the English artists.

I see a small square, the bus enters it and turns sharply to the right so as to continue its way down a long street leading out of the town. On the pavement in the middle of the square, and facing this street, I notice that a slab of paving stone has been removed, and a hole dug in the earth beneath. In this hole squats a Dutch soldier, with his rifle pointed down the street—a sniper keeping his lonely vigil. Opposite, on one of the corner houses, hangs a German plane . . . it hangs nose down over the crushed façade of the house—its great wings hopelessly disabled and its body burnt out. Its helplessness has the spent strength of a huge dead eagle: in contrast the motionless little soldier awaiting the coming of his country's enemies appears stolidly alive; he is silent expectancy—in a town suddenly hushed to a silence born of an unbearable supense.

On and on goes the bus; we leave The Hague far behind us and make for the flat open country. It gets dark: our sandwiches are eaten and we are reduced to watching a long stretch of road and listening to our own thoughts. Great fires light the distant horizon on all sides; the bus continues its monotonous hesitant journey across the immeasurable flatness of the landscape.

Suddenly we are in a wood: the bus comes to a halt among thick trees and we are told to disembark, and stick together. Just before we left The Hague, I decided that, in the event of getting mixed up with other refugees, the Company should be divided into seven groups, each group in charge of a leader who, on all occasions concerned with embarking and disembarking, would announce when his party was complete. Constant Lambert, Frederick Ashton, John Sullivan (our stage director), Claude Newman, Joy Newton, Robert Helpmann, and I were the leaders. Leaving the bus in these woods of Velsen on this dark night we hold our second roll-call and thus keep together as we follow a soldier towards a dark, heavily shuttered house. Inside is chaos: the house is crammed with refugees asleep on all available chairs, beds, and sofas. On the floor of various rooms our tired groups fling themselves down to fall into weary sleep until morning.

The next morning was bright and sunny; we were given some breakfast and left to our own devices. No one could give us any news or any instructions—it was still a game of waiting. We crowded round a wireless set and got the BBC. In England they were interviewing refugees who had just arrived from Holland on the first boats to get away. Highly coloured pictures were painted of the invasion by those who had reached England. The Company was upset: they thought of their friends and relatives and the worry that the exaggerated stories would cause them. I hinted that when they got back they should remember this incident for the sake of others who might still be left behind.

It was strange what that lovely spring day did to change the atmosphere of the previous night. By early afternoon this country house, with its proud peacocks, its artificial lake complete with swans, seemed far removed, in its wooded seclusion, from the turmoil of the rest of the country; our boys even played an impromptu football match in the grounds against the Dutch soldiers guarding us.

We spent a peaceful Sunday afternoon in a small, solid, Dutch country house with its numerous signs of secure family life. I wondered for how many years, on other such Sunday evenings, its owners had strolled by the lake throwing pieces of good Dutch bread to the glistening swans. Suddenly I wanted to know about the family; who they were and where they had gone, so hastily abandoning the pattern of their smooth lives. Did they know of the onslaught on their private rooms—whose furnishings were instinct with the intimate reminders of family friends and close relations? Did they realize that in their cool woods ugly buses drunkenly leant against the trees— sharply snapping off branches that might be in their way? My questions returned to me unanswered . . . there was no one with the necessary information, and worse, no one who cared.

Night came again, bringing back, as in a bad illness, all the fears of the night before considerably heightened now by their air of faint familiarity. At dusk the house was shuttered, and we were all bidden to go indoors. Planes and bombs were now on the increase and as the night descended we were in almost complete darkness. In the late afternoon we had been given a small meal, and we realized now that food had run out completely. We knew that it had been the last meal possible for us to obtain on Dutch soil; it had cost, anyway, the greater part of my precious £25. Once darkness had fallen the front door was continually opened to admit more and more refugees. The atmosphere was stifling, and it was difficult to find anywhere to sit down. One group of refugees wore pyjama-like convict clothes and their heads were shaven. They were Poles, who had escaped from some German labour camp. They settled themselves in a corner of one room and there in the dark they sang Polish folk-songs—until our frayed nerves unkindly wished them all back from whence they came.

About midnight we were given an order to form into long lines and to hang on to each other's shoulders; we were then told to file out into the night as our group-names were called out. "Vic-Wells" was a group-name by itself. In our hastily formed and checked smaller groups, "Vic-Wells" marched out into the dark woods as one long crocodile, with a Dutch soldier in charge. We came to our bus, packed in, and joined on to the rest of the silent convoy. There were no lights: at the head of the convoy was a motor bike with a small headlight and the same at the rear. The surrounding night sounded like fireworks at the Crystal Palace, with the appropriate accompanying flashes in the sky showing through the trees.

We now started on a slow and nerve-racking journey. Stops were frequent; they occurred whenever there was a sharp exchange of fire, either in the skies directly over us or amidst the surrounding woods. When this occurred everyone had to get down on to the floor of the bus to avoid stray bullets, shrapnel, or a possible bomb. Once more the comparative silence would return: then on again through the night at snail's pace, with the fiercely burning fires in the distance angrily illuminating the landscape.

We reached the port of Ymuiden about two hours before day-break: it must have been approximately two o'clock. A cargo boat awaited us and we were instructed to join the queue of refugees lined up to go on board. The queue stretched down the quayside, like a fat depressing snake, hugging the edge of the quay as if it drew some comfort from getting as close as possible to the dark waters. At the tail end were the refugees from Amsterdam: a monotonous message was relayed, continuously, to those further up the line—"Will some of the men come to the rear and help the Amsterdam folk with their luggage?" No one moved; the reason was obvious; no one else had been allowed to take any luggage with them! In front of me there stood what looked like a small, gloomy British commercial traveller, hunched in his

Burberry with his hat pulled well down over his ears; all at once he swung round and, charged with a sudden sense of life, he bawled in reply: "Tell the folk from Amsterdam to look after their own b—— luggage." Peace followed this undoubtedly practical suggestion.

But peace was limited to the Amsterdam folk and their luggage: dawn showed faint signs of breaking as we anxiously watched the slow progress of the queue; more anxiously still did our eyes wander to the occasional plane swooping down over the harbour, belching fire at anything it considered worth hitting: our precious cargo boat seemed an easy and tempting target. At last we reached the gangway, where anxious sailors, knowing the boat must sail before daylight, even at the expense of its human freight, hurried us on. "Vic-Wells this way," we heard again, and our numbed senses responded: mine though were suddenly crudely alert, for "this way" was the one way that I most dreaded—we had to descend a single gangway, leading down into the hold of the ship. Down however we all went, and the hold of that ship is a picture that will never fade.

Lit by a few hurricane lamps it held about four hundred people; close together they lay, or sat, on a thick layer of straw that covered the entire flooring. Sanitary arrangements were primitively set up in corners behind rough canvas hangings. At the far end was a rough couch, softly lit by an overhanging lamp, and partly encircled with some canvas draperies . . . on this lay an expectant mother in the charge of two nurses . . . everything was stilled in me for a fleeting moment, for the couch uncannily suggested a manger.

I stood at the foot of the gangway with my group, counting the other groups as they descended. Behind me a monotonous voice kept crying out "Fred—Fred—Fred," and in a sudden fit of irritation I turned round. My impatience was swiftly transformed into a feeling of deep compassion: for the man crying out so shamelessly on that cruel chaotic night for his lost friend was blind.

The Company settled themselves in the straw in the dimly-lit hold; Frederick Ashton checked each group with me. The congestion was such that it was necessary to walk across out-stretched bodies, fumbling for a clear space on which to place one's foot. I lay down, at last, in the new dinner jacket, and Fred handed me two handfuls of straw to make a pillow; I felt like a horse about to be fed.

A hazardous journey started across the North Sea that lasted for fifteen hours. About mid-morning we were allowed up on deck for some fresh air; by then two graceful, silver grey escorting destroyers were making wide patrolling circles around us. Sea breezes though for us did not last long; enemy aircraft were spotted overhead and we were ordered back to the hold.

We reached Harwich just before dark on the evening of that never-to-be-forgotten Whit Monday. Already docked was the ship that brought Queen Wilhelmina and the British Embassy over, and two fussy tugs steamed to and fro between us and the mainland. It was suddenly all over—and we were on shore. Tea and sandwiches were pressed on us by the WVS helpers, and a train waited to take us to London.

We reached the London terminus about 1 a.m. on the Tuesday morning: a silent group of relations and friends met us. The homecoming was quiet.

—from *Come Dance with Me*, 1957

MICHEL FOKINE
Les Sylphides

Michel Fokine (1880–1942) was born in St. Petersburg, studied at the Imperial school, and quickly became a star in the Maryinsky company, premier danseur in 1904, and the frequent partner of Anna Pavlova. He was also choreographing and teaching through these early years, developing the expressive style—relying more on plastique than on virtuosity—that would characterize what was seen as his revolutionary approach to classical ballet. (It's generally acknowledged that he was influenced by Isadora Duncan's 1904 performances in St. Petersburg.) His best known early works are the famous solo he created for Pavlova in 1905, The Dying Swan, Le Pavillon d'Armide, *and* Chopiniana, *the first version of what would become* Les Sylphides. *It was the ballets he made for Sergei Diaghilev's Ballets Russes that brought him worldwide fame: above all,* The Polovtsian Dances *from* Prince Igor, The Firebird, Le Spectre de la Rose, Petrouchka, Le Carnaval, Schéhérazade, *and of course the revised* Sylphides, *almost all of them featuring Nijinsky. (Fokine himself danced the Prince in* Firebird *opposite Karsavina, his favorite ballerina.) He broke with Diaghilev over Nijinsky's becoming a choreographer, and never regained his former place as the world's leading choreographer. Throughout the thirties and forties—first in Europe, then in America—he worked with many companies, creating new works (of which the most successful was* Le Coq d'Or) *and restaging his classics. When Ballet Theatre was born in 1940, he was on hand as the company's resident choreographer and to restage* Les Sylphides, *which opened the company's first season and many seasons to come. His last ballet,* Helen of Troy, *was unfinished at the time of his death. Beginning in 1921, he taught in New York, working with a number of important young dancers (see page 1234 for Pauline Koner's account), remaining a great name but never regaining his former eminence.*

The series of solo numbers and ensembles to short pieces by Chopin for the "Second *Chopiniana*" were orchestrated by Maurice Keller. I also included in the ballet the Waltz orchestrated by Alexandre Glazounov for the first *Chopiniana*. In order to save money for the charity organization, the costumes were produced by an especially economical method. From old ballets we selected the longest skirts worn by the tallest dancers and then added additional skirts, the alterations being made in our apartment under Vera's [Fokina] supervision.

On some occasions, the tickets for charity performances were sold in our apartment, and Vera—later, when she began to dance the leading roles in my ballets—managed to get a thousand rubles for the loges. But despite such prices for tickets, we still kept the expenses down to an absolute minimum.

The total amount involved in the costume reforms for *Chopiniana* (*Les Sylphides*) was twenty-five rubles. The shape of those costumes was a repetition of the contour of Bakst's costume sketched for Pavlova the previous year. The skirts were attached to the old bodices. The result was that the *corps de ballet* looked like no other that had ever been seen before.

I was surrounded by twenty-three Taglionis. I inspected their coiffures to make sure that they all had their hair parted in the middle. In later years I noticed that ballerinas in some companies tried to distinguish themselves by a differently colored chaplet on their heads. All the other dancers would wear pink wreaths, while the ballerina wore white or blue. Pavlova also distinguished herself from the rest, but not by the color of her wreath. She was an ardent devotee of my reforms and continuously asked whether her chaplet were placed correctly and if her hair style looked right.

The cast was glorious: Anna Pavlova, Olga Preobrajenska, Tamara Karsavina, and Vaslav Nijinsky. Pavlova flew across the entire stage during the Mazurka. If one measured this flight in terms of inches, it actually would not be particularly high; many other dancers jump higher. But Pavlova's position in mid-air, her slim body—in short, her talent—consisted in her ability to create the impression not of jumping but of flying through the air. Pavlova had mastered the difference between jumping and soaring, which is something that cannot be taught.

Karsavina performed in the Waltz scene. I feel that the dancing in *Les Sylphides* was especially suited to her talent. She did not possess either the slimness or the lightness of Pavlova, but in *Les Sylphides* she demonstrated that rare romanticism which I seldom was able to evoke from other performers.

Preobrajenska performed the Prelude. In this I made use of her exceptional sense of balance. She would just freeze on the toes of one foot, and in a dance almost without jumps was able to project the feeling of ethereality. One of the shortcomings of this wonderful dancer was her inclination to improvise. After dancing the Prelude exactly as I had created it, she repeated it for an encore entirely differently. She had very often done this in the old ballets, but in *Les Sylphides* I felt it was out of place. There were so many dances in that ballet that, if everyone repeated his number, there would be no concept left of the ballet as a unit.

I should like to emphasize the inadmissibility of improvisation in my ballets. To me a ballet is a complete creation and not a series of numbers, and each part is connected with the others. This is not a theory; I feel that way, for it is my approach to creation.

I did not plan to have a different ending for each dance. It just so happened that in the Mazurka Pavlova ran off the stage; in the Waltz duet she left with a *pas de bourrée* on toes; Karsavina terminated her number with a final pirouette and stopped on toes with her back to the audience; Nijinsky, after his jump, fell on one knee, with his hand extended as if to a vision; Preobrajenska froze on toes facing the audience as if imploring the orchestra to play still more softly.

All these were different endings. In her improvisation, Preobrajenska left the stage on toes, in the same manner as Pavlova was to do immediately after. Of course her improvisation did not help Pavlova, or the ballet as a whole.

I believe that his role in *Les Sylphides* was one of Nijinsky's best roles.

This ballet contains no plot whatsoever. It was the first abstract ballet. But still I would describe Nijinsky's participation in it as a role and not a part, because it did not consist merely of a series of steps. He was not a "jumper" in it, but the personification of a poetic vision. The role calls for a youth, a dreamer, attracted to the better things in life. It is absolutely impossible to describe the meaning of this impersonation and of this ballet. On numerous occasions I have had the opportunity to write the synopsis of *Les Sylphides*. I have known many critics who had a greater mastery of words, and who described it better than I did. I have read many descriptions of this ballet in programs compiled by experts—and yet I have never been able to find a satisfactory verbal elucidation of this ballet.

When I call attention to the "improvements" added to this ballet during the last thirty years, I realize that many dancers and ballet masters have not understood it either. Yet it seems too easy. Of course at times the dance is capable of expressing clearly that which is not expressible in words. But to understand, to grasp the hidden meaning of the dance—for this, one requires a special spiritual quality.

I know that there are cultured people who know the history of art and who are familiar with what the greatest minds have said on this subject, who are capable of inundating the listener with quotations—but it is plain to me that the dance has passed them by. They have not assimilated, they fail to understand the movements or gestures.

It was just the opposite with Nijinsky. I definitely know that, when I began to work with Nijinsky, he had read nothing about art, nor had he given the matter any thought. When he was a student, he would stand and watch me exercise in the rehearsal hall for a long time. While resting between exercises and combinations, I carried on a conversation with him. I knew he was a very talented boy, for at the time I was a beginning teacher and a young dancer, and was greatly disturbed that the school gave no instruction on the history and theory of art. When I talked to Nijinsky I asked him whether he was interested in this problem and in reading. No, he was not interested, and he had not yet read anything about art. Even later I never heard him discuss this subject. He was not an articulate conversationalist, but who could so quickly and thoroughly understand what I tried to convey and explain about the dances? Who could catch each detail of the movement to interpret the style of the dance? He grasped quickly and exactly, and retained what he learned all the rest of his dancing career, never forgetting the slightest detail.

The dancer partner (I am reluctant to use this term when describing the male role in Les Sylphides) is represented by a youth, a poet, entirely different from the accepted male roles in the ballet of that time. It was previously essential that all male variations include double turns in the air and end with a preparation and a pirouette. But the most important difference between the new and old classic dance was in the expressiveness. Previously, the dancer emphasized in all his movements that he was dancing for the audience's pleasure, exhibiting himself as if saying, "Look how good I am." This was the substance of each variation in the old ballets. Even at each new rehearsal of Les Sylphides I had to tell the dancer:

"Do not dance for the audience, do not exhibit yourself, do not admire yourself. On the contrary, you have to see, not yourself, but the elements surrounding you, the ethereal Sylphides. Look at them while dancing. Admire them, reach for them! These moments of longing and reaching toward some fantastic world are the very basic movements and expressions of this ballet."

My explanations were not always understood by the performers. Very often, after my persistent corrections, the dance was first performed as I wished it. But later on, the dancer would revert to the usual execution.

Again self-admiration, self-exhibition, and an attempt to please the audience would reappear.

To Nijinsky I did not have to explain this new meaning of the dance. No speeches, no theories were necessary. In a few brief moments I demonstrated the Mazurka, danced it in front of him, made a few corrections, and resumed the composition of the other variations. Nijinsky immediately—and forever—assimilated and understood all I wanted. One movement, however, became his favorite. When creating the image of the dreamer, I pictured him with long hair parted on the side and therefore, in movement, falling over one side. (Such hair styles were worn at the time of Chopin.) I introduced in this dance a movement suggesting the brushing away of a lock of hair from the face: one hand languidly reaches forward while the other performs the movement, accenting, as it were, the youth's desire to observe more clearly the apparitions around him. Nijinsky became very fond of this gesture. Without further explanation from me, he felt its genuineness for that specific moment. But—he not only never omitted this gesture in *Les Sylphides,* he introduced it into other ballets, as for instance in the role of the Slave in *Le Pavillon d'Armide,* where there was no long wig but a turban, and the movement of brushing the hair to the side was uncalled for.

I might point out that even the most talented dancers have their favorite movements and transplant them from ballet to ballet. . . .

I created *Les Sylphides* in three days. This was a record for me. I have never changed anything in this ballet and, after thirty years, I still remember every one of the slightest movements in each position. Some of the *corps de ballet* groups accompanying the dancing of the soloists were staged by me during the intermission, just before curtain time.

My faithful *regisseur,* Sergei Leonidovich Grigoriev (at the time called "Egorushka"), who looked after the administrative chores of all my charity performances, said:

"We really have to start. The intermission has been too long."

"Just a minute, one minute, I have one more group," I replied, placing the dancers on the floor and humming the melody of that part of the music where the dancers were supposed to change the position of the arms.

"Did you hear me? Did everyone understand?"

The first group was ready.

"Begin!"

That which was so hastily conceived was never changed by me. Many times haste was not only not a hindrance but, on the contrary, I created better when I did not have too much time for meditating on alternatives. I created as I felt. Art originates not from pondering but from feeling.

The "Second *Chopiniana*" made its debut in Russia, and later, renamed *Les*

Sylphides, was presented, without any changes or alterations in choreography, in Western Europe. Since then it has become the "required" ballet of every major company in the world.

—from *Fokine,* translated by Vitale Fokine, 1961

ALMA GUILLERMOPRIETO
Dancing for Twyla

One autumn day in 1969, before the start of the advanced class at the Merce Cunningham dance studio, Merce came over to me and said that there were two opportunities for teaching modern dance that he thought might interest me. One was in Caracas, with a group of dancers who were only just forming their own company, and the other was in Havana, where there was a government-funded school dedicated to modern dance.

My life in dance had been routine and predictable until then, if not exactly normal. In Mexico, my native country, I joined a modern dance company at the age of twelve. At sixteen I left my father's home and traveled to New York to live with my mother, who had moved here following her separation from my father. I kept on dancing. At first I took classes at the Martha Graham studio. In the world of modern dance the brilliant, temperamental Martha was the most revered choreographer. Starting in the 1930s, she had revolutionized not only dance but theater as well; her use of sets and costumes turned on its head every standard notion of what can be done and communicated on a stage. Her quest for a body language that reflected the deepest inner conflicts, and the way she used gestures and movements to stage great myths, centering them on the internal universe of a single woman—Medea, Joan of Arc, Eve, all of them ultimately Martha herself in any case—brought her admirers and disciples from all the arts. She was, moreover, the first creator of modern dance to devise a truly universal dance technique out of the movements she developed in her choreography. I had studied Graham technique in Mexico, and one of my reasons for moving to New York had been to train directly at the source, at Martha's studio on East Sixty-third Street.

By that time, in the mid-1960s, Martha was very old and more or less pickled in alcohol. She put in rare appearances at her own studio, interrupting even a class that one of her best dancers was teaching to hurl philosophical exhortations and wounding comments at us, mocking our lack of passion and our flabby muscles. One of my most terrifying memories is of a mute hiatus during a class when all of us stood frozen in some pose Martha had demanded while she moved through the room, pinching this dancer in a rage, giving that one a tongue-lashing. Pain was necessary for dance, she always said, and I think at that stage in her life she wanted to contribute to our training by guaranteeing that we would suffer. After a couple of years of this I felt the need for a less orthodox and oppressive atmosphere and switched to the Cunningham studio, partly because I admired Merce's work with all my heart and partly because, after Martha's, Merce's studio was the best known. . . .

Those of us who left Martha's studio for Merce's were attracted by his Apollonian temperament, which demanded concentration and intensity but rejected drama. It was mainly women who came to his little studio on Third Avenue at Thirty-third Street to take beginning, intermediate, and advanced classes, and quite a few of us were in flight from Martha. Merce's courteous distance came as cool salve on a burn, though it too had its price. Merce sometimes taught a beginners' class that started at six P.M. He didn't say much but would correct the students very patiently, and several of the more advanced dancers, including some who were already members of the company, would take the six o'clock class in the hope that Merce would at least cast a glance at them. All of us saw him as a flame flickering in a dark chapel. We spoke his name as if it were written entirely in capital letters, and we laid siege to him with our eyes. In return, he almost never said a word to any of us. . . .

One evening in Merce's dressing room one of my friends, Graciela Figueroa, mentioned that she had started rehearsing with an odd woman who had a funny name—Twyla Tharp—and she was seriously considering reaching the conclusion that the woman was a genius. That was how Graciela talked; she was the only woman friend I had who read Søren Kierkegaard and Theodor Adorno, and for years, against all logic, I was convinced that Julio Cortázar had based the character of La Maga in his novel *Hopscotch* on her. . . .

Yes, said Graciela, this Twyla woman was on the strange side, something new. A bit of a drill sergeant, but her work was very interesting: she didn't use music or even electronic accompaniment, like Merce, but total silence. At rehearsals the dancers used tennis shoes rather than ballet slippers or bare feet, and they struggled with movements that seemed improvised and *completely casual*—Graciela drove home the consonants of *completely* with a hammer and stretched *casual* out into four syllables—but in fact were diabolically hard. Twyla had suggested to Graciela—and here Graciela neighed like a colt—that she take ballet classes.

I never had the opportunity to see one of Twyla Tharp's events from the audience. Not long after Graciela started working with her, she told me that Twyla was putting together a large open-air piece called *Medley,* with sixty dancers (*sixty dancers!*—instantly I took the measure of her ambition and her madness), and it might not be a bad idea for me to audition. Two weeks later I started rehearsing with Twyla.

At eight o'clock on a balmy summer morning a breath of mist rises from the grass of Central Park's Great Lawn and drifts above it for a few fleeting minutes. It's only the evaporation of the previous night's dew, a flimsy, transparent veil that vanishes in the first breeze, but if you are fortunate enough to be dancing on that meadow at that hour, it serves to reinforce the feeling that you are floating. Perhaps the police horses that are taken out for a run then share this sensation, and so do the members of a football team who, in the distance, seem to be swimming in invisible water as they go through their complicated drills. For me, those bright mornings when we rehearsed *Medley* were the first irrefutable proof that being alive was worth it.

We rehearsed three times a week. I would emerge from the subway a little early and wait for the other dancers at the entrance to the park. Then the whole cluster of us would make our way to the heart of the park: the immense expanse of green meadow marked off at one end by a toy lake and the tower of a small pseudomedieval castle. In the evenings a Shakespeare play was performed in a modest amphitheater at the foot of the castle as part of the festival that Joseph Papp was making into a beloved summer ritual.

Twyla didn't have the slightest interest in hearing the same applause every night from that stage; nor did she covet the theater's dressing rooms, orchestra pit, and wooden bleachers that could hold almost two thousand spectators. If I interpret her thought correctly, she wanted her dancers to move across the meadow like an element of nature; she dreamed that the spectators would stand and walk among the dancers as if strolling through an orchard. She also wanted the dancers' movements to be "natural," and though there was an obvious contradiction between this aesthetic ambition and her technical demands, she meant that she was seeking an antiformal language of movement that, in following the trail blazed by Merce, would be unpredictable in its sequences and devoid of "theatrical" structure. She had decided that the work would begin in late afternoon and culminate during the slow summer sunset, with a section of movements performed not merely in slow motion but at the pace of a leaf unfolding or the sun sinking, so that our bodies would imperceptibly reach a point of stasis just as the night's first stars were appearing.

In the early sunlight and the grassy scent of morning, surrounded by a dense green wall of trees, isolated from the noise of Central Park West and Fifth Avenue, whose tall buildings framed the meadow, I felt as if my breathing were forming stanzas, the verses of a long hymn of thanks to Twyla, the park, the sun. Out of the corner of my eye I saw equestrians trotting past and football players hurling themselves through the air, and I liked to think that all of us—the horses and their riders, the athletes, and the dancers—were caught up in the delight of sharing this marvelous, improbable New York moment.

"That was awful," Twyla would say, with no smile of complicity but no impatience or rage, either. "Let's try it again." Twyla's efficiency was almost cartoonish. She arrived at rehearsals promptly, with a list of things to do during the session; she never wasted time improvising but brought whole minutes of movement already worked out and memorized. She delegated tasks immediately—"Sara, you rehearse the adagio group. Sheela, go back over section three"—and before the session was over she gave everyone instructions for the following day's rehearsal. Just as Graciela had said, there was something almost military about her, but her talent for movement was so prodigious and she was so smart, intense, and strange that five minutes into the first rehearsal she had amazed and won me over.

Twyla had the compact body of an Olympic gymnast and, like a gymnast, seemed capable of changing course halfway through a leap, suddenly ricocheting off thin air in the opposite direction. She danced as competitively as an athlete and with the same terrifying efficiency that she brought to our rehearsals. She didn't draw out her movements, seeking some hidden sensuality or languor in the spaces between them, but she did prolong to a maximum the end of an off-center arabesque, just to see how long she could maintain that impossible position. She had a perverse way of showing off her technical prowess. For example, she would do a double pirouette while revolving her arms behind her like the blades of a windmill and then immediately, without the slightest pause to leave room for applause or a sigh of wonder, slide into another equally difficult step, a leap that landed as a roll on the ground, say, and then go from there into another spin, as if to let it be known that she was after something far more exalted than our mere admiration. Her style of dancing was deadpan—but that was also her style when she wasn't moving. In her round face, with dark, round eyes, her mouth was a thin line whose ends barely turned upward to signify a smile. Her laugh was a quick bark. At the end of rehearsal she dismissed us with a "Thanks, everyone" as she looked through her daybook for her next task. She wasn't *simpática,* but she was irresistible.

Twyla's great achievements, perhaps, still lay in the future, when she became the pampered choreographer of the American Ballet Theater and conceived legendary solos for Baryshnikov and the duets she danced with him, but I've never heard anyone speak of the works of her more established phase with the same mixture of respect, astonishment, and gratitude that *Medley* evoked in its audience and its dancers. And in the intimate, devout atmosphere of that first company, Twyla forged her own dance language, an idiosyncratic mix of Fred Astaire, George Balanchine, and street cool that break-dancers and ballet choreographers alike have now assimilated so thoroughly that we see it as spontaneous and natural.

Not even her obsessive efficiency can explain how Twyla managed to keep up her nonstop creative output. Whenever she created a dance, she had to imagine, invent, polish, and memorize the whole work. She had to rehearse her own movements and work separately with each member of what she had begun to call the "core company" and with the rest of us. She had to train for at least an hour. On top of that she had to find financing for the project, obtain permits from the city and the Parks Department, design a program, and do publicity. Above all, Twyla was constantly on the lookout for studios or large, cheap spaces where we could rehearse in the afternoons. Dance nomads, we went from space to space, a different one each week, some of them so shabby that Merce's studio seemed almost luxurious by contrast.

Wearing the same tennis shoes we used for morning rehearsals in the park and the miscellaneous assortment of ragged T-shirts, worn-out leotards, and mismatched socks that became the fashion around that time, we felt divine. It was in the 1960s that decency and modesty lost all connotations of elegance, and out-landishness, self-revelation, and fanatical sincerity were eroticized: *I'm poor, make something of it,* said our clothes, and dressed in them we prepared to learn to dance in a language I called Twylish.

We learned the adagio the same way she had composed it: first the leg movements, a long series of figures—linked, broken up, knotted, and tied together again—that were sketched out with the feet. Then we worked on the second part, for torso and arms. Both halves were horrendously complicated and difficult; they offered neither rhythmic support nor logical continuity. A work of classical ballet is relatively easy to memorize because all the steps have a name and the rhythms are well known—eight-four, two-four, two-three, slow, fast, or waltzed. Even Merce held on to the practice of dividing a phrase of movement into counts "Five-two-three, turn-two-three, seven-two-three, glide-two-three, and *again!*-two-three. . . ." But Twyla, during that stage of her evolution as a choreographer, had decided to abolish rhythm. And the movements we had to learn, with their apparently arbitrary sequence full of dynamic breaks and the insolent, pop style that their very design demanded, were like nothing anyone had ever seen. Memorizing one of her pieces turned out to be like trying to learn a madman's monologue— disjointed words whose secret keys we gradually found. During those early rehearsals we could all be heard talking to ourselves: "Big step right, shift to the other leg—One! Two! Jump! And now turn and a hip thrust, head to the floor and—oops—*en dehors,* the *soutenu* is *en dehors!* Where did my arm go?"

It took us about two weeks to barely learn the two phrases of the adagio that lasted, at most, a couple of minutes. At that point Twyla told us, without a blink, that we could now join the two parts—that is, perform the leg and arm adagios together. It was like playing Ping-Pong and reciting *The Rime of the Ancient Mariner* at the same time, and some never got the hang of it.

To save time, Twyla had the core company dancers rehearse the chunks of choreography she had designed specifically with them in mind—solos, they might have been called in a less revolutionary time—with the background dancers who performed those same movements simultaneously. In addition to Graciela, the core at that time included Rose Marie Wright, Sheela Raj, and Sara Rudner.

Rose Marie, the youngest of the group, was very tall, endlessly generous, and patient as a teacher, and when she danced, she was as fresh and glowing as her name. She was the only core member who had trained entirely as a classical ballet dancer. Sheela, who was even smaller than Twyla, had enormous liquid eyes and olive skin and was perfect. Her nose was perfect, her toes were perfect, her shoulder blades were perfect. The carriage of her arms, her *developpé,* and her *relevé* were all perfect. Slender, agile, quick, and sinuous, she learned Twyla's impossible phrases on the first try and by the end of the rehearsal had already made them her own. One day she cut off the heavy jet-black braid that hung down to her waist. I believe it was an attempt to make herself uglier, because such an excess of beauty was starting to strike all of us as in questionable taste. But all she managed to do was unveil the perfection of the nape of her neck and worsen her effect on men, who gazed after her sadly wherever she went. Like Graciela, she was haunted by the specter of *la migra;* the agents of the Immigration and Naturalization Service insisted that for the good of the United States of America two of the most promising dancers in the country had to be sent back to wherever they came from.

When Twyla put her various core dancers in charge of different sections of the rehearsal, I always prayed that I would be working with Sara Rudner. The core company was perfectly egalitarian—everyone was a soloist and had to meet the same technical challenges—but we all knew that even though the title didn't exist, Sara was the principal dancer. She had the beauty of a Russian icon of the Virgin Mary, every movement of her body sketched a perfect line, as if she herself were a pencil, and she danced with remarkable spiritual intensity (without Twyla's ostentation or Graciela's dramatic emphasis, yet with a total passion for movement). But it wasn't only that: Sara, calm, warmhearted, laughing, was for me the emotional center of the group. It never occurred to me to try to dance the way she did, but if I'd been given the chance to trade lives with someone else, I would have wanted to be born again as Sara Rudner.

Twyla continued to work with the core company after *Medley,* and I went on dancing with her too because she always needed more people—six or twelve women she used as a kind of corps de ballet. I remember in particular a performance at the Wadsworth Athenaeum, in Hartford. While the core company performed the dance piece that had been commissioned by the Athenaeum, the rest of us presented a retrospective of Twyla's early choreography in the museum auditorium. That performance allowed me to reconstruct in my own body the origins of her work, which had begun five or six years earlier (and included dances as inscrutable as *Tank Dive,* in which a dancer, alone on the stage, holds for two minutes the ninety-degree angle of a diver preparing to plunge). At the Metropolitan Museum of Art we performed *Dancing in the Streets of London and Paris, Continued in Stockholm and Sometimes Madrid,* and this event received more attention from the press than *Medley* had. About fifteen dancers performed it. I didn't think this new piece was as original in its movements or as atmospherically evocative as the performance in Central Park, but I remember with gratitude and astonishment the rehearsals held in the museum after hours. It was a deliciously clandestine pleasure to practice our movements (or "tasks" or "activities," as we representatives of the avant-garde said then) in the empty space of the Spanish patio and on the great stairway at the museum's entrance. One night I couldn't resist the temptation and lightly ran my hand over a medieval tapestry.

It was during this period that Merce, feet joined and head tilted, mentioned to me one afternoon after the advanced class that there was the possibility of an offer to go abroad and teach dance.

Someone else might have felt as if she'd just been handed a bouquet of flowers: *Merce had noticed me!* I felt as if a bucket of boiling, freezing water had been dumped over my head. Merce had walked over not to say "I want you to dance with me" but "There's a gig a thousand miles away that might interest you." When I tallied up my achievements since coming to New York to dance, Merce's proposal seemed to me evidence of my failure. I was nineteen when he invited me into the advanced class, and I thought a door was opening onto the best future I could have dreamed of. Now I was twenty, which in dance-world time is a very different age, and no one had ever said to me "When you move, it enraptures my soul, dance forever." Like any young woman who aspires to be a dancer, I had no interest in being mediocre. I wanted to be used in the best possible way; I was convinced that I had great things to do onstage, that I harbored a dramatic presence of enormous force and projection. Nevertheless, I now came to the realization that I was accumulating more impediments than achievements. After so many years of training it was time for me to be something more than just a capable performer, but I was painfully conscious of my intrinsic physical limitations: my flat feet, my lack of "turnout"—the rotation of the femur in the hollow of the pelvis, which allows the knees and feet to point completely outward, like those of an iguana. I was never going to achieve technical virtuosity; that was a fact.

I haven't mentioned that I was also severely myopic; I'd never been able to get used to contact lenses, and in those days optical surgery was an experimental technique used primarily in the Soviet Union. Every morning when I woke up, the first thing I did was grope for the thick glasses that had first been prescribed for me when I was six. I felt hopelessly lost without them. Onstage, blind and exposed before the audience, I became a frightened, gray animal. I was panicked at not being able to see and equally panicked at being seen. The performance in Hartford, during which I had to appear onstage wearing only a flesh-colored maillot and the famous tennis shoes, had been a torture I would not be able to endure again. I felt that each one of the defects I took stock of every day in front of the mirror—the hips, legs, shoulders—was now exposed as if I were a side of beef hanging in the window of a butcher shop. I learned that I was a coward.

I had another carefully guarded secret. Ever since as a little girl I had chosen modern dance, I had never wanted to be just a dancer: I had always wanted to be like Martha Graham. I wanted to use my body to invent a brutal, mythical theatrical art that would be completely new. When, around the time I turned twenty, I first saw Robert Wilson's productions, I was choked with desolate, senseless rage: Wilson had ransacked my brain and stolen my ideas! His works were the same ones I had dreamed of, literally, in dreams so intense that when I woke up I wrote them all down, complete with indications for the lighting. Watching Twyla at work, so pitiless, so obsessive, I knew that I possessed no such capacity to move mountains, to sweep budgets, bureaucracies, and the lives of those around me along in my path in order to make my dreams real.

All these years later I have no way of knowing how harsh or confused my evaluation of myself was at the age of twenty. I do know that when Merce suggested I go and teach classes in a distant country, my usual state of anxiety and depression only worsened; I felt that everything—Merce's rejection, my own solitude—was conspiring to drive me away from all I had ever dreamed of. . . .

From Merce I'd received offers that I took as a rejection: Caracas or Havana. From Twyla, I'd had no more than her habitual indifference, but the friendship that bound me to the members of the company made me clutch at one last straw. I talked to Sara. "I don't know. I don't know what to tell you," she said. "Talk to Twyla."

One afternoon after rehearsal, my heart in my throat, I lingered in the studio until the others had left. Twyla was putting her practice clothes away in her tote bag, ready to go. I told her I'd been offered a position teaching dance in Cuba. What should I do? Busy with a shoelace, she lifted her eyes for a moment. "If I were you, I'd take it," she said. "You're not going to get anywhere hanging around here."

—from *Dancing with Cuba,* translated from the Spanish by Esther Allen, 2004

TAMARA KARSAVINA
Early Days

Tamara Karsavina (1885–1978) quickly became a leading ballerina at the Maryinsky, among her roles, Medora in Le Corsaire *and Lise in* La Fille mal gardée. *She danced frequently with Nijinsky and worked well with Fokine, relationships that carried over to Diaghilev's Ballets Russes, in which she was the star ballerina almost from the start.* Les Sylphides, Le Spectre de la Rose, Petrouchka, Firebird, Carnaval—*all were made for her, and her dark beauty and incomparable womanly charm won her the affection as well as the admiration of audiences everywhere. Unlike Nijinsky, she continued working at the Maryinsky during her Diaghilev years, until in 1919 she left Russia behind permanently when she married a British diplomat. Back with the Ballets Russes, she resumed some of her old roles besides appearing in new ones, such as the Miller's Wife in Massine's* Le Tricorne. *She retired to London, where she taught and generously coached English dancers— as she did Margot Fonteyn in* Firebird. *She lives on in Ashton's* Fille, *having taught him Lise's "when I'm married" mime and the famous ribbon dance. Her autobiography,* Theatre Street, *has been considered a classic since its publication in 1930.*

The *Source* gave me a very good opportunity. Lydia [Kyasht] and I were among the principal butterflies and had a solo each. Coppini addressed me affectionately as "Bambina" and was evidently pleased with my eagerness. In these early days especially, each new part was a joy, every rehearsal a sacred duty. The chief interpreters and solo dancers were often called to evening rehearsals, a call which with the majority was unpopular, interfering with their plans. I looked forward to it as to a party; it was a new and delightful sensation to be received as an equal by the artists before whom I so lately trembled.

Two brothers, Nicolas and Sergei Legat, were the leading male dancers then. Both talented, they were very good draughtsmen. An album of caricatures was just being started by them and was eventually published. Nicolas had a caustic strain in him; some of his unpublished caricatures were not without a sting, but he never told tales out of school and was very popular with the artists. The real white-headed boy of the troupe was the younger brother, Sergei, who was beloved by all; so handsome, so irresistibly good natured. A true and generous comrade, he had a rare sense of humour which never became offensive. There always occurred intervals at rehearsals when, not actually wanted, we could sit in a far corner. I became friends with both brothers; they usually beckoned me to join them. Nicolas worked at his drawings, Sergei told anecdotes, of which he knew no end. He made me repeat them, which I never could do; I usually forgot the point, which only made him laugh the merrier. Sergei used to mimic my first appearance in the class which all the solo dancers attended daily. He was late that morning and rushed in to take his place at the bar without as much as looking round. "Heavens! A funny little object drops a deep curtsy to me." He made a mock bow in answer. This incident started our friendship. My primness was a constant joke to him.

I was rather helpless in the class. The old man Johannsen never got up to show the steps; he indicated them by vague movements of his shaky hands. For a long time I could not make out what he wanted, and made constant mistakes. Besides, I was frightened of him; it made me doubly shy. There was no way of hiding behind others. Johannsen had only one eye, but Argus might have envied him, and my manœuvres never escaped him. As a penalty I was ordered forward all by myself, the cynosure of all eyes, the butt of the old man's choler. A Swede by birth, Johannsen spoke broken Russian intermingled with French. He had a vocabulary of oaths of uncommon wealth. "Pity you are weak-minded," he addressed me after each failure. "What a dancer I could have made of you but for that." He pointed to his forehead and then tapped the back of his fiddle. Epithets like "cow on the ice" rained on me. Once he was pleased with me, so much so that he called to Marius Petipa, who at that moment came in, "Come and see her *jetées en tournant*." While I exhibited my *jetées en tournant*, Johannsen muttered sadly, "What a pity! She could dance, but such a fool." Johannsen gave us very intricate steps, very difficult to fit to the music. He laid his fiddle across his knee and played pizzicato, using the bow only to point towards someone faulty, nine times out of ten to me. "I see you. Don't you imagine I can't see your bumbling feet." A small tragedy happened once; more than usually exasperated, he threw his fiddlestick at me and called me "Idiot!" On the point of bursting into sobs, I turned my back and left the room. Sergei followed me. "Come, angel, come and ask his pardon; the old man loves you. Be sensible." He led me up to Christian Petrovitch. I apologised. For the first time I saw him smile. "I taught your father," he said to me. He took my hand; it was wet with perspiration. "Clammy," declared he, "your blood wants purifying. Drink Hamburg tea. Where have you been last night?" "At a charity ball, Christian Petrovitch." "A ball indeed! We never went to balls. That is why you stumble like an old crock. No balls for a dancer."

Such was my docility that I drank Hamburg tea, and it upset me thoroughly, so much so that Father advised me to leave it off, as it was a well-known horse medicine. I realised in time that Legat must have been right; it was not persecution on the old man's part. He seemed to be constantly worrying about me. It became his habit to call me up before him to ask whether I had been to a party again and to touch my hand.

Whenever he saw me in difficulties, Sergei took me apart for coaching. He was protective to me and infinitely gentle. On his own, he sometimes gave me practice in lifts. An untimely tragic death was soon to take away everybody's darling. Not a soul but felt a blank left in our midst, a sunshine gone out of life.

The spirit of comradeship was stronger in those days than later, when the advent of new ideas brought dissension. In these humdrum years there had been unrepeatable sweetness. I feel glad I was in time to see that phase of our ballet.

The benefit night was an opportunity for paying tribute to our *corps de ballet,* greatly esteemed as a wonderfully disciplined body. It was also the fashionable performance of the year, a parade of jewels and toilettes. The performance was followed by a banquet at Cubat, which afterwards became an institution. This one was the first ever given to the whole troupe: it was also my first night at a restaurant. Restaurants were synonymous with wickedness in my mind. To the last moment I hesitated whether it would not be better to sneak away by the back door and return home. Nadejda Alexeievna teased me. "Why do you fret so? Nobody is going to abduct you. Is that what you are afraid of?" I suddenly realised I was being ridiculous. The last feeble argument I used was that it went against my principles. "Come on," she said gaily, "and bring your principles along." In spite of the principles, I could not help enjoying the party; the compliments I received, the attention paid to me, the lights, music, gaiety, the food, the like of which I had never tasted, well nigh turned my head. Besides, nobody seemed to want to abduct me; so where, after all, was the wickedness? Little pricks of conscience I felt at times, though Mother fully approved of my going. The truth was that I was a prude and a prig at that time; I had my own scheme of life built up during the years at school. I was to be a priestess of my art, uncompromising, spurning world-liness. Some fatuous Russian verses to an actress that I had read long ago impressed me by their sentiment, and I took them for my device. Translated into English, they would be something like this:—

> "No rhymes of languid poets,
> No melting sighs of swains
> The fortress of her heart can storm;
> Her art alone there reigns."

Mathilde [Kschessinska] timed her reappearances to the height of the season, allowing herself long intervals, during which she left off regular practice. In her holidays, she became untiring in the pursuit of pleasure. Fond of parties, cards, ever laughing, amazingly bright; late hours never impaired either her looks or her temper. She possessed a marvellous vitality and a quite exceptional will power. Within a month preceding her appearance, she completely subordinated her life to her work. She trained for hours, ceased to receive and go out, went to bed at ten, weighed herself every morning, always ready to restrict further her already frugal diet. Before the performance she stayed in bed twenty-four hours, taking only a light meal at noon. At six o'clock she was at the theatre, allowing herself two full hours in which to make up and practise. One evening I happened to be practising on the stage at the same time as her; I noticed a feverish glitter in her eyes. "Oh!" she said, in answer to my inquiry, "I have been simply dying for a drop of water the whole day, but I won't drink before dancing." Her fortitude impressed me greatly; I was in the habit of occasionally walking home from rehearsal in order to save my fare for buying a sandwich between the acts. I decided there and then to give it up. While at school, I always admired Matilda, and even treasured a hairpin I had picked up after her. Now I took her every word as a law.

She showed me great kindness from the very beginning. It was in the autumn of my first year that she sent me an invitation to spend a week-end at her country house at Strelna. "Don't bother about bringing smart frocks," she wrote. "We are quite rustic down here. I will send down to fetch you." Consideration of my insufficient wardrobe had troubled me; she must have guessed it. She had another considerate thought, that I might not know her secretary at the station. To spare me looking for her, she came down herself to fetch me. A small party of friends was staying in the house. As a hostess, she was at her best. The garden was quite big, and close to the sea. Within the paddock lived several goats; a pet one, who made her appearance in

Esmeralda, knew Matilda and followed her like a dog. The whole day Matilda kept me at her side, and had endless little attentions towards me. At dinner she saw me in difficulty: not dexterous enough to carve a snipe in jelly, she took my plate, saying, "Never mind, you have ample time to learn all those tricks." I had the impression that all round her fell under the sway of her gaiety and good nature. Yet, even to my uncritical mind it was obvious that there was a good deal of flattery on the part of her sycophants. Placed as she was, a great artist, rich and influential, that was to be expected. Jealousy and gossip were at all times busy with her name. I had a sense of bewilderment all the day; it did not seem possible that this charming woman should be the formidable Kshessinskaya alleged to be an unscrupulous intriguer, ruining other people's careers. What completely won me over to her side were little human touches of her character; there was more in her kindness than the attention of a hostess towards a shy girl under her roof for the first time. Some teased her on my account. "You have turned out a real chaperone, Malechka." "I am going to," she returned, "Tata is such a pet."

"Should anybody try to harm you, come straight to me. I will speak for you," she said to me later. She was as good as her word. Later, there arose an occasion for her to intervene on my behalf. I was getting considerably fewer parts; it was found out that the impression had been given to the director that the work was too much for me. A prominent ballerina [Anna Pavlova], not I fear among my well-wishers, had shown an unexpected anxiety for my health, and begged the director not to overwork me, as I was consumptive. The director accordingly, deceived no doubt by this admirably acted solicitude from a quarter where it was not indigenous, had, from genuine consideration, gradually lessened my work.

Next morning I went back to town, marvelling at what the world can hold of brilliant gaiety. The previous night I had been initiated into a new world. The garden had been illuminated with lanterns; the house had rung with music and laughter. There was a renewed zest in me as I hurried to Theatre Street, trying to be in time for my lesson. On that bright, mellow morning of early autumn, happiness almost choked me.

—from *Theatre Street,* 1931

Debut

Allegra Kent began dancing only when she was eleven. Having studied with Bro-
nislava Nijinska and Carmelita Maracci, she joined the New York City Ballet in
1953. The first ballet Balanchine created for her was "The Unanswered Question"
section of Ivesiana, *when she was just seventeen. Among the other ballets he made on*
her were the 1958 version of The Seven Deadly Sins, Episodes, Divertimento
No. 15, Stars and Stripes, Brahms-Schoenberg Quartet, *and* Bugaku, *yet*
perhaps her most famous role was The Sleepwalker in La Sonnambula *(originally*
called Night Shadow*), which he revived for her in 1960. She danced many of the*
greatest Balanchine roles—Sugar Plum, the adagio movement of Symphony in C,
Terpsichore in Apollo*—and appeared in various Robbins ballets as well (she was in*
the first cast of Dances at a Gathering*). Her career at City Ballet lasted thirty years.*

I came into the dressing room three hours early to get ready. The girls had
cleared a space for me, and I arranged the items I had acquired in the past
few days: Max Factor greasepaint, medium brown hairnets, and Dippity-Do
hair gel. I also had dark brown pencils to help me etch delicate and bold
lines, bright red lipstick, pale powder, rouge, and a small mirror to reflect
the back of my head.

It was December 12, 1952, the night of my first stage performance. One
year and four months after entering the School of American Ballet, I had been
made an apprentice so I could dance in the corps de ballet of the New York
City Ballet Company. The invitation had come from Mr. B., but we learned of
it through a secretary who called my mother. Although I had yet to take a class
with him, this was a clear message of Mr. B.'s interest in me. The School of
American Ballet did not put on performances at that time, and Mr. B. wanted
me to have some stage experience. I'd never been in a recital. I'd never put on
a tutu, snapped rhinestones on my ears, or powdered a shiny face. In fact, I'd
never put on a real dance costume. Performing was important, and Balanchine recognized that. In Russia, the children from the Imperial School were
incorporated in this ritual at a young age, as Balanchine himself had been, so
they would have stage experience.

I was intensely delighted to be made an apprentice. This was suddenly professional and real. Now I could freely watch the ballet back-stage or from an empty seat in the audience and see any program I wished. Stage technique seemed to me very different from class technique. But watching the performances had brought out new fears. I would have to be as skilled as these girls on stage. Was this possible for someone who once thought she had no special abilities and was average in all ways?

Vida Brown taught me the steps for the corps de ballet part to the second movement of Bizet's *Symphony in C*, a piece of music that Mr. B. had, in effect, discovered. The symphony was exquisite, and the section I was learning was wistful and romantic. It caught me with its beauty. I was unbearably nervous but proceeded to learn. As Balanchine ballets go, this part was particularly easy; it is somewhat of a tradition for beginners to start out in *Symphony in C,* but I didn't know that at the time. The company girls had amazing heads full of millions of steps. Would my brain ever be able to absorb all of them? I was worried about what lay ahead. It kept me up at night. Nevertheless, I learned the part in three rehearsals, with an additional one onstage for spacing, but there had been no costume or orchestra rehearsal.

I stared at the tubes and powders in front of me. I knew nothing about the ABCs of makeup, let alone "stage" makeup, or the hairdo termed "classical," with the hair pulled first back over the ears and then into a low bun on the neck.

I parted my hair in the center and draped some strands in soft locks over my ears, anchoring the gentle curve in place with hairpins. Several willful tufts could not be caught, so I glued them into submission with Dippity-Do. The cold, moist aqua gel dried stiff and dark. My bun felt as if it would come apart during turns, so I added more pins, stabbing myself and making the back of my head too heavy. Finally, I arranged a hairnet over the entire nineteenth-century nightmare.

That part was easy compared to my fake eyelashes. I nearly glued one of my eyes closed with the liquid adhesive, so Basia Walcyak, my friend in the corps, suggested her beading—jet-black wax heated and melted in a teaspoon over a candle and applied to the eyelashes.

The rest of the corps girls, most of them in their early twenties, were advanced at makeup. Professionals for years, they'd been playing with lipstick and experimenting with colors and perfecting their stage faces for hundreds of performances. Their sophistication impressed me. I looked at the girl to my right and did what she did. Then I surreptitiously glanced at the girl on my left for additional ideas. She did this, I'll do this. She does that, I'll do that. The two sides of my face were different. I created a split personality, an accidental Picasso. Another dancer had put on white eye shadow, and I copied her. The effect was Egyptian, and I looked terrible. I stared in the mirror. My bright red lips ran slightly over the boundaries. I felt dismay in my heart; when I began the evening, I had been a cleanly scrubbed fifteen.

Next, Dunya, the wardrobe mistress, gave me a pair of silk stockings that I had to split evenly at the seams, put a little diamond of material in the middle, and sew into tights that would become a well-fitting second skin. This was the tradition in ballet. I didn't split my silk stockings evenly, and the legs were not the same length; one side stretched on its own. I was too nervous to thread the needle. Time was edging up on me.

At last, I was in the wings. The ballet was underway. I would soon be out there on the strange territory of the stage of the City Center, much of me encased in the confining artifices of the ballet craft and decades of tradition. I was wearing a strangulating corset of shiny fabric with a flying saucer attached—a platter of white tulle extending from my hips. I had to dance in it and be graceful, but the tutu had a life of its own. I couldn't see my feet. I tipped it. There they were, the shoes and ill-fitting tights. I had sewn ribbons on my pointe shoes and then broke them in. Were the ribbons tucked in or had they escaped? If they had, this signified sloppiness and was not excusable. The details were numerous. Should I review the choreography in my mind? That was probably a good idea. I didn't know that the dancers warmed up again before going on stage. The first movement was almost over. There was the applause, and then there I was, part of a line of six girls doing the entrance step of bourrées, a trembling motion of the legs—tiny shimmers of dance, that resembled nothing in real life. No one does this step to board a subway— a trill of the toes that propelled the body forward with a magical motion.

The music for the second movement reached me through the acoustical barrier of my Victorian helmet. I was terrified. This was the first time I ever danced on a professional level to orchestra music and not the piano. The symphony sounded as if it were coming through water. And the lights. It was very foggy out there—a moonstone mist flowed from the beams. In the parallelogram of space known as the stage, things were different. The reflective mirror of the classroom was now the huge darker area of the audience. I could no longer see myself but had to feel and relate to the other dancers of the corps. Somehow I managed to stay in line and on my counts. With so much fear, the fun and joy were lost. It was possible that my great career idea was a mistake.

—from *Once a Dancer . . .* , 1997

La Sonnambula

O ne day I was at my favorite spot at the barre, warming up for an Oboukhov class, when I turned around and saw Erik Bruhn at the top of the stairs. How I admired his dancing and his handsome Greek profile! I smiled hello and quickly turned away because I was shy and really didn't know what to do next. But Erik did. He came over to where I was standing, shook my hand, and told me he had just flown in from Denmark to join the company for the 1959 winter season. I was impressed to see him in class so soon after that ordeal and wondered how he'd hold up to the mad workout that was soon to begin. Mr. Oboukhov entered the room and Erik went up to him, introduced himself, and shook his hand. This is exactly what I didn't do with Stravinsky once when I'd had the opportunity. Erik had lovely manners. Class began, and, after we had completed a series of innumerable jetés done at the speed of sound, Erik gave me a look of pained disbelief. I flashed my eyeballs in sympathy. Mr. Oboukhov was hovering over Erik, really enjoying himself and the effect he had on the Danish dancer. Later, when Erik did some flawless turns in attitude, I gave him a look of disbelief in return.

I was paired with Erik in a ballet that Balanchine revived for me, the one I had fallen in love with as a child in California, *Night Shadow,* now entitled *La Sonnambula.* Erik was the poet, Jillana the courtesan, and I was to play the part of the sleepwalker. I had seen the ballet twice, once in Los Angeles, with Mme. Danilova, and once in Paris, with Marjorie Tallchief, Maria's younger sister (Nijinska had told them never to join the same company).

In the ballet, a poet attends a party and is captivated by a coquette, the mistress of the host. Suddenly everyone exits but the poet. When he is alone, a sleepwalker appears. She is the unexpected presence, a mysterious person who has a secret never explained. The sleepwalker's role was a continuation of Mr. B.'s woman-in-white theme, a figure who had appeared in a younger guise in "The Unanswered Question." In this ballet, I portray a woman not allowed to live a normal life, whose husband keeps her hidden. But on this special evening she does appear at his masquerade ball. In a sur-real dreamscape the somnambulist enters and drifts across the stage with a lighted candle. My candle had a tiny, round, white lightbulb on the end. I asked a stagehand for a piece of thin orange gel and gave my flame a little peaked turban. I felt like a George de la Tour painting. The sleepwalker's fingertips see; her eyes do not. In a gliding walk on pointe, she is propelled forward. A silent alarm or air current could stop her at the very edge of the stage, but not a physical barrier. Abruptly she changes direction four times and then traverses the long diagonal of the stage with ever accelerating speed, running on pointe. She has supernatural powers and the brakes of a Rolls-Royce; uncannily, she can stop on a dime, particularly if the dime is Mr. B.'s. In some mysterious way she has escaped her imprisonment, but her route is dangerous. She floats urgently forward and backward. She pauses in front of the poet, yet she does not see him. Somehow, perhaps by echolocation, she knows he is there. She has found freedom in her dreams and, when the poet's presence is sensed, love. But her dream turns into a tragic nightmare when the host, in a jealous rage, kills the poet. In a most unusual ending, the poet's body is placed in the sleepwalker's arms, and she exits. When I first saw the ballet in 1948 and watched Danilova carry the male dancer offstage, the ending had left me stunned.

In this ballet there are no lifts for the poet, just one for the sleepwalker. The sleepwalker's carrying the poet, however, is stage magic. The choreography calls for the men to place the poet in my arms at the last moment before I back into the wings. It was really not difficult, because his whole weight was on my back and shoulders as he wrapped himself around me in a fireman's lift. This is a visual moment in ballet like a glance at the moon. It is something you want to recall, touch, and see again.

Mme. Danilova played a part in my preparing to do this role. The sleepwalker's costume was important, and with two undulating movements of her hands Mme. Danilova had told me to be sure the costume had the right kind of sleeves. Her remark was fortunate because Karinska with the sky-blue hair had already produced what looked like a Bloomingdale's nightie with short puffy sleeves. However, I misinterpreted Danilova's hand gestures—she had meant tight sleeves with tassels. Re-creating Danilova's same ripply wave of the hand, I asked Karinska for wide flowing sleeves. This turned out to be a happy accident. At the next fitting the long sleeves, like butterfly wings, were in place.

To prepare me for his choreography, Mr. B. told me not to walk in time to the music, but I found that difficult. Endlessly, I practiced three or four different ways of walking. Melissa Hayden suggested that I move forward on slightly bent legs, and that was the secret to the fluent drift. There should be no sense of a brittle shifting of weight or bouncing, just a smooth flow of movement.

Because I knew I couldn't overwork my muscles, I planned how I was going to execute the dramatic level of the role. I practiced at home, alone with the music. The transitions were very fast. This wasn't a leisurely acting job where you had time to develop a response during dialogue. In this role I had to develop my next dramatic idea on the music exactly as the conductor was playing it that night. My interpretation had to read across to the audience. If a dancer feels dissatisfaction onstage, the audience senses that, and the performance is lost.

The woman who walks in her sleep has a deep disturbance in her life. She seems to be searching for something she has lost. At the end of their pas de deux, the poet kisses her. This is a Sleeping Beauty, Balanchine style. The kiss does not wake her; nevertheless, their love for each other is sealed. After the poet is murdered, she knows what has happened and mourns, but still she does not awake. In fact, nothing can awaken her.

This ballet of nighttime arrived in my life with uncanny timing. In some deep and obscure way, Mr. B. was again using the stuff of my life by recreating for me this ballet from years before. Living with Bert [Stern, her husband] again, I was falling into a deep depression, from which I despaired I might never wake. I knew I had stepped back into misery; my marriage would never be right. Yet it would take a decade for me to extract myself.

Night is the time when dreams take over and things you want to hold on to quickly slip away. Ballets are like dreams. In both we accept the phantasmagorical as reality. But the mere fact of a pointe shoe means reality is about to be transformed.

La Sonnambula finishes like a dream in a mist with a small light traveling upward to create the illusion that the sleepwalker is carrying the poet up a staircase. Even though there is death, the illusion of her carrying him upward suggests rising above mourning. Grief is somehow transcended through the beauty of the image.

In real life, I was a sleepwalker—dance my only light.

—from *Once a Dancer* . . . , 1997

MATHILDE KSCHESSINSKA
Tsarevitch

For fifteen years or more, beginning in the 1890s, the greatest star of the Maryinsky was Mathilde Kschessinska (1872–1971)—named prima ballerina assoluta at the age of twenty-three. (Among her most famous ballets: Esmeralda, La Bayadère, The Sleeping Beauty, La Fille mal gardée.*) She was a brilliant technician, a* *sparkling charmer, and the ex-mistress of the tsarevitch, who after marrying and becoming Tsar Nicholas II supported her career, guaranteeing her undisputed authority within the company. She had liaisons with two of the grand dukes, eventually marrying Grand Duke Andrei and bearing him a son. They fled together from Bolshevik Russia, and by 1920 they were installed in Paris, where a few years later she began to teach, with great success. Indomitable and buoyant, she was remembered with fondness and respect by such pupils of hers as Margot Fonteyn.*

The Tsarevitch returned from Denmark in the autumn of 1891. From that time I only saw him by chance in the streets of the capital. Once, however, on January 4, 1892, at the dress rehearsal of the opera *Esclarmonde,* in which the beautiful Swedish singer Sanderson had a triumph, fortune granted us a fleeting encounter.

The Emperor and the Tsarevitch were sitting in the front row, while the Empress and Grand Duchesses were in the Imperial box in the middle of the Grand Tier. I was also in the Grand Tier. Leaving my box in the interval, I went downstairs, and ran into the Tsarevitch, who was on his way up, going to the Imperial box. He could hardly stop, for we were surrounded by too many people; but I was overwhelmed by the mere fact of having been able to come so near him.

I adored driving out alone, every day, with a Russian coachman, and often, as I went along the river bank, I would meet the Tsarevitch, coming out at the same time as myself. These were meetings at a distance. Yet nothing would have made me give them up. And when I developed a nasty boil on my eyelid, soon followed by another on my leg, provided with a magnificent bandage over my eye, I stoically maintained my daily outings . . . until the day when the boils became bad enough to make me stay at home. Neither bandage nor my absence had escaped the Tsarevitch's notice.

At the time my sister and I had a small bedroom of our own in our parent's house and a sitting-room prettily decorated. One evening, sitting alone at home quietly in my room, my eye still bandaged, I heard the front-door bell ring. The maid opened the door and came and told me that the hussar officer Eugene Volkoff wanted to see me. I asked her to show him into the sitting-room. This room had two doors, one leading to the hall, the other to the drawing-room, and it was through this one that I saw not Volkoff but the Tsarevitch himself appear.

I could not believe my eyes, or rather my eye, and was so overjoyed with this unexpected meeting that I was never to forget it. It was his first visit, a brief one, but we were alone, we could chat in perfect freedom! I had dreamed so often of such a meeting alone.

Next morning I received a note from him: "I hope your little eye and leg are better. Since our meeting I have been in the clouds! I shall try to come back as soon as possible. Niki."

My first letter from him! It made an enormous impression on me! I too was in the clouds.

I read and re-read that first letter until I knew it by heart. Later he wrote to me often, scattering charming allusions through his letters, like the quotation from Hermann's song in *La Dame de Pique:* "Forgive me, divine creature, for having disturbed your rest!" Indeed, the Tsarevitch liked seeing me very much in this opera, in which, dressed as a shepherdess with a white wig, I danced the pastorale in the first act. We acted Saxony statuettes and porcelain in Louis XV style. We were pushed out of the wings in twos on platforms with little wheels. Once on the stage, we jumped off and began to dance while the choir sang *"Mon cher petit ami, l'aimable et gentil berger."* As soon as the pastorale was finished we leaped back on to our platforms and were whisked back into the wings. He adored this scene.

Another time in his letter he mentioned André's love for the "Pannotchka"* in Gogol's *Tarass Boulba,* a love which made the hero forget everything, even his father and his country. I did not then understand the implicit meaning in those words, "Think of Tarass Boulba and of what André did for love of a young Polish girl!"

From then on the Tsarevitch often came to see me, always in the evening, and often with the "Michailovitchs," as we called George, Alexander, and Sergei, the sons of the Grand Duke Michel Nicolaïevitch. These evenings had a charming intimacy about them. The Michailovitchs sang Georgian songs which they had learnt during their stay in the Caucasus, where their father had been Viceroy for more than twenty years. My sister often joined us. As we were in our parents' home I could not offer my guests a meal, but I sometimes managed to serve them champagne! I can still remember the evening when the Tsarevitch undertook to perform my Red Riding Hood dance from *The Sleeping Beauty.* He took a basket, tied a little handkerchief in his hair and, in the sitting-room bathed in shadow, danced the roles of Red Riding Hood and the wolf. It also happened that one evening the maid announced the Prefect of Police of St. Petersburg: the Emperor had learnt that his son had left the Palace, and the Prefect had thought it his duty to inform the Tsarevitch without delay.

The Tsarevitch often brought me presents. At first I would not accept them, but this gave him such sorrow that I had to change my mind. These small gifts were very beautiful. On the first of them, a gold bracelet adorned with a large sapphire and diamonds, I had engraved two dates that were dear

---

* Young Polish noblewoman.

to me, that of our first meeting at the Theatre School and that of his first visit—1890–1892.

On Sundays, when I went to the Michel Riding School to watch the horse-races (my box was just opposite the Imperial box), the Tsarevitch never failed to send me flowers by two hussars, his regimental comrades, Prince Peter Pavlovitch Golitzin, whom we called Pika, and Pepa Kotliarevsky. These two officers were known as my "aides-de-camp"; they called me their "angel." When the races were over I returned home in my little single-seat carriage, proceeding slowly along Karavannaia Street towards Anitchkov Palace with the secret design of being overtaken by the Tsarevitch's carriage and having thus another opportunity of seeing him. For love feeds on such silent conversations. On the day of the Annunciation, for instance, which was the Horse Guards' anniversary, I attended the parade in one of the public's reserved boxes; the Emperor, with his suite, reviewed the regiment, but the Tsarevitch, who followed his father, had eyes for nobody but me, and I for him.

Happiness does not come without terrible awakenings. During an evening which we spent together the Tsarevitch told me of an imminent journey he had to make abroad so that he could meet Princess Alice of Hesse, to whom he was to be engaged. He had already on a previous occasion read me the passages from his *Journal* in which he described his feelings for the Princess and those for me. Everything drew him towards me. At that time he had only a fairly vague feeling for Princess Alice and saw the engagement as an unavoidable necessity. But whatever his feelings he was required by his destiny to marry a princess, and of all possible fiancées he liked Princess Alice best.

It was my first great sorrow. When he left me I remained there, powerless to move, as if made of stone, unable to sleep the whole night. The next days were terrible. My ignorance of the future in store for me plunged me into unbearable despair.

But his journey was short, and led to nothing: Princess Alice refused to change religion and to become Orthodox. Her conversion was one of the fundamental conditions of the projected marriage. There was no engagement.

When he returned we resumed our evenings, as before. The Tsarevitch was gay, full of high spirits. We were each other's own once more. My happiness can be imagined, as well as my determination to think no more of the future.

The winter season came to an end. Summer arrived, and we were ready to leave, I for my parents' estate, he for Krasnoïe Selo. The summer season promised to be a particularly happy one. It was.

Rehearsals for the summer season at Krasnoïe Selo Theatre took place at the Theatre School. My sister and I, to attend them, left our estate at Krassnitzy and returned to St. Petersburg. As soon as I entered our apartment I rushed to the piano, where the servants used to leave the letters which arrived while we were away. Sure enough, I found the precious letter which I had been expecting. . . .

On the days when there were performances at Krasnoïe Selo the artists caught the train at the Baltic Station and usually arrived in time for lunch, which we ate in the restaurant, opposite the theatre.

It was during this season that I was finally given the best dressing-room, whose two windows opened on to the Imperial Family's private entrance. I tried to decorate it as prettily and intimately as possible, with furniture in light wood, the walls hung with cretonne, and always with an abundance of flowers.

The Grand Duke Wladimir Alexandrovitch liked to attend rehearsals. He would come and sit in my dressing-room and gossip with me, greatly regretting, he added with a smile, that he was no longer young. One day he gave me his photograph with these charming words, "*Bonjour, douchka.*"* He was full of kindness and we remained the best of friends until his death.

The Tsarevitch also often attended rehearsals. Knowing the time he would arrive, I watched out for him through the window, from which I could see him coming a long way off, across the park, from the Palace to the theatre. He came on horse-back, dismounted nimbly, and at once came to my dressing-room, where we could chat freely until the rehearsal began. Then he sat in the Imperial box between the pillars, almost on a level with the stage, insisting that I should come and sit on the edge of the box, so that we could continue our confidences. He only returned to the Palace when the rehearsal came to an end and it was time for dinner.

In the evening, when the Tsar and Tsarina were to attend the performance, all the artists stood at the windows overlooking the door of honour. The Imperial landau drawn by three magnificent horses, with a Cossack sitting next to the coachman, at last appeared and we greeted the Emperor, who replied with a military salute, while the Empress gave us her most charming smile. The Tsarevitch next appeared in his own *troika*.

How many faces remain linked to these happy days! In the intervals the young Grand Dukes came to see me in my dressing-room, as did their elders: the Grand Duke Wladimir Alexandrovitch, Prince Christian, the Empress's nephew and future King of Denmark, the Grand Duke Mecklemburg Schwerin, husband of the Grand Duchess Anastasia Mikhailovna, a man of great charm with whom I was to have a deep friendship. And how many unforgettable evenings, made to delight a twenty-year-old's heart, evenings as full of fun and games as youth itself! One evening we agreed with the Tsarevitch that he should return to sup at the Palace after the show, but afterwards come back to the theatre in his *troika* and take me to Baron Zeddeler's,

---

*A term of endearment equivalent to "little darling."

at the Preobrajensky Regiment's camp, where my sister was also to go. I was to wait for him in the park, near the theatre.

All the theatre lights were already out. The alley, dark and deserted, stretched into nothingness before me. I did not dare venture there alone, and I asked a theatre attendant to accompany me. At last I heard the bells of the *troika,* furiously driven, saw the lanterns dancing, and the Tsarevitch appeared. It was a wonderful night, and we decided to go for a *troika* ride across Krasnoïe Selo. Like an arrow we drove through empty streets and avenues, carried away by the drumming of the horses' hooves, our blood lashed by the wind and our eyes filled with fleeting shadows in a star-studded sky.

At last we went to supper. Baron Zeddeler shared quarters with his friend, Schlitter. My sister was in love with Zeddeler, and I with the Tsarevitch; poor Schlitter, with no woman as his companion, had to play the solitary squire, and comforted himself with this sally: "No candle for God and no poker for the devil!" There was never such a gay supper, and the Tsarevitch stayed with us until dawn: he did not want to leave!

The last performance of the summer season ended, as usual, with a spectacular galop. I was terribly sad at the thought that these wonderful months were now over, when I had been able to meet the Tsarevitch so freely. The end of the season coincided with the end of the manœuvres: The Tsarevitch was preparing to accompany the Tsar to Denmark, from where I received warm, moving letters.

We were more and more drawn to each other, and I was thinking more and more of having a place of my own. Moreover, though he did not openly mention it, I guessed that the Tsarevitch shared this wish. I was living with my parents who, in view of my age, naturally still saw me as a child, and I longed for greater independence.

But this wish had its rub: I thought above all of the great grief I would cause my parents by leaving them. I dreaded the moment when I would have to inform them of my intentions. As a woman, my mother would doubtless understand me, but my father . . . ? It was all the more painful to approach him because I was his favourite. He was a man of principles, and his daughter's departure in such conditions was bound to be a terrible moral blow to him. I knew indeed that this was one of the things that "just is not done," but I adored the Tsarevitch, I thought only of him and of my happiness, however brief and transitory it might be.

I can still see, as I write these lines, the evening when I finally decided to speak to my father. He was sitting at the table in his study, and I waited by the door, afraid to enter. Then my sister came to my aid: she went in first and told him everything. My father was shattered: he tried to let none of his feelings appear, but I could not but feel it. He listened to my account and merely asked me if I realised that I could never marry the Tsarevitch and that our idyll would be short. I replied that I fully understood, but that I loved him with all my heart, that I did not care what happened in the future. I wanted to take advantage of the happiness open to me, even if it proved of short duration.

My father imposed one single condition: that my sister should come and live with me.

As I had foreseen, it was a great grief for my father to agree to my leaving, and I was no less grieved to cause him pain. But, whatever the cost to me, I felt relieved at having tackled that ordeal with complete frankness.

After his return from Coburg [where he finally did become engaged to Princess Alice] the Tsarevitch no longer visited me, but we went on exchanging letters. The last time I wrote to him was to ask his permission to continue using "*tu*" to him and to come to him in case of necessity.

He replied in these moving lines, which I shall never forget:

"Whatever happens to my life, my days spent with you will ever remain the happiest memories of my youth."

He also assured me that I could always go straight to him and call him "*tu*" as in the past. He kept his promise: whenever circumstances made me ask him for help, he received my request favourably and never said no to me.

My conversations with the Tsarevitch and the trust he always showed me remain among the most precious memories of my life.

He had an incomparable knowledge of the Russian language and its subtleties, and found the greatest pleasure in reading the Russian classics. In addition to being erudite and speaking several languages perfectly he was aided in his reading by an extraordinary memory. He was also an excellent physiognomist.

The Tsarevitch possessed a markedly high sense of duty and dignity. Self-mastery was one of his characteristics. He could control himself and conceal his inner feelings, maintaining this calm confidence in the most critical hour. This was not due to coldness, for in his relations he was kind, simple, and charming. All who knew him, captivated by his gentle and beautiful expression, came under his spell.

By nature a mystic and fatalist, he had the highest conception of his mission. He considered it his duty to remain in Russia, even and especially after the Revolution, and would never leave his native land: he thus paid with his own life and the lives of his family for his faith in the Russian people.

But I saw quite clearly that the Tsarevitch did not have the qualities needed to be a ruler. Not that he lacked character and will-power, but he did not have the gift of making his opinion prevail, and he often gave in to others though his first impulses had been right. But if I sometimes told him that with such a character he was scarcely made to reign, Heaven knows that I never entertained the idea of suggesting that he should renounce being Tsar.

After his engagement the Tsarevitch begged me to fix a time and place for our last meeting. We agreed to meet on the Volkhonsky highway, near the barn and some way off the road.

I came from the town by carriage; he rode there from the camp. As always when there is too much to say, tears tighten one's throat and stop one finding the words one would like to utter. What is there to say when the last moments arrive, those terrible, inexorable minutes of farewell . . . ?

When the Tsarevitch departed for camp I remained by the barn and watched him go until he was no longer in sight. He kept on turning back. I did not weep, I was profoundly unhappy, torn, and my pain went on increasing as Niki drew farther away.

Then I returned home, to the house which seemed so empty. I felt that my life was over, that no more happiness would ever come to me, that henceforth I would know nothing but sorrow, great sorrow.

I knew that some would pity me, but others would derive pleasure from my grief. I did not want compassion, but it would need courage to face the others. But all that only occurred to me later. For the moment there was nothing but terrible boundless suffering, the wrench of losing my Niki! No words can describe what I felt later when I knew that he was with his fiancée. My youth's happy springtime was over. A new life was beginning, the painful life of a woman with a prematurely broken heart!

—from *Dancing in Petersburg,* translated by Arnold Haskell, 1960

Serge Lifar
Diaghilev

One of the most controversial and commanding figures of twentieth-century ballet, Serge Lifar (1905–1986) maneuvered his way into Diaghilev's Ballets Russes at the age of eighteen. Quickly, his extraordinary looks, combined with his overwhelming ambition, won him his place as the latest of Diaghilev's "favorites," an honor he hilariously tried to deny in his well-written but utterly unreliable autobiography, Ma Vie. *Lifar, although modestly equipped as a classicist, had great stage presence, and was quickly featured in a series of vehicles, most of them choreographed by Balanchine at Diaghilev's insistence. (These included* La Chatte, Apollo, *and* The

Prodigal Son.*) After Diaghilev's death, in 1929, Lifar again maneuvered himself into a position of great power: the directorship of the Paris Opéra Ballet, a job he held until 1957, except for the few years when he was dismissed for having collaborated with the Nazi occupation. He proved an active and able administrator, reviving the fortunes and reputation of the company, although his own ballets, with which he filled the repertory, have shown almost no lasting power, and indeed look thin and derivative. (The best known are* Icare *and* Suite en Blanc.*) He was always a divisive figure, but despite his questionable character and lack of veracity, he remains a central presence in dance history.*

Now I often went to concerts, and so heard a great deal of music all through that important significant spring. Particularly I remember the Stravinsky-Koussevitzky concert in the resplendent Opéra House. During the interval I was walking timidly about in the mirror-lined pompous foyer, in which one instinctively seeks to muffle one's steps, when yet again I met Diaghilev. I bowed and, as always, wished to pass by, but he approached me and gave me a cheerful greeting. Never before had I seen him so full of joy, or smiling so kindly.

"I never thought, I never dreamed of meeting you here, my dear little flower, on the very day of our own Stravinsky! That means you really adore music and understand it!" And therewith he began to shower me with numberless kind words, such as "little flower," "little berry," "my darling good boy" . . . and all said so tenderly, with such kind simplicity, that my heart began to beat with gratitude and joy. It was the first kindness I had ever received in my life (except from my mother). *And I had received it from whom? From Diaghilev, the great Diaghilev, my God, my Divinity!*

I have always regretted that I did not, at the time, make a detailed entry in my diary, recording the whole of the ensuing conversation, for I had always had the habit of putting down in it everything that in any way attracted my attention. All I did was merely to note the main outlines. It was about women, and of Sergei Pavlovitch's jealousy in regard to them, where I was concerned. . . . Nevertheless, there was something else I noted with great completeness, and that was, that this conversation, so unexpected, so full of kindness and endearing words, did not come altogether as a surprise—as though, deep down at the bottom of my heart, I had for a long time felt that *thus it must come.*

At Stravinsky's concert I rejoiced whole-heartedly in Sergei Pavlovitch's kindness, in the charming things he had said and called me, but once I was at home, a sudden sense of fear overcame me, as I remembered all that was said in the company about Diaghilev's unusual life, his favorites and so forth.

"Can it be possible," I said to myself, "that I too am to be one of those future favorites of his, that even now he sees me in that light?" Though I was alone the thought flushed my cheeks a glowing crimson. But, immediately, I rejected every thought of such a possibility. "No, whatever you like but that, never! Never shall I become a 'favorite' ". . . . The one solution, the only issue that presented itself, was to abandon Diaghilev's Russian Ballet. But then what? For after Diaghilev, away from Diaghilev, there was no other company in the wide world that I could think of joining. . . . So I decided to abandon the dance altogether, to bury deep the greatest dream of my life: that dream for which I had abandoned all—even *her* who had clung to my sleeve, as I said good-by before leaving for Paris . . . and Diaghilev.

But to abandon the dance—was that not abandoning life too? What could life hold for me when that was accomplished? Nothing but emptiness! The world would have lost all its attraction for me. So I decided I would abandon that world for another. Once before, in Kiev, I had gone into retreat, had abandoned this world during fifteen months in order, solitary and alone, to study dancing and books. Now I would choose for myself a final retreat, a monastery cell. And so I, the incorrigible nineteen-year-old dreamer, began to dream of being a *monk* exactly as before I had dreamed of her, of Diaghilev, of his ballet and the dance. But now, it was with a poet's vision of the monastic life, with its lovely devotional seclusion, its rest and contemplation and prayer.

I had made my decision. I would remain with the Ballet a fortnight longer, until the season came to an end, then take leave of Diaghilev and enter a monastery. But yet, that world from which I was about to retire, was spreading its nets, preparing to lure me with all its snares. . . .

Then on June 20 the first performance of *Le Train Bleu* took place. It proved an immense personal success for Dolin. Before the dress rehearsal, however, Diaghilev happened to meet me in the Théâtre des Champs Elysées, and started a talk about my future. With excessive praise, and greatly exaggerating my merits, he said he considered me the most talented and capable of the male dancers in his company, and urged me to think of my career, and devote myself assiduously to working and learning.

"I want you to become my leading dancer, and I shall make you my leading dancer. Come on Monday to see me at the Hotel St. James, but meanwhile keep our conversation a secret, and don't mention it to anyone in the company."

On the twenty-fourth I called on Diaghilev as arranged, after a sleepless night, for the more I had pondered his words the more I feared the future he was preparing for me. An immense, intolerable burden of responsibility had seemed suddenly to descend with the words "most talented and capable" male dancer. It had been easy enough to dream in prison in Kiev about dancing, it was easy enough to imagine oneself leading dancer or, greatest dancer of all, when nobody paid the least attention to you, as a lad in the *corps de ballet:* easy enough while it was all far away and inaccessible; but now when, by Diaghilev's will, I was on the threshold of either a great future or a great fall . . . my head swam, not with joy or a foretaste of future glory, for that seemed infinitely remote, but with fear, lest my shoulders should never be able to bear the burden of all Diaghilev wished to impose on them. And again, I felt I must leave the Ballet, leave it now, before it became too late, for that distant monastery, by the dream of which I had so often been haunted.

In this mood, I reached the hall of the hotel, where Diaghilev greeted me with the utmost friendliness, and ordered tea for two.

Suddenly I became bold.

"Sergei Pavlovitch, I should like to talk to you."

Diaghilev smiled.

"Good, I also want to talk to you, and that's why I asked you to come and see me. . . . But what is it you want to tell me?" he says with a kind, warmhearted smile. He is obviously in an excellent mood.

Yet here I become timid again: but, overcoming that feeling, and trying hard not to look at him for fear my courage will fail, I begin stumblingly and shyly to say:

"I . . . for a long time . . . Sergei Pavlovitch . . . I have been wanting . . . I have been wanting to thank you for the season, and say good-by . . . I intend . . . I must go away next week . . ."

"Why, where do you want to go, where are you thinking of spending your two months' holiday? You know that the whole company has to be back by September 1st, and that I dislike it very much when dancers overstay their leave. Where do you intend going? I have a suggestion to make too. . . . However, tell me your plans first."

How am I to tell Diaghilev of my decision?

"Sergei Pavlovitch, it isn't for the summer I'm going away; it's for good . . . I've decided to leave the company—"

"What, what are you saying?" Diaghilev cries, turning purple and leaping out of his seat, whereupon an incredible thing happens, for he seizes the small table at which we are sitting, crashes everything on it to the floor, and begins to scream out in a choking voice, while the French, English, and Americans in the hall sit transfixed:

"What, you dare to say this to me, you ungrateful puppy? Do you realize all the ingratitude, the meanness, the insolence of what you're saying? I brought you from Russia, I supported you for two years, taught you everything, you whipper-snapper, and now, now when I need you, you tell me you're leaving my ballet! The impudence, the indecency of it! I can't believe it's your own idea, someone must have persuaded you, induced you to do it. . . . Tell me at once, which of the little sluts you are always running about with is it that is depraving you, teaching you to repay with ingratitude everything I have done to help you? I said I was counting on you in the future as my leading dancer, and so no doubt you imagined you were a first-rate dancer already. You're wrong! At present you're nothing, a nobody, and any other decent ballet company would have thrown you out long ago. I was talking of you as a future dancer, and that future is in my hands; if I want it so, you'll be a first-class dancer, if not, you'll be nothing, a speck of dust, a nonentity. . . . Well, if you want to resign, resign and go to the devil, all the devils! I've no use for such ungrateful beasts. To hell with you!"

I said nothing to interrupt Sergei Pavlovitch, but could not help looking at him with compassion, until, under the influence of my gaze, and no doubt because he felt he had had his say and was tired of shouting, Diaghilev grew calmer and continued more calmly:

"I've said a lot of harsh things: forget them and let's talk sense. . . . You really must understand, Lifar, that it isn't right, that it looks like blackmail, and that all those little girls—I saw you again with some of them at Anna Pavlova's performance, and I very much regret that you should entangle yourself with them—are doing you a disservice? I value your work, Lifar, and I won't let you go to any other company. Now what do you want? Tell me frankly and openly. Your salary isn't sufficient? You want a raise? Very well, you shall have it. . . ."

Diaghilev's outburst and the compassion I had felt, helped me to master my own feelings, and I said:

"No, Sergei Pavlovitch, it was never my intention to join some other company, and I don't want a raise. I came here, not in order to ask you for something, but to thank you for all you have done for me, and to say goodby, for I am going into a monastery."

And now a new heart-rending scene occurred, for Diaghilev dropped his heavy head on the table, and began to weep with emotion:

"So Russia, the real Russia, the Russia of the God-seekers, of the Karamazovs', still exists. But you are Alyosha Karamazov, my poor boy! Poor children, bereft of your country, but still longing for it, longing for all by which your forefathers lived!"

Then, getting up, he this time threw his arms about me, at which fresh consternation appeared on the faces of those sitting about in the hall. "Those Russians! One minute they're breaking tables and crockery, shouting at the top of their voices, and the next, for no visible reason, they're kissing each other in public!"

"For this mad, irrational impulse, I love you even more, Alyosha! But what's wrong? Why do you wish to bury your talent in a monastery, bury yourself away, commit suicide? It's sheer madness, it's impossible . . . I won't allow such an act of self-destruction. What's going on inside you? What can be behind this prompting to abandon a brilliant career, just as it's beginning to open to you?"

As well as I could, I tried to make him understand my spiritual condition, and especially the anxiety which the very brilliance of that future career now inspired in me. I said I felt hardly strong enough, and was afraid of being unable to justify his confidence, or the hopes he was building on me. "Not so long ago you said you were relying on me as your future first dancer, but today, you said I was nothing, a mere nobody, and I can't help wondering whether what you have just said isn't truer than what you said first. It's better to renounce dancing now than to turn into a failure, for that I could never survive. . . ."

"Forget what I said in anger. I have faith in you; I can see—do you hear— I can actually see you one of the world's great dancers with Spessivtseva as your partner. I cannot be, I am sure I am not mistaken about you. It was not for nothing that you interested me from the first moment I saw you, or that I have been watching you all through. There is real talent in you, and your duty is to develop it to its fullest extent. You must work, overcome all difficulties, not be afraid and try to desert. Everything must be paid for in this world. A man with determination and talent hasn't the right to be a coward, or fold his arms and give up. . . . You must work, and I, on my side, will do everything I can to lighten your task. And first you must take a long holiday to mend your health, and store up some strength for work, for at present you look like a plucked chicken. Name anywhere you like by the sea, don't worry about the details, I'll see to it all. Leave everything to me, I insist upon it, for you are the only person that matters to me in this ballet and but for you, I should have dispersed it all and retired long ago. I want to see what you develop into, I want to turn you into one of the world's greatest dancers, a second Nijinsky."

These words impressed me profoundly. Never had I suspected that his interest in me was so great, or that he could so exaggerate my capacities. I knew I could never fulfill all he expected of me, yet nevertheless I was conquered, I lost all power to resist, there seemed nothing I could say, and I relinquished myself into his strong, kind hands.

—from *Sergei Diaghilev,* 1940

Serge Lifar
Goebbels

On the morning of 1st July [1940] I was sitting at my desk in the director-general's office on the first floor of the Palais Garnier.

Suddenly repeated and hurried knocks on the door: before I had time to answer it opened and there was the *concierge*.

"Monsieur Lifar, Monsieur Lifar, a group of officers has arrived. They have asked for you. They are on their way up. I think they are important people," he said breathlessly.

Officers. In those days it was hardly necessary to mention their nationality. In those first days of the Occupation the Germans were like men who have just bought a property. They were amused with and proud of their purchase, impatient to visit it and to show it while the old owners were still on the premises.

But I scarcely had time to think. I prepared myself to play the part I had thought out a short time before. My intuition—influenced no doubt by what I had seen during the Russian Revolution where *unkempt* was synonymous with *powerful*—told me that this role was the most suited for concealing my real self and thus protecting me. So I leaned back in my armchair, put my crossed legs on the desk, and busied myself with the first papers that came to hand.

Knocks on the door. It opened. A rustling of leather and boots, a clicking of heels—the ever-present sound in those years—invaded the room. One of the visitors stepped forward, pulled himself together and shouted:

"Monsieur Lifar, *Reichsminister* Dr. Goebbels."

I forced myself not to blink at the name which hit me like a point-blank shot. So they said I had done the honours of the Opéra for Hitler whom I had not even seen, and that was enough for the BBC to sentence me to death. Now the Propaganda Minister of the victorious Reich was in my office. Although I pretended to be occupied and did not look straight at him, out of the corner of my eye I could recognise a narrow figure draped in a long, leather great-coat . . . his livid, sharp-featured, and nervous face under a crop of coal-black hair.

I remained in the position as they found me. What self-confidence the unmerited condemnation pronounced by the enemies of the "Greater Germany" gave me! What I was paying most attention to was playing effectively my part as an artistic Bohemian, ill-mannered when anything else but his art is mentioned . . . it is the only subject in the world which can arouse his wits, but for the rest a laughter-loving good fellow. This was the role to hide me, protect me from my timidity, and allow me to evade embarrassing replies and extricate myself with a pirouette. This behaviour has often been useful to me so as to unseat an interlocutor, to make him swerve his line of attack. I got up slowly:

"But I don't know him," I let drop, smiling and careless of all etiquette. "I have never met him. What does he want? What can I do for him? Is he going to come to Paris?"

Then, glancing over the six persons who were there, I recognised Rader-macher and then I noticed the minister's face change. It became inscrutable and extremely hard, his expression sharper still, under a large, intelligent forehead . . . the appearance of a sorcerer with a hooked hand.

"The *Reichsminister* is here before you, Monsieur Lifar," said the same individual who had spoken before, while the minister took a step forward with his limping gait. I felt it was time to change my tone if not my register. I got up hurriedly and walked round my huge desk.

"What, is it you, Mr. Minister? But it's not possible, I did not recognize you. We are all so preoccupied and hustled by things starting up here again . . . please sit down, Mr. Minister."

For a short time his face still remained hard and inscrutable. Then I noticed the moment when he decided to be cheerful and attractive.

"Monsieur Lifar" (the interpreter translated) "do you know that I was one of Diaghilev's first great admirers? I was present in 1929 at the first performance of *Fils Prodigue* and *Apollon* in Berlin. I was in the *poulailler*"—"the gods" but he said the word in French—"and I applauded you." I confirmed what he said. He seemed delighted, carried away by his memories of another age, another world.

"That is how I knew you, Monsieur Lifar, and I was able to appreciate your art as a dancer for which I have the greatest admiration."

I bowed but said nothing.

He went on chatting in this way until abruptly he shot at me:

"Why did you stay in Paris when everyone else made off?"

"But to defend Paris against you, Mr. Minister," I replied with a smile. "Moreover, I was mobilized at my job."

"Mobilized? But you are a Russian."

"All the White Russians were mobilized, Mr. Minister, they did their duty, as was fitting, to the country which had welcomed them."

Now he, in his turn, bowed without saying anything. Taking courage and relying, at the same time, on my "personage," I went on:

"Let us say rather that I trembled when you Germans entered Paris."

"But why?"

"Because you are the allies of the Soviet Russians and as a White Russian refugee I did not know what I should have to put up with."

"Absolutely nothing." Goebbels all at once became animated. "The Russians work in *their country* and the Germans work *in theirs*." He said *chez-eux* in French and with his two hands made an energetic gesture conveying the idea of very distinct and separated compartments. From that moment I began to have some inkling of how fragile was the alliance whose announcement had stupefied the world . . . the alliance that allowed the rapid conclusion of the conflict's first phase and led the Germans to Paris and *Reichsminister* Dr. Goebbels on an elegiac pilgrimage to the National Academy of Music and Dance.

We chatted for a good half hour in my office and then the minister expressed a wish to visit our illustrious house. . . .

We went into the Foyer de la Danse. I pointed out the portraits adorning the walls. Before that of Fanny Elssler I stopped:

"A German, Mr. Minister."

Goebbels turned round and stood before me with his forefinger raised. He said very slowly in French:

"An Austrian, Monsieur Lifar."

I still blush when I think of the lesson he taught me.

"And don't you figure among them yet?" he went on, guessing my embarrassment.

"Yes, here." I had stopped in front of a large mirror and as a joke struck a pose like that of a dancer's portrait.

Later during the visit he asked me:

"Do you like the German ballets?"

"No, not at all," I answered frankly, "I detest German Expressionism. As far as I am concerned it may be good theatre but it is not good dancing for the Dance must be free of all elements but itself."

"I know your ideas on the subject," he said with a sly smile. "I have read your book on the *Dance* written for the second International Congress of Aesthetics in 1938, Monsieur Lifar. By the way, that reminds me I'd like to see the library."

We walked across the stage. As I had wished, stage-hands were at work putting up scenery and artists were beginning to rehearse the ballet *Giselle* with Dinalix.

"We want at all costs to get the Opéra going again, Mr. Minister."

He stopped and looked at me.

"Monsieur Lifar, I've told you we appreciate very highly indeed what you are doing and we are very glad you are here. We want to help you in every way we can. The best thing we could do would be to appoint a German manager who would be in a better position to keep in touch with our departments."

"Mr. Minister, if you put in a German here, I will at once resign."

"But you are a Russian."

"Forgive me, but I am a French official."

"Ah, but then why resign?" he said, obviously annoyed.

"First of all because it is the Führer's wish that the French theatre and French art should remain in French hands. Therefore it is a choice between you or me."

"How do you know this view of the Führer?"

The idea came to me all at once. I had not seen him . . . but I retorted:

"But he himself was here last week."

Clearly Goebbels knew nothing of Hitler's visit to the Opéra and was piqued at not knowing. His face clouded over for a few instants—then he dropped the subject.

We entered the library rotunda. Dr. Goebbels took an obvious pleasure in glancing at the rows of precious volumes. With a self-satisfied look on his face he walked about in the huge room. Then, as he passed by a window, he began to shout orders in German to the members of his suite. I was alarmed and wondered what on earth could have happened and on whose head would fall the punishment for some obvious misdeed. What had happened, however, was that he had noticed in the rue Auber the name-plate of the Calmann-Lévy publishing house—which is still there. Goebbels wanted the sign-board taken down at once. By the time he stopped in front of Renoir's portrait of Wagner, he had calmed down.

"The Führer is such an admirer of Wagner, you should present this canvas to him, he would be delighted."

"Mr. Minister, you can take anything, you can requisition, you can do what you like, but I can give away nothing of the French patrimony that does not belong to me."

Goebbels walked on and said no more about the matter. The portrait has remained in its place to this day.

—from *Ma Vie,* 1965

JOSÉ LIMÓN
East Fifty-ninth Street: The Birthplace

The Mexican-born José Limón (1908–1972) arrived in New York in 1928 not knowing what to do with his life. One dance concert (with Harald Kreutzberg) was all it took to propel him into a lifetime of dancing and choreographing. He studied for years with Doris Humphrey and Charles Weidman and danced in their company before starting his own in 1946. He created his most famous work, The Moor's Pavane, *in 1949 (see page 1029), and in 1951 began teaching at Juilliard. His was the first modern dance company to survive the death of its founder: his school and company continue to flourish.*

Early in the year nineteen hundred and twenty-nine I was born at 9 East Fifty-ninth Street, New York City. My parents were Isadora Duncan and Harald Kreutzberg. They were not present at my birth. I doubt that they ever saw one other or were aware of their responsibility for my being. Presiding at my emergence into the world were my foster parents, Doris Humphrey and Charles Weidman. It was at their dance studio and in their classes that I was born. I had existed previously in human form for twenty years. But that existence was only a period of gestation, albeit a long one, longer than that of an elephant. My grandparents were equally illustrious. They were Ruth St. Denis and Ted Shawn. All this constitutes an imposing pedigree and, with the exception of Harald Kreutzberg, a very American one. Duncan was born in San Francisco, St. Denis in Somerville, New Jersey, Shawn in Denver, Colorado, Humphrey in Oak Park, a suburb of Chicago, and Weidman in Lincoln, Nebraska. *Muy americano. Muy yanqui.*

The curious thing about this birth is its posthumous aspect. My "mother," a lady of considerable and conspicuous gallantry, an incurable romantic as well as one of the formidable artistic figures in Western history, had, in the process of riding off to her latest and, as it proved, her final amorous adventure (with, of all people, a garage mechanic), had her neck broken when her trailing scarf became entangled in the spokes of the rear wheels of the automobile. Her valedictory was consonant with her courageous and indomitable spirit, "*Adieu, mes amis, je vais à la gloire.*" And there, indeed, she remains to this day. Her tragic demise took place in the fall of 1927, and since I claim to be her child and to have been born in the winter of 1929, one can only conclude that all this is one of those miracles of which only artists and philosophers are capable. Spiritually, they are fecund and procreative long after their earthly remains have returned to the native dust. . . .

Among my earliest memories as a child were the pleasures of draughtsmanship. I used sticks, pencils, crayons, brushes, and fingers to draw. A stick would do for sand or dirt. Pencils, crayons, and brushes were for paper, walls, furniture, and other handy surfaces; fingers were for the air. Drawing was compulsive. At school, when the nuns discovered I was an "artist," they promptly set me to decorating blackboards, windows, and walls with all the appropriate symbolism for Christmas, Valentine's Day, St. Patrick's Day, Easter, Washington's Birthday, Thanksgiving, and Halloween. Besides the Catholic religion, it was art that bridged the chasm separating the scared Mexican child from the slowly, but inevitably acclimatizing youth and adult. My accent may have been ridiculed, but my prowess as an artist was accepted with total and gratifying admiration. This was my chief claim to the approval of my teachers and fellow students during my entire scholastic career. It was my aunt Lupe who first teased me by calling me a second Michelangelo. It was taken for granted by everyone, including myself, that I was destined for the career of a painter.

New York art schools, art galleries, and artistic fashions were largely dominated by the French. Impressionists, cubists, modernists, surrealists, and dadaists were the models for all aspiring painters. I had the greatest admiration for Manet, Renoir, Cézanne, Braque, and Picasso. They were undisputed masters. But what was discouraging was that everyone was imitating them. By some perverse irony, perhaps as a reaction to this dominance by Paris, I found myself turning to El Greco, a painter largely ignored by my teachers in California. The more I studied his work, however, the more I came to the fatal recognition—fatal, that is, to my life's ambition—that he had done all I hoped to do and done it supremely well. New York now became a cemetery, and I a lost soul in torment. I had been earning my living by running elevators, emptying garbage cans, tending furnaces, and posing for artists and art classes. Now that bottom had fallen out of my life, I spent my days loafing or going to the movies. All ambition was lost.

It was at this point that Charlotte Vaughan, a girl from Georgia studying at Columbia University with whom I was then going, informed me one Sunday morning after our usual breakfast that she had tickets for a matinee dance recital. I had no idea what she meant by this but obediently accompanied her to what was then the Gallo—now New Yorker—Theatre. The house was packed. The lights dimmed, and the curtains rose on a bare stage hung with black velour curtains. A piano struck up the stirring preamble to the Polonaise in A-flat Major of Chopin. Suddenly, onto the stage, borne on the

impetus of the heroic rhapsody, bounded an ineffable creature and his partner. Instantly and irrevocably, I was transformed. I knew with shocking suddenness that until then I had not been alive or, rather, that I had yet to be
born. There was joy, terror, and panic in the discovery. Just as the unborn
infant cannot know the miracle of light, so I had not known that dance
existed, and now I did not want to remain on this earth unless I learned to
do what this man—Harald Kreutzberg—was doing.

In a state bordering on panic, a fear that perhaps I was too late in my discovery of the dance, I ran to all my friends for help. One of them lent me a
copy of *My Life* by Isadora Duncan. The book had just been published, and in
its pages I discovered my artistic mother. My two friends from Los Angeles,
Don Forbes and Perkins Harnley, had both attended school in Lincoln,
Nebraska, with Charles Weidman. They recommended that I look into the
school recently established by Doris Humphrey and himself, and begin my
training. I showed up immediately. The young lady at the reception desk of
the studio was Pauline Lawrence. Here, unbeknownst to me, was my future
wife. But at that moment I wasn't looking for a wife. I wanted only to
be born.

—from *An Unfinished Memoir*, 1958

NATALIA MAKAROVA
Swan Lake

*In 1970 Natalia Makarova, born in Leningrad in 1940, defected from the Soviet
Union to the West. Because of the war, she had been late to begin formal training at
the Vaganova School, but on joining the Kirov in 1956, she immediately graduated
to major roles. In the West she performed primarily with American Ballet Theatre and
the Royal Ballet, dancing a wide variety of both classical and modern roles. Perceived
as the foremost classical ballerina of her day, she is most famous for her lyrical,
romantic, dramatic performances in* Swan Lake, Giselle, *and* Romeo and Juliet.
*She has staged a number of classics around the world, most famously first the "King-
dom of the Shades" act of* La Bayadère *and eventually the entire ballet. She
appeared on Broadway in a revival of the Rodgers and Hart musical* On Your Toes,
and in 1979 published her book, A Dance Biography.

I have always remembered what Sergeyev said to me after one of my performances of *Giselle,* in London, in 1970: "I adore you in the romantic ballet, in a romantic tutu, but you have not yet found yourself in a classical tutu!"

To master dancing in both tutus is tantamount to possessing the entire classical legacy of the romantic and Russian academic schools, whose principles inspired the creations of Bournonville, Perrot, and Petipa. I began as a romantic ballerina, but after defecting, I made a firm decision to master the classical tutu.

The romantic tutu demands a special technical approach that is strictly motivated by the stylistics of romantic ballet. They are based on semitones and semiposes, and their understatement is strongly emphasized. The whole poetics of romantic ballet tend to be elusive and indefinite. In order to assimilate this style, one has to have a big, soaring jump, a free-floating torso, as if it were independent from the legs, an indefinable plasticity of the arms—*les bras inachevés*—ethereally sketched in the air, as if testing its density.

The classical tutu, as exemplified by *Swan Lake,* demands more precision in executing classical steps and does not tolerate any romantic elusiveness: all the positions are clearly defined, the extension is bigger, the arabesque and attitude are stretched to the limits, while the torso is absolutely straight. The legs are exposed, all lines are revealed, and you cannot conceal the slightest slip from the audience. The legs must express something: they have a responsibility, so to speak, for your expressiveness, a responsibility they share with the arms. And this expressiveness demands tremendous professionalism, precision in every movement. What is more, classical technique does not permit the relaxed knees that are quite appropriate for the romantic style; it requires an impeccable turn-out, otherwise one cannot achieve any precision in dance phrasing: the lines of the legs will be distorted and lose their beauty. The torso is also differently poised in the classical tutu: it stands on the working leg very firmly, and the sense of center is absolutely definite.

Finally, *Swan Lake* demands from a ballerina quite special physical qualities. It is no coincidence that in the former Maryinsky and in my Kirov, *Swan Lake* was given only to those ballerinas who possessed these qualities: soft, flowing lines of the body, long legs, expressive, elongated arms with a specific relaxation at the elbow, a clearly pronounced arch. And so certain ballerinas who could be perfect in *Giselle* or *Sleeping Beauty,* but who didn't meet these specific physical requirements, never got the chance to attempt *Swan Lake:* for instance, Irina Kolpakova and Alla Sizova at the Kirov. Whereas Maya Plisetskaya, well known for her flowing line, danced Myrtha, never Giselle, since the romantic style per se was not her forte.

In *Swan Lake,* as in *Giselle,* the second act is the key to the ballet and the most difficult in terms of style and dramatic expressiveness. But if in the second act of *Giselle* it is essential to overcome the "par terre" by soaring over the stage, for *Swan Lake* this springy, big jump is not necessary. What's more important is the flexibility of the body and the "singing" lines of the arms. Besides, in *Swan Lake* you have to feel the ground under your feet: this is the earth, a glade by a lake, where Odette is stretching out her wings as if testing her ability to take flight—a metaphor of her captive spirit, thrusting to freedom.

Technically this ballet is much more difficult for me than *Giselle,* because its basis is an intricate academic dance, fostered by Petipa and Lev Ivanov. You cannot perform its patterns differently every time: each sissonne or rond de jambe is to be executed according to the specific academic canon, established by Petipa. Due to my natural impulsiveness that sometimes makes me surrender my control over my body, I find myself involuntarily attempting to dance the given classical patterns differently each time. I seem to be trying to escape from that precision of movement which is utterly essential for Petipa's style. In Russia I had not worked on *Swan Lake* very much, and therefore its mechanical technique, implying the ability of the body to perform the same classical combinations again and again with the same precision and the same attack, never became organic to me.

In its dramatic aspect, *Swan Lake* is a real challenge compared to *The Sleeping Beauty* or *Giselle*. *Sleeping Beauty* is a *ballet féerie,* a fairy tale, devoid of the dramatic conflict with which *Swan Lake* abounds. *Sleeping Beauty* is a triumph of academic virtuosity, permeated with a youthful charm which a ballerina has to radiate. *Swan Lake* is a lyrical drama in dance requiring not only impeccable academic schooling but a special gift for dramatic acting. *Giselle* is a more aesthetic ballet, more conventional, because the naiveté of the plot gives it a certain primitive charm that excludes the genuine tragedy of human existence. Only the second act is truly dramatic—the first is a bit old-fashioned. And there is really nothing to say about the music; Adolphe Adam wrote tunes to dance to, nice for the feet, but capable of offending the ear with their operatic manner, especially to people trained on Wagner, Brahms, or Stravinsky. (The music is, after all, of the same period as Offenbach.) This is music *to which* one dances.

With Tchaikovsky, it is a matter of music *in which*—or *beyond which*—one dances. It leads you; it subordinates you to itself; it is almost beyond the ability of the body, as it makes each note concrete, to compete with it. *Swan Lake* has survived the test of time because the choreography of the ballet frequently rises to the level of the genius of Tchaikovsky's music—especially Ivanov's second act, an absolute masterpiece. The last act is, unfortunately, rather illustrative, attaining real drama and meaning for me only in John Cranko's version. I keep waiting for someone with the talent and the daring to take and read the score with fresh eyes, but to do this after Ivanov is horribly difficult. Indeed, even the finale can be worked out quite differently: what if, let's say, Siegfried kills Rothbart and perishes himself, redeeming the betrayal and paying for Odette's freedom?

Attempts have been made to interpret *Swan Lake* as a psychological drama occurring entirely within Siegfried's soul, with the image of Odette perceived only as his dream of a romantically lofty love, a last fantasy of his youthful mind to which he is bidding farewell as he enters his maturity. Odette's death is equated with the loss of youthful purity, to be followed by a wise acceptance of the prose of life, incompatible with dreams. Thus was *Swan Lake* conceived by Yury Grigorovich at the Bolshoi, but the Party ignoramuses considered his version too pessimistic, and did not allow him to realize it.

Swan Lake's meaning is unique, because through the contours of an old fairy tale the reality of life surfaces—the truth about its imperfection, about pining for true love and love's unfulfillment, which can be realized only in death (the Wagnerian idea of *Liebestod,* the idea of *Tristan*).

For me, Act II is the key. It reveals the core of the drama as well as the ballet's essence—the nature and fate of Odette.

Over many years I have read Odette differently: as a frightened, fluttering bird-maiden, in whom love for Siegfried calls human feelings to life. At the last, she awakens to the understanding that she is to be denied love by her fate. Later, I softened the bird-like features and mannerisms, got rid of the excessive fluttering, and concentrated entirely on Odette's human nature. This was another extreme that was not too satisfying to me. I wanted to find a golden mean—and I believe I finally found it. Odette is an enchanted bird-maiden who knows her fate; the Prince does not know it, but she does. She knows that the desire for love, which is inexhaustible in any living creature, the belief in love, must be marked by the trauma of failure. There is wisdom in Odette, wisdom deriving from hopelessness, from a kind of severe, penetrating view of life, but wisdom does not console; knowledge prolongs suffering—it does not alleviate it.

I hear all of this in Tchaikovsky's music. Tchaikovsky is a desperate perfectionist and therefore he is constantly disillusioned; his music is full of this romantic longing for love. It resounds in the central theme of *Swan Lake* and in the growth of the Christmas tree in *The Nutcracker,* and in all the bitterness springing from the knowledge that it is not given for one's ideal love to come into existence. These feelings are very close to me personally, and the music of *Swan Lake* says all of this to me.

In the finale, Odette is happy that she has forgiven Siegfried, happy because she has learned to forgive. This is the lesson of her love—she has acquired a human characteristic which she had not known previously and which was awakened by love. In this I see love's greatest gift: its power to purify and transform the soul. Forgiveness is more powerful than death and transcends it; it carries Odette above the cares of the world, the crafty ruses of Rothbart, and Siegfried's weakness. Odette is united with her Prince in the world beyond, wiser still, because she has come to know certain boundaries—the ultimate truth about life.

My Odette, the one I imagine, I can dance only in the Russian tradition of cantilena. Unlike many Western ballerinas, I do not in my mind break Tchaikovsky's music into measures. I do not count them, and neither do I worry about exactly fixing every position against the music or "freezing" the arabesques and attitudes. That way is, of course, quite a showy way of dancing, but in *Swan Lake* I feel that such sensationalism is all but fatal, tearing, as it does, the continuity of the choreographic texture to the detriment of its meaning. Is not the white adagio a *story* Odette tells of her captivity, of her hopes, her fears? Like any story, it requires that the narration be fluent. This is why I divide Tchaikovsky's music into phrases, not measures, trying to sing them. That is the way I was trained at the Vaganova School and at the Kirov. My way is to sing with my dancing, to make the movement itself last and finally extend itself, to "draw" the ballet phrase the way a singer "holds" the note. And this is much harder than finishing each step on the note.

Not everybody in the West approves of this distinctive Russian bel canto in dancing; many people regard it as anti-musical. For me, though, breaking of the music into separate measures is merely mechanical and thwarts the proper cantilena style of *Swan Lake*.

For all the choreographic complexity of the part, Odette suits my dance characteristics: I know that if my feet should let me down, my natural lyricism and acquired artistic habits would rescue me. I would recover, not "fall apart" on stage. Odile is another matter. I never feel sure of myself in her tutu, because for many years the choreographic outline of the part did not feel comfortable. I had no confidence in it but forced myself into it and so couldn't find the proper state of mind. There is nothing vampish about me, and it is not natural for me to play a seductress or a *femme fatale*. In Odile, I have had to discover, as an actress, that which my own nature does not possess: aggressiveness, bravado, a glory in one's own triumph. For me, Odile was like a wall of glass which I was always trying to scramble over, getting my hands bloody. This was a tremendous challenge, and it took years to overcome the barriers. I have constantly sought that inner truth that would help me find in Odile's character something similar to mine—or I would never feel comfortable in her choreography.

At first, despite all my efforts, I couldn't get rid of her traditional image, the stereotyped, one-dimensional Bad Woman. Odile became more understandable for me when I managed to see in her the mysterious stranger, reminiscent of those *femmes fatales* from the romantic poetry of Alexander Blok. I imagined her as an enchantress out of nowhere, whose ambiguous past makes her inaccessible to anyone. Odile suddenly became surrounded with a mysterious aura. But everything mysterious is not alien to me, and she emerged in my mind as a beautiful woman quite conscious of her vicious charms and her liaison with evil. According to the libretto, she is Rothbart's daughter, but I chose to disregard this convention. She might just as well be his ally, employing her natural wickedness in her own manner and to her own ends. Like Odette, she knows her destiny—to charm people with her supernatural destructive beauty, then to keep those who fall victim to it at a distance, never giving herself to them. She is playing with Siegfried, just as she has done with others—for the sake of her own amusement, in order to prove her irresistibility once again. Rothbart merely provides her with the chance to assert her evil. This approach has made Odile psychologically more understandable for me (and, I hope, more convincing for the audience). And it is no accident that some people prefer me now as Odile rather than Odette. This means that artistic and technical qualities acquired through hard work may sometimes actually appear more convincing, even stronger, to the public than innate ones.

Sometimes I am told that I have complete mastery in *Swan Lake*. But that feeling is entirely alien to me, for mastery implies something rigid, almost petrified—something hostile to art, the enchantment of which lies in its spontaneity, in the unpredictability of its movement. Of course, in *Swan Lake* I have acquired by now a certain amount of experience, certain particularly technical habits: now I am less vulnerable to the external world, to its distracting influences. I have stopped fighting with this ballet.

—from *A Dance Autobiography*, 1979

ALICIA MARKOVA

Crisis

Born Lilian Alice Marks, Dame Alicia Markova (1910–2004) was the first great English ballerina. Appearing as a child in various London shows (and billed as "The Child Pavlova"), she joined Diaghilev at the age of fourteen to perform in the Stravinsky-Balanchine collaboration Le Rossignol. *She was instrumental in creating British ballet, becoming the first prima ballerina of the Vic-Wells after having danced*

with *The Ballet Club, the Camargo Society,* and *Marie Rambert. Later, with her part-*
ner of many years, Anton Dolin, she formed several ballet companies, including Lon-
don's Festival Ballet. Her most famous role was Giselle, but she had a broad repertory,
*including several ballets made for her by Ashton (*Façade, Les Rendezvous*). In*
Dolin's reconstruction of Perrot's Pas de Quatre, *she (of course) danced the central*
role of Marie Taglioni.

After a short season at Monte Carlo, we went to Paris for rehearsals. The
proverbial springtime of that city was a tonic, and so were my companions
there. It was exciting to meet again such colleagues as Serge Lifar who had
partnered me in the Diaghilev Ballet when he was its reigning star and I a
teen-age member of the Company. Lifar had since made a huge reputation at
the Paris Opéra, partnering Spessivtzeva in *Giselle* in 1932, and continuing as
its leading male dancer and choreographer. In Paris, his Albrecht had become
so famous that it was jokingly suggested the Opéra version of *Giselle* might be
re-christened "Albrecht" in his honour!

Alexandra Danilova, too, was an old friend who had been virtually an
elder sister to me during the Diaghilev Ballet days. Now that we were both
to lead this new company, we continued our friendship on a stronger basis
than ever. Danilova had special and sparkling gifts which enabled her to
shine equally in the strict classicism of *Swan Lake* and the light-hearted Massine ballets such as *Boutique Fantasque.*

Our new *Giselle,* it was decided, should be produced for me, and the role
would be danced at later performances by Tamara Toumanova and Mia
Slavenska, when they had had time to learn it. Toumanova, of course, had
become famous as one of the "baby ballerinas" of the De Basil Company earlier in the nineteen-thirties. I was not at all reluctant to share the role, and
although in later years I could have had contracts framed which gave me the
exclusive right to dance it during certain seasons, I have always looked on
this as a pointless state of affairs. However, I did feel now that the *first* performance of *Giselle* in London should logically be mine. There were substantial reasons for this, for of the three proposed Giselles, I was the only one
ever to have danced the role so far, and over the last four years I had made
it famous in Britain. Returning as British ballerina in a mainly Russian
company—and, as we now heard, to Theatre Royal Drury Lane—I felt I
should have the chance to make a little ballet history!

Danilova supported this idea. As our brilliant First Dancer, she herself
could have laid prior claim to the role, and in this case I would have given
way. But, far from doing so, she offered to dance Myrtha in the production,
though only to my Giselle. This was a gesture of friendship and admiration

which I greatly valued; but it was also something larger. Danilova had no time for petty rivalry, and her experience told her that this was the right casting, the way to give our audiences the best. The role of Myrtha demands a very strong classical technique and dramatic flair. But, all too often, we see a weak dancer in it, because personal jealousy has precluded someone from playing "second fiddle" to the chosen Giselle. This problem, at least, we did not have. And when my points were put to Massine, our Artistic Director, he readily agreed that I should dance the first performance of *Giselle* at "Old Drury," to be followed later in the season by Toumanova and Slavenska.

So far, all went smoothly. Rehearsals were thorough, because Lifar's version of *Giselle* differed somewhat from that staged by Sergueeff. I think it was about this time that I obtained a photostat copy of Sergueeff's music score. Although this had many cuts, it was of great value, because the music of *Giselle,* by Adolph Adam, was then diamond-rare, Sergueeff and the Paris Opéra Archives being almost the only possessors of a complete score outside Russia. Now that this music has been popularized on long-playing records and played countless times over the air, we are apt to forget that once it was hidden treasure. It has, of course, been attacked by highbrows as trite and sugary; but nowadays, I think, it has many more champions. I have always been one of these, because I feel that it was not written as an attempted symphony, but as tuneful narrative music; and as such, it is a perfect accompaniment to the story, full of fine dramatic melodies.

The prospect of our Drury Lane season was, of course, tremendously exciting. This production of *Giselle* with *decor* by Alexandre Benois meant new costumes, naturally. The Ballet Russe had its own Wardrobe, so for this period, I was to have my costumes made there, instead of by the unrivalled Manya. I was duly measured for these, and a few days before the performance, I enquired how they were getting along, but was told they were not quite ready. However, soon after this, they were brought for fittings and everything seemed to be going splendidly. I told myself firmly that I was foolish to have worried, and must leave it all to the extremely competent Wardrobe. In the ordinary way, I suppose, I should have done this without a second thought. But here, after all, was a major international production, and one to which all the foremost critics were invited in strength. This Giselle was to step out, surrounded by the finest artists of her time, and in the face of such a challenge, every detail seemed of vital importance.

On the day before my performance, I arrived for the orchestra dress-rehearsal, gaily confident that the costumes would be there. But there was absolutely no sign of them! Really alarmed by now, I asked Massine if he could do anything to get the situation under control. At last a message filtered down from the Wardrobe, to say that they would be ready for certain on the day of the performance!

. . . I never like going into the theatre on the morning of a day when I am to dance *Giselle*. This is not a superstition; but Giselle's task, among others, is to create atmosphere. No modern ballerina, with a great role coming in eight hours' time, has much chance to sit gazing into a magic mirror while soft music plays. But to go to the other extreme, and wander around the theatre while cleaners are swabbing away and the plywood scenery is being hammered into place, is downright impractical. After all, Giselle must try to convince her audience that the scenery is not plywood at all, but the rich foliage of the vintage country; that behind the cottage window is a cosy parlour with a spinning-wheel, not a stage-hand in old flannel trousers and rope sandals; that the distant castle is no painting slapped on to a backcloth, but real, gleaming, and impregnable in the sunlight, with echoing courtyards and a host of retainers. So, on the day of her performance, the less Giselle wanders around the theatre, the better everything should be.

But on this July morning in 1938, feeling strong misgivings, I trailed up to the Wardrobe before noon. Lo and behold, I saw people working like beavers on my costumes, and was told they would be ready in the dressing-room in plenty of time for the performance. On the strength of this, I pulled myself together, went home to the flat and ate a large steak and vegetables! Now, of course, I should have rested, but somehow I was too disturbed.

Obviously, I told myself, it was no use getting hysterical. I must do something constructive, something that would safeguard the performance. But what? Suddenly I remembered my former costumes, worn for the Coronation Season of the Markova-Dolin Ballet. I would take these to the theatre with me, so that if the worst came to the mystifying worst. . . . I phoned Manya and asked her to come and freshen up the costumes. She was soon with me, did an expert job, and pronounced them none the worse for their long hibernation. I got down to the theatre as usual, more than two hours before the performance, to allow plenty of time for making-up and general preparation. A big gallery queue was already waiting patiently. Trying to shake off intermittent feelings of panic, I went straight to my dressing-room, all ready to breathe a sigh of relief at the sight of the costumes hanging there in their pristine freshness. But the long relaxed sigh was stifled at birth. If the costumes were there, someone had made them, like the Emperor's new clothes, invisible! I dashed up to the Wardrobe and tried the door handle. The door was locked.

. . . Slowly, deliberately, I began to make up and do my hair. The curtain was due to rise at a quarter to nine. At eight-fifteen, trying to be dead calm now, I sent "Morty," my permanent dresser and personal maid for the last three years, up to the Wardrobe. Morty, who always had everything under perfect control, returned quite harassed! Presently there was a scuffle outside and some of the Wardrobe staff came dashing in with a First Act costume.

Ready in all other respects, I hastened to put on the dress. It hung about me like a nightgown! All at once, the Wardrobe staff were apologetic, covered with confusion. Everyone suddenly remembered, with astonishment, that these costumes had been made for another dancer [Toumanova], whose measurements were totally different from mine! They had been told she was dancing the *premiere,* and I a later Giselle!

. . . Now began one of those nightmare sequences, amusing enough in books or on the stage itself, which give the sensation of doing battle with a whirling, elusive mist! In my panic, I even forgot that I had brought my old costumes. I sent for Massine, who at least had had nothing to do with the costume catastrophe, and told him that he must make an announcement. He was *not,* I said vehemently, to tell the audience that I was ill, had fainted, had fallen under a taxi, or anything of the kind. He must go before the curtain and say that I hated to disappoint them, that I was perfectly well, but the costumes had simply been made for another dancer, and therefore she must wear them. The house was crammed, and the curtain due to rise at any moment. Massine, doubtless feeling that the life of an Artistic Director is a rough one, said such a speech was impossible. In this case, I replied, speaking in the best *prima ballerina* tradition, I would go before the curtain in my dressing-gown and make it myself! As I was dealing this trump card, I suddenly remembered Manya's costumes.

But by now the mist had taken another swirl, and disclosed a mob of excited people in my dressing-room. These included Serge Lifar, my Albrecht, who had come to see where I was, and now proclaimed that he could in no circumstances allow the Bakst-type costume to be worn with the Benois *decor.* Such a thing would ruin his production!

At this point, I confess I really lost control. The curtain was well overdue, everyone was shouting at once, and the tears I now shed dissolved into my make-up, while the whole situation got gloriously out of hand. Poor Danilova, who was trying to calm me, kept telling everyone that this mad charade was taking all my strength, and that I should have none left to give to the audience! This was true enough, but the solution was becoming more and more remote. Various theatre executives stood around in white ties and tails, with distracted expressions, but no plan.

About this time, Baron, the photographer, then at the start of his career, came into the dressing-room to take a peek at all this commotion. This was his first assignment to make pictures of the glamorous world of Ballet! Close on his heels came the all-powerful Sol Hurok himself, and with him, at last, a plan. Of course, he said, I must be permitted to wear the old costumes. It was impossible to break faith with the audience! But by now I had had enough, and felt that no pep talk or coaxing could induce me to tackle the role anyway. Rather forcefully, I told everyone this.

Nobody noticed Baron slip out of the dressing-room, but he returned in a moment with a small glass of neat brandy. In rousing tones, he urged me to drink it down, to prove that I was British, show them what I was made of, and so on and so forth! I had no make-up left by now, felt as though I were made of sopping wet tissue paper, and longed for nothing more than to creep off home to my pet cat. But whether it was the brandy, or some inner rallying prompted by Baron's stout words, or a mixture of the two, I can't exactly say. Only I know that somehow, Danilova contrived to help me make up again, and to array me in the Bakst costume for Act One. They practically lifted me out of the dressing-room, while I protested with—I hope—effective sarcasm—that this was certainly an ideal preparation for Giselle!

And at this historic performance, all went wonderfully, all was triumph! Somehow the hectic games of the past hour were as though they had never been, and I knew from the applause which broke against the stage like a night-sea breaking on the shore, that, for this great audience, Giselle had come to life.

—from *Markova Remembers*, 1986

BARTON MUMAW
The End of Denishawn

Barton Mumaw (1912–2001) became a student of Ted Shawn's at Denishawn in 1931, and remained until Denishawn closed down. He was not only the company's second lead dancer, but also Shawn's longtime lover and friend. After serving in World War II, he performed in a number of Broadway musicals, including Annie Get Your Gun *and* My Fair Lady.

I arrived at the Farm in the fresh, green New England spring. I was apprehensive about my reunion with Shawn, but I need not have been afraid. He greeted me simply, warmly. His mood was somber, yet it seemed to me he had made some peace with himself. We walked our favorite path through the woods several times during the next few days, while he explained, with the frankness for which I had longed, the problems that troubled him.

Now I began to understand the reason for past behavior that had seemed heartless: Ted Shawn could not allow himself to unbend while struggling against the emotional, financial, and professional bonds that still tied him to Ruth St. Denis. Only now that he had freed himself from the most pressing of these obligations could he confide in me. I shared his very real sadness at the dissolution of the partnership that had produced Denishawn, even though I felt a guilty joy at being permitted, at last, to glimpse the whole man.

According to Shawn, and contrary to public belief, his marriage to St. Denis had been in jeopardy from the beginning, primarily because each had a different vision of dance. They shared the ideals that made it possible for them to study, create, perform, and live in harmonious, if temperamental, tandem, but at heart their differences were irreconcilable and caused continual conflict. To realize his vision, Shawn relied on organization, emphasized the importance of the school, and recognized the necessity for many dull, difficult tours if Denishawn were to survive financially. Miss Ruth, for her part, was driven to explore mystical, metaphysical, and religious areas as sources of her inspiration and fulfillment.

MANY YEARS LATER, I learned from St. Denis's dairy what her reactions had been to some of the same events Shawn had described to me. She believed that their personal crisis had begun during the 1927–28 Follies tour, when Shawn, to escape the tensions that had built between them, first suggested separate rooms. She believed the beginning of the end of Denishawn was signaled by the departure in 1925 of Louis Horst, their musical director for ten years, and culminated in the departure of Doris Humphrey, Charles Weidman, and Pauline Lawrence in 1928. As her relationship with Shawn disintegrated, Miss Ruth wrote: "It [Denishawn] has existed because of the good and true in our marriage." Without that, it could no longer exist.

Even if the reasons for it were not always openly acknowledged by the two combatants, a final battle became inevitable.

> March 8, 1932.   BB [Best Beloved, one of her private names for Shawn] came last night after a terrible boat trip from Florida. We sat up in my room and I talked first . . . I only want to unfold my latent capacities, my own being, and I want him to do the same. I want what he can do to adjust with what I can do, but it must seem to him quite otherwise. For a little while it seemed as though our whole attempt to live and work together had been worse than a failure . . . that it had been quite futile. Will he always feel that I am standing in his light? Will he always feel that I interfere with him? How awful it is. What are we doing to each other that is so wrong—I wish I knew.

At times, Shawn told me "Ruthie" felt he imposed upon her such a stultifying life that she separated herself from it completely to create programs for solo concerts or for a tour with an ensemble of girls. Shawn then carried on the teaching and occasional tours with a group of his own, until Miss Ruth returned to reassume her inspirational role in his life and the lives of their students. Throughout the Golden Era of Denishawn—the three Daniel Mayer tours of the United States, the Orient tour, the Arthur Judson American tour of 1926–27—the irresistible force partnered the immovable object, a miracle, it seemed, in view of all that Shawn was revealing to me.

> October 1931.   Teddy called and asked me not to call him Teddy! as I lowered his dignity in his own eyes! . . . It was pathetic—horrid—emotional. In spite of himself—*he* wept a little too.

> March 20, 1932.   Teddy [she still referred to him by the name] came this afternoon and we talked about my catalogue [for lessons at Denishawn House] and Teddy pointed out, very truly and strongly, that I had no right to give the impression to the public that I was continuing the Denishawn School—I was astonished and hurt deeply and terribly by the way he did it. I cried and grew quite needlessly hysterical and said, "This is indeed the end. I have made all the overtures that were possible to me. You have not met me in any real spirit of reconciliation, so we had better, indeed, agree to disagree as quietly and decently as possible."

The separation was equally painful for Shawn. He had seen his dream of Denishawn House as a great American school and theatre of the dance fall victim to the Depression. He had paid off the current mortgage debts on that dream, even knowing it was doomed. He had had the foresight to purchase a sizable annuity for Miss Ruth from their earnings of the *Follies* tour, so that she, at least, would always have enough money on which to live. Because he still felt the love for her that he would express to the end of his days, her security gave him great peace of mind.

> April "13," 1932.   Those little marks always mean 'versary [she and Shawn were married on August 13, 1914]. Teddy came to our business meeting this morning with his arms full of Gladioli. It did give me a little thrill, a warm feeling around the heart after these last dreadful inner days. I am grateful for this simple expression of love. . . .

When Miss Ruth's mother died that spring of 1932, Shawn wrote a long letter of sympathy to his "Darling Ruthie," which ended:

> I don't know just when I will be down in New York again—but if you *want* me—even for just the comfort of my presence—let me know and I will come.

It has been snowing here [at the Pillow] for three days . . . I figured I could live here more cheaply than anywhere else. But chopping wood—pouring boiling water down the frozen pump—cooking over a fireplace—practically takes up [all] one's time . . . I am still scrabbling for money for this spring and summer . . . As soon as I *do* come down to New York I will come to see you immediately.

As Shawn continued to confide in me, we drew closer than I had dared hope. With a new ease between us and a certain resolute cheerfulness, we rolled up our sleeves to go back to work. It was, as always, invigorating and companionable physical labor expended mostly on improving the Farm. We did little dancing beyond a brief daily *barre* because Shawn had, as yet, no definite plans for rehearsals or performances. In spite of his own precarious financial situation, when that of Denishawn House worsened, he invited Miss Ruth to come to the Farm that summer to work on her own things. I was amazed to see how naturally this great lady fit into our simple life.

I was to observe then, as through all the years Miss Ruth visited the Pillow, how she and Shawn, supreme egotists both, achieved an almost astral relationship that was to endure until her death in 1968. She came to the Berkshires from as far away as California, not only to perform, but, as she said, "for a talk with Teddy," or to see his new works, or to be with "the boys." At the end of one of her early visits, I was elected to drive her back to New York. She was so natural, so relaxed, during the trip that I found myself describing an idea for a dance which, in my inexperience, I thought very original. Miss Ruth listened, straight-faced, as if my inspiration really were unique, then encouraged me to get right to work to realize it.

That summer, I began to know Miss Ruth as a person, and she to know us.

June 12, 1932.   Teddy's farm—We have all sat around the supper table. Jack Cole, Campbell Griggs, a new boy [me] and Ted and I. The boys cooked a lovely supper and Teddy read Whitman. We talked and discussed while the boys listened. What else could they do? . . . It still seems all strange, though no longer am I suffering. There is no hint of any home together, and I am puzzled to know what is Truth and Love in reality, and what is still illusion. "Lose him and let him go" . . . Oh Beloved.

June 13.   I am now sitting by a table in front of a blazing wood fire. Teddy and Mrs. MacDowal [Alice Dudley's mother] and Duds and the boys are playing cards. A curious scene—a sort of "domestic" art scene: a feeling of warmth and home, and yet no core to this hustle. Or am I quite wrong, and has Teddy really found his home spirit with one of these boys? If he is really happy inside, if he has really finished the long trek with me, not as fellow artist, but as lover and a wife, then will it not be wise for me to take up the dropped divorce question as soon as is practical?

It never did become practical. Miss Ruth returned to Denishawn House and her emotional involvements there. Shawn worked on new dances in the barn-studio on the Farm to develop his ideas for an all-male company. But they remained in contact, and I was sometimes invited to dine with them in the city when they met to discuss business problems. On those occasions, even as I recognized the harmonious modus vivendi they had established, I also sensed tensions close beneath the surface. Shawn hid his worries under a mask of confidence that no longer deceived me; St. Denis smothered hers with charm. One evening Shawn praised me for the proficient way I was handling my duties. Considerably embarrassed, I protested that it was always easier to look out for another than for one's self. Miss Ruth turned the spotlight of her smile on me. "Ah!" she exclaimed, "there speaks the young philosopher." I realized then that her power of enchantment was more than the by-product of theatrical magic.

I was amused to notice that, in their dialogue, they assumed the characters they believed themselves to be with an intensity neither seemed to find to the same degree with any other person. In a social environment, both were extremely engaging. Shawn's vocabulary varied from colloquial to scholarly and his interests from ancient cultures to current events. He was a superb story-teller, with such an innate sense of drama that he seldom hesitated to improve upon facts when a compelling point was to be made. Miss Ruth equaled him in this, but with a subtlety that often concealed sharp thrusts. She could give the impression that she was withholding certain facts, that she did not wish to commit herself in words to the conclusion she implied. When they were in a room together with other people, they permitted little chance for general conversation. Everyone present had to listen to *their* views of, *their* aims for, and *their* theories about the development of that "American culture" which they wished to "give to humanity." Of course, neither Miss Ruth nor Shawn saw their attitudes in quotation marks. They were, rather, the vertebrae that made up the backbone of their lives.

On September 29, 1932, Miss Ruth reported, "A blessed, blessed evening with my beloved. . . . He was inspired in a long talk on what his vision of dance meant to him. I listened entranced. It was a new Teddy." But by the end of October, when she came up to the Farm to celebrate Shawn's birthday with us, she saw that the severance was complete: "A peaceful but quite fruitless time—I shall not go again."

There remained the painful question of what to do with the Denishawn properties they owned in common. One fall day, Shawn asked me to drive him to New York and help him through an unpleasant task. His face wore the grim expression of one who dreads what lies ahead. He explained that, in the course of previous meetings, he and Miss Ruth had amicably, if sadly, divided between them the most precious of their personal costume items: to Siva went the forty pounds of silver chains, bracelets, and belts Shawn had bought in India for his *Cosmic Dance;* to the Nautch Dancer, her green satin, gold-bordered circular skirt, belled anklets and jewelry; to the Emperor Tepancáltzin, the enormous cape of orange feathers he had worn when partnering the young Martha Graham in *Xochitl.* Each also kept those costumes in which they would perform in years to come: her *White Jade* draperies, her *Black and Gold* sari; his *Gnossienne,* his *Thunderbird;* their *Tillers of the Soil.*

Stored at Denishawn House, however, a vast accumulation of scenery, backdrops, screens, props, and ensemble costumes awaited its fate. These could not remain on the property and no other company or theatre would accept them, even when freely offered. There seemed no likelihood that the Denishawn ballets would ever be resurrected, even if dead-storage bills on the historical hoard could be paid. Miss Ruth and Shawn alone could decide what was to be done with it. That was the purpose of our drive down from the Farm.

When we arrived at Van Cortlandt Park, we found that the division of theatrical spoils had already begun under the supervision of Pearl Wheeler. (The "keeper of many keys," Shawn called Denishawn's brilliant costume designer, who was also Miss Ruth's confidante and dresser. Although he valued Pearl's indispensable talents, he had too often found her a thorn in his side because she guarded St. Denis with ferocious devotion.) Several outsize blue-and-yellow-banded wardrobe trunks stood open in the studio. Under the eyes of the household Buddha, Miss Ruth and Pearl were sorting the contents of the trunks on one side of the mirrored room. Shawn and I stood waiting on the other. As each costume, each wig, each trinket was unpacked, the two women—one tall, white-haired, graceful and the other short, heavy, gray-haired, dour—signaled one another if they wanted it. Those things they rejected were relinquished to Shawn. I added them to the collection we would take back to the Farm.

Not one of the four of us spoke a word during this dismal process. When the trunks had been emptied, Miss Ruth suddenly called out, almost gaily, "Here, Teddy!" With a final dramatic gesture, she tossed a large, pale-green square of silk in our direction—the veil around which she and Doris Humphrey had choreographed *Soaring,* one of Denishawn's most beloved dances. I reverently folded the yards of shimmering fabric and placed it with our pile of costumes, while Shawn watched, frowning. Then he looked across the room and held out his hand. "Ruthie, please—Come with me?" he asked quietly. She went to him at once and they left the studio together.

A silent, sullen Pearl and a very dejected Barton continued to stack the varicolored, varishaped materials. We looked up from our work in surprise when a student came from another part of the building to tell us that Miss St. Denis and Mr. Shawn were asking us to join them outside. Puzzled but obedient, Pearl and I followed him to the street entrance of the storage area, where two other male students had already pushed apart the double doors, exposing to the light of day the mysteries of a theatrical warehouse. Shawn spoke to us with dignity, his face expressionless, his voice steady. "Miss Ruth and I have agreed that there is only one way we can bear to bring Denishawn to an end—with fire—with a cleansing fire that will free our spirits from material encumbrances so we may each go on to achieve what we can, alone."

I heard a gasp from the students. I saw Miss Ruth reach for Pearl's hand. I stared at Shawn in disbelief. When and how had they reached this terrible decision? Before anyone could protest, Shawn seized the first roll of canvas on which he could lay his hands, hoisted it to one shoulder, and carried it to the middle of the large vacant lot adjoining the Denishawn land. Reluctantly following his lead, we men brought to him, piece by piece, fragments of the epochal Denishawn sets: the thirty-foot-high flats representing Babylonian gods from *Ishtar of the Seven Gates,* the Hopi adobe house from *The Feather of the Dawn,* the *Spirit of the Sea* rock and fishing net and green-blue backdrop, the *Cuadro Flamenco* baskets of flowers, *Job's* altar made of cartons, animal silhouettes from *Angkor Vat.* We came with armloads of shoes and wigs, of scarves and garlands, of leotards and gauzy nautch skirts, of Egyptian masks and Viennese ball dresses. The sun had set by the time we had placed everything flammable in the center of the bare ground. There, like a surrealist tower of weird angles and jutting corners, it glittered in the dim light.

Ruth St. Denis and Ted Shawn stood facing this grotesque monument to their life's work. Then she turned to him and he nodded. As in the ritual of an Indian burning ghat, where the closest relative lights the cremation fire of a loved one, he paced around the periphery of the edifice, pouring kerosene from a container. He hesitated only an instant before he picked up a makeshift torch, lighted it, and flung it into the pile.

Pearl and I stood mute and motionless and apart when Miss Ruth ran to Shawn's side as the flames crackled high around the pyre. I turned away, unwilling and unable to witness their grief. Were they listening to the *Radetsky March* while the *Straussiana* linden trees burned? Could they see Martha and Doris and all the other Denishawn Dancers rise in their Grecian tunics to vanish into the grey smoke? Would they scent remembered sandalwood and incense of the Orient beneath the stench of scorched canvas? Did they bow one last time together to the roar of applause in the roar of the flames?

Through the spark-filled dusk, I saw a figure with white hair flee toward the house. A figure with bowed head walked with wooden steps toward me. Denishawn had ended.

—from *Barton Mumaw, Dancer*, 1986

BRONISLAVA NIJINSKA
Opening Night

The formidable Bronislava Nijinska (1891–1972) was the younger sister of Vaslav Nijinsky, whom she idolized. Trained at the Maryinsky school, she resigned from the company when her brother was fired, and joined the Diaghilev Ballets Russes, where she appeared in the premieres of Petrouchka, *her brother's* L'Après-midi d'un Faune, *and* Le Carnaval. *In the early twenties, she became Diaghilev's ballet mistress, creating for him her most famous ballets:* Les Noces, Le Train Bleu, Les Facheux, *and* Les Biches. *She also choreographed the "Three Ivans" specialty number for his 1921 production of* The Sleeping Beauty. *She made ballets for many companies in the following years, including the Paris Opéra, the Colón, Ida Rubinstein's company, and de Basil's Ballets Russes (*Les Cent Baisers*). Eventually she settled in California, where she became an important teacher, of among others, Maria Tallchief and Allegra Kent, and where she created the dances for Max Reinhardt's film of* A Midsummer Night's Dream.

O n May 19, 1909, the day of the premiere of the Saison Russe in Paris, we were all very nervous and excited in anticipation of the evening. We had an early lunch and then as usual did not have anything else to eat before the performance. Many of us came to the Theater early; we wanted to be sure that we looked our best and that we should be absolutely and perfectly prepared.

Before the curtain went up everyone waited his turn to peep through the small hole in the curtain to see the public. When my turn came, not everyone was yet seated, and the auditorium and loges seemed to be swaying as some people were moving to their seats while others were sitting or standing. The ladies in their expensive furs and elaborate hairdos were wearing the latest fashion, their décolletages sparkling with jewels. They all looked young and beautiful and were elegantly complemented by the gentlemen in their black tails and white starched shirts.

As the curtain opened for *Le Pavillon d'Armide*, I was standing in the darkness behind the decor of the first scene ready with the others, waiting for the tapestry to come to life, when we were to kneel in a semicircle around the stage with our garlands of roses.

I had a painful sensation of mounting trepidation and anxiety. The whole ballet swam in front of me as if in a fog. I was very worried for Vaslav so I did not pay attention to anyone else that evening. Nijinsky remains forever in my memory, dancing his *variation* in the *pas de trois* with Alexandra Fedorova and Alexandra Baldina . . .

Nijinsky appears onstage in a long prolonged leap, *grand assemblé*, and while he is still up in the air a rumble runs through the Theater. When Nijinsky descends slowly, barely touching the stage with his feet, a sudden burst of applause erupts and he is unable to start the *variations*. Tcherepnine holds up his baton waiting for the applause to subside. The long white gloves of the ladies and the white cuffs of the men rise in swells over the Theater like a flock of white doves.

While Nijinsky waits onstage holding his pose, his whole body is alive with an inner movement, his whole being radiant with inner joy—a slight smile on his lips . . . his long neck bound by a pearl necklace . . . a light quivering of his small expressive hands among the lace cuffs. This inspired figure of Nijinsky captivates the spectators, who watch him spellbound, as if he were a work of art, a masterpiece.

Suddenly, from *demi-pointe préparation*, Nijinsky springs upwards and with an imperceptible movement sends his body sideways. Four times he flies above the stage—weightless, airborne, gliding in the air without effort, like a bird in flight. Each time as he repeats this *changement de pieds* from side to side, he covers a wider span of the stage, and each flight is accompanied by a loud gasp from the audience.

Nijinsky soars upwards, *grand échappé*, and then he soars still higher, in a *grand jeté en attitude*. Suspended in the air, he zigzags on the diagonal (three *grands jetés en attitude*) to land on the ramp by the first wing. With each *relentissement* in the air the audience holds its breath.

The next musical phrase is amazing for its dance technique—the modulation of the movement in the air, possible only for Nijinsky, executed on the diagonal from the first wing, *grands jetés entrelacés battes*.

Throwing his body up to a great height for a moment, he leans back, his legs extended, beats an *entrechat-sept*, and, slowly turning over over onto his chest, arches his back and, lowering one leg, holds an *arabesque* in the air. Smoothly in this pure *arabesque*, he descends to the ground. Nijinsky repeats this *pas* once more, like a bird directing in the air the course of its flight. From the depths of the stage with a single leap, *assemblé entrechat-dix*, he flies towards the first wing.

Nijinsky's flights in the dance hold the audience spellbound. The intensity of their admiration grows after each movement of the dance. Nijinsky ends the *variation* in the middle of the stage, close to the ramp, with ten to twelve pirouettes and a triple *tour en l'air*, finishing with the right arm extended forward in a pose *révérence*. The *variation* has been executed from beginning to end with the utmost grace and nobility.

The public screamed its appreciation and rose to applaud Nijinsky, holding him onstage after his short *variation* (thirty-two bars of music) for a period several times longer than the duration of the dance.

Already in St. Petersburg Nijinsky had amazed the public with this *variation,* but now in Paris, at the first performance of the Ballets Russes, he had surpassed even himself; he had soared away from earth into the realms of space.

Before this apparition of Nijinsky on the stage, the public in the Theater had been, as one would expect during a Gala Performance, politely restrained in its reception. Nijinsky's *variation* was the first "coup"; it jolted the public from its conventional and restrained politeness. The moment created in the Theater an unusual ambience and mood of admiration that did not cool for the rest of the evening.

During the remainder of *Le Pavillon d'Armide* each dancer and ballerina had tremendous success in the individual *variations* or *pas de deux*, and as in St. Petersburg the "Danse des Bouffons" with Rosai and the six character dancers won tremendous applause from the Paris audience.

After the intermission, Act III from the opera *Prince Igor*, with music by Alexander Borodin, was given with singers from the Imperial Theater. In the role of Khan Kontchak was Feodor Chaliapin, basso, while Vassili Charonov, baritone, was Prince Igor, and tenor Dmitri Smirnov was Prince Vladimir. In the role of Kontchakova was Yelizaveta Petrenko, who the previous year had sung a small part in *Boris Godunov*.

Act III of the opera ends with the *Danses Polovetsiennes*; Fokine had created the choreography specially for Diaghilev's Saison Russe, and it was presented in Paris with the decors and costumes executed after the designs by Nicholas Roerich.

Adolf Bolm headed the horde of wild warriors in his role of the barbaric Tartar, a role he created with such intense artistic force and danced with such unrestrained verve and *brio* that he has remained forever unsurpassed in it.

That evening we were all inspired by the excitement in the Theater and danced burning with the fire and spirit of wild untamed Tartars. In the finale of the *Danses Polovetsiennes*, in the mad rush forwards as we made to "attack" the public, I remember that I had a strong feeling that I must restrain my *élan* on the *avant-scène* or I would be thrown clear into the audience, or at least end the dance in the orchestra pit.

The *Danses Polovetsiennes* was a wild and unrestrained success.

The third part of the program was *Le Festin*, where Nijinsky and Pavlova had been scheduled to dance the *pas de deux* from *The Sleeping Beauty*, now called "L'Oiseau de Feu." Since Pavlova had not yet arrived in Paris, it was Tamara Karsavina who danced with Nijinsky.

All the *pas* were the same as when this *pas de deux* was first mounted by Petipa for the ballet *The Sleeping Beauty*. Then it was danced in a small space encircled by the many guests at the ball, but in Paris it was danced as a separate number in which the dancers had the whole stage to themselves and so had to adapt the *pas de deux* to a larger space.

The roles had been changed without altering the pattern or choreography of the dance. Dressed in the costume of the Hindu Prince designed by Léon Bakst, Nijinsky was no longer the Blue Bird but had achieved a metamorphosis from that image, created by him, into a fairy-tale Prince pursuing his beloved Firebird. His interpretation now was of a Prince so in love with the Firebird that in his enchantment he loses his human form and flies with her. He had incorporated human gentleness and sensitivity into the choreography of the role of the Blue Bird.

Karsavina was astonishing in her portrayal of the Firebird—with large, wide-open, dark eyes, tender and quivering in her dance movements like a frightened bird.

Together, Nijinsky and Karsavina were sublime, and for a long time after this performance Karsavina and Nijinsky danced as partners.

The last dance in *Le Festin* was the *Grand Pas Classique Hongrois*, to music by Glazounov. It was danced by nine couples, led by Karalli and Mordkin, and in this number Vaslav and I danced together.

The triumphant furor at the end of the performance was so great, there are not adequate words to describe the enthusiasm of the audience. They would not leave the Theater, and their ovations detained the artists for a long time onstage. We felt that the spectators had witnessed the birth of "a living art": the creation of the Ballets Russes. For we artists had ourselves experienced something great being born in us. We felt as though we were walking in the clouds, and this feeling of unreality stayed with us through the entire season.

That evening of May 19, 1909, was a historical date, but none of us at the time realized the importance of this marvelous performance, even while we treasured the joy it had given us.

—from *Early Memories,* translated and edited by Irina Nijinska and Jean
Rawlinson, 1981

A L I C E   N I K I T I N A
La Chatte

Alice Nikitina (1909–1978) was a second-level Diaghilev ballerina whose career was promoted by her lover, Lord Rothermere, who funded the 1928 Ballets Russes season. As a result, she was given the role of Terpsichore at the first performance of Apollon Musagète, *although Balanchine had created it on Danilova. (From then on, the two ballerinas alternated in the role, and Danilova consoled herself with being given the London premiere.) Nikitina also created the role of Flore in the Massine* Zéphyr et Flore, *and as she relates here, took over the central role in Balanchine's* La Chatte *when Olga Spessivtseva was injured on the day of the premiere. When she retired from ballet, she became a coloratura soprano. (Is this a first?)*

On the morning of the first night of *Chatte,* my training finished, I went to see the last rehearsal of it at the Théâtre Sarah Bernhardt.

When I arrived, the auditorium was deserted and dark. On the lighted stage, which had for all decor the black and shiny background of the linoleum, Lifar was trying out some poses and attitudes while the orchestra was rehearsing under the direction of Desormière. I learnt that the rehearsal of the ballet had been cancelled because Spessivtseva, who had twisted her ankle the night before, had to rest until the evening performance. I left the hall and had a thousand things to do, not the least one being the last fitting of the dress I was to wear that night.

When I returned in the afternoon, rather exhausted, to my hotel, hoping to have a little rest, I found to my surprise a message from Pavka; Diaghilev wanted to see me at once at the theatre. As I had not yet returned to the company since my accident, this could not be taken as an order. In spite of my fatigue I went, however, at once to the theatre, where I found Diaghilev arranging the lighting on the stage. It was exactly 4:30 p.m. When he heard of my arrival he came at once to me, dragged me into a dark recess at the bottom of the theatre. Without any preamble, but with all the charm he could muster, he said this to me:

"Alice, you must say 'Yes'!"

This was uttered in a light, jovial tone, but surprised by this approach, direct and mysterious, I replied in the same way:

"How could I do that, Sergei Pavlovich, without knowing what it is about? If you were going to ask me to marry you—would I have to say 'Yes'?"

"Yes, even if it is that, you must say 'Yes,'" he went on.

This sort of quibble lasted for some twenty minutes, Diaghilev still strong in his attack. My resistance at an ebb, I took a risk and said "Yes." At once, he burst out with:

"Alice, you're dancing the *Chatte* tonight."

I protested, saying I would be quite unable to do it, that I hadn't even seen the ballet. But to all my objections he replied: "Alice, you have said 'Yes.' So now you have to dance!"

Under these circumstances, although I was beyond myself with fright, it was best not to waste time; Lifar, who was listening in the wings, was called, and as soon as he was told what had happened we ran away to rehearse.

I was wearing a beautiful suit of beige and black mousseline which I joined up with safety pins between my legs to make trousers out of the skirt. Chernisheva lent me a pair of slippers much too big for me, and we jumped into my little Panhard and drove to the Théâtre Mogador, which belonged, like the Théâtre Sarah Bernhardt, to the brothers Isola and where we could rehearse in peace. On the way we passed by my hotel to fetch a pair of dance slippers for work and one for tonight. Luckily I always had several pairs of slippers ready.

Arriving at the Mogador we found ourselves confronted by Balanchine and Danilova, who were rerehearsing the old *Firebird,* and who greeted us icily.

"I can't permit that my ballet should be danced after only one rehearsal," said Balanchine. "If Spessivtseva can't dance it, Danilova must replace her, as she already knows the ballet."

Lifar intervened, saying that Diaghilev wished me, Nikitina, to dance tonight and we were to rehearse at once.

I explained to Balanchine what had happened and how Diaghilev had extracted my consent to dance. Balanchine ran to the telephone and when he returned he said:

"In such conditions I refuse to give my ballet."

Then Grigoriev arrived, sent by Diaghilev, and announced firmly that Sergei Pavlovich wanted us to rehearse immediately and that Nikitina was to dance the ballet from that night onwards.

But Danilova declared she needed the stage for her rehearsal, though *The Firebird* had been on the program almost since the day of my accident, almost a year ago. Lifar and I had to find shelter on the top floor of the theatre. There, in a sort of long corridor, which served as bar or smoking room, we found indescribable disorder, chairs thrown upside down, cigarette ends, empty bottles, left from the night before on the linoleum—and no piano.

It was 5:30 p.m. and not a minute to lose. We managed to sweep a little bit of free space and Lifar started to show me the *pas de deux,* humming an incredibly false tune. I tried in spite of everything to memorize what he was showing me, resolved at any price to get this crazy situation in control. For the next variation they sent me Balanchine, who, very reluctantly, showed me hurriedly the actual dance of the *Chatte.*

It was thus, on this slippery and dusty linoleum, amidst all the disorder, without music, that the greatest success of Diaghilev's last years was born and became my greatest personal triumph—that is the reason that up to now I am nicknamed *La Chatte!* At about 6:30 p.m. we were told that the stage was at last free. We scrambled down the steps and I heard at last, for the first time, Sauguet's music. I did not have the time to hear it, no time to ponder over it, just dance and dance without end until the technicians of the Mogador came to chase us away in order to install the decor for the evening performance. All we had to do now was run to the Sarah Bernhardt, where I wanted to repeat once more all the dances before the curtain rose. For the ballet *La Chatte* the floor of the stage had been covered by a sort of black, smooth, shiny oilcloth and Balanchine offered to take my slippers to Crait to have rubber soles added to them.* He had become full of understanding and was ready to do anything for me now, as a real colleague. He had at first been under some misconception, but he is, in fact, a charming individual and we have always been great friends and still are.

At the Sarah Bernhardt I had to try on the costume of Spessivtseva. Luckily our wardrobe mistress, Mme. Meyer, found little to do to it, just to take in a bit at the waist, and make it shorter, during the first ballet of the evening.

Everybody was looking out to help me, offering me this or that from their make-up box as I had not had time to take mine from my suitcase.

In a hurry I sent a message to Mme. Egorova, apologizing for not being

---

*I had danced on the slippery floor without rubber soles, as the shop was closed when Balanchine went there. This persuaded me never again to wear them.

able to come with her that night as I had invited her. I was leaving two seats at the box office but gave her no explanation so that she would have the surprise of seeing me on the stage. In fact, the rumour had spread about Paris and she was waiting for me with impatience.

As soon as the first ballet ended, I hurried, all made-up, onto the stage to rehearse a last time while strange mica figures were installed on the black, shiny floor.

A pale and slender young man with spectacles was walking nervously up and down the floor. He was making his début that night as the composer of the ballet* and behaved like a young father expecting the birth of his first baby—it was Henri Sauguet, the last discovery of Diaghilev.

I felt naturally uneasy and lost in the number of new steps that whizzed round my head. On the advice of "old hands" I had to take a sip of brandy to give me courage while the curtain was rising.

The atmosphere in the auditorium was charged; every minute seemed to weigh a ton, up to the very end, but when finally the curtain went down on a thunder of applause, I almost fainted. My nerves were snapping. The applause turned into an ovation.

The success, I thought, was more due to my courage than to my performance. I learnt, indeed, that the whole audience had been following my movements and sharing my anxiety. The tension at an end, it was acclaiming me.

Yes, the nightmare was over and I felt something wonderful taking place around me, inside me, confusing me and at the same time making me infinitely happy. Sauguet came to kiss my hand; he was touching in his gratitude and looked also relieved of the terrible weight of anxiety. The audience went on calling for curtains, merciless to my nerves. At last I was allowed to be almost carried back to my dressing-room, where already so many friends were waiting for me. Diaghilev embraced me with a radiant smile and this filled me with joy. Sert, Picasso, expressed their admiration in front of this *tour de force,* this lightning performance achieved in one hour and forty minutes.

We had supper, surrounded by friends. I was sitting opposite Diaghilev in a state of complete euphoria. This was the story of *La Chatte,* which became a legend besides being one of the greatest successes.

—from *Nikitina,* translated by Baroness Budberg, 1959

---

*The book was drawn from an Aesop fable by Kochno.

MARIUS PETIPA
A Dancer's Childhood

The central figure in nineteenth-century ballet, Marius Petipa (1818–1910) was born in Marseilles to an actress mother and ballet master father. (His brother, Lucien, was another of the most famous danseurs of his era.) After a peripatetic youth, including a family sojourn in America, in 1847 Petipa went to St. Petersburg as the Imperial Ballet's leading male dancer, and was soon assisting first Jules Perrot, the chief ballet master, and then Perrot's successor, Arthur Saint-Léon, in creating new works. His first great triumph, in 1862, was the spectacular The Pharaoh's Daughter, *and in 1870 he himself became ballet master in chief. Among his greatest triumphs were* La Bayadère, Don Quixote, Raymonda, *and the crown jewel of classical ballet,* The Sleeping Beauty. *He also restaged such crucial works as* Giselle, Coppélia, *and* Le Corsaire, *and is responsible for Acts I and III of* Swan Lake. *He has had the most profound influence of any of history's choreographers, most dramatically on the work of George Balanchine.*

On March 11, 1822, in the French coastal city of Marseilles, to Jean Antoine Petipa and his wife, Victorine Grasseau, was born a son, Alphonse Victor Marius Petipa. That was your most obedient servant. Under the conditions of the time, I could have been considered already a servant of the stage, from my very birth. My father was a *premier danseur* and ballet master, and my mother enjoyed considerable renown as a performer of first roles in tragedies. Service to art was then transferred from generation to generation, and the history of French theatre lists many theatrical families.

The role of the city in which I saw light will be limited in my biography, because neither as an artist nor as a man, in the narrow meaning of the word, did I take any kind of steps in it. I was hardly three months old when in June of the same 1822 my parents received an invitation to Brussels, whence they set out with the whole family in a travelling coach acquired by my father for this purpose.

Today, the railroad carries travellers from Marseilles to Brussels in less than twenty-four hours, but then, for the same trip, twenty-four days was not enough. The travelling carriage became a moving apartment; in it lived our quite numerous family, and I tried to occupy the least possible place, either cuddling at the breast of my mother, who fed me, or resting on her hospitable lap. Besides us and my father in the berlin (a kind of four-wheeled carriage) there were sheltered also my brother, Lucien, and my sister, Victoria. It is not difficult for the reader to surmise that I have kept no memories of this first journey of mine, and how we reached the Belgian capital.

In Brussels I received a general education in the high school (*gymnasium*), but paralleling this I attended the Fétis Conservatory, where I studied solfeggio and learned to play the violin with a comrade of mine who later became the well-known violinist Vieuxtemps.

At seven, I started instruction in the art of dancing in the class of my father, who broke many bows on my hands in order to acquaint me with the mysteries of choreography. Such pedagogical means were necessary, because in my childhood I did not feel the smallest inclination to this branch of art. To the young thinker, it seemed unworthy for men to fuss before the public in all sorts of graceful poses. One way or another, I had to overcome this great amount of knowledge, and at nine years I appeared on the stage in the ballet *La Dansomanie,* created by my father.

I first appeared before the public coming out of a magic lantern, in the costume of a Savoyard, with a monkey in my arms; my début role was that of the son of a courtier, whose name day was celebrated in the course of the ballet.

As little as my heart was inclined towards the activities of dancers, I gave way to the suggestions and admonitions of my mother, whom I worshipped, and who succeeded in convincing me that it was my duty to obey my father's will.

My educational and theatrical occupations were interrupted for two months in preparation for my first communion, which even now has great meaning in every Catholic family, and then was considered the most sacred religious duty of every Catholic, at the transition from childhood to adolescence.

Upon fulfilment of this duty, I started to dance and to play the violin again with zeal, until 1830, when a revolution broke out in Brussels. It started during a theatrical performance, after the prayer in the well-known opera *Fenella,* or *La Muette de Portici.*

At the cry of "To arms, to arms!" the tenor, Lafeuillade, still in the costume of Masaniello, rushed out into the street, where a huge crowd of revolutionaries was waiting for him.

The opera conspirator carried into reality the hero whom he played, and continued his role in real life, not even changing his costume; the stage exerted its influence on the crowd and gave an impetus to one of the greatest liberating movements of the first half of the nineteenth century.

For a full fifteen months, the theatres discontinued their activities. This was a bad time for my father. It was not easy to feed the family, being deprived of the main source of income; often we lacked the bare necessities, because my father had to be satisfied with the small amount received from two boarding schools where he taught social dance. My brother, Lucien, and I helped our father by copying music for Prince Trezine, a passionate lover of waltzes and quadrilles, which he himself composed in incredible quantity. But neither our earnings nor father's income was enough for more than a meagre existence.

Soon after the revolution started, Dutchmen were hidden in the Antwerp citadel, situated a few miles from Antwerp. The French and Belgians joined in great strength in this city, and prepared to attack the citadel.

In extreme need, and after lengthy hesitation, my father decided to rent the Antwerp theatre and take the risk, in view of the critical times, of giving a few ballet performances in this theatre, the entire company consisting only of members of his family.

We went to Antwerp. On the day following our arrival we decorated every corner and fence with posters, bringing to the attention of the public the following:

First performance of the famous company of
M. Petipa, ballet master of the grand
Théâtre de la Monnaie, in Brussels

THE MILLERS
BALLET IN THREE ACTS
Cast

THE MILLER	Petipa, father
THE MILLER'S WIFE	Petipa, mother
LISETTE (*their daughter*)	Mlle. Victoria P.
COLIN	Lucien P.
GILLES (*comic character*)	Marius P.

Male and female Peasants

The latter were supernumeraries hired in the city and trained by father. There were no lamps in the theatre. How to light it? Necessity is the mother of invention. Father ordered tallow candles to be put into large potatoes, which in turn were stuck directly to the floor, between the wings. These improvised candlesticks did their job, but at the end of the performance a small incident occurred, which fortunately ended all right, and amused the not very numerous public. From our rapid and energetic movements in the final *galop*, the potatoes became unglued, rolled onto the stage, and appeared suddenly at our feet. Several officers seated in the auditorium burst into jolly laughter, and rewarded us with loud applause. Returning to the hotel, after the performance, we, the younger generation, were still laughing, but our father and mother had no heart for laughter, crushed by the miserable receipts. In the cash-box there were only sixty francs, in all.

The following morning my father held a conference with my mother, deliberating on the question of whether we should risk giving a second performance. There were no special expectations of large receipts, but there was no other way out—we had to pay the hotel and coach, and had no money at all. Leaving to our parents the decision of this vital question, the young forces of the company, that is, my brother, sister, and I, went out into the street.

Suddenly a carriage rolled into the hotel driveway, and stopped for the changing of the horses. The doors of the berlin opened, and out stepped a gentleman. Seeing us, he approached and asked, with astonishment:

"What brought you here, children?"

It was the great tragedian Talma. He knew our family, was Lucien's godfather, and therefore kissed us all tenderly. My brother told him, in full detail, about our performance of the previous evening, not omitting to inform him of the complete absence of an audience.

We wanted to tell our father immediately about meeting M. Talma, but he forbade this, called the *maître d'hotel,* and ordered him to bring some figs. He decided on this treat because it was found everywhere because of the fashion for a dessert called *quatre mendiants,* consisting of figs, raisins, almonds, and nuts. This was a cheap, unperishable dessert, and therefore was served in all second-class hotels and on every table d'hôte.

Ordering us to turn away, so as not to see what he was preparing to do, Talma stuck three *louis d'or* in each of the three figs, which he gave us, accompanying the treat with kisses.

"Tell your father and mother that in two months I will visit them in Brussels."

He said this, seated himself in his travelling carriage, and hurried away.

Waving our handkerchiefs in farewell, we rushed into the hotel and ran up the stairs in the twinkling of an eye to tell our father the good news. There, he sprang to the window and loudly shouted, "Talma! Talma!", but the tragedian was already far away. We three, interrupting each other, choking with delight, shouted:

"Papa! Mama! Look inside the figs! In each of them are three *louis d'or*! M. Talma told us not to look, but we saw what he was doing anyway!"

Father and mother, exchanging looks, said: "What a noble way to help us."

"*Garçon,*" calls our father, "the check!"—and turns to our mother: "I will go at once to reserve places on the stagecoach which leaves at four o'clock, and you pack our things. Before our departure, we must have a good lunch."

And we all raised a sincere cry, "Long live Talma!"

—from *Russian Ballat Master,* translated by Helen Whittaker, 1958

MAYA PLISETSKAYA
The Thaw

Born in Moscow to a prominent Russian-Jewish family of dance artists, the Messerers, the young Maya saw her father dragged away forever during the purges of the 1930s and her actress mother sent to the Gulag. Adopted by her ballerina aunt, she studied at the Bolshoi and, on her graduation, was immediately accepted by the Bolshoi company as a principal dancer. Beautiful, flamboyant, powerful, and glamorous, she was a sensation from the start—as well as anathema to the Soviet apparatus that controlled her fate. She was denied the right to tour until 1959, although she was world-famous by that time, with her great roles including Odette-Odile (which she performed more than eight hundred times), The Dying Swan, Kitri in Don Quixote, *and dozens of others. Late in her career—which stretched at the Bolshoi for forty-seven years—she took up choreography, beginning with a version of* Anna Karenina, *with music by her famous composer husband, Rodion Shchedrin.*

"Foreigners will save us," Igor Moiseyev liked to say in those years. It was his motto, his mantra. He tried to console me with that aphorism, too.

They might save some people, but they only made trouble for me.

At a reception I was approached by a fair-haired, handsome young man. He introduced himself in fluent Russian. "I am John Morgan, second secretary of the British Embassy. I adore the ballet. I'm a big fan of yours."

We got to talking. Since I know no foreign languages, I could communicate only with Russian speakers.

Morgan was an amusing conversationalist. He was knowledgeable in the ballet, especially English ballet. Where what premiered, when, who was feuding with whom, who had changed partners. He had some gossip about our Violetta Prokhorova-Elvin. I was interested in it all.

"When are you dancing next?"

I told him the day after next, at Tchaikovsky Hall. A Strauss waltz in Goleizovsky's choreography.

Morgan was interested. "How can I get tickets? Will you help?"

I left two tickets for "Morgan" at the box office. Among the bouquets I received was one of white lilacs, with the card of the second secretary of the British Embassy in Moscow.

We met as old acquaintances at the next reception. I thanked him for the lilacs; Morgan praised the Goleizovsky. And suddenly, "Why are they saying that you're not going to London? How can that be?"

Because, I replied, the KGB put a red dot over my name, and that of my brother Alexander, in the theater's personnel list. (I had gotten the news as a top secret from Pyotr Andreyevich Gusev that very day; it was like a razor in my throat. And so I blurted it out.)

Morgan was unperturbed, in the British style. Not an eyebrow twitched. As if he hadn't heard.

"May I present you to our ambassador, Mr. Hayter?"

Was that going to be a help? Or a new burden? A trap?

Hayter was a tall, middle-aged gentleman. The compleat English lord. His Russian wasn't bad.

"Our side want you to come very much. The English public must see your *Swan Lake*. We shall insist."

Sensing that I had British support, I took a crazy step. I sent Chulaki, our managing director, an ultimatum. If my brother Alexander Plisetsky is struck from the trip to England (I did not mention myself), I ask to be freed from work in the Bolshoi Theater from such-and-such a date. And I left for vacation.

The letter was not smart, and harsh, of course, but it was to the point: would they really put my brother, six years my junior, through the same hell? Clearly, I was hysterical. What would I do without the ballet? Breed chickens, raise cabbages? But I was desperate.

In a thirty-second conversation, Alla Tsabel informed me over the telephone that my request had been granted. I was no longer in the theater. I should turn in my pass. Things were not good.

I spent August in Leningrad with my cousin Era. She always had a calming effect on me, like valerian drops. I traveled the length and breadth of the Hermitage several times. I stood for a long hour in the Pushkin house on the Moika Canal, where the poet slowly faded after his fatal duel. I went to Vaganova's grave. I wept and complained to her.

In the middle of August a telegram summoned me to Moscow. Minister of Culture Mikhailov wanted to talk to me. I hesitated, but went.

The conversation was conciliatory, not harsh. Why was I setting conditions? My brother was a separate issue. I should take back my impolite letter. The theater needed me.

Tsabel called my apartment on Shchepkinsky the minute I got back from the ministry, informing me that the rehearsals for London would start on August 20. I had to be at the theater; I worked there. Whether I went on the tour or not was not her concern, but I did have to rehearse.

On the first day, instead of rehearsals, we had a crowded and noisy "meeting about the trip." I was literally led, although seemingly by accident, to the meeting. A whisper in my ear: I'd do well to speak. What about? To give an evaluation of my behavior. Oh, how the Bolsheviks liked to have people repent! To humiliate themselves, trample themselves.

The theater's Party organizer, French horn player Polekh, who always wore a bow tie and makeup (after all, he was a performer), gave the first speech, and he attacked me with the might of the Party. I was this and that and a so-and-so, pushy, conceited, shaming the name of the Soviet artist.

For three hours they spoke nonsense, exposing me. Let her speak, they demanded. I tightened my lips and said nothing. Toward the end I left; I got sick of it.

But I did go through two full stage rehearsals of *Swan Lake*. Before the third one, Tsabel again: "Karelskaya will rehearse. You are not going. It is decided."

I saw black. Sophisticated Chinese torture. I rushed to make calls from Shchepkinsky. Bulganin, Molotov, Mikoyan, Shepilov, Mikhailov (friends had given me their office numbers over the summer). I didn't call Khrushchev, saving his number for a rainy day. Would it ever be rainier than this? But no one came to the phone or called back after I spoke to their assistants and secretaries. Desperately, I called the British Embassy to talk to Morgan—his number was on the business card with the lilac bouquet.

It was a switchboard. I asked for Mr. John Morgan, second secretary. Just a moment. Click. Morgan picked up the phone. I spoke disjointedly, a flow of words.

"Where do you live? Shchepkinsky, Eight? Right behind the theater? I have some brand-new books for you. About English ballet. May I drop them by this evening around six thirty, after work?"

I had made the call.

But then I got cold feet. Scared. The phone at the embassy had to be tapped. God knows what they would think. And I couldn't receive a young man alone.

I called around. I reached Nikolai Simachov, at home with the flu. "Kolya, darling, come over this evening at six. I'm getting some new ballet books. About the English. We can look at them together."

He agreed.

Morgan visited me only twice. That evening and three days later. During both brief visits I was never alone. I have witnesses. Living ones, of sound mind and good memory. We barely spoke about the London tour. Morgan assured me that everything would be all right. I'd go. No more. We leafed through the books, made silly social chitchat. Had Georgian tea with cherry jam.

But the consequences of our meetings were out of a spy thriller. A KGB car dogged my every step, twenty-four hours a day. There were always three men in the car. Their silhouettes were clear against the setting autumn sun in Moscow. Wherever I went, so went the three heroes. Eliseyev's store, a studio, an exhibit—they would park not far away. Waiting. Coming out, I'd take a taxi or get a ride with a friend, and I could see them in the rearview mirror, keeping their distance but never letting me out of their sight. All the way to my house. And then they would wait, for hours. At a distance, but I could see them clearly from the window. On duty. Fine conspirators. Just like a movie.

At first I had thought they were new admirers. I was worried. What if they were robbers? But Grisha Levitin checked their license plate and said with certainty that it was a KGB car. "What's new now?"

Everything was tied in a very tight knot. Morgan vanished. He stopped calling, he did not attend receptions. Had he left, or was he coerced? I was really frightened. I wouldn't call the Brits myself. I had been burned. This was scary.

It was not until eight years later, when I was allowed to travel, that I met secretly with Morgan when I was in London. Don't get excited, reader. Secretly from the KGB, not from the rosy, neatly pressed Mrs. Morgan and three little Morgans in their polished, clipped, and tended house with green lawns outside London. It seems that when he came to visit me in Shchepkin-sky, Morgan had parked his car near the Maly Theater. At a distance from my building. This caution must have worried the KGB—and ruined me completely. Their conclusion was clear: passionate love, Plisetskaya will remain in England, ask for political asylum. The other possibility was espionage: Plisetskaya was the new Mata Hari.

There were insubordinate people in the theater. Forty-five signed a letter in my defense to Minister Mikhailov: Plisetskaya is the mainstay of the repertoire; her presence is vital to the success of the tour. There were major names among the signatures: Ulanova, Lavrovsky, Fayer. Thank you, good people. If only you had known in your naiveté that the letter should have been sent to KGB Chairman Ivan Serov, at Dzerzhinsky Square. The letter didn't save me, but it did add kindling to the fire. Otherwise the flame of hope would have gone out completely.

Late one night Fayer called. He asked me to come immediately. I grabbed a taxi. The KGB car followed.

In a deep whisper, keeping away from his telephone, which might be bugged, Fayer told me that there had been a reply to the group letter. Not exactly a reply, but a reply . . . Not written, but oral . . . Fayer hemmed and hawed, avoiding any specifics. But it became clear to me that in order to save myself, I had to write a letter of *repentance*. To Mikhailov. The sooner the better.

I didn't sleep that night, trying to figure out what I could repent of without losing my dignity. I composed the letter as best I could. What would you have done in my place? I sincerely regret that I did not keep a draft and I cannot remember what sins besides my truly tactless ultimatum I could have blamed myself for.

And the very next day, breaking my own promise not to go to embassies ever again, I went to the Indonesian reception for President Sukarno. I was the only one from the Bolshoi who was invited. I was an attraction now, a subversive personage!

The first person I bumped into was Mikhailov. Fate. I pulled the letter out of my bag. Here, enjoy my repentance. Mikhailov's paw engulfed the letter, and he mumbled something.

A few days later he called me into his office. Gave me a long, unhurried speech. The solo aria: "It's a good letter. Courageous. Wise. Good for you. But is everything in there? Have you forgotten anything, hidden anything? Have you really understood all your actions, Maya Mikhailovna? You have a heightened interest in foreigners. That has to be taken into account . . ."

All in a smooth, steady voice, without periods or commas, but with small hitches on the letter "r," which sometimes stuck and bubbled in Nikolai Alexandrovich's throat. I could see that the minister was enjoying his own speech. It was flowing smoothly. He pushed a button to summon his secretary.

"Bring in Comrades Pakhomov and Stepanov."

I will explain who's who to the reader. Vasily Ivanovich Pakhomov was Mikhailov's deputy and had already been appointed head of the trip to England. Later he was director of the Bolshoi for several years . . . Vladimir Timofeyevich Stepanov, a soulful and not callous man, was in charge of foreign affairs at the Ministry of Culture.

The speech continued. "You have great talent, Maya Mikhailovna. A real talent, a major talent. And what did Comrade Lenin teach us? He taught us that talent must be protected. And that is why I dropped all my business to meet with you. I understand that you are suffering, perhaps not sleeping. But allow me to question which of us is suffering more. You or I, Minister of Culture Mikhailov?"

I am not angry at Mikhailov today. In essence, he was just another galley slave, like me. He was simply working two or three decks higher in the Soviet ship. It did not depend on him whether I would go to London or stay home. That was decided by a different institution. The KGB. But Mikhailov was the front man, who had to look good in a bad game. He was the visible part of the iceberg.

I ran into his wife, Raisa Timofeyevna, as I left Mikhailov's office. She was a crazy, uncontrollable woman but with a peasant's warmth and compassion. She took a most active and noisy part in her husband's work. She gave me a bear hug—the minister's wife was a large, full-bodied woman—and spoke right into my ear so that my head rang. "Nikolai Alexandrovich has nothing to do with it. We both love you. But at the KGB, Serov has mountains of denunciations of you. You have to talk to him yourself. He decides everything."

Desultorily I made my way to the coatroom for my raincoat. It was pouring. The Moscow weather matched my mood—sleet, mud, puddles, slush. My head was pounding, filled with the words I had had to listen to all morning.

Someone hailed me cheerfully in the coatroom crowd. Victor Petrovich Gontar, Khrushchev's son-in-law. Director of the Kiev Opera. I had danced *Swan Lake* there at the end of the season. He asked how things were going. Helped me with my raincoat.

"We've heard even in the capital city of Kiev that Moscow is treating you badly. I defended you at the table at Tsar Nikita's (as he called his father-in-law). Shameless men, bothering a woman. Let her go—what's she going to do? It's all that Ivan Serov's fault. Trying too hard. Little shit."

There was that name again: Serov. It always came back to him.

"Victor Petrovich, could I talk to Serov? Raisa Timofeyevna told me today . . ."

"Why put it off? Let's go call him from the ministry on the spinner." (I have to explain to the Western reader that the direct government hotline was called the spinner. Creamy beige and tubby, the telephone had the Soviet emblem on the dial. The child of Edison perfected for Party needs, it was given to the highest Soviet *nomenklatura*. Only the most select. The "top," the most "reliable.") With our coats under our arms we walked up to the third floor. Gontar looked into offices, slamming the doors. He did not stand on ceremony. He was the Son-in-Law. He burst into Stepanov's office.

"He's got a spinner. He's a good fellow, not a coward, he won't refuse."

His well-trained secretary stood up respectfully and reported, "Viktor Petrovich, Vladimir Timofeyevich is with the minister. Shall I tell the minister's secretary that you are here?"

"Maya and I will wait in his office. We're not in a hurry."

No one dared contradict Gontar. The sophistication of Soviet subordination! Gontar was merely a theater director. But . . . he was a relative. A close one. The husband of Khrushchev's daughter by his first marriage. And the denizens of the ministerial palaces knew who was a husband, a brother-in-law, a son-in-law better than the church calendar. Better than Stalin's *Short Course of the History of the Communist Party*. They never made mistakes.

Shutting the door, Gontar picked up the spinner. In the neat little directory, the size of an address book, he located the four-digit number (fortunately—or unfortunately—the all-powerful book was right next to the telephone). He dialed. And handed me the phone, gesturing that he was not there.

The line was picked up instantly. "Serov here."

The unexpectedness made me forget Serov's name and patronymic. Just a minute earlier, and quite inappropriately, I had been thinking that Gogol's character Khlestakov was also called Ivan Alexandrovich. I was losing my mind.

"Hello, this is Plisetskaya."

Serov did not respond to my greeting, nor did he say hello.

"Where are you calling from? Who gave you my number?" His voice was hoarse and infuriated. The receiver resonated. Gontar could hear everything.

"I'm calling from the Ministry of Culture . . ."

Serov interrupted harshly. "What do you want from me?"

"I wanted to talk with you."

"What about?"

"I am not being allowed abroad. On the London tour."

"What do I have to do with it?"

My voice started trembling. I was losing my nerve. He was behaving like a real boor to me.

"Everyone says that you are not letting me go."

"Who's everyone?"

"Everyone."

"Specifically?"

I lost all self-control. My vocal cords did not respond to my brain. I heard my voice, no longer my own, a stranger's hollow tones, say, "Raisa Timofeyevna Mikhailova . . ."

He was screeching like a fishmonger. "That's just what she'd like! Mikhailov makes the decisions; I have nothing to do with it."

He hung up. The conversation was over. Gontar and I exchanged glum looks. Our act was a flop. Serov was a real bandit.

A half hour later Stepanov's direct phone was removed. His innocent secretary was fired, tossed out onto the street from the ministry. The KGB knew instantly whose phone I had been using. Stepanov miraculously survived (my "diversion" took place in his absence), and to his great honor he never, not once, reproached me for my thoughtlessness.

Gontar, my dear, kindhearted Viktor Petrovich, the compassionate, noisy bull in the china shop—it doesn't matter, thank you anyway. You were a human being. Gontar, Khrushchev's son-in-law, damn it, had to pay, too. I don't know what Serov reported to Nikita Sergeyevich. But for more than two years Gontar was not allowed to cross the threshold of his powerful father-in-law's abode. His trips abroad were stopped. The disturber of the peace was punished.

I was still followed every day by the KGB car. Using up state gas, wearing down tires, making the agents' pants shiny in the seat. And people began avoiding me as if I had the plague. I was still invited to receptions, but I did not go. The one time I did go to the Kremlin—maybe someone in government would take pity and talk about my fate—I had to walk home across Moscow all alone. No one offered me a ride. I used to have to fight my way through the offers.

On October 1 and 2 *my* troupe flew off in two sections to London. There weren't a lot of ballet people left in Moscow. I was one of them.

Perhaps I have wearied you with the dates and numbers so thickly sprinkled throughout these chapters. When writing about my London epic, I kept looking into my diaries. I suppose I could have told this story more succinctly, in general outline. But I want you, my reader, to follow day by day, without haste, the path of my little Golgotha in the fall of 1956. This was the kind of "thaw" we had in Russia that year.

—from *I, Maya Plisetskaya,* translated by Antonina W. Bouis, 2001

*One of the greatest of film directors (*La Grande Illusion, The Rules of the Game*),
Jean Renoir (1894–1979) wrote a loving book about his famous father, the French
Impressionist artist Auguste Renoir, from which this excerpt is taken.*

Paris was dazzled by the Russian Ballet. While he was at work on her
portrait Renoir asked Misia [Sert Edwards] to tell him about Stravinsky.
Accompanying herself at the piano, she tried to give him an idea of the
young composer's music. "He is, in music, what you are in painting." One
evening, when the Edwardses stayed on to dinner—Misia just nibbled at her
food, whereas her husband gladly gorged himself on my mother's cooking—
they were suddenly struck with an idea. "We will take you all to the ballet!"
My father was having a bad attack of pain, and could walk only with difficulty. However, he was willing to be persuaded. My mother got dressed in
the twinkling of an eye. Gabrielle ran to the studio and put on a Callot gown
that Renoir had used for several of his pictures. Jeanne Baudot, a friend of the
Callots, had got the dresses for him, as they were "very useful for certain
subjects." The dress was out of fashion, and made Gabrielle look like a gypsy,
much to the delight of the Edwardses. I was in the party and I donned my
Sainte-Croix uniform, with its three rows of gold buttons. Edwards and
Misia were already in evening dress, as they were to meet Diaghilev at
Maxim's for midnight supper. Renoir went in his working clothes, a jacket
with a turned-up collar, a flannel shirt, a blue cravat with white polka dots,
and his cap, which he kept on for fear the cold would aggravate his neural-
gia. My mother and Gabrielle wanted to put him into his dress suit. But it
seemed too much of an effort for him, and he stayed as he was.

Edwards was a box-holder, so there was no problem about getting seats.
On arriving at the grand staircase of the theater, Renoir thought he would
have to turn back, but Edwards lifted him up in his arms, and, with Misia
and my mother on either side, solemnly carried him up, while everyone
looked on in amazement. It must be confessed that we made an odd-looking
group. The interior of the theater was magnificent. The audience which had
come to applaud or hiss these ballets that were to revolutionize the theater

was decked out in unimaginable splendor. I am not exaggerating when I say that it was more beautiful than any of my childhood dreams of the royal courts described in Andersen's fairy tales, or those of Perrault. Nor have I ever beheld anything to approach it since. The black evening clothes of the men, as they stood behind the women, enhanced their brilliance. It was like an enormous bouquet of bare shoulders emerging from pastel-colored silks. The white fire of diamonds, the barbaric sparkle of rubies, the cold flash of emeralds, the softness of pearls caressing bosoms, all shone against the smooth flesh of these women, conferring on them and, indirectly, on the entire assemblage, a sort of nobility, transient perhaps, but undeniable. They were not creatures of flesh and blood, but figures in a picture; people who are never seen walking in the street; who never catch cold, or perspire as they toil up the slopes of Montmartre in summer. All these people had their opera glasses fixed on my father, who was not even conscious of it. Gabrielle thought they recognized him, and she deplored his appearance: "With his jacket all spotted with paint, and a cycling cap, what will they take us for?" My mother smiled, touched by this confidence in "the boss's" celebrity. But Misia put the matter neatly when she observed, "Hardly half of them even know the name Renoir; but if Titian were here, none of them would even know who he was!"

Renoir was carried away by the performance, and Edwards was happy to see his friend's enjoyment. The principal piece on the program was *Petrouchka*. I cannot recall if it was that first evening that we saw *Le Spectre de la Rose,* in which Nijinsky leaped across the stage "like a bird," said Gabrielle; "like a panther," said my father.

—from *Renoir, My Father,* translated by Randolph and Dorothy Weaver, 1958

RUTH ST. DENIS
Egypta

Apart from Isadora Duncan, the most famous and influential of the early American "modern" dancers was Ruth St. Denis (1877/1878/1879/1880?–1968). She was performing as a "skirt dancer" when she stumbled upon "Oriental" dance and philosophy. Her first famous creation was Radha, *which she toured for years; others included* The Cobra *and* The Nautch. *In 1914 she married the considerably younger Ted Shawn, and they founded their joint school and company known as Denishawn, from which sprang Martha Graham, Doris Humphrey, and Charles Weidman, among others. Even after they divorced, she went on performing at Shawn's Jacob's Pillow festival until 1964. No wonder she was known as the "First Lady of American Dance."*

This was a period of extraordinarily little activity in my dancing. There were no other dancers in the company; my two little numbers contributed very little to my artistic development, and I was, on top of that, lazy. Routine has always been drudgery to me. I have seldom achieved anything in the dance except when I was so obsessed with an idea that I did not know I was practicing.

As time went on, the atmosphere, the people, the plays, D.B.'s [David Belasco's] own personality were increasingly inharmonious to my deepest self. I was not unhappy, but I was dissatisfied. My dissatisfaction and undirected energy made me loud and rollicking, which Patsy, my inseparable, did nothing to curb. I can still see us, sharing an upper pullman for purposes of economy. I seemed to be perpetually awake, sitting cross-legged at the end of the bunk, ablaze with some new idea or giggling over a new Irish story. My voice, which has always been high and penetrating, would frequently get us into trouble. Millward's tousled head would appear along the aisle, and growling protests would silence us for a while. But midnight has always found me at the zenith of my talking powers and disapproval had only a temporary effect.

I do not know what I talked about, but the stream seldom abated. It was one way of getting rid of this terrible excess energy which my small parts in the company did not begin to utilize.

Undoubtedly I was preparing myself, unknown to me, for the rapidly

approaching moment when all my perplexities would be clarified, all my
energies brought into a dazzling focus. That moment came so suddenly and
presented itself in such unexpected surroundings that I still marvel at it.

We had reached Buffalo on our way west with the *Dubarry* company.
It was a stormy, sleety day, and Buffalo is far from a romantic city. We
had ensconced ourselves in the usual drab boardinghouse. My room was a
gloomy little hall bedroom with awful red paper on the wall and only space
enough for a narrow bed, bureau, and chair. Pat and I escaped from all this as
soon as we could and went to a drugstore to get a soda. We were laughing as
usual over some joke, and sipping our sodas, when my eyes lifted above the
fountain and I saw a cigarette poster of Egyptian Deities.

It must have contained a potent magic for me. I stopped with my soda half
consumed and stared and stared. Pat at length dragged me away by force but
she could not break the spell. We had hardly reached the boardinghouse
when I said to her, "Go back and see if you can get that poster from the soda
clerk. Here's a dollar if he wants money for it."

I really suffered in the brief interval before she returned with the rolled-
up poster in her hand. What if he did not let her have it? I took it breathlessly
and hung it on the wall opposite my bed. Then I propped myself up with pillows and stared at it.

I saw a modernized and most un-Egyptian figure of the goddess Isis. She
was sitting on a throne, framed by a sort of pylon. At her feet were the
waters of the Nile with lotus growing. Her knees were close together; her
right hand was on her right thigh, while with the other hand she held a lotus-
tipped staff. The coloring was harmonious and the composition pleasing but
undistinguished.

It is only from the vantage point of maturity that I can analyze what happened to me. This seated image of Isis, a superficial, commercial drawing for
a cigarette company, opened up to me in that moment the whole story that
was Egypt.

Here was an external image which stirred into instant consciousness all
that latent capacity for wonder, that still and meditative love of beauty which
lay at the deepest center of my spirit. In this figure before me was the symbol of the entire nation, culture, and destiny of Egypt. The main concern in
the picture was, of course, the figure, its repose, its suggestion of latent
power and beauty, constituting to my sharply awakened sensitivity a strange
symbol of the complete inner being of man. It was like the white light which
contains all the colors, like the apparent stillness which contains all motion.
It was, however, not merely a symbol of Egypt, but a universal symbol of all
the elements of history and art which may be expressed through the human
body.

I cannot put into words the intensity and swiftness of this revelation. Lying on my bed, looking at this strange instrument of fate, I identified myself in a flash with the figure of Isis. She became the expression of all the somber mystery and beauty of Egypt, and I knew that my destiny as a dancer had sprung alive in that moment. I would become a rhythmic and impersonal instrument of spiritual revelation rather than a personal actress of comedy or tragedy. I had never before known such an inward shock of rapture.

Pat said she had to feed me for three days before I showed signs of coming to. I got through my part in *Dubarry* somehow, but clung very close to Pat for fear I should make some blunder with cues or costumes. I was literally obsessed, and all time spent away from the poster was a tragic loss.

The image of my dance was becoming clear and well defined. I wanted to become this seated figure who symbolized the whole nation of Egypt. I wanted to tell of the rise and fall of her destinies during the period of a day and a night. The day would show her emerging from the unknown, developing to her zenith at noon when her kings and her priests and her artists brought a nation to its prime, and then declining with alarums and wars and invasions to the time of her death. The night would be given to her concept of immortality and its processes of attainment.

I have no wish to appear more occult and mysterious than necessary, but I did have a strange intuitive understanding, far beyond anything that I consciously knew, of the great power Egypt wielded over our age and culture. I had glimpsed in the history, religion, and art of Egypt the symbol of man's eternal search for the beauty and grandeur of life. The latent, subjective side of my nature had begun to function. Visions, plans, and ideas which I had never before experienced crowded in upon me. The world of antiquity and the Orient with all its rich poetry of the human soul opened up and possessed me.

During these exalted hours Pat was my only confidante. I was afraid others would ridicule me or perhaps steal and mutilate what I knew was a great discovery.

Those fateful three days in Buffalo spun my life around like a top. Not only must I learn how to translate this new conception into movement, but I must also learn how to write about these strange new dances; I must gain some knowledge of painting and sculpture, color and line, some familiarity with archeology; I must amplify my understanding of music and costuming; and master stage direction and, above all, lighting. I suddenly discovered that all I had absorbed from D.B., when I was apparently joking and slumbering my way through the seasons, was now to be turned into rich and wide channels.

The *Dubarry* tour carried us as far as California, but even though we played one-night stands I found time to visit all the libraries I could reach and discover in their books and pictures a corroboration rather than a revelation of these new marvels. By the time we reached San Francisco I had blocked out in detail the various episodes of the dance *Egypta,* which was utterly beyond my financial powers to do at this time.

The first thing I did when I got to San Francisco is probably the last thing I shall do before I go to a better world: I searched out a photographer. I had only five dollars to spend, so I fell into the hands of a little Japanese who must have thought I was a very queer fish. In those days right-minded young ladies did not go about in bare feet, and with only a band of silk around their apparently unclothed middles. However he did his work well, and anyone who chooses may see a serious young person seated on an improvised throne, which was probably the photographer's one chair, with a dark drape thrown over it. She has on a short black Egyptian wig with a little paper lotus flower in front. Around her ankles and arms is the imitation Egyptian jewelry made out of colored beads. She is seated in the same pose as the poster and is looking as stern as a small youthful face can look when obsessed with a grand idea.

The tour closed, and I returned as fast as possible to New York and the family. I knew I had laid the foundations of what was to be my real career.

—from *Ruth St. Denis,* 1939

MARGARET SEVERN
Dancing with Nijinska

Margaret Severn (1901–1997) is best known today for her film Dance Masks: The World of Margaret Severn, *made in 1981, when she was seventy-nine. She began in vaudeville, appearing in* The Greenwich Village Follies *of 1920 and a short-lived musical called* Linger Longer Letty, *but she was clearly an accomplished classical dancer as well. According to a 1994 letter to* The New York Times, *while she was attending a performance of the Annabelle Gamson Company recreating the work of Isadora Duncan, someone said to her, "I hope you enjoy these reconstructed dances." "They were never constructed," she replied. She was then ninety-two.*

In 1931 the school I had opened in New York was just beginning to prosper when a call from Budapest, where my mother was working with the distinguished psychoanalyst and disciple of Freud Dr. Sandor Ferenczi, suggested that I come there at once, as her health was in a precarious state. I delegated all teaching to my assistant and took the first boat on which I could secure passage, hoping that I could find some way to earn my living in Budapest and remain at my mother's side. I gave a concert and was offered an engagement in an operetta, but learned that salaries were paid each night in accordance with the day's box-office receipts. As my mother was now stronger, early in 1932 we boarded the Orient Express for Paris, she coming to see that I was properly installed in a hotel before returning to her work in psychoanalysis. I wrote to her frequently, as I had always done, and the letters that she saved help me to recapture life in Paris as I observed it then.

Through my friend and former pupil Olga Kouznetsova, who had access to the Russian grapevine, I soon learned that Bronislava Nijinska was preparing a troupe to appear at the Opéra-Comique in late May and June with the great Russian bass Feodor Chaliapin and the Opéra Russe. Her company was to present an evening of ballets and to share a program with Chaliapin in Rimsky-Korsakov's one-act opera *Mozart and Salieri,* as well as provide the dances for *Prince Igor* and *Boris Godunov.* Her company was also to give a gala at the Trocadéro. Showing her no pictures of myself and uttering not a single word of English, I carefully dressed myself to look as Russian as possible when I turned up for the class that was to serve as my audition. . . .

I couldn't write you yesterday because I had a full day planned when the news suddenly came from Olga that Nijinska would hold her audition this morning and I had been warned that one of her idiosyncracies is that she likes all her girls dressed completely in black, so besides carrying out my tea program and whatnot, I had to rush around and buy the necessary things, although Olga helped by loaning me her tunic. By the time I got all rigged out in black knickers and tights and white socks (as prescribed) I felt I should go skiing or anyhow, horseback riding. The letter from Larionov was not forth-coming—he's just too vague to live, that man—so I went along with the others, sans name. There were about six girls and ten men. Her audition takes the form of a short class, which of course I found easy

enough, although she gave some Russian and Spanish character steps of a
rather puzzling origin. There was nothing in her manner to show that she
noticed me more than anyone else, but at the end she dismissed all the
others and asked if I would dance something for her. It so happened that her
pianist was the very same one I had previously rehearsed with and somebody had a book of Chopin handy, so I did one. There was no fooling Nijinska into thinking I was just any ballet girl and she displayed a great deal of
interest. Her only criticisms were that I sometimes broke my line, which is
true, and that I had evidently worked too much alone. She asked what I
wanted to do, as she would be interested to have me in the company.
I replied that if I went in the co. I would do whatever she thought I should
do. This pleased her very much because she said that all the American girls
thought they were somebody and wanted to be head of the co. right away,
and that as a matter of principle I would have to be ready to do whatever
she might wish to give me, but that I had a great deal of talent and was a
good dancer so naturally I would receive good parts. She didn't mean to put
me with the ballet girls, so to speak, but her co. was really full and she
would have to think in what way she could use me. It was evident that she
thought of giving me something special to do. So I was very meek and mild
and sweet—and she asked a great deal about what I had done, etc. and was
afraid I wouldn't be satisfied, but I assured her that I would be if I took it at
all. So I am to go to the theater on Monday to see what's what. They do not
pay for rehearsals, which are two months, and I believe the ballet girls get
something very small like 1,500 francs a month. So I can't afford to do it
unless I have a living another way, I suppose, for I surely will get very little
more, if any. The season is to be for four months at the Opéra Comique,
starting in May, and then they hope to have other bookings and continue as
a unit indefinitely. Here they will be with the Russian Opera Co, of which
Chaliapin will be the star, and there will be three nights of ballet and three
nights of opera per week. I was very favorably impressed with her personality. She is somewhat crazy, of course, but really a great artist. I could tell
that from the little she showed, and she has a marvelous technique herself.
So I would simply adore to be in the company if I could find a way to manage it. And I really believe I might eventually get a very good chance; they
say her personal likes and dislikes are very strong and control everything,
and I think she took a strong fancy to me, as I intended she should. However, she did really see my artistic sincerity and I felt the same quality in
her. So I think I could handle her all right. Did I tell you that Kyra [Nijinska,
the daughter of Vaslav Nijinsky] is to be in the Ballet? They say she treats
Kyra very badly because Kyra tries to act like she is somebody; so this opening was the most auspicious sort for me—she thinks she has discovered me
now. Well, so I shall go Monday and see what's doing. Anyhow, it was a
pleasing experience, having got up the nerve to go along with the ballet
girls and to have my merit recognized.

Monday afternoon, Feb. 22, 1932

Well, this is more fun than a picnic; if only I had a way worked out to make my bread and butter, I'd be perfectly happy. It's just what I've always dreamt of, being in a real Russian ballet. Whether I'll be in it long remains to be seen, for Olga tells me they are very suspicious because I have a school and can't understand why I want to be in the Ballet unless it's to steal all their ideas and take them back to America. Of course, I will write all the choreography down, if it's interesting. We had to stand around and wait for a whole hour this morning before anything began to happen; one girl sought a chair and Nijinska snapped at her, "If your heart is so bad that you can't stand up, you'd better go to a doctor." After which she delivered a long oration in Russian and class began; and we are called for nine tonight. The regular routine, I understand, is class every morning (at least I will save my studio rent), three hours rehearsal in the afternoon and three at night. This means about eight hours dancing a day—wonderful, if I can stand it. I guess I can, if I go well stocked with chocolate and whiskey. This morning I started to stand modestly in the rear, but everyone was acting scared to advance, so I soon found myself in my regular place, front of the class. Her steps are very good and for me were easy as pie.

Monday, Feb. 29, 1932

Well, into ye bathtub now; that Opéra Comique is one of the dirtiest places I've ever known, but I just adore it—every corner reeks with the ghosts of bygone dramas, human and theatrical, and one can wander in its long dusty corridors for hours, going upstairs and downstairs and suddenly finding oneself back where one started. I got locked in the toilet one day and I guess I'd still be there but for the fact that my trusty wallet yielded up a nail file in my hour of need, and I manipulated the lock with that.

Friday, March 4, 1932

I think Nijinska is supposed to be better than Balanchine, though both of them would like to be the one to carry the Diaghilev Ballet on. I don't think she has any money, though, and they say her husband is a bad manager. She is to be compared to Fokine rather than Diaghilev. They say she never gives solo work to new people, as she considers they need training in her way of working first. But according to present indications, Tania and I are to be the two first dancers; they say she wanted Spessivtseva but the latter has contracts in South America and I suspect N couldn't pay enough.

Tuesday afternoon, March 8, 1932

I must repeat that her choreography is simply lovely. She uses simple ballet steps to better advantage than anyone else that I know, and her dynamics are very good. But all the dancing is with quite a stiff back, with the behind protruding. Very little Fokine softness and no German writhing. A great deal of virility, passion, and severity in her movements. Also, humor, and in the Russians things, a quaint charm.

March 12, 1932

I spent most of yesterday in bed but am all right today; only the actual appearance of Nikitina does upset me a lot. It wasn't so bad being in the corps de ballet when there was no premiere, but I feel that is so rightfully my place that I have hard work to refrain from swatting her one on the nose when I see her. That she is not "working for" Nijinska is evidenced by the simple fact that Nijinska requires everybody to rehearse in black. Nikitina wears pale blue tights, deep blue tunic, red overtights, and a green and white striped sweater—and trails a perfectly marvelous dream of a coat in the dust.

March 16, 1932

There was neither class nor rehearsal tonight. The Ballet is in a sorry state, one girl having a badly sprained ankle, another had a table fall on her toe and break it, two have the grippe, one has sciatica, and one has a bad knee. I went down alone and had a lovely practice. What Nijinska gives in class is not sufficient anyhow to keep me in my high state of technique, and as there is no telling at what moment I might need said technique, I seize all extra time for practice. Tonight, for instance, I discovered I had lost a good two inches out of my back-bend; I probably won't need the bend itself, but it makes a great difference in one's general flexibility and ease of movement. This schooling is very stiff; she goes in for a sort of dramatic tension of movement which is very effective, but she overdoes it, just as Fokine over-does his softness. She includes very few pirouettes in her routine (but she clapped her hands with joy one night to see how I could do 'em—THEY can't do 'em, of course, because they don't practice enough). No toe work and nothing of a plastic nature. Very limited indeed. You gotta hand it to old Albertieri—he had them all beat for a comprehensive routine of steps. People complain of the Italian method, which provides a different set of steps for each day of the week and sticks to that, week in and week out, but when one relies, as the Russians do, on their individual imaginations and preferences to compose what they fondly believe to be a new set of steps each day, they very soon fall into a small vocabulary and omit or forget many important steps. Whereas, I says, if you stick to the good old system there is still nothing to prevent you from inserting a step of your own invention here and there if you want to. Nijinska makes one criticism of my work which I suppose is correct and that you will agree with—she says that my legs go up too high all the time. Still, their legs never go up, and they maintain a body practically always in a vertical position, with the behind protruding.

It was quite scary at the Opéra-Comique tonight, for the portion of the building in which we rehearse was in darkness with only a dim light on landings here and there, so I had to practically feel my way along the ghostly corridors, wondering the while what the best manner of addressing a rat would be if I should encounter one. I wouldn't want to offend him; on the other hand, I wouldn't care for an intimate acquaintance. The other night two girls got barricaded by two rats on the staircase because the rats sat in front of them. It seems that the rats and the girls felt a mutual distrust of one another for neither of them moved for half an hour, but finally it was the rats who took their leave first, thus permitting the girls to depart.

March 20, 1932

We finally reached the end of *Bolero* this morning. I have very little to do in it. Joyce [Berry], the English girl, came and told me it's the talk of the company that I am going to "do something" in the Variations. And Sin, Nijinska's husband, told me that Madame said that I could do my Chopin valse just as it was for the divertissements, but when I told him I had a Kreisler one, he thought he would like that better. I wonder if we will always have divertissements—I hope so for that will give me a good chance.

Tania is a niece of Chaliapin. And Nij has a twelve-year-old son who looks exactly like her brother did and plays piano. Her daughter, seventeen, is in the Ballet. Very nice girl.

Tuesday afternoon, March 22, 1932

Last night we were met at the door of the theater by Sin, who said that Nij didn't feel well and there would be no rehearsal. Of course, I went right ahead and had a lovely practice all alone. But I was so amused—just think, some forty people coming all intending to dance and when they find out that it's not obligatory, they run away as fast as they can go. This morning's rehearsal was an hour later than usual and I took advantage of this time too, so now my miraculous devotion to work is the talk of the Ballet. Aren't they silly? They all like to dance and would do anything she tells 'em, but on their own they don't have the initiative of an oyster. Two girls have now asked if they may come and practice with me—it'll be MY troupe before long if I'm not careful. I love it when I get a chance to be alone there. The place is full of ghosts, and when I practice in that old practice room, I am quite aware of the spiritual remains, so to speak, of by-gone ballerinas who sit around and watch and criticize. They are very pleased that someone sees them and heeds their remarks, and they thoroughly approve of my ambition. I am quite thrilled that I am to have the chance to do my waltz, because if I do something of my own, I am sure to make a mark. Of course, she may change her mind at the last minute.

March 23, 1932

Well, if the audience gives me as big an ovation as the members of the Ballet did last night, I shall have cause to be content. Nij arranged a very short but very snappy little dance for me in the "Variations." So far it certainly doesn't look like a leading part, but this half minute is quite likely to bring the house down. I am reminded of my half minute with the Denishawns in the Greek Theater, and Vaudeville teaches one how to do a whole lot in half a minute. The dance is one of the most brilliant and most difficult concoctions I have ever seen. It is jammed full of pirouettes, finishing with very fast fouettés, but not arranged in the usual way; it has nuances which cause it to sparkle the more. It's on toe, ¾ tempo, and just a trifle like that waltz I once did at the Hippodrome, which you have so often spoken of, only more vigorous. It is, in fact, so difficult as to be almost impossible, and I am wondering if I can really execute it all quite perfectly on the stage. If I do, it sure will be a knock-out. I certainly did it amazingly well last night, and the company couldn't contain themselves. One girl said, "When you dance, I don't BELIEVE you," and another said, "Wait till Nikitina sees that. She will be furious." They all agreed that nobody else could do it, not even Nemchinova, whom they seem to consider the best present-day technician. One especially difficult part is where, after a small very quick circle of "little turns" on toe, I suddenly stop and do a very slow relevé on one toe, lifting the other high and carrying it around from front to back, the while I remain on the one toe (fifty dollars extra) and then develop it into a very slow fouetté, increasing to a frenzy of speed for the finish. I have never attempted such fast fouettés on toe on the stage before—God help me. Nij grinned from ear to ear, and when I had done it for the last time (and with remarkable perfection) the whole troupe burst into uproarious applause. It was very amusing. They may be jealous, but they were quite carried away by their appreciation of the difficult work. They have been jabbering about it in Russian ever since. A few days ago seeing me lying down so much, they were inclined to condole me for my supposed weakness. "Poor girl, not very strong," they said among themselves. Now they are rushing to know how in the world I have such stupendous strength, and they are all going to start eating chocolate and meat right away. Ha ha ha. They say, by the way, that Nikitina can't do much but take pretty positions in adagio, so there will be danger there without a doubt.

Thursday afternoon, March 24, 1932
We have very few conversations and these are with the aid of an interpreter. It seems that Nijinksa speaks very little French anyhow. She is a little deaf and rarely talks directly to anyone, expressing herself usually to her husband, who acts as a sort of megaphone. He is never out of earshot and if he doesn't come running immediately to her "Nicolai Nicolaivitch," she shows signs of irritation. He takes precautions to keep her from getting excited, and everyone else is so afraid of her temper that I imagine they are afraid she really will go off her nut. This I can understand, but I can't understand why they are so afraid of her sarcastic remarks . . .

At the Opéra-Comique, rehearsals for the ballets that Nijinska was composing proved to be long and tiring, although not actually strenuous for me personally, as she gave me, to start with, very little to do. My problem was mostly fatigue and boredom with standing—or sitting—around, and getting very hungry as the hours dragged past. I developed a system for concealing chocolate bars in my knickers to sustain me when I felt close to fainting. All of the Russians, apparently, were afraid of catching cold, and the windows in the rather small studio where we worked were generally kept closed. The aroma from some twenty-five or thirty perspiring dancers was definitely not exhilarating.

Nijinska composed a short but very brilliant variation for me in one of the ballets and then she began to rehearse me in the principal role of *Les Biches,* but before we had got very far, Vera Nemchinova suddenly emerged out of Russia and, according to what was related to me by Mme [Ludmila] Schollar, one of the principal soloists, demanded to dance this part. Actually, she was entitled to do so, as it had originally been choreographed for her and she no doubt performed it much better than I would have done, but I was bitterly disappointed.

At the conclusion of the Paris engagement the company left for Spain, but I did not go with them. When I later heard reports of that tour, in which scarcity of money, travel hardships, and minimum success seemed to prevail, I was thankful that I had remained behind. As I had already written to my mother, "I can't help wondering if Louis [the novelist Louis Ferdinand Céline] didn't speak the truth when he said, 'You'll never get anywhere in that company. It will always be Nijinska, Nijinska, and Nijinska.'"

—from *Dance Chronicle,* 1988

MARGOT FONTEYN

Born Margaret ("Peggy") Hookham in London, Dame Margot Fonteyn (1919–1991) became one of the greatest and most loved of her century's ballerinas. She joined Sadler's Wells in the mid-thirties, and when Alicia Markova left the company, was anointed by Ninette de Valois as the company's prima ballerina, taking over the leading roles in Giselle *and* Swan Lake. *The first great influence on her (and her lover for many years) was the brilliant composer-conductor Constant Lambert. Just as important was Frederick Ashton, who created an extraordinary series of roles on her, in works ranging from* Symphonic Variations, A Wedding Bouquet, Dante Sonata, Cinderella, Ondine, Sylvia, Daphnis and Chloe, *and* Birthday Offering *to the vehicle he fashioned for her and her most famous partner, Rudolf Nureyev,* Marguerite and Armand. *Her most famous role, however, was Aurora in* The Sleeping Beauty, *which she danced at the company's opening night in New York in 1949, sealing its reputation and her own. She also danced the premiere (and made a film) of Kenneth MacMillan's* Romeo and Juliet, *with Nureyev, and it became one of their greatest triumphs, although it had been created on Lynn Seymour and Christopher Gable. Her husband was Dr. Roberto Arias, a Panamanian diplomat who was shot in 1965 and became a paraplegic. (She went on dancing until she was past sixty, in order to afford his medical bills.) Fonteyn was made a Dame of the British Empire, the chancellor of the University of Durham, and the head of the Royal Academy of Dance.*

DALE HARRIS
Snowflake to Superstar

As I write this the Royal Ballet is about to launch its fourteenth American season. For the first time since the company's debut here in 1949 the name of Margot Fonteyn is missing from the roster. There are persistent rumors that Fonteyn will give a surprise performance during the final week of the engagement. If this does turn out to be the case—and by the time *Ballet Review* appears we will all know the answer—it will only serve to underline the fact that, so far as her parent company is concerned, her long reign has indeed come to an end: making an appearance during the Royal Ballet's twenty-fifth anniversary season will be a sentimental gesture by the company's prima ballerina emerita. Either way, we are unlikely to have seen the last of her. Whether or not she actually turns up on this occasion it's a fairly safe bet that she'll dance again in New York, possibly as the *clou* of some gala benefit; as guest artist with a regional company; maybe even with the Royal Ballet—she could keep doing *Marguerite and Armand* marvelously for a while still. But she will never again be to the Royal Ballet what she was for so many years: undisputed female star (and before the advent of Nureyev, undisputed star, *tout court*), prima ballerina assoluta, a paradigm for all the other dancers. Fonteyn did not merely head the company; she typified its virtues, its sensibility. Moreover, during her greatest years—say, 1946–1965—she assumed even greater significance: she was, in effect, the embodiment of a national achievement—which is what the establishment of a great ballet company in the teeth of circumstances amounted to.

Fonteyn's career as a dancer is legend enough. She played a key role in the ultimate success of British ballet. Without her to take on the Petipa-Ivanov classics the Vic-Wells might not have weathered the loss of Markova in 1935. Without her, Frederick Ashton would probably not have developed in the way he did. For something like twenty-five years, Fonteyn was the chosen instrument of his creative will. She helped to determine the bent of his imagination. Ashton does not impose himself upon his dancers. He draws from them what they uniquely have to offer, converting their special gifts into choreography that then transcends their individual characteristics. During the intervening years, the leading roles in *Symphonic Variations*, *Scènes de ballet*, and *Daphnis and Chloe*, all originally mounted on Fonteyn, have been taken over by other dancers with great success. *Cinderella*, though made for Fonteyn, was in the end given to Moira Shearer when Fonteyn injured herself before the premiere, and Shearer danced the role very well. Yet every one of these works owed an enormous amount to Fonteyn's personal qualities: her exquisite line, her lyricism, her musicality, the radiance that suffused her simplest movements. The climax of an Ashton ballet made for her was likely to be a moment of quiet ecstasy, of inward transfiguration and fulfilment: Chloe restored to Daphnis and carried aloft in triumph, the final tableau of *Symphonic Variations*, the gentle, subsiding close of the ballroom pas de deux in *Cinderella*.

These reflect qualities that once seemed purely local in interest. It is not so long ago that the idea of a British ballet seemed absurd—not least of all to the British themselves. Fonteyn has spoken of the then Sadler's Wells Ballet's fears, prior to their first engagement in New York, that their style would not look brilliant enough to American audiences, and of the firm conviction she had that her own essentially lyrical manner would simply make no appeal on this side of the Atlantic. What had been so impressive about Ballet Theatre, the first American company to visit England after the war, was its vigor, its youthful assertiveness. *Fancy Free*, the great hit of the season, had a particularly invigorating effect during those weary days when England was trying to find her place in a changed world. Fonteyn's fears were, of course, groundless. The company made an immediately favorable impression and Fonteyn enjoyed a personal triumph. Yet without the latter, Sadler's Wells Ballet might not have established itself in the decisive way it did. Reviews of that initial season leave no doubt about the crucial part she played in the company's acceptance.

Success in America was the turning point in the history of British ballet. Before the outbreak of World War II the company made only one foray abroad, a visit to Paris in 1937 under the auspices of the British Council which brought them little éclat. In 1940, however, they toured Holland as part of the war effort (and only just missed the invading Germans), and at the end of hostilities they were sent all over Europe by a government that during the years had learned about the value of cultural propaganda in general, and about the usefulness of ballet in particular. During the course of the war, ballet in Britain attained unprecedented popularity. From an arcane ritual supported by a handful of devotees it quickly developed into surefire general entertainment. By the time peace was declared, Sadler's Wells Ballet was no longer a modest, high-minded venture struggling, in a dingy working-class suburb, to assert the validity of native art; it was a West End commercial success, it was the height of fashion, it was self-assured. Above all, it was an institution of which the whole country could be proud. Together with the Old Vic drama company it could serve to represent Britain's wartime cultural achievement. In the immediate post-war years Continental Europe applauded what had become, in effect, Britain's national ballet, an accomplishment implicitly acknowledged by the move from Sadler's Wells Theatre to Covent Garden, from, in other words, a "people's theater" to the former home of international grand opera. Yet it was America alone that, three years later, authenticated the transformation from suburban to national by making the company an international success.

New York put the last vestiges of cultural inferiority to flight, decisively transforming Fonteyn from an English girl into an English star. Lurking behind Sadler's Wells' newly won confidence until that point there was always the ghost of Ballet Russe, unexorcised even by the 1947 Covent Garden season under Colonel de Basil, in which a tatterdemalion assemblage of dancers bearing mostly Russian names moved warily through the wreckage of the Fokine-Massine-Lichine repertoire. For years Sadler's Wells had to cope with the generally held conviction that balletic quality was identical with the Russian émigré companies and that only Slavs knew how to dance. There was also a tendency to identify Ballet Russe with what in retrospect seemed to be the halcyon pre-war years. It was widely felt that the workaday present could never match up to the alluring past and that Britain was less good at culture than other nations, who would in due course reassert their old ascendancy.

A feeling of inadequacy persisted despite the fact that when, one by one, the glamorous survivors of Ballet Russe returned—first Massine, then Riabouchinska and Lichine, Markova, Danilova, and Toumanova—none of them brought revelations, only a sense of differences. Even so, it was hard for a lot of people to see beyond the progress made by the Sadler's Wells to its achievement. The quality of the latter escaped them. Cyril Beaumont in those days was always ready to invoke the past as a corrective, to find Fonteyn lacking by the standards of the pre-war Markova or Danilova. But in 1948 there was a foretaste of the changes to come, when Fonteyn danced as guest artist with the Ballets de Paris at the Théâtre Marigny and created a furore, especially in excerpts from *Sleeping Beauty*. In those days the accolade of Paris meant a great deal. It was recognition from one's cultural seniors. It signified one's arrival. The results were evident on Fonteyn's return to Covent Garden. She had a new air of confidence and greater warmth. She opened herself up to the audience more quickly. She had gained tremendously in speed and attack. She had learned the secret of the *équilibre*. Her musicality was greater than ever.

Fonteyn's American career began when she was at the peak of her powers. The dancer who ran onto the stage of the old Metropolitan Opera House on October 9, 1949, was, at the age of thirty, fully formed. *Daphnis and Chloe* was still ahead; so were *Firebird*, *Ondine*, and *Marguerite and Armand*, but in these works her inalienable qualities were deepened and refined. What she was to become in the next decade or so she already in effect was by 1949. She was without peculiarities. Edwin Denby once said he had never seen such good manners onstage. She did not assert her primacy or exploit her personality. When Toumanova—the post-war Toumanova, at any rate—made her entrance she was always at pains to distinguish herself from everyone else: with a flourish of the hand, a swift turn of the head, a more energetic scale of movement, a higher *développé*, a longer-held balance—even if the latter entailed a lot of teetering on pointe. Behind every one of Toumanova's idiosyncrasies lay the implicit need to emphasize her rank, to draw attention to her talents: she danced as if unless she exerted herself to the utmost she might have to relinquish her position as ballerina.

Fonteyn grew up in a different world. Toumanova and Baronova, her exact contemporaries, were famous stars when Fonteyn was still a beginner taking class with Astafieva. By the time Fonteyn was dancing a Snowflake at Sadler's Wells, Toumanova had created Balanchine's *Concurrence*, *Cotillon*, and *Mozartiana*, and Baronova, Massine's *Choreartium* and *Présages*. Both were veterans of transcontinental touring and of ballet politics. Both were child virtuosi, famous above all for their proficiency at fouettés. Largely through Haskell's *Balletomania*, both had already taken their place in ballet history. Fonteyn by comparison had a gentle, obscure nurture. She developed slowly, in an atmosphere of stability remote from box office demands and public adulation. She belonged to a company with its own school, a permanent home, and the need to perform only once a week. She tackled the classics gradually: *Swan Lake*, Act II, at the age of sixteen; *Giselle* at seventeen; Odette-Odile at nineteen; Aurora two and a half months later. She never had to force, either technically or interpretively. Even in her callowest days she projected a sense of confidence: she knew what her place was. Though she was always a modest dancer she was not a diffident one. She was part of an established hierarchy. In that sense she never had to make her way. She inherited the position of ballerina from Markova by command of Ninette de Valois, who found her the worthiest claimant. Her rank in the company was ordained. It came through the recognition of her merit and promise, not through the struggle to excel others. There was never any dynastic rivalry at the Wells. Grace and predestination, as interpreted by those in command, were the only factors in her success, and the only kind of success she had to consider was artistic.

It was the wartime closing of Sadler's Wells Theatre that quickened the rate of Fonteyn's development, and brought her and the company face to face with the conditions of the ordinary commercial theater: nine shows a week before enormous, often indiscriminate, audiences; poor rehearsal conditions; cross-country touring. By the mid-forties Fonteyn was giving more performances a month than she had given in an entire year before 1939. By then, however, she had already established her personality as a dancer and no harm resulted. On the contrary, she learned how to make her quiet lyricism more theatrical, how to infuse it with presence, how to add an element of surprise. Above all, she made the transition from romantic to classical ballerina. Her dancing was informed with new authority, greater inwardness, a surer command of essences. The emphasis of her Odette gradually shifted from pathos to nobility and became, as a result, more moving than ever. All the while, in fact, she was increasing her skill as an actress. She was remarkably effective in demi-*caractère* roles: as Julia in *A Wedding Bouquet*, as Ophelia in Helpmann's *Hamlet*, as the Flower Girl in *Nocturne*. In the latter she used her expressive features, especially her huge, lustrous eyes, to awaken the audience's pity. All she had to do was look beseechingly at the young man who had betrayed her and the entire theater identified with the Flower Girl's emotions—though it was the droop of her body, the tautening of her neck, and her shaking shoulders that actually moved them most. Her range, already large, became enormous: Giselle, both the Polka and the Tango in *Façade*, the gentle, lyrical flow of the White Girl in *Patineurs*; the brilliant acrobatics of *The Wanderer*, the cascading anguish of the Child of Light in *Dante Sonata*.

Fonteyn learned how to claim the attention of the new ballet audiences and how to hold it, but she never sacrificed line and she never resorted to tricks of emphasis. She made every movement expressive. She communicated utter absorption and, through it, compelled the audience's regard. When she came onstage in one of the classic roles she took possession of her domain. She looked out into the middle height of the auditorium and saw beyond the spectators into a more ideal existence. She smiled like someone with a secret to share. Fonteyn's facial expression was usually an accurate gauge of her success in a role. In parts that she never felt comfortable with she often adopted a glassy, unvarying smile that bore no relationship to the dynamics of the characterization. Swanilda was one of these roles and, later, Massine's Mam'zelle Angot. Skittishness, effervescence were never within her range. She was by nature deep. She could be funny but she could rarely be frivolous.

She had long since won the right to dance the great classic roles by dint of hard work. She maintained that right by her ability to develop. She had the gift of constantly improving. Her first attempts at a role were generally blank. Then, in almost every case, details would be gradually filled in and her conviction would grow, until she communicated complete possession of the part. She was not particularly strong, but strong enough so that few assignments ever took her beyond the limits of her physical capabilities. Only the thirty-two fouettés of *Swan Lake*, Act III, defeated her. She got through them, but they were loose-jointed, unstable, unexhilarating. But whereas a Markova would substitute a brilliant sequence of *échappés,* Fonteyn did not funk the fouettés; they were part of the role and therefore an obligation. Even after studying with Preobrajenska, who had taught Toumanova and Baronova how to do them, she never really mastered fouettés. But she never once cut them. She simply did what she was supposed to do, which was dance as well as she possibly could and thereby fulfill her obligations to the company.

In any case she didn't have the burden of stardom to carry. The star of Sadler's Wells Ballet in those days was Robert Helpmann, much more famous than Fonteyn, a bigger box office draw, and the company's dominant personality. It was really Helpmann who kept Sadler's Wells going during the war years. There were times when he seemed to be the only adult male dancer around, since, one by one, all of the other pre-war members of the company were drafted. Helpmann hadn't much in the way of technique, but his theatrical flair enabled him to carry off anything he set his mind to—even the virtuoso Blue Boy in *Patineurs* when the need arose. When Ashton went into the Royal Air Force, Helpmann turned his hand to choreography and for a time, with *Hamlet* and *Miracle in the Gorbals*, made a great success of it. As a strong personality he was the ideal foil for Fonteyn. He brought out all her womanliness. He was also a superb partner. Fonteyn developed a rapport with him that in succeeding years she found with no one else: neither Somes nor Nureyev, both wonderful partners, ever gave her the security she got from Helpmann. Somes was lacking a certain confidence in himself. Nureyev provided her with incentives to excel herself. By the time the Wells opened at the Met the Fonteyn-Helpmann partnership was a miracle of coordination. From the first bemused pas de deux in the Vision Scene of *Sleeping Beauty* to the exultant wedding celebration, there was a progression toward fulfillment that Fonteyn has never since equalled. At the climax of the last act pas de deux the sequence of turns behind the Prince's outstretched arm leading to the fish dive was so swift, so secure, you could hardly believe what you had seen. Especially dazzling was the transition between turn and fish dive; it was like a sleight of hand; it happened so fast you simply never noticed the taking up of the supporting foot.

But the ultimate proof of Fonteyn's skill was her ability to make her last-act variation into the climax of the entire evening, to transform into the apex of Aurora's good fortune a simple dance designed to provide a lyrical contrast with the grand adage that precedes it and the strong male solo and boisterous coda that succeed it. In 1949 there was no male solo and the coda was used for the Three Ivans. Fonteyn's triumph was compounded of all her virtues: the slow opening section showed off her nobly proportioned body, its perfect placement, the pliancy of her back, the clarity and continuity of her line from fingertips to feet, the ballerina head and face which gave focus to the body's expressiveness by directing the audience's attention where she wanted it to be. In the sequence to the perky violin solo, as she flicked her wrists while raising her arms she would draw the rhythm taut by raising her eyes a fraction later than her arms. The same kind of rubato informed her phrasing of the petits battements frappés to the pizzicati, so that she seemed to be toying with the music, teasing it out, flirting with it. Yet in the final section her fast, sure piqué turns were thrilling precisely because they accorded so exactly with the music's strong, driving rhythm. Fonteyn's musicality was awesome. Fundamentally innate though it doubtless was, it must have been developed by Constant Lambert, who served as Fonteyn's mentor in her early years. Lambert's conducting of the Tchaikovsky ballets was very thrilling: full-bodied, yet, because of his perfect judgment in matters of tempo and rhythm, linear, too. The combination of Fonteyn and Lambert, such as New York saw that first opening night, was uniquely satisfying. Fonteyn's great musical gift was not simply to dance as if the music welled up from inside her. She did that, but she also at will rode the music like a champion surfer, sometimes holding back, sometimes anticipating, always buoyant, impelled by and partaking of its primal energy. There were times, especially in that final variation from *Sleeping Beauty*, when one wanted to weep for the sheer plenitude of her performance.

The combination of Tchaikovsky and Petipa was ideally suited to Fonteyn's gifts. That of Tchaikovsky and Balanchine was not. The distillation of nineteenth-century grandeur in *Ballet Imperial*, presented by Sadler's Wells the year after their American debut, suited her not at all. Everything was too concentrated for her essentially lyric style. By 1950 Fonteyn was not lacking in strength or technique, but she was never able to master the dynamics of *Ballet Imperial*. She looked harried, like someone trying to follow two sets of orders at the same time, and her dancing lost its clarity. Her unease wasn't merely a question of speed. She found the slow movement as uncomfortable as the outer movements; it did not have enough expansiveness for her grand, generous, and reflective manner; its scale, its unremitting tension nullified her personality and she danced like a cypher—an effect only aggravated by Berman's white wig and pale yellow dress, which tended to obliterate her facial expression. Balanchine's visit to London made it very clear that Fonteyn was not going to be able to widen her range in any significant fashion. Before this she had made little effect in Massine's *Tricorne* and *Angot* and never worked with him again. The problem was not simply one of national temperament, since Ninette de Valois, usually thought of as the most "English" of choreographers, had been unable to provide her with a single memorable role. Even when Fonteyn took over the Betrayed Girl in *The Rake's Progress*, a part which might have been conceived with her in view, she failed to find in it a sense of conviction. Her métier was, it seemed, fixed. She would henceforth not be able to encompass with complete artistic success much beyond *Giselle*, *Swan Lake*, *Sleeping Beauty*, and the Ashton ballets, though later on she did, in fact, also make a wonderful Firebird.

What she did all this while, however, was refine, probe, and intensify. In the years that followed she purified her art, paring it down to essentials, yet in so doing she discovered an even warmer personality, an ever easier mastery over the audience. In the late fifties and early sixties her *Swan Lake* achieved its definitive form. Acts II and IV were imbued with a new tragic grandeur. Fonteyn had absorbed from the Soviet Russians, fully visible at last after years of sequestration, a series of strategies: greater freedom of movement, fuller use of the arms, a more impetuous manner of phrasing. Act III was similarly influenced. Her use of the back and shoulders was particularly seductive. She used her head, her glittering smile, to attract and to rebuff. Her eyes were wanton. She took the arabesque *penchée* at the end of the adage like an arrow flying to its mark. Fouettés notwithstanding, she wound up the excitement till it was almost unbearable.

These were years of steadily increasing popularity. In Britain her status as a national treasure was acknowledged in 1956 by Damehood, Fonteyn being the first dancer in mid-career to be thus honored. Her accolade was followed by the granting of a Royal Charter to Sadler's Wells Ballet, henceforth to be known as the Royal Ballet. It is doubtful if the latter would ever have happened without Fonteyn, though the reverse is just as true. She gave the company glamour and they gave her the opportunity to achieve it.

They gave her, above all, Ashton, who throughout the fifties was able to provide her with a series of consummate roles: Chloe, the long pas de deux of *Tiresias*, Act II *Sylvia*, The Queen of the Air in *Homage to the Queen*, La Péri, *Birthday Offering*, and Ondine. By the time Fonteyn had arrived at Ondine she was dancing with extraordinary lambency. The ballet itself was less than her role and detracted from it, but her great set pieces summed up all her allure and, especially in the climactic pas de deux in which Palemon kisses her and dies, added to it an overwhelming sense of romantic passion. But Chloe, because it forms part of a masterpiece, remains the greatest of her creations from this period, a complete, clearly articulated dramatic role which is, nevertheless, all dancing. Her eloquence in the dance she performed as a captive of the pirates remains fixed in the memory: the fear in her eyes, her shoulders hunched forward and her arms held rigid before her as she struggled to free her bound hands, her stabbing piqués forward as she begged for pity. It seemed only natural for her to awaken the pity of a tutelary god and find deliverance.

The alteration in Fonteyn's status from member of the Royal Ballet to Guest Artist which occurred in 1959, the year of *Ondine*—and which was effected, it seems, without her prior knowledge—was simply a recognition of what had actually been the case for some time. Fonteyn's career was no longer automatically identifiable with the company, and—except in America, where her box office appeal was a necessary adjunct to their success— the company no longer depended utterly on her. More and more did Fonteyn come to seem like a link with the past. The present was in other, younger hands. The future was hard to foresee. The extraordinary success of *Fille mal gardée*, first performed in 1960, was decisive in this respect. The ballet singlehandedly insured the company's rejuvenation. *Fille*, created by Ashton for Nadia Nerina and David Blair, is not only a celebration of youth, it makes use of qualities only discovered at the Royal Ballet by dancers who came after Fonteyn: impetuosity, high spirits, the sheer excitement of technical virtuosity. Moreover, it was created by the choreographer who had played a decisive role in Fonteyn's career. After *Fille* it seemed only natural that people should, seriously and frequently, talk of Fonteyn's withdrawal from the scene. There was a sense of consummation about her career, as there was about her private life. She was highly praised in Russia during the Royal Ballet's visit to Moscow and Leningrad; she succeeded Dame Adeline Genée as president of the Royal Academy of Dancing; she made a brilliant marriage. Each season looked as if it might be her last.

The advent of Nureyev changed all that. Nureyev called Fonteyn back to dancing when she was on the point of giving up. Through him she discovered fresh sources of energy. At the culmination of her career she was suddenly made aware of capabilities in herself as yet unrealized. She has spoken about the partnership with Nureyev as a challenge she accepted in full awareness of its dangers. The upshot was not rivalry. She did not compete with Nureyev. She competed with herself, with what she had been until then. From that point on she danced with unprecedented largeness of utterance, a weightier lyricism than she had ever before discovered. She threw herself into her roles as if she had nothing to lose and everything to give. What happened in 1962, the year the Fonteyn-Nureyev partnership began, was a final awakening. She took risks. Nureyev aroused the audience with his strength, his passion, his prowess; Fonteyn with her daring, the exultance that she transmitted. She was never swamped by Nureyev. Without ever developing a virtuoso technique she became, in effect, a virtuoso: she dazzled audiences with her brilliance. In *Le Corsaire* she positively devoured space. She made so kinetically vivacious a response to the music and phrased with so keen a sense of climax that you could have sworn she had performed prodigious technical feats. What was prodigious about those first three or four years with Nureyev was that in taking on a larger and more annunciative style she never purged herself of the qualities that originally made her a great ballerina. Among all the excitements of *Le Corsaire* there wasn't a moment when she did not exemplify the virtues of her classical heritage: grace, order, proportion. At her most expansive she kept her distance, never sold herself to the audience, danced with decorum and the modesty of someone who knew exactly what her limits were.

Without Nureyev none of this would have been possible. The partnership became one of the indispensable sights of the decade. Oddly enough, when Ashton came to devise a work for them both he gave Fonteyn the opportunity to be uniquely herself but gave Nureyev something far less personal. Armand is a generalized portrait of the young, handsome lover. Marguerite is the summation of Fonteyn's entire career. With infinite skill and tact it seizes on her power to excite and move the audience. *Marguerite and Armand* is a tribute to everything that Fonteyn had achieved, a fable of her attainments and inevitable decline. Unlike many of the ballets Fonteyn has appeared in during the past seven years—*Paradise Lost, Pelléas et Mélisande, Poème de l'Ecstase*—*Marguerite and Armand* is seemly. Like the "Dying Swan" for Pavlova it projects an ultimate truth in metaphorical form about Fonteyn as dancer and human being. It would be the perfect occasion for her farewell to the stage.

Those of us who feel nothing but gratitude and love toward her wish that it might come soon. The final section of Money's book is, in effect, a sustained assertion that time has stood still. It has not, of course. Some of the photographs reveal that fact. So did the performances she gave with the Royal Ballet two years ago. *Poème de l'Ecstase* showed that she no longer understands her needs. One can only hope that, at the end of her dancing days, she avoids the danger of leaving art behind her and dwindling into celebrity. She, we, deserve no less.

—from *Ballet Review,* Vol. 4, No. 6, 1974

MARGOT FONTEYN
Rudolf

When I was in Russia I had taken the opportunity to ask Mme Furtseva, then Minister of Culture, if Galina Ulanova could come to dance at the fundraising gala in aid of the Royal Academy of Dancing that was to take place in November. On returning to London from the Baalbek visit, I received a letter regretting deeply that our date coincided with an important State celebration at which Ulanova would be dancing in Moscow. This news was distressing, because it was the fourth year the Royal Academy had held this special matinée, and we were running out of attractions. Ulanova's presence would have given immense prestige to the occasion—and would have sold the tickets instantly.

Colette Clark organized the galas, with Mary, Duchess of Roxburghe, acting as Chairman. The three of us met in gloom to consider what action to take. Colette said, "I hear that Rudolf Nureyev, this dancer who defected from the Kirov, is sensational. He's just finished a season in Paris with the de Cuevas Ballet." "A brilliant idea," we said, and Colette spent two weeks chasing after him by phone. By the time she got his number in Nice he had left for Copenhagen. That was perfect because he was working in class with my old friend Vera Volkova. Messages passed endlessly between Vera and Colette, and were relayed at either end to Nureyev and me. In London, they went something like this:

COLETTE: He says he wants to dance with you.
MARGOT: I've never set eyes on him, and anyway I've asked John Gilpin to dance *Spectre of the Rose* with me. Ask Vera if he is a good dancer.
COLETTE, the next day: Vera says he's adamant about dancing with you, and that he's marvelous.
MARGOT: He sounds rather tiresome to me.
COLETTE: No, they say he's extraordinary. They say that he has such a presence he only has to walk on the stage and lift his arm and you can see the swans by the lake. I think it would be wonderful if you danced with Nureyev as well as Gilpin.
MARGOT: The more I hear of him the worse he sounds. I don't mean as a dancer, but why should he decide to dance with me when he's only twenty-three and I've never even met him?
COLETTE: Well, Vera thinks he's a genius. She says he has "the nostrils," you know what I mean? People of genius have "nostrils."

Colette dilated hers to illustrate the point. She is very intelligent, much younger than I, and has watched ballet all her life. She was always sure about Rudolf.

He gave in about dancing with me, and asked for Rosella Hightower instead. Then came another request: would Frederick Ashton choreograph a solo for him? Fred agreed nervously, saying, "I don't know what kind of solo." He needn't have worried. Rudolf knew exactly what he wanted. So all was decided, and Vera Volkova, her job completed, said, "Well, as it were, now I hand you the baby!"

We knew Nureyev was anxious to see London, so we invited him to come over secretly for three days. The press wouldn't know about it and we would give him a false name—even for the ballet world. We chose the name of a Polish dancer, Roman Jasman, who was also engaged to appear in the gala.

On the day he was due to arrive from Paris, Colette lunched with me at home. He was due at 5:30 p.m. I had to go to a cocktail party, but planned to meet them both afterwards. At 3:30 p.m. the telephone rang. "Here is Nureyev," said a voice. It was a deeper voice than I had expected, crisp, the accent pronounced. "Where are you?" I asked. "In Paris?" "I am one hour in

London airport," he replied. "Oh! We expected you later. The car isn't there. Wait where you are and I will send it at once. It will take twenty minutes." "I will take taxi," he said. "Don't do that. It's complicated. Wait where you are!" Panic! The chauffeur dashed off to the airport.

Forty-five minutes later the telephone rang again. "Here is Nureyev." "Didn't the chauffeur find you?" "No. I will take taxi." "No," I said, "ring me again in five minutes. I will try to get hold of the chauffeur there." But they could not locate each other, so I told Nureyev to take a taxi after all. It was getting late, so I dressed for the cocktail party. I remember the dress very well—it was navy pleated chiffon and had a satin ribbon round the hem and a white camellia at the neck. The reason I remember it so well is because Rudolf saw it again one year later, and immediately noticed that the satin ribbon had lost its true colour from dry cleaning. "What happened to ribbon? Looks different." He misses nothing. As he stepped out of the taxi, Nureyev seemed smaller than I had expected, probably because I was standing above him on the doorstep. He had a funny, pinched little face with that curious pallor peculiar to so many dancers from Russia. I noticed the nostrils at once.

The three of us sat over tea—five sugars for Rudolf. As I was summing him up, I could see that he was doing the same to me. He was extremely polite, sitting up rather straight but intending to look relaxed. His sentences, in limited English, were concise and clear. I said something light and silly. Suddenly he laughed and his whole face changed. He lost the "on guard" look, and his smile was generous and captivating. "Oh, thank goodness!" I said. "I didn't know Russians laughed. They were so serious when we were there." I left Colette to explain the arrangements for his incognito stay in London. Later, when Colette asked me how I had found him, I said, "I like him nine-tenths, but once or twice I saw a steely look in his eye." His face had reflected every thought, changing like lightning. Then a very cold look flashed through his eyes, just there long enough for me to catch it. Now I realize it was a manifestation of fear. I haven't seen it for a long time, as he is very self-assured these days. In the beginning, though, it was always just below the surface, ready to show itself at the slightest suspicion of attack.

Fred choreographed the new solo behind closed doors. As the curtain rose on the performance, Rudolf was standing swathed in a long red mantle. He rushed forward and threw it off to dance freely to the passionate music of Scriabin. Many people put a symbolic interpretation on the hampering red cloak, whether correctly or not I never knew, but I think Fred and Billie Chappell, who designed the costume, were more likely to have been thinking of the theatrical effect, which was terrific.

Colette and I had watched the first rehearsal in the theatre. Rudolf was a riot—not intentionally, but his character revealed itself through his dancing and everything was there, including his sense of clowning. He was actually desperately serious: nervous, intense, and repeating every step with all his might until he almost knocked himself out with the effort. From time to time he stopped to take off his leg warmers before a very difficult step; after the exertion he stopped again, let out a breath rapidly and forcefully with a sound like a sibilant "Ho." On went the woolen tights. After a few more steps he changed his shoes and put the leg warmers back on top of the woolen tights. So it went on for two hours. He was working like a steam engine. Colette and I couldn't help laughing. At the same time, I thought he would never get through the solo if he put so much effort into each movement. Surely he ought to save himself somewhere? But I hadn't counted on Rudolf's strength. I think it was from that morning that we took to him wholeheartedly. Afterwards, when I suggested he should save something in the middle so as to finish the long solo strongly, he said with what sounded like pride, "In Paris I never once finish variation!" I said, "Wouldn't it be better if you did?" He considered the point as though it were an original idea.

When it came to the gala, I visited all the dressing rooms beforehand to see if the artists needed anything. Rudolf said, "They send wrong wig!" He was preparing for the *Swan Lake* pas de deux with Rosella Hightower, and in his hand was a blond wig—a very blond wig. It was too late to change it, just before his first entrance. Colette and I agreed afterwards that if he had the success he did, which was nothing short of tumultuous, while wearing that wig, he was certainly great. I have never changed that opinion. He is great in that he is unique, not only an exceptional dancer but a unique personality, fortified by one of the sharpest brains imaginable.

The gala took place in the afternoon at the Theatre Royal, Drury Lane. At the end, the crowd mobbed Rosella and Rudolf outside the theatre. I could hardly drag her to the car as people pushed this way and that trying to touch them and get autographs. Rosella's costume, which she carried over her arm, was ripped and almost lost in the melee.

That evening there was a party at our house for the cast to relax. I admired Rudolf's patience in talking to many strangers as well as the dancers whom he knew, and it was not till the last guests were leaving that he asked to be dropped in the King's Road, which I am sure he had scented out the first day.

Earlier in the evening, Tito [Fonteyn's husband] had asked him conversationally, "What were you doing in Copenhagen?" Rudolf replied darkly, "Is story better not told." I noticed how quickly he was picking up English.

Like all dancers in Russia, who are cut off from many of the ballet contacts we take for granted, Rudolf had a discerning knowledge of English ballet acquired by a sort of sixth sense before he left home. He knew the first person he wanted to meet was Ninette de Valois, and he invited her to lunch. They got on like a house on fire. The Irish and the Tartar understood each other at sight. Her wit, shrewdness, humanity, and intelligence delighted him, and he has revered her ever since. Of course, he was just the kind of rebellious talent and engaging "enfant terrible" that she loved.

Part of his defense system when he was nervous was a penetrating criticism. We all came in for it in turn, and some of us didn't like it at all. It is quite amusing now to remember how barbed he sometimes was during the first few years. His biting remarks clashed with Fred Ashton's wit a few times, and the sparks flew. But he always acknowledged Fred's genius, and a true affection grew between them. After one such bout, when Fred had parried Rudolf's cutting remark with a lethal reproof, Fred put on his long-nosed Peruvian face, with his eyes half-closed, and said: "I gave as good as I got, my dear!" Certainly, no one has ever been known to get the better of Fred in a challenging verbal exchange.

De Valois told me that Rudolf would dance *Giselle* at Covent Garden in February, three months ahead. "Do you want to do it with him?" she asked. My immediate reaction was to say, "Oh, my goodness! I think it would be like mutton dancing with lamb. Don't you think I'm too old?" I said I would give my answer the next day. I discussed it with Tito, and we came to the conclusion that Rudolf was going to be the big sensation of the next year and I had better get on the bandwagon or else get out. I called de Valois to thank her for asking me, and accepted. I had often expressed my abhorrence of old ballerinas dancing with young men. Once again, however, it was a case of "Never name the well . . . !"

The first *Giselle* rehearsal found us both edgy. With a new partner there is some carpentry necessary to fit the two different versions together. Usually each does as he or she is accustomed to do, until there comes a section that doesn't match. Then one says, "What do you do here?" And the other says, "What do *you* do? I do this."

Most of the men say, "I will do it your way; how does it go?" Rudolf, however, said, "Don't you think this way better?" We entered into some negotiations, and each altered a few steps here and there. What mattered to me most was the intensity of his involvement in the role. Two hours went past in no time at all. I was Giselle and he Albrecht. Often he was Rudolf showing me, with infinite exactitude, how I could better do some step that I was trying to remaster now that my left foot no longer hurt. At other times he was practicing his own solos, still like the old steam engine. He literally *became* Albrecht, and there was an extraordinary harmony between our interpretations. I was deeply impressed by the unexpected felicity of working with him, and I forgot my complexes about mutton and lamb. We were happy with each other over *Giselle*.

During those rehearsal weeks I danced the complete *Swan Lake* with David Blair. It was difficult after the two-year break, but I knew the fact of dancing the most taxing of all ballets would give me more strength for the *Giselle*. I was having greater trouble than usual with the fouettés in rehearsal, and Rudolf asked, "What is your mechanic for fouetté?" I was dumbfounded by the question. I had never thought of the "mechanic"; I just did them with determination. I faltered in my answer and tried the step again. "Left arm is too back," he said, and, with that one simple correction, I recovered my old form easily. I learned a great deal simply from watching him in class. Never had I seen each step practiced with such exactitude and thoroughness. It was paradoxical that the young boy everyone thought so wild and spontaneous in his dancing cared desperately about technique, whereas I, the cool English ballerina, was so much more interested in the emotional aspect of the performance.

Indeed, when I fling myself into the rapture of, say, Juliet, and nearly overbalance the two of us, he will say, "Don't get hysterical."

Rudolf came to my dressing room after *Swan Lake*. He seemed genuinely impressed as he said, "It is very beautiful performance." But he added that, although he marveled at the way in which I did the mime scene (dating from the original production and no longer done in Russia), he thought he would not be able to do the scene himself when we danced it in the summer. He thought he would feel silly standing about doing nothing while I told the story in gesture, and added, with a touch of embarrassment, "I am afraid I will ruin your *Swan Lake*." I looked him straight in the eye and said amiably, "Just you try."

—from *Autobiography*, 1976

Robert Gottlieb
The Art of Pleasing

The stories of most great ballerinas, however different their temperaments, are basically the same. They start preparing professionally as children; their lives are ruthlessly and narrowly concentrated on their work; they have a mother to nurture them, fight for them; they inspire a powerful creative personality, who then shapes them (Pavlova had Petipa; Karsavina had Fokine; a dozen or more, from Danilova and Toumanova to Farrell and McBride, had Balanchine); and they find themselves in their forties either finished or hanging on precariously—ballerinas don't age gracefully into character roles and grandmother roles, the way talented actresses can. And they share a quality that, late in life, Margot Fonteyn identified as the one that "has helped me most": tenacity.

The life of Fonteyn, the most celebrated ballerina of the twentieth century after Pavlova, fits all these circumstances almost to the point of exaggeration. She not only started studying at the usual early age, but she was thrust into tremendous responsibility, as the leading dancer of the young Sadler's Wells Ballet, when still in her mid-teens. She not only had a famously devoted and levelheaded biological mother, known to one and all as BQ, or the Black Queen (after a character in the chess ballet *Checkmate*), she had a second ballet mother in the formidable, all-powerful Ninette de Valois— "Madam"—founder and absolute ruler of Sadler's Wells, who never wavered from her conviction that little Peggy Hookham, quickly renamed Margot Fonteyn, was the Chosen One. She not only became the muse of one of the greatest of choreographers, Frederick Ashton, but late in her career she found in Rudolf Nureyev a second if very different artistic inspiration. And although she was preparing to retire early in her forties, her connection with Nureyev revitalized her and kept her going past sixty, still in demand even if sadly diminished.

As for tenacity, she overcame what she herself called "no elevation, no extension, no instep, and feeble pirouettes"; she blossomed under the draconian conditions of having to give nine performances a week in wartime England; she gamely endured the humiliations her marriage provided, and heroically coped when an assassin's bullets left her husband a quadriplegic. And she faced a painful death with a fortitude that we can only marvel at.

But it was not only the extraordinary breadth of her career and the drama of her personal life that set her apart from her coevals, or the exceptional beauty and purity of her performances, her early technical weaknesses long forgotten or forgiven in light of her perfection of line, her exquisite proportions, her unerring musicality, and her profound identification with her roles. It was the charm she radiated, the lovability, that made her so cherished by audiences for more than four decades. As Lincoln Kirstein once remarked, "Of all the century's ballerinas, Margot Fonteyn most embodied the art of pleasing."

From the start, nothing could move Peggy Hookham from her path once she had decided on it. One of the virtues of a recent biography of her (*Margot Fonteyn: A Life* by Meredith Daneman) is that the author has been able to draw on an unpublished memoir by the Black Queen which adds considerably to our picture of Fonteyn's childhood. Little Peggy, her mother confirms, was well-behaved, self-controlled, hardworking. But when she made up her mind, nothing could change it. Many children, for instance, resist healthy diets, but not many are, as Daneman puts it, "capable of becoming ill for three foodless days" to get their way. (Meat, fish, eggs revolted her; her favorite meal was baked beans on toast.) It's fascinating to see how this quality of stubborn determination, for which Fonteyn became famous (or notorious) in later life, manifested itself from the beginning. "I learnt never to force an issue but to skirt round it," wrote her mother, herself hardly a shrinking violet. "Her will was stronger than mine if it came to a showdown."

Mrs. Hookham was the illegitimate daughter of a lower-middle-class English girl and a very rich Brazilian—his name was Fontes, which became Fonteyn when the family made it clear that they didn't want their name associated with the stage. Mr. Hookham was a fairly successful engineer, whose work eventually took him—and his wife and children, Peggy and Felix—to China in the early 1930s. In Shanghai, Peggy continued with the dancing lessons she had begun in London, and eventually Mrs. Hookham decided to take her back to England to find out whether she had real talent. That, to all intents and purposes, was the end of the Hookham marriage; he stayed on in China, was interned by the Japanese during the war, and eventually remarried. The Black Queen never looked back.

Peggy was accepted at the Sadler's Wells school—"No money you can spend on the child will be wasted," pronounced de Valois. "Unless some disaster occurs, I know she has a great future ahead of her"—and despite her weaknesses her talent was so obvious that within a year she was appearing in the corps de ballet and then, quickly, in solo roles. And when the fledgling company's one genuine ballerina, Alicia Markova, left for greener pastures, Peggy-Margot was quickly propelled into many of her roles, including *Swan Lake*'s Odette (at first, Odile was beyond her technical capacities) and Giselle. But her reception in the company had by no means been unanimously enthusiastic. Her famous partner-to-be, Robert Helpmann, found her "rather uppity, tiresomely remote for one so young, and, in appearance, rather scraggy." Frederick Ashton himself was unimpressed. He found her "strangely lacking in warmth, charm, temperament and variety. . . . I sensed a streak of stubbornness." But Madam had spoken, and Margot was soon appearing in Ashton ballets.

There was a showdown: When she failed to meet the technical demands he made on her, he grew more and more incensed, until one day she broke down in tears, threw herself on him, and burst out, "I'm trying my best; I can't do any more." He was to say that this was the moment when she "conceded" to him, and that he knew he would be able to work with her. Daneman, however, sees it differently: "Men never know when they have been conquered. To the end of his life, Ashton believed that it was he who had won the battle"—a feminist touch that perhaps owes more to Daneman's background as a novelist (and to *The Taming of the Shrew*) than to the realities of Sadler's Wells.

Even so, the most telling sections of Daneman's book are those that explore Fonteyn's relationships with the powerful people who dominated her and/or succumbed to her charm and her talent. With her mother she was respectful and obedient—up to a point. With Madam, she was *always* respectful and obedient. (When in 1954 de Valois informed her that she was to be the new president of the Royal Academy of Dancing, Fonteyn replied: "The Academy is boring, and it is absolutely not the kind of thing I am good at." "Never mind," said Madam. "It's all arranged." And that was that.) But the crucial early influence was that of the brilliant and self-destructive composer/conductor Constant Lambert, who despite his tempestuous marriage and his alcoholism was her mentor and her lover through her formative years. (In her memoirs, she mentions him only in passing—which is more than she does for several of her other lovers, with one of whom she had an ongoing relationship for ten years.)

The great emotional adventure of her life was with the man she eventually married—Roberto "Tito" Arias, the scion of one of Panama's great families, whom she first met, glancingly, in 1937, when she was eighteen. When they met again many years later, he was married, plump, the father of three children, and a diplomat. Suddenly, in 1951, there was a phone call to Atlanta, where she was performing, from New York. ("I couldn't believe it was Tito. He was talking as if we had seen each other last week, when it was twelve years since I had heard a word.") It was another two years before he turned up again, this time backstage at the Met, and the next day he announced that they were to get married; his wife, he insisted, would be pleased to divorce him. He persisted, he cajoled, he wooed, and, Reader, she married him. "I so much wanted to love," she was to write, "and it seemed so difficult for me to love." It was Tito who "rescued this human heart trapped inside the ballerina." She had already recognized that "my need to love far outweighed my need to be loved."

She certainly had found a man whom she could love more than he loved her. Tito's philanderings went beyond those apparently to be expected from a Latin aristo husband, and his cavalier disregard for her needs and comfort only pushed her to more extreme measures of self-abnegation. He was rarely there when she needed him, while she always managed to be there when he needed her. She participated without hesitation in his half-baked revolutionary activities in Panama, involving herself in adventures that were as farcical as they were dangerous—and that made headlines around the world. (Visiting Fonteyn in a New York hotel, her great friend the dancer Nora

Kaye "was astounded to find her . . . in the basement, engaged in a spot of gun-practice.")

She doted on Tito, embraced his family, forgave him, and never indicated to the world that she was suffering. His word was law: her friend Colette Clark told Daneman, "She always did what Tito said. That's what you have to realize. It's nothing to do with what she thought; she wouldn't consult her own thoughts." It was Tito who brought her into the orbit of Aristotle Onassis and Winston Churchill, Panama's Noriega, Chile's Pinochet, and the Philippines' Marcos—and to the shameful episode of Margot's choosing to dedicate her book *The Magic of Dance* to "The magic of Imelda." She had, by the way, previously accepted from Imelda a bracelet composed of seven bands of jewels—emeralds, rubies, diamonds, pearls. "What can I *do?*" she said. "I can't give it back."

The Fonteyn of the Tito years was in many ways a different person from the unaffected and collegial girl whose loyalties and affections had been so closely committed to the company. (By this time, Sadler's Wells had become the Royal Ballet.) Now she was the wife of Panama's ambassador to Britain; she was a favorite of the royal family; she was dressed by Dior, then Saint Laurent. Daneman's view of "this one and only woman who was also a great dancer" comes perilously close to idolatrous at times, but it turns distinctly caustic when Tito comes into her life: "Times had changed, and so had the company she kept. Her highly principled, sensitive nature was now diverted away from its ruling sense of duty to the public, and directed solely towards her husband."

Daneman is also uneasy about Rudolf Nureyev's effect on Fonteyn, although she credits his role in reshaping and extending her career. The book quotes approvingly the testimony of the dancer Annette Page, who was with the Royal Ballet on its extended tours of 1962 (the "happy" tour) and 1963 (the "unhappy" tour); that is, pre- and post-Nureyev. On the "unhappy tour," says Page, Margot

> behaved badly for the first time, like a sort of temperamental ageing ballerina. . . . She was the head of the company, the perfect model—up to a certain point. And that point was the arrival of Nureyev. I think she was infected by his narcissism. With his advent, the company became background—a montage. We no longer felt her support.

The Fonteyn–Nureyev partnership was to a large extent the creation of de Valois, who was fascinated by "Rudi" and understood both his value at the box office and the value of the example of his Kirov classicism to her other dancers. And of course she understood what he could do for Margot: "He brought her out, and she brought him up." But when at first Margot demurred at entering into a partnership with a dancer nearly nineteen years her junior, it was Tito who made the decisive remark: "Get on the bandwagon, or get out." "So onto the bandwagon," as Daneman recites, "at the age of forty-two, she gamely jumped." In her account of what Nureyev meant to Fonteyn, Daneman soars into the higher altitudes of prose. To his charm and bad-boyishness,

> Margot's maternal nature, so long suppressed, now rose and sprang to flower like a bloom raising its face to precious rain. . . . Even in the short time that she had known Rudolf, the earthly limitations of their bond—her marriage, his homosexuality, their disparate ages—had taught her about transcendence, and now she could base her interpretation [of Giselle] on her own spiritual resources, drawn not from the nebulous air, but from the vast, unfathomable sea of maternal passion.

Well, maybe. But all that maternal bonding doesn't deter Daneman from exploring at great length "the question which, despite its implicit prurience, none of us can, in the end, quite refrain from asking: Did Fonteyn and Nureyev sleep together?" Nor can she quite refrain from answering that question:

> When I admit that . . . yes, I *do* believe that Margot and Rudolf were lovers, you must understand that I, like the rest [of the implicitly prurient?], am telling you more about my personal prejudices and predilections than ever I could about what really went on between these two people who, as if sharing some complicit laugh, took their secret, undivulged, to their separate graves.

Having addressed the question, Daneman backs up onto higher moral ground:

> For great practitioners of the arts, whose lives are at the mercy of a vocation, the discovery . . . of a fellow aspirant both willing and worthy to give and take support along the way, is a blessing of almost mystical proportions. . . . Perhaps the most intimate union that an artist can ever forge will be with someone who shares, not his bed, but his dreams.

In other words, the question she couldn't quite refrain from asking turns out to be irrelevant. But we should never underestimate the appetite of the English for sexual gossip. Ashton and Lambert and Helpmann were particularly adept at it, and so Daneman is able to quote Ashton on Lambert's virtues: "Very good balance, very reliable tempi, very large cock." And to quote Lambert to Ashton on Margot's vaginal muscles (only he employs the vernacular term), they "are so strong that she can activate me of her own accord." But did the world really need to hear such things about a woman who was famously reticent and fastidious, and whose family and friends will presumably be reading this book? I don't think it's prudery on my part that makes me recoil, on Margot's behalf, from this gratuitous invasion of her most private life.

Still, there is considerably more to appreciate than to deplore in Meredith Daneman's biography. We will have no fuller or more canny account of the arc of Fonteyn's amazing career, and the author's background as a dancer gives her special insight into Fonteyn's qualities as an artist. De Valois, the Black Queen, Ashton, Lambert, Tito, Nureyev are penetratingly observed. (The only major figure in Fonteyn's life who seems scanted is her brother, Felix, around whom Daneman tiptoes.) Best of all, Daneman is acute on what Fonteyn was really like—the complexities of a nature that presented itself as simple and direct.

When Fonteyn deserves censure—most importantly, when she "grabbed" (her own word) the premiere of Kenneth Macmillan's *Romeo and Juliet* from Lynn Seymour, on whom it had been created—Daneman is appropriately severe: "Where is the specific, passionate endorsement of a young artist by a mature one, the generous acknowledgement that genius, when it strikes, must have its day?" She grasps Fonteyn's extraordinary capacity for denial, and knows whom to quote about it, her photographer, chronicle, and friend, Keith Money:

> Margot's way of getting through life was to have sort of steel bulkheads like a ship, and if she couldn't cope with something . . . a relationship, a problem, whatever, if she didn't solve it by dusk, it went into a box, the box went into the cupboard, the cupboard was locked and the key was thrown away.

And she quotes Fonteyn herself who, in her twenties, had told her teacher Vera Volkova: "I'm determined to be happy. If an unhappy thought comes into my head, I suppress it. I put it at the back of my head."

This talent for suppression was to see her through the stresses of her marriage, and free her to unleash the fierce—"almost maniacal"—devotion with which she tended Tito after his near assassination. Yet she was never grim. One friend remarks aptly that "she had this talent of laughing at misfortune—it was the secret of her happiness that she could laugh at the most incredible moments and make them disappear." Indeed, her laugh and her smile were among her most potent weapons. She herself noted that she may have conquered America with her smile.

The triumph of Sadler's Wells's opening night in New York, in October

1949—exactly fifty-five years ago as I write—is probably unmatched in the history of ballet in America. Fonteyn danced Aurora in the full-length *Sleeping Beauty,* and ballerina, ballet, and company were wildly hailed. She had been unknown here—the famous one was Moira Shearer, star of the movie *The Red Shoes*—but overnight Fonteyn was accepted as a great artist and a beloved personality. She was on the cover of *Time,* the cover of *Newsweek;* her performances were automatically sold out. And when she and Nureyev joined forces, her fame turned into real celebrity—"Margot and Rudi" became familiar to the general, nonballet public, like Callas, like the Beatles. They were pursued by the paparazzi. Audiences went berserk; curtain calls for the *Corsaire pas de deux* sometimes lasted longer than the performance itself.

She went on and on. Once Tito was incapacitated, her earning power became essential to their lives, since he never moderated his extravagant way of life. By the time she finally retired and they had settled down on a small, isolated farm on a Panamanian beach, the money had run out. The conditions under which they lived were extraordinarily primitive—at one point, not even a telephone. Tito's nephew reports, "They lived in something akin to destitution. Her only consideration was his welfare." She was essentially a farmer now—breeding cattle. Buenaventura, the manservant who had tended Tito for years, says she had become "*una ranchera.* A Cow Lady." Yet she could say,

> If anyone questions my happiness, will you please reassure them. I'm the happiest woman in the world. I'm doing exactly what I want to do, which is to be with Tito, in Panama, on our farm, looking after the cattle, learning how to keep the stock records and everything else, and just thoroughly enjoying myself, wearing shirts and jeans and not having to fuss about anything.

Invited to tea by the Queen and Princess Margaret, she sent her regrets: there was a cattle sale coming up, and "I don't think the Queen liked it when I said, 'I can't come because I've got to buy semen.'"

She had only a few years of this happiness. Tito died in 1989, causing scandal to the end. A well-known society woman who had been close to him—who would come to him at the farm when Margot was away—committed suicide on the day of his death. Margot had already developed the painful cancer that was to kill her. She spent more and more time in a hospital in Houston, pretending to the world that her medical problems were not serious. One friend who visited her told Daneman that "there were moments when I would go to the end of the corridor and I would listen to those screams and start perspiring and think, 'Why doesn't she die? This is not a life.'" Yet she returned to the farm, telling an interviewer, "I want to stay here till the end . . . in the place I chose to live with my husband."

There was to be one last public moment—a gala at Covent Garden organized to raise money for her. Soon afterward she retreated to Houston and, Daneman movingly recounts, "finally gave up the fight," doing it in "her own calm but powerfully disciplined way." Her stepdaughter Querube was summoned, and Margot said to her, "I've decided not to have any more treatment. That means I'm going to die, so I want you to call Felix and tell him." When the answering machine picked up, she said, "Well, give me the phone," and left a message: "Felix, this is Margot. Querube and I are here and I've decided that I'm going to die." She managed to get back to Panama, and when she died, Querube says, "She wasn't scared or anything. . . . She died like a fish, you know. A little fish. A fish receiving air."

That was in 1991. Her death was front-page news everywhere, and she remains vivid in the minds of those who saw her dance. For me, the great revelation was the radiance of that 1949 *Sleeping Beauty;* for others, it was her *Firebird* or *Giselle* or *Swan Lake* or *Marguerite and Armand,* the highly romantic vehicle Ashton created for her and Nureyev, which exploited the contrast between her contained pathos and lyricism and his febrile exoticism. For people who never saw her, there is a considerable amount of film, including television documentaries that are shown and reshown. Recently, a popular exhibition at the Performing Arts Library in Lincoln Center celebrated the impact on America of her art and her effortless projection of dignity, stylishness, and charm. She is taking her rightful high place in the history of her art.

—from *The New York Review of Books,* December 2, 2004

David Daniel
Margot Fonteyn

Whenever anyone asks me what Margot Fonteyn was like, I reply that she was perfect. Of course, she wasn't, but that is neither here nor there. She made you believe she was. And even when you understood that you had fallen in love with an illusion, you didn't feel cheated. You grew more fascinated and amazed. Her illusion of perfectness was not an act of fakery. It was the visible and tangible result of what may have been the most astute theatrical temperament of our time. Her performance of Aurora in *The Sleeping Beauty* was quintessential. No wonder, then, that her personal reading of the Rose Adagio, with its elaborate *en couronne* attitude balances, has come to supersede the choreography itself. Her "interpretation" has become the authoritative text.

Fonteyn was a beautiful woman, pale-skinned and dark-haired, and alluring without seeming dangerous or too sexy. Her refined glamour reminded you of Vivien Leigh as we know her in the movies; this vividness was softened with the sweet plainness of the young Queen Elizabeth II. She was a beauty for more reasons than the loveliness of her small head and kissably tender long neck or the generous warmth of her opening arms or the fact that her silky legs seemed not to have kneecaps. Her body was so harmoniously proportioned as to suggest that she was the avatar of an aesthetic ideal. This harmony, no less than her musicianship and her theatrical instinct, lent an appearance of rightness to every move she made, and it magnified her illusion of perfection.

Even by the standards of her day Fonteyn did not possess a virtuoso technique, although her technique was beautiful and clear and equalized throughout its range, and all of it was always available to her. But she was a virtuoso performer because she understood the function of virtuosity as a climactic heightening of a dance phrase. She had an uncanny, even eerie, sense of theatrical logistics. Her timing could take the skin off your face—she was a great musician. Unlike many of her contemporaries who exceeded her in mechanical brilliance, Fonteyn could produce a virtuoso climax whenever one was called for, and she never missed or faltered at the crucial moment. This authority, so spontaneously presented as to make you believe she had invented the dance right on the spot, only added to her aura of infallibility. Fonteyn was the real thing.

—from *Stagebill*, 1991

MARTHA GRAHAM

One of the great creative artists of the twentieth century, Martha Graham (1894–1991) transformed and expanded modern dance, and left both a highly personal dance vocabulary—the famous "contract and release"—and a repertory of powerful pieces whose fate remains undecided. After studying at the Denishawn school and dancing with the Denishawn company for a number of years, she appeared successfully in The Greenwich Follies and began choreographing on her own. By the early thirties she was a name to be reckoned with. Her first masterpiece was Primitive Mysteries (1931), and by the time of her most popular work, Appalachian Spring (1944), her name was a byword. Among her other best-known works: Cave of the Heart (Medea), Letter to the World (Emily Dickinson), Deaths and Entrances (the Brontës), Seraphic Dialogue (Joan of Arc), and the full-evening Clytemnestra (1958; see pages 444 and 1013). Her most important collaborators were her music director, Louis Horst, who was also her mentor and lover; Erick Hawkins, the first man she used in her choreography and whom she married— not a good idea; and the sculptor Isamu Noguchi, who designed many of her ballets. Among her most important dancers: Merce Cunningham and Paul Taylor. She was a major choreographer, a very great dancer—and a very complicated woman.

KENNETH TYNAN

Martha Graham

Born in Birmingham, England, Kenneth Tynan (1927–1980) had a meteoric career as theater critic, literary manager of the new National Theatre for Laurence Olivier, and author of Oh! Calcutta! Known for his flamboyant nature and lifestyle, his marriages and liaisons, and his deadly wit, he was also a great enthusiast—for Graham, as we see below, and for other larger-than-life phenomena, like Greta Garbo. He became famous in America as theater critic for The New Yorker.

Although I have heard her say: "I am not a high priestess of *anything*," she has managed to recruit an army of acolytes. They swarm about her, so many moths around her hard, gem-like flame.

In 1954 she played to thin but ecstatic houses at the Saville Theatre [in London]. Seeing her then, I was oppressed at first by her iron solemnity, but as her repertoire unfolded, one rapt female archetype succeeding another, I realised that Eric Bentley was right when he said: "The diagnostic of the dancer Martha Graham is that she is an actress"—and a great one, at that, in the line of Duse. She dwarfed her company, erasing them, even in repose, by the serene authority of her presence; one thought of the late Ruth Draper, another great performer condemned by the uniqueness of her talent to appear only in works of her own creation.

I met Graham briefly in her dressing-room, but awe confined me to mono-syllables. I had read too many daunting things about her: that "in more than one way she resembles Nefertiti" (de Mille), that her beauty was "of a formi-dable sort, enigmatic, ambiguous" and her face "an unnaturally motionless mask" (Bentley). My own first impression was of a woman who looked forty and might be four hundred, and who combined the salient physical qualities of Helene Weigel as Mother Courage and Beatrice Lillie as Kabuki Lil.

With these images colliding in my mind, it is perhaps no wonder that I kept my trap virtually shut. She did the same: what little she said was slowly and precisely articulated, eked out with large, comprehensive gestures that employed the whole arm, from collarbone to finger-tip. I felt that speech, for her, was essentially a foreign language, a Pyrrhic victory over silence.

We did not meet again until last spring, when I spent an afternoon in her New York apartment. It might be the home of a geisha turned puritan. The floor is wall-to-wall wood, polished like ice; on a low coffee-table marigolds float in a shallow bowl; Chinese scrolls speckle the walls; and the centre-piece is an ornately carved Chinese couch, ideal for meditation though not, I should think, for sleep. Small ornaments abound: talismans in jade and ebony, painted sea-shells from Japan, and a tiny bronze ram from Persia, poised for three thousand years on the brink of attempting a skyward leap.

Her hair stretched back in a high bun, Graham greeted me with both hands. Pensively, and at moments gnomically, she talked about her life and work, sipping brandy between paragraphs, using her whole body to italicise important points, and looking, whenever she paused, as if she were about to disclose some gigantic private sorrow.

She was born in Pittsburgh of Scotch Presbyterian parents, with whom she migrated in childhood to California. Her mother's family were tenth-generation Americans, and there was plenty of Sunday school in her upbring-ing: "My great-grandfather would spin in his grave if he knew I was dancing."

Although she is no longer a churchgoer, she thinks of herself as religious and keeps a Bible in her dressing room.

"I feel the Twenty-third Psalm in everything I do. And the Nineteenth Psalm, too—'The heavens declare the glory of God, and the firmament showeth his handiwork.' And later it says: 'There is neither speech nor language.' I often hear that when I'm onstage. To my mind there are three sorts of language. First of all, there is the cosmic language, which is movement. Next, there is the language of sound. And finally, the language of particular words. As my father used to tell me: 'Movement never lies.'"

She was introduced to the pleasures of theatre by an illiterate Irish nurse named Lizzie, who took her to Punch and Judy shows. Her father was opposed to dancing as a career, but he died when she was in her teens, and she promptly joined the Denishawn School in Los Angeles, where she was duly enthralled by the preaching and practice of the great dancer-teacher Ruth St. Denis. Her training completed, she moved to New York and taught for a while, but soon decided that she could not meet the demands of her talent without forming a company of her own. By 1931 she had achieved coterie fame on the East Coast, and the coterie has been spreading ever since.

The torments and anxieties of women—biblical, mythological, Victorian, and contemporary—stand at the centre of her work. "All I have ever wanted to do," she said to me, her lower jaw projecting as she paused in thought, "was to create a vocabulary that would be adequate to the past and to the twentieth century. Not one or the other, but both. I am a thief. I'll steal from anyone, and any period. But I'm not interested in television or anything two-dimensional. The stage is my area. Theatre used to be a *verb;* it used to be an *act*. But nowadays it is just a noun. It is a place."

Oriental drama and philosophy have always attracted her: "I had a Zen master when I was in California. He affected me tremendously, and I've studied Zen on and off ever since. But I don't like what they call in San Francisco 'Beat Zen.' That's just *talking* about aesthetics, and anyway I hate the word 'aesthetic.' Real Zen has to do with physical behaviour. I've always been fascinated by Oriental theatre, although I didn't go to Japan until 1956. I met one of their great, ancient female impersonators, and I went down on my knees." Swinging off her chair, Graham folded the hinges of her body in an illustrative genuflection, so that her forehead brushed the shining floor. Righting herself with equal suddenness, she continued: "I saw Mei Lan-fang when he came to America. He was the greatest Chinese actor of his time, and he always played female parts. He was that curious creature—a complete man and a complete woman."

According to rumour, Graham's sense of vocation excludes private emotional allegiances; in the words of de Mille, "one does not domesticate a prophetess." I asked her whether rumour was right, and she smiled forgivingly. "I do not believe in the cloister for the artist," she said. "An artist can live a full domestic life. I was married once, but it broke up. I wanted children, but I was told I couldn't have them without a difficult and dangerous operation. The choice I made had nothing to do with art."

She runs a school of dance in a building owned by her most faithful patron, Bethsabé de Rothschild, and there she has a family of nearly two hundred, drawn from nineteen countries. Stringently and devotedly, she moulds her pupils in her own durable image: "Out of this wonderful thing that is man, you make a world. 'We did it—you and I': that's what a great artist says to the audience. Look at Fonteyn in *The Sleeping Beauty*—such triumphant exaltation!—and Helene Weigel in *Mother Courage,* and Gielgud in *Hamlet.*" I reminded her that many of her ballets were concerned with untriumphant, even self-destructive, women. "Yes, but tragedy is a sort of triumph. Did you ever see Ulanova? She's self-destructive, and that's how she achieves—what is the word?—*illumination.*"

Graham is unimpressed by her reputation as a living legend. "The works themselves don't matter," she said as we parted, "and the legend only matters if it makes other people work. I have no opinion of myself except that I'm glad to be my own master. And if you want to know my philosophy—well, I once knew a man who told his maid that it was her sacred, bounden duty to go on scrubbing his floors. 'Mister,' she said, 'I don't have to do *anything,* except to die.'"

—from *The Observer* (London), August 18, 1963

DON McDONAGH
A Chat with Martha Graham

She received me in a white hostess gown trimmed with gold, in the middle of a busy day. She had just come from rehearsal. In less than a week she would open a major engagement at the Brooklyn Academy. As we talked the phone rang frequently, distracting her attention to one last-minute crisis after another. She handled each call politely and firmly, returning each time to our discussion despite the presence of a tape recorder. It, too, was an intrusion but, like the telephone, unavoidable. On the coffee table lay a copy of Noguchi's artistic autobiography, *Sculptor's World*. Noguchi's sets are inseparable from Graham's dances, but she had had extraordinary luck with other collaborators as well—Ming Cho Lee, Rouben Ter-Arutunian, Jean Rosenthal . . . How, I wondered, did the collaboration work? Was it possible to speak of Martha Graham "commissioning" a set? In those terms?

"Yes," she said. "Exactly. I never do it unless I am completely certain that the man I do it with is in sympathy with me and I'm in sympathy with him. And then, we never interfere with each other. Some sets I like better than others. But I never say no, I don't like it. I always say I'll have to think about it."

And with Noguchi?
M.G.: Well, of course with Noguchi I never have to say very much. I say, let me think about it—I have to get myself going on this kind of a beat. And then, because he knows in his deep Oriental way that I'm speaking in *my* Oriental way, he usually goes away and brings me back something else. You see, what he does is try to find out what it is that I am absorbed with in the dance. Of course he knows that I will never violate him as a sculptor.

D.M.: *When you say violate, you mean you would not ask for anything specific?*
M.G.: No, not entirely. I say to him that I think there's a bed here, or I think there's a chair over there, there's a place I have to sit, there's another place where I have to be. And I indicate that to him, and we show it to him.

D.M.: *The entire dance?*
M.G.: Not maybe entirely, no.

D.M.: *May I take a specific example of a set which I admire a great deal, the* Seraphic Dialogue. *What information did you convey for that one?*
M.G.: I told him what I felt about Joan of Arc, and I did not indicate anything at all. All that he did was to go and think about it. But then he took me to his studio and I saw what he had done. And it was so beautiful that I said, that's it, now we have to learn to use it. Because, you see, a set for me is nothing unless it is used. I'm not interested in a backdrop. That's why I've never used a painted backdrop. I don't want a static. Now, I'm not saying that it can't be wonderful. But I've never wanted to do it and I've never tried.

D.M.: *You actually want your set to participate.*
M.G.: It's a character in the piece. And with *Seraphic Dialogue,* when I saw it, it made such a difference to me. I had seen it, yes, in my mind and in my heart, in a certain way, but I hadn't seen the thing that Isamu would bring,

the opening of the gates and the magic. It's all Isamu's. And when I realized it could be unhinged and worked that way, well, then of course it opened for me an entirely new area of behavior on the stage.

D.M.: *About some of the spectacular props and costumes, for instance the great red cloak in* Clytemnestra. *How did that find its way into the dance?*
M.G.: I did it. I wanted it that way. I remember the day I did this thing in *Clytemnestra* in the studio. I just put pieces of cloth down on the floor, and we fiddled with it a little bit, and I talked to Isamu and told him what I thought, and then he evolved a way to use it. Now, I'd used material in movement before, but I'd not used it in the formality of design. That red thing came because I felt the necessity for it at that moment in the piece. There were nights when I used to stay at the studio and work out these things with props and costumes and so on. And Isamu went along with me. He was always so extremely aware. We had a few moments of disagreement, but we let each other alone, you know. I have this idea, and he has an idea, and he goes away and works on it, and then he asks me to come to his studio and then I see it.

D.M.: *But prior to seeing the design for Seraphic Dialogue, you had worked out in your own mind who Joan was.*
M.G.: Well, you see, I did do this piece alone. I did it with the St. Louis Symphony and I did all the characters. I danced the Maid, I danced the Warrior, and I danced the Martyr. I went off the stage and changed while the music went on. I did Helen's [Helen McGehee] part in tights and leotard. There are pictures of all of this. I did it as a solo performance. But then I realized that it wasn't rich enough that way. I realized this was a drama. So then it was that I split it off. And it was then that Isamu came into it.

Graham does not think of Noguchi as a designer. He is, she says, "a man who has made something." She owns several pieces of his, among them the "Aphrodite," which a visitor, if he is careful, is allowed to handle. Graham's apartment reflects the creative concerns of her life. It is a mixture of the contemplative and the physically active. There is a ballet barre and a mirror to the right of the front door; facing you is a four-poster couch of Oriental design. She moves easily between the two. Besides the Noguchis, her shelves hold small antique statuary of Middle Eastern origin and a number of other rare objects. At her invitation I hefted a simple blown-glass bulb mottled by eons of interment. "You're holding a man's breath," she whispered. "I'll show you where I keep my books." She did. From her books have come ideas for many, many dances. *Cortège of Eagles* came from "a book I've had for a long time about the myths and legends of Troy." For her study of St. Joan she borrowed LeRoy Leatherman's copy of the trial and read it all. ("One has to. You can't just get a pretty idea and go into it.") She is an avid reader of detective stories, "the good ones," finding in their maze of logic a constant fascination . . .

D.M.: *Now, when you are composing a new work, what happens after you've worked out the idea?*
M.G.: First, the ideas. Way back in literature, way back. Then you are stimulated. But you go to others. You're not alone in this. You go to a musician. And then comes the set.

D.M.: *What does the musician have to know?*
M.G.: I usually give him a detailed script, with all of the things in it that I've been reading, quotations from this-this-this-this-this. And then I give him a kind of sequence. Say, this is a solo, this is a duet, this is the company, and so on. I don't pin him down to time. I always tell him, if it has to be forty minutes it has to be forty minutes, and you don't have to cut off anything. Then, I never start to choreograph till I get the music.

D.M.: *You never work with the dancers at all till you get the music? A complete score?*
M.G.: No. Piano. I tell them the idea. I take all my books over and they can read about the characterizations, but when I get the score, or the piano part, then I begin to work. It might be interesting if you talked to a composer. Talk to Norman Dello Joio, talk to Robert Starer. Ask them how dancers work. I work that way. Other dancers work in another way. Now, I know in my body—it's not so young, you know, so I don't feel it so much now; this is my tragedy—but you know in your body certain things, and you know how certain things are going to go. Very difficult for me to analyze this, because it's so intensely personal that it has nothing to do with the principle, let's say, of choreography. I don't know how Tudor works. I don't know how Balanchine works. I only know how I have to work. What I do is write everything down, all of my notes, all of the readings that I've done, everything, and then boil it down to a point where I can say to a composer, Would you be interested in this subject.

D.M.: *Now supposing that when you get a piano score you find that there is far more developmental time, something that you consider subsidiary to what your main concern is. Is there any way of changing the score?*
M.G.: Well, usually I try to accept it as it is because I have found that I can learn very much from it, from another person. I don't cut, ever. If there is a deletion or an addition, I go to the composer and say, is it possible, but I have never cut a note of music or a rest of music, for the simple reason that if you do that, what are you asking for? You're asking for a mirror of your-

self. I don't want that. I want an integument from which I can get something. I'm very clear about this because I was brought up so hard in music with Louis Horst.

D.M.: *What do you mean, hard?*
M.G.: Either you accept what is written or you don't. You don't try to make the composer alter it because if you do you get a bastard job.

D.M.: *You always prefer to work with a commissioned score.*
M.G.: Yes, but I don't want something that's tailor-made. I want something that's designed.

D.M.: *The reason I ask so closely about this—*
M.G.: I don't know what you're going to say about me, but I've been warned that you're a bad boy. But that's all right, go ahead.

D.M.: *—is that William Schuman, one time on a program, was asked what it was like to work with Martha Graham. And he smiled and said that, well, you always ended up doing the right score, and he didn't know quite how it happened. Miss Graham wouldn't actually say, would you change this or would you do that, but somehow you realized, you the composer, that you hadn't done exactly what was going to be suitable. And you did go and have another look at it, and you did amplify or shorten, and then you did come out with the good score.*
M.G.: Well, that's the way I work with them. I never say I want this or that, cut that out, give me four bars here, give me four bars there. All I've had to say is, let me think about it overnight, I'm stuck. But I've never said no to Bill Schuman. I've asked, once, if I could delete a repeat, this I've asked for.

D.M.: *You want him to be engaged.*
M.G.: I want him to be engaged, for the simple reason that I want the music to be free of the choreography. I want it to exist as an orchestral piece. Now, when Samuel Barber did what was then called *Serpent Heart,** he transcribed it for orchestra to do the "Dance of Vengeance" of Medea. It took about seventeen minutes. It was wonderful. It's not the ballet, as I've done it, because that would be boring, you see. The same thing with Aaron Copland. He cut out certain things for the concert version of *Appalachian Spring.*

D.M.: *You are not interested in selecting a piece of music from the existent repertory and working with that, as far as I can see.*
M.G.: Well, the only reason that I haven't been is that I stem, not from the interpretation of music, but from the drama of an idea.

---

*Original working title, (vide *Romeo and Juliet,* III, ii, 73), later changed to *Cave of the Heart.* Barber's orchestral version is called "Medea's Meditation and Dance of Vengeance."

D.M.: *Right. I noticed in the book that Leatherman did about your career that he referred to your pieces as "plays."*

M.G.: Well, this I don't go along with, but then that's a different matter. Although it's true that *I* couldn't take a Bach or a Handel piece and do it. *Maybe* I could, but I'm not interpreting music. There's a four-way play: the idea, the music, the set, and the dance. This is what I feel I can do and have done.

I mentioned a program at Riverside Church by Yvonne Rainer and others, with film projections, slides, and recorded sound in use throughout the evening, and added that an enormous amount of expensive technical equipment is today almost indispensable. Graham agreed that "it's all become production and I'm partly responsible for that"—but it was frightening that the young no longer seemed to concentrate on "the principle which is the dance." "Why, I remember the time when I had a piano, and then there came a time when I had a flute and cymbals. Finally, I got to the point where I could have four or five pieces. Now, I'm not saying that electronics are tricks; they're not. But it has to come out of your guts."

Martha Graham, born in Pittsburgh, is Scottish and Irish on her father's side, a direct descendant of Miles Standish on her mother's. The family was Presbyterian with unscheduled infusions of Roman Catholicism largely provided by the Irish nurse, Lizzie. Dancing was not done, but Martha's decision to be a dancer was not opposed. Dr. George Graham, a specialist in nervous disorders, had died shortly before, but it was he who took his daughter to her first dance performance. They traveled from Santa Barbara, where they were then living, to Los Angeles to see Ruth St. Denis. "I know he gave me a corsage of violets on that night," Graham recalls. "I was fourteen or fifteen and my fate was sealed from then on."

D.M.: *Was Miss Ruth doing solos at this time?*

M.G.: She was doing solos. I saw her do the great ones, *Cobra, Radha*—

D.M.: *The Nautch?*

M.G.: —yes, *The Nautch,* the great ones before she became what I am now, which is to carry a company. I saw her in those great days. Of course, Ted was just coming up because he was—coming up, that's all. That sounds as though I'm bitter against him but I'm not. I'm not at all. He gave me my first chance and I'm deeply grateful for it.

D.M.: *When you went to Denishawn, you knew that you were not going to a classical ballet tradition . . .*

M.G.: I never had seen classical ballet. I never had seen another dance performance in my life. I had classical ballet training there, at Denishawn.

D.M.: *How good was it?*

M.G.: It was good, except that it was not on pointe. But I could do it. I know all of those things, how to do them, and when somebody doesn't do them, I know it. There were three aspects to the school. One was the classical ballet, one was of course the Oriental dance, which Miss Ruth had, and then there was Ted Shawn, who had drama.

D.M.: *He told me once that Miss Ruth really disliked ballet.*

M.G.: Yes, I think she did.

D.M.: *What was your feeling about it?*

M.G.: Well, what can you feel when you're fifteen or sixteen years old? You're beguiled by what you're doing. I remember the first time I ever went in to Miss Ruth for an audition. She said, "Dance for me." And I said, "But Miss St. Denis, I've never danced. I don't know anything about it." She said, "Well, you must know how to do something." I said, "No, I don't." Well, they took me because I had enough money to, frankly, pay my tuition. Then I just worked like a slave to find out what it was all about. I never let a class go by; I never let anything go by where Miss Ruth was. Well, to me she was a goddess. And in many ways, she was, regardless of what I felt. I never saw Pavlova—well, finally I did see her, on the stage. I never saw Isadora. I saw the six girls once. I never saw Nijinsky—they didn't come out there. Then, when I went to Paris, I did see Karsavina.

D.M.: *When she was dancing for Diaghilev.*

M.G.: Well—I saw her *Firebird,* but I never saw the first company, the Diaghilev company, you see, because by the time I got to Paris it was late, 1922 or 1923, and I saw what I could see. I did see *Schéhérazade,* but not with Nijinsky.

D.M.: *Were you working when you were there in Paris?*

M.G.: I was there with Ruth St. Denis.

D.M.: *So then, after the Follies—*

M.G.: Well, then I was fed up. All I had was a bad job. The first concert that I gave by myself was given because Jones and Green, who were the promoters of the Follies, wanted me to sign another contract. I'd been two years with them. We talked billing and an awful lot of money. In those days, when you got $350 a week, you know, it is quite a lot of money, pictures and everything. And I said, I want to try it myself. But they wanted me to go back, and I said, "I cannot go back. What have I got to do? What can I do from now on out?" They said, "Well, you'll have to change your style." I said, "I don't understand what style is." Well, anyway, they were sweet, but they had the Forty-eighth Street Theater. I said, "Mr. Jones, I want to do a performance, one." And he said, "All right, I'll give you the theater for the cost of it. If you lose money you ought to go right back into the Follies." I said, "All right." I did it. I did four solos. He came back to me. He said, "Girl, you've made it. You've made your expenses."

D.M.: *You don't have to go back to the Follies.*
M.G.: Well, I didn't. I went to Rochester—Eastman School. And there I began to work out things, because I'd made up my mind by that time that unless I found something to dance about, I would never dance again. Now conditions are very different. But I was not going to dance because I was very sexy. I could have done the Houris—anything—at that time. But that was not what I wanted to do. I felt there was some glory which I had never seen and had never touched. There were times, for instance in the Follies, in the old Century Theater up there on the West Side, when Duse was there. I couldn't go except to matinees, and I went to every matinee. And I remember one play, I don't even remember the name of it, where she had a son, and she wrapped her rosary around the arm of the son, and she said, "Dear God, give me the life of this child. I will do anything, I will accept anything." Well, of course he turned against her. But there was one moment, when she sat on a large chair, and this whole thing turned to her. Turned to her. So beautiful. Tears were streaming down my face, I must say. I was awfully young. Well, there were things like that, you know, that maybe somebody else wouldn't have seen, I don't know. And I remember Edith Evans doing the Nurse in *Romeo and Juliet* with Katharine Cornell. I was fluttering around, helping. I did the dances for that. And I was so touched by the Nurse because I knew that somewhere, way back in my soul, there was something about this that I couldn't quite—so I asked her once, "Would you mind, just tell me one thing, from what point did you take the Nurse's characterization, or is that too much to ask?" She said, "No, I'll tell you the exact line. 'I think it best you married with the County.'" Well, then the whole thing opened for me. The Nurse is–how many children do you have?

D.M.: *Four. Four girls.*
M.G.: Four girls!

D.M.: *Ann, Ruth, Rachel, and Amy.*
M.G.: What lovely names. Well, I'll tell you, sometimes the person that takes care of them–I'm not speaking about the mother or the father—has a tremendous influence over these little lives. It happened in my life, with

Lizzie, and in the lives of my two sisters. And then of course there were my
father's nurses from the South. And I remember, according to my great-
aunts and my great-uncles, how—and this is something I don't ever want
told, so I'm not going to tell you any more about it, because that tape
recorder is on.

D.M.: *Tell me something about Rochester instead.*
M.G.: I learned a great deal from them. I was a little embittered by them.
Mamoulian was there at the time, getting a bad deal, a very bad deal, so
when they wanted me to come back for a second year, and I walked into
that big room—it seems to me it was a tremendous room—to sign my
contract for ruining myself at a tremendous amount of money at that
time—and today!—I picked up the pen and started to write, and I put
down "M—" and I said, "Excuse me, Mr. Hanson, I cannot do it." And then
I turned and walked out.

D.M.: *What was it they wanted you to do?*
M.G.: Two things. One was, they wanted me to teach, which was utter
nonsense. They wanted me to do dances and so on. But the thing they did
not accept was that the dance was not going to go into the Eastman Theater as a revue, like Radio City, but was going to be developed as an art.

D.M.: *They did not grasp that?*
M.G.: No. And that's why I left. I came down, and I practically sold apples.
I didn't quite. You see, I knew halfway through the year when I was there
that it wasn't going to work if I stayed there for a year—I was supposed
to—and I said, please let me out. One half a year. I will take a cut in salary,
but I cannot stay; it's killing me. So I stayed for a half year, on half salary,
and then I left.

The conversation ended not because it had come to an end but simply
because there was no more time. Miss Graham had to go back to the studio.
Like an epic narrative it had begun *in medias res* and had now worked its
way back to the beginning. Martha Graham had left the Eastman School and
was going to carry Modern Dance around the world during the next four
decades. There was much more to talk about, perhaps too much. At one
point she had warned me: "You're knocking me too much." "I'll go away," I
said. "Shall I come back again?" "No, I don't think so," she said.

—from *Ballet Review,* Vol. 2, No. 4, 1968

Martha

Born in Vancouver province, Dorothy Bird (1912–1996) began studying with Martha Graham in 1930. She danced in the Martha Graham company for six years, and then with other groups, including José Limón's, as well as in such Broadway musicals as Lady in the Dark.

My appreciation of Martha grew greater every day. I was filled with an almost overwhelming mixture of awe and gratitude. As we began class with the series of basic exercises, each having its own specific purpose, I knew that this was home for me. These same exercises, which in later years would be used by dancers all over the world, were known to us quite simply as "the warm-up." One morning we sat with legs open wide, toes pointed, back straight, head balanced easily on the atlas. We rocked slightly on our sitting bones as we centered ourselves. There was always a moment of complete stillness before beginning each exercise.

We were working on the arms, using the image of powerful eagles' wings; I reveled in the feeling of strong feathers on my wings. My shoulders pressed down to bring up feather-covered elbows, as I imagined myself preparing for flight. I was absorbed in the work when Martha, glancing my way, started laughing. I thought, "Oh dear! What am I doing wrong?" Martha stopped the class.

"I see we have to work on wrists and hands," she said. "Dorothy, your hands are always anticipating shape and texture. When you take hold of a cup or spoon, the hand senses the shape, and prepares to fit the contour, and adjust to the weight before making contact. Today I want you all to over-ride that instinct. I want you to initiate the action." Martha looked straight at me. "Form your hand into a strong, aggressive fist with a firm, powerful wrist. Now, punch like a prizefighter!" I tried, but my thumb had slipped inside my fist. "The thumb," Martha insisted, "must come around outside the fingers, grasp them firmly and hold them together. The thumb acts as a brace for the fist." For the first time in my life I was able to assume a threatening gesture.

Hands became crucially important when Martha began working on what I think of as the "Circle of Pain" segment in *Seven Against Thebes*. Martha began by having us all move on a sobbing breath. We added gestures of grief, including beating with a fist, as we had done in class. It soon became apparent that we would be unable to convey the violent, intense grief that Martha envisioned.

She looked at me and shook her head from side to side. "Oh, Dorothy! What are we going to do with your ribbons? Your hand movements are *still* as lyrical and gentle as ribbons floating in the air! This is no way to communicate the powerful feelings of women whose husbands and sons are being maimed and killed on the battlefield."

I was terrified Martha was going to give up on me when she suddenly stopped cold, as if frozen. For what seemed like a long time, she did not move. Then she took a deep breath and spoke decisively.

"I want all five of you to form a circle. Lock your hands tightly together, and *don't let go!*" She had some of us sob over toward the floor, while others turned in toward each other, to give comfort and support. On the opposite side of the circle someone was rising up high, as if crying out in protest. We twisted sharply down one way, then sprang up the other way. Heads flung from side to side, up and back, then over toward the floor. The remembered rhythmic pattern of a sobbing breath silently enriched the movement. Heart-rending, shuddering sobs were torn out of us. We were cautioned always to keep the mask of the face impassive. No pained expressions were allowed. With our hands locked tightly together, we shared in this grief, just as we had once shared in the melody of "Molly Malone."

And to think, all of this was accomplished without anyone making even a single hand gesture! Martha had devised a brilliant way to include me. But that was not all. The most amazing transformation took place in me. By expressing intense feelings through my open throat, head thrown wildly back then deeply bowed, I was releasing my own agonizing suppressed emotions. I could at last express feelings I had never allowed to surface before. Martha had not just disposed of the "ribbon" problem, she had found a way to convert our individual weaknesses into a powerful, massive lamentation. The movement was strictly choreographed, but it retained the appearance of total spontaneity.

The Greek costumes Martha had in mind for us were inspired by an exquisite Fortuny gown she owned. It was made of delicate, wrinkled, twisted silk, which conformed subtly to the contours of her body. In attempting to achieve the clinging effect of the gown, but without incurring the cost, Martha enlisted our help in assembling the costumes. She took me shopping when she bought yards and yards of white cheesecloth and several shades of Tintex dye. Then she invited several of us to her apartment to work with her on the costumes. She told us to be very quiet, because she did not want her landlady to know what was going on in her kitchen. We watched Martha as, one after the other, she mixed the different packages of terra-cotta, red, and sand color dyes in a huge cauldron on the stove. She tested the color and declared, "This will have to do."

The material was divided into five sections, a length for each of us, and then placed in the cauldron of boiling dye. We took turns stirring for a long time, all the while laughing about the witch's brew we were making. We argued back and forth incessantly. "It's done." "No, it's not done." Finally, Martha determined that it had reached the desired shade. We wrung out and then tightly twisted the dyed lengths of cheesecloth and placed them in the oven, hoping to bake in the tiny, uneven pleats. It seemed to take forever to dry. We spent the time anxiously scrubbing the mess on the floor, the stove, the pot, removing all traces of the dye. Martha seemed concerned that the landlady might appear at any moment.

What eventually emerged from the oven did not at all resemble Martha's delicate, form-fitting Fortuny gown. Even though she was disappointed, Martha pushed ahead the next day. She hastily fitted and struggled to pin the stiff, scratchy, wrinkled lengths of cheesecloth with huge safety pins onto the homemade leotards we were wearing. She instructed each of us to take the costume home, sew it up, and bring it back in time for performance the following day.

The only sewing Mother had ever taught me was to sew invisible hems around linen handkerchiefs for Christmas gifts, and I could not do even that to her satisfaction. What to do with the pinned, wrinkled-up cheesecloth was beyond me. Having no notion of what or where to sew, I retreated to my room and went to sleep.

Early the next morning, the long-awaited day of the performance, I ran all the way to the Cornish School carrying my bundled-up, unsewn costume in my arms. As I ran I prayed that somehow I could slip through undetected, safety pins and all. At the school everyone was busy with a thousand last-minute details. I entered the dressing room, trying to be as inconspicuous as possible. Martha came in to personally supervise our makeup. First she had us apply a heavy layer of what she called greasepaint all over our faces and necks. It was creamy pale, almost white, and I found it horribly repellent. I felt like a clown. I was surprised when she said we would wear no rouge, and even more shocked when she told us to draw on bold, dark eyebrows. Then Martha showed us how we must paint two parallel lines to accentuate our eyes. Someone roughly drew them for me—the top line along the edge of the upper eyelids, close to the lashes, and a heavier, longer line below the lower lashes. Both lines extended beyond the outside corner of the eye, with a space between them. We placed a small patch of white between the lines at the outer corner of each eye. Martha said this was important to define the eyes and make them seem larger when seen in profile. To dramatize the eyes when facing the audience, we placed a dot of red paint where the upper and lower lids meet on either side of the bridge of the nose. Martha said this would add life to our eyes.

The most exciting part of the ritual of making up came when Martha showed us how to dress our eyelashes. We lit several candles, and then we melted slender sticks of coal-black wax in the flames. Using delicate little brushes we coated each eyelash with jet black liquid wax, adding layer after layer until our lashes glistened with small black droplets. I watched what was happening in the mirror. My eyelids were taking on the character of window shades that could go up and down! It was fascinating!

When it was time to put on our lipstick, my heart sank, and I felt slightly sick as I looked at the dark crimson color we were to use. I was used to rose-petal-pink lipstick, and that for the stage only. This was much too shocking for me even to attempt. I looked around the room, desperately wanting to escape.

Martha—who never missed anything that was going on with "her girls"—stepped briskly toward me and said to the group, "Look. This is what I want." She picked up the lipstick and firmly drew two wide red lines, one on my upper lip and one on the lower, to shape my mouth into a bold, gash-like, somewhat rectangular shape. I looked into the mirror, and looking out at me was a strange, strong, daring person. No one would ever recognize me. I found this wildly exciting!

When I heard an urgent voice saying, "Hurry! Hurry! Get into your costumes," I knew the crisis moment had finally arrived.

Terrified, I went up to Martha and sheepishly told her, "I did not sew my costume. I did not know how to sew it."

Martha was burning with anger. I knew she would be. She roughly took the costume from me and dragged it down over my head. She put safety pins into her mouth and went to work fiercely yanking the cheesecloth into shape on my body, pinning it here and there onto my leotard. She was hissing and cursing half under her breath. Anger was like fuel for her. I was not afraid. I was just thankful that she was fixing my costume so that I could be in the performance. I vaguely remember some kind of headband being tied around my forehead, just a little above my eyebrows, and I heard whispered protests about "looking like a bunch of Indians." I liked being camouflaged like a chameleon. Being transformed into a stranger from another time and place made me feel safe.

People roughly pushed Bonnie, Grace, Nelle, Bethene, and me into a line, told us to be quiet, and pulled us through a narrow passageway into the back of the pitch-dark auditorium. We took our places at the rear of the side aisle and waited for our cue. Once the music began, I knew exactly what I had to do. The slow chain of sternly disciplined abstract movements had become part of me. I wasted no time reacting to the audience, which by then was becoming aware of us as the lights gradually came up. It must have been a

startling, eerie experience for the audience to see these weirdly made-up
dancers so close to them in the ominous dim light.

Gradually we progressed in a single line. Each dancer tilted independently forward and over, head bowed toward the floor, then arched precariously up and back, with one hand placed on the heel of the back foot, and
face looking up to the far-distant ceiling. It was reminiscent of figures in an
ancient, very wild, abandoned bacchanal, but executed in slow motion. We
mounted the short flight of steps onto the stage one by one in the same two-
dimensional manner, until finally we became part of the action of the play.
Although I remember little of the actual performance, I do know that the
"Circle of Pain" segment burned with the intensity of a huge bonfire.

At the close of the performance, the five of us bowed in a dignified and
appropriate manner, as Martha had carefully coached us. We stood with our
heads held high, feet together, arms at our sides. We made a small bow from
the hip hinge, then returned to place with heads again held high. We looked
from right to left, accepting the applause simply and proudly. It was a formal
bow that was quite sexless, and it felt good to me.

After the performance, I felt as if I had climbed a mountain, and I would
never be the same as I had been before. I had experienced and learned so
much, it would be a long time before I could sort it all out or speak about it
to anyone. I carried within me the deep conviction that dance could and
should be locked into deep rivers of feelings that cannot and must not be put
into words. I looked up to Martha as if she were a figure in the Bible, Moses
perhaps. I knew that I was one of the chosen people, and I must follow her
wherever she went. . . .

Martha Graham was a pioneer like my father in the way she had turned
her back on what went before and had started from scratch to create something new and wonderful. I felt the same involvement with her that I had
experienced when helping Daddy clear the land, or sharing the chores as he
painstakingly prepared the soil for optimum growing conditions. Martha
was like a gardener, I thought. She grafted, she watered, she fed, and she
watched the movement grow. She weeded, and weeded, and weeded. I
rejoiced in being a part of this new process of growth in the dance technique. The constant creativity my father had shown on the farm, and his
devotion and care of every growing thing, was being relived in the classroom
as Martha molded movement with her bare hands. Being with Martha was
like a continuation of our communal life on the farm. A difference between
Martha and my father was that Martha never gave up.

Martha had become like a mother to me, in ways that my own mother had
never been. Toward the very end of summer, Martha sat me down, fair and
square, looked directly into my face, and asked me, "Tell me, Dorothy, what
do you know about the facts of life? Do you know how babies are *conceived*?"

"Kissing?" I mumbled, blushing crimson and wishing I were a million miles away.

"You can't come to New York City, Dorothy, without knowing how you can get pregnant! So, if no one else has warned you about this, I guess I will have to!" Martha proceeded to explain precisely how the man's seed enters the woman's womb.

—from *Bird's Eye View,* with Joyce Greenberg, 1997

TOBI TOBIAS
A Conversation with May O'Donnell

May O'Donnell (1909–2004) worked with Martha Graham first from 1932 to 1938, then from 1944 to 1952 as a guest artist. During that later period she created the crucial roles of the Pioneer Woman in Appalachian Spring, *the Chorus in* Cave of the Heart, *and the confidante in* Herodiade. *She danced at other times for José Limón and in her own company, for which she also successfully choreographed.*

TOBI TOBIAS: *How did you work on the character of the Pioneer Woman in* Appalachian Spring? *Did you make her story?*
MAY O'DONNELL: Martha gave me a great deal of freedom. Of course, I could see how she was working with the group and the stylization of the piece. The four little girls, for example, the way they moved was very much like in those early American primitive paintings—the stance, the carriage of the body. I found what path I would have to take. Her pianist, Helen Lanfer, was wonderful to work alone with on the music. Sometimes Martha would say, "Well, May, do you want me to work with you or would you like to sort of feel it out?" And I'd say, "Well, I could try something and if you like it, Martha, fine, and if you don't why, naturally, then it will come out." It was very different than in the thirties, where everything had to be so set.

TT: *What did the Pioneer Woman represent?*

MO'D: It was almost the backbone of the piece, the quality out of which the American grain could develop, a strong, outward, visionary kind of competence. It supported the whole pioneer spirit, which had lived through the trek across the country and through the great things that were happening, the hardships—the eternal spirit on which you could build a nation. Martha never spoke about this but she played with the basic material very often.

Early in the dance it was my place to look out from Noguchi's little veranda, out into eternity to the horizon, to the East and the West. And there once, right onstage (and we'd never practiced or talked about this), she suddenly gave me an imaginary baby. It was her dream child, of course, and, naturally, I took the "baby" and sat down. It was that kind of play that was so wonderful. Without rehearsing or even thinking about it, you just did what came out of the character, although you still did the same steps.

It was the same in working on *Herodiade* [1944], one of the Hindemith pieces. Martha and I were the only figures in it, and I had a sense of relationship with her. Once I knew what my character represented, I could keep in the right relationship.

TT: *Tell me a secret. What's* Herodiade *about?*

MO'D: I never asked Martha and she never told me. She never explained things; you had to build it up out of your own imagination. But I think it was about a person—Martha—facing a destiny and going back into a past, not only of one lifetime but finding reinforcement through the race itself. And I was the simple, devoted compassionate figure, having to prepare a person whom I loved even though she might be destroyed, trying to protect her from going into the unknown, which might mean death or salvation.

TT: *You say Graham didn't explain things, yet I get the impression that she created an atmosphere in which information was conveyed.*

MO'D: Yes. *Herodiade* didn't have a story; it was really a psychological relationship or adventure. I always felt it could have been Martha's own life in deciding to go into dance, that adventure, because when she did, dance was certainly the unknown field. And I let my character have the relationship one would have to Martha herself. *Herodiade* never really worked with other dancers in the roles.

TT: *The Chorus in* Cave of the Heart *[1946] was made on you. Was that another instance in which you essentially figured a great deal out for yourself?*

MO'D: That piece was of course based on a definite story, and Martha worked out the music sections so I knew exactly where I would come in musically. And also, in working her part out with Erick—she had to very definitely, naturally—and Yuriko, Martha knew where they would be onstage. So it was set up like a chess game; there were limitations as to where you would be in relationship to what and it almost dictated itself.

It opened with me standing on a Noguchi prop, actually the whole set, and Martha worked with me but at the same time gave me just enough freedom for it to be intriguing. She didn't say, "Lift your leg here and stand there." She might say, "May, if you run over to this corner on a diagonal and then take a position and hold it —" How would I run? Out of a feeling of impending terror, which was the feeling of the play. She wouldn't say, "Run by putting this foot here and put your arm there." Maybe at the end of the run I might hold my arm as if I were listening or speaking. If the moment seemed right, she would say, "Oh, that looks very good, just keep that." If she didn't like it, she would say, "If you take it on a different level—or instead of standing there, maybe if you'd drop into it." I'd watch what was going on, too, and get the feel of a reaction or a foretelling kind of feeling.

TT: *Did Graham ever say to you, "Do like this," demonstrate, and have you imitate?*
MO'D: Not very much. She would suggest you try something.

TT: *You mean she would verbally say do such and such?*
MO'D: A good deal of that, yes. When she was doing choreography she'd often sit. I know in working out *Dark Meadow* [1946] she might say, "Do a walk on a lean, maybe if your arm is here." I think she would work her part out on her own to the extent that she would get the feel of the way the piece should move and look.

TT: Dark Meadow *is another cryptic work. Do you have any idea what your role was meant to be?*
MO'D: I was called, I believe, She of the Ground—or the Earth.

TT: *I think it's been called both, actually.*
MO'D: I never saw the set until the night of the first performance, so I was a little surprised at some of the props, and Martha never spoke too much about the piece. I just knew that I was some kind of essential symbolical figure. Not the Pioneer Woman exactly, but her in a different way. It wasn't one of my favorite roles. Finally it got so that I became that figure in everything. Either very long, heavy dresses or a lot of standing around and waiting. And that became static for me after a while. It was as if I was always the serene figure, the kind angel that was keeping everything settled and quiet and happy.

TT: *Perhaps you did figure that way in her imagination.*

MO'D: I think she sort of needed that to balance off the tensions in the company because of the way she choreographed, and so many other things. For instance, if she were frustrated in trying to get a dance developed, she would build up tension with the dancers. She'd get into a frenzy and everyone would sit there and shiver and shake until it built up into an explosion. That would release her, and then she could push through.

—from *Ballet Review*, Spring 1981

NANCY GOLDNER
Primitive Mysteries

Martha Graham's first major group piece, Primitive Mysteries, *to a score by Louis Horst, was premiered in 1931, supposedly inspired by a trip to the American Southwest the two of them took the year before. Slow, incantatory, devout, it is still performed and still deeply admired.*

As its title suggests, Martha Graham's *Primitive Mysteries* enacts a ceremony. The dance passes through three stages: a prelude in which a group prepares for a rite; the rite itself, which gathers into a moment of crisis; and the resolution, which confirms the deliverance from that crisis and intimates the possibility of future ceremony. Graham calls the first section "Hymn to the Virgin," the second "Crucifixus," and the third "Hosanna." Whether one regards the girl in white a Virgin or as the body in the middle of the other bodies, every single gesture in *Primitive Mysteries* is both symbolic and a concrete expression of itself. By the time it is over, in some twenty minutes, it has become almost a definition of the kind of ceremony we regard as ritual.

Primitive Mysteries begins with fourteen women walking out of the wings, in formation of a three-sided square. They walk resolutely, heels wedged into the floor with each footstep. They know exactly where they are walking, for when they reach the center of the stage they stop dead; they have arrived. In the center of the square is a lone woman. Although distinguished by a different dress (hers is white organdy; the others, royal blue jersey with white ruffles at the hem) and by a different hairdo (hers is long and flowing; the others' in buns), what sets her apart definitively is her position in the center of the square. Her eyes downcast and her face set as a mask, she is a vessel, neither confirming nor denying hey pivotal role. The scene seems prescribed. Something or someone must stand in the center, and this figure is it.

Not quite, we discover. The group now forms into clusters. The central figure strides to each cluster, stiffly reclining into its collective torso. The cluster echoes the angles of her arms and ricochets her to the next. When she returns to the center she is still a vessel but one acknowledged by the group. With her stature now a conscious choice as well as physical fact, the group circles around her, underscoring the act of investiture. Just at the point when they begin to pick up speed, they stop dead again. The central figure raises herself from a deep knee bend. Her flexed arms return to her sides. They all march off as they had marched on.

Within the space of a breath, the group files on again, this time in jagged panels and in smaller, tighter strides. And this time, the central figure is accompanied by two women. Once at stage center, their torsos tilt toward her, their inside arms describing an X across her pelvis. Her lower body both bowered and imprisoned, she walks in place. The group echoes her walk. Her arms reach upward, becoming a funnel though which the stymied energy of her walk may pass. The group parallels her, so that the stage fills with rumbling throbs. Suddenly the two assistants step aside, revealing the central figure in full figure. She takes one step forward. That step snakes the group out of its lines and into a circle. Once again they circle in running steps; this time the runs become leaps, and the tempo builds to a stampede. Once again the action stops on a dime. They recess; then walk on for the third time.

Now the central figure is accompanied by one woman. She stands behind the woman in white, a shadow and an extension. The group jumps in quick little fountains of energy. The central figure rests on the ground while her shadow, looming above, crowns her with splayed fingers. The group falls to the ground. The two women in the center fall to the ground. Then they all rise and recess in the same formation in which they had entered at the beginning of the dance, except that now two women occupy the center of the square. The Virgin is dead; long live the Virgin.

Primitive Mysteries was made in 1931. It was revived for students in 1964 and is re-revived by Sophie Maslow for the Graham company's spring season at the Lunt-Fontanne Theatre. Graham made the dance after having spent some time in the Southwest. If one is in a fanciful mood, it is possible to see the Southwest's stark, clean outlines reflected in this dance. What is absolutely certain is that the architectural grandeur of *Primitive Mysteries* rises out of a choreographer at the peak of her incisiveness. Just as the dance is about a group of women who know exactly what they must do, so is this dance made by a woman who knows. Its austerity and purposefulness are not to be confused with Bauhaus grimness, however. Rolling up behind every jagged line is a curved line. The square becomes a circle. For every heel locked into the ground there is a subsequent spring onto the ball of the foot. The celebrants' clenched arms find release in the Virgin's full-faced, open-bodied stances, assumed once she has the group's permission to be its symbol. That first circular run, its momentum nipped in the bud, is unleashed the second time around. The tensely asymmetrical groupings of the crucifix yield to symmetry in the hosanna.

Yet despite the care with which Graham weighs dissonance against harmony, *Primitive Mysteries* is shocking for its rawness. As much as it is about the rites of passage, so is it about elbows and knuckles. The Virgin cups her hands with her fingers pressed white against one another, her knuckles bulging like carbuncles. The celebrants run with their arms locked behind their backs, their elbows rising humplike out of their spines. At other times their upper arms clench their sides while the lower arms shoot out of their hips like spikes. Or they stand full-face, arms bent back over their faces, so that all we can see are protruding elbows and fingers curling around throats. Contradicting the natural expanse of their shoulders, they straitjacket their arms into skinny Vs, so that their shoulders, and just possibly their lungs, hunch together. How can they breathe?

And how can Graham make a dance so universal in theme and so bizarre in its dance motifs? How can she show women at their most bony and yet contrive to make this dance, from a feminist point of view, the most dignified she has ever made? It has been said that once Graham admitted men to her company she betrayed her deepest instincts. This is nonsense, but there is something to the theory that whenever a woman dances with a man in a Graham work she turns neurotic. Her body shrinks into its pelvis so as to accentuate the difference in size between herself and the male. She becomes wily, feline, at best a spitfire. Her strength is predicated on smallness. With no other sex to measure up against, the women in *Primitive Mysteries* are what they are. They move weirdly all right, but on their own terms. Self-definition neutralizes them, ultimately ennobles them. Graham is too honest to make elbows beautiful. Elbows are elbows, and that's OK.

I thought that *Primitive Mysteries* was beautifully performed, though to tell the truth it would have taken awful dancing to interfere with the excitement of seeing this masterpiece for the first time. (Not even Louis Horst's tinkly score made a nuisance of itself.) The usual complaint about Graham revivals is that the dancers lack weight and psychological intensity. Hearing Graham herself on this subject would be invaluable. Lacking that, one may perhaps find a clue to her present thinking by noting that for this revival she added white flouncy ruffles to the hems of the blue shifts. In any case, I'm not convinced that *Primitive Mysteries* need be weightier than it now is; the choreography's geometric clarity says it all. Janet Eilber, The Virgin, was indeed ethereal and, yes, pretty. I thought her roundness and benign calm were in thrilling contrast to the group, although I can imagine a more statuesque dancer (does that mean weightier dancer?) in the role. Speculation about the best possible performance is somewhat idle, however, when dealing with the likes of a *Primitive Mysteries*. Its integrity is such that almost any Virgin could convince us of her symbolic power simply by virtue of the dance's design. *Primitive Mysteries* makes us believe that to stand in the center of the stage is to be powerful.

—from *The Nation,* June 4, 1977

DALE HARRIS
Dance Goddess with Feet of Clay

Martha Graham, if not exactly a legend, is at any rate a phenomenon. Two months shy of her ninetieth birthday, she is still active as a company director, a choreographer, and a teacher. Looking regal, if diminutive, in a glittering dress designed by her artistic collaborator and devoted supporter, Halston, she stood onstage with her dancers at the end of her opening-night gala at the State Theater—during the course of which her latest work, *The Rite of Spring*, was given its world premiere—and received a standing ovation from the elegant and fashionable house.

What the audience at Lincoln Center was applauding so enthusiastically, I believe, was not so much Ms. Graham's art as her character. For nearly six decades, she has been making dances and refining her style—originally a deliberate challenge to the frivolity of ballet dancing. Once a little-appreciated pioneer, a cult figure whose name until the 1960s was virtually synonymous with so-called "highbrow" art, she has persisted for so long that, despite the rejection last year of her application for a grant from the National Endowment for the Arts, the world as a whole has finally accepted her on her own terms.

The terms, as it happens, are not very demanding. One thing made clear by her only too representative opening-night program—*Seraphic Dialogue* (1955), *Acts of Light* (1981), and the brand-new *Rite of Spring*—is that her works have only a nominal connection with dance. From virtually the beginning of her career, Ms. Graham has been primarily interested not in movement or the exploitation of space, but in ideas. She herself refers to her pieces as "dance plays," which suggests that she has always had more to say than to show.

That fact has made it easy for the public to appreciate her—especially the public in search of uplift. Once the general theatergoing audience began to lose its fear of dance in the 1960s, Ms. Graham came to represent seriousness for those who wanted more than mere dancing. Unlike George Balanchine, mostly dismissed as a trivializer in those days, Ms. Graham gave people a sense of intellectual engagement.

Seraphic Dialogue, for example, is "a drama about Joan of Arc." Better yet, it is a drama about three aspects of the saint: the maiden, the warrior, and the martyr—each aspect being impersonated by a different dancer. For post-Freudians, such a conception of drama has proved very engaging, especially when used in conjunction with mythic figures like Clytemnestra, Alcestis, Circe, and Jocasta.

Ms. Graham's devotion to psychological content has helped to disguise for many the fundamental choreographic weakness of her work, the clumsiness and repetitiousness of her movement style, the lack of any sustained kinetic energy or connected dance phrasing. Particularly in her more recent works, Ms. Graham's performers do not so much dance as get themselves in and out of a series of awkward physical predicaments.

Since whatever they do is supposed to "mean" something, it becomes easy—at least, for some—to look through, rather than at, the medium of her discourse and simply ignore the insipidity of her vocabulary. The portentous titles are a help, too: *Acts of Light*, for instance, or *Mendicants of Evening*. And so are the perpetually mobile—usually tortured-looking— features of her dancers, which help to distract one from the movements they are executing.

Nothing, however, can distract one for long from what is actually going on before one's eyes during *The Rite of Spring*. Though the work in itself is perhaps no worse than the rest of Ms. Graham's recent output, so tame and prissy a realization of the theme of nature's rebirth through the sacrifice of an innocent victim is bound to seem exceptionally puny, even silly, by comparison with Stravinsky's powerful musical evocation of the universe's primal energy.

Other choreographers, of course, have failed to match the scale of the composer's imagination. Some, indeed, like Maurice Béjart and Glen Tetley, have failed dismally. But none in my experience has fallen so short in ambition: Ms. Graham seems neither to have listened to the music nor to have understood the theme behind it. Instead of creating an inexorable ritual, Ms. Graham has turned out a neat little gymnastic display, filled out with long stretches during which the leading characters gaze significantly at one another while breathing hard.

One thing is certain: This Chosen Maiden does not dance herself to death. After having been selected as the tribal victim by a tall, elegantly robed shaman, she simply expires—mostly, it seems, out of fear. Since Ms. Graham fails in any way to choreograph the fear—the victim does little more than tremble at the knees every so often—the effect is hardly convincing.

Ms. Graham herself must have realized that she was not responding to the challenge of Stravinsky's music, since in this work she has had greater recourse than usual to the distraction provided by props. At one point, a length of rope is much in evidence, though its function is never made clear, and it is soon discarded.

Much more effective on the present occasion is clothing. With his usual taste, Halston has designed some smart tribal outfits, notably the ones for the shaman and the maidens, who wear their hair in the style of the 1940s. Halston has made an essential contribution to the work's intended climax: a huge bolt of green and black material, which after the maiden's inconsequential, not to say inconspicuous, death is unfurled by what look like a pair of tribal clothiers.

By curtain fall, indeed, the atmosphere is so permeated with a sense of designer chic that the spectacle smacks more of high fashion than of high drama. In this unedifying glimpse of a sadly exhausted talent, what we are offered might better have been called *Slaughter on Seventh Avenue*.

—from *The Wall Street Journal,* March 5, 1984

RENÉE E. D'AOUST
Graham Crackers

PRACTICE MEANS TO PERFORM, IN THE FACE OF ALL

OBSTACLES, SOME ACT OF VISION, OF FAITH, OF DESIRE.

PRACTICE IS A MEANS OF INVITING THE

PERFECTION DESIRED.

—MARTHA GRAHAM

The first day of the Martha Graham Center for Contemporary Dance summer intensive, there is a large spot of dried and crusted blood in the center of the main studio floor. Advanced dancers doing sparkles on the diagonal across the floor jump before the blood and land afterward.

"Take to the air," yells Pearl Lang. She is petite, elderly, full of spine. Her gray-black hair is pulled with a small pink bow into a small chignon at the base of her neck.

One barefoot young woman lands smack on the crusted blood. Claire is usually a very careful, very precise dancer. The entire line of dancers, each waiting a turn, cringes.

Although the floor and center exercises took up an hour and a half of the two-hour class, no one cleaned up the blood. Kristi is absent. Kristi doesn't mind cleaning up blood and sometimes checks the studio floor before class. Spilled blood is a regular occurrence in a Graham class. Since modern dancers dance barefoot, often the skin tears or burns from the pressure of contact with the floor. If there's blood, Kristi gets the rubbing alcohol and paper towel and wipes the floor. She never uses gloves. Kristi also goes barefoot at Grateful Dead concerts.

It is a bold move to be absent for the first day of summer intensive, especially when company auditions will take place at the end of the six-week session. Absence means weakness. Survival of the fittest is taken to new heights in the Graham school. You must not simply survive. You must thrive or perish. If you perish, it's your own fault. The lipid content of your cellular structure is your fault, too.

Art won't come to the weak. And art isn't authentic if it doesn't bleed. In other fields, take the visual arts, for example, young people haphazardly and loosely refer to themselves as artists before they even know what it means to be touched by fire—as if without practice and guts and pain, they are already exalted simply because they label themselves *artists*. But at Graham, no pain means no gain. I dare you to toss around the word *artiste* lest you rot in hell for your audacity.

It takes ten years to make a dancer, says Martha.

Martha has been dead for two years, but summer intensive is still sacred: Pearl Lang teaches the composition class. It happens right after technique class. The dancers make up stupid twisty movements and call the amalgamation of their favorite moves choreography. Always one idiot dancer puts in a *grand jeté*—legs split, leaping high across the floor—and always Pearl takes it out.

"Yes, dear," Pearl says, "I know you love to leap, but show me something you don't love to do, and make it original."

Pearl speaks kindly because, usually, the girl has no talent. Pearl does not speak kindly to those with talent. It's a given. If you can't take it, get out. This girl, Fran, will become an arts administrator, and then she'll marry a wealthy banker named Ted who works on Wall Street for Merrill Lynch. Pearl knows not to alienate money and financial support of the arts. Fran might even think she could have made it. Usually the untalented in any field are unrealistic that way.

Pearl calls the short pieces "compositions," but the dancers call their pieces "choreography." They pronounce the "ch" as in "chore," so the word "choreography" sounds as odd as the little squirmy dance pieces look. No matter. The dancers know the pieces look odd, and they know they look like fools flailing about center floor, but they also know the little pieces of "choreography" are just a practice exercise, like copying a famous painting into a sketch book. But there's no framed picture hanging on the wall of Martha's studio; instead, there's just sweat in the air and blood on the floor. Lots of dancers have bodies that resemble gorgeous frames hanging in the Metropolitan Museum of Art—but not the Met, where Leo will end up as a has-been dancing in the Metropolitan Opera Ballet. There are plenty of dancers with beautiful bodies but no passion within. Some have ugly bodies, too. That's why they study Graham.

In Martha's studio, there is the scarred and ancient grand piano in the corner, the double doors that open to Martha's courtyard and her tree, the high, narrow windows, fluorescent lights and fan overhead, and the old barre with braces that are pulling off the wall.

The braces on the barre really need to be fixed. The barre cannot withstand the pull of weight for much longer. One brace has a screw loose, so part of it hangs limply off the wall. Ostensibly, dancers don't pull on the barre, but that is ballet. This is Graham. In Graham, dancers use the barres to pull away, to find the arch in the side of the body where one side swoops in and the other side swoops out, or to find the contraction. For that ever-present search, you face the barre, both hands on it, and pull back away from it, pretending someone punched you right in the gut—hard—whoosh, all the breath comes out of you, and you double over in pain and agony and glory and beauty. Back in Martha's day, teachers would punch you in the gut to be sure you know the real feeling. Real feeling. Real sensation. Art is no substitute for the real.

"You're a bird, an eagle," the teacher, Jacquelyn Buglisi, screams. "Let go of the barre. Fly!"

Several dancers actually let go of the barre and fall on their butts. They are the ones who always follow directions, especially when screamed in high pitch. If you hadn't been so terrified of Ms. Buglisi, you might have laughed: The ceiling is too low for flying anywhere, soon the barre will pull completely off the wall, and the humidity is so great that by the middle of class you want to plop down to the floor like the idiot dancers who actually let themselves fall on their tailbones when they didn't have to do it. Ms. Buglisi had, of course, been speaking metaphorically.

When she describes a ceremony of Native Americans who hung by their pectoral muscles in the sun, she does not specify the tribe. They wove rawhide on either side of the muscle, so the muscle took the weight of the body, and then they hung from poles. "Praise the sky!" whispers Buglisi, her face ecstatic at the thought of suffering. By the end of her class, you don't care if you sink into a little puddle of sweat: Your suffering is that great.

Again and again, you dutifully turn and face the barre the way you face a partner. The heterosexual male dancers in Graham have to be tough—if they're not, they'll be used up. Though, of course, a male partner isn't necessarily heterosexual, the role of the male in Graham is understood to be heterosexual or animal—Jason in *Cave of the Heart,* the Minotaur in *Errand into the Maze*—even if performed by a homosexual. Primarily the men function as hunks of flesh, the catalyst for the leading lady's freedom—she works against him, she hits him, she loves him; always, in the end, she spits him out. She is warrior. He is dirt. The barre has to be as solid as a man, as sturdy as a partner should be, but the studio is old, the plaster peeling, and the barre is pulling away from the wall from years of stress and abuse.

You grab the barre and pull away, the way Martha herself might have grabbed Erick Hawkins if she wasn't slapping him, your butt tight and head bowed, your back curving and your abdomen hollowed out. Please let this class be over soon, you think. In Graham, you hardly ever get to use the barre, so hanging on for dear life should be a treat.

The class where you hang on the barre is an anomaly. Graham class starts off with excruciating floor work, and the spine is supposed to be unnaturally straight, straighter than a heterosexual, so straight it looks like a Giacometti rendition of a woman in shock. All those little bronze bits are the sweat balls rolling off the body. What you don't know is that the emphasis on the straight spine in the Graham technique means that over time the natural curves of the cervical, thoracic, and lumbar regions flatten out so the spine eventually looks like a board. It means that the center of the body falls lower than in ballet technique, and it means that many Graham dancers in training flail about because the spine is rigid. That rigidity makes the arms stick out like scarecrows. No wonder everyone in Graham is looking for a center. How can you find a center if you have such distorted placement?

"We're living a long way from Bumfuck, Kansas, now, girls," Amanda announces in her British accent to the dressing room after class. She is taking off her sweat-soaked leotard and tights, exchanging them for a Lycra unitard hand sewn by Arturo. The dressing room is a long, thin room on the second floor of the Graham Center. "Where the hell is Kristi to wipe up that blood?" Amanda is black and has no boobs, and she is very thin and tall. She has attitude. But she also has passion. She'll get in the Graham Company. The Company needs a black girl this year.

Kristi went to visit her sister in Hawaii and phoned to say her plane had been delayed, but nobody believed her. Everyone suspects she stayed in Hawaii with her sister to smoke some more pot on the beach and soak up the sun. Deadheads are potheads. Everyone knows she isn't coming back. They are glad. One down.

But Amanda says, "There's always another to take her place." Except there isn't. If you consider it, life doesn't refill people who go missing. Kristi couldn't stick it out, and now the question is who will willingly take on the role of wiping up spilled blood in the center of the room before Pearl Lang's composition class. The dancers, like monks, are in charge of cleaning their own space, their own temple, but no one wants to do it. No one wants to touch HIV-positive blood. You know all dancers are promiscuous; it's a given.

This summer intensive there are dancers from Croatia and Brazil, Germany and Texas. There are a few from Oklahoma because a former Graham Company member works at the University of Oklahoma School of Dance. Other states are represented, too. There are no dancers from the African continent. Amanda is from Great Britain. There are three from Taiwan. Kun-Yang is one of them, but he won't make the Company because of his height. He's too short. There are four from Brazil. Six from Italy. Italians really love Graham. The American dancers say the Italians love Graham's pathos: her abdominal contraction. The Italian dancers say the Americans love Graham's control: her stately walk. The Italian men love sleeping with the American men, and the American women want to sleep with the Italian men.

Briget pulls on a new leotard. She wears a fresh one for each class. She always smells like Downy or Bounce. Briget has been at the school for ten years. She is a legend: "That girl who auditions for the Company every year." Someday she'll get in, even though she is too stiff and too tall, because persistence pays off. When Briget dances she looks like a sunflower that never should have tried to sway in the wind in the first place—as if a sunflower has any control over weather. No dancer has control over management, especially if half of management thinks Graham wanted all her dances to die with her and half thinks the reverse. But management in a dance company just means those who yell the loudest and are the most intimidating and have been around the longest. All the dancers are waiting for Briget's right knee to bust out. Briget's right leg wobbles on every landing. But she'll get in her beloved company first, and then her knee will bust out. Another one down.

Persistence really does pay off. If Carol Fried knows she can't break you, then she'll take you. The trouble is, most people go crazy along the way and stop dancing entirely. Daniela became the Firebird and tried flying out her fifth-story studio apartment window. Shelley understudied the role of Jason's princess, murdered by Medea in *Cave of the Heart,* and then actualized the role with a twist by murdering herself with poison. Shelley didn't even need Medea to do the dirty work. Through death, Jason's princess loses her ability to speak—though probably she never had that ability in the first place—and Shelley lost her ability to speak, too. Sometimes a dancer just plain loses it.

The other dancers call it going crackers, and if you stay around the Graham school it will happen to you, too. So get your training and get out before you become stiff and rigid and unmusical and forget your reasons for moving in the first place. When a dancer becomes a bird or something bad happens, the dancers say, "Ah, nuts." It means, "Good, another dancer out of the way"; or, "She went nuts"; or even, "Ah, nuts, it could have been me." Male dancers don't go crazy. Their penises are too needed. Often the males are homosexuals and too sweet to go crazy. It isn't in them.

In the dressing room, Amanda says it the most plainly: "Kristi couldn't take it." The dancers all nod. They can take it.

Dancers are not known for speech, which is nonetheless interesting because speech and text are very important attributes in the postmodern world of dance. David Dorfman thinks he's a choreographer and a writer, but really he simply used to be a baseball player, so he knows how to squat real well. Most dancers in the downtown scene don't have any technique, and they don't have any speech, either. The text they say is "I saw my mother" or something deep like that, and the audience is supposed to say, "Oh, wow, intense," or something deep like that. Text scrolls across a screen in something Stephen Petronio dreamed up, which looks like a scrolling message in Times Square, except it is so small and so weird and so out of place, hanging there above the stage like the Stonehenge replica in the movie *This Is Spinal Tap*, that the text means nothing at all. Neither does the dance. And the real Stonehenge is all surrounded by cement, for that matter. Who wants to dance on cement?

Dance critics think text means something and give it credence as such, but like all critics they think that everything means something even if it doesn't. Sometimes a dancer doing stupid twisty movements and speaking nonsensical text is just a dancer speaking bad text. It isn't to say that Martha wouldn't have tried techno-gadgets had she still been alive, but techno-gadgets only go so far if the dancers have nothing else to do—or, worse, if they look as if they have nothing else to do. Techno-gadgets can't do anything for a sloppy dancer or a fat one or one without any technique. Techno-realism can't make stupid twisty movements anything other than what they are. Go ahead and yell: RELEASE TECHNIQUE IS TECHNIQUE. You know it isn't. That's why Pina Bausch uses amazing dancers, trained dancers with technique, even if they only stand still or walk around in a Bausch ballet or open their legs wide and close them. Hieronymus Bosch would have adored Pina. For sure.

The spine is your body's tree of life, says Martha.

One! You're down. Two! Scoot your feet around and under and wrench yourself up to standing, don't feel the tear across your knee, ignore it, it isn't happening. Three! You're up.

"And again!" Pearl yells.

Don't think because you haven't been taught to think. Do it. Whatever they want. Again and again. You've been taught that a dancer lives to dance: Movement to a dancer is like breathing to mortal souls. You must bleed. Bleed now!

You've heard it so many times it doesn't matter if you believe it yourself. The body is aching, but you don't feel it now. You'll feel it later when you can barely lift a hand to turn the faucet on to fill the bathtub with water, and you can barely lift the box of Epsom salts and pour it into the tub. Whatever gender you are sleeping with at the time brought home the Epsom salts. Special treat. You dump the whole box into the bath and the carton falls in, too, because you're so tired you didn't hold it tightly enough. There is only tomorrow in the world of dance because goals are too far out of reach, so use up everything now.

Somehow you lift your leg over the rim of the tub, and though earlier in the day you could fall to the floor in one count, now it takes you eight counts to get your body lowered into the water. You sit holding your knees crunched up to your chest in a little huddle. It hurts too much to lean back, so you just sit there in a little ball in the water. If you are lucky, your sexual partner comes into the bathroom and clucks a little and picks up a washcloth and washes your back. Gently. Ever so gently.

After the bath, you don't have sex; you never have sex. You are too tired to have sex and too sore to have sex, and who the hell wants to explore the body at night when you've been exploring the body all day and you know where every little muscle is that isn't doing what it should? Those piriformis muscles would be great for sex because they are so strong, but you can feel your sciatic nerve ever so slightly. The last thing you want is for someone to touch you and make the nerve go on fire.

The words of the raunchier Graham teachers yelling at you reverberate in your brain all night as you lie there and stare at the ceiling: "Have an orgasm! Then you'll know life. None of you know life! Where is your contraction? Where is your orgasm? You're all frigid!"

Only the lucky ones have sex, the chosen ones, as Martha would say, "the athletes of the gods." These are the true purveyors of Martha's House—the House of Pelvic Truth. It isn't called that for nothing. Somehow the athletes of the gods are able to make all the little muscles work in their body and fall to the floor and breathe while they contract and then run and leap and look as if they do nothing but live life fully and completely in their bodies and in the dance. They have orgasms at night with a lover from a country foreign to their own. The rest just open the legs. That isn't even sex.

There is no question the will is always there—even in your bed at night, even if you just open your legs—the will to move with power and force and beauty. Martha says she never sought beauty, even though the grotesque is beautiful. When the teacher walks into Martha's studio all the students stand, quickly, and pull the feet together and squeeze the buttocks together and keep the arms long, palms in against the thighs, hopefully the thighs are not feeling or looking too big this morning, the hair should already be pulled tightly back and away from the face—it is OK if it's in a ponytail, no bun-heads here, though you might act like one.

One! You're up, standing, for the teacher. "Please sit," Pearl says, sometimes offering a little bow. Two! You sit. "And," she says. The pianist begins banging out whatever he's banging out this morning, and you are bouncing up and down, pushing your head to your feet: bounce bounce bounce. "Breathings!" yells Pearl. You breathe. Then stop breathing. This is how you start every day. For blood. For art. For Martha . . .

—from *Mid-American Review*, Vol. XXVI, No. 1, Fall 2005

HISTORICAL

M A R Y   C L A R K E
The Ballet Club

The first brochure sent out to members of the Ballet Club, printed on bright yellow paper of good quality, announced the policy: "The aim of the Ballet Club is to preserve the art of ballet in England by forming a permanent company of dancers with a theatre of its own. However important the work done by individual artists or occasional producers, continuity remains the chief need in dancing tradition* and practice. Ballets must be preserved, artists must be kept together, choreographers must have a stage and a workshop." Soon afterwards yellow postcards went out announcing the repertory for the season which was to start on 16 February 1931: *La Péri, Le Boxing, Carnaval, Les Sylphides, Aurora's Wedding, Leda and the Swan, Mars and Venus, A Florentine Picture, Sporting Sketches*. At the foot of the card, in jubilantly large letters, were the words ALL FIRST NIGHT SEATS SOLD.

The hand of Ashley Dukes was everywhere apparent in the Ballet Club literature which was despatched to members at regular intervals and always on the bright yellow paper. A true club man, one of the great personalities at the Garrick for over forty years, he enjoyed bringing the masculine arts of good writing and appreciation of good wine, good food, and good talk into the more delicate world of ballet. In April 1931 he was writing urbanely, "The Club Theatre has been re-seated with a sloping floor, to satisfy a general demand that every spectator shall see the dancers' feet." A small anthology of extracts from the yellow leaflets gives a picture of the progress being made and is also a pleasure to read. "For matinées we should like to see a small vociferous army of children—and many cheerful governesses with them.

"The exit doors are for emergency and land you in Ladbroke Road double

---

* Ashley Dukes defined tradition as meaning "classical and alive."

quick; we do not recommend them. It is more comfortable to go out the way you came in, especially as you can then visit OUR COFFEE STALL.

"We should hesitate in general to recommend one of these establishments, especially in Kensington where people go to bed much too early. But we must say a word for our own particular stall, which not only supplies a remarkable cup of coffee (black if you prefer it, or coloured with real milk), but also sausages, sandwiches, etc.

"Supper in the Foyer is therefore a distinct possibility. And if you see nobody you know . . . there is no rule of the Club against talking to your neighbour."

Kensington was one of Ashley Dukes' delights and he would write of the neighbourhood as often as about the forthcoming ballets. "Church Street is the Western Bond Street," he pronounced; "perhaps it will be the authentic Bond Street of the future.

"Art, Cultivation, being luxuries, tend to move westward in all cities (except in New York, where they leap skyward). In Kensington they pause and abide. Ours is a little theatre that can be said to have moved westward, out of the confused marketplace of nightly entertainment and into a community with an individual life and consciousness."

After evening performances, at one time, there was dancing in the foyer and on the stage to "Wireless dance music on Thursdays; radio-gramophone on Sundays (or wireless from the Paris Station)." (Such were BBC Sunday-night radio programmes at this time.)

The property was freehold, so the Mercury Theatre was from the outset in a position of "modest independence" and its development reflected the tastes of its owners. "After turning a parish hall into a theatre, we could not resist turning the dining room of the house next door into an entrance lobby. Nobody had ever done it before, at least in Kensington. And it may never be done again. The room, by the way, is sunny and pleasant these mornings, and if you live near by, you might drop in to book some seats."

Then came the development of the house next door, the decoration of the Print Room, which houses the unrivalled Rambert-Dukes collection of prints of the Romantic Ballet, and the installation of the wine bar, itself unrivalled (at least in Kensington), which Ashley made his special care.

The atmosphere was a remarkably cultured and elegant one, yet it was produced out of the hard earnings of two theatre people. Ashley's writings had built the theatre; Rambert's earnings from her school sustained the Ballet Club. Rambert drew no salary from her company until many years later (and then only on tours abroad); neither Rambert nor Ashley Dukes drew director's fees from the Mercury. Arnold Haskell, although he was a director and firm friend of the Ballet Club, had no financial rewards (or commitments) whatsoever. The dancers received a modest payment and any profits were divided among them. Markova, as ballerina, got 10s. 6d. Rambert would have brought this down to 7s. 6d., but Markova pointed out that as her shoes cost her 6s. 6d. and her taxi home (performances ended after the last bus had left Notting Hill) was 4s., she was, in fact, drawing no more than her expenses.

Rambert and her dancers toiled away all day in the studios in their old practice clothes but when the lights came on at night they were transformed into beautiful beings behind the footlights. The little theatre and its foyer were filled by an audience at once fashionable and knowledgeable. Nearly everyone was in evening dress, but in the audience (as in the company) there were always people who had neither titles nor money to offer but who brought an intense and whole-hearted love of the dance. Rambert knew them all and she valued the serious balletomane in the standing room as much as she valued Lady Oxford in the most expensive (7s.) seats. The dancers adored Lady Oxford. She was overheard to say one night, "Such nice girls. But do they have *homes*?" And every time a male dancer appeared on stage she proclaimed in her deep voice "*That's* Fred Ashton; such a nice boy." Princess Galitzine used to send the dancers cakes from Rumpelmeyer's and in *Leda and the Swan* Ashton wore, as part of his costume, a discarded feathered cloche that had belonged to the Princess.

The number of members by the end of 1932 had increased from 700 to 1,700, and a list of their names was printed and circulated in true club fashion. It makes fantastic reading. Here are a few names picked at random: Anthony Asquith, Lord Berners, Oswald Birley, Arthur Bliss, Lady Bonham Carter, Madeleine Carroll, Charles B. Cochran, Lady Colefax, the Roumanian Ambassador, Lady Diana Cooper, Douglas Cooper, Lady Cunard, Baron Frederic d'Erlanger, Beryl de Zoete, Lady Juliet Duff, Mrs. Gabrielle Enthoven, Jacob Epstein, Edwin Evans, Viscount Hambleden, Rupert Hart-Davis, Sir William Jowitt, J. M. Keynes and Lydia Lopokova, Geoffrey Keynes, Iain MacNab, Norman Marshall, Oliver Messell, Lord Moore, Montagu Norman, the Countess of Rosebery, the Polish Ambassador, Viola Tree, Geoffrey Whitworth.

The first night had been completely sold out, but the policy of presenting "seasons" of ballet at the Mercury proved to be a mistake. It was very difficult to retain the artists, for they were much in demand for work in films, revues, and musical comedies and they could not afford to turn down offers of employment. In addition, the audience tended to pack the theatre for premieres but premieres only. Arnold Haskell has recorded that on one occasion he represented one-seventh of the total audience. The policy was, therefore, changed very quickly to performances on Sundays and Thursdays, or occasional matinées, and this proved to be the right move. Scarcity value gave the performances an added appeal and the company was kept at full strength. Nearly every artist wanted to appear on Sundays and many could escape from their shows to dance in at least one ballet on Thursdays. "Here the young return on Sundays from their secular engagements to refresh themselves and their friends from the fountainhead," said *The Observer*. A spirit existed which was to breed in artists and spectators in years to come an intense longing for those halcyon years, an emotion which Ashley Dukes called *nostalgie de coterie.*

Atmosphere, *ambiance,* was all-important for the members of the Ballet Club. Ernest Newman wrote in *The Sunday Times,* "I can imagine no more delightful way of spending an evening in London just now than watching the ballets given by the Ballet Club in their charming little bandbox of a theatre in Ladbroke Road." *The Observer* spoke of "the atmosphere of Versailles . . ."

For the dancers, however, the atmosphere was something less rarefied and certainly less leisured. They were a very close little community, spending all their time together—at morning practice, at rehearsal, talking in dressing rooms ("Do you know what she *said?* . . ." "Did you hear what she *called* me . . .?"), mending tights, darning shoes, improvising, imitating, laughing, crying, quarrelling. There was always a crisis of some kind, always a clash of temperaments, or a last-minute panic that the new ballet (and its costumes) would not be ready by Sunday evening. Meals were eaten at the Express Dairy in Notting Hill Gate with such regularity that after years and years of baked beans or poached egg on toast, Andrée Howard turned hopelessly to Ashton and said, "Freddie, do you think there will *ever* be a time when we don't eat at the Express Dairy?" But Ashton, who was until 1935 the undoubted leader of the group, always spent at least fourpence more than anyone else on his food, so perhaps he did not find the diet so monotonous.

Rambert always went home to 19 Campden Hill Gardens for lunch and sometimes would take a dancer with her if she had a special problem to discuss. The dancers were all drawn into the Dukes family circle. Ashley's sister, Irene, was then in charge of the housekeeping and she contributed her share of suggestions for themes on which ballets might be made. Rambert took as much interest in her pupils as people as dancers and they, in turn, would dance for her children at parties as readily as they danced for the Ballet Club.

"She cultivated me," said Ashton, paying an informal tribute at the dinner which celebrated the thirtieth anniversary of the first Rambert season. "She taught me musical appreciation, took me to museums, plays, concerts, introduced me to her friends, gave me books to read, and recited endless Shakespeare and Racine at me." She always wanted to know where the dancers were living, what they were reading, if they were happy, if they had been to see the plays or exhibitions which she herself had enjoyed. She was quick to notice an improvement in personal appearance ("But to-day you look altogether elegant; and before you were such a *dowd*"), equally quick to seize on an intelligent remark or a witticism which she would repeat with delight for the rest of the day. "Andrée has just said the most brilliant and amusing thing . . .""I must tell you the marvellous thing that Fred has thought of . . ." She was present all through the day, driving them and encouraging them and irritating them, and the last sound they heard before the curtains parted on the evening performance was the click of her heels as she drew the curtain back at the extremity of the stage and then trotted round to the front of the house, to perch on a shooting stick* in the aisle from which she could keep an eagle eye on audience and dancers alike. It was a point of vantage and of mobility, a point of quick retreat if she needed to rush backstage in the middle of a performance and abuse some girl who had ruined, but absolutely ruined, the beautiful choreography of Fokine.

She might be the first to enthuse about a new production, but she might equally be the first to criticise. She always had (always has) an *opinion* about everything and nothing will stop her from expressing it. Ashley himself did not escape censure, and a favourite story was about an elderly member of the audience who heard her remonstrating with him and remarked with kindly concern: "That little lady had better look out if she wants to keep her job."

Rambert drove herself as hard as she drove the others. She suffered agonies of nerves before going onstage, and because there were only two dressing-rooms (one for the girls, one for the men) she infected everyone else in the room with her fright. She rested only briefly during the day, at home or on the Regency sofa in the Print Room at the Mercury. She was subject to violent headaches, yet even these she seemed to be able to subdue to the importance of the task in hand. Maude Lloyd described this "concentrated vitality" of hers as infectious, and indeed she could nearly always whip up flagging spirits or quell smouldering rebellion—a surprise word of praise could do wonders. "But this is *delightful* what you have done . . ." and the designer went on painting scenery very happily, or Andrée cut out yet another costume, or Antony Tudor began working out the next section of his new ballet.

There was never any money to speak of, and the work was guided by what Karsavina called "blessed poverty." Imagination and artistry made up for—rather, rendered unnecessary—elaborate trappings, and if the home-made costumes did not turn out quite right or were falling to pieces with

---

*Specially ordered, to the horror of Messrs. _____ of St. James's Street, with a rubber point as it was to be used in a theatre.

age, Rambert would say, as she said once to Ashton, "Do not worry, they will be lost in your beautiful movements." When Ashton wanted a decor by Marie Laurençin, she produced some old net curtains, dyed them in her bath, and persuaded him they would serve just as well. She had learned in her Paris days, and from the example of Isadora Duncan, how muslin can be wetted, folded tight, and thus pleated, and she welcomed any opportunity of demonstrating this skill. If forced to buy new materials, she always knew where to find tarlatan for threepence a yard for underskirts, allowing a layer of the best-quality sixpenny stuff for the top layer, but she was far more adept at producing garments or fabrics from her own wardrobe or those of her friends. (The pink silk blouse worn by the Prince in *Mermaid* was, according to company tradition, made from a nightdress that once belonged to Romola Nijinsky.)

Yet despite the modesty of the ingredients, the ballets which were produced were beautiful and the dancers blossomed into real—some of them into great—artists. Famous musicians were eager to play at the Mercury on Sunday evenings, and Ashley's writer friends were often to be found in the audience. The Ballet Club continued in much this way until 1939. It had its ups and its downs, its good and its bad seasons, its triumphs and its setbacks, but a clear pattern of experiment and discovery goes right through until the outbreak of war. The former parish hall accommodated in turn performances of ballets, which Rambert directed, and of plays, many of them by poets, which Ashley chose. Truly they gave to London in their tiny theatre "infinite riches in a little room."

—from *Dancers of Mercury,* 1962

THÉOPHILE GAUTIER
Letter to Heine

*A famous novelist (*Mademoiselle de Maupin*), journalist, poet, critic, Théophile Gautier (1811–1872) was also a passionate balletomane and the most influential dance writer of the Romantic era. In 1841 he was inspired by a tale of Heinrich Heine's to write the libretto for* Giselle, *featuring the great love of his life, the ballerina Carlotta Grisi.*

JULY 5, 1841

My dear Heinrich Heine, when reviewing, a few weeks ago, your fine book, *De L'Allemagne,** I came across a charming passage—one has only to open the book at random—the place where you speak of elves in white dresses, whose hems are always damp,† of nixes who display their little satin feet on the ceiling of the nuptial chamber; of snow-coloured *Wilis* who waltz pitilessly, and of all those delicious apparitions you have encountered in the Harz mountains and on the banks of the Ilse, in a mist softened by German moonlight; and I involuntarily said to myself: "Wouldn't this make a pretty ballet?"

In a moment of enthusiasm, I even took a fine large sheet of white paper, and headed it in superb capitals: *Les Wilis,* a ballet. Then I laughed and threw the sheet aside without giving it any further thought, saying to myself that it was impossible to translate that misty and nocturnal poetry into terms of the theatre, that richly sinister phantasmagoria, all those effects of legend and ballet so little in keeping with our customs. In the evening, at the Opéra, my head still full of your idea, I met, at a turning of the wings, the witty man‡ who knew how to introduce into a ballet, by adding to it much of his own wit, all the fairy caprice of *Le Diable Amoureux* of Cazotte, that great poet who invented Hoffmann in the middle of the eighteenth century.

I told him the tradition of the *Wilis.* Three days later, the ballet *Giselle* was accepted. At the end of the week, Adolphe Adam had improvised the music, the scenery was nearly ready, and the rehearsals were in full swing. You see, my dear Heinrich, we are not yet so incredulous and so prosaic as you think we appear. You said in a moment of ill-humour: "How could a spectre exist in Paris? Between midnight and one o'clock, which has ever been the hour assigned to ghosts, the most animated life still fills the streets. At this moment the Opéra resounds to a noisy finale. Joyous bands flow from the Variétés and the Gymnase; everyone laughs and jumps on the boulevards, and everyone runs to evening parties. How miserable a stray ghost would feel in that lively throng!" Well, I had only to take your pale and charming phantoms by their shadowy finger-tips and present them, to ensure their receiving the most polite reception in the world. The director and public have not offered the

---

*This work, written in French, appeared first in a Paris Journal, called *Europe Littéraire,* during 1833. In the same year it appeared in German under the title *Zur Geschichte der neueren schönen Literatur in Deutschland.* The first French edition, called *De l'Allemagne,* was published in 1835.

†It is the tradition in fairy mythology that water-spirits, however they seek to disguise themselves, can always be detected because a portion of their dress invariably appears to be wet.

‡Jules Henri Vernoy de Saint-Georges, one of the most prolific writers of *scenarii* for ballets and libretti for operas, of the nineteenth century. Among the numerous ballets he wrote, or collaborated in writing, the following are the best known: *La Gipsy* (1839), *Le Diable Amoureux* (1840), *Giselle* (1841), *La Jolie Fille de Gand* (1842), and *Le Corsaire* (1856).

least objection *à la Voltaire*. The *Wilis* have already received the right of citizenship in the scarcely fantastic rue Lepelletier. Some lines where you speak of them, placed at the head of the *scenario,* have served them as passports.

Since the state of your health has prevented your being present at the first performance, I am going to attempt, if a French journalist is permitted to tell a fantastic story to a German poet, to explain to you how M. de Saint-Georges, while respecting the spirit of your legend, has made it acceptable and possible at the Opéra. To allow more freedom, the action takes place in a vague country, in Silesia, in Thuringia, even in one of the Bohemian seaports that Shakespeare loved; it suffices for it to be on the other side of the Rhine, in some mysterious corner of Germany. Do not ask more of the geography of the ballet, which cannot define the name of a town or country by means of gesture, which is its only tongue.

Hillocks weighed down with russet vines, yellowish, warmed and sweetened by the autumn sun; those beautiful vines from which hang the amber-coloured grapes which produce Rhine wine, form the background; at the summit of a grey and bare rock, so precipitous that the vine tendrils have been unable to climb it, stands, perched like an eagle's nest, one of those castles so common in Germany, with its battlemented walls, its pepper-box turrets, and its feudal weathercocks; it is the abode of Albrecht, the young Duke of Silesia. That thatched cottage to the left, cool, clean, coquettish, half-buried among the leaves, is Giselle's cottage. The hut facing it is occupied by Loys. Who is Giselle? Giselle is Carlotta Grisi, a charming girl with blue eyes, a refined and artless smile, and an alert bearing; an Italian who tries to be taken for a German, just as Fanny,* the German, tries to be taken for an Andalusian from Seville. Her position is the simplest in the world; she loves Loys and she loves dancing. As for Loys, played by [Lucien] Petipa, there are a hundred reasons for suspecting him. Just now, a handsome esquire, adorned with gold lace, speaks to him in a low voice, standing cap in hand and maintaining a submissive and respectful attitude. What! A servant of a great house, as the esquire appears to be, fails to lord it over the humble rustic to whom he speaks! Then, Loys *is not what he appears to be* (ballet style), *but we shall see later.*

Giselle steps out of the cottage on the tip of her dainty foot. Her legs are awake already; her heart, too, sleeps no longer, for it is full morning. She has had a dream, an evil dream: a beautiful and noble lady in a gold dress, with a brilliant engagement ring on her finger, appeared to her while she slept and seemed about to be married to Loys, who himself was a great nobleman, a duke, a prince. Dreams are very strange sometimes! Loys does his best to reassure her, and Giselle, still somewhat uneasy, questions the marguerites. The little silver petals flee and scatter: "He loves me, he loves me not!" "Oh,

*Elssler.

dear! How unhappy I am, he loves me not!" Loys, who is well aware that a
boy of twenty can make the daisies say whatever he chooses, repeats the test,
which, this time, is favourable; and Giselle, charmed with the flowers' good
augury, begins to leap about again, despite her mother, who scolds her and
would rather see that agile foot turning the spinning-wheel that stands in
the window, and those pretty fingers questioning marguerites busied in
gathering the already over-ripe grapes or carrying a vine-dresser's basket.
But Giselle scarcely listens to the advice of her mother, whom she soothes
with a little caress. The mother insists: "Unhappy child! You will dance for
ever, you will kill yourself, and, when you are dead, you will become a *Wili*."
And the good woman, in an expressive pantomime, relates the terrible legend of the nocturnal dancers. Giselle pays no heed. What young girl of fifteen believes in a story with the moral that one should not dance? Loys and
dancing, that is her conception of happiness. This, like every possible happiness, wounds unseen a jealous heart; the gamekeeper, Hilarion, is in love
with Giselle, and his most ardent desire is to injure his rival, Loys. He has
already been a witness of the scene where the esquire Wilfrid spoke respectfully to the peasant. He suspects some plot, staves in the window of the hut,
and climbs through it, hoping to find some incriminating evidence. But
now trumpets resound; the Prince of Courland and his daughter Bathilde,
mounted on a white hackney, wearied from hunting, come to seek a little
rest and coolness in Giselle's cottage. Loys prudently steals away. Giselle,
with a timid and charming grace, hastens to set out on a table shining pewter
goblets, milk, and some fruit, the best and most appetising of everything in
her homely larder. While the beautiful Bathilde lifts the goblet to her lips,
Giselle approaches with cat-like tread, and, in a rapture of artless admiration, ventures to touch the rich, soft material of which the lady's riding
costume is composed. Bathilde, enchanted by Giselle's pleasant manners,
places her gold chain round her neck and wishes to take the girl with her.
Giselle thanks her effusively and replies that she wants nothing more in the
world but to dance and to be loved by Loys.

The Prince of Courland and Bathilde withdraw into the hut to snatch a
few moments' rest. The huntsmen disperse into the wood; a call on the
prince's horn will warn them when it is time to return. The vine-dressers
return from the vineyards and arrange a festival of which Giselle is proclaimed the Queen and in which she takes the principal part. Joy is at its
height when Hilarion appears carrying a ducal mantle, a sword, and a
knightly order found in Loys's hut—all doubt is at an end. Loys is simply an
impostor, a seducer who has been playing on Giselle's good faith; a duke
cannot marry a humble peasant, not even in the choreographic world, in
which one often sees kings marrying shepherdesses—such a marriage offers
innumerable obstacles. Loys, or rather Duke Albrecht of Silesia, defends

himself to the best of his ability, and declares that no great harm has been done, for Giselle will marry a duke instead of a peasant. She is pretty enough to become duchess and lady of the manor. "But you are not free, you are betrothed to another," asserts the game-keeper; and, seizing the horn left lying on the table, he blows it like a madman. The huntsmen run up. Bathilde and the Prince of Courland come out of the cottage and are amazed to see Duke Albrecht of Silesia in such a disguise. Giselle recognises in Bathilde the beautiful lady of her dreams, she doubts her misfortune no longer; her heart swells, her head swims, her feet shake and jump; she repeats the measure she danced with her lover; but her strength is soon exhausted, she staggers, sways, seizes the fatal sword brought by Hilarion and would have fallen on its point if Albrecht had not turned it aside with the quickness born of despair. Alas, the precaution is in vain; the blow has struck home; her heart is pierced and Giselle dies, consoled at least by her lover's profound grief and Bathilde's tender pity.

There, my dear Heine, that is the story invented by M. de Saint-Georges to bring about the pretty death we needed. I, who ignore theatrical effects and the demands of the stage, had thought of making the first act consist of a mimed version of Victor Hugo's delightful poem. One would have seen a beautiful ballroom belonging to some prince; the candles would have been lighted, flowers placed in vases, buffets loaded, but the guests would not yet have arrived; the *Wilis* would have shown themselves for a moment, attracted by the joy of dancing in a room glittering with crystal and gilding in the hope of adding to their number. The Queen of the *Wilis* would have touched the floor with her magic wand to fill the dancers' feet with an insatiable desire for contredanses, waltzes, galops, and mazurkas. The advent of the lords and ladies would have made them fly away like so many vague shadows. Giselle, having danced all the evening, excited by the magic floor and the desire to keep her lover from inviting other women to dance, would have been surprised by the cold dawn like the young Spaniard, and the pale Queen of the *Wilis,* invisible to all, would have laid her icy hand on her heart. But then we should not have had the lovely scene, so admirably played, which concludes the first act as it is; Giselle would have been less interesting, and the second act would have lost all its element of surprise.

The second act is as nearly as possible an exact translation of the page I have taken the liberty of tearing from your book, and I hope that when you return from Cauterets, fully recovered, you will not find it too misinterpreted.

The stage represents a forest on the banks of a pool; you see tall pale trees, whose roots spring from the grass and the rushes; the water-lily spreads its broad leaves on the surface of the placid water, which the moon silvers here and there with a trail of white spangles. Reeds with their brown velvet sheaths shiver and palpitate beneath the intermittent night breeze.

The flowers open languorously and exhale a giddy perfume like those broad flowers of Java which madden whoever inhales their scent. I cannot say what burning and sensuous atmosphere flows about this humid and leafy obscurity. At the foot of a willow, asleep and concealed beneath the flowers, lies poor Giselle. From the marble cross which indicates her grave is suspended, still quite fresh, the garland of vine branches with which she had been crowned at the harvest festival.

Some hunters come to find a suitable place of concealment; Hilarion frightens them by saying that it is a dangerous and sinister spot, haunted by the *Wilis,* cruel nocturnal dancers, no more forgiving than living women are to a tired waltzer. Midnight chimes in the distance; from the midst of the long grass and tufted reeds, will o' the wisps dart forth in irregular and glittering flight and make the startled hunters flee.

The reeds part and first we see a tiny twinkling star, next a chaplet of flowers, then two startled blue eyes set in an alabaster oval, and, last of all, the whole of that beautiful, slender, chaste, and graceful form known as Adèle Dumilâtre; she is the Queen of the *Wilis.* With her characteristic melancholy grace she frolics in the pale star-light, which glides over the water like a white mist, poises herself on flexible branches, leaps on the tips of the grass, like Virgil's Camilla, who walked on wheat without bending it, and, arming herself with a magic wand, she evokes the other *Wilis,* her subjects, who come forth with their moonlight veils from the tufted reeds, clusters of verdure, and calixes of flowers to take part in the dance. She announces to them that they are to admit a new *Wili* that night. Indeed, Giselle's shade, stiff and pale in its transparent shroud, suddenly leaps from the ground at Myrtha's bidding (that is the Queen's name). The shroud falls and vanishes. Giselle, still benumbed from the icy damp of the dark abode she has left, makes a few tottering steps, looking fearfully at that tomb which bears her name. The *Wilis* take hold of her and lead her to the Queen, who herself crowns her with the magic garland of asphodel and verbena. At a touch of her wand, two little wings, as restless and quivering as those of Psyche, suddenly grow from the shoulders of the youthful shade who, for that matter, had no need of them. All at once, as though she wished to make up for the time wasted in that narrow bed fashioned of six long planks and two short ones, to quote the poet of *Leonore,* she bounds and rebounds in an intoxication of liberty and joy at no longer being weighed down by that thick coverlet of heavy earth, expressed in a sublime manner by Mme. Carlotta Grisi. The sound of footsteps is heard; the *Wilis* disperse and crouch behind the trees. The noise is made by some youthful peasants returning from a festival at a neighbouring village. They provide excellent quarry. The *Wilis* come forth from their hiding-place and try to entice them into the fatal circle; fortunately, the young men pay heed to the warnings of a wiser grey-beard who knows the legend of the *Wilis* and finds it most unusual to encounter a bevy of young beings in low-necked muslin dresses with stars on their foreheads and moth-like wings on their shoulders. The *Wilis,* disappointed, pursue them eagerly; this pursuit leaves the stage unoccupied.

Enter a young man, distracted, mad with sorrow, his eyes bathed in tears; it is Loys, or Albrecht, if you prefer it, who, escaping from his guardians' observation, comes to visit the tomb of his well-beloved. Giselle cannot resist the sweet evocation of so true and profound a grief; she parts the branches and leans forward towards her kneeling lover, her charming features aglow with love. To attract his attention, she picks some flowers which she first carries to her lips and throws her kisses to him on roses. The apparition flutters coquettishly, followed by Albrecht. Like Galatea, she flies towards the reeds and willows. The transverse flight, the leaning branch, the sudden disappearance when Albrecht wishes to take her in his arms, are new and original effects which achieve complete illusion, but now the *Wilis* return. Giselle tries to hide Albrecht; she knows too well the doom that awaits him if he is encountered by the terrible nocturnal dancers. They have found another quarry. Hilarion is lost in the forest; a treacherous path brings him back to the place from which he had only just fled. The *Wilis* seize hold of him, pass him from hand to hand: when one waltzer is tired, her place is taken by another, and always the infernal dance draws nearer to the lake. Hilarion, breathless, spent, falls at the Queen's knees and begs for mercy. But there is no mercy; the pitiless phantom strikes him with a branch of rosemary and immediately his weary legs move convulsively. He rises and makes new efforts to escape; a dancing wall bars his passage, the *Wilis* make him giddy, push him on, and, as he leaves go of the cold hand of the last dancer, he stumbles and falls into the pool— Good night, Hilarion! That will teach you not to meddle in other people's love affairs! May the fish in the lake eat your eyes!

What is Hilarion but one partner for so many dancing women? Less than nothing. A *Wili,* with that wonderful woman's instinct for finding a waltzer, discovers Albrecht in his hiding-place. What good fortune, and someone who is young, handsome, and light-footed! "Come, Giselle, prove your mettle, make him dance to death!" It is useless for Giselle to beg for mercy; the Queen refuses to listen, and threatens to give Albrecht to the less scrupulous *Wilis* in her band. Giselle draws her lover towards the tomb she has just left, signs to him to embrace the cross and not to leave it whatever may befall. Myrtha resorts to an infernal and feminine device. She forces Giselle, who, in her capacity of subject, must obey, to execute the most seductive and most graceful poses. At first, Giselle dances timidly and reluctantly; then she is carried away by her instinct as a woman and a *Wili;* she bounds lightly and dances with so seductive a grace, such overpowering fascination, that the imprudent Albrecht leaves the protecting cross and goes towards her with outstretched arms, his eyes burning with desire and love. The fatal madness takes hold of him; he pirouettes, bounds, follows Giselle in her most hazardous leaps; the frenzy to which he gives way reveals a secret desire to die with his mistress and to follow the beloved shade to her tomb; but four o'clock strikes, a pale streak shows on the edge of the horizon. Dawn has come and with it the sun bringing deliverance and salvation. Flee, visions of the night; vanish, pale phantoms! A celestial joy gleams in Giselle's eyes: her lover will not die, the hour has passed. The beautiful Myrtha re-enters her water-lily. The *Wilis* fade away, melt into the ground, and disappear. Giselle herself is drawn towards her tomb by an invisible power. Albrecht, distracted, clasps her in his arms, carries her, and, covering her with kisses, places her upon a flowered mound; but the earth will not relinquish its prey, the ground opens, the flowers bend over. . . . The hunting-horn resounds; Wilfrid anxiously seeks for his master. He walks a little in front of the Prince of Courland and Bathilde. However, the flowers cover Giselle; nothing can be seen but her little transparent hand . . . this too disappears, all is over!—never again will Albrecht and Giselle see each other in this world. . . . The young man kneels by the mound, plucks a few flowers, and clasps them to his breast, then withdraws, his head resting on the shoulder of the beautiful Bathilde, who forgives and consoles him.

There, my dear poet, that, more or less, is how M. de Saint-Georges and I have adapted your charming legend with the help of M. Coralli, who composed the *pas,* groups, and attitudes of exquisite novelty and elegance. For interpreters we chose the three graces of the Opéra: Mlles. Carlotta Grisi, Adèle Dumilâtre, and Forster. Carlotta danced with a perfection, lightness, boldness, and a chaste and refined seductiveness, which places her in the first rank, between Elssler and Taglioni; as for pantomime, she exceeded all expectations; not a single conventional gesture, not one fake movement; she was nature and artlessness personified. True, she has Perrot the Aerial for husband and teacher. Petipa was graceful, passionate, and touching; it is a long while since a dancer has given us so much pleasure or been so well received.

M. Adam's music is superior to the usual run of ballet music, it abounds in tunes and orchestral effects; it even includes a touching attention for lovers of difficult music, a very well-produced fugue. The second act solves the musical problem of graceful fantasy and is full of melody. As for the scenery, it is by Ciceri, who is unequalled for landscapes. The sunrise which marks the conclusion is wonderfully realistic. . . . La Carlotta was recalled to the sound of the applause of the whole house.

So, my dear Heine, your German *Wilis* have succeeded completely at the French Opéra.

—letter to Heine, 1841; translated by Cyril Beaumont

DEBORAH JOWITT
Maria Theresa: Isadora's Last Dancing Daughter

It's like a fairy tale the way she tells it.

She was one of a troupe of children dancing to celebrate the electrification of the theater in Dresden. They carried heart-shaped rackets, she remembers, that lit up when put in contact with places marked on the stage floor. She was nine years old and one of the best dancers—what a disgrace that she, Theresa, should stop dead in the middle of the dance to return the smile of a woman sitting in one of the boxes. But, as she explained later to her mother, this lady looked like an angel, like . . . the statue of Demeter in the park.

The next morning the doorbell rings. There, amid the snowdrifts, in golden sandals and a Greek dress, stands Demeter. "May I come in?" asks the goddess in broken German. The door to the parlor is thrown wide, and she reclines grandly, Greek fashion, golden feet up on the stuffy, red-plush sofa. What does she want? Theresa, of course, to come and live with her and other specially chosen little girls, to be a dancer. And since her name means nothing to them, she offers them tickets to her Dresden performances. The family sees her dance, and that is that.

Theresa Kruger was one of about twenty little girls who left their homes and families in 1905 to go to Isadora Duncan's new school in Grunewald. Later, she was one of the six young women who often performed on Duncan's programs and who—given the undignified nickname of "Isadorables" by a French critic—toured the United States by themselves to great acclaim between 1918 and 1920. And would have toured another season had not Duncan, with the inscrutably harum-scarum mixture of concern and neglect, love and jealousy that characterized her relationship with her "adopted daughters," summoned them to return to her in Europe.

Theresa—or Maria Theresa, as she has called herself since she began a career as a soloist in 1921—is now the last dancing daughter of Isadora Duncan. Irma, Lise, and Margot are dead. Erica, who gave up dancing for painting around 1920, is in a convent; Anna, completely blind, lives in an institution. But Theresa of the sturdy legs, beautiful arms, wide, blunt face—the one photographer Edward Steichen considered the most gifted, the one critics praised for rhythmic clarity—endures, and, at eighty-three, likes to think she has quite a few good years of dancing left in her.

She did stop dancing for a while during the sixties, when a heart attack and the death of her husband, Stephan Bourgeois, laid her low. And, no doubt, she took some time off from performing when her two sons were born. But she was successful as a soloist, especially during the twenties; in 1934 she danced at the White House; she was giving concerts at Dance Players Studio and Carnegie Recital Hall during the fifties, when Duncan dancing was considered old-fashioned, when the modern dancers all interpreted Isadora's legacy of freedom as freedom to deal with their own times in their own way. Now there is a resurgence of interest in Duncan—among dancers, the public, and the rapidly growing group of dance scholars: we are curious to know how she danced and what she danced. We are greedy for more than descriptions, than the photographs of her with round arms raised as if to receive the sky, or drawings of her skipping in Bacchic abandon, head turned to look behind her. And so, in honor of the centennial of Isadora's birth (May 27, 1877), Maria Theresa assembled a company again, and the Isadora Duncan Heritage Group has been giving small-scale performances at the YWCA on Lexington Avenue. (There are performances next on February 24 and 25, again on March 3 and 4.)

I first saw Maria Theresa when she was giving a master class last spring at Marymount Manhattan. I remember her standing in the center of the gym wearing a long, beautifully draped lavender tunic, her dark red hair dressed in ringlets à la Grecque, her legs still strong and shapely poking out of a slit in the dress, her face . . . well, even with good bones, the face of a woman in her eighties looks *used*. She had stopped exhorting the students with a sweeping of her arm; she had stopped yelling encouraging words in a heavy German accent. She was just standing there looking bleak, while around her in a circle skipped a frenzy of young girls—a few good dancers (perhaps a shade too light, too precise), some hardworking, joyless students, and another group high on self-expression, wearing improvised tunics (checked gingham, whatever you've got), cavorting along, oblivious even to the pulse of the music. Maria Theresa looked as if she despaired of controlling what she'd set in motion and didn't much like the look of it.

But she rallied, began to toss her arms like branches in a wind. (Several of her own student assistants would rush forward, arms out, saying, "Don't, Maria," every time she'd get too active or try to stand on one leg.) Once she leaned close to me, flashed a rueful lipsticked smile, and said, "You should have seen me when I was sixty!"

Isadora wasn't a teacher; she was a pied piper. The little girls she gathered as students went to her body, mind, and soul. Even when left for long periods with Duncan's sister Elizabeth and her gymnastic exercises, even when parked for a cold winter in what Isadora believed to be a château, but which turned out to be the château's stable, with inadequate food and clothing, they remained in love with her. Ruth St. Denis bred some rebels—Martha Graham, Doris Humphrey, Charles Weidman; Duncan bred only disciples. Even when the girls revolted they did so not because they wanted to dance in a different manner but because they wanted to be financially independent, to dance solos, to interpet the great music Isadora had introduced them to. In effect, they preserved and interpeted and taught a concept of dance born at the turn of the century, in part as a reaction against confined, overstuffed, overembellished art and living. It was also a form that expressed women's freedom—not so much freedom to compete with men in the marketplace but the freedom to put away corsets, take lovers, bear children out of wedlock, and to dance like that kind of a woman (powerful, supple, fecund) instead of like some man's vision of the seductive fairy as an antidote to the respectable wife.

Maria Theresa, who today combines wisdom, innocence, and mischievousness in beguiling proportions, says that she realizes now that Isadora didn't want her girls to grow up. This had to to with the horrifying death of her own two children and the loss of a third shortly after its birth. ("She was always dreaming of children.") It also became clear that Isadora couldn't brook rivals.

A question of mine sets Maria Theresa talking about her last year with Isadora. Her talk is wonderful and, like her dancing, unhasty. When I saw her perform Liszt's *Les Funerailles*—one of the slow pieces she still dances—she walked simply and majestically onto the small Y stage, sank to her knees, and stayed there grieving for quite a while, moving her head a little, perhaps beating a hand against the floor. She used time luxuriously, confidently, allowing every change to flower organically out of her response to the music. When she talks, she keeps saying, "Well, to make a long story short . . . ," but that clearly is impossible. She cannot be diverted from a subject or made to jump forward or backward in time. The words roll on like a tide, bearing a flotsam of vivid and revealing images.

She makes you see Isadora as the girls saw her from the boat returning them to Europe—a tiny figure pacing back and forth on the jetty, a white shawl, something blue fluttering from her head. The Nike of Samothrace breasting the wind. She imitates Isadora looking them over disapprovingly and saying, "No dancing for at least a month. I have to fatten you up first; you have to go on a spaghetti tour now. Each of you has to gain five or ten pounds." (Was this only concern for her protégées' health, or did it reflect her unwillingness to appear, in her forties and quite heavy by then, with a bunch of sylphs?) Maria Theresa shows how Isadora used to twitch her mouth around "like a little rabbit" when irritated, amused, or unwilling to answer a pressing question like, "When are we going to dance?"

The summer of 1920 slipped into fall; the girls were forced to cancel their American tour; their own money was almost gone; Isadora took them from France to Italy to Greece (so that they could have the "Greek experience" that had so influenced her), but she never rehearsed with them or spoke of performing. More images of Isadora emerge: sitting at table, taunting her pianist Walter Rummel (who was evidently avoiding her bed), "Eat this slab of roast beef; it will make you *strong* and *healthy*. Drink this wine!" Then, Isadora beginning to sense that Rummel and Anna were having an affair, "She had a way of sitting quiet with only her eyes moving . . ." (Maria Theresa leans back, presses her lips together, and flicks her eyes from side of the empty Y conference table.)

Theresa was blamed by the other girls for influencing them to leave America, and she depicts herself finally flying into a rage. "I grabbed Isadora; I *shook* her. I said, 'If you don't dance with us tomorrow, I don't know what I'll do.' Suddenly she looks at me and says, 'That's the way I like it. I like it when you are so wild. Tell the girls I'll teach.'" But, although there was a little teaching after that odd summer, and a little performing, the Isadorables began to drop away until only Irma remained to accompany Isadora on her messianic, perhaps desperate, mission to Moscow. Maria Theresa tells of one last conversation. When she asked Isadora what she, Theresa, was to do in Russia: "'I want you to teach. A thousand children.' 'Oh no!' 'Oh yes.' I was appalled. I was never good at teaching children because of my bad hearing. And Isadora said, 'I don't want anyone else to dance and exploit this art. I want you to teach.'" And presumably those children in turn would be content to teach others so that, in a way, Isadora would be the unique professional, followed by generations of amateurs who would dance only for spiritual and physical enrichment.

Yet, curiously, Isadora did not, in the usual sense, teach; she inspired by music and by her own example. Irma, in her book *Duncan Dancer,* describes a session in which Isadora, asked by her pupils to break down a passage or do it slowly, found herself unable to, and took that as proof that great art couldn't and shouldn't be dissected. Irma was methodical; Maria Theresa isn't: she stimulates, sketches out general patterns, demonstrates, draws attention to the music, and has little sympathy for the unmusical, the unpoetic would-be dancers. "They should go plant cabbages."

I watch six young women in rehearsal try to feel their way into some dances to Chopin piano pieces. (Maria Theresa is at home; she has a cold, and her daughter-in-law won't let her out of the house, so the rehearsal is handled by her assistant, dance historian Kay Bardsley, once a member of the company Maria Theresa had for ten years.) The women, in a motley assortment of Greek tunics, run smoothly in loops around each other—one, then another, then another joining in. They break out of this idyllic sisterhood of nymphs to laugh and argue about who goes where just like any dancers, but

I notice that they'll suddenly drop one dance and proceed to another, as if afraid that they'd lose the spirit if they got things too tidied up all at once, or become too like one another in their response to the music. Jubilea Sebert, one of the most gifted, runs through the Chopin nocturne they call "The Angel" knocking softly on an imaginary grave and pointing the way to heaven; she does it beautifully, and the others clap for her; Bardsley laughs and says something like, "Lovely! Too bad we have to be a little more accurate." In other words, instead of learning the steps first and *then* trying to infuse them with meaning, the dancers learn the music, the feeling, the broad shape of the dance and only afterward proceed to the specifics.

For this approach you need more time than anyone has these days. "Isadora would turn in her grave," says Maria Theresa about the relatively short training and rehearsing period. She also says, "All great art is personality; movements per se are boring." Which may explain why the secrets of Isadora's greatness remain so difficult to unravel, the history of her dancers so hard to trace. Watch Annabelle Gamson perform the solos she learned from Julia Levien, who learned them from Irma Duncan. Suddenly some of the pictured poses come to life—the maenad beckons, devours, the oppressed serf wrenches her hands free of the earth and flings them wide—and they come to life, not haphazardly, but set into subtly constructed phrases. Whose phrases? Isadora's or Irma's? Isadora, everyone will tell you, never performed a dance the same way twice. Watch Maria Theresa, watch Julia Levien, whose Isadora Duncan Commemorative Dance Company is also performing this spring, and you see a beautiful sense of weight, a grandeur of spirit, a musicality—but these women are years older than Isadora at the time of her death. Watch lovely Maria Rubinate of Maria Theresa's group; she's very sensitive to the nuances of a Brahms waltz, but in the tiny curving gestures of her arms, the gentle sway of her body you see three shadowy dancers—a young girl imitating an old woman remembering the precepts of a genius who's been dead for over fifty years. And which, if any, of these group patterns were designed by Isadora? Or are even like anything designed by Isadora?

Isadora's vision of "nature," however basic it may have appeared, was a romantic, idealized one, yet it is not entirely anachronistic in a period when so many fear that the world is about to be paved over. Revivals of Duncan's work, or Duncanesque works, can, depending on the circumstances and performance, seem either naive and precious or profoundly simple and moving. To Maria Theresa, of course, Isadora Duncan is still "the central fire of the universe in the dance—flaming higher than ever!" Slyly, she quoted young Maria Theresa giving herself confidence by saying, "Well, if I am only a flame of *her* fire, that still means I must be pretty good." There is something rarified about the life pattern that Isadora set for her back in 1905. Describing with touching wonder that day Isadora first came to her mother's house, she lifts her hands and says, "It was like when Demeter entered the house of Metaneira and touched with her high head the ceiling of the house, and the ceiling was raised."

It only occurred to me years later that what Maria Theresa was saying might not have been, "You should have seen me when I was sixty,"but "You should have seen me when I was sixteen."I'm sure she was something at either age.

I'd also like to reinstate a story that had to be left out. Maria Theresa wasn't happy about how Maria Rubinate was performing one of the solos, and told her to make it slower. But how can I do that? Rubinate asked, pointing out that the speed of the taped music was fixed. "Then," said Rubinate, to me, "Maria did it. Slower." Meaning that the older woman's rich sense of the weight of each gesture created the illusion of slowness.

—from *The Village Voice,* February 26, 1979

Elizabeth Kendall
Salomé

While Ruth St. Denis was abroad (1906–1909) her conviction that dance could be artistic finally caught on in America, and a new kind of theatrical dancing was born. It was nothing like vaudeville, with jolly soubrettes in clogs, nor was it ballet, with naughty girls in tights and flounces. Those modes were too flippant in the light of serious modern theater, where the heroines of Sardou, Sudermann, Ibsen, and even Belasco moved about the stage as though in their own rooms, and revealed their states of mind by extremely naturalistic actions. Boldness in the plays' subject matter had produced this frankness in the acting, and actresses' bodies were understood to have a new license on the stage. Audiences that had seen Mrs. Fiske's *Tess of the D'Urbervilles* shiver and retch, or Eleonora Duse's *Magda* lie down and scream, were ready to watch dancing which also approximated "private" behavior, which was bold and relatively lifelike. But dancing, after stern quarantine by generations of Puritan descendants, was flammable stuff: it was fated to arrive in the form of a scandal.

On January 22, 1907, the Metropolitan Opera mounted its *Salomé* by Richard Strauss, just once, before the Met's outraged backers—J. P. Morgan, W. K. Vanderbilt, and August Belmont—withdrew it from the stage. This grave insult to an artistic institution caused the press to enter the fray, pro and con. "Salomé in her transports of rage or gross sensuality is no less respectable a person than the Saphos, Zazas, Mrs. Warrens and other red-light heroines of the contemporary stage," said *Theatre Magazine*. But her dancing—the shedding of the seven veils and the fondling of that "decapitated head"—these "sickened the public stomach." Nonetheless, Salomé's appearance in 1907 was one sign of a social and cultural upheaval that anticipated the reckless twenties. No sooner was she banished from opera than she surfaced in vaudeville, via the Met's prima ballerina, Mlle. Bianca Froelich, who had been the dancing Salomé to Olive Fremstad's soprano in the solitary performance. Plump, saucy, and Viennese, Miss Froelich simply repeated her Salomé movements in the small Lincoln Square Variety Theater, and in that context was branded a kootch dancer. A few months later, the wily Florenz Ziegfeld served up another Salomé to an elegant public in the first of his high-class vaudeville shows—the Follies of 1907. He had transformed the rooftop of the New York Theater into the Jardin de Paris. Under the city sky, amid bright new awnings and potted palms, after fifty "Anna Held Girls" had paraded in red drummer outfits, Grace LaRue had sung "Miss Ginger of Jamaica," and Annabelle Whitford had posed as a Gibson bathing beauty, the dancer Mlle. Dazié emerged as Salomé. She wore a low-slung gauzy skirt, a circle of pearls over each breast, an aigrette on her forehead, and she had four peacock-costumed girls in attendance. For Ziegfeld she perfectly embodied his theatrical strategy, which was to transform popular, even off-color, material into a new and high-class chic.

Ziegfeld had picked Mlle. Dazié because she had a certain mystery about her; before emerging as Salomé she was "La Rouge Domino," who had baffled the public for two years, cropping up in world capitals gowned and masked in red—a costume dreamed up by her publicist. In real life Dazié was Daisy Peterkin from Detroit; although she had studied ballet in Europe and could really dance on her pointes, she would have gone unnoticed without such a stunt. But now that the Follies and her Salomé were a hit, Dazié and her publicist (now her husband) seized the occasion to open a school for Salomés, two hours every morning on the theater roof garden. By the summer of 1908 she was sending approximately 150 Salomés every month into the nation's vaudeville circuits, each armed with the same routine—an incoherent mix of gestures and undulations addressed to a papier-mâché head.

A hue and cry arose on main streets, in churches, and in the press. "It grovels, it rolls in horrible sensuality . . . can we endure this indecent physical display?" No one spoke about the actual dance motions of the Salomés. Probably no one noticed them, since the shock of the Salomé costume and the Head was enough for even seasoned vaudeville audiences. Besides, they had had no experience with dance as a dramatic language; they knew only about lively steps on the beat. If any of these first Salomés was gifted, her audience wouldn't have known.

It took a clever and top-level vaudeville player to reveal Salomé's dancing potential, and she did it by showmanship. Gertrude Hoffman was born in San Francisco, and after a childhood in which she absorbed equal parts of worldliness from that city, and purity from her convent education, by the age of fifteen she was already leading the line in the Castle Square Theater operetta troupe. But she faced the same dilemma as Duncan and St. Denis: how to combine dancing with ambition. No dancers commanded much respect in the theater world. Hoffman's solution was to widen her sphere: still in her teens, she went to New York as a rehearsal director—an unheard-of thing for a woman. Soon she was coaching sixty-member shows (Oscar Hammerstein's *Punch, Judy & Co.,* 1903) and staging vaudeville routines like Elsie Janis' and La Rouge Domino's—until one night in Philadelphia in 1906 she stepped in for a sick dancer in Flo Ziegfeld's *The Parisian Model* and stole the show imitating French star Anna Held in her song "I Just Can't Make My Eyes Behave." (Held herself imitated Enrico Caruso in another scene.) As a regular thereafter, Hoffman also imitated Eddie Foy in his ballerina act and Georgie Cohan singing, until the show closed. Then she played Hammerstein's Victoria, New York's top vaudeville house, with her own "imitatrice" act, which prompted Hammerstein to send her to London to copy the biggest-drawing Salomé yet—Maud Allan's. Hammerstein hadn't thought about Hoffman's dancing skills; he hadn't picked her because she started in a dancing chorus; he simply assumed, like everybody in vaudeville, that if you were a mimic and could make your body look like somebody else's, you could also make it dance.

Gertrude Hoffman outdid herself with her first serious act in the fall of 1908, at the Victoria. In a bluish light, from the depths of a painted Eastern garden, to the sounds of a full orchestra conducted by Max Hoffman, her husband, she emerged—"garbed in the draperies and gew-gaws of a bloody age." Her legs, reviewers noticed, were daringly bare under her thin tulle skirt. A good many reviewers also noticed this time what she was doing: how she undulated around the stage, espied the head of John the Baptist, danced wildly with it, and then fell, spent—all in the space of six minutes. The Hoffman whose heavy-lidded eyes, long, thin face, and lanky body had always made an audience laugh now made it sit up and marvel. And her Salomé, begun as an imitation, became the first coherent dance creation since Isadora Duncan had left the country in 1900 and Ruth St. Denis in

1906. The new Gertrude Hoffman, aesthetic dancer, did not, however, follow her predecessors to Europe; instead she went on a national tour—and so did her imitators. This second wave of Salomés brought sophistication to even the smallest towns; it indicated to the whole country that the forces of Art and Sin had conquered Broadway and were claiming the future.

—from *Where She Danced,* 1979

Tanaquil LeClercq

Barbara Newman

George Balanchine's last wife, Tanaquil LeClercq (1929–2000), was a dancer of incomparable elegance, wit, and allure. She trained with Mikhail Mordkin until, in 1941, Balanchine gave her a full scholarship at the School of American Ballet. For Ballet Society, she appeared in Symphonie Concertante *and* The Four Temperaments; *at New York City Ballet, Balanchine created a dazzling assortment of roles for her, among them Dew Drop in his* Nutcracker *and the central Girl in White in her greatest triumph and signature ballet,* La Valse *(1951). She stood out (as she always did) in his* Western Symphony, Bourrée Fantasque *(opposite her intimate friend Jerome Robbins),* Metamorphosis, Orpheus *(as the Leader of the Bacchantes), and in the adagio movement of* Symphony in C. *Robbins created his masterpiece* Afternoon of a Faun *for her in 1953, and gave her one of her most comical roles in* The Concert. *Her career was cut short tragically in 1956, when on a European tour she was struck down by polio and confined to a wheelchair for the rest of her life. Nevertheless, she remained active, teaching at Arthur Mitchell's Dance Theater of Harlem, and writing* The Ballet Cook Book *(see page 1314) and a book about the Balanchine cat,* Mourka, *for which she also took the photographs.*

I was very young to be in the original cast of *Four Ts*; I was right out of the School. I didn't know how early it was 'til I looked up the program. If it was really '46—I thought it was '48 or '49—I would have been sixteen or seventeen.

I started with [Mikhail] Mordkin because my mother wanted me to start when I was seven and nobody else would take me. She took me to Fokine, who said, "Absolutely not. I don't take them 'til they're eight." Then we went to the School of American Ballet, at Madison Avenue and Fifty-ninth, and they said, "No, we don't take anybody 'til they're nine." So then we went to Mordkin at Carnegie Hall—my mother had seen Pavlova dance and said that was terrific—and he said, "Fine. I'll take her." I don't think children really want to study, but I liked to dance. I had been to the ballet and I thought it was very nice, I liked it. I was also taking piano lessons, which I was a dud at. I mean, you could tell right away: the kid can't play the piano, so it better be dancing.

I studied with Mordkin 'til I was about ten. Sure, I liked it; I didn't know anything better or worse. It was very peppy. It was one of those classes that everybody but the kitchen sink is in. At that time he had his own company—I saw Lucia Chase as Giselle, if you can believe it, with the Mordkin Ballet Company. So she was there in class, and I was there, and Nina Stroganova and Patricia Bowman, sort of the beginnings of Ballet Theatre— we were all mixed in together. It wasn't the way it is today at the School: children, and then children a little better. He just taught a lot of classes, I guess, and they were all mixed.

I don't know why I left. I think my mother thought it was enough, that I had gotten just as far as I could. Then I spent about two years with other people, good teachers but not known at all, and then . . . The reason I went to SAB was that we used to go to Cape Cod every summer, and there was one of those music schools with ballet and stuff, and one summer Muriel Stuart turned up there to teach the summer course with Eddie Caton. And she said, "You should go to the School of American Ballet." So I auditioned. They used to have scholarship auditions that were lots of fun; they put a number on you like a horse and then you came in and everybody looked at you.

I went in 1940, when I was still at the Lycée Français. The teachers at SAB then were Stuart and Vladimirov, and Oboukhoff came later—I was there before Mr. Oboukhoff was. Then they had guest teachers: Dorothie Littlefield taught, Danilova taught for a month or a week or something, and then Balanchine would come and maybe he'd teach for two weeks in a year. Upset everybody and then leave—you know, that kind of thing. And then Doubrovska came; she was one of my favorite teachers and one I admired a great deal. She taught toe. Stuart gave a toe class too, and the men gave adagio and variations. I was going regularly then. Often. Then every day. Class was in the afternoons after school, so I would get excused from school to go, but then the schoolwork suffered and I had to repeat the same damn class for two years. But I didn't care, not at all. School was like the piano, absolutely not for me.

* * *

IT WAS RIGHT around then that George did *Four Ts* and *L'Enfant et les Sortilèges* on the same program at the Needle Trades High School. He had professional people for all the Temperaments and Themes, except for me. It wasn't that I was so good; it just came at a time when there was nobody else. Call it good timing. If you needed a body, I was the only one. And I didn't stay in the corps because the people he had in there were worse than I was. It just happened. Ballet wasn't that popular; there weren't that many people training, and they weren't groomed the way they are now. Today, every girl in the corps de ballet has fantastic legs and feet, and in my day they did not. Now it's like a master race, but they weren't screened then, and they didn't drop you unless you were eight feet tall—everybody was there. And then, I *was* more talented than the others, and I was a little interesting, I wasn't dull. So he put me in those two things. The corps in *Four Ts,* like the girls that come in and kick, were just tall girls from the School filling in, but otherwise it was people like Mary Ellen Moylan, Lew Christensen, Gisella Caccialanza, and Elise Reiman, who teaches now at the school. They were all professionals, and they were called Ballet Society.

They couldn't have been nicer to me, telling me how to make up and how to put the toe shoe ribbons in and things like that. Everybody was very sweet. But you know that part [in *Four Ts*] where I'm in the middle and the other four women are in a square around me? One of the women, who should remain nameless, who was a lead, didn't turn up for a rehearsal. I heard through the grapevine that she had objected; she didn't want to dance with a student in the middle, or *she* wanted to be there. And then the very next rehearsal, she turned up and everything was fine. George had obviously talked to her. It was the first time and the only time I ever had trouble with anything like that, but you've got to learn sometime how people are disagreeable or envious.

He worked on *Four Ts* just about the same length of time as anything. He's the fastest choreographer I know; and also, once he sets something, he hardly ever, ever changes it. Whereas a Jerry Robbins changes every two minutes—you have so many versions you don't know what to do. But George doesn't, which is so marvelous. The only thing I ever saw him change was a little bit of *Orpheus,* where Maria [Tallchief] enters. I think she just came in and the other people danced, and then he changed it so that she started dancing when she came in.

The music for *Four Ts*? Very nice. Melodic. Easy to dance to. That's not a hard score. Certainly as opposed to Ives or something, it's child's play. Nothing was a problem one way or the other. You just count the rhythm; it's very easy. What's a little harder about my section is that in the beginning it's just piano—a cadenza or something—anyway, it's a lot of rumbles, and you don't want to get caught dancing when the piano has stopped. There's no conductor at that point; it's just you and the piano trying to stick together. And as it's not something with an even beat; if the piano finishes soon, you've got egg on your face if you're still going.

I DON'T KNOW anything about the titles of the different movements in *The Four Temperaments*—you'd have to ask George. We were just given music and our steps and a terrible costume. Everybody had just awful costumes. They were miseries. I really objected to two things in mine. I had a large nylon wig that came down to about my rear end. It had a large pompadour, and it had a white horn in the middle like a unicorn's, which made it very difficult to do all the things he had made. That was number one. Very irritating. You come to dress rehearsal, and if you swing your arm close to your head, suddenly there's a horn. The other thing was that [Kurt] Seligmann had made wings, red wings, down the whole length of the arm, fingers enclosed, and there was no place to get out. If you got in your costume and then got something in your eye or wanted to unzip yourself to get out, well, you couldn't. Once you tied your toe shoe ribbons, that was it. It gave you a feeling of claustrophobia I can't describe. All enclosed. Not even gloves with fingers—no fingers at all. It was hideous. So I remember crying, and then George came and slit a little piece on the inside palm so I had my index finger out, and that was fine. But also, it made it very hard to give your hand. When you're doing arabesque promenade, they grab for something and they don't know what they've got—it's just a big clomp of material.

And then Seligmann did two sort of papier-mâché breastplates. They were light all right, but they were large, and when you'd cross your arms, they'd go clunk. It was just most unfortunate. And I certainly was not the only one; other people were having problems too, swathed in this and swathed in that. At dress rehearsal, I got clipped, and somebody else's wig got fixed, and I think Mary Ellen got unwrapped. Imagine taking a dancer and wrapping her neck up, and then putting half Ping-Pong balls down her arms. You distort everything, there's no arm there, and it looked so beautiful in rehearsal. But we certainly did it like that at Ballet Society, and then even when we went into our black stuff, the leotards, at City Center, they tried the backdrop for one performance. It looked like bandages coming unraveled, sort of a swirl in blacks and whites and gray. It was nice—nice? It was all right. You didn't die or anything—but at least we got rid of the costumes. It was much easier with an arm free, and I remember I had that feeling that Mr. Balanchine had saved me.

You don't get pushed around so much in that section, even when the four boys promenade you. You give your arm to one, you do arabesque, then you do soutenu on your own, then you give your arm to another one, and if he's good, he stays out of your way. You do your arabesque minding your own business, unless he's a lump and knocks you off. And then there are the two boys under your arms for that lift in the finale, and it's only done twice. So you feel secure—no problems. When you're young, you don't think as much as you do later on, when you've danced more and you realize all the awful things that could happen. You just go in and do it.

I'm not sure about the different finales. I don't think the soloists were involved in that; it was the other people who had different things. I think the couples always did the glissade, jeté across, and we always did that massed group, kick, lean. At one point he had it like a circle, and they used to go up and down in waves. He said it was "my Radio City Music Hall number," sort of Florence Rogge style. I remember it distinctly, but it doesn't seem to me that I was in that circle. I wouldn't swear, but I have a feeling it was all the corps people. But my part always remained exactly the same as he originally staged it. Needle Trades was a very skinny stage that had no depth so you went from side to side a lot, and my part does go from side to side. I never worked out anything with him together. He came in and showed me what he wanted me to do, and that was it. He never changed a step. Mine was absolutely set.

As we continued to do it and we got out of those costumes, I wouldn't say I danced it differently, but I danced it better because I was better technically. I could take more chances, throw myself around. I knew the music like the palm of my hand. It was very comfy, and it was a nice fast thing—I wasn't on the stage for hours. You zipped in and zipped out and made an impression. In other words, I liked dancing it very much. I don't say that I had a different interpretation when I didn't have a costume—it was the same thing. I had the choreography and how it should look. It should look maximum, 100 percent everything: move 100 percent, turn 100 percent, stop dead. Kick legs as much as you can, straight knee, pointed toe. Zip round. Fast. Nothing slow, no adaaagio. It would be the same style to me as *Orpheus,* the Bacchantes, same idea. Kick, wham, fast, hard, big. You have certain steps that you have to do in a certain amount of time, and the certain steps give it a certain flavor. But you can't interpret because you'll be late, you won't be with the music.

I had no sense that any part of what I was doing was any more important than any other part, or that any step was pulling anything together. And if people write about it that way, I think they're wrong. I think they're just writing because they have to write. If you said to George Balanchine, "Those three ronds de jambe pull the ballet together," he would faint. He would absolutely faint. I know from having sat with him and read reviews. He said, "What is this man talking about?" Third movement Bizet [*Symphony in C*], all they're doing is plié and up, plié and up, and someone wrote something about "The Danes did it a certain way." George said, "What the hell is he talking about? All they're doing is demi-plié, up, demi-plié, up."

BUT HE DIDN'T say, nobody said to me, when we were doing *Four Ts*, "This is Choleric." They called me "LeCholeric," and said, "Ha, ha. Isn't that funny?" He said, "Oh, look at that. Your name's LeClercq and you're being Choleric. LeCholeric." That's all. That was it.

—from *Striking a Balance,* 1982

ALLEGRA KENT
Robert Gottlieb

RG: *Allegra, you were how old when you joined the New York City Ballet in 1953?*
AK: Fifteen.

RG: *And you were young for your age, weren't you?*
AK: Yes, I was young because I had concentrated on dancing, so I didn't date boys and I didn't go to baseball games or football games. Anyway, the Professional Children's School didn't have a football team.

RG: *And did you think you'd have a problem getting into a ballet company?*
AK: No, it never seemed to me I would have a problem, because my teachers were very enthusiastic about my dancing, so that gave me a lot of confidence.

RG: *Yet you started studying quite late for a dancer.*
AK: Yes, I started at eleven.

RG: *And do you feel that starting that late led to any difficulties?*
AK: Well, I think I could have started earlier, but I wasn't ready to, because

I hadn't yet seen dance when I decided to dance. I was suddenly very struck with music when I was in boarding school. I really seemed to hear it, and it compelled me to start dancing, right there at school.

RG: *Another type of person would have wanted to play music. For you, the immediate response was to move to it.*
AK: Yes. I wanted to move to it. Also, I liked running fast and jumping high, crawling low, screaming high—those kinds of things.

RG: *Do you think that this impulse to move is basic to all dancers?*
AK: It might be basic even to amoebas. [laughs] Yes, I do.

RG: *There are dancers who don't start from the music—the kind who get labeled "unmusical."*
AK: I don't know how most dancers start—I assume they hear music and they move. But if anyone wants to give me a nice label like being a "musical" dancer—well . . . !

RG: *Do you think starting so late—*
AK: Yes, I probably could have benefited from real systematic training, which I didn't have. Because I began with ex-GIs in an open classroom—grown men—and I was a little eleven-year-old. So I didn't learn the systematic strengthening of the body, the muscles to produce, and things like that.

RS: *And yet one of the things you're most famous for is your extreme extension. Isn't that true?*
AK: The minute I understood that I needed to stretch, I started working at it. I knew my muscles were peculiar and that I had to stretch them.

RG: *How did you know your muscles were peculiar? What does that mean?*
AK: I got very muscle-bound too quickly. Other people had greater endurance. I seemed to need massages from the age of twenty-one. But all muscles aren't the same; like, grasshoppers don't have the same muscles we do. [laughs] Do grasshoppers have muscles?

RG: *I never asked one.*
AK: They must be cute, those little grasshopper muscles. Quick-twitch muscles.

RG: *Did you have any sense of why you were taken into the company so young?*
AK: Well, probably they needed to fill a place. It was very small then.

There were nineteen principals and thirty nonprincipals. And the ballet mistress made fifty.

RS: *In times of trouble.*
AK: In times of trouble. And there's always trouble in a ballet company.

RS: *I remember those crazy performances of* Symphony in C, *where people would double from one movement to the next.*
AK: Yes, they'd come running on again, with slightly different expressions on their faces.

RG: *[laughs] Expressions of alarm, as I recall.*
AK: [laughs] Panting, small pants.

RG: *But that doesn't explain why it was you who was the chosen one.*
AK: Well, here's the other thing: In those days, they didn't have school performances. And Balanchine recognized that I needed some sort of experience, or else the idea of performance would just be too far away. It would never become a reality if I just kept practicing and practicing. You have to experience the stage. And my first experience of it was a little shocking because it was on a professional stage; it wasn't even a school stage. It was at the City Center, where the New York City Ballet performed before it moved to Lincoln Center.

RG: *You hadn't even been a mouse in a* Nutcracker.
AK: Later, I achieved mousedom.

RG: *But do you have any sense now what it was about you that so quickly inspired Balanchine to create roles for you? I mean, you were, what, seventeen?*
AK: Yes, just seventeen. I think that I got very wrapped up in dancing and that was visible to him. Whether I was in class or in performance, I just threw myself into it.

RG: *He always loved that, of course.*
AK: It was energy, it was love. A little wildness, a little hyperactivity. Maybe quite wrong, too. [laughs]

RS: But that never bothered him.
AK: It didn't bother him.

RG: *Because he always found a use for whatever quality interested him. The question is, what was your quality? Do you have a hunch or a clue? He obviously wasn't ever going to express such a thing verbally.*
AK: Oh, no. No.

RG: *But I think there are clues in the ballets.*
AK: We all have to be detectives in life.

RG: *Particularly with Balanchine! There are clues in the ballets that he made on you, or restored for you.*
AK: Even with paintings you have to be a detective.

RG: *You're avoiding this question.*
AK: [amused] OK.

RG: *I mean, in the first ballet that he made on you,* The Unanswered Question *[from* Ivesiana], *in 1954, you're held aloft throughout your entire time onstage, while a man who is yearning for you tries to reach you but never succeeds.*
AK: Lots of symbolism.

RG: *So you're unattainable. You're an erotic object that is unattainable. Or a romantic object that is unattainable.*
AK: Well, "neurotic" is a little—

RS: Not neurotic—erotic.
AK: Oh, erotic.

RG: *You're an erotic object that is unattainable.*
AK: I agree.

RG: *Now let's look at the famous ballet he revived for you,* La Sonnambula—The Sleepwalker—*which may be the most famous of all your roles. The same pattern—*
AK: The same pattern, and the same color costume: White. Hair down.

RG: *Hair down, but feet never really down on the floor.*
AK: There are almost no feet. It's just bourrées—up on the toes. It's sort of a magical movement.

RG: *So here is another unattainable woman, with whom a young poet falls in love, and [he] is killed for it. And she is completely unaware of him. In fact, she steps over him—*
AK: But she is aware of him.

RG: *Aware of him, but not responsive to him until she carries his dead body off the stage. And then there's* Bugaku, *which is probably the most erotic ballet Balanchine ever created—it's in essence a mating dance, wouldn't you say?*
AK: I would say it is.

RG: *But even so, it's curiously remote. It's an expression of eroticism but it's formal. You're available but you're not available.*

AK: It represents a kind of Japanese, stylized ritual.

RG: *So eight years after* The Unanswered Question, *when you're already twenty-five—*

AK: Yes, yes, it's a continuation. Of course.

RG: *And then the other most famous thing he did for you was* The Seven Deadly Sins. *On the one hand, you're the personification of every known sin, and on the other hand, you're innocent and untouched, while Lotte Lenya, your doppelgänger, is the one who expresses all the viciousness.*

AK: She does all the expressing.

RG: *Somehow you looked innocent, untouched, while embodying lust, gluttony, et al.*

AK: Yes, definitely, definitely innocent.

RG: *So to Balanchine, you were clearly an object of romantic hope, and yet you were unattainable. Innocent, almost childlike, perhaps.*

AK: [pauses] Something like that. The word *childlike*, I don't know whether that—

RG: *Well, with the innocence of a child.*

AK: Yes, the innocence of a child. It's a continuation of a Balanchine theme.

RG: *But it isn't, for instance, the theme of* La Valse, *which he made on his wife, Tanaquil LeClercq.*

AK: Yes, that's a very different story.

RG: *It's a story of sophistication and complicity.*

AK: He actually didn't want me to do *La Valse*. I did do it, maybe once or twice, but he really didn't want me to. Which is—it's odd.

RG: *I don't think it's odd. It seems very much in line with how he saw you. Now, what about the way you absorbed willy-nilly so many of the central roles of the Balanchine repertoire, like his* Swan Lake, *and the second movement of* Symphony in C, *and* Agon. *Did those come about naturally?*

AK: I was the original understudy for both Diana Adams and Melissa Hayden in *Agon*.

RG: *And did you replace Diana fairly early on?*

AK: I think so. I think I was twenty-one when I did my first *Agon* because she was injured and they had to get someone onstage. By that time, the whole ratio and balance of the company had changed. When I arrived, there were nineteen principals. By 1958 there were only three ballerinas, maybe four, and Diana was injured.

RG: *So you had to dance everything.*

AK: Everybody had to dance everything. But seasons were shorter then, so we managed to survive.

RG: *Did you ever do the real bone crushers,* Ballet Imperial *and* Theme and Variations?

AK: No. I was supposed to—I understudied them, but I never actually performed them.

RG: *Did you want to do them?*

AK: I think I did. I always assumed I was going to work up to them, technically, but—

RG: *Because they were made for formidable technicians.*

AK: Yes, they were. Supposedly, even Margot Fonteyn had trouble.

RG: *Absolutely. Margot once said to me, "Everytime I was going to do* Ballet Imperial, *I would stand in the wings and think, If I can just get through that first passage I'll be all right. But you know, I never could!"*

AK: Oh, it's killing. I had the wrong equipment in my head to do it.

RG: *What do you mean?*

AK: I mean, I was very self-defeating. People talk about panic attacks, and I probably had a few of those.

RG: *Even when you were so young?*

AK: Yes, and they got worse. Eventually I was able to calm down pretty much. Without drugs. Because, of course, now they use them.

RG: *They save people a lot of pain. But your life became fractured.*

AK: It became fractured on the outside, and then it mirrored it on the inside—I mean inside the theater. At one time I was able to keep everything separate, but then the problems sort of crossed over.

RG: *Well, you married so young and with so little experience of boys.*

AK: Really, almost none. I had changed schools many times, moved cross-country. And then I found dance and decided not to really think about "teenage werewolves" and just really to focus on dance. And also it was a kind of a loyalty to my mother not to think about boys.

RG: *She was your partner?*

AK: In a sense. But there weren't any boys available for dates, anyway. I was always running out the school door to get to a ballet class; I never stayed in school for the boys.

RG: *So when [photographer] Bert Stern came along, that was it. He decided it was you, and—*

AK: He did decide. After eight months, he decided that he would like to marry me. And I married him.

RG: *As Jane Eyre says, "Reader, I married him."*

AK: [chuckles] It's going to be a musical now.

RG: *Yes. Maybe your life will be, too.*

AK: It already has been. [laughs] "Da, da, da!"

RG: *How do you read this part of your life?*

AR: My early marriage? I was too young.

RG: *Everyone was too young to get married when they got married.*

AK: Even now, I see coming attractions of movies, and I say to myself, "I'm too young, I'm too impressionable, I can't see this movie!"

RG: *And Balanchine was famous for not wanting his ballerinas to marry, have children, et cetera.*

AK: My mother didn't care.

RG: *But Balanchine cared.*

AK: Yes, he cared.

RG: *So when you were doing this thing of getting married when you were too young and having children, to what extent were you consciously and perversely gratified that you were acting against Balanchine's wishes?*

AK: Oh, there was that ingredient. I definitely knew. [laughs] I knew what he would say. But getting married wasn't so deliberately against him; it was just . . . at that time I didn't know what else to do. I'd been living with my sister, then my mother arrived; I didn't know who in the family I should be living with. And I didn't want to live alone. So it was a kind of changing of apartments, or changing of roommates, more or less. But I didn't know anything, really, about who this roommate was going to be. He was going to be a husband/roommate. Then the children—of course, I knew how important my children were.

RG: *You wanted them.*
AK: I wanted them.

RG: *You wanted them, but also—I'm sorry—but I can't help inferring from your book that there was some part of you that needed to defy or disobey.*
AK: Well, it was the way I was—because I was always trying to be a good girl, but a good girl who was really a bad girl. And that's the way I danced, too. Because no one really taught me the rules when I started with those ex-GIs. I didn't know there were certain things you did or didn't do in classical ballet.

RG: *This matter of the good girl who's also a bad girl goes back to Balanchine's vision of you that we were talking about.*
AK: That's right, yes.

RG: *So do you think that even then you understood on some level that while you were doing what you really needed to do, which was to have children, you were also showing him that you—not he—were in control of your life?*
AK: Yes. I was.

RG: *In a way it sounds to me—I don't want to make a vulgar equation here—but you're halfway between Gelsey Kirkland, who did nothing but resist, defy—*
AK: And yet who didn't break so many dance rules.

RG: *Yes, but we're not talking about dance rules.*
AK: [chuckles] I know.

RG: *She hated Balanchine and left City Ballet. And then there is Suzanne Farrell, who made herself totally into his instrument. You're somewhere in the middle.*
AK: In a way I am. But I also saw that he liked . . . he had said to some of my teachers, "Don't tell her anything." He more or less said to me, "Don't listen to them, don't listen to anyone," because he sort of liked my instinctive approach. He wanted to see where it would go. I think this was his

pattern with dancers he was interested in—he wanted to see where their imaginations would take them in dance. Not ballet, but just dance, the real pure heart of dance. And then, after a while, he didn't want only that. He wanted everything; he wanted technical ability, too. Because he didn't want any limitations.

RG: *So he would have preferred it if you had applied yourself to technique. But you chose another path.*
AK: Mmm-hmm. I chose a series of entrances and exits. [chuckles] Very much like Anna in *The Seven Deadly Sins.*

RG: *Yet you were with the company probably longer than any other ballerina.*
AK: I think Merrill Ashley has been there over a span of thirty years, give or take eight or nine months for an injury here or there. In my case [I've taken] eight or nine months for a baby here or there. You know, if you start at fifteen and you finish at forty-five, that's thirty years. And you're still young, but you may not know what to do next, because you've put all that time into just dancing.

RG: *Some major dancers go on to teaching, coaching. And of course some women, at some point, have married and had children.*
AK: At that point, yes. In their forties or late thirties. I'd had all my children in my twenties—exactly what my mother did, although I didn't really think about that.

RG: *No, we'd really rather not believe that we're repeating our parents.*
AK: [laughs] Some people do it with variations.

RG: *It's a little embarrassing. But now you've become a writer.*
AK: I'd always written letters to my mother, lots of letters, when I was away from her.

RG: *And you'd always read books.*
AK: I'd always read, because my mother always read. Going to the book emporium or the library was very important. I loved the public library!

RG: *I grew up in one, too. Because when I was a kid, who could afford books?*
AK: Actually, once I couldn't afford a present for someone, so I went to the library and took out all these wonderful books—Havelock Ellis and

Margaret Sanger—and when I gave them to my friend, I said that at the end of two weeks I'd take them back to the library for him. He was so happy.

RG: *What a brilliant idea, but when did you start writing?*
AK: I started in 1983. I had an idea—I was thinking how many Harry Cohens there were in the entire world.

RG: *Harry Cohen, your father?*
AK: Yes, but how many other Harry Cohens there were, C-O-H-E-N Cohens. So I thought of five hundred Harry Cohen stories. Then I started to write a little bit about my family. And then I thought, Well, maybe I should try to tell my story. So I wrote some of it down. And someone actually liked it, but a lot of others didn't. They said it was too unstructured. Nor did I know you weren't suppose to use adverbs.

RG: *Who said that?*
AK: Oh, I don't know. Somebody.

RG: *Well, somebody was dumb. That isn't true at all. Words are tools; you use them when they're helpful.*
AK: Anyway, so I worked on that for a while, and I actually wrote two hundred pages and found an agent, and she sent them out. But no one in New York City wanted it, except Jacqueline Onassis [then an editor at Doubleday], who was very interested. But she thought I couldn't do it alone, so I started searching for a co-author, and then I couldn't find one, and I put it all away. In 1992, I thought maybe I'd try to tell the story again. And again, I found that I couldn't work with a co-author. I tried quite a few. And then someone said, "Why don't you take a writing course?" So I took one that lasted four days, and I showed the teacher what I'd written before, and she found a few paragraphs in there and said, "I think you can do this yourself, if you just anchor it in time." I hadn't realized that when you wrote, you had to anchor things in time—I was used to anchoring things in music. I had a book contract at this point, at St. Martin's, and I wrote a few new pages about feeling my stomach when I was pregnant—I was avocado-shaped. I wrote it like a short story. My editor said, "I like this! I think you should continue. Don't go back; go ahead."

RG: *Good advice. But I think it's very fortunate that you postponed writing the book. It gave you another ten, twelve years to digest this material.*
AK: I also asked my mother to tell me all the old stories again, so that I could think about our relationship. That was very important, my relationship with my mother.

RG: *I know that when you were younger you were far angrier than you are today.*
AK: I was far angrier. I was very bitter. Yes, I have changed.

RG: *But that's part of what gives the book its wonderful generosity—the sense that you're not settling scores, either with her or with Bert; that you're not fantasizing, that you're really attempting to grapple with your life.*
AK: Well, I tried to tell my story the way I experienced it. I mean, that's all we can do.

RG: *And I think it's a tribute to both of you that Bert has been so enthusiastic about the book despite the fact that he hardly comes across as nature's nobleman.*
AK: Yes, it's a tribute to him. I can't give myself tributes. But I can buy flowers.

RG: *It's wonderful for your kids, too, that their father accepts this book and respects your view of everything the two of you went through.*
AK: I know, it's very unusual. It's something I didn't anticipate. Before he read it I was trembling.

RG: *One of the strange things about your past is that, like many ballerinas, you danced under a name you weren't born with.*
AK: That is correct.

RG: *But your name wasn't changed to be a stage name. How did that come about?*
AK: Actually, it came about because change is something my mother believed in, all kinds of change. And she couldn't get housing in Arizona or lower California at some point during the war with the last name Cohen. There were two things against her, she said: having children and the name Cohen. Well, she wasn't going to ditch the kids, so she decided to make Cohen into Kent, and there was nothing I could do about it since I was two years old.

RG: *Your name at that time was—*
AK: Iris Margo Kent.

RG: *So when did you "de-Iris" yourself?*
AK: That sounds like something that happens—

RG: *When did you lose your Iris?*
AK: The Iris was never lost; she was cast aside for thirty years. My sister changed her name—her name was Barbara, and she changed it to Wendy

for professional reasons. She led the way and I followed. I looked at her list of rejected names, and she had "Allegra" on it. When I'd started to play the piano at boarding school—I was very enthusiastic—I noticed those little words—allegro, andante—

RG: *Andante! You could have been Andante Kent.*
AK: Yes, definitely—or furioso. And also, knowing Longfellow's poem— "Laughing Allegra." So, anyway, I chose it immediately and that was that.

RG: *How old were you?*
AK: Just eleven. I was going to a new school and that helped so much, because no one knew it was a new name.

RG: *Tell me about your first dance lessons.*
AK: It was just a class of very ordinary steps offered by some local teacher. But then I heard the music, and it was as if so many ideas presented themselves, and I wanted to dance out all those ideas, in my way but using the steps the teacher gave. It's hard to explain, but somehow I knew I was a good dancer.

RG: *That's for sure.*
AK: I could sort of see that it's not the technique or the this or the that, but some kind of . . . something. I'm not any closer to explaining it than I was then. I'll probably have to have a glass of white wine. I'm serious, though. I don't know what it is. But I was actually having such a good time! For instance, a tendu. How could anybody really get so enwrapped in a tendu? Well, I could! [laughs] Yeah, I gave my all to this tendu combination— sliding my toe across the floor in different directions.

RG: *Do you still have this feeling?*
AK: Yes, I still have this feeling. It's like . . . I'm kind of an old woman, but in class now it looks like there's one toddler at the barre. [laughs]

RG: *And that's you?*
AK: Yes.

RG: *The title of your book is* Once a Dancer . . . *Are you saying that you remain a dancer, even though you're not onstage dancing anymore?*
AK: That's right.

RG: *What does that do to a dancer?*

AK: I dance through the swimming pool. I do have to dance. It's like having breakfast.

RG: *So it's not the actual performance that you miss.*
AK: I miss that, too.

RG: *Could you dance today, professionally?*
AK: It would have to be very specialized, very tailor-made for me. I could certainly do The Mother in that very odd *Swan Lake* that's arriving—the all-boy one. And then I heard that Lynn Seymour wanted to be The Mother, and I thought, Well, we're just a year apart in age, so if she wants to be The Mother, why can't I be The Father? [laughs] Also, it would be a job. I love to work. I love assignments.

RG: *You could have writing assignments, too.*
AK: If I was given one, then of course. But I actually have an idea. It's a story about a swan—I've had it for a long time. I have to develop it. But it's for the very young.

RG: *That's OK. Do it!*
AK: I've been very distracted recently.

RG: *Well, you keep doing these things like writing books and getting married, and that will distract a person.*
AK: I'm focused enough to know that the first thing I should do almost every day is go swim. That's something I'm really proud of, my water exercises. Because I was twenty years ahead of the time when I published my exercise book, *Allegra Kent's Water Beauty Book* [in 1976]. Of course, when people say I was twenty years ahead, I say, "Twenty years ahead? The ancient Greeks were training this way for battle in the Mediterranean pond." And today, when I go into one of these little delicatessens carrying my string of water wings, people get very interested in them. Even Philip Roth has begged me for extra water wings, which I sent to him.

RG: *Just don't marry him.*
AK: I'm married already.

RG: *Exactly. So you swim every day—*
AK: And I go to ballet class, and then I'm set.

RG: *What about walking?*

AK: Walking! Well, I don't know. Walking is not my favorite exercise, although of course you have to walk. You have to walk through museums. You cannot swim through a museum, because they don't have water.

RG: *It's so unfortunate. Unless there's a Titanic Museum.*

AK: Oh, my gosh—there's someone who went down on both the *Titanic* and the *Britannic,* and survived both. What luck!

RG: *Well, luck is important for surviving a shipwreck. But it takes more than luck to achieve a long, amazing career like yours. Talent isn't enough. Hard work isn't enough. Beauty isn't enough. You also need—*

AK: You need all of those.

RG: *—determination.*

AK: Yes, plus a kind of stability to weather the ups and downs, because they do happen. Performances differ from one day to the next.

RG: *That's true about everything in life, isn't it?*

AK: Yes—there's no guarantee about the future in any part of your life.

RG: *When you're young, you don't know that. You just assume everything will keep going, getting better and better.*

AK: That's true.

RG: *But look how you've turned out as a person.*

AK: I've been very lucky. But I had to work very hard to try to overcome a lot of my problems, which got in the way of my dancing.

RG: *On the other hand, you did what you set out to do—you danced for a long time, you had three children, and you're still in there swinging.*

AK: [laughs] I'm in the swing—yes.

RG: *And you've written a really fine book.*

AK: Oh, thank you. I'm very pleased this book got out. I still can't believe it.

RG: *One critic I know who's read it told me he thought it was the best book ever written by a ballerina. I tend to agree with him, and I've read them all.*

AK: Oh, that's—I'm really thrilled to hear that. Hurrah!

—from *Interview,* March 1997

MARK MORRIS ON *MOZART DANCES*
Joan Acocella

Raised in Seattle, Mark Morris (born 1956) arrived in New York to dance for a series of modern dance companies before forming the Mark Morris Dance Group in 1980. A year later, he created his first major success, Gloria, *and quickly became the object of intense interest and approval from such eminent critics as Arlene Croce, Tobi Tobias, Joan Acocella (who has written his biography), and Alastair Macaulay. Perhaps the peak of his artistic achievement came during his years at the Théâtre Royal de la Monnaie, in Brussels (1988–1991), when he choreographed* Dido and Aeneas *and* L'Allegro, il Penseroso ed il Moderato. *Like the other major modern dance choreographers, Morris was himself a superb dancer—intensely musical, quirky, funny, powerful. He has also made dance works for a number of other companies, including San Francisco, American Ballet Theatre, and the small company he founded in 1990 with Mikhail Baryshnikov, the White Oak Dance Project. And he has successfully staged a number of operas (for the Metropolitan Opera, New York City Opera, the Royal Opera, and English National Opera).*

JA: *Your* Mozart Dances *have no explicit stories. They're abstract, or close to it. Do you think an abstract dance can ever be political?*

MM: Dancing is never abstract. It's evocative, because it's being done by human beings. If a dancer looks at something, that means something, and if he looks away, it means something else. And so, to me, whatever story there is in *Mozart Dances*—the piano *versus* the orchestra, the female soloist *versus* the women, the two male soloists *versus* the men, and also why are those men there anyway? what's happening? why does it look like he feels like that? does he?—all of that is evocative of a social situation and a sexual situation. What I feel about that situation, whether it's utopian or dystopian: that's what's being set up, and to me it's political.

JA: *You've talked in the past about sexual politics. Years ago, you said that you wanted to expand the range of expressiveness for the two sexes.*

MM: Yes, and I've done it. It's no accident that in the slow movement of the women's dance, "Eleven," the women are all standing apart from one another on the stage. They do this sort of tortured, beautiful stuff [he gesticulates], but they're always alone, because I didn't want it to become a group hug, which can happen with women, dancing to music like that. And their movement is extremely angular and powerful. Also, in the closing section of their dance, the action is all lateral and linear—thrust, drive, line. The women had a hard time with this. I had to push them to be stern, to sharpen their attack. The women, when they put on those pretty dresses and hear Mozart, tend to go soft and pastel, and to me that's dead.

JA: *What about the men?*

MM: I've had to push them in the opposite direction. Just as the women, in their slow movement, are all strong and singular and isolated, the men, in their slow section, are all together, cooperating. They dance in circles, nourishing, nesting, blah-blah-blah. They had a hard time, too, just like the women. But that's how dancers become great, by doing what's difficult for them, dancing against their grain.

JA: *It's in the slow movement of "Double" that* Mozart Dances *actually does tell a sort of story. A skinny young dancer, Noah Vinson, comes in looking quite forlorn, and the men enclose him in their circle. It's not exactly a hug, but it's poignant.*

MM: Yes, Noah does a solo inside the circle. Then he does it alone, which to me is the most tragic thing I've ever seen. But that's also because of the context. First we saw the circle, then we saw a filled circle—filled with Noah's solo—and then we see Noah's solo alone. We've learned how to see it.

JA: *Your dances always look to me half-narrative, or obliquely narrative. You come up with highly articulated gestures that seem to mean something quite specific, but one can never really say what they mean. For example, there's a movement that the dancers do while lying on the floor, with their heads angled and their arms jabbing upward. . . .*

MM: Yes! What's that? Who's ever seen that? It looks like their necks are broken. It's terrifying to me.

JA: *And there's a moment late in the slow movement of "Double" where the men are doing their circle dances and all of a sudden eight women come in, in long tarlatans, like something out of* Giselle, *and insert themselves into the men's circle. It's like a visitation from the supernatural. What did that mean?*

MM: I don't know what it means. To me it means what the music means. I don't even know what it means when the men in the circle take each other's hands and when they don't. I know that those two different actions evoke different feelings, but whatever I choose, it's not what I *set out* to do. It never is. I know what the situation is, but it's not a word situation. It's not a play; it's music. At the party after the premiere, one of the musicians came up to me and said how much he liked a certain part of the dance. He said it reminded him of how he felt when he was playing counterpoint. And I said, "You know why? Because it is counterpoint."

I think that every one of those three Mozart pieces that I used is like an opera. The ending of the last piece, "Twenty-Seven": that's the end of *Così Fan Tutte*.

JA: *How can you say that? The ending of* Così *is bewildering. It drives people crazy. And the last movement of "Twenty-Seven" seems to me the happiest and clearest thing in all of* Mozart Dances. *The dancers are paired off in male-female couples, and they do social dances. Then the men go to one side of the stage, and the women to the other side, and the two groups turn toward each other, with their hands on their hearts. It's a show of friendship, love.*

MM: You've seen it only once. Look at it again. At the end, some of the dancers place their hands on their hearts, but the others put their arms out as if they were asking a question. So it's like, "Huh?" Or, "Just a minute, I'm not finished with you." Or, "I love you." Or, "What's wrong?" That, to me, is *Così*. The reason the end of *Così* is so confusing and distressing is that the switched lovers got too close. There was too much duplicity for the problem just to be solved by an amnesty. So the opera ends in chaos. And the end of *Mozart Dances*, I think, has that same irresolution.

JA: *But if that's the case, doesn't the finale violate the spirit of its music, which is a sweet, frisky song about the coming of spring?*

MM: Peter Sellars says that in that song Mozart was writing about the spring of humankind, the spring of the Revolution, of the Enlightenment, of the Masonic ideals—the spring of Benjamin Franklin. I agree with this. That's what the music is saying, and the dance, too. It's terribly sad, I think.

JA: *Because those hopes haven't been fulfilled?*

MM: No, it's not a question of fulfillment. It's the *desire* that's wonderful. It's about hope, hope of spring, spring meaning a new opening: newness, freshness.

JA: *So what's sad about that?*

MM: I studied that concerto very hard, for a long time—two years—and as I listened to it, the spring song got sadder and sadder. There are no repeats. The score never says, "Go back here and start over." It goes straight through, and though it seems to repeat, there's always some small thing, a chord or whatever, that's different. It changes subtly and constantly. I don't know how to explain this except by the dance I made. The song is transmuted. It becomes—not bleak, but all I can say is deep.

JA: *And sad?*

MM: Yes. Everything beautiful is sad. If it's not sad, it's not beautiful. It's pretty.

—from the catalogue of the New Crowned Hope Festival (Vienna), 2006

ANTOINETTE SIBLEY
Barbara Newman

Born in 1939, Antoinette Sibley joined the Royal Ballet in 1956, and her elegance, musicality, and charm quickly propelled her to ballerina status and tremendous popularity. Her superb partnership with Anthony Dowell involved the creation of several important ballets, including Ashton's The Dream *and MacMillan's* Manon. *(She was also in the original casts of Ashton's* Monotones I *and* Enigma Variations.) *She succeeded Margot Fonteyn as president of the Royal Academy of Dance and was named a Dame of the British Empire.*

Before the *Swan Lake,* I had done *Ballet Imperial.* It was a magnificent thing, and a very great favorite of mine. It was, I think, the only Balanchine in our company at that time; very much épaulement and difficult angles, but we were used to that. But it's an extraordinarily difficult ballet, mainly because the ballerina is asked to do tremendously difficult cadenzas on her very first entrance. She comes in cold to it, half of it's the speed of light, and then you move so slowly and then quickly. It's very hard to adjust to the different tempi and to do them all right on that first entrance. In fact, you have to make your mark, like the Rose Adagio. That's it—you seal it then, and the whole performance takes off from that or not. It was my first really big role and a big success for me, and the more ballets I did, the more I liked that one still. It was such a hard ballet, it could have defeated one very much at that age, but once I could do that, I could cope with anything. *Swan Lake* became much easier—everything did.

Well, *Imperial* was such a success that de Valois said to me that she'd like me to learn *Swan Lake* and I had two weeks to learn it. And I thought, Well, how can you possibly learn *Swan Lake* in two weeks? It's nonsense. But then I thought, You can't let this drop. Maybe it won't come along again for many years. And she did sweeten the blow slightly by saying, "As you've only got two weeks, I have asked Michael Somes if he will partner you to get you through it." So I thought, I suppose I'd better try and do it in that time, so I set off to do it.

Unfortunately, we were on in the provinces then, every night in different ballets. I had to come into London before the class at 10:15 to do my rehearsals of *Swan Lake*, because that's the only time we could fit it in. The whole thing was absolutely ridiculous. It was such a worry. I hated just to do "a performance"; it wasn't a *Swan Lake* to go on and do the steps. There were certain things I knew I wanted to do and others I knew I didn't want to do. But it's such a huge undertaking at that age anyway, like climbing Mt. Everest. You hardly have time to think, let alone do your own interpretation. It was a matter of getting through it. If you'd had time to think, maybe then you'd have got into such a snit about whether you could do it or not. That's rather different from suddenly being pushed on. It's crazy to be pushed on. I wouldn't choose to do it like that if I were given the choice, but that's how it's always turned out. It seems to be my role in life for everything to come as a shock, but there you are. I was going on in two weeks for my first performance, at Golders Green, on the tour.

Well, I did my performance, and then I did another one at Streatham the next week, but with another partner. And then *Swan Lake* was completely off my list, because now we were back at Covent Garden and there was no way I was going to do it at Covent Garden, age whatever I was, nineteen or twenty. Then a month or two later, in London, Michael Somes rang me one morning when I wasn't very well—I had flu. I was married to him subsequently, but I wasn't married to him then and I didn't know him very well other than having danced with him on this one occasion and he'd rehearsed me. And he said, "Oh, you're on tonight." I thought it was a rather odd thing to say, because of course I was on that night—I was doing the pas de trois in *Swan Lake*. So I said, yes, I knew I was on, and that was the end of the conversation. I thought, Well, I might not be on anyway because I feel so gruesome, and then I went back to sleep. When he rang back to say that Margot had very kindly said I could use a bit of her rehearsal time to rehearse, I didn't know what he was talking about. And then it suddenly . . . I realized . . . He said, "Nadia's off, and you're doing Odette-Odile." I really was absolutely shattered. However, I went along and rehearsed it, and that was it; I went on and did it that night. It really was a tremendous ordeal.

Swan Lake I found very hard to get to grips with because I had a confusion:

the kind of *Swan Lake* I adored was not the kind that suited me. What I loved was the very opulent, exaggerated *Swan Lake*—Plisetskaya, back arched, legs up, crazy sort of things—Svetlana's *Swan Lake,* one of marvelous positions and very unclassical in a way. Well now, I wasn't that kind of a dancer. Whereas with *Giselle* the kind I loved was the kind I could do, I was at the opposite with *Swan Lake.* Obviously, the *Swan Lake* that suited me much more was the simpler one, because I was a simple mover. I was a *big* mover for my size, I had an expansive movement, but it wasn't an exaggerated or flamboyant movement. It was tremendously pure in a way—big but pure— and very relaxed, formal. I didn't have the swayback legs or the arms that bent backwards—I was classical-lined.

I just didn't know how to come to grips with this, so I asked [Tamara] Karsavina to help me with it. I was working on a book with her, early in my *Swan Lake* career. I told her my problem, and she said, "But that isn't *Swan Lake.* You can't do *Swan Lake* like that, exaggerated. *Swan Lake* is the purest of all the ballets." I was absolutely stunned by this. I said, "No, no. *Sleeping Beauty* is the purest of the ballets, but not *Swan Lake.*" And she said, "No, on the contrary. It is *Swan Lake* that is the purest." I then did it that way because, anyway, this is the way I had to dance. To watch it, I do love to see those crooked arms and the bent arabesques, but it isn't my way. And at least I had her saying she had always been taught that *Swan Lake* must be simple and pure.

She also helped me a lot with the mime scenes in Act II; she showed me how the mime should be done. She must have been one of the great dramatic ballerinas ever. As she did it, she became every character. When she talked about von Rothbart, she was von Rothbart, and when she talked about the mother's tears, you could almost see the mother. The way she did every ges- ture, every movement, was an eye-opener. It wasn't like saying, "You know, the English language." If you read Shakespeare, you gasp, you die. It's a flow- ering of it, and this was the same with her. I knew the gestures, but to see her do it was like listening to Beethoven after just learning the scales. She had bad arthritis, but the moment she started to move, you understood everything. She had the most beautiful eyes I've ever seen. Those eyes told a million stories. She looked up, and you died with her.

I did most of the rehearsals for that '63 production. That was Bobby Helpmann's and Fred's production, with the Prologue, where you see her as a princess before she is actually changed into Odette. You see Rothbart come and capture her and take her away, and then the ballet goes on. I think doing the Prologue slightly takes away from her wonderful, theatrical entrance in Act II, that jeté on that particular music. The audience have seen everybody else dance, as in the Prologue in the *Beauty* they've seen wonder- ful things, and now they're waiting for the ballerina. That's how I like my ballets; I'm old-fashioned about that. I like the buildup for the ballerina, and then that marvelous entrance, flying in. It was made to be like that, rather like a crown that is the final, beautiful thing of authority on a queen. I like all the trimmings.

You are a swan when you first appear, and this is why the Prince is trying to shoot you at first and capture you—he doesn't understand. It's only when he gets close to you that he realizes there's something strange about this swan: she's slightly human. Gradually you're a swan-woman, which is so confusing for him, and his confusion is why she starts to tell him the story, that her mother's tears made the lake. I think it must have been the mother that upset von Rothbart; she was somebody he wanted as a mistress, but obviously she didn't want to. So he's gotten his revenge by taking her daughter, and the mother's cried ever since—that's the lake.

It's a formal ballet, and I like the mime. I think it makes sense. Why shouldn't we know why she's a swan? It's lovely that she tells the story, and it can be so beautifully done. I don't think yet another pas de deux is valid there. In a little while, we're going to have one of the most beautiful pas de deux ever created. Why spoil it with one where you're flapping around the stage trying to escape for so long? You've already tried to escape in the beginning, before the mime. I never liked doing that version; I only liked the mime. It's not something people wouldn't understand. You get the idea. If you're watching a film in another language, you'll get the idea of it. And good heavens, it doesn't go on for very long, so you can't be that stupid not to pick up what it's about.

We had mime lessons in the School with Ursula Moreton, who was a great mime artist herself, so one was totally at home doing mime. For young people it's far harder than it is to dance, because it's mainly standing still and, with these few gestures, telling a story. But it's rather like the musicals, which you do so well in America. When we did them in England, you'd have dancing numbers, and then they'd stop and suddenly talk, and then they'd stop again and start singing—it was nonsense. But with American musicals, the singing goes into the dancing, the whole thing's one. It's the same with the mime. You don't just stand still; the gestures are all part of the dancing, but a different form than actually doing ronds de jambe.

Certainly Odette falls in love with him, in that marvelous pas de deux. You are, by then, almost a woman, but you have the mannerisms still of the swan. It's a metamorphosis, but you're never completely—or just—a woman. Now he knows the story, he knows why she's been changed into a swan, and she realizes he would do anything for her. Von Rothbart has appeared, and Siegfried must also be scared of him, but he's fighting for her. So she knows his feelings, and during that pas de deux she's getting to know him and trust him and love him. There seems to be hope. She can't quite figure out how, I don't suppose, but there is hope. And when you fall in love, you don't really think of much else—it's such a wonderful feeling.

I have done it with Benno, and he never did seem to interfere, funnily enough. A person always in the court, like a princess, would be used to never being alone, and you have to be natural when your equerry or whoever is around. Not like us mortals—if somebody else came in when we were with our loved one, we would be rather perturbed. But that's very much how it was in the court circles in those days. Benno only did the first part of the pas de deux, and it worked rather well; he would just take your arm occasionally and then give you over to the Prince. He was really rather a help, because I obviously would be rather shy dancing—or talking, as it would be—to the Prince about such deep things for, gosh, absolutely the first time. I never found him an intrusion; it seemed quite natural to a princess to have somebody else around.

A lot of your characterization comes from how you look and how you dance, which is why we get back to my problem at first. I'm a classical dancer, so I have to do it through my mold. I knew I couldn't do that Plisetskaya style, so it did take me a long time to feel the bigness of a movement. I could feel it very much in something like *Sleeping Beauty* because that's purely classical, and "The bigger the better" is the right way of doing it. Odette's very big in warmth, and I couldn't equate that necessarily with a classical line. The line of an "atti-arabesque," as they call it, an attitude-arabesque, and those arms coiled back, all those exaggerated things gave me much more the feeling of a swan than the line of Aurora. One was a swan, the other was a woman, and I wanted a swan-woman.

In the end, I related it more to the music, with sweeping movements done just in bigness and fullness. I have a very long neck, so I was able to use that, and I would always use my arms to quite good effect as a swan. Whereas the legs I never could; they wouldn't look right in those arched positions; they aren't made to be like that. So I had to do a half-change: in the top part I could do some of those, but in the bottom part I couldn't, so it had to be my very own way. Which was lovely because in the end, with every ballet, I got it to be my way. But this did take a long time.

You can't change the way you look. I am very small; therefore, I look very frail. I'm delicate. The kind of life I've led is sad in illness and things like that—one's gone through those tribulations. So one knows about sadness and breaks-up of marriages—all the things everybody knows about—but when one's lived through them, you put this into your dancing. You have to do everything as you are as a person. I couldn't change the way I look or think, no, or hear the music. So much is from how you hear the music. You couldn't do it in a gay fashion; there's nothing gay about *Swan Lake* in the second act.

I loved the black act. I thought it was wonderful. You're putting on the black costume and the black headdress and becoming a total woman, a woman of experience, a voluptuous seductress—that for me was very easy. I could always identify that side. It was how to interpret the side that my body didn't feel that was difficult, as I've explained. But Odile, never. I've always loved women. I'd always wanted, if I had lived hundreds of years ago, to have been a courtesan, in touch with all the power of the time. I wouldn't have minded doing that for a living—I would have adored it. You know, it's not like a prostitute now; it was a marvelous position to be in. You were literally in the seat of power, and you knew all the sides to every question. I've always loved that sort of woman. That's why when *Manon* came to be my ballet, it was a glove. It was my realization of all that.

Odile's wonderfully evil. The more she can do to hurt him, the better. And she's loving it, loves the power she has over anybody. She's enjoying it as much as von Rothbart. She's so beautiful, you see, and a man cannot resist a very beautiful woman however much he loves somebody else. I mean, she's overpowering. She wants him to get confused as well—it's part of her whole game—in case there's a minute of aberration when he thinks, My goodness, what am I doing?—as he does. It's in those minutes she's got to capture him back, and it's imperative then that she foil him with bits of Odette. She must confuse him all the time, because otherwise he would just know. He can't be a fool. And if you have an intelligent-looking Prince, you've got to have an intelligent interpretation yourself.

First, she's just come on and he's absolutely overcome by her. They go off. The next time you see them, they're dancing together—it's as if they're talking together—and she's seducing him. I would say he's gone off to get her a drink or take her cloak off if she had a cloak—you know, just take her around—and now he wants to talk to her. He's desperate to talk to her, find out more about her, and she's gradually letting him know as much about her as she wants him to. Von Rothbart's instructing her, saying she's doing too much or too little, or, For goodness' sake, get him now. We haven't got much time. Odette's on the way. She's really having a wonderful time using her power, and when Odette appears, the more she's got to save the situation. Von Rothbart can't. It's up to her. It's all there in the choreography. It's just a matter of doing it.

I always had to grit my teeth to do the fouettés. I never found fouettés easy. I always remember Margot saying to me, "You just go on, and you know when you go on you're going to do thirty-two fouettés. You can't allow yourself to think. You just go on to count thirty-two. That's all. You go on to get through them." In fact, in other ballets, like *Patineurs,* I could do quite extraordinary fouettés, with double turns and all sorts of things put in. So halfway through my career I thought, Maybe, if I started putting those in

Act III . . . Maybe it's the monotony I'm finding so hard. So after sixteen, I used to start doing doubles every now and then, and that I enjoyed because it was fun. I would get bored the other way, and I might start thinking I was falling apart, so it was better for me to do something harder.

Then, for the last five or six years that I did *Swan Lake,* I never did the fouettés at all. My knee was starting to play up—it would give way on me. So from then on, I did a big circle of very difficult pirouettes 'round the stage, and I found that was much more exhausting because you were having to move at such a speed rather than stay on one spot. When I would just do the black act, I would do the fouettés, but never in a whole performance because my knee wouldn't have allowed me to.

We had no leeway at all. We all did exactly the same in our own way. Nobody does an attitude or a pirouette the same, but the steps were identical. We had no choice. Whether that's a good thing or a bad thing is a different question. I do think one should have slight leeway. For the opening step in the solo, the first attitude pirouette, I always did a double instead of a single. The step's the same; I merely did a double because I found it harder to do the single and come out of it. But other than that, I didn't change any steps.

The fourth act was my favorite. I always loved that best. You change which is your favorite act and which you're doing better all the time, from one act to another, depending on what you're going through in your own life and how you're developing as a person. I found Act IV so moving. The hope gone, everything . . . the usual in life, everything just hit on the head, total disaster. Right at the bottom, literally, of the lake. Everything is falling apart around you. You see his plight, you know your plight, and yet there is that total binding love. Odette sees the whole thing in the vision. She then goes back to all the swans and tells them, because—apart from just her—she was going to save her whole kingdom with this love of the Prince. She's their queen. She's in charge of all these swans. They are her people. She was not only out for herself. They're all lost as well, and she has to tell them this. He has deceived her. He's deceived them all. It's absolutely shattering.

I did two marvelous versions of that last act. One was Freddie Ashton's with that marvelous pas de deux of hopelessness and desperation and very deep love. The other one was Johnny Cranko's; I did his version, with the most wonderfully moving pas de deux, in Munich. The Prince gets killed in the end, drowned, trying to be after her. You're alone and he's drowned. It's total disaster. I don't like the normal version that's done. To me, it's nonsense—the whole thing's awful. I hate all that Drigo; Fred's and Johnny Cranko's versions use different music, and it's far more expressive when it's all done with different music. All these other fourth acts use appalling music. They're not dramatic in any way, with the swans all piddling around.

These two fourth acts are most beautifully explicit and dramatic—for all the swans as well—and beautiful music.

Act IV is just Act II with the tragedy. She's a sad creature anyway, with all she's gone through: living as a swan, knowing that your mother's gone through hell, that all these people are also swans, and that you'll probably be like that for the rest of your life. You're already doomed. There's no way that you're a young, innocent, happy creature. You find hope and love, which makes you blossom, but then you lose all that too. No, you're obviously a sad creature. Whereas Juliet, for instance, wasn't. She was perfectly happy, because she had nothing to be sad about. Life and the circumstances she lived just gradually snowballed on her, but she wasn't doomed as we see Odette is from the start.

—from *Striking a Balance*, 1982

MARTHA SWOPE
Francis Mason

The best-known dance photographer of the second half of the twentieth century, Martha Swope was born in Texas in 1933. She attended the School of American Ballet, but was quickly singled out by Lincoln Kirstein to photograph New York City Ballet, an assignment she carried out for decades. She also was the official photographer of the Martha Graham Company and the photographer for scores of Broadway shows, including A Chorus Line, Evita, Cats, Annie, *and* Jerome Robbins' Broadway.

BR: *How did you get into dance?*
MARTHA SWOPE: I have no idea, none at all. I began to dance in Texas; then I came to New York and managed to get into the School of American Ballet. I guess that's where it all began.

BR: *What had inspired you?*

SWOPE: There was a big article about Maria Tallchief in *Life* magazine. I saw all those pictures and was awed. In some other magazine I saw an article about the School of American Ballet. It sounded OK to me, so I wrote them a letter, and they said I could audition.

I auditioned with Muriel Stuart, who looked at me and said, "Darling, you have a lovely body, but you don't even know how to stand." Well, I was floored. I had finished school, and I was old enough to come to New York. In those days, all of us SAB students in "A" class had jobs to support ourselves. We were old enough to choose, to know what we were doing. Most of us were hard up enough that we had to earn our keep. I typed for an insurance company for a while. I got tired of that, so I started trying to sew costumes, little tutus. I drew Christmas cards.

BR: *You can draw?*
SWOPE: Yes. I sold the cards to the other students. And I took pictures of my teachers, who were Oboukhoff and Vladimirov and Doubrovska and Muriel Stuart and Tumkovsky—a glorious bunch. Except for Muriel, all of them were Russian.

BR: *How many classes did you normally take?*
SWOPE: At least one a day. When I had a job, I could only do one a day. When I took the summer course, I would do three. I would get mononucleosis every spring from overwork. I had it three years in a row. I was a very thin little reed. I'm 5'9" and I weighed only 110 pounds.

BR: *You wanted to stay that way?*
SWOPE: No, I just naturally was that way.

BR: *Tallchief was still there working in the classes.*
SWOPE: There's an SAB brochure where I'm at the barre behind Maria. And I have another picture of myself at the barre behind Tanny LeClercq and Roy Tobias from the mid-1950s. They are advertising wool sweaters, and I'm in the background.

BR: *And you went to see City Ballet.*
SWOPE: Being very poor, we would go down to City Center; one person would buy a ticket up in the top balcony for $1.80 and the rest of us would go across the street to the Puccini Bar and hang up our coats. At the intermission, after the first ballet, the first person would come down with five or six *Playbills*. In our shirtsleeves, in the snow, we would take a *Playbill*

and enter City Center chatting and sit in the orchestra. There was no audience in those days.

BR: *Just a couple of hundred people.*
SWOPE: You could sit in the tenth row orchestra center.

BR: *And the performances were not so many.*
SWOPE: Two weeks. Then I was a big Angel in *Nutcracker* during the ballet's second season. That's when I began to take pictures of my teachers. I always wanted to branch out. I like to take pictures to hold on to things.

BR: *The School was still on Fifty-ninth Street.*
SWOPE: Isadora Duncan's old studio.

BR: *You still have the pictures?*
SWOPE: They're wonderful because they're so evocative of something that's gone. I loved those teachers. Each was different.

BR: *Did Stuart decide eventually that you knew how to stand?*
SWOPE: She probably came around a little bit. Of course, I got sidetracked into photography pretty fast.

BR: *How did that happen?*
SWOPE: Around 1957 Jerome Robbins came to class. By then I was in the advanced class, and Jerry was taking it to warm up for—guess what?—*West Side Story*. He is, you may not know, a very fine photographer. He has a darkroom.

BR: *Did he ever let you use his equipment?*
SWOPE: A few times. Jerry said, "Would you like to take pictures of a rehearsal of *West Side Story*?" I said, "Well, yes." So I went over to the rehearsal studio in the West Fifties. That was very exciting. I didn't know what I was doing, but they were really fun pictures. I blew up some of them for him, and he showed them to Lincoln [Kirstein]. One day in mid-plié in class at the barre Lincoln came in, towering, looked at me, and said, "I saw your pictures. I liked them very much, but you work for the company, and that's it. Be in the office Monday at such and such a time." I said, "Okay." And he strode out. Actually, Jerry sent one of the pictures to his agent. And one of them appeared in *Time* magazine. That was the first photograph by me that was published.

BR: *And at the company?*

SWOPE: I went into the office, and Lincoln told me all his dreams. He had this wonderful idea of taking pictures of the dancers around New York, like Maria Tallchief in Wall Street at dawn with the sun coming in sideways. It never happened, unfortunately. There was never a chance to get the dancers out, away from rehearsal. But Lincoln told me the plan. We did the first little program book. I photographed scenes of New York, and we superimposed the dancers against them. That was in 1958 or 1959.

Because I was known to everyone, I was always hanging around. I waltzed into rehearsals and Balanchine was always very open. We were good friends later, but even from the beginning he never minded. He was not self-conscious. "Well, here she is. Hello. How're you doing?" He would just work, and I would snap away. The first time, Eddie Bigelow called me up and said, "We need you to go over to a rehearsal." By then the company was up on Broadway at Eighty-third Street, those big, beautiful studios with sky-lights and daylight.

So I went trotting over to a rehearsal of *Agon*. I'm standing there with my little camera saying, "Let's see. If it's daylight out . . . " I didn't have a light meter. In walked Stravinsky. Those pictures turned out to be a legendary set. I was lucky. God smiled on my camera. They came out. Those pictures were in *Life* magazine.

After that, I decided that I had to follow Jerry Robbins and his Ballets: U.S.A. to Spoleto. That was the first year of the Spoleto Festival. I went to Lincoln and said, "You know, I'd really like to go to Spoleto with Jerry and would you cosign a bank loan?" He said yes for $1,270. So I flew to Rome, went to Spoleto for ten days, and then went to Paris. I was gone about six weeks on that trip. In Spoleto I met José Quintero, who brought me into the legitimate theater. He was putting on O'Neill's *Moon for the Misbegotten* with Colleen Dewhurst.

At *Life,* there was an entertainment editor named Joe Roddy. I went to him and said, "I really want to go to Europe. The Bolshoi Ballet is coming West for the first time, and I would really like to see them and take pictures in Paris." He thought this was very amusing, so he wrote a little letter to Martin Feinstein at the Hurok office, who wrote a very amused little letter to Wolf Kaufman in Paris. So after Spoleto I went to Paris. In Paris, Kaufman thought I was a real photographer and got me into the Bolshoi. So I met Ulanova and got an autographed toe shoe and took pictures and had break-fast with the Russians. Then Kaufman sent me to Avignon on the train. The French National Theater was there with Gérard Philippe. He was very nice, and I had a whole Saturday morning with him in his *Le Cid* costume.

Next, I went to the World's Fair in Brussels. That was the end. Then I approached Jean Dalrymple, whom I had met at City Center; she was very important there. I said, "I need a job. I really need the money. Is there anything I can do?" She said, "I'll tell you what you can do. Van Cliburn and his parents are coming in on the next train. I want you to meet him and take pictures of them." So I met him at the train. "Hi!" He is from Texas, he had just won the Moscow competition, and we hit it off very well. I took a picture of his folks. I even had a couple of pictures of him playing the piano, but I didn't dare do much of that.

When I went back to New York I had a lot of pictures. All of these things were coming to New York in the fall, so I went to *The New York Times* with three pictures of major events. There I was, looking like a big photographer, but actually I had an old camera. I remember one of the Russian guys saying in the wings, "Don't you have an interchangeable lens?" And I said, "What's that?" I had this little Argus with just a fixed lens. You had to put adhesive tape around it because it had a light problem. Every time you loaded it you took the adhesive tape off. I had one hundred feet of 35 mm movie film, and I'd get under the quilt and load it and take it out under the quilt.

The problem was that I had to figure out photography because I knew nothing about it. I developed my pictures in the bathroom, so that I could take prints to the *Times*. I got nervous because you're never sure your stuff will come out if you don't have a light meter. I think Betty Cage sold me a camera, a Rolleiflex. She and Jerry and Frank Moncion and Tanny LeClercq all bought cameras in Germany in 1952 when the company was there, so it was really a good camera. Betty sold me hers, and when Anatole Chujoy died he left me his, which was a twin. I've used those cameras for the rest of my career. I still have them. They're the only two I kept. I used them for dance, and they were wonderful.

I had a cyclorama built on the curve in my studio, so that I could take dance pictures. I would sit on a little stool, and I had the lighting set up. The dancers had a twenty-foot stage. I would set up my Rollei for ten feet, and I never had to focus. I could follow-focus very easily. I could just shoot. A Hasselblad blacks out as you shoot, so you don't know what you did. But if you looked in the Rollei you saw the flash and you saw the picture. I used the Rolleis until I closed my studio. I'm going to give them to someone who really wants them.

BR: *And how did you obtain technical information?*
SWOPE: I would go down to a photo store and ask them questions, and they would sometimes give me a bum answer because they just didn't know. No

one knew the field I was in, theater and dance. It is very special. So some-times I would just pick up information or ask another photographer.

BR: *Taking action photos from the stage was new.*
SWOPE: Very new. The person who was ahead of me in that was Fred Fehl, who started out in the 1940s.

BR: *Fred knew about photography before he left Vienna.*
SWOPE: And he also learned about dance and theater.

BR: *Was he helpful to you?*
SWOPE: He was always very kind and very helpful. And he loved the dance.

BR: *Do you remember what Jerry Robbins was working on when you went to the rehearsal of* West Side Story?
SWOPE: I think it was "Cool."

BR: *And since you were a dancer yourself, you knew what they were up to.*
SWOPE: I think that is why I had such access to the dancers. I could walk right in, but Jerry I would ask because he wanted to be ready. He would say, "No, come back next week." When they were not ready, they would be demonstrating the steps. Whereas with Balanchine you could walk in and right away he would be up himself dancing his heart out. And the dancers trusted me.

BR: *So you were a professional photographer.*
SWOPE: I got a little more itchy later on because if it was a new ballet and an opening night, and you were trying to get a picture because the next morning you had to be in the newspapers or *Time* magazine was sending you for a picture, you hoped you got it.

BR: *Neither Balanchine nor Robbins said afterward, "I want to see all those prints"?*
SWOPE: Never once did either one of them ask to look at them. Later, Jerry used to say, "I'd like to see the contacts," because he could mark the ones he wanted for himself. He was very generous in marking. He would mark things, and I would make him prints. But Balanchine was essentially not crazy about still photography, and he said as much: "I don't really like stills because they lack the dimension of time, so there's not movement."
On the other hand, one day in rehearsal I remember he came over to me and said, "You know, in thirty years' time that's all that will be left of us, what you're doing. You never know." And I thought, Well, my goodness, I

guess it is, sort of. Actually, I think that he felt the same way about the photographs as he did about his ballets. He didn't care if they survived him because the ballets change over time. When the creator is gone, the ballets are different. It's a fleeting, ephemeral art. He was unsentimental about his own work. Balanchine let me be there not for documentation but because I was family. This is what he said, "She's family. She's one of us." He couldn't have cared less about preservation.

BR: *And Robbins?*
SWOPE: Jerry may have felt differently because he instituted the making of films of his own work.

BR: *He started the Robbins archive.*
SWOPE: And he started the filming at the State Theater. The movies can't be shown publicly, but his ballets are all filmed. I think he cares that things last and outlive him, and finally I suppose he's right. It's your life's work. I'm working right now archiving my stuff. I do care. I want it to live.

BR: *When Balanchine or Robbins were making new pieces, you would automatically photograph them?*
SWOPE: I would go.

BR: *You would watch the bulletin board for the announcement of the cast of a new work to know what was happening?*
SWOPE: I was really on my own.

BR: *And you would photograph revivals.*
SWOPE: New dancers in new parts. I was there so often. But I also worked with American Ballet Theatre and with Martha Graham. I spread my wings. I have some pictures that go back to Sallie Wilson. Everybody wanted Sallie. Martha Graham wanted her. Balanchine wanted her.

I met Martha on *Episodes.* I hung a piece of white paper at City Center, and we had a session. I got to talk to her. Then she asked me if I would work with her company. I said yes, but then I thought, My God, I don't know anything about this. So I went over to her school and studied two years with her. I sat on the floor and did all the technique exercises. The only way you can ever know is to do it. I suppose you can train your eye, but I felt I needed to know what it was all about.

I remember the first time I saw *Clytemnestra.* I knew Tchaikovsky and Mozart—and then Halim El-Dabh! The music shrieked and moaned, and then Graham came out and didn't point her feet. I was horrified. I went down to the ladies' room with a splitting headache and lay on the couch. What is this horrible stuff? Of course, later I came to be transported. In the 1960s Graham had "Big" Yuriko and Mary Hinkson and Matt Turney and Bertram Ross and Paul Taylor. It was unbelievable. I realized that I had to get a different attitude to figure it out.

BR: *Was Graham teaching in those days?*
SWOPE: Yes.

BR: *And she knew you were studying there.*
SWOPE: Yes. I worked with her until the end.

BR: *How was Graham the dancer different from the ballet dancers as a photographic subject?*
SWOPE: She was very agreeable. She would let me come to rehearsals. As she got really older she was less enthusiastic about it, but I went anyway when she was very old, toward the end.

BR: *Maple Leaf Rag?*
SWOPE: Yes, but I also went to her home a couple of times. I took the picture of her on that red Chinese bed. We did quite a bit of work. So she was fine.

BR: *Chris Alexander told me that Martha would arrive at his studio, get in front of the cyc in costume, made up, and he would shoot away. She knew what she was doing, and he knew what she was doing. And the next day he would take the proofs to her and she would pay him cash.*
SWOPE: He photographed before I came in. Now, when I look back, I think of those early days as the dark ages in terms of the film speeds and the cameras. I remember Tri-X film in the 1950s. It was very difficult to do candid work because Tri-X had been rated ASA 100. Now, of course, you have auto-focus cameras.

BR: *You had to focus everything.*
SWOPE: And we had very slow film speeds, so it was very difficult. Martha's lighting was much more dramatic. Jean Rosenthal came out of the hospital to light the last piece in which Martha appeared, *The Lady of the House of Sleep.* It was so dark and murky. She was being kind to Martha. As a result, I never got a picture of anybody doing anything but standing there. Finally, I said something one day, and Martha asked me if I would do her lighting! I said, "But I don't know anything about lighting." I spoke to Lee Leatherman, her manager, and said, "This lighting was devised by Jean

for Martha when she was getting very old and didn't look good onstage. Now you have all these beautiful young dancers and bodies. Bring the light up!" It finally got to the point where I could shoot. The thing was, you couldn't see the dancers.

The reverse happened with Balanchine. They had that beautiful Jean Rosenthal lighting scheme. Remember the old *Firebird*? The lighting itself was a beautiful thing. But the older Balanchine got, the whiter and more overall one tone it became, daylight. It was so hot, and Suzanne Farrell was so fair and always wore white. The readings in the theater were like outdoors in summer. Balanchine couldn't see. And the lighting has stayed bright because that's the way he wanted it at the end.

BR: *But at least it helped you photograph.*
SWOPE: It certainly helped me with the faster film, the brighter light, for stop action.

BR: *And you watched Balanchine work.*
SWOPE: It flowed out of him. He would walk in and say, "Well, why don't we do this and do that?" He would do a whole ballet in one take. It was just unbelievable, what he could do.

BR: *With no nervousness and completely prepared.*
SWOPE: He could make a mistake in front of God and everybody, and it didn't bother him at all. It didn't matter to him if he left out a measure. He was very sure of what he was doing, and his faith in what he was doing was unshakable. He didn't feel grand about it, but he certainly didn't feel nervous about it. He was very straightforward as he choreographed. A lot of people have visions of a mad Russian genius creating in a hysterical framework, but no, he was more American than the rest of us. His dance making was almost like mathematics. It was logical and the music just flowed out of him. You really saw the music in Balanchine's choreography. He would sit down at the piano and play the part himself. It was almost inevitable that this movement would flow into that. He took things from the dancers' bodies, too, so that it was a true collaboration.

Balanchine was practical. If one thing didn't work, then another would. If we don't have costumes, put on a leotard! No one had appeared on the stage in a leotard before Balanchine, and he did it because there was no money.

BR: *When you photographed Robbins working on* West Side Story, *did you have any sense that it was going to be a smash hit?*
SWOPE: No. I hadn't seen that much Broadway. What did I know? He was always there and it was fun to be there. I thought it was wonderful, and it was.

BR: *You were the ideal temperament for the situation at City Ballet at the time. You fitted into the family, and what you didn't know you solved yourself.*

SWOPE: They could use an inexperienced photographer because at the time everything was young and unknown, uncharted.

BR: *You sold the pictures that you took?*

SWOPE: There was no market in the 1960s and even the early 1970s. Even in the 1960s you would go to a magazine, and they would say, "Nobody is interested in the ballet." The big dance thing was in the late 1960s. But at the beginning, no one was interested. I was just happy to be there.

—from *Ballet Review*, Fall 1998

TAMARA TOUMANOVA
Francis Mason

"The black pearl of the ballet," as she was frequently called, Tamara Toumanova (1919–1996) was, with Baronova and Riabouchinska, one of the three famous "baby ballerinas" discovered by Balanchine in Paris in the early thirties. She was born as her family was fleeing Bolshevik Russia, though the actual year of her birth is open to dispute. Her amazing dark beauty, her powerful technique (the famous fouettés!), the aura of glamour—all these made her a tremendous international star. Through the years, Balanchine created a wide variety of ballets around her, including Cotillon, Concurrence, Balustrade, *and the adagio movement of* Le Palais de Cristal *(*Symphony in C*). She was starred by Massine and Lifar, and in 1939 appeared on Broadway with Ethel Merman and Jimmy Durante in* Stars in Your Eyes. *She appeared in many companies, touring incessantly and ending up in California, where she appeared in a number of movies, including* Days of Glory, Tonight We Sing *(she played Pavlova), and Hitchcock's* Torn Curtain.

Balanchine was an extraordinary creature. How he took care of me, how he used to tell Mama what to do, to give me food, to do this, not to overdo! He presented me to the greatest names; there was not one person that he would not introduce me to. This was the beginning of my true artistic career. I really think that Balanchine looked upon me as his own child. He would play with me. For instance, after a *Cotillon,* if I had done a very good rehearsal or performance, he would go to Pasquet, a wonderful patisserie in Monte Carlo, and buy me a magnificent chocolate that I could never afford and give it to me and say, "You must eat that. That's good for you."

On my twelfth birthday, he gave me a small little gold watch from Cartier. Boris Kochno gave me an ivory elephant. Balanchine always had great respect for me as an artist, and he made great demands on me as a worker. He treated me on the same professional level. But so kind. He never raised his voice. He was always—to the end of his days—so quiet, with so much tenderness. To me he became the emblem.

Don't think that I didn't remark how all the ladies were in love with him. I saw it. Just a few weeks ago I found a diary that I wrote at the time, and I say in it, "Oh, oh, oh, Tamaravich, careful, careful." Because I understood that this was a very appealing gentleman to all those ladies. They were flirting with him, and he would take one or another out to dinner. One day Mama and I were going back home after the performance, and we had to pass just in front of the Casino, the Café de Paris, passing through to go to Des Arts de Moulin, to the room that we were renting.

I said to Mama, "Someday I will be sitting as well in that Café de Paris." Mama said, "Yes, yes, yes, when you are grown." Balanchine was sitting with one of the dancers and with Dimitriev, and as I was passing Balanchine said, "Good night and have a very nice time, have a good sleep because tomorrow we have a lot of work to do." I said to Mama, "This is disgusting. Here I am the ballerina of the company, and I can't even sit in the café." Mama said, "Young girls of your position do not sit in the café."

Balanchine knew that I was very sensitive about such things. I remember a performance of *Tannhäuser* with the great French tenor Georges Thill. Thill saw me on the stage looking at things, how the scenery was hanging, and Balanchine called me. I came and he said, "This is Miss Tamara Toumanova, the ballerina of the company, and this is Georges Thill." He looked at me and said to Balanchine, "George, this is impossible; this is a child." And Balanchine said, "And what a child!" My feeling for Balanchine is not only for a great master but for the way he handled me as a human being.

Right after *Cotillon,* he did *La Concurrence* for me, with André Derain and Darius Milhaud. During rehearsals, Balanchine would not only demonstrate the steps, he would explain the idea. For example, every time he did a choreography for me, even a brio choreography, there was always a nostalgia, a sort of tristesse. *Concurrence* ends very sad, because I go to sleep in my memories of what has happened, on my knees, with a very sad feeling. *Concurrence* is a comic competition, but as the evening comes I went on my toes across the whole stage, went to the side, went on my knees and became very sad. There was nothing to be sad about, but that is what Balanchine saw in me then.

I first appeared as a vision in a long blue dress with a large bow on the left shoulder. Then later I changed costumes and became the young girl. There was a competition of fouettés, and on each side of me there was a dancer competing to see who could do the most turns. Leon Woizikovsky was fantastic. When the competition was over, the girl was alone, the lights dimmed and I walked about on pointe, then went down to my knees and was very sad. You really didn't know if the girl was real or not. I have a feeling that she was an illusion—because she didn't belong to the crowd of the *concurrence*. There was always a tremendous fantasy in everything Balanchine did. I think that's why he touched the audience. His choreographies for me were so fine and so sensitive, and the audience—not knowing really what was happening—was touched. *Concurrence* took him about one month to choreograph.

And there was *Le Bourgeois Gentilhomme,* where I danced Lucille, who does not want to marry her intended. David Lichine was extraordinary as the Moor; he had such a personality, and Balanchine caught his quality. Lucille is terrified and a little wild, like in the Richard Strauss score. But by the end, she accepts the betrothal. Balanchine made a pas de deux in which Cleonte put his arms about me and I would shiver. It was in the music. My whole body was shivering. No one had choreographed such a moment before. The pas de deux showed the fine sentiment of the young girl. It reminds me of a medallion. I have a tiny little Fabergé medallion that was given to me when I was seven or eight years old. That's exactly what *Le Bourgeois Gentilhomme* was.

When we finished the first season with the Ballets Russes de Monte Carlo in Paris, Balanchine arranged for me, my mother, and father to take our summer vacation in Monte Carlo. Otherwise, we would never have been able to afford it. He arranged for someone very kind to give him quite a sum of money for us to go there. He wanted to work with me every single day, giving me classes every day. He also tried out new choreography, new movements, new plastic ideas. So, that summer of 1932, he started new ballets on me for his Les Ballets 1933, ballets like *Mozartiana,* and even *Errante,* which I did not dance.

The lead in *Errante* was taken by Madame Tilly Losch, who was wonderful in it and whose husband provided the money for the season. I loved that ballet very much. *Errante* was actually done in a style for me, with long hair, very dramatic. The woman tried to find her Fate, she went through much suffering, and she could not find peace. She could not find what she was looking for.

I adored that ballet, but Balanchine called me and said, "Tamaritchka, I have to talk to you about something very important. We have a very hard time with money." I said, "Yes, I know." He said, "There is a lady by the name of Tilly Losch, and her husband is very, very rich. He is now going to be the supporting power of the company." When Balanchine told me *Errante* would not be my role, I was stunned. It was like a knife in my heart. Tears started to drop. Balanchine said, "Tamarichka, don't cry. I cried so many times before I could think how to tell you. But we have no alternative." But Balanchine spared my having to show the role to Madame Losch. He himself taught her the role.

That summer it was extraordinary to see Balanchine spend his time, hours and hours, to show me how to move, how each finger should be placed. The whole morning, in these hot days of summer, he would work with me until lunchtime. This is where I really learned the essence of his genius. I was scared to death each morning because I looked upon him with such respect. But even as young as I was, I could be inspired by the music. He loved music beyond anything, and that was our link of understanding. We worked for two months. For two months, Balanchine completely devoted half of each of his summer days to me.

When I joined Balanchine for Les Ballets 1933, he played the piano for practice rehearsals. He was so charming and full of life. I had already rehearsed *Mozartiana* with him during the summer vacation. Each movement was beautifully dovetailed, like lace. It would go from one step to another, continuously. In *Mozartiana,* Christian Bérard dressed me in a black tutu, not at all short. It was between a Degas-length and a short tutu, up to the top of the knee. There were extraordinary feathers, ostrich feathers, in the hat. I represented a magnificent racehorse.

Very proud, without putting the nose up, but that look of nobility. Pride with technique. This is what Balanchine gave me. I learned from him and I understood him, and I presented it. There was no chi-chi, no figilimigilis. It was elegant, strong, magnificent, without any smiles. Balanchine did the most difficult footwork in that ballet. Everything was with dignity, but fast, very exciting, very alive. This was the first time black curtains were used for a ballet. Everything was done with lighting. Balanchine, Bérard, and Boris Kochno wanted black curtains instead of a decor. There exists a little film of my variation—Marie Rambert made it at a rehearsal during the London season.

The Paris season of Les Ballets 1933 was the most elegant ever. I remember the things that we did then, and I think, "My God, how exciting it was." We took it for granted. But Mama always told me, "Watch everything; listen to everything. Be very careful in what you choose to do." . . .

Balanchine was very religious, and this feeling that Balanchine had for a higher power was a tremendous connection with Mama. He was very much *terre à terre.* He liked to cook, he liked to buy beautiful things, but I think the base of Balanchine was the deep religion. From the very beginning he showed a quality of transferring himself away from all of us. Was it in his work? Was it during dinner? Was it during a walk or discussions? He could remove himself. And I think that the quietness with which he worked, choreographed, inspired everyone, had a great deal to do with religion.

Balanchine had two things. He had a tremendous excitement for life, and he also had that need to retire in his own world, to just go away and not hear anything. I think that's why the music helped him tremendously, by allowing him to sit down at the piano and really get away from the world with that music. I understand that very well. Since my very young days, music has been a part of me. Without music, it's impossible.

Balanchine had his own world. I think that he lived in his own world. I don't think many people really realized his sensitivity. I am afraid that some people took advantage of it. He was a very solitary person, very much apart. This is one of the most important things in life, to have your own world. If you don't have that, it's very difficult to live because you will live "outdoors."

When Balanchine played the piano, he would not even know who existed. I heard him once at his apartment in Monte Carlo play a piano concerto of Tchaikovsky. Mama and I were invited to dinner that evening, and we came early. Dimitriev was there. Balanchine never even realized we were there. He played, and I remember there were some sort of little insects around him because that time there were no screens at the windows. His apartment overlooked the Mediterranean, and he didn't even notice them because his feelings had blended so with the music. He really didn't hear us, he didn't see us, he just didn't know who existed. When he finished he turned and said, "Ah, hello." We didn't breathe; none of us breathed. After dinner he said that he had a gift for me. We all got very excited. He gave me a recording of the *Symphonic Pathétique.* I have the old records still; they are not broken. Perhaps he was preparing to do a ballet for me to the music. I think that Balanchine saw in himself and in me the same qualities. For me and my mother it was very easy to be with Balanchine. That's a very rare thing.

It is usually not so easy to be with a choreographer. You could not be in that manner with Massine or with Fokine or even with Nijinska. They adored me and made ballets for me. Massine did *Symphonie Fantastique* and *Choreartium* and *Tricorne.* He was wonderful to me. But in private life I never felt as comfortable as I was with Balanchine. He was very modest. I think he was perhaps over-modest. He was so good to so many people, even those who took advantage of him.

But there were days when we talked with him, for example, later on in Paris in 1947—or in 1944 when I was with Ballet Theatre. In the spring season he came every day to the performance, then picked us up with Mama, and we would have a lovely dinner. We would talk and he would open his heart. Not in the sense of saying whom he loved, but he would open his heart on how to live, what to expect, how hurt he was or how not hurt. I cherish that very much because he was a great master, a genius.

He worked with me on my Fokine repertory as well, *Les Sylphides, Petrouchka.* There were little things, for example even showing the use of the fingers in *Sylphides.* Balanchine had real respect for other choreographers. When I did Bronislava Nijinska's *Harvest Time* in 1945 with Ballet Theatre at the Metropolitan, he was backstage watching. I went into my dressing room, and he came and sat down and said, "You know, Tamarichka, you dance in Madame Nijinska's *Harvest Time* like Heifetz plays the violin. Your feet are like Heifetz plays the violin." For him to say that I am like a violinist, that's unbelievable. This was Nijinska's ballet. Balanchine was never jealous. People don't realize how much he admired, for instance, Tudor. He adored *Lilac Garden.* When in Monte Carlo I was learning *Les Sylphides* and *Petrouchka* and *Spectre de la Rose* of Fokine, it was clear that he knew those ballets very well.

Balanchine was a very brilliant man and he had a knowledge of what people thought. He loved to see them think differently than what he was thinking. He liked the idea of playing, having a game of thoughts. I think that that's what he liked in me and Mama and Papa, because we stood our ground. We had our own way of thinking, which he liked. He knew that with us the game would stay on a high level. For example, I never denigrated other choreographers before Balanchine to try to please him. Because that would not have pleased him. He knew that I was a very sincere person, and he knew that I loved the art to the point that I could never say, "Well, so-and-so is not as good as you are." I never did this. On the contrary, I stood, and I said, "I had a great triumph in such-and-such a ballet that had nothing to do with Balanchine." This would make him happy.

Papa had a sharp humor and I used to tell him, "Papa, be careful, these are ballet people, not military people." But when Papa said something like that, Balanchine enjoyed it because it brought him to a world he admired. Like it or not, he loved the military. Balanchine loved that strength, the ability to keep yourself going. He thought like that himself. He found in Papa an extraordinary knowledge of literature that he liked to discuss with him, about Pushkin, Lermontov, Goncharov, and Ivanov. Balanchine was very fond of my father. I even have books that he gave my father as presents around 1945–46: *Pique Dame* and *Eugene Onegin* in beautiful editions.

Both my father and my mother were very discreet in their relationships with Balanchine. Balanchine knew that anything he told them would go no further. Papa was very close to Balanchine, especially in 1939 in New York.

Balanchine was in a sentimental, difficult mood, very sad. Being the romantic that Balanchine was, he fell in love many times—perhaps not love but infatuation, the excitement. Balanchine was open with Papa, knowing it would go no further. Papa never disclosed the matter—neither to me nor Mama.

My mother understood the ballet. After watching me work with Balanchine, Massine, Fokine, Nijinska—all those great masters—she developed such wonderful taste that Balanchine, when he was creating a ballet for me, would ask her: "Mama, do you like it?" He loved Mama very much. Balanchine was alone when he left Russia; he had no family. He loved Mama and Papa because he found a family. He saw the seed of a family so close to each other, and that is why he gave his love to us, because we had a very strong family tie. When I was married, even then Balanchine loved to be surrounded with us because he felt the family feeling. It was his family.

I knew Balanchine when I was such a little girl, and I knew him when I became a grownup, and I knew him when I married. I think that Balanchine had so much; he was like an ocean. I think the waves kept coming to him, waves of extraordinary creativity, always alive like an ocean. He would not rest; he was always interested in a new phase, new ways to express. . . .

I worked with Balanchine, studied with him, took his lessons—and never in my life was I hurt by his instruction. We used to go for lunch on Sunday, and then we would go to the Foyer de la Danse—Kopeikine, Mama, and myself—and Balanchine would give me pas de bourrées, how to do them like pearls, as in *The Dying Swan.* He would look at the feet, look at the legs, look at the arms and the stature of the body. Every time I came to New York, I would run to the School of American Ballet and look forward to his classes.

I've never had any tendonitis from taking classes with him. I improved immensely, I had more speed, I had more authority, and—more important— I had a freedom of the body from the speed. Usually, when you do precise things, speedy things, your body gets cramped. But with Balanchine, it was absolute harmony of arms and body while your feet were doing those extraordinary little Scarlatti-like details. After three weeks of study with him, in the fourth week you realized that you had made a step forward, you could do more than you could before.

I think Balanchine loved teaching. I think he brought a great deal of enthusiasm to his teaching, and he was proud when the teaching was successful. I think he did not like to teach people who did not understand him. Let's face it—not everybody understands. I think he loved teaching people who understood what he was after. I remember he was teaching in Paris in 1947 for six months. At first it was only me; then when Maria Tallchief arrived it was Tallchief and Alexandre Kalioujny. What extraordinary improvement Kalioujny made thanks to Balanchine. He was very well taught by

Preobrajenska, and he was a good dancer. But he became extraordinary from what he learned from Balanchine. I have no patience with choreographers who say that they don't like to teach because it takes away from their creativity. It's not the creativity that will be taken away. It is that they don't like it, and they don't know it. Balanchine knew what he was doing.

For my gala *Giselle* in 1947, Balanchine rehearsed me every single day. *Giselle* has nothing to do with the Balanchine style, but I improved it by working with him. Leon Vayar, the French critic, said there were three Giselles in the world: Pavlova, Spessivtseva, and Toumanova. And that was after I worked with Balanchine. I became Tamara Toumanova after I worked with Balanchine. He was so extraordinary that from him I could go to another choreographer and work with him. And another one . . .

Balanchine had a tremendous admiration for the great masters, for immortal ballets. Balanchine was intelligent enough to realize that the choreography of *Giselle* was extraordinary. He was not blind. Art has no boundaries; it goes beyond personal feelings. Balanchine was enough of a brilliant man and a gentleman that he would never deny that it was a masterpiece. I know very well that we discussed the music, and very often he would say—"Oh, no, no, I—no, I don't want it." Then you would say, "But, Georgi Melitonovich, there is a melody, there is a melody, that takes your heart." "No, no, no."

Not just Adolphe Adam's music for *Giselle,* but any composer. Let's say Glazounov, and Balanchine would say, "No, no, Tamarichka, you know—no, it's nice, no, no." I would say, "Georgi Melitonovich, really. Look at that magnificent sound, this wonderful melody with which you can create." "No, no, no." But I don't think he could deny the truth. Balanchine loved beautiful things. He once brought me a gift from South America, a cardinal amethyst of such beauty. Even when he invited people to dinner, he presented his own world of living; he loved showing them a quality that was so important for him.

Balanchine was very proud of his work on Broadway. He took me to see *On Your Toes, I Married an Angel, Cabin in the Sky,* and *Where's Charley?* As I have said, Balanchine liked to play. Neither on Broadway or in the movies did Balanchine work only to make money. He adored to do movies and shows. In 1936 I was too young and inexperienced to see *On Your Toes,* so I was a bit shocked. Ray Bolger was extraordinary and Tamara Geva was marvelous in it. No one before or since has presented a star as he did Zorina. What Balanchine gave Vera Zorina and myself was the appearance of the sun and the moon. Both.

Balanchine had so many ideas that his collaborators gratefully took his suggestions for costuming and lighting. Larry Hart was dear to me, a fantastic gentleman with ideas and a sharp intelligence, and he worshipped Balanchine. Balanchine was very proud of his work on Broadway and in movies.

I remember very well in New York in 1941 the excitement of Easter coming. I had come back from Australia with the Colonel de Basil Original Ballet Russe, and Balanchine did *Balustrade* for me. It was my gift. I was dancing at the Fifty-first Street Theater, and Balanchine and Stravinsky and Tchelitchew came to every one of my performances. I danced *Swan Lake, Choreartium,* and *Symphonie Fantastique.*

We were in the third week of the season, and they came to my dressing room and said, "Tamarichka, we decided that we want to give you a gift, a diamond necklace." I look at them and said, "Well, that is fantastic." Then they said, "The diamond necklace will be a ballet of the Violin Concerto of Stravinsky. Tchelitchew will do the costumes and scenery, and you will be the one for whom it will be created." I said, "My goodness, this is more than a diamond necklace. This is beyond anything I could ever dream." We began to rehearse the ballet. Balanchine brought the recording of the Dushkin performance. He played my part for me, and he said, "Tamarichka, don't be alarmed by the sound because this is a very special sound, very clear, very pure sound, and you will understand it more when you start rehearsing it."

He called Roman Jasinski and Paul Petroff, and he started to do the choreography for the pas de trois, and you could see the extraordinary lines he would take. It was very sharp, very long, and there were movements that shocked Mama a bit. Georgi Melitonovich would turn to Mama and say, "Mama, Mama, you have bad thoughts in your mind." The choreography was different from any other he had done for me, and quite daring. I was no longer the little girl in *Fastes.* Now I was able to produce what he wanted, and it was very pure at the same time. There was absolutely no expression, which was extraordinary for me because usually I had either a dramatic or sad or coquettish expression. Here there was no expression except that very fine quality of my face, like a moon.

Balanchine said, "I will not call Stravinsky till I finish this number." He said to me, "Don't worry about it that he is not coming. He is dying to come. He wants to put his nose in, but I will not do it until it's done." When the number was done, we went into the big rehearsal room, and Stravinsky came along with many other people, including Tchelitchew. Stravinsky was absolutely enchanted. He said, "George, I think this is the epitome of whatever I thought." He did write in a book that this was the most satisfying ballet in all his career. He went into complete ecstasy.

When Balanchine and Stravinsky were together, they were like two incredible teachers. Balanchine would stand next to little Stravinsky, and they would walk together, Balanchine always saying, "Da, da, da," to him. He never said, "No." It was always, "Ah, ha. Da, da." There was such admiration for Stravinsky in Balanchine. I think that he became like a little boy in Stravinsky's presence.

The final movement of *Balustrade* was created at the School of American Ballet. I was in the second and fourth movements. The time came to have costume fittings, and then I realized what Balanchine meant about the diamond necklace. My costume was full of diamonds and rubies and emeralds. On my head there was a half-moon, a sparkling crescent, and even my shoes were jeweled. Tchelitchew gave me an original sketch for his design. The balustrade itself was white on a black curtain. I was in black. Whatever movements I was doing, you had to figure out what I was doing, and at certain points on opening night, two or three people in the audience shouted, "Ah!" or, "Oh!" because it was a shock. But the ballet was finely made, created magnificently.

At the premiere, Stravinsky conducted the orchestra, and Dushkin played the violin. What I liked about *Balustrade* was that it had a tremendous amount of long movement. Stravinsky's music had a sharpness, but it also had a continuity. Balanchine picked it up beautifully. I had tremendous adagio technique. With hard work, I had high extensions. Balanchine did not use my technical footwork. I think that he wanted to see me more or less like a strange remote being, a statue, not quite alive.

The ballet was performed only three times because my contract ended and I left the company. I went to Denham, and they had no one else to do it. *Balustrade* has been written about as though it were not a success, but that's not true. Although it was not a success in the manner of *Black Swan,* it was an artistic success, which, for me, was more important than anything else. I could not take the ballet with me to Denham because Balanchine wouldn't allow it. And Denham wouldn't want it because it had been done for de Basil. . . .

When I got married in 1944, I didn't invite Mr. Balanchine because he was in New York. Flying was not like it is today, especially in the middle of the war. My husband, Casey Robinson, liked Balanchine immensely, and Balanchine liked Casey very much. But I did not send him an invitation to the wedding because I planned to call him and say that I had been married. I was married in our church here, the Russian-Greek Orthodox church, the Virgin Mary Cathedral. The marriage was very *intime.* When I was standing at the altar after we were pronounced man and wife and receiving congratulations, suddenly I saw Balanchine. He came up to me and kissed me and congratulated Casey, even kissed him. I said, "Georgi Melitonovich, how incredible you are here." And he said, "How can I miss the marriage of my daughter?" . . .

One day I got a call from Audart, the *régisseur* of the Opéra ballet who said, "Miss Toumanova, you are on the *tableaux.* You must not have looked. Balanchine is waiting for you at the rehearsal." I said, "What are we rehearsing?" And he said *Le Palais de Cristal.* I said, "I never heard of *Le Palais de*

Cristal." "The ballet of Balanchine." Balanchine had never said a word about it, not one word. So I dressed quickly, took a taxi, got to the Opéra, dressed in my dressing room, went upstairs, and Balanchine was standing with his hand on his hip and looking at me with a half smile.

I said to him in French, "Please excuse me, Maître, I am late," and in Russian, "You didn't say anything to me about *Palais de Cristal.* I don't know what it is." He said, "You don't have to know. You just start rehearsing." We rehearsed the pas de deux of the Second Movement, which he called "the black diamond." When the ballet opened, we gave only two performances because it was already July at the end of the season. On opening night when I finished, lying back on my partner's knee, bending back to the audience, I was met with a dead silence. I said to myself, "My God, did they like it or not?" Suddenly, the whole audience just screamed. It was one of Balanchine's most extraordinary ballets.

Of course I see it differently today because I always see it in the original scenery and costumes. After that first rehearsal I said to Balanchine, "Why on earth didn't you tell me?" And he said, "Oh, I don't tell you everything." He made that pas de deux in not more than two rehearsals. It went very fast, very fast. My partner was Roger Ritz. He was very tall and a very good partner—very elegant. And Balanchine was delighted. When he finished the pas de deux, he said, "You know, Tamarichka, that's nice, that's very nice." He was very pleased. But I never saw him displeased when I created his ballets. . . .

—from *Ballet Review,* Fall 1996

LÉONIDE MASSINE

Massine (1896–1979) enjoyed the greatest success of any dancer-choreographer of the 1920s and 1930s. He was given his start by Diaghilev, succeeding Nijinsky as ballet master for the Ballets Russes, for whom his first real triumph was La Boutique Fantasque *(1919). Many of his most popular works were in the* demi-caractère *mode—*Le Beau Danube, Le Tricorne *(he danced the Miller),* Gaîté Parisienne *(he was the Peruvian)—but he also ventured into large-scale ballets danced to symphonic music:* Les Présages, *to Tchaikovsky's Fifth; Berlioz's* Symphonie Fantastique; Choreartium, *to Brahms's Fourth;* Seventh Symphony *(Beethoven). His career was on the wane in the late thirties and forties, but was restored by his choreography and his performance in the 1948 Michael Powell film* The Red Shoes *(see page 875). (Three years later, he starred in Powell's follow-up film,* The Tales of Hoffmann.*)*

LÉONIDE MASSINE
Meeting Diaghilev

One evening in December, after a performance of *Swan Lake,* a friend of mine, Mikhail Savitsky, a member of the Bolshoi *corps de ballet,* came backstage to tell me that Sergei Diaghilev had been in the audience. He had seen me dancing my tarantella, and wanted to meet me. I was naturally very flattered to be told this, as I had heard wonderful accounts of Diaghilev's company, and of the brilliant work of its leading male dancer, Nijinsky. I told Savitsky that I would be delighted to meet Diaghilev, and an appointment was made for the next afternoon at the Metropole Hotel. When I walked into the ornate, gilded lobby I felt as though I were entering a larger-than-life world of fantasy. Timidly I made my way through rows of potted palms and porters in gold braid. When I asked for Diaghilev at the reception desk, I was shown into the lift and a few moments later was knocking at his door. It was opened by a young Italian with curly black hair and beady eyes. He smiled when I gave him my name and showed me into a formal little sitting room. "M. Diaghilev will be with you in a moment," he told me.

I sat down stiffly on a plush sofa. The Italian disappeared into another room, and I heard him say, "Signor Baron, Signor Miassin is here to see you." A moment later Diaghilev appeared in a dressing gown. At first glance he appeared tall and imposing, but when I stood up I realized that he was only of medium height, but that he had an unusually large head and broad shoulders. The next thing I noticed was the streak of silver white hair, like a feather, over his forehead. Peering at me through his monocle, he looked to me like a creature from another world.

He told me that he had enjoyed my performances in *Don Quixote* and *Swan Lake.* He was looking for someone to dance the title role in his new production, *La Légende de Joseph,* and he thought I might be suitable. If his choreographer, Michel Fokine, approved of his choice, he would want me to join the company immediately. Before I had a chance to reply, Diaghilev explained that he was leaving Moscow in two days' time, and that he had to have a quick decision. He told me to go away and think it over, and to come back and see him again the following day.

When I left the hotel I was dazed and bewildered. I went straight to the Theatre School, where I told my friends about Diaghilev's offer. They urged me not to leave Moscow. Kostrovsky in particular thought it would be foolish of me to give up my theatrical career just when I was beginning to get established. He pointed out that if I joined Diaghilev's company I would lose several months of valuable experience at the Maly Theatre, where I was actually being seriously considered for the role of Romeo in the forthcoming production of Shakespeare's *Romeo and Juliet.*

I spent the next day in a state of restless indecision, at once excited by the possibility of going to Germany, France, and England, and yet afraid of interrupting my career in Russia. Although my engagement with Diaghilev's company would last for only a few months, I felt that even in that short period I might ruin my chances in Moscow. When I went back to the Metropole I had definitely decided to refuse Diaghilev's offer.

But as I walked through the lobby, I felt a sense of uncertainty take hold of me again. Going up in the lift I had to keep reminding myself of the importance of my work at the Maly, of the advice my friends had given me, of my future as an actor. By the time I reached Diaghilev's room, I had convinced myself once more that I was making the right decision. I walked in; he peered at me through his monocle, smiled, and waited for me to speak. I was just about to tell him that I could not accept his offer when, almost without realizing it, I heard myself say, "Yes, I shall be delighted to join your company."

When I look back on that moment in Diaghilev's room at the Metropole Hotel, I still cannot comprehend why, almost involuntarily, I changed my decision at the crucial moment. The only possible explanation seems to be that some unknown power, some emanation from the subconscious, took control of me, as it has done at other times when I have had to make vital decisions. It may be some quirk in my nature that causes me suddenly to change my plans after I think I have made a carefully considered decision. I was eighteen at the time.

After leaving Diaghilev, I wrote to my parents, telling them what had happened, and assuring them that I would be returning to Moscow in a few months' time. I then went to the Theatre School to say good-bye to my friends, telling them too that I would soon be back. I had no time to take a farewell of my godmother, for I had to leave Moscow the following evening for St. Petersburg. I travelled overnight in a plushy first-class compartment with Diaghilev and his Italian valet, whose name was Beppe. As I listened to Diaghilev describing Fokine's choreography, I sensed that he was preparing me for an entirely new concept of ballet. He talked about a new culture emerging from our old academic traditions, of a conception of art which was essentially his own, a fusion of music, dance, painting, poetry, and drama. Although I could not quite understand how this fusion was to be brought about, I was excited by the idea of it. Listening to Diaghilev's quiet, persuasive voice, I was impressed by the conviction and self-confidence with which he explained his ideas, but I began to wonder if I could ever reach his high aesthetic standards, and what I personally could contribute to this new form of culture of which he spoke.

The next day, in St. Petersburg, I was sent to Fokine for my official audition. I felt very nervous as I entered his room, where the only splash of colour among the carefully arranged white furniture was a mural of the Nine Muses by Guilio Romano. Fokine himself was a handsome man in his early thirties, immaculately dressed in a well-tailored English suit. There was not a hint of emotion on his sculptured, classically featured face as he greeted me with measured politeness. His manner remained distant and formal as he asked me, in an authoritative voice, to reproduce the positions in the Romano mural. For a few moments I studied the various poses, then did my best to interpret them. He made no comment, but asked me to demonstrate my "elevation." I looked round the room, wondering if there was room for me to jump, and noticed a wooden chair whose back was about three feet high. Asking him to place it in the centre of the room for me, I stood about a foot away and leaped over it, clearing it easily. Fokine smiled faintly, and told me my audition was over.

Next day Diaghilev informed me that Fokine had approved of his choice, and that I was definitely to dance the title role in *La Légende de Joseph*. During that one day we spent in St. Petersburg Diaghilev took me to a studio to be photographed as Joseph. Dressed in a white tunic designed by Léon Bakst, I was first made to pose in a kneeling position. With only a dim recollection of the story of Joseph, I attempted to assume the look and attitude of a young shepherd boy. Fokine, who was also present, suggested that I should lean back on my heels with my hands in my lap, and not look directly at the camera. For a moment, as I shifted my position awkwardly under the glare of the photographer's lights, I had a glimpse of Joseph's character, and felt I could understand his fear and uncertainty when brought before Potiphar. But as more and more photographs were taken I began to relax and assume the desired poses more easily, and by the end of the session I almost felt confident that I would be able to interpret the part adequately.

In the train to Cologne next day Diaghilev told me his plans for *La Légende de Joseph*. The libretto was by Hugo von Hofmannsthal and Count Harry Kessler, and Richard Strauss had written the music for it. This was his first ballet, and it was obviously going to be a most ambitious production, on a far higher artistic level than anything I had ever had the opportunity of seeing in Moscow. I once more felt intimidated, and began to wonder if I had the qualifications needed for such a demanding role.

Everything Diaghilev said about the ballet was illuminated by his vast knowledge of art and music. When he described to me José-Maria Sert's setting for the production, he explained that it had been inspired by the paintings of the great Venetian artists of the Renaissance period, Veronese and Tintoretto. Biblical stories like this one of Joseph were, he said, among their favourite themes, and they interpreted them on an heroic scale. I was not quite sure what "Renaissance" meant, but I was thrilled by the fervour and conviction with which he spoke, and by his complete dedication to the realization of his artistic ideals. Sitting opposite him in the train, I noticed the way his small dark eyes brightened as he talked of his plans, not as if to a new acquaintance, but more like a friend eager to share with me his hopes and fears for the future. He told me that he wanted the music and choreography in *La Légende de Joseph* to portray the architectural grandeur and monumental quality of the Venetian paintings. Listening to him I decided that he was the most cultured and yet most modest person I had ever met. In spite of his authoritative air and commanding presence he had an underlying humility and integrity which, I felt, derived from his total commitment to his art. I began to feel that all my past experience had been negligible, and that I was now embarking on an entirely new career. I felt unsure of myself, but I was exhilarated at the prospect of working with such a man as Diaghilev. As I listened, absorbing every word he said, I made a mental note to go and see the paintings of Titian, Veronese, and Tintoretto, to learn about Palladian architecture, to find out who Brunelleschi was. By the end of the journey I had begun to feel more at ease with Diaghilev. He no longer seemed as fantastic and as unreal as when I first met him. Except for his monocle and streak of white hair, his appearance was elegant but unremarkable. He wore a dark, well-cut but rather shabby English suit, and I was surprised to see that there were holes in the soles of his shoes.

—from *My Life in Ballet,* 1968

Alexandra Danilova
Massine

One of the most beloved ballerinas of the twentieth century, Alexandra Danilova (1903–1997) was trained in the Imperial Ballet School in St. Petersburg and performed at the Maryinsky until 1924, when she, George Balanchine, and several others escaped Bolshevik Russia for the West. She danced for Diaghilev until his death in 1929 and then for de Basil's Ballets Russes de Monte Carlo and the rival Ballet Russe de Monte Carlo. She was perhaps best known for Swanilda in Coppélia, *and a series of character roles created for her by Massine, most famously the Glove Seller in* Gaîté Parisienne. *Among the ballets Balanchine—whose "unofficial wife" she was at one time—created for her were* Apollo *and* Night Shadow *(later* La Sonnambula*), and she collaborated with him on versions of* Raymonda *and* Coppélia. *She also appeared in several musical comedies, including* Song of Norway *and* Oh, Captain! *From 1964 until she retired in 1989 she taught at Balanchine's School of American Ballet. At the height of her fame, she was admired worldwide for her gorgeous legs, her wit, and her glamour.*

I had many partners in the de Basil company, but as far as the public was concerned, I had only one—Massine. Everything we danced together was a terrific success. We were paired on the stage for life. As a partner, Massine was terrible. He wasn't interested in anybody else. He considered lifting a ballerina or supporting her in pirouettes not part of his job and acted as if he were doing her a favor. Like Nijinsky, like Eglevsky, he never really wanted to dance with a partner; he preferred to dance by himself. Apart from Fokine's ballets, Massine danced only his own choreography. There were duets in his ballets, but no important adagios, no pas de deux in the classical sense.

Massine always gave himself the best parts in his ballets. He was always beautifully dressed onstage. Well, I thought, why not? I didn't object. He was a first-class dancer, very passionate, expressive, with a style of his own, in some ways more a modern dancer than a classical dancer.

He was a little bit jealous of me in *Le Beau Danube,* of all the applause I used to receive after my entrance. I became famous as the Street Dancer, and my fame in the role annoyed him. Finally, we had a conversation: I told him, "Mr. Massine, we dance together; this is your choreography. So my success, it's your success—it's your ballet." He didn't see that. But after a time, he didn't bother about it anymore. If Massine was angry with me, he would pinch me on the stage while I sat on his knee or while he supported me in arabesque. I wouldn't flinch or say a word.

Offstage, we had nothing in common. I think we didn't really want to know each other. He stopped trying to woo me, the way he had in the Diaghilev company, by making erotic choreography for me. But he knew that I was a good match for him as a performer—the other ballerinas in the company were children.

Artistically, we understood each other perfectly. So when, in 1937, Massine asked me to join him in the Ballet Russe de Monte Carlo, directed by Sergei Denham, I went with pleasure.

Massine was, I think, a genius, but not as great a genius as Balanchine. Massine loved, he hated, he did everything in the extreme. By nature, he was a real artist, with volcanic emotions. He was like a monk in his dedication, ascetic and rather violent. Working with him, we were dancing for the Grand Inquisitor, who tortured people in the name of God. He had no understanding or forgiveness for dancers who couldn't do what he asked. Every dancer has his or her own best movement—one is better on the toes, another in allegro, another in adagio. Balanchine, if he wanted to make a fast variation, would cast a fast dancer. The choreography, the actual steps, depended on how you could interpret what he showed you. But Massine didn't care who you were or what you could do. If he thought you should dance adagio, you had to do it, regardless. If you turned best to the right, he would give you pirouettes to the left. When he made *Zéphyr et Flore,* he decided that Zéphyr had to jump. Zéphyr was Lifar, who didn't have a par- ticularly good jump, but Massine made him jump anyway. In *Les Matelots,* I had to dance so much on the toes, more than we ever had danced on the toes in Russia. There was a lot of jumping on pointe. Massine was unmerciful, and he couldn't have cared less. If he had an idea, he would absolutely break the dancer before he would change the step.

The result was that in Balanchine's ballets, everybody was at his best, while Massine's ballets sometimes suffered because they were miscast. . . .

Balanchine always worked very fast in rehearsals—the choreography would just pour out of him. But for Massine it was like having a baby: very hard and slow. He would pace back and forth, trying to think what to do next. He never smiled or joked during rehearsals, and he didn't like his dancers having a rest. If he could have, he would have rehearsed us for three hours straight, or longer. Massine always carried in his arms a thick book, given to him by Diaghilev. In it were mysterious symbols and writing, notations for old choreography. Massine kept his eyes on this precious book. No one was allowed to come near it, and God forbid if you touched it.

There was no softness in him. When Massine saw a woman, he had to have her. His adagio was always a conquest—the man conquering the woman, or the woman conquering the man—not a song of love, like Balanchine's. With Massine, there was no romance, not even in his ballets.

There was something dry and pedantic about his attitude toward art. When he began choreographing symphonies, he took up studying composition, because he wasn't musically very well educated. . . .

Massine's strength as a choreographer lay in the way he used the ensemble. His ballets were filled with rituals and patterns. He was very fond of hand movements and poses—hands crossed above the head or across the chest—and a lot of port de bras in groups. One group would run on and move the arms, then another three or four dancers would run on and form another group, making a pattern. He was obsessed with arrangements, creating a design on the stage. For that reason, I liked his symphonic ballets—*The Seventh Symphony,* to Beethoven, and *Rouge et Noir,* a battle of colors, to Shostakovich. I asked him what the story was behind *Rouge et Noir,* and he told me that white was for Russia, black for fascists, and red for communists. The most powerful part of this ballet was a solo for Alicia Markova, a cry—she bourréed all around the stage, changing the positions of her arms, of her body. She was weeping without tears, with her soul.

After Massine studied music composition, I could see that he improved tremendously. He found more phrases in the music to choreograph in his way, for three or four people. Massine's choreography was musical, but not to perfection the way Balanchine's was. Balanchine heard everything; he didn't miss a note. Certainly, Massine heard the music correctly, but I don't think he heard all the parts. Balanchine's steps sometimes made a counterpoint to the music, but not Massine's. Dancing Balanchine's ballets, one has to count, to be right on the music. But in Massine's ballets one could go by ear. I wouldn't say that Massine's choreography was less musical, but it was less musically detailed.

His steps were strange and sometimes awkward. What made Massine's choreography interesting was its fantastic rhythm. The rhythm was all in the feet, the way it is in Spanish dancing, which fascinated him. Where Balanchine would create a rhythm with beats and pointe work, all kinds of pas de bourrées, Massine would use heel work instead. His steps came from character dancing: the farruca, the tarantella—always ticky-ticky footwork, the talking feet.

Massine himself was not a truly classical dancer. His dancing was *demi-caractère,* and that was his style as a choreographer, too. But Balanchine's choreography was always classical: he borrowed steps from character dancing and applied them to classical ballet. Massine did just the reverse: he took classical ballet technique and applied it to character dancing. Today, Jerome Robbins does what Massine did. Even when Massine choreographed a complicated variation on the toes, like the one I danced in *Les Matelots,* it was still character dancing.

Massine's choreography depended a lot on style, and so today it looks a little bit *démodé.* His ballets are like a beautiful carpet that has faded; the years have washed away the colors. People today don't know how to dance Massine ballets, because they don't know how to dance *demi-caractère.* In the revivals I have seen, the dancers were not educated enough in character and folk dances to interpret their roles; they didn't grasp the style.

It is difficult now for people to understand how important Massine was. He widened the horizon. The 1930s belonged to him, and he helped prepare the way for what came after.

—from *Choura,* with Holly Brubach, 1986

Massine agreed to Positano for the filming, "subject to an appropriate business arrangement being made" with his London lawyer, who turned out to be Sir John Witt, chairman of the trustees of the National Portrait Gallery and son of the creator of the famous Witt Library and collector of old master drawings. We spoke on the phone. Sir John, for all I know, may have been a charming and cultured man, but my recollection after nearly thirty years is that I had never been spoken to with such patronizing condescension. If I had been the *News of the World* after a salacious story, he could not have been more disdainful. It may, of course, have been that Massine caused him so much trouble with his endless litigation and legendary meanness that Witt was trying to put me off getting involved in any way. I mentioned the fifty-guinea fee we were offering, and Witt said immediately that it was quite unacceptable. After much heart-searching, for I knew Massine to be rich and rapacious, while Sokolova and Karsavina were struggling to make ends meet, I agreed to double the figure to one hundred pounds. I had to make a special case to the BBC, who were far from convinced; Massine had appeared once on *Monitor* in an item produced by Margaret Dale, and had caused much trouble. The results had not been thought worth it, but I was getting desperate about the international element. However, nothing was agreed in time for me to link the visit to Italy with the Monte Carlo trip.

Silence fell again from Positano, and now a new element entered the argument. I was not able to afford to take a BBC film crew with me on these trips and had to hire locally. It was a chancy business; we never knew who or what we would get. At least in Paris the cameraman, Jean Crommelynck, had known what I was up to. His brother was the famous printmaker who worked for Picasso and all the other leading French painters when they produced prints or lithographs. Monte Carlo had not been satisfactory—a news cameraman with a bad case of the zoom lens—and now we were begging a crew from Italian television, the RAI, in Rome. Hirings of this kind were done under the Eurovision exchange agreement and not considered a high priority, just a courtesy, and the BBC was notoriously uncooperative with other networks' requests. When at last Massine volunteered a date, no crew was available in Rome or Naples; when the crew was available, it was the height of the August holidays, and I could find no accommodation in Positano. It seemed an endless vicious circle.

Meanwhile, after long silences, I received a peremptory telegram from Lifar: *"Vous accorderai interview sur Diaghilev 19 août à Venise à 9 heures cimetière St Michel. Salutations, Lifar."* I knew that Lifar visited Venice every year on the anniversary of Diaghilev's death and had a service said at the grave by a Greek Orthodox priest, there being no Russian church in Venice. I found the idea attractive, since Lifar had been with Diaghilev when he died in Venice in August 1929. Eventually, after a sheaf of telegrams, the pieces fitted; Massine in Positano on the seventeenth, Lifar in Venice on the nineteenth, and each with a day before to plan the interview. Crews and travel were booked, and in desperation I asked Massine if I could stay with him— my telegram ended "regret intrusion!" He agreed.

Massine's Positano home, three lumps of rock half a mile off the coast called the Isole dei Galli, had been purchased in the 1920s, for a sum equivalent to £5,000. They were later to be bought by Rudolf Nureyev. Massine returned every year, except during the war, and had made strenuous attempts to get some kind of arts centre going there. Everyone who knew him told me of his "projects." I set off on Sunday the fifteenth, flying to Naples, from where I made my way to the Circumvesuviana Railway to get a train to Sorrento, which met a bus connection to Positano, or so the Italian travel authorities in London had assured me. Of course, nothing worked; the plane was late, the train rescheduled, and the bus was on strike. I had to take a taxi over the mountains from Sorrento to Positano, arriving an hour and a half after the time I had suggested. I had no real rendezvous point—I just went down to the waterfront and hoped I would be discovered. It was the height of Ferragosto, and half Naples seemed to be on the front at the Buca di Bacco or Chez Black. I carried my suitcase down to the end of the jetty and sat on it, hoping something would happen.

In the end, after an hour or so, just as night was falling, it did. A strapping young man in the tiniest of bathing slips came up and said, in curiously accented French, *"Êtes-vous le monsieur de la télévision?"* I agreed I was, whereupon he seized my suitcase and walked into the sea, holding the case at shoulder height. Just before he and the case disappeared under the waves, he flung it into a small motor launch in which two girls were sitting. He clambered aboard and started the engine. He brought the boat alongside the quay and I jumped in. The slimmer of the two girls introduced herself in American-accented English as Massine's daughter, Tanya. The plump girl with her was a Parisian friend. We set off for the islands. It was now quite dark and we had no lights—the coastline of the Sorrento peninsula glittered behind us; ahead the shape of the larger of the three islands loomed like

Böcklin's painting which inspired Rachmaninov's *Isle of the Dead.* It was in total darkness, and Tanya explained that the generator had failed. We scrambled ashore at a small harbour, and followed a steep path up the hillside to a low building on a terrace. Voices could be heard shouting inside. We continued beyond the house along a path high above the sea to a small hut. Tanya flung the door open and said, "The guesthouse!" In the gloom I found a candle, and lit it. The room was about twelve feet square, with a bare tiled floor. There was a single bed, a window, and a washbasin whose runaway pipe stopped a foot above the floor. No water came from the taps. I sat on the bed and wondered what on earth I was getting into. Eventually I found a jug of water, freshened up, and changed from my travelling clothes.

I returned gingerly along the path to the terrace, where a group of people was sitting by two oil lamps; in the middle was a darkly attractive middle-aged woman, whom I somehow knew had been a dancer, and a Russian dancer at that. This was Massine's second wife, the mother of the girl who had met me. She had been in the de Basil company, and later became an administrator. She lived in Paris, while Massine lived in Germany, with a German companion, but obviously they still got together for holidays. Tanya, the daughter, was married to a German diplomat whose brother, Thilo von Watzdorf, I knew, since he was involved with the Diaghilev sales at Sotheby's. The Watzdorfs were very grand, and the mother of the two boys was, I believe, a member of the Luxembourg royal family. All this I pieced together that evening, with the help of the French girl, Catherine, who was, it was explained, running away from an unhappy love affair. The muscular boy who had collected my case was Belgian, a semi-literate refugee from a circus, who had been taken on to help an English puppeteer who was also staying on the island.

We sat on the terrace and talked. Everyone seemed in a high state of tension and exasperation: was it the failure of the generator, my arrival, or something else? Suddenly a figure with a lit candle and a long, old-fashioned peignoir crossed the terrace behind us. No one took any notice. She was crying noisily. "Oh, that's only Mademoiselle," said Tanya. I nodded. It was like *La Sonnambula.* We talked and talked, and drank a very rough local white wine. Eventually some raw octopus in olive oil was produced, then a Spanish omelette. Everyone tucked in. There was still no sign of Massine. I did not dare to ask. Then at the end of the meal I looked up, aware of someone else, and behind the glare of the oil lamp I saw two dark, glowing eyes, and the unmistakable face of the great man. He was polite, even charming, apologized for the confusion, said he would see me in the morning, and disappeared.

It was a perfect summer night, and now that I was used to the semidarkness the sheer beauty and romanticism of the setting became obvious. After dinner four of us—Tanya, Catherine, the Belgian boy, and I—went back down to the harbour and swam in the velvety darkness broken only by the luminous phosphorescence of the water. As we dived and splashed, a million colours glittered. I had never seen this effect before, though, of course, I remembered it from *The Ancient Mariner*. Would Massine tell me his story tomorrow? For the moment nothing could have been more romantic—Tanya was very beautiful. Voices were calling from the house in Russian, answered in French. I remembered Benois's family scrapbooks of the Crimea before the Revolution; the sense of history and continuity and Russianness was overwhelming. I can still sense the headiness of the night air and the glow of the lights on the coast as I wandered back to my curious room, and slept like a child in my narrow bed.

I was awoken by the sun streaming into the room, an easy task, since it turned out to have only three and a half walls, something I had not been aware of the night before. The fourth wall extended oddly from the ceiling to within two feet of the floor; then there was a gap through which the sea flashed, a hundred feet below. I wandered over to the house, where the pup-peteer produced some coffee and filled in some more details about who was who amongst this curious company. During the course of the day every one of those on the island got me alone to tell me of their troubles, and how hopeless and unstable all the others were. The puppeteer had been sent for by Massine for some reason, and was now a kind of prisoner, doing odd jobs, madly in love with the Belgian boy, though I did not think he was getting much in return. Tanya's marriage was on the rocks, and she was going to have to start again, unsure as to whether in Europe or America. Her French friend was a mass of giggles and tears. Obsessed with her appearance, she was overweight and kept collapsing in sobs or laughing hysterically. The Belgian boy seemed to have the least problems, living in a simple, semi-gestural world of his own. He could hardly read or write, and was often sent on errands and ended up in the wrong place. It was all quite dotty, and somehow quintessentially Russian. We toured the property; the main island was covered with unfinished buildings. There was part of an open-air theatre, a sort of barn—studios, I suppose. Of the other two islands, one was inhabited only by goats and the other had a boatshed.

At mid-morning Mademoiselle gave me a message: Monsieur Massine would see me at 2:30. She then proceeded to explain how awful he was to her, and how she could not go on as his unofficial secretary. At luncheon, where again Massine did not join us, there was a great deal of shouting. It appeared that Massine's current lady friend was in Positano, claiming her rights to visit. Madame Massine left the island, and was not seen until the next day. Although the generator had been fixed, no food of any kind was brought back by the boat; we once again ate raw octopus and Spanish omelette. I can still hear the slapping sound of the octopus being beaten on the steps of the terrace, to tenderize it.

Massine was formal, but very straightforward. There was much he wanted to say, and he had prepared it. In fact, the following day's interview came out so pat that I think he had almost memorized it. But how much would he say of his own relations with Diaghilev? I had always felt that because of Massine's quickness and intelligence, Diaghilev had been more in love with him even than with Nijinsky. He had been more companionable; he was also a very good musician. They had gone through the worst of times together during the war, dogged by money problems, but nevertheless creating works such as *Parade* and *Pulcinella, Boutique Fantasque* and *The Three-cornered Hat*. Then suddenly, in 1920, Massine had walked out on Diaghilev, without any warning, to marry the English dancer Vera Savina. It was the greatest betrayal. Diaghilev had never spoken of it to any of the people I had got to know, though Lydia Sokolova typically, staying in the same hotel as Diaghilev shortly afterwards, but on a higher floor, had overheard Diaghilev on the terrace below telling Misia Sert of his hopelessness, aimlessness, and sense of loss. Yet in the end the result was creatively remarkable. Diaghilev turned back, first to the past, and staged *The Sleeping Beauty,* and then developed Nijinsky's sister Bronislava's choreography. Though she only stayed a short time, she created at least two perfect ballets, *Les Noces,* the unforgettable evocation of a timeless Russia, and *Les Biches,* which set the whole new French mood of the company in the 1920s. Massine had been closer to Diaghilev than any of his other choreographers, for example Fokine or Balanchine. How much would he say?

The following day the crew arrived from Rome; we all dutifully ate our octopus and omelette. Madame Massine returned, saying that she had invited twenty-six to lunch the next day, and we went off to film. As we walked out onto the terrace in the blazing sunlight, Massine turned to me and said, in a voice of real fierceness, "You will ask me no questions whatever about the circumstances of my first marriage."

Afterwards, as we made to depart, with a certain embarrassment, the puppeteer handed me a piece of paper. It was a bill, for the expenses incurred by having me to stay: £7 10s per night for the room (a good room at the Waldorf at that time cost £4 17s 6d) and 2,000 lire per meal, plus the cost of sending the boat for me and for the film crew. The battle raged between the BBC and Sir John Witt for several months, and the file is full of indignant memoranda from both sides. In the end I think we paid half—no one ever got anything free from Massine. We had a long, amiable correspondence afterwards, about his wanting me to make a whole series of television programmes about his system of choreographic notation. The BBC was, in my view quite rightly, not interested. I saw Massine for the last time a year or two later at Barons Court tube station, buying a two-shilling underground ticket with a twenty-pound note. It seemed a wonderfully appropriate image.

—from *Speaking of Diaghilev*, 1997

AGNES DE MILLE
Cleopatra

The daughter of writer-director William de Mille and niece of Cecil B. De Mille, Agnes de Mille (1905–1993) forged a major career for herself as dancer, choreographer, and writer. Her best-known ballets were Rodeo *(1942) and the 1948* Fall River Legend *(Lizzie Borden), but her great fame came in musical comedy: the revolutionary* Oklahoma! *(which ran for five years),* One Touch of Venus, Carousel, Brigadoon, Gentlemen Prefer Blondes, *and others. Perhaps even more talented as a writer than as a choreographer, she has written, among other books, three volumes of dance memoirs—*Dance to the Piper; Speak to Me, Dance with Me; *and* And Promenade Home—*and a loving biography of her idol Martha Graham.*

1010 de Mille Drive
April 13, 1934

Dearest Mum,

Things get thicker and thicker, but not, on the whole, more satisfactory. I wear my feet out tramping, tramping, tramping over the cement from the costume department to the makeup, to the music, to the business offices, to the still galleries, to the stage, and back to the costumes. I suppose this is unavoidable with affairs in such confusion, but the waste of energy is distressing and exhausting.

I don't know who countermands orders, or if Cecil knows what is happening and watches to see if I can fight my way through, or whether he is too busy to notice. But I've been most deliberately served with procrastination. I've been sent to rehearse in the studio carpenter shops, where the electric saws splitting wood make it impossible to hear a piano. On my protesting strongly, I was put in an empty set (by Prince) with no piano and no space. The costume sketches have never been prepared, the scenic designs never attempted. No music is forthcoming. I've worn myself out walking all day from one department to another, on cement walks, upstairs and down, and always I've met with great courtesy (except from the business manager, Burns, an ex-waiter, and the Boss) and always nothing had been done.

The crux of the matter is that C.B. trusts no one and does not seem to take the deciding voice with expedition and certainty. Yet he insists on okaying every single item from hairpins to the still photographs that are released for my personal publicity, also all estimates of cost. You can imagine the entailed amount of waiting. He must be shown. Cecil always has to see everything finished out and completed: every eyelash drawn on his costume sketches, every muscle, particularly muscles. And if showing him necessitates the use of drapes or props his businessman, Roy Burns, holds up all outlay until C.B.'s OK is obtained.

As far as the cooperation of the other subordinates is concerned, I am being treated like a beloved sister. I get willing, enthusiastic, and friendly help at every hand. But the producer's attitude is not protective.

After our first talk, I have never been able to get his attention sufficiently to make him understand my ideas or get a decision. He has ignored my presence on the set, using the script girl for the setting of business or positions while I, a trained dancer, stand by offering suggestions to deaf ears. He has deferred right over my head to Prince on everything to do with action. He has forbidden me to hire any girls for rehearsal so that I could work out and show him the dances. At the same time he has continually announced his doubts as to the suitableness and effectiveness of my projected numbers, not in private, but in front of any members of his staff who happen to be present when his fears assail him. The psychological effect on me I needn't go into, and on the staff, which has been quick to take its tune from him.

And so we come to last Monday. On Monday afternoon Ralph Jester, the designer, brought a colored girl on the stage in one of the Lastex dresses we made as an experiment. It was not a successful one, and both of us knew it. I begged him not to show the costume, but C.B. insisted, so it was exhibited. Well, he didn't like it a bit (nor did we), or the idea which had prompted me to suggest it (which we did–I wanted something that looked carved in granite, a frieze against which I would be absolutely gorgeous). He knitted his brows; he gnawed his fist; he rocked back and forth in his chair; he snapped out questions at me. What did I think the girls could do in such a rig? He could visualize nothing. I wanted to reply that if he could visualize all they were going to do there would be no need for me around. He cut short all my explanations and continued, "It has neither beauty nor richness nor seductiveness. What will they carry in their hands?"

"Nothing," I said, "they are dancers. They use their hands for dancing."

Well, he bit his lip and shook his head and his face went stone. He demanded to see what they were going to do right then and there. I said he couldn't. I hadn't had one girl to rehearse with, not even for half an hour. (They are paid for rehearsals $5.00, by the day.) Then he ordered me to have the dance ready to show him the next day. I said that was impossible. He was angry. I stood my ground.

Christ, he said, how long was he going to be kept in the dark about what I was up to? I told him he was unreasonable, that no dance director in the world would show his work without rehearsal. Well, he said, jingling the money in his pockets, come over on the barge set and tell him about what I wanted to do there. Over there, he frowned and shook his head before I had completed the first sentence. It wouldn't be effective. I said I was convinced it was excellent else I wouldn't have suggested it. He said he wasn't, and that he was the director. Maybe I'd have my chance someday. So in desperation I myself showed him the steps. "That looks rotten," said Roy Burns, who always stands at the director's elbow whenever I wish to talk to him. "It looks dangerous," said Cecil.

I thought it did, too. It was to be a carpet of naked rolling girls through which stepped daintily the bull on whose back was to be me—naked and rolling. So far have I progressed into the spirit of things.

Well, he asked everybody's ideas on the subject until someone suggested youths pole-vaulting over the back of the bull. Then he'd had enough fun with the conversation and he went off to projection. And yet he says on all occasions that Isadora Duncan and I are the only dancers who have interested him.

I told Burns to get me ten white girls the next day so that I could show the Boss what I meant. He said I could have two girls. I appealed to C.B. He said I could have two, no more (that's $10). And that I could show him any kind of a dance in the world with two girls. "And what," I asked, "if the ten girls all did different things?"

Show them to him separately and he would visualize the assembled effect.

I sat in tears of exasperation and fatigue. Ralph Jester, the designer, kneeled on the floor beside me and begged me to alter the dance to something C.B. would know how to photograph, that he simply had no conception of what I was after. I realized that as I couldn't possibly get what I wanted I must work out something quickly that would suit his needs— and his tastes. Ralph took me out to dinner and was understanding and kind. I stayed up all night and did a new dance.

A frivolous footnote to the above distressing scene was the moment when Cecil, in the middle of the argument, had suddenly yelped, "Ouch!" The leopard which lay beside Cleopatra's bed, drugged on perfume, came to and playfully closed his jaws on Cecil's calf. The beast is kept so doped we all grew careless. Only the thick leather puttee saved Ce's leg. Even so, the teeth grazed the skin. Cecil was amused, but the keeper sternly rebuked his charge and hastened to administer another large dose of Arpège.

Friday: Well, now Colbert is playing sick (or so C.B. claims—indeed she may not be playing; in fact, the poor girl may be gravely ill), but the entire company has to lay off until she is ready to work again. This illness involves a possible loss of $10,000 (as C.B. crossly and ungallantly expresses the situation, "She always was a bitch"), the complete rearrangement of the shooting schedule, and a two-day holdup—which I feel may be good for everyone's nerves. They might be more relaxed by the time we get to the barge.

Yesterday on the set, LeRoy Prince called me over and said, "Agnes, can you find out what goes on about the barge?"

"No," I answered, "I cannot. Not anything."

"Well, shake on it," and we shook. "It's not," he continued, "as though you could call what I do dancing." ("That will be the general criticism," I almost put in, but didn't, Mom, didn't.) "But I do like to know what I'm expected to have ready."

I've made the acquaintance of the bull. He lives in the back lot, tethered in a pen. As I have always been unreasonably afraid of cows, I could see that this chore was going to present unusual tensions. At first I contented myself with hanging over the fence, making sounds that were soothing and, I hoped, bovine. But as matters have deteriorated up on the stages and workshops, I take to going to the back lot for comfort. And, yesterday, before I was aware, I was even climbing up and down his sides and leading him around (Ralph Jester had the courage and kindness to show me how). Since then I've been clinging to his enormous neck daily in a kind of animal sympathy for the strange predicament we both find ourselves in. He is a great dark tawny brute with a strangely subdued manner. It was suggested that he may be an ox. I am no expert, but as far as I can tell from a casual nonagrarian survey, he is indeed a bull, but perhaps he has been in pictures before; I think he's lost his spirit.

Yesterday, they made a camera test of me. Cecil directed. I mustn't move my head to right or left on account of my nose. I mustn't open my mouth on account of my teeth.

My bald Russian pianist (Chaliapin's accompanist, and don't you forget it) has pasted together bits of Rachmaninov and Rimski-Korsakov and I've finally assembled a dance. I don't believe it's very good, but like the bull, I have lost my viewpoint.

A.

Kenmore Drive, Hollywood
April 21, 1934

Dearest Mum,

Plenty has happened since last I wrote, and that's the reason I haven't written. It's like this—

I'm out of the picture. Walked out. And thank God, too! Never in all my life have I been subjected to greater rudeness, humiliation, ignominy, and indifference. Cecil has been unlike Cochran at his worst only in regard to money because, while not generous, he has been scrupulously honest.

Yesterday, the time at last came to show him the number—in full panoply, like a performance, at half-past eight in the evening, after the shooting was over. Two hours before the audition, the makeup department went into high gear. Ignoring bones and organs they started from scratch and worked up something quite new. As Cecil thought of things during the afternoon's shooting he phoned up his orders.

"Pull out her eyebrows." I was straightaway rendered as bald as an egg.

"Grease her hair black." (Roy Burns very shrewdly had withheld authorization for a wig until he learned whether or not I and my dance were to be retained.) "Change her lower lip." Two women and two men worked, sweating, in the little makeup room, with grim mouths. Suddenly the head cosmetician, a Westmore, said, "My God, the body makeup is streaked. Strip her and do it over." He looked stricken. "My God, if de Mille sees that!" The photographing, you will remember, was not to take place for another five days. This was only an audition I was being groomed for. Westmore looked up from my legs with a brown sponge in his hand. "You mustn't mind me, honey. Think of me as a doctor. This has got to be done. I'm the best at it. And there's no time."

There was a good deal of me to be repainted. The costume was extremely brief and affixed to me at strategic points by surgical tape.

"Hurry up. Send her down," came the call. The dressers moaned and swore and hurried. Their hands began to shake. I felt as though I were being prepared for an electrocution.

The costume was beautiful, eight yards of pleated white gauze that fanned around my painted legs exactly like the great skirts on any lotus girl in a sunbaked relief. The skirt was affixed to a jeweled halter around the groin, a wide, flat Egyptian collar, and very large eyes completed the outfit. For obvious reasons, the collar had to be rendered immovable, and this took some doing. Three times the dressers wrenched the jewels off my resisting flesh and adjusted it anew. The third time gouts of blood sprang out all over my back and shoulders. (The trained nurse took this last taping off me. And today I had to be given treatment for second-degree burns. All's well now. I add this detail because I simply can't resist it.) But "Hurry" rang the phone. They wiped the blood away without apology and glued to fresh exposure. And I thought only of pleasing a man who found me not beautiful enough to permit the turning of my head or the opening of my mouth.

Done at last and breathing imprecations and prayers, we bundled over to the stage, where the day's shooting had just ended. Cecil sat in Cleopatra's great black marble throne at the top of a flight of steps, the Sun of Horus behind his head. On his right sat Claudette Colbert, most rebukingly lovely. On his left, the public censor to remind him not to break the decency laws. In serried ranks on either hand, behind, below, ranged the cast and staff and technical force—about fifty. Better so, I thought. Fifty is an audience. No audience I have ever faced has remained altogether unfriendly. The prop boys wheeled a Steinway grand onto the black marble floor. I walked to the end of the great hall and spread my white, winged skirt behind me. It was reflected white in the polished black marble. I knew I could walk beautifully. That's one thing I can do better than almost anyone. I can walk greatly. I started toward the throne and made the first abrupt gesture.

Twice the jeweled collar broke and I had to stop for repairs. The costume department had no conception of the strength in the muscles of a dancer's back.

During the second halt, Cecil spoke quietly through the stillness. "I think the costume department owes you an apology."

"Forgive me, darling," whispered Ralph Jester, who was working at my shoulder with safety pins.

On the third try I got through. I mounted the steps to Cecil's knees and dropped the hibiscus flower I was holding into his hand, Mark Antony's hand.

Then I waited and looked up. An audience? I have faced them in four countries, in every kind of theater, big and little, intelligent and dull, but here I faced a jury. This was a new experience. No one moved. No one breathed. No one held a thought. They all suspended, waiting; a row of plates on a shelf would have made a livelier assemblage. Suddenly, the line of disks stirred, the unfaces focused, the core, the nucleus had gathered life and moved. Like ripples on a pool they circled back the decision.

Cecil was shaking his head. "Oh, no! Oh, no!" he said very slowly. "I am so disappointed! This has nothing. It may be authentic, but it has no excitement, no thrill, no suspense, no sex."

"It had beauty," said Jester, quietly. Cecil wheeled to the censor. "Would that rouse you?"

"It sure wouldn't!" said the censor heartily.

"It wouldn't rouse me," said Cecil, "nor any man. What about the bull? What's happened to the bull?"

I was standing naked under army searchlights and angry.

"What I would like is something like the Lesbian dance in *The Sign of the Cross*," he continued.

"Boy!" said the censor. "If we hadn't had the Christians singing hymns like crazy all throughout that dance we never would have got away with it."

The dance in question was in my mind a piece of the cheapest pornography. I felt I had taken enough. I blazed. "That dance was one of the funniest exhibitions I ever saw."

"That is then precisely the kind of humor we are after, baby," said Cecil, climbing down from the throne, and then remembering, he stopped and threw back over his shoulder as he left the stage, "LeRoy Prince, take this number and make something out of it we can photograph."

With that sentence he broke my contract. Five minutes later I was off the payroll. Thank God I have a prepaid berth to go home in.

LeRoy Prince moaned, "Oh honey, honey, that belly dance!" Cecil also said, very levelly on the edge of the stage: "We'll have to be very careful about the press release. This could be awkward. Try not to talk, baby, until I do; you can hurt yourself."

So the announcement in the *Los Angeles Times* today read that we had disagreed over the length of my number, and that what he had in mind was a beautiful naked woman dancing sensually on the back of a milk-white bull.

And, Mom, that just wasn't true. The bull is not milk white.

In justice to truth let me repeat that the dance is not my best. It may be lousy for all I know. I'm bewildered. He had meant to help me and I had let him down publicly. One thing I am sure of, it could have been fixed with a quiet discussion. I knew very well what he wanted, but have tried perversely to give something that interested me. Something that Martha Graham or Arnold Haskell would have praised.

Then the heavens opened and Bernie Fineman came to take me to dinner. "Good God, Agnes," he said. "You're naked! If your father could see you!". . .

The next night after my fiasco, I went to the back lot in search of a pair of work shoes I'd left in the bullpen. I was alone and I hung over the rails and stared at my late partner. There he sat, darkly couched in sweet-smelling hay, giving an odor of male assurance. He quietly chewed something healthy and simple.

"Good-bye," I said, as I picked at a splinter. The tears stuck on my enormous false lashes. "And good luck with the sexy girls." He chewed and breathed out a great snuffle of warm air.

On the edge of the lot stood a young man I had known for years. "I hear there's been trouble," he said. "I've come to take you to dinner. The gang's waiting. And we've got a bottle of wine."

"You know"—he put his arm around me in the car—"this is all not very important and what he said is not accurate."

I came to believe him.

The next day I took my new money and bought a very pretty dress and two fine hats, had my hair and nails done, then paraded around the

Paramount stages. "How well you look!" everyone remarked. "Why, you're pretty!"

I met Roy Burns outside the commissary. "Well, so long," he jauntily said. "Good luck!"

"Roy," I answered levelly, "I came here from London a trained professional and with hits in a Charles Cochran show. I came in all eagerness, mad to please, adoring my uncle and believing in him; I have been flouted and cut off on every side deliberately. I go back without a foot of film shot. Figure out what I have cost all around and what you got for it and tell me if that's good business. And then figure out the utter wastage of talent that many people think first-class and ask yourself why."

He threw his arms around me. "Forgive me; I'm nervous. You don't know the Boss. I couldn't help myself. You're well out of this."

"Good-bye, Roy, I don't wonder you're nervous. Does anyone have any fun in this place?"

He shook his head. "I'm getting ulcers."

"Back to London!"

He kissed me. He did look regretful. He did get ulcers.

What Cecil got was not the dance he wanted.

He also got a very bad press. I don't know about the financial returns. Claudette Colbert got big stardom.

Thereafter, Cecil was always unhappy and self-conscious about this episode. He stipulated when my first book was considered for a movie that *Cleopatra* never be referred to in any way (it hadn't been mentioned in the book). He had sincerely wanted to help me and he had truly been very rough. Much later, after my six Broadway hits, he greeted me fulsomely with, "Baby, you are now the greatest choreographer in the world."

"No," I said. "I certainly am not, but just possibly I am one of the best paid."

"Ah, baby," he said, looking at me with great spirituality, "there's more to it than that. You must think of other aspects. You can't take it with you, you know."

—from *Speak to Me, Dance with Me,* 1973

Limelight: Interview with Scott Eyman and Hooman Mehran

One of George Balanchine's leading ballerinas for a quarter of a century, Canadian-born Melissa Hayden (1923–2006) originated many roles for him, including Liberty Bell in Stars and Stripes *and Titania in* A Midsummer Night's Dream. *She was also in the first casts of, among others,* Agon *(the second pas de trois),* Liebeslieder Walzer, Divertimento No. 15, Episodes, *and the ballet Balanchine created for her upon her retirement in 1973,* Cortège Hongrois. *She featured as well in a series of dramatic works by other choreographers: William Dollar's* The Duel, *Frederick Ashton's* Illuminations, *Birgit Cullberg's* Medea, *and Todd Bolender's* The Still Point. *Hayden went on to a successful teaching career, working at the North Carolina School of the Arts until just before her death.*

How familiar were you with Chaplin's work before you made Limelight?
First of all, I was a moviegoer. I was a fan of his, and anything of his that was shown, I always attended, and I loved everything. I'd seen *City Lights;* I'd seen *The Great Dictator.* I thought he was brilliant, ahead of his time. He was so intuitive; you don't see movies like his today. *Limelight* touched you emotionally, and it made you laugh.

Had Chaplin seen you dance with Eglevsky at the New York City Ballet?
No, he had never seen me at City Ballet. He had seen Mr. Eglevsky often in California, at the Biltmore Theater. Ballet Theater used to play there. I'm not sure if City Ballet played there.

Was the offer to work on Limelight *made through Eglevsky or through an agent?*
I seems as though the agent contacted André and asked him if he could find someone who might look like Claire Bloom. I'm not sure if André even knew what she looked like—he initially had suggested dancers who didn't even resemble her. He must have submitted some pictures and they were rejected, and finally since I had danced with André in concerts as well as in the company, he asked me for a head shot.

"Why?" I asked.

"Mr. Chaplin's doing a movie and asked me if I could find someone who looked like the leading lady."

What followed was the agent called me to his office. I went to the office; we sat down. "Mr. Chaplin liked the picture of you. He would like you to come out and see him at his studio, with Mr. Eglevsky."

At this point, we were on a layoff from the ballet. I had nothing to lose. So arrangements were made, and we took a red-eye to Hollywod. Some-one picked us up; we stayed at the Hollywood Hotel. We were able to sleep for a few hours. I think we arrived at five in the morning, slept for a couple of hours.

At 8:30 or 9, we were told we'd be picked up by a limousine. André said, "Take your practice clothes." This was all an adventure for me. I was very nonchalant.

The studio was like a huge hangar—there was nothing there. At the end of this huge place there was a little man. A very little man. Mr. Chaplin greeted André effusively, then looked at me and said, "How do you do?" I said, "Fine," and that was about it.

I remember looking at his tiny feet. He was excited about meeting André, not me.

He had a good idea of the ballet; it was a takeoff on *Giselle* in a way, the second act. And he started to tell us about it: "Now we do an entrechat, now you lift here . . . " He was like that for an hour.

About 11:30 or 12, we had lunch at the Brown Derby, and I saw movie stars. I sat next to him. He was very chatty; nothing personal, talking about people he had seen. His brother Syd was there. Not only was Charlie looking me over, Syd was looking me over.

Then we went back to the studio, at which point, André said, "Get into your practice clothes." I hadn't eaten much lunch, but I wasn't ready to jump around on a cement floor. I got changed and warmed up.

So we played around with the part in the film where she's dancing with someone—a pas de deux. He wanted to see us do something together, you see.

Well, when you're not prepared for anything, you use the experience you already have as a performer. Since I had danced with André in a num-ber of pieces, he (André) said, "Do this step from a Balanchine, then this step from Sylphide and Fokine." And we put together a pas de deux by talking with each other.

And Chaplin would say, "Good, good, good. This is wonderful."

So we did this for an hour. I said to André, "He likes what we're doing, but I don't think he likes me. I'm stopping; I'm tired. You speak to him and ask him if he likes me. If he likes me, that's OK, I'll do it. If he doesn't, it's *finis*, right now."

I was softer in my tone than I am now, but he hadn't looked at me; I felt like anybody could have been doing this. Somebody had to show an interest in me personally.

You see, André and he had met before. André had the job; I was the one that was auditioning.

André said, "Don't worry; just get dressed."

From what I gathered, he spoke to Mr. Chaplin and he translated what I had been saying, but we never had a yea or a nay. We left the following morning.

I was still on layoff. I think within a week, the agent called me and asked me to come to his office again. "Mr. Chaplin likes you." "Gee, that's very nice." "Do you have an agent?" "No." "Well, how can we negotiate how much money you're going to get?" So I said, not really thinking, "Well, pay me what you're paying Mr. Eglevsky." And he said "OK, we'll talk to Mr. Chaplin and we'll be in touch and find out when you're free."

So the arrangement was that I was to go to California on my own. I was there three days before André was there. I got a costume fitting from a costumer in Hollywood. It was an old-fashioned kind of tutu, white, and that was all I did that afternoon.

The following morning they picked me up at five in the morning. I was supposed to have makeup starting at six in the morning in Culver City. (All the theater stuff was done on that stage in Culver City.) I went in and they gave me a sort of false widow's peak, a classical hairdo, and performance makeup.

After an hour, someone came in and said, "That's all wrong, we're shooting the audition scene." So they wiped my face off and did a normal makeup. By eight o'clock, an assistant came by and said, "You're supposed to be onstage now." I had brought my own shoes and tights—a practice outfit.

Then they took me in this little booth, a kiosk actually, and said, "This is what you have to wear. A black leotard, with black tights." I said, "Gee whiz, I've got pink shoes." It didn't matter.

It's now after eight in the morning, and I had to warm up. It took me more than fifteen minutes to do that. And here was Chaplin, this little man with those tiny feet, his sparkling blue eyes, jumping around, being very excited.

"This is where you audition," he said.

"Oh?"

"Haven't you ever auditioned?"

"To tell you the truth, I have never auditioned for anything." Now, that was a white lie, but at New York City Ballet I never had to audition. In an audition you have to have something prepared, but I hadn't prepared anything because I didn't know what we were going to be doing.

Well, here we go. "Put on the music," I said. So he started playing the music. And so I thought, "What am I going to do?"

I played around with a few steps. I was very uncomfortable; I was so unsure of myself. So I looked up ahead of me, and there was a red light on. I said, "No no, please don't film me. It will take a little time to organize." And he said, "Phew, film is very cheap."

The significance of that didn't hit me until recently when I saw that retrospective *(The Unknown Chaplin)*, where they showed how he would do seventy or eighty takes. The idea of no script and my floundering around wouldn't have bothered him at all. He was thinking, "Maybe we'll get it anyway."

From 8:30 to 12:30, that's how long I worked on the audition scene. Around 10 or 11, I was rather pleased with what I had done. I had danced well. It was about the fifth time he had photographed it. I said, "The fifth time we did it, that's pretty good; that would be very good." And he said, "No, no, do some more." Well, I did three or four more takes, and when that was over, I was tired.

"Do you want to see the rushes?" he asked me. "I'd love to." So we finished at 12:30. I realize now that what he wanted was an improvisational quality—the nerves, the anxiety, the tentativeness, and I think the scene has that.

Then there was a break, and Buster Keaton came on the set. He was sitting there carving wood, working on miniature steps, and some kind of station. "Oh, that's the One Hundred Twenty-fifth subway station in New York City," he said. "Have you ever been there? There's lots of stairs. This is what I do; it's a hobby of mine." He was waiting and working and explaining it to me—a very sweet man.

The next thing I know, he's onstage, and I watched the two of them do the scene with the drums and the piano, with Chaplin falling into the pit.

When Chaplin was doing things with Keaton, he was very intense, and his whole personality changed from what it had been with me earlier in the day. I never saw him shooting with anybody else, and it was really intense, and I was amazed. That was the first inkling I had of what the movie was about, and of what he was about.

He was very one-on-one in the circumstances of working with that person. He was very tunneled and he gave you the energy he wanted to get back.

Were Chaplin and Keaton rehearsing or filming?
That camera never stopped.

There's always been something of an urban legend to the effect that Chaplin cut out Keaton's best stuff.
I thought what they were doing was very funny. And when I saw it, I didn't think Keaton was as much a part of the film as I saw him do it at the time. On the other hand, Keaton hadn't been working for a while, and Chaplin liked him very much. Why would he do that?

Later that day we saw the rushes. I said, "Remember number five," and he said, "That's the one we're going to use."

So up to the point where you filmed the audition sequence, there was no communication between you and the actors?
I had never met Claire Bloom. I had been in London before this, and all I heard about was Claire Bloom, but I only met her after that day, when we went out to dinner.

Was Chaplin entitled to his choreography credit?
He didn't choreograph a thing; he didn't know anything about ballet. Maybe he took credit for what he was suggesting. All of our dances derived from the two of us, André and myself. And in the montage, I did that all myself. The montage took two or three hours. He just kept saying, "Do it again!"

I'm sure Chaplin knew about dance—he loved ballet, although he never spoke about other dancers—but we're talking about classic ballet. I don't know if he was ever in a ballet studio, but he could use the vocabulary of classical ballet, pliés and so forth, although he would mispronounce the words.

I danced with Balanchine and Ashton. That is a kind of vocabulary, a kind of choreography and inventiveness that belongs only to the world of ballet. I don't think he had that particular experience. He was a vaudevillian, and a lot of vaudevillians knew a little or a lot about dance, but not in a classical form; he wasn't trained in that.

Looking at the ballet again, it's slightly reminiscent of pre-war English ballet— Ashton and so forth.
Was I thinking of Freddie Ashton? I don't think so, but I had worked with Freddie at City Ballet, in *Illuminations*. Any experience you have creeps in, whether it's Robbins or Fokine. Remember that Chaplin's music is very English. I was not thinking of any one person; I was dancing to the music. I loved the music; I thought it was inspirational.

Up to this point, the relationship with Chaplin was very formal. Did it ever warm up?

When he got to know me he was much more friendly. One afternoon, he sent a car at my disposal to take me shopping or wherever I wanted to go.

I think he was basically a shy man. Eventually, when André came, after one day of shooting, he invited us to his home, and for André he had piroshki and borscht. And we met all the children.

I figured he must have liked us to invite us to the house. Oona was charming; the children were adorable, and they were all in the film.

Did you ever get the feeling Chaplin was rushed, or was he willing to spend the necessary time?

Whatever we did, we took as much time as we needed, and that was fine with him. And if you add up our footage, I don't think it takes ten minutes.

As a dancer, you were always known for seizing the stage. Did you get the feeling that Chaplin wanted that aspect of your stage personality?

He wasn't sure what he wanted. I may have looked like Claire from a distance, or the shoulder line, but he didn't know if I could deliver. He was very insecure about my being there. He had me there for three days before André came; he allowed himself enough time to work around the possibility of not getting what he wanted.

Of course, he would be insecure—he wanted something from a stranger. I think before we left, he was very happy about the sequences he made, although I didn't think André showed off as well as he could have. I knew André said during the pas de deux that he was exhausted.

André was a great partner; he liked me personally, and he liked dancing with me. André had been employed at the age of fifteen with the Ballet Russe, where he was trained by Legat, the most wonderful teacher. He probably practiced eight hours a day.

By the time he was twenty-one, he was in demand. He had big shoulders, a small waist, very short torso, beautiful hips, the greatest legs ever. His thighs were so gorgeous!

He was only insecure about his hands. "Look at these hands," he would say. "These are peasant hands." He had two sons who also had big shoulders—it was in the genes.

His personality? Oh, he was naughty! He loved running after girls and kissing them in the dressing room. He used to try that with me, at first, and I would push him away. But he was married—well married. His mother-in-law lived with him, and he loved his children. Whenever we went on tour, he would take his kids with him. He always had his children with him. André loved carpentry. He was a very good, sincere person; I just adored him.

What was your reaction on first seeing the film, and how have your feelings about the movie changed over the years?
When I first saw the film, I had been taking a ballet class, and got a message from the secretary that Mr. Chaplin wanted to meet me at the theater. It was on Broadway. He got there by taxi, and I was wearing a red cashmere sweater and gray pleated skirt. He took my hand. "I'm so glad you're here; sit right beside me." And we sat in the back, and we sat through the film.

Well, I loved it. And I thought the dance sequences were wonderful. I thought it got a little corny at the end. I remember sitting there and thinking, "Oooohhhh." And I've seen it again over the years and it's not corny; it's quite touching. See what maturity does to a person? It widens their empathetic response. I'm a cornball myself now. I cry at any movie that's at all sad. . . .

How do you feel now about your participation in the film?
Are you kidding? I'm thrilled! I feel so privileged. At the time, I didn't know what was happening; I was just excited about the experience. Chaplin himself is so meaningful. He was really a charmer—I'll always remember those beautiful, twinkling blue eyes.

—from Chaplin's Limelight *and* The Music Hall Tradition,
edited by Frank Scheide and Hooman Mehran

Pauline Kael

The Turning Point
Shouldn't Old Acquaintance Be Forgot?

The most famous, influential, and feared of American movie critics, Pauline Kael (1919–2001) began her career in San Francisco and briefly wrote for several national magazines before, in 1967, becoming film critic for The New Yorker, *a job she retained until her retirement in 1991.*

In 1943, when John van Druten's comedy-drama *Old Acquaintance* was transferred to the screen, Bette Davis played the distinguished unmarried writer living in New York who arrived in her old college town and was carried through the streets by the enthusiastic students, right to the door of her bosom buddy from girlhood days—Miriam Hopkins—who had married and was now pregnant but had never got over her catty envy of the adulation her chum received, and was busy scribbling a novel. Eventually, Davis helped Hopkins's daughter, Deedee, at a critical time in the girl's life, and the picture reached its climax when Davis slapped Hopkins and, grabbing her by the shoulders, shook the crazy, jealous suspiciousness out of her; after a lifetime of rivalry, the two women drank a toast to their friendship. For many years, a fair number of people have been longing for more of those Bette Davis–Miriam Hopkins movies, and now there is a new one, *The Turning Point,* with Anne Bancroft as Emma, the celebrated, lonely, aging ballerina with "American Ballet Company" (modelled on American Ballet Theatre), which arrives for an engagement in Oklahoma City, where her old friend and rival, Deedee—Shirley MacLaine—lives. Deedee quit her own dancing career, married, had three children—and never stopped thinking about what she had lost out on. Emilia (Leslie Browne), the oldest of her children and a promising teen-age dancer, is Emma's godchild, and when Emma begins to mother the girl—to guide her and coach her—Deedee gets riled up. The two women have a big slapfest, whamming each other until they both get the rage out of their systems, start laughing, and wind up hugging. At the end, their arms are around each other's shoulders—friends forever.

Will anybody long for more Anne Bancroft–Shirley MacLaine movies? It's doubtful. The screenplay, by Arthur Laurents, centers on the turning point in Emma's and Deedee's lives, when they made the choices—dancing for Emma, marriage for Deedee—that settled their destinies. As a device, the turning point (like that synthetic summer when adolescent heroes grow into men) is so mechanical it's an exposed construction; Laurents's girders are showing. The two women's scenes are designed to reveal what each of them gave up and what each gained—it's one little lesson after another. *Old Acquaintance* was hair-pulling high camp: it had the verve of bitchery to keep one somewhat amused. Laurents, though, writes sodden, expository dialogue in which people are forever revealing truths to each other and then explaining those truths—*The Turning Point* comes with its own footnotes. Anne Bancroft overdoes her sacrificial-artist laceration. Trying for glamour and bravura, she holds her haggard head up gallantly, with her neck drawn so taut that it pulls her mouth down. She has a gnarled, ascetic look, and the worst case of nobility in the eyebrows since Greer Garson. Garbo's suicidally exhausted ballerina in *Grand Hotel* was a ball of fluff compared with Bancroft; suffering, not dance, seems to be Bancroft's art. Shirley MacLaine plays in a snappier spirit; she gives a shrewd performance, with her own version of Miriam Hopkins's narrow-eyed avidity—the sly greediness for attention which is so transparent it's comic. And she looks great: in fighting trim. But since the movie has been placed inside a backstage ballet atmosphere, with subsidiary roles played by a dozen or more famous dancers, and with the possibility of seeing them dance, Emma and Deedee would have to be larger personalities to hold our attention. We get a glimpse of something great in this movie, and Emma and Deedee—two harpies out of the soaps—block the view.

Earlier backstage ballet films had their mad-genius Diaghilev figures, such as the ruthlessly dedicated impresario played by Anton Walbrook in *The Red Shoes*—he smoldered, trailing noxious fumes of culture. (The foreign country they all came from was really Hell.) But the whole effort here is to domesticate ballet—to remove the taint of European decadence. The ballet company was founded by the tactless, blundering Adelaide (Martha Scott—you can't get any more all-American than that), and her obsession is raising money. Most of the characters are so heartland ordinary—they're shaped to be so much like the filmmakers' idea of you and me—that they disinfect one's imagination. As soon as the dancing starts, dancers who stop our breathing become the stars of the movie: Mikhail Baryshnikov and, in a brief glimpse, Suzanne Farrell, who flies onstage—a dream on legs—during the company's annual fund-raising gala. The movie is Baryshnikov's. He plays Yuri, the Russian dancer whom the budding ballerina Emilia falls in love with, and his acting is lightly understated. Baryshnikov is so amazingly unaffected as a dancer that it is not surprising that he should also be matter-of-fact in his line readings. There are no wasted gestures, not a whisper of excess. His performance is exceedingly likable, and it gives us a chance for a semi-private look at a whirlwind in repose. He doesn't have the classically proportioned body or the stylized face of most male dance stars; his muscles are gently rounded, and his head is massive. When he's merely acting and his body is still, his huge blue-gray eyes could be gazing at another planet. He's like one of the cherubim grown up—a little puzzled about where he is but accepting it. The film never sets up the greatness of Baryshnikov: there's no fanfare. This blond-haired Russian with thick hands is simply there among the men in the company that Emma belongs to and that Emilia joins; except for the paleness of his face and those unearthly eyes, he could be a robust peasant. And with no visible preparation he's leaping into space—he's just up there, and turning. When he finishes his *Corsaire* solo, you want the director, Herbert Ross, to stop all the nonsense—the cheesy pairing, balancing, and squabbling—and just repeat the piece of film. It's like seeing a meteor streak by. There's a trace of regret mixed with your surprise and exhilaration—you haven't been able to take it all in.

The story element that will probably make *The Turning Point* a box-office hit is the romance between Yuri and Emilia. Leslie Browne is a new version of every big-dark-eyed sensitive-sprite ballerina; she has the traditional ballet baby face—a lemming in a tutu. The movie gives her showcase treatment: she is lighted to be the *jeune fille,* like Audrey Hepburn in *Roman Holiday,* tremblingly learning the meaning of love. Emilia is dancing with another partner when her eyes meet Yuri's; they dance together—a love-awakening from MacMillan's *Romeo and Juliet* (which serves the same purpose as the Jeanette MacDonald–Nelson Eddy duets)—and then they are in a bedroom together. It's tasteful, pretty, sweetly romantic, and utterly lacking in ingenuity—in the wit of romance. This stuffed, airless lyricism is just a facsimile of romantic fantasy, an appeal to teen-age swooniness.

The dancing is photographed with respect for the dancers' whole bodies, and against clear, bright backgrounds. The big screen gives it a boldness and immediacy greater, in some ways, than it might have on the stage. When Baryshnikov is in motion Ross and the cinematographer, Robert Surtees, certainly know they've captured pure joy up there on the screen. But the script—and Ross, who initiated the project, must be a partial collaborator—exploits Baryshnikov's boyish, mysteriously simple heterosexual appeal to prop up the gratuitous thesis that though the men in ballet used to be sexually ambiguous the ballet world is now as wholesome as football and Mom's apple pie. The film's approach to ballet is like a recruiting poster: join up for clean living. In the last few years, the grace and idealism incarnated in ballet, and maybe, too, its freedom from "issues," have made it almost as popular an escape from the national mess as sports. Ballet is already a mainstream art form. Would movie audiences care whether the male dancers were actually homosexual, as long as they moved with precision and refinement, and could soar when necessary? Maybe some still would; maybe there is a sound commercial instinct behind this picture's attempt to ingratiate itself by showing ballet as "normal." But it bends over backward, like gays getting short haircuts and wearing crewneck sweaters—their straight drag. (It would be more honorable to take a chance on the audience.)

The only acting with any depth is by Tom Skerritt, as Deedee's husband, Wayne, who used to be a dancer, too, and now runs a dance school with her in Oklahoma City. Skerritt (he was the Southerner who bunked with Elliott Gould and Donald Sutherland in *M*A*S*H*) has an easiness as an actor that translates to the screen as relaxed, unthreatened masculinity. Wayne is so emotionally alert to what's going on in his family that you're conscious of his awareness even when he's off camera. His simple gratefulness for what he's got makes you understand how good Deedee's life really is—and how her envy of Emma has kept her from fully committing herself to him. Everything about Wayne is convincing except the scene in which he, too, must reveal his turning point—his unsureness early in life about whether he was homosexual or heterosexual, which was resolved when Deedee and he got together. Who would dream of accusing Wayne of being anything other than what he seems? There's not a suggestion of any repressed area in him—nor, one suspects, is there meant to be. The homosexual issue is raised so it can be dismissed as a bugaboo.

The script is practically a tree of life, with dozens of characters reaching their turning points and branching off. Wayne and Deedee's youngest child, a boy torn between baseball and ballet, has his junior edition of the decisive moment. (He picks dance.) Emma's and Deedee's former suitors are part of this tree, and there are also ballerinas of several generations so we can see where Emilia will be in a few years, and where Emma will end up. And in order to dramatize the price of fame (versus Deedee's cozy family future) the film makes stupid pathos of Emma's aging—as if the possibilities open to retired dancers (teaching, coaching, choreography, management) were rackingly degrading. As the horrible example of what's ahead for the lonely Emma, there is Alexandra Danilova in the role of the ancient coach Dahkarova, but Danilova looks as vital and engaged as when she danced with the Ballet Russe de Monte Carlo in the late thirties. She's living evidence that what she gave to me and hundreds of thousands of others when she was at her height as a dancer she's still giving out, in a different form. (She shows more strength and vivacity than the young heroine's dancing does.)

Herbert Ross was himself a dancer and then a ballet choreographer, before becoming a Broadway director; after directing the musical sequences in the film *Funny Girl,* he became a movie director. *The Turning Point,* his ninth picture, is also a bow to his wife (since 1959)—the celebrated ballerina Nora Kaye, who achieved fame for her dramatic eloquence in the ballet *Pillar of Fire* in 1942, quit dancing when she was forty-one, and devoted herself to her marriage. In a sense, Nora Kaye, who served as executive producer of this film (and works with Ross on his other movies, too), has been both Emma and Deedee, in succession. She was a charter member of Ballet Theatre (now American Ballet Theatre), and Leslie Browne, the daughter of two dancers, is, in fact, Nora Kaye's godchild. Ross is not a particularly resourceful director, but his unassertive approach saves *The Turning Point*—keeps it painless; if the picture had been directed with a rigidity to match that of the script, with its gothic fix on ballet geriatrics, it would be a clanger. Ross, though, doesn't give one the excitement that a confident director can. The film has no visual sweep; the camera doesn't track with the music; it has no lift. There are too many grays and dusty pinks and faded salmon tones; the picture looks like those men who always wear dark ties with gray suits because they're afraid of going wrong. Before a scene is over—sometimes even in the middle of a word—there's a cut to another scene. At times you feel that Ross keeps shifting the scenes so you won't notice them; he half erases them. After a bit of dance, he cuts to reaction shots—to Bancroft's face, or MacLaine's—for safety. Even in the way it's made, this movie is like TV—it's the Partridge Family in Ballet Land. On this project, which he's deeply committed to, Ross is so concerned not to betray or vulgarize back-stage ballet life that he hides around corners from it. People seem to rattle about in the frame, and one could get the impression that the sets were dubbed: they have a hollow ring, as if the furnishings of a suburban home were jammed into a section of an airplane hangar.

When we go to see a ballet picture starring Bancroft and MacLaine, we don't expect a unified dance conception like *The Red Shoes,* but we do assume that the script will provide opportunities for dance which are integral to the story. Yet except for the love duet the dancing—such as that at the big gala, where we get a chance to watch snippets of dances with Peter Martins, Antoinette Sibley, Marcia Haydée, Richard Cragun, Lucette Aldous, Fernando Bujones, and others—has no dramatic function. Ross seems caught somewhere between the script's philistinism and his own love of dance. In the name of modern realism, Ross and Laurents have taken the personality and temperament out of the ballet world along with any whiffs of exotic, fetid culture. The movie makers appear to confuse realism with banality (and heterosexuality). Ross' biggest weakness is that he doesn't trust the camera enough. If he did, it would take him right to Baryshnikov, whose attentiveness to his partners and whose contradictory image—an extrovert with spiritual eyes—overpower the script's musty calculations about career decisions. One leap and he knocks this house of cards down. Ballet is romance formalized; the script uses it just as romance. The lyricism of Emilia's affair with Yuri and the mythic speed with which she becomes a star suggest the way that some fourteen-year-olds fantasize ballet—as if it were a means of arresting development between prepuberty and puberty. That's the place where Peter Pan lived.

—from *The New Yorker,* November 21, 1977. Reprinted by permission.

ALASTAIR MACAULAY
Disney's Dances

While Mickey Mouse is using a crane to haul Minnie onto his steamboat, a goat on deck eats up Minnie's fiddle and her music-sheet. What to do? Minnie tries cranking the goat's tail, Mickey opens its mouth, out pours music, and we're off! Mickey treats all the animals aboard like consenting percussion instruments, too. He plays a cow's teeth like a xylophone; he even prods a litter of six piglets busy at the sow's teats for the sound of their squeals. And *then* he turns the sow over, and uses her grunts as the next part of his score. This is in *Steamboat Willie* (1928), the first film in which Mickey burst onto the screen. It was the first fully musical talkie, and it's still glorious.

If there can be choreography without human movement, then Disney's animated cartoons surely contain some of the most blissfully inventive choreography of the century. Everybody knows that. I hadn't realised, however, how deeply dancing—and dancing to music—pervaded Disney's sensibility. But from September to November the National Film Theatre showed a season of Disney's work, from the earliest Mickey Mouse shorts and Silly Symphonies, right through to the films made by the Disney Studio after the master's death; and I was able to catch some of them. Jiminy Crickets!—as we dwarves say when hit by the shock of beauty.

Mickey Mouse—a born vaudeville artist—soon bursts into dance. Actually, Minnie beats him to it—in a slinky Latin solo with a rose between her teeth in *Gallopin' Gaucho* (1928), just before Mickey pulls her into a hilarious tango. (*Plane Crazy* and this were Disney's first sound films, but *Steamboat Willie,* his third, was released first.) At the fair in *Karnival Kid* (1932), Mickey the hot-dog seller espies "Minnie the Shimmie Dancer," as she's billed, doing her hoochy-coochy dance. It's got to be love. For *The Picnic* (1930), the two mice bring a wind-up gramophone with their hamper, crank it up, and away they dance over the meadow, spinning and tapping, the Fred and Adele Astaire of the rodent kingdom. And what good dancing. Their tap is much more characterful than Ruby Keeler's or Eleanor Powell's or Ann Miller's or, dare I say it, Gene Kelly's. Less dated, too. And their *Gallopin' Gaucho* tango is so funny because its jokes are in its dancing—Mickey pressing Minnie tight to his rodent breast as they stride their deep tango strides forever and a yard.

It's symptomatic of this post-modern age that we find high art in the popular entertainment of a bygone era. But, then, people always rated Disney high. Remarkable that when the great dance critic Edwin Denby first reviewed (in 1938) Balanchine's masterpiece *Apollo,* he called it "a ballet worth seeing several times because it is as full of touching detail as a Walt Disney." And he wrote in 1943 that "In the present film technique Disney's animals have been more successful than human dancers in giving a wide range of dance expression to movement," a judgment astonishing to us today in view of our reverence for the sublime achievement of the nine Fred and Ginger RKO movies made between 1933 and 1939. We *know* today that Astaire was the musicals' most wonderful person ever. But in 1936 Graham Greene, like others, called Astaire "the nearest we are ever likely to get to a human Mickey," and he meant it as a compliment. Mickey and Astaire were heroes of the Depression, and they remain two of the era's most shining examples of the resilience of the human spirit—cocky and sweet, dreamy and defiant.

With Disney's characters, as with Astaire, dance is just plain natural. While Mickey and Minnie dance away in *The Picnic,* the bees and flies that devour their food start to dance too; and so, in *Karnival Kid,* do Mickey's hot dogs. And the Silly Symphonies are as full of musical motion as the Mouse series. It was a thrill to discover *Monkey Melodies* (1930), with its irrepressible simian pair dancing through the jungle and finally playing an eternal pat-a-cake as they hang from a branch by their tails. Disney animals just have dance in their bones—the famous first Silly Symphony (1929) was *The Skeleton Dance*—and dance is a life force for his insects and flowers also. Flowers, in fact, are ballet: they form rings and dance on pointe, like a Petipa corps. In *Trees and Flowers* (1933), his first colour film, they do grands pliés to start the day, and in *The Goddess of Spring* (1934) they do unison pirouettes en attitude. The goddess herself, by contrast, is a Revived Greek dancer, in sandals—what used to be called "a small Isadora-and-soda."

In the latter film Disney wanted his studio artists to develop their skill at showing the human figure in motion. They never fully succeeded. His humans aren't as good—in *Snow White*—as his dwarves or—in *Cinderella*—as his cat, dog, and mice. That is, they aren't as characterful, as *human.* For oh! what human spirit his animals show. The animator Ward Kimball (creator, in *Pinocchio,* of Jiminy Cricket himself) explained, in London Weekend Television's 1988 documentary on Disney, how impressed he had been when first he saw the 1933 Silly Symphony *Father Noah's Ark.* "This wasn't just movement for movement's sake. Here was an effort to characterise." Characterization and storytelling: here Disney's own gifts became a crucial inspiration to the studio. At meetings, as he took his team through whichever film he was planning, he became every character. "Bringing dream to life" was what he was about, and he did so by means of "movement, emotion, the flow of movement, action, and reaction." (His words.) In advancing his *film d'action*—surely Noverre would have admired him—he kept advancing film technique. A chronological Disney season is an unrolling adventure story of what film learnt to do. And sometimes it's his characters who dance (as in Astaire movies), and sometimes (as in Busby Berkeley's) it's his camera. In much of *The Old Mill* (1937), hardly a thing moves at all . . . save the camera itself; and there's the film's true poetry. Here was the first use of the multi-plane camera, with its marvellous travelling three-dimensional views, passing through the cartoon landscape towards and inside the mill.

The Goddess of Spring, like *Three Little Pigs* (1933), is all-singing—another breakthrough for the movies. These are mini-operettas, and they paved the way for *Snow White* (1937), another first—a cartoon operetta ninety minutes long. I'd expected to see this movie now with the National Theatre of Brent's 1984 version in my ears. (Hacking through imaginary Disney undergrowth on his way to awaken Snow White with a kiss, Brent's Prince suddenly exclaimed: "This forest is full of *sobbing rodents*.") Well, the singing of Snow White herself is sub–Deanna Durbin. But this film is still a model of musical action. Its dances are only occasional—as in Astaire movies, it usually works from a song up into a dance—but they're highlights, as in the great house-cleaning scene and the dwarves' yodelling number.

How much some of these films say about the musical scene of their day! Both jazz and classical music were hot stuff in the early era of talkies, and Disney was as alive to this as anyone. *The Goddess of Spring* is the Persephone story; the Hell that Pluto drags the heroine down to is a jazz kingdom. In *Music Land* (1935), there's a Land of Symphony and an Isle of Jazz. One tearaway saxophone from the latter falls for the former's violin princess. Warfare ensues, as wonderful as Balanchine's *Nutcracker* battle. The Ride of the Valkyries thunders away; the Symphony organ tilts over; its pipes are used as guns; music itself is fired as ammo. But, when the two sides are reconciled, they build a Bridge of Harmony. (A year later, Balanchine, Rodgers, and Hart worked on a similar marriage of ballet and swing in the title number of *On Your Toes!*)

In *The Band Concert* (1935), Mickey conducts the *William Tell* overture. (When Toscanini saw this, he made the cinema play it again.). His gestures are so huge, he has to pull his sleeves up after each one. Then a real storm arrives, along with the one in the music, to blow the band, still playing, sky high. Disney discovered here how to let music launch a vivid fantasy and prompt that fantasy's every development. What a discovery that is. It's the essence of *Fantasia* (1940). What Disney and the conductor-arranger Leopold Stokowski do to great classical music here is wolfsbane to musical purists, of course, even in the 1982 version of the film with its re-recorded stereo soundtrack. The sections of Stravinsky's *Sacre du Printemps* are re-ordered and set to a Darwinian account of the origin of species and of evolution; Beethoven's Pastoral is accompanied by beings from Greek mythology; Dukas's Sorcerer's Apprentice is Mickey. Stokowski made many reorchestrations to heighten the film's aural brilliance, and even in the '82 version—where Mussorgsky's own *Night on a Bare Mountain* replaces the Rimsky reorchestration that was more standard in 1940—you hear extra-swoopy portamenti, extra-rolled chords, all manner of exaggerations.

But Disney's imaginings have such poetic power and aural detail that I find they justify every Stokowski re-arrangement save the pulled-about Holly-wood version of Schubert's *Ave Maria:* which Disney's haunting procession of pilgrims—lightening our darkness—nonetheless transcends. The film was made in America's big radio age of music appreciation, and *Fantasia,* bringing great music to ordinary movie-goers and suggesting the different kinds of visions that music can conjure up, was an audacious response to that. Its basic idea makes me always think at first of chapter five of *Howards End,* where Beethoven's Fifth takes E. M. Forster's characters in different ways; but really the procedure of *Fantasia* isn't a novelist's depiction of lis-teners' unprompted reactions to music, it's a choreographer's communica-tion to his audience of what music prompts in him.

Make Mine Music (1946) was designed as a popular-music sequel to *Fantasia.* When you see, in this, Disney's poetry of light, colour, and camerawork in *Blue Bayou,* you have to imagine how it would have sounded in its original form to Stokowski's arrangement of Debussy's *Clair de lune.* Instead it is marred by the soupy choral ballad to which this film fits it. Yet *Make Mine Music* includes "Peter and the Wolf." Did you know that Prokofiev (a great movie-goer) wrote this famous score with Disney in mind? Disney had considered using it in *Fantasia.* With its young-person's-guide-to-the-orchestra score, it's very much in the spirit of the day; and it's shrewd in its storytelling. Frank Staff's 1940 ballet to it, revived in 1987 by Sadler's Wells Royal Ballet, is cute—and with Disney-like moments, too—but this *Make Mine Music* version surpasses it in almost every respect. Before you see the wolf, you see his prints; and then Disney can fill the screen with nothing but the wolf's face, glaring right into the camera. The story is a natural vehicle for Disney's flair at rapid seesawing between terror and comedy. When the little bird Sasha, in an excess of glee after baiting the huge wolf, gets concussed, the wolf has its revenge—laying out its tongue like a red stair-carpet leading from the ground into the huge pillared hall of its mouth; and Sasha is so dizzy, he marches right up and in.

Make Mine Music is certainly patchy. It contains some of Disney's most corny humour—"Casey at the Bat" and, despite good moments, *The Martins and the Coys.* There just aren't enough animals. (The most marvellous part of the film is "The Whale Who Wanted to Sing at the Met." Nelson Eddy—who never sang at the Met either—sings all the voices. For Willie the operatic whale can sing with not only one voice but three. In a dream sequence at the Met, he stands onstage—he's as tall as the proscenium arch—in tuxedo and mustachios, opens his mouth with its three sets of tonsils, and sings a trio rearrangement—tenor, baritone, bass—of the sextet from *Lucia*.) A "Ballade Ballet," *Two Silhouettes,* features ballet in its most Valentine-card mood, with Tatiana Riabouchinska and David Lichine dancing through a sugary dream kingdom—while Dinah Shore sings a rumba number about "A perfect dream / Set to a theme / Lovely as you." Since the two stars are filmed in silhouette, you don't learn a lot about them from this 2-D reduction. Yet the film dances in perspective around them. The *putti* tug Riabouchinska's arabesque up and down; she runs on pointe up a path of clouds; and stars whoosh from her heel. Much better, though even more consciously fancy, is "All the Cats Join In," to a Benny Goodman jazz number. An artful crayon is seen drawing objects or wiping them out, and pages turn. But the kids in this little tale really do swing. ("When you dance with Bobby Sox,/ You dance at your own risk.") One dippy couple are joined snoozily together from the waist up; but their legs are just so crazy. And the girls are as lively as the boys: one girl picks her partner up, swings him upside down, and uses him as a Hoover.

But the sublime cornucopia of Disney dance remains *Fantasia*. When Disney heard one young artist sneering at ballet dancers, he arranged for him to watch the Ballet Russe from backstage. The artist, John Hench, came back with ballet-inspired drawings for *Fantasia's Nutcracker Suite*. (I derive this and much other information here from John Culhane's excellent 1983 book, *Walt Disney's Fantasia*.) Balanchine was around the studio when it was being made; and Riabouchinska, Lichine, Irina Baronova, and Marge Champion helped to model the steps. And when the hippo ballerina of the *Dance of the Hours* rises from the water, isn't this surely a tease directed at the 1938 movie *The Goldwyn Follies*, where Balanchine had Vera Zorina, in the Water Nymph Ballet, rise from a pool?

Disney and his studio didn't know much about music or ballet, yet they knew more than many choreographers will ever know. The Disney ear could distinguish between action music and dance music, and it prompted him to a wide range of idioms and dynamics in movement. Seldom in stage choreography do we see correspondence between sight and sound so frequent and vivid as in the *Nutcracker, Sorcerer's Apprentice, Pastoral Symphony,* and *Rite of Spring* sequences. Disney, innocently outrageous, often pursues a vision quite unlike the composer's and yet responds intently to musical detail: a wonderful paradox. Many stage choreographers this century have attempted the same, very few with anything like *Fantasia's* success. This film only triumphed at the box-office after its second re-release, in 1958, and it's possible that Disney's response to music had an impact on dance people at that time. At any rate, Disney's musicality has a fabulous naiveté that reminds me of Paul Taylor—whose 1956 *Three Epitaphs* shows a thoroughly Disney sense of shape-changing and timing, whose work has so often been about bugs, and who, in the early sixties, began choreographing to baroque music, Beethoven, and more. I can't guess what Disney would have made of Taylor's *Snow White* (1983), which I haven't seen; but I think he'd have adored the innocence and nerve with which Taylor could interweave the two tales of a dance company in rehearsal *and* a Raymond Chandler–type detective in quest of a kidnapped baby *and* fit them—so snug!—to, of all things, Stravinsky's *Sacre du Printemps.* To very few choreographers is it given—how many sub-Balanchine ballets bear this out—to take us into the world of their music and into its workings. Disney and Taylor, like Fokine (the clearest example is *Schéhérazade*) before them, developed another species of choreographic musicality—using music as a detailed soundtrack for a scenario the composer never dreamed of.

Disney is so ingenuous and ingenious in the Grandma Moses musicality of *Fantasia* that he doesn't, in his setting of the *Pastoral Symphony,* even depict Beethoven's most obviously descriptive moment—the cuckoo. But what he does provide at that moment instead—two lone centaurs brought together by the pan-pipes of three cherubs—resembles the Papageno-Papagena reunion in *The Magic Flute,* and seems to me no less fine. The drawing of the centaurs and centaurettes is too cute—it's one of the weakest things in *Fantasia*—but chances are you don't stop to think of that, because Disney's timing is so neat. A lily on the surface of the lake rises—it's on the head of a girl. Now you see her shoulders, her torso, rising from the water . . . and then this Venus Anadynomene rises a little further . . . and in the next moment you see: she's a centaurette! Beethoven's second movement has begun with tentative half-phrases in the strings; and, just as this heroine's equine lower half rises from the lake, one of those phrases opens out into full flowing shape as a melody. What an abundance of wit this movie shows! In all Greek mythology there is only one winged horse. Disney shows an entire Pegasus family, each a different hue, flying through the sky, alighting on water like swans.

Fantasia is among the most fecund of films. (Stokowski compared Disney with Diaghilev, which is not unjust.) It is one of those rare all-in-one works of art. By turns, it is abstract and figurative, terrifying and hilarous, intimate and cosmic; and it interconnects these things brilliantly. You see Stokowski conduct the orchestra; you see Mickey Mouse conduct the universe. The centaurette rises from the water in the *Pastoral*; so does the hippo ballerina in *Dance of the Hours.* Jupiter hurls thunderbolts in the *Pastoral* and then snuggles up in a cloud to sleep, and the world below is irradiated by the sun to reveal a new palette of Gauguin colours; Chernobog, the night demon of *Night on a Bare Mountain,* wreaks terror and evil on the world, only to return at dawn (like Myrtha) into his mountain and to be replaced by the *Ave Maria* dawn pilgrims, their pale lamps shining so touchingly through the enthrallingly deep, broad, travelling landscape.

And, amid these grand views of evolution, good and evil, despair and hope, the movie is at its most miraculous and musical in the tiny worlds of *The Nutcracker Suite.* Disney sent his artists not only to the ballet but to the studio's parking lot too—to get ideas from the weeds. "God is in the detail." Dewdrop fairies touching flowers (to the Sugar Plum solo); Chinese mushrooms; blossoms on the water (Mirlitons); a harem of water plants and goldfish (Arabian); thistles and orchids like the coachmen and nursemaids of *Petrushka* (Russian), autumn leaves, fairies, milkweed, frost and snowflakes (to the Waltz of the Flowers). Any good purist will turn away in horror, and any good dance fan will marvel at the numberless felicities. Such invention, such timing. It's not just that these *Nutcracker* dances are full of Diaghileviana, though that *is* part of their fun. (And Disney hears narrative cues in *The Sorcerer's Apprentice* so vividly that it resembles an early Stravinsky score written for Fokine.) And it's not just that Disney and his artists were adorable in treating ballet itself, though that's another delight. (It reaches a peak in the uproarious hippo-alligator-elephant ballet to Ponchielli's *Dance of the Hours.*) Somehow Disney with his cartoon figures takes us deep into what moves us most in dance, and sometimes he achieves it best in animation that has nothing to do with ballet. *Fantasia* is at its most heavenly in its autumn-to-winter treatment of the "Waltz of the Flowers." Leaves change color; pods open; seeds fly out and are borne on the wind; frost arrives; snowflakes skate on the ice. In a very Balanchine remark, Disney said of this film, "You will be able to SEE the music and HEAR the picture." That's nowhere more entrancing than in the way this "Waltz of the Flowers"—without showing you flowers at all—gives you the swirling rush and self-renewal of this music. (Among extant choreographies of this waltz, only Balanchine's, I believe, surpasses it.)

Fantasia recalls Balanchine's choreography in its constant development and changeover of imagery, and it celebrates "the pure act of metamorphosis," which is what Paul Valéry in *L'Âme et la Danse* defined as dance's true essence. It is brimful and bubbling with the wonder of creation, in every sense. You laugh and you wipe away tears of wonder and its springs rejuvenate you.

—from *The Dancing Times,* December 1989

ELEANOR POWELL
Interview with John Kobal

Leggy, ebullient Eleanor Powell (1912–1982) was Hollywood's most capable and successful female tap dancer. As a child, she joined the Vaudeville Kiddie Revue. Soon she was appearing in nightclubs and on Broadway, and by the mid-thirties was in Hollywood, first in The George White Scandals of 1935, *then at MGM in a series of hit musicals, including* Born to Dance, Rosalie, *and three* Broadway Melodys, *the last of which—*Broadway Melody of 1940*—featured the spectacular "Begin the Beguine" number with her co-star, Fred Astaire. Powell was married for many years to actor Glenn Ford.*

K obal: The story of Eleanor Powell's life and career is virtually a carbon of all those films she starred in, which might in part account for her success in them. Hers is the story that asks the question: "Can a little girl from a small hick town find happiness as a rich and glamorous movie star?"

She wasn't a great actress or a stunning beauty, and wouldn't claim to be either. But absolutely nobody could dance like Eleanor Powell. *Dance!* She flew. And when she tapped . . . ! She ripped across the huge musical sets conjured up as exotic backgrounds, and for a decade she stunned and exhilarated her public and the critics by an explosion of brilliance in top hat, white tie, and tails. An image she shares with the sublime Ariel of the dance, Fred Astaire. While knocking out five taps to the second, her body bent ninety degrees on itself, creating the illusion of huge sweeping arcs that left impressions in the air as she moved on, like a lighted match circling swiftly in a darkened room. And this after only seven tap lessons in her life!

She is transformed when dancing. Astaire and that musical wizard Busby Berkeley have both paid tribute to her. Contemporaries explained that she was so good because she "danced like a man." But there was more to it than that: her drive, her discipline, her total obsession with her work, these were the qualities that made one sit up. What made her distinctive was the expression and fusion of all these into something recognizable and admirable: her dancing.

For a dozen films, from 1935 to 1945, she cut a unique swath across Hollywood's soundstages to tune-filled scores by writers like Kern, Cole

Porter, and Freed and Brown. Then, still at the top, she got married to a handsome young contract artist at another studio, Glenn Ford, and virtually retired from films. Though other dancers have sprung up—Ann Miller, Vera-Ellen, Leslie Caron, Cyd Charisse, Ann-Margret—none has achieved her fame. In 1961, after her divorce from Ford and, as she says, mostly in response to being goaded to get up and do something by her teenage son, she staged a sensational comeback with a nightclub act that opened in Las Vegas and for the next four years made her a top attraction on the nightclub circuit. She could have gone on—there were offers from TV and Broadway—but, having proved something to herself, she dropped out of sight again.

With such zest and outgoing personality, the lady struck me as an unlikely candidate for mystery. She was elusive, but to find her wasn't as difficult as getting her to see me. The past is not her hang-up, nor is reminiscing her pastime. It was as a favor to a mutual friend that she agreed to see me. So there I was, one Sunday afternoon in Los Angeles, lost in a maze of little streets between Wilshire and Olympic Boulevard, preparing my excuses for arriving late. At last I hit on the right street, drove up, parked, looked about—and saw her waving to me from the top of a flight of stairs leading to her apartment in a small but pretty house on a small but pleasant street. She stood tall, bright, brimming with a contagious warmth.

EVERY DANCER IN motion pictures owes a debt of gratitude to Fred Astaire because he brought dancing to the screen in the right way. Prior to his and Ginger's films, a dancer would come on in a nightclub scene and would go into a dance and two steps later there'd be Joan Crawford's hand over the screen and a voice saying, "Come and sit down." And then the leading man sits down and looks at her and they talk some more and then suddenly everybody applauds and the dancer is bowing and that was it for him, nothing! This is what the dancer had in films, so I never had an aspiration of coming to motion pictures. My dream as a performer on Broadway was to go to Europe just like they always did in the films. Because there the artists got the *bravo!* Here it was money, money, money. Over here you last so long [snaps her fingers]. You go to sign an autograph and someone else comes out and they leave you flat—"Oh, there's so-and-so," and they're off and running and you haven't even gotten your pen out yet. To be a performer in Europe, that was my aim, not movies. But that's not how things go. . . .

Johnny Hyde was my agent at the time. I'm with the William Morris agency then and they don't have any clients in Hollywood yet. I brought them out there. Johnny comes to me all excited: "They want you for *Broadway Melody of 1936,* Jack Benny's big picture, and they want you to do a specialty."

I wasn't interested. I wanted Europe and I had had my experience with movies. Well, I said, "I want a thousand dollars"—which was more than Mitzi Mayfair and Hal LeRoy* were getting then—"and I want a part in the film as well, not just a dance or a little bit, but a role." This was deliberate. I might as well have said, "I want a million dollars and my dressing room painted in gold," because I expected them to say, "Go jump in the lake!" Instead, they sent me a script. In the original script they'd wanted me for the part Una Merkel played—which they thought would be funny opposite Sid Silvers (who was also acting as well as writing). Now I raised my fee to $1250 and Johnny was tearing his hair out, but it came back: Okay. It was for one month's work and a very good part. I'd never been offered that much before. I came out on the Super Chief, champagne and all, put up at the Beverly Wilshire Hotel, and my movie career really started.

The very first day at the studio, Roger Edens was the rehearsal piano player, Arthur Freed was the songwriter with Nacio Herb Brown, there was Mr. Mayer, Roy Del Ruth, the director, and Mr. Katz and Mr. Mannix, but I didn't know who they were. They had heard that I danced other types of dance than the tap and they wanted to see me do other work. I did toe on pointe and other things. They all got their heads down in a circle and then Mr. Mayer called me over to him and he said, very officious, "We're going to test you for the lead." And instead of being glad about it, I said, "Mr. Mayer, you can't do that." And he said, "Why?" "Because I don't know a thing about the camera. You've got a girl in this picture, June Knight, I've worked with her on the stage—she's glamorous, she's sexy, she sings, she's a good dancer. You've got $3 million, I understand, in this picture (which was a lot in those days), and you can't . . . you can't do that." And Mr. Mayer said, "Well, my dear child, you don't seem to realize that I run this studio, and if I want to make a test, I'm going to make a test." I said, "Well, you're just wasting your time." And my agent was sitting there going gray. Being very naive, not really knowing that this isn't what you do, that you're supposed to flatter him, I was just being honest.

So Mr. Del Ruth told me it was a dual role and to go home and get up on this scene and meet him tomorrow morning at 10:00 in his office. I went down the next morning and he said, "Miss Powell, what do you think?" And I said, "Well, this opening scene, Mr. Del Ruth, is supposed to be about a girl frightened to death and I guarantee you there isn't an experienced actress in Hollywood who could do *that* scene any better! The rest of it, I don't know."

They couldn't have found anything better than that part. It wasn't acting on my part so much as just being myself. Now the shy girl, the Janet Gaynor

---

*They were, with Eleanor Powell, the kid stars of Broadway in a musical together.

of Albany, the little Cinderella, was me as Eleanor Powell. When I danced, I became Mademoiselle Arlette, very aggressive!

They got Bob Taylor. I'd never heard of Robert Taylor, and I don't think many people had. He was under contract; he was getting $35-a-week jobs. They figured they'd take this young boy with the widow's peak out of stock, get all the girls excited. Bob Taylor was petrified of me—I'd been in the New York theater and he imagined me like Tallulah Bankhead. But he knew more about the camera than I did!

They wouldn't let me see the rushes. I didn't want to, 'cause Mr. Del Ruth didn't want me to see them. Suddenly one day on the set the lights were all off and Mr. Del Ruth was called upstairs. Mr. Arthur Freed and everyone else were on the set. And I went to my portable room and an hour passed. And another hour passed. A knock came on my door and Arthur Freed came in and he said, "Ellie, look, I want you to promise me that you'll never ever ever let on I told you. Well, they're all upstairs and you're doing beautifully." You know that old gag: "You're doing great, but we just need a different type." So I said, "Okay, fine, I know it." He said, "Wait a minute now. They're just afraid—meaning Mr. Katz and Mr. Mannix—that the marquee is going to read Jack Benny and that's all. Robert Taylor and Eleanor Powell—what's that? They're afraid they ought to put Loretta Young or Joan Crawford in the part and dub the dancing long shots to get the marquee value. But Mr. Del Ruth spoke up and said, 'First of all, if you take this girl off the picture, I will walk off the picture immediately. Secondly, if she isn't a star overnight, I will direct any two pictures on this lot *gratis*. That's how much I believe in this girl.'" And when I heard that, I would have walked through fire for that man!

We did this number on toe points with the Albertina Rasch Ballet, and you're not supposed to be on your toes for more than three hours without a rest. Unfortunately, we had to keep on because of the set and everything. D'you know, the blood came right through all our pink ballet slippers? And when we took our slippers off that night, they had big buckets of ice. It was like marching for days or something. I lost four toenails on the right foot on that one picture. They grew a little and I lost them again. Talk about stunts, honey! When I went down in that gun-chute thing, I didn't do it with the glove on—I forgot—and I got a burn all the way down my arm as I'm coming down. It took the skin right off my arm.

Anyway, the picture lasted four months instead of the four weeks it was supposed to. The reason it turned out so well, I believe, is that it was a very good story per se. It was a solid, dramatic story; then they embellished it with the songs and dances the way they should do every musical comedy. Set a good solid foundation and then fill in the other things instead of starting off with a song.

I was brought up there to sign a seven-year contract and Mr. Mayer is performing. All the time he's pacing up and down. He starts in by saying, "You're too tall, and you're not *bla bla bla* . . ." and he tears me down. And he says, "I have a proposition to make to you. Nobody, but nobody, gets the money and the opportunity at the same time." Which is true: if you get a big opportunity, you give a little elsewhere if you're starting out. And Mayer said that if I would work for less money on my second picture, *Born to Dance* with Jimmy Stewart, he would use all the Morris Agency clients he could, like Ray Bolger, Sophie Tucker. So I made less on the second picture and the Morris office was set up out here.

I'll never forget when Mr. Mayer came to me and said, "Ellie, how would you like to do a picture with Fred Astaire?" And I said, "You gotta be kidding!" And he said, "No, he likes the script; the money is fine. The only thing is: you may be too tall for him." You know, I'd always had an opportunity to meet Fred Astaire back in New York, but I never wanted to because I'm an idealist. I might meet him and he might do something or say something that I wouldn't like and all my illusions would go. Anyway, I didn't want to meet Fred Astaire at the racetrack back in New York or at a cocktail party. I would have wanted to talk shop. Where could I do that at the racetrack—"What do you use on your shoes? How do you do that? How do you do this?" Fred Astaire was an idol to me, but I had no idea what he thought of me.

Mr. Mayer said, "Mr. Astaire will be in Mervyn LeRoy's office at 11:00 tomorrow morning. You meet him and we'll see if your height is all right." I was there early and I said to Mervyn, "Y'know, I'm so nervous. I took a bath in Lux last night, hoping I'd shrink or something. I just hope this goes through." We were chatting a little while, and then the bell rang. Mervyn LeRoy said to me, "Quick, Ellie, go hide!" and by reflex I ran and hid behind the door. So in saunters Mr. Astaire and Mr. Hayward—Leland Hayward, who was Fred's agent at the time—and they sit down and there's a little chitchat about the weather and the races. And then Mr. Astaire said, "Boy, I'm so nervous. Do you know how she works? Does she standard record or prerecord? How long does she rehearse?" And Mr. LeRoy said, "Well, why don't you ask her! Eleanor, come on out." And I slunk out from behind the door. But the thing is, I had heard Mr. Astaire say almost the same thing I had said. Mervyn said, "I had Eleanor hide behind there because she's been a nervous wreck. She hasn't slept all night." Then the office door opened and, one by one, in walked Mr. Mayer, Mr. Mannix, all the big ones. And here's the setting: we're just chitchatting, polite company talk, y'know, and finally they said, "All right, rise!" So we stood back to back. Well, believe it or not, Fred is taller than I am—not a lot, but he's about 5'8"—so I fit in with the part. Now we sit down and everything's agreed 'cause that was the only thing—if I'd towered over him, it wouldn't have been any good.

Mr. Cole Porter was there and he handed us both a piece of paper—just a lead sheet in his own writing—of "Begin the Beguine." He plays it, we listen. Marvelous. Plays it again and everybody's listening. He hands one sheet to Mr. Astaire and one sheet to me. This is our first number supposedly—we had nine numbers in that picture. Mr. Astaire was going on vacation to London to see Adele, his sister, who was married to Lord Cavendish, and would be back in three months. I said, "Mr. Astaire, I know how important it is for you to have your own pianist." (Because your pianist, you see, becomes your everything when the only thing you have is an empty hall and a piece of music. He's the man who's going to play this and groove it and probably suggest repeating a bar or what have you.) So I said to feel free to bring whoever he wanted. And I said, "Because you're a stranger on the lot, I'll meet you at the East Gate. I have a little bungalow here which Mr. Mayer has built for me to rehearse in. Now, what time do you like to rehearse?" And he said, "Any time *you* desire." So I said, "No, no, no—you select a time." "No, no—whatever . . ." Well, it was like out of "Mr. Alphonse," you know. So I said, "Well, is 8:00 in the morning too early for you?" "No, that's fine," he said. I wasn't going to see him again till he came back, so we shake hands. "*Bon voyage,*" "Have a good trip," and off he goes.

The morning comes. In the meantime, he cannot have his pianist, according to the musicians' union—they wouldn't allow another man from another studio to come over. Naturally, we had to take my man, who was very good. I have had "Begin the Beguine" played backwards, forwards, inside out, and I have general ideas about what I would do. So I meet him at the gate and we saunter down to the bungalow. I introduce him to my pianist, direct him in to change, and he comes out and there are these two little canvas chairs and we sit. We know we have all these numbers to get, but here we are, sitting. He says, "Would you like to hear the music?" I say, "Oh, yes, thank you." So we play the music and I'm thinking, we gotta get going, we gotta start, who's going to start? "Would you like to hear it again, Miss Powell?" he says. I say, "Yes, very much." Well, to everyone around the studio it was like a heavyweight boxing match—two champs in the ring, they expect *pow!*—and here we are, sitting an hour and a half listening to a piece of music we know backwards!

We had no choreographer at all. What made it so difficult was that nobody could do what I was doing but me. Up to the time that Fred worked with me, he had always had a young lady that he could teach. And, of course, they would never say that they didn't care to do that, because that was *it*. In fact, Hermes Pan used to take the girl's part. He would work with Fred, two men together, and Hermes would be whoever the girl was—Ginger Rogers, Joan Fontaine, or whoever. Then when they'd got it all mapped out, Hermes would go teach the girl her part. When she was all rehearsed,

Hermes was Fred Astaire, still teaching her her part so that it wouldn't wear Astaire out. Then they got together for rehearsals. But me being my own choreographer and Fred being his own on *Broadway Melody,* who was going to tell who what to do?

I said, "Mr. Astaire, I have a number and there's something wrong in the middle of it. If I did it for you, would you please help me with the center part of it? It just doesn't feel right." I thought that might be one way we could get on our feet! So I did it, got to the middle, and stopped. And he jumped out of his chair real quick and said, "Oh, I see what you mean," and he did a little something and then he stopped and ran right back to the chair. So I said to him, "Mr. Astaire, what are we going to do?" And he said, "Maybe if you go over in that corner and I go over here and we just take a couple of bars and improvise—and if you see something you like, stop me. And the same if I see something." Fine.

You'd be amazed at how many things we did like. Not the same steps, the same syncopation. Finally he stopped and I fooled around and ad-libbed. "What was *that!*" he'd go, and I'd have to define what I was doing, and vice versa. Finally we got it. But it was three or four days before we started melting. Still it was Mr. Astaire and Miss Powell.

One day we did the exact same thing on a difficult piece of music in "Begin the Beguine," and he forgot and he ran over, lifted me in the air, said, "Oh, Ellie!" then put me down and said, "Oh, I beg your pardon." And I said, "Look, basically we are just two hoofers who started off in vaudeville, right? *Please* let's get down to Fred and Ellie." And he said OK. The ice was broken. I don't mean he wasn't perfectly charming after that point—it wasn't "Hi, Ellie!" "Hi, Fred!"—but we got flowing as regards the work we were doing.

If you remember "Begin the Beguine," we did that thing in the circle, counter-rhythm—we went in a circle; he went this way and I went that way. Well, we had more fun working on it! We started at 8:00, remember. My tummy made the worst growling noise—I was so embarrassed—and he said, "What time is it?" But we had no clock. D'you know, it was 4:00 in the afternoon! We had gone from 8:00 right straight through to 4:00, over and over. The poor piano player, he was absolutely dying! He had a cigarette hanging out the corner of his mouth and the two ashtrays were full. So we got a Big Ben alarm clock and we set it at 1:00. And we promised, no matter where we were, we would stop to allow this man to have time. We were crazy; *he* didn't have to be. . . .

—from *People Will Talk,* 1985 (interview took place in 1971)

MICHAEL POWELL
The Red Shoes

*Michael Powell (1905–1990) was, with Alfred Hitchcock, one of the two most orig-
inal and important—and colorful—British film directors. With his partner, Emeric
Pressburger, he was responsible for many renowned films, including* The Life and
Death of Colonel Blimp, Black Narcissus, I Know Where I'm Going, *and of
course* The Red Shoes. *In 1986 he published the first volume of his autobiography,*
A Life in Movies, *followed six years later by the second,* Million Dollar Movie.

I reminded myself that I had made two stipulations for taking on *The Red
Shoes:* the part of Vicky Page had to be played by a dancer, and a dancer of
exceptional quality; and a twenty-minute ballet, in which she would dance
the leading role, would have to be invented. A score had now been commissioned and it was time to look for the girl.

My early interest in ballet, inspired by Diaghilev and my Russian
friends in Nice, had been revived by my friendship with Bobby Helpmann
and my contacts with the Sadler's Wells Ballet. I knew that Marie Rambert
was reforming her company at the little Mercury Theatre, but elsewhere
the ballet world was in confusion after the war. Europe was rebuilding and
re-forming, but America had kept some dance companies and dance
teachers together, and it seemed to be the only likely place to find a young
ballerina who was not exactly an actress, but who could at least open her
mouth and speak the words in the script. At this point in my ruminations,
Fate in the shape of Jimmy Granger took me by the arm in the noisy
Pinewood Studios canteen. He had become a big star by now, and he aped
the handsome brute, although his friends knew him for the innocent idealist
he was.

"Micky! You're looking for a ballerina, aren't you?"

Jimmy always knew all the new girls as soon as they hit town, so I said:
"Yes, Jimmy," and waited.

"Well, there's a new girl at the Wells. She's in Bobby Helpmann's new
ballet. Go and see her. She's got it, whatever it is."

The ballet was *Miracle in the Gorbals*. It was in the repertory already, and I
would have to wait a week to see it. I spoke to Bobby.

"Oh—Moira . . . ye-e-es. You could do worse, I suppose. She's very spectacular-looking."

Bobby had read the *Red Shoes* script. I intended him to be my right-hand man all through the film.

"Do you think she could do it?" I asked.

"Mmm . . . she might . . . She's coming up very quickly. She ought to be out there dancing leads, but you know Madame."

I said that I knew Miss de Valois.

"Ye-e-es. She believes in bringing them on slowly. There's Margot too, you know . . . Ninette thinks the sun shines out of Margot's little arse. She wouldn't want anyone to stand in her light, would she?"

"What sort of voice has this girl got?"

"We-ell, she has a voice. She's Scottish, you know."

In due course, I saw *Miracle in the Gorbals*. The girl was sensational. I asked that a meeting be arranged. A month went by—Miss Shearer was at class . . . Miss Shearer was at rehearsal . . . Miss Shearer was having costume fittings—then finally she managed to fit me in between a hairdresser's appointment and a performance. I, for my part, was attending one of the vast Rank get-togethers, three hundred salesmen in the Dorchester ballroom, to be introduced to the stars and the makers of stars, directors, writers, etc., and to hear about next year's program. I had arranged to come out when I was told Miss Shearer was waiting in the ante-room. I had established a life-line of commissionaires, assistants, page-boys, to make sure that I was warned in time of my potential star's arrival. In due course, the signal came and I went out. The page-boy whispered to me as I passed him: "She's a corker, Mr. Powell." She certainly was. And is.

She was tall, with the most glorious hair of Titian red that I had ever seen on a woman. And I've seen some. She had a cheeky face, well-bred and full of spirit. She had a magnificent body. She wasn't slim; she just didn't have one ounce of superfluous flesh. Her eyes were blue. Her hands—what's the use of describing her; you all know her. After a few minutes' conversation, I offered her the part. I would have offered it to her the moment we met, but I didn't want to seem frivolous. As it was, she looked startled.

"Are you serious, Mr. Powell?"

"Quite serious. The part is yours. We don't start shooting until June next year. But you understand, you have to prepare a long way ahead."

"You too, I suppose." Silence. Then: "What are you going to pay me, Mr. Powell?"

I grinned. She was Scottish all right.

"Oh, a thousand pounds or so, and a retainer and expenses during the running-up period."

"I see. I would have to get Miss de Valois's permission, of course."

"Are you under contract to the Wells?"

"We have no contracts."

I remembered that this was true. It was one of Miss de Valois's proudest boasts: "Our dancers come to us. We don't go to them."

"Do you think she'll be sticky about it?"

"I beg your pardon, Mr. Powell?"

"I mean, it cuts both ways, doesn't it? No contract, I mean. She can hardly stop you doing what you want to do, so long as you give her plenty of notice."

"The ballet is my career, not the cinema, Mr. Powell. I must go now. Good-bye."

"*Au revoir.*" We shook hands. "When will I hear from you?" Her hand was slim and supple, like her body. She retook possession of it.

"You understand, Mr. Powell, I shall have to make an opportunity to speak to Miss de Valois. It may take a little time."

"Let me hear from you."

"Oh, and Mr. Powell. Thank you for offering me the part."

She went off with her quick stride to her many appointments. That pageboy was right. She was a corker.

Bobby Helpmann was pessimistic: "Ninette will kill it stone dead. She will think you should have offered the part to Margot."

"I adore Margot, but she wouldn't be right for the part."

"Tell that to Ninette! Margot is the prima ballerina of her company. You should have asked Margot first."

"She might have said yes."

"Yes. She might have. In any case, she would have come to me, and I would have found some clever way of talking her out of it. Oh, dear! Why didn't you let me handle it?"

A week later an agent rang up. He was not a very big agent, but I knew him. He said that he represented Miss Moira Shearer. He understood that Powell and Pressburger had offered the leading part in a dance film entitled *The Red Shoes* to his client, at a proposed fee of £1,000, plus a retainer and expenses. Miss Shearer would want a retainer of £1,000 to be paid immediately, expenses to be agreed, and a fee of £5,000 for a twelve-week film, half of it to be paid at the end of the first day's shooting and the balance on the last day.

To myself, I nodded approval. She was Scottish all right. To the agent I said, who did he think Miss Shearer was—Deborah Kerr? Anyway, we understood that she had to get permission from the Sadler's Wells Ballet, who had her under exclusive contract. Was this true? He said he would find out and come back to me. Things seemed to be trundling along in the required direction.

. . . At this point in their career, the Archers were tall in the saddle and pretty arrogant about it. . . . They seemed to have the world at their feet, or at any rate a ballerina's feet, with *The Red Shoes* next on their list. But the gods smelt hubris. Moira's agent wrote to say that she had changed her mind about doing the film.

Just as Bobby Helpmann said, it was a case of woman against woman: Scot against Irish, authority against artist. Miss de Valois was creating a national and international ballet company in the same way that Ralph and Larry had re-created the Old Vic. Her authority was based upon a mandate from the Arts Council and insufficient money. She had a small company devoted to their art and to her as artistic director, and she had three geniuses: Margot Fonteyn, Robert Helpmann, and Frederick Ashton. In the circumstances, she was keenly aware of any breach of her authority, and my direct approach to Moira had been interpreted by her as just that. Nothing is secret in a theatrical company and more particularly in a ballet company, so Miss de Valois knew all about *The Red Shoes* and who they fitted. She had only to run into Bobby Helpmann backstage at the New Theatre, which the Sadler's Wells Ballet shared with the Old Vic. Miss de Valois bided her time. After a few months, Moira asked for an interview. What happened between them was something like this:

"My dear Moira, Michael Powell and Emeric Pressburger are two very clever men, and no doubt they will do what they say they will do, although" (a little arching of the eyebrow here) "it is difficult to see how they will get any first-class ballet company to be available to them as and when they will want their collaboration. The film world is a very wonderful world, I have no doubt, and they think money can solve anything, but you and I know, my dear Moira" (a flattering inclusion, this!) "you and I know that a dancer's career is based upon three things, talent, work, and discipline, and such a break in your training could ruin—"

"But Miss de Valois, the film does not start until our holidays start. Surely it would be possible to—"

She's interrupted by a slow shake of the head for impetuous youth. "Let this red-headed beauty play the star part in a ballet film and get all the publicity and razzmatazz of a film of this kind with these two formidable young cinema men making it, and that traitor Bobby directing the ballet? And poor Margot left out in the cold when we already have an invitation to go and dance at the Met next year in New York? Not bloody likely!"

But Moira was not a redhead for nothing. "Then, Miss de Valois, you do not wish me to accept this offer?"

"My dear child! Of course you must accept it! It is a great chance for you, and no doubt these clever young men will surmount all the obstacles that I have mentioned, and perhaps they will start their film on the date they have mentioned to you. But suppose they don't start on the date that they have told you? Suppose that the film is still not finished when it is time for you to return to Sadler's Wells?"

Moira thinks this over. "But you don't object to my doing it?"

"My dear, you are as free as the air. Your holidays are your own, but naturally . . ."

A look between the two handsome women, blue eyes against steel grey ones.

". . . if you leave our organisation to do this dance film, I can't promise that I will keep your place open for you, can I?"

A pause. Then: "Yes. I see."

Bobby Helpmann was unsympathetic. "I told you so. You should have let me handle it. Now the old girl has her dander up. She talks about gratitude and devotion, discipline . . . All balls! If you offered the part to Margot and played Moira in the second lead part, she'd sing a very different tune."

"I daresay."

"Well?"

"What do you mean, well?"

"Why don't you play some lovely little black-haired actress in the part and have Margot double the dancing. Moira can dance the Russian girl, whatever her name is."

"That's old hat. It's been done a thousand times. If a dancer doesn't play the part, I'm not interested."

"Well, you won't get Moira."

"Why?"

"Because she's scared."

"Of what?"

"Losing her place in the running. Don't be dumb. She is out to take Margot's place as prima ballerina assoluta. She wouldn't give that up for all the tea in China."

"But Ninette would never—"

"Why not, with that hair and those legs? Ninette has already promised Moira the lead in *The Sleeping Beauty*. She can't keep Moira in the back row. She's very spectacular, you know."

"Well, it looks as if I'll have to get somebody else."

"You won't play Margot?"

"No, she wouldn't be right." . . .

As soon as she had made her decision, Moira regretted it. She had enjoyed our brief courtship of her. She had enjoyed being chosen for a star part by the famous Archers. She had noticed the way the company looked at her, the way they talked to her already. She was not only a potential rival to Margot Fonteyn in the Sadler's Wells Ballet, one of the top ballet companies in the world, but she was also a potential actress in the mysterious and awful world of films. And then there was the retainer that she had returned in a burst of high-mindedness, and the fee of £5,000, which would come in very handy for a girl who danced for her living.

And then there was Bobby, with his worldly-wise views, and his open scorn of her idealism and kowtowing to Miss de Valois: "Well, you are a little idiot, Moira, to believe all that stuff that the old girl threw at you. You've a perfect right to take another job in the holidays. She had no right to try to frighten you off it. The bitch! She's afraid you'll put Margot in the shade with that film publicity and that hair of yours. Drop you? That's all nonsense."

Other people were equally outspoken. Jimmy Granger was one of them. Who did she think she was to turn down a part, a dancing part, offered to her by Michael Powell himself, after he, Jimmy, had put in a word for her? She must be nuts! Poor Moira began to think so too.

Then she heard that Léonide Massine was in town, and that I had sought him out to offer him the part of Ljubov, the choreographer of the Ballets Lermontov in the film. Massine, besides playing the part, would also dance the part of the Shoemaker in the ballet. Massine was one of the great names in the history of the ballet, and Moira admired him greatly. All this without her! Moira was shaken.

Then she heard that Alan Carter and Bobby Helpmann were gathering a company together for the film. They were not going to depend upon Sadler's Wells or any other European ballet company. We were going to have our own, with Bobby Helpmann at its head.

At this point, when Moira was still hesitating, Emeric came to me. He looked more than usually mischievous. "Michael, we must find another girl for the part of Vicky."

"You're telling me, but where?"

"In America. There are plenty of ballet companies there."

"I daresay, but what makes you think I'll find another Moira?"

"Michael, have you heard the phrase 'a sprat to catch a mackerel'? It is in the *Oxford Book of Quotations*."

"You mean a red-headed mackerel?"

"Yes. You go to America, you find another girl, you bring her to England with lots of publicity to make a test for the part, and Bob's your uncle."

"Is that in the *Oxford Book of Quotations* too?"

"No, I learnt it from Bill Wall. When I say 'Bob is your uncle,' you say 'And Fanny is my aunt.'"

In America I met a lot of Russians, all with ballerinas in tow. I met Sergei Denham. He found me a girl. I brought her back to England and we announced she was going to be tested for the leading role in *The Red Shoes*—and Fanny was my aunt: Moira changed her mind.

To hell with Miss de Valois! She wanted to play and dance that part. So, is it any wonder that Emeric had such a seraphic smile when he announced that Moira Shearer was Vicky Page? His sprat had caught his mackerel.

"Not a mackerel," I said, "but a whale!"

Emeric looked pained.

"What a way to talk about a lady."

What was the name of the girl I found in New York? I don't remember. What happened to her? She's fit and well and has a ballet school in Texas.

A week later, we made a test of Moira with Anton Walbrook, who had returned to the Archers to play Boris Lermontov, the enigmatic and formidable impresario of the Ballets Lermontov.

. . . Anton conceals his humility and his warm heart behind perfect manners that shield him like a suit of armour. He responds to clothing like the chameleon that changes shape and colour out of sympathy with its surroundings. In tweeds and a Tyrolean hat with a feather, he was the perfect Viennese. In the overalls of Peter, the Hutterite, he was one of the disciples of Christ. In *Colonel Blimp,* stripped for the duel, he was the perfect soldier. Now, in white tie and tails, he was the supreme arbiter of elegance, whose approval or disapproval could mean life or death to an artist. The film would not start for several weeks yet, and then it would be on location in France, but Anton had agreed to partner Moira in the test. He was as curious as anyone else to see what he would have to deal with. Miss Shearer was surrounded by a swarm of acolytes when she came onto the exquisite little set and greeted me.

There were introductions all round, and then I said: "Ask Miss Shearer if she can spare a moment."

Syd himself went to get her. The buzzing group around her opened out and departed. She came over. Her wisp of a dress left her shoulders and arms bare, except for white gloves and a few jewels. Her cloud of red hair, as natural and beautiful as any animal's, flamed and glittered like an autumn bonfire. She wore hardly any make-up. She came with her quick stride to where I was standing with Anton, and held out her hand, saying: "How do you do, Mr. Lermontov?"

Anton's catlike eyes met her blue ones. He bent over her hand and murmured: "So glad that we are going to work together."

By now, the whole camera crew had adopted Moira. The prospect of working with her for the next four or five months did not appear to daunt them at all. Jack said: "Can we see the scene, Micky?"

It was the same one that is in the film. We walked it through and made one or two slight alterations; then I said: "Let's take it."

Most actresses, or at least most young actresses, would insist on more preparation for such an important moment in their careers, and particularly when partnered by an actor as powerful, as subtle, as Anton. He goes underneath every line of dialogue, every emotion. Moira played it straight from her warm heart and stole the scene. I made two takes. Both of them were perfect. Alas! Where is that test now? What I would not give to have it in my collection!

I said: "I would like individuals."

We shot Anton's close-ups and Moira's last. By now, the whole camera department were her slaves. They already addressed her as Moira, and made jokes that made her eyes sparkle. She was adorably natural. Anton paused by me as he left the set and whispered: "She's sensational."

In a few days we ran the tests for the executives.

Arthur said: "Did you say she had never acted before, Micky?"

John said: "Is that red hair of hers real?"

I reassured them on both points. "She's a natural. I never knew what a natural was before. But I do now. It's Moira Shearer." . . .

Marius Goring was our final casting for Julian, the young composer of the "Ballet of the Red Shoes," whose love for Vicky, combined with Lermontov's possessiveness, drives her to suicide. Marius was an old friend. He had played the young U-boat officer in *The Spy in Black,* and then the Collector in *A Matter of Life and Death.* He was really too old to play Julian in *The Red Shoes,* although he had the background, artistic and musical, for the part. The more he tried to look young, the older he looked. He was certainly not the moody, formidable young man of Emeric's dreams, but Emeric loved him too. We decided that his tact and experience would be invaluable for Moira, whose performance as an actress would certainly not be improved by some selfish Adonis. We were proved right. Marius joined the club and fell in love with Moira, and she behaved towards him with trust and affection. It was odd casting, but it worked because we were all on the same wavelength. . . .

Léonide Massine, who played Grischa Ljubov, Lermontov's choreographer, and danced the part of the Shoemaker in the "Ballet of the Red Shoes," was intensely musical, a superb mime and a good actor. He could pass from dignity to buffoonery in a flash, one moment a monk, the next a monkey. His name, his reputation, his achievement in ballet made him a formidable figure in public, and he knew how to exploit it; but in private he was a good friend who loved to pull your leg and didn't mind if you pulled his. I had worshipped him as an artist for twenty-five years of his brilliant career, and loved him as a friend for the next thirty years. We loved to work together. Together we created magic.

He had been in America during the war—he was an American citizen—and I had seen the two ballet films that he had made in collaboration with Jean Negulesco for Warner Brothers—the charming man who later made *Three*

Coins in the Fountain. But when I heard that he had arrived in London just when I was casting for *The Red Shoes* I felt that Fate had brought us together just when I needed for the film all the genius of the world. He had taken an apartment in one of those tall stone and red-brick Kensington houses, just around the corner from Barker's department store, and we met there. He was preternaturally solemn and stared at me with a look that was centuries old. I explained what we were up to and that Grischa Ljubov was based, perhaps, partly upon himself. He bowed. Then I mentioned the ballet, and explained Bobby Helpmann's part in the proceedings. The temperature of the room went down perceptibly. Massine picked his words carefully. He had nothing against the Sadler's Wells Ballet and its leading male dancer, and of course it was my privilege to appoint whom I wished as choreographer. But if he were to dance the Shoemaker in the Hans Andersen story, he would obviously create the part himself, and would want credit for doing so. I was so mad about him by now—he brought half a dozen qualities to the film which had been sadly lacking—that I strode over this minor obstacle, merely saying that I was sure Robert Helpmann would agree to this. I knew that when Bobby and Fred Ashton were beginners, they had been pupils of Massine.

Inevitably, the question of the fee came up. Massine appeared indifferent. I took a deep breath and murmured: "£10,000?"

A perceptible warmth spread through the room. I had the impression that the difficulty about who was whose choreographer was a matter for compromise: give a little, take a little. I had been conscious for some time of family noises coming from the other rooms, and at this point the door flew open and Tania, Massine's wife, swept majestically into the room. She was a magnificent creature, evidently a dancer, but putting on weight. Two children tumbled in after her: young Léonide and young Tania. I am sure that the majestic Tania had been listening at the keyhole. I was not to know that I was transforming Massine's life. In the face of fierce competition in America, where he was too well known, he had decided to bring his family to Europe, where he had many friends and a few engagements, and proposed to eke out his slender income by restaging the famous ballets of which he held the copyright. My offer was a godsend to him, and when the film became a huge success it opened a new career for him.

I went straight to Bobby and told him the Massine tale. He purred: "But of course he would say that. At his age, I don't blame him." (Massine was about fifty, Bobby about thirty-five.) "Naturally, he wouldn't want to go down a step."

"Thank you, Bobby."

"Oh! Don't thank me. It's for the good of the show, as they say. He will be just wonderful as the Shoemaker. Nobody better. As for the acting—mmmm, well, we'll see." . . .

By June, the Red Shoes Company was 120 strong and buzzing like a bee-hive. We kicked off in Paris, and true to the Archers' tradition of sharing the good things of life with everybody in our crew, we invited our French actors to join us in a tremendous lunch at a brasserie near the Place de l'Opéra. After lunch, we decided the light was not quite right on the Opéra, so we all had another round of liqueurs, with the result that we shot the only long-shot I have ever seen of the Paris Opéra leaning drunkenly to the left. Next day we shot the sequence in the Gare de Lyon. Moira was still with Sadler's Wells, and so she flew over for it and then flew back to London again. She was as busy as ever with fittings, classes, and rehearsals, and was not to join us officially until we were in Monte Carlo in three days' time. . . .

Then she flew down by the night plane. She was pretty near the end of her tether. With our fittings, and the ballet fittings, and make-up tests, she had not had a second to herself for about three weeks. She had to be up at six in the morning to start work in Monte Carlo.

"She's in the first shot. Ready at nine."

"Excuse me, Mr. Powell"—it was the wardrobe mistress speaking—"the script says that Moira runs out onto the terrace and jumps into the railway cutting, wearing the Red Shoes. But how can she be wearing them? The ballet hasn't started yet. She hasn't even tried them on."

This was a poser, but it would never do to turn tail before a wardrobe mistress. "She's wearing the Red Shoes," I said firmly. "She is wearing the full costume for the ballet, plus the Red Shoes."

"But how *can* she be," wailed the wardrobe mistress.

"You just do your job and I'll do mine," I advised her kindly. "It's the Red Shoes that are dancing her away to her death, and so she's got to be wearing them."

By now, even Emeric was against me. "I'm not sure that you are right, Michael," he said mildly. "Vicky cannot be wearing the Red Shoes when she runs out to commit suicide."

"But it isn't Vicky who's running away from the theatre; it is the Red Shoes that are running away with Vicky. We'll invent a reason for her wear-ing the Red Shoes when we get back into the studio. But tomorrow morning she wears the Red Shoes or I don't shoot the scene."

"Why not shoot it both ways?" suggested George Busby, the peacemaker.

But I already had an image in my mind of the shattered body of the balle-rina lying on the railroad track, and her Red Shoes, red with blood, and I said: "No."

Next morning we were shooting the scene in the toy railway station of Monte Carlo, which still existed then, and which I had known since I was a child. Our cameramen struggled to maintain their position as the excited and sympathetic French crowd pressed in and around the two lovers. Marius knelt between the rails beside the dying girl, and with a passionate flinging out of his arms appealed to Heaven whether this was just. Moira, with her beautiful blue ribbons and her peach-coloured dress smeared with blood, whispered: "Julian! Take off the Red Shoes."

I was desperately trying to see what was going on, when I felt an arm around my shoulders and looked round into the face of the stationmaster, who had joined the crowd. Tears were pouring down his face as he watched the dying girl, and he stammered: "*Oh! Mon dieu! C'est terrible! C'est terrible!*"

Nearly all the British critics, having failed to understand the rest of the picture, picked upon this final scene as typical of the bad taste of the Archers, and particularly of Michael Powell. Why all this blood, they asked, why all this sordid realism in a romantic and beautiful fairytale? The poor bastards had obviously never read Hans Christian Andersen, the author of the original story, in which the girl got a woodcutter to cut off her feet with his axe, with the Red Shoes still on them, and danced to Heaven on the stumps. The whole point of the scene was the conflict between romance and realism, between theatre and life. But I suspect that what they really wanted was a happy ending. Our public knew better. When Alex Korda showed the film in his private projection room to the King and Queen and the two young princesses, he told me they were all devastated by the ending of the picture, as they were intended to be, and thanked him with tears streaming down their faces for showing them "such a lovely—boohoo!—picture."

I have often thought that the difference of opinion between Emeric and myself over whether Moira should wear the Red Shoes at the end of the picture or not was typical of our two functions and our two mentalities. Emeric was the writer and knew that she couldn't possibly be wearing the Red Shoes when she runs away. I was a director, a storyteller, and knew that she must. I didn't try to explain it. I just did it. I backed up this obvious fact with a few visual touches. When a ballerina is wearing a new pair of slippers, she likes to break them in herself. And I had Moira doing this in her dressing room before Julian shows up at the door. She had no chance of changing them before she's called down to the stage, but her dresser, played beautifully by Yvonne André, has the other pair of ballet shoes of the normal peach-coloured satin in her hands, ready to substitute for the Red Shoes for the opening scene. So much for realism. I now brought the Red Shoes into play as a magical image with a power over their wearer, exactly as in the fairy tale. I went close on the Red Shoes with the camera and worked out with Jack Cardiff a high intensity of colour and light, which seemed to give the shoes life. So I invented the action where Moira takes a step towards the camera and the shoes stop her dead and then turn her round exactly as if they were the masters. The flashing light and the flaring colour get more and more intense, and she starts to run in the opposite direction from the stage. The dresser screams: "Miss Page, Miss Page!" and then: "Monsieur Lermontov! Monsieur Lermontov!" The flying figure of Moira vanishes down the stairs. Here I introduced a cast-iron spiral staircase, often found in the older theatres, set it up in the studio, and had Moira run down it. She did it in two and a half seconds.

"It's too short," said Reggie Mills, the editor.

"We must keep ahead of the feet," said Chris, the camera operator. "We'll put the camera on an elevator."

This was done. We shot it again and looked at it on the screen.

"We still don't see enough of her feet," said Jack. They made a brilliant suggestion: "What we ought to do is to have this spiral staircase on a turntable and have the turntable turning slowly as Moira runs down. This will keep her in full view of the camera all the time."

We mounted this twenty-five-foot-high cast-iron prop on an iron turntable, turned by a motor at variable speeds. We adjusted the speed to Moira's speed, which was fantastic. We shot it and ran the picture again.

"Now the shot is all right," I said, "but it's still too short."

"Simple," said Reggie Mills. "Shoot two takes and I'll cut them together."

If you watch closely, you will see where Reggie joins the two takes together, but you will have to be very quick to see it. The final length of the cut in the picture is six seconds. It gives her whole escape from the theatre, and Lermontov, a vertiginous whirling character before she bursts out of the stage door into the sunshine and to her death. There are dozens of images, cuts, and moves in the "Ballet of the Red Shoes" that have this dual significance, and this was a deliberate attempt on my part to lift storytelling onto a different level and leave naturalism behind. I do it again and again in the film. An obvious sequence, which has nothing to do with reality, is the series of shots which take Vicky in her robe and coronet, as if on a magic carpet, from her hotel to Lermontov's villa, from obscurity to stardom. I used the landscape of mountains and sea that I knew so well as if it were an audience applauding a new arrival. But enough of that. I have brought you to the first days of shooting and to Moira's transformation into Vicky Page. I had nothing but admiration for her, but, of course, I did not say so. She did everything that I asked her to do, and even suggested something of her own.

"Mr. Powell! I can jump over the balustrade onto a mattress, if you have one."

A mattress was found.

"Mr. Powell! Shall I jump like a girl committing suicide, or like a ballerina?"

I thought. "Like a ballerina."

She is only in the air for about eight frames, but it is one of the most beautiful cuts in the film. By now the camera crew were her devotees. The whole sequence of her running out and dying on the track was completed by lunchtime. Moira spent the afternoon having fittings with Mme Jacques Fath and her dressmakers for the clothes in the film. Towards six o'clock she had hysterics, went to bed, and slept for twelve hours. Her career as a film star had begun. . . .

I have said that we were shooting in continuity, so that the big *Faust*-like scene in which Lermontov and Julian fight for Vicky's body and soul was her last scene in the shooting as well as in the film. Moira had been so fêted and adored by the crew and so gratified, although puzzled, by my tacit approval that she had concluded acting was a piece of cake. Then she found herself in a tiny dressing room fighting for her life between heavyweights like Anton and Marius, neither of whom was particularly inclined to let the other steal the scene, and she lost her nerve. We rehearsed it through a long day with tempers frayed and tears and both these good actors trying to coach a hysterical Moira. I was grimly determined to get a performance out of her, but as the day wore on I began to realise that it couldn't be done. She could act with her brains and her body, but not with her guts.

"It's five o'clock, Michael," said Syd in the tactful whisper of one who watches by a deathbed.

"Send everybody home," was my answer. "We'll shoot it in the morning, made up ready at nine."

"Made up and dressed?" asked the wardrobe girl.

"Yes. And full stage make-up for Miss Shearer."

I had realised that I would never get what I planned, and that I must settle for what I could get. The two actors met me in my office, which I never used except to hang my coat in. Marius still believed that he could get me what I wanted. "Give me an hour with her in the morning and you'll see!"

I said no, we should give up trying to make a film and barnstorm our way through. In the morning, we would run through the words and directions and set up the camera for a master shot and shoot it. They would have to carry Moira through. They looked a bit shocked at this plain speaking, but after the long day they were in no condition to argue.

At 9:30 in the morning we kicked off. The selfishness and cruelty of the two men who loved and killed Vicky Page suddenly flared into reality. They mishandled Moira as if she were a beautiful thoroughbred, pulling her head savagely this way and that. Because the two men were both refined and cultivated artists, the brutality of the scene was all the more disturbing. This was no longer acting. Moira, the centre of this savage combat, got frightened, missed her cues, and started to cry. In the middle of the second take the make-up started to smear. The take ended.

The wardrobe and make-up sprang in. "She'll need a new make-up!"

"Nonsense!" I said. "Touch her up; we're going right away."

Take three came up on the number board. We were all jammed into this little dressing room set. It was abominably hot.

"Action!" I said with an intensity which surprised me. This was it. The men were terrific, and Moira turned blindly from one man to another like a broken doll between them. It was at last very moving. The mascara was running. She snatched at her lines wildly, and after Marius made his exit she seemed neither to see or to hear as Lermontov raised her to her feet and led her towards the door, saying: "Vicky, little Vicky! Now you will dance as you have never danced before."

As Moira staggered out, weeping, the whole stage burst into a roar of applause and sympathy. It wasn't art, but it was good entertainment.

—from *A Life in Movies,* 1986

DEBBIE REYNOLDS
Singin' in the Rain

Born in 1932, Debbie Reynolds won the Miss Burbank beauty contest when she was sixteen, at which time her all-American wholesome looks brought her a movie contract at Warners. Eventually she appeared in more than fifty movies, the most famous of which is the iconic musical Singin' in the Rain; *other particular successes include* The Unsinkable Molly Brown, The Tender Trap, Bundle of Joy, *and* Tammy and the Bachelor. *(Her recording of the film's theme song, "Tammy," was a number-one hit for many weeks in 1952.) Her first marriage, to singer Eddie Fisher, resulted in two children (one of them the actress Carrie Fisher) and sensational headlines when he left her for Elizabeth Taylor. Reynolds has gone on working in film, on the stage, and on TV, recently in the hit comedy* Will & Grace.

One afternoon in the early spring of 1951, I was called to Mr. Mayer's office. I took my seat as he indicated and he sat down, clasped his hands on his vest, and looked at me with a smile on his face.

"Debbie," he said, "you are a very talented little girl and I have a surprise for you today. You are going to make a picture with Gene Kelly and Donald O'Connor."

I thought, "Gene Kelly!" Every matinee I ever loved was with Gene Kelly! And Donald O'Connor!

Mr. Mayer continued, "And today Gene Kelly is coming to see you here."

Almost immediately after that, his secretary, Mrs. Koverman, informed Mr. Mayer that Gene Kelly had arrived.

"Send him in," the boss instructed.

Gene Kelly entered, greeting L.B. (as he was called by many of his employees) with a warm hello. He had the same natural charm that had totally captivated me in the Burbank movie house only three years before.

Mr. Mayer introduced us and he took a seat. Mr. Mayer, still very much the grandfather beaming with pride at the sight of two of his "children," again with his hands clasped before him, said to Gene, "So here's your leading lady."

Gene Kelly looked at me suddenly and very seriously. "Whaaat?"

Mr. Mayer repeated himself. "So here's the girl—*Singin' in the Rain*—your leading lady."

Gene stared at me and stared at me. "Do you dance?" he asked.

"No," I replied tentatively, adding, "Well, a little."

Looking at me as if he were making an appraisal, he continued, "Do you sing?"

"No." Well, I sang, I thought to myself, in that I could do harmony, but . . .

Gene looked at Mr. Mayer in shock. "L.B., w-w-w-whaaat are you doing to me?" He was very upset. Without waiting for L.B.'s answer, he said to me, "Stand up."

I stood up.

"Can you do a time step?" he asked.

"Yes, I can do a time step," I said confidently, hoping that would relieve him a bit.

"Okay." He nodded. "Can I see it?"

So I did a waltz clog.

"That's not a time step; that's a waltz clog," he corrected me with distress in his voice. I didn't know. I thought a time step was a waltz clog.

"Can you do a maxi ford?" he continued.

A maxi ford? "I don't know that car," I answered meekly.

"That's not a car; that's a *step!*" It also happened to be, I later found out, Gene Kelly's favorite step.

It didn't matter to Mr. Mayer. Gene Kelly had been told he had me and he had me. When I told Mother that night that my next film was going to be *Singin' in the Rain* with Donald O'Connor and Gene Kelly, I was bursting with excitement and anticipation. It hadn't occurred to me that I had to dance with them and be as good as they were.

However, I soon found out I should have been thinking, "Just go take gas; turn on the carbon monoxide and just close the door." Because I was about to start something more difficult, more exhausting, more horrendous than any experience I'd ever known in my short and very sheltered experience.

We started rehearsals just two weeks after my nineteenth birthday. The studio had three months to turn me into a dancer. Both Gene and Donald had been dancing all their lives. I was assigned three teachers: Ernie Flatt, who taught me tap and later became the choreographer of *The Carol Burnett Show;* Carol Haney, who was Gene's assistant on the picture and went on to star in *The Pajama Game* on Broadway; and Jeanne Coyne, who later married Gene.

For the next three months I was locked in a soundstage for seven, eight hours a day with my three teachers taking shifts. Having been a gymnast made me strong, but soon I was overwhelmed and intimidated.

Carol Haney was assistant choreographer because Gene was also directing the picture and didn't have time to do it all. Gene had certain steps he liked to do. Donald, who was working on "Make 'Em Laugh," had certain steps *he* always did; and so Carol assembled everything for Gene to approve.

Meanwhile, I was taking a two-hour class with Ernie. Then a two-hour class with Carol. Carol would go on to take care of something else, and Jeanne would come in to teach me. I was dancing eight hours a day, nonstop. That's all I did.

I had to learn every step Gene was going to use and every step Donald was going to use, in whatever sequence they put them to make the dance. I didn't know any of their steps, of course. These were very difficult tap combinations. It's a very hard thing to learn tap. You have to get your ankles very loose first. The fronts of your feet have to become like balloons. Your brain has to work very fast. It takes years to perfect. And I had three months.

Gene would come in to rehearsals, look at me, and ask me to do a maxi ford, the traveling time step, or a combination of the steps they were teaching me. He was never satisfied. I never got a compliment. Ever.

I was afraid of him. He was so strict, so unyielding, and so serious all the time. He had an enormous burden of creativity on his back. Who had time for a crying nineteen-year-old who didn't know how to sing or dance?

In my opinion, I was being thrown to the lions. At first the frustration of mastering the dance infuriated me. One day I was feeling so defeated that I flew into a rage right on the stage, shouting and swearing. I took off my tap shoes and hurled them at the stage mirror and shattered it. Everyone stopped. People were shocked, staring at me as I walked out of the rehearsal hall.

I was so ashamed of my behavior. I went home that night and talked about it with Mother, asking her to help me, to remind me whenever I was getting toward the boiling point.

After that I found myself crying on the soundstage, doing everything in my power to hold back the tears. My feet were killing me. I was so overwhelmed, so intimidated. I couldn't understand why Gene was being so hard on me. I know why now. He was stuck with me. He knew he needed to drive me and so he did. But I didn't know the word *quit*. In my mind, I just had to do it.

After we'd finish a session and I was alone on the rehearsal stage, I'd just walk around and sob to myself. My teachers were all nice to me, and even fun. But I felt inept and exhausted all the time. One day I was lying under the piano sobbing when I heard a voice ask, "Why are you crying?"

"Because I'll never learn any of it," I said, tears still rushing forth. "I can't do it anymore. I feel like I'm going to die, it's so hard. I can't . . . I can't . . . "

"No, you're not going to die," the man said gently. "That's what it is to learn how to dance."

Taking my hands from my eyes I saw a man's pant leg. I pulled myself together to look up. It was Fred Astaire looking down on me, his brow creased with concern.

"You come watch me," he said, as he lent a hand to help me up. "You watch how hard I work. I don't cry," he explained, "but I do get frustrated and upset and I'm going to let you watch."

He took me into his rehearsal hall with Hermes Pan, his choreographer, and his drummer. They were rehearsing for *Royal Wedding.* Now Fred Astaire *never* let even Mr. Mayer watch him rehearse. He was a taskmaster and I saw that. I sat and watched them work until he too was totally frustrated with what he was doing. I knew that it was time for me to leave. But I left thinking that I wasn't alone; it's hard for everybody if it's hard for Fred Astaire.

His gesture was an enormous help to me. It was another step in seeing that MGM was a university of hard work and pain and wonderful creativity.

As production grew closer, the pressure intensified. There were scenes to learn and rehearse, costumes to be fitted, and songs to be recorded. The days seemed even longer and harder. I would be so tired that instead of making the long trip back to Burbank, some nights I'd sleep in my little dressing room on the floor, with a guard stationed by the studio outside my door.

Other nights I'd stay with Lois Horne, my teacher from Warners, who lived nearby in Westwood.

Shooting began on June 19, 1951. I thought I was good at lip-synching until we went before the camera. Then the pressure was on like nothing I'd ever known. Putting the song together with the dancing takes a very special precision. They had one man on the set who did nothing but watch our lips. If there was one mistake, it was "CUT!" and we'd have to start all over again.

Now I had to remember not only the dance steps but where to breathe in my already recorded phrasing of the song. When I wasn't in front of the camera, I was off somewhere sitting listening to a record, mouthing it.

We started shooting the party number, where I did a dance with the girls:

> "All I do is dream of you
> The whole day through. . . . "

It's the scene where the girls and I are hired to entertain for the evening at a Hollywood party. The girls come in, throwing flowers in front of a big cake. The cake stops and I emerge from it.

By this time my brains were fried, my eyes were crossed inside, and my hand was squeezing my butt just to keep my concentration on the lip-synch, the steps, and the spacing. In my mind I'm thinking: "Double tap, double tap/sliiiiide tap! double tap, double tap/sliiiide tap!" My mind was racing.

Meanwhile, Gene is off camera with a microphone yelling: "SMILE, DAMNIT, SMILE!!"

Smile! I'm smiling.

"DON'T LOOK SO PANICKED!"

Don't look so panicked, I'm thinking. Double tap, double tap/sliiiide, tap! Double tap, double ta . . .

"SMILE, DAMNIT, SMILE!"

"I'm smiling, I'm smiling double tap, double tap/sliiiide . . . smile damnit, smile double tap, double tap . . .

Once in production, Gene would get mad at Donald and tear into him. "You're so stupid; you're not doing the step right! You're stupid!"

It wasn't until thirty-five years later that Donald told me the reason Gene always picked on him: It was because he was always mad at me. But he realized if he kept screaming at me I'd probably hold up production with my tears. So he screamed at Donald, who wouldn't cry.

The toughest scenes were done with Donald and Gene. Gene was in great condition. His legs were like pistons; he had the strongest thighs of any man alive. Donald was slim and not nearly as muscular but very strong. My body was strong from sports and barre work. Fortunately I didn't have to build the body, but I was still worn out.

The couch scene ("Good Morning") was the hardest scene I've ever done. Up the stairs, down the stairs. Up the couch, over the couch. We went over that couch hundreds of times. We had been shooting from eight o'clock in the morning. Gene was never satisfied. My feet were bleeding but he was relentless; take after take, he would never give up.

About eleven o'clock at night we finished a take and I just fell over. I just lay on the ground and with barely enough breath to talk, I said, "I can't do it again."

"All right! That's a wrap!" Gene said.

I was driven home that night. The next morning I couldn't get out of bed. I couldn't move. I couldn't walk.

Mother called Dr. Levy to come over and see me.

"What's wrong with you, Mary Frances?" he asked.

"I can't move I'm so tired." I felt as if I'd just crossed a desert.

He checked me over. My heartbeat was slow. "That's ridiculous!" he said. "You'll have to stay in bed for two days."

"But I can't, Dr. Levy. We're shooting a picture. . . . "

"You don't stay in bed, you may not live to finish that picture," he replied.

Mother called the studio. Hundreds of extras, musical numbers costing thousands of dollars, and Mary Frances is tired. Arthur Freed, the producer, called Dr. Levy.

"You don't understand; we have a major motion picture going here and Debbie has to report."

"No, she doesn't," said Dr. Levy. "She's exhausted and she's not going to. It's medically unsound."

"She's only nineteen years old! Get her ass in here!"

"She's staying right where she is," countered the good doctor.

Everyone flipped out. Gene Kelly, Arthur Freed, the insurance company. Dr. Blank from the studio called Dr. Levy informing him that he'd take over my case. He'd give me some "vitamin" shots and I'd feel fine.

Again Dr. Levy said, "No way. Rest is what she needs. You can keep your shots." Which probably saved my life. It was Dr. Blank who administered all the "vitamins" that got Judy Garland and a lot of other people started on the road to complete addiction.

So they rearranged the schedule for two days.

The picture was directed by Stanley Donen and Gene. Stanley handled the technical end, working with Gene in setting up the shots. Gene directed all the actors. They worked very well together.

I felt under the gun so much of the time that I missed just about anything that didn't have to do with my performance. Jean Hagen was wonderful and very nice to me. The role she played, a caricature, was not at all like Jean's personality. She modeled it after Judy Holliday. She should have won the Academy Award she was nominated for. In the picture, my character was supposed to dub the "squeaky" voice of Jean's character while she sang. Jean's real voice, however, was lovely and she dubbed herself.

I sang "You Are My Lucky Star" with Gene Kelly. But it was a very rangy song and done in his key. My part did not come out well, so my singing voice was dubbed in by Betty Royce after the picture was finished.

Shooting ended on November 21, eight months after rehearsals had begun.

Ironically, the man whose vision and instinct had made it all possible for me was no longer there. L. B. Mayer, after twenty-seven years as production head of the studio that bore his name, had been ousted in a power struggle with an ancient rival, Nicholas Schenck, the chairman of Loew's. Mr. Mayer passed through the studio gates for the last time on June 21, the third day of shooting *Singin' in the Rain*. He was replaced by producer/ screenwriter Dore Schary. Schary presided over what turned out to be the beginning of a dismal end to a long and legendary era in the history of American film.

Singin' in the Rain and childbirth were the hardest things I ever had to do in my life. The pain from childbirth was in the lower body, but in *Singin' in the Rain* it was everywhere—especially my feet and my brain. As soon as shooting was completed, I went up to Lake Tahoe for a week's rest. My friend Jeanette went with me. She'd get up in the morning, go water-skiing, play tennis, and bring me my breakfast at noon. My first day there I slept for eighteen hours.

—from *Debbie: My Life,* with David Patrick Columbia, 1988

VASLAV NIJINSKY

LINCOLN KIRSTEIN
Nijinsky

Nijinsky (1889–1950) is the most famous of male dancers. His life has inspired countless biographies, memoirs, films, ballets, and more. He was born in Kiev to Polish circus dancers (his sister was the renowned choreographer Bronislava Nijinska), and was trained at the Imperial Ballet School, where he was immediately recognized as a unique phenomenon of strength and technique. He soon triumphed at the Maryinsky, where he was the frequent partner of Pavlova and Karsavina, and in 1909 was brought to Paris by his lover Diaghilev for the first season of the Ballets Russes. (His career in Russia ended in 1911 as a result of a scandal involving his costume for Giselle.*) He was a sensational success in Europe—the central figure in Fokine's* Les Sylphides, Petrouchka, Schéhérezade, Le Spectre de la Rose, *and* Carnaval, *among others. He also choreographed two of the revolutionary ballets of the century,* L'Après-midi d'un Faune *and* Le Sacre du Printemps. *(His other two ballets were* Jeux *and* Til Eulenspiegel.*) When on a tour of South America, he married the Hungarian Romola Pulszky, Diaghilev fired him, and in 1919 he suffered a mental breakdown. From then until his death, he lived in institutions, prey to schizophrenic sexual and religious delusions—the most famously tragic figure in the history of dance.*

It may be difficult for those who have never watched a ballet class to appreciate the tedious practice and relentless correction, even of experienced performers, at the core of this vocation. In the beginning a child is mysteriously drawn to the idea or even the ideal of dancing, perhaps because he has seen a ballet and glimpsed within it a magic which is infectiously attractive. Dancers glide, spin, leap, almost fly; yet they have only two arms and two legs. If they can dance, why can't he? How soon and how well are questions that never check the determined beginner.

A genius, like Vaslav Nijinsky, did not seem particularly remarkable when he entered school except that the physical formation of his thighs, legs, and feet was promising. How these will develop past adolescence is always uncertain, but the judges who admitted him recognized a potential of athletic power. For Nijinsky his choice of career was probably scarcely in question, since he came from a line of dancers. Yet a child's personal decision to become a dancer is not important unless he has the basic capacities. With Nijinsky there was first the given body and an arresting mask; then over the years of training, his technical security progressed by what were in his case literally leaps and bounds. There have been few able choreographers who have not spent the early part of their career as brilliant dancers. Nijinsky's range was fantastic by the time he was twenty; from this came a conviction beyond competence, a promise of innate authority. What he had done and could do, he could command others to attempt.

Nijinsky has usually been discussed as one among many talents manipulated by Diaghilev, and one who, without considerable help, might never have amounted to much except for the accidental gift of expressive physique. This is true as far as it goes, for every theatrical artist is dependent for his development on the caliber of the talents surrounding him. As a student at the Imperial School, Nijinsky was taught first by the highly competent Legat brothers. He had as models the experienced performers of the Maryinsky troupe appearing in an accumulation of Petipa's repertory. His early roles were tailored to him by Fokine in the first flush of the master's freshness and exuberance. Later, when Nijinsky was deprived of Diaghilev's apparatus, his decline was precipitate while his promise was still obvious.

Before Diaghilev's enlarged career, which in the beginning centered on the visual arts and opera rather than ballet, only a small band of amateurs believed that choreography, the craft of mapping movement, could be a "major" art. It was considered a useful kind of carpentry, a skill by which a regimented corps could be moved tidily and ingeniously through charming parades that would set off the performances of the stars. It is owing to Petipa's later big ballets, Fokine's repertory before his engagement by Diaghilev, and Tchaikovsky's and Stravinsky's important scores that choreography is now accepted as equal in depth and expressiveness to the other arts.

Although his own superiority as a dancer gave Nijinsky the conviction that what he would demand of others was possible, he never in fact required excessive virtuosity, except in the matter of metrical analysis and constant counting. And his self-chosen roles in his important works were never designed to exploit his prowess. In *L'Après-Midi d'un Faune,* where he subtracted the human element to portray a creature of tense animality, he relied not on muscular expense but on rigid control through measured movement. In *Jeux* he exploited sexuality by the metaphor of a perverse sportiveness, again with little self-display and no acrobatics. He did not appear at all in *Le Sacre du Printemps.* Thus even at his height as a performer, his preoccupation was with the design of dancing rather than with his effect in the dance.

Nijinsky appeared briefly in Fokine's ballet as Narcissus, but he was not himself narcissistic. He was involved in the possibilities of human movement rather than in the exposition of his accidental personality. His was no idio-syncratic self-promotion like Isadora's, nor was he interested in the kind of historical resurrection which fascinated Fokine. His primary search was in the springs of muscular release and arrest, first within his own organism, and then through the organism of ballet as a mobile apparatus.

By the intensity of his psychological characterizations as a dancer, Nijin-sky focused a new authority in ballet that enlarged it beyond cosmetic enter-tainment, however fetching or spectacular. In his own compositions, he made audiences more aware than before of dance as design. Though Petipa, Ivanov, and Fokine had offered strong structuring, the brilliance of execu-tion by isolated soloists against opulent furnishings had tended to diminish the importance of patterning for group figures.

Although his later drawings show a draftsman's precision,* Nijinsky seems primarily to have been inspired by plasticity—the projection of forms activated in high relief. He worked in three dimensions linked to a fourth—the musico-temporal—by new and arbitrary measurement. Painted cloths against which the dancers moved in *Faune, Jeux,* and *Sacre* were rendered in the generalized terms of Post-Impressionism. For all its vaunted ethnogra-phy, *Sacre* was set in a bland, anomalous landscape which indicated an atmo-spheric surround more than any specific place or period.

If Fokine can be called a painter, then Nijinsky was a sculptor. His method was not the weaving of a tapestry but the release of forms in space. And these forms opposed the music in kinetic counterpoint as often as they accompanied, interpreted, or coincided with it. The dialectic gap precipi-tated an extra tension of contrast and surprise. For the illumination of *Jeux,* Nijinsky proposed the harsh artificial glare of electric arc lamps in early evening, as screened through chestnut trees in a city park. His taste in scenery suggested climate, air, time of day. It included the nostalgia of urban

---

*He studied drawing in Bakst's studio in private lessons and came to have a delicate and sophisticated manner of delineation.

modernity—hitherto no subject for the lyric theater, though it was already the province of Vuillard and Bonnard.

Had Nijinsky been more experienced in teaching, perhaps he could have conveyed his wishes with more tact and so reduced the friction in his rehearsals. His peers were accustomed to performing acrobatics to orchestration. He asked for another type of muscular expense that, although it was constrained by counts, bore a defeating resemblance to involuntary or at least unskilled action. At best it was walking or marching, at worst trembling or jerking. What he seemed to demand was a school of ordered fragmentation, abrupt and gauche, but on cue: quivering, shivering, spasms, ejaculations; a metaphorical hysteria which ended in assertive exhaustion and which, indeed, exhausted the patience, goodwill, and attention of his troupe.

Possibly this intensity in opposition to the alternatives of the academy contributed also to his own early exhaustion. No one before him had ever conceived that such acerbic, anguished, icy, heartless, desentimentalized gesture had any aesthetic justification, except accidentally, via pathology. Unwittingly perhaps, Nijinsky, who was increasingly on the border between super- and hyper-consciousness, tapped the deep veins of the unconscious and its imperious release through muscular momentum. In this he was neither exhibitionistic nor self-indulgent. He never, unlike later practitioners, used a simulated hysteria as a flagrant device for titillating shock. Nothing he did was improvised; everything within the confines of his design was under designated control.

Naturally, dancers who had, like him, undergone the academic discipline resented his abrasive onslaught against what was nominally known as "beauty." They were offended by his downgrading of a technical discipline that they had acquired with pain, and that for so long had been considered efficient and absolute. It was almost insulting that he did not require them to leap, spin, or demonstrate symmetrical grace. He had sighted another range, another texture, which seemed to them idiotically simple, deformed, subhuman, and ugly. Yet his own conviction and unassailable facility as a dancer, together with Diaghilev's awesome protection, enforced his single-minded aggression.

Nijinsky had to contend with two generations of able and pleasing performers who had utter confidence in their taste and training and almost no confidence in his creative talent. Today the concept of grace can be a crux for semantic or theological discussion, but when he first worked, grace spelled beauty. As many of us have mindlessly repeated, truth is beauty: "That is all ye know on earth and all ye need to know." But one oddly conditioned young Slav needed to know a great deal more. He put beauty, as defined by his epoch, mercilessly to the question. Nietzsche had already made his case for the death of God; Freud was telling terrible things of the soul; Einstein and his friends were making unintelligible jokes about relative space and bended time. Instinctively, or however, Nijinsky (with Rodin, Cézanne, Picasso, and Brancusi) for his generation murdered beauty.

Beauty always exists to be raped and revived in some other vitality by marvelous spirits who arrive armored or disguised as beasts. Such animals, seemingly blind, deaf, or dumb, propose new dimensions. They are always lurking in the forest caves of the imagination, ready and eager to violate the perennial virginity of apathy, innocence, and unthinking jealous defense of habit. Nijinsky was of this genus of marvelous monster, and it was scarcely by accident that he is most remembered for his epiphanies as slave, puppet, and faun. The nobler lyric roles considered worthy for the male First Dancer he also fulfilled in supreme personifications as *danseur noble*. His absolute virtue as a skilled artist left him free to develop his own prophetic presence past any limit so far imagined proper or possible. What he did, what he was able to do in the brief space permitted him, in the few independent works realized, established an entire field theory that ensuing decades have not begun to exhaust.

—from *Nijinsky Dancing*, 1975

JACQUES RIVIÈRE
Le Sacre du Printemps

A critic, editor, and novelist, Jacques Rivière, born in Bordeaux in 1886, was the editor of La Nouvelle Revue Française *from 1919 to 1925, the year of his death. His closest friend and brother-in-law was the novelist Alain-Fournier.*

The great innovation of *Le Sacre du Printemps* is the absence of all "trimmings." Here is a work that is absolutely pure. Cold and harsh, if you will, but without any glaze to mar its inherent brilliance, without any artifices to rearrange or distort its contours. This is not a "work of art" with all the usual little contrivances. Nothing is blurred, nothing obscured by shadows; there is no veiling or poetic mellowing, no trace of aesthetic effect. The work is presented whole and in its natural state; the parts are set before us completely raw, without anything that will aid in their digestion; everything is open, intact, clear, and coarse. . . .

Le Sacre du Printemps is the first masterpiece capable of confronting those of the Impressionists. . . .

Innovative as the music of *Le Sacre du Printemps* might be, the fact that it can be compared to that of Mussorgsky shows that it has retained a certain link to our past experience, that it is possible to find its approximate derivation. The same cannot be said for the choreography. It no longer has any ties whatsoever to the classical ballet. Here, everything has been started anew, everything fashioned on the spot, everything reinvented. The innovation is so shocking and so crude that the public cannot be denied the right—of which it moreover has made overly conscientious use—of rebelling against it. Let us therefore try, in the faint hope of accustoming the public to it, to define this innovation in some detail.

Once again, in my opinion, it consists in the absence of all artifices. As regards the dance in general, one might say that there are two types of artifices. First, those of Loie Fuller: the play of lights, floating draperies, veils that envelop the body and disguise its shape, the blurring of all contours; the dancer's chief aim is to lose herself in her surroundings, to blend her own movements with movements that are vaster and less well-defined, to conceal every exact form in a sort of multihued effusion of which she now is nothing but the indistinct and mysterious center. Quite naturally, she has been led to illustrate Debussy's "Nuages."

Against this first type of artifice, the Russians openly declared themselves from the start. They had the body reappear from under its veils and took it out from that billowing atmosphere in which it had been immersed; henceforth, our only impressions were to come from the body's own movements and from the clearly visible and distinctly outlined figure drawn by the dancer with his arms and legs. They brought clarity back to the dance. I well remember those first nights. For me, it was the revelation of a new world. It was possible, then, to come out of the shadows, to let every gesture be seen, to spell out everything in full without any mystery, and yet be profound and pathetic, holding the spectators' attention as by the most intricate and enigmatic tricks. I made a discovery in art similar to that of geometry in the sciences, and the joy that I felt was similar to the satisfaction one experiences when watching a perfect scientific demonstration. At each of Nijinsky's whirls, just after he had closed, kneeling and crossing his hands, the buckle he had opened while soaring into space, I took an immense pleasure in mentally reviewing the entire figure described by his movement: alive, pure, precise, boldly drawn, as if wrenched in one block and by force from the formless mass of possibilities. There remained no doubts, no confusion, nothing that might cause me to hesitate; rather, I felt reassured and content, like a man who takes in at one glance a system of mathematical propositions from which all possibilities of error have been scrupulously eliminated.

Nevertheless, in this dance which to us had seemed so severe, Nijinsky was able to detect yet another kind of artifice, well before we had noticed it ourselves, and he accordingly undertook to cleanse choreography of it. Having experienced a certain unease in executing Fokine's creations, he understood that they still contained a certain artfulness, a certain vacillation, some sort of inner vagueness that would have to be eliminated at any cost. Conciseness such as this could still be refined; such exactness could be carried even further. . . . From that day on, he would not rest until he himself had turned the screw, had tightened the bolts of the choreographic machinery, so that it might function with absolute precision. Those who find the feeling of something being done in a slipshod and so-so fashion extremely disconcerting will readily understand him.

First, let us determine the nature of this second type of artifice. What is there that still obscures the dancer even after he has divested himself of all accessories? The very intensity of his motion, his passage, his flight across time, the arabesque described by his movement; "he travels along a road which he destroys in the very act of his passing; he follows a mysterious thread that becomes invisible behind him; by his brushing-off gesture, by those hands that he waves in the air, by the thousand slow revolutions of his body, he gives the appearance of a magician busy at obliterating the traces of his handiwork; he will not be caught; we shall not be able to hold him fast and pin his arms to his sides, so as to survey him at leisure from head to foot."* Something interposes itself between him and us; it is that very movement of his; we see him move in a world parallel to ours but different from him; he has lost himself on his own voyage and we perceive him only through a haze formed by the accumulation of his gestures and by his ceaseless to-and-fro motion. More specifically: in the course of his first ten steps, the dancer outlines a figure that immediately thereafter tends to leave him, to escape, to go off on its own, like a melody which, once one has found its first notes, continues by itself, making its own improvisations, until it finally imposes itself on the voice that gave it birth. There is a spring concealed in it that thrusts it from its position. No sooner have the first movements been

---

*This passage is taken from a note I wrote last year (July 1, 1912) on Fokine and in which I made several assertions, which today Nijinsky obliges me not to deny entirely, but rather to surpass, just as he himself, without denying it, has surpassed Fokine.

created by the body than it seems as though, having become aware of themselves, they say to their author: "That's enough! Now we do it by ourselves!" Unchained, they regenerate each other by repetition, by redoubling, by variation, drawing from themselves an infinite abundance. The body, which at first had dictated their actions, now serves only as their support; it now is merely asked to receive and to execute them. Thus, in their hands, the body loses its own form and articulation. They rearrange it, correct it, and retouch it; they create passages in it where there had been gaps; they join its members by a graceful and unbroken line; they erase angles, fill in holes, throw bridges. From head to toe, the body in some way takes on fluidity and fullness. An added elegance casually descends and rests upon it. Like a heavily made-up actor, it is no longer recognizable. The *Specter of the Rose* offers the best example for this transfiguration. Nijinsky's body literally disappears in its own dance. The only thing that remains visible of that muscular being, with its so strong and prominent features, are exquisitely fleeting contours, constantly evanescing forms. The atmosphere in which he is submerged is dynamic rather than multicolored, but he is rendered as indistinct by it as Loie Fuller by her luminous veils. As delightful as the spectacle may be, there is in the *Specter of the Rose* a certain inner lack of truth that can no longer fail to trouble me.

The innovation of *Le Sacre du Printemps* thus lies in doing away with dynamic artificiality, in the return to the body, in the effort to adhere more closely to its natural movements, in lending an ear only to its most immediate, most radical, most etymological expressions. Motion has been reduced to obedience; it is constantly made to return to the body; it is tied to it, caught and pulled back by it, like someone being caught by the elbows and prevented from fleeing. This is motion that does not run off, that has been forbidden to chant its own little tune; motion that must come back to take orders every minute. In the body in repose, there are a thousand hidden directions, an entire system of lines that incline it toward the dance. With Fokine, they all ended in one single movement that joined and exhausted them all; rather than listening to each one, he listened to them all combined; he expressed them by substitution, replacing their varied multitude by a simple and continuous arabesque. In *Le Sacre du Printemps*, on the other hand, as many propensities and occasions as are offered by the body, as many times does the movement stop and start again; as many possible points of departure as the dancer discovers in himself, as many times does he rise again. He regains possession of himself at each instant; like a source that must successively drain all its fountainheads, he recovers his strength, and his dance becomes the analysis, the enumeration of all the body's inclinations toward motion that he can find in it. Here we discover in Nijinsky the same preoccupation as with Stravinsky: to approach everything according to its own orientation. His aim is to follow all the inclinations of the body very directly, regardless of their divergence, and to produce movement only through them. He cannot pursue them all at the same time, however, and as soon as he has followed one for an instant, he suddenly leaves it; he breaks with it and returns to seek another. A dance simultaneously faithful and cut off! Similar to our body, all the motions remain in perfect harmony with the members that execute them; they retain their meaning and conciseness; they remain joined to them as if linked to them organically. And the dancer, when we see him again in memory, instead of effacing himself behind his gestures, stands out very clearly among their multitude, like a Hindu deity among its many arms.

In Nijinsky's development of the groups one finds again the same effort to go into detail, to discover and draw out each individual command of the body. In Fokine's ballets, the groups of dancers were paired off exactly on each side of the scene; this was not the ridiculous symmetry of the Opéra, but an even distribution of masses, an equilibrium that the eye needed to seek only for the time necessary to give it the pleasure of its discovery. This was not merely a static equilibrium: it continued into the dance, no matter how intricate the latter might be; a certain kind of balance prevailed into its innermost turmoil. Each figure was conceived on the model of an exchange or a back-and-forth motion: the dancers having taken hold of a gesture would throw it one to the other, sending it back and forth, like a ball. Never did a group execute a movement that was not in response to a movement made by the opposite group; its advances and retreats, its flights and its returns were dictated solely by the actions of its partner, and intended only to compensate the latter. For this reason, attention was quickly drawn away from it: it disappeared in its dialogue with the others, and nothing more could be seen but the choreographic theme in which it moved; on the scene, there remained only a particular kind of agitation, an entirely pure form of motion. And since such a figure was too abstract to be repeated indefinitely in its essence, Fokine soon was no longer able to show his own invention except by changing the pretext and the accessories. But whether he replaced the golden fruit that the tsarinas of the *Firebird* threw to each other with daggers in *Thamar*, or with pikes in *Daphnis et Chloe*, it was a fight against the impossible; in order to rediscover the source of variety, it would have been necessary, first of all, to rediscover detail, to resume contact with the individual.

Nijinsky understood this only too well. He approached each individual group; he consulted its directions and its trends; he observed it in the manner of a scientist. He saw it arise, tremble, undulate; carried away suddenly by the thrust of its inner force; he noted its molecular formation. He discovered its instincts at the instant of their arousal; he became the observer and

the chronicler of its most minute initiatives. The dance of each group represents the movements created by him in separating each from all the others,
similar to the spontaneous combustion that occurs in haystacks. In the entire
choreography of Le Sacre there is a profound lack of symmetry that forms
part of the essence of the work. Each group sets out on its own; none of its
gestures is born of the need to respond or to compensate, to reestablish
equilibrium; it awakens and sets itself in motion apart from the others; it
glides over to its own side, drawing our attention after it. We do indeed
recapture it in the end, but only because another has seized it and carried it
away. There is no question of lack of composition; on the contrary, there is
composition of the most subtle kind in the encounters, the confrontations,
the intermingling, and the combats of these strange battalions. But this composition does not take precedence over detail, nor does it command it;
rather, it does as best it can with its diversity. The impression of unity that
we never cease to feel for a moment is the one that we experience on seeing
the inhabitants of one and the same world circulate, cross each other's path,
join each other, and separate, according to their particular inclinations, at
once familiar with and oblivious of one another.

Just now we have examined in what sense Nijinsky reacted against
Fokine; what he rejected and what he destroyed. Now we must understand
the positive aspects of his innovation. What benefit did he derive from doing
away with artifice? To what end did he break up choreographic movements
and groups? What kind of beauty lies hidden beneath this reduced and dislo-
cated dance? Without taking into account his marvelous adaptation of the
subject of Le Sacre du Printemps, it is easy to perceive where his innovation
constitutes an improvement over Fokine's dance.

The latter is inherently unsuited to the expression of emotion; one can
read into it nothing but a vague, entirely physical, and faceless joy. Indeed, in
the fluid and continuous motions of which it is composed, as in the large
arabesques of the Renaissance painters, the emotive power of the gesture, its
secret and inner force, is diluted and dissolved. On this undefined road on
which the dancer sets out, the emotions find a too easy outlet and spend
themselves in vain. Instead of the emotion being the object that the movement tries to describe and make visible, it becomes a mere pretext for
erupting into movement, and is soon forgotten amid the abundance of which
it is the source; it quickly loses itself among the repetitions it engenders. The
body sweeps everything away; its freedom reaches into the soul, demolish-
ing its innermost recesses, its resources, and its reserves.

By breaking up movement and bringing it back to the simple gesture,
Nijinsky caused expression to return to the dance. All the angles, all the
breaks in his choreography, are aimed only at preventing the escape of emotion. The movement closes over the emotion; it arrests and contains it; by its

perpetual change in direction, it deprives emotion of every outlet and imprisons it by its very brevity. The body no longer is a means of escape for the soul; on the contrary, it collects and gathers itself around it; it suppresses its outward thrust and, by the very resistance that it offers to the soul, becomes completely permeated by it, having betrayed it from without. The restraint imposed by the body upon the soul conveys upon the body a peculiar kind of spirituality that is visible in all its ways. There is a profound and constrained quality in this captivated dance: all that it loses in spirit, in animation, in capriciousness, it gains in meaning.

Fokine's dance had so little power of expression that, in order to make the spectator aware of the performers' changes of mood, they had to resort to facial mimicry: scowls or smiles. By adding and superimposing this upon the gestures, it merely demonstrated their ineffectiveness. It was merely an additional property, another type of resource needed to supplement the poverty of the language of choreography.

In Nijinsky's dance, however, the face no longer plays a part of importance; it is merely an extension of the body—its flower. It is above all the body that speaks. Moving only as a whole, it forms a block, and its language is a sudden leap with arms and legs outspread, or a sideways move with knees bent, the head dropped upon a shoulder. At first glance, it appears less adroit, less diverse, less intelligent. However, by its compact shifts of position, its sudden turnabouts, its ways of coming to a stop and shaking itself frenetically on the spot, it conveys ever so much more than the eloquent, fast, and elegant speaker represented by Fokine. Nijinsky's language consists of perpetual detail; he lets nothing pass; he seeks out all the corners. There is no turn of phrase, no pirouette, no preterition. The dancer is no longer being carried away by a trivial and indifferent inspiration. Instead of lightly touching upon things during the course of his flight, he lets his full weight fall on them, marking each by his heavy and complete plunge. He leaps in a bound upon each emotion that he encounters and wishes to express; he flings himself upon it, envelops it, and stays for an instant, to imitate it. He forgets everything so as to assume its likeness for a short while; for some time, he suffocates it with his form, blinds it by his very being. No longer obliged to fashion a link between each successive gesture, nor to think constantly of what is to follow, he leaves nothing of himself in the transition. He completely abandons himself to the invitation of the inner object; he becomes unique like the latter as he designates it by the momentary immobility of his entire body. Let us remember Nijinsky, the dancer! With what eloquence he curled himself, like a cat, around emotions! How he hovered over them closely! How well he knew how to arrange all his limbs in their image and to make himself their faithful effigy! He is both an inventor and an interpreter. All that he breaks, all that he takes away from the dance, is done to attain a realistic and complete—as if opaque—imitation of emotion. He takes his dancers, rearranges their arms, twisting them; he would break them if he dared; he belabors these bodies with a pitiless brutality, as though they were lifeless objects; he forces from them impossible movements, attitudes that make them seem deformed. But he does this only in order to draw from them all the expression they are able to give. And at last, they speak. From all those bizarre and twisted forms arises a strange materialization; they distinctly reveal a thousand complex and mysterious objects that now need only to be looked at.

Indeed, it has all become clear and easy; it has taken on the very shape of that which must be understood. Here, before our eyes, has emotion been designated, held fast, and interpreted. Here it is, like a large doll, left behind by the dancer while he goes on. What could be more moving than this physical image of the passions of the soul. How different this is from their expression through articulated language. Not that there is any greater depth, any observance of detail, or any subtleties the spoken word could not render, but by means of this tangible figure we are brought closer to them and put into their presence in a more immediate manner; we are able to contemplate them before the arrival of language, before they are pressed upon by the multitudinous and subtly varied but loquacious crowd of words. There is no need for translation; this is not a sign from which the subject must be interpreted. But though our intelligence fails to grasp it, we are there; we are present through our body, and it is the body that understands. A certain predisposition, a certain inner awareness . . . Each of the dancer's gestures is like a word that I could have said. If at times it seems strange, it is so only in the light of my thoughts, since it immediately enters into my limbs, into the depth of my organism, in a low, complete, and perfect harmony. Just as music had us absorb its narrative in "large, easily manageable pieces," it is thus that we face this extravagant dance with a peculiar barefaced credulity and with a feeling of intimacy that "goes beyond words." We stand before it like children at a puppet show: they don't need to have things "explained to them"; rather, as the show goes on, they laugh, they tremble, they understand.

Nijinsky has given the dance a power of interpretation it had lacked. But would not his effort to relate the dance more closely to the body, to cause the dance to interflow with and confine it to the bodily strength of our limbs, ultimately risk depriving it of its beauty and grace? Where, indeed, is there grace in these mean and clumsy gestures, forever held captive, forever brutally interrupted whenever they are about to soar forth? There seems to be something cacophonic in the choreography of Le Sacre du Printemps.

However, grace does not signify smooth roundedness; it is not incompatible with angular design. I claim that there is grace here, and one more profound than that of the *Specter of the Rose*, being more closely bound up with its theme. This grace is not of the independent kind; it does not come from above to alight upon objects like a bird; it is merely the outward emanation of an absolute necessity, only the effect of an impeccable inner adjustment. In the choreography of *Le Sacre du Printemps*, all has been perfected with the utmost rigor; in order to arrive at the motions, as we see them, that compose it, Nijinsky had to cultivate and develop them over a long period of time; he chose them from among the confused tangle of our instinctive movements; he preserved them from others; he gave them a slight push and led them a little farther away from the body than they would have gone on their own. In short, he patiently gave them their singular perfection, and from that achievement a new and original harmony was born. As soon as one ceases to confuse grace with symmetry and with arabesques, one will find it on each page of *Le Sacre du Printemps*; in those faces turned in profile over shoulders turned front, in those elbows held tight to the waist, in those horizontal forearms, in those hands held open and rigid, in that trembling descending like a wave from the dancers' head to feet; in that shadowy, straggling, and preoccupied promenade of the Maidens in the second scene. One will find it even in the dance of the Chosen Maiden, in the short and abortive tremors that agitate her, in her difficulties, in her frightful waits, in her prisonerlike and unnatural gait, and in that arm raised to heaven and waved straight above her head in a gesture of appeal, threat, and protection.

All during my analysis of *Le Sacre du Printemps*, I have considered the means employed by Stravinsky and Nijinsky as though they had an intrinsic value of their own, independent of the subject to which they are applied. This separation may seem artificial, and one may rightfully object that I am trying to see an entirely new technique in something that has been created for and is meaningful only with regard to a very specific work. Some will say that this angular choreography is suited only to represent the still unformed and awkward gesticulation of primitive beings. This muted music can serve only to depict the deep anguish of spring. One as well as the other is well-suited to the chosen theme; neither goes beyond it nor can be separated from it.

To this I shall reply that the sign of a true masterpiece is precisely this ability to create for its use a form of expression so complete, so apt, and so new that it becomes quite naturally a general technique. Nothing of value is invented only for its own sake. To obtain new ideas of some lasting value, it is necessary to work on a very specific object, to have the desire to express something in such a way that it cannot be confused with anything else. It is while striving for the particular, while directing all the faculties of the mind toward one small point, that suddenly, as under too strong pressure, inventions of truly considerable extent burst forth. It is from extreme urgency that true fecundity is born. Because Stravinsky and Nijinsky wanted to solve only a particular problem, they found that they had discovered a general solution. If the Cubists, in an attempt very similar to theirs, have failed until now, this is because they first sought in the abstract a solution which only later on they tried to introduce, intact and absurd, into their works.

To these considerations must be added that the germ of the choreography of *Le Sacre du Printemps* already was contained in *Petrouchka*. It is certain that Nijinsky, even though his name appeared on the poster only once, collaborated on both these works. We discover his manner in the on-the-spot dance of the three puppets, and in the so pathetic scene of the imprisoned Petrouchka. There is the same way of linking the gestures to the body, the same use of violent tremor, the same care to preserve at all times the movements' expressive power. Already then did this commitment on his part seem to be marvelously sound, appropriate, and well-adapted. Already we could not imagine that it could be applied to any other subject. And yet, how great the difference between the theme of *Petrouchka* and that of *Le Sacre*! How could one deny a general validity to the means that had served both so pertinently, and why should one not be allowed to contemplate them beyond the range of their application?

The time has come, however, to concern ourselves no longer with anything but *Le Sacre du Printemps*, and to come face to face with this terrifying work, so we can receive the particular mental shock it has the power to bestow.

Let us ask: what does it represent? What do we have here before our eyes? What happens here? The work is so rich that two levels of significance can be found in it. First of all, there is the obvious, the official and avowed meaning. *Le Sacre du Printemps* is a sociological ballet, an extraordinary vision of an age that until now had to be reconstructed with difficulty, by means of scientific documents, and which here is being set before our imagination.

Certes l'humanité antique était venue au-devant de sa soeur, et comme jadis au jour de la séparation nous nous considérions de plain-pied. *

We find ourselves in the presence of man's movements at a time when he did not yet exist as an individual. Living beings still cling to each other; they exist in groups, in colonies, in shoals; they are lost among the horrible indifference of society; they render their devotions to the god they have fashioned together, and of which they have not yet been able to rid themselves. Their faces are devoid of any individuality. At no time during the dance does the Chosen Maiden show the personal terror that ought to fill her soul. She carries out a rite; she is absorbed by a social function, and without any sign

---

*Paul Claudel, "Tête d'Or," in L'Arbre, Paris, 1914, p. 131.

of comprehension or of interpretation, she moves as dictated by the desires and impulses of a being vaster than herself, a monster filled with ignorance and appetites, with cruelty and darkness. Here we have Moloch brought back alive from the depths of the ages; trembling, he opens his maw before us. A base god, devoid of spirit! His altars are in his image: they are the stones at the crossroads of uncultivated plains; animal skulls impaled on pikes. A god that bears down upon men at the level of their heads like a leaden sky. A god who reigns on all fours, devouring his children like a cow that feeds on the pasture. Man is dominated by that which is most inert in him, most opaque and most restricted: his association with others.

But there is still a second meaning in *Le Sacre du Printemps*, something more profound, more secretive, and more hideous. This is a biological ballet. It is not only the dance of man at his most primitive stage; it is the dance that came yet before man. In his article in *Montjoie*, Stravinsky indicated that he intended to represent the coming of spring. But this is not the spring to which the poets have accustomed us, with its quiverings, its music, its tender sky, and its delicate foliage. No, here is nothing but the harshness of budding growth, nothing but the terror and "panic" that accompanies the rise of the sap, nothing but the terrifying labor of the cells. This is spring as seen from the inside; spring in all its striving, its spasms, its partition. One might think oneself in the presence of a drama acted out under a microscope: the history of mitosis; the profound need of the nucleus to break up and reproduce, the division at the core, the splitting and rejoining of turbulent matter that reaches into its very substance; large revolving masses of protoplasm; germ layers, zones, circles, placentas. We are plunged into the kingdoms of the deep; we witness the obtuse movements, the senseless comings and goings, all the haphazard swirls by which, little by little, matter rises to life. Never has there been a better illustration of the doctrines of mechanism. There is a profound quality of blindness in this dance. An enormous question is borne by all those beings that move under our eyes. It is in no way different from them. They carry it along with them without comprehending it, like an animal that keeps turning around in its cage, without tiring of touching the bars with its forehead. They have no other organ than their entire organism, and they use it in their seeking. They move hither and fro, they stop, they throw themselves forward like a package, and they wait. There is nothing preceding them, nothing they are obliged to rejoin. No ideal to be attained. One is always farthest away from them when staying with them. Like the blood that beats from within against the wall of the skull, without any motive other than its force, they demand to come out and arise. And little by little, by the sheer patience and obstinacy of their questioning, a kind of solution is created which, once again, is no different from them and which likewise interflows with the mass of their bodies that is life.

The evening of the premiere of *Le Sacre du Printemps*, there was something like a sediment at the bottom of my immense admiration, caused by a strange sadness and despondency. I felt on my heart the weight of physical matter, a mineral inertia! For the first time, I saw in the doctrines of evolution a kind of heartbreaking possibility. I discovered in myself the traces of a miserable and motionless existence: I was overtaken by the narrowness of my original state; I seemed to have been born on a day of this anguish of which I had just witnessed the prodigious spectacle. Oh! How far removed I was from humanity. How its voice had grown weak and distant to my ears. There are works filled with lamentations, with hope, and with encouragement. One finds in them ways of suffering, of regretting, or regaining faith; they contain all the beautiful emotions of the soul; one gives oneself up to them, as one listens to the advice of a friend; they have something of morality and always something of pity. *Le Sacre de Printemps*, on the other hand, is a part of the primitive globe that has been preserved without aging and that continues to live on mysteriously under our eyes, with all its inhabitants and its flora. It is a wreckage of the past, crawling with and eaten away by familiar and monstrous forms of life. It is a rock from the caves from which emerge unknown beasts, engaged in unintelligible tasks that long ago have lost their meaning.

—November 1913, translated from the French by Miriam Lassman,
reprinted in *Nijinsky Dancing* by Lincoln Kirstein

EDWIN DENBY
Notes on Nijinsky Photographs

Looking at the photographs of Nijinsky, one is struck by his expressive neck. It is an unusually thick and long neck. But its expressivity lies in its clear lift from the trunk, like a powerful thrust. The shoulders are not square, but slope downward; and so they leave the neck easily free, and the eye follows their silhouette down the arms with the sense of a line extraordinarily extended into space, as in a picture by Cézanne or Raphael. The head therefore, at the other end of this unusual extension, poised up in the air, gains an astonishing distinctness, and the tilt of it, even with no muscular accentuation, becomes of unusual interest. Nijinsky tilts his head lightly from the topmost joint, keeping this joint mobile against the upright thrust of the other vertebrae. He does not bend the neck back as some contemporary ballet dancers do. Seen from the side or the rear, the upward line of his back continues straight into the uprightness of the neck, like the neck of a Maillol statue. But Nijinsky alters his neck to suit a character role. The change is striking in the *Schéhérazade* pictures—and Mr. Van Vechten, who saw him dance the part, describes him as a "head-wagging, simian creature." Another variation is that for *Petrouchka,* where the shoulders are raised square to break the continuity of the silhouette; to make the arms dangle as a separate entity, and make the head independently wobbly as a puppet's is, on no neck to speak of. The head here does not sum up or direct the action of the body; it seems to have only a minor, a pathetic function. But it bobs too nonsensically to be humanly pitiful. In the role of the Faun the shoulders are slightly lifted when the Faun becomes dimly aware of his own emotion; but the neck is held up firmly and candidly against the shoulder movement (which would normally press the neck to a forward slant); and so the silhouette is kept self-contained and the figure keeps its dignity. Notice, too, the neck in the reclining position of the Faun. Another poignant duplicity of emotion is expressed by the head, neck, and shoulder line of the *Jeux* photographs—the neck rising against lifted shoulders and also bent sideways against a countertilt of the head. The hero in *Jeux* seems to meet pathos with human nobility—not as the Faun does, with animal dignity.

Looking in these photographs farther along the figure, at the arms in particular, one is struck by their lightness, by the way in which they seem to be suspended in space. Especially in the pictures from *Pavillon* and from *Spectre,* they are not so much placed correctly, or advantageously, or illustratively; rather they seem to flow out unconsciously from the moving trunk, a part of the fullness of its intention. They are pivoted, not lifted, from the shoulder or shoulder blade; their force—like the neck's—comes from the full strength of the back. And so they lead the eye more strongly back to the trunk than out beyond their reach into space. Even when they point, one is conscious of the force pointing quite as much as the object pointed at. To make a grammatical metaphor, the relation of subject to object is kept clear. This is not so simple in movement as a layman might think. A similar clarification of subject and object struck me in the bullfighting of Belmonte. His own body was constantly the subject of his motions, the bull the object. With other fighters, one often had the impression that not they personally but their cloth was the subject that determined a fight. As a cloth is a dead thing, it can only be decorative, and the bull edged into the position of the subject; and the distinctness of the torero's drama was blurred. Nijinsky gives an effect in his arm gesture of himself remaining at the center of space, a strength of voluntary limitation related, in a way, to that of Spanish dance gesture. (This is what makes a dancer's arms look like a man's instead of a boy's.)

An actual "object" to a dancer's "subject" is his partner. In dancing with a partner there is a difference between self-effacement and courtesy. Nijinsky in his pictures is a model of courtesy. The firmness of support he gives his partner is complete. He stands straight enough for two. His expression toward her is intense—in *Giselle* it expresses a supernatural relation, in *Pavillon* one of admiration, in *Faun* one of desire, in *Spectre* one of tenderness—and what a supporting arm that is in *Spectre,* as long and as strong as two. But he observes as well an exact personal remoteness, he shows clearly the fact they are separate bodies. He makes a drama of their nearness in space. And in his own choreography—in *Faun*—the space between the figures becomes a firm body of air, a lucid statement of relationship, in the way intervening space does in the modern academy of Cézanne, Seurat, and Picasso.

One is struck by the massiveness of his arms. This quality also leads the eye back to the trunk, as in a Michelangelo figure. But it further gives to their graceful poses an amplitude of strength that keeps them from looking innocuous or decorative. In particular in the Narcissus pose the savage force of the arms and legs makes credible that the hero's narcissism was not vanity, but an instinct that killed him, like an act of God. In the case of *Spectre,* the power of the arms makes their tendril-like bendings as natural as curvings are in a powerful world of young desire, while weaker and more charming arms might suggest an effeminate or saccharine coyness. There is indeed nothing effeminate in these gestures; there is far too much force in them.

It is interesting to try oneself to assume the poses on the pictures, beginning with arms, shoulders, neck, and head. The flowing line they have is deceptive. It is an unbelievable strain to hold them. The plastic relationships turn out to be extremely complex. As the painter de Kooning, who knows the photographs well and many of whose ideas I am using in these notes, remarked: Nijinsky does just the opposite of what the body would naturally do. The plastic sense is similar to that of Michelangelo and Raphael. One might say that the grace of them is not derived from avoiding strain, as a layman might think, but from the heightened intelligibility of the plastic relationships. It is an instinct for countermovement so rich and so fully expressed, it is unique, though the plastic theory of countermovement is inherent in ballet technique.

Nijinsky's plastic vitality animates the poses derived from dances by Petipa or Fokine. It shines out, too, if one compares his pictures with those of other dancers in the same parts. This aspect of his genius appears to me one basis for his choreographic style, which specifies sharply plastic effects in dancing—and which in this sense is related both to Isadora and to the moderns. Unfortunately the dancers who now take the role of the Faun do not have sufficient plastic discipline to make clear the intentions of the dance.

From the photographs one can see that the present dancers of *Faun* have not even learned Nijinsky's stance. Nijinsky not only squares his shoulders far less, but also frequently not at all. He does not pull in his stomach and lift his thorax. Neither in shoulders nor chest does he exhibit his figure. His stomach has more expression than his chest. In fact, looking at his trunk, one notices a similar tendency to flat-chestedness (I mean in the stance, not in the anatomy) in all the pictures. It is, I believe, a Petersburg trait, and shared independently by Isadora and Martha Graham. In these photographs, at any rate, the expression does not come from the chest; it comes from below the chest, and flows up through it from below. The thorax, so to speak passively, is not only pulled at the top up and back; at the bottom and from the side it is also pulled down and back. Its physical function is that of completing the circuit of muscles that holds the pelvis in relation to the spine. And it is this relation that gives the dancer his balance. Balance (or aplomb, in ballet) is the crux of technique. If you want to see how good a dancer is, look at his stomach. If he is sure of himself there, if he is so strong there that he can present himself frankly, he (or she) can begin to dance expressively. (I say stomach because the stomach usually faces the audience; one might say waist, groin, or pelvis region.)

In looking at Nijinsky pictures, one is struck by the upright tautness about the hips. His waist is broad and powerful. You can see it clearly in the Harlequin pictures. If he is posing on one leg, there is no sense of shifted weight, and as little if he seems to be bending to the side or forward. The effort this means may be compared to lifting a table by one leg and keeping the top horizontal. The center of gravity in the table, and similarly that of his body, has not been shifted. The delicacy with which he cantilevers the weight actually displaced keeps the firmness from being rigidity. I think it is in looking at his waist that one can see best the technical aspect of his instinct for concentrating the origin of movement so that all of it relates to a clear center which is not altered. He keeps the multiplicity, the diffusion which movement has, intelligible by not allowing any doubt as to where the center is. When he moves he does not blur the center of weight in his body; one feels it as clearly as if he were still standing at rest; one can follow its course clearly as it floats about the stage through the dance. And so the motion he makes looks controlled and voluntary and reliable. I imagine it is this constant sense of balance that gave his dancing the unbroken continuity and flow through all the steps and leaps and rests from beginning to end that critics marveled at.

Incidentally, their remarks of this kind also point to an extraordinary accuracy in his musical timing. For to make the continuity rhythmic as he did, he must have had an unerring instinct at which moment to attack a movement, so that the entire sequence of it would flow as continuously and transform itself into the next motion as securely as did the accompanying sound. To speak of him as unmusical, with no sense of rhythm, as Stravinsky has, is therefore an impropriety that is due to a confusion of meaning in the word "rhythm." The choreography of *Faun* proves that Nijinsky's natural musical intelligence was of the highest order. For this was the first ballet choreography set clearly not to the measures and periods, but to the expressive flow of the music, to its musical sense. You need only compare *Faun's* assurance in this respect to the awkwardness musically of Fokine's second scene in *Petrouchka,* the score of which invites the same sort of understanding. But this is not in the photographs.

Nijinsky does not dance from his feet; he dances from his pelvis. The legs do not show off. They have no ornamental pose. Even in his own choreography, though the leg gestures are "composed," they are not treated as pictorial possibilities. They retain their weight. They tell where the body goes and how. But they don't lead it. They are, however, completely expressive in this role; and the things in the *Spectre* picture with Karsavina are as full of tenderness as another dancer's face. It is noticeable, too, that Nijinsky's legs are not especially turned out, and a similar moderate *en dehors* seems to be the rule in the Petersburg male dancers of Nijinsky's generation. But the parallel feet in *Narcisse* and *Faun,* and the pigeon toes in *Til* are not a willful contradiction of the academic principle for the sake of something new. They can, it seems to me, be properly understood only by a turned-out dancer, as Nijinsky himself clearly was. For the strain of keeping the pelvis in the position the ballet dancer holds it in for balance is much greater with parallel or turned-in feet (which contradicts the outward twist of the thigh); and this strain gives a new plastic dimension to the legs and feet, if it is carried through as forcefully as Nijinsky does. I am interested, too, to notice that in standing Nijinsky does not press his weight mostly on the ball of the big toe, but grips the floor with the entire surface of the foot.

I have neglected to mention the hands, which are alive and simple, with more expression placed in the wrist than in the fingers. They are not at all "Italian," and are full of variety without an emphasis on sensitivity. The hands in *Spectre* are celebrated, and remind one of the hands in Picassos ten years later. I am also very moved by the uplifted, half-unclenched hands in the *Jeux* picture, as mysterious as breathing in sleep. One can see, too, that in *Petrouchka* the hands are black-mittened, not white-mittened as now; the new costume makes the dance against the black wall in the second scene a foolish hand dance, instead of a dance of a whole figure, as intended.

The manner in which Nijinsky's face changes from role to role is immediately striking. It is enhanced by makeup, but not created by it. In fact, a friend pointed out that the only role in which one recognizes Nijinsky's civilian face is that of Petrouchka, where he is most heavily made up. There is no mystery about such transformability. People don't usually realize how much any face changes in the course of a day, and how often it is unrecognizable for an instant or two. Nijinsky seems to have controlled the variability a face has. The same metamorphosis is obvious in his body. The Specter, for instance, has no age or sex; the Faun is adolescent; the hero of *Jeux* has a body full-grown and experienced. *Til* can either be boy or man. The Slave in *Schéhérazade* is fat; the Specter is thin. It does not look like the same body. One can say that in this sense there is no exhibitionism in Nijinsky's photographs. He is never showing you himself, or an interpretation of himself. He is never vain of what he is showing you. The audience does not see him as a professional dancer, or as a professional charmer. He disappears completely, and instead there is an imaginary being in his place. Like a classic artist, he remains detached, unseen, unmoved, uninterested. Looking at him, one is in an imaginary world, entire and very clear; and one's emotions are not directed at their material objects, but at their imaginary satisfactions. As he said himself, he danced with love.

To sum up, Nijinsky in his photographs shows us the style of a classic artist. The emotion he projects, the character he projects, is not communicated as his own, but as one that exists independently of himself, in the objective world. Similarly his plastic sense suggests neither a private yearning into an infinity of space nor a private shutting out of surrounding relationships, both of them legitimate romantic attitudes. The weight he gives his own body, the center which he gives his plastic motions, strikes a balance with the urge and rapidity of leaps and displacements. It strikes a balance between the role he dances and the roles of his partners. The distinction of place makes the space look real; the distinction of persons makes the drama real. And for the sake of this clarification he characterizes (or mimes, one might say) even such a conventional ornamental show-off, or "pure dance," part as that in *Pavillon*. On the other hand, the awkward heaviness that *Faun, Sacre,* and *Jeux* exhibited, and that was emphasized by their angular precision, was not, I believe, an anticlassic innovation. It was an effort to make the dance more positive, to make clearer still the center of gravity of a movement, so that its extent, its force, its direction, its elevation can be appreciated not incidentally merely, but integrally as drama. He not only extended the plastic range in dancing, but clarified it. And this is the way to give meaning to dancing—not secondhand literary meaning, but direct meaning. Nijinsky's latest intentions of "circular movement" and the improvisational quality *Til* seems to have had are probably a normal development of his sense of motion in relation to a point of repose—a motion that grew more animated and diverse as his instinct became more exercised. (An evolution not wholly dissimilar can be followed in Miss Graham's work, for instance.) And I consider the following remark he made to be indicative of the direction of his instinct: "*La grâce, le charme, le joli sont rangés tout autour du point central qu'est le beau. C'est pour le beau que je travaille.*" I do not see anything in these pictures that would lead one to suppose that Nijinsky's subsequent insanity cast any premonitory shadow on his phenomenally luminous dance intelligence.

In their stillness Nijinsky's pictures have more vitality than the dances they remind us of as we now see them on the stage. They remain to show us what dancing can be, and what the spectator and the dancer each aspire to, and hold to be a fair standard of art. I think they give the discouraged dance lover faith in dancing as a serious human activity. As Mr. Van Vechten wrote after seeing him in 1916: "His dancing has the unbroken quality of music, the balance of great painting, the meaning of fine literature, and the emotion inherent in all these arts."

—from *Dance Index*, March 1943

MARIE RAMBERT
Working on Sacre

Dame Marie Rambert (1888–1982), born Miriam Remberg in Warsaw, studied eurhythmics with Dalcroze and was hired by Diaghilev to assist Nijinsky with Le Sacre du Printemps. *Moving to London, she became in essence the first founder of British ballet, with her Ballet Club at the tiny Mercury Theatre, which she ran with her husband, Ashley Dukes. It was there that she discovered, among many other talents, both Frederick Ashton and Antony Tudor, thus changing the course of dance history. "Mim," as she was affectionately called, retained her lively humor and inexhaustible energy into her eighties, performing cartwheels to the pleasure and astonishment of her friends and guests. (I was one of them, in the mid-seventies.) Her company, whose name she changed from Ballet Rambert to Rambert Dance Company, is the oldest dance company in England, having been founded in 1926.*

Every day, after the general rehearsal, I had to stay for an hour or two and listen with Nijinsky to the score of *Sacre*. He then sketched out the movements for the next rehearsal. The rhythms were very difficult, and I had to study the rhythm with each artist individually. They soon nicknamed me "Rythmichka." There was no melody to hold on to—so the only way to learn it was to count the bars all the time. The movements in themselves were simple, and so was the floor pattern. But the basic position was difficult to sustain in movement, and the mastering of that rhythm almost impossible.

Diaghilev had a valet called Vassily Zuikov. They suspected in the company that he was so devoted to Diaghilev because he had been saved by him in Russia from a heavy sentence for some serious crime—they said it was rape in particularly sordid circumstances. Anyway Diaghilev got him off, and now his devotion embraced Nijinsky too, because he knew how precious he was to Diaghilev.

Always when in *Spectre de la Rose* Nijinsky did his last spectacular jump out of the window, Vassily would lay him down on a mattress on the floor and mop his brow and face. Nijinsky gasped and kept saying, *"Vady, vady"* (water, water), and Vassily would let him have a sip of warm water, but take it away at once before he drank too much. I saw Diaghilev sometimes there too, most solicitous, as though Nijinsky was in serious danger.

When Diaghilev went to Russia to try to arrange a season for the company at the Narodny Dom (the Theatre of the People)—which came to nothing because the theatre was burnt down before we could go there—he left behind his faithful Vassily. We couldn't rehearse for twenty minutes without Vassily coming in and saying, "Vaslav Fomich, we'd better open the window. It's very stuffy in here; it's not good for you." Then he would go out. But half an hour later he would come in again and say, "Vaslav Fomich, you know, I think it's rather draughty now; we'd better shut the window."

He was really spying on us, though there was nothing to spy on, because Nijinsky didn't take the slightest notice of me as a woman. It never occurred to him; it never occurred to me. We were only discussing the work in hand.

After rehearsals we sometimes used to go to Chez Pasquier to drink chocolate and eat gateaux, and talk about our work. We never made arrangements to go out together, but it so happened that we were mostly both ready at the same time. One day I was ready to go before he was, and not wishing to wait for him too obviously, I just went to Pasquier by myself. I had been sitting there a few minutes when in walked Nijinsky, looking as pale as a ghost.

"What on earth is the matter?" I asked.

"I very nearly killed a man."

"How can you say such a thing? Anyhow, who was it?"

"A blackguard, a brigand, who has prevented Bronia from dancing *Jeux* and *Sacre*."

"But who is he?"

"Kochetovsky!"

Bronia was Nijinsky's sister, very closely akin to him in temperament, and she was one of the best dancers in the company. Kochetovsky was her husband. Naturally I began to reason with Nijinsky and said it must all have been a misunderstanding and that Bronia would not lightly give up her role in *Sacre* and *Jeux*. Moreover, I reminded him that the previous year Bronia walked out because, although it was her turn to dance the ballerina in *Petrushka* (she shared it with Karsavina) on the opening night in London, Diaghilev had bowed to Sir Joseph Beecham's insistence that Karsavina should appear. Bronia and her husband did not return for a couple of days only—it was all patched up by then.

But Nijinsky kept repeating that through that blackguard's fault she would not create these roles conceived by him with Bronia in mind.

The next day came the official announcement that Bronia was pregnant and would not dance in our Paris and London seasons. And *this* was her husband's great crime.

When Stravinsky first came to one of our rehearsals and heard the way his music was being played, he blazed up, pushed aside the fat German pianist, nicknamed "Kolossal" by Diaghilev, and proceeded to play twice as fast as we had been doing it, and twice as fast as we could possibly dance. He stamped his feet on the floor and banged his fist on the piano and sang and shouted, all to give us an impression of the rhythms of the music and the colour of the orchestra.

It was an epic quarrel between Stravinsky and Nijinsky. But somehow or other Diaghilev managed to calm them down. . . .

It was the painter Roerich who first suggested the subject of *Sacre du Printemps*. He then worked on the theme with Diaghilev, Stravinsky, and Nijinsky. It was to be prehistoric Russia and represent the rites of spring. Stravinsky had finished his magnificent score by 1912, and we started the rehearsals with the company that same year.

Nijinsky again first of all established the basic position: feet very turned in, knees slightly bent, arms held in reverse of the classical position, a primitive, prehistoric posture. The steps were very simple: walking smoothly or stamping, jumps mostly off both feet, landing heavily. There was only one a little more complicated dance for the maidens in the first scene. It was mostly done in groups, and each group had its own precise rhythm to follow. In the dance (if one can call it that) of the Wisest Elder, he walked two steps against every three steps of the ensemble. In the second scene the dance of the sacrifice of the Chosen Virgin was powerful and deeply moving. I watched Nijinsky again and again teaching it to Maria Piltz. Her reproduction was very pale by comparison with his ecstatic performance, which was the greatest tragic dance I have ever seen.

The first night of that ballet was the most astonishing event. Already the music of *Petrushka* had provoked the absolute hatred of the Vienna orchestra when we danced there in 1912. At rehearsal they threw down their bows in fury and called it "Schweinerei." Diaghilev went down into the pit and argued with them for quite a while before they consented to play—and then they sabotaged it.

And now in Paris in 1913 at the first sounds of the music, shouts and hissing started in the audience, and it was very difficult for us on the stage to hear the music, the more so as part of the audience began to applaud in an attempt to drown the hissing. We all desperately tried to keep time without being able to hear the rhythm clearly. In the wings Nijinsky counted the bars to guide us. Pierre Monteux conducted undeterred, Diaghilev having told him to continue to play at all costs.

But after the interlude things became even worse, and during the sacrificial dance real pandemonium broke out. That scene began with Maria Piltz, the Chosen Virgin, standing on the spot trembling for many bars, her folded hands under her right cheek, her feet turned in, a truly prehistoric and beautiful pose. But to the audience of the time it appeared ugly and comical.

A shout went up in the gallery:

"*Un docteur!*"

Somebody else shouted louder:

"*Un dentiste!*"

Then someone else screamed:

"*Deux dentistes!*"

And so it went on. One elegant lady leaned out of her box and slapped a man who was clapping. But the performance went on to the end.

And yet now there is no doubt that, musically and choreographically, a masterpiece had been created that night. The only ballet that could compare with it in power was Bronislava Nijinska's *Les Noces,* created in 1923. She, like her brother, produced a truly epic ballet—so far unexcelled anywhere.

After the first night of *Sacre* was over, we were all far too excited to think of going home to bed. A great gang of us—I can't remember who we all were—went off and had a great supper at a restaurant called the Reine Pédauque. When we had finished supper, we all went in fiacres to the Bois de Boulogne and walked, and ran about, and played games on the grass and among the trees for most of the night. At about two o'clock in the morning we went to the restaurant at the Pré Catelan in the Bois de Boulogne and had yet another supper. And so went on eating and drinking and whiling away

time in the park until morning. We finished the night by having breakfast at a
dairy in Marie Antoinette's Petit Palais.

—from *Quicksilver*, 1972

Robert Edmond Jones
Nijinsky and Til Eulenspiegel

*The most acclaimed stage designer of his time, Robert Edmond Jones (1887–1954)
was born in New Hampshire and educated at Harvard. He was quickly hailed as
an original and powerful artist in his field, and for many years was associated
with Eugene O'Neill, both at the Provincetown Playhouse and for Broadway productions such as* Mourning Becomes Electra *and* The Iceman Cometh. *He also
designed such hits as* The Philadelphia Story *and* The Green Pastures. *In a feature story in* The New York Times *dated October 1, 1916, it is reported that
Nijinsky was "delighted" with Jones's work on* Til Eulenspiegel, *and that "Mr. Jones
is also reported to be delighted with the conditions under which he has worked." The
account that follows suggests a somewhat different experience for both men, but then,
as the* Times *tells us, Jones "is described by many of his friends as having the volcanic
temperament."*

THE QUESTION IS NOT YET SETTLED, WHETHER MUCH THAT IS
GLORIOUS—WHETHER ALL THAT IS PROFOUND—DOES NOT
SPRING . . . FROM MOODS OF MIND EXALTED AT THE EXPENSE
OF THE GENERAL INTELLECT.
—POE'S *ELEONORA*

I n 1916 a diffident young man from New Hampshire who was just begin-
ning to make his way in New York as a stage designer was commissioned by
Vaslav Nijinsky to design the decor for a new ballet. Up to that time no
American designer had been so honored. I was that young man, and I am

going to set down as carefully as possible my recollections of this great dancer and choreographer—now, alas! a living legend—and of an experience so novel and so startling that it altered the course of my entire life.

Not all of my story is pleasant. It is a story of two differing temperaments—of two differing cultures, really—unexpectedly and violently thrown into contact with one another. In the ballet *Til Eulenspiegel,* the artistic approach of old Russia and the artistic approach of new America met and fused for the first time in theater history. The result—it must be stated at the outset—was an instant and emphatic success. Since that day many dramatic events have been taking place in the world. Now, in this year of grace 1945, it would appear that that old Russia and new America are destined to march side by side toward a radiant future. But at the time of this association such a rapport was undreamed of, and it fell to me to bear the full brunt of the initial impact of the Russian temperament, to take it, so to speak, head on. Certain details of this experience seem to me in retrospect not unlike the custard-pie scenes in an old Mack Sennett comedy.

I shall set down my story in a series of pictures, like the "flashbacks" of a cinema, as they appeared to me at the time, without benefit of a maturer judgment. Some of the story is sordid, some of it is humiliating, some of it is outrageous. But all of it is marvelous, and all of it is alive.

THE FIRST PICTURE: It is the afternoon of a late spring day in 1916, hot and humid. I sit in the drawing room of Emilie Hapgood, the president of the now-defunct New York Stage Society. Curtains are drawn against the breathless heat. The room—all ivory-white and pale silks—is in semidarkness. We converse in low voices, waiting. Presently Nijinsky and Mme Nijinsky are announced. I see, first, an extremely pretty young woman, fashionably dressed in black, and, following her, a small, somewhat stocky young man walking with delicate birdlike steps—precise, a dancer's walk. He is very nervous. His eyes are troubled. He looks eager, anxious, excessively intelligent. He seems tired, bored, excited, all at once. I observe that he has a disturbing habit of picking at the flesh on the side of his thumbs until they bleed. Through all my memories of this great artist runs the recurring image of those raw red thumbs. He broods and dreams, goes far away into reverie, returns again. At intervals his face lights up with a brief, dazzling smile. His manner is simple, ingratiating, so direct as to be almost humble. I like him at once. Tales of unusual accomplishments and unusual ardors have clustered around this man as honeybees cluster about a perfumed flower. There was something about a scarf. There was something about a banquet. There was something about a leap through a window. There was something. . . .

But that was then and this is now. I see no trace in him of the legendary exotic. Here is only the straightforward and matter-of-fact approach of the newly appointed maestro of the Russian Ballet who has an idea and wants to see it carried out.

I realize at once that I am in the presence of a genius. What, precisely, does one mean by this word, so often and so carelessly used? Miss Gertrude Stein, who by her own account of herself would seem to know, defines it (I quote from memory) as the ability to talk and listen at the same time. This particular attribute of Nijinsky's genius is not evident at the moment, since he and I are struggling to communicate our ideas to one another in extremely halting French. I sense, however, a quality in him which I can define here only as a continual preoccupation with standards of excellence so high that they are really not of this world. This artist, it is clear, concerns himself with incredible perfections. I sense, too, the extraordinary nervous energy of the man—an almost frightening awareness, a curious mingling of eagerness and apprehension. The atmosphere he brings with him is—how shall I say?—*oppressive.* There is in him an astonishing drive, a mental engine, too high-powered, racing—perhaps even now—to its final breakdown. Otherwise there is nothing of the abnormal about him. Only an impression of something too eager, too brilliant, a quivering of the nerves, a nature racked to dislocation by a merciless creative urge. And those raw thumbs.

I show the maestro a portfolio of my designs for various stage productions. There are costume sketches for *The Man Who Married a Dumb Wife,* the stage settings for *The Devil's Garden* and *The Happy Ending,* recently produced by Arthur Hopkins, some notes for *Les Précieuses Ridicules,* the project for Shelley's *Cenci* worked out during my *Wanderjahr* in Germany. It is obvious that Nijinsky thinks that I am a beginner—indeed, I am one—but I can see that he is interested in my drawings. There is something in them that he may be able to use. We sit side by side on the carpet in the center of the shadowy room, turning over the leaves of the portfolio. "*Très heureux,*" he says, politely. . . . The couple departs. I am left in an agony of anticipation. Dare I hope? . . . Could it be? . . . I wonder . . . If only—!

ANOTHER PICTURE: I am accepted—I am a happy boy this day—and I am sent to Bar Harbor to collaborate with the maestro on the creation of the new ballet. I am quartered in a huge old-fashioned summer hotel, all piazzas and towers, with curving driveways and mammoth beds of angry red cannas on the lawns. Nijinsky lives there, too, with his pretty wife—always a little *souffrante* from the heat—and an enchanting girl baby with oblique Mongolian eyes like her father's. He practices hard and long during the day with his accompanist in the lovely little Greek temple set among the pines by the shore of the bay. In the evenings we work together until far into the night. And how we work!

Coming on the heels of the most striking series of novelties in America for the last ten years, Til Eulenspiegel *stood in a class by itself as a combination of musical, pictorial, and terpsichorean art. . . .* How shall I tell of this long-forgotten ballet, so fresh, so natural, so innocent, that flashed and vanished like a fevered dream? No critic, with the exception of H. T. Parker of the *Boston Transcript,* seems to have been able to appreciate it at the time in its true relation to the other works in the Diaghilev repertoire. It was too original in its conception, too novel, too seldom performed. Relatively few people saw it, it was soon gone, and now it is only a memory. But without question it showed Nijinsky at the very height of his creative power, and I believe it to have been one of the few genuine masterpieces—I use the word deliberately—in the entire recorded history of ballet. . . .

Nijinsky's energy, his ardor, his daring, his blazing imagination, by turns fantastic, gorgeous, grotesque, are a source of continual astonishment and delight to me. His conception of this ballet is vastly new and different. A consummate actor, he changes, chameleon-like, from moment to moment as he talks. Now he is a child, wide-eyed and mischievous, now a jeering zany, now a lover, tender and pleading, now a demoniac figure from a medieval Dance of Death. Always he is repeating the phrase, *"Pour faire rire, pour faire rire."* He summons the spirits of Breughel, of Munchhausen, of Rabelais. Gargantua and Pantagruel peer over his shoulder. Everything in this ballet is to be gay, athletic, coarse, animal. An irresistible comicality breathes through it all, a light, deft, fresh movement, a ripple of mocking laughter. At times it seems not so much a ballet as an embodied romp. *"Pour faire rire, pour faire rire . . ."*

The maestro is at my elbow. I draw. He watches, criticizes, exhorts. Together we map out the design for the front curtain—a huge sheet of parchment emblazoned with Til's device of the owl and the looking glass, all blurred and worn, like a page torn from a long-forgotten manuscript of the Middle Ages. The marketplace of Braunschweig begins to take shape in front of the brooding black mass of the cathedral, a Braunschweig seen through Til's own eyes. We fill the square with flaunting gay color. I sketch the rosy-cheeked apple-woman with her big basket of apples, all red and green and russet; the cloth merchant in his shop; the fat blond baker with his long loaves of bread; the scrawny sweetmeat seller, decked out in peppermint stripes of red and white, like one of his own candies; the cobbler carrying his rack of oddly shaped shoes; the burghers, the priests, the professors in their long robes and their ridiculous shovel hats; the street urchins and the beggars; the three chatelaines, taking the air beneath peaked hennins that tower a full six feet above their heads, their trains streaming away ten feet, twenty feet, thirty feet behind them . . . and Til himself in his varied disguises—Til the imp, Til the lover, Til the scholar, Til flouting, taunting, imploring, writhing in his death agonies. . . .

The hours fly past. Wild, eager, anxious hours.

INVITATIONS TO LUNCH and dine at the great houses of Bar Harbor are showered upon me like a rain of gold. At first I am overwhelmed by this unexpected and profuse hospitality, but I soon realize that I am being sought after only in order that my various hosts and hostesses may induce me to bring the great dancer to their tables. Some of these invitations are on a lower social plane. One morning the maestro and I are invited to the fashionable swimming pool. After our swim we dress in adjoining little wooden cabanas. I am partly dressed. I hear a light tap at the door. I open it. A middle-aged man stands there, exquisitely dressed in fastidious nuances of pearl gray which harmonize with the tones of his silvery, scented mustache. He is tall and willowy and his delicate hands are beautifully manicured. We look at one another. No word is spoken. Presently he takes a large flat case of pearl-gray leather from his pocket, opens the lid, and holds the case out to me. On a bed of pearl-gray velvet lies a mass of beautiful jewels— moonstones, black pearls, diamonds, emeralds, cabochon rubies. . . . There is an awkward silence. Time seems to run down and stand still, like a worn-out alarm clock, like a tired heart that stops beating. I hear Nijinsky putting on his shoes in the next compartment. The stranger in gray holds out his store of fabulous baubles, all glittering and flashing in the acrid New England sunlight. All at once I burst out laughing. He closes the door, turns on his heel, and silently goes away.

ANOTHER PICTURE: WE are in New York once more and rehearsals are beginning in earnest. I spend many hours with Nijinsky and his company on the bare stage of the old Manhattan Opera House. The wonderful music of Mussorgsky and Rimsky-Korsakov pervades the air. It is new to me. I breathe it in, and I tremble. I am ill with excitement. Mystical winds blow over river valleys. Conflagrations of color blaze on faraway mountains. Spilt blood dries on daggers of cold steel. Violins torture and sting. I hear cries and sobs. Always death is in the air—cruel death, bitter death. Always the eternal farewells . . . I go through the days in a dream. Can life indeed be so rich, so splendid, so passionate? Even now, after twenty-nine years, the reveries of those enchanted hours come back to me and I am lost once more in the horizons of the mysterious lands that Glinka and Borodin knew.

* * *

THE SCALE MODEL for the setting is finished. The designs for the costumes are likewise finished and approved. Now comes the first difficulty, the first sign of friction. A storm is gathering. Why is it, someone has asked, that birth is always painful and rarely lovely?

In this country when scenery is to be painted, the various "drops" and "flats" of canvas are stretched on frames, like huge easels, which hang at the sides of the scenic studios and are raised or lowered through slots cut in the floor by means of ropes and pulleys and counter-weights. In Russia, however, the method of scene painting is quite different. The drops and flats are simply laid flat on the floor and the painters, wearing carpet slippers, roam about over them carrying great pails of color and long-handled brushes, like brooms. Nijinsky, quite naturally, wishes the setting for *Til* to be executed in the Russian manner, *sur planché*. But alas there is no one in New York who knows how to paint in this style. Work is accordingly started in the conventional American manner in the West Side studios of Dodge & Castle. When Nijinsky hears of this he orders the work stopped at once.

The next picture shows the maestro riding toward the scenic studio in a taxi with me through a Negro district known as San Juan Hill, after the bloody battleground of that name in the Spanish War. A director of the Metropolitan Opera sits between us. We are silent and tense. The studio is at the foot of a hill by the Hudson. As we descend the hill a Negress is carried shrieking out of a doorway, spouting blood from a dozen razor slashes on her head and arms. A bad omen? I wonder. . . .

We go up steep, narrow winding stairs to the scene loft. This is a long, narrow and extremely high space with walls of dirty whitewashed brick. The paint frames hang from cables along the wall at either side. Tall, narrow windows are set high up at either end. The air is charged with a strong, almost nauseating smell of fish glue. Underneath the windows stand rough wooden cabinets, like bookshelves, on which are arranged dozens upon dozens of white china *pots de chambre* filled to overflowing with colored pigments in bewildering variety—gamboge, raw umber, ultramarine, orange mineral, rose madder, vert émeraude. . . . Half a dozen painters—"artists" is their traditional title—we still say, "Job for the artist!" or "Hey, artist!"— looking in their dirty white overalls not unlike a band of White Wings, hold others of these useful receptacles, into which they dip their paintbrushes from time to time, applying streaks of paint in vivid colors to the great sheets of canvas stretched on the frames at either side of the loft. It is all rather like a Freudian dream in which one sees with horror one's deepest and most forbidden repressions dragged howling into the harsh light of day. Nijinsky gives a wild look about him. His eyes swivel in his head. Is *this* the way stage settings are painted in *"les pays des barbares"*? He mutters something unintelligible. The incongruity of the occasion strikes all three of us at the same instant. We shout with hysterical laughter. The tension is broken. *"C'est vraiment très heureux,"* the maestro says with a giggle. We ride up the hill again, relaxed and friendly now. We return to the rehearsal. I am only too content to let the matter rest. But through my mind runs a phantasmagoria of conflicting images—the figure of the dreaming faun, a rose petal drifting through a moonlit window in a soft summer night, star-drenched banquets at the Lido, *répétitions générales* in Paris with languid balletomanes from the Côte d'Azur sighing and shuddering, raw red thumbs, winding stairs, *pots de chambre* splashed with hues of more-than-Oriental splendor, White Wings, rivers of blood on a sidewalk. . . . How will it end?

ANOTHER PICTURE RISES in the memory. Etched in acid, this one. I am unexpectedly summoned to the Opera House. The completed setting for *Til Eulenspiegel* is standing on the stage. I glance at it quickly as I pass. Not bad, I say to myself. I sense an obscurely hostile atmosphere in the theater. I am escorted to Nijinsky's dressing room.

The walls (I remember to this day) are papered in stripes of two tones of violent red. There is a pier glass and a chaise longue. On the dressing table a number of stilettolike knives, sharpened to a razor edge, are ranged in an orderly row. The maestro is waiting for me in a flame of rage. Torrents of Russian imprecations pour from his lips. The open door fills with frowning alien faces. Nijinsky switches to broken French. He lashes out at me with an insensate blind hate. It is a nightmare set in a blast furnace. I gather that in his opinion America is, of all countries in the world, the most backward in every aspect of its culture, that the level of artistic achievement on this side of the Atlantic Ocean is not only beneath notice but beneath contempt, and that Destiny has selected me—me!—from out of America's countless millions to symbolize, eternally and ineffaceably, everything that is most benighted in our so-called civilization. Since that day I have had occasion to hear these same views aired more than once. I still cannot believe that they are true.

Presently Nijinsky pauses out of sheer exhaustion. We go back to the stage. The setting stands there, dejected, like a child that has been punished. Swift, curt commands are issued. Stagehands hale the accursed thing from sight, swing it into the flies, flatten it against the back wall of the theater. A shattered dream, a house of cards demolished. . . . The rehearsal begins, belated and listless. The rhythms falter; the air seems duller than Saturnian lead. Suddenly there is a cry. The maestro stumbles and falls. He has sprained his ankle. He is carried moaning and cursing to his suite at the Biltmore

Hotel. "Your scenery is so bad," a dancer says to me, "that when our maestro saw it he fell down." Eager throats take up the refrain: "Yes, your scenery is so bad that when our maestro saw it he fell down."

I am a very discouraged boy indeed.

AT THE THEATER the next morning my limitations as an artist are enlarged upon by the manager of the company with an unusual clarity and a notable absence of sentiment. The principal defects of the setting, I am made to understand, are, first, that it is too shallow—it does not allow enough space for the evolutions of the dancers—and, second, that it is not high enough to give the effect of crazy exaggeration the maestro had visualized. The first defect is remedied by the simple expedient of placing the setting farther back on the stage. The second problem is not so easily solved. After a consultation (I can never forget this half hour!) it is agreed that a piece of canvas ten feet high is to be added at the base of each of the two flats which represent the houses of the town, and that this space is to be painted with an impression of foliage in broad washes of ultramarine. The flats are strung up on the frames at the rear of the stage, and with the aid of a paint boy I elongate the trees of Braunschweig, trying in vain to ignore the audible disapproval of the ensemble rehearsing below.

THE NEXT PICTURE: Two days have elapsed. The premiere has been postponed. Again I am summoned to the maestro's presence. It is evening. Nijinsky lies in bed, *maladif,* drenched in pathos, sad as a dying prince out of a drama by Maeterlinck. The little room is crowded to suffocation with the entire ensemble of the ballet, fully dressed in the costumes of *Til Eulenspiegel.* They stare at me silently with black hatred in their faces. Now begins a scene compared to which the earlier scene in the dressing room at the Opera House seems but the remote faded echo of an old refrain. This one is good. The maestro really puts his heart into it this time. The occasion—as Robert Benchley has since said of another and quite different occasion—has all the easy informality of a prairie fire. Shoes are wrenched from the feet of the *coryphées,* necklaces are torn from their throats and shattered into fragments against the walls. Unbelievable insults are hurled at me. It is like taking the lid off hell.

This, I say to myself, is what it means to have one's back to the wall, facing a firing squad. *Have you no mercy? No mercy . . .* This is what it means to be whipped at the triangles. *A low murmur ran through the ranks as the scarcely healed backs were laid bare for the second time to receive the lash. . . .* This is what it means to stand in the death cart, jolting over cobblestones, on the way to the guillotine. *Along the streets the death carts rumble, hollow and harsh. . . . The murmuring of many voices, the upturning of many faces, the pressing of many footsteps in the outskirts of the crowd, so that it swells forward in a mass. . . .*

Here I am, alone and unknown, in a little room at the Biltmore Hotel, in the midst of a lurid fantasy of the Middle Ages—a fantasy of my own making—with one of the world's greatest artists shrieking at me. There is no escape. There is no hope. This is the end. Nothing. Nowhere. Never.

Then something happens inside me. Something old and cold and ancestral rises up in me. The sense of the occasion strikes me with a kind of wry humor. As I look about me at the gaily costumed crowd I know with a definite inner conviction that this ballet will be a success. There is something about the American public, there is a quality of appreciation, a peculiarly American point of view, that even these artists, remarkable though they are, cannot yet understand. I think at this bitter moment my belief in myself as an artist is born. I will see this thing through. And then—

ANOTHER PICTURE: a week later. The dress rehearsal of *Til Eulenspiegel* is scheduled for two o'clock in the afternoon. I enter the auditorium of the Opera House by the front door. The curtain is up. On the stage stands my setting—my setting, mine!—remote, complete, fully lighted, all glowing with jewel-like blues and greens. All up and down on either side of the proscenium the great gilded boxes are filled with the dancers, dressed and painted, waiting for the ballet to begin. The circular lunette in the ceiling of the auditorium has been temporarily removed for repairs and a shaft of sunlight, pure gold, streams down across the boxes, turning the proscenium into a spectacle out of dreamland. It is exceedingly beautiful.

The boxes glitter and flame and the palaces of Braunschweig tower up out of burning blue dusk into a haze of violet and rose. A fountain of music wells up from the orchestra, a shower of sparkling notes. . . .

The torment is over. My life in the theater has begun in earnest. *Ah, light, and flame, and flowers! Ah, starry meadows beyond Orion! Ah, fields of the triplicate suns!*

The relief from the strain of the last weeks is too great. My head seems to burst. Spots and bars of gold dance before my eyes.

I faint dead away.

NOW THE FINAL picture, the first performance seen from the wings. There is a bustle, a tremor, a sickening moment of suspense. The orchestra strikes up the first bars of the music. The great curtain slides upward, sighing into the shadows far overhead, where half-seen electricians move along the light-bridges hung with many-colored lamps, like constellations of stars. An astonishing congeries of forms and colors assails the eye, grotesque, impossible figments of an imagination enchained by some ludicrous nightmare, as it were, but engrossing and appropriate beyond belief. A species of whimsicality run riot sets before the astonished vision a medieval town that never was in any age and laves it with nocturnal blue touched with shafts of crepuscular light which illuminates the inverted cornucopia roofs of tiny houses tilted at crazy angles and suggesting for all the world sheaves of sky-rockets. A wondertown in a wonderland . . . The personages might have stepped out of some Volksbuch of the Middle Ages. But there is no suggestion of coloristic disharmony within the somber scenic frame: and the light on the figurants is magical. . . . I hear a crash of applause, fierce and frightening. The little figure in green begins its leapings and laughings. There is the scene of wild lovemaking, the confutation of the scholars, the strange solo dance, swift as the flash of a rapier, the hanging of the corpse on the gibbet—and last of all, the apparition of the ghost shooting upward through a foam of tiny lanterns, like a moth veering above a sea of fireflies. . . . Then the triumph, and the cheering, like the clamor of great bells—now rapturous, now softening, melting—and the mountains of flowers, and the curtain calls that seem never to end. Nijinsky and I bow together, hand in hand. He is all smiles. As the curtain sweeps upward for the last time he murmurs once more, "C'est vraiment très, très heureux."

I go home. I am finished with it all.

I never see him again.

NOW MY STORY is ended and these memories fade into the past. The great artist who taught me so much now exists apart, away from us, in a sad world of his own. I dwell for the last time upon my strange, magical, shattering experience and remember once more what it has meant to me in the years that have passed since the creation of *Til Eulenspiegel*. It has given me a heightened and broadened sense of life. It has taught me to be true to my own inner dream, to live by this dream, and never to betray it.

And it has taught me, I hope, to be kind.

—from *Dance Index*, 1945

H. T. PARKER
The Strangeness of Til

Necessarily a mimed tale, so full and various of action and suggestion as is Mr. Nijinsky's choreographic fable, can leave but confused impression in a single seeing. First of all, it was plain last evening that Strauss's rondo of like title is no more than background to the whole, like Debussy's music in the mimed episode of the faun or Schumann's among the fancies of "Butterflies." Once and again it rhythmed the dancers and mimes as in the passage that celebrates Til's lovemaking; here and there the acute intelligence and the ingenious invention of Mr. Nijinsky gave a musical turn to the action as when the learned pedants answer the jeers of Til in a kind of scholarly counterpoint. Momentarily, too, the accent of this action was the accent of the music; but usually Strauss's tone poem was no more than background to the illusion even as was Mr. Jones's decoration. In the dim distance was the shadowy portal of a medieval cathedral, as it might be in Til's own Braunschweig. Around it in pure fantasy were topsy-turvy pinnacles of a medieval town, gabled roofs, turrets, chimney pots, dormered windows as cracked and tumbled and out of all normal semblance as the wits and the pranks of Eulenspiegel himself.

So Mr. Jones construes into decoration the ancient folk tale and the modern German tone poem. Even more fortunately and persuasively has he lavished upon the costumes his wit, fancy, readiness of design, zest for color. Peaked headdresses, comparable in height in their kind with Thamar's tower, were poised upon the heads of the opulent dames of the haute bourgeoisie. Trains of rich stuffs trailed ten yards behind them in the flaunted splendor of "position." The pedantic professors were ludicrous to see in shovel hats that were longer even than Don Basilio's in "The Barber," with their scrolls of learning tucked under their arms, with their black soutanes billowing to their pompous gait. As black under their peaked caps, with white crosses flaring at their backs, were the inquisitors, fond and foolish men, who sent Til to the gallows because he mocked at things as they are and upset the precious proprieties. To and fro among the august ladies, the learned, the bench, the rich possessors generally, went the rabble that trailed wondering and elate at the heels of Til. Coarse stuffs, dull colored and rudely caught together covered them. As often as not back and sides, as in the old ballad went bare. Greasy were their caps; slovenly was their mien. As night descended upon "the public place" where the action occurred they were alternately sombre figures of shadow or lurid figures of passing gleam. Usually, as the eye looked upon the stage, the illusion was of the swiftly turning pages of a medieval chronicle from the brushes of an illuminator who served equally wit, fancy, and the verities.

That action, more than once enriched or modulated by Mr. Nijinsky's fertile invention, followed in the main the suggestions that the imaginations of men, primed with the fact and the legend of Til, have found in Strauss's tone poem. The introductory measures set the scene, as it were, with the haute bourgeoisie, descending stately from its mansions; with the rabble streaming up from its alleys. Til opened wide the bread-vendor's basket, and the hungry were fed. Til pranced and leered about the highly respectable and highly self-conscious dames with his parodies of courtly coquetry. Til made the professors the mock of their own pedantry. Out of his long mantle, as Mr. Nijinsky swung the folds, peered ever the cloven hoof of his derision. Out of his eyes, in Mr. Nijinsky's astute and graphic miming, shone the elation of him that scores merrily off the truly good. His very steps, as Mr. Nijinsky danced them, were as the tracing of his mockery.

So far Strauss, the attributed program to his rondo, the evergreen traditions of the "merry pranks " that the composer has sent from Bavaria world-wide. Then, for climax, the wry, the comic, the modern rather than medieval, the finely touched and the finely stimulating invention of Mr. Nijinsky himself. Nightfall comes; the respectable are at home and abed; only the rabble, fed, happy, elated, intoxicated with the happenings of Til's afternoon, haunt the square. Regardless of what Strauss's music may or may not imply, heedless of the tradition that the radical Nijinsky has thrown to the winds, they acclaim and enthrone him as their deliverer. One the shoulders of the mob sits Til, enthroned, the sovereign of the wit that brings freedom, of the mockery that sends conventions and hypocrisies toppling down. Respectable Braunschweig and disregarded Strauss may endure no more. Into "the public place " troop the inquisitors; back to Til's trial and hanging comes the tone poem. Then and there he is strung up—red light of warning. But no sooner are the executioners gone than he springs anew into being, the perpetual being of the humor that bursts sham, the jeer that pricks pretension. Wistfully, prophetically—to Strauss's epilogue—the rabble eyes a perennial miracle. In fine, a mimodrama—to return to that exceedingly elastic category—like no other in the Russian repertoire; that courts a certain verity of illusion of time, place, and circumstance; yet is impregnated with an everlasting symbolism; that under medieval guise masks intensely contemporary ideas; that takes its text from Strauss's music and from the folk tale of Til and leaves Mr. Nijinsky thereon to preach the sermon; that fills the eye with pictorial illusions; the imagination with thick-coming fancies; the mind with thoughts that twinge. It is the handiwork of an intellect, invention, and fancy that shows Mr. Nijinsky more than the master dancer of his time; that offers a new and fruitful field to mimodrama; it confirms the distinction that marks the Russian ballet as one of the driving artistic forces of our time. To an eighth art almost, it goes forward.

—from *The Boston Transcript,* 1916

ANDRÉ OLIVEROFF
Nijinsky's Last Days in the Theatre

"André Oliveroff" was the nom de ballet of a young American named Oliver Grimes who fell in love with the idea of ballet from reading books, got some training, and joined Pavlova's company, dancing with her for many years. His book, Flight of the Swan, *is one of the most personal and touching accounts we have of her.*

Thanks to my friend Ptashnik I was privileged to meet Nijinsky several times and these meetings made an indelible impression on me. Nijinsky was the only dancer of his time who could be mentioned in the same breath with Anna Pavlova. He too was an absolute genius. Like Madame, he never seemed quite accountable in human terms, but whereas with Madame you always felt there was a strong cord of sanity that bound her to this world, in Nijinsky's case there was a mere thread, and if you knew him you felt this thread was liable to snap at any moment. He seemed literally not to "belong" here—there was something eerie, almost frightening, about him.

His appearance was not extraordinary; he resembled many another young Pole. He was short (surely not more than five feet one or two) and stocky. His head was small, his hair quite thin, and that face which possessed such exotic distinction in the theatre was, without its make-up, merely crude; the nose thick and bulbous, the coarse mouth lacking teeth on either side when he smiled. His eyes, at second glance, were the one notable feature of his face. Although colorless, they had an Oriental slant and an expression that was somehow arresting; quizzical eyes, at times brooding, at times full of life but always a little strange—perhaps because, like those of every genius, they viewed life at a radically different angle from anyone else's eyes.

His hands, though the fingers were stubby, were unusually sensitive and he used them constantly as he talked—the fingers held together and half-closed; his wrists were in continual eloquent motion.

Undressed, he at once lost all aspect of the commonplace. You were impressed with his force, the over-developed calf and bow-like upper-leg muscles suggesting the physical strength that was but one source of those prodigious leaps of his that won him the nickname of the Eighth Wonder of the World. The torso was fine and the neck, long and superbly modelled, was set on his shoulders in a manner worthy of Rodin or Michelangelo.

His voice was quiet and his manner (off-stage!) simple and uncommonly polite.

Two afternoons Nijinsky asked me to go to the Colon and practice with him and I seized these opportunities to study him at work. As might be expected, his method of working was peculiar. He practiced in the very darkest corner of the stage. He was feverishly concerned with what seemed to me the least important details of his technique, doing such exercises as *contre-mouvements, petits battements,* and *pliés* over and over again, interminably—and with such care and precision you might conclude they were the very marrow of his wonderful art. His pirouettes were the cleanest and the easiest imaginable, yet he was never satisfied with them. He would turn a half-dozen flawless ones, then ask me nervously, "How did I finish? Are you sure they were clean enough?"

They were obviously perfect but I could not convince him.

His *échappées* were incredible. You could only believe that some electric spring had released him into the air, which was certainly his domain—and then at his bidding brought him down again. It was no legend they used to tell—that old Cecchetti could walk upright between Nijinsky's legs when he jumped. Nor was his elevation a mere athletic feat—he seemed to soar like a bird and you were exhilarated and lifted up at the spectacle of a man rising, like Mercury, so easily and so triumphantly above the earth.

As with Madame, Nijinsky's technique was only an instrument. He could play fewer tunes upon it than she could upon hers but those tunes were unforgettable! *L'Après midi* one might almost call a refutation of technique, of its obvious aspects, that is. Actually it was the extreme understatement of a technique that was without a parallel. Nijinsky's *Schéhérezade,* his *Faune* and *Spectre de la Rose,* simply stopped criticism, made it seem impertinent and ridiculous. They were—a revelation.

He was fond of taking long walks at night, and I accompanied him several

times. It was during these evenings—spent in the more obscure streets of
Buenos Aires, where he was better able to escape from a world of which
he was desperately afraid—that I became acquainted with him; at Ptashnik's,
in the company of Madame Nijinskaya, he always seemed to be wearing a
mask. I was an eager listener and he did most of the talking, if one could call
it talking; decidedly it was not conversation, in the ordinary sense of the
word.

For he was quite incapable of "conversing." His talk, far indeed from the
logical or even the connected, consisted of a series of seemingly unrelated
phrases—blurted out or murmured, as if to himself—and often it required
an alert imagination to follow him. Dancing was the only thing in the world
he understood; the rest of living was an enigma. He was looking at life like
a stranger perplexed and harassed by his inability to account for it. He
brooded over beauty and especially over death, seemed ever to be groping
out from the world of fantasy in which he lived for an explanation of this
utterly foreign world to which he was forced to adapt himself. Any attempt
to engage him in an ordinary conversation was quite futile. The words *food,
drink, salary, clothes,* etc., were simply not in his vocabulary. At Ptashnik's I
once heard his wife ask him some question about the hotel bill; she hadn't
seen it or it had been too steep. Nijinsky looked at her blankly. "Hotel
bill . . . hotel bill . . . " He shook his head slowly. His wife might have been
speaking Sanskrit. The expression "hotel bill" did not register with him.

True, he spoke no English, and my Russian was not all that it might
have been; but I was able to get along in the Russian tongue with plenty of
others who have themselves endorsed my impressions of Nijinsky. They have
told me, moreover, that he had always been like that—it seemed difficult,
almost unnatural, for him to talk at all. It was as though, being supremely
articulate in the Dance, all other gifts of self-expression were denied him,
even the humble gift of speech. And yet in his peculiar way he spoke a great
deal. . . .

He had two dominating obsessions and these obsessions were the burden
of his talk. They were: the war (which was still raging)—and his fear of the
other members of the Diaghilev Company, a fear which I wrongly believed
at the time to be nothing more than a delusion.

His despair at the meaninglessness of the war (thrice meaningless to him
in his world of fantasy!) was overwhelming and pitiable; it amounted to a
mania, seeming to poison his whole life—a symptom and very possibly a
cause of the madness whose fearful arms were now stretching closer and
closer towards him. The war was a reiterating refrain, a leitmotif running
through his ejaculatory speech. Again and again he would come back to it.
He would pass his hand over his forehead and murmur, or exclaim furiously,
"Why . . . why is there this massacre, this murder . . . this sea of blood (he

would repeat "sea of blood," then finding no adequate phrase, end up with an illuminating gesture of those articulate hands)—all over the place . . . everywhere, everywhere the sea of blood! Why . . . why . . . ?"

This perhaps in answer to some commonplace question of mine. And then he would appear to brood, but perhaps quicken his pace, all the time muttering to himself, and I would catch a phrase here and there—"this awful murder . . . this sea of blood . . . "

He had suffered in 1914–1915. An ironical kind of suffering it was too. In the fall of 1913 he had married the daughter of a Hungarian actress; he was in Hungary with his wife when the war broke out. The Hungarian government detained him in a prison camp for eighteen months. They said they did not want him to dance for the enemy.

His life during this period would have been endurable enough save for one thing. He was treated kindly and the reason for his detention was explained to him. At first he was allowed to do pretty much as he pleased. Of course, he spent part of each day practising. One day, incredible as it may seem, his captors, observing this whirling dervish in the field, conceived the outlandish notion that he might be a spy—and these extraordinary motions of the arms and legs might be a code of signals! They promptly forbade Nijinsky to do any more "practising." From that day on he was watched more carefully and was not permitted to dance.

His one object in living denied fulfilment, he became morose. Fortunately, his father-in-law was a general in the Hungarian Army and, after repeated attempts, stretching over a year, he finally managed to persuade the government that Nijinsky was an innocent and utterly helpless artist who in all probability did not know what a signal was—and that if they didn't free him and free him soon, they would have a raving maniac on their hands. So they let him go. . . .

This long imprisonment with its idiotic restrictions must have played its part in unhinging the poor boy's mind. Certainly it accounted for his obsession with the war, "the sea of blood all over the place—the awful murder." It must be remembered, however, that Nijinsky's father died in an insane asylum.

No less than with the war was he ridden by a constant fear of his dancing associates. He lived in terror that they would kill him. I have heard people say that this fear was an hallucination, but I have reason to believe they were mistaken, though of course, in his neurotic mind, the fear was exaggerated. In Buenos Aires he never went to the theatre unaccompanied by two policemen and, once in his dressing room, he literally barricaded himself there until he was due to appear on the stage.

All the other members of the Diaghilev Company hated him bitterly. That they were jealous of him goes without saying, but aside from their jealousy they had good grounds for their hatred. In the theatre Nijinsky could be, and frequently was, a fiend. He had not the slightest consideration for anyone but himself. When he chose, he treated his fellow-dancers, and especially the girls, as so many vermin. No foul epithet in Polish or Russian was too foul for him to fling at a girl whose costume or make-up did not happen to please his fastidious eye.

"You swine, you blood of a dog, you whore!" he would cry at her, if her headdress were carelessly arranged. "I told you to wear the garland like a crown and here you dare come to me with it hanging about your ears!" Then, his voice rising to a shriek, he would fire at her a whole vocabulary of the vilest abuse.

It often happened that the lover of the girl was present during such an outburst and he would fly out at Nijinsky in one of those Slavic tempers than which nothing could be more violent. Then poor Nijinsky would look sulky and blank, as though he did not understand. "But I meant nothing by it," he would reply absently, "nothing at all. I spoke the truth, didn't I? She is a whore, as you know. . . ."

As far back as 1916, the aftermath of these scenes reached the danger point. A friend of mine, who at that time was Nijinsky's secretary and constant companion, told me that one evening in Salt Lake City, just before a performance of *Les Sylphides* in which Nijinsky was scheduled to appear, a mob comprising all the men dancers in the company came to his dressing room and threatened to do him violence. It seemed that afternoon he had insulted the girls outrageously and the men had come to make him pay for it. My friend was adroit enough to stop them. He met them outside the dressing room and told them gravely that Nijinsky was very sick and the doctor was with him now, trying to quiet him. Nijinsky had been delirious that afternoon, he explained, and was not to be held accountable for what he said. He pled with the men to go back to the wings at once—it was almost time for the show to start. Nijinsky's understudy would have to substitute for him in *Les Sylphides*. My friend finally convinced the infuriated ballet corps that he was telling the truth and they went away without so much as seeing their victim.

The wonder of it is, they hadn't killed him by 1918. Had Diaghilev not been so terrified of the sea, had he accompanied his troupe during their American tours, things might have fared better with his star. Diaghilev probably understood him better than did anyone else—besides, he knew how to hold his company together. As it was, Madame Nijinskaya was left alone to do the best she knew how with her difficult husband. She was a woman of extraordinary intelligence and tact; alas, it was not within a woman's power to control Nijinsky. . . .

The climax came one night when we were still in Buenos Aires. By accident—possibly by intention—a trapdoor on the stage was improperly fastened, and during the finale of *Schéhérezade,* when Nijinsky was turning his marvelous pirouettes in the air, with the entire company encircled about him, he stepped on this loosened door—and fell. He was not seriously hurt, but he was sure that the mishap had been deliberately planned by his enemies, and his fears were intensified a hundredfold. If only the fall had killed him, the soaring artist been brought to earth for good, and all in that supreme moment of the dance! But Fate was less kind—by far. Nijinsky rapidly sank into a profound melancholia. The greatest man dancer the world has ever known continued to exist, but in an oblivious void from which he emerged occasionally, only to imagine himself a horse, walking about on all fours.

They took him to an asylum in Switzerland, but all efforts to restore him to himself have been in vain. The slender thread which bound the fantastic world of his imagining to human things had snapped clean. And with the snapping of that thread, Vaslav Nijinsky was doomed never to dance again.

—from *Flight of the Swan,* 1932

NICOLAS NABOKOV
The Specter of Nijinsky

O ne should say that to most of the younger collaborators of Diaghilev's enterprise, like Balanchine, Rieti, Tchelitchew, and myself, Nijinsky was a kind of "Golden Age of Ballet" myth. Most of us had never seen him dance except on photographic stills. Nijinsky had left Diaghilev's company long before I came to France, and in 1916 he was stricken with an illness which made him a melancholy and mute wanderer from one Swiss sanatorium to another, and thus the most famous and the most romantic insane person of his time. We young men of the twenties had to be content with the Nijinsky stories, with which the older men of the company would treat us at every possible occasion. The most voluble of them all was Diaghilev's longtime servant and bodyguard, Vassily Ivanovitch Zuikov, a stocky, copper-bearded Mongoloid whose behavior and appearance combined the features of an Al Capone minion and an NKVD colonel. Always hovering backstage and sneaking up from behind a prop at the most inopportune moment, during, say, a balletomanic flirtation, Vassily performed the role of His Majesty's gossip collector, and protector of his personal and bodily interests. Vassily, by virtue of his long connection with the ballet, had not only acquired a unique collection of lurid stories (concerned for the most part with the amorous feats and defeats of the subjects of Diaghilev's empire), but he was also informed, with the most astonishing exactitude, of the whereabouts and activities of everyone who had even the remotest connection with the ballet.

One day early in October 1928, I went out to lunch with a friend, between rehearsals, in one of those tiny bistros with four round tables growing out of a frieze of boxwood, which cluster around the Place St. Lazare. When I arrived, I spotted Vassily sitting in the bistro's darkest corner, obviously absorbed in a conversation with a "ballet mother," one of those embittered and protectively jealous matrons who always follow ballet troupes, peddling gossip about their daughters' closest rivals. As soon as we sat down, Vassily came to our table, bent over as if he were communicating a state secret, and whispered, "Do you know that Nijinsky is coming tonight to the ballet to see Lifar dance? Diaghilev wants him to say something about Lifar's dancing, and has persuaded the doctors to let him come." He shrugged his shoulders. "But what can he say? He's mute, isn't he?"

I knew that Nijinsky was in a sanatorium somewhere in the suburbs of Paris, and I had heard that morning that Diaghilev was bragging, "I'll make him speak . . . you'll see!" The elderly Russian painter Korovin, with whom I was lunching, was appalled at the notion. "Why be so cruel?" he said. "Why disturb a poor insane man? Only to satisfy Diaghilev's colossal ego and his proprietary instincts? He likes people to admire *his* musicians, *his* painters, and particularly, his boys and girls of the ballet company. And he doesn't really care if the admirer is the Bey of Tunis or an insane genius." Korovin paused a bit and added, "Of course, this case is rather special. After all, both Nijinsky and Lifar were more or less his finds."

After lunch I returned to the opera and found Diaghilev sitting on the stage watching a rehearsal. The whole company, in tights and tutus, was spinning around in a circle to the shotlike clapping of Grigoriev's hands, "*Raz, dva, tri, tchetyre* . . . " (one, two, three, four). A little lady at the piano was turbulently banging out the Russian dances from Rimsky-Korsakov's *May Night*. Diaghilev looked angry and bored. He leaned with both hands on the silver knob of his cane, his eyes half closed, the monocle in his right eye in perilous position. After about a half hour of this choreographic *salade russe*, Diaghilev suddenly stamped his feet, knocked on the floor with his cane, and shouted angrily in his babyish voice, "Enough of that! *C'est de la merde, pure et simple!*" He turned around and yelled for Boris Kochno. "Where is Valichka?" he whined, not noticing that Nouvel was standing at his side.

"Where is Karsavina? Where is Seryoja Lifar? I can't sit around for hours waiting for Their Majesties to arrive. I must see their *pas de deux* before tonight. Tell them to come immediately." He continued to rant until Karsavina and Lifar finally appeared in costume ready to dance. Meanwhile he shouted at Nouvel, Grigoriev, and Kochno, and even at the pianist, who begged to be excused after a day's rehearsal. "I also want to go home, my dear Madame. I also am tired. Do not blame me; blame the prima donnas." As soon as the pair began rehearsing he quieted, his eyes glued to the movements of their miraculously precise and agile feet. "Boris, what time is it?" he asked in the midst of the rehearsal. "Six? My God, it's time for you to go! I told the doctors you would be there at seven." Vassily winked at me, and beckoned me to follow. "Don't you want to come with us?" he whispered. I followed them to the backstage exit.

Boris, Vassily, and I caught a taxi on the rue Auber and drove through the gentle autumnal evening light of Paris, across the rue de Rivoli, and past the Tuileries. Having reached the left bank of the Seine, the taxi turned northwards, and by the time we reached the Bois de Vincennes, the twilight had settled down and the pinkish lanterns along the road began to shine on the background of a mauve-colored sky. As we drove through the Bois, past the stone walls and bric-a-brac villas of the northern Parisian suburbs, I could not help thinking of what I knew and remembered of Nijinsky. I was a child in St. Petersburg when I first saw his photographs. The director of the Imperial Theater, the foxy-looking Prince Sergei Volkonsky, with his sixteenth-century beard and mustachios, brought them to show to my mother soon after he had returned from Paris. He also brought a series of postal cards representing Diaghilev's famous dancers, Pavlova, Karsavina, Bolm, Nijinsky, and others. I was particularly struck by two of them: Nijinsky in the costume of the blackamoor in *Schéhérazade,* his face brown, his eyes and teeth gleaming with a virile, sensual smile. He was in a pantherlike pose, about to jump. And the other: Nijinsky all covered with rose petals, his beautiful body stretched out in a languorously effete pose of an androgynal-looking youth. (I take it that in the hothouse atmosphere of Paris in 1910, this "spirit of the rose" with its absurd rose-petaled costume and suave choreography was the perfectly justified dream of a pre-Freudian ballet-soxer.)

It was perhaps because of these images that the shock of seeing Nijinsky that October night at the gate of a sanatorium in a dingy Parisian *banlieu* was more acute than I anticipated. The taxi stopped in front of the sanatorium compound, which was closed in by a quadrangle of high stone walls. Boris jumped out and asked Vassily and me to wait in the taxi. After about a quarter of an hour we heard footsteps on the pavement outside the compound; then an attendant in a long white smock and Boris appeared leading Nijinsky to the taxi. I cannot say that I did not *recognize* Nijinsky, but it was difficult to *identify* that baldheaded grayish little man (one always forgets how small dancers are) with expressionless eyes, and a sallow, sick look on his face that was accentuated by the white lights of the sanatorium lanterns. He looked more like a commercial traveler out of a job, or a schoolteacher in a small Polish mining town, than the embodiment of a terpsichorean legend. He was dressed in an oversized dark wool overcoat with a neat white scarf tied around his neck. He did not greet us, nor utter a sound.

Driving back to the Opéra I felt uneasy, as if all of us, Boris, Vassily, the male nurse, myself and even the taxi driver, were accomplices in a strangely unsavory crime. I was glad to sit near the driver, not to face the victim with his empty eyes and sick face. When we drove into the semicircular courtyard which surrounds the back entrance to the Paris Opéra, I saw that a crowd of company members were gathered near the stage door. Vassily got out and began shoving people out of the way. Grigoriev came running up to the taxi, leaped inside, and embraced Nijinsky. "Vaslav Fomitch, what happiness! *Kakaya radost,* what joy!" The whole group started for the taxi and hauled Nijinsky out. There was no response from the sick man. He remained mute, and his eyes retained their dead look. Only once did his expression change, when he stood at the foot of the staircase, and his nurse urged him to walk up. He shook his head in a curiously vehement way, and his face twitched nervously. I think that it was Boris and Vassily who carried him in a hand-chair, up the narrow stairs leading to the director's box. The theater was dark and the performance of Stravinsky's *Firebird* had begun. Only a few people in the audience could have seen the Ulyssean return of the famous dancer to his master's box.

In the box were Alexandre Benois, the painter, Nouvel, a few ladies, and myself. Diaghilev stood behind Nijinsky's seat, and leaned over to whisper in his ear. It seemed to me that a barely perceptible animation appeared on Nijinsky's face. For the first time, at least, his eyes were focused in a definite direction, and he seemed to see the dancing. Throughout the performance Diaghilev continued to talk to Nijinsky in a nagging, insistent whisper, and once or twice I heard him say, "*Skaji, skaji,* tell me, tell me, how do you like Lifar? Isn't he magnificent?" He tweaked Nijinsky's ear, poked him in the shoulder, chuckling in the tone with which elderly men, unaccustomed to infants, usually bring about a prolonged tantrum. To all of it, Nijinsky remained silent, but when the poking turned into actual pinching he mumbled something like, "*Aie, ostav,* stop it!"

I lost Nijinsky from sight immediately after the performance. He was surrounded by a crowd of old-timers, elderly Russian painters, designers, dressmakers, stagehands, ballet mothers, and aging ballerinas—all moved to tears by the sight of their idol. They whisked him on the stage, where cameras began clicking, and where a group was organized around him for the now famous photograph. It consists of Diaghilev, looking at Nijinsky with an oily smile, Benois, Grigoriev, Nouvel, Karsavina, and, as an exception to the rule of seniority, as special recognition of the princely heritage that had become his lot, Serge Lifar was added to the group.

I was unable to observe Nijinsky's reaction at that moment, but a few days later, looking at the photographs, I noticed that a vague and helplessly benevolent smile lighted his face.

A short while later, Diaghilev vanished, the crowd dispersed, and I found myself struggling through a group of dancers who were rushing out the backstage exit. Nijinsky had been carried downstairs, this time by two men in tights, and was waiting outside alone with Boris and the male nurse. On my way out I met Vassily, whose Oriental face was beaming with the pleasure of a prison warden who has just thwarted an escape. He whispered, "You see, I told you Diaghilev wouldn't get a word out of him. Serves him right."

This time we drove back in a large funereal limousine, and again I sat in the front seat but squeezed in between the driver and Vassily, whose bulging left thigh prevented me from leaning back. Vassily tried to start a conversation with the bearded chauffeur. "*Vous savez* who is inside the car? Nijinsky!" he said, obviously expecting an excited response. "*No hablo francés,*" mumbled the driver into his beard. "*Ach, on ispan yetz,*" said Vassily sententiously, and dropped into silence. I was grateful for that silence, glad to be outside again, even in that damp, opaque night which enveloped us as soon as we crossed the narrow avenues of the Bois de Vincennes and drove into the surburb of Villejuif. It was past midnight when the limousine stopped at the sanatorium gate, and the ceremony of extracting Nijinsky from his seat began again. He looked paler than before, and because his body had become as limp as an oyster, it took some time to put him on his feet. Finally, a mere shadow of a prisoner between two jailers, he walked past me toward the gate. I watched him from the car, saw him stop, turn around, and although the car's motor was on I heard him say in a gentle, halting, and somewhat tearful voice, "*Skajite yemou chto Lifar horosho prygayet.*" (Tell him that Lifar jumps well.)

—from *Old Friends and New Music,* 1951

RICHARD BUCKLE
A God Twice Buried

In spring 1950 Lincoln Kirstein was staying with me and we were getting to know each other, going to the ballet and visiting exhibitions; and the genius of Balanchine was dawning before me. On Easter Saturday, 8 April 1950, three days after the premiere of *Ballet Imperial* at Covent Garden, Lincoln and I were at a matinée of Sadler's Wells Theatre Ballet (the second company) at Sadler's Wells; we were sitting on the extreme right of the dress circle, in the second or third row. Lincoln was on the outside because of his long legs. As the curtain fell on the first ballet an attendant in uniform came down the steps to tell me that I was wanted urgently on the telephone by the *Observer*. My immediate boss, the literary editor, told me that Nijinsky had died that morning: an obituary notice was required for the next day's paper. I went backstage and asked if I could use an office to write in, and was given that of Ninette de Valois. I thought that neither Ninette, nor Lincoln, nor I would be where we were or doing what we were doing had it not been for Nijinsky and Diaghilev. Lincoln had never told me—indeed in the ten days we had known each other he had hardly had a chance to tell me—about the part he played in helping Romola with her book: so when I returned to watch the last ballet and gave him the news, remarking that if it had not been for Romola's life of Nijinsky I might never have got interested in ballet, and he replied, "I wrote it," I was astounded. "You *what?*" "I ghosted it. I helped her write it down—the first part anyway. Haskell finished it." I felt like Oedipus learning the fatal pattern of his life: it was as though Lincoln had revealed that he was my father.

Four days later I was at Covent Garden to see *Ballet Imperial* for a third time (counting the dress rehearsal). In the interval I was approached by Margaret Power. She had come to tell me that Romola was very upset because no member of the Royal Ballet had offered to be a pallbearer at Nijinsky's funeral on Friday. Dolin had been invited, and Lifar was flying from Paris: why was there no one from Covent Garden? It was absurd of Romola to be offended because, as I told Margaret to explain to her, no Englishman would dream of being so presumptuous as to *offer* himself as pallbearer at a great man's funeral. I promised to arrange something. I went straight up to George Balanchine. When he heard Lifar was coming he refused outright. No doubt he remembered how Lifar, out-Hamleting Hamlet beside

Diaghilev's open grave, had flung himself in a rage of jealousy, self-pity, and self-dramatization onto the unfortunate Kochno. Boris had been obliged to fend off the vulgar assault and was condemned to bear thereafter the stigma of having brawled over Diaghilev's coffin. After George's refusal, I asked Frederick Ashton and Michael Somes, Britain's principal choreographer and chief male dancer, who both consented to carry the coffin. Lincoln had gone to Aldeburgh to visit Benjamin Britten. Next day I telephoned Cyril Beaumont, who also agreed; and I myself made up the six.

On the morning of Friday, 14 April, I bought some lilies at Victoria Station, picked up Fred, and made for St. James's, Spanish Place, the gloomy Catholic church behind the Wallace Collection. It was just opposite my old art school, Heatherley's. When the Requiem Mass was over, the pallbearers, forewarned by the undertakers, took their places according to height: Dolin and Lifar, the shortest, in front; then Ashton and myself; Beaumont and Somes in the rear. We carried Nijinsky's coffin to the waiting hearse. I did not go on to Marylebone Cemetery to see the burial of the dancer who had changed my life.

He was not long allowed to rest in peace. Lifar had bought a plot in the Cemetery of Montmartre, and he intended vaingloriously to share it with Nijinsky. In 1953 he obtained Romola's permission to transfer Nijinsky's body to Paris. According to British law, when a body is disinterred it has to be identified. It fell to Margaret Power to perform this gruesome task in a chapel in the Marylebone Road. The inner lead coffin was then placed in a new wooden one. Margaret accompanied the coffin to Victoria Station— where Mme Legat, widow of one of Nijinsky's teachers, brought a group of her pupils to adorn it with flowers—and she sat beside it in the luggage van, crossed the Channel with it, and arrived with it at the Gare du Nord, where Lifar had promised to meet her.

Twenty-four years later, in 1977, when Margaret was dying of cancer, she climbed my eighty-two stairs in Covent Garden to tell me a few things which would otherwise be forgotten. I will give my notes just as I jotted them down the moment she had left me.

Funeral in Paris, 16 June 1953. Romola too poor to come from USA. Paul [Bohus, her cousin] was dealing in antiques in S. Francisco in a v. small way. R telegraphed would pay M's fares, hotel, red roses to be thrown *into* grave (but coffin never lowered [in Margaret's presence]). Trip cost M £70 or £80 [about $200], never repaid. M lost at Gare du Nord. Lifar never turned up. M, landed with big outer coffin w. handles, said it was *not* to go to church [having, I suppose, received instructions to that effect]. Trouble with formalities. Next day car came at 10 to her hotel for service [at the Russian church] rue Daru 10:30. Sat 2 away from Bronia, representing Romola.

Lifar bossing about, organizing people. Endless service. She pee-ed at Russian restaurant opposite. Appalling scrum at cemetery—cameras, TV. Preobrajenska clung to her, horrified. Minister, clutching vast floral tribute, held forth, hoping for photo in papers. Lifar orated. Crush and fighting. Nightmare.

—from *In the Wake of Diaghilev*, 1981

RUDOLF NUREYEV

Rudolf Nureyev (1938–1993) was the most famous and influential male ballet dancer since Nijinsky. A Tatar by birth, raised in a small town near Ufa, he only began his serious training at the age of seventeen, at the Vaganova school in Leningrad. It was Alexander Pushkin, the great teacher there (who also trained Baryshnikov), who nurtured his genius. An immediate star in Russia, in 1961 Nureyev defected from the Soviet Union at the Le Bourget airport in Paris and entered into his overwhelmingly triumphant international career—the harbinger of a new, thrilling style and the embodiment of sexual and performance charisma: a celebrity as much as an artist. His partnership with Margot Fonteyn made them the most famous couple in ballet—perhaps of all time. Among his greatest roles were Albrecht, Prince Siegfried, Romeo, Basilio, and Armand, but he danced everything, everywhere, moving back and forth between classical ballets to modern chore- oraphers like Martha Graham. His own choreography was undistinguished, and was to a large extent prompted by his desire to rework classical ballets in order to expand their leading roles for men—that is, for himself. He danced primarily for the Royal in London and the Opéra in Paris, but toured and guested relentlessly with anyone who would foot the bill. His final creation was a production of La Bayadère for the Paris Opéra Ballet, which he had successfully run in the eighties. Before he died (of AIDS), he was trying to establish himself as a ballet conductor.

Liuba Myasnikova
Some of My Memories

I first became acquainted with Rudik just after he had arrived in Leningrad. He was extremely lonely in this cold, alien town, with its inhospitable sea climate. The dank autumn days and frosty winter nights set you scurrying for the warmth and comfort of home. All that Rudik had against the frigid weather was a skimpy coat and his one little scarf. There was no cozy flat for him to retire to, only a bed in the Ballet School's student hostel. And since he was the new boy in town, Rudik was accorded a far from friendly reception.

The great Leningrad drew him out onto her streets, to her elegant facades and classical architecture. Rudik wanted to visit every museum, see every performance, go to every concert. But, most of all, he wanted to mingle with the crowd and lose himself in this fantastic town to which he had so long dreamed of coming.

There used to be a little music shop not far from the Ballet School, beside the Kazan Cathedral. It isn't there anymore, but in those days it was a quaint little establishment with a large selection of records and piano music. You could play phonographs on the store's record-player, and the shop assistant, on request, would play whatever you asked for on the piano. A friend of my mother's, Elisaveta Mikhailovna Pazhi, worked there. (Lilen'ka was our pet name for her.) She was a merry little woman from a St. Petersburg family, a wonderfully kind and cultured individual. She couldn't help but notice the shabbily dressed teenage boy who dropped into her shop almost every day. More often than not, he'd asked her to play something for him on the piano. Then he'd hang around until the shop closed and the two of them would leave together. Rudik would accompany her to the bus or tram stop, carrying her bag.

Lilen'ka and her husband, Veniamin Mikhailovich, had no children. Perhaps not surprisingly, Rudik became the object for all their unrequited parental love. They absolutely doted on him and tried to do everything they could to help him. But Rudik was independent and proud. I think he must've been born with that streak of independence and the air of imperial aloofness that he had—which meant that he'd condescend to be helped only if he felt he wasn't being denigrated. He never permitted anyone to feel sorry for him. The desire to help him, yes, that was perfectly all right, for he felt he deserved to be helped. You see, Rudik from birth believed that he had been touched by the hand of God.

Lilen'ka decided to help him out with two things. First, to find a music teacher willing to teach him free of charge. And, second, to find some people Rudik's own age so he'd feel less lonely. To accomplish this, she turned to two of her closest friends: Marina Petrovna Savva (a leading pianist at the Maly Opera Theatre) and my mother, Liudmila Nikolaevna Romankova (matriarch of our household and mother of three). Marina Petrovna, who taught both at the theatre and also at the music school, immediately agreed to give Rudik piano lessons. Her quiet beauty and entrancing smile belied her iron discipline. She always got what she wanted out of you, thanks to her gentle and mild persistence.

Not that there was ever any need for persistence when it came to Rudik. He practiced feverishly and was extremely musically gifted. Having had a little piano training in Ufa, Rudik was playing Rachmaninov's *Elegy* within four weeks. Marina Petrovna's husband, Nikolai Alexandrovich, was not only a professional violinist at the Maly Theatre but also a very amiable and kindhearted man. I'm sure Rudik very much enjoyed his visits to the Savvas—who, like Lilen'ka, had no children and so treated all their young pupils as their own.

Alas, so few of these people are alive now. But, at that time, they were all young and full of life, meeting up with each other to share their common interests and common adoration of "our dear boy." They jealously followed his every success, attending all his performances, not only those at the end of his studies but also the ones at the Kirov.

I had actually seen Rudik before Lilen'ka told us about him. Being a great fan of ballet, I not only went to all the Kirov's performances, but also to those at the Ballet School. The latter took place several times a year. A particular favorite of mine was the evening of their 1958 graduation examinations, held on the Kirov stage. The tickets cost peanuts. (During those days, theatres received state subsidies, so anyone who wanted to go could afford the pleasure.)

The Ballet School's evenings always lasted way into the night. Every student was given the chance to show off his or her repertoire. The evening would often begin with an act from a classical ballet; then the second and third acts would consist of various concert numbers—pas de deuxs, variations, character dances, and the like.

It was at one of those evenings that I first saw Rudik. He was still a student at the time—not even in his final year—and he danced the part of Actaeon from *Esmeralda*. If my memory serves me correctly, he was partnered that night by Alla Sizova. Both danced brilliantly. Right then and there, I made a mental note to myself that the Ballet School had a new star.

How I loved to hang out with those talented young dancers and follow their success from year to year. I kept all my programs and still have many of them at home, bearing the names of dancers who then went on to world fame. Rudik wasn't the only gifted young star at the Ballet School during this period. There was also Yuri Soloviev, Nikita Dolgushin, Kostya Brudnov, and, as I mentioned, Alla Sizova.

I once went with Lilen'ka Pazhi to one of those Ballet School performances. During the intermission, a rather short, elegant young man—his hair still wet from showering—came up to her. Lilen'ka introduced me to him. It was Rudolf Nureyev.

Lilen'ka asked if I could invite him over to my house for one of our Sunday dinners. I can't quite remember who was present the first day Rudik came over. It might have been only our family: my elder sister, Marina (who was just finishing medical school), my twin brother, Leonid (who, like me, was in his third year at the Polytechnic Institute), and, of course, my mother, father, and grandfather.

We "kids" were at that age when you feverishly drink in everything the world has to offer. We studied day and night, but played sports and went to every exhibition, concert, show, and museum. It was the period of the much-hailed Khrushchev "thaw," an intoxicating and thrilling time in Russia. Our whole lives were ahead of us and the possibilities seemed endless.

But back to that Sunday dinner. As I remember it, we sat down to eat around three o'clock in the afternoon, only getting up from the table around seven. My brother and I then invited Rudik to stay on and talk for a bit. The two of us liked Rudik from the moment we first set eyes on him, for he was completely unlike anyone we ever knew.

Even in those days there was a special aura about Rudik. He was very independent, but at the same time modest about himself. Having taken ballet lessons for eight years myself, it was especially interesting for me to hear him tell us all about the Ballet School and the lessons, classes, and teachers. We talked and talked long into the night.

That first meeting, which marked the beginning of our long—and sometimes complicated—friendship, is engraved in my memory forever. Rudik described it in his autobiography published in the West (in 1962), in which, out of consideration for our personal safety, he lists our surname as Davidenko in order to confuse the KGB. (My grandfather's surname was Davidenkov.) Rudik no doubt realized that our friendship wouldn't exactly endear us to the men of the "First Section." His autobiography was smuggled to me from the West, and I must confess that I enjoyed reading Rudik's reaction to our first day together:

> Suddenly I felt happy really happy.
>
> I had spent the evening with my friends the Davidenkos who had invited me to their appartment for the first time. . . . Nowhere else, up to now, had I ever found such a tranquil, cultivated atmosphere. My friend and her twin brother were both brilliant students and both very good-looking; she, very gay, with sparkling black eyes was a student in electronics . . .
>
> We had talked about everything and they showed a genuine interest in, and a wide knowledge of, subjects outside their own sphere.
>
> My life, often so meaningless to me, suddenly seemed clearly directed and orientated. For once, I felt no trace of anxiety.

The next day Rudik left for Moscow to take part in a ballet competition, where he won his first major accolade.

When we met twenty-eight years later, we reminisced about that evening. Rudik told me how he'd envied us for having been born into such a cultured family, surrounded by books and the opportunity to acquire so much knowledge. To be honest, I never suspected him of harboring such feelings. Everything that surrounded me was what had always surrounded me, like the air that I breathed. I never felt that I possessed any advantage over others. In fact, more often than not, due to my youthful self-centeredness, I spurned the family experience. Rudik didn't share our interest in politics, although he did follow closely the discussions which always tend to blaze up whenever two Russians get together. Not for anything would he allow himself to be drawn into a political debate. Nor would he discuss any topic associated with the running of our government during an interview with a reporter. I don't think it was out of fear of harming his career in those Leningrad days, or fear for his Russian friends and relatives when he was living abroad. He simply wasn't interested in politics. He was a true citizen of the world. I think he'd always been like this, from his very earliest years—even if it wasn't so apparent to me at the time. All I knew was that Rudik wasn't particularly interested in the real world. The only world he inhabited was that of the performing arts. He was ready to dance wherever there was a stage and an audience. Needless to say, he had a special relationship with the Kirov stage. . . .

Rudik's life was regulated by the strict discipline imposed by the Ballet School's hostel. They'd lock the doors at eleven and, if you missed the evening bell, they sometimes didn't let you in. Rudik's pride couldn't live with that. Although his self-discipline was almost superhuman—he never missed a single class and he put everything he had into his lessons and rehearsals—the one thing he couldn't take was outside pressure, especially when it clashed with one of his own ideas.

Marina Petrovna Savva once told me how, when she and Rudik were on holidays together in the Crimea, he had rebelled against an attempt by the people at the canteen to force him to dress "like everyone else." Rudik, it seems, had shown up there straight from the beach, clad only in a pair of swimming trunks and a red shirt carelessly knotted at the front. The manager of the canteen refused to let him in, claiming that Rudik's attire was unsuitable for a dining room. When the man asked him to put on a pair of trousers, Rudik exploded with rage and stormed out of the place, going without lunch. And he never went back there again. Rudik could imagine humiliation in almost any situation; he couldn't handle degradation and he never forgave an insult.

So our little group had to walk very lightly when it came to Rudik. We would immediately rush and try to pour oil on troubled waters whenever things began acting up. But we never really had one single group. Rather, there were actually several, with people going from the one to the other. One group had a definite intellectual inclination while another would be sports-oriented. In the former group, intellect, originality, and creativity were respected; in the latter, dexterity, sporting triumph, and physical strength dominated. It was obviously much easier for Rudik with the sports-oriented crowd, even if the guys there did sometimes make fun of him—claiming that if they ever personally chose to dance on the stage, Rudik would cease to exist. Next to these guys, Rudik really did seem small and fragile, for they were all strong, sturdy types. They went in for handball, volleyball, and hockey and were all good jumpers. Nevertheless, they were amazed that Rudik could lift up a ballerina so effortlessly. However, they rationalized that it was only because the ballerinas themselves did most of the work and all Rudik had to do was catch them. One day, they demanded that Rudik demonstrate his technique by lifting me up above his head on outstretched arms. This he did, and they followed suit. Naturally, they had no difficulties either, proceeding to take turns in lifting me. When it was all over, Rudik had won their respect. (Anyone who can do something outstanding in sports is always respected.) Thankfully, Rudik sensed their admiration and forgave them for teasing him.

On weekends, we would all travel out of town to Gorskaya, where a friend of mine from the institute—my volleyball teammate, Natasha Lavrova—had a dacha right on the Gulf of Finland. Spring days there were made for playing rugby on the shore, our feet sinking into the freshly melted snow. Although Rudik often came along, he would never join us in playing in the snow, fearing that he might injure his legs. He paid great attention to his joints and would often give his muscles a furious massage. So, while we played, he would sit and watch, revelling in the sight of us reckless young madcaps on the beach.

Rudik was distinguishable in that he was both with us and yet at the same time not with us, a participant and at the same time an observer. There were moments when I felt that he was quietly studying us all a bit. He would sometimes walk down the shore, away from all the other players, to gaze transfixed at the water and the sun. I don't know why, but one summer day remains imprinted on my memory like a photograph. We had all returned to Natasha's dacha, only to discover that Rudik had disappeared. I was worried and ran back to the shore to see if he was perhaps still lingering there. Although Rudik wasn't "my guy," I felt a certain responsibility for him and always made sure that everything was going OK with him and that he wasn't being left out of the general conversation. When I arrived at the shore, I found him there staring out over the horizon. "Rudik, what are you doing? Everyone's looking for you!" "Ssh!" he whispered. "Look how beautiful it all is." The enormous, dark red ball of a sun was slowly going down behind the gulf, its dying rays forming a crimson path on the water. It really was a fantastically beautiful scene. Rudik and I stood there in silence, admiring the otherwordly beauty of it all. Eventually, all that remained of the sun was a bloodred segment; then the sky began to darken over. We turned away and, without saying a word, plodded back to the dacha.

—from *Rudolf Nureyev: Three Years in the Kirov Theater*, 1995

JULIE KAVANAGH
A Celestial Accident

February 21, 1962: the date everyone in London's ballet world was waiting for—at least, those lucky enough to have tickets for this, the first Fonteyn/Nureyev *Giselle*. (Seventy thousand applications were turned down.) "Not even the queen could get in," bragged a clerk in the Opera House box office, while the scalpers outside were demanding £25 for a 37s.6d seat. As the curtain rose on Act I there was a wave of excitement in the auditorium. When Rudolf appeared, the standees at the back of the orchestra "moved as one body forward," but this was not the flamboyant star the London audience was expecting. "He came on stealthily," remembered Maude. "He didn't come on and say, 'Here I am. Look at me.' He wasn't aware of the audience. He was right into his role." In their combined *Observer* review the Goslings dwelled on the way Rudolf did not actively project emotion but drew the audience into the world they were creating onstage. "(This is Ulanova's style) . . . the true sign of a great artist greatly taught."

The element of nobility missing in the first Kirov performances was unmistakable that night, not only in his general bearing and the mannered elegance of his hands, but expressed in occasional telling gestures, like the way he kept pulling down his rough jerkin as if ill at ease in his peasant disguise. And yet, unlike the "playboy" of Erik's interpretation, or the "complete cad" then standard in Russia, this was not a worldly aristocrat dallying with a pretty country girl but the same intense, infatuated youth of Rudolf's Russian debut. Even when Albrecht's guilt was disclosed, he seemed immature and impulsive rather than insincere, his betrayal motivated by no more than what the Alexander Bland review defined as postadolescent instability. "It is the James Dean charm of a boy who will always be in trouble and always forgiven."

Responding to his ecstatic displays of love, Fonteyn seemed to recapture much of the youthful esprit she had been lacking for many years. "The Giselle she gave that night with Nureyev was different," wrote Clive Barnes. "More rhapsodic, more intense." Rudolf, too, was more engaged than before; no longer diverting attention to himself by capriciously adopting an inert mask during Giselle's Ophelia-like display of madness. (Even Erik— the paragon of dramatic restraint—had verged on the histrionic at this point, his performance described by Barnes as "the real thing, stark and raving.") But while still leaving it to the audience to imagine the full extent of his grief, Rudolf now disclosed his horror in "one sudden glance." To Tamara Karsavina, who was in the audience, this kind of naturalism was far too small-scale to register onstage.

> I wonder, if it was not the present tendency of the Russian Ballet towards elimination of mime gestures out of dramatic scenes which may have influenced Nureyev to be sparing of gesture. It seems to me that he missed the great opportunity of expressing grief and contrition at Giselle's grave in emotional gestures; Nijinsky's acting of the scene was more poignant.

Certainly Rudolf's underplaying was at odds with the rhetorical bombast and semaphore mime favored by the Royal Ballet, which, as Barnes pointed out, appeared to be taking part in an English melodrama while he was playing Chekhov. "Here one would ultimately concede that everyone was out of step except Nureyev." In the second act, a nocturnal reverie, there was no such disparity. On the contrary, the two dancers' symmetry of line was so remarkable that, as Ninette de Valois remarked, "You couldn't believe they both hadn't sprung from the same school." They seemed to hear the music in the same way, their instinct for filling out a phrase to their fingertips quite uncanny in its simultaneity. It was as if one were the other's shadow or mirrored reflection—"two ends meeting together and making a whole."

New elements introduced by Rudolf were also perfectly integrated; there was nothing gratuitously showy about the Russian lifts; they intensified the slow-motion, vaporous effects of the second act, making the incorporeal Giselle seem prevented from floating away only by the restraint of her partner's hands about her waist. Inspired by Rudolf, Margot had so totally immersed herself in the drama that the audience was hardly aware they were acting. Danced to the point of death by the vengeful wraiths, Rudolf lay in a state of collapse, his chest heaving with exhaustion, sweat polishing and highlighting the Slavic contours of his face. Gazing down at him for a long time as if transfixed by his beauty, Margot then half swooned when he recovered, and he carried her forward, his face brushing against hers. At the climax, when she cradled his head in her arms, a quick intake of breath was heard throughout the house.

When the curtain came down there was no applause for what seemed a minute. No one could quite believe what they had just seen: the icon of English ballet paired with a boy half her age, not the usual courtly danseur noble but an independent force who, with his huge personality and loping runs, seemed thrillingly alien and yet in perfect accord with Fonteyn. "My husband called it a celestial accident," Maude said. "To probe into its components is like trying to analyze a moonbeam." And despite her "practical, unmoonshiny qualities," de Valois agreed. "Emotionally, technically, physically—in every way. They were just meant to meet on this earth and dance together."

When the two stars took the first of twenty-three curtain calls together, "all hell broke loose." Pulling a red rose from the bouquet (sent by her husband), Margot gave it to Rudolf, who impulsively sank to one knee and covered her hand with kisses. This sudden gesture has become as legendary as their actual performance, *The Dancing Times* writing that it was the herald of a new era in ballet. Clive Barnes, with equal prescience, described it as the kind of act typical of a star capable of changing the public's attitude toward an art form: "It has happened in opera with Maria Callas . . . possibly it happened with Nijinsky. A single personality who catches the public's imagination."

To Margot it was only Rudolf's way of expressing his feelings without resorting to standard social phrases like "Thank you for your help," which seemed to strike him as stilted or false. Rudolf himself was bemused by the fuss. The tradition of what the French call *le baisse main* is alive to this day in Russia, where it remains a gesture of male esteem toward a woman (he had instinctively kissed Yvette Chauviré's hand on first meeting her). By the second performance, the dancers had clearly rehearsed and toned down the culminating moment of their curtain calls; this time it was Margot who curtsied low to Rudolf and presented her hand to be ceremoniously kissed: "It is more effective than the impulsive prototype, but it was somehow right that the first performance should have just one unique flourish to it that was never to be repeated."

The critics agreed that although Fonteyn had surpassed herself— "brilliantly, wonderfully, surprisingly," as Clive Barnes said—it was Nureyev's night. They commented on how much more polished his technique had become, praising in particular his glittering series of *entrechats*. Interviewed on BBC radio, Karsavina spoke of his unusual ability to accelerate or decelerate his pirouettes in absolute accord with the rhythm, and also drew attention to the rare elegance of his line. The feminine aspects of his movements, the hallmark high *retirés* and attitudes "tending upwards," as Karsavina put it, came as a complete surprise to Londoners accustomed to "those sturdy and violently masculine" Soviet males. From the moment he walked slowly onto the stage in Act II, his long cloak flowing behind him, an armful of white lilies held to frame his face, Rudolf was in his element—an embodiment of the Romantic image, "all lilies and languors." "The entrance was so beautiful that people were practically in tears, some of them, before he started the dancing," said Maude.

But if Rudolf had modeled his androgynous, poetic look on Nijinsky, their interpretation of the character could not have been more different. Drawing on Alexander Blok's lyrical drama *The Stranger,* Nijinsky's Albrecht was a hero in search of an unattainable feminine ideal; Giselle to him—for all Karsavina's resistance—was an abstract symbol, an alienated embodiment of his own spiritual discord. For Erik, too, these wraiths, the Wilis, were figments of Albrecht's mind— "all the things we are afraid of, that we have tried to escape." Rudolf, on the other hand, transformed Théophile Gautier's libretto into one of the great love stories. By portraying the doomed passion of a beautiful youth for an older woman, this Giselle and Albrecht aligned themselves with the more celebrated couples of nineteenth-century French literature—Stendhal's Mme de Renal and Julien, Flaubert's Madame Bovary and Léon. The mutual tenderness and poignant contrast in age had been there in the Kirov performances with Alia Shelest, but now there was a difference: Rudolf understood the meaning of romantic love.

In the film of the Fonteyn-Nureyev *Giselle* made three months later, we see to an almost voyeuristic degree the extraordinary sensuality Rudolf brought to the performance. The moment, for instance, when he tries to recapture the shape, feel, smell of Margot's hand, holding his own hands against his face with eyes closed and lips half parted; or the erotic frisson, almost too subtle to catch, as she watches him lie panting on his back, his hand stroking down his chest and hovering for a fraction of a second above the swell in his "so-white, so-tight" tights. "What we were watching was a kind of seduction," remarked the writer Brian Masters. "She responded to his *advances*—which is what they were—with a tremendous quiver of excitement which we all felt in the theater."

In fact, all Rudolf was doing was inhabiting his role to the full, acting out the Stanislavskian principles of "Emotion Memory" and the "Dramatic I" with complete conviction. "I was Albrecht, and Albrecht was in love with Giselle; on the stage I was seeing her with the eyes of a lover." From that evening on, however, audiences would interpret the ardor they saw in Rudolf as the "Real I," believing in a real-life, offstage romance. So would Margot, who sensed "a strange attachment" forming between them, despite the fact that she knew he was "desperately in love with someone else at the time." Even Erik, who had stood in the wings watching their performance, found himself overwhelmed by a confusion of private emotions and professional rivalry. "He stare. He stare. . . . He just couldn't understand that kind of success and why it should be." And instead of waiting for Rudolf, he fled from the theater. "I was running after him and fans were running after me. It was a mess."

—from *Nureyev*, 2007

ALASTAIR MACAULAY

Nureyev Remembered

It is ten years since Rudolf Nureyev died. From St. Petersburg to Monte Carlo, from Tokyo to Toronto, there have been galas, film seasons, exhibitions, tributes written and spoken and danced. (There has even been a Nureyev novel, Colum McCann's *Dancer*. It actually comes far nearer catching Nureyev's essence than the first two posthumous biographies.) Doubtless the sheer spread and quantity of these commemorations have something to do with the fact that there are two wealthy Nureyev foundations. Still, Nureyev's place in history is secure.

Nureyev travelled the globe, but for twenty-four years—1962–85—he bestowed a high concentration of his phenomenal energies upon London: first in the intensity of his association with the Royal Ballet, where he would dance a cross-section of repertory every season until 1977, and secondly in the annual Nureyev Festivals (1976–85) at the London Coliseum, in which he would dance seven performances a week for weeks on end. So it's fitting that London has done most to honour his memory. The season of Nureyev films in January at the National Film Theatre was well attended; there have been exhibitions both at the Theatre Museum and at the Royal Opera House; the Royal Ballet in April gave seven performances of a diverse Nureyev tribute.

Predictably, something is missing, even in the photographs and the films. Nureyev's most historic achievement—making both men and women dance differently, from Vienna to Sydney—could only be proven if an exhibition or film season also included a good deal of pre-Nureyev and non-Nureyev material. In photographs, you see Nureyev in front of a curtain extending an arm and proudly smiling to acknowledge the applause; but you need a memory to know how long he waited before extending that arm or smiling— how he worked the suspense. In many of the films, you see the thickness of the make-up; only if you were there in the theatre can you credit that it was submerged by his glamour.

Still, many of the photographs and enough of the films certainly show that Nureyev was a rare beauty: not the textbook Adonis that other male dancers have been, but a new extreme, a radical archetype for the changing notions of masculinity in the 1960s and 1970s. The contrast between the breadth of his shoulders and the slenderness of his waist was drastic, the same kind of drastic as the contrast between the slab-like cheekbones and the Brad Pitt mouth, with its strikingly full lips that parted to reveal so brightly fierce a smile. Nureyev had become a star just before the Beatles and Mick Jagger, and in his haircuts and those lips he was often compared to both. In the film of Roland Petit's *Le Jeune homme et la mort,* he looks like a male Brigitte Bardot.

Ballet people often speak of Fonteyn and Nureyev as if they were tailor-made for each other, but the pictorial evidence rightly proves that what made them exciting was they were as dissimilar as Tarzan and Jane. He the gorgeous prowler, she the poised cat-with-the-canary; he the luscious velvet, she the diamond; he the wayfaring brigand, she the beating heart. Though Fonteyn eloquently spoke of how much more concerned Nureyev was with technical precision than she, photography confirms that he was far less academically picture-perfect than many dancers. With Nureyev, though, how much does that matter? When Feruccio Busoni took Egon Petri, then his pupil, to hear Eugen d'Albert play, the latter was way past his prime. Petri kept making a whistling sound under his breath every time d'Albert played a wrong note—until, at the end of a piece, Busoni turned to him and said with a smile, "Don't you wish you could play wrong notes like that?" Film suggests that Nureyev played wrong notes throughout his career, but for a good many years—you can still see this—he played them heroically.

What of the repertory? Nureyev was no muse. It would be rich fare to watch all the ballets, pas de deux, and solos that various choreographers made on such individual dancers as Fonteyn, Tanaquil LeClercq, Lynn Seymour, Anthony Dowell, Suzanne Farrell, Mikhail Baryshnikov. But even if you could collect every single dance made upon Nureyev by George Balanchine, Frederick Ashton, Kenneth MacMillan, Roland Petit, Rudi van Dantzig, Glen Tetley, Nureyev himself, and others, you would find next to nothing of lasting importance. (The Royal's Nureyev tribute included a rare revival of the "Two loves I have" pas de trois from MacMillan's 1964 Shakespeare sonnet *Images of Love.* Unlike some of the non-Nureyev dances that survive on film from the same ballet, it shows how early MacMillan was already inclining to clumsy, gesture-heavy, expressionist portentousness.) Even Ashton's *Marguerite and Armand* was just a pastel sketch made occasionally tremendous by the hair-raising timing of certain moments, by the thrill of its casting, and by the febrile blaze that both Fonteyn and Nureyev could kindle. More valuable was the Prince's solo that Nureyev added to the Royal Ballet *Swan Lake* in 1962, a truly distinguished piece of work that beautifully challenged him and other male interpreters for over twenty years. (He never made a better dance. Over the next thirty years his choreography grew steadily more ambitious and less competent.) The lyrical essence this solo encapsulated is still to be felt in much of the choreography that Ashton went on to make in the later 1960s for other male dancers, notably Dowell. It was Dowell who went beyond Nureyev in making a male dancer's line poetic, whose arabesques flowed and melted and shone with yet further precision, and who took cantilena phrasing to a peak that no male dancer has ever surpassed. But Dowell, another icon of the 1960s and 1970s, would not have become Dowell had it not been for Nureyev, often present on the same stage, challenging him to greater feats.

Meanwhile Nureyev burnt himself indelibly onto certain male roles of the existing ballet repertory. Paul Czinner's film of him and Fonteyn in the *Corsaire* pas de deux is still momentous. But film's effect on the spatial three-dimensionality of dance is always flattening, its rendition of live dance musicality always blurring. You would not know from that *Corsatre* film that, at the apex of his highest leaps, Nureyev (bare-chested, in harem pants) seemed to hover—*sit* and hover, with feet tucked up under him, as if perched on a stool—in the air. Nor would you know that both of them showed timing and nerve so exhilarating that, when the Royal Ballet first programmed it as the sole centerpiece of a program, Frederick Ashton assured the alarmed Fonteyn that the applause would last twice as long as the pas de deux, and was proved right. In the Royal's 2003 Nureyev tribute, Carlos Acosta danced the solo from this *Corsaire* pas de deux, with nonchalant prowess. Yet Acosta's unforced way of dancing is the opposite of Nureyev's explosiveness. When Acosta applies exotic colour, it seems like a calculated afterthought. With Nureyev, such strokes seemed the core of his very being. With Acosta, the solo itself looks trite, obvious, even bland. Nureyev (like Callas or Sutherland irradiating Donizetti) brought more texture and dynamic excitement to this material than anybody else can ever have done. Though the whole *Corsaire* pas de deux is routinely credited to the nineteenth-century Marius Petipa, its male role must have been extensively revised in Soviet Russia; and when Nureyev danced it, I used to say that the *Corsaire* pas de deux had been choreographed on him by God. He became its sole author and first cause.

For years, it seemed as if the whole of London felt the same way. In summer 1977, if you travelled down the King's Road Chelsea or the Fulham Road, you could see eight different walls on which someone had written the name "Rudi" in letters a yard high in red, with a heart instead of a dot above the "i." Was there any doubt as to which Rudi this referred to? During the 1976–77 Royal Ballet season, straight after filming *Valentino* for Ken Russell, and while growing his hair back into his usual mane, he had danced several ballets at Covent Garden (sometimes replacing Dowell, who was injured for a year); at the Queen's silver jubilee gala in May '77, he and Fonteyn had danced the premiere of Ashton's *Hamlet and Ophelia;* and June and July had seen the second Nureyev Festival. He had launched it with the premiere of his own production of Prokoviev's *Romeo and Juliet,* dancing Romeo himself, for twenty-five consecutive performances, he had danced *Giselle* for a week (June 27–July 2) opposite Natalia Makarova or Eva Evdokimova, and for one extraordinary week (July 4–9) he had danced a mixed program with Makarova, Lynn Seymour, and Fonteyn. He danced with all three ballerinas in *Les Sylphides;* with Fonteyn, he danced their last-ever performances of *Marguerite and Armand;* and with Makarova (in heart-stoppingly exultant form), he danced performances of the *Le Corsaire* pas de deux. He had passed his thirty-ninth birthday in March 1977. Yet those *Corsaire* performances, pausing in the air, burning round the stage, blazing through pirouettes, made even senior critics feel that time had stopped and that Nureyev was still dancing as he had with Fonteyn in *Corsaire* in 1962.

Until and including that week, Nureyev was the greatest star I have ever seen. Not the greatest dancer, nor the greatest artist, but the performer who burned the brightest. He was the dance embodiment of hubris—a word that I was taught to translate as "pride before a fall." When he hurtled around the stage in one of the various *manèges* of leaps that occur in many classic ballets (the *Corsaire* pas de deux not least), you would often hear people gasp, not at the height of his jumps (though until '77 he could still show tremendous elevation), but at the risks he was taking, the angle at which he would lean. Everyone expected him to fall, to break an ankle. In my first *Swan Lake* (1975), he did fall. The audience gasped; he glared straight back and swept offstage. Then, as soon as Monica Mason, as Odile, had spun through thirty-two diamantine fouetté turns and won a wave of applause, he was onstage again, spinning in turns that seemed to compete with hers and to rebuke the audience for doubting his brilliance. Glamorous, sensual, flaring energy poured forth, from the very center of his body.

He was a Dionysus who had committed himself to an Apollonian art, and his dancing had been an act of defiance from his teens on. He liked to say that he performed better when he danced more often, even though already in '77 there were performances (notably in his own *Romeo*) when he seemed to have too much else on his mind. While there are connoisseurs who will still insist that his true prime had ended as early as 1964, most of them will agree that he was still capable of top-level performance up to that week in July 1977 when he danced with that Fonteyn-Makarova-Seymour troika. Ballet is a singularly demanding art, and no dancer can ever have driven himself harder. The quality that seems to have increasingly characterised his dancing is force, though film footage, including a *Corsaire* solo he performed when still a Kirov dancer, shows that he was never a completely pure stylist. He forced more, he encouraged others to force, and this kind of heroic straining became one of his trademarks. When Makarova—who had been another luminary of the Kirov's 1961 first tour—first danced with him in the West, she told him, "You dance like them." He replied, *"Je danse comme moi."* Essentially, such strain is alien to ballet's classicism, but Nureyev made it theatrical and (as a performer if not as a choreographer) musical. And, for years, his strain paid off: he was the most exciting of dancers even when he was the most over-emphatic. He was tempting fate; we knew it; and we had to catch his glory while it lasted.

Nureyev's hubris was punished again and again. And every time his method was, as Fred sings to Ginger, "Pick yourself up, brush yourself off, start all over again." The biggest crash came in the seventh and final week (July 11–16) of the 1977 Nureyev Festival. As soon as he took his very first arabesque, it was evident that his back had "gone." Arabesque—the position in which a dancer presents his extended line, through a straight leg, from toe to fingers—was not a position in which Nureyev excelled; but it was not one in which he had ever disappointed. Now, however, he was lurching forwards, every time. His spine had lost its strength. Nor did it ever recapture its former power.

Within months, his whole lustre seemed to drain away. One program of the Nureyev Festival of 1978 began with Hans van Manen's *Four Schumann Pieces,* a taxing vehicle choreographed for Anthony Dowell. In the interval afterwards, I remember overhearing one man say to his wife, "Good, now we'll see Nureyev." She explained to him that they'd already been watching Nureyev. *"Him?"* the husband exclaimed. "But he couldn't even *stand."* This was true; and to those of us who remembered how Nureyev could, when he chose, stand still and—because of the concentrated energy that flowed from the centre of his body even without moving—stop an audience from watching whichever dancer was performing elsewhere on the stage, it was heartbreaking. As for the *Corsaire* pas de deux, danced with a minor European ballerina, he now seemed to be like a man chasing after the last bus.

Did he learn? No. There was scarcely one important role in which he didn't go on appearing too long, there were roles (Nijinsky's *L'Apres-midi d'un faune,* Balanchine's "Rubies") which he acquired far too late, and, in London alone, he went on dancing those gruelling seven-performance-a-week Nureyev festivals until 1985, when he was forty-seven years old. When the young Sylvie Guillem made her debut at Covent Garden in 1988, her partner was Nureyev, now aged fifty, and looking it. In Paris, London, and elsewhere, he choreographed new ballets and produced old ones (skills at which he seemed to get steadily worse with the years); he directed the Paris Opéra Ballet (1983–89); he appeared in a North American tour of *The King and I*; he conducted concerts. His 1989 tour with the Rodgers and Hammerstein musical—a production in which his partner, Liz Robertson, once said she felt he never gave a single completely good performance—went on despite his responsibilities to the Paris Opéra: he ignored all the requests to return to Paris until finally he was sacked. When AIDS came, he refused to admit as much; and this too was in character. He died in January 1993. It is often said that he died young, but that is not how it felt if you had followed his career.

It's easy to overlook the fact that Nureyev was fun, but he was. Mischief was part of his lustre. And, amazing as it may seem, he could laugh at himself. The NFT season included his appearance on the Muppets TV show. I missed it this time around, but, if memory serves, the great moment came when Miss Piggy tried to seduce him in the sauna. Nureyev pouted with grim ruefulness, and said, with his finest Russian accent, "Last week I was in *Swan Lake* with Natalia Makarova. This week I am in steam bath with lady pig."

—from *The Times Literary Supplement* (London), May 9, 2003

GEORGE BALANCHINE

1904–1983

Arlene Croce

George Balanchine died at four o'clock on the morning of April 30, a matinée day. The audience filing into the lobby of the State Theater that afternoon passed between two giant sprays of white lilacs, white roses, and lilies of the valley. A recent color photograph of Balanchine taking a curtain call was in the display case. Except for TV camera crews at the stage door, there were no other signs that anything had happened. The program posted beside the box-office windows was unchanged: Jerome Robbins's *Mother Goose* and *The Four Seasons* and Balanchine's *Kammermusik* No. 2. Leslie Bailey, the New York City Ballet's press representative, was standing in a corner of the lobby, looking pale but composed. "Jerry Robbins offered to cancel," she said, "but we felt we couldn't disappoint the children who would be coming." Mikhail Baryshnikov arrived, wearing a dark-blue suit and dark glasses. "I had to come," he said. "I woke up early this morning, in a panic. I thought I must be late for something. I started to get up, thinking, I'm late, I'm late! And I couldn't go back to sleep." Lincoln Kirstein, co-founder of the New York City Ballet, passed swiftly through the lobby and stopped, noticing Baryshnikov. The two men embraced without speaking. Then Kirstein headed backstage.

Upstairs at the bar, Bob Ross, the bartender, talked about Balanchine drinking his celebrated vodka toast to the memory of Stravinsky and saying, "In Russia, we drink to the health of the guy that died." Ross went on to say, "Mr. B. was quite a belter. I served him here all the time, not vodka but Scotch. He liked boilermakers. One time, he said, 'Have one.' We clinked glasses, and he downed his in one gulp. I did, too. Then I had to pretend to be very busy under the counter. My eyes were watering. Smoke was coming out of my ears. But he didn't turn a hair."

The audience that was settling into its seats was the standard Saturday-

matinée audience—grandmothers, small children, no critics—on whom
Balanchine would frequently try out new casts unannounced. In place of the
usual pre-performance din, there was subdued chatter. Only a few musicians were warming up in the pit. Then the house went dark, and Kirstein
stepped before the curtain, holding a hand microphone, and began speaking
hoarsely but distinctly. "I don't have to tell you that Mr. B. is with Mozart
and Tchaikovsky and Stravinsky," he said. "I do want to tell you how much he
valued this audience, which is like a big family that has kept us going for fifty
years and will keep us going for another fifty. The one thing he didn't want
was that there be an interruption. So there will be none. Think of yourselves
as the marvellous, supportive, cohesive family who understands—" Here
Kirstein was drowned out by a loud electronic wail. He lowered the microphone and continued, "—who understands the family that's about to perform now."

Hugo Fiorato, the white-haired conductor, appeared on the podium, and
after a brief orchestral prelude the curtain rose slowly on the first scene of
Robbins's *Mother Goose,* which shows the dancers, in practice dress, standing
or reclining about the stage, surrounded by the scenery and props of a dozen
other ballets in the repertory. It was a perfect illustration of Kirstein's reference to "the family." One of the dancers, having the inspiration to act out the
tales of Mother Goose, reached into a wardrobe trunk, pulled out a cavalier's plumed hat (from *Harlequinade*), and clapped it on his head. In an
instant, as the other dancers were pulling out more hats, the creased old garden backdrop that has done service since City Center days was rolled down.
Then Sleeping Beauty entered, skipping rope, and the show went on.

On that weekend, there was more Balanchine activity in the city than
there would have been on any other weekend of the year. Not only was the
New York City Ballet playing at the State Theater and *On Your Toes* on Broadway, but the School of American Ballet was giving its annual workshop performances at the Juilliard Theater on Saturday and Monday, and on Monday
night American Ballet Theatre was opening at the Met with a program featuring Baryshnikov's revival of *Symphonie Concertante,* a Balanchine ballet that
was introduced by School of American Ballet pupils thirty-seven years ago.
The stir of dancers in and around Lincoln Center was intense. And their
emotion united them, perhaps, as never before. Wherever one looked, there
seemed to be dancers meeting and embracing wordlessly. At the Juilliard
Theater, the students who would be dancing on Saturday evening began
dress rehearsals at ten o'clock that morning. They rehearsed two Balanchine
ballets they had probably never seen—*Valse Fantaisie* and *Western Symphony.*
Many of them had never even seen Balanchine, except from a distance, having grown up at the school in the years when he was following a curtailed
schedule under close medical supervision. Like the rest of Balanchine's

organization, the students had lived with bad news of Mr. B. almost daily since last November, when he entered Roosevelt Hospital. Now, on the fatal Saturday, they worked with their teachers as if it were any other day, and the rehearsal went smoothly. The only voice to be raised was Robert Irving's, repeatedly admonishing the student orchestra not to watch the stage. That night, at eight o'clock, the performance went on after Kirstein, flanked by Jerome Robbins, Peter Martins, and John Taras, made another brief speech from the stage, thanking the audience for "this school and your support of it." Kirstein continued, "We know that this night George is probably teaching the angels to tendu. The *angels,* who don't need to rehearse."

Kirstein also spoke to the Saturday-night audience a block away at the State Theater, and he would appear onstage at the school performance on Monday night, reassuring the audience each time of the continuity of the Balanchine tradition and, each time, wearing in his lapel the silver lyre pin designed by Balanchine for the Tchaikovsky Festival. On Saturday night, the closing ballet at the State Theater was *Symphony in C,* conducted by Gordon Boelzner before a packed house. Suzanne Farrell and Peter Martins appeared in the great adagio and finished to a storm of applause. They took two bows. They took a third. Then, as the audience began to demonstrate, they ran off and did not return for another bow. In the finale of this ballet— surely the most exhilarating finale ever devised by Balanchine—there comes a moment when the profuse invention of the choreography clears away like mist and the stage turns into a classroom, its three sides lined with young women doing battements tendus while the four principal ballerinas compete like dervishes in the center. In this moment, at once the simplest and the most complex moment in the ballet, Balanchine seems to be outlining both his dream for American ballet and the foundation necessary to achieve it. Then, the vision having been disclosed, the happy dazzle of invention resumes, mounting and mounting until, with an abrupt flourish, it ends. This time, the dancers took call after call from the standing, shouting audience. It was an ovation that Balanchine, had he been backstage running the curtains, might have been glad to acknowledge himself.

A lifelong communicant of the Russian Orthodox Church, Balanchine died the day before Palm Sunday, on the feast of the resurrection of Lazarus. At the funeral, Bishop Gregory Grabbe pointed out the coincidence in his eulogy, and he went on to praise Balanchine as a devout Christian who had prepared himself for death. The Cathedral of Our Lady of the Sign, at Ninety-third Street and Park Avenue, was overcrowded; the funeral service was long, and the humid air was thick with the scent of flowers, incense, and hundreds of burning candles. When the service ended, shortly after noon, the candles were extinguished, and for an hour or more the mourners filed by the open coffin, some pausing to kneel, to kiss the ribbon printed with a prayer which lay across the forehead, to kiss or touch the hands, or to leave a flower. Some chose just to pause and pass on. Among those who approached the casket, one by one, were great and famous dancers—dancers young and old—whom Balanchine had nurtured. The beautiful little faces were crumpled with grief. The crowd overflowed onto the staircase outside and into the courtyard, two stories below. As the church emptied, it was impressive to see six generations of ballerinas descend the stairs. Many were weeping. Some children of *Nutcracker* age wept, too, though they were too young to have known the man—only the legend. The mass of mourners dispersed; a few hundred lined the stairs or joined the crowd that had gathered on Ninety-third Street. At length, the closed coffin appeared in the doorway and, accompanied by the tolling of a bell and the chanting of the cathedral's small choir, was borne along the balcony, down the stairs, through the courtyard, and out onto the street, there to be placed in a waiting hearse and covered with a blanket of gardenias. It was the ending of *La Sonnambula* in reverse. As the cortege rolled away, heading toward Long Island, where the burial would take place, it was impossible not to think of the ballets in which Balanchine staged his own death. Besides *La Sonnambula,* there was *Orpheus* and *Don Quixote* and *Robert Schumann's "Davidsbündlertänze,"* and, most awful and explicit of all, his setting of the last movement of the *Pathétique* symphony. And there were dozens more in which the fact of mortality was held out to us not in sorrow or anger but in the calm certainty of transcendence. If the readiness is all, then the Bishop was right, and Balanchine died a happy man. It was only that his dancers and his audience could not bear to let him go.

—from *The New Yorker,* May 16, 1983

Honi Coles

1911–1992

Mindy Aloff

Charles "Honi" Coles was born in Philadelphia and became a celebrated tap dancer, appearing at the Apollo Theater in Harlem and working with Charles "Cholly" Atkins in a partnership that lasted nineteen years. On Broadway he appeared in Gentlemen Prefer Blondes, Bubbling Brown Sugar, *and, in 1983,* My One and Only, *for which he won a Tony Award.*

Charles "Honi" Coles, the venerated tap dancer, died recently at the age of eighty-one. He happened to be black, and he happened to be great; but the main reason to go to his funeral is that you think you can bear it. There are so many funerals these days of dancers cut off in their prime that you've stopped attending them to protect yourself from becoming callous, or from overdosing on pain. But here's a man who lived a long, full life, and who gained the recognition he deserved when he could hear it, too. It turns out to be the best funeral you ever attended—full of wonderful dancing, music, and storytelling—and you walk back to your office full of energy and hope. Then you tell your colleagues about it, and they start to wise you up about reality.

If they're already in the dance-world loop, they shake their heads and say something like, "Yes, I loved his dancing. And what a mensch he was, and what a teacher. It's a shame that someone like that, a real New York treasure, is going to drop away into oblivion." And you start to say, "No, no," and you wave your arms in protest. And they say, in a cool, level tone, "Think about it. He wasn't famous enough."

Wait a minute. Honi Coles got a Tony, a funeral at which the mayor of New York delivered an oration, and a sixteen-inch obit in *The New York Times:* he must have created a stir outside the field of tap dancing. So you buttonhole some acquaintances outside the dance loop. "Who was Honi Coles?" they say. You take a breath. And, hurtling forward toward cultural connection, you answer, "Remember *Sir Gawain and the Green Knight?* There was the Green Knight, who was Sir Gawain's hero, and then there was the old guy in the back room, who was the real thing—the precedent for the Green Knight. Honi Coles was that old guy for tap dancers." Your acquaintances look at you with a mixture of affection and pity. They say, "*Sir Gawain and the Green Knight?*" Or, trying to be friendly, they ask, "What did you think of that piece on Mort Zuckerman in the *New York Observer?*"

No one has time anymore—that's what you hear in New York. And it's true, even at funerals. I was late to Honi Coles's funeral because I got two phone calls at the last minute. Mayor Dinkins was later than I was. He began his speech with an apology: he had to speak at another funeral.

But Honi Coles always seemed to have time, all the time in the world. When he was dancing, the musicians could multiply the tempo on a count, and he'd swing right along with them and still look as if he were waiting for a chauffeur to pick him up (a chauffeur in a stretch limo: Honi was aristocratically tall, with lean, long legs). When he wanted to encourage a dancer, he found the time for a pat on the back. With dancers who showed promise, he took the time to tell them where they'd messed up. Tap dancing is essentially a soloist's art form, but Honi turned it into human conversation. He made an instantaneous connection with audiences, which may account for why people who never met him can't resist calling him by his nickname. At his physical prime, he sported one of the faster pairs of legs in the business, but an observer wasn't likely to think, "Wow! That guy's fast!" One thought, "Hey, that guy's talking." His dancing represented what tappers strive for: to lay down iron as if it were feathers, to cut the steps, to make music, and have it all translate as a person sharing what's on his mind.

As a dancer, Honi was entirely self-taught. During the depths of the Depression, he went into a studio every day for a year and gave himself tap lessons; when he concluded his course, he was ready to dance. When he enjoyed success as a performer in the 1940s and '50s—in partnership with Cholly Atkins or touring on his own—he didn't forget his friends. When the jobs dried up in the 1950s and '60s, he went to work as manager of the Apollo Theater in Harlem. At the Apollo, he helped any dancer who showed an appetite to learn, and as a mentor he was color-blind, sex-blind, and impervious to celebrity. His protégés include women and men, whites and blacks, people you've probably never heard of and household names like Gregory Hines.

At the funeral, Hines related a lifetime of moments. Now forty-six, he met Honi some forty years ago, at the Apollo, where the Hines brothers—Gregory and Maurice—used to whip up audiences to a frenzy with their tap dancing and drumming. As story followed story, the words gelled into a split-screen mental movie—of Honi Coles growing older and Gregory Hines growing up.

There was Gregory, the sassy prodigy, who barked orders at a stagehand to get his drum set into the wings, and Honi, the headliner, who came into the boy's dressing room and said, "Don't you ever talk to Henry like that again, or to any stagehand—white or black—who's trying to make you look good out there. One day, you'll look around and the drum set won't be *on* the stage." There was Gregory the movie star, who had top billing on Francis Ford Coppola's *The Cotton Club,* a film where Honi had a supporting role. "Francis adored Honi," Hines said. "At one point in the movie, I was having trouble with a scene. I was supposed to break down over something, and I couldn't get it. Then I had an idea. I said to Francis, 'Let's have the guy beat up Honi Coles. That would make me really upset.' And Francis said, 'Never! I will never touch a hair on Honi's head. We'll have the guy beat *you* up.' And that's what they did."

Three weeks before Honi Coles died, Hines visited him for the last time, and asked the dance student's ultimate question of a teacher. "Honi," he said, "who was it? Who was the best?" (Honi's answer was John Bubbles, the virtuoso of rhythm tap.) At the end of the hour, Honi began to fail. Hines—who is the most famous living tap dancer in the world today—pleaded in a boyish voice, "Honi, before I go, tell me something to help my tap dancing. Give me advice."

At this point in his remarks, Hines paused. Then he said, "Honi gave me a real aggravated look." Hines paused again: "And he told me, 'Gregory! Don't just rattle around in the middle of the stage. Move about, do pretty things. *Then,* rattle.'"

—from *The New Republic,* December 21, 1992

La Goulue

1866–1929

Janet Flanner

Born Louise Weber in Alsace, La Goulue rose to be "Queen of Montmartre," famous for her outrageous cancan at the Moulin Rouge and immortalized by Toulouse-Lautrec in his first poster and in other paintings and drawings. La Goulue translates as "the glutton," and her appetite for alcohol, above all, led to the inexorable downward spiral of her life.

The death in misery of La Goulue, one of the great *demi-mondaines* of the nineties, petted cancan dancer of the then devilish Moulin Rouge, model for Toulouse-Lautrec in some of his most famous cabaret canvases, and general toast of the whiskered town, afforded her a press she had not enjoyed since her palmiest days. La Goulue (Greedy Gal) was born Louise Weber, daughter of a cab driver; she was a pretty, full-fleshed blonde of the mortal Olympian type popular with the gay Edwardians the world over. Rising by natural stages from the sidewalk to the ballet of the Moulin Rouge, her triumph came when bankers and Impressionists drank champagne from her shoe. She did the split amidst the sixty yards of lace trimming her stylish long skirt, and starred in the quadrilles in the arms of her famous partners: Valentin-le-Désossé (the Boneless Wonder), Grille-d'Égout (Sewer Gate—and very popular in his period), and a lady known as Nini Patte-en-l'Air. La Goulue achieved a private *hôtel* in the Avenue du Bois and even lived in what had once been the property of her famous predecessor, Païva, fashionable mistress of Napoleon III. It was from this discreet mansion that La Goulue was invited to dance before a gentleman who afterward literally covered her with banknotes and turned out to be the Grand Duke Alexis. She had charm, a dazzling complexion, and wit. It was the last great heyday for courtesans, and she made hay.

Then came her fall. She went to jail after some lark. She became a lion-tamer in a street fair. She became a dancer in a wagon show; Toulouse-Lautrec painted curtains for her, but she forgot them in some barn and the rats gnawed at them.* Then she became a laundress. Then she became nothing.

A month ago she reappeared; fat, old, and dancing drunkenly in a few feet of a remarkable documentary film about the ragpickers of Paris—called, after their neighborhood of wagon shanties, *The Zone*. Her last interview was given to the weekly *Vu*. After the first glass of brandy of the interview she took out a cracked mirror; after the third glass she recalled her cab-driving father. After the fourth she remembered the Grand Duke Alexis and, on the promise of a box of face powder, even remembered her son, who had died in a gambling den. A few weeks later her ragpickers took her to a city clinic, where she too died, murmuring as if declining a last and eternal invitation, "I do not want to go to hell."

—from *The New Yorker*, 1929

---

*They later turned up, cut into salable sections, in the shop of a dealer; purchased by the Louvre, reassembled and restored, they now hang in the Jeu de Paume.

HANYA HOLM

1893–1992

Christopher Caines

Hanya Holm was born in Germany and studied with Dalcroze before beginning work with Mary Wigman, whom she followed to America in 1931, when she began to teach and choreograph here. Her own company lasted until 1944, but although she both danced and made dances, she was best known as a teacher. Her greatest popular successes came as the choreographer for Kiss Me, Kate, The Golden Apple, My Fair Lady, *and* Camelot.

Hanya Holm died this spring, just shy of her hundredth birthday. There are many who knew her much longer, much more deeply, more thoroughly than I, and I don't doubt that many books and monographs and reminiscences about her life and work will soon appear. Still I have a small offering to make.

I studied with Hanya for eight weeks during what turned out to be the last session of her summer school at Colorado College in Colorado Springs, in 1983. It was that summer that enabled me to find the courage to become a dancer. After I had moved to New York in 1986, I would occasionally visit Hanya, by then largely confined to her apartment in the West Village. Since I had just finished college with an intensive course in German, which I didn't want to erode too fast, and since her eyesight was too poor to allow her to read much, I would sometimes converse with her and read to her in German from the writers I was then painstakingly plodding my way through—Rilke and Kafka (*"ein sehr negativer Mann"* said Hanya—a very negative man). She would matter-of-factly correct my pronunciation, and recommended that I take up "Heine, beautiful Heine" instead. I loved her and I know she enjoyed seeing me and was concerned for my progress through life, but I was also painfully shy with her. I wish I had gone to visit her more often.

Most people's Hanya stories are all about things that Hanya said—her idiosyncratic Germanicisms, her spontaneously goofy wit, her aphoristic logic. But many other friends and colleagues will recall her half century of sayings in America much better than I; I only want to write a little about how she sat.

Even in her tenth decade of life in a human body on this earth, even in ill-ness, Hanya never merely sat on, and certainly never in, a chair. She allowed a chair's horizontal surface to support her sit-bones as a matter of structural convenience, a minimal necessary concession to gravity. Her back might hardly touch the back of a chair where it reclined lazily behind her. Her physical relationship with a chair was courteous, respectful, but she always made it look unnecessary. She allowed the chair to accompany her seated-ness, and that was that.

It is hard to find the right words. To speak of Hanya's posture sounds wrong, etymologically at least, because there was nothing posed, or positioned, or placed about her. Her body was unself-conscious: she was not arranged. I could speak of her bearing or her carriage, and the old-fashioned tang of such words might seem to suit a little better the demeanor of a lady born in the late nineteenth century. Yet Hanya never gave the impression as she sat of bearing or carrying anything, of having any burden to be borne. There was nothing in her, such as those words suggest to me, of bringing with her body something that was not of her body to begin with.

Hanya didn't so much have "noble bearing," or "refined carriage," or "ele-gant posture"; her body seemed to speak little of her social class and her-itage, but rather of her life as a woman, a dancer, an artist, a teacher. Beyond this, Hanya's body bespoke her spirit, which I suspect might have arrived at the same place even had her life been completely different, even if she had become not an artist, but, say, a welder or an archaeologist. The truth is, Hanya Holm simply sat up straight.

Perhaps it was not so simple. Hanya gave the impression of sitting, not merely straight, but absolutely straight. Yet not ramrod straight, bolt upright, strong as iron—these familiar metaphors are all wrong in their unyielding hardness. There was instead in Hanya a sense of effortless command, of coex-istence with gravity, of lively energy steadily renewing itself, rising from the depths of her spine to the top, an endless supply. Her way of sitting was still and animated at the same time, pure, simple, each bone constantly reasserting her uprightness.

In this way Hanya's way of being in her body, like everyone's in some sense, moved into the moral dimension. Looking at Hanya you saw the whole woman, her vital integrity, a sense of dignity so immense and profound that the word *dignity* seems too small, too weightless to capture it. Her spine, I felt, rendered her completely, each bone poised and ani-mated with the struggles and sorrows and triumphs of her life. Her mar-velously expressive hands and face revealed the nuances of her character and thought, but Hanya's spine presented her being, her self, more clearly, more unequivocally than I have ever seen in any other woman or man.

Her body also spoke of her patient endurance of age and illness and frailty. Her spine said, *I am. I accept. This is what is. This is the truth.* I asked her once, since she seemed not to enjoy recorded music too much, or television, could not see to read, and did not always have or want visitors, what she did all day sitting by her window overlooking Eleventh Street. *"Nur Sitzen und Denken,"* she said—just sitting and thinking.

"Finden Sie nicht, das es langweilig ist?" I asked—Aren't you bored?

"No," she said slowly, changing to English. "There are still a lot of things to be thought."

—from *Movement Research Performance Journal* 7, Fall/Winter 1993–94

RUTH ST. DENIS

c. 1880–1968

Walter Terry

"Miss Ruth" is gone, and with her passing one might think that an era in dance, in the theater itself, had come to an end. I think not, for what she dreamed and what she did will influence the world of dance, the arena and the temple of theater, for untold years. Ruth St. Denis, "Pioneer and Prophet," as her husband and partner, Ted Shawn, called her in a now-historic two-volume book he wrote in 1920, died last month in Hollywood, her home for many years.

She was, by my very careful calculations, ninety-one years old—Mr. Shawn is quite sure she was eighty-nine and others were certain she was ninety-three—and she never once faltered in a career which spanned an incredible seventy-five years as a professional dancer. Indeed, she danced for my amateur movie camera just a year ago on her patio and only five months before she died she seemed indestructible. The final heart attack (she had had some comparatively mild preliminaries) which hospitalized her had irked her (she was too busy to waste time), and the subsequent stroke which paralyzed her she never knew had happened, for it occurred in her sleep.

"Miss Ruth," as she was known to dancers of all ages from New York to New Delhi, was born or blessed with what can only be described as a divine instinct for flawless movement. But she had a brain, too.

As a child, on the New Jersey farm where she was born, she danced in the sunlight and in the rain. She also, at eleven or twelve, sat in a tree and read her three favorite books, Mary Baker Eddy's *Science and Health,* Kant's *Critique of Pure Reason,* and Dumas's *Camille.* This sounds indigestible, but, esthetically, she digested the three, and her great art, her great wit, her great wisdom partook of this wild trio of influences.

She was both reverent and irreverent—with God, the former, and with mere mortals, the latter—and she was sensuous yet spiritual (this baffled the critics in 1906). She had a self-assurance that was so great that she envied no one—she knew she was a genius and she believed it to be God-given— but she looked upon her only rival, Isadora Duncan, as her idol, and she always said that without Ted Shawn there never would have been the Denishawn schools and companies which, for nearly two decades, guided the course of dance in America.

What do I remember or know about Miss Ruth? I know that in 1938, when I was a youth, I spent my hard-earned money to travel from New England to New York City to see her dance at a big do at Rockefeller Center called Dance International. At that time, to me, she was history, she was very old, and this would probably be my last time to see her dance. For thirty years I've watched her dance, and she always laughed when I said, "Miss Ruth, I come back every year because I keep thinking it may be the last time—not for you, but for me!"

What can I tell you about Miss Ruth? In 1893, she was a skirt dancer, a high kicker, one who did splits in a variety show for which she was paid $11 a week. In 1894, she got $20—for eleven shows a day. In 1898, she danced in toe shoes for a show called *Ballet Girl,* although, in her own words, she had had "only three lessons from Mme. Bonfanti, and before I had mastered three of the possible five positions of the feet, I was asked to leave the class." Duncan had also deserted the same class at about the same time (1896).

Miss Ruth was a good hoofer, a good actress, and Belasco, the famous producer, "canonized" her from little Ruthie Dennis into Ruth St. Denis. When show business was slack, she earned money as a model and once entered a six-day bicycle race at Madison Square Garden, where she came in sixth (later she won a championship). Incidentally, the bicycle she used was a gift from an admirer, the famous architect Stanford White. Mother St. Denis would not permit her daughter to accept jewelry from a gentleman, but she approved the bicycle!

Although she was successful as a show business dancer and, for five years, as an actress-dancer with Belasco, she was restless and unwilling to settle for her much-admired high kicks—"I didn't really kick like chorus girls do today; I raised my leg to my ear and then let it descend very slowly. No one else could do that"—and so as far back as 1896, while attending the Packer

School in Brooklyn for a brief period between shows, she experimented with a dance which has its roots in the classicism of ancient Greece. But it was ultimately the Orient which gave Miss St. Denis the inspiration for her dance rebellion, while Isadora Duncan found her sources in the Greek concept of beauty.

Today, ethnic influences and classical inspirations are everywhere in our theater, but it was not so at the turn of the century. Jack Cole, the dancer-choreographer, has seen the journals which Miss Ruth began in the 1890s, and he once told me, "We used the word 'genius' too loosely. But when you read what Miss Ruth wrote about the dance that surrounded her and what her visions were of what dance could be—and with no one to guide her or teach her or believe in her—then you know that you are in the awesome presence of genius."

Miss Ruth had, indeed, been born into a dance age which she described as "moribund." Ballet was at its lowest ebb in America—even male roles in ballets such as *Coppélia* were danced by women *en travesti*—and a dance art which could equal the best in painting, sculpture, literature, and philosophy did not exist in America. Ruth St. Denis changed all that.

Miss Ruth's particular heresy was that she made dances in which steps were less important than the movements of a breathing, sensitized body, and that she wanted to dance about God. Since America, in its churches, had long since forgotten about, if it ever knew, "David dancing before the Ark of the Lord with all his might," or Jesus's admonition, "We have piped unto you and ye have not danced," or the psalm which says, "Praise him with timbrel and dances," Ruth St. Denis turned to a culture which celebrated deity in terms of dancing: India.

But Egypt gave her the clue. While on a Belasco tour, she saw a poster advertising cigarettes. The figure on it was that of the goddess Isis. She made her roommate go back to the drugstore and get it for her. She brooded on it, she lived with it, and she said to herself, "No, I don't want to be an Egyptian dancer; I want to be Egypt herself from dawn to dusk, from life to death, the Nile, the feather of truth weighed against the human heart."

This *Egypta* was much too expensive to produce at first—it was done in 1910, though it had been conceived in 1904—so she made her historic debut as a concert dancer at the Hudson Theater in New York in 1906 in a program composed of *The Incense* (which she was to dance for the rest of her life), *The Cobras,* and the ballet *Radha,* all inspired by India. Not one was authentic in the ethnic sense, for all she knew about Oriental dancing was what she saw at Coney Island and what she found in encyclopedias. She herself was the first to say that *Radha* was about a Hindu goddess dancing a Buddhist theme in a Jain temple! Yet so perfectly and profoundly did she capture the intent of the sacred dances, the rhythmic philosophies of India, that she achieved a double triumph: for America, she re-established the right of dance to mirror the deepest feelings and highest aspirations of man himself; and for India, she was responsible, in many ways, for the renascence of ancient dance heritages in that ancient land. Indeed, on the two-year tour of the Orient which she, Ted Shawn, and their Denishawn Dancers performed in the mid-1920s, the Eastern dances which she and Shawn performed were received with unparalleled enthusiasm.

After her New York and Boston debuts in 1906, Miss Ruth toured Europe and met with her greatest success in Germany, where, if she had stayed, a theater would have been built especially for her. In 1909, she returned to her homeland in triumph and became the first dancer to appear in an engagement of dance recitals at a Broadway theater. Her personal repertory grew, expanding to countries other than India and even into dance-dramas and abstract dances without ethnic colors. Her Japanese *O-Mika,* which used dance, music, and spoken drama, heralded the great American musical theater, which was to come in such works as *The King and I,* or even *West Side Story* (although she would not approve the harshness of the theme), for she envisioned total theater.

In 1914, she met Ted Shawn, engaged him as her partner, and married him. Total theater and total dance education (ballet, Oriental, primitive, European modern dance, Delsartean principles of meaningful motion) were their special contributions to a great new age of dance, along with producing a number of towering talents, among them Martha Graham, the late Doris Humphrey, and Charles Weidman. When they separated after fifteen years of marriage (they were never divorced), each to go his own way artistically (Shawn is founder-director of the Jacob's Pillow Dance Festival), Miss Ruth turned more and more to the dance and religion.

In her years of seeking to build a liturgy of dances comparable to the vast liturgy of existing music, she was in the services of all faiths—Buddhist, Jewish, as well as her own Christian religion. She took her dance duties to religion seriously, but she was never puritanical (she disliked puritans intensely); she was always theatrical and her wit was spiced with a marvelous bawdiness.

When I visited her last summer, she said to me, "My cricket,"—she called me that because she said that the title "critic" was much too forbidding—"I really have been a faithless wench for so long that I'm trying to reform at last. I've always worshiped three gods—the God in Heaven, the god of art, and the god of physical love. Now that I'm very, very old, I know that my art and my energies must be in the service of the God in Heaven." Then she slapped me on the back and added, "As for physical love, that belongs in my past, but don't think for a moment that I don't *think* about it!"

When I talked to her by phone just a few weeks ago to ask about her health—"pretty chipper," she said—she added, "Dear cricket, do you mind if Mother pontificates for a bit? I have danced for nearly all of my ninety-one years and I believe more than ever that dance is the language of man at his highest. This language can guide man to self-realization and not simply to organization—which is just a nice word for 'power.' And I would say—still pontificating, mind you—that man is an emanation of God if he is anything at all."

Those were the last words I heard her say. Shawn called me to tell me of her passing, and, though choked with grief, you could sense the understanding smile when he said, "And you know Ruth was Ruth to the last. There were four heart specialists by her hospital bed and one said, 'Miss St. Denis, would you please stick out your tongue?' and Ruth retorted as you might expect she would, 'Which of you four distinguished gentlemen should I stick my tongue out *at?*'"

I once called her "half-mystic, half-mick," and she loved it. The world of dance called her "genius." She was all three, as heady and unlikely a combination as the three books she read while perched in a tree. Behind her is a fantastic record of dance accomplishment. Ahead is a world theater which will be forever in her debt.

—from *The Saturday Review,* August 17, 1968

ANNA PAVLOVA

The most famous of all ballerinas, Anna Pavlova (1881–1931), the illegitimate daughter of a poor laundress and (probably) a Jewish father, began her studies at the Imperial school at the age of ten. Despite certain physical limitations and technical weaknesses, her dance genius was so unmistakable that by the age of twenty-five she was named a prima ballerina of the Maryinsky. She was delicate, lyrical, hypnotic, with her greatest early successes in classical works such as Giselle *and* La Bayadère *(and in the solo Fokine created for her in 1905,* The Dying Swan, *which became her signature role). After a brief moment with Diaghilev's Ballets Russes, she danced only for her own company with her own repertory, much of it salon pieces like* The Dragonfly. *She toured relentlessly, obsessively, covering hundreds of thousands of miles in her mission to bring ballet to the world. Her name became—and has remained—synonymous with the art form she embodied.*

KEITH MONEY
Anna Pavlova

There are some names that loom so large and imperishable in one's life that they are icons, safely international, and to find oneself involved with one is a bewildering affair indeed. Scratching away at a daubed monument, looking for hints of original color—one needs to excuse oneself for treading where so many others have trodden, for exhausting the ground still further. It seems an intrusion.

I knew the *name* Pavlova as a child. Growing up in New Zealand, the country that produced the meringue cake which carries her name, was sufficient to ensure that, at least. Though a helping of Pavlova cake seldom came my way, it was strange and wonderful when it did: all that shattered meringue, and thick cream, and weirdly transparent green slices of Chinese gooseberry! And a hint of passionfruit—that was the trick. There was always the odd seed, hard and elusive. Only now do I understand that no chef could have struck a better balance for the subject of his homage: a delicate and fragile thing, cool yet faintly exotic in appearance. An attempt to take it apart leaves one with a disconcerting collapse of the whole. The slivers of meringue are like ice floes on the Neva; the passionfruit leaves a haunting after-taste. It is vivid, and yet . . . what was the shape?

Years after my greed for Pavlova cake subsided there came a vague realization that the name represented something else: a touchstone for dancing, for theatrical excitement. Why did every ballerina have to present her art upon a stage already shadowed by this woman? Was she a talisman or an avenging ghost? One day in the early sixties, in a room full of cheerful chatter, my eyes strayed to a glass-fronted cabinet of books. I opened one of the doors and took out a volume; it was illustrated with numerous sepia plates. From nowhere, the owner of the book was at my side. "Isn't she beautiful? I'm sure no one else could *ever* look like that." Since this remark was made by Margot Fonteyn, it made me realize that each generation seeks and finds its own idols.

Two years later, I was asked to do a book on Anna Pavlova. I refused. Several years later, the same suggestion was made. Again I refused. Four years after that, the suggestion was put to me again. I was beginning to feel that the name would not go away. It lurked there, very blurred, but frighteningly large, like a grotesque shadow cast by a small lamp. At a time when I was talking to Robert Gottlieb of Knopf in New York (in retrospect, about everything *but* Pavlova) I was aware of something: that I was ducking away from a shadow while he was focusing on a concept. He thought I should exorcize the shadow, and he was prepared to encourage the exorcism. He kept all his numerous misgivings to himself and proceeded on his agile way among the crags and pinnacles of the publishing world. Somewhere in the deep ravines, I was left to face the enormity of such rashness.

For a year I merely read related material, and it soon became apparent that no sequential document of Pavlova's life existed, although related memoirs abounded, some enormously self-serving, others less so. The books directly about Pavlova tended to dissect her, examining different aspects of her in isolation from the whole. After a lifetime in the company of Anna Pavlova, Victor Dandré had produced a book that was utterly devoted, very detailed, and ultimately like the Taj Mahal: a monument symbolizing an ideal. It seemed to me that I should commit myself to the orderly progress of a paper chase. If clues led me to a dead end, I would go back until I found the main trail again; I would plunge in at the beginning, and try to emerge at the end. It proved engulfing: the existing books were revealed as outcrops of a vast substructure, veins of ore that ran in all directions, seemingly without end, twisting and turning and doubling back on themselves, layer upon layer. After five years I am still unearthing caches of related material; only now, my capacity for surprise is somewhat reduced. And here I have halted; I must lay out the evidence. In doing so, I know something of the feelings of the Don as he faced up to the looming shape on the plains of La Mancha and—at the very moment when the giant came into focus—found himself upended. The quarry is more diverse, bigger, stronger, more surprising, and, yes, more human than any single thing has a right to be. But even if we cannot capture the creature, we must try to mark her passing; her phenomenal energy alone would deserve a monument.

IN A SPAN of twenty years, Anna Pavlova managed to be observed closely by millions of people around the world. Unlike a movie star with hundreds of alter egos spawned across different prosceniums at one and the same time, Pavlova could not tell her tale but that she drew fresh breath each time she told it. For her there could be only one stage at any one time; but there were—literally—thousands of them, and she graced them all. She was constantly expending her physical resources at a fever pitch, and just as constantly she managed to renew them. She did it in the great capitals of the world and she did it, with the same degree of energy, in provincial towns and grim seaports.

Pavlova often turned her back on security and on adulation from people in high office, so we know that she was promoting something more than just herself. She was really selling Art, as a faith, and she was careful not to get too deeply enmeshed in the semantics of its exact nature. She longed to find beauty in the world and to distill its essence. If, in the process, she came across cruelty and ugliness, then she did not flinch; she merely set about finding an antidote, and her laboratory for this happened to be the stage. She was lucky in having a medium of expression that vaulted language barriers, but within its confines she had a very precise, difficult, and esoteric language of her own to contend with: the language of nineteenth-century classical ballet. She had been painstakingly schooled in it—all her early life had been entirely governed by a desire to master its strange complexities—yet she was one of the first to join in the expansive reforms that swept in with the new century. So, contrary to popular myth, she was not a reactionary at heart. She did things her own way, recognizing her boundaries; and if others later raced on more daringly, she respected their right to do so, while reserving her own right to avoid what seemed to her to be excessive modernity. Two-thirds of the way through her life, she was sometimes thought to be old-fashioned—but it was in the way that a genuine Chippendale chair is old-fashioned: expressive, timeless in quality, and always being copied.

History is so often a matter of interpretation—legend made plausible.

From the moment of her untimely death Pavlova was swept along, a fugitive occupant in some phantom troika harnessed to Gossip, Apocrypha, and Hearsay. True, she wrote her message in the waters; but it was a powerful message, and we seem to have been cavalier about recording its author's achievements. She was in her time the most famous dancer in the world; and for all the extraordinary numbers of people who actually saw her dance, there were countless others who knew her name and what she stood for. She also happened to have been Russian, yet the late Natalia Roslavleva, an indefatigable researcher of Russian ballet history, could write in a letter: "Nothing much is known about Pavlova; she was never really talked about." The eminent Soviet ballet historian Vera Krasovskaya, in her book about Pavlova, felt the need to employ a *belles-lettres* fantasy. Yet she did turn to contemporary newspaper accounts for information, and in this way uncovered much about the vital first ten years of dancing—years that had all but evaporated in the mists surrounding the legend.

When Pavlova died, it was headline news around the world, but even in that first week the facts were becoming clouded: in Paris, a Russian-language magazine printed the wrong day in the caption for a cover picture. We can forgive the memorial card for her funeral that gave her age discreetly wrong; they were printing what they had been told. But printing her first name wrong? To take another instance from that same week: her partner of thirteen years, Alexandre Volinine, when asked how they came to work together, replied:

> In 1910 Diaghilev took me to London in the Russian Ballet along with Nijinsky and Lydia Lopokova. At the same time Pavlova and Mordkin were dancing for Charles Frohman at the Globe Theatre. A year later Mordkin was ill, and Gatti-Casazza took Pavlova and me to the Metropolitan Opera.

It is hardly giving things away to say that in Volinine's statement there is only one correct fact—Mordkin was ill—and even that is not in its correct context.

Memoirs play strange tricks with facts. Victor Dandré, Pavlova's husband (who failed to provide legal title to that relationship after Pavlova's death), wrote a book that was devotedly detailed, and yet he describes with apparent firsthand knowledge a London season during which, in fact, he was in St. Petersburg—and under arrest. Pavlova's last words on this earth have become almost as famous as the costume she was asking to be prepared, and yet there are reports, written within hours, none of which mentions those words (which she may very well have murmured), but which do mention a phrase even more haunting.

Even the facts of her birth are obscured. For the date, we can take an entry in the registry book of the St. Petersburg Military Hospital, which gives us 1881 and January 31 (February 12 new style). In the catalogue of a 1956 exhibition it was said that a birth certificate giving 1882 was in the Constance Paget-Fredericks Memorial Collection in California; there is now no trace of such a document. When Anna Pavlova became widely known in St. Petersburg society, there was speculation about her background. Was she really the daughter of reserve soldier Matvey Pavlov? She seemed to have the look of a well-bred Jewish girl. Pavlova, in 1910, was telling reporters that she had been born in St. Petersburg, that her father was a minor official who had died when she was only two, and that as a result she and her mother had lived in straitened circumstances, relying on a small pension. When Pavlova was a ballet student, it was noticed that she disliked her friends addressing her as "Anna Matveyevna," which was the normal patronymic for a daughter of Matvey Pavlov. The girl seems to have instilled an understanding that a polite fiction, "Anna Pavlovna," was more acceptable to her. (This confused the administration; in records of the company one can tell which writer knew Pavlova well, and which one didn't; she was A. P. Pavlova to some, and A. M. Pavlova to others.) This ambiguity certainly suggests illegitimacy, and the likeliness of her Jewish blood compounded a social stigma. In St. Petersburg at that time such ancestry carried a hidden threat of potential banishment from principal residential districts—if the government took it into its head to enforce its own statutes.

In the Leningrad State Theatre Archives there is a document in the form of an official pass issued to the mother of Anna Pavlova on October 10, 1899, stating that Lyubov Feodorovna Pavlova, from the village of Bor in the province of Tversk, and wife of reserve soldier Matvey Pavlov, is discharged into towns and cities of the Russian Empire. Discharged? The word *uvol* is employed in the decree. It was probably a bad choice of word by some minor clerk; however, it has a stern connotation: the equivalent of being dismissed, or even expelled. Lyubov Pavlova is listed as being married, with a daughter, Anna, by a first marriage. The inference is that Matvey Pavlov, in 1899 at least, was still living. This was a time when wives of peasants did not have the right to leave their husbands without their permission, and a husband had an automatic right to bring a wife home by force, should he so wish. The document makes it clear that Anna is not Matvey's offspring, but it cannot be regarded as evidence that an earlier marriage ever took place. The mother's profession is given as washerwoman, her faith Orthodox, and her age forty. This would mean that she had her child when she was about twenty-two. Lyubov's pass was valid for one year. At the time it was made out, the new season at the Maryinsky—with the new graduate, Anna Pavlova—had been under way for a month, so the daughter at least had a salary of sorts to contribute to a joint dwelling. From one account we know that Pavlova's mother was in St. Petersburg in 1900; yet by the autumn of that year Anna was said to have in her employ a personal maid. This makes one wonder if the mother's pass was not renewed in October. It is difficult to imagine the mother and the maid both catering to a young dancer's needs, and one does have to remember that the world of ballet in St. Petersburg almost dictated that personable young dancers received (and considered) the attentions of admirers. A modestly conventional mother could only have cramped this style, unlike a maid, who would be circumspect in such matters and whose salary in any event would probably come from her mistress's admirer.

Either Matvey Pavlov was content to be abandoned by his wife in October 1899, or he had already done the abandoning. We know that Pavlova acquired from her mother all the outward trappings of Orthodoxy: icons (particularly of the Virgin), the festival of Christmas, and sanctuary in the sign of the cross; but she seems also to have acquired a clear knowledge of a Jewish background. The intensity of the mother's cloak of Orthodoxy is not surprising in the light of Russian anti-Semitism, but the daughter seems to have absorbed the Scriptural teachings as well as a dichotomy of background. She absorbed it, and she also concealed part of it. A member of a wealthy Jewish banking family, Poliakoff, has been reported as saying once that he was the half brother of Anna Pavlova. If this points to a liaison between Anna's mother and Lazar Poliakoff, we might assume that Lyubov was in that family's employ. Even if Anna's natural father was of reasonable means, the financial support for the poignant outcome of the union appears to have been minimal. Perhaps it was the support that "died" after two years.

Victor Dandré fills in details of Pavlova's early years. The baby had been born two months premature, and she was such a frail mite that she was christened without delay—on February 3 (o.s.), Saint Anne's Day. She was kept wrapped in wool swaddling, but one might guess that her survival had as much to do with the will of her spirit. Dandré said that the child was removed to the care of a grandmother in Ligovo, "in order to improve the health of the little girl." This summer resort, fifty miles from St. Petersburg, may have been less prone to waterway miasmas, but it can hardly be considered a climate's divide away from the city. One imagines the young mother was simply unable to care for the child adequately, having to return to work. In her own fragmentary memoir, first published in 1912, Pavlova displays a deep romantic attachment for her grandmother's cottage and its surroundings, yet she never specifies that it was Ligovo; and though Dandré says that it was there that the local teacher instructed her in Russian and Scripture, Pavlova herself implies that the visits to "the country" were only summer expeditions, when their own belongings had to be transported in a van from the city. It was not a case of the grandmother having died, because Pavlova mentioned her as being alive at the time of an interview toward the end of 1910. The implication is that their frugality of life was such that there was no spare furniture in the cottage. Dandré published a photograph of a dacha of three or four rooms, with an auxiliary lean-to, but it was certainly not isolated; there were adjacent buildings on the same road, behind a picket fence and a screen of birch trees.

We know for certain that the single most important event in the whole of Anna Pavlova's life took place in the city, and we should learn of it in her own words:

> When I was eight years old, I heard that we were to celebrate Christmas by going to see a performance at the Maryinsky Theatre. I had never yet been to the theatre, and I plied my mother with questions in order to find out what kind of show it was that we were going to see. She replied by telling me the story of "The Sleeping Beauty"—a favorite of mine among all fairy tales, and one which she had already told me countless times. When we started for the Maryinsky Theatre, the snow was brightly shining in the reflected light of street lamps and shop windows. Our sleigh was noiselessly speeding along the hard surface, and I felt unspeakably happy, seated beside my mother, her arm tenderly enclosing my waist. "You are going to enter fairyland," she said, as we were being whirled across the darkness towards the theatre, the mysterious unknown. . . .
>
> As soon as the orchestra began to play, I became very grave and attentive, eagerly listening, moved for the first time in my life by the call of Beauty. But when the curtain rose, displaying the golden hall of a wonderful palace, I could not withhold a shout of delight, and I remember hiding my face in my hands when the old hag appeared on the stage in her car driven by rats. In the second act a swarm of youths and maidens appeared, and danced a most delightful waltz. "How would you like to dance this?" asked my mother with a smile. "Oh," I replied, "I should prefer to dance as the pretty lady does who plays the part of the Princess. One day, I shall be the Princess, and dance upon the stage of this very theatre."

But of course. Anyway, it makes a charming scene, even if one wonders how Aurora's entrance came to precede the waltz. The important thing is the sunburst in the child's mind; it is quite likely that she had never heard an orchestra play before, and the impact must have been staggering, given that she was already eight years old. We are left to consider how the mother's housekeeping budget encompassed the price of two seats in the Tsar's theatre, and whether the sophisticated entertainment was suggested, and paid for, by an interested well-wisher. The result of this Christmas outing was that the child pestered her mother until she was taken for an interview at the Ballet School. There they were told that Anna would have to complete her tenth year before she could audition. For two frustrating years she seems to have skipped about the woods at Ligovo, waiting for the all-important tenth birthday. Like many an only child, she was very dependent on her own resources, and she had the time to observe natural things without distraction, since there was often no one to talk to. At these times she expressed herself in movement; it was her medium.

A photograph of the little Anna at about six years of age shows an alert child, fully engaged with the camera's presence. She is composed rather than posed, with legs crossed in a naturally elegant manner. Her bonnet and parasol may have been studio props, but she is dressed prettily, and though obviously a fine-boned child, she looks perfectly healthy. Three years later she has acquired a solemn and introverted expression; it is something more than the stillness required by a slow photographic exposure. It seems to be the mother who appears alongside her. But the child's expression is not simply a reaction against the adult's presence; it seems more a look of contained rebellion against the confinement of the static pose she has been made to adopt. There is no communication with the camera—more a resentment at its intrusion. This is not a child with any intention of winning friends. The bangs of earlier years have gone, and the auburn hair is brushed back severely, revealing an almost unnaturally high hairline. Another picture, about three years on, suggests that there had been some attempt to alter this trend; the hair has been cut, and the natural slight wave has sprung into life. There are signs, too, of bleaching from the summer sun, but already the hair is pulled back again, in a manner that suggests the discipline of a school. The expression is proud and the manner detached, and only the natural upturn to the corners of the mouth avoids a look of sullenness. But the eyes are lifted much more, and though the turn of the head still dismisses the camera, the gaze seems to be leveled at some distant horizon beyond the confines of the studio. Her ears have been pierced, and she is wearing earrings designed like a snowdrop cupped around a pearl. They are still in evidence eight or nine years later—but the young Anna has a locket and a brooch, as well as a surfeit of bows. She is dressed to impress.

At the time of her tenth birthday, the child achieved a return visit to the Ballet School, and though there were doubts expressed about her physique, she gave enough hint of promise that the examiners were won over. Her acceptance at the academy can only have been a boon to the hardworking, hard-pressed mother; the school removed at a stroke all financial responsibilities for the girl. Pavlova wrote in 1912:

> Every Sunday my mother came to see me; and I used to spend all my holidays with her. During the summer we always lived in the country. We grew so fond of our little holiday cottage, that even now we have not the heart to

give it up in favour of some more comfortable abode. And I am writing
these pages on a table upon the verandah, amidst surroundings which I love
because every feature reminds me of the days of my childhood.

So the early years would seem to have been reasonably happy ones, despite
the inherent loneliness of her situation.

As a student, Pavlova was talented and also different. She looked thin by
the standards of the day, and in an effort to remedy this she swallowed the
regulation issues of castor oil with less fuss than any of her fellows. For such
an apparently slight creature she had strong hips and thighs and a thorax that
was not particularly waisted, so that the body, though immensely supple,
flowed "all of a piece." Her thin ankles and exceptionally arched insteps gave
an illusory brittleness to her figure, while the setting of the head on a very
clearly defined neck contributed to this suggestion of frailty. It was a body
that fooled the Maryinsky selectors, and it went on fooling observers. Her
muscles were steely; she was actually a racing machine, a hare.

Pavlova's story is one of willpower and dedication underpinning an unwavering belief. Her natural talent, the curious poetry of her body, was so outstanding that nobody could ignore it, even though the idiosyncrasies were
disquieting to some. By the time she was eighteen or nineteen she seems to
have begun to realize that a camera might be friendly toward her, that
she could conspire with it; she has sensed that she can contact an audience
through the lens. The moods swing from the flirtatious to the contemplative,
and whereas the childhood photographs tend to shut out the observer, the
subsequent ones seem to imply that Pavlova is now prepared to share even
the somber moods. In many hundreds of photographs, there is a talent for
communing with the camera so rare in its consistency that today she could
have become a top fashion model. She wore clothes with a faultless understanding of their potential. On her, any hat seemed a desirable model. Under
it, the face was a mysterious confluence of planes and angles. It is difficult for
us to realize that this exotic quality was at that time considered disturbing, at
odds with the reigning ideals of feminine charm. She suffered from being
thought "not beautiful," and this attitude, frequently expressed, seems to
have contributed to a certain defensiveness in her character.

Her temperament was a churning mixture of things, volatile and timid.
She never acquired the artificiality that could conceal her shifts in emotion,
the roller-coaster swings from gaiety to melancholy, which seems in her case
to have been something more than "Russian" temperament. The pattern of
her moods would today arouse a suspicion that she was a manic-depressive.
In an interview in 1910 she put the emphasis on the melancholic side of her
nature: "I was born in St. Petersburg—on a rainy day. You know, it almost
always rains in St. Petersburg. There is a certain gloom and sadness in the

atmosphere of the Russian capital, and I have breathed the air of St. Petersburg so long that I have become infected with sadness."

The adult Pavlova could behave like a child, giving vent to her feelings quite openly, and her inability to channel these currents and divert them into a more acceptable lagoon of social manner made many people wary of her; to them she appeared "difficult." If she felt at ease with someone, she could be the epitome of friendly warmth, but she often seemed hypersensitive and tense, like some forest creature forever alert to signals. She processed stimuli instantaneously and did not block the counter-reaction; this often led to sudden tears, flushes of anger, or merry explosions of joy. The fact that she did not learn to process these emotions in the usual manner may actually have helped her stage personality, because the sincerity of her feeling transferred itself readily to an audience. She had good native intelligence and deep humanity, but she did not have an intellect based upon being well-read, and as a result she suffered a lack of communication in the company of those who had this learning. With them she sometimes retreated into shallow coquetry, not because she was superficial but because she needed an armor.

Pavlova had a rare affinity with birds. In many ways she was like a bird herself in her day-to-day deportment: quick, darting hand movements, a straight-legged walk, and swift turns and inclinations of the head when the dark brown eyes focused brightly or were suddenly averted if she wanted to shield her own reaction. Her voice was birdlike too—a high chirrup. She had that waxy pallor so often associated with dancers, but hers was a skin that took the sun well if given a chance. Notwithstanding the propensity of photographic retouchers in an era that smoothed away all signs of strain, Pavlova's neck did have a natural soft cushioning unusual in dancers. In the latter part of her career her weight fluctuated slightly, according to stresses, climate, and physiological changes, but the costumes she wore were either of the draped variety or tutus so elaborate by present-day standards that it was the extremities—the amazing feet and ankles, and the arms with their wonderful plastique—that claimed the attention. In the latter part of her career, after visiting the Orient, her stage make-up became heavier and more stylized: a whitened mask with great triangles of eyes shaded in violet, and lips of deepest crimson that took on a strangely sardonic cast when she acknowledged applause.

Relationships were difficult for Pavlova: a mixture of loyalty, dependence, and trust that sometimes fractured because she could not always take into account the stresses that her own unnatural and fragmented life placed upon others. She sought and found a surrogate father, one whose adoration was so secure that she could fight furiously against it, knowing that she would be forgiven. She was brought up in an age, and a setting, that taught girls that sexual activity was an obligation, something to be faced up to, and there were signs that she never entirely overcame this indoctrination. In the Ballet School this was by the example of elders, some of whom seemed to owe their advancement to the care with which they picked an admirer. Pavlova was not of a mercenary inclination; nor was she prone to fall in love easily—though she certainly knew what romantic love could be. The lack of it through much of her life seems to have cast a shadow over her spirit. She never had a child, and this too was felt by her to be in the nature of a penalty.

How to chart the course of such a strange and unremitting odyssey? Pavlova's voyages were global, and the effect she had on the history of dancing is incalculable. She took places by stealth or by storm; either way, they never forgot she had been there. In each audience there was usually one person who felt, at the end of the evening, that his life was going on an entirely different and previously unimagined course. Such people were converts. In the age of the airplane, can we begin to imagine traveling over 400,000 miles by train and steamer?

There came a point in Pavlova's career at which world events finally played a decisive hand in the direction of her aims. Previously she had brushed through the edges of conflict and carried on, but the conflagration was finally too great. We can see Pavlova's caravan falter, and then, like some pioneer group realizing that its old base is irretrievably gone, move off again, knowing that the act of living is in the moving, not in the arriving at some new home or in the thought that the progression is finally curving back to hallowed territory.

This book too changes at that point. Because Pavlova survived by carrying with her such secure, even unshakable, traditions, I have thought it vital to try first to discover her surroundings and the influences that formed her. Even if her progress seems now to have been meteoric, that is because so much detail has been pared away subsequently. She did not leap center-stage at one bound and dismiss all rivals. She was surrounded by talent of varying order, some of it exceptional, and unless we understand something of that conjunction, we cannot measure her true strength. Pavlova is often presented as some disembodied head of thistledown, skimming along above rougher pasture as if she had never come from that base. This is quite wrong. She grew out of a dense and competitive field, and she flowered in much the same way as her fellows.

After the psychological juncture in her career—which was arrived at in 1917—the progression became a sort of divine madness, and the reality of what was going on can at best be suggested. One hopes that by then, a determined reader will understand the full implication behind the mere mention of a country or a brutally stark itinerary, and know that Pavlova's energy never faltered. She was a missionary for her art and she served it faithfully, above everything and everyone.

—from *Anna Pavlova,* 1982

A K I M   V O L Y N S K Y

Anna Pavlova

Pavlova has a phenomenal arch, which she almost dares not bend entirely when she lifts herself on pointes. If she were to extend it, she'd break her foot. The arch, which promotes take-off, provides force to the push, although the muscles and tendons of the leg, heel, and knee play the major role here: The aerial throws of the body are managed exclusively by them. Nijinsky's arch is average, but due to the elasticity of his tendons, he flies across the stage like a bird. Kschessinska's foot is almost flat, but in stockings she dances perfectly. There is no doubt, however, that at the barre or in the middle of the hall, the oval of the foot, which is especially balanced, is beautiful. Pavlova's arch is only partly a result of her school exercises. Nature itself in its generosity endowed her with plastic features which, as they developed, provided the external image of this major talent of our day. But still more of Pavlova comes from God than from nature. When you watch her dance you can't help feeling that her art, though not perfect in all its details, is directly connected to her emotional make-up. Her choreographic features are wrapped in inspiration, which alone is evident. All the rest seems trivial.

Pavlova's foot is charming, small, and narrow. The structure of her leg is right, but somewhat concave in the knees. Her knee-caps almost touch. That is why Pavlova lacks the perfect turnout, which one finds in Trefilova; but her knee depressions do not give her a single line. Her small beat is not pure. Thus her passage downwards or upwards along the diagonal of the stage with the fleeting contact of the feet higher than the knee joint, called, in the language of ballet technique, simple or double *brisé,* as well as the rather low take-offs of her body, such as *entrechats quatre* and *royale,* are not managed entirely well by Pavlova. Her knees are not impeccable either in her *attitudes* or her *arabesques;* the knee-cap does not provide a horizontal line with her foot, but often hangs much lower. The sole of her foot is therefore raised to the ceiling and can be seen by the spectator, which is totally alien to the classical dances of the French school.

Pavlova's legs are lanky and muscular, as if they were taut, like a goat's. Their lightness is extraordinary. She can do any step she wants with them, any *battement,* any leap from one foot or from both. But for all the inadequacy of her turnout, her *batteries* during her movement in the air are brilliant. They become beautiful only at high altitudes from the floor.

Because she is able to fling and throw out her legs whenever she so desires, Pavlova produces the impression of an artist with extraordinary elevation. But there is an illusion here which is easier to understand than to follow. The perfection of her dancing flows from another source. Her deep and even plié, the swiftness of her leap, her *ballon,* give the sensation of the fluttering of wings high in the air. But in reality, Pavlova's elevation, if strictly measured, would not outdo Vaganova's. In this regard, next to her even Elsa Vill could dance without a loss to her reputation. Of course, I'm talking about the height of the leap. The jumps themselves are astonishingly beautiful, not only in the character but in the poetry of their lines. Before us is a major talent, filled with hymns to Apollo and dithyrambs in honor of Dionysus.

Throwing her legs slightly back, Pavlova spreads herself in the air like a wild bird. And on stage she flies at rapid speed up and down, obliquely, near the floor, against all logic, against all the laws of gravity, with her widely opened, dark brown eyes in which fire burns.

Given her resilient, albeit not strong back, Pavlova's pirouettes cannot be considered first-class—in this respect it is Trefilova's art that has achieved greater perfection. Here, obviously, besides an inborn talent and a natural equilibrium of the legs, which is not found in a passionate nature, a firm back is required. However, doing a pirouette with her partner, Pavlova spins at such a quick tempo that the spectator can in no way count the number of turns she produces. In the whirlwind of her movement, it always seems that only one circle has flashed before our eyes.

Pavlova's body is lissom and light. Her shoulders are ravishing, they slope down with soft muscles the color of ivory. Her arms are too extended at the elbows and lack the semicircular lines that make the *arabesque* and *attitude* beautiful, but they are lively and tremulous. Her hand is strong and not pomaded, although the fingers are short, prehensile, and square, like a Botticelli madonna or like the late Vera Kommissarzhevskaya. Moreover, her entire image conveys the impression of an undeveloped little girl who is ready to twirl almost pointlessly, merely from an excess of enthusiasm. Before the ballet she does no exercises, yet she flies right onto the stage on her cold feet, warming them up during her activity. In general, she does not prepare on the day of the performance. She drinks champagne and chatters away capriciously and randomly. Other dancers have a bite six hours before a performance and then lie on a couch with their legs stretched out; two hours before they go on stage they're already beating out their *battements*. Pavlova furiously flits around all day. She has breakfast and then eats nothing until the evening. But fifteen minutes before the curtain goes up, she quickly gulps down five ham or roast-beef sandwiches. And then she flies onto the stage.

I have said far from everything about Pavlova. The image of this inspired artist needs to be gleaned from her dancing itself, from her first-class art.

—from *Birhevye Vedomosti (The Stock Exchange News)*, 1913

Walford Hyden
The Genius of Pavlova

Best known as Pavlova's musical director and the author of a successful book about her, Anna Pavlova: Genius of the Dance, *British-born Walford Hyden (1892–1959) studied at the Royal Academy of Music and went on to a long career as a conductor and composer.*

Pavlova knew only too well that the secret of perfection is in unremitting attention to detail and hard work. Many a time on our tours I have arrived at the theatre at nine-thirty in the morning, for a rehearsal called for ten o'clock, to find her already there, practising, doing her exercises on the stage. It was strange to see her, a solitary, delicate creature, pirouetting in the half-darkness of a vast empty stage, in a chill and deserted theatre. The rest of the Company would arrive, and begin "warming up" for the rehearsal. Woe betide any girl in the Company who neglected her practice exercises, or was not properly "warmed up" before a rehearsal of a performance! There would be no sympathy from Madame if an accident happened. "Why did you not loosen up properly?" she would say bitingly. "It serves you right. You will not be so lazy next time!"

An amusing incident occured once in Australia when Pavlova was practising in the early morning by herself. A stage carpenter told her to get out of his way and go to practise somewhere else! With her perfect understanding of theatrical niceties, Pavlova was not affronted. She went meekly away as directed. "The man was quite within his rights," she commented afterwards, and that settled the matter, as far as she was concerned.

She was not always so meek. During rehearsals of dances in which she did not appear personally, Madame would keep warm by exercising at the side of the stage, using for a bar anything that came to hand, but watching the rehearsal keenly all the time. At unexpected moments, often when everybody else concerned thought that things were going very well, her voice would ring out sharply, "Do that again!" or "That is all wrong!" I have known her to insist on rehearsing for an hour and a half a movement which takes only *ten seconds* in execution.

Sometimes she was at variance with her ballet-master—or even her musical director! As regards ballet, she was always ready to listen to Fokine or Clustine, but I recall one stormy scene in which Pianowsky resigned because of a difference of opinion from Madame. There were occasions, when, out of sheer devilment, it seemed, she absolutely would not give way, though she knew herself to be in the wrong. Once on tour in Germany her partner Novikoff ventured to suggest that Madame was exerting herself unnecessarily in a certain movement. She knew at once that he was right, but she would not alter her method. She continued to do the movement in her own way. She gave the *most difficult rendering* of the step. But this, too, was characteristic of her. She was obstinate and wrong often enough; but she never spared herself.

She was thorough, unbelievably thorough, in the preparation and rehearsals of her ballets. When audiences applauded the apparent spontaneity of the Ballet's movements, very few in the front of the house could have imagined the discipline and endless routine of rehearsals by which that perfection had been attained. Every movement, every gesture, every position on the stage had to be exactly as Madame wanted it, and she would keep the Company at rehearsal until her effect was achieved. Even the lighting effects she did not leave to the good intentions of the electrician. Pavlova herself would go out into the auditorium during rehearsals and make the most careful notes and comments on the lighting of the stage in each theatre we visited.

I remember one occasion on which she rebuked members of the Company who were dancing in Hungarian costume because they did not have a sufficient number of necklaces! Every ribbon, every detail of costume and make-up, had to be as perfect as the execution of the steps and movements in the dance itself.

She was likely to become excited when things were going wrong. She expected people to understand her when often, in her excitement, she could not explain what it was that she wanted. In Russian, French, German, or English, she would remonstrate and attempt to explain, tossing her head, stamping her feet with impatience. For example, if she wanted certain alterations in the music, she could not always convey to me what she wanted because she did not know the technical expressions necessary. On such occasions she would work herself up from a slight impatience to a condition of raging frenzy. The storm would pass, as storms do; but she was not the only one who could become excited. I do not mind admitting that once, in Buenos Aires, I lost my temper and gave as good an exhibition of Russian "temperament" as could be expected from a naturally phlegmatic Staffordshire man. I remembered my football days, and kicked a musical score from the orchestra onto the stage!

If she could become excited when things were going wrong, she could become equally excited when something pleased her. When a member of the ballet did a step particularly well, Madame would jump about like a little girl, clapping her hands with merriment and delight, and excitedly calling out "*Harascho!*" (Good!)

She was sensitive to anything that could affect her attitude towards her work. Often I have seen her at rehearsal, not in the usual practice dress, but in a ballet skirt with bodice and a little shawl. It would have been easier to wear a practice dress, but she never took the easier way. We may surmise that the fluffiness of the ballet skirt gave her something, a quality of lightness, a feeling of elation, which made even her practice or rehearsal an expression of an art and not a dull discipline.

To be praised by Madame at rehearsal was a prize well worth the winning, but in her endeavor for perfection in everything, she was not always just in her censure. She was inclined to be whimsical in exerting her authority. I have known her, for example, say to a girl in her Ballet, "What a terrible make-up! For goodness' sake alter it at once!" Not knowing exactly what Madame wanted, the girl would retire to the dressing room and reappear in due course with exactly the same make-up as before. Whereupon Madame would say, "There! You see! What a vast improvement!" Yet Anna Pavlova won the genuine esteem and respect of those working with her, quite apart from the respect due to her unquestionably supreme art and the authority of her world-famous name. . . .

To work with her was like being a disciple of a Messiah. She regarded herself as infallible. She was structurally incapable of understanding that other people could not see things from her point of view—or, indeed, that there could possibly be any other point of view than her own. She would become almost hysterical when contradicted and would suffer from depression afterwards. In one of these moods, her maid once said to her, "Sometimes, Madame, there are two opinions, and both are right. Other people are entitled to have a different opinion from yours, and still not be wrong!" Pavlova was astonished at this simple dictum and pondered over it for several days. Then, with the air of one experiencing a great revelation, she said, "You are right. I have never realized it before. It is quite possible that even when people contradict me they are not deliberately trying to annoy me. I will try to remember this in future, but it will be difficult."

But, as a rule, it was no use remonstrating with her. She would lose her temper and become an inferno of incoherence, abuse, insult, and imprecation.

She was impatient enough with anybody who could not learn a dance immediately, yet she was oh, so slow herself to learn anything new! The music had to be repeated *ad nauseam* before she could remember the steps. Then to make matters worse, after she had learned the dance perfectly, she would proceed to introduce her own variations in tempo. A conductor would develop eye strain, heart strain, and nerve strain, trying to synchronize the orchestra with her frantic feet. She was aware of this difficulty, of course, and took an impish pleasure, sometimes, in trying to make a fool of the conductor by suddenly jumping out of her position after giving preliminary indications that she was going to hold it for some moments.

No dance was ever the same twice. If she felt well, her dancing was uncontrollable—even by herself. She was a being possessed. If she felt at cross-purposes with the world and herself, she was just as likely to be sulky in a dance as not. The audience, of course, would not detect her sulking. But for the man trying to follow her musically, it was obvious enough.

Yet she was always likely to lose her temper with the other dancers, or with one of them, if *their* dances did not happen to synchronize exactly with the music and the movement of the rest of the ballet. Her favourite term of abuse was to call one of the girls in such circumstances a "cow"—than which there could scarcely be any epithet more injurious to a ballet dancer, who, theoretically, has little resemblance to that useful animal. But the Company understood Pavlova and could put up with her fits of temper and her abusiveness, because they knew that in a few moments she was just as likely to become excessively gracious and affectionate. The Company knew, too, the terrible strain under which she lived and worked. . . .

. . . It was thus by precept and by example that Pavlova inspired the whole of her Ballet with the principle that as far as dancing is concerned it is impossible to work too much. She would impress upon them, by precept and example, that no one's technique is so perfect that it cannot be improved by hard work and relentless practising. Because she worked like a slave herself, it was impossible for anyone to grumble behind her back that she was a slave driver. If the girls practised only three-quarters of the time that Pavlova herself practised they would have been giving more time each day to their work than any other dancers in the world. There were compensations in this life of devotion which Pavlova compelled from those who were associated with her—the satisfaction that everything humanly possible was being done to achieve perfection; the satisfaction of a performance so finished in its details as to give pleasure to the dancer herself; for the audience would never realize subtleties of technique and difficulties of execution, so effortless did they become in the Pavlova Ballet as the result of perpetual drilling.

Besides, if anyone in the Company did not like Pavlova's methods, he or she could leave and go somewhere else, where life would be less strenuous. Because this grand principle exists, weaklings were excluded from the Company of Anna Pavlova.

—from *Pavlova,* 1931

Sol Hurok
Pavlova

The next season began my long and unforgettable association with Pavlova. I made that entire first tour with her, and not for business reasons. At the end of that coast-to-coast tour, after the triumphs in the big cities and the struggle to put on a show in the little towns, after the uncomfortable hotels and the sleepy taxi-rides to catch early trains and the long train rides that demanded all our resourcefulness to keep ourselves and each other from boredom, I knew Pavlova.

I knew her tears as well as her laughter. I knew her stoic devotion to her work, to her company, to her audience. And I knew her unsatisfied heart.

The truth is that Pavlova was never married. I myself married her off in the press. In 1925 the newspapers printed a story I gave them, announcing for the first time that she had been married to Victor Dandré—some of them called him her accompanist—seventeen years before.

Anna Pavlova was the daughter of an unknown father and a simple woman living outside St. Petersburg. She never saw her father, although once, sitting in a park in Calgary, she told me that he was a Jew. It was virtually all she knew about him.

Her gift alone saved the young Anna from a lifetime of poverty-stricken anonymity. The shrewdness of the Czar's Government in picking jewels out of the mire of its own neglect of the people brought the little girl to the Imperial Ballet School. From there on she made her own way. She was never one of a group; always she stood alone. Even with Diaghilev she did not stay long. One season, and she was off in search of her solitary destiny.

When she was a young newcomer in the glittering world of Theatre Street in St. Petersburg, Victor Dandré came into her life. He was the son of a landowner in Poltava, a gilded youth in a position of some responsibility in the Czar's diplomatic service. Like all the young men of his class in the capital, he was a fanatic balletomane. He had been one of Preobrajenska's beaux. When Pavlova emerged from the Imperial School and began to be noticed in the Ballet, he devoted himself to her career. He arranged concerts for her, showered her with flowers and gifts.

He spent—for one of his position—vast sums of money on her, and presently it appeared that it was not all his own money. Some of it was the Czar's. When he was arrested, Pavlova came at once to his rescue. Whether she loved him then or not, she could not—being Pavlova—see him sacrificed for his devotion to her. She used her influence, of which a prima ballerina assoluta in St. Petersburg had a great deal, to get him out, and put him in charge of her business affairs. They left Russia together.

For Dandré it was forever. Even had he been permitted to return, his bitterness against the old regime, his inability or unwillingness to understand the new, were an effective barrier to his ever going back. For Pavlova it need not have been forever, for any regime would have embraced her, and she herself longed to return. But Dandré stood in the way.

He managed her affairs scrupulously, but without brilliance. He himself admitted that her American tours were the most profitable, and the reason was clear. His was a road-show mentality; outside the United States Pavlova was poorly presented. . . .

Knowing her hunger, and not infrequently her despair, I found it all the more tragic that a heartless fate should have bound her for life to Dandré. Whatever the romantic attachment she might have felt for him when she was a young untried ballerina and he a gallant admirer in St. Petersburg, it had long vanished when I knew her. He was coldly correct, with a stubborn concern for minutiae. Even while she admitted the usefulness of this virtue, she found it a constant irritant. The rigid conservatism of his class possessed him to the point where nothing new, no change of any kind was desirable, or indeed possible to him. When she talked with yearning of going back to

Russia, when she grew eager and animated over news of the progress of the Soviets, his fleshy face turned stonily pale. He wanted none of it.

At first the drama of his disgrace for her sake was enough to bind her to him. Later he became so necessary to her career that she could not imagine continuing without him. In his mind alone were recorded the thousand details of management; in his hands the solution of the thousand little problems of the company, the tours, the finances.

Once, indeed, he left her. It was during her second season with Mikhail Mordkin, either 1912–13 or the next year. In the middle of the season Dandré walked out and took the boat back to London. When we were on tour there were weeks when she did not speak to him. But she could not cut herself off from him entirely. It would have been like cutting herself off from her work.

For his part, it seemed to me that he was afraid to let her stop working. It was always Dandré who egged me on, each season, to get the contract signed for the next.

She talked of taking a year off, of enjoying life. She talked of a villa on the Riviera, where she would do nothing but bask in the sun, tend her flowers, and cook delectable Russian dishes for the Novikoffs and me. She even talked of someday having a child. But the child remained a dream child, the villa a dream villa, and even the beautiful year of just living—all were dreams that never came true.

Dandré was always planning for the year to come, the tour, the repertoire. Even before the season was at its half-way mark, he was suggesting to me that it was time to discuss next year's business. And I, sorely tempted—as who would not be, by a contract with Pavlova's name on it?—would go to her.

"Coming back next year?" I would ask, as we sat over a supper in some American town.

She would shrug, and her answer was without enthusiasm. "What else is there to do?"

—from *Impresario,* with Ruth Goode, 1946

CARL VAN VECHTEN
Pavlova at the Met

March 1, 1910

More than two-thirds of the boxes at the Metropolitan Opera House were still filled with their occupants at half after 12 last night. It was not a performance of *Götterdämmerung* without cuts that kept a fashionable Monday night audience in its seats, but the American début of Anna Pavlova, the Russian dancer from the Imperial Opera in St. Petersburg. Mme. Pavlova appeared in a revival of *Coppélia*, which was given at the Metropolitan for the first time since the season of 1904–5. As this was preceded by a performance of *Werther*, the ballet did not commence until after 11, and it was nearly 1 before it was finished.

However, Mme. Pavlova easily held most of her audience. It is safe to say that such dancing has not been seen on the local stage during the present generation. If Pavlova were a regular member of the Metropolitan Opera Company it would also be safe to prophesy a revival of favor for the classic ballet.

The little dancer is lithe and exquisitely formed. When she first appeared just after the curtain rose there was a dead silence. She received no welcome. She wore the conventional ballet dress and her dark hair was bound back with a blue band.

After the first waltz, which immediately follows her entrance, the audience burst into vociferous applause, which was thereafter repeated at every possible opportunity. Pavlova received an ovation of the sort which is seldom given to anybody at this theater.

And her dancing deserved it. To begin with, her technique is of a sort to dazzle the eye. The most difficult tricks of the art of the dancer she executed with supreme ease. She even went further. There were gasps of astonishment and bursts of applause after several of her remarkable feats, all of which were accomplished with the greatest ease and lightness.

Grace, a certain sensuous charm, and a decided sense of humor are other qualities which she possesses. In fact, it would be difficult to conceive a dancer who so nearly realizes the ideal of this sort of dancing.

In the first act she was assisted at times by Mikail Mordkin, who also comes from St. Petersburg, and who is only second to Pavlova as a remarkable dancer. Their pas de deux near the end of the act was perhaps the best-liked bit of the evening. It was in the second act in her impersonation of the doll that Pavlova disclosed her charming sense of humor.

At this time it is impossible to write any more about this dancer, but there is no doubt that she will prove a great attraction while she remains in New York.

March 2, 1910

The second appearance at the Metropolitan Opera House of the two Russian dancers, Anna Pavlova and Mikail Mordkin, was undoubtedly the feature of the performance which was given there last night for the benefit of the pension and endowment fund of that institution. The auditorium was packed for the occasion, and the total receipts were somewhere in the neighborhood of $15,000.

Very late in the evening before these two dancers had appeared in Delibes's ballet *Coppélia*. Last night they appeared alone without the assistance of the somewhat ragged corps de ballet of the Metropolitan Opera House in two divertissements, which were so entirely different from anything they had done in *Coppélia* that anyone who had seen their previous performance would have had difficulty in recognizing them.

Such dancing has not been seen in New York in recent years, and last night's audience manifested its feeling as heartily as had that of Monday evening.

Early in the evening the curtains parted on a woodland scene which left a large open space on the stage. The orchestra played an adagio of Bleichmann's. First Mordkin darted onto the scene dressed as a savage. Pavlova followed him. The two danced together and then alone. Mordkin whirled for long seconds on one foot, with the other foot pointed at right angles from his body. He did another dance, in which he shot arrows from a huge bow behind his shoulder. The celerity, the grace, the rhythm of his terpsichorean feats were indescribable in their effect.

Pavlova twirled on her toes. With her left toe pointed out behind her, maintaining her body poised to form a straight line with it, she leapt backward step by step on her right foot. She swooped into the air like a bird and floated down. She never dropped. At times she seemed to defy the laws of gravitation. The divertissement ended with Pavlova, supported by Mordkin, flying through the air, circling his body around and around. The curtain fell. The applause was deafening. Again and again the two were called before the footlights.

Later in the evening the two danced again to music from a ballet of Glazounov's. This special divertissement was called *Autumn*. The music was gay and furious in its rhythm. The two in Greek draperies dashed about the stage, veiled in a background of floating gauze. The music became wilder and wilder, and wilder and wilder grew the pace of the two. The bacchanalian finale, in which Pavlova was finally swept to the earth, held the audience in tense silence for a moment after it was over, and then the applause broke out again. The curtain calls after this dance were innumerable.

March 18, 1910

Mlle. Pavlova and Mr. Mordkin introduced two new dances to this public at The New Theatre yesterday afternoon. Both of the new dances were better suited to the smaller stage of that theatre than *Coppélia*. In the first Pavlova danced alone to Saint-Saëns's *Le Cygne,* played on the solo violin with a harp accompaniment. This dancer's poetic conception of the swan was an achievement of the highest order of imagination. It is the most exquisite specimen of her art which she has yet given to this public.

Immediately after, to the accompaniment of Chopin's C sharp major waltz, played on the pianoforte, Mordkin and Pavlova danced a pas de deux in early nineteenth century costumes. This was as beautiful in its way as the other dance. The two will be repeated to-night at the New Theatre.

October 16, 1910

To say that history repeated itself yesterday afternoon at the Metropolitan Opera House, when Pavlova and Mordkin reappeared with their own company, to give for the first time here a program all by themselves, would be to express the case very mildly, indeed. It might almost be said that history was made on this occasion. It is doubtful if such dancing has ever been seen on the Metropolitan stage save when these two Russians were here last season, and it is certain that there never has been more enthusiasm let loose in the theatre on a Saturday afternoon than there was yesterday.

The program included two complete ballets and several divertissements, and from 2:30 to 5:30, with intermissions now and then, Pavlova and Mordkin gave exhibitions of their highly finished and poetic art.

The afternoon began with a performance of Adolphe Adam's ballet *Giselle,* which has never been given before on this stage and probably not often in New York, although it was seen here in 1842, one year after the original Paris production, which occurred at the Opéra, with Carlotta Grisi as the unhappy heroine. . . .

The music is gently fragrant, a little faded here and there, but a pretty score, and one of Adam's best. Cuts were made freely. In fact, almost one-half of the music had been taken out, and this was probably for the best, as far as present-day audiences are concerned. There was one interpolation. In the first act a waltz from Glazounov's *Raymonda* was introduced, which was very much as if some conductor had performed *Also Sprach Zarathustra* somewhere in *Fra Diavolo.*

Mlle. Pavlova yesterday revivified this honeyfied and sentimental score of Adam's, full of the sad, gray splendor of the time of Louis Philippe. Grisi is said to have been gently melancholy in it, but Pavlova was probably more than that. Her poetic conception of the betrothed girl's madness when she finds that her lover has deceived her, and her death, came very close to being tragic. It is almost impossible to describe the poetry of her dancing in the second act, where as one of the Wilis she engages in the wildest sort of measures under the forest trees.

Mr. Mordkin had no dancing to do in this ballet, but in appearance and action he was superb. For some reason the program referred to the Wilis as "fairies," which can scarcely be regarded as an accurate translation.

The second part of the program consisted of divertissements beginning with a very pretty performance of Liszt's Second Rhapsodie by Mme. Pajitzkaia, and the corps de ballet. After this Pavlova and Mordkin danced the adagio of Bleichmann and the Tchaikovsky Variation, in which they were often seen last year. After the bow and arrow dance, with which this divertissement concludes, it seemed as if Mr. Mordkin would never be able to leave the stage, the applause was so deafening and so long continued.

Some Russian dances followed to music from Glinka's *A Life for the Czar,* not by Tchaikovsky, as the program stated, and this section of the program was completed with the *Bacchanale* from Glazounov's ballet *The Seasons,* in which Pavlova and Mordkin swept the audience almost literally out of their chairs. This dance to many reaches the heights of choreographic art.

The ballet which concluded the program was called *The Legend of Azyiade,* and was doubtless suggested by a performance of Rimsky-Korsakow's symphony *Schéhérazade* as a ballet at the Paris Opéra last summer. However, Mordkin had arranged for this occasion an entirely different story and the music was taken from many sources although some of the themes from Rimsky-Korsakow's symphony were retained. Among the dances introduced was one from Bourgault-Ducoudray's opera *Tamara,* distinctly Persian in character, and quite extraordinarily sensuous in its rhythm and tonal monotony. Several other composers, including Chaminade and Glazounov, were called upon to contribute.

Pavlova as the captive princess was as bewitching as possible, and Mordkin was so beautifully king-like that many in the audience were heard to condemn the escape of the captive princess at the close as an unhappy ending.

—from *The New York Times,* 1910, reprinted in *Dance Index,* 1942

Ryūnosuke Akutagawa
Russian Ballet in Tokyo

*Known as "the father of the Japanese short story," Ryūnosuke Akutagawa (1892–1927)
is best known as the author of "Rashōmon," the story that gave its name to Kurosawa's
famous film. (Actually, most of the film's action comes from the author's best-known
story, "In the Grove.") Akutagawa committed suicide at the age of thirty-five.*

*A*marilla, *Chopiniana,* and seven dances including *The Dying Swan* were the
Russian Ballet I saw.

Amarilla was disgusting. First, the scenery was unpleasant. The colour of
the woods, the sky, and even the stone balustrade were impossible. Secondly,
the libretto was artificial and unpleasant. The love of a beautiful gypsy girl
and a count has a Watteau-like charm, one might say, but I was overwhelmed
by its poisonous sweetness. If at the opera you do not like what you see, you
may close your eyes, but at the ballet if you close your eyes it is a catastrophe.
Thirdly, the gypsy girl of Anna Pavlova was disagreeable, exaggerated, voluptuous, hysterical even. In a word she was decadent. The society to which
this art was born, the society in which such an art is admired, is, giving a
favourable account, a world of sexual abnormality. I am not a moralist. . . . I
even have some respect for violent lust. But I do not sympathize with abnormal, feeble, disguised lust. . . . As soon as the curtain fell I rushed to the
foyer cursing Anna Pavlova, the Imperial Theater, and the magazine . . . that
engaged me to produce an article about this performance. . . .

After *Amarilla* came *Chopiniana.* I was indifferent to that, too. The impression of the stage was just like a handkerchief box or the picture of a
European story book cover. Fortunately, this ballet has no story. . . . Moreover, to see the dancers dressed in white and moving here and there in a
bluish spotlight is a beautiful sight. Although I was indifferent, mentally I did
not feel the positive unpleasantness I felt when I saw *Amarilla.* Physically,
I felt dizzy a couple of times. To watch Western ballet dancers turn like
tops or soar in the air is not good for one's health. . . . Fortunately, I felt
only dizziness, but there was a gentleman groaning under the table of the
smoking-room when I went to the foyer in the intermission. He told me he
was Russian-Ballet-sick—in the same way as one might be sea-sick. . . .

My vitality was recovered when I saw the seven dances, which included *The Dying Swan*. Gradually, from the stage "art" began to radiate its dim lustre as moonlight through the mist. *The Dying Swan* was beautiful—at least, more beautiful than the Japanese translation of the words "The Dying Swan" suggests. Seeing Anna Pavlova dancing, one feels bonelessness before skill. In fact, we Japanese have never seen such a freely flexible body other than that of a boneless man; but, of course, a boneless man is grotesque. The feeling of grotesqueness remained within me; I felt nervous and ridiculous. . . . However, when I saw *The Dying Swan* it was strange how the feeling of bonelessness disappeared suddenly. As I gazed upon the arms and legs of Pavlova, the neck and wings of the swan seemed to emerge, accompanied by the wake and ripple of the lake; I even heard the soundless voice—I could not believe my senses. Pavlova became magnificent. The feeling of decadence remained, but I could overlook it. I had seen something beautiful. I could not complain. Pavlova was good. . . .

My impression of Russian Ballet as a whole is as follows. Russian Ballet contains a sinister vagueness, never found in *The Dying Swan*. This sinister vagueness is vivid, barbaric, full of sunlight; it smells of rye, and is very close to the Orient. It has not the powerful, accomplished form of *The Dying Swan* as yet, and it is evident in various dances from time to time. I admire *The Dying Swan* because it does not have the power to make me uneasy. I have experienced the breeze of that exquisite world alongside French poetry, but the sinister vagueness felt before lacks the delicacy of this breeze.

These formidable Russian geniuses all have this sinister vagueness in their powerful veins. Understanding Russian Ballet this way, I think it has tremendous possibilities. In retrospect, I feel I was careless to have ridiculed *Amarilla*—even if I did not like it.

—from the Japanese journal *The New Stage Art,* 1922

PRESENT AT THE CREATION

APOLLO
Alexandra Danilova

Apollo—*originally called* Apollo Musagète—*was Balanchine's first master-piece (he was twenty-four), and the key ballet in the development of neoclassicism in dance. The newborn Apollo must choose which of three muses is to be his, and his choice is Terpsichore, the muse of dance. Balanchine's* Apollo *was created for Diaghilev's Ballets Russes in 1928, to the exquisite score by Stravinsky. It remains a central work in the repertory of countless ballet companies around the world.*

*A*pollon Musagète, which George choreographed in 1928 to a score by Stravinsky, is now regarded as a landmark in dance history, a ballet that gave birth to a new era. *Apollo* seemed to us different and a little more difficult than George's other ballets, and revolutionary for the simple reason that at times we had to dance on flat feet—that was astonishing.

Balanchine's idea for *Apollo* was that the three muses would be in love with this god. They have, as the French say, *un béguin*. It was an attraction between them, but cool, god-to-god, it was admiration, not passion—passion is human. In order to show that they are divine—superior, not ordinary—there could be no passion between them.

Apollo was Lifar, who by this time was a marvelous personality on the stage—it was a personality Balanchine had given him. The muses were Tchernicheva as Calliope, the muse of epic poetry, Doubrovska as Polyhymnia, the muse of mime, and Alicia Nikitina and I alternating in the role of Terpsichore, the muse of dance.

Lifar was a beautiful youth who couldn't dance in a purely classical style. But when Diaghilev requested a premiere for him, George had no choice but to use him. Faced with a premier danseur who wasn't classical, Balanchine created what we now call the neoclassical style.

After the opening, Apollo's birth, came a pas d'action between Apollo and the three girls. In much of the ballet, the three muses dance and stand with their feet together, parallel, instead of in fifth position, and this gives *Apollo* a different, more natural kind of beauty. Apollo gives each of the muses a gift. When he gave me the lyre, I was to appear to be very flattered because it meant that I was the epitome of dance. I always made sure that my first step as I walked away carrying the lyre was very light. Each of us danced a solo variation. Mine was last, and right afterward I danced the pas de deux with Apollo. Then came the coda, when we all walked upstage in some kind of ritual and went to Zeus, who is the god of the gods.

Some people tried to read something special into my role as Terpsichore, but at the time I didn't think anything of it: one of us had to be the goddess of dance, and it can't have been a very difficult choice for Balanchine, because the other two were definitely not Terpsichores. And if Balanchine was in love with a dancer, she became Terpsichore for him, his inspiration.

In rehearsals, I had to separate myself from him, to behave as one of the dancers, not as the choreographer's girlfriend. But in a way this was easy. In the studio, our relationship was different. I had so much respect for George that I just turned myself over to him as material to work with. Whatever he ordered, I tried to give him.

George would come to rehearsal with a definite plan in mind, but the details, the actual steps, he would mold on the dancers. He could choreograph them right there, straightaway, because he knew the capacity of each dancer so well. He would show me what he wanted me to do. If it didn't work, he would say, "All right, then I will simplify it or make it different." The movements in *Apollo* were unusual and intricate, but the style and the sense we could pick up from Balanchine, because he always demonstrated.

Balanchine in rehearsal was not like any other choreographer I have ever worked with. The steps just poured from him. But with *Apollo,* he had trouble, and he couldn't put his finger on it. He worked and worked on Terpsichore's variation. It didn't click, and I could feel that it wasn't right somehow. When we got to Paris, Diaghilev still wasn't satisfied with it and decided to cut it. Stravinsky came and said, "Where is Terpsichore's variation?" And Diaghilev said, "Choura doesn't feel very well and she isn't doing the variation tonight." It still wasn't what it should be, but Stravinsky was upset that it had been cut, and I think Balanchine was, too. By the time the next performance was scheduled, Balanchine had made some changes in my variation that improved it: he added some soft, light, quick sissonnes, with the arms open.

But for that performance, I *was* sick and couldn't dance. Diaghilev was very upset. "I brought this on Choura," he said. "She got sick because I said she was." But I danced the next performance, including the variation, and the new choreography worked fine.

There was a big to-do about our costumes. They were changed again and again, until finally Chanel gave us Grecian tunics made of tricot, a knitted material that took nicely to the body. They were very classic, very beautiful.

I was Terpsichore, but my only premiere was in London. One day during rehearsals, Diaghilev came to me and said, very openly, "Choura, you will have to give your part to Nikitina to dance in Paris." Lord Rothermere, her benefactor, had given Diaghilev a big check to help pay for the season, and one of the terms of his gift was that Alicia have a new ballet to dance. The premiere was to be in Paris. Well, I wasn't very happy about it, but there was nothing I could do. Besides, I reasoned, London was as important a city for ballet as Paris. I could tell Balanchine was upset, though he never said anything to me.

Apollo was a very hard ballet for me, because I had to stay on the stage all the way through, from my entrance until the end. We stood in a line, waiting our turn to dance our variations. I was last. When Tchernicheva finished her variation, Doubrovska and I jumped forward. When Doubrovska finished her variation, I jumped forward and began mine. The other two muses went offstage, they could run to the wings and collapse and breathe, the way all three of them do today. But I stayed on the stage all the time until my variation, and then I immediately started the adagio. Doubrovska and Tchernicheva didn't come back until the coda.

Apollo was difficult for Lifar, too, because it was such a new approach, different from anything he had ever danced before. In the pas d'action, he had to partner all three of us together.

Today, it's a different ballet. For one thing, the steps for Terpsichore's variation are different. What I danced was lighter, smaller, and quicker. I did fifth, arabesque, fifth, arabesque—nobody does that anymore. And then I did sissonnes—my version was jumpier than the one they dance today. Balanchine changed it when Suzanne Farrell learned the part, because she couldn't jump so well—she's taller than I am, and she couldn't move as fast. For example, in the first part, she goes down in plié and turns on a bent knee in arabesque where I did sissonne en tournant, jumping and turning at the same time. It's the same movement, really, but with a different accent—my accent was up, hers is down.

The adagio I did was the same as every Terpsichore's, but lately I notice that dancers tend to emphasize the angular aspects and accelerate everything in between, which I didn't do. I tried to do one movement like the next, always light, in harmony, so that the angular positions didn't jump out at the

audience. Balanchine was doing something new, but he was not simply trying to shock.

Also, when we all went on the toes and then off the toes onto our heels, I
was as light on my heels as I was on my toes. Now dancers go very light on
the toes but then stamp their feet when they go on their heels. We didn't do
that, and I don't think Balanchine wanted it to be done that way. The idea
was to make all these things part of a whole, not to show the contrast
between them. Going up on the toes was what everybody expected to see in
a ballet, going down on the heels wasn't, but we didn't call attention to it, by
making one movement graceful and the other movement awkward—we
gave each movement equal weight. Our job was to make it look as if we
went on our heels all the time, as if it were not a big event, no more unusual
than opening and closing the arms in pirouette.

We were the first ones to interpret Balanchine's movement, to find that
path. The steps were very difficult to perform. It was for the second generation to take what we had done and build on it. After seeing somebody
else perform a role, you can think, "Oh, I know how I can do it better. . . ."
The dancers who came after us in *Apollo* could look to our performances and
copy what we did or dismiss it. That was their privilege, but not ours—
we had a hard enough time grasping that new style and finding a way to
express it.

On opening night, we all felt the excitement of being in on something
new, regardless of whether we had a success or not. We had molded this ballet ourselves. When we did *Apollo* at the Opéra in Paris, some people were
applauding, some were booing, but it didn't matter—we knew that we had
done something great.

—from *Choura,* with Holly Brubach, 1986

BALLETS 1933
Diana Gould Menuhin

*After leaving the de Basil Ballets Russes, George Balanchine created Ballets 1933 to
present his own new choreography. It lasted for one brief season in Paris and London,
with the money coming from a rich Englishman, Edward James, who wanted to give*

his wife, the Viennese ballet / exotic dancer Tillie Losch, a ballet company to star in. Balanchine featured her in two of the six new works he created: L'Errante *and* Les Sept Péchés Capitaux *(also with Lotte Lenya, whose husband, Kurt Weill, provided the commissioned score). His other new ballets were* Mozartiana, Les Songes, Fastes, *and* Les Valses de Beethoven. *Among the other dancers were Tamara Toumanova, Roman Jasinski, Pearl Argyle, and Diana Gould. Artists who participated included Pavel Tchelitchew (who designed the decor for* L'Errante*), Christian Berard, and André Derain and the composers Darius Milhaud and Henri Sauguet.*

Massine's choreography was basically romantic, large-scale, somewhat like Brahms tinged with the Rockettes at its least worthy, wonderfully expressive and danceable at its best—totally other than Balanchine's work, which was more finely tuned and more private. In Massine's later works for the de Basil Ballets Russes, he was using bigger and bigger canvases, symphonic music, exploiting the exciting techniques of the so-called baby ballerinas, Toumanova, Baronova, and Riabouchinska; so when one looks back across the years to his epoch of the thirties and compares those last two Diaghilev choreographers, one sees that Massine's tradition lies in a direct descent from the *Esmeraldas* and the *Corsaires,* whereas Balanchine marked the beginnings of a completely new vision of the dancer. He was the future; Massine was the final flower of the past.

That, I imagine, was what caused Balanchine's breakaway from de Basil's Ballets Russes. The great good fortune that Edward James was looking for a framework in which to show off his wife, Tilly Losch, and perhaps inject a little life into his failing marriage was the catalyst that brought about Les Ballets 1933.

From the Ballets Russes, Balanchine brought with him the lovely Tamara Toumanova, all of thirteen—or was it fifteen? Anyway, I do remember celebrating her fifteenth birthday repeatedly over the years, which makes it difficult to be exact. What one can easily be exact about was that she was very young, very beautiful, and had that marvellous rock-hard technique that Preobrajenska gave her and Baronova. Together with Toumanova he brought several other "defectors," among whom was Tchinarova of the wonderful long black plaits. Tamara Sidorenko (later Grigorieva) was also with him, a lovely dancer with an enviable memory who could pick up three or four parts in each ballet after watching them once.

With Roman Jasinski as principal male dancer and a little padding from the vast pool of dancers to be found in the various Paris studios, Balanchine had a small but strong company which suited his needs, for he had no use for the old-style corps de ballet, which to him represented a dreary frieze that filled in blank spaces, dressed the stage, and permitted the soloists to catch their wind in the wings.

For Edward, with all his taste, his real vision for painting, it was an ideal moment to try to make a company in the image of Diaghilev, with fresh productions in which great composers and designers created each ballet as a composite whole. I had known him slightly when I understudied Tilly in the part of the Nun in *The Miracle,* and Tilly of course I knew well: naughty, mischievous Tilly with her huge ice-blue eyes and her beautiful, erotic arms and hands; Tilly who ran circles round the fresh-faced, eternally boyish Edward; Tilly who was the despair of Balanchine, who found his inspiration totally blocked when it came to devising a ballet for her; Tilly who finally triumphed in *L'Errante* and *Anna-Anna* (as *Les Sept Péchés Capitaux* was retitled for London).

Balanchine and Edward James wanted, after the Paris season, to bring the company to London—a stroke of luck for me. Equity demanded that two English soloists and two other dancers be engaged, so Rambert offered Prudence Hyman and myself plus Elisabeth Schooling and Betty Cuff. The start was ominous. Pru and I had no sooner arrived at Calais than it appeared we were illegal, as no one had thought of giving us a "permis de travail," and customs refused to let us go one foot further for fear of our polluting France as illegal immigrants. Furious, I asked for the telephone, rang Edward at the Prince de Galles, luckily found him, whereupon he apologized, saying he would send someone down by early morning next day. Pru and I had a marvellous dinner in the Hotel Terminus, famed for its pommes de terres soufflées and, thus assuaged, climbed into bed (very dingy and a bit suspect) and slept like logs. Next day, permit arrived, we went on to Paris, where Pru and I would be staying at my grandmother's.

Following morning we four presented ourselves with apprehension to Balanchine, holed up in a very small studio with a linoleum floor, no ventilation, and the thermometer mounting toward ninety degrees outside (one-hundred degrees inside). We were received coolly, George giving us all a sharp look of appraisal with that ornithological head of his. Trim and neat, he was dressed like Massine in black alpaca trousers and a white shirt, but there the similarity ends: no banked fires, no blazing eyes—very cool face, highly intelligent look, aquiline nose, so that the whole head resembled two profiles neatly stuck together.

He launched into the barre, conducting from the upright piano on which he played wonderful improvisations of jazz and semi-classical mixtures. But he was obviously all set to kill the newcomers, to grind them into the dust if need be. Not twelve battements on each side but fifty, and the same with every other combination. We came to a slow and steady boil, agonizingly determined to keep the Union Jack flying. After that punishing barre, complicated enchaînements with George pounding away and us sweating from every pore.

At last we were freed and able to take in our colleagues. Toumanova was thirteen? Fifteen?–anyway, almost still a child, with a beautiful Georgian face atop a rather plump body. Poor lamb, her mother had wrapped her in rubber, with the result that we used to stand her in an enamel basin when she stripped, and the sweat poured off her in floods. She was sweet and warmhearted, and we soon became friends.

At the end of that week, Balanchine suddenly smiled and we knew we'd been accepted. We moved out of the Black Hole of Calcutta and were transferred to the rehearsal room above the stage at the Champs-Elysées and began being allotted roles. Tilly was there, looking a little out of place, and we must have appeared, if not formidable, certainly a little alien to her, for all of us were in our teens, all highly trained technically, and this must have been the first time Tilly had had to compete with such a company. Trained only in the Central European school of modern dancing, she had carved herself her own special and very successful niche in the Cochran revues in London and finally, a year before, as the Nun in *The Miracle*. A beautiful mover with very supple and expressive hands, she relied upon her own brand of sensuality and so was not exactly equipped to face such a band of young and strong dancers.

In the end the Tilly problem was more than successfully solved in two works. *Anna-Anna* was a typically thirties-Berlin production concocted by Kurt Weill and Bertolt Brecht on the subject of the seven deadly sins. Some of us loathed it because any leftover dancers (like yesterday's cold meat) had to pull on huge cloaks which covered the head as well and rush on brandishing poles vaguely and exuding either sin or the punishment of same— Tamara Sidorenko and I never did find out what we were doing. And in *L'Errante,* Payel Tchelitchew and Balanchine, having draped the stage with four kilometers of white silk and flooded it with very ingenious lighting, put Tilly into a marvellous dress of emerald green satin with a great wide train, which we would gather up in the wings and let fly as Tilly ran on looking suitably bewildered. (When we got to London, yet another of those rows endemic to the ballet erupted when the theater firemen at the Savoy insisted that the white silk be fireproofed and it all turned a dirty yellow.)

To be working at last in Paris, in the very theater, the Champs-Elysées, that had seen the premiere of *Sacre,* was thrilling. The rehearsals were strangely spasmodic, sometimes in the afternoon, sometimes at night. As one was never sure what was going to be rehearsed, one simply turned up— and anyway, to watch Balanchine at work was no time wasted. I remember one rehearsal in the upstairs room to which Josephine Baker came, almost unrecognizable with clothes on and no bananas.

Gradually the ballets took shape: *Mozartiana, Les Songes, Les Sept Péchés Capitaux, Fastes,* and *L'Errante,* to which George suddenly added a sixth: *Les Valses de Beethoven.* Based on the Greek myth about Daphne's spurning of Apollo, it was choreographed mainly for Tilly and Jasinski. A rich and not very gifted South American called Emilio Terry designed a dotty decor and hideous costumes. There were the four elements: Earth, Air, Fire, and Water. I was Earth, in a deplorable sort of chiton in Bovril-colored chiffon (Old Mother Manure, I called myself). I would stand dismally for hours while the magnificent Karinska, dripping amethysts, draped and redraped, muttering the while, somewhat hampered by a mouthful of pins: "Ach, Boje moi! Kak oojasniya"—which, meaning "Oh my God, how awful!," did nothing to cheer me on my way.

On the opening night, trembling with nerves, we were still awaiting the head-dresses backstage, the audience clapping with impatience and panic all around. At last Karinska arrived in a flurry and a taxi. She handed me a monstrous sort of cairn at least two feet high and made of plaster and mud. I put it on my head, tears pouring down my face, and appealed to George. Mine was the first solo, and I was to be found reclining on something or other (a plaster couch, I think) extremely uncomfortable as the curtain lifted, from which I had to spring into fourth position on pointe, flinging the top half of my body back as far as it would go (Balanchine had discovered that I had a double-jointed back). What was to happen to this monument on my head is anybody's guess and very obviously *my* funeral. Fortunately, George lifted the thing off, wiped my tears, gave me a kiss and a gentle push—"Go on—go on, Dianotchka"—and I ran, knees knocking, to take up my lonely position onstage and try not to listen to the mounting anger of the derisive applause. Despite lovely solos for Prudence as Air, Sidorenko as Fire, and Ouchkova as Water, the ballet did not set the theater alight and was dropped. No one really minded, for the difficulty of turning Daphne into a laurel bush proved insurmountable. I remember a whole lot of messing about with green branches made of paper leaves, Tilly trying to hold them in such a way that it would appear that the metamorphosis from nymph to shrub had really taken place; not all the wistful wonder and rolling of those ice-blue eyes by Tilly did much to convince the very chic audience that it was not a rather sorry affair. Farewell, Mother Manure!

The real excitement began much earlier, though, when we got out of the rehearsal studio and onto the stage and into our dressing rooms. At last one saw the various collaborators Boris Kochno, Balanchine, and Edward James had brought together: André Derain, with his enormous, casklike belly and his jolly bulging eyes; "Bébé" Bérard, all mince and wince (he was perpetually having toy rages and being offended); "Pavlik" Tchelitchew, with his beautiful, haggard, romantic face; "Nika" Nabokov, a marvellous Russian with a mane of dark blond hair and witty blue eyes. These latter two would take me all over Paris on various purposeless and very Russian outings to see friends who were usually absent or to chatter with American expatriates and have tea. (Tchelitchew would read my hand: "Dianotchka, you have the palm of a very old lady!") And there were Henri Sauguet, always smiling and pleasant, and Darius Milhaud, a big, lemon-colored face and dreamy black eyes. All of them would be walking up and down the stalls or watching their ballets, discussing changes and adjustments with Balanchine; and I realized how privileged I was to belong to this moment of creation: not one stale, taken-out-of-the-cupboard-and-dusted-over ballet; all fresh or rarely heard music, fresh designs, fresh ideas. It is an earnest of Kochno's grip as well as Balanchine's genius that any of it came to fruition. There were moments when one felt a certain lack of roots, of the security that the well-tried ballets gave, a sensation of giddiness at the almost blinding vision, the newness of it all—so many conceptions, so many precarious births, so much peril taken quite calmly. For I cannot recall one angry word from George as he took us through the steps, the enchaînements, the solos, the pas de deux, adjusting, readjusting here and there. One day, while we were walking together in London, he said, "You know, to my mind, ballets should be only topical—disposable. Once they have lasted a season, they should be thrown away." I expostulated, finding the idea a little troubling—a step too far away from the ancient crustaceans.

After Paris, with its "Assistance très élégante," we arrived in London to perform at that stiff little theater the Savoy. By then I was dancing the Demi-Monde in *Songes* and the blue Saltateur in *Fastes*. Edward, fearful of the coming competition from de Basil's Ballets Russes at the Alhambra and hearing of a projected appearance of Serge Lifar at the Aldwych, nobbled the latter to join us and give a number of performances to be inserted on various nights. Lifar brought with him Nikitina, Doubrovska, Slavinsky, and a few other leading members of the defunct Diaghilev company. At Lifar's first performances with us, he raised the fury of both audience and critics by performing *L'Après midi d'un faune* in solitary grandeur, without the lovely frieze of nymphs. Edward approached him; they had a resounding row and came to blows in the foyer of the Savoy Hotel, after which pleasant exchange Sergei relented sufficiently to allow the presence of the chief Nymph, a role I had learnt from Woizikovsky, and to accept me. All afternoon I hung anxiously about the theater hoping for a rehearsal; finally, I went to Lifar's dressing room in frightened desperation. No rehearsal, no time—just do the part—enter the stage from the OP (opposite prompter) side *there,* he said, jabbing at the score. Nasty fellow! So I went on, trembling. Unfortunately, Sergei had not been to class since Diaghilev's death some four years before, and had developed a fine wobble in the very difficult parallel stance on demipointe, in which idiom the whole choreography is written. Facing him, nose to nostril, while he yawed from side to side, I was forced to fix my eyes on the proscenium arch to keep my own balance and not look at the malicious glare from those eyes of his, moving from east to west like the hand on a metronome.

I have never enjoyed a performance less. Nor did it improve with the two subsequent performances. Sad to get such an opportunity and to be so disillusioned. Lifar had gone to seed and was evidently proud of it.

I have zigzagged from London to Paris to London and back, because, seen down the wrong end of a telescope of almost half a century ago, scattered memories weld the two seasons together, making an all-over whole in which the contrasting elements, while to a certain extent melding, nonetheless emerge clearer as the flesh of immediate experience falls away and the bone structure remains.

Paris had been a heady few weeks, watching the evolution of so many recently conceived ideas as they took form and put on substance; being instructed in new rules by Balanchine; seeing the coming-together of composer, designer, librettist, and choreographer, all creating from scratch, as it were. *Mozartiana* alone used an old score intact; the music for *Les Valses de Beethoven* was odds and ends orchestrated by Nabokov; while *L'Errante* was a pastiche of Schubert, including the "Wanderer" Fantasy, put together by Koechlin.

The impression that remains is one of a season of great distinction that was more like an exhibition in motion than a run-of-the-mill ballet season with its draconian hours of work: class, rehearsal, and eight performances a week, entailing fifteen hours a day minimum. Here we danced on specific nights; the repertory was small: six ballets to start with, five when *Valses de Beethoven* was dropped. Balanchine worked with a loose hand—no shouting, no commands, simply showing the steps, correcting, adjusting with a precision and a musical perception that were the joy of any dancer who has had to struggle with intractable arrangements illfitting the measure and the rhythm, cutting across phrases and melodies, twisting instincts and one's mind in the process.

Here was a logical and utterly musical mind. After all, Balanchine had first studied music in Russia, and it showed in everything he created. He used the human body as a musical instrument, preferring the female dancer to the male, and above all the tall dancer, who interpreted his long lines the better. One has only to recall Doubrovska in *Le fils prodigue*, where he pulled her lovely legs like so much soft toffee, to recognize the innovations that he, supported by Diaghilev, had introduced already in those last years under that magician—and start again to wonder how much further forward this modern development would have gone had not Diaghilev died comparatively young and creative ballet in the big companies gone to earth and nearly to dust?

Which brings me to the final curtain of the London season. Jasinski had injured his foot, so to my delight Balanchine danced with me in *Songes'* Demi-Monde sequence (wrongly attributed to another dancer in the beautiful program-cum-catalog of the Brighton exhibition). . . .

Another, less fond memory is of the Savoy, where most of the dressing rooms are out of earshot of the stage. Unaware that *Fastes* was about to begin, I was happily slacking when Balanchine burst in and said, "Diana, the Ephèbe!"—as we then called the Saltateurs. He shovelled me into the tights while I smeared my face with blue; fastening my hipbelt, I tore out and down the stairs to hear about two bars remaining before my entrance from the upstage OP corner. Panting, I dashed across behind the drop and erupted onstage only to find in my nightmare that I had come on about two bars early and almost collided with my partner, Tamara Sidorenko, as the other Ephèbe (all-over peach). With a twist in midstage we managed to avoid a head-on crash, but I shook with anguish until I could get offstage and apologize to both George and Tamara. It is one of the classical bad dreams of all stage people to miss an entrance, and I had virtually done so; I loathed the Savoy Theatre even more after that.

After the final performance we had a party in one of those Bloomsbury hotels where dancers always stayed, partly because they were inexpensive and cozy and partly because they turned a blind eye on those strange combinations and permutations that comprise the looser terms of "marriage" according to the Russian code.

Balanchine took me for a walk round and round the square afterwards in the warm July night. "Dianotchka," he said, "today a man came to see me, an American man, and said he could offer me a school and company if I go to America—would you please come?" Longing to say yes but young and frightened at such a long leap into what might be the dark, this idiotic English virgin said no. Even though we must have circled that square a dozen times and Balanchine pleaded and I was torn in two, my fear and my cowardice won, and sadly we returned to the hotel and said goodbye.

History knows the rest: the American was Lincoln Kirstein, and Balanchine, deservedly, never looked back.

—from *Ballet Review,* Fall 1988

CLYTEMNESTRA
Paul Taylor

Martha Graham's most ambitious dance work, Clytemnestra *premiered in 1958 at the Adelphi Theater in New York. The commissioned score was by Halim El-Dabh, the decor by Isamu Noguchi. The cast included Graham in the title role, Bertram Ross, Helen McGehee, Ethel Winter, Yuriko, and Paul Taylor.*

The overture is starting and the curtain's soon to levitate. Other dancers and I are waiting in the wings, some chatting nervously, others trying to get in the mood to, as it says in the program, rape Troy. Tiny Martha is standing alone upstage center on a blue-carpeted ramp, looking very calm. In fact, her stillness might be taken for complacency, even boredom. But it's not. She's a monumental mote, a doughty dot, an electron at the quiet center of a spinning atom. Her hairdo is towering higher than usual, and her giant eyelashes have been heavily beaded with wax. Protruding from under her brocaded skirt is a big toe which, either from so many years spent dancing or from being crammed into too many small shoes, or both, has grown in an unnatural direction, crowding neighboring toes, and now slanting sharply outward. Eyes cast down in Buddha-like contemplation; her face is as durable as a porcelain mask, one that is to express Clytemnestra's story of treachery, murder, disgrace, and final rebirth. Her concentration breaks for a moment, and she turns her head to the wings to hush us with a queenly hiss.

I've probably mentioned that my feelings for her aren't simple? Love, awe, fascination are spliced to a dimmer view, and, once in a while, stresses tug at my commitment to her. Yet, right now, seeing her stand so monumentally, so alone, I feel nothing but admiration for this small, feisty woman who, for at least thirty-two years, has been lifting dance to new heights. Besides, her knowing eyes have seen something wonderful in me, and I'm determined to be worthy.

Two curtains lift, one after the other (overpaid stagehands finally get the order right). An interesting but not quite Mycenean throne sits downstage right. There are two singers, one at each side of the apron. A third curtain—

a row of vertical golden bands—rises, and Martha stands revealed. The audience scrambles to their feet and welcomes her warmly.

Drowned out by this ovation, Halim El Dabh's music becomes inaudible. Considerable delay before Martha's first move. When the commotion quiets, she begins a series of repeated clenched-hand gestures and in-place treadings, almost matching herself to the corresponding thonks in the music. When the music goes on to something else, however, she soon goes right along with it, doing only one or two thonks too many before regaining her bearings.

Precision in a lesser dancer is not nearly as great as Martha's inaccuracies. Personally, I like her mismatching of steps to music, for then the steps don't seem so obviously phrased. I also enjoy seeing her choreograph her body into snarls and then find such wonderful ways to get out of them.

But right now I'm putting my mind on the rape of Troy. It's the only part of the dance when I'll need to be in unison with the other dancers, and it's quite a challenge. Something about the way I move—shades of timing, force of attack, not sure what—makes me stick out in a group, and even though I've worked hard at it, fitting myself in has been a problem. Maybe it's because my approach or mental outlook isn't the same. Being an ex-swimmer, I remember how nice it feels to press against water. I can't resist using air in the same way. Counterbalancing the imaginary weight of space makes my body feel that it's accomplishing something. Though I've tried many times to dance with less pressure and weight, that always feels weak, willowy, and extremely stingy. Martha's probably just about given up on me being in unison, and, to tell the truth, I don't really mind. But tonight I'm determined to do my best to rape Troy exactly like all the other guys.

They dance great—Bert Ross, David Wood, Gene McDonald—even the others who only get to clutch spears, tote dead bodies off, and such. Except for David, all of us are six feet or over; all move forcefully and archaically; all conform to the concept of a flat, two-dimensional figure that seems to be Martha's idea of a man. Naturally, her dances stem from her own point of view. We're usually stiff foils, or something large and naked for women to climb up on. A few of us would like to be more 3-D and think that less beefcake would be a good idea, but have been scared to say so.

The girls—Ethel Winter, Helen McGehee, Matt Turney, Yuriko, and the newer ones, such as resplendent Ellen Siegel—are all terrific, too. Helen, usually cast in ingenue roles, is wonderfully wiry and vengeful as Electra; Yuriko, movingly dramatic as Iphigenia; Ethel, glorious as Helen of Troy; Matt, always a favorite with audiences and company members alike, makes a gracefully broken and appealing Cassandra (unison dancing isn't her strongest point, either, so she's easy for me to identify with).

All of us have been thoroughly trained at Martha's school in a methodically developed vocabulary. We are seasoned performers with strong techniques and understand Martha's choreographic aims clearly. None of us are all that young; the majority have had college educations. Most of the men started their training later than the women, in our early twenties.

What happens for two hours after *Clytemnestra*'s opening curtain is to be described, photographed, analyzed in depth, and stored in libraries for future reference. There seems little left for me to add, except a few unrecorded, and probably unimportant, impressions. Most have to do with feelings and sensations difficult to describe, ones that, even if described, may seem unlikely; yet they're true, or as true as remembered feelings can be.

Inside, at a million m.p.h. or more, corpuscles are zipping around and filling me with a sensation of great speed. Otherwise, I'm experiencing a feeling of superslow ooziness. This, of course, has little to do with actual rates of speed but is because of something that, for lack of a better term, I'll call the dancer's clock. Focus or concentration makes time different for when you dance and for when you don't. No ordinary timepiece, like a drug, this clock stretches stage seconds, implanting eons in between—also compresses performing years into an outrageously short span. So I'm both speeding and oozing at once, scooting through space, slithering through time, eating it up and savoring each swallow. A flick of the foot and I'm airborne.

Bright stage light is coming from all angles. Clinically. Like under a microscope, or on a vast, borderless desert. Basking there. Adding to the hot light, internal rays are traveling out through each of my pores.

Besides the music, such sounds as street traffic, murmuring from the wings, and burbling from the plumbing are magnified to a high pitch. Lint on a drape, the flavor of sweat, the odor of a stagehand's ground-out cigar are noticeably present. Hearing, sight, taste, touch, scent have become paranormal. Present is also a sixth sense—let's call it will power. I can will myself into midair, hang there forever. By means of another, even more mysterious power, I'm able to control what the audience sees, can direct their eyes to any particular part of my body: my left shoulder . . . my right elbow . . . both bunions at the same time. Anywhere. When a dancer is hungry, determined, or motivated enough, anything is possible.

Steps are Aegisthus's voice. Lunges bellow, spins scream, skitterings whisper insidiously. From someplace down low a carefully controlled spasm ripples up through torso, arm, and finally out through the tip of a recently acquired limb—Aegisthus's black leather whip. It's as if he's saying, "Look, everybody. Slime! Fury! Sadism! Dementia!" There is no doubt in my mind that I've been given a franchise on wickedness.

Great greedy gulps from an empty Noguchi wine cup. Rapturous reelings, slow darts. While in the midst of a cartwheel, I study the details of an upside-down proscenium. Hedonistic burning sensation of soles whisking across boards. Softness of a leap's superslow spongy landing. Softness of blue-carpeted ramp against rump. Softness of featherweight Martha in my arms.

For her safety, I shift into low gear, support her gently, treat her as spun glass. According to the whorls of my fingertips, her silky-smooth veil feels roughly corrugated.

Wantonly, we plot the murder of Agamemnon and the usurpation of his throne.

Aegisthus motions: "There is the dagger. Take it."

Queen motions: "Oh no, I could not possibly."

Aegisthus motions: "Sure you can. Just let me help you to place your hand on it. It's over here in a pocket of the throne somewhere. Somewhere here. . . . Rats! The stupid prop man's forgotten to preset it. No, here it is after all. Grab on, O Queen."

Queen motions: "Mercy, it does feel nice. I do like daggers."

Aegisthus motions: "Wait a minute. Your dress has gotten caught up on something. May I be of assistance? There. Now you can go do your dagger dance."

Leaving me sitting on the throne with the purple veil in my lap, she begins a long, demanding solo. Since I'm downstage in bright light, it might be easy to draw the audience's attention away from her, but this wouldn't be cricket.

I've figured out that I'm here because she needs a strong presence onstage, a kind of energy bounce to help keep her from lagging, to be a presence for her to battle. I should keep alive for her, stay in character, yet do nothing distracting. I've placed a safety pin to mark a place in the veil that I'll be needing to hold in order to manipulate it right. Keeping my face down so that it's in shadow, I slowly, unobtrusively inchworm the cloth through my fingers, maintaining the tension until, safety pin found, her solo completed, I fling the veil over both of us and spin her off.

When the curtain goes up on Act III, Clytemnestra and I are draped over her bed. She's having a bad dream. I'm going to be there for thirty minutes or so, so I've tried to get myself into as comfortable a position as possible, which isn't simple, the bed being not exactly a bed but one of Noguchi's stony and treacherously tilted abstractions.

I'm sleeping the best I can when suddenly, from out of the blue, Martha starts pummeling my stomach. I'm thinking that maybe she's come up with better things to do than the planned ones—something that the older dancers have warned me about. (Ad-libbing at premieres is not unknown.

Later on, things get more precise.) I flick her fists away, then roll over and go back to sleep. She likes it when you play along with her. She soon comes back to pummel some more, and I keep flicking, rolling over, and trying to keep myself from falling off the bed. After a while she leaves me alone and goes off to dance with Bert, Helen, and Gene.

After the final curtain, on her way to her dressing room, she says, "Pablo, I noticed what you were doing on the bed. Naughty! Let's keep it in."

Clytemnestra is a resounding success. Both public and press immediately accept it as a masterpiece. Among many other tributes, Martha is praised for her merciless integrity (no mention of merciless pins) and for being a colossal figure in a theater of her own intellectually preconceived goals. John Martin of the *Times* writes that "the girl still holds promise." A more heartening and sincere tribute could scarcely be paid to her.

Her company is also extolled, and I'm singled out for praise. My part of the duet, with partial thanks to the safety pin, is deemed a deep characterization. This is very gratifying, since my role, though an important one, isn't as large as I would've liked and could have been lost in the shuffle.

The last performance over, I pack theater gear, return to wet sneakers, cold loft, Tabby's mouse patrol. . . . Within a batch of fan mail is an eviction notice from the Housing Authority, accusing me of illegal living. I relegate it to the trash basket and hide the hot plate.

—from *Private Domain*, 1987

FIREBIRD
Maria Tallchief

There have been numerous treatments of Stravinsky's magnificent Firebird *score. The first, and most historically important, was Fokine's version for Diaghilev's 1910 Paris season. In 1949, Balanchine acquired from Sol Hurok the splendid decor Chagall had produced for Ballet Theatre and staged a new version for his then-wife, Maria Tallchief, and Francisco Moncion. Tallchief's blazing performance and Balanchine's exciting choreography gave New York City Ballet its first smash hit, turning around the public's perception of the company.*

One night George and I were dining at the Russian Tea Room when Sol Hurok, the Russian impresario and a regular at the restaurant, approached our banquette and sat down. Mr. Hurok was a bear of a man who wielded a lot of influence in the world of music and ballet. Russian artists in particular were his passion. For some reason, whenever he saw me he always made a big fuss and acted as if he had discovered me. Actually, the` dancer he discovered was my sister, Marjorie. It was he who arranged for her to join Ballet Theatre after watching her in class with David Lichine. He always seemed to confuse us, as if mine was the career in which he had played an important role.

"George," he said, getting comfortable in the banquette, "don't you think it's time to have your wife dance *Firebird*?"

The question seemed to drop from the clouds, but George nodded and said, "Yes, why not?"

"Ah, wonderful, wonderful." Mr. Hurok sighed.

My reaction was pure terror. Until then most of the Balanchine ballets I had appeared in were works with which audiences were unfamiliar. Yes, parts I had danced in *Ballet Imperial* or *Baiser de la fée* had been performed by others and had their own tradition, but only a few people had seen them, and I couldn't really be compared with anyone else.

A well-known classic, *Firebird* was Stravinsky's first major success. Michel Fokine choreographed the ballet in 1910 in Paris, and Tamara Karsavina danced the title role. For years the ballet was associated with Karsavina's name. Later, several versions of *Firebird* were presented in America, including one at Ballet Theatre in 1945, in which Alicia Markova enjoyed success in the title role and for which Marc Chagall designed the highly praised sets and costumes. Could I live up to that memorable interpretation?

By the time that Mr. Hurok brought up the subject, a revival was ready to move beyond the planning stage. As usual, only money stood in the way: George and Lincoln had been told by Mr. Baum that the City Center budget wasn't large enough to cover the costs for a ballet like *Firebird*. The price of the decor alone would be astronomical. The person who made the production possible was Mr. Hurok. As it turned out, it had been he and not Ballet Theatre who paid for the Chagall sets and costumes in 1945, and so they belonged to him. Once the production dropped out of the repertory, Hurok put them in storage. George admired Chagall's designs and wanted them for his production. If he could obtain them from Hurok for a reasonable fee, the City Center's limited budget wouldn't be a problem.

After the conversation at the Russian Tea Room, George persuaded Mr. Baum to telephone Hurok. A deal was quickly struck: The fee for the sets and costumes was $4,500, a sum that Baum could afford.

* * *

FALL 1949 WAS a busy time in the New York ballet world. Ballet Russe de Monte Carlo and Ballet Theatre had seasons and both sold well, but the true excitement was the opening of the Sadler's Wells Ballet from England. Appearing in America for the first time, the company was dancing the complete *Sleeping Beauty* at the Metropolitan Opera House on opening night in a season that included several other classic ballets. Before the company had danced one step, advance order requests for tickets were breaking box office records. People were excited about seeing the British dancers. Moira Shearer, one of the principals, had become world famous because of her role in the movie *The Red Shoes,* and of course George and I were personally acquainted with Margot Fonteyn, Sadler's Wells's leading ballerina.

Typically, George wished the company well. He never viewed the competition as a threat. He believed that the more good ballet in New York, the better, and he hoped the Sadler's Wells repertory might even pave the way for audiences to appreciate our *Firebird.* But he wasn't taking any chances. Our production had to be perfect.

The story of *Firebird* is simple. Prince Ivan captures the mysterious Firebird who gives him a magic feather so he'll release her. He can use this feather to call her whenever he's in danger. Ivan falls in love with the Tsarevna, who becomes imprisoned by the monster Katschei. Using the feather, Ivan summons the Firebird, who helps him kill the monster. The marriage of Ivan and the Tsarevna is celebrated in a grand processional.

When we started rehearsing the ballet, George sketched a few steps and outlined my gestures to show me how he wanted me to move. I watched him closely and did my best to follow his gestures, but I was having trouble. In order to keep me from exaggerating my movements, he started imitating the way I was flapping my arms. Upset, he flailed about energetically and threw his back out. He could hardly walk and had to cancel rehearsal. He then went home and lay down on our bed. That night was the Sadler's Wells opening he'd been anticipating with great enthusiasm. He could barely sit up straight. It was my fault, I thought, but he never blamed me.

That night, Lew Christensen escorted me and George stayed home in bed. Lew had recently joined New York City Ballet as ballet master. He had danced for the American Ballet in the 1930s and was devoted to George, who, in turn, adored him. I was glad he was my date for the opening.

The atmosphere at the Metropolitan that night was fraught with excitement. The audience expected something out of the ordinary, and they weren't disappointed. As soon as the curtain rose, everyone was astonished. *The*

Sleeping Beauty sets and costumes by Oliver Messel were colorful and opulent; the British dancers performed the mime sequences with great authority; the Tchaikovsky score, played in full for the first time, added to the magic. But Margot made the greatest impression of all. She was radiant as Princess Aurora. I'll never forget the effect she made during the rose adagio. The audience was in ecstasy. Most of the evening, I sat in my seat with a knot in my stomach.

Oh, I thought. The next big opening in town will be our *Firebird*. How will it compare to this?

I was miserable.

When I got home, George wanted to hear all about the evening. He was delighted. *The Sleeping Beauty* was a favorite; he was happy it was beautifully received.

IN THE MORNING, George was still in pain, but had recovered sufficiently to work. He was keen to finish the pas de deux. It was fascinating to get inside his mind. The port de bras he was devising were sinuous and Oriental in atmosphere. The partnering was especially intricate, including a precarious moment that Frank [Francisco Moncion] and I knew would give us trouble later when we danced it on unfamiliar stages if we didn't have enough time to rehearse it properly. George refused to stop to explain each detail or make adjustments. By late afternoon of the next day, we were starting on my entrance variation.

At the time, George had been teaching class every day, giving very difficult combinations in addition to instructing us. As soon as he started creating my solo I realized he was including everything he'd been teaching in the studio in one endless variation. He had always warned against using class to choreograph, but this time he wasn't taking his own advice. The long variation contained a succession of turned-in movements that reflected the music and suggested a frightened bird in flight, and had to be executed quickly and effortlessly. I knew it would be necessary for me to build a reserve of stamina for this variation because for two minutes all I did was jump. What made it even more difficult was that the variation went into the pas de deux without a break.

George finished the variation the next day, then began setting the section in which I danced the berceuse, the scene that occurs after the Firebird has helped the prince defeat the monsters. Most of the berceuse is made up of pas de bourrée, a delicate traveling step, embellished by beautiful port de bras. In this section, however, the arm movements contrasted with those of the pas de deux. They were simple and traditional—the kind I'd studied with Nijinska—and revealed the tender, lyrical side of the Firebird. The berceuse quickly became my favorite part of the ballet.

Once he was finished with the Firebird's choreography, George went to work on the "Dance of the Princesses" and the scene with the monsters. Left alone, I went into another studio and worked on the variation by myself, using old, scratchy 78s, doing the steps over and over, trying to master them so that onstage I'd be able to perform them in one seamless flow. Working so hard I began to feel as if *Firebird* were going to be my death. As opening night approached I started feeling ill. I was pale and losing weight. Elise Reiman became worried.

"You have to eat more, Maria. You look like a skeleton."

"I'm trying to, but it hurts to swallow."

I was also having trouble breathing. Now George became concerned. I knew what he thought of doctors, but he wanted me to see one. It was tonsillitis. My tonsils were inflamed and they had to be removed as soon as possible. The doctor said he could perform the surgery on a chair in his office. George accompanied me on the day. After the operation, I fainted dead away. George took me home in a cab and sent me straight to bed. I lay there for two days trying to get the sleep I needed to recuperate, but I was so worried about *Firebird* I hardly rested at all.

THE FINAL DRESS and lighting rehearsal for *Firebird* was scheduled for the morning of the premiere, November 27, 1949, and it was painful. I was still feeling the effects of the tonsillectomy and was moving slower than usual, but I arrived at the theater before dawn to be ready for rehearsal at 7 a.m. I never really knew why we had to be there so early. The company danced on Mondays and Tuesdays only, and the ungodly hour was most likely the only time the theater was available.

A morning person, I didn't mind starting work at that time. What's more, I knew we desperately needed to rehearse. We hadn't danced the ballet with the orchestra, my costume was still being made, and this would be the first time that the Chagall decorations would be hanging in place.

Frank Moncion and I presented ourselves onstage, and George told us to begin. Unbelievably, not only was this the first we were doing it with the orchestra, but it was the first time the production was lit. All that shone on me was a single golden follow spot. It created the effect George wanted, but it took getting used to because it made a rim of light around me beyond which I couldn't see a thing, not even Frank.

When the music started to play we began to dance. Once my variation was over I started feeling better. Frank, however, was in agony. It was hard for him to get going at that hour, and since it was dark onstage, having to grope around made it even worse. Surrounded by blackness, with brilliant spotlights blinding us, we found that the difficult parts now seemed impossible. Later I discovered that George had specifically requested dim lighting. He was afraid that if the Chagall sets were brightly illuminated they'd detract from the dancing.

Nevertheless, the rehearsal was progressing smoothly. After the first arabesque, I turning to face Frank and giving him my hands, I performed a glissade, a traveling step. Then after a preparation, while he continued moving, I went flying through space and threw myself into his arms. The force of my jump almost knocked him over. Somehow he managed to catch me, but he staggered from the shock. George had invented the movement; there seemed to be no balletic term to describe it adequately.

I thought to myself, Thank God for all those tumbling classes at Mr. Belcher's.

But Frank was quite upset. He had a fiery temperament, and acted as if I had smashed into him on purpose. He sulked for the rest of the rehearsal, refusing to speak. I guess it was his way of dealing with his nerves, but it unsettled me. Everyone else was rather nonchalant. No one said, "Oh, that was wonderful, Maria," or "What a lovely variation," or "It's going to be great." I was sure we were headed for disaster.

I left the theater and went home to rest. Often after class and rehearsal, I'd go back to our apartment to lie down and relax my muscles, but I was never able to sleep. The thought of what was ahead of me on any given night would always keep me awake. After a few minutes I'd jump up and rush back to the theater. As soon as I arrived, I'd do my own barre, then practice the most difficult steps I had to dance that night and hope all would go well.

The day of the *Firebird* premiere, I wasn't home more than ten minutes before I ran out the door and rushed back to the City Center. My costume had arrived from Barbara Karinska's studio, and I tried it on. It was the one element of the *Firebird* decor that hadn't been designed by Chagall.

As soon as I tried it on, Madame Karinska and George began fussing over me, tugging and pulling. They didn't like the way it fit, but nothing they did improved it. They also didn't like the headdress, which had arrived ten minutes before curtain and was pinned in place. By then it was too late to change anything. Standing in the wings, I realized that I had never rehearsed in the feathered crown, and I worried that it might fall off. But what could I do? The curtain went up and I jumped out onto the stage.

Once the ballet began, I stopped thinking about good or bad, success or failure, and just danced as well as I could. In spite of all my practice, the variation was very difficult, and I was completely out of breath. But when we started the pas de deux, I felt secure. Standing upstage, I took an extra breath and then made the flying leap into Frank's arms. Suddenly there I was being held by him upside down, my head practically touching the floor. An audible sigh rose in the audience. We heard it. It was as if they could barely believe what they had seen. One second before I had been at one end of the stage standing upright, yet now here I was at the other side, suspended in Frank's arms. No one could see how it had been done. I must have flown.

This was one of the effects George had worked so hard on in rehearsal, and the way he had been able to create that moment was astonishing even to me. I'd become this magical creature, the Firebird, yet I knew I had become the Firebird because George had made me the Firebird. His genius had never been as clear to me as it was in that instant. When we finished the pas de deux the audience applauded so loudly that Frank and I were stunned. We hadn't expected it.

In fact they seemed to be enjoying everything—the scene with the princesses and the monsters, the berceuse, and the final tableau, the wedding scene. In that scene, the music swells to a glorious finish, but since there's no movement and all is still, it's as if there's a hush when the curtain falls. When it did, we all stood there in a state of shock. It was over! But calls had never been rehearsed, and nobody knew quite what to do.

Then the curtain rose again, and as long as I live I'll never forget the roar. A firestorm of applause erupted in the City Center, and the audience was on its feet clapping, stomping, and shouting. We just stood there, dumbfounded. People were screaming, "Bravo!" shouting themselves hoarse. It was pandemonium. The theater had turned itself into a football stadium, and the audience was in a frenzy. In the mezzanine a group of people was standing in the aisles, and every time the curtain came down they started calling out my name until it went up again: "Tallchief! Tallchief! Tallchief! Tallchief!"

When the curtain fell for the ninth or tenth time, they were still cheering. We were all in a daze. Then George took my arm to lead me out in front for a bow. Before going out I looked around for Frank but he had disappeared. He probably thought we weren't going to have any more calls and had gone back to his dressing room. So George and I were out there alone. Perhaps it was fitting that it was just the two of us.

—from *Maria Tallchief,* with Larry Kaplan, 1997

A MIDSUMMER NIGHT'S DREAM
Edward Villella

After the West Coast tour, Balanchine announced that he was choreographing Shakespeare's play *A Midsummer Night's Dream.* My assumption was that I was going to be cast as Puck. I still thought of myself as more of a demi-caractère dancer than anything else and was convinced that this was how Balanchine still saw me. I was in for a surprise. When the casting was announced, I was listed for the role of Oberon, King of the Fairies. I thought there must be some mistake, and I wondered, what could be going through Balanchine's mind? But I took it as a great compliment and hoped he was trying to stretch my range. I was eager to begin working, but found myself waiting around at rehearsals, doing nothing. Oberon is a presence in *A Midsummer Night's Dream,* but except for his big set piece, the scherzo, he's incidental to a lot of the dance action. Balanchine basically choreographed around me. The full company was called to rehearsals on a daily basis, and a great deal of activity was going on in the studio as Balanchine created the first act. But there was nothing for me to do. Once in a while he'd come up to me and say, "Oh, you have an entrance here, but we'll do that later."

I'd shrug and sit down. I never got used. After a while, I would lie down under the piano and doze. I'd fall into a deep sleep and snore away peacefully while all the creativity buzzed around me. Waking up, I'd begin to worry. Was I being treated fairly? But I believed that Balanchine was confident enough in me to postpone our work. He knew I'd pick up the part fast. Still, I felt I was being overlooked. I got more worried when I realized that the pas de deux and the solos were set and everyone had steps but me.

Less than a week before the premiere, Balanchine started choreographing the scherzo in which I had a bravura variation, but most of what he came up with was for the children, young SAB girls. What he gave to me seemed thrown away, even though I could see that the steps themselves were phenomenal—and phenomenally difficult.

"You'll do this and you'll do that," he said as he showed me the steps, "and then you'll make your entrance here and go off and then come back again."

Then he went back to work with the students. The next day, the same. "You know, you'll do couple of steps here," he said. "Don't worry, we'll fix. We'll do later."

I was perplexed. But Stanley Williams had returned from Denmark and was teaching now at SAB.

"How's it going?" Stanley inquired. "What's it like?"

"I don't know," I answered. "Frankly, it's a real pain in the ass. You know, he's choreographing all this great stuff on the kids. They've got the best music. He's hardly doing anything for me."

"But what kind of role is it? Oberon, King of the Fairies . . ." Stanley smiled.

"Please don't make that joke about 'King of the Fairies.' I've heard it too many times."

He was serious now. "Okay. But tell me what it's like."

"Well, I have entrances and exits, but I don't do much."

"What about the scherzo?"

"I start something, and then I run offstage, and the kids come on. And then I come back on and do something and go off again."

Truly, I was in the dark. At no time during rehearsal did I dance the variation from beginning to end. We did it in sections, and the concept of the role was obscure to me. I never sensed the impact of the choreography.

A few days before the premiere, Balanchine pulled the variation together, finalized my exits and entrances, and told me where to mime the action. I had never done mime before in my life.

"Well, now you call Puck," he said.

I did what he asked.

"No, dear. Is this way." He demonstrated in a perfunctory manner and then walked off. I tried to copy what he had shown me. But the manner of the role was completely foreign to me: it was a style I'd never seen, no less ever had to perform. It was not in the New York City Ballet tradition; no one in the company had any previous experience with it at all. I had no idea how to call someone onstage by miming, or how to speak and emote with my face and my eyes, my arms and my hands.

The following day was a full technical run-through of the ballet, the biggest production the company had done since *The Nutcracker:* scenery and lights, orchestra and children, and costumes. It was pandemonium. Nearly everyone was wearing a wig, and nearly all the wigs were coming loose and falling off. The children were getting caught up in the scenery, everyone was bumping into one another, and there wasn't enough space in the wings for so many people to move around freely.

Dressed in a bejeweled tunic with close-fitting sleeves, wearing a flowing, fifteen-foot-long cape and a headpiece, I felt completely out of my depth. The material for the cape was exquisite and delicate. It had a windblown quality and cost two thousand dollars. In today's market, it would cost closer to ten thousand. I had never worked with a cape before and found myself choreographing its movements so that it flowed after me as a continuation of my gesture. I had to devise a way of moving so that I didn't get caught up in the material, or trip over it. The entrance with the butterflies, the young SAB students who carried my train behind me, also had to be coordinated. If they didn't keep up with me as I entered, the cape would jerk my neck and pull me backward off-balance. And the top I wore also presented problems. Made of heavy brocade, and further weighed down by the jewels sewn into it, it fit tightly, with little give or elasticity.

The rehearsal finally started, and I managed to get through the ballet. But I felt as if I were sleepwalking. Every so often during the first act Balanchine would cry out to me, "Now, you enter now! You come on *now*! Oberon! Now!" I came on and danced or looked around.

"What happened, what happened?" I asked when the rehearsal was over. "What did it look like?" I hadn't a clue as to what went on.

A day or so later, Lincoln Kirstein approached Stanley. "Stanley, Villella's going to ruin the ballet," he said. "He doesn't know what he's doing. Too much sleeping under the piano. Balanchine thinks he's going to ruin the ballet. Can you talk to him?"

"Isn't anyone else talking to him?"

"No."

"Why?" Stanley asked.

"Because he's so difficult."

Stanley said, "He's not difficult. Just talk to him."

Lincoln shook his head. "No. He's very difficult, and no one can talk to him except you. Will you do it?"

"Of course," Stanley said. "Sure."

Stanley searched me out. When he found me, he came up to me and asked, "What do you think of the role?"

"I don't have a clue, Stanley," I said. "I hardly know what I'm doing. They taught me all this stuff as of yesterday."

"Well, Lincoln asked me to work with you."

"Great."

"He said Balanchine thinks you're going to ruin the ballet."

"He—!"

Stanley cut me off. "Let's go up to the studio and work."

The first thing he said to me in the room was, "Show me what Mr. B told you to do."

I said, "Well, I come in here. Oberon is looking for Puck. I stop and turn around and call him."

"When?"

"On this count."

"Well, what did Balanchine say? How would you call him?"

"He said, 'Look this way and turn this way.'" I showed him. "'And then you call Puck.'"

"Okay. Show me how you call him."

My words accompanied my gestures. "I walk out, and I look around, and no one's there so I call him."

Stanley shook his head. "No one is going to be able to see that. You have to do it deliberately so that it's visible to the audience. Onstage you have to make the statement and let it rest for a moment so the eye can absorb it." He demonstrated the proper way to do it. I was fascinated. I could see that I had to slow down the movement, give it weight.

Stanley walked me through the ballet start to finish, analyzing the character with me, working out gestures that would be appropriate. Oberon is a monarch. He has to have a regal presence. He's willful, mischievous, not sinister, but spoiled, petulant, used to having his own way. I also got insights from Misha Arshansky's makeup, which he created after talking to Balanchine. The makeup was elaborate but not beautiful. There's an otherworldly, alien-being, elfin quality to Oberon, but he has innate grandeur. He's as much creature as he is a character. At rehearsals I watched Balanchine carefully. He just naturally expressed the character in his carriage, the tilt of the head and the bend of the torso. Finally, the character formed itself in my consciousness.

In further sessions, Stanley and I then went through the steps of the scherzo. Careful analysis of the variation brought the character into focus even more. The variation, I realized, tells you everything: the lightness and speed, the darting quality of the attack, reveal it all. It was full of bubbling little delicacies. Oberon's explosive, but not destructive. Balanchine saw the character in terms of his duality: "scherzo" and "power." This is the big challenge of the variation, to have the power of the jump as well as the requisite speed, and it's probably why people have had so much difficulty with the role. They can summon up the power, but not at the high speed required by the music.

The very first pose Oberon strikes is in fourth position, and the choreography that follows makes a vivid impact. It's majestic in its way. Oberon executes the steps and flies off. In the second sequence of the variation, he does a series of brisées ouvertes, behind. What I tried to do is not move any part of my upper body, just let my legs do all the work, as if I were floating, buzzing over the tops of the trees or above the ground fog.

The final segment of the variation is a sustained line of steps, after which Oberon moves backward, skimming the stage. He's flying over the forest.

Stanley and I went over the variation again and again, and we refined it so that we really understood it. He said to me, "Do you realize what an incredible role you have?"

I did now. It was simply a wonderful variation and I was flattered. I felt that it did three things: it assured me that I could jump and beat and turn; that I could do these things with power and speed; and that I could be purely classical. The fun part was making Oberon a little bit devilish while retaining the classical conception. I had to achieve and project a long, extended line. Dancing at such a level of intensity—and at such velocity—I had to be careful not to tense my muscles, not to hunch my neck and shoulders. Nothing in this role can be done abruptly. No shortcuts can be taken. The steps must be elongated; in preparation for the jump, the plié must be articulated in its entirety. I was beginning to understand the concept of slower being faster: in order to dance quickly, I had to take the time to articulate everything to acquire the speed. . . .

By the opening night of *A Midsummer Night's Dream* I felt fairly confident. When the curtain went up, I went out and gave everything I could. In a way I felt inspired. In the performance, I tried to sum up everything I had learned about the part in my first entrance with Oberon's first grand gesture. My mother told me that on opening night she didn't recognize me when I came out onstage. She thought Oberon looked six foot two. The scherzo stopped the performance, and I received a prolonged ovation. Madame Karinska, a Russian who designed most of the costumes for Balanchine, announced at the party after the premiere that I had scored the biggest success of the evening. . . . That night I was already sore, and the morning after I could barely move. I got up early and went straight to the theater just to get my body going. I knew it was going to take some effort.

No one had shown up yet. The theater was completely empty. Deserted theaters can be cold and empty places, especially in the early hours of the day. All that was lit up this morning was one bare bulb way up in the flies. I walked to the back of the stage near the big loading door, which opened onto Fifty-sixth Street. Steam pipes protruded from the wall, which was covered with crumbling concrete. I held on to one of the pipes and tried to do a few battements tendus. My attention was diverted by a noise, and I turned around and saw Balanchine, who had almost bumped into me.

He had just arrived, wearing his worn and wrinkled trench coat, and carrying a newspaper under his arm. He saw me and nodded and kept walking on his way. Then he stopped, he turned around and looked at me. He walked up to me slowly.

"You know, last night you danced excellent," he said. "Excellent." He stepped closer to me and put his arm around my shoulder. "Excellent." Emotions turned over in my chest. He was certainly not given to such expressions, and not to a man. I was terribly grateful. I felt that he was trying to shorten the distance that had sprung up between us. He nodded, removed his arm, and walked away. Those words were the greatest compliment that Mr. B ever gave me.

—from *Prodigal Son,* with Larry Kaplan, 1992

THE MOOR'S PAVANE
Pauline Koner

José Limón's best known and most enduring work, a compressed retelling of Othello, *had its premiere at Connecticut College in 1949. The music was by Purcell, the costumes by Pauline Lawrence (Limón's wife). Limón himself danced the Moor; Betty Jones, his wife; Lucas Hoving, the Friend; Pauline Koner, the Friend's Wife.*

We stood there on the darkened stage, nervous, intense—in a tight cluster centerstage—a breathless moment—the center spot fading in, our joined hands slowly reaching upward. *The Moor's Pavane* had begun.

There was electricity in the air, on the stage, in the audience. The final chord, two arms reaching forward palms open, the quivering silence crying "This is the tragedy of the Moor." Blackout. A dead hush, then thundering applause. Bravos. *The Moor's Pavane* was born. We stood there slightly stunned, dripping wet.

It was a hot night in August 1949 at Palmer Auditorium of the Connecticut College for Women. This was the second season, there, of the famous dance festival which had originated at Bennington College and had been transplanted to New London.

Until that moment we didn't know whether the piece would be a success. We had worked feverishly till the last minute. I remember Pauline Lawrence, José Limon's wife and costume designer for the company, giving me the heavy orange velvet costume with a voluminous organdy underskirt only the night before dress rehearsal. The dress had a ten-inch additional length in back. When I said, "Pauline, this is impossible," her answer was, "You can handle anything." Panic-stricken, I begged Lucas Hoving to rehearse with me in the costume for the sake of mutual self-preservation. We worked after our regular rehearsal until 4:30 a.m. so that I might literally choreograph for the skirt.

Now as we stood there on the stage, taking bow after bow, my one thought was, "Thank God no costume disaster." I didn't fall flat on my face, and Lucas had skilfully avoided stepping on the dress. The "bravos" continued and it dawned on us, "We have a success."

The Moor's Pavane is very dear to me. First, though it was never public knowledge, José and Doris always allowed me to choreograph my own roles. This worked well for all of us. It kept me creatively active in the company repertoire, saved valuable time, and since my personal style complemented José's, it made for an interesting collaboration. I could offer sharpness, attack, and speed to José's grand, noble, and heroic movement. So aside from the general satisfaction of a successful work for the company, there was a sense of personal creative fulfillment as well. Though I performed the work from 1949 to 1960, I never tired of it. Each performance was an artistic challenge. What subtle nuance could I add, how further enrich the character? As a matter of fact, after being away from it for seven years, I found it as challenging and satisfying as ever when it was revived with the original cast for a performance at the White House in 1967.

The Beginning

It was spring 1949. José announced a new work based on *Othello*—José as Othello, Lucas Hoving as Iago, Betty Jones as Desdemona, and I as Emilia. Though José preferred in the program listing the titles "The Moor," "His Friend," "The Friend's Wife," "The Moor's Wife," in rehearsal we always used the actual names. He decided for the sake of clarity to use only the central plot—Iago maliciously planning to prove Desdemona's infidelity by producing her handkerchief which he claimed to have discovered in another man's possession.

Rehearsals started in New York. Unfortunately, I had other commitments. José decided to begin without me, with Ruth Currier standing in for the unison parts. We would work on my sections when I arrived at New London. He planned the work in a most fascinating way—a suite of formal court dances broken by incidents which revealed both the characters and the plot.

When I arrived, he showed me what he had blocked so far. Somehow what I saw did not convince me dramatically. The handkerchief motif was not clearly defined. That evening, after rehearsal, José and I sat on a large rock at the entrance of Connecticut College and analyzed the matter. We traced a series of dance moves which would create a dramatic sequence.

1. Betty would drop the handkerchief during one of the formal dances, and I would find it.
2. I would then do a short solo highlighting the handkerchief, bringing it into sharp focus.
3. This would be followed by a duet with Lucas, showing him the handkerchief, teasing him, flirting with him, till he would snatch it away.
4. Now he would have the proof (which Emilia does not realize) to show to José, in a duet, where he would produce the handkerchief, convincing Othello that Desdemona has betrayed him.
5. Finally, when Emilia accuses him of murder, he (Othello) would show her the handkerchief.
6. With the realization that Iago was the source of the villainy, she would denounce him.

In the play Iago kills Emilia but José used only a symbolic approach leaving the figures of Iago and Emilia as players pointing up the tragedy to the audience. Now, even in this capsule version of *Othello*, the handkerchief theme was logical and convincing and could motivate the dramatic climax needed to make the ballet credible. I took the handkerchief speech from the play, as a key to Emilia's character and as a motivation for my solo, and began work.

> Emilia: "I am glad I have found this napkin:
> This was her first remembrance from the Moor:
> My wayward husband hath a hundred times
> Woo'd me to steal it: but she loves the token,
> For he conjured her she should ever keep it,
> That she reserves it ever more about her
> To kiss and talk to. I'll have the work ta'en out,
> And give't Iago: what he will do with it
> Heaven knows, not I;
> I nothing but to please his fantasy."

We then worked on the duet with José choreographing Lucas' role while I, using the character as a point of departure, filled in my parts. There were experiments, many discussions among us about the characters and, of course, as always, changes. Finally we were near the end of the work. Time was running out. José was suffering from the usual summer session fatigue, the studio was hot, and inspiration had run dry. At this point Doris Humphrey, our artistic director, with her extraordinary sense of dramatic timing and creative genius, came up with a brilliant solution. The murder would not be revealed. Facing the audience, Iago would spread Emilia's skirt as a screen to hide the act. Then wheeling about, she would suddenly discover Desdemona dead.

I always got gooseflesh at these final moments. José showing me the handkerchief, my taking it and burying my face in it, the realization, the accusation of Iago, a final lament over the body of Desdemona, then (again a suggestion of Doris') the sudden wheeling away of Lucas and myself to opposite downstage corners—to be drawn back with a gesture faintly reminiscent of prayer to the prostrate figures of José and Betty—the sudden drop of body and hand to chest, a sob—then the slow reaching forward of the arm to the audience, the inner anguish, the open palm saying—

"This is the Tragedy."

The Characters

With a source so well known, it was important that each character should be carefully thought out and finely etched. It is essential for the dramatic content of the dance that there be as much contrast as possible. Anyone who has studied the play will undoubtedly find this to be Shakespeare's intent.

Othello: Strong, noble, honorable, emotional, frank, trusting, credulous, believing implicitly in the honesty of Iago. To Othello, honor was a sacred possession.

Desdemona: Pure, gentle, innocent, helpless, her love absolute, accepting her fate without comprehension.

Iago: Evil, for the sake of being evil; malicious, coldly calculating, conniving, treacherous, absorbed in manipulating people at any cost, all covered by a suave exterior.

Emilia: More problematic because of strange contradictions in the text. To understand her character one must try to fill in some background of her life and relations with Iago. Her character needs elaboration.

In various performances of the *Pavane* which I have seen these past years, I sometimes find Emilia distorted and out of true character, thus disturbing the balance and shape of the work. I have read criticisms which applaud her as "sensual, conniving, malicious" and in league with Iago. I have even read, with astonishment, critical complaint that one or another Emilia was not conniving or sensual *enough*.

Sensuous, yes, for her many speeches about men prove her a woman of the world, knowledgeable and cynical about men and their treatment of women. I'm afraid that very often the words *sensual* (given to overindulgence of physical desires) and *sensuous* (influenced by sense impressions, sensitive to beauty, voluptuous) are confused. Whether changes in interpretation of the role of Emilia evoke this response, or whether the criticism has driven performers to see her as such, I'll never know. But this I do know, during my eleven years of performance, I don't think the words *sensual* or *conniving* were ever used to describe Emilia in a piece of criticism. I had not conceived or choreographed the role with that motivation.

RATIONALE FOR THE CHARACTER OF EMILIA

In her handkerchief speech quoted above, one realizes that Emilia found the handkerchief and did not steal it as Iago had begged her. She calls him her "wayward husband," recognizing he is no angel. She also knows it is precious to Desdemona and intends only to have it copied and then return it. She has no idea why he seems so anxious to have it, but wants to please him.

> . . . . What he will do with it
> Heaven knows not I;
> I nothing but to please his fantasy.

One can hardly call that conniving. On the contrary, Emilia seems totally innocent of her husband's design. When she shows him the handkerchief and teases him (since he constantly badgers her), he snatches it from her, refusing to tell Emilia why he wants it, and roughly sends her away. It seems to me that, knowing Iago, she is well aware that it is hopeless to try to retrieve it at this time, so she lets it be.

The one line in the play which has led some annotators to suppose that Emilia plotted with Iago occurs when Desdemona asks if she knows the whereabouts of the handkerchief. Emilia answers, "I know not Madam." This seems strange and is obviously a lie. Why should a good friend and confidante lie? My feeling is that she is too embarrassed to admit that Iago has taken it from her against her will, and since she hopes to retrieve it, she avoids the truth, for the moment. She has no idea of the serious implications and importance of the handkerchief; she is simply playing for time. Again when Desdemona asks Iago why Othello is accusing her, Amelia says to Iago,

> I will be hang'd if some eternal villain
> Some busy insinuating rogue

> Some cozening slave, to get some office
> Have not devised this slander.

Would such a speech exist if she were co-conspirator? Should she protest Desdemona's innocence to Othello by vouching for every moment of Desdemona's actions? Finally, where would the dramatic climax and the excitement of the final scene be without Emilia's devastating realization that she has been the dupe of Iago? She has been his innocent tool. She is in fact the catalyst of the tragedy, by revealing the truth and denouncing Iago, though it means her own death.

Evil and conniving indeed! Rather, warm, worldly, sensuous, mature, compassionate (to me the only compassionate character in the play) and devoted to Desdemona. This is the way I understood and played her.

—from *Ballet Review,* Vol. 8, No. 4, 1980

PARADE
Arthur Gold and Robert Fizdale

It was about Parade *that the poet Apollinaire coined the word* surrealism. *This ballet about a circus sideshow—concocted by Jean Cocteau, who invited Erik Satie to write the music and Picasso to create the decor—was premiered by Diaghilev's Ballets Russes at the Théâtre du Châtelet in Paris in 1917. It was a tremendous event, if not a tremendous ballet.*

On May 18, 1917, in the third year of the war, the curtain of the Théâtre du Châtelet rose on that concise, mysteriously telling ballet *Parade*. At last Cocteau had succeeded in astonishing Diaghilev with a brilliantly original scenario. In so doing, he helped to provoke a scandal which he liked to think was almost as satisfyingly tumultuous as that of *Le Sacre* itself. "Our wish," Cocteau wrote, "is that the public consider *Parade* as a work that conceals poetry beneath the coarse outer skin of slapstick. . . . *Parade* brings together Erik Satie's first orchestral score, Pablo Picasso's first stage decor,

Massine's first Cubist choreography, and a poet's first attempt to express himself without words." There were those in the audience who recognized *Parade* as a milestone in the history of the arts. But others felt that such frivolity at the height of a tragic war was so unpatriotic that its perpetrators should be deported. *Parade* was announced as "a *ballet réaliste* by Jean Cocteau," but for the program notes Apollinaire invented a new word, *sur-réalisme* (super-realism), to describe its magical fusion of decor, scenario, music, and dance, which he felt had a poetic reality more intensely valid than reality itself.

For this ballet Picasso painted a lyric front curtain: an Italianate landscape as a background to an alfresco meal served by blackamoors to a Venetian boatman, a bullfighter with a guitar, and a group of circus performers in harlequin costume. The scene is dominated by a pale Pegasus licking its foal. A winged ballerina stands poised on the horse's back. The curtain rose on a Cubist evocation of New York skyscrapers set at crazed angles. Even more astonishing, two end men, "managers" encased in towering Cubist constructions, presided over the sideshow booth of a cheap travelling fair. One by one the acts were presented to lure passers-by inside. The performers, appearing in eccentric mimetic dances, included a pair of acrobats, a dizzy American flapper, a fire-eating Chinese magician (danced by Massine), and that old circus trick: two men as a horse. In his infectiously brash and jazzy score, Satie had written the *Ubu Roi* of music. Brushing the past aside, he composed a work as seemingly simple and repetitious as a baby's rattle. On closer study the score reveals a mathematical asymmetry and a spare orchestral transparency that are the emblems of a new aesthetic. The ballet is light and comic, but it has resonances that are still with us today. It influenced a new generation of French composers and anticipated *musique concrète*. And it opened the path to ballets that deal with everyday life.*

The events leading to the creation of *Parade* were even less dignified than the ballet itself. In fact, the making of *Parade* was an almost farcical example of the backstage intrigue that seems as fundamental to a ballet company as the five positions. In-fighting and behind-the-scenes treachery made for a power struggle that Cocteau was to refer to as the "greatest battle of the war." He might with greater accuracy have called it a comedy of bad manners. Appropriately, it began on June 28, 1914, the day that Archduke Ferdinand was assassinated. On that day, as we have seen, Misia [Sert] had Erik

---

*In 1973, fifty-six years after its creation, when *Parade* was revived by Massine for the Joffrey Ballet in New York, it was still startlingly fresh and innovative. At that time Massine said that he had re-invented many of the steps. He added, "I was just a young greenhorn when I first choreographed it."

Satie play his music for Diaghilev, and planted the seed for a Satie ballet in Diaghilev's mind; but the scheme had to be put aside with the outbreak of war. At that time the eccentric composer's original talent was recognized only by those in the know: among them Debussy, Ravel, and Stravinsky, all of whom were influenced by the hypnotic purity, the anti-Wagnerian aspect of Satie's music. A refined and subtle spirit, Satie was always desperately in need of money and recognition. His wit, his charm, his pince-nez, his stiff collars, and his dozens of umbrellas are as legendary as his daily bottle of brandy and his terrifying readiness to take offense. Paul Morand, who met Satie at Cocteau's apartment, wrote that he looked "like Socrates: his face is made of half-moons; he scratches his billy-goat's beard between every two words. . . . Above all, he wants to give the impression of being crafty . . . the semi-failure, the man whom Debussy has always crushed and who suffers from that."

In 1916 Diaghilev, responding to Misia's continued enthusiasm, again took up the idea of a Satie ballet. The alert was sounded and Cocteau pricked up his prehensile ears. Still smarting from the failure of his ballet *Le Dieu Bleu* and the frustrations of the abandoned *David,* Cocteau at twenty-seven was determined to fulfill Diaghilev's historic injunction: "*Etonne-moi, Jean!*" Here at last was his chance to "astonish" Diaghilev, to climb back on the Ballets Russes's bandwagon. According to the young artist Valentine Gross, Satie and Cocteau had met at her home as early as October 1915 to discuss working together. Now they agreed that Cocteau would devise a scenario for the ballet Satie was to write. But how to break the news to Diaghilev, who had never asked for Cocteau's collaboration? Through Misia, of course—and so the intrigue began. At Cocteau's suggestion they decided to conceal this first meeting from Misia, for they all feared that she would try to destroy any ballet not hatched under her wing. (As Diaghilev was in America, it is likely that Misia was behaving in a more proprietary way than usual.) In any case, Cocteau was convinced that Misia had intrigued against him in his abortive collaboration with Stravinsky. It was soothing to the young poet's vanity to blame her rather than face the fact that neither Diaghilev nor Stravinsky had ever shown any enthusiasm for *David.* Through Cocteau, Picasso was later chosen to design the sets and costumes—his first work for the theatre. It was a coup that Cocteau, not unnaturally, boasted about for the rest of his life.

As in many theatrical collaborations, everyone connected with the ballet wanted top billing and credit for originating the ideas. In an atmosphere of shifting loyalties no one drew the line at lies and subterfuge. Backbiting and bitchery were the order of the day. Misia, usually helpful, became meddlesome. Satie, the benign Socrates, became malignant. Picasso, whose only loyalty was to himself, behaved treacherously to Cocteau. And Cocteau, who said, "The art of life is to know just how far to go *too* far," went even farther. As Diaghilev wisely observed, "In the theatre there are no friends."

The letters that flew back and forth during the planning of the ballet read like an eighteenth-century epistolary novel. There is a conspiratorial, *Liaisons Dangereuses* tone in the correspondence between Satie and Cocteau and between each of them and Misia and Valentine. The ladies were the *commères*, the two end women of the offstage minstrel show that preceded *Parade*.

The conspiracies begin on a courtly note.

SATIE TO MISIA

May 1916

Chère dame,
What you said to me, at your house, about the "Ballets Russes" has already produced a result: I am working on a thing that I plan to show you very soon and that is dedicated to you as I think of it and as I write it.

All this, dear Madame, gives me the greatest pleasure. Are you not a magician?

SATIE TO MISIA

[n.d.]

Chère dame,
I am coming on Tuesday, isn't that right? If so, not a word to the others about what I've prepared for you. My little idea for the "thing" has ripened so well that I could play it for you right to the end. (There's a bit missing in the middle but I count on you not to tell anyone.) And I want it to please you. . . . Diaghilev is not a man to go back on his agreement, I imagine?
Bonjour chère dame,
E. S.

SATIE TO COCTEAU

April 25, 1916

Cher ami,
Forgive me—sick—grippe.
Impossible send word except by telepathy. All right for tomorrow. Valentine Gross tells me marvellous things. You are the *idea* man. Bravo!

Satie to Cocteau

June 8 [1916]

Cher ami,

For heaven's sake stop worrying, don't be nervous. I am at work. Let me do it my own way. I warn you, you won't see the thing until October. Not a note before that. I tell you so under oath. Will it be all right if I mention that you are the author of the scenario? I need to. Madame Edwards is all for the project. . . . You *must* trust me.

Cocteau to Misia

[n.d.]

Chère Misia,

A letter from Erik Satie absolves me from my vow of silence. One evening in your house, by thrilling coincidence, Satie asked me to collaborate with him at the very moment I was about to ask him the same. That little miracle happened in the presence of Valentine Gross, who thus learned of the matter. I kept the secret until I was sure that the work was well on the way, having suffered from being overhasty with Igor. This was also Satie's explicit wish. Moreover, though nothing is left of *David, David's* failure surely served to make possible the birth of the new work—there are mysteries that are beyond human understanding. You will be the first to hear it, so I am telling you about it at once—dropping my incognito *(for you alone)* the moment Satie asks me. We won't take less than your "love"—mere "approval" would kill us poor Arcueil-Anjou minstrels.* It is a very short work which resembles the composer—everything goes on behind the eyeglasses.†

After receiving Valentine's "lying letter," Misia wrote to Cocteau, who was shuttling back and forth between Paris and his military duties at the front. As she received no answer—perhaps for once he was at a loss for words—she wrote again.

---

*Satie lived in the working-class suburb of Arcueil, Cocteau in the fashionable rue d'Anjou.

†According to Francis Steegmuller's remarkable biography of Cocteau, "It is not certain that this letter was ever sent. It is not among those which Misia prints in her memoirs. Two slightly different versions exist, both formerly among the papers of the late Valentine Gross Hugo, to whom Cocteau apparently submitted the drafts for approval. . . . Valentine once told the present author that she herself had sent a lying letter, composed by Cocteau, assuring her that it was at Misia's house rather than in her own that *Parade* had really been conceived. Perhaps that took the place of anything signed by Cocteau himself."

In Valentine Gross's copy of Misia's memoirs, opposite a quotation from a Cocteau letter—in which he wrote, "My meeting with Satie was all lightness and happiness"—Valentine pencilled an indignant "What lies!"

Misia to Cocteau

Paris, Sunday, June 1916

Mon cher petit Jean,

. . . I answered your letter after receiving a long letter from Val[entine] about Erik Satie and you. I will just tell you again that I already knew about this collaboration. Although I have not said anything to E. S., I know that if he wants to do something for Sergei, your presence would be useless. I shall pass over this however. . . .

I expect Sergei this week and hope to work all this out once and for all. Satie comes to see me fairly often and I still have great hopes of him. He is both candid and crafty and I hope he will disentangle himself from the wretches who surround him. . . .

Igor passed through Paris on his way to Spain to see Sergei (who came back from America on an Italian boat loaded with munitions but preferred DEATH to the dreadful boredom of America and just couldn't wait). So he went to Spain where he has been with Stravinsky ever since.

Therefore I asked Stravinsky to support Satie and he was so enthusiastic that he even thought of combining this project with the new work that was commissioned from him by Polignac [*Renard*] to make a short and perfect evening. . . .

I embrace you with all my heart
Your
Misia

Tell me as much as possible about yourself.

Understandably, Cocteau was upset to hear that Diaghilev did not want him, but it was always Misia's way to be brutally frank. The tone of her letter shows, however, that her frankness had nothing to do with her affection for Cocteau. Her first concern was to convince Diaghilev to put on a ballet by Satie; her second and more delicate task was to soften Diaghilev's attitude toward Cocteau. Evidently she succeeded, for when Diaghilev finally gave him his chance, Cocteau wrote from the front to thank her.

Cocteau to Misia

[n.d.]

. . . Your letter arrives as if by carrier pigeon and reassures my heart. Far from everyone, in the land of cannibals, one is tortured and begins to doubt even the most faithful. . . . Satie is an angel (well disguised). . . . My part of the work doesn't make things easy for him—quite the contrary. If only our collaboration could move you the way it moved me the day I told him what he must write. . . .

I can guess from his postcards that things are going the way I most want them to.

Cocteau was in for a disappointment that he could not blame on Misia. He may have received encouraging postcards from Satie, but at the same time Satie, far more crafty than he was candid, was telling Valentine Gross that things were not going at all the way Cocteau thought they were. Valentine, moreover, was passing the information along to Cocteau.

COCTEAU TO VALENTINE

July 30, 1916

. . . I feel terribly alone and anguished—I beg you to let me hear from you, exorcize the devil, see Satie, learn what is going on. If this thing fell through it would be the end of me.

SATIE TO VALENTINE

August 8, 1916
Tuesday, 3:12 p.m.

It's happened! I've broken with Aunt Trufaldin [Misia]. What a bitch!

Of them all only Satie had cause to be angry with Misia, for she had committed the cardinal sin of interfering with his creative activity—and with the possibility of his being paid for a new composition. One can only suppose that Satie had played parts of *Parade* for Misia. She loved his *Trois Morceaux en Forme de Poire* with its alternating sections of expressive lyricism, hypnotic stillness, and high-stepping music-hall gaiety, but his new style may have alarmed her. *Parade*'s daring ingenuousness, its single measures repeated endlessly like a wallpaper design, made what seemed to her an aesthetic rather than a musical statement. And she might well have been afraid that Diaghilev would find it more gaga than Dada. She made no secret of the fact that she and Diaghilev might prefer to use some of Satie's old pieces instead of the new work. "Satie is old—let him stay old—it's so good that way," she was heard to say. It was enough to infuriate any artist. Satie was deeply hurt and began to call her names that fell below the standard of his usual exquisite wit. Misia was demoted from "*chère dame*" and "magician" to "Aunt Trufaldin" after the deceitful servant in the *commedia dell'arte*. Like naughty children, Valentine and Cocteau joined in the game. From now on in their correspondence with Satie, Misia was not only "Aunt Trufaldin" but

"Abortionist," "Sister-in-Law," and "Aunt Brutus," while Sert, of course, became "Uncle Brutus." And Satie's *mot,* "Misia is a lovely cat—so hide your fish!" was soon being repeated all over Paris.

As for Cocteau, it must be remembered that Diaghilev had never asked him to work on the Satie ballet, any more than he had asked him to collaborate with Stravinsky. In both cases the young poet had pushed himself forward uninvited, behind Diaghilev's back, and then felt betrayed when he was not made welcome. Besides, Cocteau had stepped on Sert's toes (and Diaghilev's!) when *Le Mot,* the magazine he and Paul Iribe published, attacked *La Légende de Joseph* in a jingoistic display of anti-German feeling. That Misia continued to promote Cocteau's cause with Diaghilev after that was a gesture of real friendship on her part. Despite these complications, some progress was being made.

COCTEAU TO VALENTINE

August 9, 1916

Very good day's work with Satie. Erik-Trufaldin catastrophe not serious and very serious.

COCTEAU TO STRAVINSKY

August 11, 1916

Satie and I are collaborating on something for Sergei, since Sergei, despite the abyss that I feel divides us, is still the only impresario with genius.

COCTEAU TO VALENTINE

August 13, 1916

My dear Valentine,

Nothing very new except that Picasso keeps taking me to the [Café] Rotonde. . . . Misia is now inseparable from Apollinaris [Apollinaire]. What is she up to with him at Maxim's? She has quite abandoned Saint-Léger for him. Our good Satie . . . is composing marvels for me and refuses to see Aunt Brutus. A long letter to Igor S. in which I let him know that I am far from being a party to inept intrigues. To tell you the truth, Diaghilev—that Italian tenor—finds it clever to attribute to me all the blunders of the quai Voltaire [Misia], all due to my influence, he says—and naive Igor accuses me of treachery.

Still, it's a great thing to be in the thick of the dog fights of great art.

JOINT POSTCARD FROM COCTEAU
AND SATIE TO VALENTINE

August 24, 1916

Picasso is doing *Parade* with us.

COCTEAU TO VALENTINE

August 31, 1916

Picasso and Satie get on like Misia and Sergei. Picasso is moulting, undergoing a transformation—Saturday night we begin real work.

Little did Cocteau realize the ominous undertones of Picasso and Satie's burgeoning friendship. When he brought off his great coup and arranged for Picasso to do the decor for *Parade,* Cocteau could not have anticipated the game of musical chairs that followed. Picasso had his own ideas for the scenario and Satie preferred them to Cocteau's. Picasso and Satie felt that in "their" ballet, Cocteau's "presence would be useless," just as Misia and Sergei had thought in the first place. It was civil war in the none-too-solid ranks.

COCTEAU TO VALENTINE

September 14, 1916

. . . Make Satie understand, if you can cut through the aperitif fog, that I really do count for something in *Parade,* and that he and Picasso are not the only ones involved. . . . It hurts me when he dances around Picasso screaming, "It's you I'm following! *You* are my master!" . . . Does he hear anything I say? . . . calm him in his inordinate hatred for the Aunt. Sh! Burn this, for the work is going ahead, and that's the main thing. Picasso is inventing marvels.

SATIE TO VALENTINE

Thursday—September 14, 1916

Chère et douce amie—

If you knew how sad I am! *Parade* is changing for the better, behind Cocteau's back! Picasso has ideas that I like better than our Jean's! How awful! And I am all for Picasso! And Cocteau doesn't know it! What am I to do? Picasso tells me to go ahead, following Jean's text, and he, Picasso, will work on another text, his own—which is dazzling! Prodigious! . . . Now that I know Picasso's wonderful ideas, I am heart-broken to have to set to music the less wonderful ideas of our good Jean—oh! yes! less wonderful. What am I to do? What am I to do? Write and advise me. I am beside myself.

SATIE TO VALENTINE

Wednesday, September 20, 1916

Chère amie,

It's settled. Cocteau knows everything. He and Picasso have come to terms. How lucky! Did I tell you that I got along well with Diaghilev? Still no money from him. Our "Aunt" is in Rum—I mean Rome.

COCTEAU TO VALENTINE

[September 22, 1916]

. . . You were probably worried about Satie—let me quickly set your mind at rest. Caught between Picasso and me, our good Socrates from Arcueil has lost his bearings—our different vocabularies make him imagine that one of us is talking white and the other black. Have decided with Picasso to lie to Satie so that he'll be able to go ahead without getting confused.

COCTEAU TO MISIA

[n.d.]

Dear Misia,

Come back soon—I'm impatient to hug you and to laugh and kiss away a thousand misunderstandings that have been exaggerated by distance and fatigue. Very good meeting with Sergei and Massine—the latter's fresh intelligence and general air I like very much. I have the impression that Sergei likes our work and that he understood perfectly the seemingly very simple motivation I provided for the union of musician and painter. I stand between them, giving a hand to each. . . . For the first time I feel myself in rapport with Sergei—a very nice feeling.

SATIE TO COCTEAU

[n.d.]

My "sister-in-law" is no longer dangerous, I think. What luck!

Finally, in February 1917, Diaghilev invited Cocteau, Satie, and Picasso to come to Rome to work with Massine on *Parade*. "Will I really go?" Cocteau wrote Valentine. "I wonder: Aunt T. is in charge! ! !" Go he did; but Satie, despite the fact that he had been shopping for luggage, remained behind. When asked if he knew Rome, Satie replied, "By name—only by name." From Rome, Cocteau wrote Misia, "Picasso amazes me every day. To live near him is a lesson in nobility and hard work." But there was one more problem to be worked out. The possibility that Cocteau might be called back to France to resume military duty disturbed Diaghilev, who felt that *Parade* could not be completed without the poet's help. At last Cocteau had made himself indispensable.

COCTEAU TO MISIA

[n.d.]

Dear Misia,

Reassure Sergei that if my stay here upsets the War Ministry too much, since the work is going very well (Massine soaking up my ideas) no matter what Diag thinks, my absence could no longer hurt *Parade*. . . .

It's boring to be far away from you.

Apparently Misia spoke to Berthelot at the War Ministry and succeeded in extending Cocteau's leave.

COCTEAU TO MISIA

[n.d.]

Dear Misia,

. . . Thanks for Berthelot. Sergei was really worried that I might leave the work incomplete. I think you will be happy with it.

The Chinese magician is done. Massine was supposed to play the acrobat but he demonstrated the role of the Chinese with such talent that I begged him to dance that role. . . .

Write a little postcard, you are my *other* family, you know that, and just the sight of your handwriting moves me. Bakst has a cold—he buys special handkerchiefs that "don't excite the nose" and is living in a brothel. He explained to us . . . that when young he posed as Antinous at drawing school since at that time he looked as much like Sarah Bernhardt as two peas in a pod.* Sergei nearly died laughing and the meal was interrupted as the waiters were doubled up with laughter themselves. . . .

I shall return soon in spite of Sergei. . . . Uneasy far from home. In the Pincio I dream of the quai Voltaire.

Embrassez Mons. Sert

Jean

At last *Parade* was completed. When, at the first performance, Misia and Sert "received" in the foyer of the theatre—Misia in full regalia, with a silver tiara—Cocteau could not resist saying that she looked like the mother of the bride. As the ballet unfolded, Misia might well have been reminded of Cocteau's behavior during the past year, for the characters he had

---

*According to Paul Morand, Bakst was "a rumpled, tubby man with spectacles, sparse red hair, a ridiculously dapper military mustache, and a comical lisp."

devised hawk their wares in much the way that Cocteau himself had done in selling his act to Satie and Picasso, to Misia and Diaghilev. Like his characters, Cocteau had used coquetry, sleight of hand, acrobatics, and slapstick, with that overlay of mockery that was his own cynical, slightly sinister veneer.

All the same, by this time Misia and Cocteau had made up their differences. She was to remain his close friend for life, while Valentine Gross broke with Cocteau six years later. And Misia and Picasso became so attached to one another that he asked her to be a witness at his wedding to Olga Kokhlova, one of Diaghilev's Russian dancers, and godmother to their son Paolo. Valentine married the artist Jean Hugo, a great-grandson of Victor Hugo, with Cocteau and Satie as best men. The couple had met in Cipa's apartment, where Jean first saw Valentine seated on a leather sofa under a portrait of Misia's father. Jean Hugo became one of Misia's closest friends, but Valentine never liked her. When Misia's memoirs were published after her death, Valentine was still complaining. Spitefully she marked the margins of her copy with short, corrective splutters of rage.

After the reviews of *Parade* appeared, Satie, who never forgave a slight, sent an insulting postcard to a critic who had treated his score harshly. *"Monsieur et cher ami,"* Satie wrote, "you are nothing but an ass-hole and an unmusical one at that." The critic sued for libel and Satie was sentenced to a week in jail. His friends were horrified, and Cocteau was not above turning to "Aunt and Uncle Brutus" for help. Cocteau's was the last word, a postscript to the intricate parade of letters.

Cocteau to Misia

Poor Satie. Were you told that we *all* stopped by to see you after the verdict? Satie did not want to bother anyone beforehand (alas!) as he thought the matter was not very serious. . . . What's to be done? If only he could be kept out of prison. . . . Just now Sert telephoned. I've told him to arrange something. . . .

Fortunately something was arranged, either by Misia and Sert or by the combined efforts of the group. Satie was given a suspended sentence and spared the humiliation of going to jail.

—from *Misia,* 1980

PETROUCHKA
Alexandre Benois

Born in St. Petersburg in 1870 to a family of distinguished architects, Alexandre Benois studied for the law while becoming an accomplished watercolorist. At the end of the century he joined with a group of like-minded artists and critics, including Sergei Diaghilev and Leon Bakst, to found a new and highly influential magazine, Mir iskusstva (The World of Art). *By 1901 he was the scenic director of the Maryinsky and the Moscow Art Theatre, and a few years later he joined the Ballets Russes venture, eventually designing the decor for Diaghilev's* Les Sylphides, Giselle, *and* Petrouchka *(for which he also wrote the libretto), among other ballets. From 1918 to 1925 he was Curator of Paintings at the Hermitage museum, after which he moved to Paris, designing scores of ballets, operas, and plays throughout Europe until his death, in 1960.*

I was back again in St. Petersburg when I received a letter from Diaghilev which greatly perturbed me. Its contents were approximately the following: he did not doubt that my decision was final, and yet, in view of certain *exceptional* circumstances, he addressed me again in the hope that I would forgive the insult I had suffered and once more join my friends. The exceptional circumstances were that, only a few days ago, Stravinsky had composed and played to him a sort of Russian Dance and another piece which he had named *Petrouchka's Cry,* and that both these compositions were, in every sense of the term, works of *genius.* They had both had the idea of using this music for some new ballet, but no story had as yet been devised. They had only conceived the idea of representing the St. Petersburg Carnival and of including in it a performance of *Petrouchka,* the Russian Punch and Judy show. "Who else but you," wrote Seriozha, "could help us in this problem?" Therefore they had decided to apply to me and Seriozha expressed the assurance that I could not *possibly* refuse.

Seriozha certainly had every foundation for his assurance. Petrouchka, the Russian Guignol or Punch, no less than Harlequin, had been my friend since my earliest childhood. Whenever I heard the loud, nasal cries of the travelling Punch and Judy showman: "Here's Petrouchka! Come, good people, and see the Show!" I would get into a kind of frenzy to see the enchanting performance, which consisted, as did the *balagani* pantomimes, in the endless tricks of an idle loafer, who ends up by being captured by a hairy devil and dragged off to Hell.

As to Petrouchka in person, I immediately had the feeling that "it was a duty I owed to my old friend" to immortalise him on the real stage. I was still more tempted by the idea of depicting the Butter Week Fair on the stage, the dear *balagani* which were the great delight of my childhood, and had been the delight of my father before me. The fact that in 1911 the *balagani* had, for some ten years, ceased to exist, made the idea of building a kind of memorial to them still more tempting. They perished under the on-slaught led by Prince A. P. Oldenburg* against alcoholism (the common folk certainly gave themselves up to the Russian Vodka-Bacchus at the Butter Week Fair!).

Besides the duty I felt I owed to Petrouchka and my wish to "immortalise" the St. Petersburg Carnival, I had yet another reason for accepting Seri-ozha's offer—I suddenly *saw* how this ballet ought to be presented. It at once became plain that Guignol-Petrouchka screens were not appropriate to a stage performance. A year before we had tried to arrange a similar *Petrouchka* performance with real people in the Arts Club, but although Dobuzhinsky had put much of his wit into the production, it turned out to be rather absurd and on the dull side. The effect of big, grown-up people acting with their heads over the edge of a curtain and little wooden legs dangling below, was more pitiful than funny. The effect on the stage of a real theatre would have been still worse; a ballet would have been entirely out of the question, for what could a ballet artist do if he were not allowed to use his "natural" legs? Once the screens were abolished from the stage, they had naturally to be replaced by a small theatre. The dolls of this theatre would have to come to life without ceasing to be dolls—retaining, so to speak, their doll's nature.

The dolls should come to life at the command of a magician, and their coming to life should be somehow accompanied by suffering. The greater the contrast between the real, live people and the automatons who had just been given life, the sharper the interest of the action would be. It would be necessary to allot a considerable part of the stage to the mass of real people—the "public" at the fair—while there would only be two dolls, the hero of the play, Petrouchka, and his lady.

Soon I decided that there should be a third character—the Blackamoor. In the street performances of *Petrouchka* there was invariably a separate intermezzo, inserted between the acts: two Blackamoors, dressed in velvet

---

*The Prince had perhaps a special dislike to the noisy *balagani* because they took place under the windows of his palace. The *balagani* were transferred from the centre of the town—the Tsaritsin Loug—to the Semeonovsky Place, where they soon ceased to exist.

and gold, would appear and start unmercifully hitting each other's wooden heads with sticks. I included a similar Blackamoor among my "chief characters." If Petrouchka were to be taken as the personification of the spiritual and suffering side of humanity—or shall we call it the poetical principle?—his lady Columbine would be the incarnation of the eternal feminine; then the gorgeous Blackamoor would serve as the embodiment of everything senselessly attractive, powerfully masculine, and undeservedly triumphant. Having once visualised the complete drama in my mind's eye, and foreseeing what an interesting collision of contrasted elements must inevitably ensue, how could I refuse Seriozha's proposal that I should help to interpret it as a ballet on the stage? I fully believed what Diaghilev had written when he claimed that the *Russian Dance* and *Petrouchka's Cry* were works of genius, and was still further encouraged. How could I maintain my stubbornness and my attitude of "injured pride"? I gave in and informed Seriozha that I accepted his proposal and had forgiven all grievances; I was once more entirely with him and Stravinsky.

Several weeks later Seriozha arrived in St. Petersburg. My scheme was accepted with enthusiasm. We met daily in Diaghilev's flat in Zamiatin Lane where, at the traditional evening tea with *boubliki,* we discussed the "forthcoming" *Petrouchka.* At one time I let loose my imagination and the subject began to swell into something beyond bounds, but gradually *Petrouchka* took shape and fitted ultimately into four fairly short acts, without any intervals. The first and last acts were to take place at the Carnival Fair; the two middle ones were to show the interior of the Conjuror's theatre. The puppets that had come to life in the first act, under the magic spell of the Conjuror, were to continue living a real life in their own quarters, where a romance was to begin between them. *Petrouchka's Cry,* which Seriozha now described to me in detail, was to fill the first of the two intimate acts; the second was to be devoted to the Blackamoor. The detailed action had not yet been decided.

Stravinsky arrived in December on a short visit to his mother and I was at last able to hear the two fragments which had been the "beginning of everything." Igor played them to me in my little dark-blue drawing-room; the piano was my old, fearfully hard Gentsch, the same instrument (the poor old fellow had since had his abnormally long tail chopped off) on which Albert used to tell me the story of the little boy caught by the devils. What I now heard surpassed my expectations. The *Russian Dance* proved to be really magic music in which infectious, diabolical recklessness alternated with strange digressions into tenderness—then, after a culminating paroxysm, came to abrupt end. As for *Petrouchka's Cry,* having listened to it about three times, I began to discern in it grief, and rage, and love, as well as the helpless despair that dominated it. Stravinsky accepted my comments, and later on this program, that was constructed *ex post facto,* was worked out by me in full detail.*

Today, when I listen to the music of this second act of *Petrouchka* and watch what the artist is expressing, more or less successfully, in his gestures and mime—*demonstrating* the absolute co-ordination of action and music—it is difficult even for me to believe that the music was not written to a set program, instead of the program being subsequently fitted to the music.

We continued to collaborate, actively and harmoniously, in the creation of the new ballet, in spite of the fact that we did not meet again till the spring of 1911. Stravinsky went back to Switzerland to live with his family while I remained in St. Petersburg, but we kept up a constant interchange of letters. The subject was acquiring definite shape. The dramatic situation produced by the "hopeless love" of the "poet" Petrouchka in the second act was counter-balanced in the third by the undeserved passion awakened in the Ballerina by the foolish Blackamoor. Their personalities began to take definite shape, and when I heard the music of the "Blackamoor's room," I invented his mono-logue in all its absurd detail: the playing with the coconut, the coconut's resentment at being chopped open, etc. The Ballerina appears at the moment of the Blackamoor's wild, religious ecstasy before the coconut. At the cli-max of their love-making, when the enamoured Blackamoor is almost ready to devour his charming visitor, poor Petrouchka, mad with jealousy, rushes in, but, as the curtain falls, the Blackamoor pushes out his ridiculous rival.

The last part of the third act foretells the final *dénouement.* Similar scenes are supposed to go on inside the tiny theatre, passions grow, and at last the pathetic, luckless lover reaches a fatal end. It was essential to carry the finale outside the intimate surroundings of the previous two acts; to set it among the Carnival crowd, at the fair where, in the first act, the puppets had actu-ally been brought to life. I was delighted with Stravinsky's idea of introduc-ing a party of *riageni*† into the street crowd. This was a regular feature of the Russian Carnival, which could not do without such a "devil's diversion." All sorts of "creatures of hell" and even the Devil himself were to appear among these masked visitors. At the climax of the drunken revelling, Petrouchka's cries were to be heard coming from the conjuror's theatre. Petrouchka rushes out into the crowd, trying to escape from his infuriated enemy, but the Blackamoor overtakes him and puts an end to his existence with a blow from his curved sword.

This was the general plan of the finale, but we only began working it out

---

*It was then that I imagined the black room where the wicked conjuror imprisons his puppet—now, alas, fully conscious of its surroundings.

†*Riageni* were masked revellers, in traditional dress, who, at times of Festival, enjoyed special privileges.—*Trans.*

when Stravinsky and I met again in Rome. The composer reached the height of tragedy in the final few bars expressing Petrouchka's agony, his piteous goodbye to life. To this day I cannot listen to it without the deepest emotion. The very moment of death—when Petrouchka's soul departs to a better world—is expressed in an unusual and very successful way. A broken sob is heard—produced by the throwing on the floor of a tambourine. This "unmusical" sound seems to destroy the spell, to bring the spectator back to "reality." But the drama of the Conjuror who has dared to put a heart and a soul into his toys does not end so simply. Petrouchka turns out to be immortal, and when the old magician disdainfully drags the broken doll along the snow in order to mend it (and again torment it), the "genuine" Petrouchka suddenly appears in miraculous transformation above the little theatre, and the terrified Conjuror drops the doll and turns to flight.

The finale did not come to Stravinsky at once, and he had to search and use different combinations for it. He finished composing the music only a few weeks before the performance. We were staying at the same hotel in Rome for nearly a month, and every morning I used to hear from my room a confused tangle of sounds, interrupted from time to time by long pauses. This was the maturing of the last bars of the fourth act. . . . When everything was ready, *Petrouchka* was played to Diaghilev and me from beginning to end. Diaghilev was no less delighted with it than I; the only thing he argued about was the "note of interrogation" upon which the ballet score ended. For a long time he would not agree to it, but demanded a more traditional solution—a curious proof of how strongly influenced Diaghilev was by "academic prejudice" even in 1911!. . . .

The first rehearsals of *Petrouchka* took place in the same Teatro Costanzi. We had to hurry to be in time for Paris and therefore decided to begin the production before the music was quite finished. As the management of the theatre could not find a more suitable building, the rehearsals had to take place in the restaurant of the theatre. The floor was covered with soiled crimson cloth, on which our artists had to dance and sometimes lie. The weather was terribly hot and everybody suffered from it, most of all Fokine, who was always moving, and Stravinsky, who for hours performed the duties of a pianist—for who but the composer himself could read the complicated manuscript or simplify the music to make it comprehensible to the dancers? Even Fokine used at moments to have difficulty in mastering some of the rhythms (which were indeed unusual) and memorising the themes, now so well known and in those days so "daringly original." Seriozha, immaculately dressed from early morning, appeared almost daily at these rehearsals. He looked extremely tired, for the burden he had taken on himself was weighing heavily on him and the coming season in Paris would demand a still greater expenditure of energy and strength.

The rehearsals of *Petrouchka* went steadily ahead when we reached Paris. The costumes and decor (perfectly executed from my sketches by Anisfeld) arrived from St. Petersburg, everything was in order, our work progressed at full speed . . . We had now to think of the program and to decide the question of who was to be considered as the author of the newly born work.

My enthusiasm for Stravinsky was so great that I was ready to efface myself completely out of reverence for his genius; the initiative of the whole enterprise, indeed, belonged to him—I only helped to endow his enchanting music with tangible, scenic form. The subject of the drama, the characters and development of the action and most of the details were mine, but all this seemed a mere trifle in comparison with the music. So when Stravinsky at one of the last rehearsals asked: "Who is the author of *Petrouchka?*" I answered: "Of course it is you." But Stravinsky would not agree to this and protested energetically, saying that it was I who was the real author. Our *combat de générosité* ended with both of us being named, and here again out of reverence I insisted on his name being placed first. My name appeared a second time in the score, for Stravinsky dedicated *Petrouchka* to me, a fact which touched me deeply.

—from *Reminiscences of the Russian Ballet,* translated by
Mary Britnieva, 1977

PILLAR OF FIRE
Sono Osato

Pillar of Fire *was the first ballet created in America by Antony Tudor after his arrival here in 1942. It became one of Ballet Theatre's greatest critical and popular successes, making a star of its thrilling protagonist, Nora Kaye. An intensely psychological dance-drama about a young repressed woman,* Pillar *was set to Schoenberg's* Verklärte Nacht *and had decor by Jo Mielziner. The Young Man was danced by Tudor's lover, Hugh Laing; the Older Sister by Lucia Chase, the head of the company; the Younger Sister by Annabelle Lyon; the Friend by Tudor himself. Also in the large cast: Maria Karnilova, John Kriza, Rosella Hightower, Donald Saddler, Muriel Bentley, Jerome Robbins, and Sono Osato.*

Along with rehearsals with Fokine, who had joined the company to choreograph *Bluebeard,* and the hectic touring schedule, we were also working on a new ballet by Antony Tudor. I knew, of course, that Tudor was an outstanding choreographer whose talent had first been recognized through his ballets for Ballet Rambert in England. Over the years, we've become accustomed to hearing tales of Tudor's caustic wit and sometimes hurtful remarks to his dancers, but my experience was different. I had only the briefest day-to-day contact with him, so I didn't have the chance to really get to know him. But even during the creation of this one ballet, I felt that his work gave me a picture of his profoundly personal views of love, hate, and compassion. At the time, Tudor was still a young man of thirty-four, just gaining momentum as a leading force in American choreography, with little time to develop complex personal and psychological analyses with every member of his cast. Being called to rehearsal, I was more curious than nervous. I had no idea how Tudor wanted to use me, or what he had seen in my dancing that made him want to work with me. I knew nothing about the way he worked, about the ballet he was making, or about the role I would have in it.

When I entered the rehearsal hall, Tudor was standing calmly before a group of six dancers. His body was straight but strangely passive, his neat head resting on his long neck like a bird's. "Don't forget," he was saying, "you are Lovers in Innocence. You live in a small town. It's dusk and you're going to the corner to get a soda." As the three couples repeated their steps, he reminded them to be relaxed and casual in order to establish the mood of a particular time and place. Tudor seemed satisfied with the dancers' response to his evocation of the scene.

I was baffled. Totally ignorant of the period and setting of *Pillar of Fire,* I could not understand what a corner drugstore was doing in a ballet. But as the days passed, I learned that we were in a small American town just after the turn of the century. The ballet was not about princesses or magic birds or sylphs; it was about a young woman's repressed emotions and her eventual release from frustration through reciprocated love. No one ever defined those themes in words, but no definitions were necessary. Before our eyes Hagar's torment and subsequent peace emerged slowly and inexorably from the flow of movement.

In the central role of Hagar, Nora Kaye became someone I'd never seen before, a woman who bore no relation to the funny, good-natured girl who squashed bedbugs with me on the road. The moment she heard the opening bars of the recording of Schoenberg's *Verklärte Nacht* which Tudor used for many rehearsals, Nora closed herself off from all external stimuli. Sitting on the front stoop (a rehearsal-room chair), her spine rigid with tension, her feet flattened against the floor as if pushing it away, she was transformed. Slowly she raised her right hand to smooth her hair, and I shivered. In that single gesture she established her character indelibly. Deeper and deeper Nora dug into herself to help Tudor find the woman he wanted to create.

Out of her twenty-one years she drew an awesome understanding of repression, loneliness, and frustration, maintaining the many emotional levels of the character even as she performed the most difficult technical feats. At one moment, she had to arch backwards suddenly while balanced on pointe, then contract her torso sharply forward and walk ahead without jarring or stumbling. Flexing her steely spine like a whip, Nora mastered the convolutions of the choreography as smoothly as she portrayed the twists of Hagar's mental anguish.

As the Young Man from the House Opposite, Tudor cast Hugh Laing. Hugh was extravagantly handsome, with brooding dark features. He moved with supreme arrogance, his stark sexuality the foil for Nora's vulnerability. Pitting one against the other, Tudor created a pas de deux that was an explosion of sexual desire, intense and unrelenting. He molded their pas de deux into an emotional, psychologically charged dialogue. When Hugh left Nora prostrate on the floor, his walk alone spoke volumes, expressing at once his indifference to her shame and a passion devoid of tenderness. Though graphic, the artistic subtlety of this passage completely removed it from vulgarity. Tudor welded acting so closely to dancing that the explicit eroticism of the encounter was expressed wholly in choreographic terms.

Rosella Hightower, Muriel Bentley, Miriam Golden, and I were cast as Lovers in Experience, partnered by Jerome Robbins, Donald Saddler, and Frank Hobi. At times I split away from the group and danced with Hugh. The unrestrained, sensuous movements Tudor gave us emphasized Hugh's lasciviousness and lust.

In some way, each character was itself and a whole world as well. The wary movements Tudor conceived for Lucia [Chase] as Hagar's Eldest Sister revealed a conformist, subject to the social pressures that so ruthlessly motivate human behavior. Lucia was beautiful in this part, the embodiment of sober elegance. Moving with the dignity befitting the responsible eldest in the family, she was at once a prisoner of conventional morality and its staunchest advocate.

As the Youngest Sister, Annabelle Lyon epitomized the libidinous adolescent, rubbing her hand across her open mouth whenever a man approached, then tossing her dark hair flirtatiously. Cruel to Hagar in a casually frivolous way, Annabelle, with an unforgettable mastery of nuance, etched the bold outlines of the heartless, mature woman the Youngest Sister would become.

Tudor worked very slowly. He would often stand for a long time lost in thought and gazing into the air, one finger on his lips. When a sequence did not flow exactly as he had envisioned it, he remained calm, at times accepting suggestions the dancers offered to make the steps more manageable. Having begun dancing and choreographing relatively late, he lacked the facility for composing that enabled Fokine or Massine, after years of experience, to reel off combinations of steps as quickly as they could speak, and sometimes quicker. This is not to do Tudor an injustice. He is as great an innovative genius as they, in his own way. In those silent moments of searching, Tudor was creating a dance vocabulary that had never before been used for ballet.

—from *Distant Dances,* 1980

PRIMITIVE MYSTERIES
Dorothy Bird

It is well known that, at this time, both Martha and Louis [Horst] each taught us separately in their respective classes that not one movement from one dance would be acceptable or appropriate in any other dance that was being newly choreographed. This concept that no movement could be transplanted from one dance to another was taken from nature.

Louis told us again and again, "Just as an oak leaf would never be found on a maple tree, because each seed, each acorn, has its own individual growth patterns, so movement must grow organically, naturally, and spontaneously from the core of an idea."

So it followed that the specific character of a walk appropriate for a new work, *Primitive Mysteries,* had to be found. The walk was to be the seed of the style. In quiet, unpressured rehearsals with her group, Martha meticulously analyzed the coordination of the body as she searched for the precise dramatic quality that would best communicate to the audience exactly what she had in mind. Her patience was inexhaustible. During countless hours of rehearsal, over a period of months, we walked side by side in groups of three or four, without holding hands but with the knuckles of our cupped hands pressed lightly against the knuckles of the person next to us. Once she placed a broom handle across the backs of our shoulders to hold them flat as we walked in groups of three as a unit. Martha decreed that no one should lead, and no one should follow. With no word cues or sounds of any kind, we progressed from walking to an easy loping run, which developed into a wild, free run, similar to the run of untamed horses, hair flying, like the hair of women running in a painting by Picasso. Then, without an outside cue of any kind, we slowed down, changing smoothly to a walk that gradually became slower and slower until we were almost not moving at all, and finally, gradually, we came to a stop. It was exciting to be absolutely still after the wild run, and to be a part of the trio that moved as one.

Using peripheral vision, we could see our bare, flexed feet come forward and hang in the air for a suspended second before a hushed footfall could be heard as we forged forward. We pushed the ground backward under our feet, and the impetus impelled us boldly forward. There was nothing tentative about it. We went so far as to practice walking in the surf at the newly opened Jones Beach on Long Island. First we pressed just our feet through the water, then up to the knee, then up to the thigh, and finally the whole body. When we returned to the studio we could draw upon the distinct muscular memory we had absorbed through thrusting our whole body forward against the surf, then being dragged back by the undertow. We had rehearsed so much that, even when I walked alone, I felt as if I were being carried forward as one of three, with a feeling of buoyancy combined with a momentous thrust.

After a while, all our differences in size, shape, temperament melted away. The group had become one person, with the feeling extending to Martha as being one of us. It seemed as if we even breathed as one. Each of us carried our own weight, but the whole was stronger than the parts. The walk Martha finally found had in it none of the ruthlessness of *Heretic* nor the laughter and abandon of *Rustica*. This hushed and silent walk, which permeated the fiber of everything we did, became the key to *Primitive Mysteries*. Uncluttered by sets, props, and elaborate music, this enigmatic walk would not only introduce the cast of characters, it would also transport the audience in their imaginations to a different time and place, where they would see something they had never encountered before. The walk was like a piece of cloth onto which the story would be embroidered.

When Martha finally allowed Louis to come into the studio to see what she had created, they decided that all the entrances and exits should be executed in silence. When Louis wrote the melody and it was united with the dance, the release from the intense concentration of the silence swept us into a feeling of joy that burst out of us explosively. The music was not merely decoration, or something we would copy. It was an integral part, an active partner, emphasizing and clarifying each movement. It supported and defined the dance.

The costume Martha created for herself for *Primitive Mysteries* was a masterpiece of simplicity. I was alone with her in the studio when she made it. First she took one large section of heavy, stiff white organdy and cut it into two equal squares. I rather think she had been treasuring this organdy for quite some time. She placed a corner of one of the large squares between her breasts, and pinned it to her leotard. As it fell down in a diamond shape toward the floor, she made a decision about how long she wanted this dress to be. I placed a safety pin to mark the length, near her ankles. She unpinned the corner attached to her leotard, and placed that large square of white organdy on the floor. While I firmly held the point still, she carefully folded the organdy, first in half, then quarters, then eighths, thus pleating the fabric like a fan that when folded closed was four or five inches across. With a large pair of shears, she quite simply cut a curve across the lower corner where it had been marked for the length. We unfolded the organdy, and again pinned the top corner at a point between her breasts, anchoring the fabric to her brassiere. We did the same thing with the other square, this time pinning it to the back of her leotard. We put two large safety pins down the side seams to close the skirt around. Martha reached down to the floor and picked up the two curved triangular remnants that she had cut from the squares. She placed one triangle on her shoulder, and moved it around until she was able to create a sleeve and something covering her breast, then did the same on the other side. We pinned the pieces in place, and in almost no time at all, it was basted together. Her costume was complete and was never changed.

It was during this period of time, when we were getting ready to perform *Primitive Mysteries,* that an intriguing letter came for me in the mail. My name and address on the envelope were not written in script but instead were printed rather awkwardly in an uneven, labored manner. I was puzzled by this. When I opened the envelope I found a short note, also printed in the same way. As I unfolded the note, a ten dollar bill fell out. This was exciting! The message said, "Dear Dorothy, I hope you will use this money to buy some good, healthy meals. I hear you are not eating properly." It was signed "From an Admirer." There was also a postscript, "I will be sending more money from time to time." How thrilling! An admirer! Dinners cost fifty cents at that time at Alice McAllister's on Eighth Street. Ten dollars would buy a lot of meals.

I immediately showed Martha the letter. She held it in her hands, looked at it carefully, and took out the ten dollars. She was clearly as puzzled as I had been. After a moment or two, she said slowly and rather thoughtfully, "You know, Dorothy, it may be from someone rather strange. It might even be from a lesbian!"

I had only just recently heard this term, and it sounded a bit scary. Martha paused before continuing, "Of course, it would be absolutely wonderful for you to have lots of delicious dinners." Another pause. "But if you did that, then you would be inclined to feel obligated, and I know that you would not want to feel obligated, would you?"

Martha stared first at me, then at the note, and remarked, "There's no return address, is there? So we can't send it back, can we?" Then she smiled at me for a moment before saying, "Dorothy, why don't we just use the money to buy the materials we need for the group's costumes for *Primitive Mysteries*? We could do that today. That would be absolutely grand, wouldn't it?" She used those words a lot at that time—"absolutely grand."

I was shocked and a little disappointed by Martha's suggestion, but she was holding fast to my ten dollar bill. It was true that I would not want to feel obligated to anyone "strange," and this way Martha would not have to feel indebted to Louis for money. Louis sometimes said that Martha was reckless about the way she spent the money he was loaning her. I felt it must have been humiliating for Martha to have to ask Louis for money, so it made me glad to agree to give Martha the ten dollars for costumes.

We immediately went downtown together to shop. In keeping with her established rule that costumes for the group could cost no more than one dollar each, Martha headed straight to the remnant tables. Her hands moved over each of the materials, feeling which ones would stretch, which were rough, and which had movement in them. Martha liked jersey. Finally, she settled on some large remnants of tubular jersey, enough for the whole group. It was a color I thought of as Virgin Mary blue.

That evening Martha cut a length of jersey for each of us, and one by one we stepped into our jersey tube. She pinned a pleat over one hip, and carried it up onto the shoulder. The pleat was sewn straight down the front from the shoulder, over the breast, to the hips. There was no fitting in at the waist or under the breast, but it was fitted closely around the rump. The neck was square, the sleeves short, and the skirt was cut off at an awkward length. We looked very solid. I believe she wanted us to look like the little wood carvings or clay figures she had brought back from New Mexico. The one thing that she surely did not want was for us to look graceful or seductive.

The preparation for *Primitive Mysteries* that had taken so many months was to culminate finally in public performances at the Craig Theatre in New York City. There was tremendous pressure as performance time drew near. The stage was available to us for only a very limited amount of time. Looking at what had been prepared in the studio, and then transferred to the stage, was a devastating experience for Martha. There was so little time to clarify and adjust spacing. Martha became a holy terror, tearing everything apart, respacing, and rechoreographing.

She developed the most frightful headache. When we took a break, she and Louis sat together in the audience for consultation. She called out for me to come and rub her neck, and try to relax her knotted muscles with my "healing hands," as she called them. I stood behind her seat, trying to ease the tension for her, while she and Louis immersed themselves in urgent discussion. Together they searched desperately for ways to solve problems as they arose. Louis pressed always for abstraction and purpose. Nothing could be done for decorative effect. I felt privileged to hear Martha and Louis talking freely in front of me, as if I were a member of their family. Louis drove Martha forward and encouraged us to be patient and keep going. He was a bulwark of strength for everyone as we prepared for the premiere.

On the day of a performance, Martha always washed her hair and brushed it for nearly an hour, working Vaseline into it to thoroughly coat it. The Vaseline made it shine and hold together. Her hair was not sticky, but it was heavy. She wore it long and thick and cut off straight across in back, and it would swing out, extending her movement range. For *Primitive Mysteries,* the members of the group wore the black hair nets from *Heretic,* so that no hair showed at all. I had to hide my fair hair with two heavy black nets in order not to break the feeling of anonymity.

The audience for modern dance was very limited at that time, but each of Martha's concerts was considered an event. Sculptors, painters, composers, writers, actors, directors, and stage designers all flocked to see what she was up to. The theater was filled with celebrities and patrons of the arts. Many came prepared to give support for perhaps unpopular, but promising and important works. Others came to criticize. No one knew what to expect.

The lights were lowered. The curtain opened. The entrance for *Primitive Mysteries* made a powerful visual statement. The sudden impact of the walk caught the audience off guard and captured their attention. It was important that they first see the One in White walking with the group, all of us moving together in silent unison. Martha's tremendous presence carried us with her. Her white organdy costume instantly established the mood of her character as virginal, angelic, innocent.

With the first note of the flute, the youthful, delicate, vulnerable heart and soul of the dance was revealed. Martha swung her legs out, almost as if skipping in a childlike fashion, then floated softly, running high on her bare feet, from one small group of friends to the other. The members of each group in turn cherished her, supported her, framed her with sharp designs before sending her with loving care, gently but firmly, across the stage to others waiting eagerly to receive her. Gradually, strange and darker sounds began to ring out like church bells. Hints of the Gregorian chants that Louis loved could be heard. As Martha continued the childlike skipping walk back and forth across the stage, she quite clearly was drawing strength, first from one group and then the other, as the music grew more compelling.

My group was seated solidly on the floor, in a line placed squarely across the upstage area. We were like primitive carved stone figures of the ancestors—the generations. When the somber, cathedral-like chords rang out, we rocked fiercely, turned, and knelt sharply as we folded ourselves over into the most compact shapes. As the music grew in strength, we rose, rocking to our feet. I felt that in the act of standing we had become part of the present. Now we used a more full-hearted version of the theme walk, moving jubilantly, joyfully, with a singing feeling as we came forward, and back, and forward again to join in the "Hymn to the Virgin."

Because of the discussions I had overheard during rehearsal, to me it was not Martha onstage—it was an echo of Mary, the Mother of Jesus. When Martha walked forward between two lines of dancers, I accepted the idea without hesitation that she was recalling and suggesting the One who walked on water. I shared the memory and cherished it as she did. With each step, she first raised a foot in front of her, then paused a moment before taking the next step. This allowed one of us, starting consecutively from the back of the line, to drop down and reach a cupped hand forward to place it underneath her foot as if ready to support her weight in the air. At the moment someone placed a hand under her foot, Martha would reach out to touch the face of a girl on the other side of her. With this caressing gesture, she distracted the audience from seeing the hand slip away from under her foot as she stepped down and allowed the next hand to come into position. Martha was like a magician, who knows how to capture the eye of the audience and make them see precisely what she wants them to see.

At another point, Martha sat serenely on the floor, her gown spread out to cover her raised knees. Her lap had suddenly become a resting place to receive the body of a dancer who descended gently in a softly spiraling back fall. Martha rocked the dancer back and forth, as if Michelangelo's *Pietà* had come to life. This vision dissolved just as suddenly as it had appeared. The figure in Martha's lap rose to stand behind her in a wide, deep plié, then spread out the fingers of her two hands into a fanlike shape behind Martha's head. To some, this movement may have suggested a circle of light, a halo, or the points of a crown. To others, it might have represented His crown or an illustration of the Virgin Mary as seen in Sunday school. To me, it was a marvelously colored aura.

When the music of the "Hymn to the Virgin" suddenly stopped, the group—with Martha again one of us—calmly, deliberately, silently assembled and made our formal exit. We took a breath, reassembled, and returned to the stage once more in total silence for the second segment of the dance. "Crucifixus" was urgent, close-knit, and staccato. With the first note of the music, our arms and heads were jolted up. They remained in that position, as if frozen with distress, while we focused up toward that imaginary point where a figure had once hung, suspended on a cross. There was one among us whose head was not held high, one who did not, could not, look up. This was the One in White. Her hands were cupped, raised in a gesture that shielded her eyes from the terrible sight that transfixed the rest of us. A tall girl stood on either side of her to guide and support her in her blind horror. The three edged slowly but steadily forward, as if treading water.

Again and again each small group of the rest of us pressed forward, then fell back, to try to see better. This was done first from one angle and then from another, until at last we were all assembled at what I always imagined was the foot of the cross. Our twisted fingers came up in silent empathy, to feel and shape out the crown of thorns. There ensued a still, silent, seemingly endless moment. When at last the One in White flung her arms wide to suddenly uncover her eyes to see, the first of us broke out of our frozen stillness into a huge, massive, deliberately crashing leap. One after another, the dancers joined in a leaping circle around her, everyone crying out silently for her. As we ran, our arms were wrenched up in back of us in a feeling of self-flagellation, our bodies contracted over. I felt my face, as it thrust forward, was a mask of shared agony and horror.

The momentum gathered. The tempo increased furiously. When at last we stopped, abruptly, we had encircled Martha, who was sitting on the floor. We all tipped forward, head to the ground, perhaps paying homage. As we rocked backward, the One in White slowly, effortlessly, ascended straight up in a moment of near levitation. The timing had to be perfect to create the illusion of "the rising" in an obscure, delicate, subtle way. Sophie Maslow once admitted to me, "I give Martha a little push from the back, just to get her started up. It's our secret," and she smiled.

After this quiet ending, we all walked offstage quite simply and took a deep breath. Then we returned for the last small segment, "Hosannah!" Without "the rising," how could we have shared such a joyful, buoyant, radiant finale? As we walked offstage for the last time, there was a pause, and then the sound of shouting and clapping came like an explosion. An extraordinary ovation followed. It was a tremendous embrace for Martha and her dancers, affirming that what we had all felt for a long time was also being experienced by the audience.

—from *Bird's Eye View*, with Joyce Greenberg, 1997

LE SACRE DU PRINTEMPS
Lydia Sokolova

Born Hilda Munnings in England, Lydia Sokolova (1896–1974) joined Diaghilev's Ballets Russes in 1913, the first English ballerina in his company. Her most important role was as the Chosen Maiden in the Massine version of The Rite of Spring *(1920). She also appeared in the original productions of* La Boutique Fantastique *and* Le Bal.

It is generally agreed that the *Sacre du Printemps* contains the longest, the most exhausting, and the most difficult solo dance of all ballets—that of the Chosen Virgin, which I created in Massine's ballet. This amazing choreographic work was started in the unromantic surroundings of Liverpool. I can truthfully say that I am the only living person who knows, and remembers, the original version of the *Danse Sacre* in its entirety. I little thought when I was appearing in Nijinsky's *Sacre du Printemps* in Paris, when it was howled down, that seven years later I should be creating the role of the Chosen Virgin in the same ballet with Massine's choreography, and that it would be my biggest achievement.

The very first step arranged by Massine was possibly the most famous in the whole dance. This, like all of them, had a very complicated rhythm. The step was repeated thirteen times, but it came so near the end of the dance, and after a series of enormous jumps, that by the time I had to execute it I was almost in a state of exhaustion and was long past counting the number of times I had to do it; consequently I was assisted by Woizikovsky, who prompted me by counting aloud up to thirteen.

As Massine and I seemed to work together so harmoniously, the actual creating of the steps came very easily to him. After two or three rehearsals, Diaghilev and he decided that it would be wiser if we were separated completely from the usual routine of everyday work, and so the two of us returned alone to London. Massine decided he would have to divide the dance into phrases, some long and some short. This was because this particular work of Stravinsky has no set dance formula: for instance the first step repeats itself seven times, the second five times; then comes a small echo of five, executed by the *corps de ballet;* the next step repeats itself seven times, the next five, the next sixteen, and so on. The dance is danced completely separate from the orchestra in rhythm and phrasing; but it had to be danced so perfectly in rhythm and detail that on three occasions I had to meet the orchestra on two beats, where there was a definite pause in the music. If either the orchestra or I were early or late, it had to be faked by my missing or adding one movement. During the whole time I danced the *Sacre,* the orchestra and I met on these three occasions perfectly only at two performances, both of which Eugene Goossens was conducting. The whole dance was so intricate that the only people who could possibly have known were Massine and myself.

To arrive at such absolute rhythm it was necessary to spend hours practising the dance with a metronome. As I have said, my rhythm was completely different from that of the orchestra; I could only take my cue from the first beat of the conductor at the beginning; and after the three pauses when I met the orchestra, I used to remember how many times I had repeated each step by pressing a finger down into the palm of my hand each time I did it.

I used to find it a terrible nervous strain, during the first act while I was preparing in the wings, and during the first part of the second act where I had to dance with the *corps de ballet,* hearing the powerful Stravinsky music which was so completely different in interpretation from the dance which I knew I had to perform a little later. All the time I was concentrating so profoundly on what was to come, that it was a great mental effort to force myself to listen to and count what I had to dance with the *corps de ballet.*

As the moment drew near for the enormous group of about sixty people formed by the ballet to move back, leaving me alone in the centre of the stage, I could feel the cold perspiration gathering on my hands as I stood with fists clenched. The tensity of that moment was overpowering. At such a time it is impossible not to feel the absolute contact with a huge audience, as there always was for the *Sacre.*

With my eyes fixed on a red "Exit" light at the back of the theatre, without allowing them to blink, I lived the role of the Chosen Virgin of the Sun, completely spellbound in the part I was playing. As the huge group moved back to the count of twenty, I knew the moment had arrived, when with one upward beat of the conductor my ordeal was to begin.

Those who know the music of this famous dance will remember how it works up to an absolute frenzy. This was interpreted by Massine by huge jumps round and round the stage, until at the last moment, like a deeply inhaled breath, I held myself poised on my points, before literally collapsing exhausted in the middle of the stage. The sensation following the dance was indescribable. The nearest description I can give is that my heart was bursting and that I felt I could never recover my breath again.

Always Woizikovsky and Hoyer were the ones who pulled me up and stood me on my feet, and I can honestly say I was all but unconscious until the curtain had fallen and risen three times.

—from *Dancing for Diaghilev,* 1968

SERENADE
Ruthanna Boris

Serenade *was the first ballet George Balanchine created in America—he used*
Tchaikovsky's Serenade in Strings *and his students at the new School of American*
Ballet. The first performance was out of doors, on the estate of Felix Warburg, on
June 9, 1934. By the time it entered City Ballet's repertory, in 1948, it had under-
gone many changes, but throughout its career it has remained one of the best-loved
dance works of our time.

Among the students participating in the creation of Serenade *was the very young*
Ruthanna Boris (1918–2007), who was one of the first students at Balanchine's new
School of American Ballet. She went on to an illustrious career as a dancer—the first
American ballerina to star in the Ballets Russes de Monte Carlo, from 1942 to
1950—and a choreographer, her best-known work being Cakewalk *(1951) for the*
New York City Ballet. In her later years she taught, mostly on the West Coast, and
grew increasingly interested in dance as therapy, eventually becoming president of the
California chapter of the American Dance Therapy Association.

After several months of uninterrupted class schedules there came the
moment we were awaiting: finishing technique class as usual, Mr. Balanchine
stood up from his seat on the watching bench while we brought the last
grand battement down into fifth position, each toe touching the floor, light,
soundless, each Achilles tendon pliant, stretching, guiding the heel, lower
metatarsal arch, upper metatarsal arch and its five toes firm into the final-
fifth position, *demi-plié, relevé,* stay–stay–stay while the finalizing arpeggio
and its overtones flowed from the piano, diminished to a whisper, faded and
was gone. Mr. Balanchine then did something unusual.

He stepped up onto the bench, stretched both arms out toward us, palms
open and out like a welcoming greeting. His eyes moved over all of us standing there sweating in fifth position—he looked at one after another, no one
was left out. There was a suspended moment of stillness. I felt a rising tide of
expectation in my body, in my blood, in the studio, spreading through the
bodies and bloodstreams all around me. He spoke softly, without emotion:
"Gentlemen, you are excused. Ladies, take rest, fifteen minutes, come back

to studio, we will make some steps." He waved his hands in dismissal, went to the piano and began a conversation with Ariadna Mikeshna.

That invitation—"take rest" . . . "we will make some steps" could mean only one thing! We, his chosen American dancers, were about to begin work on a new choreography made on US! The American Ballet was about to happen!

We rested in a state of unanimous excitement, laying ouselves out on the floor of the dressing room, our legs propped all the way up to our buttocks on our lockers. There was none of the usual talk or gossip—it was a time to savor silence steeped in feelings too deep for words.

Fifteen minutes later we assembled again in Studio "A." Ariadna Mikeshna came in, carrying her briefcase, sat down at the piano, took out sheets of music, spread them on the music stand where she studied them with care. We gravitated to each side of the studio, draping ourselves along the bars, waiting. We were about to become a real ballet company! It was a Holy Day. Mr. Balanchine appeared in the open doorway, looked around at the bars and his waiting dancers, smiled, came through the space, closed the door behind himself, walked slowly, thoughtfully to the middle of the studio where he stopped.

He appeared to be having a conversation with himself; his lips were moving but no sound came out. He walked the distance between the center of the studio and the center of the watching bench but did not seat himself; he looked all around again, from one of us to the next, from bar to bar; then, striding purposefully, he walked over to the bar on studio right, lifted Kathryn Mullowney's arm off the bar, put it through his own arm, walked her to the direct center of the studio, turned her to face the mirror, disengaged her arm, and returned to stand at the watching bench.

He repeated this process over and over. One by one he chose a dancer from the bar and escorted her in the manner of a cavalier to a place in the design he was making. A picture emerged: lines extending from studio right to studio left were being formed; first, a line across studio center, two dancers on either side of Kathryn Mullowney; next, a line of four behind that line; then two dancers behind that line with a wide space between them; and, finally a line of four in front of the center line of five. I was standing at studio right, looking at what was happening in the mirror, seeing it from the front: the center line spread across the width of the studio, from right to left; all the dancers in the lines of four in front and behind it and the line of two at the rear could be clearly seen—no one was behind anyone else, each body had its own visible position and its own surrounding space. It was totally unlike any group placement I had ever seen—the usual a faceless set of straight lines dancing behind a soloist. Mr. George Balanchine was making lines where everyone could be seen!

I noticed Annabelle Lyons, standing, waiting as I was waiting, across the studio at the left side. She looked as unhappy as I felt. We were the two smallest dancers in the group of seventeen who had been in class that day. It was common knowledge that tallness was especially interesting to Mr. George Balanchine. The grouping I saw in the mirror looked complete. I couldn't find a nook or cranny where Annabelle and I might be smuggled in. My despairing heart told me "You will be an understudy. Be brave. Maybe someone will break her leg."

Mr. Balanchine studied the design he had made carefully; then, he jumped up onto the watching bench, rubbed his hands together gleefully, looked directly at the center of the studio, and announced—distinct, commanding— "ROOTANABELLA!"

We came flying and stood together in front of him. He stepped off the bench, took my arm, and escorted me to downstage right, in front of all the lines, returned and escorted Annabelle to downstage left, in front of all the lines, then he resumed his position—standing facing his now completed arrangement. Annabelle and I had become the front line in an assemblage of dancers standing in lines, put together so that every single body could be clearly seen.

He walked slowly back and forth in front of us, speaking slowly, thoughtfully, conversationally. He told us about his student days in Russia—how he had to run from building to building on the way to class every day because "it was revolution, bullets in street"; how he made "small company—four dancers, me one"; how "after revolution Soviet wants ballets for politics. I want to make dancing, not politics. I take my company away—leave Russia— go to Germany—find Ballets Russes Sergei Diaghilev—he give us work— we stay in Germany." We listened, respectful and anxious; he had never talked to us about himself before—mostly his talking was about how to do what we were working on.

Little by little his talking became more like a report—less conversational, more charged with feelings of anger and distress: "In Germany there is awful man—terrible, awful man! He looks like me only he has moustache— he is very bad man—he has moustache—I do not have moustache—I am not bad man—I am not awful man!" He went on and on about this awful man in Germany and his moustache, how they looked alike but he did not have a moustache. It seemed to me he was tasting his words and trying to get past them. To the best of my memory no one knew what he was talking about. We were adolescent and young adult ballet dancers, mostly American, mostly aware of the dance world, unaware of governmental affairs in the world beyond it. Radio and movies were then fairly primitive, television did not yet exist. Only sophisticated, well-travelled, alert American political observers might have understood what he was talking about during his increasingly impassioned words that morning in late 1933.

The talk was getting boring. Who cared about an "awful man" in Germany? We wanted to dance! Where were our steps? However, our manners, despite a lack of knowledge about an awful man with a moustache in Germany, were native, trained to venerate a balletic voice of authority; so, we remained at attention, listening and wondering what he was talking about and what it had to do with dancing.

Suddenly he paused, fell silent, drew himself up and proclaimed "When people in Germany see that man they do this"—his right arm shot out in front of him, raised diagonally up toward the ceiling. He continued, speaking softly, leaving his arm exactly where it was "But, you see, I am not bad man, I do not wear moustache—maybe, for me, you do this." He moved his arm to the right side, still held in a high diagonal. His voice went on "Now, put together feet, side by side—now, turn face, eyes look at hand. Now, maybe hand is tired, hand falls down." His hand slowly relaxed its stiff salute; his finger-tips, then hand, then wrist softened and dropped until his wrist was completely bent, the hand suspended from it. He continued "Now head is tired, cheek rests on left shoulder, wrist rests right side forehead, hand falls down, rests front of left shoulder, head change, rest on right shoulder, hand, arm fall down, meet left hand, make position *preparation,* feet make position one, arms position one, arms position two, *battement tendu par terre à la seconde,* right foot, close foot position five front, arms again position *preparation,* and, we dance!"

He had shown all the hand, cheek, head, and arm positions as he spoke them; we had picked up and moved along with him, just as we had been practising to do in all our technique classes for all the months we had been working with him. He continued after "we dance!" giving us the unison opening phrases of movement; then, he turned to face us, saying "Maybe you will show me?" We returned our feet to the parallel position from which everything had developed; he signalled Ariadna Mikeshna, who told us "I will play introduction before curtain; when I tell you 'Now' it is time to begin; you will be in your beginning position when the curtain goes up." She waited until Mr. Balanchine had taken his seat on the watching bench, and, with a wide, warm collegial smile in our direction she lifted her hands, brought them down to the keys, and played the opening measures of the Tchaikovsky *Serenade for Strings.*

It did not go perfectly the first time we did it. We all realized there was much refining and polishing ahead, but! we were on our way. We were told "We go on. Tonight you will think, you will close your eyes and you will see what we do today. Tomorrow we will practice. Soon you will know exact what to do." He roughed out half of the first movement that morning, configuration after configuration for groups, small solo *encha*înments interspersed between them, lots of running, weaving in and out between each other, sudden pictures made by interwoven arms, varieties of body level in relation to the floor, always moving, always connected in time and space.

That night, as I lay in bed mentally rehearsing all I had learned in two one-hour rehearsals, that morning, counting the ten-minute "speech" before the dancing began, the wonder of his way of making dancing filled me with a swelling sense of mystery. The words he had said, the image of an awful man with a moustache who looked like him transformed into an opening of sad reverie that became a dance of gracious connections and beauty! The dancing that seemed to pour out of him as he worked among us had reminded me of a spider spinning a web. I looked up at my bedroom ceiling and said "Whatever you are, wherever you may exist, you were with us in Studio 'A'

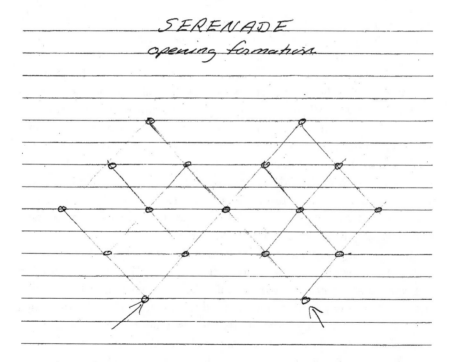

NOTE: When I was preparing these pages I wanted memory confirmation about the exact number of dancers in each line. I asked two of Mr. B's dancers who are among those he trusted to stage his ballets: Una Kai and Francia Russell both danced with his New York City Ballet during its formative years, sixteen or so years after his original *Serenade* was composed. Here is the opening formation: Una drew the grid; Francia concurred, saying "It is perfection itself." Although an audience sees it from the front, as I did, looking in the mirror, it is actually based on diagonals. The two little arrows in front are Annabelle (stage left) and me (stage right). I had told Una about the day he began; she drew the arrows and sent a note saying "Your place!"

this morning. I want to understand why he said what he said and did what he did. Maybe sometime I will."

Two-hour rehearsals, between classes, were added to our daily schedule after that day, Monday through Saturday, with special three-hour rehearsals on Sundays, preceded by a half-hour warm-up *barre* given by Dorothie Littlefield. Until then my understanding of required rehearsal behavior had been limited to a sense of obedience—to pick up what was shown and strive to do it in an immediate technically correct replica of the model. Mr. Balanchine did not model his steps clearly, carefully, or technically—he indicated them, moved through them fleetingly, often giving body and arm positions by name at the same time. He ran, jumped, turned, changed direction, made combinations of classroom steps that looked like improvisation instead of technical practice. He gave positions following swiftly after each other that blended one into the next—he often looked like a kaleido-scope—fluid, flexible, free. He went all the way down to the floor and then bounded up into the air—he kneeled, stretched up to standing, wove our arms and torsos in and out of linkings with each other. As I watched him darting among his dancers, placing arms, tilting heads, curving torsos, he made me think of a bee among flowers—he looked serious and happy at the same time—when he was pleased with a result of his exertions he giggled his dry little giggle. We became participants in his process—he shared his pleasure when making dancing with all of us. There were times his combina-tions seemed to surprise him—he asked "You can do like this? You say to me if is comfortable, not comfortable"—"You must say to me about if you can do *en pointe*. I am man—I do not go *en pointe*." I felt he trusted us—loved working with us—wanted us to have as much to do with what he made for us as he did. Rehearsing with Mr. George Balanchine, day after day, became a never-ending discovery of new ways to dance.

One morning he completed the first movement of the dance we had been learning by the end of our first rehearsal hour. He set a configuration that returned each of us to our original place and position in the opening picture—legs parallel, right arm upraised toward stage right, heads turned to the arm, eyes looking up at uplifted hands. One dancer was missing—Annabelle had missed class that morning, had been absent from the rehearsal. Her place was empty. He looked nonplused; then, re-rehearsed what he had done. He gave us a ten-minute break at that point. Annabelle arrived for the second hour; he reviewed the ending; and, once we all were in place and beginning the last arm, head, eyes movements, he brought her in from stage left rear, wandering through the lines, looking for her place, finding it, assuming her arm position, looking up at her hand; then, he had us all drop our arms, turn away from her, and slowly begin to exit into the wings off stage right; and, at the same time he brought Bill Dollar (the most accomplished male dancer) in through the moving bodies, to Annabelle, reach for her upraised hand, bring it down to his shoulder, and together they began the second movement, a *Waltz,* turning, dipping, flying together in a wide circle on the now empty stage.

He went on, bringing us back in groups, until the stage was full of dancers waltzing in constantly changing formations, finally coming together for a mass exit off stage right, whirling and waltzing. It took a few more rehearsals to complete the *Waltz:* the morning he reviewed it, after it was fairly well cleaned and polished Heidi Vossler fell down during the exit, far downstage right. She scrambled to get up but Mr. Balanchine stopped her and said "No, you stay, others go." He put Kathryn Mullowney together with Charles Lasky (who was tall, strong, and handsome); he placed Charles in front, bent forward from the waist with Kathryn draped over his back and had them enter from upstage left in that position, moving on a diagonal toward Heidi. He fussed with their positions a bit, then had Kathryn wrap her downstage arm around Charles's chest and cover his eyes with her upstage hand. It made an interesting, dramatic picture as they slowly advanced toward Heidi, lying stretched out on the floor; that was the beginning of the last movement, the *Elegy.* After rehearsal I asked "Mr. Balanchine, how did you think of that position for Kathryn and Charles Lasky? It's very interesting and dramatic." He smiled and whispered, as if it was a secret, "You know, Lasky, he is very near-sight. I thought he does not see, so, maybe more comfortable if eyes have cover and Kathryn looks where to go." It was my turn to giggle, which I did as I whispered back, "Thank you for telling me. That's a neat idea—it makes a lot of sense. You made Heidi's accident and Lasky's nearsightedness into a beautiful passage—the same way you turned Annabelle's absence from rehearsal into the beginning for the *waltz.* I love you, Mr. Balanchine! I love the way you work—I love the way you teach us—I want to be a choreographer just like you!" He looked at me very seriously, took my hands and held them together in his hands, and said "Yes, little one, you can love me but you must not worship me. Always remember! When I pull the chain on my toilet it is for the same reason you do." He smiled, released my hands, and said, "Now you eat your lunch."

—Previously unpublished in this version

PROFILES

COLONEL DE BASIL

Sol Hurok

Born in Lithuania, Vasily Grigorievich Voskresensky found it useful to adopt the name Colonel Wassili de Basil (1881–1951). He was an émigré Cossack colonel who had relocated to Paris, entered the art world, and become director of L'Opéra Russe. Somehow in 1932 he joined forces with René Blum to co-direct the newly reborn Ballet Russe de Monte Carlo, and a few years later maneuvered Blum out of the organization. (Blum was to to die in the Nazi camps.) The de Basil Ballets Russes, with a constantly changing cast of choreographers and dancers, toured the world under constantly changing names until de Basil's death. (During the war, it performed mainly in Australia and South America.) To a large extent, it was his company, with its glamorous Russian stars, that cemented in the American mind the identification of "ballet" with everything "Russe."

Early in 1932, René Blum joined forces with one of the most curious personalities that modern ballet has turned up, in the person of a gentleman who wished to be known as Col. W. de Basil.

De Basil had had a ballet company of sorts for some time. I first ran into him in Paris, shortly after Diaghilev's death, where he had allied himself with Prince Zeretelli's Russian Opera Company; and again in London, where the Lionel Powell management, in association with the Imperial League of Opera, had given them a season of combined opera and ballet at the old Lyceum Theatre. With ballets by Boris Romanoff and Bronislava Nijinska, de Basil had toured his little troupe around Europe in buses, living from hand to mouth; had turned up for a season at Monte Carlo, at René Blum's invitation. That did it. De Basil worked out a deal with Blum, whereby de Basil became a joint managing director of the combined companies, now under the title of Ballet Russe de Monte Carlo. A season was given in the summer of 1932, in Paris, at the Théâtre des Champs Elysées.

It was there I first saw the new company. It was then I took the plunge. I negotiated. I signed them for a visit to the American continent. A book could be devoted to these negotiations alone. It would not be believable; it would fail to pass every test of credibility ever devised.

I feel that this is the point at which to digress for a moment, in order to sketch in a line drawing of de Basil, with some of the shadows and some of the substance. Unless I do, no reader will be able to understand why I once contemplated a book to be called *To Hell with Ballet!*

To begin with, de Basil was a Cossack and a Caucasian. Neither term carries with it any connotation of gentleness or sensitivity. De Basil was one of the last persons in the world you would expect to find at the head of an organization devoted to the development of the gentle, lyric art of the ballet. Two more dissimilar partners in an artistic venture than de Basil and Blum could not be found.

René Blum, the gentle, cultured intellectual, was a genuine artist: amiable, courteous, and fully deserving of the often misused phrase—a man of the world. His alliance with de Basil was fore-doomed to failure; for one of René Blum's outstanding characteristics was a passion to avoid arguments, discussions, scandals, troubles of any sort. Blum commanded the highest respect from his artists and associates; but they never feared him. To them he was the kind, understanding friend to whom they might run with their troubles and problems. Blum's sensitivity was such that he would run from de Basil as one would try to escape a plague. René Blum, you would say, was, perhaps, the ivory-tower dilettante. You would be wrong. René Blum gave the lie to this during the war by revealing himself a man of heroic stature. On the occupation of France, he was in grave danger, since he was a Jew, and the brother of Léon Blum, the Socialist leader, great French patriot, and one-time Premier. René, however, was safely and securely out of the country. But he, too, was a passionate lover of France. France, he felt, needed him. Tossing aside his own safety, he returned to his beloved country, to share its fate. His son, who was the apple of his father's eye, joined the Maquis; was killed fighting the Nazis. René Blum was the victim of Nazi persecution.

Let us look for a moment at the background of Blum's ballet collaborator. The "Colonel" was born Vassily Grigorievitch Voskresensky. In his native *milieu* he had some sort of police-military career. Although he insisted on the title "Colonel," he certainly never attained that rank in the Tsar's army. He was a lieutenant in the *Gendarmes*. After the revolution, in 1918, he turned up as a captain with Bicherakoff's Cossacks. Later on he turned naval and operated in the Black Sea.

There is an interval in de Basil's life that has never been entirely filled in with complete accuracy: the period immediately following his flight and escape from Russia. The most credible of the legends surrounding this period is that he sold motor-cars in Italy. Eventually, he turned up in Paris, where my trail picked him up at a concert agency called *Zerbaseff,* which concerned itself with finding jobs for refugee artists. It was then he called himself de Basil.

At the time I met him, he had a Caucasian partner, the Prince Zeretelli whom I have mentioned, and who was a one-time manager of the People's Theatre, in St. Petersburg. It was this partnership that brought forth the Ballet and Opéra Russe de Paris, which gave seasons at the Théâtre des Champs Elysées, in Paris, and, as I have mentioned, at the Lyceum Theatre, in London.

Let me first set down the man's virtues. De Basil had great charm. By that I do not necessarily mean he was charming. His charm was something he could turn on at will, like a tap, usually when he was in a tight spot. More than once it helped him out of deep holes, and sticky ones. He had an inexhaustible fount of energy, could drive himself and others; never seemed to need sleep; and, aiming at a highly desired personal goal, had unending patience. With true oriental passivity, he could wait. He had undaunted courage; needless, reckless courage, in my opinion; a stupid courage compounded often out of equal parts of stubbornness and sheer bravado. He was a born organizer. He intuitively possessed a flair for the theatre: a flair without knowledge. He could be an excellent host; he was a *cordon bleu* cook. He was generous, he was simple in his tastes.

Yet, with all these virtues, de Basil was, at the same time, one of the most difficult human beings I have ever encountered in a lifetime of management. This tall, gaunt, cadaver of a man had a powerful physique, a dead-pan face, and a pair of cold, astigmatic eyes, before which rested thick-lensed spectacles. He had all the makings of a dictator. Like his countryman Joseph Stalin, he was completely impossible as a collaborator. He was a born intriguer, and delighted in surrounding himself with scheming characters. During my career I have met scheming characters who, nevertheless, have had certain positive virtues: they succeeded in getting things done. De Basil's scheming characters consisted of lawyers, hacks, amateur managers, brokers, without exception third-rate people who damaged and destroyed.

It would be an act of great injustice to call de Basil stupid. He was as shrewd an article as one could expect to meet amongst all the lads who have tried to sell the unwary stranger the Brooklyn Bridge, the Capitol at Washington, or the Houses of Parliament.

De Basil deliberately engaged this motley crew of hangers-on, since his Caucasian Machiavellism was such that he loved to pit them one against the other, to use them to build up an operetta atmosphere of cheap intrigue that

I felt sure had not hitherto existed save in the Graustark type of fiction. De Basil used them to irritate and annoy. He would dispatch them abroad in his company simply to stir up trouble, to form cliques: for purposes of *chantage;* he would order them into whispered colloquies in corners, alternately wearing knowing looks and glum visages. De Basil and his entire entourage lived in a world of intrigue of their own deliberate making. His fussy, busy little cohorts cost him money he did not have, and raised such continuous hell that the wonder is the company held together as long as it did.

De Basil's unholy joy would come from creating, through these henchmen, a nasty situation and then stepping in to pull a string here, jerk a cord there, he would save the situation, thus becoming the hero of the moment. . . .

De Basil and his methods became increasingly aggravating. His chicanery, his eternal battling, above all, his overweening obsession about the size of his name in the display advertising, were sometimes almost unbearable. He carried a pocket-rule with him and would go about cities measuring the words "Col. W. de Basil." Now electric light letters vary in size in the various cities, and there is no way of changing them without having new letters made or purchased at considerable expense and trouble. I remember a scene in Detroit, where de Basil became so obnoxious that the company manager and I climbed to the roof of the theatre and took down the sign with our own hands, in order to save us from further annoyance that day.

All of this accumulated irritation added up to an increasing conviction that life was too short to continue this sort of thing indefinitely, despite my love for and my interest and faith in ballet both as an art and as a popular form of entertainment.

—from *S. Hurok Presents,* 1953

THE MARQUIS DE CUEVAS
Agnes de Mille

Married to a Rockefeller heiress, the eighth Marquis de Cuevas (1885–1961), born in Santiago, Chile, poured a fortune into a series of ballet companies, beginning with the International Ballet in America, in 1944. Employing a roster of important dancers and famous choreographers, the company held together until the death of the marquis in 1961. In that year, Rudolf Nureyev, having just defected from the Soviet Union, performed with the company's latest, and final, avatar, the International Ballet of the Marquis de Cuevas.

The Marquis de Cuevas was a man of vast wealth and unlimited enthusiasm for the ballet, a combination to set local impresarios' pulses racing and manners tripping. Like a tropical hummingbird, however, he buzzed about teasingly, only to elude all efforts at capture. Why he chose to build a ballet company we can only guess, but he did.

His entry in Anatole Chujoy and P. W. Manchester's *The Dance Encyclopedia* reads:

> De Cuevas, Marquis George (eighth Marquis de Piedrablanca de Guana de Cuevas), American patron of the arts, b. 1886, Chile, of a Spanish father and Danish mother (American citizen since 1940), d. Feb. 22, 1961, Cannes, France; m. Margaret Strong, granddaughter of the late John D. Rockefeller; sponsor of the Masterpieces of Art exhibition at the N.Y. World's Fair (1939–40); founder and director of Ballet Institute (1943) and Ballet International which made its N.Y. debut in 1944.

Suddenly and most unnecessarily in October 1943 the Marquis announced his very own new company, a large, permanent company with unlimited financing. He decided to waste no time in slow developments. He bought the old but lovely Columbus Circle Theatre and completely renovated it, including the prettiest crystal chandelier in New York. It was a wonderful gala theater, white and gold with crimson velvet. The stage was a bit small, but the company took a pleat in *Sylphides* and squashed it into view, although the corps de ballet lines came out rumpled. Nijinska was hired for new works, Salvador Dalí did the scenery, and Gian Carlo Menotti contributed his first fine big score, *Sebastian.*

Oh, how had de Cuevas managed to escape the baits and snares set by so many suave tongues? People had appealed to his artistic instincts, to his ambition for fame, to his concern for young artists, to his zest for creating, to the paltry arithmetic of possible financial developments. All to no avail. He wanted to have his own company all to himself, his own way, one that would bear his name. There followed on the instant a gnashing of teeth and the prediction of doom and bankruptcy. Dancers stood to gain, of course, but they had no voice in any of these matters. They just quietly rushed to sign up.

The Marquis soon had dancers enough. What he needed was choreographers, and in a dragnet operation, he approached all of us, every one. His emissary was a young Greek named Yolas who had been the dancing partner of Theodora Roosevelt. After several years of touring with moderate success, Roosevelt had given up dancing, married the young painter Tom Keogh, and started her brilliant career as a novelist (*Meg, The Double Door*). Yolas cast about for other activities and found the Marquis.

Rehearsals were held daily at Studio 61 Ballet Arts in Carnegie Hall. The Marquis arrived to supervise, frequently took charge, and on occasion, growing remarkably exercised over points of discipline, jumped onto the floor to act. Diana Adams once told me with goggle eyes of the morning when the Marquis discovered that the star, Viola Essen, had absented herself without explanation. He flew into a passion and backed Yolas right across the room, denouncing him in French for failing to keep order. The dancers stood by, astounded. Finally the Marquis, who was considerably shorter than the large Greek athlete, grabbed Yolas by the earlobes and banged his head against the wall several emphatic times.

"Marquis, Marquis," groaned Yolas. "Pas de scandal!"

"Don't be an ass," said the Marquis tartly, punishing his skull once more. "The dancers don't know I'm scolding you. They can't understand what's going on. I'm talking French."

Yolas, no doubt chastened, came to me with a royal summons. I begged off time and again, but finally the great black Hispano-Suiza with the crest on the doors waited for me in Fifty-seventh Street. I was led into it directly out of a morning class, at the outlandish hour I had deliberately and uncivilly designated as convenient for my lunch. Yolas and I progressed on feathers to the East Sixties, where a butler flung open the house door. I was led up hushing rugs to the first or drawing-room floor and left in a long narrow salon, where I sat gingerly on the edge of a baby-blue satin chair. Yolas went to fetch his master while I contemplated a naked amorous Bouguereau nine feet high. Suddenly there was a scream and the Marquis was with me.

"A *biche*! A *biche*! She has ankles like a *biche*!" he shrieked, and sat down opposite me, staring with satisfaction at my legs, which were decorously and nervously crossed. This was a flattering start, and I simpered prettily and rapidly recrossed my ankles several times.

The Marquis himself had very neat ankles, and his slender, delicate feet were shod in custom-made glove-kid boots. He was a trigger-tight little person, all black and white, and as he gazed at me with his agate eyes he seemed to be mentally biting his nails. Now and then a small flame winked in the opaque pupils. It gave promise of life but was no clue to emotion. He leaned forward or jerked with nervous excitement, and swung around and rotated on his blue satin chair as on a trapeze—and his voice was shrill. He wore the beautifully cut black alpaca trousers of a Spanish dancer and a shirt buttoned down the side of the neck like a Russian officer's but of the color chosen by Mussolini and Franco as suitable to their ideas. Since we were in the middle of the war and were battling most terribly with legions of fanatics in just this color, I didn't find his choice endearing. But I would guess that he had no personal convictions and found it merely teasing to be provocative.

With a series of yelps and shrieks he expatiated on his plans, which were in essence grandiose. At the moment he wanted me, and that I had other commitments and affiliations made no matter. He wanted me. He was, he informed me, going to have me. "But," he shouted with a giggle, "I am an autocrat. I am a true dictator. I tell the choreographers what to do."

"Which choreographers do you tell what to do?"

"All—all. Nijinska don't mind."

"Does she not? Well, now, who would have thought!"

"No. And when Romanov restages *Giselle,* he have no time for all details. He fixes the feet like so." The Marquis de Cuevas indicated the choreographer fixing the dancers' feet individually, a sight I have never been privileged to witness. "But he forgets the heads and I fix the heads. I run up and down the lines and fix heads like so, and so, and so . . ." He made a gesture of fixing heads reminiscent of the man who used to turn flapjacks in the window of Child's restaurant.

"Monsieur le Marquis," I said quietly, "I don't permit anyone to fix the heads in my rehearsals."

"No? You'll see what a help it is! I'm a dictator—absolute as to taste."

"I'm pretty sassy myself in my own rehearsals."

"Oh, we understand each other perfectly. We're going to get along."

This joyous conclusion was cut short by the entrance of the Marquise, a quiet, unobtrusive, brown-haired lady with very sad eyes and a gentle voice. I naturally presumed she would be our hostess, but after murmuring the amenities, she melted away. I never saw her again.

The Marquis had waved a hand and announced, "My wife." He then seemed to suspend all animation until she was gone.

"Now for lunch," he said, bounding up. Yolas, who had sat throughout unspeaking, jumped up on his strong legs and began to look interested. We were ushered into a long and superbly appointed dining room. At a table that could easily have accommodated forty, three places were laid—rather sparsely, I thought—at the entrance end, as though the butler had made sure that we could not get too firm a foothold in his domain.

We had hardly started on our cold sliced lamb and lettuce when angry voices were heard below. The butler whispered. The Marquis said, "Tch! Tch!" and "Pardon," threw down his napkin, and went to attend. Yolas attempted to make some sort of small talk and passed me cold lamb repeatedly. The shouting rose to the point of violence. There were several piercing screams.

I asked, "In God's name, what's going on?"

"Katya Gelesnova and her mother are suggesting a higher salary," explained Yolas.

"But I know Katya well. She is a gentle, kind, and quiet girl. She would never shout like that."

"That is not Katya. That is the Marquis—and her mother too, of course."

We finished lunch and then our host returned, smoothing down his hair and looking brisk. The butler had removed all traces of the meal. We sat facing a bare table. The forks and knives were assiduously taken away on a silver salver. The Marquis had not eaten a bite.

"Oh," he wailed, "I want something to eat."

The butler inclined punctiliously. "Too late," he said.

"Oh, Thomas," said the Marquis to his retreating back, "just anything, just something. I'm hungry."

Thomas barely turned. He stood with the implements for eating protectingly withdrawn in his far hand. "I have to set tea for thirty people, sir, and I'd better get at it." There was real rebuke in his tone. Both sentences were rebuking, in different ways.

"Anything," the Marquis begged. "On a tray, in my bedroom—anything. Some little tea, je vous en prie . . ."

Thomas looked exhausted and left.

I tried to understand what kind of ballet company the Marquis was planning and what his modern repertory was to consist of. He was distraught and unfocused, and he kept looking first at the door through which he had reappeared from his financial exercises and then at the door through which all hope of lunch had receded. Finally he said, "Ah!"

The tray had arrived—a small black tin tray such as is used in third-class cafeterias, presenting a kitchen cup and a small tin teapot with a teabag hanging out of it. Four saltines lay on a thick white crockery plate.

"And now, sir, if you please," said the butler, literally sweeping us out of the room. The doors snapped to behind us, and I got the impression of enormous activity suddenly released. Battalions of servants were swinging around that great table with Sèvres cups and crested plates.

The Marquis carried his own tray, although Yolas courteously offered to help. It weighed little enough, God knows. We made our way upstairs to the Marquis's bedroom. This was a surprise, a cross between a side chapel in a Latin American church and the corner of a nineteenth-century French museum. The pièce de résistance or center of focus was quite properly the bed, a narrow pallet with very high foot- and headboards of Spanish wrought iron entirely interlaced, festooned, and looped with stage jewelry—bracelets, necklaces, earrings, tiaras, and rings of diamonds and pearls, emeralds and rubies, as thickly massed as in the window of a junk shop. The effect was both grotesque and frightening. The pallet was quite simply and chastely covered with a zebra skin.

On the wall opposite the door was a splendid pen-and-wash drawing by Dalí of a very naked young man. Facing the bed was an equally aggressive naked youth by Sandro Botticelli. When I took this in, my jaw dropped, or rather it would have if I'd thought to shut it after viewing the bed. I had just discovered that one could go on saying no without closing one's mouth. Every horizontal space supported a memento or objet d'art, either precious or peculiar but always extraordinary. Crucifixes and rosaries, fine snuff-boxes, jeweled intaglios, goblets, madonnas, superb little missiles, phallic symbols, were scattered everywhere. This was a room straight out of Gautier's lushest daydreams.

Under a large glass bell in the corner, reposing on a velvet cushion, was what I thought I heard the Marquis designate as his wedding wreath. He may have said it was his wife's, but I thought he said it was his, and by this time I was bewildered enough to accept any statement. The wreath was of exquisite wax orange blossoms, a little bent, a little dusty, and obviously quite old, like the wreath of a holy effigy. About the whole room there was the air of a crypt made cozy with superstition. At the side of the bed was a massive door, leading, rumor said, into the next house, which the Marquis had bought for guests and friends. This door figured in Theodora Keogh's *The Double Door.*

The Marquis perched on a little carved chair of fine seventeenth-century workmanship, drank his unappetizing tea, and tried to get a definite commitment from me. But I was not so far gone that I would make a promise, and the conversation frayed out while my eyes rolled round and round that extraordinary room. At some mysterious moment my host seemed to know that the audience was at an end, and he politely but firmly terminated the interview. I hastily agreed that I had a rehearsal I must hurry to.

As I made my way down alone, I saw Thomas through the dining room door, placing the thirty-fourth gold-painted porcelain dish on the lace cloth. He looked at me coldly as he laid a heavy embossed spoon at its side, and an egg-fragile cup. I hastened out. From the mistress and her apartments there had been neither signal nor sound.

—from *Portrait Gallery,* 1990

However Ninette de Valois started her career—and the story has often been told—and at whatever point in it, whether at the very beginning or later, she became conscious of a mission or determination to found a national ballet in Great Britain; and whatever period of time must pass, in her calculation, before her undertaking reaches its high summer and begins to wane: there can be no doubt that she, of all persons occupied with any one of the arts today, has made the most elaborate plans, employed the greatest number of people, and worked on the grandest scale.

Being in some ways of a modest disposition, I never expect celebrated people to recognize me until I have been introduced to them four or five times. At luncheon recently with Ninette de Valois I wondered if she remembered our first meeting in 1936, and was fairly sure she did not.

I was an art student at that time; and between sessions of drawing buxom matrons or Italianate strong-men in the nude I would invent ballets and design the decorations for them. Gordon Anthony, the photographer, de Valois' brother, arranged a meeting between us, so that I could show her my sketches; and it was at his apartment in Cromwell Place opposite South Kensington Station, not in the studio which had once been Hoppé's and Millais's, but in the front sitting-room with its pink concealed lighting, its bookencased bed, radio-gramophone, and Pimm's No. 1, made with cider instead of lemonade, that I was first privileged to exchange a few words with the great woman, already familiar by sight, and shake her by the hand. As I can remember nothing she said about my work I now suppose her remarks must have been a miracle of diplomatic evasion: at any rate, she missed the chance of launching me immediately as the English Bakst, and we continued to be introduced intermittently for ten years. . . .

It was not until the second season of the Ballets des Champs-Elysées in London, at the Winter Garden Theatre in 1947, that I realized Ninette de Valois knew me by sight. She spoke to me in the bar; and I asked her if she did not like Babilée in the *Blue Bird*. "I have three dancers who can dance it better than him!" was her reply. Rudely I demanded, "Why do we never see them?"

Towards the end of that year Ninette de Valois and I began lunching together at irregular intervals and I came to know her better. These luncheons nearly always took place at the Dog and Duck, a pub at the corner of Frith Street and Bateman Street, two doors away from my office. It was patronized by film people from Wardour Street, journalists from *Time* and *Life,* film and theatrical dressmakers, loaded with jet and uncomfortable cameos, and of course a steady clientele of local business men. At night, customers in the little saloon bar, which was lined with the most gorgeous coloured tiles, Assyrian in effect, could sometimes enjoy the apparition of an artiste from the Casino Theatre imbibing bitter in full make-up. Upstairs there was a small restaurant, which served luncheon only, and there my friend Fina would dispense the most delicious plain English food that was ever served in exotic Soho.

Ninette de Valois has a reputation for being austere and forbidding: she is certainly, and of necessity, a strict disciplinarian within her company, and she has a somewhat baleful eye. Considering that she spends about a quarter of her life prostrated with migraine it is a wonder she is not more savage still. I found her gay and natural, full of gossip and frank disclosures. She would often stop short in the middle of a scandalous piece of unwritten history to exclaim "Now, this is not for publication: I don't trust you!"—then continue as before. She always got very excited relating something she thought funny, and would repeat the point several times with evident delight. She interrupted constantly, and I would occasionally notice that we were talking simultaneously about two different subjects. All things considered, although I was a critic—and therefore presumably a sworn enemy of Sadler's Wells— and although I knew *absolutely* nothing about ballet and was full of the most dangerous ideas, and although she had once stamped her foot and thrown a copy of *Ballet* right across Mr. Beaumont's shop, Ninette de Valois and I got on very well together.

One day I arrived a few minutes late for luncheon to find Miss de Valois already seated at our table, reading *Ballet Today* with an air of deceptive calm. I did not realize she was crouched to spring. Suddenly like a hungry puma she was at my throat. "How *dare* you write such a notice about *Job* in the *Observer?*" Unaware that the short piece I had done on her famous ballet, newly revived, could be construed as "a bad notice" I was taken completely by surprise: I gaped. She was in a blazing rage: stopping short only at blows, she continued to storm at me throughout the meal—to the evident interest of the other customers. I had said John Piper's settings were "mottled"! How dared I insult a *great painter,* and after she had taken me only a month before to see his designs being executed in the workshop? Mottled! I had said in the same notice that Helpmann's *Hamlet* had "worn thin"! *Hamlet* was a fine ballet; and Lewis Casson had told her it had had a profound effect on the theatre in general. I had said "Ashton's *Symphonic Variations,* the company's only successful new creation since the war, received the warmest applause"! Who cared about the applause? I was invited to criticize, not to record the reactions of the audience! Finally I had said that it was "a failure of our national ballet that it turned its successes into 'classics' by over-repetition"! Nobody could turn anything into a classic which wasn't one by right. I was an ignoramus; I neither knew nor cared anything about ballet; and I was only interested in trying to be clever.

Some of this was true. I had not at that time learned the knack of expressing myself properly in the two hundred words which were all the *Observer* then allowed me. When so much must be omitted, it is easy to leave out the wrong things; and one's condensed, elliptical remarks can give a false impression of one's opinion or cause offence through the absence of qualifying epithets. However, I still consider that Piper's settings *were* mottled; and that he is not a great artist. He is a charming topographical and landscape painter, without the proficiency, much less the mastery, that a *great* painter must have in painting figures.

The storm continued for an hour or more; but before returning to Covent Garden my stern monitress, like the just parent who administers correction for a misdeed and then agrees never to mention it again, said "Pax, Dicky," and smiled.

I have a very special sympathy for her: that is to say I *feel with* her, and understand her motives and ambitions more often than not. I envy her her varied and fascinating job—so much more fun than sitting in a stuffy room stringing words together to make English prose; and I think, though she may not, that my career as a critic and editor has from the beginning been dedicated to serving the same great cause as hers, if at times in a roundabout and peculiar way.

I see Ninette de Valois as the standard English lady, the daughter of an officer and a gentleman. She is of the same race as Jane Austen and Florence Nightingale, with some of the qualities of each. Brought up to be clean, neat, fair-minded, economical, and industrious, a woman of this type would be suspicious of any eccentricity or exaggeration, yet not without enjoyment of a secret giggle at the absurdities of the vicar's wife or at the odd habits of foreigners. She would be reliable and resourceful; getting her young brothers off in good time and properly equipped to school; improvising games at a children's party, yet even when the gaiety was at its height not omitting to tell Billy to stop picking his nose; coping admirably with an awkward situation at the village fete; and, *in extremis,* knowing instinctively the right thing to do if the ambulance broke down during an air-raid, or if, on a civilizing mission into the heart of Africa, the native porters started a revolt. Yet with all her good sense, conventional outlook, and quiet efficiency, there would perhaps be a romantic spark waiting to be kindled inside this woman, so that if the right breeze blew at the right time she might be off over the hills without a hat or gloves, like one of E. M. Forster's heroines, and end up, very likely, being burned at the stake, married to the gardener, or even, to the dismay of her relations, wearing tights on the stage.

If it was this romantic spark, this moonshine, this "artistic nonsense" that turned Edris Stannus into Ninette de Valois and set her twirling round the stages of Great Britain as a dancer, it was the practical, unmoonshiny qualities inherited from military and empire-building forbears that made her persevere and excel in her profession; and if it was another glow of the romantic spark—call it inspiration—which made her conceive the almost impossible ambition of transforming half a dozen girl pupils into a national ballet, it was the squire's daughter in her, the woman of sense, thoroughness, foresight, and efficiency, who carried the endeavour through years of trial and poverty to glorious success. From the marriage of inspiration and discipline works of art are born.

—from *The Adventures of a Ballet Critic,* 1953

SENTA DRIVER: STOMPING OUT A NICHE FOR HERSELF
Deborah Jowitt

A member of Paul Taylor's company from 1967 to 1973, Senta Driver (born 1942) struck out on her own to found her own company, called Harry, which she ran and for which she choreographed until 1991. Since then she has been active in many fields: as a writer (particularly about choreographer William Forsythe), a member of the boards of both Dance/USA and the Dance Notation Bureau, and as a registered nurse.

I walked into the dimness of Washington Square Methodist Church and saw this dancer I knew, Senta Driver, telling a small boy that all he had to do was to keep saying the multiplication tables in his head. Then she strapped him onto her back in a sling that held him facing away from her, said "I'm ready," to whoever was running the lights, and started striding heavily back and forth across the church on diagonal paths.

The work was called *Melodrama,* and this 1975 dress rehearsal preceded the debut of Driver's company, Harry (pragmatically subtitled "dance and other works"), which will be performing in BAM's LePercq Space from October 24 to 28. *Memorandum,* another dance on that early program, is still the piece that people usually bring up when Driver's name is mentioned. What happened is this: Driver strode on in a dark jumpsuit with a black veil over her face, made a cryptic warding-off gesture toward the direction she'd come from, and began to pace resolutely in a circle. Resolutely and weightily. Driver is a medium-sized woman and long-bodied rather than long-legged; she's not plump, but she gives an impression of solidity and force. Anyway, every time she came past a certain point in her circle, she uttered the name of a famous ballerina. As she inexorably moved up through history, you could learn something about each dancer from Driver's enunciation. "Marie TagliOni," she breathed reverently, while she flashed the name of Fanny Elssler, the legendary sylph's rival, in a way that called up a more vivacious, less ethereal dancer.

I was much taken with Driver's audacity. And by something more unusual. Her sense of history. Clearly she was a minimalist. Clearly she was a conceptual artist. But she was—and is—interested in matters that do not interest choreographers one might otherwise be tempted to link her with—Laura Dean or Lucinda Childs or Trisha Brown. Things, too, like performance styles, personas, dramatic situations treated as "material," not unlike the way in which, in Harald Lander's ballet *Etudes*—a showy paean to virtuosity and ballet training—an excerpt from the story ballet *La Sylphide* is presented as material. (Many choreographers who consider themselves up-to-date would resent being mentioned in the same breath as *Etudes;* Driver understands the point and doesn't seem to mind the comparison.)

During the course of a long conversation, Driver brings up—pertinently and sympathetically—Pheobe Neville, Meredith Monk, Merce Cunningham, Douglas Dunn, Trisha Brown, Laura Dean, Twyla Tharp, Martha Graham, Pearl Lang, Jane Dudley, Grethe Holby, Bill T. Jones, Martine van Hamel, Natalia Makarova, Felia Doubrovska, George Balanchine, Mathilde Kschessinska, Anna Pavlova, Marie Taglioni, Peter Anastos. She goes to so many dance performances that people used to take her for a critic. (Although she does refer to a particular critic as "one of the outstanding interesting dummies of the field," she is benign on the subject of critics. Thinks most of us—me in particular—aren't harsh enough and that "people who rail against critics imagine that everyone else in the audience has *humming* going on in his/her head.")

Few choreographers considered radical have spent so much time examining the past they're determined to make a break with. Driver says that she once wrote in a notebook, "History is a nightmare from which I am trying to escape." Now sitting in her apartment, which is very colorful and multifocused compared to her dances—or maybe it's just that it hasn't processed *its* history—she balances a coffee cup, and modifies that outcry: "I am aware of history. I respect it. I'm trying to find where it belongs and how to use it without repeating it." And she adds firmly, "I have never seen any reason to continue unless I could do something that was original."

Driver thinks that she really began her career in the audience, although while a Latin and philosophy major at Bryn Mawr, she started coming into New York and taking a class once a week (which, she says, she naively thought was enough). She racked up a couple of summers at the American Dance Festival and, hooked, took off for Ohio State, where she'd heard the training was good, and picked up an M.A. in dance. (She always acknowledges her debt to the head of Ohio's dance department, Helen Alkire, who, she claims, formed her taste and judgment, taught her to be both disciplined and open to whatever came along.)

Her ambition was—had been for some time—to dance with Paul Taylor. She got into his company very soon after she left Columbus, and stayed there from 1967 to 1973, although she characterizes their relationship as "stormy" ("He fired me in 1970, but I wouldn't go"). Taylor once said "Senta talks a lot," and it's her guess that he mistrusts excessively verbal people. Which she is. Most of Driver's best roles in the Taylor company were ones she inherited from other dancers. She remembers Taylor asking her why she didn't want to look like herself in *Aureole* instead of like Sharon Kinney. Driver, typically, felt that she had a commitment to history, to preserving the Taylor style of a certain year by dancing as much as possible like the dancer on whom the role had been made. This stance may have puzzled Taylor; I find it noble.

Finally out of the Taylor company, ordered to rest for several months because of the tendinitis in both her ankles, she read and thought about choreography. "I had to consider, 'what can you do that someone else isn't already doing very well?' I loved the kind of work Paul did. I loved dancing it. And it was important to me, *for me,* not to do anything like that—not to make a career doing the pieces he forgot to do. Since Douglas Dunn had already covered lying still, the only thing I could do was to walk. I'd take three-hour blocks of time in the studio, and since I tended to sleep to avoid doing anything, I made a rule for myself that, if I wasn't dancing, I'd walk continuously, because I *had* to use the time." (She was encouraged to find that Laura Dean had undergone a similar period.) When her feet hurt too much to walk, she crawled or rolled. Out of this came *Memorandum* and, after that, *Melodrama.* "The number-one thing I did in the studio was to walk around and around," she says wryly. "And then I had this big breakthrough and began to walk diagonals."

Since the debut of Harry, Driver has made a number of witty and provocative works—many of which, she is aware, have literally provoked, *infuriated,* some members of the audience. Some of the pieces have involved intrepid and pungent juxtapositions of sound and dance: two dancers walking as fast as they can around a five-spoked pattern, while Tom Johnson provides an excited commentary on their supposed competition ("The Star Game"); three deadpan dancers executing phrases of bold, blunt movement while, on tape, lighting designer Tom Skelton calls for a myriad of light and sound cues for a final rehearsal of José Limón's *Missa Brevis* ("Board Fade Except"); dancers slouching around dispiritedly while a soprano walks among them singing the lyrics of some Gilbert and Sullivan songs—sweetly and sincerely, as a manifesto instead of a joke ("In Which a Position Is Taken and Some Dance"). Who but Driver would end a dance with a long kiss between two performers ("Sudden Death")? Or have a woman, elaborately coiffed and wearing early twentieth-century practice clothes, perform a dramatic solo on pointe while sitting on a revolving piano stool? ("The Kschessinskaya Variations" is usually performed as part of "Two Dances from Dead Storage.")

Driver's interest in weight—your own, someone else's, and how to deal with it—has surfaced in many of her pieces. Watching a Driver dance, you usually hear the pound, thud, slap of feet against the floor. You notice people carrying each other, people standing on each other. Driver says this isn't meant to look cruel or political, contrary to what some spectators think, it's simply a matter of finding out how much weight you can support, of accepting another person's weight as a burden you must cope with. And the idea that women can be strong, can carry men, has become a major factor in her work. So has its concomitant: that men can be carried, can be presented as sex objects, can do the kind of precise, detailed dancing they're often not expected to do. It may be this skeptical attitude toward conventional gender-deportment that has led her to collaborate on what promises to be a diverting new work with Peter Anastos, formerly one of the directors of the Ballets Trockadero de Monte Carlo, a gifted choreographer and—as the legendary Olga Tchikaboumskaya—no stranger to paradoxes of gender. He too is obsessed by dance history.

I go to Driver's studio—well, only hers for a year, isn't it beautiful, she says enviously—to watch class for the company and a few others. Driver, as is usually the case, is collected, good-humored, and full of energy—not a hair out of place. (I think that she works hard to counteract the impression that might be produced by her soft, round, pretty face—the kind that often seems to go with a more indulgent attitude toward life.) Here are the members of Harry. Jeffery Clark, who's tall and long-legged, with an innocent face and the chest and shoulder development of a crack swimmer; Rick Guimond, smaller and thinner, with limber flyaway legs and a way while performing of looking at the others as if they really interested him; Nicole Riché, compact, technically adroit, with unusually powerful and well-defined back and arm muscles for a small woman; Peg Conner Hewitt, strong too, but softer, with a cheerful face and untidy hair.

It's some class. A few of the long sequences the dancers perform while sitting on the floor have the swinging kind of vitality that's in keeping with Driver's respect for early modern dance, "for what Martha started with in the '30s: weight, simplicity, starkness." Nothing looks usual, everything looks arduous and physically suspenseful: the weighty, fluid arm gestures ("not neat," she calls, "but rich"), the way the dancers can make a leg move by throwing it from the hip joint, the push-ups, the intricate rhythms. Then, while Senta works in a corner with a newcomer, Jeff puts the others through a long combination performed while standing on the head, which ends with a terrifying dismount, in which the dancers topple to the floor in one piece, like trees. "I thought the body would look good up there and have a good time," says Senta, shrugging, and it's true that *I'm* the only one wincing. The dancers are also perfecting what Driver calls "preparation for point-work." Barefoot.

All this turns out to be stuff that's in her new work, *Primer.* And now you can understand why Driver says with a grin, "Marathon running has created an atmosphere in which my work should flourish." It has to do, she says, with finding out what the body can do, with maybe taking it a little farther. She's interested in violence—not in the sense of brutality or sadism, but as a violent expenditure of energy, even to the breaking point. Like the Graham of the '30s, she's scornful of prettiness, "Pretty starts at the ankle and goes all the way out to the toe and that's it." What Graham wrote in 1928 might almost have been written by Driver today: "Virile gestures are evocative of the only true beauty. Ugliness may be actually beautiful if it cries out with the voice of power."

Driver isn't arrogant about her work or inconsiderate of her audience. Of her recent *Theory and Practice,* she says "it turned out to be a two-week workshop. It's my work of that year, but it shouldn't be on the stage." She's begun to think about ways to provide relief from the prevailing intensity of her dances; she's investigating passive movement. Certainly her preoccupation with force and intensity sets her apart from most contemporaries, who are interested in a more laid-back, underplayed style. (Even Driver's casualness is controlled.) So does her way of altering material through stylistic changes—often theatrical ones, too—rather than movement changes. I call her a maverick, and she says with a certain irony, "Am I lucky enough to be in a new slot? After all, I'm hardly the first person to do many of these things."

Driver is getting plenty of recognition these days; the company is doing quite well; she got a Guggenheim last year. She says she has no right to complain. But she does sometimes wonder where she belongs. "People who examine the current generation of choreographers do not examine me. Places that present what I consider my kind of work seldom present me. . . ." I'm touched by her puzzlement. It would be highly unfair if someone as scrupulously concerned as she is with the past, present, and future of dance didn't end up as a chapter, a page, or a very lengthy footnote in the dance histories of the next era.

—from *The Village Voice*, October 22, 1979

BOB FOSSE: DANCING AND THE DARK
Joan Acocella

Bob Fosse (1927–1987) began in Hollywood and almost reluctantly moved to Broadway. He had a spectacular career as a choreographer of musicals, beginning with The Pajama Game *("Steam Heat") and including* Damn Yankees *(where he met his future wife and muse, Gwen Verdon),* Sweet Charity, Pippin, Redhead, Chicago, *and* Cabaret. *Within a single year, he won the Oscar for Best Director for the movie version of the latter, a Tony for* Pippin, *and an Emmy for* Liza with a "Z." *His semiautobiographical movie musical,* All That Jazz, *won the Palme d'Or at the Cannes Film Festival.*

If, today, you go to see a dance act in a night club, it may well start with a single light trained on the stage, a single white-gloved hand jutting out, a single rear end gyrating meaningfully, and, then, as the lights go up, a pair of eyes staring at you as if to say, "I know what you're thinking." If you switch on MTV, chances are you'll see the same thing: the glove (Michael Jackson), the cold sex, the person eyeballing you as if this were all your idea. There is an imp of the perverse at loose in mass-culture dance, a spirit that has little to do with the blowsy cheer of old-time night-club numbers, not to speak of the innocent jitterbugging we used to see on television. One could say that this is just part of post-modern culture—its toughness, its knowingness. But it is also something more specific: the heritage of Bob Fosse, who was Broadway's foremost choreographer-director during the late sixties and the seventies.

That it *is* a specific style—one you can look at and say, "There's Fosse"— tells us something about the era in which this man worked. The period from the forties through the seventies was the heyday of the choreographer-directors, a group that included Agnes de Mille, Gower Champion, Jerome Robbins (above all), and Michael Bennett. These were people who believed that the meaning of a show could be contained in its dancing, and that the show could be fueled by the energy that comes only from dancing. One by one, they changed the American musical, bending it away from its European-operetta roots. De Mille made it realistic, vernacular—fellers and gals getting together at clambakes. Robbins, in *West Side Story,* made it urban, modern, with sneakers and social problems. Fosse made it something else altogether, no longer even a representation of life but a kind of emanation from the lower brain—edgy, unwholesome.

He had a personality to match. By the late sixties, Fosse was the kingpin of the American musical. He had a string of hits behind him, and more to come. Soon he began directing movies, and showed himself, as Pauline Kael said, a prodigy in that medium. He went into television, too, directing the wonderful *Liza with a Z,* which, together with his movie *Cabaret,* made Liza Minnelli a star. In 1973, he won the Oscar (for *Cabaret*), the Tony (*Pippin*), and the Emmy (*Liza*) all in one sweep. He was at the top. Yet nothing could have persuaded him of this. He never learned to occupy his fame—never bought the suits, learned the tone, got comfortable. On the contrary, to the end of his career he regarded himself as an outsider, someone who'd snuck in off the street. According to his biographer Martin Gottfried (*All His Jazz,* 1990), Fosse had lunch almost every day at the Carnegie Delicatessen with the playwrights Paddy Chayefsky and Herb Gardner. He would order a beer and a pastrami on white with mayo (he was a midwesterner) and then push the sandwich away, drink the beer, and pour out his miseries. "Everything he does he thinks it comes out of bullshit," Chayefsky said. "It's a game, a phony."

But that was only half the story. The other half was that everyone else was a phony. As Fosse once said to a *Times* reporter, "I alternate between these terrible states of thinking I'm a fraud and this raging ego." He was an uncomfortable soul, and looked it: runty, slope-shouldered, with a caved-in chest. He dressed mostly in black—a style not fashionable in his time—and often had a hat pulled down over his brow. He said this was to cover his thinning hair, but it may also have been to hide his face. Out of his mouth, almost always, hung a cigarette. ("There was a sort of groove in his lip where it sat," the choreographer Donald McKayle says in Kevin Grubb's 1989 book on Fosse, *Razzle Dazzle*.) In 1977, when Herb Gardner's play *Thieves* was being filmed, the director needed someone to play a street junkie. Fosse volunteered, and was perfect. In some measure, he just had to be himself.

Fosse died eleven years ago, but he is making a comeback. *Fosse: A Celebration in Song and Dance,* a revue directed by Ann Reinking and Richard Maltby, Jr., will open in New York next month. Meanwhile, the revival of his 1975 musical *Chicago* is in its third year at the Shubert Theatre, and the English director Nicholas Hytner is gearing up to make a film based on the show. In these productions, unlike the MTV trickle-down, one can see Fosse's style in its pure and narrow form. Gottfried quotes the *Daily News* drama critic Howard Kissel saying that Fosse's dances reminded him of "things that crawl under a rock," but they don't always look that way. Sometimes they look like a bad dream or a George Grosz drawing. What they seldom resemble is any dancing ever made on Broadway before Fosse got there.

IT IS OFTEN SAID that Fosse's roots were in vaudeville, and this is partly true. He was born in 1927 on the North Side of Chicago. The father was a Hershey's-chocolates salesman, the mother a housewife; the family was large, normal, and Methodist. Fosse's primary dance teacher was a vaudeville aficionado, and paired the twelve-year-old boy with another boy in a tap act called the Riff Brothers. At first, they played "presentation houses" (movie theaters with live acts), along with Elks and American Legion meetings. Soon, however, they graduated to Chicago's strip clubs— the Silver Cloud, the Cave of the Winds—and it was that world, far seedier than vaudeville, that printed itself on Fosse's imagination. His work is strewn with low-life types: pinup girls, taxi dancers, sequinned dames flashing their thighs at men with cigars.

The strip clubs gave Fosse more than his subject; they supplied the emotional field. The strippers toyed with Fosse. They took him on their laps and licked his ears. Some probably did more with him. (He later claimed that at age fifteen he was named in a divorce suit brought against a waitress in one of the clubs.) But during the day, at Roald Amundsen High School, he lived the life of an innocent, clean-cut teenager. He played sports; he got good grades; he was voted Most Popular Boy in the class. No one at school knew how he spent his evenings. His parents didn't know, either. He told them he had club dates, but he didn't say what kind of clubs.

Gottfried believes that this situation created a serious, lifelong division in the choreographer's mind, and though the theory sounds pat, Fosse's work bears it out. As it is said that he got his start in vaudeville, so it is said that the subject of his work was sex. But it wasn't really sex: it was sleaze, fraudulence—the idea of something being passed off as respectable when it is really cheesy and cheap. Sex was merely the example, the thing most likely to poke its head up from under the surface and say that the surface was false. Fosse was in psychoanalysis during the fifties, when he came of age as a choreographer. He was one of many artists in that decade—Tennessee Williams, Martha Graham, John O'Hara—who believed that beneath the Eisenhower/*Reader's Digest* world being sold to them was a censored inner world, a Real Truth, and that sex was its leading edge.

Fosse broke into show business the usual way: Broadway choruses, road shows, small parts in Hollywood musicals. (If you rent *My Sister Eileen,* you will see what a wonderful dancer he was—fast, ebullient, charming.) In the 1953 film of *Kiss Me, Kate,* he got a break. He was to dance in a brief duet, and Hermes Pan, the movie's choreographer, let him design it. This gave him ideas, and the actress Joan McCracken, his second wife (he went through women fast), pushed him further. She persuaded George Abbott, at that time Broadway's foremost director of musicals, to use Fosse as the choreographer for his upcoming show, *The Pajama Game* (1954). *Pajama Game* was a hit, so Abbott rehired Fosse for *Damn Yankees* the following year. Fosse had arrived, very fast.

Much of his choreography for these two lovable shows was in the wholesome Agnes de Mille mold that dominated Broadway dancing at that time. Even so, we can see Fosse's style being born. In *Pajama Game* there is a famous number, "Steam Heat," for three people who, in keeping with the song's title, look less like people than like a plumbing system. They jerk, they bob, they hiss, they clap, in perfect syncopation. Here we see the automatism that was to be so much a part of Fosse's mature work. Nevertheless, "Steam Heat" is still a human sort of dance. It's an act being put on by three amateurs—pajama-factory workers—at a union meeting. They're delighted with what they're doing; when they're applauded, they're goofily grateful. Though "Steam Heat" is about sex, it has no slyness. On the contrary, part of the charm is seeing these factory workers dream about a hot experience that they know about only from songs on the radio.

Still, Fosse was trying to get down. For *Damn Yankees,* he created an actual striptease, for a little devil named Lola who was attempting to seduce a big, dumb baseball player. Lola was played by the up-and-coming star Gwen Verdon, who had been trained in Hollywood by Jack Cole, foremost maker of the erotic/exotic dances (Rita Hayworth in Greek draperies) that red-peppered the films of the forties and fifties. Through Verdon, it is often said, Fosse was influenced by Cole—emboldened to make sex dances, of which "Whatever Lola Wants," Verdon's strip, is the first example. But here, too, sex is subverted by innocence. Lola *tries* to seduce her ballplayer. She does everything that Jack Cole did: casbah, flamenco, you name it. But she tries too hard. To see her struggle out of her pedal pushers on the floor and then, with a jaunty flourish, whip them through the air like a matador's cape is to see a strip act gone badly wrong—gone comic. Verdon, with her generous figure and huge charisma, may have been Jack Cole's premier sexpot, but by the time she got to Fosse she was also a wonderful comedienne—human, fleshly, decent, with an ear-to-ear grin.

With the help of Verdon, who was by then Fosse's mistress and whom he would marry in 1960, Fosse got his first job as director-choreographer, on the 1959 musical *Redhead*. (The producers needed Verdon as their star, and she insisted on Fosse as her director.) Thereafter, he would direct most of his shows and movies. At the same time, the darkness that was to affect so much of his later work began to set in. You can see it emerging in the superficially upbeat *Sweet Charity* (1966). Fosse adapted the story from Fellini's *Nights of Cabiria*—he converted Fellini's prostitute heroine into a dance-hall girl— but Fosse's Charity (Verdon again) had none of the dignity of Cabiria. She was a cheerful little fool in a heartless world, and at times Fosse seemed to side with the world. The show both started and ended with Charity's being thrown into the orchestra pit. (It was supposed to represent a pond in Central Park.) This actually looked sadistic, and to insiders who knew that the Verdon-Fosse marriage was coming apart it no doubt seemed more so.

For *Sweet Charity*, Fosse created a new, harsher sex ballet, "Big Spender." It shows the women in the Fandango Ballroom, Charity's place of employment, standing behind a rail, displaying themselves to the customers. They are done up to look as cheap as possible: all spray net and fringe. They barely move. One snaps her fingers; one hooks a weary thigh over the rail. Now and then they sing, but mostly they whisper: "Hey, big spender, spend a little time with me." You sense that anyone who spent a little time with one of these women would have to go to the doctor afterward. The number is supposed to be a comedy, but it's a grim one—the Silver Cloud strippers as seen, with full terror, by the Most Popular Boy in the class.

THE GRIMNESS CAME, in part, from Fosse's life at that time, and before. "I'm afraid of failure," he told a TV interviewer, "afraid that the ideas I have, I don't have the talent to execute. . . . I threw up twice a day when I was a performer. Now I throw up three times a day." "Flop sweat," the sweat you get into when you think you've got a flop on your hands, was for him a permanent affliction. On occasion, according to Gottfried, it practically immobilized him. In 1960, when he was working on a show called *The Conquering Hero*—this one *was* a flop—Verdon said that he paced back and forth in their hotel room clutching a cheap Mexican statue of Jesus and screaming at it, "Why don't you help me?" Even when he had a success, he thought it was a failure. In 1973, when he won his Oscar/Tony/Emmy triple crown, he told his friends it was all a sham: "I fooled everybody."

The world was a fraud, and he was a fraud. Didn't his own work prove this? What Fosse loved best about show business, and what he did best, was the razzle-dazzle—the sequins and girls, the flash—but this was also the thing that made him feel cheap. So, as if to rise above it, to "frame" it, he made it cheaper, but this just made him feel cheaper still. When he looked at others—particularly at those who worked in ballet, a form in which he had never been trained—he felt like showbiz trash. He owed his dominance of Broadway in the seventies to the fact that Jerome Robbins had decamped to New York City Ballet to work with Balanchine. Of Robbins and Balanchine, Fosse said to *Rolling Stone,* "They talk to God. When I call God, he's always out to lunch."

Around 1969, he had suffered a great humiliation, with his first film-directing assignment, the movie version of *Sweet Charity*. The film was a failure, and Fosse, always prone to depression, feared that he would never work again. Then, in 1971, Verdon, whom he had cheated on almost throughout the marriage, asked for a separation. He moved out, and began living very hard. He took Dexedrine to wake up and Seconal to go to sleep. He generally drank his dinner (double margaritas). He smoked four packs of Camels a day. He also went through scores of women, often dancers in his shows, often two at a time—that is, two in bed at the same time. He had a five-year liaison with the dancer Ann Reinking, but she got the same treatment as his wives. He worked obsessively, at times hysterically. Verdon, in an interview, described him in rehearsal as a kind of monster: "His face changes. He gets ropey looking. His eyes sink into his head. . . . I've worked in insane asylums and the inmates don't look as weird as Bob." (Dexedrine no doubt did its part here.) He rehearsed dancers till they dropped, and pushed himself even further. "I had to work twice as hard as everyone else to be half as good," he said.

He hid none of his troubles. He blithely discussed his drug habits with a reporter from the *Times*. When his mother died, he told the *Post,* "I think there would have been nothing better than to have had an affair with her. I think everyone ought to have an affair with his mother." He was one of those people, often veterans of psychoanalysis, who feel that if they admit their sins they are somehow absolved of them. And why not? For—as this line of thinking goes—doesn't everyone commit the same sins? He wasn't so much a bad man as a truth-teller in a hypocritical world. In 1974, when he had a heart attack and almost died, this conviction seems to have hardened. He had gone to the edge; we hadn't. He knew the score, and he was going to tell us.

Hence the Luciferian righteousness that hangs like a low cloud over much of Fosse's later work. In the four movies that he directed after *Sweet Charity*—*Cabaret* (1972), *Lenny* (1974), *All That Jazz* (1979), and *Star 80* (1983)—the heroes are all refractions of himself: corruptees, but more honest than the world that corrupted them. In these movies, the very camerawork banners its brave candor. *Lenny* opens with a long closeup of a pair of lips. We don't know whether they are male or female, let alone whose they are. What we see is just lips: speech, sex, appetite. We have the sense that if Fosse could have gone past the lips—to the tongue, the gullet, the mucous membrane—he would have, in search of a better, wetter truth. His Broadway shows, too—*Pippin* (1972), *Chicago* (1975), *Big Deal* (1986)—all used low life as a metaphor for life. Even in the 1978 *Dancin'*, which had no book, he supplied as much raunchiness as he could. In one number, "Dream Barre," a ballet class turned into a frank scene of copulation.

But the most interesting product of Fosse's late world view, because it is the most abstract product, was his choreographic style—a sort of *ne-plus-ultra* extension of the sex-oiled machine of "Big Spender." In the classic Fosse dance of the seventies, the dancers are seen in tight formation, and they don't actually move much. (As Arlene Croce once wrote, "Footwork has about as much to do with Fosse style as lariat-twirling.") The focus is on isolated gestures—a shoulder roll here, a finger splay there. The body part that gets the most action is the pelvis. It jerks, it wags, it oozes. Meanwhile, the dancers remain coldly removed. Their faces are often covered by hats. Their backs are stiff; to bend, they have to tilt. They look like mannequins, or Martians.

Furthermore, they are rarely characters in a drama. In the Broadway choreography of the fifties and sixties, the songs and dances were supposed to emerge naturally from the stage action. One minute the heroine was hanging out the wash; the next minute she was dancing. Fosse followed this rule up through the sixties, but then it started to look corny to him. So, in an interesting proto-postmodern shift, he reverted to his vaudeville roots, making dance numbers that were confessedly numbers. In much of his later work, there is little or no story to humanize the dancers, or to objectify them. We can't separate them from ourselves, can't say, "That's Laurey and Curly." They come from nowhere, or—as Fosse, with his *hypocrite-lecteur* philosophy, appears to be saying—from within ourselves.

IT WAS IN THIS LATE, dark-minded period that Fosse created some of his best work, most notably the film of *Cabaret*. Just as in *Damn Yankees* he got Verdon, with her stubborn humanness, to save the strip act, so Fosse—working, it seems, against his instincts—uses Liza Minnelli to rescue *Cabaret* from what could have been its wallow in Weimar decadence. Minnelli plays

Sally Bowles, an American entertainer working in a cheap Berlin night club in the thirties. Early in the movie, Sally sings "Mein Herr," in which she tells her man that she is leaving him because it's not in her nature to be faithful, and that she means to screw her way across Europe. The staging is straight out of Fosse's late trick bag: lots of bowler hats and spread-eagled chorus girls. But if this is corruption it is seriously undermined by Minnelli's wholesomeness. She tears around the stage like a child. She waves her arms, wags her fanny, has a good time. Above all, like Verdon, she shows her body to us in a frank, happy way. In the last chorus, those big legs of hers span the stage like a suspension bridge. "Mein Herr," as it happens, *is* about corruption: Sally will indeed leave her man, she will screw her way across Europe (or at least Berlin), and, as others in the film come to oppose Nazism, she will not. She will be lost. But in Minnelli's stage manner we see the preciousness of what will be lost: innocence, fun, life. She is not the film's only saving grace. In *Cabaret,* unlike other Fosse productions, evil is not a naughty little thing (sex, drugs). It is the Third Reich. Between that reality and the big, blooming girl on whom it bears down, Fosse manages to make corruption look like something more than just his personal bugbear.

Chicago followed soon after. Developed from the same sources as the 1942 Ginger Rogers movie *Roxie Hart,* it tells the story of how Roxie, a floozie if ever there was one, parlays a murder rap (she shot her boyfriend— "He had it coming," she says) into a career in vaudeville by batting her eyelashes at the press and the jury. Most of the other characters are worse than Roxie: her lawyer, who can get anyone off for a fee; her jail warden, who can supply anything for a fee; her prison mate, Velma, a hard-as-nails babe who competes with Roxie for press coverage. In keeping with Fosse's late antirealism, the musical is staged as a vaudeville show: one after another, the characters come forward to sing their venal tales, while in the background the chorus dancers bump and grind in panties and chains.

This is about as low as Fosse ever went, and it's very funny. Verdon, the original Roxie, probably made it more so. But even the revival, which first starred Ann Reinking (Roxie) and Bebe Neuwirth (Velma), is endearing. It doesn't leer at you; it can't. The characters are too extravagant in their vulgarity. *Chicago* was Fosse's first and last *satire* on cynicism. It may also have been his satire on himself. "Razzle Dazzle," the show's most famous number, begins:

> Give 'em the old razzle dazzle,
> Razzle dazzle 'em. . . .
> Give 'em the old hocus pocus,
> Bead and feather 'em.
> How can they see with sequins in their eyes?

In Fosse's work, corruption always needed some solid counterweight in order to work artistically. Corruption alone is a corrupting subject; it brings out our righteousness and our salaciousness and nothing much better. In order to look serious, it has to be placed against some idea of goodness. That is what Verdon brought to the shows she worked on with Fosse, and what Minnelli gave to *Cabaret*. (As for *Chicago,* the show actually laughs at corruption, and thus restores the balance.) Fosse clearly sensed this need. It was he who directed Minnelli, he who chose Verdon as his leading lady. But he never wholly got the lesson through his head; he just went back and forth between doing the job right and doing it wrong.

A FINE EXAMPLE OF THE LATTER is *All That Jazz,* his embarrassing movie autobiography of 1979. The film's hero, Joe Gideon, is a famous Broadway and Hollywood director, with a life just like his creator's. (Fosse coauthored the screenplay.) The strip-club apprenticeship, the discarded wife, the drug addictions, the heart attack—it's all there. Fosse went so far as to cast Reinking, his betrayed girlfriend, as Gideon's betrayed girlfriend. But he didn't just portray his life; he mythologized it. A beautiful angel of death, Jessica Lange, keeps turning up in Gideon's dressing room; the movie concludes with Gideon's being zipped into a body bag. Fosse may have recovered from his bypass surgery, but he was damned if he was going to end his testament on such a benign note.

Four years later, Fosse made his last movie, and in it, inexplicably, he not only cast aside the two-bit satanism of *All That Jazz*—and of so much of his work—but actually indicted it. *Star 80* is still lurid enough, God knows. It was based on the much-publicized story of Dorothy Stratten, the murdered *Playboy* playmate. Stratten was a waitress in a Vancouver Dairy Queen when a small-time hustler named Paul Snider laid eyes on her and decided she should be in *Playboy*. He got her in there and intended to push her higher, into movies, with himself as her manager. But his plan backfired: Stratten got into movies without him, and then abandoned him. *Star 80* is hard to describe, because it is so appalling. The rejected Snider blew Stratten's brains out with a shotgun; after that, he sodomized her corpse, on a special table he'd painstakingly constructed for that purpose. In the film, the story is repeatedly intercut with shots of Snider doing this. Actually, we don't know what he's doing. All we see is his agonized, sweat-bathed, blood-smeared face. But we know, we know, that something terrible is happening. At the end, we find out what it is.

Many reviewers, and many filmgoers, were repelled by *Star 80*. But it is a compelling piece of work, a portrayal of sex as utter nullity, power without meaning. All the energy in the film—imagination, hope, effort, anguish—

belongs to Snider, the putative villain, and it is all aimed at a brick wall, the blank, passive Stratten (Mariel Hemingway). Here Fosse at last went beyond the idea of corruption. In this story, there is no innocence to corrupt. (According to the movie, Snider wasn't Stratten's first.) There is just ambition, with sex as its vehicle. But the most radical thing about the movie is that it takes the point of view of Snider. "I somehow identified with him," Fosse told *Rolling Stone*, "because he was trying to get in. . . . I know that sense of them all knowing something I don't know."

Star 80, more than *All That Jazz*, was Fosse's autobiography, the story of his insecurity, and of his fascination with sex, which, in this movie, turns to dust in his hands. When Eric Roberts, who played Snider, was having trouble with the role, Fosse instructed him to play it as Bob Fosse. Gottfried tells the story: "'Look at me,' Bob demanded. 'Look at me!' and he glared at Roberts. 'If I weren't successful . . . —look at me—that's Paul Snider. That's what you're playing.'" That Fosse should have seen in Snider—a pimp, a loser, a murderer—the image of himself is amazing, but he never lacked for boldness, or for self-hatred.

In 1987, at the age of sixty, he collapsed on a sidewalk (another heart attack) and died. It is hard to detect his influence in today's new musicals, for the movement he was part of has vanished. Apart from Tommy Tune, there are no choreographer-directors left on Broadway. When a show needs dances, the director calls one of a group of capable journeymen—Susan Strohman, Graciela Daniele, others—who are lively and upbeat, good at period style, and seemingly content with those virtues, as are the directors. Even leaving aside Fosse's tone, the sheer individuality of his choreography is not what is wanted now. His imprint is easier to trace in the mass culture— in those music videos and night-club shows, and in dance movies. When in *Fame* and *Flashdance* you see the fast cutting, the isolated body parts, you are seeing the spirit of Fosse. He may have influenced advertising as well. Fashion models who look lacquered or drugged or dead—Fosse is probably in the background here.

He was better than his inheritors, or at least more ambitious. In, in, he tried to go. In *Lenny*, he trained the camera on the lips; in *All That Jazz*, he filmed open-heart surgery—the pump itself. (He had to get special permission from the patient.) Though his motivation often seems naive he was nevertheless interested in who we actually are. What is forbidden? What is true? Almost everything he did was unpleasant. His work was tacky, pushy, obsessive. He was a hophead. Yet he was a moralist, of a generation that had little hope of innocence. He was clearly drawn to innocence; its presence, or its mourned loss, is at the center of his best work. He toys with it, undermines it, reembraces it, pushes it away again—a struggle that at times seems oppressively personal. With all artists, we have to deal with the business of personality versus art, neurosis versus imagination. With Fosse, the imagination is smaller, the neurosis bigger. Still, he was an artist.

—from *The New Yorker*, December 21, 1998

LINCOLN KIRSTEIN
Richard Buckle

Kirstein accepted the invitation to put up at my house. On March 25, staying at the Bedford Hotel, Brighton, where I wrote the first pages of these *Adventures*, I cabled to him on board the *Queen Mary*.

> *Expect you between ten and midnight Tuesday. Tell taxi Bloomfield Terrace off Pimlico Road not Paddington.*
> *—Dicky.*

How much of one's self can one reveal by post? Even those of us who specialize in self-knowledge and wield the most facile of pens are probably ignorant of—and therefore unable to describe—the personal peculiarities which make us, as hosts, guests, friends, or lovers, just what we are. Even if we are aware of being charming, boring, overwhelming, or irritating, we may not know what makes us so. I have always believed, for instance, because my mother once told me, that my voice is monotonous when I read prose; but until I heard it recorded I had no idea how deliberate and affected it sounds.

I was prepared, therefore, for the possibility of some physical singularity turning me against my "pen-friend" Kirstein. I could never—except perhaps on a desert island—be friends with someone who made a champing noise when he ate, or wore a certain kind of overcoat.

Because of his seniority and his superior education, because he had studied philosophy and art history, because I knew him to be the patron and theorist of a whole new school of painting, and above all because he was the founder of American ballet, I looked upon Lincoln Kirstein as a mentor or elder brother, with respect. I consider myself less than half educated. That I made little progress in writing Latin verses, prematurely gave up Greek, resigned mathematics forever after passing my School Certificate, and had no training in logic: these I have always supposed to be the reasons for my ill-disciplined mind, difficulty in concentration, and consequent slowness in literary composition.

Our mutual friend, Frederick Ashton, to whom anything that is not a bouquet is a bomb, and who will never really feel quite safe till he has been buried alive in Turkish Delight, had told Kirstein I was unkind, spiteful, and dangerous. Now, I may be bad-tempered and intolerant, but I have a kind heart and a capacity for affection; and I forgive readily. I am also extremely sensitive to what people think of me, though I try not to let this affect my conduct. Lincoln Kirstein is of German descent, and he likes to fit the human race into pigeon-holes. We juvenile delinquents all have our labels. If, for instance, we possess big ears, wide pelvises, and spatulate nails, he will expect us to grow hysterical in time of war, be hopeless over money, and worship our mothers. I think I have tended, in Kirstein's mind, to remain in the category Ashton originally helped to prepare for me. Having cast us for our roles he is reluctant to make changes. I am a talented but worldly villain: but Kirstein readily tolerates meanness, egoism, and immorality if he believes one has a responsible function to fulfil in the all-important history of art.

Although he had expressed his violent disapproval of "interior decoration" I took the risk of having my spare bedroom redistempered, as there was a damp patch on the ceiling. The maple-wood bed, in which my grandfather Sandford and three of his sisters had been born, was suitably hard; and the engravings of ancestors after Reynolds, Hoppner, Leighton, and Watts, which hung on the walls, seemed the very antithesis of the *chi-chi* he despised. In a bookcase stood Saint-Simon's *Memoirs* in twenty volumes, uncut.

On the evening of Tuesday, March 28, Michael Somes's first ballet, *Summer Interlude,* was having its first night at Sadler's Wells. I did not, therefore, go to Waterloo to meet Kirstein, the time of whose arrival depended on the docking of his liner at Southampton; instead, I returned home to prepare a meal. Ashton was to wait for the train; and both Balanchine and Andrew Sykes were joining us for supper.

It may be imagined with what feelings of pleasurable alarm I poked the fire in the red room and stirred the salad dressing. (I had been so excited during the ballet that, although the impression it made was distinctly favourable, I could not remember a single movement five minutes after the curtain went down. This made it difficult to write three hundred words of sense for the *Observer.* Several people, however—and this very rarely happens—came up subsequently and said how much they liked what I had written.)

Ashton missed Kirstein at the station, and I was alone in the house when his taxi drew up. There he stood on the doorstep, tall, burly, with very little back to his short-cropped head, his dark eyes peering, probing through gold-rimmed glasses: like an enormous chicklet with a mission, unsure how he was going to be received in the cynical world of men. Before we had finished bringing in the luggage or paying the taxi he had broken open a suitcase and was spreading out a hundred large new photographs by George Platt Lynes on the floor of the hall. He described to me the wonders of Balanchine's *Orpheus,* the words pouring in an elemental torrent from his lips, as if life were too short to waste any time before inspiring me with his ideals and enlisting me in the cause. Overwhelmed by these buffeting transatlantic rollers, my inquiries about his journey and whether he would like a bath were utterly submerged. In some ways the elder brother proved to be a wild, uncouth, and impetuous youngster after all: but his sincerity put my conventional good manners to shame.

The other guests arrived in due course and we had supper by the fire. It turned out that Kirstein did not like champagne, but he liked dry martinis, so no harm was done. The evening must have passed off well as I can remember nothing more about it.

One great difference between Kirstein and myself which became evident during his first stay of just under three weeks was in our methods of work and the amount we did. He did twice as much as I. When I am writing I sometimes lie in bed for hours, looking straight ahead of me, before setting pen to paper. The interruption of a telephone call can set me back for a whole morning. Then I have a *bourgeois* dislike of working at night, particularly in London. I do not mind writing from breakfast until seven in the evening, with a break for luncheon, but after that hour I like to relax. Kirstein, on the other hand, can settle down at his typewriter no matter what the time of day or night. He will sit for a moment in thought, take off his glasses, pass a hand over his eyes, and then rattle away without pause for two hours. After a charge round the block, a rest on his bed, or a handful of raisins he is ready for more. I have often fallen asleep to the busy music of his typewriter in the small hours, to be awakened by the same sound at six in the morning. His energy, his enthusiasm, constantly poured out in a breathless, unrelenting flow of speech, sometimes had the effect of exhausting me not only mentally but physically. My brain and body rebelled and I got cross. Thus I must often have seemed to fit into my predestined pigeon-hole—a lazy, hedonistic, spiteful dilettante, too well-born to work hard, too materialistic to have any ideals, and too selfish to be sympathetic. I was English and he was American. We were both in a sense artists, and consequently self-centred. Somehow, though, in spite of this, we managed to be friends. How exhausting his personality could be in a genuine state of eruption I was to learn during the summer.

Kirstein's life passes in a ceaseless activity because he daily devises new projects to work on. During his stay he was, of course, preparing the way for the summer season of New York City Ballet, both with the people at Covent Garden, with the English Speaking Union, and with the American Embassy. At the dress rehearsal of *Ballet Imperial* I introduced him to Peggy van Praagh and John Cranko. The consequence of this meeting was a visit to Sadler's Wells, and great plans were made for an interchange of choreographers between his and their companies. *The Witch* and *Trumpet Concerto* were the outcome. He arranged with the Institute of Contemporary Arts, then in an embryo condition, for a show of his Symbolic Realist painters to take place simultaneously with the American ballet season. Osbert Sitwell was enlisted to open the exhibition. This was to be followed up in future years by a continual process of inter-fertilization between American and British art. There were no American pictures in the Tate Gallery: this must be remedied—and within a few months it was. Kirstein spent a weekend at Aldeburgh with E. M. Forster, who was an old friend, and Benjamin Britten, whose music he had been the first to use for ballet ten years before. I think he tried to conjure a new ballet out of them, but they were busy working on *Billy Budd*. He met Lucian Freud and began to plan bringing an exhibition of his work to New York. Freud and Francis Bacon he claimed as Symbolic Realists. He met some of the English critics of ballet and spilled out before them the gospel of Balanchine and the new American classical ideal. All the time he was inciting and indoctrinating me. I was a ready pupil.

Certainly he wanted to be loved, as we all do; and he urgently needed to convince others and himself of the righteousness of his artistic ideals; he desired, naturally, appreciation from the right people. Otherwise, I believe, he was and is innocent of all worldly ambitions. He cared nothing for comfort or luxury, thought it wrong to spend money on clothes, furniture, or *bric-à-brac,* and considered that the pictures he bought from time to time were entrusted to him for a brief period only, on their way to a museum. Innocent he was and is. Yet this single-minded missionary, like the Jesuits under Elizabeth, frequently found it necessary to adopt worldly disguises, to feign and to fight ruthlessly for his cause. How can one persuade a bloated oil-magnate to buy the work of a starving genius unless one speaks the same language as he? Sometimes boasting, sometimes base flattery may come in useful. Kirstein hates to mix with worldly people who bore him, but he forces himself to do it in pursuit of an aim. He will exaggerate shamelessly to arouse interest and focus attention. Because he is a highly intelligent man, and one set in authority, people believe what he says. I always did at first. Occasionally, to achieve some object or to fit himself more easily into the scheme of things his latest project has rendered temporarily inevitable, he resorts to self-dramatization. One day I have heard him say that every penny he ever inherited or ever will has been spent on the ballet company: that it is up to them now to carry on, for he has a bare pittance left. The next day he is Kirstein, the rich Jew, to whom nothing is impossible; who, if only one will obey him faithfully, holds the key to all the kingdoms of the world, and the glory of them. I have witnessed these metamorphoses and heard these two stories regularly alternating; and I have no idea which is true.

—from *The Adventures of a Ballet Critic*, 1953

NICOLAS LEGAT
Alan Carter

The elder of two highly talented brothers, Nicolas Legat (1869–1937) was a major dancer at the Maryinsky, performing all the great classical roles and partnering all the great ballerinas, from Kschessinska to Pavlova. His aptitude for teaching and choreographing was recognized early; by 1902 he was assistant ballet master to Petipa, and by 1905 he was director of the "Class of Perfection." In 1910 he and his brother, Sergei, became joint ballet masters in chief, but by 1914 he had left the company, at odds with the modernizing efforts of the management. (He was replaced by his rival, Fokine.) Legat worked throughout Europe, and by 1926 had established an important school in London. One of his most celebrated students, André Eglevsky, collaborated on a book about him called Nicolas Legat: Heritage of a Ballet Master, *in which this tribute first appeared.*

The atmosphere in the very high-pitched Baron's Court studio (it had been built for a monumental sculptor) was mysterious, and I immediately felt like a royal duke in a vast palace ballroom. Round the walls were a number of very funny colored caricatures of ballet dancers and personalities. The master was prodigiously adept at evoking likenesses of faces and bodies and the studio was much enlivened by this graphic humor. He was also a considerable musician, playing the piano extempore for all his classes, and twanging a merry balalaika on Sundays in concert with an orchestra of emigré White Russians. Sometimes the studio resembled an exotic musical instrument museum with balalaikas of all shapes and sizes draped around the walls.

To my lasting sorrow I did not learn Russian, and my dear master did not learn English, except for a few pidgin phrases, graphically expressive, but not always explicit in their meaning. Contrary to present practice, he allowed visitors to watch the classes. We sometimes had a bevy of distinguished impresarios, ex-dancers, theatrical agents, fans, and mothers watching from a row of tip-up theatre seats installed for that purpose. Legat would sometimes turn to one of these onlookers sitting nearest to the piano, and whisper loudly what he thought of a particular pupil. Once he said to a doting mother, "She verra goot dancer but . . . not today . . . not tomorrow . . . not in hundred years!" Neither mother nor daughter returned again to sample the master's wit or knowledge.

Undoubtedly a considerable number of students did not return after one or two classes. Legat seldom made any comment or correction until the pupil had a chance to assimilate the structure of his lessons, and this might take up to a year. Indeed many of us were so confused and deflated by our obvious non-comprehension of the master's simplest directions that we had to steel ourselves in order to continue. But Legat noticed our discomfort and encouraged us with, "Leetel by leetel." I, at least, was totally won over by his patient quietness. Sometimes one of the pupils would be on form in pirouettes, and shower the audience with beads of sweat. Legat would recommend an umbrella. Or ill-fixed hair-dos would disintegrate in lethal volleys of hairpins peppering the spectators. Legat would lift the lid of the piano and hide his head while continuing to play with the other hand. Occasionally he would rise from the piano with stately purpose and cross the studio with deliberate step to demonstrate or give a judicious prod in the appropriate hip or back or head or muscle of an offending dancer. On the way back to the piano he would invariably crack a joke in Russian which made those who could understand double up with hysterics. Gradually I began to get the gist of his jokes, but too vaguely alas to recount.

His English never advanced beyond basic pidgin. He used a few picturesque words to formulate his conversations. These took me months to understand, but finally made sense. Such expressions as "tore-darn; lyka sorsaage; stronk-bak; worr tis dis; gut-boie; you no spik my vife, she no understan." These injunctions, coupled with onomatopoetic additions, were used more or less to cover all exigencies. Crazily enough they did. Being able to accompany his own lessons on the piano, he was able to guide the pupil by the rhythms of the steps, a facility he acquired over years as a first-class ballet-master of stars of the first rank.

Legat taught a subtle *épaulement,* which gave lightness and quickness even to gargantuan dancers. He explained how an almost imperceptible change in the angle of the hips could effect pirouettes and balance. He taught where to focus the eyes when turning; how to correct or give special accent on turning step; how to add *battu* to almost every known step; how the arms must always be perfect in shape from any angle; how and where to accent standard combinations; and how the body's weight can be used like a pendulum. Whatever he taught, it was always infused with the idea of classicism, of perfection, and not of trickery or strain or gimmickry. That was what impressed me then, and impresses me even more now. Indeed I find myself rethinking steps and combinations of steps in his way, as if he were still guiding me. He also taught me the importance of shape and form: a chair balances because it remains in its shape, whereas a piece of string falls limp; or facial strain betrays incorrect use of the neck and diaphragm muscles.

He taught me the double *tour en l'air* which had evaded me for some time. Suddenly one day I could do it—and not only to one side. Because of his insistence on training equally both right and left, I was able to pirouette or turn or jump equally in both directions. In spite of the very considerable technical improvement generally amongst dancers, I am still horrified by the absurd pedagogic attitude of even very famous teachers of ballet who perpetrate, "Do it the best side dear. No point in doing it the hard way." This is like advocating swimming with the right leg and arm only. Of course everyone tends to be one-sided, but then education of any kind is supposed to teach one what one can't do, or doesn't know. Anyway, for myself, after training with Legat, I did not have to distinguish between right and left, for they were trained equally.

I have always followed Legat's teaching, although I do not copy him. That is what he taught: to rethink, understand, and develop, but not to copy. Each body has its own beauty which must learn to conform to the technique in its own way. Technique itself is a living, growing thing, and must adapt and encompass new things. A master is greater than a method, because the master can adjust and change to suit the contingency. A master must visualise perfection and transmit it to his pupils; this is classicism. If I am nonplussed by a technical point, I try to rethink it through his eyes. Legat's way was the classical way. It takes longer and requires great care and thought, but it provides a better and finer solution than any glossing over method or rule of thumb. Pupils must be guided and not bullied; they must learn to contribute with mind and body, and not be desiccated sausages. Frigidity is anathema to art. The body and the mind must be flexed and flexible.

All the leading Russian dancers had worked with Legat at one time or another in Russia, and all the emigrés visited him and revered him, at first in Paris and then in London.

On one occasion the huge studio was further enlarged and a stage built at one end for a performance. An astonishing number of famous dancers appeared to honor the master. Even his wife returned and interfered, between practicing *développés* with weights attached to her legs. The music was beautifully chosen and played on two pianos, Vladimir Launitz sharing the accompanying with the master. In retrospect one number still amazes me. It was for six girls, I think, all famous dancers—and now teachers. The choreography was abstract and would even appear to be modern today, I believe; certainly post-Fokine.

But now the dear old man was beginning to decline. He felt the cold. The one anthracite stove heated a few feet of one end of the vast room, while Legat froze at the other. His wife sometimes popped in and out and seemed to irritate him, although he was always well-mannered and good tempered. There were days when he could not give the Class of Perfection, and his wife took over. It was not the same. She was energetic and by no means without ability and knowledge, but her mind was not classic. Truly she taught some of the master's tricks of the trade, but, as I thought, in exaggerated forms, and usually to students long before they were ready for such advanced work.

Time was running on. I was almost sixteen; time to look for a job. Ninette de Valois auditioned me for the Wells, the Vic-Wells Ballet. She laughed with Irish frenzy when she saw my *grand battement*—above hip-level—something unknown among English male dancers of that era. Later she exploded into fits of spastic-like choreography when she "experienced" my pirouettes! They were numerous, multiple, and equal to the right and left. She was by no means a fan of Legat's, although she admitted that he was a great teacher. Her irascible, forceful nature could not allow the old man's masculine approach. I suspect, too, that his wife had offered terrible and unforgettable insults to "the Irish woman with the French Royal Family name, and her terrible English amateurs." This was a great pity. Legat could have given the English Company a great deal in the early days, not least the nobility of style and attack which has since taken so long to acquire. It is an example of her greatness, I think, that Ninette did engage me on the spot, and offered me thirty shillings per week, in spite of her disapproval of the master.

Legat was upset, but understanding. He was often bed-ridden and seldom able to take even his Class of Perfection. I returned whenever possible to take classes and to see him. He recovered sufficiently at one point to visit my family's house. He played on my piano and insisted that I play to him afterwards. Then we improvised a duet: "Vera gut; not lika sor-saage!"

A little later Madame Legat gave an enormous party in the big studio, but the old man couldn't make it. I went to see him in his bed. He was uncharacteristically unshaven, both face and pate. He tried to talk to me, but was soon defeated by the deafening row from the party above that made the rafters shake with merriment. He spoke in Russian; Anna Roje translated. I was lost in a sea of tears and unspoken thought. There was nothing I could do but rush out of his room and get the Baron's Court tube to go home. Even on the underground I could still hear the gaiety of the party.

A short time later he died. André Eglevsky stood vigil all night over the coffin in the great studio. An enormous painting of Pavlova, one of his favorites, leaned outwards precariously from its hook on the wall, as if flying over his body like a guardian angel. Then came the Russian church service. We all stood; no chairs or pews. The great bass voice of the priest and the incredibly sonorous choir penetrated the gloom. A lot of people, many weeping, including the widow, were there. In my youthful sincerity I felt surrounded by crocodiles. So many of those people had said such bad things about the old man. Now they filed round the church, queueing up to kiss his body. I held my mother's hand tight and tried not to cry. Tears, I felt, were shed by his enemies. Humor and the perpetuation of his teaching would be more useful and more sincere to his memory.

The famous caricatures on the walls of the studio seemed more poignant and precious; a wisp of hilarity in death—Til Eulenspiegelish! Unquestionably he is still part of me.

—from *Heritage of a Ballet Master*, 1978

CARMELITA MARACCI
Agnes de Mille

Supposedly born in South America, but according to her husband, actually born in Goldfield, Nevada, Carmelita Maracci (1911–1987) was a singular presence in the world of dance. She studied both ballet and Spanish dance and somehow merged them in her mesmerizing performances. (John Martin, dance critic of The New York Times, *wrote, "Here is a mistress of ballet teaching and style who never dances ballet, of Spanish dance who never does Spanish dance. Both styles are merely materials out of which she fashions an art that is purely personal, purely subjective in its creative approach, and utterly unique.") Maracci was one of the most important teachers of her time. Among her students were Cynthia Gregory, Allegra Kent, and Agnes de Mille, who recalls her in the following profile.*

I had heard about Maracci from many sources, but the first time I saw her was in 1935, when I went to take a class from her in Hollywood, on Highland Avenue. She was dressed in a little knitted bathing suit, and she sat upright on the edge of her chair, her insteps crossed precisely before her (she had the most beautiful feet in the ballet world). She was smoking. She had tiny hands with long quick fingers, the nails extravagantly long to facilitate castanet playing. She was very small, doll-like, and compact; she had the most attractive small figure I had ever seen. She had, in fact, the perfect dancer's body: a small torso with narrow, trim shoulders and a high chest, and long arms and legs for line. Her black hair was nailed, Spanish style, in a knot at the back of her head.

I have said she was doll-like, but there was no hint of prettiness in the face. Her large mouth peeled back from strong biting-teeth, and was held, not like Martha Graham's in patience against the world or open in ecstatic acceptance, but in wide aggression and abandonment to emotion. Maracci had the head of a rather precocious monkey, or of a wicked marionette. Under the bald, hard, round forehead, her eyes were large and flecked with yellow lights like an animal's. It was an angry little head, proud and passionate—the head of a Spanish gypsy. She always held it curbed in, as though she had a bit in her mouth, the cords of her neck jutting out in strong vertical lines. She always looked out under flickering lids, as though she were about to bolt.

She suggested comparison with Graham constantly: the masklike face, the fixed, aloof gaze, the sudden unleashing of energy. But whereas Graham seemed universal, and on stage even monumental, with the limitless power of the primitive, Maracci was quick, nervous, small, and explosive. The eyes flashed with amusement or scorn. The voice rang out in flat, broad southwestern speech. "Oh my goodness!" she said the day I met her, in washday Bakersfield impatience. "Show some gumption! You look like limp lettuce leaves. What do you think you're doing?" She threw down her cigarette and ground it out on the studio floor with the toe of her pink satin slipper. "Now, let's get going!" Up came the chest; the spine tautened. Her neck and head assumed the tension of accumulated force that is a dancer's preparation. The long arms moved to fourth position, her knees galvanized, and she was off on cold legs, without a plié or an excuse me, in a series of the most astonishing chaîné pirouettes one could ask for, revolving as fast as the eye could follow, as smooth as silk unwinding from a spool. Her lungs were filled with smoke, her thighs relaxed from sitting down. She stopped in arabesque, erect like a T-square, the straight supporting leg planted on its delicate point, the structure of her body balanced and counterbalanced, sinew against bone against height against sinew, hanging in the air, tension counterbalanced on tension. The lovely, tense foot, like the hoof of a deer, was adequate to all, attaching itself to the bare floor and permitting the body to branch and flower above. She posed there on pointe, in defiance of gravity, until her knee got tired, and then, and only then, she allowed her heel to touch ground. She had remained immobile, from full flight, for about fourteen seconds.

"Glory be to God!" I murmured. The girls just stood and looked. We gaped.

"Well!" said Carmelita with a throaty chuckle. "That was pretty good. I think I'll have another smoke on that one. Now, how about some of you trying?"

I'll tell you something extraordinary. We did not match her performance, because there were only four or five people in the world who could. But we did much better than we had ever done before.

One day Anton Dolin visited her class. Carmelita rose from her cigarette, winked at her girls, and unleashed a series of entrechats six, interspersed with entrechats huit. Dolin had not been capable of these since he was thirty, and Igor Youskevitch and André Eglevsky would have had to stretch their thighs a bit to duplicate it. Today I believe only Mikhail Baryshnikov could match it, and possibly some Soviet male stars, and only one woman in history, Adeline Genée. Carmelita sat down, breathing a bit hard, her nostrils flaring, and asked Dolin for a light. I dare say his hand shook a trifle as he offered it. "It nearly sprung me," said Carmelita later, "but I figured I had to do it. He'd heard I was a technician."

"Stretch your feet," she would yell suddenly, sitting on the floor at our ankles and taking the offending member in her strong, surgical fingers. "Isn't that a good pain? I like to feel pain like that. That kind of pain is accomplishment."

We left at the end of an hour and a half, not too tired. Her classes were designed for exhilaration, and she had the great pedagogic faculty of helping us each day to do one thing we had not done before. After her students left she would change her slippers and reenter the empty studio for a little practicing herself, alone—something very few ballet dancers will force themselves to do, it being too drearily exhausting. Carmelita was the only great dancer I ever knew who worked without a coach. She also practiced two hours of castanet and heel work daily. All this was in addition to her composing.

She always said she had been born in Montevideo, Uruguay, but her husband discovered after lengthy and arduous searching (when applying for Medicare) that she had been born in Goldfield, Nevada. Her mother had lied about this. Carmelita never mentioned her father, who was her mother's second husband. Although Carmelita was not an only child, she grew up like one, because her mother drove off an older stepsister and encouraged Carmelita's older brother to leave home.

Carmie was her mother's spoiled darling. Her mother owned a nine-foot Steinway on which she played very well, and it was to her music that Carmie danced, from the moment she could move—danced before she could walk. Her very early formal ballet training began when she came to New York from California and studied with Luigi Albertieri and Enrico Zanfretta. She also studied Spanish dancing with Hypolito Mora. She made her professional debut in California, with a small troupe headed by Alexis Koslov, then she started on her own in San Francisco. At the same time she began teaching, to earn money.

When I first knew her, she was living and working in a cottage that had been built out of one of the rooms in my old school, the Hollywood School for Girls. I hung about and tagged along whenever I could, because I found the atmosphere of the house comforting. There was always a group of radicals, malcontents, and indigent writers, intermingled with painters and dancers, waiting to be recharged by Carmelita's personality, for she was great fun to be with.

Carmie did all sorts of interesting extracurricular things. She was a superb cook. She drew well. She sewed exquisitely and could make her own costumes. Most especially, she showed me how to enjoy a city when one had no money at all; she took me to Chinatown, Japantown, Negro Baptist churches, Spanish services in the Old Mission Church (where in the 1850s my grandmother George had been schooled by Spanish nuns), night court, and dollar day on Hollywood Boulevard. There were alluring cities within our city, and as Carmie revealed them, they were irresistible. All these were to be had for nothing, and I'd grown up right there without knowing anything about them!

We practiced and talked and shopped together and went to parties and improvised outrageous dances. We fell into glooms and were encouraged by our hangers-on. She never seemed to have doubts about her work, as I had about mine. Shortly I found out why.

Up to this point I had not seen her dance. I had heard rumors, but these were so extravagant that I gave them little credence. The night before she entrained for a San Francisco concert, she asked me to watch a rehearsal, so after my work I snatched a peanutburger by the roadside and walked up the crunchy drive-way to her studio. The fresh, moist night air fanned through the garden leaves as I went, along with the sound of the piano, alive and unnaturally distant as always when heard outside at night. Carmie seemed to be alone with her pianist and a large Spanish hat. I sat in a corner quietly. She pulled herself up from the floor and said she might just as well do the dances right off—so she did.

It is no ordinary experience to discover one evening that an intimate, a
known, well-loved, daily companion, has genius and stands outside of the
standards we set for ourselves. The person speaks with the usual voice,
laughs with the ordinary expression, and then, without transition or warning, becomes a figure of magic. I have known this experience three times in
my life, with Antony Tudor, with Sybil Shearer, and with Carmelita. It is a
very humbling experience, involving as it does some of the fastest reorienta-
tion a person can be asked to make, and strong discretion, because one is
brought up sharp against the knowledge that the other fellow has known the
score all along.

That evening my jaw dropped. I sat in the studio where I had done a daily
practice for six months, where we had had parties, Christmas and birthday
celebrations, and long, long talks. The place smelled of wood and floor wax;
the trumpet vines tapped at the windows. Carmelita walked on incredibly
high heels to the center of the room and sat down on a kitchen chair. She said
to the pianist in her plain western dancing-class voice, "I'm ready, I guess."
And it began. The great experience.

Not in Covent Garden during a Ballet Russe gala, when Kschessinska,
Sokolova, and Danilova stood on the same stage, not in Pavlova's presence,
not in the Bolshoi nor the Kirov, not in Graham's concerts, not in the most
dazzling opera houses of the world have I experienced more. This girl
worked with thunder. The dance she showed me was her "Cante Jondo," or
"Deep Song." These notes were made at the time and record exactly what I
saw and thought that night.

She begins the dance as she begins so many—sitting, her head snapped forward, her arms hanging like ropes to the ground. In the maw of her spread
knees, her torso waits, ready, until the ground becomes vital under her
heels. A shudder of energy twitches through her feet, jerking her knees and
spasmodically lifting her head. She is ready. The ground takes possession of
her. Her insteps quiver; the heels ring out nervously. Long shudders pass up
her body—the head rolls on its supporting shoulders. She rocks on her
hams, the weight of her head, of her back, is carried on arms thrust square
against the knees, braced square, of a piece, resisting.

Then, like the splitting of wood, the earth-anger erects her and throws
her out into space. She wrecks herself against the surface of the world. Her
knees double up, jackknife fashion. She spikes at the ground with her heels.
Her head rears back, her chest lifts, as she drills and drums. Doubling and
straightening, wrapping and slapping, she flays the air in naughty rage. See
the clavicles close and open under the taut skin. The cage of her little ribs
works like a bellows. Her fingers poke and stick. Flecks of foam are dashed
from her teeth. Her sturdy legs trot and strike like the hooves of a pony.
She can kick up the ground all right! She can slap the air again and again.

She can lash out at the sky, a merry hard time, a tattoo from hell. Olé, Carmelita!

This is a punishment. This is the anger of the dust, the wrath of the grave. The weakening pulse shudders through her body. Her eyes roll back—her fear becomes audible. "Ay!" she cries, and her teeth cannot hold the quivering lips. "Ay!"

This was the year the civil war got well under way in Spain. Carmelita was brought up as Spanish. She felt an anger in her bones, in her tight young sinews. She raged at the stones and dirt, the waste and dirt of death. "Ay!" It is done.

After the dance I walked to her quietly and put my arms around her. "Carmie, I didn't know."

"I'm glad you like it," she said. "I think it's good, myself." Then she laughed with a matter-of-fact, throaty chuckle that seemed to cut through all hyperbole.

She didn't do this dance very often, because it took too much of her strength. There were others: "Live for the One Who Bore You," sitting on a revolving piano stool from which she never rose; "La Pasionaria," about the inspirational miner's wife, the voice of the Spanish revolution, which got audiences screaming; "Dance of Elegance," a savage satire, an animalistic, monstrous caricature of a ballet dancer preening; "The Nightingale and the Maiden," from Enrique Granados's *Goyescas,* which Jerome Robbins described to me as the most beautiful solo dance he had ever seen. In this dance Carmie's castanets made the sounds of the bird's song, much as they became the sound of the surf curling on the long shore in another of Granados's lyric pieces, "Shells of the Sea Wind."

Plainly and simply, Carmelita's best dances were the most passionate and powerfully devised solos I have ever seen. She worked in the spirit of great caricature, being more of a grotesque than a satirist. She played with cruelty in a manner suggesting Goya and Toulouse-Lautrec.

Her line was visually flawless.

She baffled criticism because her technique fell into two categories: ballet, which, although impeccably correct, was not classic in style, and Spanish, which was virtuoso in its range but highly unorthodox in form and flavor. She had no wish to perpetuate aesthetic traditions and used only those stock gestures so deeply imbued with emotion as to have become, under her manipulation, original. Like the internationally known Spanish dancer Argentina, she made tradition.

At the time I first knew Carmelita, John Martin of *The New York Times* predicted international glory. So why didn't everyone hear about her? Why did she miss her career? She presented one of the most tragic and interesting paradoxes in all of dancing.

When Raquel Meller, the greatest Spanish *diseuse,* came to America, I was told there were fifty Spanish café singers back home quite as good. I am bored with hearing about the pianists who play as well as Gieseking or Rubinstein. What if they do? Have they arranged their lives so that they can perform for me under auspicious circumstances at prearranged times? I want the core of their hearts, foaming and red, between eight-thirty and ten-thirty, in a comfortable place of assembly near my home. For this I am willing to pay a small sum and go out to the auditorium. Between the perfect performance achieved in privacy and the blinding happenstance produced at my convenience, on my terms, is a spiritual and psychological gap as great as that which lies between great talent and not much. Only the giants leap the chasm.

Carmelita had imagination, verve, energy, and fascination. What she did not have was the ability to cope with the practicalities of her career, nor did she get herself assistants who could. She was a fugue of neuroses. I never knew a person to have so many megrims and vapors—her various decays came and went like passing moods. I arrived for class one day to find her sitting in the sun, knitting and moaning. She had developed cancer of the stomach, she informed me. She didn't think, however, she would care to see a doctor. I made three different appointments, and went three separate times to fetch her in my sister's car, before I finally got her under a trained eye. She did not have cancer of the stomach.

She nearly always got laryngitis the day before a concert. She was usually prostrated afterward. She could not be made to keep an appointment. If it was social, you could bet she wouldn't show up. Many a dinner I watched cool on my table until at last her husband phoned to say that she had a headache, or felt she must put in one more hour of rehearsing, or was forced to interview a critic, or . . . but does it matter? If she was not the hostess, she would not show.

But she never once taught a bad class or, having reached the stage, failed to perform superbly and like no other contemporary. The tragedy was that these occasions were so few.

In the late thirties Erin O'Brien Moore, an actress-pupil growing impatient with the public's indifference to Carmelita, gave her $35,000—in those days a tidy sum—to come to New York for two concerts. She also procured her a manager—not one of the best ones, but the best one to be persuaded to manage an unknown. He was, incidentally, Erin's lover. Before Carmelita reached New York, Erin broke with the lover, but she failed to notify Carmelita of the change in her personal affairs. Maracci took exception to the manager and to the treatment accorded her, including her modest hotel accommodations. She expected to be hailed as a world-famous celebrity, like Argentina. She was not Argentina, the manager pointed out, and he was not prepared to fulfill Erin's promises. Carmelita was abandoned. She tongue-lashed all concerned. She turned on Erin viciously. The manager was no longer emotionally obligated and was disinclined to do anything helpful. Carmelita left New York forlornly and went back to California. She did not, however, return Erin's money, that having been spent on rehearsals, preparations, and fares. She salved her conscience for the failure to repay the debt by never forgiving Erin. But Erin forgave Carmelita, and at her next public performance murmured, "More beautiful than ever" as she walked up the aisle.

Carmie later came back to New York and was scheduled to give a concert at the YMHA, but she developed a septic throat the night before and had to cancel. This was, of course, momentous news in her life, but not, as it turns out, in the public's, because on the very day of the cancellation, December 7, 1941, we returned home from the auditorium's closed doors to learn that Japan had just bombed Pearl Harbor.

After the war I suggested that Ballet Theatre produce a suite of Carmelita's dances. After months of remonstrating and arguing, she was prevailed upon to come east again and rehearse the Ballet Theatre corps de ballet, which she did assiduously. They were fascinated, as everyone always was. The painter Rico Lebrun designed sets and costumes that were outstandingly fine in themselves, but they did not help the dance movement. The music was orchestrated.

Alas, Carmelita's solo dances, although left unchanged in their pristine beauty, did not assimilate into a larger piece. At the first performance the audience was puzzled and not a little put off by Carmelita's austere, sardonic personality, and on the whole was tepid in its response.

I met Oliver Smith, the codirector of Ballet Theatre, in the foyer. "What shall I tell her? Whatever shall I say?"

"You'll go back," said Oliver, in his heartiest Broadway fighting manner, "and give her a pep talk, as you would on any opening night to any pro. She can pull this piece together. You know she can. The material is there. It just wants the doing. But she'll have to get at it and work very hard, very fast."

So I went back to her dressing room, where Carmelita sat wrapped in a huge dressing gown, enormous-eyed and shuddering with nerves, and gave her a pep talk, as I would to any professional, and produced in no time a collapse. She had to be carried out of the theater by Don Sadler, one of her dancers, while her faithful acolytes addressed me in terms of sorrow and rage: "What did you think you were doing?" She terminated the season and went back home. I don't think she wrote to me for several years.

Then, in the late forties, Sol Hurok, the great manager, came to her. Argentinita—not Argentina, but another popular Spanish dancer—had just died of cancer. Hurok offered Carmie all of her unfilled dates, and Carmie, I felt very unwisely, jumped at this opportunity. In effect, it was no opportunity. Argentinita had been a traditional dancer, splendidly fine but orthodox. Carmelita Maracci was bittersweet and very particular in her appeal. She was an acquired taste. The audiences didn't know what they were looking at.

In addition there was the Maracci point of view. Carmelita took up causes like a street fighter, and she used this tour to propagandize her latest interest, which was at the moment loyalist Spain (later it was ending the Vietnam War). As later, she went to exaggerated extremes. Lee Freeson, her husband, suddenly found he could not meet his payroll, because Carmie had secretly instructed her concert management to send half the box office receipts to the Spanish refugees. The transaction was kept secret because she was afraid Lee would not approve. He did not; he had bills to pay.

The performances on the Hurok tour were successful enough while Carmelita herself was onstage, but dull when she was off it and the assisting group of three girls and one boy were forced to carry the show. One night in St. Paul a lone drunk, losing interest like many others, rose and began to burlesque the dances, prancing up and down the aisles. The audience welcomed the diversion and started to call out encouragement and laugh. Carmelita was in her dressing room, changing for the next solo. Her three girls were left alone with the hubbub, fervently going through one of Carmie's irate, merciless, and deeply felt anti-Franco numbers, "Spain Cries Out." Carmie heard the uproar and rushed half-dressed to the wings.

"Pull down the curtain," she screamed.

"Don't do it," said Lee. "It's only one drunk. The ushers will take care of him."

Carmelita became hysterical. "Close the curtain! Close the curtain!" She clawed at the curtain man's arms.

The curtain descended, to the amazement of the dancers and audience. Carmelita returned fuming to her room, denouncing in loud tones the decriers of loyalist Spain, the savages who could not understand a serious statement of the passion of our times.

Her fulminations were cut short by the enraged entrance of one of the backers. "Where is this Maracci woman?"

Carmelita stood at bay. Then she let loose in gutter terms, viciously and brutally, the full extent of her primal rage. She attacked the man personally and all of the people of St. Paul, their intelligence, their lack of ideals. Forty years after the episode she still referred to "the drunken audience jeering at Spanish heroes."

Carmie manufactured this quarrel. She was determined on martyrdom; she sought it, she wished it, she needed it—immolation at all cost, no matter how unnecessary, no matter how ineffectual. She would have it. Well, she had it.

That concert was terminated then and there, and so was her entire career. The management phoned Hurok's New York office as soon as they could get through and refused flatly to pay her fee. They also canceled all the remaining Hurok concerts for the rest of the year and threatened to maintain the boycott indefinitely. Hurok, of course, was frantic, and immediately repudiated Carmelita Maracci's contract. She was sent home with very little money, and her name was placed at the head of a blacklist.

She had done for herself.

MANAGERS SAY THEY want reliable clients. They also say they must give the public what it wants. One thing is certain, they want no trouble.

Yet I believe that anyone who prefers practical cooperation to genius is a fool. Back and forth across the country every year trek the girls and boys who will do what they're told, give what they're asked, comply, conform, and adapt. All they do is corrupt public taste, drive interested people from the theaters, and make shabby and flat a fierce and magic calling. Do any managers know what the public wants? A good part of the public really wants a public hanging or a ceremonial deflowering. The rest of the public could not possibly say what it wants. People simply want to be moved.

What goes toward the building of a great career? I should say sixty percent of the requirement is character, by which I do not mean a kind heart. Rather, I mean durability, stead-fastness, and realism. Above all, realism—as well as talent. There is no substitute for talent. Talent, however, can lie moldering for lack of common sense. It takes realistic courage to wade into the welter of crossed ambitions, tastes, and greeds involved in the theater and distill from the ferment what one desires. The work involved is rough, and the perils of demoralization and cheapening arise daily. Very many great artists must by their nature work in private, but these should not choose theater as a medium.

All dancers have to use other people as collaborators. The conflict is therefore generated right in the moment of creation. Dancing must have collaboration and help; help is people, and people are trouble. The point where the great artist and the great careerist fuse is on the public stage at eight-thirty sharp.

Most creative artists are neurotic, as most people are neurotic; I believe that creative artists are no more neurotic than anyone else. But they are more noticeable. However, I think it is possible to make another generalization: those with a great gift generally have in their character a certain instinctive protection of the endowment, so that while it may be deflected, tortured, or delayed, it is seldom destroyed. Carmie was a tragic exception.

Repeated collapses are usually contrived to hide flaws, weaknesses in the talent, and their inevitable exposure. In Carmie's case there was no flaw. Her talent was immaculate. Why then did she insist on withdrawing? What was she terrified of?

Tantalizing, magical hazards provided her with a staunch excuse for not standing up to her test and being counted. Behind these perils, which she almost cherished and which she certainly supported, she could hide. She could not put the blame on others. She had evaluated herself as of unmatched worth; she did not ever have to diminish this appraisal, not while she could hide behind other circumstances and other people.

Carmelita sometimes failed to meet an obligation because she could not pay her taxi fare to the date. Several times Lee came to me for money, always at the last moment. But this was not the real reason for defaulting. We all knew it. Money alone could not answer her need. At the beginning I could give her none, because I had none. Later, when I had a little, I of course sent her some. But once she made the appeal herself. I went to Jerome Robbins for additional help, and he asked if this was to be a regular thing with her. I had to admit that it probably was, so with the money I finally sent Carmelita a letter. In effect I said that I thought she had one of the greatest gifts I knew, but that she had not enjoyed the success she certainly deserved. I, who had a much smaller gift—and I meant this quite sincerely—was getting the most out of it, I felt, because I had had a psychiatric analysis. I had Jerome Robbins's permission and Martha Graham's permission to say that they both had had analyses, and I suggested that Carmie try one for relief and clarification.

The letter I got back almost burned the paper, after which Carmelita didn't write a word to me for six years. She thought my suggestion was wickedly mocking. The fault obviously lay in the perverted taste of the public and the venality of the management.

After her St. Paul experience she retired to a studio and spent the rest of her life in raging against management, against American taste, against her colleagues, against whatever. She broke off with nearly all her friends because she scolded so bitterly about their politics, their way of life, their taste. Most of her students, including Cynthia Gregory, Christine Sarry, William Carter, and Paul Godkin, testified that the steel and brilliance in their own technique came from Carmelita, but after a while they did not dare go near her. Either she quarreled with them or she demanded their entire time and service, which none of them could afford. Carmelita rehearsed two or more years for every concert, and while her personal performance sharpened, her assistants were bled juiceless—she sucked them dry. She never forgave them when they left.

Over the years Carmelita wrote many letters, most bitter, some directly scolding, all eloquent. I submit a few random paragraphs.

> I think that a technique should be subordinate to the idea, and of late the opposite is true. . . . I don't want to see a well-trained dancing army in government hire who leap without question.

> I am tired of the dancing department store, where people come and go and buy leg secrets and a hint of how they can do a better fouetté soufflé— in other words, a length of this and a yard of that. . . . I am not a pedagogue trying to prepare fodder for the dancing machines.

> No one speaks of content, and Martha Graham looks embalmed. The ballet polish she has used in the last ten years has completely ruined her awkward wonder of the early years. The photograph of her with Gerald Ford made me gag. And Baryshnikov is surely the Mrs. Miniver of the day, in disguise.

> The terrain I traveled was not the studio floor, for my world led me into Goya's land of terror and blood-soaked pits. . . . The life I lived could not make me a dancer of fine dreams and graveyard decor . . . so I danced hard about what I saw and lived. I was not an absentee landlord. I was one of the dispossessed. I was a gypsy.

And years later:

> I live in anonymity. I can barely remember that I once danced. Some photographs reassure me.

> I was a rotten soldier, Agnes, and it is you who want people to be good ones. [I don't remember ever saying anything to this effect.] I am more of an anarchist than ever. I could never have danced as I did if I had been an obedient servant.

> I am changing my profession in November. I am stopping teaching after forty-eight years. I'm going to write. I hope it isn't too late.

Thirty-five years after the St. Paul evening, she still alluded to the tragic event with all the venom in her soul:

I have not forgotten St. Paul, Minnesota, nor have I forgotten my cruel dismissal and mismanagement. . . . No one should be given the power that Hurok knew to ruin another person, but it is natural that people preferred silence, since they might have hurt their chances of being managed by the powerful one.

Whether or not Carmie wrote anything beyond letters and scraps I cannot say. There were other things she could do. She drew cartoons, extraordinarily pungent line drawings of ballet dancers. Rico Lebrun thought she had a future as a caricaturist. "I am a dancer," she said, closing the subject.

She cooked extremely well, making dishes for her studio parties that were legendary. Lee told me she used long needles to inject wine into meat, then let it marinate for two days. She contributed articles to *Gourmet* magazine and was offered an annual stipend to be on its staff. "I am a dancer," she said, turning the offer down.

But she didn't dance.

As the years went on, she developed bad arthritis, until she had to teach from a wheelchair (which she could do with wonderful effect). Terry Orr told of her later teaching:

One of my first memories is doing pliés and making rain-drops fall from the sky. She didn't show you how you had to create the rain. Twelve people in the class might have twelve different variations, which shocked me, because suddenly my arm wasn't going from second position to the first, and then opening to the second again. Another time I remember is when she opened up a book after we had done pliés and tendues and started talking about poetry. After an hour and fifteen minutes had gone she made us come into the center for grand battements and we then did turns for the next fifteen minutes and that was the end of the class.

But that day was not about learning to do pirouettes. That day was learning about poetry.

A time of being free with dance! In ballet you don't get that chance very often, but that was exactly how I learned to pirouette. She created different arm movements, such as putting our hands behind our backs. She was the first one who taught me how to control centrifugal force. It was the first time I could do six or seven pirouettes, while at first I was doing only doubles or triples. After that I started loving the sensation, of turning much more. When I went back home to San Francisco, I could do nine turns. (Walter Terry wrote of me that I was the Rudolf Nureyev of the West because I was jumping and turning in a way that had not been seen often.) To the lay reader this may not designate any radical change, but to the dancer, to depart from orthodox controls is as frightening as the loss of the thumb in piano playing.

Riddled with pain, Carmelita was carried about her house in her husband's arms. Then, most sinister of all, she began to feel that she was distorted by her disease (and she was), that she was a mockery of what she had been. She became a recluse. People who really loved her took to dropping by without warning, trapping her into a meeting, and after their departure Carmie would have weeping fits. Through it all her faithful husband did the housework, maintained his own business (selling rare manuscripts), and took the brunt of her incredible angers and vagaries. One never knew what to expect with Carmelita. Up to the end she sent the most enchanting cards and little presents, made phone calls, offered gifts of homemade cookies or similar delicacies, but any definite plan to see her met with repeated frustration, in spite of her ardent protestations.

In 1987 Carmelita had a massive heart attack. She was taken to the cardiac department of Cedars of Lebanon Hospital, but she would not listen to the doctors or do as they said because, naturally, she distrusted them. They allowed her to go home, mainly, I suppose, because under the circumstances the hospital could do nothing for her.

There was a second attack. This time Lee was desperate. Once again she went to the hospital. Her doctor came back only on the condition that she would obey him. Being sufficiently terrified, she complied. On returning home she stopped eating, which is a solution for almost every problem. Then one night she said she would like some fish. Lee gave it to her, then watched the television news as she lay quietly dozing. After the news he went to her; failing to rouse her, he discovered that Carmie had left him. She had died.

At the mortuary he had to identify the body—a legal imperative. Reluctantly he looked, and there, he told me, lay a little girl, at the most thirteen or fourteen years old, absolutely pure, incorporeal, weightless, a spirit. He thought she would float from the room. He had seen nothing like it in his life. This was the essence of la Maracci, a born dancer, a great one who had concealed herself, hidden somehow until this moment in an ambuscade of deceit, trouble, disease, and ugliness. Now she had escaped.

CARMELITA MARACCI IS barely remembered today. She is given hardly a paragraph in the dance histories and memoirs. Nonetheless, there are those who saw her in the thirties and forties, and like the notes of the nightingale about which she danced with her singing ebonies, she sounds in our memory sweet and clear, pure and crystalline. *Olé*, lost lovely voice, *olé*, our Carmie.

—from *Portrait Gallery,* 1990

ALICIA MARKOVA
Agnes de Mille

Madame Marks, as she used to be called at Ballet Club, knew her own wishes. She never shared her dressing room with another woman. She insisted that every costume be cleaned each time she wore it. (Costumes almost invariably belong to the company, not, as in opera, to the star performers, and two or three ballet stars have to share the same dresses.) Nora Kaye came offstage one night during *Romeo and Juliet* and held out her arms for the next costume, a cloth-of-gold robe. She was informed that Markova had visited the theater that afternoon and that on her instructions the overeager dresser had sent the costumes to the cleaners; there would be no further changes during the current performance. On hearing this news, Miss Kaye's face was, as they say, a study.

At that time Markova lived sparsely in unmodified hotel rooms, without a personal maid. She had instead a kind of acolyte—neither dresser nor maid, but a humble young professional who ran errands, stood by, listened, sympathized, handed things, and worshiped. This person was always present and silent. Besides her recompense she received instruction and coaching in ballet technique and the daily opportunity of watching genius. Markova always talked in front of her as though she were not there, with regal imperviousness to human criticism; two or three intimate attendants constituted for her complete privacy.

It goes without saying that her discipline about sleep, food, and drink was rigid, continuous, and lifelong. She did not smoke. Her only real expenditure was on ravishing clothes by name designers, but these did not include furs or jewels. She held herself to a severe budget, permitting herself a first mink coat only after the South African tour in 1949. About twenty-five years of dancing paid for this. She always supplied all her own tutus (to ensure their freshness), her own headpieces and accessories, and, of course, all slippers and tights—a very sizable expense. She rarely entertained.

Dolin seemed to live high and fancy, but he was doing public relations for both of them, and Markova paid for half. It was always Dolin who held court in his dressing room for columnists, civic functionaries, movie stars, and fans, talking his way through cold cream and towels. His dressing room had the air of a levee, but he usually remembered to point out the quiet little figure, already cleaned up and dressed impeccably, sitting in attentive silence. . . .

Alicia came to the theater as a rule before anyone else. For a gala she was in and out of the place all day, but for each routine appearance she was on hand at least three hours ahead of time. Her room seemed as businesslike and as prophylactic as a surgery. The dressing table had pristine, dainty skirts and spotless cloths laid over the makeup. On a white-covered table lay her shoes, pair by pair, long and exceedingly narrow (triple A). Markova's feet were flawless—white, supple, and unmarked. Most dancers' feet look like the ace of clubs: gnarled, jointed, skinned, bruised, and blackened, with horny nails and rubbings and scars that have bitten into the tissue. The feet of dancers who dance barefoot cannot be imagined; they are hoofs. But Markova gave her feet solicitous, almost medical, care, and they were dreams.

She took ten minutes to put on her shoes. She cleaned everything she owned every day. She puttered and fussed and mended, the acolyte sometimes helping her clean, sometimes watching her. But often Alicia was alone and wanted it so. She was like a young mother assembling her first layette, cutting off connections with the world. She was already beginning to connect with the audience. They did not know this. It was afternoon still; many of them were at their offices. It would be an hour yet before they got ready for dinner.

After some while of this meandering, Alicia put on practice clothes and her makeup base and went onstage for a lesson from her coach, Vincenzo Celli. Celli put her through an hour or two of everything he could think of. In lieu of a barre, she hung on to the wardrobe trunks or the tormentors. Other members of the company appeared and started practicing, but apart from her. When she left the stage to go to her dressing room, she was dripping. Her acolyte waited with a towel, for from now on she had to keep in a light sweat. (Her audience was probably now having cocktails.) She sponged off and finished her makeup. She gave half an hour to her hair.

Twenty minutes before curtain she stripped and got into her all-silk tights. I have seen Alicia stripped. She had no body at all. She had no bust, no stomach, no hips, no buttocks; she had two long supple arms and two long strong legs, joined by a device that contained in the most compact manner possible enough viscera to keep her locomotive. She was utterly feminine but as incorporeal as a dryad. Her slenderness, her lack of unneeded flesh, was a rebuke to everything gross in the world.

The tights were held taut by elastics and tapes that wrapped around her twenty-one-inch waist (this was long before the time of elasticized stockings and tights). Her toes were swathed very exactly in lamb's wool to prevent shoe friction, and the priceless little mummies were then inserted into the flawlessly clean satin boxes, which were glued to her heel. (Pavlova used spit in the heel of her shoe, in the old tradition; Alicia used LePage's glue—it is stronger.) Then the ribbons were sewn; she had to be cut out of her shoes after a performance. Five minutes before curtain she stepped into the tutu. As the orchestra started she walked onto the stage. It always took four men to help her with the flowers on the return journey.

Classification is silly. Many stars are flabbergasting artists, quite different and mostly blessedly contemporary. When performers reach this standard of excellence, choosing between them becomes a matter of personal taste. But John Martin of *The New York Times* dared to risk his very considerable reputation by writing, "[Markova] is not only the greatest ballet dancer in the world today, but very possibly the greatest that ever lived"—a claim impossible to substantiate, but eye-catching.

I happened to be backstage the day after Martin's incredible pronounce-ment was printed. In my minor way, I was going through the process of warming up, quieting down, and cutting off from daily life. I passed Alicia's room. She was standing alone, rubbing the toe of a slipper with a piece of gauze soaked in benzine.

"Alicia," I said, slipping onto her sofa, "tell me something. As one woman to another, how does it feel to read in a newspaper a statement like Martin's— 'the greatest ballet dancer of all time'?"

"That's very well and good," said Alicia, placing the slipper precisely beside its fellow, drawing her silk dressing gown up neatly, and sitting down with crossed ankles. "It's easy to write something like that, but it's I who have to live up to it. What am I to do the next day, I ask you? I said to Celli, I must work all the harder. I mean, ducky, the audience is going to expect something after reading that bit. It will be hard lines if I let them down. There's always the next performance to think of. That's what I said to Celli."

Alicia had at the time reached the age (not a great one) when in the days of Russia's Imperial Ballet the stars were forcibly retired and pensioned, but she was dancing better than ever, with virtuosity and an enormous brilliance of dynamics and power. Instead of slacking off with the years, she seemed to be attaining greater and greater physical and emotional strength and achiev-ing subtler and more exquisite refinements of style.

Building her reputation had been hard; maintaining it was harder. When Pavlova danced, she was the only great ballet star most of us had seen, and she brought with her the excitement of revelation. The theaters of Markova's day bulged with dandy technicians, and the beady eyes out front were knowledgeable and blase, while in the wings stood those ready and able to crowd the star off center spot. If Markova seemed at times mettle-some to the girls and boys who worked with her, she was only fighting for her position and her future. One mistaken step from an assistant, one hand on a wrong light lever, undid a hundred hours of practicing. Markova might have had the proverbial nervous temper of a ballerina; she also had the responsibility. She might have seemed fragile, childish, and gentle, but cross her will, or turn on the wrong light, or make a damaging mistake in tempo, and you would know why Britain had withstood the blitz and held Gibraltar and girdled the world, and lasted as long as any other country in recorded history.

After an ovation, this airy, fairy, feathery little thing was known to place an armful of white orchids deliberately on the floor, pass silently and exquisitely over to where the head electrician waited uncomfortably, and break him.

She was acclaimed the greatest ballet dancer for just one reason: she intended to be.

—from *Portrait Gallery*, 1990

OLGA SPESSIVTSEVA
Anton Dolin

Considered by many to be the true successor to Pavlova, Olga Spessivtseva (1895–1991) suffered one of the saddest lives of any twentieth-century dancer. Immediately recognized both at the Imperial Ballet School in St. Petersburg and in the Maryinsky company as a singular talent, she quickly ascended to major roles such as Giselle (her most famous creation) and Odette-Odile. For a while she danced with Diaghilev's Ballets Russes, leading the company in its brave but failed 1921 production of The Sleeping Princess *in London. In 1916 she went to America with the Ballets Russes, dancing with Nijinsky, and although rooted at the Paris Opéra Ballet from 1924 to 1932, she toured with many companies through Europe and South America. In 1937 she suffered the first of her nervous breakdowns—she had always been considered fragile and unstable. She was hospitalized in New York in 1943, and remained institutionalized until 1963, when friends, led by Anton Dolin, had her removed to the Tolstoy Farm in Rockland County, New York, where she lived quietly until her death at the age of ninety-six. To add insult to injury, she was resurrected as the central character of Boris Eifman's unfortunate* Red Giselle.

Two weeks before Christmas, I returned to New York. I had an apartment on Fifty-eighth Street. Quite a Ballet House at that time. Mia Slavenska and her mother, Freddy Franklin, and Alexandra Danilova were among the many dancers living there. A few doors away was the Windsor Hotel, where Alicia [Markova] had her suite, and one other great artist who had arrived from South America to tour the Northern States under Sol Hurok's management, Encarnacion Argentinita. What a joy it was to see this truly wondrous Spanish dancer again. We were to see much of each other for the next years, both in and out of the theatre.

Another dancer living, or, as she said, existing, in New York was Olga Spessivtseva. Immediately I arrived from Chicago, I went to call on her at her apartment at the Salisbury Hotel, where I found Olga in a far from peaceful state of mind and mood. I was horrified at the change in her and by much of what she said to me. "I cannot stay here. I die here. Anton, they poison me." She made a movement to the fireplace. "There, look, smell, Anton, the poison fumes. I will not stay. I tell to Mr. Brown, give me my passport. I will go back to Russia. He will not. Why? Why?"

I tried to calm her, to tell her there was a war on in Europe. She did not seem to understand what I said, or to take any notice of my arguments.

Two days later, the telephone bell by my bedside rang very early in the morning. I took up the receiver to answer it. It was Olga. "I must see you now, at once. I go to change my hotel." I promised I would come for her at ten o'clock. As I saw by my watch, it was six-thirty. I tried to sleep till nine o'clock, but my brain was troubled with the thoughts that kept recurring. A few minutes before ten o'clock I went downstairs to the lobby. Olga was sitting there, huddled, staring blankly before her. It was only later I learned that she had been there since her call to me hours before. As a matter of fact, she had telephoned from the reception desk. I thought that the call had come from her apartment at the hotel. She seemed to be looking at me through dazed eyes, tired, and with dark shadows under them. I can still hear myself saying, "Olga, Olga, what is it?"

"I go. I go to the Savoy Plaza. Take me. I will go to my old room there, No. 341. It is safe, I know. Take me, take me, now, *now*."

Her voice rose. I quietened her, and led her out of the hall to the street. The lights were against us crossing Sixth Avenue. She did not stop. I took her arm in mine gently, firstly to prevent her from being killed and, secondly, to escort her across the Avenue when the lights turned green.

"Do not touch me, Anton. I am the *prima ballerina* of the Paris Opéra. I am not a whore. *Je suis* Olga Spessiva!"

The lights changed, and she was across the street and on her way to the Savoy Plaza. We arrived together, and there was a dreadful scene at the reception desk. Room 341 was occupied. She should have no other. It was all a conspiracy, one more conspiracy against her. With great difficulty, I eventually got her back to the Salisbury Hotel and into what I hoped was the safe keeping of her guardian, Mr. Brown, who was there.

I talked to him for a few minutes. He seemed helpless. He didn't know what to do. It appeared that Olga would see nobody but me. She would stay nowhere but at the Savoy Plaza, but was finally persuaded to be moved to another hotel. She had refused to see any of her other friends of the Ballet—and there were many in New York at the time, Pierre Vladimirov and his wife, Felia Doubrovska, Ludmillar Schollar and her husband, Anatol Vilzak, among them—who had not only been with her in *The Sleeping Beauty* during those wonderful evenings at the Alhambra Theatre, but were her classmates at the Maryinsky Theatre, Leningrad.

A week later I was dining with Constance Collier at her apartment, when I was called to the telephone. I was not surprised, for I had left a message at the desk of the Van Dorn that if I was wanted, this was where I could be found. A strange voice spoke to me. "Is that Mr. Dolin? I am the doctor at the Roosevelt Hotel. A lady is asking for you, a Russian lady, Mr. Dolin. Spessiva or something. I am afraid she is not well, and if you can come at once, perhaps you can help."

I explained the situation to Constance, who was very sympathetic, rushed over to the Roosevelt Hotel, where Olga was now living, asked for the room number and went up. As I entered the elevator, I knew instinctively that what I had been so afraid of had happened. When I entered the room, Olga was sitting on the bed, a tragic, demented creature, looking exactly like Giselle, the role which had been her greatest portrayal. Mr. Brown was standing by the window. The doctor was by the telephone near the bed. The situation needed no explaining, not even by the doctor, who, however, insisted upon telling me.

Olga had been fighting with Mr. Brown, or so she said. He had hit her. She pointed to a mark on her forehead. There was no sign of any bruise that I could see. She herself had picked up the telephone and called for the house doctor and the police. Unhappily, they had both arrived.

"This lady, Mr. Dolin, tells me you are an old friend. She refuses to answer any question I ask her. Only that I should get you here. I do not know you, sir, but, happily, she did keep saying 'Telephone Van Dorn, Fifty-eighth Street.' You know the rest."

I talked, or rather tried to talk, with Olga. She kept repeating over and over again, "He hit me. This is my home. I stay here now. This room. I will not go from here, not go. Look at my face, it is hurt."

I had to explain, upon further questioning, that Mr. Brown was not her husband, no relation at all, but a dear friend. I also was no relation, but had been her dancing partner in London, who she was, etc., etc. It meant little to the doctor, who faced, as he had been, with situations before, found this one a little more difficult, and more unusual. Olga kept repeating in French, Russian, and English who she was. "I am Giselle. I am Olga Spessiva of the Paris Opéra. *Prima Ballerina*. This is my home. I stay only here."

It was terrible, and the doctor's patience was coming to an end. He had his duty to perform and, in his opinion, Olga was far from normal. And her remarks, sense to me, were far from sense to him. "If this lady will go quietly with you from this hotel I will commit her to a private home for a few days, otherwise I have no alternative but to commit her for observation to Bellevue Hospital. That, Mr. Dolin, is the law of New York. This lady has made a disturbance, called the police, and we have an ambulance downstairs in the street. We must take her by force if she will not leave with you quietly and with no further fuss."

Those were his words, but words and the law meant nothing to Olga Spessivtseva. I pleaded with her. At moments, she was calm. Then suddenly she would raise her voice, pace the room for a few moments, sit down upon the bed and, like a child, look at me with her large, sadly demented eyes.

It was no use. She would not budge. And Mr. Brown and I were asked to leave her room. Then the doctor, aided by two police officers and the ambulance attendant, had to take her by force out of the bedroom, through the corridor, and down to the waiting ambulance.

Mr. Brown and I stayed in the corridor. It was a dreadful scene, and to this day I can hear her pitiful cries: "Save me, Anton. I am not mad. Save me. You are my partner. Anton . . . Anton. . . ."

Later, Mr. Brown and I took her clothes to the hospital. As we waited in the psychopathic ward, they brought in a man who had jumped from a twenty-storey window and was all broken to pieces. He died in front of us as we stood there talking to the nurse about Olga's belongings. It was horrible.

For the next five days, Olga was kept under observation and then the doctors decided that it was not a complete mental breakdown but a bad case of menopause, and they would be glad to release her to a private sanatorium to which, now quiet and rational, she agreed to go. Mr. Brown was able to arrange this.

Towards the end of March 1941, I went to see Olga at White Plains and found her quiet and, within reason, ready to talk, though she still had the air of a child, and in her eyes was the unspoken question, "What is next? Where to now?" "Why did you not save me, Anton, why?" I heard her say that distinctly, and I tried to answer quietly that I had no power, no authority to do anything, except to try to persuade her to leave the hotel with me. She did not seem to understand what I said to her. It had been a very sad afternoon, but I had the reassurance of the doctor in charge that, after many weeks of quiet and rest, she had every chance of being discharged and would enjoy a normal return to her life.

I prayed very hard for her that Sunday and asked the Almighty God, "Why, why did all this have to happen to Olga?"

I spent a most wretched Christmas and New Year and hope and pray that I may never go through anything like it again. . . .

IMMEDIATELY AFTER MY arrival in New York [in 1943] before we were due to begin dancing for our first season at the Metropolitan Opera House, I telephoned the sanatorium at White Plains to inquire after Olga Spessivtseva. To my surprise I was informed she was no longer there and then, to my horror, that only a few weeks previously, she had been sent to the State Hospital for the Insane at Poughkeepsie. That was all the information they could give me. Just those few heartbreaking words.

I went at once to the Essex House Hotel on Central Park South, to find Mr. Brown. That was his last address, and I had seen him there before I left for Mexico, when we had talked about setting up a trust fund for Olga and he had asked me then whether I would act as a trustee. I had agreed to this, making a stipulation that he and two other people would constitute a board of control. He told me that there was a sum of money at a bank in New York to pay the large fees due to the White Plains Private Home each month.

When I inquired for him at the reception desk of the Essex House Hotel, I was told: "Mr. Brown dropped dead of a heart attack some five months ago."

Days later, not without difficulty, I contacted his lawyer who was living in Brooklyn and made an appointment by telephone to meet him. With trepidation and much misgiving I made my way to his office, where a stormy, useless encounter with the executor of Mr. Brown's will took place. Mr. Brown had left his fortune to his only sister and the executor could not see why *she* should now be responsible for the welfare of Olga.

"I understand the lady is a mental case and her removal to a State asylum and becoming a charge of the State is the only thing possible."

He laughed and brushed aside my threat of creating an open scandal by giving the story to the papers. To him Olga meant nothing. He said, "She was just the mad mistress of my late client, Mr. Brown."

I returned to my apartment, thoroughly defeated and dejected. It was impossible for me to make the journey to Poughkeepsie until the Metropolitan season was under way and I had a free day either from rehearsal or a performance. Finally I went to Poughkeepsie and found the Home in which Olga was a patient. I tried to tell the doctor in charge quickly who I was but, what was more important, who Olga was and what her position had been in the world of the Ballet for, as I found out at once, he knew little of her background.

He took me to see her. It was dreadful. A dozen poor demented women were gathered together in a dimly lit room. Olga sat quietly, away from the others. She saw me, got up, looked around for a second, then ran like a scared and frightened animal into a corner of the wretched room. Nothing would persuade her to come to me or speak to me. I saw in her eyes and in the way she behaved the tragic and false feelings she felt about me. In her mind I had betrayed her. Later, when I spoke to the doctor again, he verified it to me as part of her depression and persecution mania. She had called my name to help her when she was moved from White Plains. Tragically for her, for me, I could not hear her.

Before leaving the hospital, I exacted a promise that she would be moved to more private quarters and that her case would be more thoroughly gone into. I went to see her again two weeks later and took with me all the books and photographs I could find about her and of her, to show to the doctor and the nurse in charge of her. I begged that she should be released and sent to a private home. I was informed that that would be impossible unless a fund of several thousand dollars were set up to ensure her maintenance for at least three to five years. She was now a State charge and unless this guarantee were forthcoming, nothing could be changed.

I made one last appeal. I was earning a salary in America. I was free. I would marry her. Would that obtain her release and give her into my charge?

"No, Mr. Dolin," I was told. "The State does not allow by law the marriage of an insane person, and Miss Spessivtseva is of unsound mind. Her recovery is problematical, and it will be a long affair."

I wrote to the Russian Embassy in Washington and received a short, curt reply to the effect that when Olga Spessivtseva had left Russia, her political statements and her friends at the time were alien to the policy of the U.S.S.R. Through a State attorney provided for her, I had now obtained some more information and also been given the address of Olga's mother, who lived in Leningrad. I wrote to her. Weeks later, I had an answer from Olga's brother, who told me that their mother was dead but that he would be happy to look after his sister if it could be arranged for her to make the journey to Russia.

I had hoped that once the war was over, the Paris Opéra would be able to do something, but again it seemed impossible. The ghastly tragedy was made so much greater by the fact that Olga was so little known in America in comparison with London and Paris.

A few months after the end of World War II, I made another visit to Olga. This time, she seemed more rational and talked quite quietly with me for a while. During the first year of the war, she had so often expressed to me her wish to return to her mother and Russia. Then I did not realise how sad and tormented her poor brain was. "Anton," she would say, "why Mr. Brown not give me my passport? I go from here to Russia, to my mother. Why he not give it me?"

"There is war in Europe, Olga. It is not possible. Please believe me."

"There is not war. Here there is war. Noise. I cannot, I will not stay. You must find and take my passport. I go to Russia."

Now it would be possible to send her in charge of a trained nurse on a boat to the land of her birth. I tried to tell her sympathetically that her mother was dead, and that I had a letter from her brother. Would she like to read it? Would she be willing to go back to Russia?

Her whole being changed, and her voice rose as she began: "No, I stay here. Here I am Mahomet. These are my subjects. Here I reign. I am Odette, Queen of the Swans. I do not go back to Russia. No Russia. No! No! No!"

The nurse in charge arrived by now and I was told that Madam must be left alone. All this excitement and talk was bad for her. Poor Olga! It seemed that nothing could penetrate to her sick brain, or she would not permit it to do so.

Whenever I am in New York, I try to see her. I always telephone to find out how she is. And always I wonder how much longer her torment will continue.

The years have passed since that terrible evening in December 1941. Few days in my life have gone by, whether before going to sleep or on waking up, that I have not heard those cries and relived those first two hours at the Roosevelt Hotel. At times it would be impossible to sleep, and when I did eventually doze off, I would wake up bathed in perspiration, the nightmare of that evening with me, and the cries of Olga Spessivtseva still ringing in my ears. I think I shall hear them until I die!

—from *Autobiography*, 1960

MARY WIGMAN
Sol Hurok

The leading force in European modern dance during the interwar period, Mary Wig-
man (1886–1973) studied with Rudolf Laban and Dalcroze before starting her own
company and school. She was thought of as the princess—or queen?—of Expres-
sionism in dance, her fame and influence nearly as great as Martha Graham's. She
brought her group to America in 1930, under the aegis of impresario Sol Hurok, who
here narrates his experiences with her. Her disciple Hanya Holm stayed in America
and spread the word.

W hen I brought Wigman to America, shortly after the Great Crash, she
was no longer young. She had been born in Germany, in 1886, and could
hardly have been called a "baby ballerina." Originally a pupil of Emile Jacques
Dalcroze, the father of Eurhythmics, whose pupils in a "demonstration" had
kindled Wigman's interest in the dance, she did not remain long with him.
Dalcroze himself, at this stage, apparently had little interest in dancing.
However, he established certain methods which proved of interest to certain
gifted dancers. The Dalcroze basis was musical, and his chief function was to
foster a feeling for music in his pupils. Music frustrated, handicapped,
restricted her, Wigman felt. Individualist that she was, she left her teacher in
order to work out her own dance destiny. There followed a period of some
uncertainty on her part, and, for a time, she became a pupil of the Hungarian teacher Rudolf von Laban, who laid down in pre-war Germany the foundations for modern dance. Unlike Isadora Duncan, Laban had no aversion to
ballet. As a matter of fact, he liked much of it, was influenced by it; was
impressed by the Diaghilev Ballet, was friendly with Diaghilev, and became
an intimate of Michel Fokine. His later violent reaction from ballet was certainly not based on lack of knowledge of it.

At the Laban school, Wigman collaborated with him, and having a streak
of choreographic genius, was able to put some of Laban's theories into practical form. However, Mary Wigman's forceful personality was greater than
any school and, in 1919, she broke away from Laban, and formed a school
of her own. She abandoned what were to her the restricting influences of
formal music, as Isadora had abandoned clothing restrictions. A dancer of

tremendous power, like Isadora she had an overwhelming personality. Again, like Isadora, all this had a tendency to make her pupils only pale imitations of herself. Wigman's public career, a secondary matter with her, actually began in Dresden, in 1918, with her *Seven Dances of Life*. Dresden was her temple. Here the Teutonic Priestess of the Dance presided over her personal religion of movement. German girls were joined by Americans. The disciples grew in number and spread out through Germany like prose-lyting missionaries. Wigman groups radiated the gospel until one found schools and factories and societies turning out *en masse* for "demonstrations" of the Wigman method. I have said that Wigman found music a deterrent to her method.

On the other hand, one of the most important features of her "school" was a serious, thorough, Germanic research into the question of what she felt was the proper musical accompaniment for dance. Her pupils learned to devise their own rhythmic accompaniment. In her show pieces, at any rate, Wigman's technique was to have the music for the dance composed simulta-neously with the creation of the dance movements—certainly a new type of collaboration.

In addition to forming a *"schule,"* where great emphasis was laid on *"span-nungen,"* perhaps best explained as tensions and relaxations, she also created a philosophical cult in that strange hot-house that was pre-war Germany, with an intellectualized approach to sex.

I had known about her and her work long before I signed a contract with her for the 1930–1931 season. Pavlova had talked to me about her and had aroused my curiosity and interest; but I was unable to imagine what might be America's reaction to her. I was turning the idea over in my mind, when there appeared at my office,—in those days in West Forty-second Street, overlooking Bryant Park,—a young and earnest enthusiast to plead her case. His name was John Martin. . . . Martin's earnest and special pleading on behalf of Mary Wigman moved me and, as always, eager to experiment and present something new and fresh, I decided to cast the die.

The effect of my first announcement of her coming was a bit disconcert-ing. The first to react were the devotees. There was a fanaticism about them that was disturbing. It is one thing to have a handful of vociferous idolators, and quite another to be able to fill houses with paying customers night after night.

When I met Wigman at the pier on her arrival in New York, I greeted a middle-aged muscular Amazon, a rather stuffy appearing Teutonic Amazon, wearing a beaver coat of dubious age, and a hat that had seen better days. But what struck me more forcibly than the plainness of her apparel was the woman herself. She greeted me with a warm smile; her gray eyes were large, frank, and widely set; and from beneath the venerable and rather battered hat, fell a shock of thick, wavy brown hair. She spoke softly, deeply, in a completely unaccented English with a British intonation.

There was no ballet company with her, no ship-load of scenery, properties, and costumes. Her company was made up of two persons in addition to herself: a lesser Amazon in the person of Meta Mens, who presided over Wigman's costumes—one trunk—and her percussion instruments—tam-tams, Balinese gongs, and a fistful of reedy wind instruments; the other, a lanky, pale-faced chap with hyper-thyroid eyes, Hanns Hastings, who composed and played such music as Wigman used.

On the day before the opening, I gave a party at the Plaza Hotel as a semi-official welcome on the part of our American dancers, among whom were included that great pioneer of our native contemporary dance, Martha Graham, together with Doris Humphrey, Charles Weidman, and, of course, that champion of the modern dance, John Martin.

Much depended upon Wigman's first New York performance. A tour had been arranged, but not booked. There is a decided difference in the terms. In the language of the theatre, a tour is not "booked" until the contracts have been signed. The preliminary arrangements are called "pencilling in." The pencil notations are inked only when signatures are attached to the contracts. If the New York *premiere* fizzled, there would be no inking. I had taken the Forty-sixth Street Theatre, and the publicity campaign under the direction of my good friend, Gerald Goode, had been under way for weeks.

It was a distinguished audience and a curious one that assembled in the Forty-sixth Street Theatre for the opening performance. It was an enthusiastic one that left at the end. I had gone back stage before the curtain rose to wish Wigman well, but the priestess was unapproachable. As she did before each performance, she entered the "silence." Under no circumstances did she permit any disturbance. She would arrive at the theatre a long time before the scheduled time of the curtain's rise, and, in her darkened dressing-room, lie in a mystic trance. Later she danced as one possessed.

If the opening night audience was enthusiastic, which it was, I am equally sure some of its members were confused. At later performances, as I stood in my customary position at the rear of the auditorium as the public left the theatre, I was not infrequently pressed by questions. These questions, however they may have been phrased, meant the same thing. "What do the dances mean?" "What is she trying to say?" "What does it all signify?" I am not easily embarrassed, as a rule. The constant reiteration of this question, however, proved an exception.

For the benefit of a generation unfamiliar with the Wigman dance, I should explain that her dances were, as she called them, "cycles." In other words, her performances consisted of groups of dances with an alleged relationship: a relationship so difficult to discern, however, that I suspect it must have existed only in Wigman's mind. The one dance that stands out most vividly in my mind is one she called "Monotonie." In "Monotonie," Wigman stood in the dead center of the stage. Then she whirled and whirled and whirled. As the whirling continued she was first erect, then slowly crouching, slowly rising until she was erect again; but always whirling, the while a puny four-note phrase was endlessly repeated. Through a sort of self-hypnosis, her whirling had an hypnotic effect on her. In a sort of mystic trance herself, Wigman succeeded, up to a point, in inducing a similar reaction on her public.

But what did it mean? I did not know, but I was determined to find out. Audience members, local managers, newspaper men were badgering me for an answer. To any query that I put to Wigman, her deep-throated reply was always the same:

"Oh, the meaning is too deep; I really can't explain it."

—from *S. Hurok Presents,* 1953

JEROME ROBBINS

Generally considered the greatest of American ballet choreographers, Jerome Robbins (1918–1998) was also the greatest of Broadway's choreographer-directors. Having practiced making dance pieces at Camp Tamiment, in the Poconos, and appearing in the chorus of various Broadway shows, Robbins joined the new Ballet Theatre in 1940, and in 1944 created for the company his first ballet (and a huge hit), Fancy Free. *In 1949 he joined Balanchine at New York City Ballet, for which he danced—most impressively, in a revival of* The Prodigal Son*—and choreographed, on and off, until his death. Among his biggest successes there were* The Cage *(1951),* Afternoon of a Faun *(1953),* The Concert *(1956), and on his return from Broadway in 1969,* Dances at a Gathering. *(In 1965 he had created a version of Stravinsky's* Les Noces *for American Ballet Theatre.) He also for several years toured with his own company, Ballets USA. On Broadway, his first show—*On the Town, *based on* Fancy Free*—was a hit. Among other successes to follow:* High Button Shoes, *with its Keystone Kops ballet;* The King and I, *with its "Small House of Uncle Thomas" ballet;* West Side Story *(he won Oscars for direction and choreography for the movie version);* Gypsy; *and the greatest success of all,* Fiddler on the Roof. *In 1989 he returned to theater with a retrospective show called* Jerome Robbins' Broadway, *which ran for a year and a half.*

MINDY ALOFF
Jerome Robbins

Of all the ways in which a ballet can be said to live, perhaps the most profound is that, on a hearing of the music alone, the stage events ineluctably flood back. When Jerome Robbins died on July 29, reportedly at the age of 79 (like a number of facts about his career, even this one can be questioned), I tried to think which of the thirty or so of his ballets that I have seen (of the some sixty works that he made for the ballet stage) prompted such remembrances. By "stage events" I mean more than costumes, decor, and general situation: I mean specific steps and gestures keyed to specific musical passages. For me, there are three works, all from early in his career: *Fancy Free* (1944), to a score by Leonard Bernstein; *The Cage* (1951) to Igor Stravinsky's Concerto in D for string orchestra; and *Afternoon of a Faun* (1953), to Claude Debussy's *Prélude à l'Après-midi d'un Faune.* Many moments from many other of his works are in my mental storage as well, but they exist quite independently of their musical support, and the music itself doesn't invoke them. These three are autonomous, organic worlds.

Of them, I think that *Afternoon of a Faun*—a pas de deux for a boy and a girl in a rehearsal studio—is also a great dramatic ballet, and the best that Robbins ever made. The plot is minimal. The girl enters the studio where the boy has been warming up. They practice ballet partnering before a mirror that we are asked to imagine. (It occupies the "fourth wall" of the stage.) The boy spontaneously kisses the girl on the cheek. She leaves the room. Yet absolutely every detail of performance matters: the way the girl holds her head on her entrance, the way the boy touches her, the way she covers her cheek with her hand after the kiss, the rate at which he settles back on the floor when alone. The ballet is selflessly warm; it almost arrives at the psychic place where Balanchine's ballets begin. That is, it is not "about" anything other than the action it presents. It is not the residue of some larger story which has been boiled down to ten minutes, but the story itself. This also seems to me one kind of extreme in Robbins's work: the capacity for projecting, in theatrical contexts, real, intimate, romantic love. Of this, *Afternoon of a Faun* is a unique example.

The Cage, in contrast, represents another extreme: Robbins's capacity for presenting theatrically, with analytic detachment, real public scorn. In the case of *The Cage,* the subject is hatred: two ballerinas, two danseurs, and a female corps de ballet impersonate a mating ritual among a species or culture in which the females kill and eat the males. (Today, *The Cage* tends to be characterized as a ballet about the insect kingdom specifically, but its early program note read: "There occurs in certain forms of insect and animal life, and even in our own mythology, the phenomenon of the female of the species considering the male as prey. The ballet concerns such a race or cult.") It is a cold-blooded fantasy presented cold-bloodedly, without any context of transformation, as for example, Martha Graham provided for her avenging Medea and Clytemnestra. Even without spiritual light, however, *The Cage* manages brilliantly to convey the illusion of a hot process. Its visual and dramatic symmetries—two queens, two lovers, two deaths—its switchblade gestures and stabbing marches on pointe are so clearly wedded to the music's perfectly calm relation of hysteria that one can still sense in it the excitement of choreographic invention burning away everything that brought the ballet about, except for what Edwin Denby once called its "horrifying succinctness."

Where did *The Cage* come from? Robbins famously pronounced that "if you observe closely you must realize that it is actually not more than the second act of *Giselle* in a contemporary visualization"—although, since no man lives, it would have to be *Giselle* from the point of view of the peasant Hilarion, and without the transfiguring love for Albrecht that leads Giselle, herself, to rebel against the Wilis and save him—without the element that makes *Giselle* what it is. Lincoln Kirstein thought that Robbins was looking closer to home, to the repertory of the New York City Ballet, for which *The Cage* was fashioned and which has never contained a production of *Giselle*. In *The New York City Ballet*, his memoir of the company which appeared in 1973, he wrote that "it is impossible to imagine *The Cage* without a double image of the bacchantes' final fury in *Orpheus*," although, he added, "the metrical division which Robbins gave his hive of horrid creatures is due as much to Stravinsky's syncopation as to Balanchine's structure." (Alas, Kirstein's observation must be taken on faith: the original choreography for the bacchantes in Balanchine's *Orpheus* is no longer performed.)

Denby had yet another suggestion in a review in 1952:

> The dramatic pressure of *The Cage* is extraordinary. It devours the notes, it die-casts the gesture; when the curtain comes down, as [Virgil] Thomson said to me, there isn't a scrap left over. I was fascinated by the gesture—so literally that of the important Broadway people at parties and in offices. Bothered to be caged in with them, I looked around unhappily. No exit.

Then he added an offhand remark that has curiously stood the test of time as a more general truth about Robbins's oeuvre for the ballet stage: "But the murderous power that led to the climax and beyond—I couldn't really sense it in the force, the propulsive force of the gesture. I felt it outside the characters."

Some version of the word "outside" inflects the conversations of many dance-goers who know Robbins's work well. There are the stories his ballets apparently enact, and the stories one feels they are really enacting. Frequently, that second level of story turns out to be an account of his admiration for other people's ballets, notably Balanchine's, to which Robbins liberally referred with reverence over much of his career. Robbins could also, on occasion, summon up the Russo-American repertory in which he performed as a valuable character dancer during his early years with Ballet Theatre in the first half of the 1940s. If you want to see him truly evoke *Giselle*, one of Ballet Theatre's staples in those years, you might look at the section of his comic masterpiece, *The Concert, or, The Perils of Everybody* ("A Charade in one act" from 1956), in which the triangle among Giselle, Albrecht, and Myrtha, Queen of the Wilis, is reproduced in the triangle of a concertgoer, a dreamy young woman in the audience who excites him, and his jealous spouse. This lunatic Punch-and-Judy sequence remains funny on its own; but the fun originates in the exacting way it reproduces and simultaneously mocks the conventions and stereotypes of a ballet that, itself, mocks nothing.

It may be that the outsider, or the role of audience member, is one key to Robbins's most memorable invention. It is certainly the basis of *The Concert*, which depicts the antics of an audience at a piano recital; of *Moves* (1959), a work without a score, in which the cast twice lines up at the edge of the stage as if to walk out into the audience or confront us in some way, then each time melts into a dance movement; of the unforgettable late moment in *Dances at a Gathering* (1969) when, after nearly an hour of solos, pas de deux, and little group encounters to Chopin, the dancers come together, pause as an ensemble, and gaze upward at some ineffable thing passing overhead, momentarily yet steadily, like a cloud or a plane. Outsiders who watch presume insiders who are watched: one of the wittiest elements of *Afternoon of a Faun* is that the couple inspecting their images in the "mirror" are literally training their sights on the audience. When Robbins uses the proscenium stage opening this way—as a mirror for reality and reflection (and he does it in several of his ballets from the 1950s)—the theatrical effect is immediate and spellbinding, as if he had found some rent in time and space that would heal a basic separation among human beings. After one viewing, however, it remains an effect, a tool borrowed, I think, from certain works by Anna Sokolow—another choreographer for whom Robbins displayed affection.

Still, when he creates the figure of the outsider as audience member *within* a ballet, the result is always charming and magnetic, the way a backstage musical can be (Robbins choreographed and directed *Gypsy*, the ultimate backstage musical). I think of *Ma Mère L'Oye (Fairy Tales for Dancers)*, from the New York City Ballet's Ravel Festival, where the dancers start off lounging in practice clothes, listening to tales of Mother Goose, then, in a home-spun manner put on a little show to reenact some of them. The path to performance, the ballet seems to say, is through the role of an audience. The best section in the labored whole of *Ives Songs* (1988) is the bench dance for "three little girls" in adult bodies, squirming as they wait for a small-town concert or theatrical to begin. The movement is deliberately awkward, yet the behavior carries the authenticity derived from decades of watching dancers and audiences and children. When Robbins turned his dancers into kids, he made those kids real. In a recent interview, the ballerina Allegra Kent—who performed in Robbins's works and originated the part of the girl in yellow in *Dances at a Gathering*—especially commended the way Robbins treated actual children in his work, whom he never failed to use with playfulness (as in his choreography for the smallest mice in Balanchine's version of *The Nutcracker,* on whose nightmare scene Robbins collaborated) and dignity (as in *Circus Polka,* where he sent forty-eight girls from the School of American Ballet cantering through amusing and delicate configurations as a ringmaster—originally impersonated by the choreographer—cracks a whip). Kent also singled out a moment in the Broadway musical *The King and I* (1951), which Robbins choreographed, where the king's children are brought forward to meet Anna. "It was all in their stance," she said. "The special effects were very simple and very deep."

No figures of the audience in Robbins's ballets are more beloved by the audience who observes them than the two young women in *Fancy Free.* It is they, sitting at a table in a bar, for whom the three sailors perform their self-revealing variations, like dancers auditioning for a couple of producers. Without them—that is, were the sailors only dancing for themselves and the bartender—the scene would have no dramatic interest; and although the women don't dance during this section, their slightest reactions powerfully affect the feeling of the whole. These girls of *Fancy Free* not only suggest the acting strengths of Muriel Bentley and Janet Reed, their originals at Ballet Theatre; they also indicate in the most concentrated way the gifts as a choreographer-director that Robbins would go on to exhibit spectacularly in Broadway musicals.

Fancy Free, with a score commissioned from the wunderkind Bernstein, launched Robbins's creative career with a bang. An instant hit with Ballet Theatre audiences, it remains in active repertory more than a half-century later. Right off the bat, it crystallized Robbins's omni-competence, ambition, and obsession with gestural detail. It also displayed the strengths that he possessed as a dancer: observers who saw his original rhumba-like solo as the third sailor say it has never been bettered. (Robbins's charisma as a performer would lead Balanchine to, among other things, revive his *Prodigal Son* in 1950 with Robbins in the title role.) Kent, who met Robbins when she was eleven, in the class of Carmelita Maracci, speaks of his performing abilities with unabashed admiration—both on stage and in the rehearsals of his own ballets, where he would demonstrate exactly how he wanted a part performed. "He was magnetic to watch," she said. "He had a way of moving that wasn't based on anything technical, particularly—more of a quality. Everyone in rehearsal just couldn't wait to watch him dance."

Fancy Free opened a treasure door not only for Robbins, but for the American musical stage. The score led to subsequent Robbins and Bernstein collaborations for the ballet, such as *Facsimile* (1946) for Ballet Theatre. (Steeped in the collaborators' experience with Freudian analysis, *Facsimile* failed as a dance, although the score still stands up.) Within less than a year of *Fancy Free*'s premiere, Robbins and Bernstein joined with Betty Comden, Adolph Green, and George Abbott to produce a Broadway musical, *On the Town,* based on *Fancy Free*'s scenario. In our age, when ballets and musicals are routinely recycled from the movies, the origins of *On the Town* seem the stuff of which a dance fan's dreams are made.

From this show, another hit, the collaborators went on in various permutations to enrich the Broadway musical over the next decade, with such shows as *Look Ma, I'm Dancin'* (1948), *Call Me Madam* (1950), *Wonderful Town* (1953), *Bells Are Ringing* (1956), and *West Side Story* (1957). Indeed, the full story of Robbins's monumental contribution to Broadway has yet to be authoritatively chronicled. The Library of the Performing Arts—whose Jerome Robbins Archive of the Recorded Moving Image was established in 1965 with a small portion of Robbins's royalties as the author of *Fiddler on the Roof* (a show he also choreographed and directed)—lists him as a contributor, sometimes the chief choreographic contributor, to shows that are frequently credited to others. Robbins consulted as a show doctor on many more projects than are usually associated with him: *The Pajama Game* (1954), for instance, whose choreographer of record was the young Bob Fosse, a virtual Broadway unknown. In his biography of Fosse, *All His Jazz,* Martin Gottfried recounts how Robbins contradicted the director, George Abbott, who wanted to dispense with the Fosse number "Steam Heat" because it stopped the show. Abbott's trademark was a musical with an invincible continuity, where all numbers contributed to the ultimate effect of the whole; furthermore, the dancers of Fosse's music-hall turn were, at that time, also unknown (Carol Haney, Buzz Miller, and Peter Gennaro). Robbins argued that the number was too good to excise, and it is thanks to him that "Steam Heat" survived to become one of the most well-known and well-loved numbers that Fosse ever made.

This anecdote about Robbins and Fosse is not the only example I have found of Robbins's backstage generosity on behalf of a colleague. And his establishment of the archive at the library was an act of generosity benefiting thousands of individuals he would never know. As a number of individuals who did know him cautioned me, there was a kind side to Robbins. During the first two-thirds of his career, however, there was also a dark, tyrannical side, especially visible, it seems, in his treatment of dancers and subordinates. In sum, the dividing line for how he treated his colleagues in the theater and the ballet was whether or not he could fire them. If he couldn't, he could still prove a colossal pain in the neck in his effort to control the tiniest details of a production out of the self-assurance that he knew what would work for an audience, but he extended professional courtesy. If he was their boss, however, he could wound them terribly, and because he was an astute student of psychoanalysis, he could humiliate them to the core, frequently in public rehearsals. Although the harshest stories about Robbins are not published, some very harsh ones are: in the interviews that Barbara Newman conducted for her book *Striking a Balance,* for instance, or in Dorothy Bird's memoir, *Bird's EyeView: Dancing with Martha Graham and on Broadway.*

The ballerina and choreographer Ruthanna Boris, who knew Robbins from his years as an aspiring choreographer for Max Liebman at Camp Tamiment in the Poconos during the late 1930s and during the early 1950s at the New York City Ballet, believes, as she said in a recent interview, that he suffered from some undisclosed emotional torment which his work for the stage exacerbated, and which he licensed himself to unleash on others in a studio setting. The issue is not Robbins's genius as an artist. Frequently he did know what would provoke a particular audience response, and on Broadway, especially, his knowledge was not only admirable, it was also bankable. The question is whether the sum of his art was worth the human cost it exacted; it is a question one asks as well of the careers of Antony Tudor and Martha Graham, for similar reasons.

Although Robbins left no published autobiography, no picture of himself from the inside, he did go on record in 1981 in an interview with what Doris Hering calls, in her entry on him for the *International Encyclopedia of Dance,* a "credo":

> One thing I have absolutely no patience with in the theater is anyone who works in it without being a completely dedicated artist and professional in all senses of the word, bringing to the theater not only the talent, but also coming equipped with technique and craft. I feel that if someone doesn't have an insane love for the theater, he shouldn't be in it.

Laudable as this passion sounds, it must also be set beside the fact that, unlike choreographers as diverse as Graham, Tudor, Fosse, and, extensively, Balanchine, Robbins's works did not, on their own, develop the career of a single significant dancer. Even individuals who performed his ballets particularly well—in recent years at New York City Ballet, Kyra Nichols, Robert La Fosse, Jean-Pierre Frohlich—were either formed elsewhere before he found them or developed as artists in other repertories. This is a particularly sad fact since Robbins possessed one of the keenest eyes for dance talent, particularly among youngsters, in the history of ballet. Yet he seemed unable to envision what they might do to grow as dancers; his expertise was to use, sometimes with consummate assurance, qualities they already possessed. This end-stopped insight may be linked to his apparent lack of interest in teaching or in company management. His own short-lived company, Ballets: USA, did not lead him to widen his skills as a leader outside the rehearsal studio and the stage. His legacy of hope to his field was the other choreographers whose work he fostered or inspired: Fosse, Michael Bennett, Eliot Feld, and—it may be suggested—the valedictorian of the class, Twyla Tharp.

Jerome Robbins was a tangled person, with many mysteries. (Not the least of them is how, once he had given the names of colleagues to the House Un-American Activities Committee, he managed to survive, indeed thrive, in the theatrical milieu of New York, where his appearance before HUAC was bitterly resented.) Even so, none of his complications would be of the slightest interest as more than a footnote to history were it not for the work that he sacrificed so much good will to bring into being. Without his art, he is just Jerome Rabinowitz, one more New Yorker who came of age during World War II and cruised into its Golden Age with driving ambition, ironic defenses, and, somewhere far inside, a heart. But he was almost never without his art. During her summer at Camp Tamiment, Boris explained, Liebman encouraged a number of young theater artists, many of them unknowns, to contribute their skills to shows and cabarets, and he provided a bus from Manhattan to convey them there. Boris took a seat on the bus behind two guys with heads of thick dark hair. After a while, one of the heads turned around and introduced himself.

"Hi," he said teasingly. "I'm Eddie Gilbert, and I'm the scenic designer." "Hi," Boris answered, in kind. "I'm Ruthanna Boris, and I'm the choreographer." Slowly, the other head turned around and said, in pointedly measured tones without a touch of humor in them: "My name is Jerome Robbins, and *I am the choreographer.*"

—from *The New Republic,* September 14 and 21, 1998

Tobi Tobias
Bringing Back Robbins's Fancy

Jerome Robbins's first ballet and a sensational success, Fancy Free *(1944) put on Ballet Theatre's stage three sailors on shore leave in New York and the three girls they try to pick up. The boys were John Kriza, Harold Lang, and Robbins himself, with his famous* danzón *number. The two lead girls were Janet Reed and Muriel Bentley. Score by Leonard Bernstein, decor (a neighborhood bar) by Oliver Smith,* Fancy Free *made Robbins a star and morphed later that year into the brilliant musical* On the Town *and eventually into the Gene Kelly movie.*

TOBI TOBIAS: *They call* Fancy *officially your first ballet but you had actually made some dances before, hadn't you?*

JEROME ROBBINS: I'd made some dances before, yes—sketches. I had made a tiny little ballet, maybe, one that ran six minutes or ten minutes or something like that. This was in the late '30s, up in Camp Tamiment, the summer borscht-circuit place. And that came about because I first started doing solos for myself. Then I did some duets, and then I wanted to do something bigger. But *Fancy* was the first—I'd say it was the first real *ballet* I did.

TOBIAS: *What was Tamiment exactly? What kinds of people were working there?*

ROBBINS: It was a summer adult camp up in the Poconos. They had a rather large entertainment staff, especially for those times. It was run by Max Liebman who used to do *Your Show of Shows.* It was my first paying job as a dancer. And there I met Imogene Coca, Danny Kaye. I worked with Anita Alvarez, who was one of Martha Graham's major dancers at the time. The Bird sisters, Bill Bales, Ruthanna Boris were there. Everyone came in and out of that place. And it was an extraordinary training field. We had to do three different shows each week. There was a big revue on Saturday night. There was a nightclub show—on Thursday night, I think. And on one other night there was a sort of vaudeville-style show. So we got a chance to do just about anything we wanted to do.

TOBIAS: *Now when you joined Ballet Theatre—that was 1940—you started proposing ballets to them?*
ROBBINS: I don't think right away—no. I was too busy absorbing. But I think that after two or three years I began submitting scenarios. They were rather elaborate. I still have some of them. Five-act ballets. *(Laughter.)*

TOBIAS: *For instance. Describe one.*
ROBBINS: *(Pause.)* No. I don't think so. *(Laughter.)* I still have some of those scenarios. I guess I was anxious to choreograph, not right away, but after a while.

TOBIAS: *Now those were turned down—the first few—and* Fancy *was taken.Why?*
ROBBINS: Well, very simply, I went to speak to Anatole Chujoy and I think it was he who said, "You know, Jerry, why don't you devise something small, with a few people and one set? Something that maybe they could do with not too much expense if they're going to try you out."

And then I was a friend of a woman named Mary Hunter who at that time ran a group called the American Actors Company. And working there at the time were Tennessee Williams and Joe Anthony and Perry Wilson and Horton Foote and a lot of people who went on to become actors, directors, and writers. And when I was talking with Mary about it she said, "You know what's a wonderful subject—*The Fleet's In,* the Paul Cadmus picture." And I looked at that and I thought, Well, maybe I can do something on that subject.

But more than that, I had just spent I don't know how many years dancing with Ballet Theatre at the point where it was completely Ballet Russified. And for one whole year I did not get out of boots, Russian bloomers, and a peasant wig. And I thought, "Why can't we do ballets about our own subjects, meaning *our* life here in America?" And it was sort of anti–Ballet Russe that the sailor subject came up.

TOBIAS: *What makes a ballet an American ballet?*
ROBBINS: A lot of different things, according to different people. In this case, by "American ballet" I meant subjects of our own land rather than Russian fairy tales.

TOBIAS: *Is there something that would be different in the movement too, though?*
ROBBINS: Well, that's a sort of general question. I can only answer in terms of *Fancy Free.* Yes, it was, because it was about our life and our social life also. So therefore it included our social dancing. As the Russians used their folk dancing, I used ours.

TOBIAS: *I remember your saying recently that there is never a single element that you can pinpoint and say, "That made me do that ballet," but that there are always many things—I imagine some of them unconscious. But can you say what some of the things were, that you haven't mentioned yet, that got you going on* Fancy?

ROBBINS: Well, you know, I did it during the war years, when the kinds of people I described in the ballet were all around us. At that time we were dancing at the old Metropolitan Opera House which was situated at Thirty-ninth–Fortieth Street and Broadway, and Times Square was right there and that was all bubbling out over us. We saw it everywhere we looked—the kind of incident, the kind of people, the kind of kids that were dancing then. I can't give you an answer on that further than that right now.

> Muriel Bentley: *I remember, from my sojourn with Ballet Theatre, all of us going to a lot of parties, and that Jerry would watch the people dance. It's incredible. It's constant research with Jerry. At that party he would stand at the side—he still does—and watch how the people dance and how they are and what they are.*

TOBIAS: *People said in articles at the time* Fancy *was made that you actually set out to observe sailors, sailors and their girls, in New York and on tour.*

ROBBINS: Well I didn't *set out* . . . I just always observed it about me. No matter what the subject is that you're interested in, you go searching for it. When I was doing *Dybbuk,* I looked up old books on magic. When I was doing *Goldberg Variations,* I was studying the baroque period. But there are some steps in the ballet that I actually saw sailors do in a bar.

> Janet Reed: *Jerry picked up on everything that was going on all around us. I didn't actually witness this, but someone, Johnny or Jerry, told me that the little episode in Jerry's solo, the rumba, where he pretends to dance with a girl who isn't there—someone told me he got the idea from seeing a drunken soldier pick up a chair in a bar and dance with it as though it were a girl. Then once, on tour, look- ing out a train window, we saw planes flying in a shifting, triangular formation, and Jerry choreographed that into the opening sailors' dance. And one time—we were in Bloomington, Indiana, walking down the street on the way to the theater, and Jerry said, "I wonder what would happen if—" and he described the girl run- ning and suddenly jumping and the boy catching her. He just talked his image of it as we were walking. I let him walk on ahead a little ways and I said, "You mean like this?" and I ran down the street and jumped at him. And he had to drop his bag and catch me. That's in the pas de deux we did together.*

> Harold Lang: *When we were in New York, between rehearsals and performances at the old Met, often Jerry, Muriel, and I would be wandering around Times Square*

and Jerry would point out, "Did you ever see one or two sailors? No, you always see three. There are always three together."

ROBBINS: And I—yes—would watch the way they would do all those bravura posings that I was talking about in the rehearsal today.

TOBIAS: *I remember you were telling the dancers that the sailors at that time had images of themselves. What kind of images?*
ROBBINS: Well, everyone that went into the armed forces felt that he had to behave the way the public expected him to behave. A sailor in New York had to be cocky. He wanted to appear not to be afraid of the city, especially if he came from out of town. Once you put on the uniform, that's the way you behaved. Just like young kids who come into the ballet company; you'll see young girls who come into the New York City Ballet take on attitudes of the rest of the company because they think that's the way they should be. . . .

TOBIAS: *Now when did Oliver Smith and Leonard Bernstein come into the picture?*
ROBBINS: Well, Oliver had heard I was doing a ballet and he came to me and asked whether he could design it.

TOBIAS: *He was not yet affiliated with Ballet Theatre at the time?*
ROBBINS: No, not as an artistic director. He was just a designer.

TOBIAS: *And what kind of collaboration did you have? The scenario you wrote describes the set to a certain extent. Did you have input further than that?*
ROBBINS: Oh yes. Oliver likes to work with me. He feels he does his best work because I keep pushing him and pushing him until he does something better than he just did—moved it on a bit.

TOBIAS: *How was Bernstein chosen to do the score?*
ROBBINS: Well, I'd written the scenario—that rather detailed one, as you've read—and then I had to find a composer. And I took it to a lot of people who turned it down. Finally there was a composer in Philadelphia named Vincent Persichetti who looked at it and said that he thought that he couldn't write it, but that he knew of a young guy in New York who could—Leonard Bernstein. And he gave me an address and I went to the address when I came back to New York and it was an empty lot on Fifty-second Street. So I could not find Lenny. By chance, I mentioned it to Oliver and he said, "Oh, I know Lenny. He lives at Carnegie Hall. I'll give a call and see if we can go up there." So we did. He introduced us to each other. Lenny played me part of his yet unplayed *Jeremiah*

symphony. I gave him my scenario to read. We decided to go ahead and work.

TOBIAS: *Wasn't your scenario unusually specific—just short of Petipa to Tchaikovsky on* The Sleeping Beauty?
ROBBINS: Well, I had to have something to show people the kind of ballet I wanted to do. I had to describe it. I mean, I was an unknown. I had no track record at all. The only thing Ballet Theatre had allowed me to do was some dances for a movie in Mexico. They had seen that. And I think Charlie Payne somehow felt that I was talented, and Nora [Kaye], and there was enough "underground" feeling going on that possibly I could do something. But the only reason I finally got to do *Fancy Free* was that some ballet they had planned to do had conked out. And then they turned to me and said—"Can you get this ready?"

TOBIAS: *When you wrote that scenario had you actually visualized the movement?*
ROBBINS: The steps, no. The qualities, yes.

TOBIAS: *Talk about the collaboration between you and Bernstein. You were not in the same place, right?*
ROBBINS: No, we started talks in the same city, which was New York, but I was on tour with the ballet company, and he would write a piece and send it to me with a record so I could hear what his intentions were.

TOBIAS: *He sent you the notated music plus a record?*
ROBBINS: He sent me the piano copy of it, it wasn't orchestrated yet. And a record.

TOBIAS: *With him playing the piano?*
ROBBINS: With him and Aaron Copland playing the piano, as a matter of fact.

TOBIAS: *I hope you have those records.*
ROBBINS: I do too. I don't know where the hell they've gone. And I would get to work on it. If I had a problem I would call or write him from out of town. I remember we had differences over the second variation, the one that was Johnny's, which I didn't understand at all when I first heard it; didn't get it. So in a case like that he would explain it more, and say what he felt about it, and then I'd start to see the light of it. And I'd say, "I think this—" And this kind of work went on, backwards and forwards this way, until I was able to come to New York. . . .

TOBIAS: *Where were you over that period of time? And how long did it go on?*
ROBBINS: We opened in spring so it must have been over that whole late fall and winter.

TOBIAS: *What parts of the country were you in?*
ROBBINS: Oh gosh. I decided that our tour was booked so that when we got finished, if you drew a line from city to city over the map of the U.S.A. it would spell out "S. Hurok." *(Laughter.)* It was absolutely a crazy tour— very, very difficult now when I think back on it. Mostly one-night stands. War years—which means that we had no trains. When we did get a train we were all crowded into one coach. We traveled mostly on buses, some- times all night long. We didn't have food, because there was no food on the train. If there was, it was served to the troops, whichever branch hap- pened to be traveling. But I don't think I noticed any of that. I think I had my head in the score the whole time. And was figuring out the counts and the accents and the themes and where they went and how they were to be worked out.

TOBIAS: *At what point in all this did you bring in actual bodies to work on?*
ROBBINS: On this tour. And with my best friends then. I teamed around with Johnny Kriza and Harold Lang and Muriel Bentley and Janet Reed. It was sort of like working with your home team.

TOBIAS: *Did you deliberately stay away from established stars?*
ROBBINS: It wasn't that I avoided them. I wanted to work with the ones I picked. The ballet wasn't meant for "stars."

TOBIAS: *Is there, would you say, a lot of the original dancers themselves in the ballet—as dancers, and as people?*
ROBBINS: I imagine so. I think Johnny's variation is certainly based on Johnny.

TOBIAS: *What was he like, Jerry?*
ROBBINS: Well, there was an incredible sweetness about that man. And not in an icky way. He just was generally nice and kindhearted and light. And wistful. There was a wistfulness about Johnny too. And humor. *(Long pause.)* I liked him a lot.

Bentley: *Jerry really caught Johnny in that role—the sailor who always paid the check. Somehow Johnny always picked up the check. Johnny was the sweet one. Johnny was the good one. The one who just loved to dance, loved going to parties, loved to drive his car out on tour, loved people. He was a good dancer. He was not a brilliant dancer. He was a terrific performer. He gave a lot of himself. He didn't care how much money he made as long as he could get out on the stage and dance. He was kind. He was simple. He was generous. How do I describe Johnny Kriza? I'm very partial. I was madly in love with him. He was loved by a lot of people. There isn't another one like him.*

ROBBINS: Johnny was the second sailor. The first sailor was this extro-verted, bravura boy—Harold Lang danced that. He had a formidable tech-nique. Not a classical, *danseur noble* technique, but still a very strong one, and yet he was unusually limber. No one has been able to do that double air turn into the split the way Harold Lang did it. Which was straight down with the feet—one in front and one in back, and the arms out to the side. When he landed he looked like a jack.

Lang: *I think he took out of us what would be—not exploitable, but usable. Jerry himself had a good Latin feeling to him, he saw Johnny as being lyrical, kind of dreamy and sweet—a country boy, and I guess he saw me as a show-off. He put in all the things I liked to do: pirouettes, air turns—a lot of high movement, exten-sions, and jumps. Jumping on the bar, things like that: it seems like I'm always on the furniture. One day we were rehearsing in a Los Angeles studio and I was stretching in a split and Jerry looked at me and said, "Could you do a double air turn and come down into a split?" And I said, "I don't know, let me try." And I did. And he began laughing and said, "That's part of your variation."*

ROBBINS: Those three variations, you see, were for three distinct, different people. The third boy, the one I danced, was sort of a New York sharpie—he thought. Latin influenced.

TOBIAS: (Laughter.) *Is that how you saw yourself then?*
ROBBINS: *(Laughter.)* No, that's how I decided to make that character. Span-ish dancing and character dancing were close to me and I was good at them, so maybe I threw it that way, for myself.

TOBIAS: *You trained in a lot of dance forms, didn't you? You studied ballet . . .*
ROBBINS: I studied ballet, I studied Spanish dancing. Ballet came in later. I started as a modern dancer, and studied Graham technique, and Doris Humphrey's, and—God, I forget who else, just a whole slew of them. And then I studied ballet. I studied with Nimura. I don't remember what else, but if there was something around, I'd study it. *(Laughter.)*

TOBIAS: *Has most of the other stuff found its way into your work in one way or another?*
ROBBINS: I don't know. I suppose it has, but certainly not consciously.

TOBIAS: *In* Fancy *there's a lot of street dancing, social dancing. What are some of the things that are typical of that time?*
ROBBINS: Well, the Lindy of course. Boogie-woogie. Shorty George. Then there's a lot of theatrical dancing, you know, like waltz clogs, time steps, Shuffle Off to Buffalo. And then my variation, which is really based on a *danzón*—a Mexican dance—but we call it the rumba.

TOBIAS: *Was it hard to choreograph yourself into the ballet?*
ROBBINS: I'll tell you something, I hadn't finished my variation by opening night.

TOBIAS: *It sounds like Martha Graham.*
ROBBINS: Right. I just hadn't done it. Hadn't finished the last part of it. And I think I used Michael Kidd sometimes to stand in for me, so I could see what I was doing. (He took over my role, when I left the company.) But that's the only way I could see what was happening. Now I can't imagine how I did it—choreographing it and being in it too. But I did do it.

TOBIAS: *Now what about the two women? Are the personalities very different?*

Bentley: *That role is me—the first girl. That is a character by the name of Muriel Bentley. She was sharp, she was knowing, she was not a whore, she was bright, she was smart. Patent leather. Jerry used to describe that girl as patent leather. Black hair, slicked up, and carrying a red pocketbook.*

Reed: *Muriel's movement was more big city—sharp and staccato; she was a real rhythmic virtuoso. I guess my girl was a little softer, sweeter. Long red hair hanging loose. Every girl I saw do it after me I thought was too tough and hard, consciously trying to be sexy. Which I didn't think was right. . . . I never really thought of that girl as anyone but myself.*

ROBBINS: Muriel's a New Yorker; Janet isn't. In a way that sums it up.
My relationship with Muriel went way, way back. I think she's the person I know longest in the ballet world. I met her during a rehearsal of *Prince Igor. (Laughter.)* It was being put together for some one-time occasion, I don't know where. And there was a point where all the Tartar warriors filed in and out between the girls. We each ended up behind a girl and the girl had to lean forward and then bend back over the boy's shoulder, and the boy was supposed to lift her up. The girl who was in front of me leaned forward and as she started leaning back she stopped, looked at me, and said, "Think you can manage it?" *(Laughter.)* And that was Muriel.

TOBIAS: *And what about Janet?*

ROBBINS: Janet I met later, in Ballet Theatre. I'd seen her first with Eugene Loring's company—Dance Players. And thought she was so wonderful. And then when she joined Ballet Theatre I knew that there was material I wanted to work with. And I used her a lot while she was in the company. I did *Interplay* with her. *Fancy Free.* And then when she joined New York City Ballet I used her there.

TOBIAS: *What was the feeling amongst the group of dancers as you were all preparing* Fancy?

ROBBINS: Hard work. Mostly. Muriel will tell you how many times she broke down and cried because I was pushing her so and yelling at her, and it had to be exact.

Bentley: *It was just six to eight months of sheer torture for me—those rehearsals making* Fancy. *Jerry picked on me constantly. I was the patsy. Hal came in for it a little bit maybe, but Johnny and Janet—they had it easy, they were the golden ones. He adored them, and maybe he knew he couldn't get away with that kind of thing with them. But not me. Anytime Jerry was unhappy with me, he really let me have it. I took it all. I never answered him back. I didn't have it in me. It was hell.*

I'll tell you the crowning glory. You know that part—my entrance, where I walk and I'm stopped by the three sailors. I would practice on the street. And Jerry would watch me walk and would comment on the way I walked. He would make me do it over and over again. I was under constant scrutiny. Then, when we finally showed the ballet to Sol Hurok for the first time, I made my entrance—walked, stopped, looked at the three boys, and Jerry halted the whole rehearsal and said, "You look like you're walking down the street to get a salami sandwich." And I froze. And cried.

I cried a lot, I can tell you, working on that ballet. But you know something, everything Jerry did for me was right for me. In fact, the best roles I had in my career—in Fancy Free, Interplay, *three Broadway shows—were made by Jerry Robbins. Now, looking back, I think he felt that in badgering me and belittling me he could make me perform better. I never agreed with his tactics but I really think that's what he meant to do. At the time there was never one moment when I thought I could look at Jerry and say, "Did you really like it?" But when I finally retired I said to Jerry one night, "I don't even know what kind of dancer to tell people I was." He said, "You just tell them you were a good one."*

ROBBINS: It was a very intense work period. The relationships between us had already been established long ago and those just went on.

Bentley: *When we were not rehearsing, we were very close friends. All of us, really close friends. We laughed, we cuddled on trains, we had good times.*

ROBBINS: In those days we played the army game together. Because there were no rooms on tour and because we got paid so little—for instance, we'd get to Bloomington, Indiana, and this company of eighty people would descend on the hotel lobby and the desk clerk would go berserk with all this signing in and registration and then the lobby'd be cleared and they'd look down and they'd find that there were only maybe twenty people registered. And we would double up, of course, in rooms, and take mattresses off the beds and sleep four in a room that was registered for one.

TOBIAS: *So you know each other quite well.*
ROBBINS: We know each other quite well.

TOBIAS: *While you were in the process of making* Fancy, *did you have regularly scheduled rehearsals?*
ROBBINS: Oh no, it was grab as grab can. Any free time we could get. Anyplace they could find room for me I went into. We would rehearse in hotel ballrooms or nightclubs. Sometimes with no music, only counts, sometimes with the phonograph, sometimes with a pianist, if we could get one. But no one could play jazz. Finally, I remember, I got permission to leave the tour—either in Cincinnati or Cleveland, one of those C's—and Janet and I came back to New York to work on the pas de deux.

> Reed: *The company was someplace in Ohio. We had been doing a lot of one-night stands. If there was a chance for Jerry to choreograph at all it was in a different, unfamiliar studio each time, sometimes in theater basements, working around the packing cases. Finally Jerry and I got on a train and came back to New York and we worked every day in the same studio. Leonard Bernstein came and played—improvised and composed right alongside us while the pas de deux was being choreographed. I loved every moment working with Jerry—it was marvelous. It was very demanding, though—an awful lot of time and energy spent on small details. I remember one day having worked for I don't know how long—towards the end of the day we were so exhausted that every time we tried to do a lift we would collapse on the floor and giggle. We were just getting slaphappy tired. Lenny was there that day and we all laughed together hysterically.*

TOBIAS: *When you finally got into the same city as Bernstein was there still stuff to be ironed out with the music?*
ROBBINS: Oh yeah.

TOBIAS: *What kinds of things?*

ROBBINS: Well, he hadn't finished the score completely. You know, where I wanted something to be longer or something was too long or . . . It was that kind of collaboration.

TOBIAS: *And was it an easy relationship between you, about the changes that needed to be made?*

ROBBINS: Oh yes. I mean, sure, we had differences, but that was a healthy part of the collaboration.

TOBIAS: *How much did your concept of the dance change, if at all, from the scenario stage to the finished ballet?*

ROBBINS: Well, I remember in the initial scenario that I wrote, which I showed to Mary Hunter, that I made some reference to the war being an element in the background of the ballet. I think that there was a newspaper in the bar which someone opened and you saw some headline about it, but I felt that was a little too heavy. Or maybe when I showed the scenario to Mary she suggested it was a little too heavy, and obvious, and so I cut it out. I think it had something to do with the relationship between the boy and the girl in that pas de deux.

> Reed: *It was World War II. The whole attitude of so many young people at that time was very disoriented. And we were living right in the middle of it: On tour, when we could get a train, the Ballet Theatre cars would be hooked up to the troop cars. All those soldiers and sailors and ballet troupes, in strange places and different towns. We were uprooted, and although we had a very carefree attitude, we were also very tentative about relationships. There was a certain brashness and carefree feeling mixed with a sensitive, almost timid quality. We were all so terribly young, not necessarily young in years, but kind of innocent, and rather lonely. Our attitude was one of wanting to be close to one another but knowing that it couldn't last. So that there was this constant reaching out, but knowing that it was only temporary. Can you see that in the choreography, in the pas de deux?*

TOBIAS: *On the whole, did the movement come out more or less as you had originally imagined its qualities to be?*

ROBBINS: The qualities, yes—and sometimes I was surprised and delighted by the movements. . . . Well, it's nice. Making any piece of choreography is a nice experience if it moves, if it goes on. It's starting with nothing and then building something. And then the materials that you've created help you make the next materials. It becomes an organic thing.

The thing I *don't* remember with *Fancy* is ever getting stuck. I don't remember hitting a snag where I didn't know how to get out of it. Or hitting a block at all. And I don't remember that even with *Interplay,* which I did the next year. I think by my third ballet I began to see what the problems were. *(Laughter.)* Up until then I didn't—I just went ahead and did it.

TOBIAS: *Do you look back on that with regret, or nostalgia?*
ROBBINS: Oh, and how. Right. Naiveté works for you. There's also a certain amount of bottled-up energy which you've got inside of you, dying to get out. The more ballets you do, in certain ways the more difficult it can become. You're just along further, and you know more. There are more traps to be seen which you weren't aware of the first time.

TOBIAS: *Is it a pressure, as well, being known to have made some wonderful ballets? That you feel each one has to be more special and inventive than the one before?*
ROBBINS: No. That sounds like you're talking about the Broadway field. Whether you're going to do another hit show or not. Has Michael Bennett got another smash or will so-and-so top himself this time? No, we're in a repertory system and I take as my motto Mr. Balanchine's advice. He says, "Do a ballet, do another ballet, do another ballet, do *another* ballet, then do another ballet, then do another ballet, then maybe you do a really good one." *(Laughter.)*

TOBIAS: *I wasn't counting.*
ROBBINS: Neither was I. But his idea is, do them. The important thing is to do them. Don't count on whether it's going to be a good one or not. That's not your job. Your job is to do them.

TOBIAS: *Are there any sections that were originally in the dance that were taken out?*
ROBBINS: Did I cut anything? No. I think originally I thought the whole ballet was going to be fifteen minutes.

TOBIAS: *And it's . . . ?*
ROBBINS: Almost a half-hour.

TOBIAS: *It always seems like—no time at all. It just happens, and it's wonderful.*

TOBIAS: *Was there any indication, before the opening, that* Fancy *was going to be a winner?*
ROBBINS: As a matter of fact no one looked in at rehearsals. I don't know if Lucia [Chase] had seen anything till we got it up to the point of stage rehearsals. Nobody saw it until about two weeks before we opened. And

then by chance a press representative of Hurok's came to watch it. And then he started to say, "Oh, I think there's something there." And began to spread the word around.

TOBIAS: *What was the opening night like?*

ROBBINS: Well, of course we were excited as hell. I remember just before—I had gotten dressed in my costume, came down on stage, and was doing a few fast pliés to keep warm, when my side zipper broke. And it was the best thing that could have happened because it gave me a sense of concentration. I had to get somebody and have it sewn up, I had to be still, and I collected myself that way.

Once we started there was a lot of reaction from the audience that we didn't expect—just didn't know there were laughs there, or jokes there, or that they would catch every moment that we had worked on so carefully. And then a terrific reception for it which really surprised us. It was thrilling. *(Laughter.)*

> Bentley: *It was an enormous success for all of us, the most incredible feeling. I cannot tell you how many times Johnny and I looked at each other, incredulous:"Jerry is going to go out and take another call. Jerry's going to take another call."*

> Reed: *I think we set a new record in curtain calls that night. Twenty or twenty-five. Something really fantastic.*

> Lang: *By the time we got on we had been rehearsing not just* Fancy Free, *but other ballets, and performing as well. So by that night we were down to skin, muscle, and bone, and sheer nervous energy—which sometimes makes a dancer dance better. I don't think I was really aware of the extraordinary reception of it. A year later someone played a recording they'd made of the music—and you could hear the audience's reaction—the delight: laughter, and all that applause. And I thought, Wow, that must have been exciting. Wish I'd been there.*

TOBIAS: *You and the dancers weren't anticipating anything like that response?*

ROBBINS: No, we were shocked opening night. We were absolutely floored by it. We didn't know it was going to be what it was. As I remember, they had scheduled it for an opening performance and the next one was not scheduled until at least a week later. And by that time all the reviews came in. And we read them, and by the second performance we were so nervous that each of us fell down. I fell down right away, as soon as I came on stage. Later on Johnny fell down. Later Harold fell down. We were just like that with tension.

TOBIAS: *Did the extraordinary success of* Fancy *change your life a lot?*

ROBBINS: Oh yes, of course. Because suddenly where I had—Up until that point where I was sort of wanting to get in, suddenly I was not only in, but sought after. And that was very shocking. I remember being very surprised by the first interview I had where someone asked me, "Well, what do you think the future of American dance is, and where it lies?" And I thought, My God, I don't know anything about it. I'm just out of the corps de ballet. I don't have a theory about it. Why are they asking me these questions? You know, suddenly I was supposed to be a guru about all these things and have opinions about them, which I didn't have. Suddenly I was being invited to see shows where before I couldn't afford to buy a ticket. Scripts were suddenly being thrown at me, to do shows. I couldn't help but go through some pangs of: *Wait* a minute. I tried to get into the shows as a dancer. I couldn't even get in to see the producer or the casting agent. Now suddenly everyone is saying, "Come, come, come. Be a part of what we're doing now." So anyway there was a lot of joy, a lot of elation, and some little edges of irony and resentment that this all changed so radically.

TOBIAS: *So you felt there should have been some interim phase?*

ROBBINS: It was a shocking change. From nothing to—to everything. And I wasn't prepared for it. I think really what happened, when I think back on it, now, was that somewhere in my early life I had thought that all my career and personal problems would change once I was a success. Well, here I was a success and although there was much more opportunity and attention, none of my personal problems changed. I realized I had to look somewhere else rather than to being well known and accomplished, to straighten out inside of myself.

TOBIAS: *Who were some of the dancers that you've particularly enjoyed seeing in the sailors' roles, subsequent to the original cast?*

ROBBINS: You'll have to remind me who's danced it. It's been going on for some thirty-five years. I remember I liked Paul Godkin in my place. Tommy Rall was wonderful in Harold Lang's place. Terrific in that. Eliot Feld was very good. . . . You know, I feel very reluctant to talk about "others" who have danced *Fancy Free*. The truth is, after the first few years I didn't always follow its castings. I loved Mischa's [Baryshnikov's] recent performance, and I'm sure there are others also—Fernando Bujones, Terry Orr, and so on—but I may be leaving out many that I've liked.

TOBIAS: *What about some of the women who danced it?*

ROBBINS: When I ran the film we have of the original cast, what was surprising to me was how the third girl, who was danced by a girl named

Shirley Eckl—I don't know what's happened to her, where she is—how remarkably clear she is in that film. It was taken from the balcony of the Met and it's a fuzzy, grainy film, and sometimes you can't tell which sailor is which, but Shirley's accuracy and projection are amazing.

This might be interesting to you. I still receive all of ten dollars a performance royalty on the ballet from ABT. It was never increased over all the years.

TOBIAS: *What do you do with all the money?* (Laughter.)
ROBBINS: I remember it was such a big hit at the opening that Hurok extended the Met season for two weeks and played it almost every night. And *he* volunteered to add to the royalty. He was going to give me fifteen dollars, more, per performance.

TOBIAS: *You should have taken it—*(Laughter.)
ROBBINS: As a matter of fact I said no. He said, "Why not?" I said, "Because that's the contract I made with Ballet Theatre and the next one'll be different."

TOBIAS: *Was it?*
ROBBINS: It was.

TOBIAS: *Has any company other than Ballet Theatre danced* Fancy?
ROBBINS: No.

TOBIAS: *What gave you the idea to mount it on the New York City Ballet?*
ROBBINS: Well, last year, when we did the sailors' variations for the School of American Ballet benefit. . . .

TOBIAS: *What gave you the idea to do it then?*
ROBBINS: I'd always been thinking we ought to do it sometime or other. That we ought to do those variations. And occasionally it crossed my mind whether we should do it here or not and I always thought, Oh, it's going to be so difficult to do. And it's true; it is very difficult to do.

TOBIAS: *Is that because, as we were saying at the rehearsal, it's so jam-packed with movement?*
ROBBINS: Not jam-packed. Detailed. Not only the movement but the acting that goes on, and the timing of the acting. And then, once having learnt it, how to relax on it, so that it doesn't look like it's forced.

> Reed: You know the part where the boys come walking around and meet in front of
> the door to the bar and the two girls slowly turn and recognize one another, and

then they go into a fast, chattering sort of thing? Well, that was a very touchy spot and we constantly had to work on it. The problem was not anticipating it, so that the reaction would look unrehearsed. It took such concentration and discipline to keep your mind off the fact that you knew what was coming. You really had to play tricks with yourself to make it happen fresh each time, to keep the timing natural.

TOBIAS: *You had said at one point that, in this production for the New York City Ballet, you're trying to go back to the original. How has the ballet changed over the years?*

ROBBINS: What happens, as a part is handed down, is that each person, maybe, likes a certain step that you do, or a certain passing step that you do, and that might suddenly get emphasized. The next person who learns it, learns it with that as an accent. And then the person after that hits it twice as hard, so the steps can change that way very easily. For the most part, though, it's kept pretty well in shape.

TOBIAS: *Are you retrieving the original just in your own head or is the film some help to you? Can you read from that film?*

ROBBINS: Oh yes. Especially a dancer who knows what is meant, you see. We study it and study it. So that's a godsend, to have that film. Really a godsend.

TOBIAS: *Will you make more film, now, once you get this set?*

ROBBINS: Yes, I'll videotape it. For sure.

TOBIAS: *Aside from steps, have things about* Fancy *changed since the 1944 version? Is there a sense of atmosphere that's changed too?*

ROBBINS: Well, you know, as with any ballet after its first performances, it's hard for other people who dance it to catch all the intimate qualities that happened while you first worked on it. The original cast discovered all the things that I discovered as we were doing it. And they didn't know the result. Dancers coming in now already know the result and quite often they're playing that result. And so its's hard for them. I think the hardest thing is to find the warmth and intimacy that the original cast had with each other, that relationship of three buddies who always bummed around together, always had this terrific affection and support for each other— who knew each other well.

—from *Dance Magazine,* January 1980

Jerome Robbins and Edwin Denby
Dances at a Gathering

The ballet that marked Jerome Robbins's return from Broadway to New York City Ballet in 1969, Dances at a Gathering *was greeted as a masterpiece. An hour long, and danced to a group of eighteen Chopin piano pieces, it presents ten dancers in solos, duets, trios, and other configurations, yet they are clearly all part of a community—the community of dance. The original cast was led by Edward Villella as the Boy in Brown, Patricia McBride as the Girl in Pink, and featured other such stars as Violette Verdy, Allegra Kent, Kay Mazzo, and Sara Leland.*

Robbins's Dances at a Gathering *is a great success both with dance fans and the general public. And it is a beautiful piece. But it wasn't planned as a surefire piece—it wasn't planned at all before hand, and began by chance as Robbins explains in the interview (taped shortly after the official premiere) which appears on the pages that follow.*

The ballet is set to Chopin piano pieces and the program lists ten dancers but tells you little more. The curtain goes up in silence on an empty stage. It looks enormous. The back is all sky—some kind of changeable late afternoon in summer. Both sides of the stage are black. Forestage right, a man enters slowly, deep in thought. He is wearing a loose white shirt, brown tights, and boots. He turns to the sky and walks slowly away from you towards center stage. You think of a man alone in a meadow. As he walks you notice the odd tilt of his head—like a man listening, inside himself. In the silence the piano begins as if he were remembering the music. He marks a dance step, he sketches a mazurka gesture, with a kind of pensive vigor he begins to improvise and now he is dancing marvelously and, in a burst of freedom he is running all over the meadow at its edge. Suddenly he subsides and more mysterious than ever, glides into the woods and is gone. Upstage a girl and boy enter. At once they are off full speed in a double improvisation, a complexly fragmented waltz, the number Robbins speaks of as the "wind dance."

As one dance succeeds another—the ballet lasts about an hour—you are fascinated by the variety and freshness of invention, the range of feeling, and by the irresistibly beautiful music which the dance lets you hear distinctly—its mystery too. You see each dancer dance marvelously and you also see each one as a fascinating individual—complex, alone, and with any of the others, individually most sen-

sitive and generous in their relationships. The music and the dance seem to be inventing each other. For a dance fan, the fluid shifts of momentum are a special delight. For the general theater public Robbins's genius in focusing on a decisive momentary movement—almost like a zoom lens—makes vivid the special quality of each dance, and all the charming jokes.

But it is a strange ballet.

Our talk began before the tape machine arrived. Robbins had been telling me how the ballet developed. He had been asked whether he would care to do a piece for the 25th Anniversary City Center Gala, May 8th. Delighted by the way Patricia McBride and Edward Villella had been dancing The Afternoon of a Faun, he thought he would like to do a pas de deux for them—perhaps to Chopin music—and he accepted. As he listened to records and became more and more interested in the possibilities—it occured to him to add two more couples—and he began rehearsal. In the course of rehearsals however, all the six dancers he had chosen were not always free, so he went on choreographing with four others, using those who happened to be free. Gradually he made more and more dances, but without a definite plan for the whole piece. When about two-thirds of the ballet was done, he invited Balanchine (who had just returned from Europe) to rehearsal. At the end of it he turned to Mr. B and said, "Don't you think it's a bit long?" Mr. B answered, "More. Make more!" He did.

Robbins said to me, "As you see, there are still never more than six dancers dancing at once." He told me that as the dances and relationships kept coming out of the different pieces of music and the particular dancers available, he began to feel that they were all connected by some underlying sense of community (he said, laughing, "Maybe just because they were dancers") and by a sense of open air and sunlight and sudden nostalgia perhaps.

We spoke of one of the many lovely lifts—this one at the end of Eddie's pas de deux with Pat where it looks as though he were lifting a sack onto his shoulder and, up on his shoulder the sack suddenly changes into a beautiful mermaid. Robbins explained how it came out of a sudden metamorphosis in the music. And he illustrated how the lift is done.

We were talking of Villella's gesture of touching the floor in the final minutes of the ballet, and Robbins mentioned that he was perhaps thinking of the dancers' world—the floor below, the space around and above. I was saying that I liked that gesture better the second time I saw it because it was slower and I wondered if he (Robbins) had changed it. At that point the tape begins:

ROBBINS: No, that's just a very subtle thing of acting and where the human being is at the time. I think two weeks ago, at the preview, Eddie was under more difficulties and pressures—down more—and perhaps that made the difference.

I think the ballet will seem different in almost every performance, not vastly, but shades like those you saw, they will happen, depending on the dancers. You said it, I remember, way back—the dancers read (in a review) what the ballet is about, then they change because now they *know* it (they know it in words)—before they just *did* it. And that can happen—there was a modesty and a sort of not knowing in the first showing. They may start to think now that maybe they should do it more like what everyone says it is. I don't know what to do about that except to ask them not to.

I always tell them to do it for themselves, and to think of "marking" it—Don't think of doing it full out.

DENBY: *Well, that's another quality the ballet has. I was very happy to see that with Eddie who is used to "doing it full out"—he does that very beautifully, it's not vulgar selling at all—he's not forcing it. But the inner business he also does very well—in* Giselle. *He's remarkable, you know, wonderful.*

ROBBINS: I like watching ballets, anyway, best of all at rehearsals when a dancer is just working for himself, really just working. They are beautiful to watch then. I love to watch George's [Balanchine] work that way. Just love to.

DENBY: *How beautiful everything is before gets its name.*

Did I hear you say that Melissa [Hayden] will be covering Violette [Verdy]?

ROBBINS: Yes, I think she'll be marvelous.

DENBY: *And so is Verdy. Someone told me that you're working to add a much longer number for her. So I said, "Oh, wonderful."*

ROBBINS: I haven't been around ballet for so long, I forget how scuttle-butty it gets around here. If you say to someone, "I want to work with you tomorrow," the next day someone asks you, "Are you doing a new ballet?" It already has gotten that big.

But it was nice working with them. I did enjoy it very much. Patty McBride, I just *love* working with her.

DENBY: *Yes, she's remarkable . . . And I am very happy about what you did with Bob Maiorano. Because this year he's suddenly become a very good dancer wherever I look at him. He was beginning last year and all of a sudden, there he is,—now you can really see it.*

ROBBINS: Yes.

DENBY: *He has a marvelous Italian beauty of gesture. Maybe he was afraid of it all this time. The arm is so heavy the way he moves it. But the weight is right for all of them—the boys especially.*

ROBBINS: Bobby Weiss, have you seen him? In one of the performances he is going to do Johnnie Clifford's part.

DENBY: *He was wonderful in a school performance last year, too. Especially in the end of* Sylphides *when he lost his nervousness in the finale. He looks as though he were not letting go as much as is his nature.*

ROBBINS: He is beautiful when he lets go. In rehearsal, I just made him go.

DENBY: *Clifford was remarkable too; he is so positively there. But it's not so simple. There is also something private about it. And Tony's [Blum] great—so much livelier that he's been often.*

ROBBINS: That's the fun of having another choreographer work with the dancers. Like in Ballet Theatre, Eliot Feld was doing a ballet, and I looked at his dancers and thought, now, those are people I by-passed, but he saw something in them and brought out another whole aspect of them. It's always charming. But every choreographer—Agnes [de Mille] has people she works with I can't see—people I work with that she can't see. That's nice for the dancers, isn't it?

DENBY: *And for the choreographers if you are going to travel around. You should try out your dances on the Russians. I'm sure they would like to have a dance of yours, they like to gather things—archives in their minds. It would be so much fun.*

ROBBINS: I'm going to Russia. I *would* like to see if I can get it either to the Bolshoi or Kirov. I would like to see them dance this. I really would. It might finally turn out to be a peasant parody, you never know (laughter)— that folk part of it—I was surprised.

DENBY: *I was surprised that people made so much of it, because the dancers are always so elegant. They might be landowners, if they were anybody in Europe.*

ROBBINS: At first I also thought they were very elegant people, maybe at a picnic, maybe doing something—their own thing.

And also to me—and this I'm being very careful about—I don't want it to be a big thing—but the boys and the whole period are very hippyish.

DENBY: *At first you had the beards. I was quite pleased with that.*

ROBBINS: The boys still had them at rehearsal because of the long lay-off. Tony had long hair and a moustache and John Prinz had long hair and a beard and it was marvelous looking. It really affected what I was doing. I liked the boots—and the sketches are much more hippy than they appear on stage in the sense of belts and open blouses for the boys and long hair and ballooning sleeves. There is something in the nature of knowing who they are and having love and confidence in them.

DENBY: *Competence . . . ?*

ROBBINS: Confidence—which I feel is in the work, finally. Loving confidence in themselves and in the other people.

DENBY: *That is in there very strongly.*

ROBBINS: It has some strangenesses in it too, I'm sure, but I can't yet quite see it. Every now and then I look at a step and think that is a very odd step. There is a strange step that Eddie does in his solo—he should play with it the way one does this (hand gesture).

DENBY: *There was an 8-year-old Negro boy in the street and he was running; he suddenly started throwing his feet around—with such pleasure.*

ROBBINS: I saw something nice in the park. Near Sheep Meadow there was a black boy and a white boy, both happened to be wearing blue. The black boy had a blue sweat shirt and the white boy had a blue sweater and open collar. They were running toward each other and it was more than a game. They ran and reached out hands. Not just shook hands, because that's what it was about, but they took hands and swung around each other with their heads thrown back with laughter. And then let go and embraced each other. Oh, it was so beautiful, I was thrilled by it. There was so much rapture and ecstacy and friendliness and openness about it. Then they quieted down and began talking. (laughs)

DENBY: *There are things in the ballet that are a bit gruesome. And, you know, very interesting.*

ROBBINS: Gruesome?

DENBY: *It's partly in the lifts, partly sometimes in the way the boys treat a girl.*

ROBBINS: Well, opening night there was an accident. I want to be sure you know that it was an accident. There was a place where Sally [Sara Leland] was being swung around and they fell off the lift and it turned into a—it looked like she was in outer space—like she'd been released from a capsule. She was just swirling around. Horrifying for a moment. But there are?—I don't know, I can't tell.

DENBY: *It's definitely in the music. It's much stranger than one . . .*

ROBBINS: Yes, than one thinks.

DENBY: *Than one is supposed to think.*

ROBBINS: There's a nocturne. I began late listening to one nocturne—it was like opening a door into a room and the people are in the *midst* of a conversation. I mean, there's no introduction, no preface; it's like a cut in a film; it's almost like Chopin had finished the previous nocturne, finished it properly, and there was a fade-out. And suddenly (clap) you're on somebody's face who's talking. But in the middle of a sentence! You don't even get "and then," it's right in the middle of a word and he's very strange, really quite strange. He knew a lot, I think. Much more than I thought before I began. It was fascinating that way—just like some connection happened between all those sounds that he thought of, and where I was at.

DENBY: *The movement through a piece is always so interesting, and that you catch so well and do so many things with.*

ROBBINS: I listened to a lot of recordings, different people playing the same piece. I used mostly Rubinstein and Novaes and some Brailowsky. I listened to some of the Dinu Lipatti. Then it was enough for me and after that I knew I would start to get confused. There are hardly any liberties taken at all—I would say none. Only one where at the end of Eddie's first dance it's marked *fortissimo*—da da da *whoosh*—I don't even know if it's Chopin's indication—I choreographed it that way—and Eddie was gone, *whoosh*. I didn't like it, it was a little obvious, like I was trying for a hand and the piece was trying for a hand, I thought there was something else there, so I took it on retard and soft, and let him take that poetic thing he does there. The dancers are beautiful.

DENBY: *Gordon [Boelzner] plays it very well because he also plays it for movement, without those extra questions of pianism.*

ROBBINS: There are no sentimentalities.

DENBY: *If you were listening to the music at a concert you might want more nuances, but this way you don't because the dancers are doing it, the nuances.*

ROBBINS: And he's tireless, that boy. It's fantastic. He plays it all day long, and does the other rehearsals, too. Some of those pieces are killers. I suddenly thought, "Look at a Chopin concert"—They play a piece and go off and rest. They do maybe half an hour or twenty minutes and go and have a fifteen-minute intermission. But he's tearing off those études written for these two fingers. You know about the one Eddie dances to—the little fast one—sort of chromatically going up and down the scale? Well, Chopin devised it to give these two fingers which are the weakest, a work out.

DENBY: *I am so glad you didn't orchestrate it. Not that it would be possible, but there's that temptation.*

ROBBINS: I got worried for a while before we got it down on the big piano because it began to sound very hollow to me. And, I thought, well when people come to this big theater and they have just seen a big ballet with a lot of marvelous sounds, the piano is going to sound like a little rehearsal piano. But it doesn't, where it is. It seems it fills the house and sustains—a good combination, I think, between what you are seeing and what you hear.

DENBY: *It isn't miked?*

ROBBINS: No, not at all!

DENBY: *And you're so glad to see him too. I wondered whether he can see the dancers.*

ROBBINS: Most of them, but not the ones on the side of the stage he is on. But there is a place where we have a mirror—rigged way up high on the wings so that if he looks up he can see someone come in for just a cue. And I thought Tom Skelton did a very good job in a very little time. He did the lighting.

DENBY: *Some of it looks ominous, sometimes. I mean weather. It changes. I suppose you wanted that too. I liked it.*

ROBBINS: I didn't mean it to look ominous, but I suppose that vast sky, it is almost like nature changing on you. You're a little worried about what is going to happen next, it doesn't matter if it goes up or down. It's just that it changes. Everything changes.

I didn't know it was going to be that long a ballet or what it was going to be. I originally thought, we'll do it using the wings and the cyclorama because it's just going to be a pas de deux. But by the time it was all done, I thought, wow, who should do a set? Is it Jane Freilicher, or is it one of those watery sort of places, or is it——? Now I'm used to the way it is. I don't know if I want a set, or anything softer around the edges. That's a very hard line, those black wings. But once it starts, I don't suppose you are particularly aware of it anymore.

DENBY: *When you watch you realize that there are woods there, and you're in a meadow and there are trees.*

ROBBINS: Isn't that funny, odd how that all got evoked. My names for the dances themselves, for instance, the second dance for John Prinz and Allegra [Kent], I call it "wind waltz" because to me they are like two things that are on the wind that catch up with each other. There is something about air—breezes which are clawing them and pushing them almost like two kites. And "walk waltz" or "the three girls" to me is somehow in the woods. On a Chekhov evening. It just is, I can't see it any other way. It has that quality.

DENBY: *The whole piece is a Chekhov piece. There are so many things suggested and not explained. The business of looking around at the end is the trickiest. I didn't like it at all the first time. Yesterday I didn't mind it so much. It is like looking at an airplane, I think of missiles and war.*

ROBBINS: They must do it very softly. That is almost one of the hardest parts to be able to do. It is very hard for them just to walk on and be confident and just raise their heads or eyes and look at something without starting to make it dramatic. I keep telling them, "Relax, don't be sad, don't get upset, just see it, just whatever you want to pick, just see. It's a cloud passing, if you want. Take it easy on it, don't get gloomy."

DENBY: *It's because they all do it together.*

ROBBINS: Together—right—they all follow one thing. And that upset you? You thought it was airplanes and missiles?

DENBY: *The atom bomb comes in and everything else. The sort of thing about Hitler attacking Poland. Your mind gets full of ideas that you don't want, that don't have anything to do with the piece.*

ROBBINS: If I had to talk about it all, I would say that they are looking at—all right—clouds on the horizon which possibly could be threatening, but then that's life, so afterwards you just pick up and go right on again. It doesn't destroy them. They don't lament. They accept.

DENBY: *That's what I told myself: It must be that they are looking at clouds—clouds rarely go that fast, but it might be a storm coming up and they're wondering if it's going to happen.*

ROBBINS: That section, it was the last piece I did, though. I spent about two weeks after I finished the bulk of the choreography—it was almost all done about two weeks before the eighth of May. But that last two weeks I spent in arranging, trying to get the right order. Not only who danced what, but also that sense of something happening—making the dances have some continuity, some structure, whether I knew specifically what it was or not.

At one point I had the scherzo finishing the ballet and the grand waltz opening it. All different sorts of ways. It was just—it was a marvelous sort of puzzle. Here I have all these people and these situations and know they belong to each other—now let me see how. It was almost like rearranging *things*. And suddenly a picture was there. I am surprised by a lot of it. I am very surprised by the reaction to it. I didn't expect it at all. Something is there that I didn't know I was doing.

DENBY: *The reaction?*

ROBBINS: To the ballet.

DENBY: *That everybody liked it so much.*

ROBBINS: So much. The questions you are asking me about it seem to— I was originally going to call it *Some Dances*. That's all they are, just a series of dances. But something else takes over.

DENBY: *I don't know that the title is exactly the best.*

ROBBINS: It's a hard one to find. I was going to say *Dances: Chopin, In Open Air,* but that isn't the right title. In French *Quelques Danses* is nice, but in English *Some Dances* is sort of flat. If you say *18 Dances* or *19 Dances,* it divides them into compartments.

DENBY: *And it's of no consequence. Once you see the piece, you figure it is a piece. That end is quite prepared for all along when it happens. You really didn't want a big dance at the end. Since they are walking so much anyway, it is natural to make the end out of that.*

ROBBINS: Also the end of it had to come out of the scherzo, that very restless piece which ends with them all sort of *whoosh* running out— disappearing like cinders falling out into the night, and it couldn't end there, either. That's not the end of it, that's not how I feel about these people—that they went *whoosh* and disappeared. They are still here and they still move like dancers. They are a community. They take—what's the Italian word?—"a passegiata"—they take a stroll, like in an Italian town, around the town's square at sundown. They may have felt a threat, but they don't panic, they stay.

I was very touched by Maria [Tallchief] last night. She was moved by the ballet, and I suddenly realized how much it meant to me that she *was* and that it pleased her, because she is such an image in my mind of what a dancer should be, and I can't think of her as a cinder which went *whoosh* and was gone.

So coming hack after the scherzo to the stage and the floor that we dance on, and putting your hand on it—if it's the earth or a ballet dancer's relationship to a wood floor—*that* somehow is the ending I knew I had to get to somewhere. Very little of this was conscious, Edwin. I don't like to make theory afterward. I'm just trying to get at it—there may be seven other reasons I'm not mentioning, well, you understand.

DENBY: *I don't want to pull it out of you—*

ROBBINS: Well, besides, you have your thoughts about it anyway.

DENBY: *Of course. Everyone is very happy that you've done a ballet again.*

ROBBINS: So am I.

DENBY: *And the dancers are happy. And it's nice you want to do some more.*

ROBBINS: I'm surprised. I didn't know which I would do or how I would do. It's almost like an artist who has not been drawing for a long time. I didn't know how my hand would be. And I was so surprised that the dances began to come out and began to come out so gushing, in a way. And I worked in a way I hadn't worked before. Whether I knew the details or not, I pushed through to the end of the dance. I sort of knew where it was going, and then I'd go back and clean it up and fill it up. Quite often the dancers weren't even sure how they got through the steps to the next step. But they went with me. Well, what I started to say was that I was pleased to be choreographing again and to have it coming out, and it's given me a sort—it's unplugged something. And I want to do a lot of ballets, I want to go on and see if I can work a little bit more the way I've worked this time—that sort of trusting the intuition more than self-controlling the intuition. I'd like to see what happens with some other kind of music now. That music I feel I am very identified with and always have been. It may go all the way back to my sister's dancing days as a Duncan dancer. I think a lot of that's in there.

DENBY: *I imagined you and your sister at the piano—you were seven or eight. The first thing that came from it was* The Concert *which, the first time, I was quite offended by.*

ROBBINS: (laughs): I made up for that.

DENBY: *I miss it now. I'd love to see it. But your jokes this time are adorable.*

ROBBINS: I love them in the section where they're posing, just love them . . .

I had a researcher call me from a magazine to ask me some questions. The first one was something very close to this: "Where do you place your newest ballet in the mainstream of the trend of abstract dancing today?" (laughter) I've also been asked, "What is the relation between *Les Sylphides* and your ballet?" Well, I guess we used the same composer.

DENBY: *Did you use any of the same pieces?*

ROBBINS: No, I didn't except one, the adage that Tony and Pat do, the third dance. Evidently, that music was used as the man's variation at one point, which I didn't know. It's a lovely piece.

DENBY: *You told me that you are going to do another Chopin ballet.*

ROBBINS: I've finished one nocturne and I've about three-quarters of another one, and I have an idea for a third. I've started them and want to see how they come out. One for Millie, one for Allegra, and I think one for Kay Mazzo.

DENBY: *She's beautiful.*

ROBBINS: Isn't she lovely?

DENBY: *Sally is wonderful. She gets more and more of that giving-without-thinking.*

ROBBINS: She has a kind of toughness, not tough as much as a practical quality. But then I'll say something and can see in her eyes that she's suddenly grasped it, and you can see it explode inside her—such joy.

DENBY: *The dance of the girls comes off so wonderfully. Allegra is wonderful all through.*

ROBBINS: That's the way about all of them. At so many rehearsals, they didn't dance all out. They sort of walked. That's how I got Eddie to do that first variation the first night. He came into rehearsal and had to save himself for the performance and just marked through it. I ran back and said, "Now, that's what I want." The same with Allegra—when she marks something, she shows you what it is. I don't think they realize how trained they are—so clear. Like someone with a great voice who can whisper and you hear it. And that's what you see. And that's what they do.

DENBY: *They are so completely clear, it's extraordinary how clear they are because whatever is passing through is never a blur or an uncertainty or a conventionalism.*

Postscript from Robbins to Denby (sent the following day from Stockholm where Robbins was supervising final rehearsals of Les Noces *for its June 6 premiere with the Royal Swedish Ballet. He went from there to Moscow to attend, by invitation of the U.S.S.R., its International Ballet Competition.)*

May 27, 1969

Dear Edwin:

Something bothered me terribly after we met—one of your remarks about the people looking up and watching something cross the sky at the end of the ballet. You said something about planes—A bomb—war today, etc. and it jarred me very much. I couldn't figure out "the why" right away—but then I did on the trip over. First of all I feel you are imposing a terribly out-of-context meaning to what they are seeing. The ballet stays and exists in the time of the music and its work. Nothing is out of it, I believe; all gestures and moods, steps, etc. are part of the fabric of the music's time and its meanings to me. I couldn't think of planes—A bomb, etc. Only clouds—and the flights of birds—sunsets and leaves falling—and they, the people's reactions are all very underplayed, very willing to meet whatever threat is *in the music.*

Well, those people knew their disasters—felt them, maybe felt that at a certain time their being would come to an end—but they faced it as a part of living.

I hadn't thought of *all* of this when I did it. All I knew is that they weren't afraid, had no self pity, and stayed—didn't leave.

And I do feel that last piece is the logical end of the whole ballet. To me it is very much the only possible result of all that's come before.

. . . Stockholm is lovely, limpid skies at midnight—looking clear and blue as a New York fall—It was so good to see you—*J*

—from *Dance Magazine,* July 1969

THE SLEEPING BEAUTY

Thought of as the acme of the classical style in ballet, The Sleeping Beauty *came to life in 1890 at the Maryinsky, with its sublime score by Tchaikovsky and superb choreography by Petipa. For many Russians—Balanchine, Pavlova, Benois, and others—it was the touchstone of their art, never to be surpassed. It is based on the Charles Perrault version of the traditional fairy tale, and its underlying message— the eventual triumph of harmony, as personified by the Lilac Fairy, over wickedness (Carabosse)—gives it a depth of meaning few ballets can convey. The original Aurora was Carlotta Brianza; other famous interpreters include Spessivtseva (in Diaghilev's 1921 London production), the Kirov's Irina Kolpakova, and most renowned of all, Margot Fonteyn, whose signature role it was. Its influence on the art of ballet is pervasive, most obviously in Balanchine's classicism, built on Petipa's. The former's* Theme and Variations *is, for instance, an homage to* The Sleeping Beauty.

FREDERICK ASHTON
The Sleeping Beauty

In the first place I would like to say that my knowledge of Petipa's ballets is limited. The ballets of his that I am familiar with are *Swan Lake* and *Sleeping Beauty*, which I know in their full versions, and I have seen versions of *Raymonda* and *Don Quixote*, which, though based on Petipa, were obviously not authentic versions. That, together with excerpts from *Paquita* and *La Bayadère*, is alas the full extent of my knowledge of his works.

Personally, I find *Sleeping Beauty* the most interesting choreographically. It is a marvel of construction, form, and climax, and of all the scenes in the *Beauty* I find the Prologue the most exciting. What is fascinating to me, apart from the choreographic steps, is the construction of this scene which, like a beautiful edifice, is built up and up to its final glory. It is remarkable the way that he devises all the entrances leading up to that of the Lilac Fairy and the

Cavaliers, and only then does the glorious Pas d'Action commence. This, in itself, is a great climax, which is then lowered, like a receding tide, only to overflow the stage again with the entrance of Carabosse, and if ever there was a reason for the preservation of a mime scene this is it.

It is wonderful the way that the mime scenes are included in his work, usually after there has been a great deal of dancing, and they are properly placed there to rest the spectator and the eye.

These mime scenes, in my opinion, are most carefully placed in the general construction of the scene, and I am not of the opinion that they should be heightened into a form of dance, thus destroying all Petipa's original intentions. Mime is only tedious in the hands of a boring performer, but in the hands of a proper artist of the theatre, the gesture can be just as eloquent and thrilling as any passage of dance; in other words, it is the way that these scenes are done that matters.

After the exit of Carabosse there is a telling decrescendo of the whole atmosphere, while the company re-assembles itself for the glorious final group, in which the Queen walks to the cradle and thus points the whole future action onto the baby Aurora. This is a most masterly stroke of theatrical genius, a *coup de théâtre*.

The same climactic conditions occur in the first act, in which the scene gradually builds up to a great expectancy for the arrival of the young Princess, further ascending to the wonderful Pas d'Action of the Rose Adagio, ending with the re-entry of Carabosse and the Princess's temporary demise.

Both the Prologue and the first act are poetic realism at its very highest. From there Petipa takes us into the world of dreamlike, lyrical fantasy, which suggests the long slumber of the Princess.

I find the last act least satisfactory, with the introduction of all the fairy characters coming to the wedding; but nevertheless we are in the world of poetic realism again, and out of this come two superb choreographic compositions in the Blue Bird and the Grand Adage. Here again the great sense of climax in the Adage is purely choreographic, as distinct from the production climaxes in the other acts.

I experience, in a good performance of the Grand Pas de Deux, all the great dramatic emotions of love and life and death and even, paradoxically, that of a great bullfight (where one is apt to experience all emotions), and this Pas de Deux is inadequately performed unless it has a sense of high drama in every attitude.

I can truly say that I have learnt more from the lessons that these ballets have to offer, than from any other choreographic experience of my life, and I frequently return to re-study their construction and form when I am contemplating ballets on a major scale myself.

I might add, just as a footnote, that my favourite variation in the entire choreographic repertoir is what we call the Finger Variation in the Prologue. This never ceases to arouse in me a response and excitement.

I think that it is necessary to maintain Petipa's ballets as far as possible, and as far as one knows, just as he created them. By this I mean that there should be some system by which they are preserved, so that they could be remounted actually as near as possible as they were, and with no deviation of style.

In our two companies I have preserved one production of *Swan Lake* like this, and another that we have tampered with, trying to bring things more up to date and heightening passages that we considered tedious, and in the end I must frankly say that I don't think we have done any better. I am of the opinion that it is better to leave a choreographer's version of his own ballets to speak for themselves, or re-act totally against them. Things can be old-fashioned and dated, but many masterpieces are dated in the right way, and I think it impertinent to tamper with these. I do not like to see hotch potches of Petipa's work with another choreographer imposing his own, often trite, ideas on established masterpieces.

I think it much better that they should attempt completely new versions, but of course in the end these are doomed to failure, for who would be able to overtop the arrangement of the Rose Adagio, for instance?

I also believe that they should be danced in the style of dancing for which he conceived them. In this I was lucky having witnessed performances of both Trefilova and Spessivtseva in *Swan Lake* and *Sleeping Beauty,* and of that Queen of the dance Karsavina in *Raymonda.* This was purity of dancing with no exaggeration of Port de Bras, or mannerist interpretations, which one is apt to see these days.

Petipa's ballets will always be the crowning jewels in any company that possesses them, and they should be preserved with a reverence due to their stature, and for the edification of future generations.

—from *The Sleeping Princess* by Gordon Anthony, 1939

CONSTANT LAMBERT

Tchaikovsky and the Ballet

The English composer and conductor Constant Lambert (1905–1951) was a driving force in the early years of the Vic-Wells (later, Royal) ballet company as musical director and artistic adviser. He wrote several ballet scores (including The Rio Grande, Horoscope, *and* Tiresias*) and was a nonpareil conductor of ballet music. Many people credited his conducting (particularly of* The Sleeping Beauty*) with being a substantial element of Sadler's Wells' 1949 triumph in New York. He also had tremendous influence on Margot Fonteyn, whose lover and mentor he was in her formative years. He was also the author of a brilliant collection of essays,* Music Ho! A study of Music in Decline.*

The reasons why Tchaikovsky's genius was ideally suited to the ballet are obvious. The classical ballet offers no opportunity for the long-drawn-out symphonic developments, the intellectual expositions and summings-up, which were notoriously Tchaikovsky's weak spots. On the contrary, it calls imperatively for what I have described as his three great gifts—lyricism, colour, and a sense of dramatic effect. Tchaikovsky's melodies are essentially tunes rather than symphonic themes. They are direct and final statements, not the premises of a lengthy argument. That is why his melodic faculty is seen to such great advantage in the medium of ballet. The subjects of his symphonies are usually excellent considered on their own, but he himself was conscious of the fact that their subsequent development was often forced on them after they had come to a natural close.

In the ballet his tunes come to a natural close, and then some new variation or piece of action demands a different tune, with the result that his ballets are devoid of any padding. In the whole range of music I know of no greater example of melodic fecundity than the score of *The Sleeping Princess*. The Prologue alone contains more material than the average composer puts into a whole opera. And not only are the tunes good in themselves (it is difficult to think of a theme more completely satisfying than that associated with the Lilac Fairy), they are ideally written for the body. This purely physical element is far too often ignored by the modern ballet composer. No composer would sit down to write an opera without some knowledge of a consideration for the human voice, yet he will blithely sit down and write a ballet without any consideration for the limbs that are eventually going to execute it. Tchaikovsky's tunes not only sing themselves, they dance themselves, and they present an unparalleled combination of musical value and practical suitability.

It must be admitted that at times his skill in writing to the demands of the choreographer leads to a sequence of musical ideas that would not be congruous in the concert-hall. For example, the middle section of the *pas de deux* in the second act of *Lac des Cygnes* is so ideally suited to the choreography that in the concert-hall it is as ineffective as some of the illustrative passages in *Petrouchka,* and Tchaikovsky, in my opinion, made a mistake when he included it in the none-too-well-chosen orchestral suite. But these moments (Aurora's solo in the first act of *The Sleeping Princess* is another example) are not only rare but excusable. Generally speaking, one is astonished at the way Tchaikovsky was able, without any spiritual compromise, to adapt his melodic gifts to the precise style and scale demanded by the occasion.

To vary the scale or dimensional unit of one's melody is even more difficult than to vary its style, but Tchaikovsky never fails us in this respect. Take the long sweeping line for solo oboe in the prelude of *Lac des Cygnes,* Act II, with its evocation of desolate frozen spaces, and compare it with the deliberately jerky and constricted little tune which represents the four cygnets. Or again, compare the easy, nonchalant line of the villagers' sunlit valse in *The Sleeping Princess* with the breathless, fluttering cross-rhythms of the snowflake valse in *Casse-Noisette.*

Tchaikovsky's unerring sense of theatrical style is shown not only in his thematic material but in his orchestration. A particularly happy example of this is provided by the variations for the six fairies in the Prologue of *The Sleeping Princess.* (Incidentally, those critics who complained about the absence of a seventh fairy in the present revival should remember that she was added by Diaghilev for his Alhambra revival and had no place in the original score.) Within the space of five minutes or so Tchaikovsky provides six entirely different types of tune, six entirely different types of rhythm, and six entirely different types of "lay-out" on the orchestra. Not only is the orchestration brilliant in itself, it is invariably of the type that aids, not impedes, the dancer. How well one knows the type of modern ballet orchestration in which the essential melody and rhythm of the music (to which, it must be remembered, the dancer can necessarily give only partial attention) are obscured by over-ingenious counter-subjects and passages of *remplissage* which may tickle the composer's eye but confuse the executant's ear. Tchaikovsky's orchestral texture is far from being bare, but it is never confused. It is notable not only for its sense of colour but for what may be called its sense of perspective. We always know exactly which is the foreground and which the background. Take, for example, the Breadcrumb Fairy variation (*miettes qui tombent*) in *The Sleeping Princess*. The character of the dance is established by a pizzicato tune over an accompaniment of softly accented and beautifully placed chords on the trombones. To these are added first a smooth counter-subject on the 'cellos, then a series of wood-wind trills. The final combination of all four colours is delightful, yet the separate elements never interfere with each other, nor is the main outline ever obscured.

An entirely different type of orchestration is provided by the highly original symphonic *entr'acte* representing the Princess asleep. This is in every way a technical *tour de force*. The persistent sleep is ingeniously suggested by a continuous tremolo C on second violins, against which we hear first of all the sleep motive from the end of Act I (a chromatic progression of chords somewhat reminiscent of Rimsky-Korsakoff in style), then the motives of the wicked fairy Carabosse and the Lilac Fairy, and finally the main motive of the piece, an oboe tune of haunting beauty. Every harmonic change which can be wrought round the continuous C as pivot is employed, and the orchestration, astonishingly unorthodox for the period, shows equal resource. The colour throughout is curiously veiled, and it is fascinating to the musician to notice how Tchaikovsky gradually works up from a thread of sound to a full but *muffled* climax. Anyone can bring off a rousing climax in the brilliant style, just as anyone can create an effect of darkness by using only the lower registers of the instruments, but to create this twilight world in which the whole scene is overshadowed yet every detail crystal-clear is the work of a master-hand.

The fact that Tchaikovsky's three ballets are separated by a number of years makes a comparison of their scores of particular technical interest. *Lac des Cygnes,* the earliest, is effectively, but on the whole rather crudely, scored. There are one or two exquisite moments of colour, notably in the slow preludes and in most of the music associated with Odette, but, generally speaking, the orchestration is laid on with a shining trowel and the ear becomes a little fatigued by the recurrence of the same type of flamboyant tutti in each act. It was not until later, in the *Sleeping Princess* period, that Tchaikovsky learned how to obtain the utmost sonority from the orchestra without ever degenerating into noisiness.

Casse-Noisette, one of his last scores, has extraordinary technical interest for the musician, particularly in the earlier scenes. There is hardly a page without some remarkable *trouvaille,* and there are one or two fascinating and successful experiments in tone colour which even to-day have not been followed up. It is a great pity that only the popular and comparatively conventional suite is readily available, for the student (and for that matter the professional) could learn far more from the first act. Those who imagine that

Rimsky-Korsakoff was the only progenitor of the *Oiseau de Feu* type of scoring should listen carefully to the nightmare scene in *Casse-Noisette,* which still has the power to astonish and must have been a revelation at the time it was written.

Speaking, as I said, from the purely technical point of view, *Casse-Noisette* is the most finished and ingenious of all Tchaikovsky's scores, but I still find the score of *The Sleeping Princess* a more inspiring one. *Casse-Noisette* is a score one delights in analysing, saying, "How clever to have used the flutes that way, what a good idea to double that up with the coranglais," and so on, but listening to *The Sleeping Princess* one is rarely made conscious of any particular device—the orchestration, like all great orchestration, is so essentially a part of the whole conception that we cannot separate technique from inspiration. The orchestral texture is not applied from without, it grows naturally from the very soul of the work. This complete artistic unity is what places *The Sleeping Princess* above Tchaikovsky's other two ballets. *Lac des Cygnes* has the fresh spontaneity of youth, but also some of its crudity. *Casse-Noisette* has the uncanny *expertise* which only comes at the end of a man's career, but shows in places a flagging vitality. *The Sleeping Princess* is one of those rare works of art written when both technique and inspiration are in their prime.

I have dwelt on the purely orchestral contrasts between Tchaikovsky's three ballets because they are a symbol of the even more striking emotional contrasts between the three. People talk glibly of Tchaikovsky's "ballet style" without realizing that in each of his ballets he has created an entirely different emotional world (a fact which can readily be appreciated when numbers from *Casse-Noisette* are mistakenly introduced into *The Sleeping Princess*).

The world of *Lac des Cygnes* is, curiously enough, a human one. In spite of all its artificialities, in spite of the Gothic mummery of its scenario, the ballet has a very direct emotional appeal, an appeal which may be compared to that exerted (in a more powerful way) by *Romeo and Juliet* or *Francesca da Rimini. Casse-Noisette* arouses no emotional problems. It is the perfect child's picture-book and, like all good picture-books, can be returned to again and again. Not even the dirty thumb-marks left by innumerable bad performances of the suite can dim the brightness and charm of its colours. There are some toys of which a child never tires.

The emotion evoked by the music of *The Sleeping Princess* is of a very different order, and belongs so essentially to the world of music that it is difficult to express or suggest in words. The melancholy which, for all its outward gaiety, the ballet occasionally arouses is not the same as the melancholy aroused by the symphonies. We do not need to read Tchaikovsky's life or letters to realize that these are the works of an unhappy frustrated man whose only escape from ever-present melancholy was either bitter anger or vicarious gaiety. When I say "only escape" I am speaking of him as man rather than artist. As artist he was on certain occasions (and to my mind *The Sleeping Princess* is the supreme instance) able to escape into a world of pure and timeless beauty which has been attained by only a handful in the history of any art. The difference between the emotional world of Tchaikovsky's concert works and that of *The Sleeping Princess* is best realized by comparing the second subject of the slow movement of the Fifth Symphony with the tune for solo 'cello in the second act of *The Sleeping Princess* when the Prince sees Aurora in a vision. The purely physical similarity between the two tunes is astonishing, but they inhabit entirely different psychological worlds. In one, Tchaikovsky is crying for the moon; in the other, he is content to gaze at its beauty.

The comparison may seem to many too exalted, but I feel that *The Sleeping Princess* stands in relation to the rest of Tchaikovsky's work as *The Magic Flute* does to the rest of Mozart's. Both are magical works in the fullest sense of the term, and both have a serenity of spirit which is due not to any monastic withdrawal from life but to a fuller comprehension of its enduring values. The human woes and passions of Don Giovanni and Donna Elvira, of Romeo and Juliet, are left behind, and the lovers meet calmly as in a dream. The old fairy-tale phrase "and they lived happily ever afterward" for once seems true, for in *The Sleeping Princess* Tchaikovsky has suspended time as magically as the Lilac Fairy herself. Even the nostalgic *Panorama,* in some ways the most moving number in the score, has nothing in it of the *lacrimae rerum* which is the dominant note of Delius's idyllic and melancholy music, entranced by the beauty of the moment yet obsessed by the realization that its beauty is ephemeral. It reminds one more of the land which "seemed always afternoon." Such a world of art is sternly denounced by some modern critics as being "escapist," and certainly those who expect ballets to have a "message" will not find much to please them in *The Sleeping Princess.* Ballet, to my mind, is of all mediums the least suited to conveying a message, and that is why it provides so welcome an oasis in a world where writers, painters, and composers keep on sending one messages whether one wants them to or not. "Escapism" in art may not be so bad a thing after all. The realm of the imagination which has given us the landscapes of Claude and Poussin, the poetry of Coleridge and Keats, the *Magic Flute* of Mozart and the finest pages of *The Sleeping Princess,* may well prove more enduring than the platform from which are hurled to us the urgent polemics of the present day.

—from *The Sleeping Princess: Camera Studies,* 1946

ARLENE CROCE

The Sleeping Beauty

The Royal Ballet's production of *The Sleeping Beauty,* new last year, just doesn't work. I think they've forgotten it's a fairy tale and accepted too meekly the proposition that spectacle on the stage isn't as interesting to modern audiences as stories about lovers in which the boy gets to dance as much as the girl. It's suspicious how many of the Royal's evening-length ballets tell the same story about enchanted or doomed lovers, with the dance scenes appropriately divided into His and Hers. The rest of the production tends to drop into low relief while one or another popular dance team hogs the foreground. *The Sleeping Beauty* has a narrative sweep and a spectacular tradition utterly different from *Swan Lake* or *Nutcracker* or *Romeo and Juliet,* yet the principle behind these various productions seems to be that they should all look as much alike as possible and keep the stars out front all night long. The male star of *The Sleeping Beauty* gets to do the same meditative largo solo he does in the first act of *Swan Lake,* and in all these ballets there now seems to be one pas de deux too many. The superfluous pas de deux in *The Sleeping Beauty* not only sounds like *Nutcracker* (Ashton used music originally discarded by Petipa, part of which Tchaikovsky later recast as Christmas-tree music) but looks like it, too, with the dancers moving in the broad parallel steps that Nureyev uses for the last-act duet in his version of *Nutcracker* (in which, incidentally, Nureyev has given himself and his ballerina two roles apiece).

Because it also looks like an Ashton pas de deux, it's interesting to watch, but it interrupts the ballet at the worst possible moment, when the audience's attention should be not on the lovers but on the awakening of the castle—the lifting of that century-old cobweb and the bestirring of the court into fresh activity. These are the things that I ask to see in *The Sleeping Beauty* because they are there in Tchaikovsky's music. It is all there—his magical intimacy and his expertly judged distances, too—in the moment when the Prince bends down with his kiss of life. We see the private moment, and then we "see more" as the music begins that withdrawing motion in which, with a mighty relief, all nature stirs and wakes. Actually, we should see this, or something close to it, on the stage, but unless you're very quick you'll miss the little clump of waxworks royalty on their throne being whisked out of sight in mid-yawn. The action is much too simple for what the music is doing—

which may be the reason the audience giggles and then hastily recomposes itself when it realizes it's going to get another! a new! pas de deux.

If we're lucky, we see it performed by Antoinette Sibley and Anthony Dowell, on whom it was set, but we may wonder why on earth it was set on them in this ballet. It would look better out of context. The music that Petipa discarded is entr'acte music (which it becomes in Balanchine's version of *The Nutcracker*). Originally, it was to bridge the moments between the Panorama and the Awakening. We have followed the Prince's long journey to the sleeping forest, and now we await the lifting of the spell. To compose a pas de deux to this music is not to misuse it—like so much of Tchaikovsky, it is very serviceable dance music—but the kind of dance music it is, is not the kind of dance music that characterizes the ballet; and the kind of choreography that goes with such music is not Petipa's kind of choreography. Ashton's pas de deux, even when danced by Sibley and Dowell, makes no sense as part of the production; it's a rupture in style. Tchaikovsky's ballet is not so far from us in time that its conventions can be violated even if they cannot be reactivated. The same with Petipa: you can stick with him or abandon him completely, but you cannot cancel him at convenient moments. It's surprising to see a choreographer like Ashton, so sensitive to period style in his Garland waltz and in the new "Fairy of Joy" variation, collaborating in such a blunder.

This isn't the only blunder in the new production. In general, the ballet strikes me as badly edited, indifferently staged, and decoratively coy. But the entr'acte pas de deux is a key weakness and one from which the production never recovers, unambitious though it may be. There were plenty of holes in the old version, but it held the stage. This one barely holds the attention. It doesn't, as seems to be its wistful intention, reconstitute Tchaikovsky in a lazier, more domestically fragrant English vision of an Arthurian romance; it only punishes and confines him in a theatrical perspective more suited to the dimensions of a Delius or a Sir Arnold Bax. The production is at best a handsome caprice; at worst, it is an insult to the militant sincerity of Tchaikovsky's imagination and of his temperament, which was Russian, pessimistic, and aristocratic to the core. I don't find any of these qualities at variance with the "French" delicacy, the ecstasy and childlike directness of emotion which are mirrored in this music. I do find them at variance with the peculiarly faithless spirit of the production and can only conclude that the people responsible for it either (a) haven't listened to the story Tchaikovsky is telling, (b) don't know how to produce it, or (c) imagine they can tell a better one.

a) *Haven't listened.* Tchaikovsky's music throughout the ballet is, like Dickens's writing, protocinematic in its pacing of events and in its clear and continual opening-up of imaginary perspectives through which the action assumes color, size, and detail in our minds. It makes you *see*. The extraordinary visual suggestiveness of Tchaikovsky is present in other scores of his, too—in *Swan Lake* notably, but also in music not intended for the stage: the *Manfred* Symphony, the orchestral suites, the overture-fantasy *Romeo and Juliet* are especially tantalizing. The difference between *Swan Lake* and *The Sleeping Beauty* is that in the latter ballet Tchaikovsky's natural powers of visual suggestion are focused in the second-by-second shaping of a dynamic theatrical fantasy that could really be expressed on the stage. *Swan Lake* suggests more about the dance theatre than that theatre can express, which may be why it's the favorite ballet of people who have never seen a ballet. The one ballet of Tchaikovsky's written without Petipa's collaboration, it did not find its form until it was revised under Petipa's supervision, and in Ivanov's conception of the swan it acquired a transfixing image. Yet even today its poetry seems more hypothetical than real. *Swan Lake* is a dramatic poem written for a medium that does not exist.

The Sleeping Beauty, on the other hand, was written for a theatre capable of the kind of ambient spectacle that was overtaken by the movies. Strangely, the score is faster and more fluid than *Swan Lake*. If the fantasy in *Swan Lake* is still largely mental and abstract, in *The Sleeping Beauty* it is of an absolute pictorial distinctness, the stage pictures now melting and flowing, now packed with detail, now void and still with one figure moving toward us as if in closeup. One of the wonders of the score is the extent to which it suggests the plasticity of theatre—suggests separate resources of dance, pantomime, and architecture, and suggests also what the secret potency of their proportions is. Of the fairies, Carabosse only mimes. The others only dance. The Lilac Fairy alone both mimes and dances. The speed we move at in this imaginary world would be impossible without the particularized sensation we get from everything in it. The abrupt shifts in scale the ballet makes between intimacy and grandeur, the many shifts in mood and subtle leaps in rhythm, are movielike in their flexibility, yet they are every one of them of and for the stage, exactingly composed to the requirements of the particular theatrical technique it takes to render them. One could not make a decent movie of *The Sleeping Beauty*. I may describe its effects of speed and emphasis and contrast as movielike; one might as well say they are dreamlike. It is only description, a metaphor for their emotional reality.

Metaphorically, then, I suggest that Petipa wrote a script and Tchaikovsky directed it. The score is the ballet. We still have some of Petipa's dances and they are glorious. We have, besides, in the Royal Ballet production some exceptionally careful restorations. What we do not have is the details of Petipa's actual production—his mise en scène—but even if we had nothing, we have the music for which he provided an excruciatingly detailed minutage. This was expert dramaturgy. This was precision engineering in the ballet. It is what Tchaikovsky produced on orders from Petipa ("Give me four bars of yes and four bars of no, three-four time")—not only filling out the expressive content of a scene but flooding it with meaning—that is our main text. In a sense, the ballet comes to us pre-staged. When in doubt, we need only listen for a cue.

When we listen, we realize that we are in the grip of a master dramatist who with equal skill places us now within his characters' minds and hearts, now on a great height viewing the design of an allegory as it unfolds. Thus, in Act I, the music cries out with Aurora when she is stricken, a few moments later drawing down the deep, sweet darkness of her sleep and the sleep of an entire kingdom. In the next act, the music by its pronounced early-eighteenth-century intonation places us in another world a hundred years later and gives us a sharp, almost satirical depiction of the kind of court life out of which the Prince steps. The present production suggests not the slightest sense of the passage of time, and its hints of decadence are limited to having the Prince borne on in a sedan chair. The characterization of the Countess (formerly so interestingly vicious, especially in Julia Farron's performance) is limited to having her borne out, rather early, in the same chair. Scenically, it is exotic to the point of having no point, suggesting some odd country where people wear furs and disport themselves in the middle of a slag heap. The period is the same as in the Prologue and Act I—and in the pre-Raphaelite wing of the Tate Gallery.

After the Vision Scene, Tchaikovsky gives us a wonderful moment when the Prince's heart leaps in his eagerness to be off on the journey that will take him to the woman whose existence has just been revealed to him. This music—so crucial to the Prince's character (in the score Tchaikovsky writes, "Désiré implores the Lilac Fairy to take him to Aurora") and so suggestive, in its agitato reprise of the Rose Adagio theme, of the pairing of his destiny with Aurora's—used to be given by the Royal Ballet and given again when Tchaikovsky has it recur after the kiss. In the later years of the former production, it was given only the second time. Now it is not given at all. Similarly with that moment in Act I when the Lilac Fairy reclaims Aurora's life from Carabosse. The transition—the modulation toward the light and peace that the Lilac Fairy stands for—is cut.

The passages that I have cited take only a few seconds, yet their omission deprives us of vital links in the action. These minor cuts, like others that occur throughout the ballet, are harder to understand than the major ones that dispense with whole characters like Gallison the tutor or Red Riding Hood. Such penny-wise deletions have the effect not of tightening up the action but of forcing it in fits and starts. The directors undoubtedly think that twentieth-century audiences are quicker of eye and instinct than nineteenth-century ones. If that is true, it is true only in relation to twentieth-century entertainments. When we are going at nineteenth-century pace, we need nineteenth-century detail. We don't accept abridged editions of Dickens. We don't cut out and frame bravura patches of Delacroix's brushwork because the action painters of the fifties sharpened our fancy for such things. But we do cut the scenario of *The Sleeping Beauty* without regard for a dramatic structure which carries us up to and away from a succession of climaxes carefully distributed over the course of a long evening. Interfering with that structure shortens the clock time of the ballet but not that other time in which the ballet happens in the imagination of the audience. When structural cuts are made, we experience a disintegration of our nervous sympathy that makes the ballet more difficult to endure than if it had been allowed to happen in its own time. We open the first act hard on the Garland Waltz, omitting the scene with the knitting women that prepared us for the fatal spindle. We start Act III with the Polonaise. But such is our folly that the ballet actually seems to grow longer. The new *Sleeping Beauty* is not only dramatically perfunctory, it's a bore.

b) *Don't know how.* I suspect the knitting-women scene was cut not because it saved time but because the directors of this production didn't know how to put it right. A truncated version of the scene Tchaikovsky wrote, it always looked frantic and crabbed and unintentionally somewhat hilarious. Here were these three crones down near the footlights with their elbows pumping to beat the band. Couldn't the designer, Henry Bardon, or whoever it was who put those ladies with their beautiful medieval tapestry screens into the Prologue, have found a way to get them back into the first act? Anything would have been better than introducing and hastily dispatching a harmless old lady whom we've never seen before and who doesn't even turn out to be Carabosse in disguise.

In producing *The Sleeping Beauty,* the hardest part is knowing where to put the intermissions. In that respect, it's harder to produce than *Swan Lake,* in which usually only the last act is anti-climactic. The great series of stumbling-blocks is in the second, Vision-Panorama-Awakening-Wedding, half of the ballet. Compared with what lies ahead, the Prologue and Act I go like a song.

The dilemma lies in deciding whether to sever Act II from Act III after the Vision Scene or after the Awakening. If after the Vision Scene, the Panorama may or may not be given by the orchestra as a prelude to the next act. It may or may not be played to a dropcloth (as it was in the Bakst version for Diaghilev*), but the chances of staging it are next to impossible because the stage is already burdened with machinery for the transformation that must

*From contemporary accounts of the Bakst production it is clear that no break took place between the Awakening and the Wedding, although one most certainly did occur either before or after the Panorama. Cyril Beaumont

take place between the Awakening and the Wedding. If the break occurs after the Awakening, as in the original production and the present Royal one, the big transformation scene can come with the end of the Vision Scene, leading into the Panorama and then out of it to the Awakening. But here the ballet runs the risk of an anticlimax much worse than *Swan Lake*'s. Even if the audience can be coaxed back into the mood of the lakeside story after the glittering ballroom scene of *Swan Lake*, in *The Sleeping Beauty* there's no story to get back to. Another difficulty is that for *Swan Lake* Act IV Tchaikovsky wrote not enough music, while for *The Sleeping Beauty* Act III he wrote almost too much. In *Swan Lake*, the story, unless pieced out by additions to the score, winds up almost in the fashion of an epilogue. In *The Sleeping Beauty*, the dance divertissement of the Wedding Scene is such a sharp departure from the kind of spectacle we've been watching all evening that it's almost like another ballet—almost like *The Nutcracker*, in fact. But *The Nutcracker* has only two acts. It's hard to get a fresh grip on our attention so late in the evening—and then ask us to watch anything close to a full suite of the dances that Tchaikovsky wrote for Aurora's wedding. My memory tells me that that is exactly what the Kirov did ask us to do, but then the Kirov didn't bloat the previous act with an irrelevant pas de deux. (It put its irrelevant pas de deux in place of the Vision Scene.) And the charm and novelty of the Kirov's Wedding was worth staying for. The Royal's present production calls us back from intermission for a Wedding the only apparent purpose of which is to hurry up and finish the ballet.

Most people object to this new Wedding not only because it's so curt and claustrophobic (it takes place in a kind of *Ivanhoe*-like mead hall or pavilion with a diminishing perspective like a wind tunnel) but because the festivities are unbalanced between classical and character dances. There is only one character dance—Puss in Boots and the White Cat. I agree with the objection, but then I object to the cats, too. Out of so much that is so seldom seen, I would have preferred Red Riding Hood, or Cinderella, whose music is so lovely. But the strongest objection that can be made to this act is that it has obviously been worked on with an exasperation known only to people who have seen it and dealt with it too long from the inside and are now looking worriedly at their watches. Yes, the hour is late. Florestan and his sisters were charming (whoever invented them?), but they've been replaced by somebody and her brothers, who dance to even less of the music that

---

suggests that the break came after, and that Bakst actually contrived to stage the Panorama, a very vivid one in Beaumont's description, right after the Vision Scene. But, as in many descriptions of *The Sleeping Beauty*, it is not clear whether the vivid pictures we get are of things that actually happened on the stage or of things suggested to the mind of the writer by the music. Sacheverell Sitwell, another constant observer of that 1921 production, states explicitly that the Panorama *followed* the intermission, and that it consisted merely of the music played to one of Bakst's dropcloths, in the manner of an entr'acte.

Tchaikovsky wrote for this episode. The Bluebirds (so called) come on much too soon and do a fussily worked-over version of their formerly beautiful dance, and then there are those damn cats. Here's the grand pas de deux (what, again?), and before you have a chance to notice the absence of the Three Ivans and be grateful for it, the ballet is over. Not enough charm, wrong kind of novelty.

What shows appallingly in this act—exasperation and exhaustion—shows also, I think, in the big decision to stage the Panorama in Act II. This decision forces everything that follows onto a downhill path—the phony pas-de-deux ending of the act, the anticlimax of Act III. It needn't have.

For the twenty years that the Royal had to dance it (1946–66), the production that Oliver Messel designed served every purpose but this: it had nothing to show for the Prince's journey by water, with its long cantilena gradually subsiding into the murmurs of the enchanted forest. This journey (the Panorama) the company now stages for the first time with one of those dry-ice mists that covers the stage (in preparation for which the whole of the act takes place behind a scrim). The stage becomes an underground river; the Prince steps into a small motorboat driven by an anonymous helmsman and chugs off to the Tunnel of Love. A ripple of green light on the scrim shows us the movement of water while concealing a change of scenery.

This is exciting in a whimsical sort of way, but the idea uses itself up too quickly. Karsavina tells of a Panorama of 1895 in which a succession of sights came into view. One of them was of hunters and hounds frozen in their tracks by the spell in the middle of a great park. The mixed-media proponents of the sixties have lived in vain if dry ice is all we have to challenge the painted forests and living tableaux of the nineties. Why not an actual movie on the scrim (a better excuse for a scrim) instead of a stage effect that is exhausted long before the music? If the Royal had used a movie or a series of projections for the Panorama, the stage would have been left clear for the only transformation scene that really matters—the one between the Awakening and the Wedding. And the way would have been open to try something really novel and worth trying in an era when even movies are getting longer: the presentation of Acts II and III, Vision through Wedding, without a break. At the very least, a movie would have allowed the Prince really to go somewhere. Where he goes is back to the set of the previous act. The script has him fight off some monsters (giving the unnecessary impression that Aurora is being held captive when it's enough that she's comatose), climb a wall, and at length bestow the kiss that revives her for their big new pas de deux. The awakening of the court is barely indicated, and the curtain drops on the diminuendo ending of the pas de deux.

The comic-book excitement of this scene doesn't compare, to my mind, with what used to happen in the old Messel version. There, to a succession of light-changes, with details of the castle and its surroundings getting ever clearer and larger to the eye, the Prince simply crossed and recrossed the stage, and in a few moments he was standing in the bedchamber. It was the very ease and freedom of his entry that thrilled—as if all this had lain for a hundred years asleep, awaiting only his appearance to be brought back to life. The Messel version also had a diminuendo end to the second act, but it came earlier, when the Prince embarks on his journey with the Lilac Fairy. The Royal then used to give the Panorama music (sometimes) as an overture to Act III, which commenced with the approach to the castle and continued through the Awakening to the Wedding, a brilliant transformation scene in which we were allowed not only to watch as the entire court participated (as Sacheverell Sitwell wrote of this production, ". . . the veil lifts, the cobwebs and the mists are dissipated and we behold the palace of the Sleeping Beauty in all its pristine splendour") but also to settle ourselves for the great dance divertissement that is to come. It was all one superb theatrical gesture, from the moment the curtains parted on the sleeping forest to the moment when, on a brightly lit "pristine" stage, Florestan and his sisters stood in place for their pas de trois. The ballet then rose to its natural peak in the bridal pas de deux.

Any great classic has three separate lives: what it was for the men who made it, what it meant to the history of its art (i.e., its "legend"), and what it became in the process of revival. Sometimes a revival is so successful or so important historically that it starts another series of incarnations—a sub-classic, as it were. The model for the Messel production of 1946 was obviously Diaghilev's London revival of 1921, but it is doubtful whether the directors of the company at that time sensed the significance of what they had in *The Sleeping Beauty*. They thought they were prolonging the afterglow of the Maryinsky twilight (Diaghilev had already done that) when in fact they were seeing the dawn of a great new classic for English dancers. At her New York début in 1949, Ninette de Valois wanted to open not with *Beauty* but with the contemporary ballets by herself and Robert Helpmann which to her represented English dancing. But she did open with *Beauty,* and the result of that opening was that the ballet became more important to the life of the company than any other. Still the company didn't see what they had. They kept it up loyally, believing both the people who said it was a "museum piece" and those who said it was an English classic, really. It was all a great strain. The present production capitalizes on the ballet's "Englishness" but in the dreariest way possible. It's like a revolution carried out from within by petty bureaucrats bored with their jobs. And considering how long the English have been in the *Beauty* business (thirty-one years if you go back to the Nadia Benois production of 1939; longer if you start with Diaghilev's passing of the torch in 1921), it's no wonder that they should have become more than a little bored with it by now. Besides, the Messel production was falling apart, and not for the first time. So the Royal called in Peter Wright, an all-around Mr. Fixit of ballet, and said, Give us something new, make it English if you can, and while you're at it . . .

c) *Tell a better story.* Don't destroy the ballet, Mr. Wright, just make it "now." They would have done better to call in Zeffirelli or Visconti. Mr. Wright's reputation is inscrutable. The story his production tells is one of simple lack of confidence—in the ballet, in the company. In a sense, it's the inside story of the company and something of a scandal.

It's understandable if the company had really come to identify the Messel production with the ballet that Tchaikovsky and Petipa created and to assume, furthermore, that it was theirs for the changing. This was the ballet in which Margot Fonteyn reached international stardom, pulling the company up after her. Fonteyn was *Beauty. Beauty* was the Royal. And the Royal didn't believe in *Beauty* as much as it believed in Margot. Now, with Fonteyn on the threshold of retirement—panic. Smash the image. If international audiences were silly to rave over just one ballerina out of a stageful of spectacle (such as it was), the Royal makes matters worse by reducing the spectacle still further and splitting the action between female and male stars. It's a His-and-Hers ballet. The ballerina still possesses Act I with its Rose Adagio and variations. In Act II, Florimund gets a new solo (we've had Her, now let's have Him) and, after the Vision Scene, gets to ride around the stage in that little boat and fight monsters. And to make sure our interest isn't taken by extraneous persons, the Lilac Fairy, a five-star general in the former production, is broken to the rank of master sergeant. The role of Carabosse loses almost all its force for no longer being played *en travestie* and on wheels (wooden wheels, as I recall, on which the black coach bore down like a thundercloud upon a suddenly foolish, suddenly dear little court). The idea of Carabosse as a heavily aged, insulted old queen was simple dramatic counterpoint; you didn't need a star to put it over, although star mimes would often be cast in the part—Frederick Ashton, Ray Powell, Stanley Holden, Alexander Grant. In the old days, Robert Helpmann would often double the role with Florimund.

And you don't need a star for the Lilac Fairy if the production treats her as one. It's wonderful how in the Prologue Mr. Wright contrives to keep losing her by changing all the diagonals. Once the apex of any triangle, the capstone of any arch, the Lilac Fairy is now more like the fairy nobody invited than Carabosse is. The seventh fairy whom this production adds to Petipa's train of six takes a lot of the play away from her. Mr. Wright does the rest. And her movements following the Awakening bear all the earmarks of "We've got her on, now how do we get her off?" Of course, in Maryinsky days the Lilac Fairy was a star, Petipa having assigned the part to his own daughter and Tchaikovsky having clearly made her prominence and importance one of the major motifs of his score. Musically and dramatically, the ballet is a duel between the Lilac Fairy and Carabosse. In this production, they are barely tolerated.

Still, and for all its mangled notions of hierarchy, the Prologue is the best part of this show. It's the one act that still looks like *The Sleeping Beauty,* that still has space and light in it. I think it also looks like a beehive. But the oddities of decor and costume are just fanciful enough to be interesting in a positive way; they don't spoil things as much as they will later. And the grand design of Mr. Wright's new-style *Beauty* ("It's just a story of young love, folks") hasn't yet emerged.

With all the protection they get, the current young Auroras and Florimunds of the Royal Ballet don't make a more exciting show of their parts than they did in the old production. Except for the dull entrance she now has to make, the ballerina's part is basically no different from what it was before. You'd think that, with Tchaikovsky setting the scene, no ballerina's entrance could be really dull, least of all this one, and yet . . . In place of the exciting entrance Aurora used to make—a fake one followed in an instant by a real one—we now see her come over a bridge and down some stairs. The old entrance was like nothing else in ballet. The new one is, too—it's like everything but ballet (operetta, Broadway, old film musicals). If Mr. Wright thinks he's making it easier for a ballerina to live up to our expectations by toning down her entrance, he isn't; he's making it harder. But maybe he doesn't think he was toning it down, maybe he thinks he was toning it up? With Mr. Wrights like this, the Royal Ballet doesn't need any Mr. Wrongs.

Anthony Dowell, obviously the star for whom the new Florimund was choreographed, is the finest classical stylist before the public. In the Vision Scene, he really seems to be seeing an apparition come and go. (Nureyev, charming everywhere else, looks as if he's playing hide-and-seek.) The new bits focus on Dowell's specialties as a dancer. When he and Miss Sibley do the new pas de deux, we see two stars who have already been typed—Sibley as the fearless plunging instrument of Dowell's archery as in *The Dream*—and who will be doing *The Dream* forever because that is what people are paying to see.

The Sleeping Beauty isn't, of course, about one star or two but about a parade of stars. It's the grandest classic a company can own. I used to think the English dancers in the old version most wonderful at the very end, doing the mazurka (the leads don't join in now—infra dig) and getting quite carried away with it until Tchaikovsky interrupted them with his heavy anthem. Then they would all line up and pose as much like Russian royalty as they could. But it wasn't the Romanov court and it wasn't Louis XIV's; it was the

Court of St. James's. Or it was all three at once. I don't see these things any more. The production wants me to see something else—Camelot, I guess. All this Franco-Russian energy forcing a briar rose.

Since I've rhapsodized certain of its effects, I want to make it clear that I don't think the Messel production was all that much better. (Franklin Pangborn voice: "Thank heaven! If I see one more colonnade or one more plashing fountain on the stage of this theatre, I think I'll scream.") But its horizon was right. The fake opulence of 1946 should have led on to something more nearly real in the 1970s; it was a halfway house, not the dream castle itself. Significantly, the new production was staged on the eve of the twentieth anniversary not of its London but of its New York premiere. New York was the making of the company, they say; but it was the start of the unmaking of the ballet. I remember a remark of Richard Buckle's at the time, something to the effect that "the fate of a company is poised on the slender point of one ballerina." Is that what *The Sleeping Beauty* had become? Not really, but everyone thought so. Since we can't do *Miracle in the Gorbals,* dear Margot, it's all up to you. Was it? Not really, but everyone thought so, Margot most of all, perhaps. I wasn't there, but I believe she was perfectly splendid; and we and the company and the ballet are in debt to her to this day. Fonteyn's magnificent effort made fine publicity, but its effect was finally narcotic. The ballet went to sleep, snoring over its press notices by the library fire.

It was in New York that everything began to go wrong, at first subtly, then drastically. In its second most important reincarnation in our time, a masterpiece was being surrendered—ruinously—to a whole new legend. *The Sleeping Beauty,* that dear old crock, had saved the company when it didn't want to be saved, it wanted to shine in vital modern works. The male dancers of the company, gaining strength after the war years, grew tired of having to worship the star image that the part of Aurora had become. And the company's notorious policy of scaled casting—putting stars in support of the stars who were really Stars and dropping everybody down a peg when the lowercase stars danced in place of *the* Stars—kept things permanently on ice. This pecking order has ruined the life of more than one ballet, and it stops careers dead. Ann Jenner has advanced to dancing a Bluebird to Fonteyn's Aurora rather than just to Sibley's or Park's, but we should have seen Jenner as Aurora years ago. By the time we do, there'll be another potentially great young dancer being held back at Bluebird level. And if you don't think it matters to a dancer which "great" part she gets to do in *Beauty,* ask one. Ask the Lilac Fairy. The company in 1970 has become more anxiously star-conscious than ever; it has even rescaled its greatest classic to the proportions of secondary stardom—the whole thing has been dropped into lowercase. Naturally, it isn't terribly exciting in performance.

All ballet companies are crazy, but each is crazy in its own way. It's almost justice that the new production has gone to Rossetti and Burne-Jones for its visual style. All these years asleep and *Beauty* wakes up bonkers.

ON THE CLOSING NIGHT of the engagement, we had to endure from Sir David Webster one of those traditional Royal Ballet curtain speeches which rehearse the early circumstances of the company's début in New York more than twenty years ago. These English-Speaking Union speeches are accepted in good grace by the audience as the obligatory fatuities they are; nothing could be more harmless than hands-across-the-sea and all that. But ah, these English. Give them half a chance and they'll always slip it to you. Ninette de Valois, a past mistress of the needle, used regularly to congratulate the stupid Americans on their ability to appreciate fine classical dancing (meaning her). I remember the speech of hers that ended the Royal season that followed the first New York season of the Bolshoi Ballet. How relieved she was, she said, to find that New Yorkers could still love the Royal after we'd seen the Bolshoi. And Sir David this year chose to remind us yet again (we've heard it dozens of times) how, long ago, he'd been offered a "most unsuitable theatre" for the first appearance of the Royal in America, and how he'd held out for the Met, and how the rest was history, etc. Even if you didn't know that the theatre in question was the New York City Center, which, unsuitable or not, became the home for fifteen years of the New York City Ballet, the remark was ungracious. One may mention the unheated guest room to one's host, but one doesn't go on mentioning it for twenty-one years, especially if one has never slept in it. But do these people think we have no ballet life of our own, nothing to warm us on the cold winter nights when the Royal (or the Bolshoi) is out of town?

This is a crucial year for the Royal Ballet. Ashton is stepping down; the entire company is being reorganized under new directors who are going to have to decide what course the company takes in the next decade. Signs of disrepair and demoralization were evident in the season just past. There is a lot for the Royal to do. Let them stick to their knitting women.

—from *Ballet Review,* Spring 1970

ALASTAIR MACAULAY

The Big Sleep
THE SLEEPING BEAUTY AT ITS CENTENARY

With no other ballet could the idea of a centenary be so resonant. There is, for one thing, that hundred-year sleep in the ballet. And the ballet itself is full of different layers of history, of different centuries. Its own performance history, studded with such dates and places as 1890 in St. Petersburg, 1921, 1939, and 1946 in London, is a crucial thread of the history of the art. And, then, survival and rebirth are among its subjects.

Pasternak said that he loved Pushkin's poetry because it was "full of *things*"; and this surely is true more of *Beauty* than of any of the old ballets. It is alive with the variety not only of ballet but also of life itself: as when in Petipa's—or, better, Balanchine's—Garland Dance in Act I the stage is full of men, women, and children; or when peasants and courtiers all dance in the farandole. It can be a great ballet in the theatre, but it is elusive—far more so than *Swan Lake* or *The Nutcracker*. During the seasons when there is no great *Beauty* to watch, however, it remains a marvellous *idea* of a ballet to run through in one's head—which is the only place where some details will probably now ever happen, such as the effect described in my favourite sentence from Petipa's scenario, when Aurora and the court awaken: "The dust and cobwebs disappear, candles illumine the room, the fire flares up in the fireplace." This clinching stroke, like many others in the ballet, might well belong in a novel—like the master of ceremonies whose hair is torn out and who, because it can never grow again, wears a fantastic wig ever after; or the foolish well-meaning knitting-women; or the hunt and the game of blind man's buff (subjects painted by Fragonard); or the journey by water through the sleeping forest; the arrival at the enchanted palace. The ballet is alive with the excitement of what nineteenth-century music-theatre could do. The *panorama mobile* of the Act II water-journey, which never works today as Petipa and Tchaikovsky intended, was based—like a similar journey in Act I of Wagner's 1882 *Parsifal*—on an earlier *Beauty* ballet: the 1829 *La Belle au bois dormant* by the librettist Scribe, the composer Hérold, the choreographer Aumer, and the designer Ciceri. And Petipa would have been influenced too by the precedent of Jules Perrot's 1849 *ballet-féerie* tale of a heroine over whom good and evil fairies conflict, *La Filleule des fées*—one of the first ballets revived by Perrot for Russia (in 1850) and one of his most unusual.

Three or four different centuries seem to exist at the same time in *Beauty*. The Prince and his retinue dance an eighteenth-century minuet; the awakened courtiers dance in Act III (according to the ballet's plan) a seventeenth-century sarabande; and the music of every act of the ballet is steeped in the great dance of the nineteenth century, the waltz. Primarily *Beauty* is about Versailles and the spirit of Louis XIV. Louis, who as a young man had seemed a young Apollo to the diarist John Evelyn, who took his famous Sun symbol from ballet and who was never seen to make an ill-considered or ungraceful gesture, made Versailles a court whose life of ritual and etiquette was described as "a perpetual ballet." But *Beauty* is also, in Act II, about the eighteenth century—about the endurance of Versailles after Louis; and it suggests also the replication of Versailles in Imperial Russia. At the ballet's last climax, the old French anthem "Vive Henri Quatre" rings out. Now, at Covent Garden, the Lilac Fairy returns with her retinue to the stage; but what Vzevolozhsky, Tchaikovsky, and Petipa had in mind here was "Apollo in the costume of Louis XIV, illuminated by the sun and surrounded by fairies." (Not the Sun King as the Sun God, but vice versa!) This symbolic gesture makes the full historical suggestion of the ballet clear: it is about the continuance of the classical ideal (Apollo) by way of the Sun King and the emergence in France of ballet—and by implication, as crystallized in Tsarist Russia. At that point at the Kirov, today, fountains suddenly burst forth—reminiscent of Versailles and of the Tsar's summer palaces. But Apollo, the Sun King, the eruption of fountains—these are symbols that only have force if *Beauty* demonstrates the enduring life of academic dancing. You should sense the ancient Greek ideals of proportion, balance, and harmony, and the vitality of bodily line as it evolved through the French and Russian academies as the ballet's lifeblood. The ballet says, as Diaghilev did, "Classicism evolves."

History is peculiarly present in the ballet's very steps. Just look at the Rose Adagio. Don't pay too much attention to the balances; they only became a canonical part of the role in the West with Margot Fonteyn in the forties.* But look at the positions involved before, during, and after those balances. Aurora, in profile to us, prepares—her left leg stretched before her in croisé tendu front. Then, as she takes a Prince's hand and arches one arm above her head, she raises that leg and keeps it angled behind her in effacé attitude back: which she sustains throughout the promenades, the balances, and the successive Princes. Finally, as she lets go, she opens that same

---

* "When I first did the Rose Adagio, I did not do any of those sustained balances; I cannot even remember when they first emerged. Although I never saw Markova do *Sleeping Beauty,* people described to me how she would maintain marvellous balance while changing hands with the various suitors, so then I started experimenting. The greatest difficulty is to manage to do it without making a great fuss; it is only really valid if one can make it seem as easy as getting off a bus." Margot Fonteyn in Keith Money's *The Art of Margot Fonteyn.*

leg into first arabesque, her head and upper body now stretched towards the audience.

Those three positions, which characterise Aurora throughout the ballet, derive from different eras. The tendu front we associate with the minuet and the eighteenth century; the attitude with the 1820s neoclassicism of Carlo Blasis; and the long-stretched line of the first arabesque with the late nineteenth century, with the era of the Imperial Russian Ballet which produced *The Sleeping Beauty*. Aurora, daughter to King Florestan XXIV, embodies the whole Versailles spirit of classical-academic codification that pervaded Louis XIV's Royal Academies—and its subsequent development. The tendu front, the attitude, the arabesque are signal events in every version of *Beauty*'s choreography, Russian or Western. Russian productions emphasise the baroque flavour of the ballet, with powdered wigs and a particular period flavour given to such older ingredients as that tendu front.* The importance of the attitude to *Beauty* has been widely acknowledged; and those balances have made it more so. The first arabesque is no less vital. In the long-lived 1946 Covent Garden production, with designs by Oliver Messel, the ballerina in her very first entrance would run on at the back, strike a first arabesque, and run off the other side, before re-entering in her lively first dance.† Aurora emphasises first arabesque in her big Act I violin variation,‡ and in each of her supported adagios—the Rose Adagio, the Vision Scene, the Wedding.

And when Aurora sleeps, ballet—formal, turned-out, classroom dancing; the *danse d'école*—sleeps. Ballet has existed before her, with her fairy godmothers; and it exists around her in her attendants and, later, her wedding guests. But, until she reappears as a vision, the only dancing that occurs at all is the court dances and the peasants' farandole. Dance continues; for a hun-

---

*The particular importance of this tendu pose to the Russian tradition of performing this ballet is confirmed by its presence in photographs of Anna Pavlova (in heeled baroque shoes, in Bakst's 1916 designs) and of Olga Spessivtseva's Aurora (in pointe shoes, in the 1921 Diaghilev-Bakst production); and by its presence in Balanchine's most *Beauty*-inspired choreography—*Theme and Variations*.

†Aurora's entrance in Act I has been the subject of much confusion and revision. I believe that in the 1890 St. Petersburg production she entered down a flight of steps, and that it was the 1921 Diaghilev production that added the "false entry" of Aurora running along behind a colonnade at the back of the stage. (In a 1984 interview, Frederick Ashton told me that this was the one specific image he had of Olga Spessivtseva in this production.) The 1939 Vic-Wells staging, like Soviet productions, used the flight of steps; the 1946 restored the first entrance along the back as in Diaghilev's staging; the 1968 revision reverted to the flight of steps. I do not recall the entrance in the short-lived MacMillan staging; Ninette de Valois restored the run along the back for the present, 1977 staging—but with Aurora stopping for only a little pose, such as in fourth position on pointe. The first arabesque seems to have been invented for the Messel production—and then to have been relegated to oblivion. (In the designs for Act I that are currently in use at Covent Garden, there is not space for Aurora to show a first arabesque.)

‡Vera Trefilova, according to Mary Skeaping, "in the variation stressed the arabesque allongée at the beginning and she stretched and stretched forward and then came out of it into attitude pose, with less emphasis on the chassé and glissade which came in between." (*A Conversation with Mary Skeaping*, Peter Anastos. *Ballet Review*, vol. 6 no 1.) This is very much the way that Fonteyn, by all accounts, phrased the variation; Antoinette Sibley has often spoken of how easily Fonteyn just "walked" from position to position here, whereas she, Sibley, "just had to" stress all the transitional steps.

dred years, however, ballet vanishes. That's why the structure of the ballet is spoilt if modern producers allow the Prince to dance either an allegro ballet solo during the Hunt scene or an adagio one immediately after it. It is part of the ballet's poetic impact that, when the Prince discovers Aurora, he discovers ballet. When Aurora appears as a vision, she enters dancing, as she had in Act I; and when the Vision fades, we don't see ballet again until Act III. Throughout *The Sleeping Beauty,* ballet's existence is imperilled—by the curse and then the spell. One of the work's themes, then, is the rebirth of ballet.

And isn't this the history of the art of academic dance? Ballet dies, again and again, or seems to. People have always been saying "It's all over, it's gone"; and they've often been right, inasmuch as what they've known as dance has come to an end. In 1739—just about the implicit time of *Beauty's* second act, and soon after the Paris debut of the bounding sixteen-year-old virtuoso ballerina La Barbarina—a French play had an old man conversing with his daughter on dancing old and new. He adheres to the dancing of Lully's day: "People used to dance; now they jump." (She replies: "People walked, people ran, but they didn't dance; it's only in our day that people possess this art . . . This is the real era of dance.") Ballet died again with the French Revolution; and again with the decline of the Romantic era; and again with the combination of the First World War, the Russian Revolution, and, in 1929, the death of Diaghilev. And now, after the deaths of George Balanchine and Frederick Ashton in the 1980s, we are witnessing another such death of ballet.

"She's dead!" Carabosse proclaims in Act I after the spindle has pricked Aurora's finger and she has fallen lifeless. General consternation and dismay, while Carabosse vanishes in a puff of smoke through the floor. Enter the Lilac Fairy, taking her time. "Can't you remember *anything?*" she mimes. (She does so at Covent Garden anyway; it's one of my favourite pieces of silly mime.) She goes on to remind them of her counter-prophecy. ("Oh, yes, *now* we remember," they all seem to say to each other.) It's comic. It's also beautiful, for she is saying, "She is not dead, but sleeps."

Aurora is not the only character in mythology who wakes from an enchanted sleep. Her story recalls that of Rip Van Winkle and, in the Nibelungen Ring story, that of Brünnhilde. (It was a coincidence that Perrault's original 1697 story of "The Beauty in the Sleeping Wood" was retold for English readers in Andrew Lang's *Blue Fairy Book* in 1889, while the ballet was in preparation. But in 1876 Tchaikovsky *had* seen Brünnhilde's awakening in the Bayreuth premiere of Wagner's *Ring* cycle.) All these stories, however, have important differences. Aurora's awakening isn't like that of Rip van Winkle, who wakes to a sense of misplacement and nostalgia. It's more like that of Brünnhilde, who has been laid to sleep and surrounded with a ring of magic fire that only a fearless hero can enter; when Siegfried does so, he wakens her with a kiss; she wakes to joy. The charm and the significance of Aurora's story are that the old world sleeps and wakes with her.

And, when she wakes, she gives the Prince her hand. The bestowal of hands—an image of betrothal—is one of the key choreographic signs of the ballet, and it is the sign that is emblazoned on the ballet's great adagios. We first see supported adagio while Aurora is in her cradle, when the fairy god-mothers, using their partners' support, show the attitudes, arabesques, and pirouettes that will become part of Aurora's adagios.* And more than giving Aurora a vocabulary, this adagio is the first choreographic demonstration of chivalry in the ballet. (Like the adagios that Aurora then dances in each act, its melody takes its flow and rhythm from the Lilac Fairy's theme.) The his-tory of supported adagio is not clear (there are hints of it in the way Fanny Elssler is described as using the support of her sister, Thérèse), but its spirit derives from the medieval concept of courtly love. And it seems now that *Beauty* is the first ballet to have made it central to our concept of classical ballet. A man helps a woman to perform on pointe feats that otherwise she could not do in that manner: in particular, long phrases in which she changes direction and shape while remaining on one pointe. This becomes noble and eloquent in Petipa, as later in Balanchine, because we are shown, elsewhere and during the adagio, the considerable extent of what the ballerina can do without support.

Aurora is not only the most classical heroine from the old repertory, she is also the most modern. As in the plotless Ballet of the Twentieth Century, Aurora is a heroine who hardly ever mimes, whose emotional inner life is not made important to us, who seems only to exist in terms of academic movement. And her steps make her real to us—make her the heart of the ballet. Like a work by Balanchine, this is a theme-and-variation ballet; as Feodor Lopoukhov may have been the first to note, Aurora takes steps and floor-patterns from each of her godmothers. Roland John Wiley has written in *Tchaikovsky's Ballets* that the sound world of Act III is less magical, more materialistic than that of the Prologue and Act I; the harp is replaced by the piano. Likewise Lopoukhov, whose Petrograd staging of *Beauty* was of immense importance, observes that whereas only effacé positions and en dehors movements are used in the Prologue and Act I, croisé and en dedans become part of the choreographic texture in Acts II and III, as if part of the shadow cast by Carabosse. The new world does not have the unclouded radiance of the old one. But it has more wisdom, as we see with Aurora's

---

*I base this on the assumption that the presence of cavaliers in the Prologue adagio as seen at the Royal Ballet is authentic Petipa. The Kirov and Bolshoi Prologue adagios, however, omit cavaliers from the choreographic climax, and instead have a striking line-up of fairies *un*-supported on pointe. Whether or not this was Petersburg Petipa, it probably became Petrograd Petipa, for Balanchine took that image and built on it in *Theme and Variations*.

dances, which rise to their most complex and various in her great third-act variation.

I spoke of the present death of ballet. Right now *The Sleeping Beauty* is one of the surest victims. Its inner life has steadily faded in Kirov, Bolshoi, and Royal performances during the last twenty years; nor has any other company definitively picked up its torch. But *Beauty* has always been a work in progress. When the current Covent Garden production was new, Ninette de Valois went on making improvements for the first nine months; and I'm always moved to think of her words then—"We must get it *right*." There are features that were so finely developed by post-Petipa generations—such as Fonteyn's balances—that they have now become part of the ballet. The hundred years of the ballet's performance history also contain several rebirths. The Diaghilev staging was surely one—the most influential failure in dance history. ("I have been fifteen years too early with this production," he said.) Only four years had passed since the Russian Revolution. How moving that Diaghilev, the originator of "Étonne-moi" and all that, should have chosen that moment to turn to this, of all the old ballets from lost St. Petersburg. Like Aeneas fleeing from Troy with the *penates,* the home-gods, of his old city, Diaghilev was, with his *Sleeping Princess,* rebuilding St. Petersburg in the West. Just as Ninette de Valois would later take those *penates* and made them central to Royal Ballet tradition. Just as Vzevolozhsky, Tchaikovsky, and Petipa had already taken Versailles and rebuilt it in St. Petersburg. Classicism not only evolves; it migrates.

—from *The Dancing Times,* May 1990

PAUL TAYLOR

One of America's great choreographers, Paul Taylor (born 1930) started dancing at Syracuse University, which he attended on a swimming scholarship. Soon he was noticed by Martha Graham, whose company he joined and for whom he danced many major roles, including Aegisthus in Clytemnestra. *In 1954, while still with Graham, he founded his Paul Taylor Dance Company, now in its fifty-fourth year. During his Graham years, he was "borrowed" by Balanchine to create a solo in* Episodes, *and then invited to learn* Apollo *and stay on at City Ballet, an offer he rejected. As a dancer he was a commanding presence—resembling, as Clive Barnes put it, "a doe-eyed Superman." His first notable piece, 3* Epitaphs, *was made in 1956, but the work that brought him unanimous and lasting acclaim was the 1962* Aureole. *Through the following forty-odd years, he has produced an extensive list of masterworks, in every mood, many of them designed by famous artists such as Robert Rauschenberg, Jasper Johns, and Alex Katz, and lit by Jennifer Tipton. Among his best-known works: the savage* Big Bertha, Esplanade *(a company signature piece),* Cloven Kingdom, Diggity, Arden Court, Le Sacre du Printemps (The Rehearsal), Last Look, Sunset, Company B, *and* Promethean Fire.

CLEMENT CRISP
Paul Taylor

It was love at first sight. During the 1950s and '60s, Dame Margot Fonteyn used to organise a gala matinee every year in aid of the Royal Academy of Dancing, of which she was then president. Her name was sufficient to guarantee that the dancers whom she invited were happy to appear in these jolly events, where a legion of hatted ladies were joined by eager balletomanes for an afternoon of usually blissful dance. Rudolf Nureyev made his first and sensational London appearance at one of these in 1961, and three years later Paul Taylor and his company were invited to appear. Taylor's presence in London was part of a brave sequence of American modern dance troupes whose visits to London owed much to the enterprise of Robin Howard and Francis Mason, then cultural attaché at the American Embassy. So, on the afternoon of November 17, 1964, at the Theatre Royal Drury Lane, the curtain rose on *Aureole* with Taylor and his artists buoyed up on the Handelian air, angels in some brighter dream.

We had already seen Martha Graham, Alvin Ailey, Merce Cunningham, and splendid and fascinating—or bewildering—they were. But what Taylor offered in *Aureole* was something different: dance which lived in its music as a bird in the air, and the buoyancy, the airiness of the movement, in its choreographic phrases as in its performance, was immediately lovely. Here was dance which proposed an image of its dancers, of humanity, as courteous, loving, generous-spirited. Civilised. Oh, so civilised! How could one not fall in love with, respond with utter delight to, such choreography, such performers—such Americans—and with Taylor as dancer, too, grand in physique, and as springing, as light-footed, as light-spirited, as his dances. (I felt—I think we all felt, as critics and commentators—this same joy when Carolyn Adams first appeared with the Taylor troupe. Not since Alicia Markova had there been an artist who trod the stage so lightly, who seemed to deny gravity—in every sense of the word—as her dance raced and soared above the stage.)

There followed London seasons by the Taylor company in which we could understand, and learn to love even more, the range of his choreography, the power of his imagination, and above all, the force of his humanity; which did not mean flag-day displays of dance in aid of some aesthetic or social good cause, but dance which spoke about how we were, how we might be—for good or ill—and how we should be. Taylor, speaking for the angels, also knew (and knows) how to talk of the devil. I am reminded of the fact that Taylor has made boxes, rather like, but wholly unlike, those made by Joseph Cornell. In them, found objects are meticulously placed (Taylor's eye is that of an artist-painter or sculptor in his choreography, too) to suggest a location or a view of the world in which these found objects were discovered.

Years ago he sent me a box composed of things he had gathered on the shoreline in Cape Cod. I do not know the place, yet because of the box, I do know it. Taylor's choreographies can sometimes be seen as resembling these boxes. From the life of his nation, from the concerns of his time, he finds objects, incidents, manners, tendencies, joys, and warnings, which fire his creative imagination. The resultant dance works become pictures of American life or perspectives on society, grave or happy, and sometimes both at the same time.

Far too many choreographers today—damn them—make thunderous

comments—damn them again—on Life, which always has a capital letter in their thinking. As a critic based in Europe, I am faced almost every week with some abomination run up by one of the Euro-trash gang who dominate the "contemporary" dance scene here. From France and Sweden, from Russia and the German tanz-theater, from Spain and from the sluices and lowlands of Holland, and from the depths of the Belgian provinces, there lurch monsters. (Their creators make Baron Frankenstein seem like a plastic surgeon dedicated to making the ugly beautiful.) These dance works are hysterical, coarse-grained, unmusical, thumpingly pretentious, and lapel-gripping in their tedium.

Taylor's work is, I suspect, as "engaged" in its concerns about humanity as any of these detestable products of angst and bad choreography. But Taylor, first of all, makes dances rather than polemics or disgruntled commentaries. And it is the variety of his observations, the wide and unpredictable range of his creativity—What will he do next? Which trap will he spring from? Be sure it is not the expected one!—his receptiveness to musical ideas (for he is supremely musical in the shaping of his dances) that give Taylor's dances their vividness. I love especially his daring, that high-wire insouciance that enabled him to use Stravinsky's *The Rite of Spring,* a sacred dance text, not as yet another piece of sacrificial mayhem—and Lord!, the mayhem the Euro-gangsters commit with it—but as a work layered with ideas about cops and robbers, about a dance troupe, and with references to Nijinsky. Like some transcendental conjuror, Taylor kept producing surprises, glittering dance ideas and theatrical marvels, from a non-existent top hat. As choreographic virtuosity I know of few works to beat it.

That he can be tearingly funny, exquisitely light in heart and dance, we have seen in such soufflé triumphs as *Public Domain* or *Funny Papers* or the recent *Offenbach Overtures.* (Can one ever again take a duel seriously?) That he can be profoundly serious without seeming portentous, that he can dare and win in using the greatest music, we know from such works as *Orbs* (to late Beethoven quartet movements) or *Mercuric Tidings* (to Schubert symphonies) or *Guests of May* (to Debussy) or in his version of *The Rite of Spring.* About *Orbs* of 1966, I must here interpose a memory. Taylor brought it to London. In it we see the progress of the seasons cast in noblest dance, or (in the case of Autumn) as a wedding celebration with Taylor himself as the priest, having an oddly difficult time with a turkey. I looked, and was knocked out by its power. I had to return the next night to see it again and sat with a friend, a distinguished academic who, as the piece progressed, suddenly turned to me and said: "It's like watching God at work." Not blasphemous as comment, but searchingly true since the piece's theme was cosmic, concerned with the planets and the seasons. This daring is one of the signatures of Taylor's work—daring to use certain music, daring to treat of certain themes in dance, and then shaping dance perfectly to his ends.

Taylor is a cool-eyed, cool-headed observer of the worst aspects of human behaviour, and withal, compassionate in his observations. It is a common critical attitude to see Taylor's work in terms of blackest black and whitest white. Not, I feel, so. His works have colour, unexpected shafts of feeling, be they of joy or sheerest terror (as in *Last Look*) or as commentary upon the awfulness of sufferings in medieval life shown in *Agathe's Tale* or *Churchyard*. Taylor can certainly view the world with an unwavering gaze. *Big Bertha*, as a portrait of American social manners gone fearfully wrong, is chilling; the early *Scudorama*—I still see a curling wave of movement that crossed the stage—looked at mankind as shown, soulless, in Dante's *Inferno*; *Last Look*, which one can interpret as behaviour after an atomic disaster, chills utterly. (I remember leaving a Paris theatre after a performance and rushing to a café for a reviving cognac.)

Taylor also sees with a certain weary despair the awfulness of religious intolerance and of religious manipulation of people: *Speaking in Tongues* makes a fearful point, as does *The Word*, with its view of religious intolerance and doctrinaire obedience. And yet, as Oliver Edwards said to Dr. Johnson: "I have tried too in my time to be a philosopher; but I don't know how, cheerfulness was always breaking in." I suppose, ultimately, Taylor's work is coloured by hope, by belief. It is yea-saying, whatever the evils that dog man's footsteps (and they range, chez Taylor, from the crippling and deformed limbs of *Churchyard* to the breakdown of a family in *Big Bertha*).

That this is so is owed in part to Taylor's taste in music. As wiser men than I have remarked, only one differentiation matters: there is good music (be it Bach or Cole Porter) or bad music (be it Albrechtsberger or Lloyd Webber). Taylor knows only good music. It speaks to him, and he listens and makes dance that is beautiful, heart-lifting—think of the sublime *Lento* duet from Haydn's *Seven Last Words of Christ*, or his assurance in using Bach for *Promethean Fire* or that apotheosis of walking and sliding that is *Esplanade*, where our pedestrian activity is made joyful, fascinating, and then suddenly mysterious and emotion-riven in a family portrait. Taylor, like Balanchine, like Ashton, and like an awfully few other choreographers, hears music, then gives it a dance-form that never—never ever—betrays it.

Thirty years ago, Mary Clarke and I were asked to write a book about how choreography was made. We talked to a dozen dance-makers, not least Paul Taylor, who was in London with his company for a season at Sadler's Wells Theatre. The tour had been exhausting for the dancers and glorious for the audience, and among many things, Taylor made one statement that seemed to us absolutely indicative of why we loved his work so much. "It is important that a dance be a dance." Taylor's dances are dances, not messages, or protests, or arid exercises in moving people over the stage. Taylor makes dances that are, first and foremost, and last and always, about what the human frame can do when inspired by music, when liberated by technical prowess, and then shaped in action by a master. (His own dancing was superb: his grand physique—at six feet one inch he could command space in extraordinary fashion—was allied to a marvelous fluidity and something which I think of as buoyancy: his solo in *Aureole* was a formidable exercise in the changing of shapes, of impulse, of rhythms, which Taylor cast in what seemed one long, ravishing phrase. Subsequent performers have danced it well; none has so suggested that the dance was made on a single miraculous impulse that its inner variants of steps and positions could be so smoothly and musically stated.) What Taylor showed was danced *bel canto*. And as important ultimately as the dance itself was Taylor's stage presence: something joyous, generous, life-affirming, marked his path over the stage, and his belief in the dance itself.

Taylor's dance works are, in his own felicitous phrase, "Food for the eyes." They are about dancing, but in that dancing we discern multiple layers of behaviour, of meaning, of ways of making comment or delineating action. (In *Company B*, the Andrews Sisters' songs are perkily or sentimentally there; behind them Taylor discerns their period quality, their wartime resonance, and what war might mean to the men and women who heard them when they were new. We time travel as we watch, know sorrow as well as brighter feelings, and suddenly feel the terrible chill of bereavement.)

Paul Taylor speaks to us in his dances about ourselves. He makes jokes, he mocks, he despairs, he is compassionate, he produces throwaway lines and makes indictments. Supremely, he tells us about dancing. About what dancing can do as just dancing, about what dancing reveals of the human condition, and about what the human condition is, and might be (ideally or tragically.) His messages are dances (and his dances are sometimes messages—but not always), and we see and understand, or see and laugh and overlook, and need to respond to his every comment. He speaks also about himself, as an artist who must make movement because he cannot do otherwise. He looks. He sees—and how he sees! And how clearly he sees! He listens and fleshes out music for us. It is something about his very Americanness that seems to me to be so typical, beneficent, aware. In the extraordinary half-century since he started to dance and make dances—think of the political and international and social changes during those fifty years, and marvel at what we have lived through—Taylor's choreography has been engaged. Our world is the world of his dances—not on always very obvious terms, and without tub-thumping or carrier-pigeon message deliveries, but through awareness and spiritual grace and compassion. His work has been a light in the world. His dances have fed our eyes in the most generous, grandest fashion.

—from the program for the Paul Taylor Dance Company's
fiftieth anniversary, October 14, 2004

PAUL TAYLOR
Aureole

Aureole (1962) was Paul Taylor's first great success. A lyrical pure-dance piece, set to the music of Handel, it was created for the American Dance Festival, which generally featured the more Expressionist work of José Limón and Martha Graham. Today it is danced to acclaim around the world.

At this time—'62—modern dance is still keeping its distance from lyricism, "pure" or unexpressionistic kinds of dance, and reassuringly melodic music. There are a few exceptions—José Limón and Pearl Lang have done pieces that are primarily movement structures meant to match their Bach scores. But most modern choreographers are still oriented to asymmetrical angularities and use music such as Bartók or Wallingford Riegger—modern, but not too modern. *Aureole* has been commissioned by the American Dance Festival, where anything old is out. Unable to resist quirkiness, and always eager to ignore trends, I've accepted Handel, hoping to rankle anyone at the festival who thinks modern dance has to limit itself to modern music and weighty meanings. Am also hoping that a change of diet will be good for both audience and myself.

In another way, the dance is an attempt to get what I've learned in Louis Horst's classes out of my system. As Louis would've wanted, the dance's steps have been limited to a few basic seed steps—themes to vary in speed, direction, sequential order, and any other way that might make them seem less redundant. My favorite step in *Aureole*—a certain run with flyaway arms—is a direct and intentional steal from Martha's *Canticles for Innocent Comedians.* It may be a little off, but it's the closest I could come.

Something about simplicity has been on my mind. No puzzlements for folks to ponder, no stiff-necked pretensions from classic ballet, or even any of its steps. Just old-fashioned lyricism and white costumes. By the way, Dr. Tacet,* who's designed and sewn the costumes, isn't happy about having to use the elastic from Jockey shorts for the girl's waistbands, or about me substituting a white bathing suit for tights. And he pouted some when I ripped his ruffles and suppository-shaped decorations from the girls' skirts and tossed them into a trash can.

The dance's many entrances and exits are an attempt to give an illusion of a larger cast than five and to open up the stage space so that the dance will seem to be happening in a larger one than is bounded by the proscenium. The best parts of *Aureole,* to be seen only backstage, are the dancers' hurtling races through the dark crossover in order to make their next entrances on the opposite side of the stage. There are likely to be graceless collisions with unwary stagehands, the dancers' onstage expressions changing into ones of something less than angelic serenity.

As far as choreographic invention goes, and virtuosity, there isn't much of that in my duet with Liz Walton, but at this time there isn't a high premium put on these things. Even in this "pure" piece, feelings are foremost. "Dance" is a meaty word, and, naturally, there's more to it than firework displays. The duet is built on my own feelings for Liz—part fantasy and part real. As she changes from a cute kid with scrawny shoulder blades into a radiant woman, my admiration is on the upswing. I intend the duet to be easy and warm, also formal and distant. It's hard to say if the formal part is fantasy and the easy part real, or vice versa. Liz and I never discuss it, but the duet is a reflection of a real relationship, one that, as usual, is loaded with inexplicable duplicities.

The solo for me isn't set until the rest of *Aureole* is finished. This is due to procrastination pure and simple. I've told myself that the other dancers must first be well rehearsed and secure in their parts. But now rehearsal time is running out, and the long solo, which I'm beginning to wish in the worst way wasn't so long, is set on the commuter train to Adelphi, where I sometimes teach. In order not to attract attention, I stay in my seat drawing little stick figures in a pad and later copy the anatomically possible ones with my body. It's like learning a dance by mail—deciphering one of those Arthur Murray Teaches Dancing in a Hurry footprint diagrams. The main difficulty lies in keeping the flow going by passing through, rather than hesitating in, each position. It's been irksome to see other dancers lock themselves in to

---

*A pseudonym for himself.

positions as if to say, "Get this, everybody, I'm perfect—think I'll hold this pretty arabesque awhile longer in case your slow eyes don't notice." Though I'm able to get the hang of it, the matter of flow, as well as other things particular to the way I move, may become a problem if the role is ever taught to someone else.

The solo, done almost entirely on the left foot, is also unusual in that it's an adagio. Usually, in classic ballet anyway, adagios are danced by women. Though I haven't intended to get too involved with meaning, the Handel has a hymnlike sound, and, to amuse myself more than for any other reason, I've made the part as if it's to be performed by some kind of earth father who goes around blessing things. Doesn't travel much, but indicates expanding space with développés of arms and legs toward the four cardinal points. If done in a gestural way, these slow-motion semaphores may give the effect of being in an open plain which extends beyond the theater and out into the stratosphere. I have myself a pretty big image—Father Nature, religion, and the cosmos. The balances are deceptively simple—the solo's hardest part is the entrance in silence. It's a simple walk from the wings to stage center which has to be unselfconscious, friendly, and seem inevitably right. No matter how often I've practiced it, this easy walk scares me to death. It's going to strip me of dance steps to hide behind and leave me stark naked.

When *Aureole*'s premiere is only a few days off, four of its sections have been set, but not the fifth and final one. By my bending Horstian rules, the seed steps have become unreasonably transmuted beyond recognition. They're twisted backwards, sideways, and inside out. I've hit the bottom of the barrel and can't think of one more blessed way to vary them for the finale. How to fill up the remaining music? I tell myself what I once learned from Bob Rauschenberg—that the easy way is best—and go over to the rehearsal tape machine to snip off the pesty last movement.

Just then Edwin Denby comes into the studio to see a runthrough. He often treks to nickel-and-dime performances and ratty studios, where, if asked, he offers hesitant and gentle criticism. It's late morning, and he's probably been up all night writing poems in a microscopic hand, then left them to walk his thin frame and long feet from West Twenty-first to Thirty-eighth, perhaps savoring some noteworthy examples of ironwork façades along the way. Another guess is that he's arrived with no change in his pockets, he being the city's softest touch. Also generous with his time to many unestablished dance makers like myself.

Bet [Bettie de Jong] offers Edwin some coffee and shoos the studio cat from the middle of the floor. Tabby's always underfoot and loves to bask in beauty in the golden rectangle of light that falls from the skylight. Tail twitching, the cat saunters off in dignified retreat, then veers around to take a picturesque pose on Edwin's lap.

After we show the dance, Tabby seems unimpressed, but Edwin blinks cheerfully.

"Well, what do you think?" I ask, deep down preferring a couple of choice compliments, not criticism.

He answers mildly. "I think that perhaps it could be even better if a little something is added to finish it off."

"But, Edwin, there's no time! And ending this way gives more importance to the duet. It makes an unexpected ending."

This is wishful thinking. I know he is right.

Wishing us luck on the premiere, he apologetically nudges Tabby off his lap, rises, then shyly backs out the door.

With little time to lose, the dancers and I tackle a concluding apotheosis, or coda. Unable to bear the dull prospect of more tinkering with the same old used-up steps, I throw together the first that come to mind. A bunch of dizzy tilts, turns, breakneck cavorting. Even if the dance is no good, at least we'll have a workout.

And then on a bright day in August, Bet packs our costumes and magnetic orchestra into one small case and we all train up to New London. During the trip she completes a pair of tights she's been knitting for me, needles clicking away like Madame Defarge's. Dark-eyed Sharon Kinney is looking nicely complementary sitting next to Renee Kimball's fair splendor. Liz is radiating enthu-siasm, and Dan prattling. I'm a million miles away and scanning fields for butterflies—whites and sulphurs to match the fluttering ones in my stomach.

Arriving at Connecticut College, seat of modern ferment, ivied asylum of creative sweat, we go backstage to hug our lighter, Tommy Skelton. He smiles and bobs his Adam's apple up and down for us, looking a lot less skeptical of me than he had in this same place ten years ago. It's a homecoming. Merce and his troupe are the resident company this summer, along with José and his. I trust that Tommy's student stage crew will be more adept than I was. They're beginning to look awful young. Larry Richardson, who's pulling curtain, will one day, like me, be taking to the road with a group of his own. Here we are, all one big family. Am supposing that I can put up with a little generational repetitiousness.

The gang and I are to share a program with Katherine Litz, a dancer of delight whose solos are delicate flights of whimsy, a phantasmagoria dreamed up by an eternal ingenue. She does dilapidated aristocrats, fragile souls at their toilets in the twilight, romantic matrons with girlish tremors. My favorite is a dithering enigma in a sack. She never ceases to cheer her audiences, never seems to mind that her work isn't widely recognized, and never mentions her solitary struggles to continue work that deserves higher acclaim. We, her friends and fans, are nuts about her, but sometimes there are a few in the audience who seem confused by Katy's ladies. Let's face it, these are insensitive jerks. No art and no genius can ever be without touches of haziness and mystery. It's a big honor to be sharing the same program with her.

At the dress rehearsal in the darkened Palmer Auditorium a large piece of plywood has been placed across the back of some center seats. On it is Tommy's usual clutter of cue sheets, shaded desk lamp, metal ashtray brimming with Gauloise butts, and something new—a flashlight. Also as usual, Tommy's headset has gone stone deaf, and so technology is being replaced by primal shouting. "Put another amber gel on the special that's over stage center," Tommy calls to the crew.

Preoccupied with a sense of impending doom, I've finished a long warmup and, curious to see what Tommy has up his sleeve in the way of lights for *Aureole,* jump down off the apron and grope up the aisle. Noticing the flashlight, I ask nervously, "Does that mean you're expecting the light board to blow?"

"Nar," he twangs. "Your solo's going to be lit dark. It's for you so's you can see your way around the stage while you're dancing. I'll have a giant spotlight follow Dan."

"Skeleton, I'd have thought by now you'd have gotten rid of your New England twang. Hey, what's that ugly rope dangling down over there stage left? And what's that wrinkle in the eye? And why does this proscenium look so slanted?"

"Don't worry. Everything will be fixed by tonight. We'll have the audience all lean to one side so the proscenium will look straight."

Tommy's wit knew no bounds. Right now, though, I'm thinking he's not so funny. "Dancers, come out onstage so we can see what your costumes look like under light," I call, wondering how everyone can be so cheerful when we're about to dance the worst mess since spaghetti.

Tommy says, "Paul, how do you like this sunshine effect? Pretty gorgeous, huh?"

"Everybody looks yellow. If I'd wanted Orientals, I'd have gotten some in the first place."

"But that's the color of sunlight. We mix green light with lavender and out comes sunlight, see?"

"Yeah. I see green and lavender edges on their faces. Can't we just have plain white people in plain white light? Let's dump the sunshine this time. Also that soft focus you use for ripe old stars. Who needs it anyway?"

In professional lighting circles uncolored light is considered poor taste. Tommy, like his teacher Jean Rosenthal, favors shaded depth over flat visibility and has learned to mix his palette not like a painter's but according to unfathomable laws of light. However, more out of friendship than out of artistic beliefs—"compromise" being another word for "friendship"—he humors me by yanking all the gels.

After the dress rehearsal, I go downstairs to a dressing room where I make up to fateful ticks of my watch, indulging in as much fear and insecurity as I want. Involuntarily, my left big toe is twitching a little dance of its own. Can't help wondering if that might be a sign of approaching insanity. I get up to put on a dry dance belt, put it on upside down, take it off, put it on wrong again, sit down, get up, sit down. (Recollections need to be somewhat choreographed.) Noisy watch tells me to get into costume. I skid into Bet's room next door and say in a totally expressionless voice, "My costume. I can't find my costume."

With a double gesture, one hand denoting pity, the other disdain, Bet replies, "Oh, *Paul*—you have it on!"

How stupid of her to be so clever. Dutch Treat was always saying annoying things. Miss Treat is her other name. And she peppers her food too. Heavily.

What happened, and how *Aureole* felt to perform, are things that are nearly impossible for me to describe. To pare it down to basics: the curtain lifts, we depart from this world, find a far more vivid place, and then the curtain closes.

Toweling off quickly, reveling in relief for being not too tired to still walk, the dancers and I grope for each other's hands and force our leaden feet to scamper back onstage for a speedy bow before the audience gets a chance to escape. I'm making an effort not to look overly humble when a tidal wave crashes into us. They liked it; we like them—in that order. Catching a sideways glimpse of Sharon, I notice her brown eye brimming.

Friends and faculty come backstage to say complimentary things. Pal Babe's hand appears from between two people, offering me his program. On it are written the numbers of bows for each dance. By *Aureole* is a circled "12." Across the cover is lettered "I like Katy best." The Babe, bless him—tact was never his strong suit.

Wonderful Merce drops by to say he's thought my dancers wonderful, and grand José is gracious and supportive. Other than the experience of dancing itself, these rewards are best.

None of the troupe has any idea that this has been the first performance of a piece that we'll be dancing hundreds and hundreds of times. On five continents, in world capitals and Podunk towns, in North African desert heat, at the edge of Alaskan glaciers, in the moonlit Parthenon's shadow, under banyan trees. With happy hearts and grapefruit ankles we're to dance it in Rotterdam, Rosario, Riga, Rio, and Istanbul—in more corners of the globe than you can shake a leotard at. *Aureole* is to be performed in big, fancy opera houses and on shaky postage-stamp platforms, on slick parquet and splintery planks, on wax and linoleum and broken glass. It's to be danced with amoebic dysentery, Montezuma's revenge, bleeding hearts, and yellow jaundice, with sprained backs, split soles, torn ligaments, popped patellas, and a hernia or two. The usual. Orchestras of all ilks will play astounding tempi, often the correct ones. Magnetic tapes waver and sputter out, but the dance persists. We're to get quite tired, yet Handel never falters. He's our novocaine.

There are to be garlands of jasmine, too, often looped around our necks by almond-eyed strangers. At times paupers or great fortresslike socialites come to say that they've been touched in some meaningful way. Kings, queens, and bag ladies are to see it.

Today it's strange to imagine the many *Aureole*s that are danced by other companies, casts in many places, mostly dancers I've never met whose limbs move through the same shapes as ours, and who've probably grown similar calluses. God bless their poor little bare toes.

—from *Private Domain*, 1987

NANCY DALVA
Sunset

Six soldiers on leave, or simply walking in a park, encounter four girls dressed in white. The deeply evocative dappled set is by Alex Katz, the music is Elgar's Serenade for Strings *and* Elegy for Strings, *interrupted by a series of long plangent cries of a loon. Premiered in 1983,* Sunset *is to many people Paul Taylor's most moving work.*

The artist Alex Katz has designed the decor for some fifteen of Paul Taylor's dances, among them *Sunset,* the elegiac wartime dance first performed in 1983, and currently in revival at City Center. These particular designs are more like a Katz painting than most of them—the flat sky of the background, in subtle gradations of pale aqua, dappled with aqua leaves and marked with the suggestion of tree branches is like the ground of one of his paintings, in which there is no real distance, and everything exists in painterly equilibrium. The dancers, too, appear large in scale, and plain in outline. The men's costumes are an amalgam of the Basque and the American: chinos, tan shirts, sleek brown shoes, and red berets. On their sleeves are round patches in green and yellow. These colors, and a pretty blue, are echoed in markings on the dresses for the women, which also involve an expansion of scale: the white summer frocks are marked with big, infrequent dashes, or "x"es, or dots, one color to a dress, as if to differentiate them, but not too much. The backdrop consists of two pieces, set at an angle, so that space is broadly triangular. Along the left side runs a simple iron fence.

That this design exactly echoes in form, but not in content, the set for *Fancy Free*—there is even a barred fence where the bar is—Jerome Robbins's very different dance about men in uniform, is one of those interesting coincidences that occur sometimes in the theater. Another parallel is the three bounding servicemen who first dance on in the Taylor, although they are quickly joined by three more. But that's about it.

If you're in the mood, and don't get carried away wondering about the Freudian symbolism of the red handbag snatched by one of the sailors, *Fancy Free* can make you laugh. No matter what your mood, *Sunset* will make you cry because the plentitude of its relationships—among the band of brothers, and among the men and women, who are both girls and angels—suggests impending loss. The piece is one of sustained lyricism, perfectly matched to its music, Edward Elgar's *Serenade for Strings* and *Elegy for Strings*. (The plangent quasi-programmatic suggestion of the scores is very much like that of his *Enigma Variations,* which drew from Frederick Ashton the great ballet of the same name.) But then, too, there are the loons.

Part way though the piece, after the soldiers meet, gambol with the girls, play games, enter and exit and re-enter and re-exit in various combinations, darkness begins to fall. The Elgar stops, and nature takes over, and the sounds of dusk. One man lies prone, soon to crawl towards a central grouping. It's possible that this is a break into reality. We may be seeing the future—perhaps the battlefield. We may be in the future. Or, we may have relocated, and the scene that follows may be yet a third place: heaven. It doesn't really matter how you interpret it. I've thought a lot of different things over the times I've seen it, when I've thought at all, because the feeling is so clear that it isn't really necessary to think, and the feeling is always the same. As Taylor said ruefully in a conversation before the performance, a war dance never goes out of style.

The performance I saw at City Center was the first for the current cast, and it was particularly plain-spoken and clean. For example, a marvelous duet for two men, when danced formerly by old Taylor hands Patrick Corbin and Andrew Asnes, had an interesting element of soft shoe, swift and graceful. The current performers, Robert Kleinendorst and Andy LeBeau, are less Fred Astaire and Gene Kellyish, and more like, say, guys from a gas station engaged in a fast, clear, light-footed drill. Both ways of performing the piece work, but it was perhaps the very lack of personality in the current incarnation of *Sunset* that made its structure so clear and interesting.

For within that Alex Katz flat world with its close-up vanishing point, Taylor exercises a whole different three-point perspective—a moveable one, as if the dance is a series of paintings, seamlessly melded. This notion naturally leads one to the thought that the work is cinematic, but it really is not, because the camera ruthlessly chooses what you see. Rather, Taylor takes the auteur sensibility and works it out in the theater, guiding you to see what he wishes, when he wishes.

Certainly traditional choreographers have always done this, but their devices are transparent—dancers in the ballet stack up like castles of sugar cubes, or spread out like battalions. Taylor uses far fewer elements, working off center or on center, down stage or up or across or in any combination of where—in other words, he is a modern choreographer.

—from *danceviewtimes*, 2004

HOLLY BRUBACH
Moving Pictures

For Paul Taylor's New York season last spring, the gala opening-night attraction was the revival of his *From Sea to Shining Sea*, a sequence of tired-out patriotic tableaux, with a cast headed by Mikhail Baryshnikov, Rudolf Nureyev, Gwen Verdon, Hermione Gingold, Betty Comden, and Adolph Green. It was sometimes hard to see the forest for the trees. We got Baryshnikov crossing the Delaware, Green landing at Plymouth Rock, and Verdon stitching up the Stars and Stripes.

But when, the following night, Taylor's dancers took over the roles parceled out to celebrities for the first performance, *From Sea to Shining Sea* became a different dance altogether. It's this version that audiences will be seeing as the Taylor company performs the work, without celebrities, on tour.

The gags, some of them side-splitting and all of them over before you know it, became its substance (whereas the substance the first night was the cast), and the marvel of it was that Taylor had managed to weave out of all these scenes a whole piece of dancing. What makes his "Living Pictures," as he calls them in the program, succeed on their own terms where more traditional *tableaux vivants* would surely fail is a point of view.

Something is amiss. The spikes on the Statue of Liberty's crown are bent, as if vandals have been here before us. When the figure of Liberty reappears in the name of God and country, it's with a man sprawled across her lap— as the *Pietà*. Mae West, Marlon Brando, and the Ku Klux Klan all pass through. The weary soldiers hoisting the flag at Iwo Jima are barely able to stand up themselves. Men in bathrobes and women in curler bonnets wander the stage, dejected; we watch them brush their teeth. In a scene straight out of *Route 66*, or *The Flintstones*, or both, Elie Chaib drives an imaginary convertible past a hitchhiker, screeches to a halt, backs up, picks her up, and drives off; the wheels are played by two curled-up dancers turning somersaults, backward when he shifts into reverse. The *Mayflower* runs aground on Plymouth Rock (the rock played by a dancer), and the Pilgrims, as they set foot on American soil, are greeted by an Indian of the Cigar Store tribe. "How!" he says, and, according to the best classical ballet tradition, launches into a long, fast mime speech, which starts out something like "Fish gotta swim, birds gotta fly . . ." and in no time progresses to a curvaceous woman and a four-letter verb, in Italian.

Choreographed in 1965, *From Sea to Shining Sea* has all the earmarks of its time—antiwar sentiment, slouching posture, moral fatigue. The dance survives because it's wittier than it is sullen, and it's hard to imagine any other choreographer working today who could carry off such an assignment. Or who would want to—this picture pamphlet looks static compared with the dancing that audiences have come to expect. Why go to see a ballet if its choreography isn't anything we couldn't do? (Not surprisingly, it was *Arden Court*, a new dance-packed piece that looks as if it were made at 33½ and performed at 78 rpm, that brought down the house and walked off with the season.)

Many resourceful choreographers turn, at one time or another, to painting and sculpture for inspiration. But when the original source finds its way into the finished dance, it's generally as a paraphrase rather than a direct quotation, a position rather than a pose. Vaslav Nijinsky's *L'Après-midi d'un faune,* from Egyptian reliefs, is one, and the most obvious, example. Frederick Ashton's *Foyer de Danse,* after Degas, is another. Homages to Thomas Eakins (*Eakins' View,* by Rodney Griffin) and Alexander Calder (*Under the Sun,* by Margo Sappington) are in the Pennsylvania Ballet's repertory. In a TV documentary, *Martha Clarke Light & Dark,* Clarke shows us the photograph of Baron de Meyer that inspired her *Nocturne.* But Taylor's choreography, when he isn't borrowing scenes from history books or paying tribute to Nijinsky with an Egyptian-style frieze of his own, is every bit as vivid as when he is, and as visually original as the work of most painters.

In Taylor's *Polaris,* the only set (by Alex Katz) is a huge eight-foot cube, an aluminum-tube frame at the center of the stage. The dance is performed twice through—the second time by a different cast, to different music, with different lighting, which makes the cube glow first silver against a dark blue field, then bright white, like the heat of a star, against blackness. The choreography never strays far, and the steps that take place inside the cube are magnified by it. *Polaris* begins with one dancer standing at the cube's center, facing us, and four others, one at each corner, facing her. They shift and climb over one another inside as if they were shut in a stateroom; they spiral-turn around the corner poles. An overhead light shines in, like a hot spot in an interrogation chamber. The dancing, by reiteration, takes on a magical, ritualistic quality: this is the sequence of events defined by this cube, this space.

This set, Taylor says, came first, before the choreography: the cube was the premise for making the dance. The cart carrying the set also came before the horse in two other cases. "I was over at Alex's studio and we were looking out the window, into the buildings across the street," Taylor recalls. "People were doing things—you'd see them and then miss their action as they went from room to room and window to window, and then they'd reappear. So that was the idea for *Private Domain,*" in which we glimpse the dancing through three arches in a flat drop curtain at the front of the stage. And, again, "Alex called me one day and said, 'I've got an idea for a set—dogs all over the stage.' I said, 'Great. We'll do it.'"

In that dance, titled *Diggity,* we see eight people wending their way through an obstacle course of twenty-five cut-out dogs—standing, sitting, rolling over, playing dead. The dogs stay put; the people—jumping, skipping, hopping in *arabesque*—dwell in a stratosphere just above the dogs' heads. Midway through the piece, two men roll out a giant-size cabbage that falls flat to reveal Linda Kent behind it. She dances a solo that announces itself as seductive, with arms flung open, an arched upper back, syncopated hips—movements that read as wild abandon—but in the end is overwhelmed by its own wholesomeness. This bit has about it the earnest, straight-to-the-audience sales pitch more typical of the Miss America Pageant's talent competition than of a Paul Taylor dance; it's out of place not only in *Diggity* but in the entire repertory. But just as we begin to get bogged down in its incongruities, the solo ends, the giant disc is lifted behind the dancer, and we see, painted on the flip side, a sunflower. The only possible logic for this non-sequitur is purely visual.

It's not just occasional moments that strike us as odd in Taylor's work, it's whole dances. His instinct for the unexpected is infallible. None of the preconceptions we bring to other kinds of dancing—to classical ballet, for example—do us any good when we're watching his choreography: the equilibrium we find in symmetrical arrangement, the reassuring knowledge that the dancers will eventually return to certain time-honored formations (the soloist in the center, set off by the corps) are missing completely. So is our notion of who dancers are.

Not all ballet dancers look alike, of course, but their bodies are shaped by the classical technique along similar lines, as if according to the blueprint for some superior race. Onstage, they acquire a universal identity that enables one ballerina to represent all women. Unlike ballet dancers, who generally have long, well-stretched, diagonally formed thigh muscles, loose-jointed hips, feet with a strong high arch for good spring in a jump, and, in women, a secure position on pointe, Taylor's dancers have haunches. Their strength runs along the front, not the back, of the legs, and when they jump, they lift themselves by the power in their thighs. The women have bosoms, the men are beefy. Their flat-footed speed, which is pure locomotion, brings to mind the Road Runner. The bodies of these dancers haven't been stylized—or idealized, as ballet dancers' have—by any uniform system of training; they seem instead to have been chosen for their singularity, in all shapes and sizes.

The governing principle in classical ballet is, traditionally, beauty. Every individual dancer aspires to certain standard positions. Turnout, in addition to facilitating a greater range of motion, shows us the most interesting lines of the legs. But this flattery, presenting the body at its best, is no concern of Taylor's. His dances, as a result, look determinedly honest, and innocent. We see fewer lines, more shapes. Classical ballet has a visual tradition all its own, and dancers trained in it look as if they had stepped out of a ballet. But Taylor's dancers look like people, and the images he makes have more in common with painting and sculpture than with other kinds of dance.

In *Tablet* (1960), *Le Sacre du Printemps (The Rehearsal)* (1980), and *Profiles* (a thumbnail sketch for *Sacre,* in 1979), Taylor explores his fascination with flat, two-dimensional dancing. His *Sacre* pays tribute to Nijinsky, who choreographed the same Stravinsky score the first time around, with positions in the style of *L'Après-midi d'un faune*—knees bent, with the legs and feet in profile and the torso twisted front, palms out and fingers curled under at the knuckle. Two women at a dressing table mirror each other's movements; we watch the final, sacrificial solo in a rehearsal-studio mirror upstage. John Rawling's costumes and set, all black, white, and gray, except for an occasional red prop—a bag, a dagger, a baby's bunting—give this *Sacre* the look of a cartoon filmstrip. The somewhat hazy plot is a detective yarn, set in Chinatown. The Egyptian reliefs that inspired these same positions in Nijinsky are twice removed and buried beneath other references.

The picture Taylor presents in *Nightshade* is drawn in indelible ink. The idea, according to Taylor, came from etchings by Max Ernst. Like a nightmare in slow motion, the events unfold with an inevitability that's at the same time terrifying and fascinating; it's hard to imagine a more horrific dance. The horror lies in its ambiguity, and just after its premiere in 1979, reviewers made a desperate—but unconvincing—attempt to account for its action, as if by doing so they could reason away the dread that takes hold of us in witnessing it. But whatever *Nightshade* is about, its subject isn't nearly as clear as its images.

There are six people in Victorian dress—the women in long skirts and bonnets, the men in tailcoats—and two characters who are distinctly not human: one, a quick-moving sprite (Carolyn Adams), whose ankle bands and short "grass" skirt made of colored ribbons are vague reminders of a medieval jester's costume; the other, a hulking man (Elie Chaib), dressed all in black, with a black face and a black moplike wig—a witch doctor or a mysterious voodoo god. He struggles with a fair-skinned, red-haired woman (Karla Wolfangle), dressed in a loose black negligee—and prevails. The apparition of this woman dragged by the feet, seemingly nude, with her nightgown hanging down around her shoulders and her head in a big wicker basket, invariably provokes uneasy laughter from an audience until, as the image persists and the laughter subsides, we find ourselves reluctantly considering the suggestion of rape. But suggestion is as explicit as *Nightshade* ever gets, and the dancing moves on without ever resolving the issue or the image.

By lanternlight, we watch two men crouched over a woman lying on the floor; another woman, as if testing for death, lifts her wrist and it falls back to the floor, lifeless. The gesture is repeated—another thud. The sprite sits perched on the black man's shoulders and, for a moment, for no good reason, we take heart. He whirls like a dervish. Then, without warning, she drops from where she sits and, her ankles around his neck, hangs limp, swaying upside down. In this awful final image, whatever it signifies, we recognize the vindication for our fears.

—from *The Atlantic Monthly,* September 1981

PAUL TAYLOR

Why I Make Dances

No one has ever asked me why I make dances. But when flummoxed by the financial difficulties of keeping a dance company afloat, I sometimes ask it of myself. Dance makers are most often quizzed this way: Which comes first, the dance or the music? This conundrum was answered most tellingly by the celebrated choreographer George Balanchine, who said: "The money." Nobel Prize winner Orhan Pamuk has often been asked why he writes. The savvy answer in his "My Father's Suitcase" was so meaningful and struck such a chord of recognition in me—his devotion, his steadfastness, his anger— that it caused me to ponder my own reasons for doing what I do. Motivated by Balanchine's sensible quip and Pamuk's candid perceptiveness, this is how I might reply:

To put it simply, I make dances because I can't help it. Working on dances has become a way of life, an addiction that at times resembles a fatal disease. Even so, I've no intention of kicking the habit. I make dances because I believe in the power of contemporary dance, its immediacy, its potency, its universality. I make dances because that's what I've spent many years teaching myself to do and it's become what I'm best at. When the dances are good, nothing else brings me as much satisfaction. When they aren't, I've had the luxury, in the past at least, of being allowed to create others.

From childhood on, I've been a reticent guy who spends a lot of time alone. I make dances in an effort to communicate to people. A visual medium can be more effective than words. I make dances because I don't always trust my own words or, for that matter, those of quite a few others I've known. I make dances because working with my dancers and other cohorts allows me to spend time with trustworthy people I'm very fond of and who seldom give me trouble. Also because I'm not suited to do the jobs that regular folks do. There is no other way I could earn a living, especially not at work that involves dealing face-to-face with the public. I make dances because crowds are kept at a safe distance. That's what proscenium stages are good for.

Dance making appeals to me because, although group projects and democratic systems are okay if they work, when on the job I find that a benevolent dictatorship is best. I don't make dances for the masses—I make them for myself. That is, even though they are meant to be seen in public (otherwise, what's the point?), I make dances I think I'd like to see.

I'm not above filching steps from other dance makers, but only from the best—ones such as Martha Graham and Antony Tudor—and only when I think I can make an improvement.

Although there are only two or three dances in me—ones based on simple images imprinted at childhood—I've gone to great lengths to have each repeat of them seem different. Because of the various disguises my dances wear, viewers sometimes mistake them for those made by other choreographers. My reaction to this depends on how talented I think that person is. Imitating a chameleon has always come easy. Maybe it's genetic, or a protective artifice. The only identity that bugs me is that of the lauded personage. This is because the responsibilities demanded by fame are nuisances that I could easily do without. Ideally, my work would be anonymous.

Stylized lies (novelistic truths) for the stage are what the medium demands. I love tinkering with natural gesture and pedestrian movement to make them read from a distance and be recognizable as a revealing language that we all have in common. Of particular interest is the amorous coupling of men and women, as well as the other variations on this subject. In short, the remarkable range of our human condition.

Whenever a dance of mine is controversial it brings me much satisfaction. One of my aims is to present questions rather than answers. My passion for dance does not prevent me from being terrified to start each new piece, but I value these fears for the extra energy they bring. Getting to know the music I use is a great pleasure even though toilsome. After making sure that the rights to use it are affordable, each piece needs to be scanned, counted out, and memorized. Since I've not learned to read scores, this can take an awful long time.

I make dances because it briefly frees me from coping with the real world, because it's possible to build a whole new universe with steps, because I want people to know about themselves, and even because it's a thrilling relief to see how fast each of my risk-taking dancers can recover after a pratfall.

I make dances, not to arrange decorative pictures for current dancers to perform, but to build a firm structure that can withstand future changes of cast. Quite possibly I make dances to be useful or to get rid of a chronic itch or to feel less alone. I make them for a bunch of reasons—multiple motives rooted in the driving passion that infected me when I first discovered dance. The novelist Albert Camus said it best:

A man's work is nothing but this slow trek
to rediscover through the detours of art
those two or three great and simple images
in whose presence his heart first opened.

—from *The Wall Street Journal*, February 23, 2008

TEACHERS

MERRILL ASHLEY
Class with Balanchine

Merrill Ashley (born 1950) had an extraordinarily long and productive career with New York City Ballet. Known for her brilliant allegro technique and sparkling attack, she commanded the most difficult ballets in the repertory—Ballet Imperial, Theme and Variations, Square Dance—but also inhabited major lyrical works such as "Emeralds" and Swan Lake. Balanchine created two ballets for her, Ballo della Regina and Ballade, and today she coaches and stages them, and other Balanchine works, for City Ballet and companies around the world. Although she officially retired as a dancer in 1997, she has gone on making welcome appearances as Carabosse in Peter Martins's Sleeping Beauty.

As a new corps member of the New York City Ballet, I attended Balanchine's classes partly because I felt I should and partly because I knew that my feelings of relative ignorance were well founded and I needed to learn all I could. In every class, Balanchine brought up many technical points that were new to me, but he rarely explained them in full detail, and my eye was not yet sharp enough to detect the subtleties in his demonstrations.

Another difficulty I faced was his frequent request that the same step be done differently from one day to the next. It took me a long time to realize this wasn't an inconsistency in his demands but was instead his attempt to give us a broad range of skills to choose from. He wanted us to be in complete control, not forced by our bodies' habits to move in one particular way.

One thing was immediately clear to me: Balanchine wanted a high level of energy in every movement. It made no difference whether we were moving slowly, quickly, or not at all. We had to be aware of every part of our body and make it look alive.

He tried to make us understand that principle when he taught class at the School of American Ballet. (I was a student there for four years, until 1967, when I was asked to join the company.) He wanted to see the energy contained in our bodies even when we were standing still at the barre. He liked to draw a comparison between a cat ready to pounce and one sitting in the same position. There is no movement in either, but one can sense the energy and alertness in the cat that is ready to pounce. We too had to be ready to pounce!

I dwelled constantly on the mysteries and frustrations of class with Balanchine. I took his classes, except when they conflicted with the advanced class taught by Stanley Williams at the school. It was reassuring to work in a class where I felt in close harmony with the teacher, as I did in Williams'. I began to hear, however, about up-and-coming young corps members who never missed Balanchine's classes. It made me wonder whether I should not be doing the same thing. Soon I realized that my only hope of stimulating Balanchine's interest was to learn to dance the way he wanted, and that could be done only in his classes. They might not be comfortable or reassuring, but that was where my future lay. I couldn't just *say* I was committed to him. I had to *be* committed. It took me a little while to understand the obvious, but finally it became clear. Many never understood.

Company class was given then, as today, in the "main hall," a large studio, supposedly with the same dimensions as the stage of the State Theater. But, since the studio was enclosed by four windowless walls, it seemed a much more confined space. Everyone complained about the dim fluorescent lighting that strained our eyes and gave us a sallow, sickly look. How nice it would have been to have natural sunlight and a glimpse of the outside world. Balanchine, too, had wanted windows; but the architect would not relent, feeling they would spoil his design. We would have appreciated the benefits of fresh air, too, for the air in ballet studios becomes stale very quickly.

Barres lined the four walls. Space was at a premium, but no one had yet thought to put portable barres in the middle of the floor. When the room became unbearably crowded, tall ladders were dragged in and used as makeshift barres. A few dancers used the piano for support, but Balanchine permitted that only when there was no alternative. (He did not like to see a piano used as a barre or a resting place for anything other than music. He said a piano was not a piece of furniture but a beautiful instrument that should be treated with care.) The floor was covered with battleship gray linoleum, which I found easy to adjust to after the slippery wooden surfaces of the school studios, but the main hall lacked the springiness of the stage or the floors at SAB. (This was later corrected.) There were tiles missing from the ceiling, and during rainstorms we would dance around the large plastic garbage cans we had placed in the middle of the studio to catch the dripping rain. (That, however, has never been fixed.)

I always arrived a minimum of fifteen minutes before the scheduled starting time: 11:00 a.m. This was not to get a desirable spot at the barre—such maneuvering by a newcomer would not have been appreciated—but simply to warm up, for we all knew it was foolhardy to launch into a Balanchine barre with cold muscles. His was not like one of those comfortable, leisurely barres given by other teachers to massage the muscles and reassure the egos of their temperamental devotees.

Each dancer had his favorite place at the barre, and as a newcomer I naturally had to defer to everyone. At first I found a place in the middle of a side barre, but from there I frequently had trouble catching Balanchine's words. He spoke softly, for he felt he would lose his voice if he spoke up all the time. Later I switched to the opposite side and moved a little nearer to the front. That was the beginning of my long march to the front of the class.

Balanchine would usually arrive ten to twenty minutes late. When he entered the room, everyone fell silent and was immediately ready to work. He almost always appeared in good spirits—he was not a moody person— and he enjoyed spending a minute or two exchanging words with the pianist or one of the dancers before class began.

He was very fond of colorful western shirts, which he sported in denim, prints, satin, and silk. I was fascinated by the contrast between these distinctive shirts and and the nondescript "work pants" he wore, when teaching or choreographing. He often wore his regular street shoes during class and rehearsals (when choreographing he wore either his street shoes or light, flexible dance shoes), but, no matter how stiff or heavy the shoes, they never seemed to interfere with his innate grace when he walked about and demonstrated steps. If he had just come from a meeting, he might appear in a jacket with a scarf loosely knotted around his neck. The jacket immediately went over the back of the pianist's chair, but it was a little while before he removed the scarf and rolled up his sleeves to show he was ready to get to work with us.

Balanchine rarely varied the plié combination that started the barre; a simple "and" to the pianist or an expansive thumb-down gesture with one hand, meaning "go down," was all we needed to start our deep knee bends, or grands pliés. He wanted us to bend our knees and come back up in one perfectly smooth movement, and he wanted a minimal amount of music to accompany the movement—just chords would do. Throughout the rest of class, if the pianist played music with too many notes in a measure, or played too loudly, Balanchine would stop and remark that the pianist was working so hard that *we* could easily believe that *we* were working hard, too. He would then ask the pianist to play soft chords so that the movement of the dancers' feet could be heard. Balanchine could tell as much, and sometimes more, from the sound our feet made than he could from looking at them. He could literally "hear the dance." Generally he snapped his fingers or tapped his foot to indicate emphasis or the timing, although he sometimes also slapped his thigh. If he wanted to stop the action at any time, he clapped his hands, but repeated clapping was an expression of irritation.

After grands pliés came many battement tendu combinations. Balanchine believed tendus were the foundation of a dancer's technique. "If you just do battement tendu well, you don't have to do anything else."* At first it was hard for me to grasp how—by merely sliding the foot out from fifth position along the floor as far as it would go to either the front, side, or back, while maintaining contact with the floor, and then returning it to fifth position—we were doing a step that would influence our every move on the stage and largely determine whether our technique was precise or sloppy or something in between. Eventually, I realized how right he was.

Tendus came in several varieties, but Balanchine liked to give simple tendus first. It seems perverse to call them simple, for they were by no means easy, especially the way Balanchine wanted them done. I strained my ears to catch all the details that Balanchine gave so lavishly, if at times inaudibly. At first I thought that he and the teachers at SAB were after the same thing but that Balanchine was just being more emphatic and insistent. Then I realized there was a world of difference: Balanchine pointed out many more details and he meant exactly what he said.

The easiest corrections to understand were those about fifth position and about where in relation to one's body the toes should rest on the floor when the leg was extended out as far as it would go with the foot fully pointed. That was the tendu position, the stretched position, which was not supposed to vary one iota when we did a succession of tendus in one direction or another. For example, each time we moved our foot to the front, he wanted it to go to exactly the same spot on the floor, in line with the center of our bodies. The same rule governed our tendus to the back and the side. The foot and leg had to be well turned out and the foot had to have light contact with the floor as it slid out and returned. And all the while he was scrutinizing our fifth position to see if the heel of one foot was even with the toes of the other foot and to be sure that both feet were nestled together. He would often stand next to a newcomer and say, "Don't you know what the fifth position is, dear? Didn't anyone ever tell you? Where did you study?"

---

*Quoted by Maria Tallchief in *Ballet Review*, Winter 1984, p. 25.

Of course, he knew perfectly well that the dancer had studied at his school, but with that question he made his point, with devastating effect.

The most difficult corrections had to do with everything that happened between fifth position and the tendu position. But at the time, these corrections having to do with the in-between positions were often too subtle for me and they just passed over my head.

Balanchine, like everyone else, knew that perfection was not of this world. Yet what he thought was humanly possible was much closer to perfection than we could ever have imagined. He cared about the most minute details of these tendus. The timing was perhaps the trickiest part of all. I struggled mightily to retain everything he said and hoped that somehow, someday the words would filter through my anatomy and come out looking like perfectly executed battements tendus.

Since at first I had only a vague idea of what the finished step should look like, I watched others in class and tried to learn from them. Many had been there for years, but quite a few seemed even farther from the mark than I. How could that be? Did they not hear what Balanchine was saying, or did they hear but not understand? Or was it that they understood but couldn't be bothered to make the effort?

And what an effort it was—as well as *painful*. Balanchine taught tendus through the use of extremes: very slow and very fast tempos; many repetitions; and a great expenditure of energy. He took the same approach as one might take to tongue twisters: by starting slowly you have a chance to think about each element, and then build up speed. He normally gave a minimum of sixteen tendus in each direction—that is, a total of forty-eight with each leg—to begin with. These were usually done at an extremely slow tempo, alternating legs all the time: first sixteen to the front with the right leg, then sixteen to the front with the left leg, and so on to the side and back. Then the tempo would quicken with each new combination. We'd have eight front, side, and back with the right leg and then the same with the left. Then faster still: four front, side, and back with each leg. There was no rest between sides or between combinations, so by the time he gave two or one in each direction with each leg, our muscles were burning and dancers were groaning and sometimes giving up altogether.

Throughout all the repetitions at accelerating tempos, Balanchine wanted the mechanics and timing to remain intact; the foot was to be presented in the tendu position as beautifully as if we had all the time in the world. He also wanted us to get used to expending vast amounts of physical energy, and he liked to draw an analogy between energy and money. If you have plenty of money in your pocket, he would say, you have the choice of whether to spend it or save it. But if you have no money, you have no choice. It's the same with energy. If dancers are accustomed to expending energy, then they are free to determine exactly how much energy to use on each step. But if they are always sluggish in class, it's impossible suddenly to become dynamic on the stage when it's needed. The theory was elementary, but it took dogged perseverance before correctly executed tendus became second nature to us.

While I understood Balanchine's methods, I couldn't help wondering what he was really after as he worked to get us to perfect these tendus. Were all these niceties just a matter of aesthetics? Was it just that he wanted tendus done his way, whereas another choreographer might want them done another way, if he cared about them at all? The answers to these questions came slowly, but I had to be patient and thoughtful.

I gradually realized that each time I made a movement with a straight leg, I was doing something related to a tendu. Whenever I started to move a straight leg either away from or toward my body, it was almost always because I was either about to take my foot off the floor or place it on the floor. My foot then had to make all the adjustments that were necessary between the weight-bearing and pointed positions. That is precisely what happens in tendus, and the tens of thousands that I had done had given me great familiarity with these intermediary positions of the foot. For that reason I was able to present my working foot beautifully and make sure it was turned out as I put my weight on it or transferred my weight smoothly from one foot to the other. Tendus had also taught me how to start and stop the movement of my legs quickly and easily. In fact, it was an ideal step for the development of fast movements in general, because of the relative simplicity of the step.

Whenever I started or ended tendus in demi-plié, I was learning how to move from step to step by bending and straightening my knees in the most efficient and beautiful way possible. The only things that tendus did not pre-pare me for were movements of my leg in the air with a bent knee (fondus served that purpose) and movements of my leg in a circular pattern (ronds de jambe prepared me for that). Those four basic exercises at the barre, with all their variations, prepared us for practically any movement we would have to make while dancing, and when I finally grasped that simple but elusive truth, Balanchine's great insistence on these exercises made much more sense to me.

We proceeded quickly with the different tendus and other remaining exercises at the barre, which took no more than twenty minutes altogether. There was often a link between the exercises at the barre and what was given in the center. If, for example, Balanchine spent extra time at the barre on demi-pliés and grands pliés, there was reason to suspect that all those knees were being made to bend for a purpose: lots of jumps with special attention to the takeoffs and landings were coming in the center.

Throughout the barre Balanchine walked around the room, eyes darting about, his mind racing; he was noticing our flaws and deciding how to correct them. The steps at the barre were calculated to make our legs move in all the ways they would have to move during the work in the center: front, side, and back; up and down; slowly and fast; and clockwise and counterclockwise. He might stop by a dancer and adjust the position of an arm or leg, head or foot. If a verbal correction failed to produce the desired results, he might plant himself right by the dancer, who had the choice of either doing the step properly or hitting Balanchine with his leg or foot. It certainly was an effective way for Balanchine to get what he wanted. He did this most frequently when he was trying to get us to move directly to the front, side, or back or to make sure our fifth position was right. Often he used his hands and arms to imitate the movement he wanted us to make with our feet and legs. He wanted them to be as dexterous as his hands and arms, although he never said so directly. The clearest analogy he drew was with an elephant's trunk; our legs were supposed to look flexible, even boneless, but at the same time to maintain their control and strength just as an elephant's trunk does.

When it was time to move away from the barre to the center of the floor, the class, perhaps forty strong (about half the company), divided into two groups, with the more experienced dancers going to the front of each group. The groups then took turns occupying the entire floor for two or three minutes in four or five rows of four or five dancers each. Balanchine took up a position in front of the class, walking from side to side to get a better view of everyone, giving corrections as he went. He might concentrate briefly on one dancer, bending over slightly for a better view of the feet. If he had to reposition a part of the body, he did so. If he could correct verbally, he did, but if that did not work he demonstrated the step himself. Many of the subtleties that were so hard to comprehend from verbal instructions alone were plainly visible when he moved. You could learn much just by watching him. He always put us to shame with his grace and finesse. Never have I seen *any* dancer move as beautifully as Balanchine. The quality of movement that he had in every type of dancing was extraordinary. But sharp eyes and ears were constantly needed to absorb everything there was to learn.

Class usually ended a little late, around 12:10 or 12:20 p.m., for Balanchine was not a clock-watcher. If he became involved working on a particular point, he wasn't going to stop simply because the clock said class was over. The appearance of a ballet mistress, or gentle prompting from her, sometimes reminded him that he was running into rehearsal time and had better end class. He would always end proceedings a little suddenly, with a "that's enough" accompanied by a sweeping gesture. Brief but appreciative applause would follow for a few seconds—a practice he didn't like but was never able to stop.

—from Dancing for Balanchine, with Larry Kaplan, 1984

ALEXANDRA DANILOVA
On Teaching

Students can always sense which teachers care about them and which do not. I love my pupils and try to show them understanding. Some are shy and need encouragement; others are what I call "blue jays"—they think well of themselves and go all the time to the front row, where they will be seen. I tell my pupils, "You must come forward and fight for your place. You must not be soft. The angels do not come down and get you. You must step forward and nominate yourself."

There must be a thread of good will, a feeling of warmth and fondness, that extends from me, the teacher, to each student. It is important that they know that I care about them, not because I tell them so but by the way I work with them. I don't hesitate to criticize my pupils, but I never insult them. Sometimes I scream at them, but always with love.

I dislike teachers who try to work their way into the souls of their pupils and become their friends. A good teacher should not be afraid of being unpopular. If there is a step your pupils are afraid of, you must give it to them over and over again, until finally they say to themselves, Oh, this teacher annoys me so, I will do the step, just to make her stop. I believe that there should be a respectful distance between a teacher and her pupils, but the respect should not be founded on fear. The teacher who inspires fear in her pupils is working against herself, because her students, if they are scared, will be too tense to dance well. Instead, I think, a teacher must win the respect of her pupils—you must prove to them during the course of the lesson that you know more than they do, that they have something to gain from you, and once you have done that, they are yours. If you have a pupil who can't do two pirouettes, you must tell her what to do in order to turn.

"All right," you say, "your way isn't working, so now please try it my way." And if you help her, if she does two pirouettes correctly, she will place her confidence in you from then on.

Class begins at the barre. When I began to teach, Mr. Vladimirov told me, "The human body is a delicate mechanism, like a racing car—you must warm it up carefully and thoroughly before you race it." It is at the barre that you warm your muscles and get your bearings. You find your balance there—you can concentrate on certain movements, to get the feel of doing them correctly, before you stand on your own two feet in the middle of the floor. The barre gives you a third leg—you begin class with three legs and then you finish with two.

Even though the exercises follow the same pattern every day, I watch my pupils carefully when they are at the barre to make certain that they are executing the basic movements and positions correctly. Each day, I begin with half pliés in first and second position, then deep pliés: grand plié, port de bras, grand plié, balance. First, second, fourth, and fifth positions—one side, then turn the other way. Next I do battements tendus, first with pliés, then without pliés, then quick battements tendus—always varied, never set. These are followed by battements tendus jetés.

At the School of American Ballet, we don't insist that the children turn out the legs too much the first year, because if you force the turnout before they have the strength to maintain it, they roll over on their feet. But in the second year, we demand more and more turnout, particularly at the barre. At the barre, where you are more or less stationary, you can work more turned out than in the center—you don't need to maintain your turnout in motion, and you have the help of your "third leg" for support. So beginning in the second year, we require that our students turn out more than is comfortable for them, until finally they reach a perfect fifth position—the toe of each foot exactly even with the heel of the other.

Some people disagree and say that the second year is too early to ask for a perfect fifth position, that the children are too young. It's true that in the beginning, fifth position is difficult for them. But children are soft—you can take their legs in your hands and just turn them—and I give them exercises that turn out the heel, the thigh, the whole leg. For instance, I do battements tendus with a plié in fourth position, then relevé, to develop the turnout in the thigh. I demand good turnout as soon as possible, because if dancers acquire it early on, it stays with them. For the rest of their lives, a perfect fifth position comes automatically.

I teach classical exercises, and I demand that they be done exactly as they should be done. If students want to be serious, the teacher must pay close attention to details, because in classical ballet if a fifth position isn't right, it's wrong—there is no room for interpretation. But if people want to do pop-ular dancing—to go on Broadway, for example—then it doesn't matter so much how their fifth position goes. (Lately, it has become fashionable among the older students and some members of the company, the New York City Ballet, to exaggerate the fifth position and overcross the feet—I call this "tenth position," and I refuse to accept it in my classes.) It is up to my pupils after they finish school how they do the movements, how they execute fifth position, but during my class, they must do it precisely right.

After battements tendus, I give ronds de jambe—first, par terre; then grands ronds de jambe en l'air. This is the movement—développé and carry the leg all the way around, from the front to the side to the back—that develops height in extension. I proved this to myself when I was teaching in Dallas. I ran an experiment in my classes: we did grands ronds de jambe reg-ularly, and my pupils all had big extensions.

When I was growing up in the Theatre School, a high extension was con-sidered vulgar, and even Margot Fonteyn never raised her leg higher than her waist. It is only because of Balanchine, who wanted the leg higher, that dancers have begun to develop their extensions, and I personally agree with Mr. B. The leg in développé should not be stopped; if it is, the movement becomes stiff and mechanical. Instead, I think the leg should just go, reach-ing upward; the movement must be free if it is to be graceful.

Most dancers today think that a high extension comes from stretching, and they stretch and stretch—they tear their muscles, stretching them far-ther than they have the strength to support. This stretching has become an obsession—just because Mary can stretch her legs behind her ears, so must everybody else in the class! My students come to class and first thing, they do hard stretches. I warn them constantly: "If you want to stretch, do it after exercises at the barre, when your muscles are warm and limber." I say this over and over, I bang my head against the wall, but they don't listen. They tear their legs apart. I see them sitting between rehearsals in grand écart, in a split, and say, "Why don't you do your two pirouettes that are not so hot instead? Why don't you work on something that is important? How high can you do développé? Higher than your head?" It becomes ridiculous.

Instead of so much stretching, I give my pupils exercises that concentrate on the muscle at the top of the thigh, to control the leg—slow ronds de jambe, or grands battements. A grand battement by itself is not enough, because you can kick the leg and never hold it. I make my pupils hold the leg at the top, to build strength at the height of their extensions.

These are exercises that must be done correctly and with care; otherwise they can overdevelop the muscles of the thigh. Looking back, I realize that many of the girls I grew up with at the Theatre School had big calves and thighs, overdeveloped because they had overworked those particular muscles.

Mr. B., when he taught, was always very conscious of which muscles he was working and was careful not to abuse them. Sometimes, for example, he would make us do sixty-four battements tendus, but he would break them up—sixteen on one side, sixteen on the other side, sixteen and sixteen, or variations, not all the same and not all in one gulp. I don't allow my pupils to "sit" in any position or to abuse their legs with harsh accents. "Don't force the movement," I tell them. "Just do it gently." The movement should always be soft and very elastic.

After fondus and frappés, I do adagio and then petits battements sur le coup de pied, to warm up the knees, then ronds de jambe en l'air, which I save for last because they require a highly complicated use of the knee and you must be very warmed up in order to do them correctly. I give rond de jambe en l'air en dehors, en dedans, with a plié, sometimes with a jump—everything, always different.

I take teaching very seriously, and I like to sit in on other teachers' classes to see how they go about things differently. Many teachers become famous for their methods—Cecchetti, for instance—structuring their lessons a certain way or giving the same sequence of exercises every Wednesday one way, every Monday the same. But to my way of thinking, it's a mistake for a teacher to settle on a system like that. The exercises at the barre are like the Bible, more or less the same wherever you go. But the exercises in the center of the floor vary greatly from one teacher to the next, and that is where the true art of teaching lies. In the center, you must get your student on balance, make her turn, make her jump, make her graceful, make her dance.

In the center, I begin with adagio, then battements tendus and fondus, usually in combinations with some sort of fancy pirouettes. There are students who are afraid to turn—for their benefit, I lead up to pirouettes gradually. I structure my class in such a way that they are prepared to turn. "What is a turn but a balance?" I tell my classes. It is all in the placement, which is very important—only dancers and flamingos stand so much on one leg.

I give my pupils the opportunity to practice their balance first at the barre, by ending nearly every exercise combination with a balance. This is the way we were taught in Russia, where good balance was admired to the same extent that a high jump, for example, is admired today. Anna Pavlova used to take a position and stay by herself, unsupported—that was one of her tricks, and ballerinas everywhere copied her until eventually it became boring. Somebody once described to me another ballerina's performance.* "You must see her to believe it," he told me. "She stays so long on one toe!"

---

*Editor's note: Toumanova.

Well, I thought, so what? I am too busy dancing. These long balances that used to bring down the house and bring the performance to a halt are out of fashion now, no longer in good taste; but dancers must still learn how to hold a long balance, for the sake of their pirouettes. I was taught by Mme Egorova and M. Legat to do balances at the barre and half-turns to practice my placement, and I do the same for my pupils, so that full pirouettes, doubles, triples, and turns in sequence come more easily in the center.

But to be a really good teacher, one must be also a psychologist, able to build in your pupils the confidence they need to dance without hesitation or holding back, to help them overcome their fears, to soothe their minds. They are anxious because they are not sure that they will do the turn, and already they doom themselves. "If you fall," I say, telling them what Mme Vaganova told me, "you will sit on the floor—it is right underneath you. It won't be like falling from the second story."

. . . At the end of the lesson, pupils should want to do more. That is what my teacher M. Legat told me. Some dancers say, "Oh, we had such a marvelous class, I can't move." Well, from my point of view, that is a very bad class. Class is for teaching people how to do things; the idea is not to exhaust them and leave them with their tongues hanging out, like dogs who have been taken for a run around the block. A good class is one that seems too short. "Ah, what a pity," you say. "The lesson is finished already."

—from *Choura,* with Holly Brubach, 1984

MARGOT FONTEYN
My Teachers

During my unusually long career I must surely have attended more classes with more teachers than any other dancer in history. Even in the early years at Sadler's Wells we had several guest teachers. My favourite was Stanislav Idzikowski, affectionately known as Idzi, a brilliant dancer who had been with the Diaghilev Ballet. He was diminutive, dapper, and precise, speaking rather good English with a clipped Polish accent. Severe but never unkind, he knew exactly what he expected of his pupils and explained clearly how to achieve it. He demonstrated all the steps himself, even in pas de deux class, and he could deftly swing one into a lift supported with only one arm. What incredible strength and knack to partner, so airily, lumpy teenagers taller than himself! Forty years later he is still as slim and precise as ever, his face scarcely changed at all. I do not remember ever seeing him without a waistcoat to his neat grey suit.

Another teacher was unusual insofar as she never even pretended that dancers were supposed to follow the music. She only cared that we should learn to jump high. "Stand up in the air, turn round and then come down" was her preferred way of setting an exercise. Finding that, not unnaturally, we came down to the ground sooner than she wished, she would start to shout, "Don't listen to the pianist; she is only there to play. Stand in the air. Don't listen to the music." She brought a favourite pupil from her private school to show us how to jump, but the poor girl, overcome with embarrassment, landed badly and sprained her ankle. We never did succeed in standing in the air.

There was one teacher who made ballet so incredibly boring that I made every effort to do the opposite of what she told me. In the end, as an antidote, I began going secretly to take private lessons with Lydia Kyasht, who had been Karsavina's classmate and friend in the St. Petersburg ballet school. Kyasht filled the room with movement and music and I was happy to find dancing once more a thing of grace.

Nicolai Sergeyev was by far the oldest and most demanding teacher. A wizened little man but quite erect, with upright grey hair, the ghost of a moustache and wearing thin-rimmed glasses, his well-kept clothes hung rather loosely about his body. . . . His classes were in the very old tradition and quite killing, but his sharp eyes noticed any slackers and his little malacca cane would come down with a light whack on the calf, or jab at some muscle that was not working to his satisfaction. To gain a breather we would try to inveigle him into conversation, but his French and English— and some said his Russian—were very limited. Someone would ask, "How did you like the new ballet last night, Mr. Sergeyev?" He would reply, "No good moderna ballett! Publica like classica ballett. Classica ballett good." It did not matter what new ballet it was, they were all no good. The same went for what he thought of as the younger generation of ballerinas: "Pavlova no good"; "Tamara Karsavina no good"; and so on. Only his favourite, Loukom, who danced at the turn of the century, ever got a word of praise. Heaven knows what he must have thought of us! But he was oddly indulgent, and I was very fond of him; he brought so much atmosphere of the old-style ballet school to Sadler's Wells Theatre. . . .

In those pre-war days we received no pay for our six weeks' holiday. Nevertheless, we somehow managed to go off to Paris to study with the famous

Russian ballerinas of the last Czarist days in St. Petersburg. There were three of them living in exile, each with her own ballet school, and each offering different qualities as teachers of the prerevolutionary period before Vaganova collated and standardized a system for training under the Soviet régime. Senior of the three, and the one to become my favourite, was Olga Preobrajenska. She was small, about four foot ten in height, with a slightly hunched back, a face full of character, and an impish sense of humour. This was the woman whom Gontcharov, in Shanghai, told me had terrified all her students because of her severity and terrible temper. Naturally I was most apprehensive of attending her class until I found that, at the age of sixty, she was considerably mellowed, though still able to get extremely angry. Her daily class followed a very set pattern, to which one quickly became accustomed, though the pianist, another little *émigré* old lady, never could get it quite right. "Pourquoi *poum—poum—poum?*" complained Preobrajenska towards the piano. "Je veux *Poum—Poum—poum—po-poum!* No *Poum— Poum—Poum!*" And she would turn back to glower at the class until someone danced especially well, when she would rediscover her smile. As a matter of fact, none of the Russian teachers adhered to strict musical patterns. The accompanist was expected to lengthen some measures and add a few flourishes at the end of a phrase as required. Conductors were expected to do the same thing, pandering to the dancer's whim, and this created some rather unmusical traditions. In the English ballet, however, we were brought up very strictly and subjected as likely as not to a curt reprimand if we dared to ask for a change of tempo. Constant Lambert was not a man to be ordered about by a handful of ballet dancers. He understood ballet as a genuine marriage between music and dance, with music the senior partner.

Preobrajenska had always been the poorest of the three teachers. She told me that she had only succeeded because she watched every role in every ballet so that if a ballerina was suddenly taken ill she would be able to replace her instantly. Now, in exile, she was the only one who did not have her own studio. She rented one at the extraordinary Salle Wacker rehearsal rooms at Place Clichy. This building in the Montmartre night-club area consisted of steep iron staircases and small studios, two or three to a floor, each with its piano pounding out a conflicting tune for a different group of dancers. It was a long climb to Preo's studio on the fourth floor, but once there one found a light room with windows on two sides and a big mirror covering the whole third wall. Parents or visitors could sit near the piano. It was said that M d'Artemovsky, brisk, white-haired, with a little moustache, a little paunch, and a monocle, who acted as her secretary, welcoming one effusively and collecting the money, had been cheating her for years, stealing most of the profits and giving her just enough to live on. She was a darling. I worked very hard with her, learning much about presenting oneself to the audience. *"Regardez publique,"* she would shout, indicating the mirror. "Don't look at the floor, look at public."

She taught all day, with a short lunch break, during which she had a morsel to eat before climbing onto a chair to put the crumbs out on a high windowsill for the birds, whom she loved much more than humans. There was a peculiarity about her main class of the day for professional dancers. At the end of one hour and a half the door was opened to allow the children in to start their junior class at the barre. Meanwhile our class spent fifteen or twenty minutes in the center of the room, practicing the difficult fouetté turns (featured in *Swan Lake,* Act III) for which the pianist accompanied us. This meant that the children got on as best they could against our music and with scant attention from Preo. My mother used to puzzle over it. "I see the children with terrible faults getting no correction. I can't understand at what point they turn into the accomplished dancers of the senior class. I just cannot make it out," she said.

The ballerina Mathilde Kschessinska, by marriage La Princesse Romanovsky-Krassinsky, was a completely different personage. She lived with her husband, the Grand Duke André of Russia, in fashionable Passy, where they had a charming little villa on a private road, and she had her own private studio nearby. The studio was modern, clean, elegant, light, and airy. Photographs of her best pupils adorned the walls above the positions they normally occupied at the barre. Pride of place beneath the picture of Tatiana Riabouchinska was offered to favoured visitors to her class.

Kschessinska, about the same age as Preobrajenska and also as diminutive, was very upright, with a rather aristocratic face, long straight nose, and the most coquettish, sparkling eyes. By contrast to Preo, who invariably wore the same brown dress, school-tunic style, over a white short-sleeved knitted blouse, she had a variety of different-coloured floral chiffon dresses made to the same becoming pattern and worn with a matching single-coloured chiffon bandana tied round her coiffured grey hair. Everything about her class was happy, smiling, enchanting, light, and free. She had, after all, charmed the last Czar when he was a young cadet, and had become his mistress. Later she was protected by the Grand Duke Sergei Mikhailovitch, who covered her in jewels and built for her the small palace that Lenin was later to find so appropriate for his famous balcony speech to the revolutionary crowds. It was on an Italian holiday with my beloved Princess Astafieva that Kschessinska had fallen in love with the Grand Duke André and conceived the child she was somewhat embarrassed to bear while still protected by Grand Duke Sergei. Not daring to reveal the true situation she continued dancing on her return to St. Petersburg—but had her costumes cunningly altered, and changed the direction of certain steps so that she should never be seen in profile from the Imperial Box. She loved parties, jewels, and gambling, even though this high life was incompatible with the daily routine necessary for a Prima Ballerina Assoluta. Therefore she cleanly—and cleverly—divided her life in two. Four weeks before a performance at the Imperial Maryinsky Theatre—now the Kirov—she closed her house to guests, followed a strict régime, practiced for hours each day, and retired early at night to prepare herself for the triumph of her appearance and for the several encores which the Grand Duke requested by a nod of his head from the box.

When the curtain fell on her last *révérence* she resumed the lavish entertaining in her palace and the bewitching of handsome men. At times she retired with the Grand Duke to the country estate he had given her, for a restful summer idyll.

As an exile in Paris, after gambling away in Monte Carlo the fortune and jewels with which she escaped from Russia, she was still vivacious, captivating, full of life and allure. Her lessons were unusually musical and were bent on charming an imagined audience behind the wall of plate-glass mirror. She was really a delight. June Brae, who loved Kschessinska's style, was always one of her favourite pupils. I loved her, too, but found it difficult to choose between her, Preo, and Lubov Egorova, third of the famous Paris teachers.

Egorova, perhaps ten years younger than the other two, was married to one of the Troubetskoi princes, and she, too, had her own studio, near the Place de la Trinité—not as fashionable as Passy and not far from the Montmartre area. Egorova was taller, more like Astafieva in build, dark-haired, and full of the dignity and soul of old Russia. I felt her to be very warm-hearted, but remote. It was as though the other two had remained children at heart, while Egorova had grown up and experienced the sufferings of the world. As a teacher there was a depth of emotion in her class arrangements, particularly in the long adagio sections, that no one else I know has offered. I felt a deeply respectful adoration for her.

—from *Autobiography*, 1976

ALLEGRA KENT

Nijinska

My mother and I stood in the open doorway watching. A thin girl was practicing fantastic pirouettes that I remember to this day. I was awed by the beautiful bodies and their clean and smooth movements. A secretary pointed out Belita, the ice-skater, and Vera-Ellen the movie star. The names meant nothing to me except that they were famous people who wanted the best training. I was in the right place. I was surprised, however, by the number of grown men in the class. They were former GIs, all doing complex steps and combinations. The GI Bill covered the study of ballet as well as college.

The Yellow Pages had helped us locate the studios of Bronislava Nijinska, the sister of the illustrious dancer with the extraordinary leaps, Vaslav Nijinsky. Madame, as she was called, a plump, nice-looking woman in black lounging pajamas with a long cigarette holder (an outfit that never varied), stood off in a corner with a pianist. She was counting in Russian; I would hear *"ras, va, tri"* from all my Russian teachers for the next thirty years. Her husband was simultaneously translating everything she said into English. She had great authority and was single-minded about what was going on in that room. The world began and ended right there at that moment. Extraneous aspects of life didn't exist for her. I was impressed.

Even though I didn't know what ballet dancing looked like, let alone how to do it, Mother had again enrolled me in an intermediate class. For her, it was never necessary to start at the beginning. Once again she was exercising her reckless courage through me, but I was in a state of dazed happiness. At last I was where I wanted to be.

I changed into my two-piece sleeveless sunsuit and met Irina, Madame's daughter, who would be my first teacher. She also was in black lounging pajama pants but with a flowered top. Mother told her how little I knew about ballet, but that didn't seem to matter, and I joined the large class of perhaps forty people. I looked at the ex-GIs who were so big next to the young girls in the class. These men had been through a war and all that that meant, and I was an extra-small eleven-year-old, but strangely that didn't make me uncomfortable or self-conscious. My yearnings had brought me here, and eleven is a receptive age for a child, no longer a baby and not yet a teenager. I assumed that the mixed group was typical.

From my experience in Florida, I knew that a ballet class started at the barre, so I took a place near a window and waited for the class to begin. This time I understood that a turnout was not a turn-in. Mother was sitting on a long bench at the back of the studio already engaged in earnest conversation with another mother. Was their gossip about me? No, not yet. Today Mother was my investigative reporter.

Class began with pliés. These I could do, but as we progressed to more complex steps, I felt discouraged. I tried to imitate the steps the others were doing, but the movements were too advanced. The obvious became a reality: I hadn't had the basics. I threw all of my energy into concentrating. My body had to do what the other bodies could do. But I was about two years behind everyone else, and my athletic abilities didn't help me as much as I had thought they would. I also couldn't understand the instructions, because Irina spoke rapid-fire English with a heavy Russian accent, and she indicated only vaguely, impressionistically, what she wanted. I looked at Mother. She was now talking to a mother seated on her other side.

Still, I wasn't going to give up as I had in Florida. I had the utmost faith in my ability to dance, and I was convinced I would catch up. In some ways, I'm glad I didn't start at the beginning. The pace might have been too slow, and dry technique might have dampened my spirit. This was top-of-the-line training. Had it been less than that, I might have wasted years and been ignorant of what the best can give.

At the end of the class, Irina gave a repeated pattern of step, step, leap—or as she called it, jeté—in a circle around the large room. I immediately did this combination with a free, powerful style, jumping high. This was the athletic side of dance I understood. What I had been doing on my own was already in the dance vocabulary. Then I looked around. For my size, I was jumping higher than anyone else. Although I was unable to do some of the more basic steps, the most difficult moves came easily. And I knew I could learn the rest, it was merely a matter of time. I had the beginning and end of class in place; I would have to learn what needed to be done during the middle. But the moment I made my mighty jump and flew higher than anyone else, I knew this world would be my life.

So that I could learn to leap in a more balletic way, Mother arranged for a few thirty-minute private lessons with Irina. Mother and I believed years could be compressed into a half hour. During these sessions, Irina told me that her uncle Nijinsky used to crouch slightly in his preparation and then spring to full height at the peak of a jump. This enhanced the elevated look of his grand jetés. I understood that dance is partly based on illusions and magical effects.

I worked ferociously, embarking in all innocence on a systematic and accelerated crash course. I increased the number of regular classes I took and copied the imagery as best I could.

Because Irina's English was almost incomprehensible, I took out books from the public library to learn the names of the steps. I read an illustrated book on the fundamentals of ballet, a biography of Pavlova, and books on dance history. I read about Fokine and Massine. There was very little space given to the name George Balanchine. I also read a softcover pamphlet called *The ABC's of Ballet* by Lincoln Kirstein. (I never told him about this.)

Apparently I caught up, because Irina told me I was ready to begin pointe work some six months after starting her class. Most young dancers cannot wait to get on pointe, but I contradicted her. I had read that two years of training were necessary first. As a compromise, I said I needed another month. After a total of seven months of hard work, I began lessons on pointe.

By the second year, I took classes from Bronislava Nijinska herself. She used a set barre, which meant that the same exercises were done every day to the same music. One piece by Burgmüller was played for grand battement, and when I hear the piece today I think of Mme. Nijinska, the woman who told us "arms cannot be like spaghetti." One day in class, she asked me to try to push her arms around. I exerted great effort, but they wouldn't budge. She wanted me to see her underlying strength and power, which ballet requires in order to project its airy look. She wanted me to understand that the light look of dance was merely the surface of the sculpture—there was a mixture of steel and quicksilver at the heart. Madame herself was on the heavy side, but, in a demonstration of how to hold the body, the men who lifted her were amazed at how easy she was to raise from the floor. This was the dichotomy—the achievement of fragility and delicacy meant a core of strength. Butterflies are not weak.

Madame couldn't stand anyone chewing gum in her class, but she never directly confronted the person who was doing it. Instead, in a surprising move, she would deflect her anger toward another target. In flight, with feathers extended and her black lounging pajamas flapping against her legs, she would rush over to an innocent spectator and accuse him or her. I think she always chose a timid soul to point out how upset the real offender should be. The accused visitor never understood what was happening. After class, Madame would explain her tactics to the bewildered onlooker; it seemed this was some variation on Russian etiquette or some law of the steppes. Another forbidden action was whistling, which Madame considered bad luck in the studio or theater. I would remember these things thirteen years later when I danced in her native country.

After class we grouped around her, and she hugged and kissed us with great emotion and warmth. We had tried to be dancers, but that was over, and now we were once again human beings who needed affection. She told us that when she was young she had never fussed over pointe shoes—she'd wear anybody's if they were the right size. To dance was all; the equipment was incidental and shouldn't be overemphasized.

From her, I also learned not to fear competing with men. Toward the end of class one day, Madame took my hand. The men had just done a big jumping step across the floor and covered an enormous amount of space. Now the two of us, an old woman and a child, were going to do the same. I looked in Madame's face. She was gloriously ready. She signaled for the pianist to start. We would not be outdone by the male dancers—or anyone, for that matter. I looked at the corner of the room. That's where I was going. And so we were off and flying. We did it: "Very good," Madame said in Russian, smiling wildly. For her, life was really only a series of moment-by-moment triumphs in dance. She was absolutely her brother's sister.

—from *Once a Dancer ...*, 1997

PAULINE KONER
Fokine

The Fokine home and studio was a white stone mansion on Riverside Drive and Seventy-third Street. In the winter a permanent tornado swings around the corner of Seventy-second Street and sweeps up the street. Coming down that street in winter I had to lean with all my weight against the wind. The interior of the house was elegant in European fashion with an entrance foyer, marble staircase, and iron balustrade spiraling to the second floor. At the base of the staircase hung a life-size portrait of Fokine in the costume for *Panaderos* and, farther up, hung a smaller portrait of his wife, both painted by Fokine. To the left of the staircase was a carved armchair flanked by a marble-topped table which held the class book we signed as we entered.

When I arrived for class, cold and breathless—sometimes with frost clinging to my eyelashes and the wind still whistling in my ears—I often heard Fokine playing the piano. He was a sensitive musician. I took the tiny elevator to the fifth-floor attic, a bare dressing room with a few plain chairs.

If you were lucky to find a free chair, you could hang your clothes on it. If not, the floor would have to do. In a terror about being late, I struggled into my pink tunic with underpants to match (leotards and tights in class were unheard of at that time), taped my blistered toes and heels, slipped into ballet shoes, and rushed to the fourth-floor studio, a small room equipped with a barre.

Fokine entered class with a brisk bouncy step, trim and vibrant. "Good afternoon, ladies," in a heavy Russian accent. At forty-six he was strikingly handsome; his baldness, revealing a finely sculpted head, enhanced rather than detracted from his appearance. The side hair brushed forward softened his face with its high forehead, arrow-straight nose, and piercing gray eyes shadowed by bushy eyebrows. His strong chin was mellowed by a sensitive mouth that curled in the corners. This balance of strength and softness was evident in other aspects. He had a sly sense of humor which could be droll or bitingly sarcastic. At times those gray eyes could take on a steely look, and I was sure there was a temper I would rather not see unleashed and a stubbornness that could harbor a grudge. Although he was only five feet eight inches in height, I always thought of him as tall. He had a way of holding his body that projected height. He had a lightness and buoyancy, tempered by a strength and sharpness, that made everything he did unique. I could easily imagine how his young students at the St. Petersburg Imperial Theater School must have worshipped him and vied for his attention. He admitted to having had an entourage and loving it.

In class Fokine was adamant about the details of his style. He never permitted a flexed foot in beats. His grand rond de jambe was with a slightly arc-shaped leg, rather than the straight leg, with the knee well turned out. To test the line of the leg, he would put a straight-backed wooden chair at the side of the body where the knee would be in space. The rond de jambe had to be executed without the slightly bent knee touching the top of the chair. He showed us that if the knee turned in at the side or if the leg dropped too soon as it moved to the back, it would touch the chair. He insisted on an arm shape that today has completely disappeared in ballet technique. When the arm was held to the side, the palm faced down with a slight arching of the waist. The fingers were never very separated but reached into space in a rippling curve with the thumb long and tucked under the palm. Fokine always talked about tapering the hand and the need for it to continue the flowing line of the arm, a profile shape that was far more interesting as a design than simply seeing the flat of the palm. Furthermore, to emphasize flow, he wanted the hand to move in slight opposition to the arm. This kept the wrist and fingers alive to the very last movement.

For me, the most important element of the Fokine style and technique was the total awareness of the body. The spirit of the movement was as important as the mechanics.

"I want you to use entire body, always," he said. "If you keep torso stiff, you are not dancer. You look like broomstick." He loved the diagonal line and asymmetry. The reason so much of ballet movement faced front, he claimed, was that in early days it was forbidden to turn your back on royalty.

When barre was finished, I crammed my feet into my toe shoes, which I hated, and trooped with the others down a dark, back spiral staircase to the third floor, then down the marble staircase to the second floor, where the Ampico grand piano stood on the landing. The main studio on the second floor was a magnificent room, running the width of the house. Floor-to-ceiling french windows faced the Hudson River, allowing the sunset to pour in. A crystal chandelier hung in the center of the room, and wall sconces framed by gold-painted molding hung on the walls. At one end was an elegant marble fireplace. Centered on the opposite wall was a gold-framed mirror, the only mirror we had to check our positions.

In this studio we did center floor-work: the adagio, allegro, and finally Mr. Fokine gave us combinations, sometimes whole excerpts from his ballets. For me this was the most interesting. I could let loose and dance. My class was intermediate-advanced. There was a young stringbeany girl whose legs I envied. Her name was Nora Koreff (we later knew her as the famous ballerina Nora Kaye). I would look at her and think, My body is all wrong; I'm too short. I hate my legs, but, thank God, I have a long neck and long arms. Nora was one of the most determined hard workers in the group, taking two or three classes a week. I always wondered why, when it was the fashion to change your name from American to Russian, she did the reverse. Of the others, Esther Rosen, who was my friend, danced for years in the Radio City Music Hall Ballet. Betty Eisner, renamed Betty Bruce, was a headliner in Broadway shows. Annabelle Lyon, an exquisite, delicate dancer, was in Ballet Theatre for years. She and Nora were in the original cast of Antony Tudor's *Pillar of Fire*. The miniature Leda Anchutina, a brilliant technician, married André Eglevsky and later helped create his school. Orest Sergievsky and William Dollar came to some classes. At times we caught glimpses of Patricia Bowman, star of the Roxy, Radio City, and Broadway, or Paul Haakon, who, at the age of sixteen, was already a professional dancer with an established career.

I never took class with a sense of routine. I was bubbling with excitement. The anticipation, the thinking, the taking, was a special event. My whole life revolved around it. Exposure to Fokine was less a technical development than an artistic experience. Whatever technique I had, I got from him: but more important in Fokine's classes, I learned to *dance*. Technique was acquired by the need to perform as classroom exercises excerpts from *Petrouchka, Carnaval, Les Sylphides, Firebird,* and *Les Elfes.*

Fokine always sang for our classes, never at a loss for a melody from Tchaikovsky, Chopin, Schumann, or music remembered from his own student days. We had no regular accompanist, but the Ampico piano was a very special instrument. It was a grand piano of excellent quality, yet its special feature was that it was equipped to play, electrically, piano rolls recorded for it by the leading pianists of the time. After learning a dance to Anton Rubinstein's "Romance" or a section of Fokine's *Les Sylphides,* Fokine would turn on the Ampico. Imagine dancing in class to the world's greatest pianists! Since I was sensitive to sound, it was ecstasy for me, and it helped, I am sure, my musical phrasing and dynamic response.

From the start, I hung on to every word Fokine said and watched every move he made. The depth of his emotional color, the passion with which he attacked a phrase, taught me more than just doing an entrechat six. Fokine hated the use of virtuosity for display; every movement had to fulfill its purpose, his vision of the dance as a whole. I worked hard on my technique and learned to do entrechat six with great ease, but only as a means to an end. It was not the *doing,* it was the *dancing* I craved. He rarely complimented us, but his eyes and his smile were enough for us to know. He often stopped to explain in detail why he had developed his stylistic changes. For him, all his movement had "motivation." He was the first person I ever heard talk about the "harmony of line." For him, arabesque meant a sense of flow in space, a crescent shape parallel to the floor, extending from fingertip to toe without any break of line, a sense of reaching, a need to go forward, a sense of floating or soaring in space. An attitude was the vertical opposite, a reaching up to the sky, but again the ever-present flow of line from fingertip through body to the arc-shaped leg tapering toward the earth. Fokine's use of the head was special; its elegance in repose, with its slight tilt up, the lift from chest, through throat to chin to complete a movement. He insisted that the flow of movement be continued through the head and through the hands into space: "Reach into the space. Don't stop movement at neck or wrists. I want whole body alive, be involved with smallest movement—expression of whole being."

Fokine gave us long phrases so we could sense the shape of the movement as a whole. When he demonstrated an excerpt from one of his ballets, there would be a sudden transformation. The years dropped away as he swept through the studio with a light, fleet urgency of movement to evoke a sense of delicacy, of fragility, that covered the gamut of dynamics. He could convince us that he was Petrouchka, or the Moor, or the Ballerina through an instantaneous change. He could be a diaphanous sylph, then a Greek shepherd, or an oriental slave. His body seemed to take on a different shape and proportion for each role; even his face changed. Sometimes he stopped for a moment and looked out the window, and there was a distant look in his eyes of a long-remembered time: the time of his greatness when these works were first danced by Pavlova, Nijinsky, Karsavina. I could feel his wistfulness. How frustrating it must have been to watch us, a bunch of adolescents, all shapes and sizes, struggling through his masterpieces. I can see him showing us the moment from *Carnaval* when Pierrot tears out his heart—his twinge became visible as he said, "I cry." To watch him offer his heart as a gift to Columbine was to realize what he meant by dance characterization. It was not pantomime; it was real.

—from *Solitary Song: An Autobiography*, 1989

Suki Schorer
Balanchine's Teaching

One of the leading teachers at the School of American Ballet, Suki Schorer (born 1940) joined New York City Ballet in 1959, and quickly won Balanchine's admiration both as a dancer and a potential pedagogue. She became a principal through her agile quickness and charm, creating such roles as the Butterfly in A Midsummer Night's Dream *and Pierrette in* Harlequinade. *Almost from the start, Balanchine had her giving lecture-demonstrations around the city and teaching class, and upon her retirement she became a full member of the SAB faculty. Her deep understanding of Balanchine technique and style is demonstrated in her detailed book* Suki Schorer on Balanchine Technique *and in SAB's annual workshop performances, for which she has staged some three dozen ballets.*

It is the teacher who must find a way to obtain maximum effort and constant striving to master every aspect of the technique while allowing the dancer's individual gifts to develop. Yes, Mr. B wanted a tall, slender body, a long foot, good turnout, high extension, extreme quickness, mastery of every step in the vocabulary, refined musicality, and on and on . . . and yet, it was the dancing *person* who finally engaged his attention. Even though they must constantly insist on the best possible execution of the entire technique, teachers need to remember where it is to be used. They must remember that they are not drilling soldiers or training circus performers and that very few ballets call for dolls or robots.

Mr. B taught clarity, musicality, purity of form, and simplicity. Any overt display of personality was superfluous; there was no place for any play-acting or hard sell. "Don't pretend to dance," he would say. He wanted the dance to speak for itself, guided by the music. The result could be romantic, chic, passionate, sad, elegant, sensual, mysterious, flirtatious, witty, etc. When the choreography called for the dancer to go onstage and take a pose before starting, Mr. B wanted us to walk quickly or run to place and set ourselves immediately to dance—no slow processional to place in the grand ballerina manner. "Run like a sandpiper," he said, meaning fast legs and feet and no noise. When the dancer had finished, he wanted a brief, modest bow and then quickly off. We were not to stand out there and woo the house for more applause.

Mr. Balanchine's classes had only one purpose: to prepare us to dance his ballets better and more in keeping with his aesthetic. Balanchine was the one who said, "I don't teach health." Class was not a generalized warm-up or conditioning, not even the barre. The company schedule allowed no time for that, even had he been willing. We were expected to start class ready to work full-out on the technique of classical ballet, meaning that some of us had to warm up before class began. The purpose of class-work was to give our movement the qualities required for a beautiful and interesting performance. The goals were refinement, control, articulation, and the highest possible levels of skill and finesse, all aimed at making real, if only briefly, the idealized beauty of the human body.

We worked on perfecting the movements specific to ballet. Balanchine thought of classical technique as a language with its own vocabulary, rules of grammar, capitalization, punctuation: A stop in fifth was like a period, dance phrases were separated by implied commas and connected with pliés, and so on. Whatever the specific aspect we were trying to develop, he made sure we never lost sight of its function in the overall scheme.

It's as if the dancer speaks with her legs and feet. To Mr. B, the clarity of steps, all steps, was equivalent to good enunciation. Just as a person speaking has to say each word clearly for the complete meaning to be conveyed, so too Mr. Balanchine made us understand that each gesture, each step had to be clearly legible for the audience to see and appreciate the beauty of the movement as a whole. Even when we were working most intensely to extend ourselves in one way or another, to do a certain step as we had never done it before, we could not throw away what came before, nor what followed. Participating fully in the present moment really meant participating fully in each of the many moments.

Mr. B would remind us that the Greek orator Demosthenes had to put pebbles in his mouth and practice speaking aloud to learn to enunciate clearly. Otherwise, how could he address the Athenian assembly? In the same way, we needed to learn to clearly and beautifully articulate our movements; otherwise, how were they to be seen across the orchestra pit and to the back of the house, to the top of the house? So we repeated them over and over in a variety of combinations and at the widest possible range of tempos.

Mr. B often used very simple combinations to remind us what classical form entails—for example, échappé sauté, jump to second and jump back to fifth. He could start by correcting anyone whose starting fifth position was not exact (feet crossed and glued together, no toes sticking out, legs properly turned out). Next, he would watch to see if we made a good plié and then, when we pushed off the floor, that we took ourselves into the air with the chest lifted and the hips up, and then he would look to see if our legs had opened—POW!—to second position (an immediate, precise second; no splitting way out and pulling back into second), and if our feet had pointed instantly, as we made a beautiful picture in the air. Finally, he would see if we landed on the tips of our toes and came down through our feet in second position, bringing our heels forward (with the same precise spacing between them) and knees side, with the weight over the balls of the feet. "No noise! Like bird landing on eggs," he would say, "catch yourself and descend." Jumping from second back to fifth would be looked at with the same care. And, of course, the upper body and the timing all through. If the details in the dancing are not precise in class, there is a great risk that the steps will lose their distinctive character when the dancer is onstage. . . .

Balanchine did not like to theorize, even about something as central to ballet aesthetics as the turnout. If pushed in an interview, he would simply say we turn out because it is beautiful. But when I was preparing to take over the New York City Ballet lecture demonstration program, I felt I needed something more to tell the public, so I went to him and asked if he could explain to me why ballet dancers turn out. Mr. B got up and, putting his feet in a tight little "V" and mimicking a bulky woman tilting forward, said, "In the old days, dancers wore long dresses with bustles, they had big hips and breasts, and they hardly moved, maybe just a minuet with a little bit of turnout." Widening his "V" and mimicking a fashionable lady closer to our time, wearing a romantic-era tutu, he said, "Then the dresses got shorter and we turned out more and we danced more." Opening his feet to a correct first and standing up as straight as he wanted us to be, he said, "We really move. Now we dance in leotard and tights, we are thin, and people see the whole body." He thought for a moment and said, "We turn out for the same reason poets write beautiful poetry." I thought, writing poetry is harder than writing prose. Poetry is stripped down to the essentials, and it is beautiful. We strive for the same effect dancing in leotard and tights.

This is not to say that Mr. Balanchine did not use the "natural" flexed foot and "natural" parallel feet in his choreography. In the First Theme of *The Four Temperaments,* for example, the dancers flex their feet and then point them to show even more beautifully the stretched foot. They also turn their legs in and then out to show the contrasting lines. On the stage, in his ballets, Mr. B used what was needed to obtain the desired effect, but in class he developed our classical technique.

—from *Suki Schorer on Balanchine Technique,* 1999

Richard Thomas
Interview with Barbara Newman

For many decades, Richard Thomas (born 1925) was one of the most important teachers of dance in America. In the fifties he danced (with his wife, Barbara Fallis) in the New York City Ballet, appearing in the first casts of such ballets as The Nutcracker *and* The Concert. *He and Fallis opened their own school, the New York School of Ballet, which, with the help of Lincoln Kirstein, eventually moved into the old premises of SAB. In later years, he taught in various schools and with various companies, most prominently Eliot Feld's Ballet Tech.*

You're writing about teachers or you're writing about teaching? It's hard to write about either of them, because teaching has to do with . . . God knows. I don't know what. I have a hard time about the whole business.

First of all, I'm retired. I teach only in this school [the Ballet Tech School]—I won't teach anywhere else—because I have no attitude here from anybody. When I came here the boys and girls who are now the company were 10 or 11 years old, I started that class. These children that I'm teaching now . . . Fortunately they have not seen anything and unfortunately they have not seen anything. It's a double whammy. They have never had the opportunity to see great dancing, but then, where would you see it anyway? That's what's so upsetting to me.

Now, I was never a very good dancer. I had a certain amount of talent, I'd had a lot of athletic experience as a boy and the wonderful thing for me was I really wasn't a child when I started. So I studied with my mind rather than just visually aping, like young people tend to do when they start out very young. I don't think children should ever go to ballet school 'til they're 11, 12 years old, 13, because it's so repetitive and they just mimic. Well, I was not a child, and I went to the class and I listened and I learned my lessons.

You have to understand, one of the most important things when I started dancing, which was in the '40s, there were no bad teachers in the United States. There may have been some regional people who ran up to Chicago and took ten lessons in ballet and went back and taught in their dancing school, but as far as I'm concerned that was legitimate, because they were bringing something back to town that might inspire a child to leave and go off someplace else. I was a tap dancer when I started out, and my tap-dancing teacher went up to Edna McRae or Harriet Hoctor in Chicago and she'd study for six weeks and come back and teach the routines that she had learned.

So I was lucky. But when I talk about teachers, I'm not talking about little regional dancing schools. I'm talking about Seattle, Los Angeles, Chicago, San Francisco—there, there were no bad teachers. Mary Day was in Washington, Leila Haller was in New Orleans. In New York City, if you couldn't make this class you could go to that class, and you went to a good teacher because there were no bad teachers. I came in on the end of the time of Fokine, who was from the Imperial school, and of Mordkin, who was from Moskva. They were both acceptable schools, but as Danilova would say, "Thanks God, I came from the Imperial school." Did you ever see that wonderful lecture she did years ago? She talked about, "There were two great ballet masters," before her time, actually, "there was Marius Petipa and there was Bournonville. Bournonville went to Denmark, and Petipa, thanks God, came to Russia." And I always thought, "Yeah, I know right where you're coming from," because they were both from the French school, but one encompassed the whole art form and the other had his own thing.

All of my schooling . . . the same with my wife . . . our schooling was right out of St. Petersburg, the Maryinsky. The great bulk of the schooling at the Imperial school was Cecchetti, and it was Petipa, and it was Johansson who was Danish [trained], and it was the Legat brothers [Nikolai and Sergei]. One taught one thing, another taught another thing. But you have to realize that the Italian school is the only basic intellectual school of ballet. All of the science of ballet technique came from the Italian school, and everybody else took from them. Now, most of the Russians didn't speak very much English, so consequently they didn't teach verbally a great deal, except to make a lot of noise and stomp around . . . and instill in you an attitude about what it was. But they didn't have the vocabulary to really analyze. You know, everybody laughs now when you say "perch turn." Well, those Russians translated piqué as "perch," Fokine taught you to do "perch turns" and "perch arabesque." It wasn't a vaudevillian attitude about ballet—they had no English. And nomenclature is a very interesting thing. I hear that in Australia now everybody has to call everything the same thing—your vocabulary can only be one way. I went to Celli, I went to Vilzak, I went to Oboukhoff, and nobody called anything the same thing. But they all taught the same thing, all of my teachers, everybody. It was presented totally different from one teacher to the next, but in its theory it was the same.

I'm not talking about style. There is no style in teaching classical ballet. A school must never have a style. You can teach styles, but you must never teach a style, because the style of your dancing changes with the choreographer you work for. You must never be schooled in one way of performing, because then you lack scope as a dancer. You have to be able to do whatever, and years ago we were very lucky because we had such sterling choreographers, and every time you danced for one of them it was all different. Fokine had a port de bras—there are a thousand port de bras—and Tudor had almost no port de bras, because he loved the sternum and this wonderful feeling of movement and he wanted to keep your arms out of the way. Makarova could never do the Tudor ballets, because she couldn't get rid of the port de bras and only use the arm as a gesture, for a statement, not for dancing.

So the teachers all presented it differently, but each one gave you a spirit to dance. Mme Nijinska was wonderful. First of all, she walked into the lesson, and you never knew how it was going to go. She had a set barre, which was the Italian barre, fifteen minutes, bip bip bip, and it was over. Then you came into the center floor, and you did all the Cecchetti exercises, forward and back, and she would give a very pretty adagio, and that was it. We had already gone through exercises that *had* to set you up, because then she started to choreograph. She would show her pianist what music she wanted, and then she would go here, go there, you do this, then we jump, entrechat six, soutenu, snap, snap. The class would be over and she'd still teach—I mean, she'd go on giving these things, "You come from this side, and you come from that side, and we all do. . . ." They were adults in her class and most of them were dancers. I was an exception, because . . . well, I was a teenager but not a dancer by any stretch of the imagination, so I was gasping! She made you hold your arms in a proper place and she would smack you . . . My dear, she bruised people all the time. She hauled off and hit me once because I was lazy—I was doing passé and I had my toe here, leaning on my knee, and she smacked me so hard my ears rang.

Have you read her memoirs? Isn't it the prettiest thing you ever read? I saw the manuscripts, because Irina [Nijinska] pulled them out and showed me. You could have hung the calligraphy on the walls. I never realized, until we went through all the books and papers, what a phenomenal education Nijinska had out of that Imperial school, in literature and art, in music, everything. She was just a fat little woman who couldn't speak English and screamed and yelled, and people hated her. Do you know that she was coming to teach for me on Eighty-second Street? Irina said, "Mama said she would love to come and teach, but you would have to give the barre. If you will do the barre and the first center floor, then she will teach the lesson." And then she died. It was heartbreaking for me, because I wanted all my kids to see this woman, who was a paragon. She was Women's Liberation before there was any such word, and she was one of the most inspiring people I've ever been in the class with, because she was so in love with what she was showing you and doing and wanting you to do. She would stand in the middle of the room like a little round ball and take a preparation and hit second position, relevé turn, relevé turn, relevé turn, and pirouette, pirouette, pirouette, and she was an old lady. And what she couldn't do she would come and beat out on your skin. She'd take her hands like this and mark it on your body and sing the rhythms. She wanted you to get all the musical nuances out of the steps, not just pas-de-bourrée. She and Balanchine had the greatest understanding of the musical significance of the vocabulary. Of course she did not teach it like he did, because she didn't have the words— she choreographed it but she didn't speak it.

When I went to the New York City Ballet, towards the end of my dancing career, and he was there teaching, for me it was like a postgraduate study of classical ballet. First of all, he taught just like everybody else from the same school that I'd always studied with. But he had the most phenomenal sense of the musical nuance of every bit of the vocabulary, so that it became a language with expression, each step had expression. And the wonderful thing . . . Everybody hated the fact that you'd go to class and he might only do rond de jambe in the air. After the first few pliés, you'd spend the whole rest of the class doing ronds de jambe in the air, one way or another. And everybody would go, "Aggghhh!" but I thought, *Isn't this wonderful, because I'm learning thousands of wonderful things about what this is*. And I always liked to teach that way, which I think is why a lot of people who ended up choreographing used to like to study with me, because it gave them a sense of ballet as a means of expression. You can do anything with the ballet vocabulary, there are so many things that you can tell.

* * *

LET ME TELL you about teaching. I never thought I would teach until I knew that I wasn't a dancer anymore. First of all, I really wanted to be a dancer and if you want to be a dancer, that's what you want to do with your life. It never occurred to me, Will I be able to pay the rent? Will I be rich? Will I starve to death? Will I have a car? No. I never gave it a thought. I just wanted to be a dancer, and the idea of being a dancer to get famous or to be rich. . . . I mean, it didn't enter into it. I wanted to do that, I wanted to be Vaslav Nijinsky. A lot of the problem we have today is that most young people are so interested in the fame and fortune side of being a dancer that they're defeated before they start. And, as I tell my children [students] all the time, I never knew a great dancer that was dumb, but I've known a lot of famous ones that were stupid beyond hope. It just depends on what you want: do you want to be a dancer or do you want to be famous?

And teaching is like dancing—there's no point in going into teaching for money. I started teaching back when I was still dancing with the Alonso company, and Fernando [Alonso] was trying to develop a school. He went to an orphanage and took ten little boys, of a certain age with a certain facility, very much like they're doing here. He brought them to the school twice a week to take ballet class, and he put me in charge of teaching them, I guess maybe because of my background. Not that I was any great dancer, but I did have a good background of teachers. I taught them twice a week, and I enjoyed it.

THEN I LEFT the Alonso company, came back, joined the New York City Ballet company. And then, when I left City Ballet company in '58 and joined the circus and left the circus and came home, then I really was not working and I wanted to teach. I came from the theatre. I knew something very special that meant a lot to me. Why would I go do anything other than that? When I stopped dancing a lot of people said to me, "You're going to choreograph, aren't you?" and I said, "No." "Well, why not?" I knew I couldn't choreograph—you have to have a talent to choreograph. That's part of the trouble with the choreography today. All these people get to the point where they have to stop, so they start making ballets, which are, you know, noxious and impossible.

Harry Asmus opened a little school off Broadway and Fifty-fourth Street, and I taught for him. He was at that time teaching at the High School of Performing Arts, and all these kids came up from there. How well taught they were I don't know, but they always had a flair about them and they were a joy to teach. I knew what I was doing because I was just doing what I had been taught all my life. I was never a creator, ever—as a teacher I never created anything—and I didn't try to form my own theories about anything, because there aren't any new theories. There is no "Cecchetti system." Cecchetti was theory. It was stylized because the style he was teaching was the only format for performing at that time, everybody danced like this. But that doesn't mean that when you teach the Cecchetti school, the Italian school, you have to do all this funky stylization—that's not what it's about. The Cecchetti school is about the theory of classical ballet, just what I was teaching today.

After Harry Asmus, I was teaching at June Taylor [Dance School], and that was like being a prostitute. Sol Lerner said, "You go in the room, there's a pianist, you take on all comers. If there's one student or there's 20 students, it doesn't matter. You take 'em." And I did. I found out that you teach whatever comes in the room, and I probably developed security as a teacher at the June Taylor school, because I taught all day long. And on Saturday, I used to get up at 7:00 and hie myself over to Brooklyn. Marjorie Mazia, who is Arlo Guthrie's mother, had a school in Sheepshead Bay, and I used to go over there and teach, from like 9:00 in the morning to 12:00 or so, and get on the subway and run back to June Taylor's and teach from 1:00 until 5:00 or 6:00 at night. That's when Lupe Serrano left Ballet Theatre school and came to study with me, and I was teaching the June Taylor girls, big, hippy, tough ladies, by the same rules, same principles absolutely. Now, if you don't learn something from that, you'll never learn anything.

Then . . . I never wanted to go to the Joffrey school, Joffrey asked me to come and teach. Bob was wonderful, but the Joffrey Ballet to me was always a mediocre company because . . . Bob never left Seattle artistically. He studied with Mary Ann Wells, who was a very fine teacher, but . . . You know, I can be persnickety about a lot of things, but I can also hootchy-kootchy, and Bob couldn't. He couldn't do both and you have to, because, like I tell the children, "You're studying ballet, but the theatre's a gigantic world. It goes on forever." The first time I was to teach a 5:00 class, Eddie Caton was coming out of class and he said, "Dickie! You're gonna hate it! They can't dance on the music." And he was right, they couldn't, it was mind-boggling. John Prinz studied with me at Joffrey's, and I said, "I like having you in class, but you must go to the School of American Ballet, because there is no future here." I told Christine Sarry the same thing, "Go to Ballet Theatre. You gotta get out of here." I sent Eddie Shellman to Dance Theatre of Harlem. Bob Joffrey hated my guts—I threw them all out.

But I stayed until I went with the company to Russia. Bob dragged me off . . . He said, "You have to go with us, because we have no ballet master." I said, "I'm not a ballet master." He said, "Well, it doesn't matter, you have to come, because you can give company class and you can help rehearse the ballets." I said, "I don't like to rehearse ballets," and he said, "Well, you *can,* and

I have no one else." When we came back from Russia, I left Joffrey and went to Ballet Theatre and taught the 6:30 advanced beginners class. Of course that didn't make Mme Pereyaslavec and Bill Griffith and a lot of people happy, because I started out with like seven people and then all of a sudden I had twenty or thirty. Then a lot of other people came in just to listen, and it got too crowded and there was no place for me there. And that's when Barbara and I went over to Fifty-sixth Street and moved into the old Matt Mattox school, and Eliot's [Feld] father did all the paperwork and all the lawyer work to get us going—we didn't have a nickel. We had nothing.

At the same time I was teaching in Philadelphia for Barbara Weisberger at Pennsylvania Ballet. Getting on the train to Philadelphia and teaching all day long, twice a week. When I was in Philadelphia, Barbara taught on Fifty-sixth Street, and when she was in Philadelphia I taught on Fifty-sixth Street. How else was I going to make a living? I didn't have enough money to open a school and run it without working, and Philadelphia was paying me pretty well. We wanted a school in the city and I had all these people saying, "Open your own school."

You know, we didn't leave City Ballet under the best circumstances. There was a big blowup fight and we left, and then I started all the teaching business. But when George [Balanchine] was moving to Lincoln Center, Lincoln [Kirstein] sent a message to me saying, "Dickie, do you want the school on Eighty-second Street and Broadway?" Now, Ballet Theatre was dying to get in there, Joffrey was dying to get a hold of the premises, everybody wanted it. Lincoln wrote me a letter, and said, "Do you want the school? Because if you do, it's yours." And everybody was pea green with envy.

I don't know why they did it. Well . . . George liked me as a teacher. It's not a humble thing to say and I like to feel like I'm a humble man, but I'm probably the only teacher today who teaches what George Balanchine taught. You think SAB would be surprised to hear that? Well, they would, but they don't know what they're doing. No. George expounded to certain people on certain things to enable them. He never gave them an overall . . . It wasn't like when Oboukhoff did this at SAB and Vladimirov did that and Muriel Stuart did this and Doubrovska did her thing and Balanchine would come in on a Friday or Saturday and do his. That was already really thinning out. And you have to replace those people because they die, and they did die.

So George Balanchine and Lincoln Kirstein gave me that big school, and they said, "We can't just let you walk in there, so you have to pay us $1,800 for what we leave." I said, "I don't have $1,800," and they said, "It doesn't matter—$100 or $200 a month." Not for the lease. I went right in behind them on my own lease, and I just paid them $1,800 as fast as I could. The barres were left, the mirrors were left, the lockers were left, everything was left. Cockroaches forevermore.

And then we were stuck, yes, stuck, because we never had any money. We never had backers. We never had anybody. Which was OK, because I think that's the way to go, frankly, and I'm not a very subservient person. But we had the school and we did some very good work there. There were a lot of good minds and good people and good thoughts, and I have no hard feelings about anything that ever happened up there. We had good children's classes, from the area up there, and they sent me a lot of children from the School of American Ballet. They'd say, "No, we can't take you, but you should go up to the New York School of Ballet, because Mr. Thomas will have room for you." All the modern dancers never, ever left my school, and Lupe and Toni [Lander] studied with me until they retired. I was very fortunate at one period to have a class of brilliant dancers who were students. That was Toni and Lupe, Royes [Fernandez], Bruce Marks . . . They didn't come to me just because you have to take class every day—they came and studied with me and listened and tried out things. Maybe they agreed with me, maybe they didn't, but they all came to my class and tried—they all fell down, they all stood up, they could do this, they couldn't do that, and it was a great era in my teaching career. It was probably the most satisfying time of teaching adults, when all those people were there, doing it.

MY SCHOOL CLOSED in 1985, and that was part of the times' change. I have no hard feelings about the school being gone. It was a good time for it to close, it was on its last legs because of a lot of things. It was always a big financial hassle. I had a very hard time escalating the price of classes for the student body, because I didn't understand how they could be waiters and pay. The financial situation in New York . . . I would have been paying almost $10,000 a month rent, and I never had the kind of school that could meet that. I had a hard time paying $3,000 and then going up to like $4,500—that was not easy for me. We didn't have schools like Steps when I started, there were no grind houses back then, not at all, no, no, no.

The world has changed. We live in the '90s. Nobody in this world really chooses to analyze anymore who or what they are as a student or as a person or as an artist. *Artist* is an easy word to bandy about, but I don't really find much artistry around, because it's gone with the '90s. It's a done deal and it's over, and it's kind of sad. It will come back, the phoenix will rise. It always does—it's happened before. When everybody realizes how boring it is, something's got to change. I do not go to the ballet at all. I can't go to see City Ballet and I can't go to see Ballet Theatre for the same reason. I was in both of those companies, I know all the ballets and . . . they change the steps. But also, I cannot go to the ballet because it bores me. The last thing I went to see at Ballet Theatre, I saw a Tudor program, and they did *Dim Lus-*

tre, and I've never been back, because the dancers, whoever they were—not memorable, for certain—I don't think they knew who Proust was. I don't think they ever read Proust or ever knew what the phrase "remembrance of things past" could mean or ever heard that unbelievable music, because they danced the ballet like they were a little embarrassed. And when she runs and she drops her handkerchief and then he comes along and picks it up . . . the audience laughed.

Oh, those ballets are dead. I really and truly feel that we did the last *Les Sylphides* that I'll ever see. Just the tempi alone . . . I sit there now and think, It's going to stop. When you think of the finale of *Sylphides,* it's not andante, it's not pretty. It's a whirling mass, and those nuances have gone. I know the nuances of a lot of wonderful ballets—*Coppélia, Giselle* . . . I know more about *Giselle* than anybody alive, because I watched Alicia Markova night after night after night. I was on the stage in so many *Giselles* that if I ever wrote down all the ballerinas who I sat and watched go mad . . . Barbara had a wonderful way with coaching steps and stuff—I don't. I can only do it as a teacher. Coaching is a different thing, and companies aren't interested in that anymore. I couldn't be responsible for those ballets unless I had my own company, because as I said, I'm not subservient and people don't put up with me easily, and I need . . . always did . . . a lot of help. So the companies don't want me.

They could take my dancers maybe . . . They don't even want my dancers, because my dancers are too good and they're not persnickety enough. These kids have a hard time with refining themselves for certain things, because unless they see a reason for it, which they don't with Eliot because Eliot's ballets are so contemporary, they see no particular need. Since the first classes here become the company, they want to be in the company. That's their vision of where they're going, and they don't know about Ballet Theatre or anyplace else. They don't know who Greta Garbo is. But if you're talking about teaching, you have to talk about Greta Garbo. You have to talk about Margot Fonteyn. You have to remember that Beryl Grey was one of the most beautiful Lilac Fairies ever. You have to know that that happened. We tell them. We talk about it, and there will be one or two who listen. Somebody listens. I will not teach adults again, but I teach children because . . . Some of it's selfish. I love classical ballet and I love the theory of classical ballet and I get to see them do things that I know they should do, and that makes me happy. It's also very good for me, because I'm in my seventies and it makes me use my head. I work crossword puzzles on the train, which makes me use my head, I judge dogs all over the country, which makes me use my head, and I teach ballet, which is what I love more than anything in the world, and that makes me use my head. It also makes me use my body, to some degree. I don't try to do anything in class, because it's not nice for a student to see a teacher stumble around. Your age will modify how much you can do and what you can do.

The nicest thing in this school . . . I have never taught anyplace before where there wasn't one child that I couldn't stand, but there's not a child here that is not captivating in one way or another. See, they come from no place and from no background, which is wonderful, because then you don't have to deal with any background. There are certain other things you have to erase. You have to erase if they want to be "blaaack" or they want to be "Spanish." Whatever they want to be, they can't bring it in my lesson, and I immediately inform them, "Leave your attitude outside my classroom." If you teach, you don't give class—you have to teach a lesson. If you have a lesson, you have x number of students. If you have x number of students, you're responsible, personally, for each one of those little lives. You are responsible for the future behavior of young people on their own, of tomorrow's citizens, and that's an important thing to take into consideration.

I threw out a whole bunch of girls the other day, because I said, "You can't come into my class with those fingernails. I'm teaching an art form here, and you can't dance on the stage with those nails because you'll hurt someone. You have to cut them all the way back and make them nice and rounded, keep them clean, but you can't wear them that way. You may not wear makeup and eye shadow in my class. I won't have it. You cannot wear all that mess. That's not what we're about here." Nobody can teach them to dance—only God. You can only teach technique, and if you're going to teach technique they have to be prepared to cope with technique, which means they have to be as streamlined as a Georg Jensen knife. There can be nothing hanging out. I just want to see you. I don't want to see costumes—that's for the stage. I have a lot of trouble with the boys and the hair. You know, the black kids like all the funky hair, and I tell them how awful and ugly it is and how I hate it. It's like earrings—I tell them, "You can only have one hole in each ear. More than one hole is mutilation, and I'm not into mutilation so you can't do it."

But you see, even if they hate you for it, it implants a seed that will produce sooner or later. You don't just teach jeté battu—you have to teach deportment. You have to teach, "Don't put your elbows on the barre. Don't lounge. Don't yawn in my face, it's rude." Now, in most schools, for instance in Russia or, I'm sure, the Royal Ballet School, no child would ever yawn in class. They certainly didn't when I was in the Soviet Union, but then, they come from a totally different background. They're frightened to lose the place in the school and they are taught manners. They certainly lose them fast enough after they get to the graduating stage. I was there in 1963, and they wore their bathrobes in company class, and when the teacher gave grand plié, some of them faced that way, some faced the other way, some did it with straight legs . . . No. If you go to a lesson, even an adult, even a finished dancer must conform to the classroom, because it's the only thing that saves his hide in the years to come. I know that from Fonteyn, from Danilova, from Markova, I know that from every great dancer I ever saw on the stage. They never came into the lesson and did their own thing. They came into the lesson, no matter who the teacher was, and did what they were told. So I think if you're not born to teach you shouldn't, because it ain't a job. It's not a job because it encompasses too many things. The only reason I teach now is because . . . not because I see a future for the students particularly, but because there is more to it than perch turns.

—from *Grace Under Pressure*, 2003

Tobi Tobias

The Quality of the Moment: Stanley Williams

The preeminent teacher of male dancers in the West for the latter decades of the twentieth century, Stanley Williams (1925–1997) was born in Copenhagen to a Danish mother and English father. He trained in the school of the Royal Danish Ballet and joined the company, where he enjoyed a successful if not spectacular career. By 1950 he was teaching (eventually Peter Martins, among others), and—having been a guest teacher at the School of American Ballet beginning in 1960—he was invited by Balanchine and Kirstein to become a full senior member of the staff in 1964. There he trained not only pre–City Ballet boys but worked with the greatest male dancers of the time, who made pilgrimages to his class—from Erik Bruhn and Nureyev and Baryshnikov to Edward Villella, who credits Williams with saving his career. (He had girl students as well—Darci Kistler, for one.) In 1981 he staged for City Ballet an homage to his dance upbringing: Bournonville Divertissements.

"Only connect . . ."
        —E. M. Forster

As usual, Stanley Williams is standing in the center of the studio—a huge space filled with raw morning light, his head cocked to one side, his gaze

directed inward as if he were listening to an interior voice. The dancers, dotted along the barres that rim the room, are paused in the kind of charged
silence that denotes ardent attention. Williams takes a breath, imperceptible
but for its lifting the breastbone, stretches his arms high—like a condor's
wings—on diverging diagonals, glances at the pianist who intones a single
note, then begins to stroke the ground with one foot in exquisite little
circles of motion. Rond de jambe par terre: one of the first three actions a
ballet dancer learns, and continues attempting to bring somewhat nearer to
perfection for the balance of his life in the theater.

The studio is in the School of American Ballet, which provides the New
York City Ballet with most of its dancers. In Williams's advanced men's class
this morning is Peter Martins, the company's reigning premier danseur, and,
in between barre exercises requiring the utmost physical concentration and
finesse, the two make tiny jokes in Danish, their common native language. In
the same class tomorrow will be Mikhail Baryshnikov, artistic director of
American Ballet Theatre, matter-of-factly taking his place among some two
dozen youths in the final years of their preparation for the stage. With his
two or three sessions a day at SAB, in the course of the week Williams will
meet several times as well with the intermediate men—boys, really—and
with the junior and senior sections of the academy's celebrated advanced
girls, creatures with limbs like thoroughbreds and faces like flowers.
Williams is a self-contained man of trim build, middle height, middle years.
He is rightly held to be one of the most extraordinary teachers of his
generation.

To the outsider, and even to the student not attuned to his approach,
Williams's classes may seem cryptic. For one thing, they are minimally verbal. A token word or two, perhaps just what sounds like no more than a
cluck or a grunt, a rapid flutter of the hands, and an exercise is set. To a certain extent this is commonplace dancers' shorthand, but even what Williams
does say is more likely to be a metaphoric clue to execution—how to think
about a step—than a literal instruction.

Williams's thinking about steps appears—deceptively—unconventional.
Actually it dwells at the very heart of classical academic dancing, but it is
indeed rarefied. At least it makes conventional methods look primitive by
comparison. Williams never occupies himself with the daily housekeeping—
straighten that knee, gaze forward, suck in the gut—of dance training. The
drill-sergeant technique and its cousin, the governess style, which teaches
prim correctness, are alien to his reflective nature. So is the popular method
that carries a class on the sheer physical thrill of moving, urging the dancers
on to bigger and bolder efforts with battle cries and flamboyant music.
Williams is working at a far more abstract level. He is absorbed with the
intrinsic quality of a given step or dance phrase—its unique look and feel; its

shape, its rhythm, the quality of its energy. For him, the authentic conception of an action puts a dancer halfway on the path to its proper execution.

One of his basic tenets has to do with the flow of energy, which must never be jagged, never slacken, never die. The dancer must move through the positions or poses ordinarily thought of as constituting a particular step, not rely upon them as way stations. Even when the body is momentarily in stasis—the pauses that give meaning to motion—it must continue to emanate this inexhaustible vital force.

Most of the time, Williams comes at this effect musically. A series of multidirectional tendus, throbbing battements sur le cou de pied, or unwinding chaîné turns may be compared to a single wave length of sound, a steady stream perturbed only by the even oscillations natural to it. "Listen to the pulse." Williams often returns to the comparison of the voice, vibrating in the singer's throat. He asks his dancers to be aware, simultaneously, of the individual short phrases and the overarching long phrases that constitute an exercise or an enchaînement. Time and again, he disconcerts their pedestrian notions of rhythm by dividing the typical eight-beats-each-way chore of a barre exercise into five-plus-threes, or by displacing the customary emphasis so that the feet are opening instead of closing on the downbeat. "Don't pay any attention to the step. Hear the timing. Our technique comes into the body by timing." Williams's rhythmic and musical ideas are most clearly projected when he is working in tandem with his preferred pianist, Lynn Stanford, who supplies their ideal accompaniment. It ranges from simple but subtly varied tones for the barre exercises, to infectious, rhythmically idiosyncratic improvisations in jazz and rag modes for the more exuberant traveling work. The way in which the dancer's ear must become alert and sensitized to this unusual sound track parallels the way in which the body must work.

What Williams does say in so many words can seem, on superficial examination, perverse. In order to get the visual or kinetic effect he wants, he instructs by contraries. On jumps he'll warn at the instant of take-off, "Don't jump," because he's after the buoyancy that is a gift of the prefatory plié, not gross thrust. On turns, in pursuit of the single frontal image in which the dancer appears magically suspended, rather than a whirling blur, he cautions, "Don't turn." "Am I confusing you a little bit?" he inquires, tilting his head quizzically.

He denies himself the luxury of abundant verbal images and the ones he employs stay strictly within the frame of reference of the human body. But they are oddly striking. To get the airborne dancers' feet arrowing correctly he reminds them that, aloft, they are on pointe. Or: "I see you have two arms, girls. But you should have only one. From the fingertips right across the chest to the other set of fingertips. One arm."

The enigmatic character of Williams's teaching style is belied by the lucidity of its results. So precisely do his disciples learn to isolate the quality of action needed for the core elements in the vocabulary that to see them reiterating a step in unison is often to have the nature of that step revealed as if for the first time. It's breathtaking to watch a whole room of them in solemn slow motion, angling first one way then the other, dipping creamily backward into fourth position, then loosing the energy into a swirl of pirouettes. The piano tolls like a faint echo of bells and there's no other sound but the balls of the feet spinning against the floor, a rhythmic whisper like sea waves receding against sand.

Williams's classes have an organic feeling to them, with good reason. They are not, like some conscientious teachers' syllabi, carefully outlined in advance, but allowed to grow out of concerns that manifest themselves in the immediate flow of activity. A mental image of a step that currently preoccupies him, or a dancer's unconscious revelation of a particular quality of movement, will provide the theme for a class, and for ensuing sessions—so that a series of lessons is vitally linked—until Williams has explored the theme to his satisfaction, exhausted its usefulness. At that point another theme will emerge to take its place. *Peter Martins*: "I've studied with Stanley since I was a boy and to this day, whenever I'm free, I take his class. Why? Because he is constantly renewing himself. He is constantly reconsidering the material of our métier and finding a fresh way to approach it. He is never what he was before, but always evolving new insights and explanations to intrigue you."

At some lessons Williams will zero in on a single student because that young dancer's entire mode of moving has enkindled his imagination; then he will work to analyze and communicate the essentials of that information to the rest of the group. This laser-beam attention is often impersonal on Williams's part; after an hour's devotion to an amazingly fluent, stork-legged girl, he couldn't, when requested, tell her name. That he senses a great deal about the students as individuals, however, is illustrated by his consistently directing the bulk of his efforts to those who display the eagerness and openness that permit teaching to happen. High-level receptivity might be Williams's first requirement in a pupil.

Other attributes can be listed in a Williams canon of dancers' virtues—for example, concentration. Until the dancer gathers his attention and focuses it steadily on the matter in hand, discerning the *real* matter in hand, no learning is possible. This kind of centering is particularly difficult for adolescents; it is even harder for teen-agers under the pressure of competing for the few open places in the most exclusive ballet company in the world. That these students are so frequently willing to sacrifice brilliance of effect to the kind of nuance they are only beginning to understand is an indication of the trust Williams elicits.

Then there is the question of will. The plentiful measure of irony in Williams's temperament is at its most evident when he explains, as if it were the simplest matter on earth, that one must make this or that part of the body do as one bids it. In pirouettes the toe must remain placed just so on the opposite knee—throughout a quartet of slow-motion revolutions if necessary; in attitude turns, the same toe must be extended firmly onto an imaginary plane in the air—and Williams requires the dancer to command this to happen. "It won't stay," he shakes his head sadly at a slipshod foot and its abashed owner, "if you don't make it."

Williams is not an unrealistic teacher, though. One of the salient features of his pedagogy is its juxtaposition of an uncompromising vision of the ideal and human sympathy—for the body's fallibility, the often absurd youth of his pupils, and the inch-by-inch way in which knowledge is won. "It's closer, but it's still not quite—," he remarks to an ethereal thirteen-year-old who, on a fourth attempt, has almost articulated the kinetic quality with which an arabesque penchée must—not descend but extend, then float up as if it were not hauled up, nor even lifted up, but appear to have arisen of its own accord. Williams takes in the last, wavering finish, reads the message in the child's dark, bewildered eyes, and says soothingly, "I know, but I have to tell you these things now, and later, when you're stronger and have more experience, then it will come."

It's a given that a dancer is a kind of angelic day laborer; the amount of brute physical work he must accomplish daily is legion. But under Williams's tutelage one doesn't earn more than basic credit for the muscles' dogged persistence. "You can practice forever," he sighs, half to unseen hearers—the ghosts of practitioners past, perhaps—half to the earnest *perpetua mobile* in the back of the room who repeat everything three times over, "but if you don't practice right. . . ." Then, abruptly shifting a keen gaze to the youngster next to him, "You have to do it right. Otherwise," he explains with tender patience, "you don't benefit." At this juncture, inevitably, one or two in the class stop flailing their limbs about or driving themselves like gyroscopes and stand stock still, the younger ones open-mouthed, and give every appearance of meditation. The dynamic American dancer Edward Villella, who credits Williams's teaching as a central factor in his education, recollects, "Stanley taught me to understand that, assuming a reasonably appropriate body for the work, seventy-five percent of dancing is mental."

Equally, Williams demands risk—not just athletic pluck but the spiritual mettle that permits relinquishing what is safe to dare the unknown. He pinpoints the extra second in place a boy is allowing himself where a soaring leap alights only to swerve into a whirlwind of turns. "You shy away from the crucial moment," he chides. "To see you with both feet rooted into the ground like that is so—dull. Try it again." Face belligerent with panic—"Now, don't be afraid of it"—the boy launches into the combination. "Do it all the way," Williams calls at the danger spot. The boy stumbles, grimaces—"Ye-e-es?"—begins a third time—"There," Williams signals—makes a fleeting, coherent mark in space that evokes gasps from several watchers, and lands to exchange a long look with the teacher who says quietly to him, "—and little by little the body learns."

AN OLD FRIEND has said about Stanley Williams: "He is in many ways a quite private man; he keeps his life on the other side of the curtain." Indeed it is difficult to persuade Williams to think autobiographically. "I really don't live in the past," he protests. "I'm not that sort of person. So suddenly, when you bring up a question, it all rolls by. So many different things come into my mind. I have a hard time figuring out—when did this happen, and what was really the reason for that. . . .

"I had, I guess, a happy childhood," he reflects, puzzling, as he often does, over how much truth can remain in anything that happened "so long ago." An account of his youth should be illustrated by Degas sketches—of horses and dancers. Danish on his mother's side, Williams was the grandson of a well-known horse trainer who frequently traveled to England to buy thoroughbreds for his clients. His English father was in the same business, had been a jockey as a youth. Williams was born in England in 1925 and lived there until he was about seven, in Newmarket, "the middle of nowhere." Relocated in Denmark, he'd spend Sundays, he remembers, "watching the races at a wonderful track north of Copenhagen. I loved the horses; they were beautiful creatures."

And he was one of those kids—countless dancer-stories begin this way—who was always scampering about. "From the time I was three or four, when an organ grinder came to play in the street, you know, with his little hat to put the money in, I would run out and jump around to the tune, like his little monkey, and follow him away." His mother, telling this as a party anecdote, encountered a dancer who suggested, "Why not try him in the ballet?"

"The ballet" in Denmark is the Royal (to foreigners, the Royal Danish) Ballet, housed in the venerable Royal Theatre on the King's Square—theater, studios, administrative offices, and academy under one roof, and sheltered by the protective benevolence of state support and an artistic tradition that reaches back two centuries. Here a youngster may enter before his tenth birthday, receive both a theatrical and academic education, and, if he continues successful, become an aspirant (company apprentice) at sixteen, attain full company membership at eighteen, retire at his peak on a lifetime pension, or continue his performing career indefinitely thanks to the wealth of mime roles the RDB repertory cherishes.

Williams entered the Royal Theatre at nine. "The audition was very simple. You take your shoes and socks off and they look at your feet. Then you walk, and march. Next, they play some music and see if you can move in time to it. We did a little polka, a little waltz, and that was it. I loved it from the day I started. Instinctively I realized that was what I wanted to do."

The program of ballet training Williams entered was rigorous and old-fashioned. Six days a week, year after year, first in the younger, then in the older group of boys, he went through the Bournonville "class" assigned to that day, each with its unvarying sequence of exercises and enchaînements set to prescribed music. The system, which seems tragically arbitrary, was devised after the great nineteenth-century ballet master's death, in an attempt to preserve his work; for decades the RDB practiced it like a religion. Williams was instructed in this method for seven years by Karl Merrild, "a military type—he taught with a stick, you know—a strong disciplinarian. He wasn't an imaginative teacher, no, but he injected a lot of energy into the work. And of course the style became second nature to us.

"So, every morning we would have our ballet class, which was followed by a free period when we did our homework, ate lunch, ran around a little. Then, in the afternoon, school, right on top of the building. We were always being taken away from our lessons, for rehearsals, because they used the children all the time then in operas and plays and ballets, so our education suffered. But it was an incredible life, in the theater, being exposed to all the classics—music and drama as well as dance. With the performances so many nights and traveling back and forth—home to theater—we never slept enough. And when I could rest at home I was always running off to do sports with my other—neighborhood—friends, because I needed that side of life too. There always had to be something—else."

After a mid-adolescent crisis—a stripling growth spurt causing severe postural problems, the career salvaged through the help of an astute gymnastics teacher—Williams duly became an aspirant and, in 1943, graduated into the company. Svend Kragh-Jacobsen, Copenhagen's senior dance critic, describes Williams's development as a performer: "He had acquired a very nice and clean style. He could do the things right. He had excellent 'tenure,' épaulement, and very nice feet. Very Bournonville. He was a handsome boy, and rather a quiet boy. You didn't notice him primarily for his temperament at the start. And then something extraordinary happened. Leonide Massine came here—it was in 1948—and set his *Symphonie Fantastique* on our company. The performance was wonderful, especially for one very young man, Stanley Williams, as the Jailor. This is in a passionate, witchy episode—with fantastic things happening. And there suddenly was Stanley with this *furioso* temperament and fire and force. This very nice and correct and not-too-passionate boy suddenly cracked open as a dramatic dancer. But, instead of building on this, the Theatre never really used him in that way again."

Although Kragh-Jacobsen's account may be heightened by his robust abilities as a raconteur, and by the intimate-mentor relationship critics abroad enjoy building with the artists they write about, a work film of the production confirms the idea of this raw, and surprising, theatrical force. Williams did get one more opportunity to display his dramatic gifts, when he played Mercutio in the *Romeo and Juliet* Frederick Ashton made for the RDB. Henning Kronstam, who was an incomparable Romeo in that work, remembers Williams's death scene as "moving and beautiful" although not quite up to the portrayal of Frank Schaufuss—"a different type: big, handsome, and tough"—in the first cast. Kronstam, who is the RDB's present director, concurs with Kragh-Jacobsen's idea that Williams never overcame a certain reticence as a performer, "perhaps because Stanley is a perfectionist. That little extra plus that makes the audience scream and roar is not his form of dancing." Niels Kehlet, the RDB's senior male virtuoso, and once Williams's student, suggests that Williams didn't have that overwhelming love and hunger for performance that overcame diffidence. "Frankly, he always seemed a little nervous onstage; you could always see it in a funny little trick he had with his thumbs."

Without exception, eyewitnesses praise Williams's purity in the Bournonville ballets. In the course of his career he laid claim to an impressive group of Bournonville roles, among them the pas de six from *Napoli,* the pas de deux from Act II of *Kermesse in Bruges,* Wilhelm in *Far from Denmark,* the ballet master in *Konservatoriet,* James in *La Sylphide*. Harald Lander, who directed the company from 1932 until the early '50s, made frequent use of him in his own ballets which were then plentiful in the repertory— "things the outside world will never have heard of," Williams jokes; "only *Etudes* made it internationally."

That Williams never attained the level of a Kronstam, a Kehlet, or an Erik Bruhn is explicable not merely in the light of his natural limitations as a performer but by his type and by his competition. In looks, line, and physical temperament he was a demi-caractère dancer, not a *danseur sérieux,* to use the old term, the classical "princely" type Bruhn came to embody so sublimely. Neither did he possess Kronstam's Romantic-hero qualities nor Kehlet's ebullience and pyrotechnical skill. When, in 1949 Williams was elevated to soloist status (the only official distinction the RDB makes from the ensemble), four of his peers were promoted along with him. They were Schaufuss, Poul Gnatt, Fredbjørn Bjørnsson, and Bruhn—a formidable group. By the early '50s the company included Kronstam, Flemming Flindt, and Kehlet.

In the end Williams's onstage career was prematurely curtailed by injury—a torn Achilles tendon—which limited him to less strenuous dancing roles, and mime parts in which he excelled. But nearly a decade before he gave his farewell performance, as Dr. Coppélius, his interests had been diverted in good meaure to teaching.

To hear Williams tell it, he happened into his real vocation by accident; one is tempted to apply the Denby line: "the sort of accident that happens to geniuses." In 1949, he says, Lander asked casually, "Would you come and help me teach the children in the school?" "So of course I said yes"—unquestioning deference to official power is still evident in Danish institutions—"and I assisted for a few months, after which"—Williams chuckles—"Lander never turned up again, so it was my class. Next was, 'Stanley, I have a meeting. Could you just go in and teach the company girls?' Now that was a big step because I was still quite young and I had grown up with a lot of them. It was hard for me to be an authority there. But that's the way it built. I don't know why Lander picked me, but I must say I liked it—teaching. It gave me such a satisfaction—to tell you the truth, that performing never did."

At the time Williams was giving his first classes, the insularity of the Danish ballet and its Bournonville-based pedagogy was already being penetrated by Russian influence. When Williams was just an aspirant, studying under Lander, he was exposed to bits and pieces of the foreign method and style that Lander had brought back from his own observations in the Soviet Union. After World War II, when European travel once again became possible for Danish dancers, Williams himself visited Paris where legendary émigré instructors such as Preobrajenska and Egorova gave lessons to an international clientele at the Studio Wacker. At home, Lander, recognizing both the value of the Soviet system and his own inability to assimilate and transmit it, invited Vera Volkova to become ballet mistress to the Royal Danish Ballet. The event proved to be a pivotal one for the company. Under Volkova's instruction, which was rooted in the Vaganova method—a codification of time-honed Soviet practices—the RDB was to gain the technical prowess that would enable it to join the mainstream of twentieth-century ballet. (This was accomplished at the inevitable cost of some of its most fragrant and fragile virtues—those having to do with the nineteenth-century charm of the Bournonville repertory.) Volkova's coming to the Royal Theatre in 1951 was also a critical event in Williams's career: One of the most inspired and effective teachers of her era, she apparently discovered in Williams an ideal apprentice, first, and subsequently a like-minded equal.

Niels Kehlet: "She had tremendous knowledge about dancing, and a great love for dancers. She had wonderful taste, and the most fanciful imagination.

She was always using images. Your hands should open"—unconsciously, his fingers unfurl—"like flowers. Or you were carrying a ten-øre piece [a tiny, glittering coin] on the breastbone. Use the neck like a horse—bend it, and move it up, bend it, and move it up"—suddenly so stallion-likes the nostrils might be flaring. "Now that she's gone [Volkova remained with the RDB until her death in 1975], we have these little jokes among us, about little flower here and little horse there." His eyes flash with passionate affection, and fill. "It's the way we remember her.

"She had a very clear eye. She saw and she understood. She could correct the smallest things, invent ways for you to discover how to do them right. But it was more than that. She had figured out, and she showed you, where the movement cane from—where the impulse lay, and how it felt as it traveled through your body. She was not interested, you see, in dancing by rote. Oh, she demanded a lot of hard work, but she was never a rigid or arbitrary disciplinarian. In between the most difficult combinations in her classes she'd put something just to move—that little piece of cake.

"She was a complete teacher. Always here. Always helping us with any and every aspect of our work—or, instinctively, leaving you to your own devices when you were trying to experiment for yourself. And personally—she had my total confidence. I could talk to her about anything, private, and I knew it would stay safe with her. She was a singular influence, and not just for me."

Williams: "She took a liking to me. She felt I had a talent for teaching. She would talk to me, until four in the morning. . . ."

Kronstam: "She did it after performances. She was staying at the Palace Hotel at that time and Stanley would come in dead tired in the morning, because she had been teaching him all night how to teach. Showing him what was right and wrong."

Williams: "I would ask her questions about specific things and she would answer—"

Kronstam: "I think she danced for him. Because that's what she did for me when *I* started teaching—lifted up her skirt and showed me the position and how to do and what to do and which things to use in order to get what she wanted out of the company at that time."

Williams: "She made me consider in a very professional way what I knew and what I didn't understand. But mostly we would just talk about *ideas* about dancing and teaching."

Kehlet: "You can't repeat other people's ways of explaining different aspects of technique and how to accomplish them. You can learn somebody's methods, yes, but what makes a great teacher is that he absorbs the influence and gives it his own interpretation."

Williams: "She made me start thinking about what I was doing. In the old days in Denmark when somebody retired from the stage he would just start giving classes. They were never taught the skill of teaching. So they would just give the same old steps every day. There was no thought or imagination behind it at all. Volkova taught me—I owe her such a great deal—to use my imagination."

Shortly after Volkova's advent on the scene, Lander left the RDB in the aftermath of a scandal over his alleged personal misconduct. The affair divided the company, with peripheral parties, among them critics, taking sides; it even became a public issue. Subsequently, while Lander pursued his career abroad, administrative power in the company shifted from one faction to the other and the directorship changed hands twice. During these difficult times, Volkova remained chief teacher, with Williams her right-hand-man, although he was favored with objectively better assignments under Niels Bjørn Larsen's administration than under the Frank Schaufuss regime. Most important, Williams was not overly distracted by the involuted, virulent political situation. He managed to develop steadily and serenely in his own vein, offering classes of exquisite simplicity which required the dancers to consider the very essentials of their technique. Kehlet remembers: "I was in my early teens when I first came into Stanley's class. We had been dancing our asses off for years, but we had absolutely no comprehension of what we were doing, and no placement. I could do fouettés, but I didn't know what first position was. Stanley took us back to basics and made us get it right, and I shall be forever thankful to him for that." To this day, it's this Shaker-furniture distillation of fundamentals that draws seasoned artists to Williams's class for regeneration.

Paths cross fortuitously. In 1956 the New York City Ballet was completing an engagement in Copenhagen when one of its principals, Tanaquil LeClerc, was stricken with polio. She was then married to the company's guiding force, the choreographer George Balanchine. "It was a terrible thing," Williams recalls. "For three months she was in the hospital, couldn't be moved, and Balanchine remained behind with her. Sometimes he would turn up at the theater early in the morning and watch me teach the children's class. I thought, boy, he must be bored silly with this. Then I would go downstairs and watch while he staged his *Serenade* and *Apollo* for our company, and it made this enormous impression on me—it was flabbergasting—to see how he got the dancers to do what he wanted with the choreography. Then, just when he was leaving Denmark, he came up to me and asked if I would give him my home address; I never thought to ask why. And I never heard from him. Four years later—that long—Erik Bruhn returned to us after a guest appearance with the New York City Ballet and told me Mr. Balanchine had said to him, "You know, you have a teacher in Denmark I would like to invite over here, but I can't remember his name." "Oh," Erik said, "you must mean Stanley."

"My first class for them was at the old City Center. The company hadn't moved yet to the State Theater. I found the office, someone pointed me down a flight of stairs to where I could change, showed me the studio. I peeked in. The whole company was there. I was terrified. I had never taught in English before. I was saying to myself, Stanley, you must be crazy to be trying this."

Edward Villella: "Naturally Mr. B has an incredibly quick eye for spotting talent. Do you know what he said to me about Stanley that first day? 'He knows how to make people move.'"

Williams: "There was no pianist. Mr. B said, 'No, dear, you're better off—' snapping his fingers. And introduced me, and watched for ten minutes, and went away. I don't know how I had the nerve, how I managed, but if I must say so myself that first class was a success."

The success proved to be sustained. Again the next winter Williams was invited to return for a month of guest teaching, during which he typically gave company class in the morning, two lessons daily at the School of American Ballet, and a pre-performance warm-up. His classes were crammed with devotees, and dancers flocked to him out of hours for extra coaching.

Villella: "His teaching was a revelation tome. He had investigated the technique—exhaustively—discovered where different kinds of movement came from. Physically, there was a wonderful simplicity about his material, coupled with an immensely refined musicality. His teaching was precisely and carefully structured and elucidated. It was my salvation.

"You see, I was operating under a tremendous disadvantage. I wasn't like the others. I had lost four years of my dancing life—in a maritime college, where I was welterweight boxing champ. And that's how I danced, like a pugilist. All bunched up. When I got out of college and came into the company, I had mistakenly tried to make up for lost time, worked like a frantic fool for two or three years, and that's how Stanley found me: a body that was taut and tight and short-muscled and spasmed. Understand, I never disagreed with Balanchine—his insight and understanding are beyond everything—but his company classes couldn't help me. They were too sophisticated, and the speed—. I needed to go back to the core of things and work slowly—elongate—so my mind and my muscles could figure it all out. I was in desperate straits when Stanley came to the New York City Ballet, and I was overwhelmed by what he offered. I just opened myself up to him completely."

Although Villella's needs may have been unique, the impact of Williams's teaching that he describes was widespread. Among those indelibly marked by it were Robert Weiss, currently a NYCB principal, and his wife, Kathleen Haigney, a former company member. Both encountered Williams for the first time in their mid-teens, a stage of development over which Williams

exercises an almost hypnotic effect because the student has become sufficiently mature physically, intellectually, and emotionally to deal with the
kind of knowledge Williams is offering, while being still relatively free from
restrictive habits of mind and body and contrary persuasions.

Haigney: "I had been dancing just from feeling—sort of bashing around.
Suddenly there was Stanley asking me to think, to discriminate, to use specific muscles for specific actions. To grasp the distinctive quality of a movement. It was more cerebral than what I was accustomed to; at the same time
it made immediate sense to me. The results were what I wanted, instinctively, from my own dancing, but could never have arrived at without him."

Weiss: "I was a kid who was interested in a million things—the sciences,
acting, and playwriting—and not particularly in ballet. All I liked about dancing was the athletics—flying around and seeing how many pirouettes I could
do. It took Stanley to show me that it was an art. It wasn't just the scrupulous
intelligence of his whole approach in class, but conversations, about anything
and everything, in which he spoke to me as if—as if I were an adult."

Haigney: "One of the most significant things about Stanley's teaching is
that he doesn't impose. Which is why every one of his dancers is an individual. The accomplishment isn't pasted on top of you. It comes slowly, and
from the inside. The things he suggests to you are quite small, and subtle.
You take the information into your body and you assimilate it, and after a
while the accumulation just starts to well up from within, and it emerges as
a coherent technique. When it happens that way, you feel as if you did it—
he's helped, but you did it—and that gives you confidence. He gives you the
power to believe in yourself."

As Weiss's and Haigney's comments suggest, Williams's teaching, like
most memorable instruction, makes little distinction between matter and
manner, between the transmitting of practical and conceptual knowledge
and the establishment of a mutual and profound human contact. More even
than he is valued for his material, a stellar teacher will be remembered for
his "self." This personal impression may be effected by a variety of means: by
charismatic example, by vivid and rigorous exhortation, or, as in Williams's
case, by the setting up of an intimate, often unspoken communication.
Because of the intentness of his looking and listening, and his unconscious
projection of his own integrity, it is nearly impossible in his company to lie
or tell half-truths—either with the body or the mind—and it is in this atmosphere of "uncovering," made easier by Williams's sensitivity and natural
kindness, that consequential learning begins.

Perhaps that is the real message in Lise la Cour's remembrance. "I first
really knew Stanley when I came into his class at thirteen in the Royal Theatre. He saw everything. You couldn't for one moment do something he
didn't notice. First he made us very stretched and strong—put a force into

us. But then he'd say, 'Don't just stand. Move! Dance!' He can make people do things they never did before. When we left him to go as aspirants into the company we really thought we were better than the grown-ups. We felt we could command the world—at sixteen.

"It's funny, looking back. He never uses so many words when he's making the classes. In the beginning it wasn't too easy to understand him because he wasn't *telling* you so much. You had to *sense* the meaning. Still, I always thought I understood what he said when he said it, and yet I probably understood it better afterwards. Years later, maybe, you'll be doing a step and remember what he was suggesting to you about that movement, and apply it for the first time. He puts something inside you to stay forever.

"I don't think you can get a better person to work with in ballet than Stanley, and I don't think you can find a better friend. He's a very serious person. I don't mean he is never joking and laughing, but that he is serious about life. And positive. He is never saying that things are easy, not that. But that the whole world is so wide and you can use the things in it, and learn. He was beautiful in his mind.

"I felt especially close to him when my husband [Peter Martins] was going to leave for New York, and it was a question about whether I should leave too, with Nilas [their son, presently a student at the RDB], or make the separation complete. It is very comforting to talk with Stanley because he can help you to see a good point of view.

"I wish Stanley wasn't so far away now and I wish we could have more time together when he's visiting. There's not so much more to be said because the rest is how it so often is when you're with Stanley—feelings without words."

The official reaction at the Royal Theatre to Williams's acclaim in New York was typically ambivalent: pride and grudging pleasure in the honor accorded a native son by ranking international artistic powers, coupled with an unwillingness or inability to acknowledge the special talents that made the honor so deserved. In 1963 the Theatre administration asked Williams either to settle down in Copenhagen, taking no more leaves of absence, or to retire from the stage. Williams was content enough to end his performing career, but found himself being offered a teaching arrangement hardly commensurate with his gifts. (Williams's gentlemanly code does not allow him to come even this close to criticizing his titular superiors; the information must be pieced together from observers' reports.) With today's hindsight over the era of Flemming Flindt's direction of the RDB (from the mid-'60s through 1978), Williams also doubts that his own devotion to the concerns of classical dancing would have had a welcome influence over the repertory hellbent on garish modernization.

Then, beckoning from the other side was America: New York, making a fair claim to be dance capital of the world, and, especially, the Balanchine orbit. "Seeing the Balanchine ballets danced by the company they were created on, seeing Balanchine himself teaching—can you imagine," Villella exclaims, "the impact that would have on a mind like Stanley's? It stimulated curiosity and exploration and growth. He'd had the Bournonville schooling, then Vaganova through Volkova—what an incredible background! And now Balanchine. And it was being inside and in the middle of things. At night, in the theater, to watch a piece that has just been choreographed by the greatest inventor of our time, and the next morning to be working in the classroom with the dancers who were in that ballet—inventing, himself. Because we all reached out to him to articulate what we were doing. Of course his teaching expanded in that environment. The vitality was catalytic."

Williams chose. In 1964 he took up Balanchine's offer—a permanent appointment at the School of American Ballet. "To be very honest," he confesses, "there was not so much I regretted leaving in Copenhagen." Ironically, from 1966 until 1980 he returned to the Royal Danish Ballet every August as a guest instructor, and, even at this late date, there are those in the company who express reservations about his "controversial" methods. Back in Copenhagen, he teaches in English.

Williams's early years in New York were a vortex of activity. The cosmopolitan excitement of New York, a fervid response to Balanchine's creativity, the alacrity with which American dancers responded to his teaching—these elements produced an atmosphere in which, according to Villella, Williams's particular genius didn't so much evolve as explode. "It wasn't merely a question," Villella explains, "of Stanley's giving classes, watching our performance, and then quitting—breaking off the contact— for the day. It was a whole life of hectic and exhilarating investigation. Intense work and wild friendship—a bonding between Stanley and those of us who were traveling the same path. I remember sitting in the old Carnegie Tavern with him, night after night, eating and drinking until two or three in the morning, and talking about technique—we could spend hours discussing tendu battement, how you lift an arm, where a double tour begins and ends. And analyzing the performances—in every aspect: choreography, music, style, the dancers' execution. We were immersed in it, you see, day and night."

Eventually, Williams's influence in the New York City Ballet may have appeared to undermine somewhat Balanchine's own, rightful, artistic leadership, and a delicate redistribution of power was effected in the course of which Williams withdrew from his direct involvement with the company and concentrated his efforts in the school. A good deal of comment and speculation on the subject has been made—both on and off the record—by some of the people interviewed for this story, and others who were caught up in what they perceived as a conflict of loyalties. The issue, rather like the RDB's division over the Lander controversy, is one of those complex tangles perhaps best left alone once peace has been made with the passage of time, because it is essentially a family affair, setting at painful odds people whose lives are bound together. One questions Williams on the subject only obliquely—his gentleness and tact are both object lesson and defense—and his response is perhaps the most elegant and touching of any: "I could do just so much and I supposed—this is only my own idea, I never asked—that Mr. Balanchine preferred me to focus my energy on the generation coming up. And, you know, he did a wonderful thing, Mr. B. Through all these years he let me learn my own way. He never once said to me, 'No, such and such is wrong and I don't want it.' All he's ever done is suggest; then it was up to me. Because if I had felt pushed, I would have been afraid ever to try anything. He just gave me that little corner in the school and let me develop."

Most of Williams's colleagues agree that his personality has undergone a radical change over the years. As a young man he was markedly gregarious. Henning Kronstam recalls "a Stanley always in the middle of a large crowd of people, laughing and yelling. Still today I think of all the good times we had together." *Villella*: "When I first knew him, Stanley was a man full of verve and humor. He'd be doing this work at white heat all day, be in the theater every night, then out—everywhere. Socially he was in tremendous demand. People would invite him to parties, pretend they were just happening, but they were really parties in his honor."

Gradually, however, Williams withdrew from this animated existence to a life that was self-contained to the point of appearing reclusive. *Kronstam*: "He is completely different from what he was. I suppose it wouldn't be a wonder if he'd really used up all his mad young years. They've really been used." *Villella*: "All that heightened living and working—the two were inextricably tied up—well, it was fantastic, but it was also a phase we had to pass through to get to the next place." *La Cour*: "People wonder—what happened?" *Villella*: "I think that's what's happened to Stanley. He's gotten to the next place." *Williams*: "It was too much. I began to find that my mind wouldn't function the way I liked it to. So I had to change my life a little bit around. Some of my old friends, maybe, don't understand. But we have to live according to what is most important, and for me it was to continue my work." One is reminded of the passage in *Howards End*: "As for theatres and discussion societies, they attracted her less and less. She began to 'miss' new movements, and to spend her spare time re-reading or thinking, rather to the concern of her Chelsea friends. . . . She had outgrown stimulants, and was passing from words to things. It was doubtless a pity not to keep up . . . but some closing of the gates is inevitable . . . if the mind itself is to become a creative power."

Teaching is an ongoing, seemingly endless process that is as even and cyclical as the passage of the seasons. To think of a teaching career as a succession of landmark events is essentially to apprehend it mistakenly. Nevertheless, Williams's progress has been studded with little festivals, as it were, among them the annual Workshop Performances in which the School of American Ballet showcases its students in productions staged by its faculty. Williams's traditional contribution is a piece of Bournonville choreography, and some highlights over the years have been the pas de deux from *Flower Festival in Genzano* with a very young Gelsey Kirkland and Robert Weiss (1968); *Konservatoriet*—Bournonville's evocation of the Parisian dance studios he visited as a youth—for Fernando Bujones, Marianna Tcherkassky, and Lisa de Ribere (1970); and, in 1977, *La Vestale,* with Patrick Bissell and Victoria Hall playing the roles of ballet master and pupil first danced by Bournonville himself and his fourteen-year-old protegée, Lucile Grahn.

These yearly Bournonville displays resulted in Williams's mounting a cluster of them for the New York City Ballet in 1977. Initially the *Bournonville Divertissements* comprised the Ballabile from *Napoli,* the Act I pas de deux from *Kermesse in Bruges,* the pas de trois from *La Ventana,* the *Flower Festival* pas de deux, and the "gypsy" pas de sept from *A Folk Tale.* Subsequently the Tarantella from *Napoli,* the *Wilhelm Tell* pas de deux, and the Jockey Dance from *From Moscow to Siberia* were added, although not all the items are performed at any given showing under the umbrella title. What was most significant about Williams's production was not the transferral of the charming and effervescent nineteenth-century Danish choreography to a twentieth-century American stage in reasonably accurate form—although bastard versions elsewhere make one grateful for mere faithfulness to history. Williams's triumph lay in the brilliantly workable compromise he effected between the amiably tempered, tradition-reflecting style with which the RDB renders these passages and the broader, bolder, sharper attack of the NYCB's native body language. Williams proved that Bournonville's ingenious arrangements of steps could survive even a radical translation of time and environment, that Bournonville was writing choreograph choreography to last, not comedies of manners doomed to fade with their period. He also demonstrated, inadvertently perhaps, the kinship between Bournonville's obsessive fascination with steps and their patterning, and his trust that such material alone might make dancing worth watching—and Balanchine's. The stars of the show turned out to be Peter Martins, RDB-bred and re-educated in the Balanchine repertory, and a bevy of Williams's students, just a few years out of school.

Williams is in demand beyond the confines of the NYCB and its affiliated academy. In the autumn of 1980, for example, he went to American Ballet Theatre at the invitation of Mikhail Baryshnikov, to stage the *Flower Festival* pas de deux and the trio from *The Lifeguards of Amager* and to teach a month of company classes. "We did some good work together there, I think," Williams reflects. "I thought I was very well received, coming like that as a stranger"—he goes on, sliding familiarly from reportage to teasing. "Of course there were one or two familiar faces over there," alluding, although he's not likely to specify, to Kirkland, Bujones, and Tcherkassky, who had become principals at ABT. "I'm always glad to see my old friends, find out how they're developing, but, you know"—slyly shifting to another theme and a sudden, sober tone—"I don't indulge in nostalgia for the past. I am interested is the next generation, in the continuity; in the—," he looks sharply into the middle distance as if what he were about to mention had the perceptible form and texture of a glissade or a cabriole—"I'm interested in the quality of the present moment."

Should Williams care to look back, a list of his indebted students would be studded with yesterday's and today's stars. Nureyev, Hayden, Verdy, Wilde, Tomasson, Ashley, Duell, and the fledgling Kistler can be added to those already named here. Williams will barely help in compiling such a list. "Fame has never meant anything to me. How can I put it so that it doesn't sound—. I have worked my whole life consistently, and whatever I've done has been absolutely the same. Teaching is every day, year out and year in. Anyone who suddenly comes and compliments me, to flatter me, I don't really like it. Oh, it's nice when people say nice things about you, but it distracts me. It pumps the ego. I am working best when my ego is entirely— not there. The moment I'm aware of doing something right or something good, the moment I begin to feel a little superior, it takes away from my rapport with the dancers. And this communication is critical. Because it's teamwork that puts this knowledge into the body—whether I'm working with professionals or students. I'm not the center of importance; it must be them." Williams is probably quite right in thinking that reportable credits may be the first to vanish from the true record of his influence, and what will remain, something far less clearly measured or defined.

. . . It's late afternoon on a wintry day at the turn of the year. The light is fading in the grey sky and the Juilliard lobby is nearly deserted. A leggy girl of about fifteen, with a sweet, blank face, stands by the elevator bank, waiting to be carried to the SAB studios on the third floor. Unconsciously, she starts doing her demi-pliés. In her scruffy down jacket, worn corduroy trousers, muddy Adidas, the girl is anonymous; she could be any one of the hundreds of hopeful ballet nymphets harbored in New York. But the pliés are not anonymous. The slim body moves buoyantly down and up, down and up, with an unbroken flow of energy. One arm is angled over a bulging dance bag, but the other curves gently out and in, out and in, in a serene, wave-like accompaniment. The effect is that of two soft, clear voices singing a cappella, in harmony. These are unmistakably "Stanley's pliés."

—from *Ballet Review,* Spring 1981

TWYLA THARP

One of the most innovative, productive, and successful of modern American choreographers, Twyla Tharp (born 1941) has tried just about everything, and triumphed at most. After graduating from Barnard, Tharp—who had studied with Graham and Cunningham—joined Paul Taylor, and two years later, in 1965, formed her own company. Her own brilliant, loose, edgy, dynamic style of dancing, both aggressive and funny, has set the tone for her 125-plus creations, from the early successes (The Fugue, The Bix Pieces, Eight Jelly Rolls) *through her breakthrough into ballet, first with* Deuce Coupe *for the Joffrey, to the music of the Beach Boys, followed by* As Time Goes By *and* Sue's Leg. *One landmark was* Push Comes to Shove, *for Baryshnikov and ABT, in 1976. Others have been* Nine Sinatra Songs, In the Upper Room, *and "The Golden Section" from* The Catherine Wheel. *She created the dance for several important movies—*Hair, Ragtime, Amadeus—*and had a tremendous success on Broadway with* Movin' Out, *to the songs of Billy Joel: 1,331 performances and every conceivable award. She has written two books, and is now back to choreographing full time—most recently for ABT, Pacific Northwest Ballet, and Miami City Ballet.*

NANCY DALVA
Twyla

Twyla" wraps itself around you like a boa, languorous, loopy, bendy, swoony. "Tharp" starts off soft and low with a purr, then pops up and punches you—pow!—smack in the solar plexus. You're seduced, smitten, doubled over, gasping for breath, and you haven't even shaken hands yet. *Twyla Tharp.* (It's the perfect name.) There are many artists who deal contradictions, who revel in them, in fact. Contradictions of mood, for instance, are many a choreographer's stock-in-trade. Happy, sad. Funny, pathetic. Light, dark. Yin, yang.

The yolk, the egg. As anyone who has seen her perform knows, Twyla Tharp simply *is* contradictory—scrappy and elegant, combative and malleable, ironic and (however much she likes to deny it) romantic.

At first, one might have supposed her idiosyncratic choreography sprang from her compact, low-down body and its idiosyncratic wiggle-and-melt ways. Now—having seen her, with a variety of companies, work her way through a staggeringly broad inventory of music, formats, techniques, and idioms—we can see that her choreography springs also (as all choreography springs) from a particular temperament and cast of mind.

This, then, is the best Tharp irony, the most delicious contradiction: if there is something inherently antagonistic in Tharp, or in Tharpian structure, there is also something abundantly optimistic. (Even off-balance, aggressively sustained, is another kind of balance.) In her work we have the wish, and the proof, that dissimilar and divergent elements can be marvelously and distinctively united. Hers is, willy-nilly, a utopian vision, hopeful and humane. *E pluribus Twyla.*

—from *Dance Ink,* 1994

Twyla Tharp
Push Comes to Shove

Shortly after *Sue's Leg,* I met with Lucia Chase and Oliver Smith, co-directors of American Ballet Theatre, and their associate, Antony Tudor, in a very large, fairly intimidating, sumptuously appointed, and appropriately high-up corner office in a Chase Manhattan Bank building. Wasting no time, Miss Chase asked me to make a ballet for Mikhail Baryshnikov, Gelsey Kirkland, Martine van Hamel, the entire chorus and ensemble of the company . . . and, oh, could I maybe find something for Fernando Bujones? Equally quick, I said I would consider the offer, but if I agreed, my fee would be ten thousand dollars for a three-year exclusive license.

Lucia gasped. "Young lady," she said, recovering her self-possession, "that is a great deal of money." No one in the ballet set out to make money. Balanchine often gave his works away. Just who did I think I was?

The two men tried covering their surprise at my audacity, Tudor in particular looking as though he had just swallowed a whole chicken with all its feathers. I explained that I supported myself and my son and that while I was honored by their invitation, I could not afford to work for less. Further, I would not commit until I had seen Baryshnikov in a rehearsal. I wanted to be sure he would be able to do new work. I had seen him perform *Giselle* already and had been properly impressed. Physically, he was adorable—a short, muscular, manly body, an innocent, worldly face; his dance technique was perfect, genuine and dominating; his stage manner was admirable—he had generously and warmly stepped into the shadows when the spotlight was on his partner. But performing beautifully in the nineteenth-century ballets was one thing. I needed to judge for myself whether he could do anything else, physically and emotionally, and how willing he would be to put himself on the line. My cool response masked my real reaction. As Tudor probably guessed, I didn't really doubt Misha's artistic commitment or ABT's financial one. I already knew Misha himself had proposed the idea after seeing *As Time Goes By,* and the company was going to give him everything he wanted.

It was myself I doubted. Could I pull it off? Making a ballet for Mikhail Baryshnikov was a tall order. Yes, he guaranteed great exposure for the choreographer working with him. But notoriety can harm as well as help: if the work failed, the choreographer, not Misha, would be blamed because he was already an untouchable. Since his defection in the summer of 1974, he had received enormous publicity, including the covers of both *Time* and *Newsweek* in the same week. The publicity, combined with his reputation as one of the century's premier—if not the greatest—dancers since Nijinsky, in addition to his profound sex appeal, made him a forbidding collaborator. Before the official announcement of my commission, I ran into Alvin Ailey. Alvin was larger than me in size, reputation as a choreographer, and experience. He just looked down at me and said with sardonic amazement, "Are you really going to do a ballet for Baryshnikov? You've got to be nuts. You'll be eaten alive."

Still, with the courage of the naive and the willfulness of the ambitious, I attended a rehearsal to see up close what all the hoopla was about. I came into the rehearsal a bit late, so there was no formal introduction. I crept around the edge of the space to my empty and waiting chair. Misha was rehearsing lifts with Gelsey Kirkland. Gelsey was evidently unhappy with the lifts, but Misha kept doing them the same way: I was apparently witnessing a standoff. Then suddenly, just after Gelsey had stopped the pianist with a soft wave of her hand to go back for maybe the fourteenth pass, Misha paused and, instead of following her to the upstage corner, turned a cartwheel and a somersault and landed at my feet—literally—arms outstretched somewhere around my knees. And such a grin. The one thing I had not expected from the great Russian ballet stylist of our time was acrobatics and clowning. But then, I didn't know Misha yet. "Take me," he was saying. "I promise I'll never become boring or predictable." Well, what was a girl to say?

We rehearsed in the old ABT studios on West Sixty-first Street, an ingeniously designed space that included an overhead walkway, letting you view the action in four large studios below. I asked for the last studio, the fifth, because it was not accessible to the walkway: concentrating on new and foreign ways of moving, Misha didn't need the extra trouble of thirty little faces analyzing each move. Those who were hopelessly and desperately in love with the body and the image would have to wait for him at the downstairs door.

Almost instantly, two things became very clear about Misha. One, he was unbelievably eager for new movement, trying anything I did with complete sincerity and heart. And two, his concentration span was practically nil. After two or three minutes he would phase out, his eyes glazing over; he would pace the room as though the walls were confining him, then turn and go up close to the mirror, looking into his own eyes as though he were suffering amnesia and searching for a way to recognize himself. Frowning, he seemed to be saying, "Where am I? Who am I?" My heart went out to his bravery and pain. As he wandered toward the mirror he would run his fingers through his thoroughly drenched hair—in mid-July, the room was a hotbox with the fans turned off for fear his muscles would cramp—drawing it back off his face, but also to touch himself, "pinch" himself: "Am I really here?" Without language to distract him—earlier plans of learning Russian in two weeks had been abandoned after my first look into a beginner's primer—I clowned, waited, futzed, until I caught his eye with an interesting move and he returned.

Partly his inattention was the result of an intense, lonely culture shock. But his wandering was also due to fatigue. In Russia, he performed rarely; one performance a month was not uncommon in the large Kirov company. This problem was compounded by the structure of ballet classes, the morning exercises made into brief combinations that don't develop aerobic or muscular endurance beyond what is required for the short variations in the ballet repertoire.

Misha began to understand the logic of my movements. While I wanted a literal, athletic heroism from him, capitalizing on his unsurpassed virtuosity in the male domain of ballet—jumps, multiple pirouettes, batterie—I wanted it in a new form. At first, Misha couldn't locate his balance off center, and his face would cloud when I asked for turns and large jetés that twisted or lay far back from his supporting leg. Then I would demonstrate the movement I wanted, and, as though he had ingested my body, he would mime my action perfectly (trained in acting and music as well as dance at the Kirov, Misha was an excellent mime, and he always loved becoming characters—including me). Actually it was easy for him to pick up my movements because our proportions are uncannily similar. Slowly, he also learned how to come out of the strange movement, watching me catch my weight just a little lower than normal, or in turning, reverse my momentum a hair before usual, coming to understand that the trick was in the timing— actually, I'd never left my center; I'd simply shifted it—a relief because it meant this new movement was not going to end up with him hurling himself untended into space.

And I began incorporating parts of Misha into the dance, embedding his idiosyncrasies into the work, using as a signature for the opening variation one of his particular gestures: he dips his head, runs his fingers through his dripping hair, then tosses his head back. This delighted him, for this gesture and this dance were his and his alone, and it was a desire for such freedom and personal expression that had drawn him to the United States in the first place.

When we began working, I intended setting the ballet to Bach's Partita Number 2 in D Minor. Sublimely musical, Misha knew intuitively how to take his pulse from the Bach—pulling back from it, digging under it, soaring with it. But the music was getting a little heavy: I wasn't sure the American public—or I myself, for that matter—was up for such deep soulfulness from the Russian guest in our midst. The rehearsals had begun to drag. Misha's thirst for artistic adventure, to be the first one there, was something I associated in my mind with his love for ice fishing: To witness his artistic process was like watching a man sitting patiently on a fjord in the middle of nowhere, just him and the frozen water, waiting for a fish to take the bait, for days, maybe weeks—any length of time so long as the mission was complete. In this regard we were alike—we both liked being on the edge of nowhere—but sometimes his tenacity would turn into petulance, intransigence for its own sake; there would be flashes of rivalry, and I could sense a stalemate brewing. Then we would both instinctively know it was time to recess to the water cooler, and there, at a safe distance from the studio, on neutral ground—and unable to speak the other's language, thank God— we'd waste no time talking it out. We'd simply look at each other, see ego coming out of our ears like steam, and laugh it off. A little hug and back we'd go, into the fray, pushing and racing each other toward another unique combination of our individual personalities, striving for that new boundary where the body has never yet been. . . .

Misha was scheduled to leave soon for a three-week barnstorming stint and, to get the ballet as thoroughly prepared as possible, we worked on duets in addition to his solos. His partner was Gelsey Kirkland, a wonderful dancer whose work habits drove me crazy. First of all, she always arrived at least half an hour late. The habit was worse than a mere irritation—her tardiness threw the whole ballet off schedule. But this was just the beginning. Once in the studio, she had to make the right selection of practice skirts, of which she kept a seemingly never-ending supply in her bag—long chiffons, short taffetas, plus thousands of barrettes and three or four pairs of leg warmers, all of which she had to pin, fold, and otherwise beguile into shape. And then the ankle still hurt, after all this.

It was this ankle that finally parted us. Always claiming she was frail—though somehow I found this suspect, because she was a workhorse when she wanted to be, pushing herself nonstop with a fierce commitment that even I found extraordinary—Gelsey asked to be released from the ballet because of her injury. But I wondered how much she really wanted out because of her temperament, her fear that this was going to be Misha's ballet, not hers. This wasn't my plan. I was determined that everyone in the ballet be shown to the very best of his or her abilities, and I very much wanted to explore Gelsey's natural love of movement and her exquisite New York City Ballet technique, but her bottom-line fear of anything beyond her control made working with her an agony.

So now we had to find another partner. Natalia Makarova was the likely next choice, but there were problems with her. Rumors circulated, claiming friction between her and Misha. Misha said he'd go along if I wanted her, but I didn't: From the upper ramp that looked down into all the studios, I could easily see that she was temperament in spades. Her passion was also the wonder of her dancing. A wild, free spirit, she was capable of altering movement to her own divine purpose. But while this habit was great for her onstage, I decided her way of working might be something of a tension provoker in my rehearsals, so I decided to forgo the opportunity of working with her just yet. Instead I opted for a much less famous, lovely dancer of exactly the right size and proportions for Misha to partner, and one who would be grateful for the opportunity. Marianna Tcherkassky, a beautiful, small, dark-haired woman, fit the Gelsey mold but was much sturdier. I had a feeling she would need to be.

I drafted a drama for the ballet. Misha was a womanizer, and being perverse, I decided to give him his wish: every woman in the company. There would be two principals, the little one, Marianna, and a big one who towered over him, capable of squashing him, a terrifying, dominating Myrtaesque figure in juxtaposition to Marianna's lovely petite coquette. Martine van Hamel fitted this image perfectly; she was a gloriously expansive and still very feminine beauty, extraordinarily strong on pointe and capable of enveloping space in a way that ordinarily requires a masculine drive.

In addition I would give him the chorus—a double chorus, eight girls in each—for whom I developed some of the most difficult movement in the piece. I like to side with the underdog, and I figured that the valiant among them would view this as a challenge, a promise of a future beyond the chorus and into larger things. Meantime, the chorus would be a little less boring place to be.

Then I changed the music. Inspired by Misha's birthday—the same as Mozart's—I decided to exchange the baroque for the rococo. I chose Haydn's Symphony No. 82 in C—"The Bear," an appropriate choice, I thought, for a Russian. The four movements would be the dramatic "acts" of the dance. The first would introduce Misha and his two dates—big and little—and end in an impasse: each would have to show more of her stuff. The little one, with the entire chorus as reinforcement, got the second movement (my double-chorus concept fit nicely with the music, which was essentially a series of variations). The third movement belonged to the big one, with the rest of the ensemble and her own cavalier (Clark Tippet in the original cast, one of the rare members of ABT with some modern dance in his background). Then Misha crashes this party—the fourth movement—and wins everyone in the ballet, another instance of art imitating life since he had already captured the heart of the dance world.

But what of Misha's original reasons for wanting to dance in America? How did they fit into the ballet? I sat at a restaurant alone on Thanksgiving and contemplated this Russian so in love with American pop culture. Astaire was his idol—not a strange choice for a dancer. To Misha, Astaire was a mortal elevated to godhood, not the other way around: the Apollo descended, that generic heavenly being that so many of Misha's ballet roles called for. Could I get more of this quality into the ballet for Misha? What of the Broadway part of Misha who wanted to dance Jerome Robbins's musical comedy and jazz? Did we have any of that in the ballet for him? We Americans wanted to see him dig his teeth into our culture.

But I saw no opportunity for this in Haydn. To broaden Misha's range in the piece, I decided to start with him introducing the whole circus to come. Taking a page from *The Raggedy Dances,* where I had combined Mozart with Joplin, I mixed the Haydn with Joseph Lamb, a successor of Scott Joplin's. These were frontiersmen of jazz, America's pop culture, and this beginning was where Misha would start.

As I studied the Haydn fourth movement for the nine thousandth time— I wanted to be completely prepared for Misha's return because we would have very little rehearsal time before the premiere—the title occurred to me: *Push Comes to Shove.* A little trashy for such a grand institution as ABT, but then maybe a posh audience would be grateful for a little funk. Besides, there was a yin and yang to the words—as well as the obvious sexual hook—that suggested the juxtapositions in the ballet: the old classical forms of ballet versus jazz and its own classicism, the East of Misha and the West of me (though which of us was push and which shove was up for grabs). Then too, there was a personal reference I knew would please Misha: the name of the great Kirov instructor, responsible for Misha's development from the time he first entered the academy as a child, was Alexandr Pushkin.

So that's where we were when Misha returned: same material, completely different music, two paramours and two choruses instead of one, the responsibility of hosting the whole event resting on Misha's shoulders, and a joke for the title of his premiere piece. If he was shocked he didn't let on. Part of our deal always was: up for anything.

We started working on the Lamb rag, transforming this Apollo into Astaire, by moving his weight down, centering him further back into his legs. Working into his new character, Misha looked horrible, hideously out of whack, his poor feet, locked into their tightly confining black slippers, trying to learn parallel movement, syncopated timing, and a new, lower-to-the-ground balance, all in one fell swoop. But instead of being daunted, Misha took delight in his clumsiness. Soon he had stopped looking in the mirror—because what he saw there was too awful. Instead he began to visualize the movement for himself through its feel, reveling in the dangerous risks.

At the same time, we worked on the two solos I had given him before he had left. Misha had put the time on the road to extraordinary use. He had parsed the movement by himself, working out the transitions in his own way. His solutions were breathtaking. He was learning to maneuver around an ever tighter base, and the precision and audacity of his leaps and pirouettes astonished me. Everyone watched his rehearsals for the moments of greatness, all of us feeling we had participated in making him ours, changing him from our guest into a cousin. If you were a dancer you could not but love him. He was just that good.

The last touch was a hat. Misha would enter fondling a bowler, establishing his character with a single dramatic prop: He was the lovable rake. And in the course of the ballet he would live up to his reputation—every woman would be his, and we would approve. (Some feminist I turned out to be.)

Then it was time. Misha and I exchanged opening-night presents—he gave me a nineteenth-century crystal pendant shaped like a very fat heart with a diamond center; I gave him two photographs of himself taken in rehearsal—the orchestra struck the first (as requested) slightly off-key note, the curtain rose, Misha sauntered into the spot.

He was nervous, but the actor in him quieted the dancer, telling him to focus on his role, and the hat. He introduced the two women, and the audience started to fidget: "Is she going to cheat us? This guy hasn't gotten off the ground once."

Then the Haydn began, and there's nothing but darkness onstage, as I delay the inevitable for as long as possible. At the very last moment the spot hits him and he's off. He circles, runs his fingers through his hair, paces, gathers himself, and he's in the air. It was a moment every dance aficionado hopes for—a moment in dance history. From there on he's in perpetual motion, soaring, spinning, feet flying, back working overtime, releasing as much energy during his two variations as any audience has ever seen from any dancer, while never compromising his technical purity. Martine and Marianna follow, each with small solo passages in the first movement as well, during which Misha, unbeknownst to either woman, observes them from upstage. We begin to see the dramatic question is not which woman he will choose but whether he will pick any at all. When, at the end of the second movement, Marianna pulls Misha in from the wings and confronts him with the whole chorus, he's only momentarily overpowered by this ocean of femininity; within moments he's vanquished them.

Martine dominates the third movement, and the company gets an opportunity to look as strong as possible, setting a high mark for Misha to top, which he does at the start of the fourth, entering on the deep diagonal with double sauts de basque, flying higher than anyone has ever seen and still keeping his bowler on his head with a free hand and a big grin on his face. Enter chorus, ensemble, and soloists together, and from now, wherever Misha goes, he seems to be in the way, about to be trampled, his life in imminent danger. Ringleader as clown and underdog—a favorite role for those of us who are short—he tries to maintain order, getting bashed and ignored as he tosses out hats for everyone. Finally the whole chorus bears down on him and the music stops: He pauses with both arms formed into a cross over his head, warding off this swarm of vampires. Then the music resumes and so does the little one, interjecting herself between the girls and him, saving his life. Then everyone else pours in to celebrate the final chords, Haydn thoughtfully ending the symphony about twelve times. On the last of the finishing flourishes, Misha tosses his own hat high in the air, and dozens of other hats, snuck onstage in the last moments of skittering chaos, fly up to meet it, celebrating his battering, bruising, incontestable triumph: "Hats off, gentlemen, a winner!"

—from *Push Comes to Shove*, 1992

MIKHAIL BARYSHNIKOV
Push Comes to Shove

Twyla Tharp's 1976 Push Comes to Shove, *also the title of her autobiography, was a great success for ABT—a landmark collaboration between the quintessentially American modern artist Tharp and the quintessential Russian classicist of our time Mikhail Baryshnikov. And it served to redefine them both. The music is ragtime plus Haydn. The wit comes from the play between Tharp's loose, jazzy American style and classicism.*

When I first saw Twyla Tharp all I could think of was "You probably have to be born here to do it." This whole melange of classical ballet, jazz, tap, social dancing needs a special technique and a special accent that seemed so foreign to me. Strangely enough it was not the steps, not the movement, in Twyla Tharp's work that first attracted me, but her ideas about the music, her attitude toward music. I had seen the two works she had created for the Joffrey Ballet, *As Time Goes By* and *Deuce Coupe,* and was very struck by her personal understanding of music. It wasn't until I began to grasp how she worked musically that I could really concentrate on the "language" of the pieces. And as I began to understand and be able to take in that language, it was so unexpected and marvelous that I was swept off my feet. It was obvious to me from the beginning that her work was *serious,* and had a highly developed, *willed* style. Seeing her ballets opened up a whole new world of possibilities for the use of classical ballet steps.

I first met Twyla in Spoleto in 1975, where I had gone to dance John Butler's *Medea.* It was while watching Twyla perform her *The 100's* there that I saw how refined and delicate and impossibly difficult her vocabulary is. The most important thing about Twyla's work is that it is very controlled and classical in its intent. It never speculates and it's never arbitrary, and her demands in relationship to the music are more specific than almost anything I have ever done.

As I began to work with her I found things very difficult technically. The body movement is often slightly off balance—on purpose, of course—something completely foreign to my very straightforward, classical way of moving. There are many turns off balance, and there is a lot of off-balance work that demands a very strong demi-pointe and very strong ankles. All of this work in the legs and feet is played off against an extreme flexibility in the upper body. In Twyla's work the body can switch direction in the middle of the beat for any given movement. She not only has these changes in the arc of each movement, as well as complicated variations of them, but the choreographic structure is very broad, all over the stage, and performed at top speed. So the breathing is very difficult. As you are dancing you feel like a fish in the sand.

As I said, musically Twyla is extremely precise. We worked for hours and hours on the phrasing, which was very intricately developed. The flexibility of the body and the complexity of the movement parallel the flexibility of the phrasing—which also goes in and out, on and off the beat. When Twyla began working on *Push Comes to Shove* she created most of the movement for my main solo to a piece by Bach, and after the music was changed to Haydn, most of the original movement was kept. Working on this solo was like going to the moon and back again, hours and hours and hours of very technical rehearsals, repetition over and over again. Twyla takes it for granted that the choreographer and the dancer can do a single *enchaînement* three thousand times to get it right. I had never had the habit or discipline to do anything so many times and with such concentration of energy. In classical ballet I more or less know what the possible is, but in this case I had no idea what I could or couldn't do. Twyla pushed me and encouraged me to accomplish many things I never would have dreamed I could do. She is a genius in the studio at keeping the energy level high and productive, and giving the dancers the moral strength to get to what she demands. I always had the feeling in the beginning that I was out in a boat that had no sail, doing forbidden things. She herself moves so beautifully, and there she was asking me to do it too. It was like a professional flautist saying to a professional pianist, "You're a musician; here, play this instrument the way I do." Except that while Twyla and I have basically the same instrument, my tone is not as beautiful as hers for *her* "music."

Push Comes to Shove is a tour de force. It's so meticulously constructed, so theatrically perfect. If you watch it carefully you see the seriousness of the piece, the seriousness of the intent. Many people say Twyla "gives them what they want." Well, she does. But her work also springs from complete dedication to an idea. In *Push,* for example, the balance is between two kinds of music. The rag with its jazzy upbeat rhythms is so skillfully attached to the Haydn that one can only think, well, yes, of course, that's the way it has to be. The opening section, which is set to the Joseph Lamb rag for Martine, Marianna, and myself—it's a calling card from Twyla to the audience: "This is where it all comes from, this is *my* tradition." That parentage is immediately established, an unpretentious, highly charged American-classical way of dancing. And then we move on to Haydn, but as we move from music that is Twyla's naturally to music that might not be, we see that her attitude toward the Haydn is as classical as the Haydn itself. She can work with it, push with it, play with it; she feels up to Haydn. The rhythmical structure of the dancing in the Haydn section is perhaps more developed and more complicated than anything I have known. Twyla's not afraid of the work, and attacks it, catches the fluidity and jazziness in the score. But she doesn't play with the music coyly. She takes it for what it is, and makes it into something logical and beautiful.

A lot of the work I first did in the West was new to me. But nothing was as new, as different, and, thank God, as inevitable as *Push Comes to Shove*. It's lovely that it was a big hit. But, more important, it was really new. For all of us.

—from *Baryshnikov at Work*, 1976

NANCY GOLDNER

Nine Sinatra Songs

It doesn't matter if you think that the best thing about Frank Sinatra's voice is the color of his eyes. In *Nine Sinatra Songs* Twyla Tharp has transposed his sleepy-time voice and cozy songs into a suite of dances bursting with sexual vitality. That vitality isn't due to the specific gesture or attitudes of the duets Tharp has set to the songs, however, but to their fullness of expression. Never has Tharp worked in so bold or accessible a spirit. In this dance you can sense the flood gates of her arteries opening, and the movement pours out with lushness and intensity. In a season (at the Brooklyn Academy of Music) whose repertory considered the music of Fats Waller, David Van Tieghem, Telemann, Willie Smith, Glenn Branca, and Jelly Roll Morton, the songs of Sinatra figure as the intermission break. Yet it might be the very simple-mindedness of the Sinatra material that allowed Tharp to go, in Sinatra's lingo, all the way.

Almost all the way. If Tharp threw her obsession with choreographic complication to the wind, she didn't chuck her mind as well. Ironic humor often rears its head. But rather than double-cross the lyricism and sexiness of the dances, Tharp's double-edged point of view validates the dances, making them sensible as well as rhapsodic. We know that the dance recognizes its material with open eyes. Some of the songs are dumb, and all contain fantasy at bargain-basement level. The dumb songs Tharp can do nothing about, so with an occasional barb she exposes them by having the dancers literally act out the lyrics. When Sinatra declares in the pseudo-tough song "That's Life" that he's going to pick himself off the floor, Shelley Fredont gets picked off the floor by her partner. Tharp works the cliché into a virtuostic maneuver, and it's the virtuosity of that moment that allows her to win her point honorably. She makes us forget (almost) the lyric by involving us so completely in the dance.

As for the level of fantasy with which Sinatra seduces his audience, Tharp transcends it pure and simple. "One for My Baby (And One More for the Road)" turns the sentimental notion of Sunday-morning blues into a stunningly torrid exploration of bonelessness. The bonelessness associated with one drink too many is Tharp's starting point. She enlarges the feeling to include, ultimately, the bonelessness that comes with an extended bout of love-making. This duet is a tribute to Sara Rudner, to her unique ability to move as if drenched in sable. That the very bonelessness and soft abandon of Rudner's dancing places her in amusingly indecorous positions is a testament both of Tharp's unflinching wit and of her faith in her prima ballerina. Not for one second does Rudner fail to enthrall, not even when she's splattered all over the floor.

I guess that "One for My Baby" is my favorite duet of the suite because of Rudner, yet each of the seven duets makes its point with a force appropriate to the content of the song; and each of the duets makes a different point, too. As a suite of dances, then, *Nine Sinatra Songs* deals logically with a form that more often than not is a random anthology. Two of the dances—one serving as a mid-point demarcation and the second as the finale—are for more than one couple. Set to different recordings of "My Way," they are reprises in the sense that they recall back to the stage the dancers we've seen in previous duets. The odd thing about these group dances is that they're not group dances. Retaining the character of their duets, each couple dances in isolation; they dance their way. Tharp's unwillingness to make her ensemble pieces for an ensemble was at first disconcerting to me, because it meant forgoing structural contrast. One loss is another gain, however. In having the dancers exist in mutually exclusive spheres, with eyes only for each other, Tharp says something about love. What she says is simple but true, and it's worth saying.

—from *The Saturday Review*, February 1984

Deborah Jowitt

Tharp Against the Whirlwind

Watch the kamikaze critic attempt the ultimate daredeviltry: nose-diving into Twyla Tharp's *The Catherine Wheel*—a dance-theater piece so huge-scaled, so active, so fierce, so densely layered and cross-referenced that you sit in your seat hardly able to move, unaware of your breathing for the whole of its seventy-eight-minute development. The suite of songs and instrumental pieces written for *The Catherine Wheel* by David Byrne of the Talking Heads, which comes to us via fastidiously engineered tapes, combines Byrne's voice with a variety of instruments and electronically produced effects. But because the percussion instruments usually lay out a strong rock beat and several of the songs seem to whirl around on themselves, the effect is of a powerful, almost ominous storing up of energy that only occasionally relaxes or explodes.

The Catherine Wheel features the same embattled family that populated Tharp's *When We Were Very Young* (1980)—scrappy, ambitious, ineffectual mother (Jennifer Way); feckless, lecherous, charming father (Tom Rawe); bully/baby son (Raymond Kurshals); flouncy, calculating daughter (Katie Glasner). The expanded household includes a flirty maid (Shelley Washington) and a twitchy little "pet" (Christine Uchida in a furry vest). A dreamy poet (John Carrafa) gets mixed up with them—I think because they have this pineapple that he wants. (Wait, better not bring the pineapple up yet.) Then there's a Chorus, of which the family is sometimes part, and a Leader (Sara Rudner). The Chorus expands the family's brawls into full-scale war, echoes or initiates themes—making them more efficiently abrasive—and comments on the action like the chorus in a Greek tragedy. Within the chorus parts, another "play" occurs that has to do with disruption, with the crowd turning against its leader, with nastiness, violence, and, finally, a cleaning up and a restoring of order: all the wrenching, spinning, swaggering, wind-milling dancing slotted into balanced contrapuntal patterns between Santo Loquasto's ranks of steel poles.

Then there's the pineapple. Pineapple as forbidden fruit, as object of desire, as confidant. Pineapple as hand grenade. Pineapple as god—plucked golden from a gilt heaven, disguised as a humble pineapple, sometimes ignored or treated disrespectfully, getting larger and more imposing, destroyed, gathered up in pieces, and at last enshrined on a little golden wheel and hung again on that shimmering cluster. Who would have thought, ten years ago, that Twyla Tharp would ever be investigating the uses of symbolism? (Hang in there, Martha Graham, we may be coming full circle.)

Then there are the wheels. Everywhere. Huge bicycle wheels seen in shadow form, carried across the stage. Inscrutable wheeled objects that descend from the flies, like working models of some unfathomable machine (Santo Loquasto as Leonardo da Vinci). A suspended rack with wheels and down-pointing spikes on which Leader and Chorus keep trying to impale the netted bundle of pineapple chunks. It sticks, then with a double clank, the machine drops the load. (It's your burden; you keep it. And don't let it touch the ground if you can help it.) A small tacky living room sits briefly on stage in a wheeled cage. And wheels—as velocity, as spinning in place—accumulate in the dancing: cartwheels, pinwheels, dancers spread-eagled overhead (St. Catherine was slated to be broken on the wheel, but it fell apart at her holy touch), dancers as fireworks, spewing stars onto a black sky.

So (don't tell me you don't get it)—Tharp gives us violence and aspiration, death and transfiguration, dance as both demon and dispeller of demons. And everything washing over everything else, so you see the lineaments of one idea through another, just as you see pieces of the action in shadow-play behind Loquasto's gray-white silk curtains, behind the antics of live performers. And in the black depths of the stage are things you can barely see.

Tharp has made the drama ride a ceaseless base of dancing. The performers keep their feet moving, their hips swiveling, their knees pulsing no matter what they are telling each other with their gestures and facial expressions. People trying to settle the affairs of their lives while on a treadmill, on a dance floor, or an erupting world. The first night I wondered if the fluid, ongoing pulse of Tharp's movement mightn't be antithetical to the development of drama. The second-night performance was cleaner and more pointed, and I found my way more easily through the hugger-mugger of scenes like this one: Brother tap dances ineptly (Mother has taught her kids how to do this and pass the hat), Sister vamps, Mother tries to rent Sister out to Poet, and Poet pretends to go along while waiting for his chance to steal Pineapple. In scenes like this you yearn for a few more small sharp gestures.

There are some amazing scenes. "Down, down we go / Fall through, fall through the cracks," growls Byrne; and Washington, as the maid, has some kind of horrifying fit—making big motions of grabbing and uprooting and thrusting away, of sinking down and rising up. And all the time, her face is doing a carefully structured dance of demented grimaces—tongue hanging out, or teeth bared and eyes rolling. Lust too long balked by subservience and frustration finally explodes in a gibber of rage. Or there's the bumbling, farcical mustering of the family for battle. Poet skips lightly around the perimeter. Mother has to point him in the right direction.

Wriggly, itchy little Pet aligns herself with Father, then, perhaps remembering his penchant for humping her publicly, knocks him out and bounces delightedly up and down on him. There's the bitter, looping adagio in which the couple, reconciled, attempts to dance together while their children (Orestes in overalls and windbreaker, Electra in a ruffly jumper) try to pry them apart and get in on the cuddling. There's the phenomenal Rudner, first coy and mischievous and jivey, later spinning and leaping in horror (over what she's started?), shaking her head as if she wants it to fall off. Toward the end, she and the black-garbed people with red masks tied over their eyes seem to be wallowing in evil, and there's nothing bumbling about *their* combat. Grab Rudner, turn her upside down, spin her around. And she seems to expect, even crave, this violence. When the curtain first went up, we saw dark silhouettes of the Chorus—leaderless—going through a cyclical, going-no-place pattern of throws, lifts, punches. Maybe they were practicing for this moment.

But as Byrne opens a twang of glowing chords on top of the running beat, and all the blackness lifts to reveal a golden curtain textured like giant bamboo stalks and Jennifer Tipton beams brightness onto the stage, Carrafa, Washington, and Uchida spring into sight—golden athletes in silk clothes. As all the dancers reappear in twos, threes, singly, violence is transmuted into dancing. Dance as battlefield, the dancer as warrior. Not even in the *Brahms Paganini* has Tharp made dancing as astonishing as this. It flashes, cuts like swords, spins in air. It gleams with fearlessness, with risk, with trust, with glory. You won't ever have seen people so beautiful, so brave, so engaged with the moment and their individual places within the intricate web of exchanging partners, throwing and catching each other. It's Graham's vision of the dancer as celestial acrobat on another level. These dancers cannot pause to affirm self-image: there's the beat of the music to be shattered into twenty intricate motions of legs, body, arms, head; there's a colleague falling from the skies who has to be caught; another leaping high—duck and let him sail over.

Dancers keep pouring onto the stage and flashing away. No posing, no preparing blunt the impetus or stall the twisting, shimmering current. How can William Whitener keep his footing with leaps, twists, and spins so savagely fast and whipping that he is perilously close to being out of control? How can Richard Colton let one leg swing out and down while he's in the middle of a multiple pirouette so that you think one foot will hook around the other and trip him? How can Shelley Washington leap straight up and believe that Kurshals, several feet away and busy with some other phrase, will catch her as she plummets floorward? How can any of them—Mary Ann Kellogg, Shelley Freydont, John Malashock, Keith Young, and all—*do* what they're doing? Those who had roles in the first part bring their characters into this fray, but dissolve their gestures into the virtuosic dancing. In fact, probably every move you've seen all evening is here. Transmuted.

In the program, Tharp lovingly lists each dancer's name for every appearance he or she makes in this "Golden Section": "Way and Carrafa, Young, Rawe; Young; Young, Glasner, Freydont, Colton . . ." Every ten seconds onstage has a lifetime of dancing in it and deserves recognition. As Byrne's "Light Bath" reprises, Uchida begins to dance alone more quietly than anyone has danced for a long time. Several times she throws herself into the wings and arms catch her. The blacking out of lights leaves her held up in mid-wheel, half out of sight. Perhaps our dance will be moving to another part of the universe, irretrievably shattered, sucked into a black hole, expelled somewhere else beyond imagining.

"Twyla Tharp's subject is not your life or hers. . . ." Arlene Croce wrote that in 1971, and it seemed true then. I think Tharp's subject has always been life, only she chose to make the form of her dances embody those concerns rather than doing any deliberate storytelling. The strongest parts of *The Catherine Wheel,* to me, are those in which form and dramatic intent are one—as they are in the paradigmatic "Family Loop" quartet already mentioned—and the weakest those in which costume and mugging have to tell the story because the steps don't. In the first section of *Short Stories* (music by Supertramp), Washington, Kurshals, Whitener, Carrafa, Glasner, and Kellogg can express a novel's worth of emotions about pairing up, eyeing others, quarreling, finding new partners because a ballroom (or prom floor or disco) tidily provides steps, pretext, and structure. In the second section, violence spills over—no more tender dancing, punctuated by wary pauses and brusque gestures—and Kellogg is hurt, raped and killed perhaps, by the three men. The dancing continues. To Springsteen's apocalyptic cries (". . . down in Jungleland") two other couples—Rawe and Way, Rudner and Malashock—accidentally stumble into other pairings, like joggers in the park who bump into contact. Two beautiful, drastic duets promise reconciliation, but the dance ends with silent angry conversations, expostulating gestures, bitter shoves. And here we go again. Compared to the smooth blurry dancing in *The Bix Pieces* (1971) the dancing Tharp's making now is like a blade, honed and polished—slashing, jabbing, slicing curly pieces out of the air. Maybe the increasing violence and risk in her work is intended as sympathetic magic. If you can top the whirlwind, will it subside?

—from *The Village Voice,* September 30–October 6, 1981

GEORGE JEAN NATHAN
On the Ballet

*The acerbic theater critic George Jean Nathan (1882–1958), the purported model
for Addison De Witt in* All About Eve, *was notorious for his wit, mordancy, and
strong opinions. With H. L. Mencken he co-edited* The Smart Set *and co-founded*
The American Mercury, *as well as maintaining for many years a column for the*
New York Journal-American.

What I am about to say will probably result in the denunciation of me as
an obnoxious philistine, fit only for the company of halfwits and admirers of
the art of Sir Walter Besant. However and nevertheless, I risk the indignation and say it. It is this. I offer you all but a relatively small portion of the
modern art of the ballet for one American nickel. The remaining collop I'll
keep for myself and, as for the considerable rest, if you haven't the nickel
handy it is yours on the cuff.

I don't suppose this commercial transaction would be of any particular
public interest if it were not for one fact. And that fact is the enormously
increased American interest in the ballet during the last few years, not only
in New York but in many other cities. Only in Australia, peculiarly enough,
where a single ballet troupe not long ago enjoyed an unprecedented run of
eight months in the three or four leading cities, has a greater increase in
curiosity been manifested.

What leads me to my spuriously generous offer is the conviction that
much of the modern ballet is a hybrid that is gradually getting to be less and
less real ballet and more and more a freak form that vouchsafes all the
beauty and grace of a one-armed Ubangi toying with a squab. There are

exceptions, true enough, but the majority of the exhibits that I have honored with my attention impress me as being little more than very bad short plays, most of them with a minimum of sense, performed by mute actors suffering from incipient attacks of arthragra but doggedly determined that the show must go on.

In some instances, indeed, the nonsense has reached such a point that dancing in any genuine sense has been practically eliminated and has been supplanted by something that looks to any intelligent layman like a cross between an invisible doctor testing the cast's knee reflexes and the plebes' drill ground at the Culver Military Academy. William Saroyan's *The Great American Goof* is a case in point. Not only is there no dancing in it worthy of the name, that is, outside a hospital ball for arteriosclerosis patients, but American speech has intermittently been provided the hoofers who, being foreigners, speak it like so many chipped Berlitz Russian and Swedish records. Supplement all this with scenery projected by colored magic-lantern slides which periodically act like jitterbugs and mingle an intended factory scene with a previous Ritz salon, or whatever it is meant to be, and you begin to get a faint idea that if you lay out that nickel I was talking about you will get the bad end of the bargain.

If, furthermore, you imagine that the aberrant Saroyan has been picked upon as a too easy horrible example your imagination needs looking into by a psychoveterinarian. There are a dozen boys and girls whose exhibits come pretty close to matching his, and another dozen who run him an even race.

Take a look, for instance, at something called *Mechanical Ballet,* by Adolph Bolm. Originally manufactured for the movies, it may be acceptable Hollywood but in any other place where bloom æsthetics on however modest a scale it is likely to impress the beholder as a paraphrase of Eugene O'Neill's *Dynamo* concocted by the Minsky family and performed by their uncles, cousins, and nieces, in tights. It is possible that a stage full of characters called Dynamos, Gears, Pistons, and Fly Wheels all jumping up and down to an accompaniment of bangs and clangs from the orchestra may be art in the minds of the more frenzied balletomaniacs, but to any slightly more realistic mind it seems to be merely a lot of obstreperous imbecility.

Or turn to the number called *Dark Elegies.* This one is the brain-child of Antony Tudor and consists in an effort to combine choreography with Gustav Mahler's song cycle, *Kindertotenlieder.* Inasmuch as Mahler composed his music after the death of a particularly beloved child and inasmuch, further, as it reflects his deep and intimate sorrow, the idea of accompanying it with a troupe of kickers and posturers comes about as close to the obscene and ridiculous as is humanly imaginable. The only analogous mixtures I can think of would be *Uncle Tom's Cabin* with whites in the Negro roles and Negroes in the white or a ballet founded on the *Internationale* and danced by a stageful of Republican senators.

Or, still again, for another example out of the humbug car-load cast your eye upon something called *Hear Ye! Hear Ye!* Fabricated by a Miss Ruth Page with the connivance of Nicholas Remisov, this one seeks to dance a murder trial into a ballet. After flashing a number of tabloid scareheads on the curtain–"Murder in a Night Club," "Who Is Guilty?" etc.–we are vouchsafed a courtroom with judge on bench, jury in box, and a gross of wooden dummies representing the public in the spectators' seats. Attorneys for the prosecution and defense get busy and then a series of flashbacks show seriatim the shooting of a male hoofer by a chorus girl, and the shooting of the selfsame hoofer by his male partner, each of the potshots being equally fatal. After each murder the jury proclaims the particular shooter guilty. At the conclusion, it turns out that a stray maniac did the dirty work, and the lawyers shake hands.

Now, gentlemen, I ask you! If such stuff, whatever the music and choreography, is appropriate ballet material, I resignedly await the day when we shall be treated to a ballet danced to the annual report of the Commissioner of Street Cleaning or choreography visited upon Jan Valtin's home life.

The more recent urge to Americanize the ballet has been responsible for some curios that outcurio almost anything this side of a believe-it-or-not museum. We have had everything from ballets showing roadside gas station operators imitating Nijinsky, as in the exhibit by the late American Lyric Theatre, to ballets displaying Russian dancers or their equivalents cavorting in far western ghost mining towns. Where the fatuity will stop, no one can tell. The time may not be distant when they will be laying the scene of *Schéhérazade* in Columbus, Ohio, and when they will be having *Hommage aux Belles Viennoises* danced by the Four Inkspots.

The Messrs. Cole Porter and Gerald Murphy, otherwise honorable, have a lot to answer for. It was they who, nineteen years ago, inaugurated this sort of absurdity. Their job was called *Within the Quota* and was the first ballet with an American theme set to music by an American composer. I take the liberty of quoting the plot of the masterpiece as it has been succinctly recorded for posterity by that eminent antiquarian, Mr. Cyril W. Beaumont:

"An immigrant lands in America and before him pass, against a giant reproduction of an American daily newspaper, a cavalcade of American types–part real, part mythical–with which he is already familiar through visits to the cinema. His pleasures in these types is interrupted by a figure who assumes in turn the character of Social Reformer, Revenue Agent, Uplifter, and Sheriff. Finally the immigrant makes the acquaintance of the World's Sweetheart with the inevitable result, which brings the ballet to its conclusion."

That one is thrown in for extra good measure with the others, and all for the same nickel.

—from *The Entertainment of a Nation,* 1942

Max Beerbohm
A Note on the Ballet

Sir Max Beerbohm (1872–1956) was known as a superb parodist and caricaturist as well as the theater critic whom George Bernard Shaw chose to replace himself at The Saturday Review, *where he labored from 1898 to 1910. His most famous books include* Around Theatres, *a collection of his reviews;* Seven Men, *a series of invented biographies;* A Christmas Garland, *a group of devastating parodies; and his one novel,* Zuleika Dobson.

May 19, 1906

Ballet, as an art-form, inspires me with less of delight than of affectionate interest. It was at its perihelion in the time of our fathers. And for all men the time of their fathers is the most delicious time of all—just near enough to be intelligible, just far enough to seem impossible. I am glad I never saw Grisi, glad I never saw Taglioni. Their names would not make such music for me, had the vision been vouchsafed. Nor would those pale-tinted portraits of them, still to be seen in out-of-the-way places—Taglioni floating through a glade; Grisi perching on the boards with the tip of one foot—touch so agreeably in my bosom the chords of pathos. I am glad the tradition of the ballet has not been lost. I like to see the "haute école" not quite disestablished, after all these years, by skirt-dancers and cake-walkers. But the æsthete in me rejoices less than the sentimentalist. As a representation of life, ballet fails for me. I am a writer, and thus a lover of words, and where no words are is a void for me. At least, there is a void where words might have been but are not. In a painting I do not feel the need of words, for they are excluded by the nature of the art. But they are not excluded thus from ballet. Their exclusion, the substitution of mere gesture, is quite arbitrary.

There is no essential reason why ballet should not, like opera, have words. It gains nothing by the sacrifice, and (for me) loses nearly all. There is (so far as I, in a theatre, am concerned) no reality in a wordless representation of life. And, however fantastic be a representation of life, it ought to awaken a sense of reality—a fantastic sense of reality. Ballet not merely gives me no illusion: it conveys no meaning to me. Here, I admit, its failure is due partly to a defect in myself. A man ought to be able to master the meanings of formalised gesture. When a ballerina lays the palms of her hands against her left cheek, and then, snatching them away, regards them with an air of mild astonishment, and then, swaying slightly backwards, touches her forehead with her finger-tips, and then suddenly extends both arms above her head, I ought of course to be privy to her innermost meaning. I ought to have a thorough grasp of her exact state of mind. Friends have often explained to me, with careful demonstrations, the significance of the various gestures that are used in ballet; and these gestures are not very many; and I have more than once committed them to memory, hoping that, though I could never be illuded, I might at least be not bemused. But, after all this trouble, the next ballet that I have seen has teased and puzzled me as unkindly as ever. Is it that gestures were given to the ballerina to conceal her thoughts? Or is it merely that the quickness of the hand deceives the eye? Unable to catch for one fleeting instant the drift of the lady's meaning, I concentrate myself on her merely visual aspect. And here, again, I am disappointed. Of course it is very wonderful that a woman should be fashioned—or rather, should have contrived to fashion herself—thus. How many hours (I have often asked myself), on how many cold grey mornings, and in what large, bare, locked room, at the back of what house, must have gone to the making of this strange shape? Nature is not, of course, a conscious artist. She aims at usefulness, not at beauty. The reason why arms are slighter than legs is not, I presume, that any first principle in beauty demands that they should be so. Arms are slighter than legs because they have not to sustain the burden of the body. And thus we, who know no first principle in beauty, and derive our ideas of beauty through what we know to be useful, would be really repelled at sight of a woman whose arms preponderated over her legs. Such a phenomenon might be achieved if a woman were trained from childhood to walk on the palms of her hands. Suppose, on the contrary, a woman who had been trained from childhood not to use her hands and arms for any purpose whatsoever. She, too, would be unsightly. The meagreness of her arms, in proportion to the rest of her, would seem to us unlovely. And yet her arms would be not more meagre in proportion to her legs than are the arms in proportion to the legs of a ballerina. I do not say that the structure of a ballerina is an offence against abstract beauty; for I have no means of knowing what abstract beauty is. But certainly this structure jars my æsthetic sense, as being an obvious deviation from what is natural. It is natural enough that a woman should dance sometimes, just as it is natural that she should walk, sit, lie down. But it is unnatural that dancing should be the business of her life. And Nature takes vengeance by destroying her symmetry, by making her ridiculous. Poor ballerina! Is it for this that she has been toiling, toiling, day by day, in that large, bare back-room—toiling to become physically ridiculous? That is a question that has often asked itself in my brain during the performance of a ballet. All those trippings, and pirouettings, and posturings at incredible angles, are very wonderful of course, and are paid for at a very high rate. If the ballerina is not extravagant, she will be able to retire into private life, with a comfortable income, before old age shall have overtaken her. She will be able to cease to be ridiculous. Meanwhile my heart goes out to her. It comes in again quickly. There had been no need to pity her. Regret is all that was needed. Such power of thought as she may once have had was long since absorbed into her toes. She does not know that she is ridiculous. Her fixed smile is no assumption to hide an aching heart. She really fancies that she is admirable, admired. And so she is, in the way that a performing dog is admirable, admired. It is wonderful that a dog can learn to behave more or less like a human being. It is wonderful that a human being can learn to cut capers seemingly beyond human power. But dog and human being alike cause in us—in those of us, at least, who are a little thoughtful—more of sorrow than of pleasure. My sentimentalism rejoices in the survival of the ballet. But my humanitarianism is revolted by the survival of the ballerina . . . Mlle. Genée? Ah no; I grant an exception there. No monstrous automaton is that young lady. Perfect though she is in the "haute école," she has by some miracle preserved her own self. She was born a comedian, and a comedian she remains, light and liberal as foam. A mermaid were not a more surprising creature than she—she of whom one half is as that of an authentic ballerina, whilst the other is that of a most intelligent, most delightfully human actress. A mermaid were, indeed, less marvellous in our eyes. She would not be able to defuse any semblance of humanity into her tail. Mlle. Genée's intelligence seems to vibrate to her very toes. Her dancing, strictliest classical though it is, is a part of her acting. And her acting, moreover, is of so fine a quality that she makes the old ineloquent conventions of gesture tell their meanings to me, and tell them so exquisitely that I quite forget my craving for words. In *Coppélia,* which is now being enacted at the Empire, Mlle. Genée has a longer and better part than she has yet played. And the delight she gives us is accordingly greater than ever. . . . Taglioni in *Les Arabesques*? I suspect, in my heart of hearts, she was no better than a doll. Grisi in *Giselle*? She may, or may not, have been passable. Genée! It is a name that our grandchildren will cherish, even as we cherish now the names of those bygone dancers. And alas!

our grandchildren will never believe, will never be able to imagine, what
Genée was.

—from *The Saturday Review* (London), May 1906

GRACE CURNOCK
Pavlova Goes Shopping

MADAME PAVLOVA MAKING FINAL PREPARATIONS
FOR HER COMING TOUR

*Venez faire des emplettes avec moi demain, je vous en prie, j'ai tant de choses à
acheter pour ma t`ournée de province.*

Toujours à vous, Anna Pavlova

W ho could resist the invitation? Anna Pavlova in the theatre is an unapproachable wonder. "In the life," as she expresses it herself, she is a dear little
friend, as little like the typical artist as can be. A little pathetic sometimes
and the least ready to assert her own wonderful individuality of any woman
I have ever met. But with rehearsals for the opera and for her own tour, even
apart from the performances, she is so seldom "in the life" that the chance of
going shopping was seized with delight by both of us. So we set forth after
many alarms and false starts two hours later than we meant to, and finally
had to let the purchasing time brim over into a second day.

And how it rained!

Madame Pavlova, a quietly garbed little lady, ran from her motor-car
across the wet pavement of Oxford Street, through the wide-open doors of
a great shop. With the actions of a sensitive child she appealed with shy indecision to me. "Où commencerons-nous? Where do we begin? But how many
people here today!" Her white-gloved hand sought to hide itself in my muff.
As she disappeared into the lift not one among the crowd of buyers at the
counters seemed to realise that the shyly moving figure in sensible "wet
weather" boots was the greatest of all Russian dancers, the woman whose
every moment is a delight, and whose charm is without equal on the stage.

Mme. Pavlova does not court notice off the stage. She wishes to be recognised only across the footlights. Her audiences she adores while she is dancing for them, but Mme. Pavlova the dancer remains at the theatre or in her studio. In her own home, with her friends, in her own hours, in what little while she has all to herself, she is Anna Pavlova, the gentle woman, shunning unnecessary publicity and intent upon passing through the crowds of people as unobtrusively as possible.

But, like a child, she enjoys to shop. Like a child she notices every detail and criticises as she goes, naively and with easy wit. Her great eyes, which have "the colour of ripe, dark-brown cherries," seem eager for fresh impressions, yet yearn wistfully for kind faces and for affection for their owner not as a dancer but as a "real" person.

A Real Fairy

The first time I saw her off the stage was in her dressing-room at the Palace Theatre. She was still dressed in the softly falling drapery she had worn in the *Valse Caprice*. The applause of the audience was still humming from the house. Those who had watched breathlessly the dance of a Grecian boy and girl, the glide and flicker of feet that never seemed to touch the floor, the supreme art of her invisible but severe technique, each footstep a note of music, wanted their idol back again. But she was upstairs, those great eyes seeming to beg sympathy from two children who had been of her audience and sought the joy of seeing her "alive." "A fairy, a real fairy," breathed one little girl—the dream of her six years come true at last. But Anna Pavlova put her arms out to the child and bent until the waves of her dark hair touched the English flaxen curls. She kissed the rosy baby lips shyly as one child kisses another, and then, with a mother arm around her, "My little one, my little one," she said, "it is beautiful to be so young and gentle." She talked softly in French to the little ones, speaking with the pretty singing accent of the Russians and interposing Russian words of endearment. Her hands caressed the eager little faces and she received the child-love her eyes had sought. "I am glad she is not a fairy, after all," said the baby. "She is quite young, like we are."

Again I remember when some friends presented her with a dainty wrapper, a soft thing of silks and broideries. She wrapped herself in its draperies and ran about her dressing-room. "I shall never take it off, never. I shall keep it until the end of my life, it is soft and lovely. I kiss it. I—" "Madame Pavlova, please." The Russian troupe were finishing their National dance, and the *Bacchanale* was nearly due, so the wrap must go for the time with other delights—go for the joy of dancing, itself a happiness of youth. The old in heart cannot dance.

And then to be a child again, a real child, and "go shopping." To be a child with no knowledge of the value of money, but to buy dearly, or "bon marché," just what one wants. "I think," said Anna Pavlova the child, as she wrapped herself in an ermine stole and smoothed the soft whiteness of the fur with her cheek. "I think that everything is so bon marché in this London, and here in this shop so chic. I will have this for Dublin; do you like his little black tails? So, please, I would like it." She did not stop to ask the money equivalent. And the furs went down to the waiting car.

"I really am certain—and I do not say it as a compliment to you cherie, or to anyone—that the shops in London are the most agreeable in the world. There is no rush and bother. I go to buy something; it is shown to me at once, tidily from its own box or cupboard. Everything is good; even the cheapest things are worth having. I have never been shown rubbish in a London shop, as I have been in other great capitals. I like, too, the idea to let me wander about a shop—such as this house of Selfridge—without worrying me to choose all the time."

"Now, shall we dress ourselves in paletots just to find one I can wrap about me going to and from the theatre? Will you ask for me please?"

A Hypocrite in a Cloak

Now when Madame Pavlova says "Please" and throws a quick sideways glance from her dark eyes to see how I take the request, I must needs play spokeswoman for her. She pretends that English is beyond her and gazes as if deaf and dumb as long as I am by to speak for her. Presently I move away to examine a cloak more closely. When I come back the hypocrite is talking English quite quickly and well understanding the attendant's replies. She looks like a child discovered in mischief, and hastily wraps herself in a cloak of soft silk, grey-green in colour, with deep collar and cuffs of grey fox. "Is it the size for me?" she asks, as she turned this way and that in front of the long glass. "Oh do say, shall I have it? Do you not believe that such a paletot as this will be warm for me? I can wear it in the day or night. It is an economy to have such a beautiful coat. I buy it at once." But she bought another for travelling as well.

Another shopper passed while we waited for the lift. She had a tiny dog in her arms. "Oh! that little dog. I cannot have it. It is so like my dog." "Yours is a bulldog," I said. "That is a toy Pom. I see no resemblance."

"Now you laugh at me. Well, I will tease you presently. It reminds me of my dog. Left behind this time in Russia. He is ill, in character, but not wicked. I do not know what to do with him. He is badly brought up—'mal élevé.' His wife, too, is the same. It is I who will bring up their children. They will be proud parents to have such a friend for their little bulldogs, small—like that." Pavlova's hands measured an imaginary dog the size of the toy Pom.

"You are a bad friend to come shopping with," she went on. "You make us do too much talking."

"Quickly, then, what shall we buy next? Hats?"

"You think I need buy other hats? Vraiment! Well, perhaps in the country, in the train or on the boat for a tour of four months I must have several new ones. But is not this I have on charming? I found it when I came through Paris. Just grey chinchilla and little fluffy white feathers. Now do you think £26 was too much? Someone told me that it was a terrible price. But how pretty and comfortable!"

So she tried on hats one after another, turning for approval, speaking sweetly to the girls who waited on her, asking for their opinion, flitting from one glass to another, moving her head and body to try the effect of some particular chapeau in half a dozen dainty poses. Selfridge's millinery department ceased to be a shop, it became a studio, a stage on which moved the most graceful figure in Europe, and the assembled attendants composed an admiring audience, though compelled to silent applause.

TEA

"Somebody looks," whispers the shopper, timid once more. "Come away quickly, let us have our tea." We fled to the Palm Court, Anna Pavlova speeding up the stairs like thistledown in spite of the wet-weather boots, I following, feeling all arms and legs, and arriving at the top quite breathless. "Sometimes we cannot wait for the lift," she said, "these tables are taken so quickly. Let us sit behind a big tree with our backs to everyone. Smell the violets on my muff."

Over tea she told me once more that it had been the dream of her life to conquer London. And now, having conquered London, she is going to tour the provinces to conquer there, too, before her fresh triumphs in London next spring.

"You know what my dancing is to me," she said. ("Oh, do let me do the tea!") "But no one in England can know how we work at the Imperial Conservatoire in St. Petersburg. Oh, to do anything above the ordinary requires infinite patience and such hard work. I was nine [sic] at the time of my admission to the institution. For eight years the pupils are not allowed outside the walls of the buildings except during the summer holidays, and the course of studies we have to go through is as comprehensive as it can be. Yet, in spite of the hard work I am sure there is not one pupil who regrets having gone through the apprenticeship. As soon as the students show the necessary talent for music, acting, and dancing they are given a place in the ballet. The next step, which comes after several years of hard work, is the chance to appear at the Opera in a solo dance. It had always been a rule that no one could be made a ballerina until she had been a soloist for seven years, and I regard it as a very great distinction that I was appointed after four years. But all the training is good and dancing is a fine art.

"After these years of probation the dancer must strike her own line. It is then, and only then, that individuality should assert itself. For my own part, I thought the old conventional ballet could be modernised to a very great extent, and made to interpret the human emotions almost as effectively as music, painting, or any other art. It was then I attempted to render by rhythmic poses and gestures such pieces as Rubinstein's waltzes, or fragments from the work of Delibes, Chopin, Tchaikovsky, Saint-Saëns, and other comparatively modern composers."

"My Own School"

"Next summer I want to found a school of dancing in London. I want to train some English children, just a few. It will be the most delightful and charming thing in my life. I will be with them and see their talent grow. We will dance together.

"It is so great a pity that there is no institution in England like our Opera House. Some of the children I have seen would have great success if they were properly trained. But you have a teacher here, another there, all on so small a scale. There would be great dancers among the English if they knew the dance. It is, of course, a question of character, of temperament, of physique. Each country has its own art, I think. An art that belongs to its people. We Russians, in Petersburg, are dancers. In Paris it is the drama, and so forth. Oh! my friend, I have a little rehearsal for the Opera in twenty minutes, and I have many more things to buy. May we come again tomorrow? I have so few opportunities to buy nice things. For me it is always la scène—the stage."

"If you are going to be pathetic," I said, "I shall leave you quite alone in the lift, and you will not be able to find your way out of the shop—"

"You are thoughtless for all those other dancers waiting for me. We will come again. Tomorrow I will be quite another lady."

And the next day Madame Pavlova was "quite another lady." We were to start from the hotel at eleven o'clock. At twenty minutes past a parcel arrived—a gown, rich black velvet with barbaric splashes of colour at throat and waist, yellow and green, and red worsted worked in a bold design. "The sun is shining. I must wear a new gown." She slipped into the elegant little frock and announced that she was ready.

Madame Anna Pavlova was gay, the sun after a long night's rest had buoyed her up.

CHARM OF MODERN SHOPPING

"I did enjoy yesterday," she said as she settled herself in her automobile. "London shopping is more fascinating every time. How much we did on such a rainy day. So many things of different character and for different occasions all in one shop. In Vienna I would not have accomplished nearly so much, for I should have been in six shops instead of only one. In Paris my automobile would have been up and down the Rue de la Paix, to the Louvre, everywhere. I should only have found one thing and I should have been late for rehearsal. I should have been shown all the things I do not want, have been worried by inferior articles because they were bargains, and have finished very unhappy.

"Everything is good in England, and your shops are best. I have never done so much shopping since I came to London. All the summer at the Palace Theatre I had no time; always rehearsals for "the scene," many performances, fresh dances, as well as my favourites, my snowflake ballet of children. You remember how hard we worked all that summer weather. I could not go to shops. I used to say to a girl friend I have, "Hilda, go to buy for me, my clothes are finished. I must have something cool to wear. You are thin like I am. What fits you will fit me." She did shop so well. But this time I have been able to try on everything I have wanted to in the shop, before these long glasses, one thing after another, quickly, until I have found what I want."

All those things she could not "try on" in the shop itself she loaded onto the arms of the assistants, and we retired to the convenient little "fitting rooms," gathering more loot as we went. Dressing up is a great game, whether to children or grown women. Madame Pavlova was an example of the fact. She danced round the little room in one costume after another, suiting her mood and actions to the dress she donned. A "tailor-made" is severe and requires, if not dignified, at least quiet and sober movement; in a rest gown one may repose in graceful attitude before a long glass; and a rich evening gown for a "dinner of ceremony" should be criticised while one passes with stately grace on the arm of "my host."

It was all great fun, but withal to be taken seriously.

For the Tour

The first department we came to when we again entered Selfridge's was devoted to hosiery. Stockings, stockings, everywhere. Beautiful hose in soft silk, gold-coloured, rose-tinted, crimson as the sunset, hung on stands, and the counters were laden with piles of multi-colours. Madame Pavlova made all speed to seat herself at such a delightful place. "Now," she said, "I must buy plenty of stockings and gloves to wear in Dublin and Newcastle. Do you think they will like my dancing in Dublin? Mr. Mayer, who is organising the tour, tells me so much of the Irish audience. I am looking towards it all so much. It would astonish you if you knew how many stockings I use in the year. More for 'the scene' than for 'the life.' All these are silk stockings. I wear silk for my dance—I must—but for my life—have you any in cotton, please, like these?"

Shoes of Gold

Madame Pavlova put out one of her wonderful feet and showed a stocking of finest lisle thread. "But, I do not know, when I think again, these are so fine, so light and how charming: the least expensive suit me best. I will have some golden silk stockings to wear with some gold shoes. We will have the shoes presently."

A few pairs of white silk daintily embroidered up the front were also chosen, but for all ordinary occasions the little lady bought lisle thread, unadorned by aught but silk clocks. She does not like openwork or "lace" stockings, for they are not becoming to the leg. She is altogether very neat and quiet in her footwear.

"Did you ever try to wear silk gloves," she asked me. "They are terrible—so—so—so scrunchy? Yes, what a good word."

I think that Madame Pavlova would have spent all the time at her disposal buying stockings if she had not looked around suddenly and discovered quite close to her—sweets and bon-bons!

So we bought, if not enough for four months, at least enough to send to all the children she knows in London, and some for friends in Russia—"that they may know English sweets," and "some for myself." And here is another fancy of Anna Pavlova, and here again she differs from every other girl or woman I ever knew. She does not like chocolates. "But," she said irrelevantly, with a look of rapture on her face, "I do like the grapes I have had in London this week. Oh! lovely big Muscats and such flavour, so splendid. We have big grapes in Petersburg, but not like those I eat here.

"I will tell you," she ran on, "something else I have liked to find here and have bought very much of. Silverware. The most beautiful things are made in silver in England, and whenever I wish to send some very nice present to my friends in Russia I send silver. When I went back at the end of the summer I took many large parcels with me. And now I cannot resist the attractions of a silversmith."

Madame Pavlova adores a good perfume like all women, but she is not extravagant in its use and chooses with much care. The English makers are the best, she thinks, and sets her faith on one particular distiller for his sweet pea perfume and another for the arum lily scent.

Before we finally left the shop of many attractions, Madame Pavlova attempted to make a calculation of what she had purchased, used many pieces of paper, and finally gave up the idea.

"We will look at all the things at tea-time at the hotel," she finally decided.

Two Russian lady's maids worked hard all the evening arranging the purchases, two clever maids who make all the costumes the wonderful ballerina wears on the stage, working from designs. Madame Pavlova superintends all their work, examining and criticising, making vivid suggestions and being very particular over minute details.

Did ever such a charming creature of varying moods as Anna Pavlova come to London before? I doubt it.

—from the *Daily Mail*, November 2, 1911,
reprinted in *Anna Pavlova* by Keith Money

LINCOLN KIRSTEIN
Alec: or the Future of Choreography

Just as a preponderance of great dancers in the past has been female, most of the choreographers have been male. The male principle, by instruction and design, has determined the executive prowess of girls and women. A few famous male dancers have been grateful for dances designed by ladies. There are familiar parallels in other fields; lady painters have been far between, though if few, yet frequently exquisite. Lady composers of music are more of a rarity, but cantatrices are legion and actresses are numerous. Female architects are scarce; choreography is the fluid architecture of human mass in space and time.

At the present (1953), we are suffering from a paucity of choreographers. From this we have suffered for four hundred years. The combination of gift and authority which saves time at rehearsal—for the dancer must know what he wants to have done, and can at once teach other dancers to do it, determining that a new work gets itself on a given stage at a given night—is rare. It is rare today as it always has been. It might be curious to consider exactly how it might be rare tomorrow.

While almost anyone with three years of training in the classic academic theatrical discipline (ballet) can be expected to string together steps that may be read as some sort of dance, few students develop into dance-designers. The nature of the strength used in performing, in absorbing the patterns of others in order to appear clearly in a large design with other dancers, takes an energy that at its most effective is seldom inventive. The assimilation of a chain of tricky steps, the need to perform well and project personally, exhausts other potentials in the pattern-making, which many good performers otherwise may well have had. Few ballet-masters have not been at one time efficient performers; their knowledge of performance, the fact that they too have been actually successful in pleasing the public, gives them the necessary confidence to demand intense performance in others, and permits the given troupe of performers to submit to their highly personal schemes and patterns.

Boys are not lucky with dancing; their parents too often feel it is fine for their sisters, but sissy for themselves. It is a little better off now than it was ten years or twenty-five years ago, but it still is not very good. It is now decent for a male child to practice the piano, but to move his whole body in time to music is still considered questionable. A boy may paint with impunity, sing for the radio, and almost act (for films), but there is little cash connected with dancing; our practical Puritan inheritance has franchised the uses of the male body for professional sport, not for dancing. However, some boys still dance, and some very young ones are now dancing. From this less than a handful will come the one or two choreographers of the nineteen-sixties and seventies. They are in schools today. Maybe they are presently so young that they don't even mind being in classes where almost everyone else is a girl. Maybe their pride can survive the atmosphere of the awkward minority. Maybe they can stick long enough to graduate into a more advanced group, where there are more boys, on the verge of appearing on the stage. Then the moment will come when they must face being sucked into Broadway or television, even though on a part-time basis at first, eventually being lost to their serious and trying craft.

Should they survive up to the age of seventeen, they face the military draft. At the moment when, after long years of tiresome training, they are getting to feel a trace of confidence, they must have known for quite a while that time must be taken out for the wars. Some will feel it as an End. Others must have so strong a direction that they will realize that even two years out, backed up by honest previous training is by no means an irreparable discouragement. But let those draft-boards who take this setback lightly compare a similar truncation in training in the education of any young ballerina; for two years,—a girl of seventeen stops dancing. Who can expect her ever to be a first dancer?

So, with all these unfavorable and unhappy conditions in mind, let us project the career of some young choreographer, who, in 1953, at the age of seventeen-plus, can't wait for the draft, nervously volunteers for the Navy, is accepted, and even after many months, each of which seems like ten years, still hopes that he can dance. Let us call him Alec Lasagna. His mother was of Swedish descent, his father Italian. She was a dietician; he was a contractor. She believed in manual and physical training; he loved the opera. Their only son hated boxing, but was good on the parallel bars. He had no voice, but played the piano. He was entered in the High School of Performing Arts, in New York City. This caused some domestic difficulties. His father's concrete-mixing plant was on Long Island, but Alec showed such promise and such passion for his work that he was permitted to live with an aunt in Manhattan. His classes with Lillian Moore and the keyhole sight he caught at once from her of the grand styles of the past gave him enough corroboration of his own instinct to determine his subsequent career.

Alec will have been born too late to have seen much of the bona fide Russian ballets of the thirties and forties. At the age of eight he caught a performance of Alexandra Danilova in *Le Beau Danube*. This proved the same sort of vocational revelation that Anna Pavlova combusted over the provinces of the world forty years before. Watching her waxen limbs, feeling that fierce concentration of freshness, delight, and power, he knew he was Called. He saw Youskevitch in *Giselle;* he knew he would never have cheekbones as high as that, nor a profile so nobly, sadly elegant. He despaired. Later, he saw Margot Fonteyn as the Sleeping Princess; he knew he could never support so weighty a spirit of such impalpable graciousness. He was humbled. In 1950 he saw Maria Tallchief as the Firebird. He was dazzled and excited as if her turns had set turning in him something that would never stop until he could actually pirouette the obsession out of his system. He knew what he wanted: perfect power in perfect repose, hidden mastery, dominion, without apparent domination—the strength of the silent waters building up steadily purring dynamos in a dam whose walls were music and whose electricity was muscle. He wanted to become a Choreographer.

The Navy was no nightmare; he found sheepishly that he thoroughly enjoyed it. He passed a few terrible moments, but after Boot Camp at Great Lakes, where he spent most of the time playing the piano for the massed choir-practice, he found himself at the Boston Navy Yard, attached as yeoman to a ship in drydock. He had a sympathetic Chief who collected L.P. recordings. And later he would have had just enough sea-duty to make him feel almost like a sailor. More weekends than he could ever imagine would have been spent in New York. Then he will have discovered Balanchine.

He will still have clung to the idea that he is a dancer; yet he had hardly danced except in school. There, he had been strongly attracted by the Modern Dance; it seemed completely digestible; the idiom he could grasp at once, and composition with the few elements at hand seemed easy and satisfying. There was no endless road to virtuosity. Quite broad effects were not impossible to project with happy speed. And at this epoch he would have been a bit of an intellectual. His young girl-friends did not approve of Balanchine; there was no Soul there; all his ballets were the same; Balanchine did not care about dancers much, and never thought about boys. Balanchine had no psychological overtones, and never seemed to have been influenced by Joyce, Yeats, or Kafka. All the Balanchine ballets were only about dancing. It took the perspective afforded by the Navy to show Alec that the ballet was indeed chiefly about dancing, and that probably he would never be much of a dancer.

Alec was discharged early in 1954. Veterans of the Korean campaigns who wanted to dance as a career, unlike those of the war before, had no rights under the G.I. Bill, which reformed itself to eliminate beauty-schools and dancing-schools. Alec had little money. But his father had been successful, building ranch-houses near Syosset. Alec's mother felt the boy deserved a chance at his own aims, after two years out. He entered the School of American Ballet. His first interview was unsatisfactory; by now quite tall, he looked much older than twenty. His previous training seemed to count for little; practically he might just as well start all over again. He was placed in a class with small children; his first real friend was a boy of ten, grimly serious, in whom Alec saw himself, ten years before. But somehow, he was able to make a private game of this starting-all-over. He tried to wipe his mind into a blank. He became, for the purposes of his boring classes, a child again. Doggedly he pursued the conquest of Correctness, but there was little release in action. Must it all be *this* tiresome? Could he stand it? Doubts that he had never permitted to arise before now started to betray him.

But there is little of any directed energy lost, and that gift or power which made him want to dance in the first instance, yet robbed him of early chances to perfect his prime instrument—his body—soon enough to ensure its virtuosity compensated him with a rare capacity for analysis. Alec found he enjoyed the pleasures of his mind. He started to think. He began to make first steps towards thinking with his body. He came to comprehend that

choreography was not a projection of the personal designs of the choreographer as performer, but rather of a pattern-maker for quite other performers whose physiques and personalities bore slight resemblance to his own.
Because he would never appear as first-dancer, because he had long known
he was no Youskevitch, the normal incipient narcissism remained vestigial in
him. He would never have to please the public in his own person. He heated
up his pride for others. He attempted to analyze for himself what was the
essence of the choreographic secret. Was dance-design to be pretext for performers, or some pattern superior to performance? He inspected the ballets
in the current repertory; he tried to find out why other ballets had been
dropped. This was his homework. He reduced the structure of each ballet to
formulas. He dissected them as if they had been anesthetized on a table
before him. He read books. In the memoirs of the Diaghilev era he discovered how much accident, hazard, expediency, opportunism, and irrelevance
went into the collaborations that created ballets which, in spite of their
dubious provenance, nevertheless remained in the repertory for years. He
pondered the fact that many works, famous at their debut, evaporated when
robbed of their original casting, and that other works, stronger than their
stars, were continually reproduced for two or three decades, in three or
four companies in five or six revivals.

Alec will have to have outside help, having little money. At first he will
have taken a job, part-time, as an usher in the Radio City Music Hall. He
had, it is true, been offered the position as a dancing-master for a small class
of more-than-well-to-do children whose mothers wished to spare them the
dangers of working with other children of their own age who might become
professional. Alec will have correctly estimated that labor so parallel to his
own interest, yet in which he was not genuinely interested, would tend to
exhaust him emotionally even more than physically. Ushering at the Music
Hall was more fun than controlling spoiled children. But, God knows, it will
have been absolutely tiring too.

Robbed of his chances under the G.I. Bill, he naively addressed himself to
the great educational foundations, of whose inspired benevolence and liberal policy he was increasingly to hear. He set himself to apply for some category of fellowship or scholarship to enable him to study, not as a dancer,
but as a choreographer. He could not seem to arrange appointments to see
anyone in authority at the James Foundation. The Ford Foundation was
clearly too big to bother with. The gentlemen at the Rockefeller Foundation
would have been surprisingly kind and encouraging had he wanted to write
a survey of the state of choreography in the Eastern Atlantic States (and the
Maritime Provinces of Canada) between 1911 and 1951. For this he could
have received a thumping grant-in-aid. But he merely wanted to become a
practicing choreographer, alas, and there was no precedent or existent for-

mula whereby the Foundation could risk half-a-dozen thousand dollars on so precarious a project.

Anyway and every way, he will have persevered. After analyzing the peripheral needs of the ballet school and the ballet company, he made himself increasingly useful in a growing number of small ways. He answered the telephone for dancers in rehearsal. He checked toe-shoes and learned the secrets of individual feet. By bringing coffee to dressing-rooms, he got to know dancers. He became indispensable. He was promoted to presenting on stage the flowers sent by the dancers' admirers. He had never admired the delivery of flowers by the stage-servants at the Metropolitan Opera House. He asked Maria Tallchief how she wanted her flowers to be handed to her. She rehearsed him. He analyzed the size and weight of each bunch; he had a firm step and a charming bow. He groomed himself carefully; he made his face up in a healthy non-professional tan. Soon the company gave him a tuxedo. Nowhere, before or since on the American stage, will bouquets have been offered with such confident elegance.

As the seasons passed, he approached a modest academic correctness in his own dancing. He felt the muscles in his legs harden. He even began to watch the position of his arms. He found that girls' arms are not boys' arms. He started to note the difference between the style of his instructors: the older graduates of the Imperial Russian schools of the pre–First War, and the dominant manner of the later Balanchine ballets. He tried to find where the Fokine influence left off, and the new, dryer style began; he found that the new style was even older than Fokine, and yet could not have come into existence without the smoother freedom of the romantic philosophy. Alec thought all the time. He thought with his mind as a working mechanism, just as his body was a working machine. He developed his machinery by listening and by seeing. There was always an L.P. recording being played somewhere: he started to analyze the choreography of instrumentation. He haunted the opera. He tried to figure the placement of breath in dramatic singing and the phrasing of breath in dramatic dancing. He considered of what music was made, and which music was most made for dancing. His were no discoveries to change the history of criticism; they were simply the start of preferences to project a style. He looked at sculpture and small objects. He tried to penetrate the secrets of static plasticity, and the sense in three-dimensional torsion and balance. Human and animal anatomy began to absorb him; he saw how frontal design could capitalize on the meaning of masses of muscle, how muscle described form, and how the proper presentation of forms intensified the sense in the rapid shifts of design which the interlacing bodies made in the frieze and braids of dancing. He looked at sculpture and small objects, in the Egyptian wing at the Metropolitan Museum and at the Cloisters: an ivory whip-handle of a leaping horse; a portable altar of the whole story of the Journey of the Magi in twenty-four miniature tableaux. He found that static plastic is a facet of the diamond sphere of motion. He slowly came to realize that choreography is an echoing of order, that all order is a reflection of a superior order, that all important art is religious art, and that he would never be merely a decorative artist. This was a tremendous decision, because he began also to see that in our time order has been all but overwhelmed by obsessive idiosyncrasy, personal mannerism, and the egomaniacal vogues that atrophy the mind and deform the ego by self-indulgent improvisation and ignorant accidental choice.

Alec would be a bright boy; he was also a good boy, and this goodness would be apparent. At first he would claim only the amused tolerance of the other students and dancers; then, their affection; finally, their respect. At the beginning, he will have asked their advice about the execution of small steps and their combination; this was both flattering to the artists and useful to the apprentice. He will have found out quickly that combination is the commencement of invention, that certain sequences cannot combine harmoniously, and that certain suites have a magnetic inevitability. He would discover whether or not his limited palette, or small chords of steps, jumps, kicks, twists, and turns were grateful in execution, as well as feasible. Other dancers would try them for him. And this was all pursued according to his deliberate plan. From elementary advice requested, within two years, he would find himself prescribing little variations, so that when he would have his first chance to compose a *pas de deux* for actual performance (for a benefit for the Endowment Fund for a library at the High School of Performing Arts, where he had started his own training), he would find that even professional dancers were quite willing to submit to his patterns. He did not, in the first place, waste their time. He knew what he wanted. And if this *pas de deux* (to music by Mendelssohn) will not ever have replaced any of the grand duets of Petipa or Balanchine, nevertheless the number was neatly designed, made its own sense, and—what was even more promising—had its own ironic commentary on the style of Balanchine and Petipa.

For Alec was not an original. In him nothing emerged that had not been seen before. Everything he thought and did came from some attributable source that he frankly traced and acknowledged. Without much natural brilliance, he knew he was working not in a loosely original, but rather in a tightly traditional, field, and that he was slowly (but surely) pushing into a part of that tradition. His first little *pas de deux* amounted at once to a graduation exercise (for himself as apprentice ballet-master), a thesis on developed dance-design in the mid–twentieth century style, and a tasteful comment on the wry dryness and elegant intimate domesticated formality of the later Balanchine. It was a triple-exposure, but a bit more than a snapshot, for it made a clear and sensitive composition. There would be no doubt about it. Alec would have artistic and theatrical authority, for he had developed his body in training, and he would have schooled his mind past most of the demands one would have ordinarily expected of it.

So let us leave this luckless boy on the verge of a promising career. Luckless, but well-trained, with the gifts of head, hands, and heart, who would be absorbed into the New York City Ballet Company, as assistant to its Administrative Director. Lew Christensen, who had been a skillful performer himself, realized in Alec a variant of himself at half his age. It was Christensen indeed who proposed to Alec the music for his first full-length ballet. This was a suite of six pieces drawn from Handel's *Royal Fireworks* music. Christensen assigned him a few dancers and a few rehearsal hours from the company's working time. Alec knew his dancers of old, and he wasted no words or minutes. His ballet was accomplished within three weeks, though the company was even then performing. He took his soloists and worked the group numbers around them, fitting it all together as he could, but it was sufficiently clear in his own mind before he started so that his joinery was cleanly achieved. Balanchine would have been busy; he would have seen Alec around backstage, but would certainly not know his name. But Christensen asked him to look at the finished *Fireworks,* which involved three first dancers and a corps of eight. Alec conducted his rehearsal as if he were a cabinetmaker offering a commissioned dining-room table. Balanchine would not be slow to see that the piece was nicely turned and well-finished and would stand up under the weight of an ordinary meal. He would give orders to Madame Karinska for the eleven dresses to be created forthwith. Jean Rosenthal invented a modestly ingenious device whereby, in Alec's finale, a pyrotechnical display showered the dancers, whose pirouettes seemed to combust into Fourth-of-July sparklers.

In *The New York Times* of the following morning, John Martin will have written:

> Young Mr. Lasagna is definitely worth watching. The miniature fireworks display of last evening may well prove more than an explosion of a packet of penny-crackers. Underneath the apparent informality, there is strong structure, wit and some delicacy. It would be surprising if in his debut, Alec Lasagna has not created that rarest of theatrical properties, a valid repertory piece.

And Walter Terry, in the *New York Herald Tribune,* would be even more enthusiastic:

> Make no mistake about it, Alec Lasagna is a young ballet-*master.* His *Fireworks* is a youthful ballet master's-piece. To be sure, there were more than a

few moments when *his* master, Balanchine, was fleetingly evoked, but the overwhelming impression was of a luxurious kinesthetic security.

And so, a new choreographer will have been born. It must be recalled here that Alec knew he would never be a star dancer, that he was too tall to dance, that he started very late, and that he joined the Navy. And after his first success, there will have been offers from television, the films, and Broadway, and all the attendant demons that beset each brilliant career. But possibly his authority, which was growing unshakeable, the pleasure he will have been able to take in his mind, and above all his sense of anti-decoration, of superior orderings, will have made him a ballet-master of use to the profession.

—from *Dance News Annual,* 1953

PAUL TAYLOR
An Early Interview

Hello, this is Bethpage Bulova-Trit calling for the *San Bernardino Gazette.* Is this Paul Tylor?

Uh, yes, I think so. Only it's Taylor, not Tylor.

Might you speak a little louder, please. Your voice sounds awfully distant. Am I disturbing you?

Uh, no, not at all. I was expecting something sometime.

It is now exactly five o'clock. My publication arranged this interview last week with your press representative. You knew about this, did you not?

Mmmmm.

Hello, hello, are you there? It is exactly five and I am Bethpage Bulova-Trit calling from San Bernardino. My periodical is featuring an article on modern dance.

Oh, now I get it. This is five o'clock.

Yes indeed, it is exactly five in the morning. Is this the noted choreographer to whom I am speaking?

So it's five on the nose, right? And Friday morning already.

Pardon me but this is Wednesday. Would you prefer me to call back later?

Yes. I mean no. It's fine. I'm awake now.

Then I may proceed with my questions?

Shoot.

First of all, what is your view of the latest trends in the world of creative dance; secondly, what is your evaluation of the golf carts our city manufactures; and thirdly, how do you feel about your company performing here?

No kidding, is it? That's nice. I hear it's really exciting to be in San Luis Obispo. Lots of earthquakes and stuff.

Indeed it is. However, this is San Bernardino. Have you not heard that we have far more earthquakes than in San Luis Obispo?

I heard they can be pretty damaging all over the place.

Oh my yes! It is quite thrilling. You should see how our chandeliers and porcelain quiver. Why sometimes even the typewriters walk themselves right off the desks. I myself write with a genuinely antique Remington, you know. The keyboard was designed for the sight impaired and has all capital letters. But please, Mr. Tylor, I have a number of interesting questions for you and a deadline to meet.

Call me Paul if you want. Your name is Trip, right? Sounds familiar. I think maybe we've talked before.

How extraordinary of you to remember! Except I am now Mrs. Bulova-Trit, not Trip. I once attended a master class taught by you in 1963 at the Manifest Destiny Day School where I was enrolled as a girl.

Oh sure, now I remember. But weren't you a boy in the cast of a kids' dance recital there?

Yes, that is more or less true. I was cast as a boy in the recital but, when in your class, my cast was a plaster one. You expressed concern and wanted to help. You kept saying "Bend it, bend that leg! Why won't it flex, you poor little guy?" You do remember that, Mr. Tylor, do you not?

I've always wondered why your leg was so white and so much fatter than the other one. I thought you'd be limping for life. Does it bend now?

Yes, thank you. May we return to my prepared questions?

Right, enough chitchat. Let's get on with it.

My next question concerns your artistic efforts, a subject which could be of interest to many of our readers. Please describe your Creative Process in detail.

My what?

Your Creative Process, the particular method you employ when forming dances.

Oh that. Well, my creative progress . . .

No no, not your creative progress, your creative PROCESS. If you like, we can get to the progress part in a moment, but first to the Creative Process.

Oh, that. Well, what about it?

Precisely to which system of choreographic creativity do you subscribe?

You want me to say how I make up dances?

Please do. I shall quote your each and every word.

Sorry, but I can't say anything about that. They don't let me.

Well, for heaven's sake, why not? Who does not let you?

The choreographers' union. It's very strict about that kind of thing. There'd be a lot of plagiarism if us dance makers went around telling everybody how we make up our dances.

I see.

Ask something else. I bet you'd like to know what I eat for breakfast.

Oh, all right. What are you having?

Nothing. I never eat breakfast. What time is it now?

It is exactly four minutes and twenty seconds after five. What will you be having for luncheon?

I don't eat that either.

Dinner?

No time for dinner. I go to bed early.

And what time would that be?

I don't know exactly. Us dance makers refuse to be clock-watchers no matter what the union says.

But then how long do you sleep?

Well, let's see—counting naps, plus the time it takes to be fully alert, and adding everything all together, I'd say the total time is usually about as long as I'm actually lying flat-out.

I see. Do you dream much?

And how! That's when I do my best work.

You mean to say that your Creative Process ocurs in your sleep?

No, not my creative process, my digestive process.

Forgive me, but did you not say that you refrain from taking meals?

I said breakfast, lunch, and dinner, nothing about snacks. Maybe you'd like to hear about my digestion. I'm kinda proud of it.

Ah, so you have an unusual digestive system?

You said it! Sorry if this sounds like bragging but I'm practically the world's eighth wonder. My stomach has been written up in several medical journals, and *The Guinness Book of Records* is even after me. Just now, in fact, I thought it was them calling.

Really? Just what is it that makes your stomach so special?

It's like this: I used to have a huge beer belly but now it's the flattest thing you ever saw. It's so flat nobody can figure out how it digests anything.

My goodness, that is an unusually flat stomach. What happened to your old one?

First off, half of it ate itself up, see? And then the other half scrunched down into practically nothing.

No! Not really?

Yep. I used to need suspenders to hold my pants up but now I'm back to belts.

Marvelous! No more out-of-style braces.

Right. And nobody can snap them anymore either. Plus my fly is reachable. But maybe you'd better forget I said that last thing.

Yes, mentioning your fly does seem a bit personal. However, my readers will need to know if you sleep with anyone.

Come again?

Do you sleep with someone in the nude?

I sleep in my pajamas under a blanket, sometimes two, only the top one sometimes slides off.

Come now, are you not begging the question?

Okay, if you must know, I usually have a lot of cracker crumbs in bed with me. But let's keep that under wraps. Haw haw, what a good pun!

Indeed, I shall not tell. Be assured that it will be our little secret. Well now, I believe that covers everything.

Covers everything—that's a good one too! Thanks for calling, Mr. Trip. It's been swell talking with you. Keep on bending that leg.

Thank you, thank YOU, Mr. Tylor. Should I have any further questions, might I phone again? Hello? Hello?

—Previously unpublished

TANAQUIL LECLERCQ
The Ballet Cook Book

GEORGE BALANCHINE

Take one-half of an untoasted Thomas' English muffin, cover it generously with sweet butter, say about a quarter of an inch, spread a layer of excellent black caviar over the butter, at *least* one inch thick, and cover with the other half of the muffin. If you can't afford lots of caviar, better to forget the whole thing."

That is my husband's notion of an ideal sandwich. Since I have been married to George Balanchine, many of my tastes have undergone a change. But a liking for caviar sandwiches is not among them. I am more the peanut butter and jelly type.

My husband's love of caviar started when he was a small boy in Russia. He would often beg his mother for it, chanting, "Mama, Mama, caviar, caviar!"

"No dear," she would reply, "it bites." Priced at ten rubles a pound, it was the pocketbook that felt the bite, but my husband envisioned every little black egg equipped with sharp teeth wanting to nip at him, and his enthusiasm dwindled for a time.

Returning to Russia much later, in 1962, "Mr. B."—as his associates call him—immediately inquired after the beluga, the best caviar-producing sturgeon, and was told, much to his dismay, that these fish are rapidly disappearing. It seems that the Government has erected across the Volga a large dam that impedes the fish's yearly swim up the river to spawn.

Nothing daunted, the beluga hurl themselves in frenzy against this obstruction until the river flows red and is choked with dying fish.

The untoasted English muffin used in my husband's favorite sandwich is meant to approximate a bread which, to his great joy, he found still being baked in the Russia of today. These *Kalachi,* as they are called, were originally the bread of the "street cleaner." They come in the shape of a purse with a handle. The handle is grasped while eating and later sanitarily thrown away.

Now a raw English muffin reminds me of nothing (except the necessity of getting it toasted as soon as possible). The smell of caviar likewise reminds me of nothing (except maybe the cod liver oil forced on me as a child). Without partaking of it myself, however, I have learned from my husband a few do's and don'ts about the selection and serving of this delicacy.

They go like this: don't ever buy caviar from a delicatessen, where it has probably been hanging around for years. Do buy it if possible at a gourmet specialty store, most cities have them now. If your store receives its caviar packed in a barrel, do select the caviar from the middle of the barrel because the caviar at the top tends to be dry, and that on the bottom, oily and pressed. Do serve caviar cold (keep it in the refrigerator, or it can be set in a bowl of crushed ice). It may be accompanied by crustless *white* toast or melba rounds, but never, never serve caviar on any dark bread or with chopped onions or hard-boiled eggs. Unless, of course, it's bad caviar, or you don't like the stuff. . . .

On Sundays around noon, in Weston, Connecticut, where we own a small prefabricated house, and seven and one-half acres of tenderly cared-for land, my husband will lay aside his weekend implements, and, after a morning of mowing, spraying, fertilizing, watering, mulching, pruning, staking, plant-ing, and transplanting, come into the kitchen, hungrily muttering to him-self, "I am going to make eggs like Mama used to."

In order to do that he requires pumpernickel bread. Now the word "pumpernickel," Mr. B. swears, is a corruption of the French *"pain pour nickel"* (bread for a nickel), a most unlikely idea which is not to be corrobo-rated anywhere. On the other hand when I consulted so classic a sourcebook as Alexander Dumas' *Dictionary of Cuisine,* I confess that the explanation offered there struck me as even harder to swallow than my husband's.

Dumas tells the story of a Frenchman who owned a horse named Nick. The horse being extremely hungry one day, his owner went to an inn and thus asked for bread with which to feed it: *"Donnez-moi du pain pour Nick."* (Give me some bread for Nick.) He was duly awarded some coarse black bread, and somehow *"pain pour Nick"* became world-famous as pumper-nickel. (The horse must have told everyone.)

Eggs Like Mama Used to Make Them

2 tbs. butter	Seasoned salt
2 slices of Munzenmaier's	Ground pepper
pumpernickel bread	Dill weed, or fresh dill,
4 eggs	chopped
Cheddar cheese	

Melt butter in skillet. Tear bread into bite size pieces and fry lightly on both sides. Break in eggs, dot with slices of Cheddar cheese. Add seasoned salt, pepper, and dill and cook covered until done.
Serves 2.

Mr. B.'s Sweet Kasha

Kasha made from cream of wheat or farina is known in Russia as *mannaya-kasha*. The word *mannaya,* means manna—spiritual or divine food—and served as a dessert it is divine.

Dessert or no, it constitutes one of my husband's special late-at-night snacks. He whips the cream of wheat into a large dish, takes it to a closet where all manner of provisions are kept, and it returns minutes later buried under an avalanche of confections, different combinations of goodies every time.

1½ cups milk	Apricot jam
½ cup cream of wheat	Melba sauce
2 tbs. sweet butter	2 ounces slivered almonds,
1 tbs. sugar	flavored with ½ tsp.
Pinch salt	almond extract
1 8¾-ounce can Bartlett pears	1 cup heavy cream

Combine milk, cream of wheat, butter, sugar, and salt in a saucepan; cook, stirring constantly until mixture comes to a boil. Cover, lower heat, and cook until very thick, stirring frequently. Divide mixture among 4 dessert dishes, placing pears on top. Spoon apricot jam on top of pears, and trickle Melba sauce over jam. Sprinkle with slivered almonds, and pour a little heavy cream over.
Serves 4.

Ladies are advised to remove their mascara before trying the next recipe. Tears are unavoidable. Mr. B. fairly bawls while preparing this specialty of his.

Horseradish Ice Cream

⅔ cup grated fresh horseradish	1 tbs. sugar
4 heaping tbs. sour cream	Pinch salt

Combine grated horseradish with remaining ingredients stirring well. Pack into a wet bowl and freeze until firm. Unmold and cut into pie-shaped wedges. Serve with boiled beef, corned beef, tongue, pigs' knuckles, or fish in aspic.

Russian Easter

To give you even a vague idea of what goes on around our house around Russian Easter is simply not possible. A white linen table cloth and candles are of course placed on the table, but most important of all there must be hyacinths and Easter lilies to intermingle their fragrance with that of the food. And there is the rub (the first of quite innumerable rubs)! Have you ever tried to buy Easter lilies two weeks after Easter? For the Russian and the American versions of the holiday, like as not, may fall at least that far apart.

All that ceremony! All that preparation! All those highly complicated once-a-year specialties! No, I shall not even attempt to convey the bustling enormity and confusion which Mr. B. and I somehow manage to undergo, and even survive, when the time comes. Whatever it is that sustains the two of us, whatever it is that is needed to carry *anyone* through this annual project, is contained in my husband's general philosophy of a true cook's qualifications:

"No matter what he does, he must not rush, yet he must not be late, and the finished product must be exquisite. You need patience, and finally you have to appease your public's appetite. Besides this, it should be inexpensive enough to be accessible, and, in itself, the whole must be pretty and there must be a lot of it."

KULICHI

5 packages granulated yeast	18 egg yolks
½ cup warm water	1¼ cups sugar
1 tbs. salt	5 cups sweet butter, melted
3 cups sugar	17 cups sifted flour
6 cups milk, scalded	1½ cups raisins
8 cups sifted flour	½ cup currants
1 tbs. saffron	1 egg yolk
¼ cup vodka	1 tbs. water
4 vanilla beans	
15 cardamom seeds	ICING
¼ cup sugar	
2 tsp. almond extract	Juice 1 lemon
2 cups finely chopped	1 cup sugar
blanched almonds	

Dissolve yeast in water. Add salt and 3 cups sugar to milk and stir to dissolve. Cool until lukewarm and stir in dissolved yeast and 8 cups sifted flour. Cover with a towel and allow to rise 1½ hours.

Meanwhile prepare the following for use later on: dissolve saffron in vodka; slit vanilla beans, scrape out insides and combine with crushed cardamom seeds and ¼ cup sugar; combine almond extract with almonds; beat egg yolks until thick and lemon colored; gradually add 1¼ cups sugar and continue beating until well blended.

Add egg yolk mixture to yeast mixture and stir. Blend in butter and flour alternately, stirring well after each addition. Strain saffron vodka, adding the clear liquid to the yeast mixture. Add remaining ingredients, except egg yolk and water, and blend in thoroughly. The dough will be sticky. Turn out on a lightly floured board and knead 45–60 minutes until the dough is elastic.

Place dough in tall, cylindrical molds to half fill. Place towel over and allow to rise in a warm place until dough reaches just to top of mold, about 2½ hours. Combine egg yolk and water and brush tops of kulichi. Bake at 350°F. about 1 hour or until dry when tested with a cake tester. Cool slightly, remove from molds, and allow to cool on racks.

Combine lemon juice and sugar and stir over low heat until sugar melts and the mixture is transparent. Pour over tops of kulichi allowing icing to run down sides.

Yields 3 kulichi.

PASKA

4 packages cheesecloth
10 lbs. unsalted skim milk
     cottage cheese
9 vanilla beans
3 tbs. sugar
2 cups finely chopped blanched
     almonds
2 tsp. almond extract
1 lb. salted butter, softened

4 lbs. sweet butter, softened
9 cups sugar
2 dozen egg yolks
1 cup sugar
1 lb. cream cheese
¼ lb. currants
1 lb. white raisins

Wash cheesecloth in boiling water and wring out. Line 3 large colanders with three thicknesses of the cheesecloth leaving excess around sides. Place cottage cheese in colanders, fold cloth over top, and lay inverted plate on top of the cloth. Put heavy weights on the plate and place the colanders on top of bowls to drain at room temperature overnight.

Meanwhile prepare the following ingredients for use: slit vanilla beans, scrape out insides and combine with 3 tablespoons sugar; sprinkle almonds with extract; cream butter and 9 cups sugar; beat egg yolks until thick and lemon colored; add sugar gradually, and continue beating until well combined.

Remove cottage cheese from cheesecloth and, along with the cream cheese, rub through a medium-fine sieve into a cauldron. Add the remaining ingredients including the vanilla pods and stir with a wooden spoon to combine.

Half fill a large roasting pan with water and place over two burners. Place a large trivet on the bottom of the roasting pan and set the cauldron on top of the trivet. Heat, stirring often, until the mixture is heated through, about 2 hours. Remove from heat and cool to room temperature. Remove all vanilla pods. Pour mixture into paska molds, flower pots, or colanders lined with cheesecloth. Fold cloth over, place weights on top. Set over a bowl, making sure molds are elevated to allow for drainage. Refrigerate three days. Unmold and serve.

G. Balanchine

SIR FREDERICK ASHTON

When Sir Frederick Ashton, now artistic director of the Royal Ballet, first arrived in New York City to choreograph his ballet *Illuminations,* based on selected poems by Rimbaud, I was delighted. For I was to portray the role of Sacred Love in one of the episodes and looked forward to dancing unencumbered by much costume.

When I was little, you see, I used to puzzle over a reproduction of the famous painting *Sacred and Profane Love,* wondering which was which. Was it the nude that was sacred, or the figure fully attired? I had to be told that the exposed epidermis symbolized virtue.

Now, however, my hopes of very little costume were not to be realized. Cecil Beaton had designed for Sacred Love a calf-length costume, tights, toe shoes, sleeves, neck-ruff, and even a hat, while Profane Love cavorted around the stage bare-legged and minus one toe shoe. What heaven! How I envied her the part—one slipper off—what a relief to the toes.

As it turned out I couldn't have been more wrong. After every performance, Profane Love would give vent to a string of profanities. It seems that in the heat of the role, she would forget which foot was shod, and like as not wham up on the wrong point, onto the bare foot, bruising all five nails. Far better to be sacred, though burdensomely costumed, I thought.

During his sojourn in New York, Sir Frederick sampled mightily of our cooking, and he left these shores with certain fond memories of the native cuisine. These were the American specialties that he particularly fancied: clam chowder, corn on the cob, vichyssoise (New York style), a salad of avocados and tomatoes (with the skins taken off), and a sandwich made of sliced avocado and peeled, chopped walnuts.

Back home in England Sir Frederick is partial to another foreign dish, kedgeree. This originally was a Hindu conglomeration, and in India is a stew consisting of rice, meat, vegetables, and eggs. Outside its native habitat it has become a dish of fish, with eggs, spice, and rice (which almost makes a rhyme), the meat and vegetables seeming to have departed.

K E D G E R E E

½ cup rice
½ lb. cooked smoked
    haddock (see note)
¼ cup butter
2 hard-cooked eggs, cut in
    large chunks

1 tsp. curry powder
½ tsp. salt
¼ tsp. nutmeg
Pinch cayenne
1 tsp. chopped parsley

Cook rice according to package directions; keep warm. Remove skin and bones from fish and flake. Melt butter in skillet, add fish, rice, eggs, and seasonings, cooking until thoroughly heated. Mound on a heated serving dish and garnish with parsley.
Serves 2.

Note: Cooked white fish may be used instead of smoked fish.

At the Covent Garden Theater, in 1735, there was inaugurated something called the Sublime Society of Steaks. The Sublime Society was formed when an actor named Rich cooked an impromptu steak for a Lord Peterborough. His Lordship was so enthusiastic over the steak that he proposed forming a society and repeating this gladsome event every Saturday henceforth. The Society continued to meet at Covent Garden until the fire of 1808, when things became too hot even for steaks. The beef was then removed to a new location, and it was not until many years later that the Society was dissolved. Somewhere I have read that the original grill on which Mr. Rich broiled his first steak is still in existence.

Be that as it may, were any peer of the realm to taste Sir Frederick's Beefsteak Pudding there would be a new society formed: a Sublime Society of Beefsteak Puddings. Sir Fred would be the inevitable choice as chef, and he would have no time left in which to choreograph, and otherwise administer to the Royal Ballet's needs.

B E E F S T E A K   P U D D I N G

¼ lb. beef suet
2 cups flour
1 tsp. salt
2 tsp. baking powder
Cold water
1 lb. round steak, cut in cubes

1 sheep or beef kidney, cut into
    small pieces
1 tbs. flour
1 tsp. salt
¼ tsp. pepper
¼ cup stock
Parsley
1 cup beef gravy

Grind beef suet using the finest blade. Combine suet with flour, salt, and baking powder. Toss with cold water, using a fork, until a dough is formed. Turn onto a lightly floured board and knead a few times. Roll out ⅔ dough to fit a casserole. Line casserole and set aside.

Toss steak and kidney in flour seasoned with salt and pepper. Put into the casserole and add the stock. Roll out remaining dough and use to cover the casserole. Pinch edges together to seal. Place a cloth over the top of casserole and around sides. Set casserole on a rack in a large Dutch oven; add 2 inches water and steam 4–6 hours. Serve in casserole garnished with parsley. Pass gravy separately.

Serves 4.

Waste not, want not, as the saying goes, and Sir Fred never does—be it bread or kilts.

Our company had a dozen authentic kilts stored in the warehouse, left over from an unperformed ballet. Such waste could not help but weigh upon Mr. Balanchine's conscience, and he used to ponder occasionally how he might put them to good use. He had just seen the tattoo in Edinburgh which had given him the germ of an idea. An appropriate score, however, was lacking.

What to do? he queried Sir Fred and, like the knight he is, Sir Frederick came galloping to the rescue. "There's a Mendelssohn symphony that should just suit your kilts," he replied. And following his suggestion, we used our kilts and produced *Scotch Symphony*.

He's a clever man with the leftovers, all right. You, too, may follow Sir Fred's advice; use your stale bread, and produce Bread Pudding.

Bread Pudding

2 tbs. currants	1 tbs. plus 1 tsp. sugar
3 thin slices buttered bread	1 cup milk, scalded
1 egg	Nutmeg

Wash currants well and dry. Trim crusts from buttered bread and cut slices into cubes. Place half the cubes in a well-greased 8-inch pie plate, sprinkle with currants and top with remaining cubes. Beat egg, add sugar and scalded milk, stirring to combine. Strain and pour over bread and currant mixture. Allow to soak 30 minutes. Sprinkle with grated nutmeg. Bake at 350° F. until a knife inserted in the center comes out clean, about 30–40 minutes.

Serves 2–4.

To Sir Fred there is a definite resemblance between the art of choreography and the art of cooking. "A good ballet is only a good ballet," he remarks, "when all the ingredients are right and, like a cake, unless there is enough baking powder it doesn't rise." The ingredients are very important, he affirms, in both cases. Food he likes to be simple and well presented and pleasing to the eye as well as to the palate. No cookbook, whatever its particular scope, dare omit a rich, heavy, succulent, traditional Christmas recipe from its pages. Who among my contributors, I was wondering, would supply this indispensable formula? Just when I had begun to despair, Sir Frederick stepped forward with a recipe for plum pudding. As the British might put it, and in a phrase that seems highly suitable under the circumstances, Sir Frederick came through in pudding-time.

For "pudding-time" is when pudding is obtainable and has come to mean any lucky or fortunate time.

Sir Frederick reminds us of the ritual that always takes place around September, during the making of the pudding for Christmas. When the mixture is ready, and when all the little silver trinkets have been put in, everyone in the house-hold is supposed to stir the mixture and wish *hard* for his heart's desire. After which the pudding is steamed for hours, then tucked away until Christmas morning when it is reheated.

Should you be unwilling—even for the sake of Noël—to entrust your cherished jewels to the vagaries of the steaming process, you can still capture the true Yuletide spirit of the recipe by carrying out the stirring and wishing ceremonial.

PLUM PUDDING

½ lb. suet, finely chopped	¾ cup chopped blanched
2½ cups bread crumbs	almonds
1¼ cups brown sugar	2 tsp. nutmeg
1½ cups currants	¼ tsp. salt
1½ cups raisins	6 eggs
¾ cup mixed candied fruits	½ cup brandy
	Silver trinkets, to taste

Combine suet, bread crumbs, brown sugar, currants, raisins, candied fruits, almonds, nutmeg, and salt in a bowl. Beat eggs in another bowl and stir into dry ingredients. Add brandy to mixture, and stir in trinkets. Cover and allow to stand overnight.

Pour into 2 buttered casseroles or earthenware dishes. Wrap each casserole in a floured cloth and set aside. Bring 3 inches water to a boil in 2 medium saucepans with tight-fitting lids (see note). Set a trivet on the bottom of each pan; place casserole on top of trivets, cover tightly and

steam 6 hours, adding water when necessary. Remove from pan, cool slightly, and unmold. Serve with hard sauce (recipe below).
Yields 2 puddings.

Note: One large roasting pan with a tight-fitting lid could be used to accommodate the 2 casseroles.

BRANDY HARD SAUCE

¼ lb. sweet butter   Brandy
1 cup confectioner's sugar

Cream butter until fluffy. Gradually add sugar, beating well after each addition. When all the sugar has been added, flavor as desired with brandy. Serve with plum pudding.

Before closing the Ashton dossier, it may perhaps be in order for me to acknowledge a very personal indebtedness here. To do so, however, I must first recount a little tale of long, long ago—1950 to be exact. It was then that Mr. Balanchine went to England to stage *Ballet Imperial* for the Royal Ballet, at that time known as the Sadler's Wells Ballet. And while in London, he stayed with Sir Fred as his house guest.

Recently, talking over those good old days together, my husband turned to Sir Fred and said, "You know you really taught me something." Eavesdropping on this conversation, I half expected he was about to make public a useful pointer on choreography, or perhaps the management of difficult ballerinas, or at the very least a good horticultural tip (Sir Fred raises beautiful roses). "Yes," continued my husband, "you taught me *always* to pile up the dinner dishes in the sink and run water over them before your charwoman arrived."

From an American housewife and/or charwoman: many, many thanks, Sir Frederick Ashton.

—from *The Ballet Cook Book,* 1966

PERMISSIONS

Grateful acknowledgment is made to the following
for permission to reprint previously published and unpublished material: